ENCYCLOPEDIA

❧ OF ❧

SOUTHERN

CULTURE

CHARLES REAGAN WILSON
& WILLIAM FERRIS

Coeditors

ANN J. ABADIE
& MARY L. HART

Associate Editors

Sponsored by
The Center for the Study of Southern Culture
at the University of Mississippi

ENCYCLOPEDIA

OF

SOUTHERN

CULTURE

VOLUME 2
Ethnic Life–Law

☆ ☆ ☆ ☆ ☆ ☆ ☆ ☆ ☆ ☆ ☆ ☆

ANCHOR BOOKS

DOUBLEDAY

New York London Toronto Sydney Auckland

An Anchor Book
PUBLISHED BY DOUBLEDAY
a division of Bantam Doubleday Dell Publishing Group, Inc.
666 Fifth Avenue, New York, New York 10103

ANCHOR BOOKS, DOUBLEDAY, and the portrayal of an anchor
are trademarks of Doubleday, a division of Bantam Doubleday
Dell Publishing Group, Inc.

Encyclopedia of Southern Culture was originally published in hardcover
in one volume by the University of North Carolina Press in 1989. The
Anchor Books edition is published by arrangement with the University
of North Carolina Press.

Both the initial research and the publication of this work were made possible in part through a grant from the Division of Research Programs of
the National Endowment for the Humanities, an independent federal
agency whose mission is to award grants to support education, scholarship, media programming, libraries, and museums, in order to bring the
results of cultural activities to a broad, general public.

Book design by Chris Welch

Library of Congress Cataloging-in-Publication Data

Encyclopedia of Southern culture / Charles Reagan Wilson & William
Ferris, coeditors; Ann J. Abadie & Mary L. Hart, associate editors.
—1st Anchor Books ed.
p. cm.
"Originally published in hardcover in one volume by the University of
North Carolina Press in 1989"—T.p. verso.
Includes bibliographical references and index.
Contents: Vol. 1. Agriculture–Environment—v. 2. Ethnic Life–Law—
v. 3. Literature–Recreation—v. 4. Religion–Women's Life.
1. Southern States—Civilization—Encyclopedias. 2. Southern States—
Encyclopedias. I. Wilson, Charles Reagan. II. Ferris, William R.
F209.E53 1991 975'.003 90-973
CIP

ISBN 0-385-41546-X

"Tell about the South. What's it like there.
What do they do there. Why do they live there.
Why do they live at all."

WILLIAM FAULKNER
Absalom, Absalom!

The *Encyclopedia of Southern Culture* was
produced through major grants from the Program
for Research Tools and Reference Works of the
National Endowment for the Humanities, the
Ford Foundation, the Atlantic-Richfield
Foundation, and the Mary Doyle Trust.

The publication of this volume
was made possible by the
Fred W. Morrison Fund of the
University of North Carolina Press.

CONTENTS

CONSULTANTS

AGRICULTURE
Thomas D. Clark
248 Tahoma Road
Lexington, Ky. 40503

ART AND ARCHITECTURE
Jessie Poesch
Department of Art
Tulane University
New Orleans, La. 70118

BLACK LIFE
Thomas C. Holt
Department of History
University of Chicago
Chicago, Ill. 60637

EDUCATION
Thomas G. Dyer
Associate Vice President for
Academic Affairs
University of Georgia
Old College
Athens, Ga. 30602

ENVIRONMENT
Martin V. Melosi
Department of History
University of Houston
Houston, Tex. 77004

ETHNIC LIFE
George E. Pozzetta
Department of History
University of Florida
Gainesville, Fla. 32611

FOLKLIFE
William Ferris

Center for the Study of
Southern Culture
University of Mississippi
University, Miss. 38677

GEOGRAPHY
Richard Pillsbury
Department of Geography
Georgia State University
Atlanta, Ga. 30303

HISTORY AND MANNERS
Charles Reagan Wilson
Center for the Study of
Southern Culture
University of Mississippi
University, Miss. 38677

INDUSTRY
James C. Cobb
Honors Program
P.O. Box 6233
University of Alabama
Tuscaloosa, Ala. 35487-6322

LANGUAGE
Michael Montgomery
Department of English
University of South Carolina
Columbia, S.C. 29208

LAW
Maxwell Bloomfield
Department of History
The Catholic University of
America
Washington, D.C. 20017

LITERATURE
M. Thomas Inge
Randolph-Macon College
Ashland, Va. 23005

MEDIA
Edward D. C. Campbell, Jr.
Virginia State Library
11th Street at Capitol Square
Richmond, Va. 23219

MUSIC
Bill C. Malone
Department of History
Tulane University
New Orleans, La. 70118

MYTHIC SOUTH
George B. Tindall
Department of History
University of North Carolina
Chapel Hill, N.C. 27599

POLITICS
Numan Bartley
Department of History
University of Georgia
Athens, Ga. 30602

RECREATION
John Shelton Reed
Department of Sociology
University of North Carolina
Chapel Hill, N.C. 27599

RELIGION
Samuel S. Hill

Department of Religion
University of Florida
Gainesville, Fla. 32611

SCIENCE AND MEDICINE
James O. Breeden
Department of History
Southern Methodist University
Dallas, Tex. 75275

SOCIAL CLASS
J. Wayne Flynt
Department of History
Auburn University
Auburn, Ala. 36830

URBANIZATION
Blaine A. Brownell
School of Social and Behavioral
Sciences
University of Alabama at
Birmingham
Birmingham, Ala. 35294

VIOLENCE
Raymond D. Gastil
48 E. 21st Street
New York, N.Y. 10010

WOMEN'S LIFE
Carol Ruth Berkin
Baruch College
City University of New York
17 Lexington Avenue
New York, N.Y. 10010

FOREWORD

Can you remember those southern elder men who "jes' set" on their favored chair or bench for hours, every day—and a year later they could tell you at about what time of day someone's dog had trotted by? And the counterpart elderly ladies, their hands deeply wrinkled from decades of quilting, canning, washing collective tons of clothing in black cast-iron pots, in which at other seasonal times pork fat was rendered into lard, or some of that lard into soap? These southern ancestors, black and white, have always struck me as the Foundation Timbers of our South, and I think that we who were reared and raised by them, and amongst them, are blessed that we were.

I consider this *Encyclopedia of Southern Culture* the answer to a deep need that we resuscitate and keep alive and fresh the memories of those who are now bones and dust, who during their eras and in their respective ways contributed toward the social accretion that has entered legend as "the southern way of life," which we continue today.

It is a culture resulting from the antebellum mixture of social extremes based on the chattel slavery that supported an aristocratic gentility; in between the slaves and planters a vast majority struggled for their own survival. Centuries of slavery were abolished by an indelible war whose legacies continue to haunt us. The southern memory is of generations of life, of the good and the bad, the humor and the suffering from the past. The southerner does not sentimentalize but only remembers.

Out of the historic cotton tillage sprang the involuntary field hollers, the shouts, and the moanin' low that have since produced such a cornucopia of music, played daily, on every continent, where I have been astounded at how much I heard of the evolved blues, jazz, and gospel—as well as bluegrass and country—all of them of direct southern origin.

Equally worldwide is southern literature. Writers took the oral traditions of the South—the political rhetoric, preaching, conversational wordplay, and lazy-day storytelling—and converted them into art. The latest addition to southern literature is this *Encyclopedia*, no small part of whose greatness, I think, is that it is compiled by many researchers who did not simply read books but who rubbed shoulders with those whom they interviewed and recorded and studied. They walked and talked with the sharecropper farmers, the cooks, the quiltmakers, the convicts, the merchants, the fishermen, and all the others who make these pages a volume of living memories.

The region and its people have undergone dramatic changes in the last decades, overcoming much, although not all, of the poverty of the past, and they are now sharing in the nation's prosperity. Old ways that divided the people have fallen away to be replaced by new dreams. The hard lessons from the past are not forgotten in this *Encyclopedia*. I testify that this *Encyclopedia of Southern Culture* mirrors the very best of what has lately come to be called "the new South." Never before have such volumes been produced by a team so committed to distilling and presenting our southern distinctiveness.

Alex Haley

ACKNOWLEDGMENTS

||||||||||||||||||||||||||||||||||||||||||||||||||||||||||||||||||||||||||||||||||||||||||||||||||||||||||||||||||||||||||||||||||||||||||||

These volumes could never have been completed without the assistance of countless individuals. The coeditors and associate editors wish to thank our consultants and contributors for their planning, researching, and writing of articles. We should note that Raven McDavid helped to plan the Language section before his untimely death in 1984. Clarence Mohr's work on the early design of the *Encyclopedia* provided the basic organizational structure for the volumes. Many scholars reviewed articles, made suggestions for improvements, and verified factual material. Richard H. Brown, of the Newberry Library in Chicago, advised wisely on *Encyclopedia* matters, as with other projects of the Center for the Study of Southern Culture. Howard Lamar offered sage counsel on the *Encyclopedia* from its earliest planning stages. Research assistants Elizabeth Makowski and Sharon A. Sharp supervised the review and verification of entries, assisted by numerous teaching assistants and volunteers, and also served as staff writers. Editorial assistants Ann Sumner Holmes, Ginna Parsons, and Karen McDearman Cox supervised final production of copy and served as endless sources of good advice and varied skill. Lolly Pilkington read the entire manuscript with a skilled eye. Teaching assistants in the Department of History and the Southern Studies program spent much time in the library checking and rechecking information and reading galley proof. Personnel in the John Davis Williams Library of the University of Mississippi often came to our rescue, and we are grateful to the many archivists and librarians across the nation who assisted us with obtaining illustrations. Special thanks are due the staff of the University of North Carolina Press, especially its director Matthew Hodgson, editor-in-chief Iris Tillman Hill, managing editor Sandra Eisdorfer, and Ron Maner, Pamela Upton, and Paula Wald.

The *Encyclopedia of Southern Culture* was produced with financial support from the National Endowment for the Humanities, the Ford Foundation, the Atlantic-Richfield Foundation, and the Mary Doyle Trust. The Graduate School and alumni and friends of the University of Mississippi donated required funds for a matching NEH grant in 1983, and the editors are grateful for their assistance. Donors include: The James Hand Foundation by Kathleen Hand Carter; Mrs. R. R. Morrison, Jr.; Mrs. Hester F. Faser; David L. May; James J. Brown, Jr.; Lynn Crosby Gammill; First National Bank of Vicksburg, Mississippi; The Goodman Charitable and Educational Trust, Hallie Goodman, Trustee; Dr. F. Watt Bishop; Robert Travis; Mrs. Dorothy Crosby; Christopher Keller, Jr.; Worth I. Dunn; Wiley Fairchild; Mrs. Eric Biedenharn; John S. Callon; Betty Carter; Shelby Flowers Ferris; Mary Hohenberg; Mr. & Mrs. John Kramer; Samuel McIlwain; and Prescott Sherman.

INTRODUCTION

The American South has long generated powerful images and complex emotions. In the years since World War II, the region has undergone dramatic changes in race relations, political institutions, and economic life. Those changes have led some observers to forecast the eventual end of a distinctive southern region. Other scholars and popular writers point to continuities with past attitudes and behavior. The *Encyclopedia of Southern Culture* appears during a period of major transition in the life of the South and is in part a reflection of these changes. It examines both the historical and the contemporary worlds of southern culture. The *Encyclopedia*'s editors have sought to assemble authoritative, concise, thoughtful, substantive, and interesting articles that will give scholars, students, and general readers a useful perspective on the South.

SOUTHERN CULTURE

The *Encyclopedia*'s definition of "the South" is a cultural one. The geographical focus is, to be sure, on the 11 states of the former Confederacy (Alabama, Arkansas, Florida, Georgia, Louisiana, Mississippi, North Carolina, South Carolina, Tennessee, Texas, and Virginia), but this tidy historical definition fails to confront the complexities of studying the region. Delaware, Kentucky, Maryland, and Missouri were slave states at the beginning of the Civil War, and many of their citizens then and after claimed

a southern identity. Social scientists today use statistical data covering the "census South," which includes Delaware, Maryland, West Virginia, Oklahoma, and the District of Columbia. The Gallup public opinion polling organization defines the South as the Confederate states plus Oklahoma and Kentucky.

Moreover, the realities of cultural areas require a broadened definition. Cultural areas have core zones, where distinctive traits are most concentrated, and margins, where the boundaries of the culture overlap with other cultural areas. The *Encyclopedia*'s articles explore the nature of both these core areas and margins in the South. The borders of the South have surely varied over time. In the colonial era Delaware was an agricultural slave state with a claim of being southern. Maryland was a southern state, sharing much with its neighbor, Virginia, in a Chesapeake subculture. Maryland did not join the Confederacy, but soldiers from the state fought in the Confederate armies and one finds Confederate monuments in Baltimore. St. Louis was a midwestern city and the gateway to the West, but southerners have also claimed it. The Mississippi River culture tied St. Louis to areas of the Lower South, and southerners have often been associated with it. John F. Kennedy once said that Washington, D.C., was known for its southern efficiency and northern charm. Carved from an area of Maryland as a concession to southerners, Washington was a slaveowning area and was once a center for slave auctions. Later, under Woodrow Wilson, a southern-born president, the nation's capital became a racially segregated bastion reflecting southern regional mores. Washington has also long been a center for southern black migration, an educational mecca for blacks, and a center for black musicians, artists, and writers. Most recently, geographical proximity to Appalachia has made Washington a center for the performance of such other expressions of southern culture as bluegrass music. Contemporary Washington, however, appears to be less and less "southern," and urban historians consequently omit it from the list of regional cities (and thus there is no separate entry on Washington in the *Encyclopedia.*

Contributors to the *Encyclopedia* at times transcend geography and history when examining questions of regional consciousness, symbolism, mythology, and sectional stereotyping. The "South" is found wherever southern culture is found, and that culture is located not only in the Deep South, the Upper South, and border cities, but also in "little Dixies" (the southern parts of Ohio, Indiana, Illinois, and parts of Missouri and Oklahoma), among black Mississippians who migrated to south Chicago, among white Appalachians and black Alabamians who migrated to Detroit, and among former Okies and Arkies who settled in and around Bakersfield, California. This diaspora of southern ethnic culture is also found in the works of expatriate southern artists and writers. Although Richard Wright and Tennessee Williams lived in Paris and New York, respectively, they continued to explore their southern roots in their writing.

The South exists as a state of mind both within and beyond its geographical boundaries. Recent studies of mythology suggest that the New York theater in the late 19th century and Hollywood in the 20th century have kept alive images, legends, and myths about the South in the national consciousness. One can view the American South and its culture as international property. The worlds of *Roots, Gone with the Wind,* blues, country music, rock and roll, William Faulkner, and Alice Walker are admired and closely studied throughout the world. The South has nurtured important myths, and their impact on other cultures is a vital aspect of the *Encyclopedia*'s perspective. In the end, then, the *Encyclopedia*'s definition of the South is a broad, inclusive one, based on culture.

These volumes focus specifically on exploring the culture of the South. In the 1950s anthropologists Alfred Kroeber and Clyde Kluckholn cataloged 164 definitions of culture, suggesting the problems then and now of a precise definition. To 19th-century intellectuals culture was the best of civilization's achievements. Matthew Arnold was perhaps the best-known advocate of this Victorian-era ideal, and H. L. Mencken—the South's nastiest and most entertaining critic in the early 20th century—was also a believer in it. Mencken argued in his essay "The Sahara of the Bozart" (1920) that the upper-class, aristocratic southerner of the early 19th century "liked to toy with ideas. He was hospitable and tolerant. He had the vague thing that we call culture." Mencken found the South of his era severely wanting, though, in this ideal of culture. He saw in the South "not a single picture gallery worth going into, or a single orchestra capable of playing the nine symphonies of Beethoven, or a single opera-house, or a single theater devoted to decent plays, or a single public monument (built since the war) that is worth looking at, or a single workshop devoted to the making of beautiful things." Mencken allowed that the region excelled "in the lower reaches of the gospel hymn, the phonograph and the chautauqua harangue."

The South of Mencken's day did trail the rest of the nation in the development of important cultural institutions; but today the South, the nation, and the world celebrate the "lower reaches" of southern culture. This judgment on the value of the sounds and words coming from the region reflects 20th-century understandings of culture. Anthropologists have taken the lead in exploring the theoretical aspects of cultures. Edward Burnett Tylor gave a classic definition of culture as "that complex whole which includes knowledge, belief, art, morals, law, customs, and any other capabilities and habits" acquired by the members of a society. For students of culture, the goal was to study and outline discrete cultural traits, using this definition to convey the picture of a culture. During the 20th century another major anthropological theory of culture emerged. Kroeber, Bronislaw Malinowski, and Ruth Benedict stressed the study of pattern, form, structure, and organization in a culture rather than the simple listing of observed traits. Patterns could include customs associated with food, labor, and manners as well as more complex social, political, and economic systems.

Recently culture has been viewed as an abstraction, consisting of the inherited models and ideas with which people approach their experiences. The theory of social structure, first developed by British anthropologist Alexander Reginald Radcliffe-Brown in the 1930s and 1940s, stressed that culture must include recognition of the persistence of social groups, social classes, and social roles. The structuralist theories of Claude Lévi-Strauss attempt to apply abstract mathematical formulae to society. Although social anthropologists avoid the term *culture*, they have insured that the study of culture not neglect social background.

The theoretical work of Clifford Geertz is especially significant in understanding the definition of culture developed for the *Encyclopedia of Southern Culture*. Geertz defines *culture* as "an historically transmitted pattern of meanings embodied in symbols, a system of inherited conceptions expressed in symbolic forms." Through culture, humans "communicate, perpetuate, and develop their knowledge about and attitudes toward life." This contemporary definition stresses mental culture, expressed through symbol systems, which gives human beings a framework for understanding one another, themselves, and the wider world. Culture patterns, including material, oral, mental, and social systems, are blueprints for organizing human interaction.

The *Encyclopedia of Southern Culture* is not intended as a contribution to the general study of culture theory, although awareness of theories of culture has been useful background in the conceptualization of the volumes and in the selection of topics. The volumes attempt to study within the southern context what 20th-century humanist T. S. Eliot said, in *Notes towards the Definition of Culture*, was culture—"all the characteristic activities and interests of a people." Articles in the volumes deal with regional cultural achievements in such areas as music, literature, art, and architecture. The broader goal of the volumes is to chart the cultural landscape of the South, addressing those aspects of southern life and thought that have sustained either the reality or the illusion of regional distinctiveness. The volumes detail specific cultural traits, suggest the cultural patterns that tie the region together, point out the internal diversity within the South, and explore with special attention the importance of social structure and symbolism. Above all, the volumes have been planned to carry out Eliot's belief that "culture is not merely the sum of several activities, but a *way of life.*"

Eliot's definition of culture, then, can be seen as a working definition for the *Encyclopedia of Southern Culture.* In order to foster interdisciplinary communication, the editors have included the full range of social indicators, trait groupings, literary concepts, and historical evidence commonly used by students of regionalism. The criteria for the all-important selection of topics, however, have been consistently to include the characteristic traits that give the South a distinctive culture.

A special concern of the *Encyclopedia* has been to identify distinctive regional characteristics. It addresses those aspects of southern life and thought—the individuals, places, ideas, rituals, symbols, myths, values, and experiences— which have sustained either the reality or the illusion of regional distinctiveness. The comparative method has been encouraged as a way to suggest contrasts with other American regions and with other societies. One lesson of earlier regional scholarship has been the need to look at the South in the widest possible context. The editors of the *Encyclopedia* have assumed that the distinctiveness of southern culture does not lie in any one trait but rather in the peculiar combination of regional cultural characteris-

tics. The fundamental uniqueness of southern culture thus emerges from the *Encyclopedia*'s composite portrait of the South. The editors asked contributors to consider individual traits that clearly are unique to the region. Although some topics may not be uniquely southern in themselves, contributors have been asked to explore particular regional aspects of those topics. Subjects that suggest the internal diversity of the region are also treated if they contribute to the overall picture of southern distinctiveness. The Cajuns of Louisiana, the Germans of Texas, and the Jews of Savannah, for example, contribute to the distinctive flavor of southern life. Their adaptations, and resistance, to southern cultural patterns suggest much about the region's distinctiveness.

The question of continuity and change in southern culture is another central concern of the *Encyclopedia.* Contributors have examined themes and topics in an evolutionary framework. Historians represent by far the largest group of contributors to the project. The volumes do not attempt to narrate the region's history in a systematic way, a task ably achieved in the *Encyclopedia of Southern History* (1979), but contributors from all disciplines have developed material within an appropriate time perspective. As Clifford Geertz has written, culture is "historically transmitted," a fact that is especially relevant for the study of the South, where the apogee of cultural distinctiveness may well have been in an earlier period. Because the *Encyclopedia* focuses on culture rather than history, historical topics were chosen because they are relevant to the origin, development, or decline of an aspect of southern culture. Given the historical shape of southern cultural development, one would expect less material on the colonial era (before there was a self-conscious "South") and increased concentration of material in the Civil War and postbellum eras (perhaps the high points of southern cultural distinctiveness). Nearly all articles include historical material, and each overview essay systematically traces the development of a major subject area. In addition, such selected historical entries as "Colonial Heritage," "Frontier Heritage," and "Civil War" are included with a cultural focus appropriate to the volumes.

STUDY OF SOUTHERN REGIONALISM

The *Encyclopedia of Southern Culture* reflects a broad intellectual interest in regionalism, the importance of which in the United States is far from unique when seen in a global context. The struggle to accommodate regional cultures within a larger nation is an experience common to many Western and Third World peoples. Despite the contemporary developments in transportation and communication that promise the emergence of a "global village," regionalism is an enduring reality of the modern world. The Basques in Spain, the Scots in Britain, the Kurds in the Middle East, and Armenians in the Soviet Union are only a few examples of groups that have recently reasserted their regional interests.

Although public emphasis on the United States as a cultural melting pot has sometimes obscured the nation's enduring regional heritage, the study of regionalism has long been a major field of scholarship involving leading authorities from many academic disciplines both in the United States and abroad. The *Encyclopedia* is part of the broader field of American Studies, which has dramatically evolved in recent years from a focus on such regional types as the New England Yankees, the southern Cavaliers, and the western cowboys and Indians. Since the 1960s studies of black life, ethnic life, and women's life have significantly changed the definition of American culture. In the 1980s the study of American region, place, and community—whether it be a Brooklyn neighborhood or a county in rural Mississippi—is essential to understanding the nation. In the context of this American Studies tradition, the *Encyclopedia* focuses on the American South, a place that has influenced its people in complex and fascinating ways.

Significant bodies of research exist for all major regions of the United States, but by almost any standard the American South has received the most extensive scholarly attention. Since the 1930s virtually all aspects of southern life have come under increasingly rigorous, systematic intellectual scrutiny. The *Encyclopedia of Southern Culture* is a collaborative effort that combines intellectual perspectives that reflect the breadth of Southern Studies. Sociologists, historians, literary critics, folklorists, anthropologists, political scientists, psychologists, theologians, and other scholars have written on the region, and all of these fields are represented by contributors to the *Encyclopedia*. Journalists, lawyers, physicians, architects, and other professionals from outside the academy have also studied the South, and their contributions appear in these volumes as well.

Students of the South operate within a well-developed institutional framework. The proliferation of academic journals that focus on the South has mirrored expanding disciplinary boundaries in regional scholarship. The *Journal of Southern History*, the *Southern Review*, the *Southern Economic Journal*, *Social Forces*, the *Southern Folklore Quarterly*, the *Virginia Quarterly Review*, the *South Atlantic Quarterly*, and the *Southwestern Political Science Quarterly* are only a few of the titles that have specialized in publishing material on the region. The contemporary era has witnessed a dramatic expansion in the publication of books on the South. The University of North Carolina Press was the first southern university press to publish an extensive list of titles on the South, and by the early 1950s the press alone had produced some 200 studies. Works on the region are now published by university presses in every southern state and find a ready market with national publishers as well.

Research on the South has led to greater appreciation of the region's internal diversity, which is reflected in the study of smaller geographical areas or specialized themes. Such recent periodicals as the *Appalachian Journal*, *Mid-South Folklore*, and *South Atlantic Urban Studies* illustrate the narrowing geographical and topical focus of recent scholarship on the South. Overlapping interests and subject matter shared among regional scholars have exerted a steady pressure toward broadening disciplinary horizons. Meaningful cooperation among disciplines is complicated by differences of vocabulary and method, but students of the American South demonstrate a growing awareness that they are engaged in a common endeavor that can be furthered as much by cooperation as by specialization. Such periodicals as *Southern Quarterly*, *Southern Studies*, and *Perspectives on the American South* have established forums for interdisciplinary study.

In recent years regional scholarship has also influenced curriculum development in colleges and universities. Leading institutional centers for the study of the South include the Center for the Study of Southern Culture at the University of Mississippi, the Institute for Southern Studies at the University of South Carolina, the Institute for Southern Studies at Durham, N.C., and the Center for the Study of Southern History and Culture at the University of Alabama. Appalachian study centers are located at, among other places, the University of Kentucky, East Tennessee State University, Appalachian State University, Mars Hill College, and Berea College. The Institute for Texan Cultures is in San Antonio, and Baylor University launched a Texas Studies Center in 1987. The Center for Arkansas Studies is at the University of Arkansas at Little Rock, while the University of Southwestern Louisiana's Center for Louisiana Studies concentrates on Cajun and Creole folk culture. These developments are, again, part of a broader interest in regional studies programs at universities in other regions, including the Center for the Study of New England Culture at the University of Massachusetts at Amherst and the Great Plains Center at the University of Nebraska.

The *Encyclopedia of Southern Culture* grows out of the work of the University of Mississippi's Center for the Study of Southern Culture, which was established in 1977 to coordinate existing university resources and to develop multidisciplinary teaching, research, and outreach programs about the South. The center's mission is to strengthen the university's instructional program in the humanities, to promote scholarship on every aspect of southern culture, and to encourage public understanding of the South through publications, media productions, lectures, performances, and exhibitions. Center personnel administer a Southern Studies curriculum that includes both B.A. and M.A. degree programs; a Ford Foundation–funded, three-year (1986–89) project aimed at incorporating more fully the experiences of blacks and women into the teaching of Southern Studies; an annual United States Information Agency–sponsored project for international scholars interested in regional and ethnic cultures; such annual meetings as the Porter L. Fortune Chancellor's Symposium on Southern History, the Faulkner and Yoknapatawpha Conference, and the Barnard-Millington Symposium on Southern Science and Medicine; and a variety of periodicals, films, and media presentations. The center administers these programs in cooperation with the on-campus departments in the College of Liberal Arts, the Afro-American Studies program, and the Sarah Isom Center for Women's Studies. The University of Mississippi and its Center for the Study of Southern Culture provided the necessary institutional setting for coordinating the diverse needs of the *Encyclopedia*'s hundreds of participants.

Recognizing both the intellectual maturity of scholarship in the American South and the potential role of regional study in consolidating previously fragmented academic endeavors, the *Encyclopedia* planners conceived the idea of an interdisciplinary reference work to bring together and synthesize current knowledge about the South. Scholars studying the South have been served by

a number of reference works, but none of these has had the aims and perspective of the *Encyclopedia of Southern Culture*. The 13-volume series, *The South in the Building of the Nation* (1909–13), which attempted a comprehensive survey of the region's history, was the closest predecessor to this encyclopedia. Other major works include the 16-volume *Library of Southern Literature* (1908–13), Howard W. Odum's monumental *Southern Regions of the United States* (1936), W. T. Couch's edited *Culture in the South* (1936), and, more recently, the *Encyclopedia of Southern History* (1978), the *Encyclopedia of Religion in the South* (1984), and the *History of Southern Literature* (1986).

Like any major reference work, the *Encyclopedia* addresses the long-range needs and interests of a diverse reading audience. Before launching the project the editors consulted extensively with leading authorities in all areas of American Studies and Southern Studies and sought additional advice from directors of comparable projects. Planning for the original single-volume edition began in 1978 with the compilation of a working outline of subjects that had received frequent attention in major studies of regional culture. During the fall of 1979 some 270 U.S. and international scholars received copies of the preliminary topical list, together with background information about the project. Approximately 150 of these scholars, representing a variety of disciplines, responded to this mailing, commenting upon the potential value of the proposed volume and making suggestions concerning its organization and content.

In 1980 the Center for the Study of Southern Culture commissioned several scholars to prepare detailed lists of topics for major sections of the volume, and to write sample articles as well. The National Endowment for the Humanities supported the *Encyclopedia of Southern Culture* with a 1980–81 planning grant and grants covering 1981–83 and 1984–86. The Ford Foundation, the Atlantic-Richfield Foundation, and the Mary Doyle Trust also provided major funding. Full-time work on the *Encyclopedia* began in September 1981. The content of the volume was divided into 24 major subject areas, and the editors selected a senior consultant to assist in planning the topics and contributors for each section. During the fall and winter of 1981–82, the consultants formulated initial lists of topics and recommended appropriate contributors for entries. In general, the consultants were actively involved in the initial stages of planning and less involved in later editorial work. Project staff handled the paperwork for assignments. The editors sent each contributor a packet of information on the project, including the overall list of topics, so that contributors could see how their articles fit into the volume as a whole. Authors were encouraged to make suggestions for additional entries, and many of them did so. When contributors were unable to write for the volume, they often suggested other scholars, thus facilitating the reassignment of articles. The editors assumed the responsibility for editing articles for style, clarity, and tone appropriate for a reference book. They reviewed all entries for accuracy, and research assistants verified the factual and bibliographical veracity of each entry. The senior consultants, with their special expertise in each subject area, provided an additional check on the quality of the articles.

ORGANIZATION AND CONTENT OF THE ENCYCLOPEDIA

The *Encyclopedia of Southern Culture* is a synthesis of current scholarship and attempts to set new directions for further research. The *Encyclopedia*'s objectives are fourfold: (1) The volumes provide students and general readers with convenient access to basic facts and bibliographical data about southern cultural patterns and their historical development. (2) By bringing together lucid analyses of modern scholarship on southern culture from the humanities and the social sciences, the *Encyclopedia* is intended to facilitate communication across disciplinary lines and help stimulate new approaches to regional study. It attempts to integrate disparate intellectual efforts and represents an innovative organization and presentation of knowledge. (3) The volumes can serve as a curriculum component for multidisciplinary courses on the American South and provide a model for scholars wishing to assemble similar research tools in other regions. (4) Viewed in its totality, the *Encyclopedia* locates the specific components of regional culture within the framework of a larger organic whole. At this level, the volumes attempt to illuminate the nature and function of regionalism in American culture.

The editors considered an alphabetical arrangement of articles but concluded that organization of information into 24 major sections more accurately reflects the nature of the project and would provide a fresh perspective. Cross-references to related articles in other sections are essential guides to proper use of the *Encyclopedia*, enabling readers to consult articles written on a common topic from different perspectives. Sections often reflect an academic field (history, geography, literature), but at times the academic division has been rejected in favor of a section organized around a cultural theme (such as social class) that has become a central scholarly concern. In general, the sections are designed to reflect the amount and quality of scholarship in particular areas of regional study. Articles within each section are arranged in three divisions. The overview essay is written by the *Encyclopedia*'s consultant in that section and provides an interpretive summary of the field. That essay is followed by alphabetically arranged thematic articles and then by alphabetically arranged, brief topical-biographical sketches.

Although the editors and consultants conceived each section as a separate unit, sections are closely connected to one another through cross-references. The titles of major sections are brief, but the editors have grouped together related material under these simple rubrics. The Agriculture section thus includes rural-life articles, the Black Life section includes articles on race relations, Social Class includes material on social structure and occupational groups, and Industry includes information on commercial activity.

Several sections deserve special comment in regard to their organization and content. The Black Life section (Vol. 1) contains most, though not all, of the separate entries on southern black culture. The editors placed Richard Wright and Ralph Ellison in Literature (Vol. 3) to honor their roles as central figures in *southern* (as well as black) literature, and most blues musicians are similarly

found in Music (Vol. 3). But the list of biographies in Black Life is intended to stand on its own, including individuals representing music, literature, religion, sports, politics, and other areas of black achievement. The *Encyclopedia* claims for southern culture such individuals as Mary McLeod Bethune, Ida Wells-Barnett, Arna Bontemps, and James Weldon Johnson, who traditionally have been seen as part of black history but not southern culture. The separate Black Life section is intended to recognize the special nature of southern black culture—both black and southern. Black culture is central to understanding the region and the *Encyclopedia*'s attempt to explore this perspective in specific, detailed topics may be the most significant contribution of these volumes toward understanding the region. Although the terms *Afro-American* and *Euro-American* are sometimes used, *black* and *white* are more often used to refer to the two major interrelated cultures of the South. These terms seem the clearest, most inclusive, and most widely accepted terms of reference.

The Women's Life section (Vol. 4) has similar aims. Many thematic articles and biographies of women of achievement appear in this section, which is designed to stand on its own. Scholars in the last 20 years have explored southern women's cultural values and issues, and their work provides a distinctive perspective on the region. Gender, like race and social class, has set parameters for cultural life in the South. The section includes articles on family life, childhood, and the elderly, reflecting the major responsibilities and concerns of women. The inclusion of these topics in this section is not meant to suggest that family responsibilities were the sole concern of women or that men were un-involved with family, children, and the elderly. The articles usually discuss both male and female activities within the family. Scholarship on family life has often focused on women's roles, and family matters traditionally have played a significant part in women's lives. Most of the Women's Life section is concentrated, however, on concerns beyond the family and household, reflecting the contemporary scholarship in this area.

The Education section (Vol. 1) presented especially difficult choices of inclusion, and again, a selective approach was adopted. The flagship state public university in each southern state is included, but beyond that, institutions have been selected that represent differing constituencies to suggest the diversity of educational activity in the region. Berea College, Commonwealth College, the University of the South, and Tuskegee Institute each reflect an important dimension of southern education. The inclusion of additional school entries would have departed from the *Encyclopedia*'s overall guidelines and made a four-volume reference work impossible.

The History and Manners section (Vol. 2) contains a mix of articles that focus on cultural and social dimensions of the South. Combining topics in history and manners reflects the editors' decision that in a reference work on cultural concerns, history entries should deal with broad sociocultural history. There are, thus, no separate, detailed entries on Civil War battles, but, instead, long thematic articles on the cultural meaning of battlefields, monuments, and wars. The article on Robert E. Lee discusses the facts of Lee's life but also the history of his image for southerners and Americans.

Overview essays in each section are interpretive pieces that synthesize modern scholarship on major aspects of southern culture. The consultants who have written them trace historical developments and relate their broad subjects to regional cultural concerns. Many specific topics are discussed within overview essays rather than through separate entries, so readers should consult the index in order to locate such material. As one might expect, major subject areas have developed at a different pace. In such fields as literature, music, religion, folklife, and political culture, a vast body of scholarship exists. In these areas, the *Encyclopedia* overview essays provide a starting point for those users of this reference work interested in the subject. Such other fields as law, art, science, and medicine have only recently emerged as separate fields of Southern Studies. In these areas, the overview essays should help define the fields and point toward areas for further research.

Most thematic, topical, and biographical entries fall clearly within one section, but some articles were appropriate for several sections. The Scopes trial, for example, could have been placed in Religion, Law, or Science and Medicine. Consultants in Black Life, Music, and Women's Life all suggested Bessie Smith as an entry in their categories. The article on cockfighting clearly related to the Recreation section but was placed in Violence to suggest how recreational activities reflect a culture of violence. The gospel music articles could have appeared in Religion, but the editors decided that Music was the most appropriate category for them.

Much consideration and consultation with authorities in relevant fields occurred before such decisions were made on topics that did not fit perfectly into any one section. Readers should rely on the index and cross-references between sections to lead them to desired entries.

Biographies focus on the cultural significance of key individuals. The volumes do not claim to be exhaustive in their biographical entries. Rather than attempt to include all prominent people in a subject area, the editors decided to treat representative figures in terms of their contributions to, or significance for, southern culture. In selecting individuals, the goal was to include biographies of those iconic individuals associated with a particular aspect of the region's culture. Consultants identified those major figures who have immediate relevance to the region. The editors and consultants also selected individuals who illuminate major themes and exemplify southern cultural styles. Persons in this category may have made special contributions to southern distinctiveness, to cultural achievements, or to the development of a characteristic aspect of southern life. The Music and Literature categories have been given somewhat fuller biographical attention than other subject areas, a decision that is warranted by southern achievements in those areas. In addition to the separate biographical entries, many individuals are discussed in such thematic articles as "Linguists" or "Historians," which outline contributions of key persons to certain fields. Readers should consult the index in each volume to locate biographical information on southerners who appear in that volume.

The *Encyclopedia* includes biographies of living persons as well as the deceased. It is especially concerned with regional cultural issues in the contemporary South, and the inclusion of living individuals was crucial to establishing continuities between past and present. Entries on Bill Moyers and Charles Kuralt, for example, help readers to understand that the journalistic traditions of the South have been extended into the television age.

Selecting approximately 250 individuals for inclusion in the *Encyclopedia of Southern Culture* was no easy task. The list of potential individuals was widely circulated, and the choices represent the informed judgment of our consultants and contributors, leading scholars in the field of Southern Studies. The selection of biographies was made in light of the *Encyclopedia*'s overall definition of culture. The goal was not to list every cultural trait or include every prominent individual in the South but to explore *characteristic* aspects of the region's life and culture and to show their interrelationships. The biographical entries are not simply descriptive, factual statements but are instead intimately related to the broader thematic and overview essays. Biographical entries were meant to suggest how a representative individual is part of a broader pattern, a way of life, in the American South.

Interdisciplinary study has become prominent in a number of scholarly areas, but in few is it as useful as in the study of region. The interrelatedness of such specific fields as politics, religion, economics, cultural achievement, and social organization becomes especially obvious when scholars study a region. Interdisciplinary study of the South is a means of exploring humanity in all its aspects. The intellectual specialization of the modern world often makes this study difficult, but the editors of the *Encyclopedia* hope these volumes will promote that goal. Scholars exploring various aspects of the South's life now compose a distinct field of interdisciplinary Southern Studies, and the *Encyclopedia* joins those scholars in common effort to extend the present bounds of knowledge about the South.

The Editors
Center for the Study of Southern Culture
University of Mississippi

EDITORS' NOTE

The *Encyclopedia* is divided into four volumes and 24 major subject areas, arranged in alphabetical order. A table of contents listing articles in each section is found at the beginning of the section. An overview essay is followed by a series of alphabetically arranged thematic essays and then brief, alphabetically arranged topical-biographical entries. Readers are urged to consult the index, as well as the tables of contents, in locating articles.

When appropriate, articles contain cross-references to related articles in other sections. Material is cross-referenced only to similar-length or shorter material. Thematic articles, for example, are cross-referenced to thematic articles or to short topical articles in other sections but not to longer overview essays. Topical-biographical entries are cross-referenced to topical-biographical articles in other sections but not to

longer overview or thematic essays. Each cross-reference to related material lists the section in small capital letters, followed by the article title. If the entry is a short topical-biographical article, the title is preceded by a slash. The following example is a cross-reference to, first, a thematic article and, then, a topical-biographical entry, both in the Folklife section:

See also FOLKLIFE: Storytelling; / Clower, Jerry

Every effort was made to update material before publication. However, changes in contributors' affiliations, in biographical data because of the death of an individual, and in the names of institutions, for example, could not be made after the book went to press.

ETHNIC LIFE

GEORGE E. POZZETTA

University of Florida

CONSULTANT

☆ ☆ ☆ ☆ ☆ ☆ ☆ ☆ ☆ ☆

Overleaf: Tomochichi and his "nephew" Tooanahowi, from an untitled William Verelst portrait (1734)

ETHNIC LIFE

||||||||||||||||||||||||||||||||||||||||||||||||||

Although the South received far less foreign immigration than other sections of the nation, the region throughout its history has contained a heterogeneous population by world standards. Too much has been made of the cultural homogeneity of the South. Not only did the region share in migrations that linked America with the rest of the world, it also assisted in shaping national attitudes that defined the role and place of ethnic and cultural minorities in American life.

The existence of ethnic and cultural minorities in the South occasioned two different but interrelated sets of adaptations. On the one hand, groups possessing distinctive customs and lifestyles helped to shape the general regional culture. On the other hand, the region profoundly influenced the internal cultural adjustments that newly arrived groups underwent as they dealt with the wider society. The relative balance of this give-and-take dialectic has varied over time and space, depending on a variety of factors including transportation networks, topographical conditions, agricultural possibilities, particular cultural preferences, and outside historical events. Significant variations also depended on whether groups settled in urban or rural locations. Additionally, it must be borne in mind that the South has seldom, if ever, possessed a single cultural unity. The region typically has been composed of a cluster of subregions, each with a distinctive cultural style, so every generalization made about the South must be qualified by a recognition of these realities.

Formative Ethnic Patterns. The colonial South received its initial cultural imprint from the settlers who first populated its lands. The majority of these people came from the British Isles, principally Scotland, Wales, Cornwall, and Ireland. These simple geographic designations, however, masked substantial diversity. Ireland sent Catholic immigrants from the south and Presbyterian Scotch-Irish from the north; Scotland contributed quite distinct Highlanders and Lowlanders.

Almost 75 percent of the colonial South's population was composed of these "Celtic" elements. Even though they initially possessed diverse cultural and religious characteristics, a set of shared cultural values came to predominate with time. According to historians Grady McWhiney and Forrest McDonald, the resulting regional lifestyle was characterized by "a pastoral economy based upon open range herding," an avoidance of sustained hard labor, belief in the traditional values of rural hospitality, and acceptance of personal violence. Furthermore, 16th- and 17th-century folk styles characterized the music and much of the craft of these people. In music, for example, they contributed to the development of a distinctive sound that became part of America's musical heritage through the "country and western" tradition. Remnants of Celtic culture, then, survived

3

to influence the development of a southern culture.

Cultural adaptation of these settlers stemmed in part from early patterns of internal migration. As the 18th century advanced, the northern tier of the region received people from the Middle Atlantic zone (particularly from Pennsylvania and Maryland). Many of the Scotch-Irish settlers, for example, moved to the largely unpopulated middle and western portions of the Carolinas and Virginia in this manner. Wherever they settled, they farmed, fought Indians, and brought a rough "frontier culture" to the region. German settlers followed similar routes as they spilled down the Shenandoah Valley on the "Great Wagon Road." These newcomers generally engaged in more settled farming than their Celtic neighbors and exhibited a greater degree of cultural hegemony in their religions. Whether they were Mennonites, Moravians, Lutherans, or Reformed, church buildings quickly appeared. Their cultural and religious strength allowed such communities as Staunton, Bethania, Wachovia (Winston-Salem), and Salisbury to take root. These new towns often encouraged a further southward drift of population as the peopling of the region continued.

Port cities served some colonial settlers as entry points. Charleston, S.C., for example, set an early pattern that other coastal locations emulated. This bustling city not only served as a conduit for individuals bound inland but also attracted a heterogeneous population of its own. Charleston contained sizable numbers of black slaves and French Huguenots and smaller totals of Sephardic Jews, Germans, Spaniards, and Scotsmen. Such diversity set the pattern for similar developments later in Savannah, New Orleans, and Baltimore. In each

case, the result was a cultural blend uncommon in more rural inland locations.

Occasional instances of direct group settlement also occurred in the colonial South. The German Moravians of Georgia and North Carolina established rural colonies, which, though short-lived, allowed for the creation of a cultural unity not possible in either more diverse urban settlements or more scattered farming areas. Small clusters of Swiss (Mennonites), Dutch, Swedish, and Spanish settlers briefly dotted the region as well, but were generally of less importance than the Germans.

Throughout the colonial period, and indeed beyond, white southerners were forced to deal with racial minorities in a more long-term and socially significant fashion than citizens of other regions. The presence of large numbers of Indians and blacks was, of course, of fundamental importance for the development of the region. These groups profoundly influenced the nature of southern customs, political institutions, racial beliefs, and cultural practices. Indeed, it is difficult to conceive of the South—even the contemporary South—without reference to them.

White southerners encountered Indians from the very earliest period of settlement. Unlike the coastal tribes of the North, southern groups were well organized and populous. Hence, they resisted encroachment more fiercely and persisted longer as a cultural presence. As a result, a long, intense period of contact, lasting until well into the 19th century, led to the partial "Indianization" of the region. Certain crops— corn, tobacco, and some herbs—trace their origins to Indian cultivation. In addition, various pottery and basket-weaving styles transferred to white society, where they still survive in certain locations, as do many Indian folktales and wildlife stories. Many southern place names (Chickamauga, Chattanooga, Alachua, Chattahoochee, etc.) are Indian in origin, and American English is sprinkled with many other linguistic carryovers. The physical presence of Indians themselves in areas of the South, of course, lends diversity to the human condition of the region. Vestiges of tribal cultures (dances, costumes, and rituals) are rare but can still be found in places such as the Seminole tribal areas of southern Florida and the Lumbee sections of North Carolina. Finally, the amount of intermarriage that has occurred between Indians (and blacks) and southern whites can never be known exactly, but undoubtedly such marriages have been considerable.

As important as Indians were, the antebellum South increasingly focused its attentions on blacks and the problems of slavery. Considerations involving immigration and ethnic group development slipped below the level of immediate public concern. Two exceptions bear mention. In major port cities such as New Orleans, ethnicity continued to exert an influence. New Orleans had been a distinctive southern city because for a century or so after its founding Anglo-Saxons (British Americans) were an ethnic minority within a predominantly French-Spanish culture. Many different cultural traditions and population strains enriched New Orleans during its antebellum history (French, Acadian, Spanish, African, Irish, etc.). A distinctive "Creole" culture evolved and persisted with remarkable strength into the 20th century. The city's vigorous blend of cultural patterns can still be seen in its architectural styles, linguistic adaptations, musical forms, food

preferences, and religious observances. Even after the Civil War New Orleans continued to add to its population diversity. Sicilian laborers settled in substantial numbers, Jewish merchants peddled their wares, Chinese workmen operated small laundries, and Slavic immigrants staked out claims to the oyster industry. Each of these groups added new ingredients to the city's cultural mix.

Just as the South mirrored the nation in its ethnically diverse urban areas, so too did it participate in the periodic outbursts of nativism that swept America. Antiimmigrant sentiments intruded into the antebellum South, and on this level one finds the second exception to the region's seeming lack of public concern for ethnic issues. The most vivid political and social manifestation of this trend was the rise of the Know-Nothing party in the 1850s. Representing the culmination of two decades of growing anti-Catholic sentiment, the party appeared in various parts of the South. In

Grusset Saint Sauveur, Femme Acadienne (1800)

Louisiana and Maryland anti-Catholic campaigns succeeded, and the Know-Nothings captured political office and established nativist newspapers and organizations. Election confrontations with Irish immigrants in Memphis, Louisville, and Baltimore also served to heighten tensions. Indeed, for a brief period after 1856 the Know-Nothing party became something of a southern institution. In that year the party's presidential candidate, Millard Fillmore, received his greatest support from the region. Concerns centered on foreign immigration, however, were soon erased by the mounting sectional crisis.

Recruitment of Immigrants. The return of peace after 1865 resulted in the creation of new contexts for the entry of various groups into the South. A regionwide effort to replace newly freed slaves with white European immigrants generated substantial organizational and promotional activity, though few actual results. Immigration enthusiasts succeeded in establishing a few colonies, and occasional work gangs of Irish, Italian, and Slavic immigrants crisscrossed the region. Some settlement "spin-off" resulted, as in the case of the Chinese areas of Texas and Mississippi, the Polish communities of Texas, and the Italian and Slavic enclaves of Birmingham, Ala., but no enduring transformations of the southern work force took place.

Nevertheless, the immigration campaign did solidify attitudes that defined the place of foreigners in southern society and assisted in determining the positions former slaves would occupy. Paradoxically, the campaign itself and its meager success led many potential immigrants to regard the South as un-

desirable. Because southerners recruited immigrants to replace blacks, they often relegated them to the same social and economic status as the freedmen. Hence, immigrants occasionally suffered social discrimination, vigilante violence, and even peonage. White foreigners quickly learned that to remain in the region and gain acceptance they must adopt local attitudes toward race. Immigrant leaders soon advised individuals to avoid the South.

Rebirth of Nativism. Even as the recruitment campaign failed, an upsurge in national nativist sentiment swung white southerners decisively to the side of the antiimmigrant cause. For their part, blacks had recognized from the beginning the threat foreign immigrants posed to their future and opposed further movement. Thus, by about 1910 both major elements of southern society shared the same negative attitudes toward immigration, although they had arrived at their positions by different paths.

The rekindling of nativism after 1890 had again forced southerners to confront directly questions dealing with foreign immigration. The pseudoscientific racialism (eugenics) that characterized this outburst of nativist activity merged neatly with southern cultural views on superior and subordinate racial structures. Sporadic outbreaks of violence against foreigners in the South made headlines. Italians and Jews were the most common targets, with the 1891 lynching of 11 Italians in New Orleans easily constituting the most dramatic episode. The region also resonated to the mounting tide of religious nativism that gained momentum after 1910. Located in rural, small-town America generally (and the South most particularly), this nativism coincided with the rise of religious fundamentalism.

By the second decade of the century, southern spokesmen, in Congress and elsewhere, were among the most articulate nativist advocates. Populist leader Tom Watson spread a message of papal intrigue and Jewish depravity, at first in his own publications and later in the U.S. Senate. Wilbur Franklin Phelps's virulently anti-Catholic *The Menace* reached a million circulation by 1914. The rebirth of the Ku Klux Klan after 1915 gave a vigorous institutional base to these attitudes. The Klan shaped the region's political culture by endorsing nativist platforms in various local, state, and national elections, sometimes with successful results. Although the hooded empire declined by the late 1920s, many of the antiimmigrant viewpoints it sponsored remained (albeit without a significant institutional foundation and often buried beneath other concerns). Disruptions to the region's equilibrium, however, have often served to bring these nativist assumptions to the surface of public attention. Hence, southern culture continues to be responsive to the presence of ethnic and minority groups.

Migrant Workers and Immigrant Communities. By the 20th century certain portions of the South could already look back to long traditions of migrant labor involving foreigners. Louisiana's experiment with Sicilian sugar harvesters, for example, fostered the spread of Italian cultural patterns in the state. Parts of Texas, Louisiana, and Mississippi had employed the services of Mexican agricultural workers for decades with similar results. Transient gangs of harvesters, pickers, and general field hands followed well-defined routes across the

area, carrying with them a rough camp culture. Songs, tales, and poems emanating from this migrant life often endured for years, unwritten and passed from camp to camp by word of mouth. The transiency of the migrations, however, served to reduce their cultural impact on the region.

Southern Florida vibrated to different crosscurrents as migrants from the insular Caribbean probed the peninsula for economic opportunity. Farm workers and general laborers from Barbados, Jamaica, Trinidad, and Haiti made annual treks to engage in seasonal occupations, and they could regularly be found in dredging operations, canal building, railroad construction, and agricultural work. In some cases, handfuls of temporary workers remained behind and formed nuclei of settlement, which attracted permanent settlers later in the century.

Although the North has typically contained those areas of dense foreign settlement that so worried nativists, they were not completely absent from the South. Some urban locations attracted sufficient immigrants to create a "critical mass" of population, permitting different patterns of cultural adjustment. The case of New Orleans has already been mentioned, but it was not unique. In Tampa, Fla., for example, foreign population was concentrated enough to create a distinctive cultural unity. Cuban, Italian, and Spanish immigrants were able to erect complete institutional structures in their Tampa settlements, which included foreign language newspapers, mutual aid clubs, immigrant banks and stores, and churches. Such concentrations also nurtured the creation of elements of "high culture"— music, theater, reading and debating groups, literary clubs, etc.—which were typically not possible in more scattered locations. Finally, such large immigrant quarters allowed immigrant cultural expressions to spill over into the host society more easily and with greater permanence. This was particularly true of foods, linguistic adoptions, and musical styles. These patterns have continued to the present day and can be seen at work in the Cuban and Haitian sections of Miami, the Arabic quarters of Jacksonville, Fla., and in numerous Mexican *barrios* of Texas cities.

Although large-scale foreign settlement most commonly occurred along the coastal periphery of the region (especially since the 18th century), immigrants did not overlook interior locations entirely. Occasionally, an immigrant group existed in such settings in sufficient numbers to create a unique cultural landscape. The German sections of south-central Texas are a case in point. Arriving both before and after the Civil War, German immigrants moved vigorously into farming activities, often buying previously tilled lands. Because they were numerous and maintained their cultural bonds, they were able to exert an uncommon influence on the region. In terms of architectural styles, farming techniques, familial patterns, religious practices, and voting preferences, these locations still testify to the enduring impact of German settlers.

Various Gypsy groups have claimed the roads and fields of the South as their territories. Though relatively little is known about them, there appear to be four major groups—Continental European, English, and Scottish Gypsies, and the Irish Travelers (each with subgroups). The Travelers exhibited a typical pattern of development. Arriv-

ing sometime in the 1850s from Ireland, where they had engaged in a number of itinerant occupations, Travelers moved south and specialized in horse and mule trading. Although they follow different trades today, they continue many old cultural practices, including a migratory lifestyle, seasonal occupational preferences, special language forms, and strong endogamous marriage patterns.

Similarly, a number of racial islands or "isolates" have added to the cultural diversity of the South. Often bearing pejorative local names such as Red Bones, Brass Ankles, or "Cajans" (as used in south Alabama), what most often characterizes these groups are allegations of racial crossovers (white with black or Indian or both) in their historical pasts. Ostracized by the dominant white society and occasionally by black society as well, these self-conscious groups have occupied a very marginal position in society. As a result they have developed distinctive cultural patterns, usually featuring a high degree of "clannishness," suspicion, and distrust toward outsiders. In these last characteristics they resemble the mountain people or "hillbillies" of Appalachia and the Ozarks.

Different dynamics explain the origins of ethnic pockets that were created by "target migrants," those who sought out a specific locale. Usually appearing along the coastal areas of the region, these settlements most often owed their beginnings to economic factors. The Greek community in Tarpon Springs, Fla., is an example. Begun in 1905, when an enterprising Greek sponge merchant discovered unusually rich areas of deep-water sponges, the settlement quickly attracted hundreds of experienced Greek divers and their families. Immigrants quickly outnumbered natives and soon thereafter a Greek Orthodox church appeared, along with Greek restaurants, groceries, clubs, and retail businesses. The cultural ambience of Tarpon Springs, with its Greek foods and colorful religious festivals, continues to attract visitors who find the old world style appealing. Smaller clusters of Portuguese, Filipinos, Dalmatian Yugoslavs, and, more recently, Vietnamese followed roughly similar patterns of settlement, adaptation, and cultural persistence in the South.

The passage of national restriction laws in the 1920s and the economic grip of the Great Depression drastically reduced the inflow of European immigrants and migrants from Mexico and the Caribbean. The movement of Mexicans into the South, however, revived after World War II and soon came to outstrip earlier totals. As a result, a vigorous Chicano culture evolved in the region. Though concentrated in Texas, Chicanos spread throughout the South, bringing with them distinctive styles of music, food preparation, and family practices. More recently, Chicanos have developed a political culture that has perhaps best been symbolized in the charismatic figures of union leader Cesar Chavez and San Antonio mayor Henry Cisneros.

Contemporary Patterns. Although the South failed to share heavily in the immediate post–World War II movement of displaced persons and refugees, the region has come to play an important role in immigration. Indeed, by the 1970s the South had become one of the principal immigrant receiving areas of the nation. Vietnamese exiles, Mexican migrant laborers, Cuban "boatlifters," Haitian refugees, and other Latin Amer-

ican immigrants have gravitated to the South in unusually heavy numbers, at times overtaxing the abilities of local areas to accommodate them. Accordingly, some areas of the region have shown renewed manifestations of antiimmigrant sentiment, much of it apparently economic in motivation.

At the same time, the South has received a large and still growing influx of second- and third-generation ethnics from northern locations seeking jobs or retirement homes. Coupled with the increased Asian and Latin American presence, this movement has redrawn the cultural map of many areas, especially the cities. Miami, Fla., for example, with its large Cuban sections, bordered by Haitian, Jamaican, and Afro-American quarters (which include thousands of other Central and South American peoples), and its populations of Jewish, Italian, and Slavic transplants from the North, resembles New York City of a century ago. In the future, therefore, ethnic and cultural minorities will play a greater rather than a lesser role in molding the cultural fabric of the region.

See also ART AND ARCHITECTURE: French Architecture; German Architecture; BLACK LIFE: African Influences; Appalachians, Black; Creolization; Immigrants and Blacks; Indians and Blacks; FOLKLIFE: / "Hillbilly" Image; GEOGRAPHY: Ethnic Geography; Indians and the Landscape; Ozarks; / Cherokee Settlement; Cuban Settlement; INDUSTRY: Industrialization in Appalachia; LANGUAGE: French Language; German Language; Indian Language; Mountain Language; Spanish Language / Conch; Indian Trade Languages; LITERATURE: Appalachian Literature; MUSIC: *Música Tejana*; / Balfa, Dewey; Jimenez, Flaco; MYTHIC SOUTH: Appalachian Culture; RELIGION: Appalachian Religion; Ethnic Protestantism; Jewish Religious Life; SOCIAL CLASS:

Appalachia, Exploitation of; WOMEN'S
LIFE: Appalachian Women; Indian Women;
Mexican Women

George E. Pozzetta
University of Florida

Lucy M. Cohen, *Chinese in the Post–Civil
War South* (1984); John Cooke and Mackie
Blanton, *Publications of the Committee on
Ethnicity in New Orleans*, 4 vols. (1978–);
Leonard Dinnerstein and Mary Dale Palson,
eds., *Jews in the South* (1969); Eli Evans,
*The Provincials: A Personal History of Jews
in the South* (1973); Russell L. Gerlach, *Im-
migrants in the Ozarks: A Study in Ethnic
Geography* (1976); James Haskins, *The Cre-
oles of Color in New Orleans* (1968); Charles
Hudson, *The Southeastern Indians* (1976);
Rosan A. Jordan, George F. Reinecke, Jo-
seph V. Guillotte III, and H. F. Gregory, in
Louisiana Folklife: A Guide to the State, ed.
Nicholas R. Spitzer (1985); Terry G. Jordan,
*German Seed in Texas Soil: Immigrant
Farmers in Nineteenth-Century Texas* (1966);
Lewis M. Killian, *White Southerners* (1970);
James G. Leyburn, *The Scotch-Irish: A So-
cial History* (1962); John Shelton Reed, *One
South: An Ethnic Approach to Regional Cul-
ture* (1982); *Southern Exposure* (November–
December 1985); Arnold Shankman, *Am-
bivalent Friends: Afro-Americans View the
Immigrant* (1982); Henry D. Shapiro, *Ap-
palachia on Our Mind: The Southern Moun-
tains and Mountaineers in the American
Consciousness, 1870–1920* (1978); Nicholas
R. Spitzer, *Southern Exposure* (Summer–
Fall 1977); Stephen Thernstrom, Ann Orlov,
and Oscar Handlin, eds., *Harvard Encyclopedia of American Ethnic Groups* (1980);
George B. Tindall, *The Ethnic Southerners*
(1976); David E. Whisnant, *All That Is Native and Fine: The Politics of Culture in an
American Region* (1983); Walter L. Williams, ed., *Southeastern Indians since the
Removal Era* (1979); J. Leitch Wright, Jr.,
*The Only Land They Knew: The Tragic Story
of the American Indians in the Old South*
(1981); Klaus Wust, *The Virginia Germans*
(1969). ☆

Caribbean Influence

The culture of the southern coast, especially the Gulf Coast from Texas to
Louisiana and down to south Florida,
owes much to the African-Latin culture
of the Caribbean. The Caribbean cultural area that has influenced the southern United States covers three island
chains. The Bahamas includes about
3,000 mostly unoccupied islands stretching within 50 miles of the Florida coast
and then southeast 760 miles to the Dominican Republic. The Greater Antilles
includes Cuba, Puerto Rico, Hispanola
(with Haiti on the western part of the
island and the Dominican Republic toward the east), and Jamaica, a commonwealth nation in the United Kingdom.
The Lesser Antilles lies to the east of
Puerto Rico and includes the Virgin
Islands, Leeward Islands, and Windward Islands; this archipelago ends
northwest of Caracas, Venezuela, at the
Netherlands Antilles. The Caribbean
cultural zone also includes Costa Rica,
Nicaragua, El Salvador, Belize, Guate-
mala, Panama, and Honduras—all of
which touch the Caribbean and are
united to the islands by ethnic composition, language, religious institutions,
political instabilities, broad historical
experiences, and economic problems.

Southern United States ties to this
area have been historical, economic,
ethnic, diplomatic, and military. The
Gulf coastal areas of the American
South and the islands share a semitropical physical environment and a history
of colonial development. The North
American Gulf Coast was first explored
and settled by France and Spain as an
offshoot of their exploration of the islands. Louisiana had sugar plantations

resembling those on Santo Domingo (Hispaniola). Companies shipped bananas, coffee, and other products to the docks of New Orleans in the late 19th century, and today close economic ties remain as oil from refineries in Puerto Rico, bauxite from Jamaica, cocoa produced in the Dominican Republic, and illegal drugs from Colombia enter the United States through ports.

The Louisiana Gulf Coast was among the first areas of the South to experience Caribbean cultural influences. The *Islenos*—Spanish Canary Islanders—came to Louisiana from Cuba in 1777, introducing a long Spanish presence. They still fish and trap in Saint Bernard Parish, eat their distinctive foods such as *caldo*, and sing Spanish ballads. The Louisiana Purchase in 1803 led to the arrival of increased numbers of Americans, mostly from the Southeast, in Louisiana, but their influence on the area was diluted as a result of another population migration. Ten thousand French planters, their slaves, and free people of color fled Santo Domingo during and after the revolution that began with an uprising in 1791 and led to the establishment of a black republic, which was launched 1 January 1804 in what is now the nation of Haiti. This migration introduced many of the central cultural customs and institutions of southern Louisiana. Voodoo, gumbo, jambalaya, zydeco music, street dancing to Afro-Latin rhythms, shotgun houses, Creole cottages, the prevalence of festivals, and a Creole language (a language of French words within a system of African-derived grammar and pronunciation) have all been traced back to these early refugees.

The Louisiana Gulf Coast thus developed its abiding diversity of ethnic and cultural life partly because of the Caribbean influence. The Caribbean also played a part in the creation of a distinctive black southern folk culture. As far back as the 1700s blacks in the Low Country of Georgia and South Carolina, especially on the Sea Islands, created distinctive patterns that were African in background but that also reflected island ways. Scholars have shown Caribbean influences on southern basket styles, pottery, and music and dance. Zora Neale Hurston, who was from Florida, set out to study black folk culture in the 1930s, and her research led her first to the American South, then to Louisiana specifically (*Mules and Men*, 1935), and then to the Caribbean, where her fieldwork in Jamaica and Haiti resulted in *Tell My Horse* (1938).

The event that best symbolized the Caribbean's image for 19th-century southern blacks and whites was the Haitian Revolution that began in the late 18th century. The island had long been an important trading partner for the young American Republic, and some Americans, especially antislavery advocates, praised this uprising when it began in the early 1790s. But Americans, and southern whites particularly, became fearful as the rebellion against the French became increasingly bloody. It nurtured growing racial fears of southern slaveowners during the Jeffersonian era and was cited for decades afterwards as a terrible vision of a bloody postemancipation world in the South. Americans welcomed refugees from the island, but this was accompanied by a growing uneasiness among Virginians and South Carolinians. Charleston residents complained that the slaves brought by refugees from the island were insolent and potential carriers of rebellion. An era of increased slave unrest did occur after news arrived of the racial conflicts on the island, the most serious case being Gabriel Prosser's rebellion in the summer of 1800 in Richmond.

In the two decades before the Civil War some southern slaveowners looked upon the Caribbean as the potential locale for expansion. Stephen Vincent Benét called it the "purple dream" of a Caribbean empire. Americans of the time who considered the area were generally disturbed by the poverty, disease, political instability, and miscegenation they saw, but white Christian slaveowners—assuming the "white man's burden"—saw it as a challenge to bring "civilization" to the downtrodden while expanding slavery's influence within the United States. Cuba was to be the key to a tropical empire, based on either outright annexation of the Caribbean Islands or the creation of colonies managed by southern whites. This was regarded as progress for the unfortunate people of the islands and for the civilized world, which would then have plentiful and stable supplies of sugar, coffee, fruits, and rice. The United States government never supported the southern imperial idea. Charismatic Mississippian John Quitman advocated private military adventures in the area, but cautious moderate southern leaders disapproved. Filibusterer William Walker did gain control of Nicaragua in the mid-1850s, briefly introducing slavery there before his "reign" ended at the firing squad.

In the contemporary South the Caribbean cultural influence is seen most dramatically in Florida. The development of Florida dates back to the turn of the century. Henry M. Flagler had a vision of the state as a sunny playground for the leisured class, and his Florida East Coast Railroad promoted tourism and ties with the Caribbean Islands.

Palm Beach grew around a resort hotel, the Breakers, and Flagler extended his railroad farther south to Miami and then in 1913 (at a cost of 700 dead workers on construction crews) to Key West. The importance of the Caribbean even at this early date was apparent when Flagler proposed building a railroad bridge to the Cuban capital, Havana.

The military played an important role in tying this southern subregion to the Caribbean. It was a point of departure for U.S. Army troops going to Cuba in the Spanish-American War in 1898, for Marines occupying Haiti in 1915, for airplanes taking part in the 1961 Bay of Pigs invasion of Cuba, and for American troops invading the Dominican Republic in 1967. The U.S. Navy has long sent its ships and personnel between Florida ports and the islands.

Up to the 1960s the development of southern Florida was culturally an Anglo vision of the good life in a semitropical world. Aristocratic yachtsmen, retired middle-class elderly from northern and midwestern cities, blacks and poor whites from the adjacent Deep South, violent mobsters, and well-off Jews from New York City dominated the culture. Jackie Gleason's television shows of the early 1960s were taped at Miami Beach, opening with shots of the city skyline while the announcer proclaimed the beach "the sun and fun capital of the world." Miami was throughout the 20th century the stepping-stone to the Caribbean, but before the 1960s it clearly faced north, its development based on luring business and people south.

The post-1960 South in general has undergone dramatic and wrenching change, but south Florida has experienced a particularly traumatic change involving a geographical redirection in outlook. Its culture and business now face south. Jaime Raldos, for example, the former president of Ecuador, once called Miami "the capital of Latin America." The watershed event in this new Caribbean connection was the 1959 Fidel Castro revolution in Cuba. There had been earlier waves of Cuban immigration to Florida, particularly to Tampa, but the events of 1959 sent a distinctive group of generally well-educated, skilled, politically conservative, upper- and middle-class exiles to Florida. Some were obsessed with returning to their island homeland and became involved in a life of intrigue and conspiracy that began to cast dark shadows on the area's sunny image. Watergate burglars were Cubans from Florida. When despotic heads of state in Central America or the Caribbean were toppled, many headed for Miami. That city's banks have come to hold many fortunes of the wealthy to the south. Gun dealers are a prominent part of the Miami landscape (Gun City, Inc., is typical) and are suppliers to the Caribbean. Joel Garreau has surveyed south Florida's business life and characterizes the importation of illegal drugs as its number-one industry, with Colombia in particular sending marijuana, cocaine, and methaqualone. Violence from the "cocaine cowboys"—an affectionate name for Colombian drug dealers—periodically erupts on Miami streets. The new television image of south Florida is the violent, flashy *Miami Vice*.

The Caribbean connection has given Florida cities a new cultural vitality and diversity, but with an increasingly dominant Hispanic style. More than 40 percent of Dade County's population is Hispanic, and Miami has become a Spanish-speaking city. Its Little Havana, Calle Ocho Street, and festival

Carnaval Miami each March are new symbols of Latin influence, as was Xavier Suarez's election in November 1985 as the first Miami mayor from its Cuban community.

The contemporary Caribbean influence on south Florida includes, however, more than its Cuban population. The first boatload of black boat people from Haiti arrived on American shores at Pompano Beach, Fla., 12 December 1972, and the island has sent over 50,000 refugees to those shores since then. These refugees are a national problem, but south Florida and other areas of the American South have experienced a particularly acute crisis with their arrival. These have been generally poor, desperate people, and their arrival has strained Florida's ability to deliver health care and social services. Many of them now work as low-paid migrant workers along the Atlantic Coast from Florida to Virginia. Their neighborhoods in Miami and elsewhere represent a different cultural landscape from native blacks and whites, or the Cubans from the last two decades. Voodoo, French-influenced Catholic rituals and images, foodways, and other aspects of Haiti's culture have again, as after the Santo Domingo revolution, become a part of a subregion of the South. The same racial fears directed against black-skinned people are also heard today as in that earlier period in the South.

Charles Reagan Wilson
University of Mississippi

William L. Barney, *The Road to Secession: A New Perspective on the Old South* (1972); Joel Garreau, *The Nine Nations of North America* (1981); Bob Hall and Jim Clark, *Southern Exposure* (May–June 1982); Winthrop D. Jordan, *White over Black: American Attitudes toward the Negro, 1550–1812* (1968); Lester D. Langles, *The Banana Wars: An Inner History of American Empire, 1900–1934* (1983), *The United States and the Caribbean, 1900–1970* (1980); Nicholas R. Spitzer, *Southern Exposure* (May–June 1982). ☆

Indian Cultural Contributions

||||||||||||||||||||||||||||||||||||||||||

Indians seem to have affected southern culture little, but in fact the Native American legacy to the South is extensive. Narratives of 16th-century Spanish conquistadors describe populous Indian towns, powerful regional chiefdoms, copper ornaments and weapons, wooden carvings, hieroglyphics, picture writing, and large truncated temple mounds. Much of this was associated with the southeastern ceremonial complex, which was also known variously as the eagle, hawk, buzzard, or southern cult. It was part of the Mississippian cultural tradition. Flourishing in the centuries before Columbus's voyage, in what became the Cotton Kingdom in the early 19th century, Mississippian culture represented one of the most highly developed civilizations north of Mexico. This was the era of the mound builders, who constructed temple mounds up to 100 feet tall, with religious and political structures on their flat tops. Frequently there was not just a single isolated temple mound but several spread over acres in planned clusters. The organized labor necessary to construct these mounds implies a structured political organization. Coastal Indians, such as the Algonkians

in Virginia and the Calusa in Florida, whom Ponce de León, Menéndez de Avilés, Sir Walter Raleigh's colonists at Roanoke, and John Smith encountered, were on the periphery of the maize-growing Mississippian heartland and the high culture there.

Much of this culture and many of the Indians themselves were destroyed before Englishmen ever made a permanent settlement at Jamestown in 1607. New diseases introduced by Europeans and Africans were the culprits. Pandemics wiped out entire tribes and linguistic families. Warfare and enslavement of Indians also took their toll. For several centuries between Ponce de León's 16th-century voyages and the early 19th-century removal of the southern Indians beyond the Mississippi River, the South was inhabited by three cultures—Indian, African, and European. These three peoples interacted with one another, modifying each other's culture. Despite prodigious population losses, during much of the period before western relocation the Indians were relatively numerous, and they had a considerable impact on whites and blacks.

Perhaps the most significant Indian contribution to the South—and the world—was in agriculture. Journeying through the South in George Washington's time, a traveler could notice fields of tobacco and corn, with pole beans climbing the stalks of the latter; these had long been familiar sights to the Indians. Plows might have turned the soil on large plantations, but plain white farmers often raised crops without a plow's benefit, using Indian methods. The Native American influence easily can be appreciated when considering maize (Indian corn). It is no accident that grits, hominy, hoecake, and corn bread are southern dishes typically consumed in areas where Mississippians formerly lived. Sweet potatoes, squash, beans, and many other favorite items of the southern diet are Indian in origin. James B. Duke's 19th-century cigarette machines laid the basis for a major southern industry, but Indians had cultivated tobacco long before that. Tea, to take another example, was the most common nonalcoholic southern drink until the 19th century, and not all of it was imported from the Far East. Made from the southern holly (*ilex vomitoria*), yaupon tea was extensively consumed. Though eventually overshadowed by coffee and colas, the Indians' yaupon tea enjoyed a revival among southerners during periods of economic distress throughout the 19th century. This tea was the Mississippians' "black drink," their standard beverage in rituals and social gatherings. Europeans and Africans manifested keen interest in native medicines and cures, and a considerable portion of folk medicine in the South appears to be of aboriginal origin.

Indians made other major contributions to the material culture of the South. Recent archaeological discoveries permit a closer look at modifications in early white material culture, particularly its pottery. After European contact, Native Americans continued to produce large amounts of pottery in the usual fashion—coiled and handworked, shell-tempered, and stick- or pebble-burnished. This or similar pottery has come to be known as colono-Indian ware. Large amounts have been unearthed at sites throughout the South. Planters, wealthy merchants, and the governing elite dined and entertained on delft, majolica, and other imported china, but the middle and lower classes, including slaves, regularly used colono-Indian pottery. Mention should also be made of clay tobacco pipes. When George Washington and his circle called for their pipes, they were long-stemmed clay ones, modeled after those used by the Powhatans. Aboriginal baskets and mats appeared in colonial households, and are still prized by modern southerners. Colonists appropriated part of the Indians' dress as frontier clothing,

Alfred Boisseau, **Louisiana Indians Walking along a Bayou** *(1847)*

used the dugout canoe for transportation, and even lived at times in Indian-style houses. Some scholars attribute a popular 20th-century, good-health institution—the sauna—to the hot houses and sweat houses of Mississippian times.

Indians also contributed to the oral lore of the South. They put such euphonious names as Rappahannock, Altamaha, Talladega, and Mississippi on the landscape. Settlers borrowed aboriginal words to describe unfamiliar objects. Early Jamestown residents borrowed from the Powhatans, for example, words such as moccasin, matchcoat, terrapin, opossum, raccoon, chinquapin, chum, hominy, pone, and tomahawk. Southern folklore has been enriched by the stories of Pocahontas's rescue of John Smith, Sequoyah's invention of a syllabary, William Weatherford (Red Eagle) and Andrew Jackson in combat during the 1813 Creek War, and the Cherokees on the Trail of Tears.

From the early colonial period onward the southern Indians interacted with black slaves. With mounting recent interest in the African heritage and pan-Indianism, scholars have shown little concern for the effects the two groups, living side by side in the South for centuries, had on one another. The evidence is overwhelming, though, that over the centuries Africans and Indians did not remain separate but for a long time associated and intermingled, in various ways influencing each other's development. Southern Indians were enslaved, especially in the 17th and 18th centuries, with males sometimes shipped to the West Indies and women and children left behind. In contrast, African slaves imported into the South in this early period had a higher ratio of males, and they often took Indian slave wives. Miscegenation led to the

Native Americans' genetic contributions to the appearance of the new Afro-American in North America. There were other cultural ties. Though okra was an exception, much of modern soul food is Indian. Black English may owe a debt to remnants of Mississippian language. Assuredly this was true regarding black folktales: Mississippians had their own version of Brer Rabbit long before Africans arrived in the South.

The Indian influence has also survived among whites. Despite statements to the contrary early in southern history, extensive Indian-white miscegenation and intermarriage occurred. One can now find a governor of Virginia and a president of the United States proudly proclaiming descent from Pocahontas. Some Indians in the Old South were planters who modeled themselves on the white gentry. Some of Red Eagle's children, for example, were wealthy Alabama cotton planters who, like other southern Indians, lost their slaves and much more during the Civil War. Stand Watie led a brigade of Cherokee followers in the Confederate cause, participating in battles in the Indian Territory and at Pea Ridge in Arkansas. Watie became a brigadier general for the Lost Cause. As discussed earlier, southern material culture and oral lore, like southern history in general, would not have been distinctive without Native American influences.

In one fashion or another many people identifying themselves as Indian remained in the South after the removal of the major tribes to the Indian Territory in the 1830s. In recent times their presence has become more obvious. Cherokees, Choctaws, Seminoles, and Miccosukees have preserved their language and some aspects of their culture. Others, such as the Lumbees in North Carolina and the Creeks in the Florida

Panhandle and southern Alabama, have lost all knowledge of their native tongues. The number of southerners who call themselves Indians seems, nonetheless, to be increasing, and in a variety of ways they are asserting their Indian identity. Moreover, consciously or not, southern whites and blacks perpetuate ancient Mississippian customs as they eat grits, smoke tobacco, read about Brer Rabbit, and possibly even sit in a sauna. One cannot escape the Indian legacy, which is far greater than suggested by the lonely temple mounds still dotting the South.

See also ENVIRONMENT: Plant Uses; FOLK-LIFE: Basketmaking; Folk Medicine; / Brer Rabbit; Okra; HISTORY AND MANNERS: / Jamestown; Soul Food; Trail of Tears

J. Leitch Wright, Jr.
Florida State University

Maxine Alexander, ed., *Southern Exposure* (November 1985); Gary C. Goodwin, *Cherokees in Transition: A Study of a Changing Culture and Environment Prior to 1775* (1977); G. Melvin Herndon, *North Carolina Historical Review* (Summer 1967); Charles Hudson, *The Southeastern Indians* (1976); Winthrop D. Jordan, *White Over Black: American Attitudes toward the Negro, 1550–1812* (1968); J. Anthony Paredes, in *Social and Cultural Identity: Problems of Persistence and Change*, ed. Thomas Fitzgerald (1974); John R. Swanton, Bureau of American Ethnology, *42d Annual Report* (1928), *The Indians of the Southeastern United States* (1946). ☆

Indians before 1700

||||||||||||||||||||||||||||||||||||||||||||||||

The first humans to inhabit the South were Paleo-Indians, who had spread over North America well before 10,000 B.C. Most archaeologists agree that the ancestors of these people migrated from Asia to America by way of a connecting land bridge between Siberia and Alaska between 10,000 and 30,000 years ago. During the Pleistocene "Ice Ages," when the climate was much colder, these wandering bands of big-game hunters traveled lightly with few possessions besides their basics for survival: fire-making tools, bone- or stone-tipped spears, and domesticated hunting dogs. They lived in extended family kin groups of about 20 to 40 people.

About 8000 B.C. a warming of the climate caused the extinction of many of the large mammals upon which the Paleo-Indians depended. As new environments began to form, the people living in them adapted in response to local conditions. The peoples of eastern North America, from the Great Lakes to Florida, evolved the Archaic culture, relying heavily on fishing, small-game hunting, and collecting shellfish and wild plants. They did not move often, and the Archaic Indians produced more material goods than their ancestors. About 2000 B.C. people of the coastal Georgia area independently invented pottery, which allowed for year-round storage of food. Pottery and other inventions led to the transformation of plant collecting into agriculture.

The Woodland period emerged in the Ohio River Valley about 1000 B.C. A new way of life began for most southeastern Native Americans and it lasted into the 19th century. Woodland Indians had a mixed economy of agriculture (corn, beans, squash, pumpkins, sunflower seeds, and other foods) and forest use (hunting, fishing, wild plants). Men hunted and women did the farming. Probably because their economic role was so important, women had high status, with kinship relations organized around extended-family matrilineages. Increased population and leisure time led men to develop craft specializations and religious ceremonies. The Woodland peoples paid particular attention to funeral rites, burying their dead in large earthen burial mounds. Bodies were carefully dressed and provided with food and tools to take with them into the afterlife. Objects of artistic and religious value were traded over an extensive territory, ranging from Florida to the Rocky Mountains and Great Lakes regions.

The next cultural explosion occurred in the lower Mississippi River Valley after about A.D. 700. This Mississippian period saw a further evolution of Woodland forms as well as a strong cultural influence from the Indians of Mexico. Through contact along the Gulf of Mexico, elements of the great civilizations of Meso-America reached the South. In fertile farmlands of large river valleys, the Mississippians developed towns around ceremonial centers consisting of huge mounds. Unlike the earlier Woodland burial mounds, these earth structures were built as high platforms for religious temples. Major temple mounds survive today, most notably at Etowah and Ocmulgee, Ga.; Moundville, Ala.; Emerald Mound, Miss.; and Spiro, Okla.

The various Mississippian city-states developed a high standard of living based upon intensive agriculture. Prosperity allowed the rise of an artistic class, as well as a high class of religious leaders. The growth of population meant that competition for the best valley farmlands increased to the point that organized warfare arose among the independent towns. Moats and palisades were built around the towns, and people lived in rectangular wood and plastered houses either inside or near the defenses. Mississippian tribes were stratified societies comparable to European city-states.

Mississippian culture, unique to the South, reached its height between A.D. 1200 and 1600, but several Indian states maintained this way of life into the early European era. French explorers wrote detailed descriptions of the Natchez Indians of Mississippi and Louisiana, who probably best exemplified the culture.

During the 1500s and 1600s the complex Mississippian societies declined drastically, due mainly to tremendous population decreases brought about by the introduction of Old World diseases. Europeans brought numerous foreign germs with them, left over from the plagues that earlier ravaged the Old World, and Indians had no immunity to them. Epidemics of smallpox, diphtheria, scarlet fever, measles, yellow fever, malaria, and other diseases rapidly killed from 50 to 90 percent of Native Americans. The successive waves of diseases, begun with the earliest explorers, helped destroy Mississippian culture.

As the large Mississippian towns declined, Indians living on the fringes reverted to Woodland ways of life. Native society now focused more on language-related ethnic or national groupings. The four main cultural subdivisions were: (1) Algonkians, probably the original settlers of the South, scattered down the Atlantic Coast from Canada to North Carolina; (2) Muskogeans, spread over a huge area of the central South from the Gulf Coast to Kentucky; (3) Iroquoians, who had migrated into the southern Appalachians and the Carolinas sometime between 100 B.C. and A.D. 1000; and (4) Siouans, scattered in pockets through different areas. Little is known about other language and cultural groupings, because they became extinct so early in the colonial era.

Depopulation produced a crisis among southern Indians that provoked a revolution in ethnic identity during the colonial era. As small bands were decimated, survivors joined a nearby larger group to form a new "tribe." The larger groups were suffering their own population losses and thus welcomed additions. Where there was no predominant tribe, individuals from numerous bands tended to coalesce into small multitribal communities. These diverse groups sometimes adopted a European trade language as their only mutually understandable language and gradually absorbed more European and African culture, through contact with individual whites and escaping black slaves. This process accounts for the rise of numerous new "tri-racial isolates" in various areas of the South by the 18th century and also helps explain the fluidity of ethnic identity in the changing Indian "tribes."

Walter L. Williams
University of Cincinnati

Charles Hudson, *The Southeastern Indians* (1976); Wilbur R. Jacobs, *William and Mary Quarterly* (January 1974); Jesse Jennings, *Prehistory of North America* (1974); Wendell Oswalt, *This Land Was Theirs: A Study of the North American Indian* (1973). ✩

Indians, 1700–1840
||||||||||||||||||||||||||||||||||||||||||||||||||

European contact with American Indians in the South over two centuries dramatically changed native societies. The first, most critical revolution in Indian life was due to disease. Though massive depopulation occurred in the 1500s and 1600s, severe epidemics continued to decimate Indian societies through the 18th century. Small tribes of the coastal areas were often completely wiped out by disease, warfare, and enslavement.

The larger native nations of the interior were protected from this onslaught by their greater population and their distance from white settlements. In fact, they began to prosper from European contact in terms of trading furs (especially deer) for manufactured goods (metal tools, firearms, cloth, alcohol). The Cherokees, Creeks, and Choctaws in particular drew on the resources of their own large territories and served as middlemen in the trade with Indians farther west. Because they were able to play off rival traders from the English coastal colonies, Spanish Florida, and French Louisiana, the interior southeastern Indians occupied an important economic and diplomatic position.

While the fur trade was revolutionizing Indian material culture and making hunting more important to native economics, warfare also became more important. Many coastal groups had earlier escaped white expansion by migrating west to join the interior nations or by leaving the area entirely (Tuscaroras to Pennsylvania and New York, Shawnees to Ohio, Yamassees and others to Florida). As various groups were pushed west, they clashed with previous native occupants. This, combined with competition over hunting territory and raiding for captives to sell to the English as slaves, vastly increased intertribal warfare in the colonial era. Europeans encouraged the use of native peoples to

General Dance of the Natchez Indians, *from* Le Page Du Pratz, **Histoire de La Louisiane** *(1785)*

do their fighting for them, a tactic that reduced Indian population further. The Indian nations had become so dependent on European trade that they could not avoid involvement in European national rivalries in the Second Hundred Years' War. Yet they skillfully used their position in a complicated balance-of-power diplomacy.

Changes in the mid-18th century undermined these successful native adaptations based on trade and military alliances with the Europeans. First, as game declined, Indians had a diminishing product to trade for the European goods on which they had grown dependent. Second, by the Treaty of 1763 the French were forced to surrender their North American empire and Spain gave up Florida to the English. Indians

no longer had the opportunity to exploit European rivalries. After the British evacuated the South in 1781, and other Europeans abandoned their claims to the new United States, Indians were left in a precarious situation. Their last attempt to use white rivalries was during the War of 1812, but the British abandonment of native interests left them without allies. Though the new national government was weak and was forced to recognize Indian sovereignty in treaties, the white population was bent on expansion over native lands.

Despite their weakened economic and political situation, the interior Indian nations had managed to avoid cultural disintegration. Much of their 18th-century daily life continued to reflect aboriginal patterns. Communal agriculture, carried on by women, was still the basis of their food supply. Though stone tools and pottery were largely replaced by manufactured goods, and politically independent towns were unified under national governments, the basic cultural elements—language, matrilineal kinship, social patterns, and religions—remained primarily indigenous.

During the early 19th century even these cultural elements came under attack, primarily from missionaries, government agents, and "mixed bloods." Economic and political decline meant that some Indians were in a mood to listen when missionaries told them to save themselves from further decline due to "God's displeasure for following pagan lifestyles." Those Indians who already had white relatives, through intermarriage with frontier traders, were particularly susceptible to missionary propaganda. These "mixed bloods" (who were completely accepted as Indian because of matrilineal descent) were expected to deal effectively with whites, because of their familiarity with white ways. A new class of acculturated Indians, led by "mixed bloods" and mission converts, began adopting Western culture as part of a new peace policy of accommodation designed to gain American respect. By proving to whites that they had become "civilized," they hoped they would suffer no more land losses and could coexist in peace.

By the 1820s the Cherokees, Chickasaws, Choctaws, and Creeks were becoming known as the Civilized Tribes. They adopted Christianity, set up schools, and elected national governments at least outwardly modeled on the United States. Prosperous "mixed bloods" practiced cash-crop agriculture based on black slave labor. Slavery was seen as an indication that the Indians were "civilized." Much of the incentive for setting up centralized governments, other than the need to deal in a unified manner with the United States, was to enact laws enforcing slavery.

As the traditional communal-agricultural towns disintegrated and more Indians owned their own private family farms, they turned to the national councils rather than the old town councils. Society became disjointed and in flux. Missionaries led their converts not only to reject traditional ceremonials in favor of Christianity, but also to take English patriarchal family names, to use the English language, and to adopt white styles of clothing and housing. Even more importantly, European ideas of private property, inheritance, and wealth destroyed the old classless homogeneity. Classes of rich and poor emerged. Naturally, traditionalists—probably the majority—felt uncomfortable about this new departure, and each nation became factionalized. They all wanted to hold on to their remaining lands but were divided by repeated U.S. government pressures for land cessions.

Though the Supreme Court ruled in *Cherokee Nation* v. *Georgia* (1831) that the Indians were outside the control of state jurisdiction, Georgia and other states pressed for expansion over Indian lands. President Andrew Jackson pushed hard for Indian removal to the West. One group after another of eastern Indians was forced to sign removal treaties, exchanging their homelands for the promise of permanent self-government and possession of new lands in Indian Territory (Oklahoma). In vain the Indians pleaded for the United States to enforce its earlier treaty promises and Supreme Court decisions, but removal acts continued to be passed under Presidents Jackson and Van Buren. The removal of the Civilized Tribes proved that fears of "hostile savages" were not as important as white land hunger. In several of the removals, Indians were marched on winter "trails of tears," in which thousands died.

The last Indian holdouts in the South were the Seminoles. A group formed in the late 1700s from Creek, Yamassee, and other tribes who had fled to Spanish Florida to get away from white settlers, the Seminoles were united in their resistance to the United States. Southerners were not especially interested in Seminole lands, but they were threatened by the Seminoles' taking in runaway black slaves. Seminoles had resisted both acculturation and pressures for them to return their black allies. War broke out in 1835 and became one of the most costly and frustrating the United States ever fought. It did not end until 1842, after the United States commander captured Seminole leaders by violating a flag of truce. Once the national government promised to let the blacks accompany them to Indian Territory, the Seminoles agreed to remove. Though hundreds of Seminoles hid in the swamps and refused to leave (as occurred with other Indian tribes also), the completion of Indian removal allowed white southerners to expand into new lands and solidify their slave economy.

Walter L. Williams
University of Cincinnati

Robert Berkhofer, *Salvation and the Savage: An Analysis of Protestant Missions and American Indian Response, 1787–1862* (1965); Grant Foreman, *Indian Removal: The Emigration of the Five Civilized Tribes of Indians* (1953); Michael Green, *The Politics of Indian Removal: Creek Government and Society in Crisis* (1982); Charles Hudson, *The Southeastern Indians* (1976); Wilbur R. Jacobs, *Dispossessing the American Indian: Indians and Whites on the Colonial Frontier* (1972); Duane King, ed., *The Cherokee Indian Nation: A Troubled History* (1979); James O'Donnell, *Southern Indians in the American Revolution* (1973); J. Leitch Wright, Jr., *The Only Land They Knew: The Tragic Story of the American Indians in the Old South* (1981). ☆

Indians since 1840
||||||||||||||||||||||||||||||||||||||||||||||||||

Because the majority of Native Americans were forcibly removed from the Southeast in the 1830s, southern Indians have been split geographically. The removal treaties set up Indian Territory (modern-day Oklahoma) as their permanent homeland, with federal guarantees of full ownership of lands and internal self-government. The Cherokees, Chickasaws, Choctaws, Creeks,

and Seminoles were each granted a separate area. Though they were bitterly factionalized on the removal question (especially the Cherokees), the transplanted nations made remarkable progress in reestablishing themselves in the new lands during the 1840s and 1850s.

The Civil War tragically reopened factional disputes as those families who had cooperated with removal (led by "mixed blood" slaveowners) favored allying with the South. The withdrawal of U.S. troops, continual delays in federal treaty payments, and more favorable treaty terms from the Confederate government strengthened the pro-South Indians. Treaties of friendship were signed in 1861, and Confederate Indian regiments were organized. Along with Texas troops they terrorized pro-Union and neutral Indians, who fled to Kansas. Death and destruction occurred in the Indian Territory's severe guerrilla warfare, which laid waste to the countryside.

In 1865 the United States ignored the Unionist Indians, but imposed new treaties that punished southern Indians even more than the Confederates. Not only was slavery ended and blacks made citizens of the nations, but the Indians lost half their lands (the western half of Indian Territory was taken for settlement of Plains Indians) and the federal government imposed more restrictions on tribal governments. Indian governments were deeply divided because of wartime loyalties and new questions concerning white and black squatters on their remaining lands. These internal divisions weakened the Indian nations precisely at the time when the United States was putting most pressure on them. Congress and the courts set policies in the 1870s and 1880s that abrogated past treaty guarantees, forced the tribal governments to accept railroad landgrants, and transferred legal matters from native to federal courts.

By the 1890s Congress had abolished communal landholdings and substituted individual allotments, and then it abolished the tribal governments altogether. In 1907 Oklahoma was admitted as a state. Although some acculturated Indians did well financially, many traditionalists lost control over their lands through legal proceedings declaring them "incompetent" or through illegal graft and intimidation. Traditional Indians isolated themselves in rural communities on economically marginal lands, while their government "guardians" or white settlers reaped bonanzas from oil discoveries. The 1936 Oklahoma Indian Welfare Act attempted to reestablish tribal governments, but with only mixed success. By the 1970s these governments had become more active in attempting to deal with continuing impoverishment among Oklahoma Indians.

Meanwhile, native peoples remaining in the Southeast suffered other problems. Some of these groups (North Carolina Cherokees, Florida Seminoles, Mississippi Choctaws, Alabama Creeks) represented only small portions of the removed nations who managed to escape removal by settling on isolated, economically marginal lands; others, who had never been pressured to remove, continued to reside in long-settled areas of Virginia (Chickahominy, Mattaponi, Pamunkey, Rappahannock), the Carolinas (Catawba, Lumbee, Haliwa, Coharie, Waccamaw), and Louisiana (Houma, Chitimacha, Tunica, Coushatta).

Whatever their origin, each native community isolated itself and survived by developing a localized subsistence economy. If whites became interested in Indian lands, they tried to dispossess the natives by lowering them to the status of landless blacks. This process culminated in guerrilla resistance during the 1860s by the Lumbees, the largest southeastern remnant. By the late 19th and early 20th centuries, as agriculture and timbering expanded in the South, more Indians lost their lands and were forced to become sharecroppers or wage laborers. Their local subsistence economies were destroyed, and their living standard declined as they entered the cash economy.

Up to this time southeastern Indians had continued to follow their traditional lifestyles, with many aboriginal activities predominating among the removal escapees and a mixed Indian-European-African folk culture among the nonremoved groups. Once they lost their independent economy, acculturation to modern white-dominated society oc-

Deaconness Harriet M. Bedell with Seminole Doctor Tiger and a small boy, Florida, 1936

curred. Indians suddenly expressed great interest in Christianity and education, as they struggled to control their own institutions (mainly the church and the school) as an ethnic group within the larger society. Several federally unrecognized groups attempted to gain treaty status as a means to protect their landholdings and legitimize their Indian status. Federal reservation Indians, especially the Cherokees, had to deal with a more diverse population because of white intermarriage and government-forced acculturation policies.

The 20th century has seen a steady increase in acculturation, due partly to intermarriage and government policy but more significantly because of outside employment. Especially since World War II more Indians have migrated to take jobs off the reservation, and some of them have abandoned a distinct tribal identity to merge into the larger urban society. Ease of automobile

travel has encouraged this migration, as well as a reverse migration of white tourists to visit Indians. On the Cherokee and Seminole reservations in particular, much of the economy has become dependent on tourism. Television has also encouraged acculturation.

Yet even as Indians' lifestyles have become more like those of other southerners, their identity as Indians persists. The majority of them are not disappearing into the larger society as assimilated individuals. Instead, both reservation and unrecognized Indians are emphasizing their distinctiveness through revitalization of cultural traits (language, music, mythology, clothing, crafts) and a sense of a shared past in their kinship relations.

Better education has promoted more community organization and political-legal activism. This has also exposed southern Indians to other Indians outside the South and has promoted a Pan-

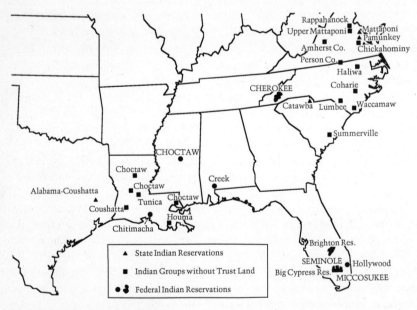

Southern Indian Reservations

*Source: Charles Hudson, **The Southern Indians** (1976)*

Indian identity. By ending their isolation and attaching themselves to the larger Indian movement of the last two decades, they have preserved their Native American identity. If an Indian community has managed to retain at least some landholdings, and a sense of general community and kinship, its ethnic survival seems assured. The South will continue to be, as it has in the past, an area of three cultural and racial groups.

See also BLACK LIFE: Indians and Blacks; GEOGRAPHY: Indians and the Landscape; LANGUAGE: Indian Language; / Conch; Indian Trade Languages; WOMEN'S LIFE: Indian Women

Walter L. Williams
University of Cincinnati

Jesse Burt and Robert Ferguson, *Indians of the Southeast, Then and Now* (1973); Angie Debo, *And Still the Waters Run: The Betrayal of the Five Civilized Tribes* (1972); W. McKee Evans, *To Die Game: The Story of the Lowry Band, Indian Guerrillas of Reconstruction* (1971); H. Craig Miner, *The Corporation and the Indian: Tribal Sovereignty and Industrial Civilization in Indian Territory* (1976); Theda Perdue, ed., *Nations Remembered: An Oral History of the Five Civilized Tribes, 1865–1907* (1980); Walter L. Williams, ed., *Southeastern Indians since the Removal Era* (1979). ☆

Mountain Culture

||||||||||||||||||||||||||||||||||||||||||||||||

The inhabitants of the southern mountains do not refer to themselves as "hillbillies"—a pejorative that first appeared in print during the early 20th century. Nor do they call themselves "mountaineers" or, more politely, "highlanders." They simply refer to themselves as "just plain folks," which is precisely what they are—the descendants of the plain folk of the Old South.

Historian Frank Lawrence Owsley first drew attention to the mass of southern whites who lived outside the plantation economy and who composed the bulk of the antebellum southern free population. Dubbed the "plain folk" by Owsley, these agricultural masses included small slaveholding farmers, slaveless farmers, herders who ranged their livestock on the public domain, and the more substantial tenant farmers. Although some of these small-scale agriculturalists eventually joined the ranks of planters, most aspired "to acquire land and other property sufficient to give them and their children a sense of security and well-being." In addition, most plain folk practiced a "grazing and farm economy," meaning a "diversified self-sufficient type of agriculture, where the money crops were subordinated to food crops, and where the labor was performed by the family aided by a few slaves."

By 1860 these plain folk could be found throughout the Old South from Delaware to Texas, but they were especially prominent in the southern mountains—the Blue Ridge Mountains, the Cumberland-Allegheny plateaus, and the Ouachita ridges—where they composed the vast majority of the mountain inhabitants. Before the Civil War, these plain folk of the southern mountains attracted minimal attention. Their lives differed little from those of the plain folk who lived elsewhere in the Old South.

Antebellum plain folk were, above all, economic generalists. During the course of a single year, a family might engage in such varied activities as hunting, trapping, collecting, home manufacturing, livestock herding, subsistence farming, and growing cash crops. The key to their economic life was the herding of livestock on the unfenced range and the growing of corn on temporary fields claimed from forests. Free-range herding provided meat and surplus livestock for sale. Corn cultivation offered food for families, fodder for livestock, and cash, if the corn were distilled. Together livestock and corn furnished the subsistence base for a distinctive life and culture, the outline of which one finds in travelogues, reminiscences, and oral tradition. Plain folk lived in depressed rural neighborhoods, called "settlements," where many of their neighbors were also their kinsmen. They occupied houses built of horizontal logs cut from neighboring forests, and they usually fashioned their own agricultural implements, household furnishings, and even garments. They patronized mills, stores, and evangelical Protestant churches in crossroads hamlets. And they periodically visited the county seat towns to shop, trade, vote, and socialize.

The Civil War and the postwar cotton boom shattered this antebellum culture. Cotton plantations encroached on the unfenced rangelands. Planter-dominated state legislatures enacted laws forcing plain folk herders to fence in their livestock. The day of the free range having ended, plain folk in the cotton and plantation belt turned to cotton growing, borrowing money for seed and fertilizer as well as for food and clothing to last them until harvest and market. If cotton prices were high, they paid off their debts. If prices were low, they became debtors, often losing their farms in

the process. Landless plain folk then joined the growing mass of tenant farmers and mill workers. Antebellum self-sufficiency and economic independence gave way to postbellum poverty and economic dependence.

In the southern mountains, however, the postbellum southern economy could not establish itself. Poor soils, rugged terrain, and unpredictable frosts hindered the spread of cotton culture. The mountains remained an isolated enclave of plain folk. But during the late 19th century, a series of family feuds, including the storied Hatfield-McCoy vendetta, focused national attention on the previously little-noticed southern mountain regions. The first "discoverers" were journalists, but they were soon followed by missionaries, educators, and a host of scholars. These outsiders found a world of log cabins, log barns, split-rail fences, ox-drawn plows, homemade furniture, and spinning wheels—all the familiar attributes of American pioneer life. Many of these observers reported that they had been carried back to the time of Daniel Boone, Davy Crockett, and Lincoln's boyhood. By the 1890s academic visitors were proclaiming the southern mountains to be a retarded frontier still bearing the stamp of 18th-century existence. By entering the southern mountains, one could hear archaic words, listen to traditional ballads, be regaled with folktales about the supernatural, and view the last frontiersmen plowing their corn and rounding up their razorback hogs.

The last frontiersman stereotype of the 1890s soon gave way to a more lasting hillbilly image. Following the defeat of Spain in 1898, the United States became a minor colonial power, shouldering the "white man's burden" in Puerto Rico and the Philippines. Concern for the primitive people of the world, however, was not confined to areas outside the continental United States. Some uplifters turned their attention to the mountain folk of the South, believing them to be as lost in ignorance and poverty as any foreign people of color. After all, they feuded with their neighbors, believed in witches, raised broods of children, practiced incest, and avoided work—except to distill illegal moonshine whiskey. In short, they were "hillbillies."

The term *hillbilly* first appeared in print in 1900 in the New York *Journal.* The word soon appeared in a spate of early 20th-century mass media articles and novels, purporting to describe the life patterns of the southern mountain people. The term even circulated among the mountain people themselves, serving as a jest or as an insult. For instance, a mountain string band, journeying to New York in 1925 to record dance tunes for Okeh records—a label that pioneered in recording white southern music—was asked by the record producer for the name of their group. Heretofore, producer Ralph Peer had simply termed the recordings of mountain music "Old Time Tunes." But in this instance, one band member facetiously replied, "We're nothing but a bunch of hillbillies from North Carolina and Virginia. Call us anything." Peer wrote down "Hill Billies" as the band's name.

On the group's return trip to New York, the members expressed second thoughts about their new title. As one musician later recalled, "Hillbilly was not only a funny word, it was a fighting word." The band's records, however, achieved such success that despite misgivings about the group's name, their music and the word *hillbilly* became

inextricably linked. "Hillbilly music" remained a disquieting term, however, and no one proudly proclaimed himself to be a hillbilly.

Southern mountain people had been predominantly agricultural in the early 20th century. They grazed their livestock on the unfenced range and grew corn in fields claimed from wooded hillsides. Every range cow needed a minimum of 15 acres of woods pasture for a year's forage, and when a hillside field eroded, farmers would abandon the old field and clear new ground from the wooded slopes. Mountain agriculture thus required an abundance of forest land.

After 1900 forest lands were no longer abundant. Mountain families, with their high birthrates (children were needed to work on the farms), tended to produce more young farmers than the land could accommodate. As farms grew smaller because of population increase, productivity and average size of farms declined. And after 1900 extractive industries—mining and logging—began to compete with agriculture for the remaining lands. Timber and coal companies purchased entire valleys and mountain slopes. Lands that had once been grazed or farmed were left deforested and denuded.

Mountain agriculture could therefore no longer support the growing rural population. During the 1910s and 1920s many mountain families migrated westward to Texas and Oklahoma, hoping to continue their way of life as tenant farmers. Others abandoned farming altogether, settling in logging camps and coal towns. In the era of the Great Depression many migrants returned to the mountains they had left, surviving on tiny hillside farms. During and after World War II, out-migration accelerated as hundreds of thousands of mountain people sought jobs and homes in the industrial cities of the Midwest and South. In leaving the mountains these plain folk abandoned their traditional way of life based on livestock herding and corn cropping. They transferred aspects of the mountain culture, though, to northern cities such as Cincinnati, Detroit, and Chicago.

Today, the southern mountain region is primarily a land of government forests, cities, tourist centers, coal towns, and modern commercial farms. It scarcely resembles the rural, agricultural landscape of 1900. The world of plain folk, from which the hillbilly stereotype is conjured, has all but disappeared. Yet the pejorative and its demeaning images live on. Southern mountain people, in all their diversity, do continue to share one common attribute: they resent the "hillbilly" stereotype. They continue to regard themselves as "just plain folks."

See also BLACK LIFE: Appalachians, Black; FOLKLIFE: "Hillbilly" Image; GEOGRAPHY: Ozarks; / Northern Cities, Whites in; INDUSTRY: Industry in Appalachia; LANGUAGE: Mountain Language; LITERATURE: Appalachian Literature; MUSIC: Country Music; MYTHIC SOUTH: Appalachian Culture / Appalachian Myth; RELIGION: Appalachian Religion; SOCIAL CLASS: Appalachia, Exploitation of; WOMEN'S LIFE: Appalachian Women

Augustus Burns
John S. Otto
University of Florida

Harry M. Caudill, *Night Comes to the Cumberlands: A Biography of a Depressed Area* (1963); Archie Green, *Journal of American Folklore* (July–September 1965); James C. Klotter, *Journal of American History* (March 1980); Forrest McDonald and Grady McWhiney, *American Historical Review* (December 1980); John S. Otto and Augustus M. Burns, *Journal of American Folklore* (April–June 1981); Frank L. Owsley, in *The South: Old and New Frontiers*, ed. H. C. Owsley (1969); Henry D. Shapiro, *Appalachia on Our Mind: The Southern Mountains and Mountaineers in the American Consciousness, 1870–1920* (1978); David E. Whisnant, *All That Is Native and Fine: The Politics of Culture in an American Region* (1983). ☆

Nativism

||||||||||||||||||||||||||

In the United States nativism—that is, hostility toward immigrants based on the belief that they threaten traditional American culture, institutions, and social order—has been rooted in racism, anti-Catholicism, antiradicalism, and anti-Semitism. Throughout the 19th century nativism flared in the North while it sputtered in the South, only to become a southern preoccupation in the 20th century as it abated in the North. Southern nativism, however, represented more than a response to immigration, for foreign immigration to the South was never sufficient to pose imminent danger to southern cultural norms or homogeneity. For southerners unsure of their place in a changing America, nativism provided a language of protest, a catch-all for deeper cultural and social fears regarding changes brought on by any external force. In the 20th century politicians and professional hate groups, especially the Ku Klux Klan, often used nativist rhetoric to capitalize on southern anxieties regarding modernization or federal interference in local ways, thereby sustaining nativist interest even in the absence of a significant foreign presence.

Political nativism in the form of the Know-Nothing movement in the 1850s made an appearance in the Old South, but, unlike nativism in the antebellum North, it did not fracture politics or influence social policy significantly. Old South Know-Nothingism lacked the ideological underpinnings of its northern counterpart, owing its existence largely to the demise of the two-party system during the slavery controversy. For former Whigs casting about for a means to oppose Democratic rivals, the Know-Nothing party fit nicely.

Anti-Catholicism, a staple of nativist thought in the North, appeared sporadically in the southern movement. Indeed, in the heavily Catholic sugar parishes of Louisiana, which were also former bastions of the Whig party, Know-Nothingism enjoyed its greatest strength. Catholic French Creoles of New Orleans embraced nativists as allies against the Irish newcomers who challenged their political and cultural power in both church and city. Here the Know-Nothing party ignored most traditional nativist appeals, focusing rather on local issues of law and order and economic development. After the party gained power in the late 1850s, it proved unable, and perhaps unwilling, to reform the city's morals and promoted railroad and street improvements instead. Likewise, in Baltimore the ascension of Know-Nothing candidates produced no changes in governmental controls over immigrants.

Know-Nothingism did attract individuals who feared immigrants, religious diversity, or any change in southern ways. Various editors who attacked im-

migrants and Catholics repeated old canards about popish plots and European corruption that were part of the republican heritage of America. Their impact, however, was confined to cities where immigrants competed with native-born southerners for social, economic, or political space. Louisville, Memphis, Baltimore, and New Orleans had sizable immigrant populations by the late antebellum period, and election disorders involving the Irish in these cities fueled nativism.

Nativism remained shallowly rooted in the Old South because immigrants were few outside of the cities and because the immigrants in the region soon adopted local norms on slavery and conservatism. Also, the politics of slavery intruded to push southerners away from nativist concerns. During the Civil War immigrant contributions to the Confederacy further discredited negative views of the foreign born, and after the war the whites' need to stand together on matters of race and home rule supplanted questions of ethnic or religious differences. For a time, nativism almost disappeared.

From 1865 to 1907 most southern state governments actively sought European immigration. Planters, eager to replace exslaves with supposedly more reliable, docile, and cheap laborers, became the principal immigration boosters. Chinese workers were brought to Mississippi and Louisiana cotton fields and southern Italians to Louisiana cane fields, but neither group proved any more tractable than the exslaves. Freedmen and their white Republican allies generally opposed efforts to pit immigrants against blacks, and nativism never prospered under black or Republican auspices in the South, diminishing even further after the return to "home

rule." As late as the 1890s many southerners spurned nationally organized nativist groups, such as the American
Protective Association, because they
were identified with the Republican
party. Immigration, not nativism,
seemed the way to white rule.

By the first decade of the 20th century, however, official attitudes encouraging immigration for economic reasons
masked a powerful nativist surge from
below. Throughout the 1890s numerous
incidents against immigrants revealed
the deep-seated class and cultural tensions in southern society. Previously,
nativist violence had been sporadic and
confined to cities, but in the 1890s the
attacks increased and spread across the
rural South. In 1893, for example, night
riders in Mississippi burned the property of Jewish landlords, and in Louisiana debt-ridden farmers wrecked the
stores of Jewish merchants. In 1896 in-
vaders twice burned the Catholic church
in the Italian settlement at Tontitown,
Ark. Several lynchings of Italian immigrants occurred in lower Louisiana.
Most spectacularly, 11 Sicilians were
lynched in New Orleans in 1891, following the mysterious death of the police chief. Although the hangings
created an international furor, the local
authorities and newspapers applauded
the mob's action.

Regional nativism, as distinct from
isolated local expressions, developed
slowly, but by the early 20th century it
had experienced revolutionary change
and growth. Attacks on Jews and Italians pointed up the class basis of the
new nativism, for Jewish merchants and
landlords and Italian workers symbolized the altered economic and social
order of the "New South." Nativism,
like Populism, represented another response to industrialism. The Farmers'

Union especially criticized the policy of
importing Asian and southern European
workers and demanded tight immigration restrictions. The black press in the
South endorsed the argument for restriction. Significantly, almost every important southern politician who claimed a
populist lineage and constituency converted to nativism. Cole Blease, "idol
of the cotton mill operatives," made nativism a political shibboleth in South
Carolina in 1908. Tom Watson, in
1912, helped to establish the Guardians
of Liberty, a Protestant-nativist organization, and with his Jew baiting in
1915 contributed mightily to the lynching of Leo Frank, an Atlanta Jew who
had been convicted of murdering a
young woman in his pencil factory in
1913.

Racism went hand in hand with populist nativism. Until the 1890s southerners rarely invoked race in nativist
arguments, except to insist on the unity
of the white race. But the new immigrants, especially Jews and southern
Italians, deviated too far from accepted
norms. Italians caused particular concern because they worked alongside
blacks in the fields, thus further demeaning their "white" status.

Racial nativism gained strength from
a new concept of American nationalism
based on pseudoscientific thinking that
divided Europeans into different
"races" rather than nationalities and,
inevitably, encouraged the notion that
one "race," the Anglo-Saxon, was superior. The South readily accepted the
celebration of Anglo-Saxonism as the
font of true Americanism. A nationalism
so defined permitted the South to return
fully to the nation it had once left, but
on terms assuring its social prominence.
Pseudoscientific racial arguments in the
North blended with, indeed vindicated,

southern arguments in defense of white rule over "colored people." Southern participation in the nation, then, was partly due to a nationalism of race.

The people's representatives in Congress echoed the racial theme. Led by Oscar Underwood of Alabama, they compared the "pure whiteness" of the older immigrants with the new immigrants' tainted mixture of "Asian and African blood." Armed with racism and the new nationalism, southern congressmen became ardent immigration restrictionists. The xenophobia of World War I and its aftermath reinforced the southern commitment to immigration restriction. During the 1920s southern congressmen played critical roles in the passage of restrictive legislation that for some 40 years thereafter effectively stemmed immigration from Europe and Asia. By the 1920s the South had become the most nativist region of the country, even as the small percentage of immigrants in the region continued to decline.

Religious nativism further propelled southern xenophobia. Born of the union between the rural, small-town revolt against modernism and the historic Protestant American distrust of Catholics and Jews, this was a nativism of faith and history rather than science. Wilbur Franklin Phelps of Aurora, Mo., galvanized religious nativism with his diatribes against alleged Catholic perversions and plots, which he exposed through his widely circulated weekly, *The Menace*. Other rustic publishers from such diverse places as Magnolia, Ark., and Moravian Falls, N.C., assisted. All bespoke the militant rural fundamentalism, the war against the moral laxity and secular liberalism of the cities, that marked religious nativism. The southern fundamentalists' fail-

ure to slow the spread of modernism and science only intensified their outlook.

The Ku Klux Klan played upon such frustrations with its anti-Catholic, anti-Semitic, antiimmigrant messages. The Klan's Bible thumping and patriotic breast-beating were exaggerated, if sometimes violent, expressions of what many southerners believed about the need to restore old-time religion and old-line groups to prominence. Several states responded to anti-Catholic pressures by considering official inspection of Catholic facilities, and Georgia actually enacted a law to supervise convents and monasteries. Sidney J. Catts rode anti-Catholicism into the governor's mansion in Florida in 1916, and Methodist bishop James Cannon, Jr., caused the first significant break in the Solid Democratic South when he mobilized fundamentalists against that party's wet, Catholic candidate, Al Smith, in 1928.

Religious nativism reached its peak in the 1928 election and ebbed slowly thereafter. By 1960, with southern voters helping the Catholic John F. Kennedy win the presidency, the political punch had gone out of anti-Catholicism. Among many factors, the narrowing of the European immigrant stream after the 1920s and the rising income and educational levels in the South made nativist fears seem superfluous, as did the post—World War II ecumenical movement and the conservative alliance of the Catholic church and southern evangelical churches on such social issues as family maintenance, abortion, and law and order in the South.

In the 1970s, however, the widening of the Asian and Latin American immigrant flow revived nativism in the South. Many Latin Americans remained in the region as migrant workers or laborers in low-wage jobs. Competing with white and black southerners for jobs and social services, they met increasing racial and religious nativism as, once again, the interests of southern economic boosters and lower-class southerners clashed. Compounding the new nativism was the post–World War II struggle of southerners against federal intervention in local affairs, a product of the civil rights movement. From the 1960s through 1980, federal policy advocated cultural pluralism and, consequently, encroached upon the local community's traditional monopoly over schools and other instruments of social control and cultural maintenance. Hostility toward new immigrants in many southern communities in the Gulf states, where Latin Americans and Asians congregated, derived from both the traditional taproots of southern nativism—racism, antimodernism, religious fundamentalism, and economic rivalry—and the resurgent antifederalism in the region. Thus, the federal government's programs for bilingual education or employment of immigrant refugees seemed to agitate both nativist and localist sentiments in the South. Further, the federal government's willingness to accept refugees from Asia and the Caribbean antagonized southern communities forced to receive them. The Cuban "Freedom Flotilla" of 1980 and the Haitian refugees who followed aroused fears of crime and disorder that subsequently spread from Florida across the Gulf states. The desperation of the refugees notwithstanding, they were unwelcome because many southerners were feeling the pinch of recession and the stresses of rapid social change.

Refugees from Asia also found their way to the South in the 1970s. They located in some odd places, broadening the immigration issue's geographic reach. Indochinese Hmong tribesmen, for example, clustered in Selma, Ala., and Memphis, Tenn., and Vietnamese peasants settled in Bucktown, La., and Seabrook, Tex., among other places. Hostility toward the Asians arose quickly. It was largely economic in tone, although racism and ethnocentrism also contributed. New Orleans's sizable Vietnamese community excited resistance from blacks who feared job competition, and violence erupted. Along the Gulf Coast and on Lake Pontchartrain in Louisiana struggling white shrimpers and fishermen resented competition from the Vietnamese, who were partly outfitted with government assistance and, perhaps worse, who worked too hard. In 1978, in Bucktown, La., and in Corpus Christi, Tex., whites attacked the Vietnamese fishermen and burned their boats. The Ku Klux Klan entered the fray, dusting off old racial and religious nativist arguments to remind southerners that the Vietnamese were colored and often Catholic.

A national debate emerged in the mid-1980s from the "New Immigration." Congress debated but did not pass the Simpson-Mazzola bill, which proposed curbing the flow of illegal aliens by applying sanctions to employers hiring them but also granting amnesty to aliens in the United States before 1982. These most recent nativist rumblings lack force or direction in the South itself, though, and remain almost entirely peculiar to the Gulf area. The eagerness of hate groups such as the Ku Klux Klan to exploit nativist fears, however, bodes ill for the South's accommodation with immigration and social change, for large numbers of immigrants will continue to come, illegally or not, to the South because of its physical proximity to Mexico and the Caribbean. Whether the South will reemerge as the most nativist region in the country will depend on how much southerners choose to rise above their history.

See also BLACK LIFE: Immigrants and Blacks; Race Relations; LAW: Frank, Leo Case; MYTHIC SOUTH: Racial Attitudes; SCIENCE AND MEDICINE: Racism, Scientific; VIOLENCE: / Ku Klux Klan, History of

Randall M. Miller
St. Joseph's University

Jean H. Baker, *Ambivalent Americans: The Know-Nothing Party in Maryland* (1977); Ray Allen Billington, *The Protestant Crusade, 1800–1860* (1938); John Higham, *Strangers in the Land: Patterns of American Nativism, 1860–1925* (1965); W. Darrell Overdyke, *The Know-Nothing Party in the South* (1950); Arnold Shankman, *Ambivalent Friends: Afro-Americans View the Immigrant* (1982). ☆

APPALACHIANS
||||||||||||||||||||||||||||||||||||||||||

The Appalachian Mountains range southward from Quebec and Newfoundland to Alabama. The central and southern highlands—consisting of the Blue Ridge and Smoky Mountain ranges, the Allegheny and Cumberland plateaus, and the Great Valley in between—are frequently conceived as a distinct sociocultural region known as "Appalachia." More than 10 million people live in the mountainous sections of Maryland, Virginia, West Virginia, Kentucky, Tennessee, North Carolina, and Georgia.

Appalachia is often portrayed as an arrested frontier, a geographically isolated subculture, and a reservoir of culturally homogeneous, white Anglo-Saxon southerners. Appalachians are commonly stereotyped, both favorably and unfavorably. Sometimes Appalachians are pictured as proud, fiercely independent, and God-fearing southerners. Conversely, they are portrayed as fighting and feuding, barefooted and backward, ignorant degenerates, downtrodden by centuries of isolation, inbreeding, and poverty.

The discovery of Appalachia as a distinctive cultural region was prompted in the mid-1870s by local color writers such as Mary Murfree and John Fox, Jr., who explored in fiction and travel sketches such mountain themes as conflicting Civil War loyalties, moonshining, and feuding. Later, educators and social reformers such as William G. Frost and John C. Campbell defined Appalachia as a social problem area deserving of uplift by church home missions and private philanthropy. Their depiction of Appalachia as a distinct cultural entity was subsequently reinforced by social scientists seeking to identify and catalog Appalachian subcultural traits. The idea that the region has a distinct identity was given further credibility by creation of a federal policymaking unit in the 1960s, the Appalachian Regional Commission. Actually, however, few people in the southern mountains identify themselves as Appalachians.

Appalachia is best viewed as a set of heterogeneous rural areas providing people and resources to eastern, midwestern, and southern cities. Though stereotyped as isolated and backward, many portions of Appalachia have been heavily industrialized since the late 19th century, providing lumber, coal, oil, gas, textile, and chemical products.

Prior to industrialization subsistence agriculture supported rural communities that stressed personalistic, familial, puritanical, and democratic values. It is doubtful that rural mountain culture was distinguishable from that of the rest of the nonplantation South.

Appalachia was initially settled by English, Scotch-Irish, and German migrants. Few blacks were present prior to the Civil War. Despite claims of ethnic homogeneity, industrialization brought diverse ethnic populations into the mountains. One study reveals that more than half the new jobs in southern West Virginia coal mines between 1890 and 1910 were filled by southern and eastern European immigrants. Southern blacks augmented the labor force in the following two decades, and in southern West Virginia they comprised roughly one-fourth of its total workers. Although the Appalachian black population has been declining since World War II, it has been very significant in some localities.

See also EDUCATION: / Campbell, John C.; ENVIRONMENT: / Appalachian Mountains; MYTHIC SOUTH: / Appalachian Myth

Dwight B. Billings
University of Kentucky

Harry Schwarzweller, James Brown, and Joseph Mangalam, *Mountain Families in Transition* (1971); Henry D. Shapiro, *Appalachia on Our Mind: The Southern Mountains and Mountaineers in the American Consciousness, 1870–1920* (1978); David E. Whisnant, *All That Is Native and Fine: The Politics of Culture in an American Region* (1983). ☆

ASIAN GROUPS

Asian Americans are rarely associated with the South. According to the 1980 census the South contained about a third of the nation's total population (33.3 percent), more than half of its blacks (53 percent), nearly a third of its whites (31.3 percent), more than a quarter of its Amerindians (26.2 percent), and just over an eighth of its Asians, as shown in Table 1. Yet the nearly half-million Asians recorded by the census are many more than most Americans imagine. Most of these Asians are newcomers to the South, but significant numbers of Asians have been there since Reconstruction.

After the Civil War, amidst chimerical fears and hopes about the disappearance of black labor, many southerners talked about bringing in Chinese to replace the freedmen, and a few actually did so. The best-known example of such talk came at an 1869 Memphis convention that urged southerners to cooperate "with the apparent leanings of Providence" and import "pagans . . . of the Mongolian race" for work and "to bring to bear upon them the elevating and saving influence of our holy religion." The proposal was to import laborers from both California and the Caribbean (chiefly Cuba) at $100 per head with payment of $8 to $12 per month. A few thousand such laborers were brought to the South—chiefly to Alabama, Arkansas, Mississippi, and Louisiana—and employed in railroad construction, sugar refining, and the growing and processing of cotton. Some 200 Chinese were brought to work on the Houston and Texas Central Railroad and more than 900 on the Alabama and Chattanooga; 147 worked the Millaudon sugar plantation near New Orleans. In some instances wages were supplemented with opium. Chinese labor never became a significant factor in the regional economy, although newspapers frequently speculated about it. By 1880

Table 1. *Asian Southerners—1980 Census*

Census Div.	Total	Chinese	Filipino	Japanese	Asian Indian	Korean	Viet- namese	Hawaiian & Pacific Isl.
U.S.	3,500,636	806,027	774,640	700,747	361,544	354,529	261,714	241,435
South	469,762	90,616	82,596	44,636	83,586	70,375	80,240	17,713
% in South	13.4%	11.2%	10.7%	6.4%	23.1%	19.9%	30.7%	7.3%
Del.	4,132	1,004	813	426	1,075	495	205	114
Md.	64,276	14,485	10,965	4,805	13,705	15,087	4,131	1,098
D.C.	6,635	2,475	1,297	752	950	338	505	318
Va.	66,209	9,360	18,901	5,207	8,483	12,550	10,000	1,708
W.Va.	5,194	881	1,313	404	1,641	587	253	115
N.C.	21,168	3,170	2,542	3,186	4,718	3,581	2,391	1,580
S.C.	11,807	1,388	3,697	1,414	2,143	1,390	1,072	703
Ga.	24,461	4,324	2,792	3,370	4,347	5,970	2,294	1,364
Fla.	56,756	13,471	14,212	5,565	9,138	4,673	7,592	2,105
Ky.	9,971	1,318	1,443	1,056	2,226	2,102	1,090	736
Tenn.	13,963	2,909	1,901	1,657	3,195	2,237	1,391	673
Ala.	9,695	1,503	960	1,394	1,992	1,782	1,333	731
Miss.	7,412	1,835	1,442	687	1,163	576	1,281	428
Ark.	6,732	1,275	921	754	832	583	2,042	325
La.	23,771	3,298	2,614	1,482	2,873	1,729	10,877	898
Okla.	17,274	2,461	1,687	1,975	2,879	2,698	4,671	903
Tex.	120,306	25,459	15,096	10,502	22,226	13,997	29,112	3,914

Source: U.S. Dept. of Commerce, Bureau of the Census, *Race of the Population by States: 1980* (1981).

the census found fewer than 1,000 Chinese in the whole South; in 1910 there were just over 3,000. Most of these had found their way into urban occupations, especially in laundries and restaurants, that were typical for Chinese of that era.

A different pattern developed among the several hundred Mississippi Chinese. With the decline of plantation agriculture, planters ceased to furnish staples to their black tenants on credit, and enough cash began to circulate that an opportunity for the independent merchant was created. Many Chinese in the Delta capitalized on this opportunity by opening small grocery and supply stores. Although providing goods and services to a largely black population, the Mississippi Chinese were careful to avoid identification with this socially inferior group. Three sets of public schools—white, black, and Chinese— were often set up, and a Chinese Baptist Church was established. Occupying a strategic position in a racially stratified society, Chinese throughout the Deep South have retained a cultural identity, absorbed by neither black nor white communities. Living in far-flung communities and cut off from the clans, *hui kuan* (secret societies), and temples characteristic of urban Chinatowns, they have relied on the nuclear family and the family-owned business to nurture and maintain this distinctiveness.

Although culturally intriguing the Chinese were not numerous in the South. In 1910, 3,299 Chinese lived in the southern states as a whole, and Mississippi's 257 made it the fifth most populous census division, after Texas (595), Louisiana, Maryland, and the District of Columbia. One further early increment of Chinese to the South occurred in 1917 when General John J. Pershing brought about 500 Chinese-Mexican refugees to San Antonio. By 1940 only about 5,000 Chinese were found in the South.

Japanese Americans entered the South in largest numbers during the World War II era. The 1940 census found just over 1,000 Japanese southerners, with a few hundred Texas rice farmers constituting the only significant community. Massive if largely temporary infusions of Japanese Americans occurred as a result of government actions during the war. Two of the 10 War Relocation Authority camps for the Japanese, Rohwer and Jerome, were on marginal land in Arkansas that had belonged to the Farm Security Administration. Almost 16,000 Japanese Americans from the West Coast were incarcerated there between 1942 and 1945. Starting in late 1942, more than 5,000 Japanese American recruits, many of them from Hawaii, were trained at Camp Shelby, outside of Hattiesburg, Miss., where they became the 442nd Regimental Combat Team. Again, educational arrangements were adjusted so that the few Japanese American children were educated separately from both whites and blacks. And, finally, several

Chinese grocery, Vicksburg, Miss., 1975

dozen Japanese American students were accepted by southern colleges and universities, largely in the Upper South. Few of these Japanese stayed in the South: the 1950 census found just over 3,000, whereas Chinese southerners numbered more than 10,000.

The increase in Asian groups since 1950 has been spectacular, with by far the greatest part of it coming in the 1970s. The 1970 census found 114,623 Asians in the South; a decade later the figure was 469,762, an increase of 310 percent. The reasons for the increase are threefold. First, many Asian American professionals have been drawn to the South, as other Americans have been, by the benign climate and the thriving economy. Second, the relaxation of immigration restrictions in 1965 has made it possible for relatively large numbers of Asians to come to the United States. And third, the continued involvement of the United States in Asian wars has increased the nation's Asian population in two ways. Since the mid-1940s servicemen, including many southerners, have been marrying Asian women and bringing them home, so that in some southern states adult Asian American women outnumber men by a substantial margin, reversing the previous sex ratio. In addition, American involvement overseas made the government receptive to Asian refugees, particularly from Southeast Asia.

Asian southerners today range from fourth- and fifth-generation Americans to persons newly arrived; from highly educated professionals and technicians to persons barely literate in their own language. The more recent immigrant groups, especially the Indochinese, have shown a greater propensity to come to the South than have the longer established Chinese, Filipinos, and Japanese.

Referring to the Southeast Asian peoples who were under French colonial rule from the late 19th century to the mid-20th, the term *Indochinese* includes the culturally and linguistically diverse Vietnamese, Cambodians, and Laotians. Before 1966 *Vietnamese* was not even a designation in immigration and naturalization statistics, suggesting the relatively low level of Indochinese immigration.

The fall of Saigon in the spring of 1975 dramatically changed the situation. Approximately 130,000 refugees from Vietnam, Cambodia, and Laos more than quadrupled the United States Indochinese population. Initially received at resettlement centers such as those at Fort Chaffee, Ark., and Eglin Air Force Base, Fla., they were eventually settled by church-affiliated or state sponsors. Fearing the social and economic consequences of massive concentrations in any one area of the country, the government favored diffusion. Some 9,000 were relocated in Texas, 5,000 in Florida, and 3,000 in Louisiana. Widely separated rural settlements, however, proved to be too isolated and within less than a year refugees began to move in significant numbers into adjacent cities, especially those with already established immigrant communities.

Given its Catholic-French heritage and waterland topography, the New Orleans metropolitan area, not surprisingly, attracted many recent arrivals. In 1980 Louisiana ranked behind only California and Texas as a haven for refugees, listing its Indochinese population at over 9,000. The Versailles community in east New Orleans, still possibly the largest concentration of Vietnamese

in the United States, has become a socially stable community supporting traditional culture in the form of front-yard herb gardens, a Buddhist temple, and Vietnamese markets.

In other parts of the South tensions between local residents and Indochinese refugees have sometimes complicated resettlement. Often involving fishing rights, as in the Texas coastal community of Seadrift, these tensions have erupted into violence. The Indochinese continue to be a relatively mobile population with a preference for settlement in California and the southern states of Texas, Florida, and South Carolina.

Korean settlement in the United States has been concentrated on the West Coast and in Hawaii, but Koreans settled in New Orleans beginning in the early 1960s. Most of them were professionals, including university professors, architects, engineers, and musicians. The Korean community in New Orleans is served by a Korean American Friendship Association, two Korean restaurants, a supermarket, and a Korean Christian church. Little formal research has been done on Koreans in other areas of the South, although one dissertation has studied the acculturation process among Korean residents of Georgia.

Roger Daniels
University of Cincinnati

Russell Bearden, *Arkansas Historical Quarterly* (Winter 1982); Lucy M. Cohen, *Chinese in the Post–Civil War South* (1984); John Cooke, ed., *Perspectives on Ethnicity in New Orleans* (1979); Roger Daniels, *Comparative Studies in Society and History* (1983); Don Chang Lee, "Acculturation of Korean Residents in Georgia" (Ph.D. dissertation, University of Georgia, 1972); James W. Loewen, *The Mississippi Chinese: Between Black and*

White (1971); *Mississippi Triangle* (film by Christine Choy, 1983); U.S. Department of Commerce, Bureau of the Census, *Race of the Population by States: 1980* (1981). ☆

CAJUNS AND CREOLES
||||||||||||||||||||||||||||||||||||||||||||||||||||||

The French founded Louisiana in 1699. At first, only a few forts perched precariously along the rivers of the frontier, but a society of French colonials eventually developed. Those born in the colony called themselves *Creoles*, a word meaning "home-grown, not imported," to distinguish themselves from immigrants. Between 1765 and 1785 the Acadians arrived in south Louisiana. Exiled after French Acadia became English Nova Scotia, they isolated themselves to reestablish their society along the bayous and on the prairies. By the 19th century the varied French cultures, enriched by the Native American Indian tribes and immigrants from Germany, Spain, Italy, Ireland, England, and the new United States, created a people who came to be called *Cajun*. The descendants of African slaves added ingredients of their own and improvised a language, a culture, and an identity, which they called Creole.

In 1803, when Napoleon sold Louisiana to Thomas Jefferson, the territory, which stretched from the Gulf of Mexico to Canada, was divided. Artificial, arbitrary boundaries ignored cultural regions and historical settlement patterns. The new state of Louisiana included the piney hills of the north and east, populated by English-speaking farmers; the bayous and prairies of the south, where French-speaking Cajun and Creole farmers lived; the rich alluvial plains along the Red and Mississippi rivers, home of planters; and New Orleans with its multilingual, multicultural urbanites.

When the time came for statewide laws to be enacted, Louisiana's cultural and linguistic diversity strained the state's arbitrary borders. Early versions of the state constitution made valiant attempts to legitimize the French language. By the turn of the century, however, the battle cry of President Theodore Roosevelt, "one nation, one language!" thundered across the land. The approach of World War I induced a quest for national unity that suppressed regional diversity. Beginning in 1916, when mandatory English language education was imposed throughout the state, children were punished for speaking the language of their fathers and mothers in school. French was discouraged in campaigns against illiteracy. Over several generations Cajuns and Creoles were eventually convinced that speaking French was a sign of cultural illegitimacy. Those who aspired to the language of the future, of the marketplace, became more American than the Yankees. Western swing, for example, replaced Cajun music in the dance halls, while black Creoles, who had preserved their language and traditions largely in isolation, were increasingly diverted toward the national civil rights movement as their most pressing struggle. The discovery of oil fueled an economic boom, which brought both groups out of the 19th century just in time for the Great Depression. First shared by horse-drawn buggies and horseless carriages, Huey Long's new highways and bridges opened the countryside and linked the bayous and prairies of south Louisiana with the rest of America.

South Louisiana was humming down a newly paved road toward homogenization. But was this the right road? Stress cracks appeared on the social surface: alcoholism and suicide among musicians and artists; juvenile delinquency among children who could no longer speak for their grandparents because of the language difference and would no longer speak to their parents because of television; self-denigration among a people who now called themselves "coonasses."

Then, in the late 1940s, the tide seemed to turn, particularly, at first, among the Cajuns. Soldiers in France during World War II discovered that the language and culture they had been told to forget made them invaluable as interpreters and increased their chances for survival. After the war returning GIs, aching from foreign wars in faraway places, sank into the hot bath of their own culture. They drank and danced to forget. Dance halls throughout south Louisiana once again blared the familiar and comforting sounds of homemade music. The glowing embers of the Cajun cultural revival were fanned by political leaders like Dudley LeBlanc and Roy Theriot who used the 1955 bicentennial of the Acadian exile as a rallying point for the revitalization of ethnic pride (along with their own careers). The message of 1955 was that the Cajuns had survived the worst; their culture and language, though injured, were alive.

In 1968 the state of Louisiana officially fostered the movement with the creation of the Council for the Development of French in Louisiana (CODOFIL), designating former U.S. Congressman James Domengeaux its chairman. But the movement was not without problems. CODOFIL found itself faced with the monumental task of creating a quality French language education program. Older Cajuns who

once wrote "I will not speak French on the schoolgrounds" a few thousand times learned the lesson well and avoided inflicting on their own children what was long considered a cultural and linguistic deficiency.

The mandate of CODOFIL, as a state agency, covered the entire state. CODOFIL was forced to press only for establishment of French as a second language in the elementary schools. A dearth of native-born French teachers compounded the problem, and CODOFIL opted to import teachers from France, Belgium, and Quebec as a stopgap. This, along with a broad program of cultural exchanges, brought the Louisiana French experiment to the attention of the Francophone world. Meanwhile, activists on the home front felt that the indigenous language and culture were once again being forced into the shadows as many Cajuns dutifully echoed past criticisms, apologizing that their language was "not the real French, just broken-down Cajun French."

The Cajuns were no longer alone. France, Belgium, and Quebec became interested in fanning the fires of self-preservation along the bayous. They invested millions of *francs* and *piastres* to create a life-support system in the hope that French culture and language might ultimately survive in south Louisiana. Along with money and teachers have come hordes of tourists eager to visit this long-lost, long-forgotten "exotic" place where, against all odds, French has somehow survived. This contact with outsiders has shown the Cajuns that, contrary to their childhood lessons, their French "works just fine" to communicate with folks who speak "real" French. And now that institutionalized segregation has diminished, black Creoles as well are increasingly interested in preserving the French parts of their culture.

Visitors to south Louisiana invariably bring their own cultural baggage. French Canadians, for instance, who seek in Cajuns a symbol of dogged linguistic survival in predominantly Anglo-Saxon North America, find virtually no Anglo-Franco confrontation and an absence of animosity in cultural politics. The French who seek vestiges of former colonials find instead French-speaking cowboys (and Indians) in pickup trucks. They are surprised that the Cajuns and Creoles love fried chicken and iced tea, forgetting this is the South; that they love hamburgers and Coke, forgetting this is the United States; that they love cayenne and cold beer, forgetting this is the northern top of the West Indies. American visitors usually skim along the surface, too, looking in vain for traces of Longfellow's Evangeline.

Black Creole culture involves more than the obvious confluence of African and French heritages. Before the Civil War, most black Creoles were slaves on French plantations, but others, called *gens de couleur libres*, held positions in the business and professional communities and sometimes owned their own plantations and slaves. Further, many generations of intermarriage by blacks with whites and Native Americans produced an intricate internal caste system within black Creole society based on skin tone, dialect, and family history.

The most consistent element in south Louisiana culture may well be an uncanny adaptability. Cajuns and Creoles have always been able to chew up change, swallow the palatable parts, and spit out the rest. This adaptability has become the principal issue of cultural survival in French Louisiana. Earlier, change had been slow, organic,

and progressive. Now, much of it is imported at a dizzying pace. The fight to save the language looms large because many fear that if it is lost, the culture will go with it. Can the culture be translated into English without loss of cultural identity? To be sure, Cajuns and Creoles will eat gumbo and crawfish forever, but is "Jolie Blonde" sung in English still Cajun music?

In the midst of this debate are signs of renewed vigor. Young parents are deliberately speaking French to their children. Authors choose to write in French. Louisiana teachers replace imported ones. Even a few movies have been produced locally in French. Cajun music, once dismissed as "nothing but chanky-chank," has infiltrated radio, television, and the classroom. Zydeco king Clifton Chenier, who recently brought home both a Grammy and a National Endow-

Cajun accordionist Wayne Toups with his father, Emery Toups, Rayne, La., 1978

ment for the Arts Heritage Award, has inspired a new army of black Creole musicians. With festivals and recording companies at the local and national levels, young musicians are not only preserving the music of their tradition but improvising to create new songs for that tradition. Contemporary musicians, however, would be less than honest if they pretended they never listened to the radio. They import the sounds of rock, country, and jazz today as they did blues and French *contredanses* earlier.

Cajuns and Creoles are constantly adapting their culture to survive in the modern world. Such change, however, is not necessarily a sign of decay, as was first thought; on the contrary, it is more likely a sign of vitality. Because the early effects of Americanization were too much too fast, the melting pot boiled over. But the cooks of south Louisiana culture have since regained control of their own kitchen and continue to simmer a gumbo of rich and diverse ingredients.

See also GEOGRAPHY: Ethnic Geography; Foodways, Geography of; LANGUAGE: French Language; MUSIC: Cajun Music; Zydeco; / Balfa, Dewey; Chenier, Clifton

Barry Jean Ancelet
University of Southwestern Louisiana

Barry Jean Ancelet, *The Makers of Cajun Music: Musiciens, Cadiens et Creoles* (1984), with Mathé Alain, *Southern Exposure* (Summer 1981); Glenn R. Conrad, ed., *The Cajuns: Essays on Their History and Culture* (1978); Jon L. Gibson and Steven Del Sesto, eds., *The Culture of Acadiana: Tradition and Change in South Louisiana* (1975); C. Paige Guittierrez, in *Ethnic and Regional Foodways in the United States*, ed. Linda Keller Brown and Kay Mussell (1984); William Faulkner Rushton, *The Cajuns: From Acadia to Louisiana* (1979); Nicholas R. Spitzer, *Southern Exposure* (Summer–Fall 1977). ☆

CATAWBAS
||||||||||||||||||||||||||||||

The majority of the Catawba Indians live on a small state-owned reservation near Rock Hill, S.C. Others live in nearby towns, and some live elsewhere in the United States. The name *Cataba* is mentioned in the records of the Juan Pardo expedition of 1566–68, along with over two dozen other names of Indian groups who lived in upper South Carolina and western North Carolina. Present-day Catawbas are no doubt the genetic descendants of several of these groups, as well as of others, but why *Catawba* was the only one of these names to survive is unknown.

In the latter half of the 18th century, the Catawbas included people from several Indian societies that had been shattered by warfare and epidemic diseases. For a while they served as a buffer between the South Carolina colonists and the northern Indians. At the Indian Congress at Augusta in 1763, they were granted a reservation measuring 15 miles square (144,000 acres). However, by the time of the American Revolution, their population had dwindled to 300 or less, and they were unable to retain control of their reservation.

By 1852 the few Catawbas who survived were living on what is now called the "Old Reservation," some 630 acres of their original reservation, subsidized by a small pension from South Carolina. Most of them lived by sharecropping, as well as by making and selling Indian pottery. They used traditional materials and techniques, but the forms in which they made their pottery were designed to appeal to the tastes of tourists and curio hunters: pipes, animals, pitchers, vases, and toys. In the late 19th century a few Catawbas became Mormon converts, and as time went on more and more of them converted, so that today most Catawbas are Mormons.

Their most outstanding spokesman in this century was Samuel Blue (1873–1959), the last person who was fluent in the Catawba language. Wearing a Plains war bonnet, Chief Blue was a familiar sight in Rock Hill, and he periodically made appearances before the South Carolina legislature to plead for more assistance for his people. After Chief Blue died, the Catawbas appeared for a time to be on the verge of social dissolution. But this trend appeared to reverse itself in the late 1970s and early 1980s, when the Catawbas sought legal redress for the loss of their 144,000-acre reservation.

Charles Hudson
University of Georgia

Charles Hudson, *The Catawba Nation* (1970). ☆

CHEROKEES
||||||||||||||||||||||||||||||||||

Of Iroquoian origins, the Cherokees migrated into the southern Appalachians over 2,000 years ago. Following a Woodland way of life, which was later influenced by the Mississippian culture, they depended on farming, hunting, and gathering wild plants. Cherokee society was practically a matriarchy, with women owning the property, leading family life, and doing the farming. Men spent much time away on the hunt, in warfare, and in dealing with outsiders.

Each independent town had its own council, but the Cherokees were held together by the clan system's extended kinship ties.

Each town council was made up of a priest, who was a leader without any powers beyond his persuasive abilities, and seven elder men chosen by the women of each clan. The council operated by consensus, regulating relations with other towns and tribes, and organizing religious ceremonials. Cherokee religion did not emphasize the idea of a god, but instead focused on the spirituality of everything in existence. Spirits of animals, plants, water, earth, and sky were all equal to humanity. This view promoted respect for the ecosystem, which humans had no right to dominate or misuse.

The major annual religious event was the Green Corn Ceremony, held in thanksgiving to the corn spirit, at the first harvest of the major food crop of the Cherokees. The cornfields were owned communally, with each woman helping to grow the crops and everyone taking as much as they needed from the common store of grain. There was no private property nor hoarding of food. Cherokee values emphasized equality, generosity, and sharing. Private possessions were ritually destroyed each year and at the death of a person. These practices produced a society without class differences and with little need for formal laws. Social harmony was kept by social pressure and by negotiation between matrilineal clans.

By the late 1600s European influences heightened men's importance, with the increase of the deerskin trade and accompanying warfare with other Indians competing for that trade. Cherokee diplomats dealt skillfully with English and French officials, alternately allying and trading with one side against the other. This role ended when France withdrew from America, and Indians were left with no one to play off against the British. In addition, the Cherokees were weakened by smallpox epidemics, which severely reduced their population in the late 1700s, precisely at the time that white settlers began moving into their lands. Several Cherokee towns, in reaction to the Americans' land hunger, allied with the British during the American Revolution. British defeat left them in an even weaker state.

The new United States signed several treaties in which the Cherokees gave up claims to parts of their homeland in exchange for promises of payment and guarantees of control over their remaining lands. With the end of warfare by the 1790s and under the influence of Christian missionaries and white traders who had married Cherokee women, more Indian men shifted to farming cash crops, sometimes using black slaves. In the early 1800s an acculturated minority emerged as leaders in establishing a national government. These "progressives" favored a white lifestyle, based on a plantation economy and adoption of European clothing, manufactured tools, and housing. They supported a newspaper and printing press, based on a syllabary invented by Sequoyah. By emphasizing their conversion to Christianity, "civilization," and pacifism, they hoped to retain their lands and coexist in peace with whites. This peace policy, however, was overcome by increasing white land hunger. President Andrew Jackson sponsored a removal treaty in 1835 that was renounced by most Cherokees, yet approved by Congress.

The removal of 16,000 Cherokees in 1838 was devastating, with 4,000 dying on the Trail of Tears. When the survivors reached Indian Territory, they received little assistance. Factionalism emerged during the Civil War as the slaveholding minority favored the Confederacy, and in 1865 the United States forced the war-ravaged Cherokees to cede half their lands and accept more federal control. By the late 1800s Congress had revoked earlier treaty promises, and in 1898 it abolished the Cherokee government altogether. Through intermarriage with whites, Cherokees in this century have merged into Oklahoma society, but traditionalists still isolate themselves in backwoods communities that have retained a strong Cherokee identity.

Meanwhile, in the North Carolina mountains, about 1,000 traditionalists on economically marginal lands managed to escape the 1838 removal. After 1870 the federal government gradually extended recognition to them. They are the largest federally recognized reservation in the South, with a growing population now over 8,000. Since the 1940s tourism has been an important, if undependable, part of their economy. Even as acculturation takes place, their Indian identity is growing, and traditionalists among both eastern and western Cherokees are becoming more influential in their tribal governments.

See also GEOGRAPHY: / Cherokee settlement; HISTORY AND MANNERS: / Trail of Tears

Walter L. Williams
University of Cincinnati

Charles Hudson, *The Southeastern Indians* (1976); Duane H. King, ed., *The Cherokee Indian Nation: A Troubled History* (1979); Theda Perdue, ed., *Nations Remembered: An Oral History of the Five Civilized Tribes,*

1865–1907 (1980); Walter L. Williams, ed., *Southeastern Indians since the Removal Era* (1979). ☆

CHICKASAWS
||||||||||||||||||||||||||||||||||

The Chickasaws in late pre-Columbian times numbered an estimated 4,000 and claimed a territory astride western Kentucky, Tennessee, northern Alabama, and Mississippi. Most Chickasaw lifeways resembled those of their neighbors—Choctaws, Creeks, Cherokees, and Natchez. Chickasaws are related to Choctaws; their language, the Muskogean, except for mild dialectal differences, is the same. Early European observers described these Indians as "tall, well-built people, with reddish skin, raven black hair, and large, dark eyes." They had a strong warrior tradition, and their incessant wars with neighboring tribes led them to replace losses in combat by adoption of captives and absorption of tribal remnants. Chickasaw men were hunters and warriors first and farmers only on occasion. Chickasaw women and Indian slaves performed the menial tasks of clearing land, caring for crops, and gathering firewood.

During the 18th century Spaniards, Frenchmen, and Britons vied for Chickasaw support in their drive for control of the lower Mississippi Valley. Traders from Charleston won the Chickasaws to a British alliance. Between 1720 and 1752 French armies from New Orleans invaded Chickasaw territory to force these tribesmen from the British orbit. Each invasion ended in French defeat. Chickasaws served with British armies in the lower Mississippi Valley during the Seven Years War. Chickasaws also supported the British during the American Revolution, fighting in Tory armies in the West against American insurgents.

Soon after 1800 Chickasaws came under the influence of missionaries and white neighbors settling on the margins of their territory. Indian youth attended mission schools, became literate, and eventually ascended to positions of tribal leadership. Several became slaveholders and developed productive plantations on tribal lands.

Through successive treaties with federal officials, Chickasaw leaders ceded tribal territory in western Tennessee and Kentucky so that all that remained by 1830 of their once vast domain was a residual area in northern Mississippi and a fragment in northern Alabama. By the Treaty of Pontotoc in 1832, and an amendatory treaty in 1834, the Chickasaws agreed to sell their eastern lands and remove to Indian Territory. In 1837 Chickasaw and Choctaw leaders signed the Treaty of Doaksville whereby the Chickasaws accepted a home in the Choctaw nation. In 1855 a treaty with the Choctaws permitted the Chickasaws to establish a separate union in south-central Indian Territory. They adopted a constitution providing for an elective council, a chief executive designated governor of the Chickasaw nation, a judiciary, and a public school system. In the antebellum period the Chickasaws sustained themselves by farming, stock-raising, and frontier trade.

During 1861 the Chickasaw nation joined the Confederate States of America, and Chickasaw companies fought in several campaigns against Union troops in the Indian Territory. The Chickasaws were required to undergo Reconstruction, which included freeing their slaves and altering their constitution to provide equal civil and social status for freedmen.

Pressed by the Dawes Commission

during the late 19th century to adopt allotment in severalty, Chickasaw and Choctaw leaders finally submitted by signing the Atoka Agreement in 1897. The following year the Curtis Act set forth the process for dissolving the Chickasaw nation, and in 1907 the Chickasaws were absorbed into the new state of Oklahoma.

Arrell Morgan Gibson
University of Oklahoma

Arrell Morgan Gibson, *The Chickasaws* (1971); John I. Griffen, ed., *The Chickasaw People* (1974); Daniel F. Littlefield, *The Chickasaw Freedmen: A People without a Country* (1980). ☆

CHOCTAWS
⸎⸎⸎⸎⸎⸎⸎⸎⸎⸎⸎⸎⸎⸎⸎⸎⸎⸎⸎⸎⸎⸎⸎⸎⸎⸎

The Choctaws are today one of the largest tribes of Native Americans in the South. They speak the Muskogean language as do the Creeks and Chickasaws, whom they resemble. In historical times the Choctaws and related tribes occupied central and southern Mississippi. With the establishment of French settlements on the Gulf Coast in 1699, the Choctaws were rapidly plunged into a complicated colonial rivalry between European powers. They were generally allied with the French against the English and their allies, the Chickasaws. Although neutral during the American Revolution, the Choctaws, during the Creek War and the War of 1812, demonstrated their loyalty to the new American nation by fighting on the side of Andrew Jackson against the Creeks and the Spanish in Florida. In spite of this effort, they were the first major southern Indian tribe removed to Oklahoma.

Although the Treaty of Dancing Rab-

Choctaw women, Mississippi, 1930s

bit Creek in 1830 permitted individual Choctaws to remain in Mississippi, most were denied the land promised under the treaty. The Choctaws in Oklahoma and Mississippi fought on the side of the South in the Civil War and suffered from the impact of that conflict. The Mississippi Choctaws were finally legally recognized by the federal government as an Indian tribe in 1918. The Choctaw nation established in Oklahoma following removal came to an end with statehood in 1907, but a Choctaw tribal government still exists there.

Although outstanding agriculturalists, the Choctaws lacked distinguishing customs to excite the interest of travelers or scholars. They attained a degree of political centralization, but otherwise their activities were undramatic. As a result, they have received less scholarly or popular attention than other tribes. They were second only to the Cherokees in adopting European institutions, and early descriptions of their traditional culture are limited. They are best known for a detailed origin legend, their music and dance, and stickball. To a large extent they have continued to retain their language, dances, and ballgame and basketmaking skills. The Choctaws, and other southeastern tribes, contributed corn and hominy to the regional diet. The Choctaws probably contributed the use of sassafras in Louisiana French gumbo. Perhaps their most distinct characteristic has been an ability to adapt, yet remain distinctively Choctaw.

John Peterson
Mississippi State University

Angie Debo, *The Rise and Fall of the Choctaw Republic* (1934); John Peterson, in *The Southeastern Indians since the Removal Era*, ed. Walter L. Williams (1979); John R. Swanton, *Source Material for the Social and Ceremonial Life of the Choctaw Indians* (1931). ☆

CREEKS

||||||||||||||||||||||

Historically, the Creek (Muskogee) Confederacy was the dominant American Indian political and military force in the present-day states of Alabama and Georgia. The native economy rested upon maize, beans, and squash cultivation and hunting and fishing. Politically the Confederacy consisted of several dozen autonomous chiefdoms, or towns, organized internally on the principle of matrilineal descent coupled with a prestige system based largely upon distinction in warfare. Religious life revolved around a ceremonial calendar culminating in the Busk, New Fire, or Green Corn Ceremony in late summer. Following sustained contact with whites in the late 17th century, the Creeks became increasingly dependent upon commercial hunting and trade, resulting ultimately in dependency, indebtedness, land cessions, and complicated entanglements with competing European powers in the Southeast. After the American Revolution the United States relentlessly pursued a "plan of civilization" for the Creeks that included greater centralization of authority in the "Creek Nation," precipitating internal divisions culminating in the Creek War of 1813–14 and the eventual subjugation and removal of most Creeks, then totaling about 20,000, to Indian Territory (Oklahoma) by 1840.

Despite the 1830s removal, a few Creek Indians managed to remain in the Southeast, particularly some of those who had remained friendly to the United States during the Creek War. Their descendants today number several thousand, and most are assimilated into the general population. Near modern-day Atmore, Ala., however, a sufficient concentration of unremoved Creeks remained to sustain a viable Indian community to the present. These Creeks, largely isolated and ignored by federal authorities throughout most of their history, have maintained a cohesive community through informal social and political mechanisms. Formally organized as the "Poarch Band of Creeks," the group actively pursues a program of community betterment, cultural enrichment, and political action.

This latter-day resurgence of the Poarch Creeks began in the 1940s and 1950s when Chief Clavin W. McGhee (1903–70) spearheaded a drive for improved educational opportunities for his people and directed a land-claim suit against the United States, efforts in which the Creeks eventually were successful. By 1984 there were approximately 1,300 enrolled members of the band headed by an elected Tribal Council. Many band members now live in cities, as do many other Indians, but over half the Poarch Creeks reside in the vicinity of the Tribal Center, near the sites of federal allotments received by "Friendly Creek" ancestors under terms of the 1815 Treaty of Fort Jackson, which concluded the Creek War.

Since the early 1800s the Poarch Creeks have become acculturated to white ways, yet some elements of native culture and language have survived. Once objects of discrimination, the Poarch Creeks lately have begun to transform their identity as Indians from a local stigma to a national asset. Since 1971 the Poarch Creeks have sponsored an annual Thanksgiving Day powwow at their community center attracting craftsmen, dancers, and others from tribes in Oklahoma, Mississippi, Florida, and North Carolina, as well as thousands of non-Indian spectators. Since 1977 the Poarch Band of Creeks has been a voting member of the National Congress of American Indians, and their tribal chairman, Eddie Tullis, was elected vice-president of the Congress in 1983. In August 1984, following a process begun in 1975, the Poarch Band of Creeks was officially acknowledged by the United States as an Indian tribe, historically related to but politically distinct from the modern Muskogee (Creek) nation of Oklahoma, and, thus, entitled to all the rights and privileges of other federally recognized Indian tribes under United States law.

J. Anthony Paredes
Florida State University

J. W. Fritz, *Federal Register* (Number 5, 1978); J. Anthony Paredes, in *Indians of the Lower South: Past and Present*, ed. John Mahon (1975), and in *The Versatility of Kinship*, ed. Linda S. Cordell and Stephen Beckerman (1980); Frank G. Speck, *American Indigena* (1947). ☆

CREOLE
||||||||||||||||||||||

Few ethnic terms in North American society have been as controversial or as sensitive as the term *Creole*. Coined by the Spanish and Portuguese who ventured into the New World, the word originally denoted individuals born in the colonies of European parents. Under the restrictions of this connotation, the term should have fallen from disuse with the cessation of colonial immigration.

Within Louisiana, the disparities between the predominantly Latin culture of the original settlers and the predominantly Anglo-Celtic culture of the late 18th and 19th-century newcomers served to encourage the perpetuation, evolution, and expansion of the term Creole. By the 19th century it had become synonymous with "native." In both the noun and adjective forms it embraced all objects indigenous to Louisiana, from cabbage to cotton, and all people, regardless of hue, whose families were native to the Louisiana colony. Its application to people appeared in one of three forms: Creole, Creole *de couleur* (which denoted Creoles with African or Indian admixtures), and Creole Negro (which denoted blacks of unmixed ancestry). By definition, the term was so inexclusive that it barred only those born outside of Louisiana.

Varied restrictions upon the usage of the term have been attempted, within segments of Louisiana society, since at least the late 19th century, and a considerable degree of misunderstanding over the term has existed outside the state. The most commonly encountered circumscriptions suggest that a Creole *must* be of "pure" white ancestry, is necessarily wealthy and aristocratic, and is rooted in the Delta country of lower Louisiana. Travelogs of past generations, penned by those who sojourned chiefly among the upper classes of New Orleans and the sugar planters of the surrounding countryside, were perhaps initially responsible for this limited concept of the term. From their romanticized portrayal of Creole society, there has blossomed (in the words of one Louisiana historian) "a veritable cult of the Creole . . . for those who look so longingly to the past" in which "their kind . . . ruled . . . with a grace and charm long since lost to the modern world."

Simultaneously, the widely read works of the 19th-century Louisiana writer George Washington Cable, and those of a great number of his successors, have left much of Anglo-American society with the impression that Creoles are uniformly poor in worldly goods, quaint in customs, and mixed of blood. The latter misunderstanding has been propagated to a great degree in the 20th century by those of mixed racial heritage who seek to escape prejudicial injustices by identifying themselves as Creoles rather than by the term black, which is more commonly applied to their counterparts outside of Louisiana.

The only restriction that has been applied to the term *Creole* that has been customarily agreed upon by most segments of society is the exclusion of those individuals more commonly known as "Cajuns." Even this limitation, however, is arbitrary, in light of the degree to which the two groups have intermarried. In 20th-century America, Creoles with "Cajun" ancestry and "Cajuns" with Creole ancestry are probably more the rule than the exception.

In consideration of the ambiguity that surrounds what is principally a question of evolving semantics, the safest definition of the term may well be the classic Louisiana compromise: A Creole can be anyone who says he is one.

See also LITERATURE: / Cable, George Washington; URBANIZATION: / New Orleans

Gary B. Mills
University of Alabama

Elizabeth Shown Mills, *Louisiana Genealogical Register* (March 1977); William J. Thomas, *Wichita State University Bulletin* (February 1973); Joseph G. Tregle, Jr., *Journal of Southern History* (February 1952). ☆

CUBANS
||||||||||||||||||||||

Cubans constitute the largest Hispanic group in the southeastern United States. Although Mexicans are primarily concentrated in the Southwest and Puerto Ricans in the Northeast, Florida contains the nucleus of the Cuban community in this country. In 1980 more than half the 803,226 persons of Cuban origin in the United States resided in Miami's metropolitan area.

The concentration of Cubans in Florida has a long history. As early as 1831 Cuban cigarmakers were working in Key West, Florida's southernmost town, whose Cuban population increased throughout the 19th century. Starting in 1886, cigar manufacturers from Cuba, led by Vicente Martínez de Ybor, established factories on the outskirts of

Tampa. The immigration of Cuban cigarmakers to the area increased dramatically during the height of the Tampa cigar industry (1886–1910), resulting in the founding of Ybor City, which survives to this day as a neighborhood within the metropolitan area of Tampa.

But by far the bulk of the current Cuban-origin population of the United States immigrated after 1959, the year in which the revolutionary government headed by Fidel Castro rose to power and began transforming the country's political, economic, and social institutions. Miami has been the principal destination of those postrevolutionary migrants, although important communities have also arisen in the New York City–New Jersey metropolitan area and in Los Angeles, Puerto Rico, Spain, and various Latin American countries. Miami bears the imprint of the large Cuban presence. The Cuban community has served as a magnet for other Latin American immigrants, so that in 1980 one of every two Miami residents was of Latin American origin.

The relatively high proportion of professionals and entrepreneurs among the Cuban immigrants has contributed to making Miami's Spanish-speaking population an institutionally complete ethnic community. Its members can work, shop, bank, dine, and be entertained in establishments in which Spanish is the principal language. This institutional completeness, coupled with the predominance of first-generation immigrants among Cuban Americans, has made possible the retention of many cultural traits from the country of origin. Evidence of this retention can be found, for example, in religious practices. Most Cubans in the United States are Roman Catholics, and others adhere to religious beliefs that have Afro-Cuban

origins. Communitywide cultural events held by Miami's Cubans, such as Carnaval, art and music festivals, and the Three Kings' Parade, are all reminiscent of similar events once held in Cuba. The proliferation in Miami of grocery stores and restaurants that cater exclusively to Cuban dietary tastes is yet another example of the tendency to adhere to cultural traits of the country of origin. As expected, however, the younger generation, largely born in the United States, exhibits a substantial degree of assimilation to the cultural patterns of this country.

In 1980 the widely publicized Mariel sealift brought some 125,000 Cubans to the United States and dramatically increased the number and visibility of Cubans in this country, and especially in Florida. While Cuban immigration has slowed to a trickle since the termination of the sealift in September of 1980, the conditions that gave rise to it persist, and it is not unimaginable that the Miami Cuban community will be replenished with new arrivals in the years ahead.

See also GEOGRAPHY: / Cuban Settlement; URBANIZATION: / Miami; Tampa

Lisandro Pérez
Louisiana State University

Thomas D. Boswell and James R. Curtis, *The Cuban-American Experience: Culture, Images and Perspectives* (1984); Richard R. Fagen, Richard A. Brody, and Thomas J. O'Leary, *Cubans in Exile: Disaffection and the Revolution* (1968); Lisandro Pérez, in *The Harvard Encyclopedia of American Ethnic Groups*, ed. Stephen Thernstrom, Ann Orlov, and Oscar Handlin (1980); Eleanor Meyer Rogg, *The Assimilation of Cuban Exiles: The Role of Community and Class* (1974). ☆

FRENCH
IIIIIIIIIIIIIIIIIIII

French presence in the South has been concentrated historically in two places, Charleston, S.C., and Louisiana. Beyond those two areas French influence has been so slight, insulated, or ephemeral as to be of negligible significance. The largest community was Henri Castro's settlement of several thousand Alsatians in Medina County in western Texas in 1844, but it left only a local imprint.

Even the celebrated South Carolina manifestation is little more than a historical memory. Beginning in the 1680s and continuing through most of the 18th century, a total of not more than 2,000 French Huguenots, fleeing persecution by Catholic authorities in France after Louis XIV's famous revocation of the Edict of Nantes that had protected French Protestants for nearly a century, took refuge in the recently founded English colony of South Carolina. Most of them settled in or around Charleston, where they quickly became the backbone of that important colonial city's business and financial class. With religion no bar and their language rapidly eroded, they were assimilated by the predominantly English population. Though they were of vital importance to the economic life of early South Carolina, they left no real ethnic legacy—nothing, for example, in the way of an architectural or linguistic heritage.

An important reminder of their presence is in the great number of Huguenot surnames found today throughout the South, carried there as the Huguenots' descendants joined other southerners in the classic migration to new territories that populated the Deep South. Another reminder is the Huguenot church they established in Charleston. After having its membership fall nearly to the point of extinction in the 1950s, the church is again viable today, its following enlarged as a result of renewed ethnic awareness during the 1960s and 1970s.

In Louisiana, on the other hand, 572,262 people in 1970 reported to the census takers that their mother tongue was French. An estimate of 450,000 Louisianians in 1980 had French as their mother tongue—slightly more than 1 out of every 10 people in the state. Of those, 291,137 still speak it, in one degree of fluency or another. That represents the largest concentration of French-speaking natives with an indigenous ethnic tradition in the United States.

All of them—save 5,000 or so foreign-born French-speaking immigrants of the recent past and their children—are the descendants of one or some combination of five French-speaking groups that largely made up Louisiana's colonial and antebellum population. The first group came from Canada or directly from France and settled in New Orleans, up to the Mississippi River, and along what are now the Mississippi and Alabama Gulf coasts. Toward the end of the 18th century that early population began to style themselves *l'ancienne population* in distinction to newcomers who were flooding into the colony. Some of the newcomers, or *les français étrangers*, emigrated directly from France, but great numbers, some of them free people of color, came from the French West Indies and Santo Domingo, particularly after revolutions there in 1791. The colonists also brought in many black African slaves who quickly learned French and became the third group. In the latter decades of the 18th century Acadians, or Cajuns as they came to call themselves, immigrated to Louisiana from Canada after the British conquest there and settled as small farmers and woodsmen in the swamps and along the bayous southwest of New Orleans. And throughout the 19th century continuing waves of emigrants from France, the fifth group, poured into Louisiana, and particularly into New Orleans, keeping it a predominantly French-speaking city until the Civil War and a largely French-speaking one until World War I.

Although reminders of historical French presence remain in some outlying areas of the great expanse of French territory that constituted the Louisiana Purchase—most notably at Saint Louis, Mo., Mobile, Ala., Biloxi and Natchez, Miss., and Natchitoches and Baton Rouge, La.—these are limited mostly to remnants of an architectural and town planning legacy, to a larger Catholic presence than normal for the South, and to numerous French family and place names.

In south Louisiana, however, a pronounced French influence continues. In addition to Catholicism and to French, which is spoken today by about 373,500 Cajuns as well as around 76,500 people in New Orleans, Cajuns maintain an architectural tradition, typically modern adaptations of a four-room, story-and-a-half, frame cottage with a narrow incorporated front porch; a rich folklore of sayings, superstitions, cures, songs, and tales; Sunday community dances called *fais-do-dos*; and a kind of poker called *bourré* in which even penny-ante stakes can suddenly rise to hundreds of dollars on the flash of a single card. They have also institutionalized and refined into a high athletic skill racing in pirogues, which are long, narrow dugout canoes. They have their own music, a unique French-folk-country-western-blues combination, and their own cuisine, hearty, highly spiced seafood, fish, crawfish, and game dishes that carry a distinctive French undertone and that have recently become increasingly popular across the nation.

In New Orleans the Creole tradition and the tradition of "creolizing" natives of whatever background, and newcomers as well, also remains pronounced. New Orleans retains a viable local architectural tradition, the origins of which are French. And the city remains distinctly Catholic in tone, though now predominantly Protestant in numbers. New Orleans cooking, a rich, delicate cuisine that is essentially an adaptation, developed largely by black chefs, of traditional continental French dishes to local ingredients and seasonings supplied by the city's various 19th-century immigrant groups, is world famous. In addition, the city has developed a public culture, a way of life—best known but by no means limited to its expression in the celebration of Mardi Gras—that is also traceable to French colonial origins.

New Orleans's antebellum free black population, almost entirely French speaking, was not only the largest in the Deep South, but the only one anywhere in the South to develop a full-fledged high culture of its own. It included a coterie of poets, novelists, historians, and musicians and supported its own theater, newspapers, several schools, and a small symphony orchestra. That culture maintained continuing contact with France; Edmond Dédé, for example, served as conductor of the Bordeaux symphony for 25 years, and Victor Séjour had a number of his plays performed on the Paris stage. Moreover, the free black population and its descendants furnished most of the state's black leaders during Reconstruction and the latter 19th century, and in the course of the 20th century has exported such talent to the rest of the South, most recently in the examples of Atlanta mayors Maynard Jackson and Andrew Young, both of whose families have roots in New Orleans.

See also ART AND ARCHITECTURE: French Architecture; LANGUAGE: French Language; URBANIZATION: / Charleston; New Orleans

Jerah Johnson
University of New Orleans

Glenn R. Conrad, ed., *The Cajuns: Essays on Their History and Culture* (1978); Arthur Henry Hirsch, *The Huguenots of Colonial South Carolina* (1928); Jerah Johnson, *Contemporary French Civilization* (Fall 1976). ☆

GERMANS
||||||||||||||||||||||||||||

Although one of the largest "ethnic" components of the American population, Germans (that is, those emigrants from the area of Imperial Germany, the states forming Germany in 1871) as a group never assumed cultural importance for the entire southern region. German immigration to the South encompassed too broad a time span, was too irregular, and drew from too many diverse sources within "Germany" to impose a single cultural order anywhere. Still, large numbers of Germans settled in the southern region from the colonial period through the 19th century, and within their areas of concentration they built and maintained German subcultures that thrived into the modern era in several instances, at least in attenuated forms.

In the 18th century thousands of Germans moved along the great wagon road from Pennsylvania into the Virginia backcountry, the Carolinas, and even as far south as Georgia. German-speaking sectarian groups, such as the Salzburgers in Georgia, the Swiss Germans at Purrysburg in South Carolina, and the Moravians in North Carolina, augmented the "German" presence in the colonial period. German cultures proliferated in rural areas for more than a century, but they began to weaken in the 19th century because, after 1800, few immigrants arrived to renew them. Economic and social forces intruded on Germans' isolation or drew them into the larger commercial and social world of the antebellum South. Individual German groups, often religious in character and organized by colonizers seeking refuge and prosperity in America, continued to venture to the South in the 19th century, following the good reports of land and nature from such German promoters and travelers as Gottfried Duden, whose tract on Missouri stimulated a rush of Germans there.

Various German societies that formed after 1830 to colonize America looked to the South for land. Among them were the Auswanderungs Gesellschaft, which planned a settlement in Arkansas, and the Rhein-Bayerische Gesellschaft and the Mainzer Adelsverein, among several, which established German colonies along the Brazos River in Texas and elsewhere. These societies were particularly attracted to the southwestern region, but with the opening of western lands, the economic and social dislocations caused by the Civil War, and the shift in the sources of German immigrants generally by the 1870s, the South no longer appeared inviting to prospective agricultural colonies. Various entrepreneurs and southern state governments responded to pressure from planters who wanted to replace black workers with German and other immigrants after the Civil War, but few Germans responded to their appeals and those who did remained only briefly in the South. Except for a handful of successful experiments in recruiting, such as the work of John G. Cullman in bringing Germans to Cullman County, Ala., German farmers had ceased to enter the South by the late 19th century.

During the 19th century the character of German immigration changed significantly. Beginning with the great immigration waves to America in the 1840s, Germans came to the South through the port of New Orleans, often arriving on the cotton ships trading between New Orleans and Bremen. Many of the immigrants moved up the Mississippi River in search of jobs or land to settle in the Midwest, but many also remained in New Orleans or the river towns and cities to work on the levees, on railroads, on the docks, or as laborers and artisans in the towns. In cities such as Memphis and Louisville the German population swelled to more than 10 or 15 percent of the total city population in the 1850s. Meanwhile, other Germans left northern ports to seek work in Richmond's iron industry or went to other industrializing towns in the upper South. For a brief moment, German immigrants contributed to the "modernization" of southern urban life, adding cultural diversity, ethnic politics, Old World arts and crafts, and an infrastructure of social and cultural organizations to city life. The urban Germans developed a rich associational life throughout the South. In Richmond, for example, a German rifle club, *Turnverein*, Schiller society, benevolent soci-

ety, drama club, choral group, and free thinkers' congregation brought German culture to the city. In Memphis, as late as the 1870s, the German population of no more than 4,000 persons then supported 18 benevolent and fraternal societies, a fire company, eight lodges, five militia companies, several theater groups, and a host of religious and social associations. Even a small German population, as in Mobile in the 1880s, could boast at least a German school, a charity organization, a choral society, a gymnasium, and a Lutheran church. German newspapers sprang up in every southern city, and German heroes and festivals were celebrated in print and parades as recently as the early 20th century in some places.

The strong associational life of the Germans reflected their numerical and cultural significance in the cities, but also their weakness. The diverse origins of the German population combined with class and religious differences to separate the Germans among themselves. So, too, did rivalries between old and new settlers, between the German "intelligentsia," who derived their identity from European liberalism, and the poorer, new immigrants, many of them Catholics, who showed greater respect for authority. These and other differences explain the proliferation of German associations, for each group inclined toward its own kind. No single German cultural imprint was possible under such conditions.

By World War I any viable German culture that remained was rooted in the southern countryside. In subtle ways the intensive agriculture of German farmers created a specific cultural landscape, particularly in the rural German enclaves of the Shenandoah Valley of Virginia, in scattered communities in the

Carolina Piedmont, in Cullman County in Alabama, in south-central Tennessee, in the Arkansas Ozarks, along the Missouri River in Missouri, and in several pockets in eastern Texas. Because Germans viewed their farms as permanent homes rather than speculative investments, they have tended to farm them more intensively than non-Germans, with greater per-unit productivity and locational stability. In addition, they traditionally have exhibited relatively higher rates of landownership wherever they have clustered in numbers. German ethnic subcultures, with their high religiosity, family centeredness, and conservative values, grew in rural areas, nurtured by German agricultural societies, social clubs, fraternal and benefit associations, the local German churches, and, as late as the 1950s in a few instances, a German-language press. Rural isolation and German churches served as the twin pillars of German ethnicity for over a century or more, but since World War II mass communications, improved roads, changed market conditions, and consolidated school systems have combined to erode rural German distinctiveness.

Even those German cultural traits that have persisted did so only because they were modified somewhat to meet local conditions. Most German farmers have accommodated to local social, economic, and physical environments. Germans have followed southern practices both in the production of staple crops for the market economy and in the selection and treatment of livestock. They also abandoned their Old World village settlement patterns for the dispersed settlement habits of America.

German building and crafts further displayed the syncretic, dynamic qualities of German-American acculturation generally. In building large barns and substantial homes Germans adapted to local architectural styles and used available building materials. In the 19th century, for example, German settlers in Missouri and Texas first built with logs, which were both inexpensive and practical, and put up houses in the American style. In time, Germans constructed frame houses resembling those in the areas from which they had migrated. They also used stone widely, especially in Missouri. In cities with German craftsmen and German population concentrations distinctive brickwork traditions also developed, but by the early 20th century German urban design and construction had yielded to standardized American conventions and styles. In rural areas a Missouri-German, Texas-German, or Shenandoah-German vernacular style evolved, but everywhere the great diversity of German backgrounds among settlers and craftsmen produced much artistic and architectural variety within any given area. Little distinctive regional furniture or decorative art emanated from southern German settlements, as it did from Pennsylvania Germans, although sectarian groups such as the Moravians of North Carolina established their own folk expressions and, as in the Shenandoah Valley, rural isolation and German population density kept alive *fraktur* writing, basket weaving, and pottery making for several generations after immigration.

In rural areas German churches conducted services in the native tongue and ran schools that resisted the English monolinguistic culture. German publishing houses serving Lutherans particularly and the German language press proliferated throughout the 19th century, imposing a standard German idiom on German readers. Lack of funds, teachers, and readers, along with wider

Schmidt Brothers saloon, Fredericksburg, Texas, date unknown

commercial contacts beyond German settlements, however, contributed to the weakening of German language institutions by the end of the century. Bilingualism entered the German churches via lay insistence, and English rapidly replaced standard German in the marketplace. Still, various spoken German dialects survived in isolated communities as the language of informal social intercourse.

In the cities the heterogeneity of backgrounds among Germans caused them to adopt the formal *Hochdeutsch*, used in churches and in the press and sprinkled with American usages, more readily than their rural counterparts. The urban Germans' more frequent and sustained contacts with non-Germans also rapidly forced them to become a bilingual people. Indeed, many German associations regularly conducted their affairs in both English and German by the late 19th century. Small numbers of German publicists and nationalists lobbied for German language maintenance, and educated, affluent urban Germans supported German-speaking theater and high culture in Richmond, Charleston, Memphis, Nashville, and New Orleans, among other places. But the bulk of the German population gravitated toward American entertainments and speech as the natural concomitant of their work and dispersed residence patterns within the cities.

Enough "German" restaurants, *Maifesten* and other festivals, folk art objects and architecture, and, especially, Lutheran and Reformed churches survive to recall a German contribution to southern life, but, save for the rural enclaves, German identity now exists largely, and then often dimly, too, in memory.

See also ART AND ARCHITECTURE: German Architecture; LANGUAGE: German Language

Randall M. Miller
St. Joseph's University

Kathleen Neils Conzen, in *Harvard Encyclopedia of American Ethnic Groups*, ed. Stephen Thernstrom, Ann Orlov, and Oscar Handlin (1980); Russell L. Gerlach, *Immigrants in the Ozarks: A Study in Ethnic Geography* (1976); Terry G. Jordan, *German Seed in Texas Soil: Immigrant Farmers in Nineteenth-Century Texas* (1966); John Nau, *The German People of New Orleans, 1850–1900* (1958); Charles van Ravenswaay, *The Arts and Architecture of German Settlements in Missouri* (1977); Klaus Wust, *The Virginia Germans* (1969). ☆

GREEKS
||||||||||||||||||||||

Although Greeks in the South are not numerous and comprise only about 10 percent of the total Greek American population, Greek southerners form a distinctive element in Greek American history. The first Greeks to settle in America—about 400 souls—were indentured servants brought over by a Scottish entrepreneur to New Smyrna, Fla., in 1768. The first Greek Orthodox church in the United States, Holy Trinity, was established in New Orleans in 1864. A Greek Orthodox religious commune—the Malbis Plantation—was founded in 1906 in Baldwin County, Ala. Tarpon Springs, Fla., underwent a metamorphosis in 1905 with the arrival of 500 Greek spongers. The Greek character of Tarpon Springs has been unique in America and remains well defined today. The American Hellenic Educational Progressive Association (AHEPA) was established in 1922 in Atlanta, Ga. The AHEPA became the leading Greek American fraternal organization.

The major wave of Greek immigration to the South—as elsewhere in the United States—occurred in the early decades of this century. Like their counterparts outside the South, the vast majority of these early Greek arrivals were

A Greek American deep-sea sponge fisherman, Tarpon Springs, Florida, 1944

males seeking their fortunes in America. Most came with the intention to return to the old country where they would lead lives of comfort from their American earnings. Because of their relative success, the Greek immigrants to the South, however, realized much earlier than their compatriots in other parts of the United States that America was to become their permanent home. This also meant that internecine political conflicts, which marred much of Greek immigrant life in this country, largely bypassed the Greeks of the South. To a degree even greater than their non-southern compatriots, Greeks in the South established small businesses, notably restaurants, and generally prospered. Greek emigrant women came over in substantial numbers after World War I. The children and grandchildren of those early emigrants have, in the main, moved into professional, white-collar, and upper-middle-class vocations.

Greeks in the South quickly established stable communities whose focal point was the Greek Orthodox church. By the mid-1980s there were 90 Greek Orthodox churches in the region. Some 100,000 persons of Greek birth or ancestry now live in the states of the old Confederacy. About half of these are "southern Greeks," descendants of the early immigrants. The others, especially in Texas, Florida, and northern Virginia, are migrants to the Sunbelt—part of the national pattern occurring since the 1950s.

An indigenous Greek American community, as opposed to a Greek immigrant colony, first developed in the South. The southern variant thus became the prototype of the Greek experience in America.

Charles C. Moskos
Northwestern University

Alexander Karanikas, *Hellenes and Hellions: Modern Greek Characters in American Literature* (1982); Charles C. Moskos, *Greek Americans: Struggle and Success* (1980); Theodore Saloutos, *The Greeks in the United States* (1964). ✩

GYPSIES
||||||||||||||||||||||||

Well represented among southern ethnic minorities are the Romani people (*Rom*, or *Gypsies*), who maintain their distinctive language and way of life while remaining outside mainstream society. All Romani groups trace their ultimate heritage to 9th- or 10th-century India, but subsequent westward migration into Europe and thence to the Americas has scattered the original population, giving rise to a number of distinct ethnic subdivisions within the overall race. In the South, several of these subdivisions are represented, particularly the Romanichals, or Gypsies, who came from the British Isles, and the Vlax (*x* like *ch* in German *Achtung*), who arrived later from southeastern Europe.

The first Gypsies to reach the Americas came with Columbus on his third voyage in 1498 and were presumably from Spain. The first to reach North America were probably those banished to serve in the Virginia plantations by Cromwell in 1664. The transportation of British Gypsies to the American colonies continued sporadically until the mid-1800s, and the French began similar deportations to Louisiana after 1700. Spanish shipments to the same territory followed a proclamation issued in 1749; Gypsies came as redemptioners from Germany to Pennsylvania, New York, and New Jersey following the Thirty Years War, and some of them eventually made their way south. The Vlax Gypsies began coming to America in the middle of the 19th century when 500 years of Gypsy slavery in the Balkan states ended.

Romanichal Gypsies live throughout the South, probably numbering between 50,000 and 100,000. Particularly large communities are found in Texas, Arkansas, Georgia, Louisiana, Kentucky, and the Carolinas. Many are homesteaders who own much land and at the same time follow a variety of occupations such as horseraising, blacktopping, roofing, and paving. Others involved in these occupations follow an annual migratory business circuit and move from campground to campground living in motorized trailers. The Vlax Rom have little to do with the Romanichal population, whom they outnumber by perhaps five to one.

Romani culture, for both groups, re- quires that social contact with non- Gypsies, whom the Vlax Rom call *gadjé* (singular *gadjó*) and the Romanichals *gorjers*, be kept at a minimum. Gypsies avoid calling attention to ethnic identity and keep a low profile. Much of this reluctance is a reaction to the prejudice that operates against Gypsies at both the popular and administrative levels. Gyp- sies have not had the wherewithal to challenge the stereotype of Western tra- dition that portrays them in a generally negative light, and they have little mo- tivation to draw attention to their ethnicity. One Mississippi law states that "gypsies . . . for each county . . . shall be jointly and severally liable with his or her associates (to a fine of) two thousand dollars"; another law in Geor- gia requires that "upon each company of gypsies engaged in trading or selling merchandise . . . $250 is to be col- lected." As a consequence, while Rom- ani culture in the South is vigorous and in little danger of disappearing, the general public is hardly aware of it.

In recent years two independent movements, one sociopolitical and one evangelical, have begun to bring changes within the Romani population. The former has resulted in the creation in Florida of a national journal, *Ro- manija*, the purpose of which is to bring news of national and international Gypsy-related matters to the Romani population. The evangelical movement has also led to the establishment of a newsletter, *Romany Fires of Revival*, which is sent out to some 600 families in Louisiana. Romani churches, both Vlax and Romanichal, are now found in many southern cities including Atlanta and Houston.

See also FOLKLIFE: / Traders

Ian Hancock
University of Texas at Austin

Irving Brown, *Gypsy Fires in America: A Nar- rative of Life among the Romanies of the United States and Canada* (1924); Ian Han- cock, *American Speech* (Fall 1986), *The Pa- riah Syndrome* (1987); Andrew A. Marchbin, *A Critical History of the Origin and the Migration of the Gypsies* (Ph.D. dis- sertation, University of Pittsburgh, 1939); Anne Sutherland, *Gypsies: The Hidden Americans* (1986); John N. Wilford, *New York Times* (14 October 1986). ☆

HAITIANS
||||||||||||||||||||||||||||||

Before the independence of Haiti in 1804, many emigrants from the island came to settle in the South. As early as 1526 slaves from Hispaniola were brought to South Carolina. In the first half of the 18th century, colonists and free people of color immigrated to Lou- isiana. Some of them, like the mulatto Stephen LaRue, remained in New Or- leans; others, like Jean Baptiste Point Du Sable, moved to the Midwest or the East Coast.

In 1779 a battalion of 800 volunteers from Santo Domingo fought against the British troops at the battle of Savannah, Ga. These courageous men contributed in their own way to the strengthening of American independence. However, the first major wave of emigration from the island took place during the Haitian Revolution of 1791–1803. During this period more than 15,000 immigrants, including French planters, free people of color, and slaves, settled in Louisi- ana. A few thousand more went to Charleston, S.C. Some came to the

United States after an interim stay in Cuba, Jamaica, or Trinidad. This explains why they were able to immigrate to the South even after the independence of Haiti. For the year 1809 alone, 2,731 whites, 3,102 free people of color, and 3,226 slaves—all former residents of Santo Domingo—came to New Orleans. The immigrants helped to restore the agricultural industry of Louisiana and made outstanding contributions in the arts and in New Orleans's cultural life. Writer Charles Gayarré wrote that "among the refugees who sought an asylum in New Orleans, was a company of comedians from Cape Français, who opened a theatre a short time after their arrival. From that circumstance dates the origin of regular dramatic exhibitions in New Orleans." They also played an important role at the elementary and secondary school levels. A few of them opened schools and others became school teachers, thus contributing to the maintenance of the French language in Louisiana.

The arrival of the slaves and free people of color contributed to the spread of the Creole language and voodoo practices in the South. Haitian Creole became part of the speech community in Louisiana and found its public expression through occasional voodoo dances and Mardi Gras songs. Marie Laveau, whose parents were emigrés from Santo Domingo and who married consecutively two Haitian immigrants, was known as the Voodoo Queen of New Orleans. In addition, slaves and free people of color brought with them the knowledge of traditional medicine, and they continued to participate in the activities of the Catholic church, thereby enlarging the population of black Catholics in Louisiana.

The early Haitian immigrants have left their mark on the military and architectural history of the South. For example, Joseph Savary headed the Second Battalion of Men of Color who fought in 1814–15 under the command of Andrew Jackson. Savary became the first black to hold the position of second major in the U.S. Army. In Old Charleston and in the French Quarter in New Orleans, the immigrants built French-style residences as well as shotgun houses.

During the 19th century and the first half of the 20th, Haitian immigrants came sporadically to the South, more particularly to Florida, almost every time a Haitian president was ousted from office. Because of the prevalent practice of racial discrimination in the South, however, they kept a low profile and their presence was not felt by the larger community.

The administrations of François "Papa Doc" Duvalier (1957–71) and Jean-Claude "Baby Doc" Duvalier (1971–86) resulted in the largest group of Haitian immigrants settling in the South, mostly in the state of Florida and more particularly in the Miami area. These new immigrants consisted mostly of individuals who came with a tourist visa and overstayed. Since 1972, however, numerous boatloads of refugees from Haiti and the Bahama Islands have arrived in Florida and requested political asylum. Many of these immigrants were placed in detention centers or refugee camps in or near Miami. Pending the clearance of their application for political asylum, most of them were released in 1982 to their sponsors after a long legal battle (*Haitian Refugee Center, Inc.*, et al. v. *Immigration and Naturalization Service et al.*). In the meantime, the population of "Little Haiti," a Haitian enclave in Miami, has continued to grow. It remains the commercial, religious, and cultural center of the Haitian community in the South.

See also FOLKLIFE: / Shotgun House; LANGUAGE: Gullah; RECREATION: Mardi Gras; URBANIZATION: / Miami; New Orleans

Michel S. Laguerre
University of California at Berkeley

Rodolphe Lucien Desdunes, *Our People and Our History* (1973); Charles Gayarré, *History of Louisiana: The Spanish Domination* (1866); Michel S. Laguerre, *American Odyssey: Haitians in the United States* (1983). ☆

IRISH
||||||||||||||||||||

The first important Irish migrations to the South came from Barbados to the Carolinas in the 1680s, Cromwell having sent many thousands of Irish to that island three decades earlier. During the next century many thousands made the move to the South directly from Ireland—some as self-financed emigrants, far more as indentured servants, and many who were transported for crimes or rebellious activity. Others went first to Philadelphia and migrated thence southwestward along the valleys. By 1790 people of Irish extraction, not counting the Scotch-Irish, constituted about one-eighth of the white population of the South.

The Irish were nominally Catholic, but in 17th- and 18th-century Ireland fewer than a third ever attended mass. The absence of Catholic churches in the South except in Maryland and in Charleston was thus of little consequence to them. Indeed, the Irish suffered little or no culture shock on being transplanted to the American frontier. For the most part they blended in with the Scotch-Irish and the Highland Scots—peoples with whom they had shared traditions and ways for centuries.

After the potato famine of the 1840s a new and larger wave of immigration to America began, and though most by far went to the North, as many as 100,000 may have gone to the South. In 1850 some 25,000 Irish lived in New Orleans alone, constituting a quarter of the city's population. The postfamine Irish had a considerably different experience in the South than had their colonial predecessors. Unlike the earlier Irish, they had been thoroughly reduced to the peasant class before they migrated; lacking money, they could not easily obtain land, and in the South of the 1850s there was but minimal demand for their labor. Nonetheless, they were enthusiastic supporters of the Confederacy, providing five general officers and Irish units for eight southern states. Not until after Reconstruction were they absorbed into the mainstream of southern life.

See also FOLKLIFE: / Traders; MYTHIC SOUTH: / Celtic South

Grady McWhiney
Texas Christian University

Forrest McDonald
University of Alabama

David Noel Doyle, *Ireland, Irishmen, and Revolutionary America, 1760–1820* (1981); Earl F. Niehaus, *The Irish in New Orleans, 1800–1860* (1965); Michael J. O'Brien, *Irish Settlers in America: A Consolidation of Articles from the Journal of the American Irish Historical Society*, 2 vols. (1979). ☆

ITALIANS
||||||||||||||||||||||||||||

From the importation of Venetian glass-blowers to Jamestown in 1622 to the Spoleto Festival in Charleston in the 1980s, Italians have added to the diversity and vitality of the South. Italians migrated to southern states in four distinct phases, reflecting American demands for labor, international labor patterns, and peninsular politics.

Between the age of exploration and the Civil War, Italians appeared prominently in southern history, but their notoriety derived from individual exploits rather than group endeavors. Giovanni Verrazzano charted the Atlantic Coast, and Henry di Tonti explored the southern interior. Italians helped explore and settle St. Augustine, San Antonio, and Savannah. William Paca of Maryland signed the Declaration of Independence, and Thomas Jefferson counted the intellectual Phillip Mazzei as a friend and teacher. Jefferson also persuaded a number of Italian sculptors and architects to help with the building of the Capitol. The New Smyrna experiment on the eastern coast of Florida offered the largest concentration of Italians in the South prior to the late 19th century. The experiment began in 1763 when an English physician, Andrew Turnbull, imported 1,500 Italians to labor on his plantation; the Minorcans and Italians soon rebelled, however, and the survivors scattered. On the eve of the Civil War, few southern states boasted many Italian residents; Louisiana numbered 915 and Mississippi 121, but all other states counted fewer than 100 Italians.

During the second stage, between the war and 1920, relatively few Italians migrated south, compared to the mas-sive numbers concentrated in northern cities. A handful of Italian agricultural communities in the South, however, attracted much attention. The most noteworthy and successful of those rural experiments was in Arkansas. Between 1895 and 1897 about 1,200 Italians from northern Italy were recruited to replace black laborers in Sunnyside, Ark. The experiment failed almost immediately, but a faction, led by Father Bandini, resettled in what is today Tontitown. Other colonies claiming varying successes included Bryan, Tex., and Valdese, N.C.

Louisiana attracted more Italians than any other southern state in the early 20th century. Between 1880 and 1914 as many as 16,000 Sicilians migrated to the sugarcane fields and strawberry farms. New Orleans counted 5,866 Italians in the 1900 census. Sicilians there quickly dominated the fruit and vegetable markets—as they would in many cities. Italians thrived in the commercial and agricultural fields of Louisiana, in spite of vicious nativist violence, which took 19 lives in the decade of the 1890s.

Industrial enterprise characterized the third phase of Italian migration. Italians from Bisacquino, Sicily, sought their fortunes in the steel mills of Alabama. In 1890 Jefferson County included 130 Italians, a figure that increased to 2,160 by 1920. Italians constituted the largest ethnic group in Alabama, as in Louisiana. In Birmingham they labored as unskilled steel workers, and, in typical fashion, they organized 13 mutual aid societies and branched into truck farming and small family enterprises.

Tampa, Fla., offered a unique setting for Italian immigrants—Ybor City. Founded in 1886 by the Spanish financier Vicente Martínez Ybor, Ybor City had evolved as the cigar capital of America by 1900, having over 100 cigar factories offering employment to 10,000 Cubans, Spaniards, and Italians. Several thousand Sicilians, after abandoning an ill-fated sugar colony at St. Cloud, Fla., arrived in Tampa between 1882 and 1920. In Ybor City they learned Spanish, rolled cigars, flirted with and embraced radical ideologies, organized unions, participated in a series of strikes, and eventually achieved an impressive amount of economic mobility as grocers, dairymen, and fruit vendors.

The second- and third-generation Italian Americans' migration to the Sunbelt, especially Florida, constitutes the fourth—and still active—phase. A number of salient trends appear in the developmental stage. Cities without historic Italian immigrant communities, such as Atlanta and Miami, have attracted thousands of Italian Americans in recent years. These midwestern and northeastern migrants have imported their social and cultural institutions, and today organizations such as the Sons of Italy and the National Italian American Foundation can be found throughout the South.

See also URBANIZATION: / New Orleans; Tampa

Gary R. Mormino
University of South Florida

Alexander De Conde, *Half Bitter, Half Sweet: An Excursion into Italian-American History* (1971); Jean Scarpaci, *Italian Immigrants in Louisiana's Sugar Parishes* (1981). ✩

JEWS

Southerners have often stereotyped Jews as "eternal aliens" who refuse to weave themselves into the fabric of southern culture. They largely have been ignored as newcomers who have not made any meaningful contribution to southern society.

Jews, however, are not new to the South. In 1800, for example, Charleston, S.C., had one of the largest Jewish populations in America; over 1,000 lived in South Carolina alone. For over 300 years Jews, individually and in small groups, have established themselves throughout the region in a myriad of cities, towns, and villages, some of which they helped to establish. Indeed, until the post–Civil War period, the centers of American Jewish life and the sources of many social, cultural, and religious institutional changes shaping the character of all American Jewry were found in Charleston and in Savannah, Ga., which had gathered a Jewish community as early as 1733. Not only did Jews living in the South set the course for American Jewish tradition by leading the Jewish Reform Movement, they helped mold southern traditions as well.

Though Jews never composed more than 1 percent of the South's population, few phases of the southern experience and few places in the South escaped their influence. Individuals such as Mordecai Sheftall of Savannah and Francis Salvador of Charleston stood among the southern leadership during the American Revolution. After the Revolution, Jews such as Abraham Mordecai, who is credited with founding Montgomery, Ala., moved westward, occasionally joining other Jews who had been living along the Mississippi since the early 18th century. David Yulee of Florida and Judah P. Benjamin of Louisiana were instrumental in bringing their territories into the Union and later were no less influential in taking their states out of it.

Having crossed vast chasms of culture, Jews adopted not only southern folkways, but the full range of political opinions and passions of their Gentile neighbors as well. Jews such as Rabbi Maximillian Michelbacher of Richmond could be counted among the defenders of all southern institutions including slavery. Not only did Jews fight in the Confederate regiments, they assumed positions within the Confederate military and political leadership, including the offices of surgeon general, judge advocate, quartermaster general, and secretary of state.

After the Civil War, Jews contributed significantly to the recovery of the South. They started as peddlers and shopkeepers, and many rose to the ranks of the most prominent and influ-

A rabbi, Alamo, Georgia, c. 1854

ential businessmen. Outstanding examples were the Rich brothers in Georgia, the Sanger brothers as well as Neiman and Marcus in Texas, Godchaux in Louisiana, Psitz in Alabama, the Maas brothers in Florida, and the Levine brothers in North Carolina. Jews assumed an active role in their communities' social and civic life, thereby continuing a tradition begun by Mordecai Sheftall when he helped to establish Savannah's Union Society, one of the first charitable and interfaith ventures in the United States. As leaders, Jews became involved in all branches of government at the local, state, and national level. Adolph Ochs, who was from Chattanooga, developed the *New York Times* into the great American newspaper; his mother, Bertha, was a charter member of Chattanooga's United Daughters of the Confederacy.

To be sure, the anti-Semitism that southerners inherited as part of Christian culture appeared sporadically in the form of quotas, social restrictions, and strong words. Exclusion could be found from the Mardi Gras in New Orleans to the local country clubs. Nevertheless, the active involvement of Jews, past and present, in southern culture shows that the South has not been a monocultural society, existing apart from the American melting pot. Nor, with a very few notable exceptions such as the Leo Frank case in Georgia, has it been an altogether violent, savage place in which minorities live fearfully at the mercy of drunken white bigots. In South Carolina, for example, Jews experienced real freedom after over a millennium of religious, civil, and political persecution. Georgia can boast of having elected David Emanuel in 1801 as the country's first Jewish state governor, and Florida sent David Yulee to Congress as the country's first Jewish senator. Some Jews even saw the South as a possible homeland for their people. The "Galveston Project" in the early 20th century helped send more than 10,000 eastern European immigrants into the region as a base for future growth, and earlier, in the 1880s, a much smaller group tried to establish a Jewish communal colony in Sicily Island, La. Jews in the South, in short, have reflected, and added to, the region's overall complexities.

See also LAW: / Frank, Leo, Case; URBANIZATION: / Charleston; Savannah

Louis E. Schmier
Valdosta State College

Leonard Dinnerstein and Mary Dale Palson, eds., *Jews in the South* (1973); Eli Evans, *The Provincials: A Personal History of the Jews in the South* (1974); Nathan Kagnoff and Melvin Urofsky, eds., *"Turn to the South": Essays on Southern Jewry* (1979); Carolyn Lipson-Walker, "Shalom Y'all: The Folklore and Folk Traditions of Southern Jews" (Ph.D. dissertation, Indiana University, 1986); Louis E. Schmier, ed., *Reflections of Southern Jewry: The Letters of Charles Wessolowsky, 1878–1879* (1982). ☆

LUMBEES

Lumbee Indians are the largest tribe east of the Mississippi River; they are also the largest federally unrecognized tribe in the United States. More than 40,000 Lumbee live in Robeson and adjoining counties in southeastern North Carolina.

The origin of the Lumbee people is cloaked in mystery, but some scholars trace the Lumbee ancestry to the Cher-

okee, the Tuscarora, and the eastern Sioux. Many historians support the "Lost Colony Theory." According to this view, the Lumbee are descendants of John White's Lost Colony who left Roanoke Island between 1587 and 1590. These people probably mixed with the Hatteras Indians who lived near Roanoke. Historian Samuel Eliot Morison believed that the dangers and difficulties on Roanoke Island led the Lost Colony settlers to move among the friendly natives of Croatan, near Cape Hatteras. They probably found few supplies on the Outer Banks, and around 1650 the Croatan tribe likely migrated to southeastern North Carolina. Scotsmen began to arrive in 1730 in what is presently Robeson County, where they found a mixed Indian-white group living like Europeans.

The Lumbee, a nonreservation people, were free prior to 1835, when the revised North Carolina constitution disfranchised free Negroes and mulattoes. The Lumbee were also deprived of their political and civil rights because they were not white and were regarded as dangerous. A number of Lumbees served in the Continental army during the Revolutionary War and fought in the War of 1812, but during the Civil War the Lumbee were denied the right to fight as soldiers. Many were taken, however, to Fort Fisher, N.C., where they worked as forced laborers. Knowing working conditions there were intolerable, some Lumbee refused to leave their homes for the infested swamps at the fort. At the beginning of the war the Indians of Robeson County favored the Confederacy, but by the end of 1863 they had come to view the government as oppressive. Allen Lowrie, a Lumbee, had 10 sons and all refused to serve the Confederacy as laborers at Fort Fisher, although, if given the opportunity, they would have been willing to serve as soldiers. On 3 March 1865 Allen Lowrie and his son William were shot by soldiers. According to Lumbee legend, they were forced to dig their own graves. Allen Lowrie's 18-year-old son, Henry Berry, witnessed the killing of his father and brother. Seeking justice, he imposed a reign of terror on the whites of Robeson County that continued for the next 10 years. The Lowrie War had its impact for decades to come. Today an outdoor drama, "Strike at the Wind," portrays the folk hero Henry Berry Lowrie.

In 1885 the General Assembly of North Carolina passed an act to provide for separate schools for the Croatan Indians of Robeson County. The segregated school system continued until the 1960s. As a result of the law, Croatan Indian Normal School was established in 1887, the forerunner of Pembroke State University. Today it has an enrollment of more than 2,000 students with 65 percent white, 20 percent Indian, and 15 percent black.

In the 1880s the Lumbees also formally organized churches, although they had been following Christian teachings for over a century. The Burnt Swamp Baptist Association became the chief church group among members of the tribe; in the 1980s Methodist, Holiness, Assembly of God, and other churches are also found.

From the 1880s to World War I, Lumbees from Robeson County went to Georgia to work in the turpentine industry, but by 1917 most had returned to North Carolina. Lumbees served in the armed services during World War I, but they returned home to farm cotton, corn, or tobacco. During the Great Depression most Lumbees were tenant farmers, day laborers, Works Progress Administration workers, or landlords renting out their own land. The migration to cities like Baltimore and Detroit that had begun earlier increased during World War II. Those who remained in North Carolina faced intimidation in the 1950s from the Ku Klux Klan, although Lumbee protesters broke up a Klan demonstration in 1958 and showed increasing assertiveness of their rights thereafter.

Today, most Lumbees in North Carolina are farmers, with flue-cured tobacco the chief money crop. Increasing interest in Indian heritage is seen in Pembroke's "Indian Day" homecoming on 4 July.

Adolph L. Dial
Pembroke State College

Adolph L. Dial and David Elidades, *The Only Land I Know: A History of the Lumbee Indians* (1975), and in *Indians of the Lower South: Past and Present*, ed. John Mahon (1975); W. McKee Evans, *To Die Game: The Story of the Lowry Band, Indian Guerrillas of Reconstruction* (1971). ☆

MEXICANS

Mexican Americans (Chicanos) live in every southern state. However, their greatest impact on the South has been in Texas, where they number over 3 million, make up more than 20 percent of the state's population, and comprise some 30 percent of the national Mexican-descent population. More than half the residents of such Texas cities as Brownsville, El Paso, Laredo, and San Antonio are Mexican Americans, who are also growing in number throughout the entire South.

The average Mexican American is

young, Roman Catholic, bilingual in English and Spanish, and native born in the United States to parents themselves born in this country. Chicanos are about seven years younger than the national average, and approximately 90 percent belong to the Catholic church. English is the primary language of Chicanos, but an estimated 75 percent speak (but do not necessarily read) Spanish, and about half use Spanish at home.

Mexican Americans entered southern life in two ways—through annexation and through immigration. They first became part of the South via the emergence of the Republic of Texas. In 1822 Americans, mainly southerners, began to settle in the northeastern corner of Mexico, which had just won its independence from Spain. Mexico hoped these immigrants would become a loyal, integral part of Mexican society. However, in 1835, supported by some native Mexicans who also opposed the central government, the settlers revolted and in 1836 established the independent Lone Star Republic. When the Republic joined the United States as the state of Texas in 1845, the 5,000 Mexicans in Texas became the South's and the nation's first large group of Mexican Americans.

Although Mexicans first entered the South through annexation, their ranks have expanded both through relatively high birth rates, compared to other Americans, and through continuous immigration. In contrast to most other immigrants into the United States, Mexicans have not had to cross an ocean. The 2,000-mile Mexican border with the United States has generally functioned more as an avenue than as an obstacle, with people constantly flowing back and forth across the frontier, including the long, winding Rio Grande River, which forms the Mexico-Texas border.

Mexican immigration during the second half of the 19th century was relatively modest. However, that immigration trickle turned into a flood as a result of the 1910 Mexican Revolution, which drove thousands of Mexicans north for sanctuary in the United States. At the same time, growing economic opportunities in this country, including Texas, attracted Mexicans. Immigration increased through World War I and the 1920s. The coming of the Great Depression and the drastically reduced job market in this country sharply curtailed Mexican immigration and led to the Repatriation Program, through which some 500,000 persons of Mexican descent were voluntarily or involuntarily shuttled to Mexico. The end of the Great Depression and the start of World War II brought another migration reversal, establishing a pattern of major Mexican immigration into the United States that continues to the present.

Within the Mexican American experience, Texas has held a special place. On the negative side, Mexican-Americans in Texas have traditionally had some of the lowest indices among Mexican Americans nationally, in such areas as jobs, income, poverty, and educational attainment. Moreover, discrimination against Mexican Americans has taken harsher and more virulent tones in Texas than in most other parts of the country, partly as a result of the strife-ridden beginnings of the state's Anglo-Mexican relations during the Texas war for independence.

On the positive side, Texas Mexican Americans have taken a strong leadership role within the Chicano community nationally. For example, such major national Chicano organizations as the League of United Latin American Citizens and the American G.I. Forum began in Texas, as did the Partido de la Raza Unida (PRU—United People's Party), formed in Crystal City, Tex., by José Angel Gutiérrez. *La Prensa* of San Antonio, founded in 1913, is the oldest Chicano newspaper still operating.

Texas has also been a launching pad for Mexican Americans who work in the agricultural migrant stream, which stretches into the Midwest and the Pacific Northwest. Spreading throughout the nation in this way, tens of thousands of Texas Chicanos have settled around the country. There they have formed *barrios* (communities or neighborhoods) of transplanted Texas Chicano society and culture.

The core of Chicano society is the *familia* (extended family). Mexican Americans generally have a strong sense of familial, rather than merely individual, identity, and individuals feel a deep sense of family obligation. Moreover, particularly in traditional Chicano families, the roles of the father, mother, children, grandparents, and other relatives are more sharply defined than is the norm in the contemporary United States. One special feature of Chicano family life is the practice of *compadrazgo* (godparentage), which involves the assumption of serious obligations toward godchildren.

Chicanos have contributed to southern culture in many ways, ranging from tacos to *teatro* (theater). Texas Mexican Americans have been in the forefront of the development of Chicano literature and visual arts. San Antonio has been the site of the annual national Chicano Film Festival. In a more popular vein, Mexican food—especially such popular dishes as tacos, tostadas, enchiladas, carnitas, and tamales—has increasingly become a feature of southern life.

The many varieties of Chicano music include that unique southern form, the Tex-Mex music of south Texas (also known as *conjunto* or *música norteña*). An outgrowth of early 20th-century Chicano contact with the music of German Americans, particularly in New Braunfels, Tex., Tex-Mex music has evolved over the years as Chicanos have added their own instrumentation and musical variations to the basic German polka rhythm. Traditional Tex-Mex *polkeros* still feature the accordion and bass. However, more contemporary Tex-Mex groups use horns, drums, and electric instruments, integrate jazz, rock, and country- and-western elements, and sometimes use lyrics to portray and comment on the Chicano experience.

Chicanos are becoming an increasingly visible, vocal, and significant part of the South, as well as of the United States as a whole. Possibly the best symbol of the growing importance of Chicanos is the 1981 election of Henry Cisneros as mayor of San Antonio—the largest city ever to be led by a Mexican American.

See also MUSIC: *Música Tejana;* / Jimenez, Flaco; URBANIZATION: / San Antonio; VIOLENCE: Cortez, Gregorio

Carlos E. Cortés
University of California at Riverside

Rodolfo Acuña, *Occupied America: A History of Chicanos* (1981); Leo Grebler, Joan W. Moore, and Ralph C. Guzmán, *The Mexican-American People: The Nation's Second Largest Minority* (1970); Joan W. Moore with Harry Pachón, *Mexican Americans* (1976). ☆

MULATTO

The term *mulatto* is the most commonly used and the most ambiguous of all the racial designations that have evolved in the Americas. In current usage and in that of certain societies of the past, it broadly denotes anyone with a visible physical mixture of light and dark ancestry. Historically, it was but one of a multiplicity of terms coined to describe almost every conceivable mixture that resulted from the introduction of Europeans and Africans into the Western Hemisphere.

The principal terms that have been used, and their most common definitions, are

MULATTO	½ white	½ black
QUADROON	¾ white	¼ black
OCTOROON	⅞ white	⅛ black
SAMBO	¼ white	¾ black
SACATRA	⅛ white	⅞ black
MESTIZO	½ white	½ Indian

Even in Catholic New World societies, where infant baptismal registrations have been customary for centuries, the application of racial terms has been exceedingly imprecise. Exact genetic mixtures have often been difficult to identify, and popular confusion has existed over the meaning of many of the terms. Mulatto, as previously indicated, was corrupted to include sundry mixtures of black and white as well as, on occasion, those of mixed Indian-white ancestry.

Synonymous with the word *octoroon* there developed *sang-melée*, which literally translates as "mixed blood"; both were convenient terms to denote individuals whose darker color was but barely visible. *Mestizo* evolved into *mus-*

tée, which in early Anglo-America was popularly used to denote a mixture of black and Indian. Yet another term, *griffe*, was variously used as a synonym for *sambo* or—like mustée—applied to those of mixed Indian-black heritage. In popular usage within historical documents, such terms as mulatto are frequently followed by the phrase "in color," indicating that appearance rather than precise genetic mixture was the criteria for racial designation.

Application of the term *mulatto* to individuals or families of African ancestry has traditionally continued as long as a visible mixture remains. The application of special racial designations to those of Native American descent has been less rigorous; individuals of less than one-half Indian blood have more commonly been identified with the color of the society in which they mingled, and the term *mulatto* is seldom applied to them in current usage.

Gary B. Mills
University of Alabama

Gary B. Mills, *The Forgotten People: Cane River's Creoles of Color* (1977); D. Jose F. Pujol, *Guia del Propietario de Terrenos, Poseedores y Denunciantes de Baldios* (1879); Joel Williamson, *New People: Miscegenation and Mulattoes in the United States* (1980). ☆

OKIES

Throughout the 20th century the migration of white southerners to the industrial regions of the North and West has served to highlight cultural distinctions between the South and the rest of the United States. The experience of southerners who settled in the Great Lakes industrial belt and formed quasi-ethnic "hillbilly" enclaves there is well known. Less well understood is the parallel experience of white southerners who moved westward to California during the 1930s and 1940s.

The so-called Dust Bowl migration of Okies and Arkies to California during the Great Depression marked the first large-scale introduction of southern whites into that state. Drawn by attractive images of life in California, and fleeing economic hardship in the cities and farms of the western South, more than 400,000 people left their homes in Oklahoma, Texas, Arkansas, and Missouri during the 1930s and headed west. They were followed during the subsequent decade by at least 600,000 more migrants. But it was the initial Dust Bowl migration that proved decisive. Arriving in California at a time of severe economic and political crisis, the first wave of migrants triggered a reaction that set the stage for the emergence of a distinct Okie subculture in California.

Californians responded with unexpected hostility to the Dust Bowl migrants. Their central concern was economic: the newcomers seemed to pose a threat to scarce jobs and resources. But the intensity of the Californians' response showed that the migrants were also perceived as culturally alien. Their southern accents, their style of dress, and their extreme poverty set them visibly apart from the native population, who treated them as an inferior ethnic group. Disregarding the diversity of their origins, Californians labeled all the newcomers Okies and heaped upon them the kind of abuse and prejudice normally reserved for nonwhites and foreign immigrants.

That prejudice provided the context for a separate Okie social life in California. Drawing together defensively, many of the migrants settled in separate neighborhoods called "little Oklahomas," where they set up their own Southern Baptist and Pentecostal churches, listened to "hillbilly music," and remained for the most part alienated from the larger population. In that way an Okie subculture based on values and institutions brought from the western South gradually took shape in California. In time, the term *Okie* took on a new and more positive significance as former migrants learned to embrace their separate status and express an aggressive sense of pride in their southern heritage. Today, nearly a half century later, most of the differences between Okies and natives have disappeared, but evidence of a separate subculture survives. In certain California communities the children and even grandchildren of former migrants still speak with distinctly southern accents and talk proudly of what it means to be an Okie.

James N. Gregory
University of California, Berkeley

James N. Gregory, "The South Moves West: The Dust Bowl Migration and the Emergence of an Okie Subculture in California" (Ph.D. dissertation, University of California, Berkeley, 1983); Walter J. Stein, *California and the Dust Bowl Migration* (1973); John Steinbeck, *The Grapes of Wrath* (1939). ☆

SCOTCH-IRISH
||||||||||||||||||||||||||||||||||||

The Scotch-Irish are usually thought of as descendants of Lowland Presbyterians who settled on the "Plantations" established in the north Ireland province of Ulster by James I in 1609. Actually, Scots from the Hebrides had been in

Ulster for many centuries before that; they constituted a Celtic subculture that was neither quite Irish nor Scottish. By the early 19th century they had become the industrious and frugal Presbyterians of the stereotype, but their massive migrations to America had taken place earlier. Scotch-Irish filled the southern backcountry from the late 17th century until the Revolution, and there they were able to retain many of their ancient ways. As much as any group, they stamped the South with its enduring traits. They have been characterized as a leisurely folk who preferred herding to tillage, telling tall tales to accomplishing, talking and listening to reading and writing; they have been seen as improvident and disdainful of accumulating worldly goods; they were said to be violent and tending toward extremes of apathy or enthusiasm in politics as in religion; they appeared at once clannish and hospitable, oriented toward the extended family rather than toward an abstract community.

Upwards of 250,000 Scotch-Irish migrated to America before the Revolution. Many went to the Carolinas and some went to upper New England, but most landed in Philadelphia, whence they moved southwestward in a steady stream. From 1776 until the end of the 19th century they comprised the largest single ethnic group in the white population of the southern interior. During the Revolution they were fiercely anti-English, as they had always been, and they provided a disproportionate share of the soldiers in the Continental army—as they would do in all America's wars during the 19th century. They had the reputation of being fearless, impetuous, and undisciplined soldiers. In politics, never having acquired the English habit of obedience to central

authority, they were intensely local-minded. Most therefore opposed ratification of the federal Constitution, and they formed the backbone of the Jeffersonian Republican party and, later, the Jacksonian Democratic party.

See also MYTHIC SOUTH: / Celtic South

> Grady McWhiney
> Texas Christian University
>
> Forrest McDonald
> University of Alabama

R. J. Dickson, *Ulster Emigration to Colonial America, 1719–1775* (1966); James G. Leyburn, *The Scotch-Irish: A Social History* (1962). ✫

SCOTS, HIGHLAND

The first appreciable settlement of Highland Scots in the South began in North Carolina in 1732. During the next three decades they trickled in; after 1763 the flow became a great wave. Between then and 1775 probably 20,000 (of a total of 25,000 coming to America) settled in the South, half or more in North Carolina. At first the Highlanders lived in compact areas isolated from others, and they preserved their accustomed ways. During the American Revolution they were Loyalists almost to a man; in Virginia, Loyalists were referred to as "the Scotch party." After the war many left for Florida, the West Indies, or Nova Scotia, but they were more than replaced by a new wave of immigrants: perhaps another 25,000 Highlanders migrated to the South between 1783 and 1789. In 1790 Scots constituted a fifth to a third of the white population in the southern states, though most of these were doubtless Scotch-Irish. One more wave was yet to come: during the five years after the Napoleonic Wars, between 5,000 and 10,000 Highlanders settled in northwestern Alabama and northeastern Mississippi.

Historically, western Highlanders had moved back and forth between the Hebrides and Ulster, north Ireland, home of the "Scotch-Irish," and culturally the two were virtually indistinguishable. In the American South both continued to live much as they had in the Old World, preserving a leisurely lifestyle based on open-range animal husbandry and a minimum of crop raising. As the population moved westward, they usually led the way, with the result that perhaps half the people in the trans-Appalachian and Gulf Coast South were of Highland Scots or Scotch-Irish extraction.

Scottish influence remains in the modern South through family names, remnants of the language, a few folk festivals celebrating customs, such as The Highland Games and Gathering of Scottish Clans at Grandfather Mountain, N.C., and a simple consciousness in some people of the ethnic identity.

Grady McWhiney
Texas Christian University

Forrest McDonald
University of Alabama

Ian C. C. Graham, *Colonists from Scotland: Emigration to North America, 1707–1783* (1956); John P. MacLean, *A Historical Account of the Settlements of Scotch Highlanders in America Prior to the Peace of 1783* (1978); Duane Meyer, *The Highland Scots of North Carolina* (1961). ☆

SEMINOLES
||||||||||||||||||||||||||||||||

The Seminole Indians of Florida have historically presented a unique enclave of tribal-traditional culture within the broader context of southern society. Yet these seemingly changeless people have proven highly successful in modifying aspects of their lifestyle to accommodate major shifts in the milieu.

The Seminoles were originally constituent elements of the Creek nation who had migrated southward to Spanish Florida during the early 18th century. The tribal name is derived from the Creek term *simano-li* (after the Spanish *cimarrones*) meaning "wild, runaway" as applied to plants or animals. It was extended to identify those Indians who went to live in the wild country or frontier. The Seminole towns, actually independently governed kinship units, moved primarily to escape political domination by the Creeks, as well as to avoid the encroachment by white settlers from the seaboard. In Florida they developed a prosperous lifestyle based on their Creek cultural origins. They retained a highly developed town life and distinctive sociopolitical organization, augmented their basic agriculture with extensive cattle herds, and perpetuated traditional ceremonies such as the Green Corn Dance as a source of spiritual values and social cohesiveness.

The Seminoles also evolved new cultural patterns that set them apart from other tribes—and often placed them at odds with southern whites. In Spanish Florida they were virtually free of the pressures for land, trade, and religious conversion that most southern tribes experienced. This limited culture contact left the Seminoles to develop as a fiercely independent people. During the

British period (1763–83) in Florida the Seminoles developed close trade and political ties to the English and supported them in both the Revolutionary War and the War of 1812. The Seminole towns also became havens for runaway slaves from southern plantations. Blacks became fighting allies as well as a source of technological innovation in Seminole life; blacks also incurred the enmity of southern whites who harbored a long-standing fear of an Indian-black alliance.

When Florida became a U.S. territory in 1821, missionary groups did not rush to proselytize the Seminoles in the same manner as they had attempted to transform the Cherokees. Perhaps the Florida tribesmen were perceived as too incorrigibly pro-British, pro-black, and anti-American to live with in peace, or more likely were dismissed as "savages" who were totally unreceptive to "civilizing and Christianizing" influences. In either case, the Seminoles were not afforded an opportunity to assimilate in peace. Caught up in the maelstrom of Jacksonian removal policy, they were forced to choose between fight or flight. Led by Osceola, most Seminoles opted to defend their homeland in a guerrilla war from 1835 to 1842. Another Seminole war occurred from 1855 to 1858, but the U.S. Army gradually captured most of the members of the tribe.

The remaining Seminoles settled in the forbidding swamp and sawgrass region of south Florida known as the Everglades. There they lived in secluded island camps, cultivated subsistence plots, and supplemented this by hunting, fishing, and gathering. In the last quarter of the 19th century, white traders moved to the periphery of the Everglades and carried on a thriving business with the Indians. Moreover,

Seminoles were easily accepted in the egalitarian frontier communities that grew up around trading posts at Miami, Fort Lauderdale, and similar locations.

By World War I the social and economic status of the Seminoles had drastically declined. Drainage projects in the Everglades seriously depleted animal life, and the market for pelts and hides collapsed at home and abroad. The arrival of railroads in the 1890s brought waves of settlers who took up lands formerly occupied by Indians. The Seminoles soon became a poverty-stricken, landless minority.

The Great Depression affected the Seminoles as severely as any minority in the South. Fortunately, a federal reservation, which had been opened in 1926, became the locus of relief, employment, and health and education programs for many Indians. By the late 1930s two rural reservations were also opened and became the hub of a Seminole cattle enterprise. These reserva-

George Catlin, **Osceola, the Black Drink, a Warrior of Great Distinction** *(1838)*

tions afforded safe havens for the renaissance of tribal life.

The modern era of the Seminole tribe began in the 1950s, when a federal charter was issued allowing them to elect officers and conduct business affairs with government supervision. Today the tribe is virtually self-regulating. Such business enterprises as tax-free cigarette sales and high-stakes bingo games on the reservations have brought negative reaction from many quarters, yet federal courts have upheld the legality of these Seminole ventures. Moreover, as Indian leaders point out, traditional tourist attractions are no longer economically viable in a period of shrinking federal assistance to the tribe. Thus, Seminoles are undergoing yet another transformation as they seek their niche in the modern South.

Harry A. Kersey, Jr.
Florida Atlantic University

Harry A. Kersey, Jr., *Pelts, Plumes and Hides: White Traders among the Seminole Indians, 1870–1930* (1975); John Mahon, *History of the Second Seminole War, 1835–1842* (1967); Walter L. Williams, ed., *Southeastern Indians since the Removal Era* (1979). ☆

SPANISH
‖‖‖‖‖‖‖‖‖‖‖‖‖‖‖‖‖‖‖

Spain was the first European power to establish and impose a culture upon the aboriginal inhabitants of the American South. Ponce de León's discovery of La Florida in 1513 encouraged the Spanish Crown to explore the mainland. Expeditions by *conquistadores*, most notably Narváez and De Soto, ended in tragedy. Spain failed to establish a permanent

colony until the founding of St. Augustine in 1565.

Spanish explorers reached as far north as Virginia, and the Spanish presence contributed to the founding of Pensacola, Mobile, and New Orleans. A vigorous Franciscan missionary system across the South added to the Spanish influence. Spain was ultimately unsuccessful in maintaining its empire, ceding Louisiana (which it gained in 1763) to France in 1800 and Florida to the United States in 1821. Another area of the modern South, Texas, remained a part of the Spanish borderlands until Mexican independence in 1821.

Despite the inability to sustain settlements in the United States, Spanish culture infused the South with a distinctive spirit. Spanish ways influenced the legal systems, land-use patterns, traditions of self-government, and economic affairs of states like Louisiana, Texas, and Florida, which were once under Spanish control. Spain's Roman Catholicism provided the first European religious influence on the southern landscape. New Orleans, after the fire of 1788, was rebuilt in the Spanish design, characterized by wrought-iron grillwork, shaded patios, arcades, and fountains. The Spanish also added to the cosmopolitan nature of Louisiana, most notably in the Delta, where Isleños from the Canary Islands farmed in settlements such as New Iberia. Today the Spanish language in Louisiana survives only on the Delacroix Islands.

Spanish settlements were rare on the eve of the Civil War; only Louisiana claimed more than 1,000 Spanish immigrants. Beginning in the 1850s, the pace of Spanish emigration quickened due to economic, political, and diplomatic tensions, as Spain wished to increase its loyalist population abroad.

Key West emerged as a significant refuge during the Ten Years War in Cuba, 1868–78. A number of Spanish cigar manufacturers relocated their beleaguered factories in Key West, creating a thriving American institution with the skills imported from Cuba and Spain.

Later, during the mass influx of "new" immigrants, 1890–1921, relatively few Spaniards entered the United States, and even fewer migrated to the South. Spain encouraged emigration to its own colonies, especially Cuba, and Florida became a safety valve for Hispanics on that island. Tampa, Fla., evolved into the greatest Spanish-American enclave outside New York City. In 1885 Vicente Martínez Ybor and Ignacio Haya, after considering offers from Galveston, Mobile, and Pensacola, chose Tampa as the new center for their cigar industry. Ybor City, organized as a company town in 1886 and soon incorporated into Tampa, attracted thousands of Latin *taba-queros* (Spanish, Cubans, and Italians). By 1900 over 1,000 Spanish workers had settled in Tampa, providing the organizing genius for the city's 100 cigar factories. In contrast, the next largest Spanish center in the South was New Orleans, with 493 Spaniards. By 1920 almost 4,000 Spaniards (and 5,000 Cubans) had created a cohesive Latin culture in Tampa.

Spaniards transplanted to Tampa their traditions from the homeland. In 1887 Spanish doctors organized *La Iguala*, the first of many medical cooperatives in Tampa; these group enterprises aroused antipathy from the American medical establishment. Spaniards also erected magnificent clubhouses to house their mutual aid societies, Centro Español and Centro Asturiano. These societies provided complete medical care with the erection of modern hospitals amid a thriving cultural milieu. During the Spanish-American War in 1898, the U.S. Army took over Centro Español. During the New Deal, the only Spanish-language theater sponsored by the WPA was in Ybor City. The stringent immigration quotas imposed in 1924 severely curtailed the Spanish population flow to America, an act especially injurious to the Spanish because of the imbalance of men over women.

A small but forceful group of Spanish anarchists coalesced in Ybor City between the 1890s and 1920s, serving as social critics and intellectual leaders. They supplied a class ideology that helped shape a labor consciousness of lasting power. Moreover, through their clubs, newspapers, educational work, and debating forums, they articulated a leftist orientation to the social problems of the day. By the 1920s the radical edge of the Ybor City labor movement had dulled. The labor wars of attrition had taken their toll, as had vigilante police tactics, especially evident during the long strikes of 1901, 1910, and 1920 and the Red Scare, 1918–19.

See also URBANIZATION: / Tampa

Gary R. Mormino
University of South Florida

R. A. Gomez, *The Americas* (July 1962); *Southern Folklore Quarterly* (1937–41) for articles pertaining to Spanish folkways in Tampa; Glenn Westfall, "Don Vicente Martínez Ybor, the Man and His Empire: The Development of the Clear Havan Industry in Cuba and Florida" (Ph.D. dissertation, University of Florida, 1977). ☆

SYRIANS AND LEBANESE
|||||||||||||||||||||||||||||||||||||||||||||||||||||||||||||||||||||

Ninety percent of the population of Syrians and Lebanese in the South is Christian and 10 percent Muslim. The Christian sects include the Maronites, the Melktines, and the Chaldean Catholics (affiliated with Rome) as well as the Eastern Orthodox and numerous Protestant groups. Most of the original Arab immigrants, who arrived between 1878 and 1948, were from the Syrian Province of the Ottoman Empire, which included the Mt. Lebanon district. They called themselves Syrians, identifying more specifically in terms of their region of origin, native village, or religious sect. The term *Lebanese* was not used until the independent republic of Lebanon was created in 1946.

Among the earliest immigrants to the United States from Syria were those who escorted a shipment of camels purchased by the federal government to help facilitate travel in the undeveloped Southwest. On 14 May 1856 a cargo ship, the *Supply*, brought the first 33 camels to Indianola, Tex. The camels adjusted to the varying climatic conditions and continued to be used in the Southwest until 1875.

The Arbeely family, who became known as the first family to immigrate to this country from Syria, arrived in 1878 and spent the next three years in the South. Two sons remained in Austin, Tex., when the rest of the family moved to New York. Two of Dr. Arbeely's sons later founded the first Arabic language newspaper in the United States called *Kowbab Amerika* (The Star of America).

Most Syrian and Lebanese immigrants were unskilled laborers and farmers. They came hoping to earn money quickly and then return home. Some returned to Lebanon or Syria temporarily but most remained in this country. A network was quickly established that attracted relatives and others from a native village to a particular city here.

The concentrations of Syrians and Lebanese in the South developed slowly but otherwise followed the general patterns of American settlement. Early settlers tended to gather temporarily in colonies, with sizable communities existing only in cities. Significant concentrations remain in Atlanta, Ga.; Birmingham, Ala.; Miami, Fla.; and New Orleans and Shreveport, La. One reason the South did not attract many Syrians and Lebanese at first was the lack of industrialization. Those who did not establish businesses of their own sought employment in the factory centers of the Northeast and Midwest. During the Depression, because of the lack of business opportunities throughout the United States, almost 50 percent of the Syrian and Lebanese immigrants went to the southern states, where many were able to find farm work.

The Syrian and Lebanese immigrants to the South did not consistently follow the usual economic pattern of initially earning a living by peddling. New Orleans in 1920, for example, had 20 Lebanese peddlers but 15 well-established merchants. Many families operated their own businesses, most of which were economically successful.

Today the Syrians and Lebanese in the South are well integrated into larger communities, although they are generally quite proud of their Syrian and Lebanese backgrounds. Ethnic culture is preserved through clubs and churches. Festivals and holiday celebrations focus on ethnic food and folk music. The most popular foods include *kibbee, tabouli, humous, baba ganouj, baklawa,* and *kahwee.* Two musical instruments used by the Syrian and Lebanese Americans are the *oud,* a string instrument related to the lute, and the *dulbeky,* a small drum. Two styles of dancing that have been retained are the *debke* (a line dance) and belly dancing.

Noted Syrian or Lebanese southerners include Dr. Michael DeBakey, Houston heart surgeon; Dr. Adel Yunis, professor of medicine at the University of Miami; U.S. Congressman Abraham Kazen from Texas; Florida State Senator James R. Deeb; and Alan Jabbour, director of the Library of Congress American Folklife Center.

See also SCIENCE AND MEDICINE: / DeBakey, Michael

Dena Shenk
St. Cloud State University

Louise Seymour Houghton, *The Survey* (July–October 1911); Philip M. Kayal and Joseph M. Kayal, *The Syrian-Lebanese in America* (1975); Alix Naff, in *Harvard Encyclopedia of American Ethnic Groups,* ed. Stephen Thernstrom, Ann Orlov, and Oscar Handlin (1980); Afif I. Tannous, *American Sociological Review* (June 1943). ☆

TRAVELERS
||||||||||||||||||||||||||||||||||

Often referred to as "gypsies," the population calling itself the Travelers has quite separate origins from the true Gypsies, the Romani people, yet shares a number of characteristics with them. Living in settlements from Texas to Florida, the Travelers are descendants of Irish and Scottish Traveler families who began to arrive in the South during the 19th century, probably with the influx

of Irish forced to leave their land because of famine. Records are scant, but some Irish, and particularly Scottish, Travelers may have arrived even earlier as indentured laborers to the plantations. Each Traveler community, numbering together perhaps 20,000, interacts with others—and with the Romanichal population to some extent—but each staunchly maintains its distinctiveness. Like the Romanichals, Travelers have their own ethnic language and have traditionally engaged in horse trading, paving, and other specific occupations. There are frequent references to the "Irish Travelers" in the southern press, but the most complete studies are those of Jared Harper.

See also FOLKLIFE: / Traders

Ian Hancock
University of Texas at Austin

Ian Hancock, *American Speech* (Fall 1986); Jared Harper, "The Irish Travelers of Georgia" (Ph.D. dissertation, University of Georgia, 1977), *Proceedings of the Southern Anthropological Society* (1972); Edwin Muller, *Reader's Digest* (July 1941); George Ryan, *Ave Maria* (18 March 1967). ☆

VIRGINIA INDIANS
||||||||||||||||||||||||||||||||||||||||||||||||||||||

Virginia's surviving Indians fall into two categories: communities (about 1,200 people) descended from the Powhatan tribes on the Coastal Plain, and scattered mountain populations (size uncertain) whose diverse tribal origins are now lost. All of these groups lack federal recognition as Indians.

The Powhatan Indians encountered large numbers of European settlers earlier than any other North American Indians except the southwestern Pueblos. They have been culturally adjusting since 1607, so their present state may show what the future of other tribes will be.

By 1700 the Powhatan tribes had lost nearly all their land to Europeans. Today, there are only two reservations left in Virginia, with about 125 persons in residence and land totaling some 1,000 acres. However, treaties and reservations are not outdated relics of the past to Virginia's Indians. The Pamunkey and Mattaponi are intensely proud of their treaty of 1677 with Virginia, and they are deeply attached to their communally owned land, even though most of them must commute to work off-reservation and some of them own nearby land privately. These tribesmen are equally at home with private and communal ownership. More importantly, the reservation land has never been owned by non-Indians, so it is "home" in every sense of the word. The nonreservation Indians have continued to live near one another, keeping their sense of community alive. Some of them have occasionally tried to reestablish their lost reservations and treaty rights.

By 1800 all Indian groups in Virginia outwardly resembled their non-Indian neighbors, except for their physical appearance. They farmed, hunted, and fished as they had always done, but now they lived in log cabins or frame houses, spoke only English, and attended the Baptist church. They had adopted these customs gradually, without pressure from government or missionaries. Their apparent assimilation, together with their near-landlessness, protected them from any attempt at removal to Oklahoma, but ever since 1800 they have had to face charges that they are not "real Indians" anymore. Rumor, in the absence of reliable documents, classed them as Afro-Americans.

Virginia was like the rest of the nation in her attitudes toward non-whites and like the rest of the South in her willingness to translate these attitudes into law. Virginia's Indian-descended people had to defend their civil rights by fighting against the "free black" label before the Civil War and against the "colored" label afterward. For nearly a century after the war, Virginia society became increasingly segregated and polarized, and the Indians struggled to establish themselves as a third race. The coastal groups set up their own tribal churches and schools. After 1900 the nonreservation groups formally organized as tribes with state Corporation Commission charters: the Chickahominy (now split into Eastern and Western Bands), the Upper Mattaponi, and the Rappahannock. But credibility remained poor even for the reservation people. The civil rights movement ended much of the harassment, but it also took away those hard-won tribal schools. Recent access to federal ethnic-heritage funding has helped to restore that essential part of the modern "Indian" identity.

Today's Virginia Indians are moderately prosperous country—and now city—folk who remain unique in the state because of their long perspective on American history and their feelings of kinship with Indian people nationwide.

Helen C. Rountree
Old Dominion University

Helen C. Rountree, *The Chesopiean* (June 1972), *Journal of Ethnic Studies* (Fall 1975), in *Southeastern Indians since the Removal Era*, ed. Walter L. Williams (1979). ☆

WEST INDIANS
||||||||||||||||||||||||||||||||||||||||||

The assimilation of black emigrants from the British West Indies has been complicated by the need to adapt to patterns of racial stratification. Nowhere has this condition been more pronounced than in the southern states. Nevertheless, thousands of West Indian immigrants established homes and found new opportunities in the postbellum South. The flow of West Indians became regular after the Civil War and was directed primarily toward Florida, where 2,189 foreign-born blacks lived in 1880. They formed one stream in a growing migration from the British West Indies that carried newcomers to Michigan, New York, and Massachusetts. Because of its proximity to the island homelands, Florida was a major point of entry from which West Indians fanned out to settle in neighboring states. By 1900 over 7,500 black immigrants, 37 percent of the foreign-born black population, lived in the South Atlantic and South Central states. As the influx continued, the West Indian population in the South Atlantic states alone grew to nearly 13,000 by 1930.

A sizable proportion of the newcomers were skilled workers and most had sufficient schooling to read and write English. Other young adult males came to take jobs in agriculture and construction during the labor shortages of World War I. Over 3,200 laborers from the Bahamas arrived to work on government construction projects in Charleston, S.C., and on the truck farms of Florida's east coast.

Although the West Indian population in the South grew substantially in the early 20th century, West Indians were migrating in greater numbers to the cities of northeastern states such as Massachusetts and New York. Industrial and commercial jobs were more available there than in the South, where the proportion of West Indians employed in rural jobs was 10 times higher than in the Northeast. Because of the structure of a labor market with rigid racial barriers, the South could not attract as many West Indians as the Northeast. Thus, the share of black immigrants who lived in the southern states shrank from 37 percent in 1900 to 15 percent by 1930.

The group life of West Indians in the South was profoundly affected by proximity to the home islands. The West Indian community of Florida provides a valuable case study. The relative ease of going home from the peninsula produced a high rate of return migration. A third of all departing black aliens in the 1920s left from Florida.

The migratory flow between the West Indies and Florida kept alive attachments to home-island traditions. Many West Indians worshipped as Episcopalians and revered the British royal family. A study of West Indian immigrant life indicated that the cultural forms persisting strongly after migration were customs relating to death and burial, courtship and marriage, spiritualism, folk narratives, and a semitropical diet. The West Indians stressed and displayed proudly their English traditions, partly to differentiate themselves from native southern blacks and to impress whites with their cultural sophistication. Unwilling to exchange an identity as a British subject for American citizenship under Jim Crow law, West Indians in

Florida became naturalized at one-half the rate at which West Indians in New York were becoming citizens.

Even during the post–World War II economic expansion and lessening of racial discrimination, West Indian immigrants avoided permanent settlement in the South. The West Indian population in the South grew only 8 percent from 1960 to 1970, while in the Northeast it more than doubled in size. Unlike the communities of the Northeast, those in the South contained a much higher proportion of transient males, which produced a gender imbalance that limited endogamous family formation. In 1960, while the sex ratio was nearly even among West Indians in the Northeast, West Indian males in the South outnumbered females by three to one. The difficulties of maintaining permanent employment and finding marriage partners may have discouraged newcomers from flocking to the South. Also, West Indian immigrants may have wanted to avoid the pressure of merging with the southern black community, and so chose to settle in Boston or New York City where they could be identified as another immigrant group. Still, by 1970 over 17,000 West Indians had made their homes in the South, and in the subsequent decade newcomers arrived on the currents of legal and illegal migration from the Caribbean. They and their forebears who had settled in the South added to the region a distinctive pattern of racial assimilation in which the conditions of immigration superseded the heritage of slavery as a factor shaping the process of adjustment.

Reed Ueda
Tufts University

Ira Reid, *The Negro Immigrant* (1939); Thomas Sowell, *Race and Economics* (1975); Reed Ueda, in *Harvard Encyclopedia of American Ethnic Groups*, ed. Stephen Thernstrom, Ann Orlov, and Oscar Handlin (1980). ☆

FOLKLIFE

WILLIAM FERRIS

University of Mississippi

CONSULTANT

☆ ☆ ☆ ☆ ☆ ☆ ☆ ☆ ☆ ☆

Overleaf: Doris Ulmann photograph of a weaver, Shooting Creek, North Carolina, 1930s

FOLKLIFE

||||||||||||||||||||||||||||||||||||||||||

Southern folklife is the heart of southern culture, and its traditions are intimately tied to the region. Southern communities and states define themselves through folklife as do the region's racial and ethnic groups. As southerners increasingly acknowledge their folk roots, they link formal learning at the university with traditions learned in the home. They join the South's written and oral heritage to create a more complete portrait of her culture.

Southern folklife includes music, narrative, and material culture traditions that are passed on orally from generation to generation. These traditions have diverse roots in Anglo-American, Afro-American, ethnic, and Native American cultures. Interest in southern folklife has grown rapidly since the 1940s, when Benjamin A. Botkin's *A Treasury of Southern Folklore* and several other ground-breaking folklife studies were published. Sociologists at the University of North Carolina's Institute for Research in the Social Sciences in the 1930s and 1940s produced pioneering regional studies materials, including such massive works as Howard W. Odum's *Southern Regions of the United States* (1936), which incorporated aspects of southern folklife into a general portrait of the region. Scholarly journals like the *Journal of American Folklore*, which began at the turn of the century, intermittently included articles on southern folklife, and in 1937 the *Southern Folklore Quarterly* provided an important outlet for information on the South and paved the way for later periodicals such as *Mid-South Folklore*, which began in 1973.

During the 1970s the Library of Congress American Folklife Center was launched, and sent a team of folklorists to develop a project in Georgia. The National Endowment for the Arts Folk Arts Panel and the National Endowment for the Humanities Special Projects Division provide significant support for folk musicians, festivals, and scholarship in the South, and state folklorists have developed valuable research throughout the region. Also during the 1970s three important folklife projects developed in the South. Foxfire in Rabun Gap, Ga., Appalshop in Whitesburg, Ky., and the Center for Southern Folklore in Memphis, Tenn., did significant work in North Georgia, Kentucky, and Mississippi, respectively. Their films, records, and books have been widely used in the study of southern folklife. In addition, graduate programs in folklife now exist at the University of North Carolina at Chapel Hill, the University of Texas in Austin, and Western Kentucky University at Bowling Green.

Contributions to Southern Folklife. The origins of southern folklife and the cultural contributions of blacks and other racial and ethnic minorities have increasingly been recognized. British-derived contributions to southern folklife have been clear, but the African roots of black folklife were questioned by scholars earlier in this century. In response, Melville Herskovits clearly documented the survival of African folk roots in his classic study, *The Myth of the Negro Past*, which was published in 1942. Since that time extensive research on black music, tales, and folk art and crafts has shown their relationship to Africa; and the study of black folklore has focused predominantly on the South. For example, the 1978 bibliography entitled *Afro-American Folk Culture* lists 1,428 articles and books focusing on the South, as opposed to 375 focusing on non-southern communities. This growing body of research balances the view of the respective contributions Africa and Europe have made to southern folklife. African and European folklife were both reshaped in the South, and the interaction of these black and white traditions created important new styles of music, tales, and art. Blues and country music, for example, influenced each other as black and white musicians shared musical ideas. Scholars are also exploring the contributions of Native Americans to southern culture and their legacy to black and white southerners.

Southern folklife is also the legacy of the southern working class. Poor white and black sharecroppers and factory workers expressed themselves through music, tales, and folk art distinctively different from the music, literature, and art embraced by wealthy black and white classes in the South. Ballads and blues, folktales, and quilts are closely associated with poor whites and blacks, whose cultures are symbolized by the dogtrot and shotgun house, respectively. By contrast, classical music, the novel, and portraiture are associated with wealthy whites and blacks, whose

culture is symbolized by the columned Georgian mansion. Though separated in many areas by caste and class, southerners nonetheless established significant cultural exchanges across these lines. Formally taught writers and artists were drawn to and inspired by folk artists and performers whose skills they admired. The result was a merging of southern folk and academic cultures from diverse backgrounds that in time produced extraordinary literary, musical, and artistic achievements in the 20th century.

Understanding how Old World cultures, the American South, and individual artists shape folklife contributes to an appreciation of their diverse influences on southern folk traditions. Many of these traditions are defined through occupational lore. Truckers, railroad engineers, miners, sailors, and cowboys as well as doctors, lawyers, and students all have important folklife traditions. Each group has folksongs, tales, and superstitions that reflect its identity. Sailors' superstitions focus on the weather, while students' superstitions deal with final exams and term papers. Both groups use folk belief to control events that directly affect their lives.

Age is also a major influence on folk tradition. Children, adolescents, adults, and old people develop different bodies of lore based on their stage of life. Children's games are an example of a folklife genre identified with two age groups. In communities where old people have contact with children such games are shared between the old and the young. A grandmother, for example, may recall games she played as a child and teach them to her grandchildren. Ghost stories and lullabies are other forms of folklore that older people use to entertain children. Elders also pass on countless rituals and traditions associated with marriages, births, funerals, holiday celebrations, manners, and social relations. Family photos, diaries, oral histories, and genealogies help preserve families' folkways and strengthen intergenerational ties.

Gender also shapes folklife in significant ways. Quilts are closely associated with the lives of women who make them, and the women's movement has repeatedly acknowledged the contributions—often anonymous—that quilt makers made through their needlework. The folksongs, tales, and crafts of women express a feminine perspective. Female blues singers, for example, complain about their men as predictably as bluesmen sing of their problems with women. Southern women's folklore often derives from the traditional home-centered roles that long defined women's sphere of activity. Folk beliefs about choosing a spouse, bearing children, and maintaining a home have certainly changed in the last several decades, but southern women continue to incorporate elements of folk wisdom even as they forge new family and work patterns.

Oral Lore. The storyteller is a familiar figure in southern culture. Every community has its "crackerbox philosopher" who entertains and teaches through folktales. These folktales are an important part of southern literary and folk heritage. The folk sermon is a narrative form central to the Protestant religious service. Black and white preachers trained "by the spirit" rather than "by the book" lead congregations in both rural and urban communities. They frequently use chanted verse forms to heighten the emotional intensity of their performance. Anointing with oil, faith healing, snake handling, speaking in tongues, and baptism by immersion are at times included in these services. Preachers draw on a rich array of biblical stories and images to illustrate their sermons. Belief in voodoo, which originated in West Africa, has at times influenced black religion and its lore. African belief systems were overlaid with Christian tradition beginning in the early 1800s with the Great Awakening.

Folktales. Folktales tell a fascinating story of southern culture. In trickster tales a small trickster outwits a larger person or animal. Joel Chandler Harris popularized Brer Rabbit, the best-known black trickster, in his *Uncle Remus Tales*. These animal tales evolved from Africa and are still told today. Black tricksters frequently outwit whites in protest tales. The signifying monkey and Stagolee are contemporary black tricksters who appear in long epic poems called toasts. The toast is a highly obscene form popular in prisons and urban black neighborhoods. Both tricksters and the tales in which they appear have been popularized on records by comedian Ruby Ray Moore and in songs such as "King Heroin" by James Brown. Interestingly, Anansi, the spider trickster who is a favorite in African and Caribbean cultures, did not survive in the United States.

The tall tale is a narrative form often associated with Texas and the frontier in which events appear larger than life. In southern tall tales men outrun deer and wrestle alligators and wildcats in displays of uncommon strength and power. A well-known Appalachian cycle of tall tales is known as the Jack tales. In these tales the protagonist, Jack, defeats giants and outwits the Devil. The tales are derived from Europe and offer an interesting comparison to Afro-American tales.

Folktales are a key to understanding southern humor, and popular comedians have developed comic styles based on folk narrative forms. Dick Gregory builds performances using Afro-American trickster tales, while Jerry Clower uses tall tales drawn from his rural white Mississippi roots. Each develops popular humor based on folktales from black and white southern cultures. Their performances demonstrate the humorous appeal of southern folktales to the American public.

Music. Music is the best-known area of southern folklife. Its links to European and African Old World roots and its impact on contemporary music are both important. Musical forms such as the Anglo-American ballad and the Afro-American blues are shaped by Old World traditions, by southern cities and rural communities, and by individual artists who perform them. Anglo-American ballads brought to this country by British colonists have been widely collected in Appalachia and the Deep South. British ballads like "The Unfortunate Rake" reemerged in the South as "St. James Infirmary." The ballad's narrative verse form evolved in country music, which was first recorded on 78 rpm "hillbilly" records by performers like Jimmie Rodgers, who is regarded as the "Father of Country Music." Later Hank Williams, Johnny Cash, Loretta Lynn, and many other country singers popularized country music through their recordings and performances on WSM's Grand Ole Opry in Nashville, Tenn. Hank Williams's songs celebrated the small nightclub, or honky-tonk as the symbol of a faster urban life and often expressed longing for the simpler ways of the rural South.

Bluegrass is a recent white music sound that develops complicated fingerpicking styles on guitar, mandolin, and banjo. Bill Monroe and the Bluegrass Boys and Lester Flatt and Earl Scruggs have been among the most popular bluegrass performers. Their musical "breakdowns" introduce high-speed runs on instruments in pieces like "Cannonball Special," which is a standard at concerts.

Afro-American blues has an equally rich heritage. With roots in spirituals and work chants, the blues lyric verse form emerged after the Civil War and was first recorded in the 1920s on 78 rpm "race" records. These early country blues recordings featured artists such as Blind Lemon Jefferson and Charley Patton, who performed with acoustic guitars. As blacks from the Mississippi Delta and other areas in the South moved north to Memphis, St. Louis, and Chicago in the 1930s and 1940s, B. B. King, Muddy Waters, Howlin' Wolf, and other artists developed an urban blues with faster rhythms and amplified instruments. B. B. King epitomizes a performance style that individualizes the music's sound. King's blues evolved from African musical roots shaped in the Mississippi Delta where he grew up, and to this tradition King adds his personal style as a blues artist using the distinctive voice of his guitar, Lucille. Both rural and urban blues artists sing of lost love and of racial suffering. Their music began as one of the few escapes blacks found from their hard labor in the fields and factories of our nation. Like his ancestor the African griot, the bluesman became—and remains—a spokesman for the suffering and the aspirations of his people. Blues reached a large white and black audience in the South in the 1950s through Nashville radio station WLAC, which featured disc jockeys "John R." Richbourg and William T. "Hoss" Allen.

Although jazz has long outgrown its

folk roots and modern progressive jazz has become America's most sophisticated popular music, Dixieland jazz is still heard widely. Dixieland is associated with New Orleans, and some of its original performers can still be heard at the city's Preservation Hall nightclub. Jazz funerals are a familiar tradition in New Orleans. When a musician dies, a jazz band plays a slow dirge as mourners march to the cemetery. After the burial the band leaves the cemetery playing fast-tempo pieces, recalling the dying musician's request in the "St. James Infirmary": "Put a jazz band on my tailgate, and let's raise hell as we travel along."

Black and white sacred music evolved from roots in the Great Awakening, when itinerant preachers brought religious music to the South. Four-part, shape-note singing of traditional hymns that were "lined out" was common in black and white congregations. Shaped notes in the form of rectangles, triangles, diamonds, and circles proved a simpler system of reading music and were widely used by singing teachers. These teachers "lined out," or read each line before the group sang it. The shape-note hymns of four-part sacred harp singing are still performed in the Deep South and are being revived in New England, where their roots date back to the revolutionary period.

At the turn of this century a faster paced gospel music emerged and has steadily grown in popularity. Gospel music is often performed by white and black family groups such as the Blackwood Brothers and the Staple Singers. White and black sacred music, like country music and blues, was first recorded on 78 rpm hillbilly and race labels. Today southern gospel music has an enormous appeal and can be heard throughout the nation.

Ethnic folk music reflects the rich diversity of southern cultures. Cajun music of Louisiana and norteño music of Texas are two major southern ethnic musics, and both were performed on 78 rpm records sold to ethnic audiences. These early performances have been reissued by the Library of Congress and commercial record companies on long-playing albums as part of the growing interest in southern ethnic music. Contrary to the melting-pot theory, these recordings clearly show how southern folk music is preserved in the region's ethnic neighborhoods and communities. Contemporary performers such as Dewey Balfa and Flaco Jimenez have brought renewed popularity to these ethnic musical forms.

Southern folk performers thus reshaped their musical heritage from Africa and Europe and created new sounds of country, blues, gospel, and ethnic folk music. Each of these folk musics in turn has had an enormous influence on contemporary American music. Popular traditions of early rock and roll, folk, and rock are heavily influenced by blues and country music. Elvis Presley, Bob Dylan, and the Rolling Stones "covered" pieces by black blues artists that became hit tunes on the popular charts. Michael Jackson's fame is built on his early Motown performances with the Jackson Five, performances heavily influenced by urban blues rhythms and dance styles. Even classical composers such as Aaron Copland and William Grant Still have developed techniques and tunes from southern folk music.

The role of southern places in shaping folk music is particularly interesting. Harlan County, Ky., is famed for its white ballad singers and the South Carolina Sea Islands for their black Gullah culture, while the Mississippi Delta produces an unending stream of blues artists. These areas and, more broadly, the Upland and Lowland South, define culture zones in which black and white folklife varies in distinctive ways. White singers in the Deep South such as Jimmie Rodgers, Hank Williams, and Johnny Cash are heavily influenced by blues because they grew up among, and often learned music from, black people. Their Upland South counterparts such as the Carter Family and Lester Flatt and Earl Scruggs were part of an Upland South region with a smaller black population and a greater British-derived cultural influence than the Deep South.

As performers moved from rural to urban areas, important musical associations with cities developed. Nashville is known for the Grand Ole Opry and its "Nashville sound," while Chicago, the "windy city," is celebrated by urban black singers. Detroit is the home of the Motown sound, and Memphis produced the first rock-and-roll recordings of Elvis Presley on its Sun Record label and important rhythm-and-blues and soul artists on Stax Records. As white and black southerners moved to urban industrial centers beyond the South, they carried country and blues musical traditions with them. Their neighborhoods in Chicago, Cincinnati, and other cities represent a southern diaspora in which the region's music continued to thrive. The Chicago urban blues, for example, is closely tied to the Mississippi Delta, where many of its musicians were born.

Since the 1950s, organizers of folk music festivals throughout the South have rediscovered older performers and have encouraged young artists to continue their musical traditions. Many southern musicians were first recorded by folklife field-workers such as John A. and Alan Lomax, who traveled in the South and gathered large folksong collections, which are deposited in the Library of Congress Archive of Folk Song. Since its establishment in 1928 distinguished scholars have directed the Archive's efforts to collect and study folksong. Through their efforts, the Archive has produced over 60 longplaying records, many of which feature Native American, Afro-American, Anglo-American, and ethnic music from the American South.

While field-workers like the Lomaxes gathered and studied folksongs, the record industry issued thousands of commercial folk recordings dating from the 1920s. Afro-American "race," white "hillbilly," and ethnic commercial records are a significant complement to folksong archives. Commercial issues were often recorded by field units of companies like RCA that traveled to remote southern areas in search of undiscovered performers.

An important tie developed between southern folk music and southern social change as labor and civil rights leaders repeatedly used southern folk music to support their causes. In the 1940s folksingers like Leadbelly and Aunt Molly Jackson drew widespread support through their music and influenced young white musicians such as Pete Seeger and Bess Lomax Hawes, who sang with the Weavers and the Almanac Singers. This music was chronicled by *Sing Out!* magazine and appeared on the Folkways label issued by Moses Asch. During the 1960s the civil rights movement mobilized popular support with the folksong "We Shall Overcome," and gifted black vocalists such as Bernice Johnson Reagon organized the Student Nonviolent Coordinating Committee's Freedom Singers in support of the movement. The folk music revival of the 1960s also established a national audience for southern protest songs popularized by Joan Baez and Bob Dylan.

As Americans turned to their musical roots, southern performers at the Newport Jazz and Smithsonian Folklife festivals grew in popularity. These and small regional festivals in the South continue to be an important public platform for southern folk music.

Because of recent discographies, studies of the recording industry, and large record collections, commercial recordings now are a major resource for study of southern folksong. Important archives of these recordings can be found in the South at the Country Music Foundation in Nashville, the Blues Archive at the University of Mississippi in Oxford, the Tulane Jazz Archives in New Orleans, and the John Edwards Memorial Foundation at the University of North Carolina at Chapel Hill.

A distinguished body of international research on southern music has encouraged further folk-music scholarship, the development of institutional archives, and federal support for both scholarly study and performance. A jazz appreciation movement began in Europe shortly after World War I, and for several decades the systematic collection of jazz records and the publication of works and periodicals devoted to the music took place almost exclusively in Europe. While Alfons Dauer in Austria analyzed African polyphony and rhythm in jazz in his *Der Jazz* (1958), Paul Oliver in England expanded blues scholarship through *Blues Fell This Morning* (1960), *Screening the Blues* (1968), and *The Story of the Blues* (1969). The Institut für Jazzforschung in Graz, Austria, and the *Folk Music Year Book* in England reflect the continuing European interest in southern folk music.

Material Culture. Southern houses, barns, folk art, and crafts—known as material culture—have been increasingly studied by folklorists over the past three decades. Much of this work is based on models developed by European folklife scholars whose extensive study of material culture is developed in open-air museums. Building on this European research, scholars study house types such as the dogtrot and shotgun and their respective roots in Europe and Africa. By measuring and photographing structures and their locations across the southern landscape, one learns how architecture is influenced by and in turn defines the American South. The cabin, for example, may be built with stones or logs depending on its location.

Folk crafts such as basketmaking also vary in pattern and material as the location and ethnic culture of their makers change. White-oak baskets made by whites in Appalachia, pine needle baskets made by blacks in the Georgia Sea Islands, and cane baskets made by Choctaws in Mississippi demonstrate how pattern and materials can vary.

Craftspeople learn their skills through apprenticeship with older members of their community. Their traditions are often maintained within families through father-son or mother-daughter relationships, which quilter Pecolia Warner describes as "fireplace training." Recycling of used materials

Rural barn, Hickory Flat, Miss., 1968

is common in folk crafts as old clothing is reused to make quilts and automobile tires are transformed into planters for flowers in the yard. Both function and aesthetic change when such materials are recycled by the folk artist.

Stoneware pottery has often been produced in southern communities by the same families for generations. Potters' kilns and wares were once familiar throughout the region, and many potters are now reviving the tradition. "Face jugs" made by the Meaders family in north Georgia have been a favorite topic for folklife scholars and filmmakers. These face jugs and other southern stoneware pottery are now prominently displayed in folk art collections throughout the nation.

Quilts are the most colorful example of southern folk crafts. Quilts made by southern whites present a more controlled design than the asymmetrical Afro-American "crazy" quilts with their juxtaposition of bright primary colors such as red and yellow. In each tradition the quilter uses stitched bits and pieces of cloth to evoke colorful images. Events from both biblical and community history are often included in quilts, and quilted blocks at times present a narrative sequence of events that range from literal to abstract images.

Afro-American paintings, clay sculpture, and carved walking canes frequently use the snake motif, which is known in West Africa as Damballah, the snake god of the vodun religion. Images of other animals familiar in West African and southern black animal tales also appear in Afro-American folk art. African conjure canes are clear prototypes for Afro-American walking canes with carved faces at their top. These visual connections between African and Afro-American folk art parallel similar Old and New World links in black music and folktale traditions. The work of contemporary black artists like Romare Bearden has a striking similarity to the collages of folk painters. Bearden works with narrative themes in his paintings and acknowledges the influence of folk forms such as quilts on his work.

A strong sense of place influences southern folk artists. Their work reflects memory, imagination, and visions that shape an internal place as a balance to the literal rendering of landscape into art. These artists often stand apart as children and observe others their age, and childhood memories of landscape, homes, and family provide a foundation for later work. There is an urgency in the folk artist's work, as each artist freezes this memory of life before it changed. Theora Hamblett remembered the old hickory trees her father planted, and she painted them as they stood before they were "slain." "I don't go back out there. I don't want to see that. My favorite trees are all gone," she said. But the trees stand remembered and preserved in their full beauty on Hamblett's canvases. By depicting memories through art, the artist frames his or her culture into recognizable units. Pecolia Warner's quilts stretched across her bed and Theora Hamblett's paintings on her walls preserve the memories of their makers and enable the viewer to see life through the artist's eyes.

The internal sense of place recalled in the artists' memories is expanded and enriched by their imagination. Images are rendered greater than life and give the art suggestive rather than literal power. Literal and imaginary worlds merge as imaginings become part of art. The more interesting level of the artist's internal place involves dreams and visions. This level appears during sleep or in semiconscious states, and its revelation haunts the artist until released through art.

In developing folk art, repetition, balance, and superimposition of materials are particularly important. When artists repeat the same visual idea, repetition is never exact. Rather, variations are shaped on the same theme. Artists thus develop incremental repetition in their work as they unveil variations with each piece. Balance and symmetry are important in quilts, needlework, and painting—all of which often focus the eye on the central image. Theora Hamblett's paintings of her dogtrot home, the structure she knew as a child, focus the viewer's eye through a central hall with two rooms on either side to the seed house beyond. Superimposition of materials is basic to mediums such as painting, needlework, and quilting, where oil paint, stitches, and cloth pieces, respectively, are attached to a primary surface. Through superimposition of materials folk artists increase texture and three-dimensionality. Each animates his or her work with bursts of color and shapes that draw the viewer's eye to unexpected, sometimes frightening images.

At times folk artists insert themselves more literally into their work through self-portraits or signatures. They take the license of introducing the audience to the art's creator. Artists' homes are filled with their work, and a visitor moving through each room feels watched by their work. Within this world the artist locates a space where at certain times he or she works. Artists find their spot and from it produce objects that soon decorate their homes and those of their friends. Their art draws the community together as people gather and comment on new pieces by the artist. An important affinity is felt for animals and the natural world. The artist's eye wanders from barnyard animals to creatures such as crawfish, alligators, and bullfrogs. Artists are curious about animal life and sometimes imagine themselves as the animals they portray.

Old photographs are another important resource for folk artists. Photographs offer a glimpse of ancestral faces and establish the expression of a person posing. The frozen, wide-eyed stare familiar in old photographs is at times recaptured by artists in a literal rendition of a photograph.

Folk artists and their images unveil a moving portrait of the South and suggest how landscape and season inspire artists to share real and imagined worlds with their neighbors. Their art is a special gift offered to friends, to those who know, who will understand. It leads into a sacred place where one sees and marvels at familiar, everyday beauty transformed by the artist's hand. Like Pecolia Warner's quilt on a cold night, folk art offers beauty and shelter.

Folk Medicine. American folk medicine traditions have been particularly strong in the South, where such practices still thrive, though perhaps less so than in pre-World War II eras. Among mountaineers of Appalachia and the Ozarks, Native Americans, and rural blacks of the South, folk medicine practices have flourished only partly because of lack of access to modern medical care. Folk healers embody and act on their communities' concepts of life and death, health and illness. Thus, they act as trusted confidants within a system of beliefs, a system that may clash with that of the white medical establishment. For example, many types of African healing practices were used among slaves in the

South, and some masters designated certain slave women to be plantation nurses. Vestiges of these practices still influence black folk healers. Folk medicine practices of many rural black southerners also remain strongly rooted in voodoo, an amalgam of African beliefs and French Catholicism brought to the United States by Haitian blacks in the 1700s. Likewise, the conjurer-curer role that is still important among Cherokee Indians in the Southeast reflects adherence to a variety of rich—and non-Anglo—traditions.

Practices of folk healers in the Ozarks and Appalachia have foundations in fundamentalist Protestant beliefs, with much reliance on scriptures as an integral part of cures. Unfortunately, many studies of folk medicine overlook religious or spiritual components and merely list remedies, plant sources for concoctions, and "superstitions" about illness. Folk healers and their patients also have received relatively little attention, but the *Foxfire* books and some recent academic investigations have provided fresh insights. Increasingly, the wide range of southern folk healers has been recognized, ranging from herbalists, bone setters, and granny women (midwives) to faith healers, psychic healers, spiritualists, root doctors, and conjurers, among others. Only recently, too, scholars have noted the crucial roles women have played in the South as folk healers and as teachers of traditional folk medicine practices. Urbanization and modernization have diluted the importance of folk healing in many southern locales, yet many practices still flourish. For example, one Alabama herbalist was in such demand that he drew the attention of *Wall Street Journal* reporters (8 July 1985), and many drugstores in the Lowland South have special sections stocked with ingredients for conjure bags and other voodoo components. For many poorer southerners, especially, folk medicine practices—and the beliefs they represent—remain important adjuncts to health care.

Traditional Customs. Folk customs and rituals helped to structure living in the South. The rural cycle of life so pervasive until recent times developed pronounced seasonal rhythms for people on the region's farms and rural areas. Spring planting and fall harvesting, corn shucking and hog killing were only a few of the occasions with ritual meaning. Southerners have valued family and kin, and the family reunion remains a popular regional custom. Families often develop their own unique traditions, sometimes drawing on regional foodways, recreational activities, and religious commitments.

Traditional customs are often associated with rites of passage, the special events of childbirth, marriage, and death. Rituals such as the shivaree, honoring the newly married couple, and the "sitting up," a modified wake honoring the dead, once were popular in the South, although they can be traced back to Old World traditions. Calendar customs are holidays celebrating annual events. Christmas has been traditionally an especially important holiday in the South, evoking some true folk traditions within families and local communities, whereas Thanksgiving was associated more with New England. Southern blacks had distinctive folk celebrations for Emancipation Day and Juneteenth, the day on which the end of slavery was celebrated in Texas.

Festivals are communitywide celebrations of annual events. Many festivals are not true folk events. The Mardi

Gras in New Orleans, for example, has become a commercial enterprise, yet it had folk origins, and rural Cajuns in southern Louisiana continue traditional celebrations of the carnival spirit. In the modern South the term *folk festival* is widely used to describe the numerous annual occasions for performances of folk music and dancing and for the display of folk art and crafts.

Religion has long been a major source of custom and ritual in the South. Frontier camp meetings emerged after the Cane Ridge meeting in Kentucky in the late 1790s, and afterwards revival meetings, river baptisms, brush arbor encampments, sacred harp and gospel singings, dinners on the church grounds, and church homecomings were common occurrences for southerners, black and white. Civil rights protest marches and meetings had pronounced aspects of folk ritual drawn from the southern black church.

Food has been a significant yet often overlooked aspect of southern folklife. The region's people have an enduring attachment to certain foods, such as country ham, fried chicken, biscuits, and corn bread, and to ways of food preparation, especially frying. The consumption of black-eyed peas on New Year's Day is a common custom of southern blacks and whites, both of whom, in fact, share an appreciation of regional cuisine. Subregions within the South develop their distinctive foodways, such as the Cajuns with their crawfish dishes and southwesterners with their beef and Mexican dishes.

Folklife and Literature. The emergence of southern folklife closely parallels the birth of southern literature. Europeans traveling in the South, like Tocqueville, noted the rugged beauty of the southern landscape and were equally fascinated by local inhabitants whose language and colorful folkways reflected this landscape. As the region developed, its identity was influenced by places such as the Mississippi River, where folk heroes like Mike Fink inspired a rich body of river lore.

Mark Twain built on this lore and consciously integrated southern dialect, superstition, and folktales in *The Adventures of Huckleberry Finn*. Twain listened carefully before writing, and his love for the folktale and southern humor is evident in the novel's accurate description of the river's inhabitants and their folkways. Through the life of Jim and Huck on their raft, he also explores the relationship of white and black culture, an ever-present theme in southern folklore and literature. Twain saw the art of storytelling as central to his fiction.

Twentieth-century southern writers such as William Faulkner also pay close attention to regional culture and its folk roots. Faulkner portrayed his "little postage stamp of native soil" in a series of novels that create a mythic Yoknapatawpha County. Within this county he presents a southern *comedie humaine* through the voices of white, black, and Native American characters whose lives span over a century in their small Mississippi community. Pat Stamper, a horse trader in *The Hamlet*, is modeled on horse and mule traders whose wit and storytelling skills attracted Faulkner. Like these traders, Faulkner admired the mule, who, he wrote, would "work for you ten years for the chance to kick you once."

Ralph Ellison taps the rich vein of southern black folklore in *The Invisible Man*. As he shifts the novel from the rural South to Harlem, he effectively shows the spectrum of southern rural and northern urban black folk experience. Ellison stresses that blacks are a people "of the word" and argues that any study of black culture must begin with black folklore. He uses folktales, the sermon, and blues to structure his novel, and like Twain and Faulkner he focuses on the white-black issue as the central theme of his fiction.

Alice Walker is a part of a new generation of southern writers who base their fiction on folk traditions. Walker greatly admires Zora Neale Hurston, the black folklorist and novelist whose *Mules and Men* is a classic portrait of black folktales and voodoo. Walker draws on folk roots as she presents blues singers, voodoo doctors, and quiltmakers through her poetry, short stories, and novels. Her most recent novel, *The Color Purple*, features a female blues singer, Shug Avery, in a moving description of black culture and its folk roots.

Southern folklife offers a rich, complex vision of the region as seen through its music, tales, and material culture. Southern places and their inhabitants are defined and shaped by this folklife. The appreciation of contemporary southern art, music, and literature is also enriched by study of folk traditions that influence them.

See also BLACK LIFE: Preacher, Black; / Hurston, Zora Neale; GEOGRAPHY: Foodways, Geography of; Log Housing; HISTORY AND MANNERS: Foodways; LITERATURE: / Ellison, Ralph; Faulkner, William; Harris, Joel Chandler; MUSIC articles; RELIGION: Folk Religion; Preacher, White; SOCIAL CLASS: Poverty; WOMEN'S LIFE: Children's Games; Healers, Women

William Ferris
University of Mississippi

Barry Ancelet, *Musiciens, Canadiens et Créoles/ The Makers of Cajun Music* (1984); John Beardsley and Jane Livingston, *Black Folk Art in America, 1930–1980* (1982); Benjamin A. Botkin, *A Treasury of Southern Folklore* (1949); Simon J. Bronner, *Grasping Things: Folk Material Culture and Mass Society in America* (1986); Jan Harold Brunvand, *The Study of American Folklore: An Introduction* (2d ed., 1978); John Burrison, *Brothers in Clay: The Story of Georgia Folk Pottery* (1983); Richard M. Dorson, *American Folklore* (rev. ed., 1977), *American Negro Folktales* (1967), *Buying the Wind: Regional Folklore in the United States* (1964), ed., *Handbook of American Folklore* (1983); Alan Dundes, *Mother Wit from the Laughing Barrel: Readings in the Interpretation of Afro-American Folklore* (1973); Dena J. Epstein, *Sinful Tunes and Spirituals: Black Folk Music to the Civil War* (1977); David Evans, *Big Road Blues: Tradition and Creativity in the Folk Blues* (1982); William Ferris, ed., *Afro-American Folk Art and Crafts* (1983), *Blues from the Delta* (1979), with Mary L. Hart, *Folk Music and Modern Sound* (1982), *Local Color: A Sense of Place in Folk Art* (1982); Henry Glassie, *Pattern in the Material Folk Culture of the Eastern United States* (1968); Daniel Hoffman, *Form and Fable in American Fiction* (1961); Bruce Jackson, *Get Your Ass in the Water and Swim Like Me: Narrative Poetry from Black Oral Tradition* (1974), *The Negro and His Folklore in Nineteenth Century Periodicals* (1967); Alan Lomax, *The Folk Songs of North America* (1960); Bill C. Malone, *Country Music U.S.A.* (1968), *Southern Music—American Music* (1979); William Lynwood Montell, *The Saga of Coe Ridge: A Study in Oral History* (1970); Américo Paredes, *A Texas-Mexican Cancionero: Folksongs of the Lower Border* (1976); Vance Randolph, *Ozark Magic and Folklore* (1964), *Pissing in the Snow and other Ozark Folktales* (1976); Sharon A. Sharp, *Women's Studies International Forum* (October 1986); Nicholas R. Spitzer, *Louisiana Folklife: A Guide to the State* (1985); John F. Szwed and Roger D. Abrahams, *Afro-American Folk*

Culture: An Annotated Bibliography of Materials from North, Central and South America and the West Indies, 2 vols. (1978); Jeff Todd Titon, *Early Down Home Blues: A Musical and Cultural Analysis* (1977); John Michael Vlach, *The Afro-American Tradition in Decorative Arts* (1978); Wilbur Watson, ed., *Black Folk Medicine: The Therapeutic Significance of Faith and Trust* (1984); Eliot Wigginton, ed., *The Foxfire Book* (1972), ed., *Foxfire 2 (1973)*. ☆

Aesthetic, Afro-American

||||||||||||||||||||||||||||||||||||||||||||||||||||||||

This tradition is an open-ended one that favors extensive experimentation in a search for novelty. This is an aesthetic of freewheeling improvisation and innovation, and the art works it generates and the cultural contexts in which it operates are marked by a distinctive dynamism that can be regarded as indicative of black cultural values. This dynamism stems from an ever-present delight in the surprise value of new, not completely anticipated discovery.

When commenting about his elaborate ornamental ironwork designs, Philip Simmons, one of the foremost Afro-American blacksmiths still practicing his craft, noted: "It isn't always a thing gonna be set in your mind and when just half way you can see you ain't gonna like it. . . . You think you like it to start, [but] it isn't always you like something that you can visualize. . . . I may not like these scroll[s] when I start but still I see it that way after puttin' it in and I see where I can improve it." These words about composing a piece of wrought iron art give a glimpse of a crucially important aspect of black culture, for they reveal how its traditional

art forms are enacted. What Simmons says about ironwork other black artists have said about music, dance, and many other expressive forms: namely, that the preferred shape of a specific work will only be known when it is completed.

As Simmons indicates, the black folk artist himself may at midpoint sense that something is amiss in his performance, but, rather than starting over completely, he will work with what he has until a satisfying pattern emerges. The artist is then doubly rewarded for his effort in that both his product and his creative process are enjoyable. In the end, he has a beautiful item and has solved his problem of composition by playing with it.

The Afro-American aesthetic encourages the exploration of new possibilities such as unlikely blendings of motifs, inversions of common patterns, and the layering of embellishments on standard forms. Black quilters can make quilt tops that have much in common with Anglo-American patterns, but when they enact their most distinctive artistic codes their bed covers can be spectacularly different after only a minor adjustment of a "normal" quilt motif. Consider, for example, the commonplace log cabin quilt square, a block composed of small, concentrically arranged strips that are usually no larger than one foot on a side. Many of these blocks will be set into a grid to form a quilt top. Black quilters employ this particular motif in an ordered and precisely geometric manner, but they can also make the log cabin so big that one block alone will constitute the entire quilt top. They may also skew the center of the block to one side and select high effect colors that are rarely employed by Anglo-American quilters. Such a quilt when viewed from the perspective of the Anglo-American aesthetic would seem strange or flawed or even so lacking in aesthetic quality that it could only be referred to as "crazy." Closer consideration, however, reveals that such a quilt, which seems random, misshapen, and crazed, does in fact have an order, albeit not an order marked by the same meticulous, geometric precision employed by white quilters. The black quilt, when harshly evaluated, might be read as a distorted white pattern, but when viewed from the perspective of the Afro-American aesthetic its randomness, its off-balance composition, and its deviance from the "norm" should be read as playfulness, as willingness to test the norm, as a strong desire to find novelty within the familiar.

Such quilts manifest the same spirit of innovation and improvisation that is encountered in Philip Simmons's ironwork. In the midst of composition and performance the artist gathers new insights about previously unconsidered possibilities. If judged as positive, these possibilities become "improvements," and they are used to convert the usual quilt or ironwork or song or dance step into something unusual. Thus, Afro-American works have an emergent quality to complement the open-endedness of their design. Improvisations, testings, or improvements are compiled to produce an additively composed artwork. Because this additive approach is incremental, even piecemeal, the final goal is not often seen from the outset of the creative process. Later, at some critical, even magical point, when an acceptable shape begins to emerge, it may seem that the work almost creates itself. In an instant, seemingly random elements come together and appear as powerful, evocative, or beautiful.

It is not surprising, then, that many black folk artists speak of a visionary episode as the source of their work. The plans for their creativity, they say, come in dreams, mysterious voices, prophecies, or spiritual visitations: that is, from some external force over which they have no control. Clay sculptor and bluesman James "Son" Thomas reports: "The dreams just come to me. If I'm working with clay, you have that on your mind when you lay down. You dream some. Then you get up and try." Leon Rucker, a carver of fancy walking sticks, explains his ideas in the following manner: "The idea came with the voice of the man. Now who was the man, I don't know but I say he must have been a god 'cause man couldn't do a thing like that just by himself." Gravestone maker William Edmondson while lying in bed received a command to carve from his "Heavenly Daddy." Soon after that communication he experienced another extraordinary event: "I looked up in the sky and right there in the noon day light He hung a tombstone out for me to make." Beneath such diverse statements is the Afro-American aesthetic that encourages its proponents to experiment spontaneously and somewhat randomly until they seize upon an order that suits them. That order will seem marvelously self-generated even though it is the artists who are actually responsible.

Improvisation is sometimes perceived as a symptom of the decline of tradition; it is thought to signal the demise of historically sanctioned standards. When a form changes constantly, it is assumed that its traditional base must be unstable and its aesthetic impact must be weakening. This is not the case in Afro-American culture where novelty is expected as the norm, where the rules of artistic composition are loosely rather than rigidly enforced, where the creator is expected to stand out from his community. There is thus a strong sense of individuality in black folk expression. Cultural license exists for black artists to do whatever they do in their own way. Blues singers today often refer to standard numbers by famous traditional celebrities such as Robert Johnson or Charley Patton as "my own" even though the original authorship is well-known to all. They are expected to remake the tradition and in fact they do transform old favorites with the addition of their own new elements. Sonny Matthews explains: "I will sing their songs, but I will put the words my way. If he have a word do one way, I'll change it and put it another. That's the way I do most of my singing." Philip Simmons in like manner claims: "I like doing *my own* work." A strong sense of self, then, enters black folk art and is responsible not for the demise of tradition but for its perpetuation. The aesthetic of improvisation promotes a freedom to explore the limits of one's imagination, encouraging each would-be artist to examine fully the creative formats of his or her community. Such freedom could lead to chaos and confusion, but this is not the case, for most artists exercise their options for self-expression conservatively and modestly, observing that the past is a valuable and useful resource. They negotiate between their sense of self and their sense of society. Their creativity involves a measure of compromise between what they think is good and what their audience will accept as good. Because the shape of these negotiations is similar to the testings and probings required for the composition and performance of black expressive culture, the Afro-American aesthetic seems to consist not simply of the rules for creativity but also of the rules for living.

See also ART AND ARCHITECTURE: Sculpture; MUSIC: Blues

John Michael Vlach
George Washington University

Ralph Ellison, *Shadow and Act* (1972); William Ferris, ed., *Afro-American Folk Art and Crafts* (1983), *Blues from the Delta* (1979); Leroi Jones, *Blues People: Negro Music in White America* (1963); Linn Shapiro, ed., *Black People and Their Culture: Selected Writings from the African Diaspora* (1976); John Michael Vlach, *The Afro-American Tradition in Decorative Arts* (1978), *Charleston Blacksmith: The Work of Philip Simmons* (1981). ☆

Aesthetic, Anglo-American

||||||||||||||||||||||||||||||||||||||||||||||||||||||||||||||||||||

A shared aesthetic dictated much of the look of the South's man-made landscape. White British settlers brought with them guiding principles of order, balance, and proportion. The Anglo standard for good proportion—apparently intuitive but actually acquired by traditional learning—was the "Golden" or "Greek" oblong. It measured two units on the short side to three on the long side. According to one aesthetic primer, this perfect rectangle "is more beautiful than a very long, narrow oblong, in which the breadth and length vary so greatly that they do not seem to be related." This folk aesthetic of what constitutes proper order and proportion is represented in the basic southern folk house—the single pen, usually a rectangular unit (with roots in West Britain). Variations on this unit, like the double pen, dogtrot house, and I house, extend the rectangular image. Indeed, at the earliest settlement of Jamestown the most efficient housing would have been large multifamily dwellings, but instead the settlers insisted on small, single-family rectangular houses. The predominance of the rectangle as a basic constructional concept, in fact, extended also to dining and art, for the table was typically rectangular and so was the frame for paintings.

The ideal three units of the oblong's long side is manifested in a preference for two identical design elements flanking a different central one. The windows of the typical folk house are symmetrically placed around a central door. The southern mountain cabin typically has the fireplace in the center of the far wall, rather than in the corner where the Scandinavians preferred it. The Anglo preference for the bilaterally symmetrical pattern is indeed a contrast to African, Gothic, and Italianate architectural styles. Beyond architecture, the American design of gravestones and dress, even the arrangement of food (meat, potatoes, vegetables) on the dinner plate, follows the bilaterally symmetrical pattern as well. In the English language sentences are rectilinear, reflecting symmetry and a design of threes: beginning, middle, and end; subject, object, and verb; past, present, and future.

The symmetrical aesthetic stems from a geometric projection of the human body as an ideal form; faces and bodies are designed symmetrically. The regularity expressed helped nurture within southern culture a sense of order, balance, and harmony. Anglo-rooted and southern-based country music, for ex-

ample, is noted by its rhythmic regularity and evenness; it also represents politically a conservative attitude. The so-called English barn is another example of the Anglo geometric aesthetic: it contains two bays around a centrally placed passage. The entrance is on the nongable end to emphasize the ordered rectangular facade.

The rectangle is the key form in the Anglo-American aesthetic, reflecting the opposition of two equal pairs. Even the Stars and Bars consists of two crossed rectilinear bars that form a field of solid colored pairs. The double-doored double pen, a pair of rectangular units, is the limit of folk architectural extension; a triple pen is not found in the Anglo folk repertoire. The house might be extended by placing a double pen over the first pair, thus forming the so-called I house, or an L or T extension can be put on the back to preserve the binary facade. The special case is the addition of a central door and hallway that projects an image of bilateral symmetry. Inside a rear door is typically paired in line with the front door, and, even in a single pen, a light partition often divides the cabin into two rooms. The basic Anglo-American house consists of a Golden Oblong with central front and rear door and symmetrically placed windows.

Again, there is geometric projection of the human body in the binary aesthetic—paired arms, eyes, and legs. In fact, in language people use this reference when saying "on the one hand, on the other." Binary thinking goes further, from artifact to worldview. The classic binary oppositions of North and South, upland and lowland, and black and white show the place of aesthetic not as ornament but as a central, socially important idea. Indeed, "separate but equal," a common guiding doctrine of an earlier South, was an aesthetic principle as much as a social one.

In addition to a concern for shape, the southern Anglo-American aesthetic stresses a natural look. The pronounced image of an agrarian South finds characterization in the country-gentleman ideal borrowed from the English. The folk painters and tale tellers of the South have shared a long tradition of celebrating its rusticity. This means more than depicting the adored everyday activities of the country church and farm; it reflects an overarching aesthetic stressing man's close ties to nature. The emphasis may be partly explained by southern settlers' need to adapt to a geography and climate most unlike their point of British origin. The look of the folkbuilt landscape thus more often blends into the environment than clashes with it.

Natural materials add to the appeal of artistic products. Wood is especially favored for its look and feel. Whittlers refuse to paint their wooden chains to make them more realistic; the natural wood, they will tell you, *should* be shown. Baskets, houses, and pottery commonly display soft, natural colors. Figures made from corn husks, bedcovers in a honeycomb pattern, and instruments made from skins or gourds are among the mainstays, for instance, of a 1937 survey of southern handicrafts by Allen Eaton.

The pride expressed by southerners in the naturalistic appearance of their objects is coupled with an aesthetic preference for objects shaped or controlled by hand. The title of a recent Mississippi folk art exhibition was, in fact, *Made by Hand*. The persistence of handicrafts such as chairmaking, whit-

tling, and quilting, even in the face of factory goods, makes an aesthetic statement in favor of handmade quality. Although some observers associate this predilection with southern cultural conservatism, another more plausible interpretation relates the value seen in handwork to the connections—both to nature and to other people—provided by the aesthetic control and emotional compassion of human touch. Like the symbol of ample "time on your hands" reflected by traditional southern storytelling, handworked items represent for southerners the value of close attention to the object and a sense of leisureliness.

Although the form and feeling of southern material folk culture are varied, the major British inheritance did find prominent expression. A set of coherent aesthetic principles emerged in the southern experience. They were not identical with, or exclusive to, the Anglo antecedent but drew inspiration from general principles of proper order, balance, and proportion. Yet scholars disagree over how many of those principles were imposed on non-white or non-Anglo southerners. Some, like folklorist John Michael Vlach, see a major African presence on the landscape, whereas others, like folklorist Richard M. Dorson, argue that the European culture in America transformed or eliminated most of the cultural traditions of blacks and Indians. Identifying distinctive, multiple aesthetic systems of ethnic origin, however, does not contradict the existence of a dominant southern aesthetic. Despite different, frequently overlapping, identities expressed aesthetically, a predominant influence on southern folk design has been those aesthetic principles based on a combination of an Anglo-Celtic heritage

Pieced quilt showing Anglo-American aesthetic form, Oxford, Mississippi, 1973

and new demands of the American scene.

Simon J. Bronner
Pennsylvania State University
Capitol Campus

Simon J. Bronner, *Grasping Things: Folk Material Culture and Mass Society in America* (1986); Richard M. Dorson, in *American Folklore in the New World*, ed. Daniel Crowley (1977); Allen H. Eaton, *Handicrafts of the Southern Highlands* (1937; reprint, 1973); William Ferris, *Local Color: A Sense of Place in Folk Art* (1982); Henry Glassie, in *The Study of American Folklore: An Introduction*, ed. Jan Harold Brunvand (2d ed., 1978), in *Folklore and Folklife: An Introduction*, ed. Richard M. Dorson (1972), and *Folk Housing in Middle Virginia: A Structural Analysis of Historic Artifacts* (1975); Warren Roberts, "Folk Architecture," in *Folklore and Folklife: An Introduction*, ed. Richard M. Dorson (1972); John Michael Vlach, *The Afro-American Tradition in Decorative Arts* (1978). ☆

Arts and Crafts

Southerners have produced a wide variety of arts and crafts. Men and women, blacks and whites, Native Americans and ethnic groups have all contributed to the region's traditions. The Appalachian white, rural Afro-American, Native American, and Moravian ethnic traditions are among the best documented in the region.

Folk painting includes works sometimes called primitive or naive, such as the work of Clementine Hunter in Louisiana, Nellie Mae Rowe in Georgia, Theora Hamblett and Luster Willis in

Mississippi, and Minnie Evans and Minnie Reinhardt in North Carolina. Distinctive pottery traditions can be found in North Carolina, Georgia, and east Texas. Among the South's most famous potters are Lanier Meaders of north Georgia and Burlon Craig of North Carolina.

Carving of stone and of wood has been a frequently practiced craft and includes the documented stone carvings of animals and angels by Tennessean William Edmondson, the sculpted clay skulls of James "Son" Thomas of the Mississippi Delta, and the wooden walking sticks of Victor "Hickory Stick Vic" Bobb in Mississippi. Ironworking has included utilitarian products with aesthetic dimensions. Philip Simmons of Charleston is the best-documented among many examples of black craftsmen who have used iron to make art.

Basketmaking provides a good example of the existence of the three ethnic-artistic folk art and craft perspectives in the South—Native American, Afro-American, and Euro-American. Each used somewhat different materials and designs. The Mississippi Choctaw baskets, the Afro-American Sea Islands baskets from South Carolina and Georgia, and the baskets from Appalachian rural areas are well known to collectors and scholars. Other craftsmen in the South have specialized in creating musical instruments, including Louis Dotson (guitar) of Mississippi and Homer Ledford (dulcimer) of Kentucky. Women have produced distinctive and distinguished textiles, including quilts (Pecolia Warner of Mississippi and Harriet Powers of Georgia) and needlework (Ethel Mohamed of Mississippi). "Sewing" encompasses many specific techniques. The regional arts and crafts tradition would also include chairmak-

ing and furniture making, weaving and spinning, Indian beadwork, jewelry in general, rug making, leather work, glass work, toy and doll making, and countless other activities.

Like those found in other regions, folk arts and crafts in the South are rooted in the traditional values of communities and families. Embedded within folk objects, made with skill and designed for beauty, is a conservative desire to preserve the ways of an honorable past, believed still to have worth in the present. What southerners are saying in a material mode when they fashion quilts or baskets or churns is that the people from whom they learned their craft were good, decent, and intelligent folk worthy of imitation. Thus, contemporary artisans turn their talents to making objects whose designs may be a century old. They repeat again, rather than create anew, so that tradition will survive, so that their sense of group is more pronounced than their sense of self. These patterns, which are seen in all folk societies, are repeated in folk society in the South.

From the colonial period until the first decade of the 19th century, most American artifacts were made by traditionally trained artisans. But throughout the 19th century these same goods came to be made more often in factories by large numbers of workers using machines. Industrialization and the factory system took hold first in New England, however, and did not reach the South in any appreciable manner until after World War I. Hence, in the 20th century the number of folk artisans in the South is significantly larger than in other regions. Consequently southern folk arts and crafts today enjoy relatively high visibility and homemade items are often presented as emblematic of the region.

What one really sees in coverlets and carvings is a national pattern that has simply survived longer in the South than elsewhere.

Although the various genres of traditional art and craft are found all over the country, southern examples have some distinctive features. Southern stoneware vessels, for example, are sealed with a wood-ash or alkaline glaze not found in other regional pottery-producing areas. Its characteristic runny finish, variously called "Shanghai" or "tobacco spit" and found from North Carolina to Texas, but nowhere else, can be used to distinguish a Deep South style of ceramics. Other glazes and glazing techniques have been carried into the South, but the alkaline glaze has remained exclusively in its original territory.

In patchwork quilting many block patterns such as "log cabin," "double wedding ring," "drunkard's path," or the ubiquitous "nine patch" are shared across regional boundaries. However, southern blacks, in addition to using block patterns, have also composed quilt tops with strip units. As a consequence of this ethnic tradition, southern quilting as a whole is quite different from quilting done in other regions; it includes an Afro-American as well as an Anglo-American approach to quilt composition and design.

Until the 19th century the slat-back chair was a piece of sitting furniture common in all parts of the eastern United States. At that point other chair types became popular in the North while the slat back remained the most typical southern "settin' " chair. Subsequently, it underwent a number of modifications: most notably its rear posts were curved backwards and their front surfaces were shaved flat, producing the so-called mule-ear motif. Southern furniture making thus evolved a distinctive chair type at roughly the same time its earlier form was nationally distributed. To identify the "southernness" of southern folk art and craft, then, one must be aware not only of national patterns but also of very minute and specific attributes of an item's materials, techniques, and social history. What is uniquely southern about an item may consist of a minor detail, important mainly to the maker of the object.

A folk society is often, although not necessarily, a rural society. Because the South has only recently been open to major industrial development, farming remains quite prominent and rural agrarian values are widespread. Life on a farm is, above all, marked by making do with whatever is at hand, and craftsmanship of either the production or repair variety is part of the daily routine as handwork helps supplement the marginal finances of a small, family-owned farm. The economic benefits of traditional know-how mean that craft activities are not archaic, quaint survivals. Rather, they are necessary, useful, and practical ways to live, independent of urban control, and they make one proud of inherited skills. The decorative touches that grace rural homes and yards in the South likewise manifest a spirit of independence. Quilts and bottle trees and tractor-tire planters and whirligigs and walls covered with newspaper and magazine cutouts all convey the message that life can be brightened with means that are close to home. Homegrown art, it is asserted, is as good as any other.

Visitors to the South in recent years, imagining the place to be peopled with exotic "hillbilly and cracker" personalities, have expected southern folk art to be extraordinarily deviant. Indeed, one can find southern artists without conventional studio credentials who have created highly innovative works. Walter Flax of Yorktown, Va., has his fleet of almost 150 battleships and cruisers; Charlie Field near Lebanon, Va., decorated a whole house, inside and out, with polka dots; and Eddie Owen Martin of Buena Vista, Ga., made a stepped Aztec pyramid in his backyard. But these people, though they are southern and artists and possibly members of folk communities, are not southern folk artists. Their efforts reflect private visions and fantasies rather than a shared folk heritage. In looking for folk art, one looks not for spectacular expressions but for the regular and commonplace, confirming the ordinary rather than celebrating the novel. A culture is kept vital by the mutual agreement of the members of a group, not by the efforts of a lone individual. In communities and families folk art and craft are perpetuated in the South.

See also ART AND ARCHITECTURE: Sculpture; ETHNIC LIFE: Indian Cultural Contributions; Mountain Culture; RELIGION: / Moravians

John Michael Vlach
George Washington University

Carl Bridenbaugh, *The Colonial Craftsman* (1950); John A. Burrison, *Southern Folklore Quarterly* (December 1975); William Ferris, *Local Color: A Sense of Place in Folk Art* (1982); Henry Glassie, *Pattern in the Material Folk Culture of the Eastern United States* (1968); John Michael Vlach, *The Afro-American Tradition in Decorative Arts* (1978). ☆

Basketmaking

Basketmaking is a dynamic craft with ancient roots. More than one basketmaker has proclaimed that baskets trace their origin back to Moses in the bullrushes, and, indeed, woven baskets of various fibers are an essential cross-cultural craft known in practically every civilization from antiquity to the modern day. The craft has retained a position in the constellation of cultural traditions in communities and families through lean times and good in every part of the South. Basketmaking is well-embedded in the distinct yet related traditions of southerners of Native American, European, African, Caribbean, and Asian descent.

There are three major traditions of southern basketmaking: Native American, Afro-American, and Anglo-American. Of these, the black basketmakers in the Georgia and South Carolina Sea Islands have long been admired for the beauty and quality of their coiled grass baskets, whereas less attention by scholars or the public has been paid to Native American baskets (arguably the most intricate and finely made by any civilization) and to those in the white traditions. Even less attention has been paid to Asian basketmaking traditions in the South.

The various culturally determined forms, materials, and modes of construction (essentially a process of weaving, plaiting, or coiling) indicate a rich exchange between peoples over the generations, but distinctive characteristics remain within each group. Indian peoples favor split reed, willow, and grasses, as do black craftsmen, but incorporate colorings and special designs in the woven container. Certain baskets made by black makers are not known among Indians or whites and may echo West African or Caribbean traditions. Anglo-Americans have always favored straight-grained hardwood stock for baskets, chiefly white oak and hickory. Pure function and physical rigidity mark the work of culturally conservative white craftspeople, while playful ornamentation in color scheme often highlights the work of Indian and black American builders. White-oak basketmaking of the Anglo southerners is similar from the Virginia Piedmont across the mountains into Missouri, Arkansas, and Texas, while the work of Native Americans differs from the coastal areas of the South to the western edge of the region (where some of the tribes lived separately for countless centuries).

The purposes to which baskets are put are as numerous as the chores of

Craftsman making a white-oak basket, Sharon, Mississippi, 1972

daily life. Baskets take whatever shape is necessary for their function. All are artifacts of flexible woven material and are used to gather, hold, measure, transport, store, and sort everything from eggs and seeds to babies and firewood. Southern baskets are created from every kind of useful plant and wood: from cornshucks, straw, grasses, branches, stalks, cane, bark, vines, pine needles, hickory, ash, willow, and oak.

Among the regional types are cotton baskets made and used by both black and white people in southern agriculture, fish traps for mountain streams, Choctaw corn sieves, and Sea Island Afro-American flower baskets. Some basket types—such as the Choctaw basket of split dyed cane, black South Carolina coiled grass basket, and white riven and ribbed oak egg basket—require great labor and intricate skill. Others are easily made from gatherings of vines, grasses, or branches.

Craft revivals have played an important role in southern basketmaking. Movements of the 1920s and 1930s were fostered by various foundations, craft guilds, and New Deal agencies that sought to document and interpret southern life and work. From the 1960s to the present, basketmaking has been nourished by the folklife studies movement, folksong revivals, back-to-the-land enthusiasts, the *Roots* phenomenon, tourism, Foxfire-like projects, and a return to the craft by older artisans in retirement.

The interest in country things and "primitive" artifacts at rural auctions and art galleries reflects the growth of outside markets for traditional baskets that, in spite of philosophical misgivings of some scholars, has encouraged the continuation and occasional rebirth of authentic basketry. Adult craft classes and recreational programs also foster basketmaking in the modern South, allowing one to learn to produce a basket under proper tutelage.

Modern machines cannot produce a satisfactory "traditional" basket. Despite 19th-century attempts, the failure of technology to create good, inexpensive baskets in factory settings helped generate demand for the development of other cheaper containers, from paper sacks to plastic bags and glass jars. The domination of cheap sacks and bags has encouraged the decline of basketmaking, a craft that flourished when baskets were genuinely needed in society and that still can flourish among a small group of knowledgeable workers.

The process of craftsmanship is a fluid, dynamic one of constant if unnoticed inspiration, innovation, and alteration as builders encounter inviting technologies, new outlets, and new ideas in aesthetics, design, decoration, and function. If the basket made by Earl Westfall in Howard County, Mo., in 1969 holds magazines in a parlor rather than kindling by the hearth, the artifact remains a vivid and stable testament to a rich legacy, and it remains a traditional basket no matter what its present function. While one may mourn the loss of the old-timers, theirs is a craft of life, not death, and baskets will continue to be produced in response to the vicissitudes of cultural expression.

Basketmaking is well suited to the workshop or spare room and is a convenient way to supplement income from other jobs. Other factors, however, such as the difficulty in obtaining suitable wood or fiber or even high-quality tools, have inhibited the growth of the craft in some areas. Without a proper market outlet or the patrimony of the museum,

there would be little incentive to retain the old skills so laboriously learned and manifested in basketmaking, nor would conservative, unassertive craftspeople come to the attention of researchers, collectors, nontraditional imitators, and businessmen. Some, like the late Jim Nicholson of northern Virginia (coming from a long line of basketmakers), continued making white-oak baskets and selling them from the hood of his car on the highway shoulder.

Basketmaking has always been central to the life of all economic classes and groups of people in the South. Baskets today are considered art or handsome functional artifacts. Some basketmakers continue production in traditional contexts for traditional purposes. Although there are few "traditional" makers at work today, the craft continues, ever changing but still a characteristic feature of the cultural landscape of the South.

See also ENVIRONMENT: Plant Uses; ETHNIC LIFE: Caribbean Influences; Indian Cultural Contributions

Howard W. Marshall
Missouri Cultural Heritage Center
University of Missouri at Columbia

Gerald L. Davis, in *Afro-American Folk Art and Crafts*, ed., William Ferris (1983); Allen H. Eaton, *Handicrafts of the Southern Highlands* (1937; reprint 1973); Howard W. Marshall, in *Readings in American Folklore*, ed. Jan Harold Brunvand (1978); Otis T. Mason, *Aboriginal American Basketry: Studies in a Textile Art without Machinery* (1904); Sue Stephenson, *Basketry in the Southern Appalachian Mountains* (1977); Mary Twining, in *Afro-American Folk Art and Crafts*, ed. William Ferris (1983). ☆

Cemeteries

||||||||||||||||||||||||||

The South has two major distinct cemetery types, urban and rural. Urban cemeteries are less regionally distinctive because they exhibit a greater degree of cross-cultural exchange. National trends in sepulchral art, cemetery design, and botanical landscaping are more obvious in the burying grounds of Savannah, Charleston, Atlanta, and New Orleans than in the small graveyards of the more prevalent rural communities. Moreover, the rate of innovation is more rapid in the urban context, often creating cemeteries that represent an eclecticism difficult to classify into meaningful types. The rural burial grounds, however, more aptly express the region's peculiar attitude toward the proper disposal and veneration of its deceased.

Southern rural cemeteries are modest in size, averaging between two and five acres. The rural South had two general graveyard categories until recent times—the family cemetery and the loosely identified community cemetery, with or without the association of a church structure. The family cemetery is not uniquely southern; however, it is found more frequently in the South than in other regions of the United States. The distinctiveness of the plantation as a southern land-use phenomenon certainly fostered the use of private burial plots. The lag in urban development also promoted the regional predisposition toward family cemeteries.

By far the most common southern cemetery is the public graveyard associated with the hamlets and crossroad settlements that pepper the landscape. The cemetery may or may not be adjacent to a church; indications are that some of the older, more established burial grounds preceded any church association by many years. These southern graveyards had common traits. Excluding for the moment any urban innovations or ethnic peculiarities, several definitive characteristics lend a distinctive regional stamp to southern rural cemeteries: (a) decided preferences for location of the cemetery site, (b) preferred species of vegetation, (c) axial grave alignments, (d) diverse innovations in decoration, and (e) cults of piety.

One term suggested for this distinctive regional burial ground is the Upland South folk cemetery. Widely associated with the uplands found throughout the South, it is found scattered across the South from central Texas to the Atlantic Piedmont and from the Ohio Valley to the Gulf fringe. A number of its characteristics have been shared by rural blacks as well as whites; a major distinction between the two is that the black cemeteries tend to be less well cared for than those of the whites.

Rural folk graveyards show a marked tendency for hilltop location. Wherever feasible, these cemeteries will be perched on the very summit, or, if not on the summit, on the crest of a ridge or well up the side of any slope or inclined plane. The sacredness of hilltops is recognized as being of great antiquity, but locals rationalize cemetery location in terms of drainage.

Certain species of vegetation have evolved by long use as "cemetery" plants. Evergreens are a particularly obvious example, with dominant species being the eastern red cedar, various pines, or oaks. Evergreens are symbolic of immortality. In addition, a wide variety of shrubs, perennials, and annuals are also common. Arborvitae, roses, azalea, spirea, and various lilies abound. Species of vegetation will, of course, vary somewhat with environmental differences across the South.

Graves in southern rural cemeteries are almost always aligned along an east-west axis with the head toward the west and the feet to the east. Sacredness associated with direction is another Old World trait of great antiquity. The alignment of graves is not always cardinally accurate, though. Rather, the graves are placed in what is perceived to be an east-west direction; actually, it is more southeastward than eastward. The orientation of graves has a strong religious component, rationalized as proper so that the faithful will rise to face the risen Christ on Judgment Day. Jerusalem lying to the east is also of some significance.

Innovativeness of decoration in southern rural cemeteries covers a broad spectrum of traits. In general, there is a well-established tradition of "making do." Grave mounds are covered with shells, dishes, personal artifacts (such as favorite mugs, eyeglasses, medicine bottles, and the like), or other paraphernalia. Coffee cans or fruit jars covered with foil make suitable flower containers. A particularly eye-catching, homemade container is made by cutting an aqua, or white, gallon detergent bottle in half. A hole is cut in the bottom center, the neck of the top half is inserted, and the cap screwed on. The resulting container has a broad enough base to resist easy toppling and will hold an abundant array of flowers. Children's graves display a phenomenal array of personal items. Favored toys, marbles, animal or diverse-shaped figurines, or stuffed animals may be encountered. There appears to be less difference

among graves of black and white children than among those of adults. Dishes, for example, are seldom broken on white adults' graves, whereas some scholars hold that the African trait of breaking pottery is especially evident on black adults' graves. Evidence of the latter is, however, very restricted and may prove less characteristic with continued research.

Other grave artifacts are symbolic of occupation or of the tragedy responsible for death. The use of a toy log truck on the grave of a young adult was the family's way of respecting his love of trucking, even though the young man died as a result of a freak trucking accident.

Shells used for grave decoration have a wide global distribution and date from the far past. Originally associated with pagan fertility symbolism and rites, the shell appears to have been absorbed into Judeo-Christian symbolism through the Romans. It is widespread throughout rural southern cemeteries as a decoration. Most often the shells are freshwater varieties of clams or mussels. Where available, they include various whelks and conchs. Shells are placed along the crest of the grave mound, randomly spotted or sometimes totally blanketing the grave; other times a single conch or large whelk may be placed near the head. There are pagan overtones, even psychological ones, but the southerner is seldom, if ever, cognizant of why shells are used, recognizing only that they are attractive.

Other decorative practices include the use of white sand for grave plots or even for covering entire graveyards. Various tombstone styles are represented as well, although the introduction of commercial stones has not been uniform across space or time. The grave shelter is an unusual decorative form.

The typical shelter is a rectangular structure with open sides, picket fencing, gable roof, and with gables at the head and foot of the grave. This practice is not found among blacks, and its prevalence among whites remains inexplicable. It has experienced a morphological evolution and appears to be a matter of preference; distribution is widespread across the South.

Cults of piety express veneration of deceased family members. One of the most widespread of these cults is graveyard workday, once again a phenomenon more prevalent among whites than blacks. Graveyard workday is an annual event where all people with relatives in a particular cemetery gather to clean the cemetery. Activities include scraping all grass from the cemetery (creating a stark visual contrast with surrounding woodland or field), mounding all graves, raking or sweeping all debris from the grounds, righting fallen tombstones (when present), and mending fences to keep animals out. Associated with this daylong event is "dinner on the grounds," light courting, business dealing, and general renewing of family bonds and friendships. Thus, graveyard workday serves multiple functions within the community, much the same way that southern funerals are family-strengthening affairs.

The traditional southern rural cemetery described still exists, although decreasingly so. As the South has urbanized and become more accessible via the automobile and blacktop road, ideas and attitudes concerning proper disposal and care of the dead have changed. Within towns especially the traditional cemetery landscape has given way to the memorial garden concept conceived in California and diffused eastward across the United States. The graveshed has all but disappeared,

graveyard workday has been supplanted by perpetual care, decoration is relegated primarily to the artificial flower, and the naked graveyard with its mounds of earth has been replaced by parklike expanses of grass. Yet some locales doggedly adhere to traditional folkways, and cemeteries there are a curious blend of elements from both ends of the spectrum. Large, sweeping expanses marked by family plots, some of which are still scraped and have mounded graves, remind one that the landscape of the dead is not as static as one might initially perceive.

Thus, the South has one of the most varied cemetery landscapes found anywhere in the United States. There are still pristine examples of the folk graveyard; there are black cemeteries embodying a number of the same cultural traits found in white graveyards; examples of aesthetically appealing memorial gardens can be found in nearly all modest-sized southern towns and certainly in the cities. Across this range of sacred space one finds evidence of pagan ritual and symbolism, traits having greater geographic distribution than the South, a strong Old World influence (probably more European than any other), and more unanswered questions than definitive conclusions. For all this, however, the southern cemetery remains an important element of the cultural landscape. It remains a barometer of the economic and social viability of a community and a looking glass into the southerner's innermost feelings about proper burial and veneration of the dead.

See also BLACK LIFE: Funerary Customs, Black

D. Gregory Jeane
Auburn University

D. Gregory Jeane, *Journal of Popular Culture* (Spring 1978); Terry Jordan, *Texas Graveyards: A Cultural Legacy* (1982), *Southwestern Historical Quarterly* (Janurary 1980); Fred Kniffen, *Geographical Review* (October 1967); Fred A. Tarpley, *Southern Folklore Quarterly* (December 1963); Robert Farris Thompson, *Flash of the Spirit: African and Afro-American Art and Philosophy* (1983); John Vlach, *The Afro-American Tradition in Decorative Arts* (1978). ☆

Childbirth

||||||||||||||||||||||||||||||||

The first stage in the cycle of human life, childbirth, is universally recognized as a period of crisis. Until recently, the distressingly high mortality rate of both mothers and babies at childbirth and the lack of professional health care resulted in the universal usage of traditional strategies and behaviors to prophesy and protect mothers and babies. In the South, folk beliefs, customs, and medicine associated with childbirth derived from more diverse sources, developed more fully, and endured longer than in any other region of the United States.

The 18th and 19th centuries saw the amalgamation of Native American, Afro-American, and Euro-American folk remedies and beliefs in the South. Although the spread of black medical knowledge was limited somewhat by harsh laws in the antebellum South, on many large farms and plantations black midwives played a significant role, even when white men and women were officially in charge of plantation health. Before the advent of modern hospitals, medical doctors, and adequate transportation, trained and untrained white and black midwives, granny women, or female neighbors assisted during home births. Prenatal care was almost nonexistent. Even when doctors and hospitals were available, many women in the rural South preferred to give birth at home with the help of midwives.

In each phase of the birth process—conception, gestation, delivery, and postpartum—southern families sought to insure the health and intelligence of babies and the safety of mothers through prophecy, strict control of environment, and principles of homeopathic medicine ("like cures like"). Many southerners believed that it was possible to determine or control the sex of an infant at conception. Some southerners believed that a baby boy was assured if the father kept a leather string in his pocket during conception; the side to which the female turned following intercourse (to the left for girls and the right for boys) was also believed to be effective in determining the sex of an infant. Other folk beliefs surround the gestation period of pregnancy, such as the notion that the pregnant female who crosses a threshold or begins to climb stairs using her left foot will have a girl, but if she does so with her right foot, it will be a boy.

One of the oldest beliefs about childbirth is based on the concept that the events occurring while a woman carries her baby have a direct effect on the fetus. Southerners believed and continue to believe in prenatal influences. It is thought that a pregnant mother's experiences—of fright, deprivation, contact, or craving—may be manifested in her child's habits or physical marks. In the past, mothers-to-be were warned to look only on beautiful things during pregnancy. If a pregnant woman was frightened by a snake, her baby would weave when he or she walked. If she saw her husband bleeding a mule, her baby would be marked with a blood-red birthmark. A birthmark on an infant also was attributed to a mother's unfulfilled craving for a particular food or overeating of a particular food during pregnancy. Often dietary allergies, aversions, or preferences in a child were and still are credited to a mother's prenatal behavior. A child's disposition could be affected positively or negatively prior to its birth by the mother's own disposition and aspirations for the child; if a pregnant woman was ill-natured during pregnancy, her baby would share her mean-spiritedness. Some believed that if a pregnant woman looked at a dead baby or spoke the name she intended to give her baby before its birth, it would be stillborn. Names were carefully chosen because it was believed the baby would have characteristics similar to his or her namesake.

To hasten labor, herbal teas were offered to the woman or pepper was blown in the mother-to-be's face. The most difficult and dangerous phase of childbirth, delivery, and the concerns about this process provoked many protective and divinatory practices. An almost universal technique used during labor consisted of placing a sharp instrument—a knife, scissors, an axe—on or under the pillow or bed of the laboring woman "to cut the pain." This was the most prevalent method for alleviating the pain of labor among southerners, although the ingestion of certain herbs or of that most popular of southern soft drinks, Coca-Cola, was believed to be efficacious in the relief of labor pain. Southerners believed it was inappropriate and a bad omen for the father to be present at the birth, although in some areas of the South the presence of the father or some article of his cloth-

ing was often utilized to transmit male strength to the female in labor. In rare instances, the southern man followed the primitive custom of the "couvade"—taking to bed as if bearing the child himself.

One of the most persistent and widespread beliefs about childbirth, which still endures among some southern black people, concerns the psychic powers of babies born with faces covered with a veil or caul, the membrane of the amniotic sac. The belief prevails that these babies will possess the power to foresee the future and to see and hear ghosts. In the case of excessive bleeding during and after delivery, several common verbal formulas, including a section from the book of Ezekiel, were recited. The delivery phase of the birth process ended with the careful and traditional disposal through burning or burial of the placenta, membranes, and cord. These disposal methods were believed necessary for the future well-being of infant and mother.

The less medical science knows about a condition, the more likely traditional medical beliefs are to survive. In recent decades in the South childbirth has evolved into a highly institutionalized, bureaucratized, and safe procedure. This evolution in modern medical practice has replaced, for the most part, the alternative traditions of folk medicine. Today, by and large, the southern way of birth is the American way of birth. The bearing of a child is circumscribed by how-to books and classes, hospital deliveries, and modern medical practice. Yet even now the medical practices of childbirth, woven from the knowledge of Europeans, Africans, and Native Americans, are not entirely dead, particularly among working-class families in the South.

See also SCIENCE AND MEDICINE: Health, Public; Health, Rural; WOMEN'S LIFE: Healers, Women

Carolyn Lipson-Walker
Bloomington, Indiana

Marie Campbell, *Folks Do Get Born* (1946); Karen Cox, in *Foxfire 2*, ed. Eliot Wigginton (1973); Josephine B. Currie, *Mississippi Folklore Register* (Spring 1978); Ronald G. Killion and Charles T. Waller, *A Treasury of Georgia Folklore* (1972); Harry Law, *Tennessee Folklore Society Bulletin* (December 1952); Alice H. Murphree, in *Southern Anthropological Society Proceedings, No. 1: Essays on Medical Anthropology*, ed. Thomas Weaver (1968); J. Hampden Porter, *Journal of American Folklore* (April-June 1894); Vance Randolph, *Ozark Superstitions* (1947); Carroll Y. Rich, *Journal of American Folklore* (July-September 1976); Lawrence S. Thompson, *Kentucky Folklore Record* (January-March 1959); Newman I. White, ed., *Frank C. Brown Collection of North Carolina Folklore*, vol. 6 (1964); Gordon Wilson, *Tennessee Folklore Society Bulletin* (June 1965); Peter H. Wood, *Southern Exposure* (Summer 1978). ☆

Clothing

||||||||||||||||||||||||

Don Yoder specifies four characteristics of folk clothing: it is immediately identifiable and distinct; it identifies the wearer to the outside world as well as to the community; it is prescribed by the community; and its forms are dictated by the community's traditions. For these reasons, folk clothing has always served as a potent symbol of the South.

In the southern United States clothing styles fall along an elite-popular-folk-continuum. Elite clothing includes the one-of-a-kind creations of haute couture. Popular clothing includes both mass-produced and homemade garments designed with an eye to current fashion. Folk clothing, whether purchased from catalogs, small-town stores, or made at home, is not seen as subject to the whims of fashion. Early journals and diaries, magazine pictures, and photographs document traditional clothing in the South. By and large, the dress of southern subsistence farmers, tenant farmers, and Appalachians did not differ notably from the dress of rural people of other parts of the United States, especially of the Midwest and Great Plains. The Wisconsin clothes in the photography of Charles Van Schaick are not notably different from the clothing worn in Kentucky and Arkansas photos from the same period. The Walker Evans Farm Security Administration photographs of Alabama and Mississippi farmers reveal the same sort of clothes as the Dorothea Lange and Russell Lee photographs from Oklahoma, Ohio, Idaho, and California. Even the warmer climate of the South did not necessarily dictate lighter clothing in summer, though it did create less demand for warm clothing in winter.

Nevertheless, some distinctive styles and garments have developed in the South. Joseph Doddridge, in describing the mode of dress he saw on the Appalachian frontier in the revolutionary period, speaks of "the hunting shirt . . . a kind of loose frock reaching half way down the thighs, with large sleeves open before, and so wide as to lap over a foot or more when belted. . . . The bosom of this served as a wallet to hold a chunk of bread cake, jerk, tow for wiping the barrel of the rifle, or any other necessity for the hunter or warrior. The belt . . . was always tied behind." The hunting shirt, which seems to have been a civilian adaptation of the military coat, was usually made of cloth rather than of deerskin, because wet leather is clammy and cold. It was worn over another shirt, also long, but opened only at the neck. This inner shirt was the ancestor of the modern "soft-collar" shirt and also of the night shirt.

Through much of the 19th century, work clothing for rural men consisted of trousers, high boots, a soft shirt, a vest, and a broad-brimmed hat. For women it consisted of a long full dress, an apron, ladies' boots, a bonnet, and perhaps a fichu (a light triangular scarf draped over the shoulder). Black women favored a turban or bandana. In New Orleans this took the form of a *tignon*, an elaborately folded madras square worn around the head, reminiscent of African women's head coverings.

Between the Civil War and World War I there was a shift to bib overalls for men and to prints and shorter skirts for women. Mills in the Upland South provided inexpensive ready-made clothing, but shirts and dresses were frequently made at home from the white or print cotton sacks that staples such as rice and flour were packaged in. Women often wore men's shoes.

Specific occupations often necessitated special clothing. Tanners, cobblers, carpenters, tailors, and smiths in the South, as in other parts of the country, wore distinctive aprons. Street vendors often wore unconventional clothing, such as smocks, sashes, or sailor's jumpers, to distinguish themselves. Of all occupations, however, the cowboy produced the most colorful American folk costume. The cowboy early adopted the choke-barreled, copper-riveted blue canvas pants manufactured in San Francisco by Levi Strauss and the broad-brimmed hat by J. B. Stetson of Philadelphia. The rest of the cowboy's working outfit consisted of a collarless shirt, a bandana for a collar, high-heeled riding boots, and perhaps a vest and chaps. Cut like Indian leggings, chaps were leather for protection in cactus country and were fur or hair in rainy or snow country.

Florida cowboys were slow to adopt the full southwestern regalia. Early photographs show broad hats and jeans but also regular soft-collared shirts and laced boots or wellingtons. Perhaps more dress conscious than most occupational groups, cowboys developed clothing-related customs and superstitions, such as avoiding yellow shirts, setting the hat down brim-side up "to hold in the luck," and avoiding placing the hat on a bed.

Much folk clothing is sewn, but stockings, mittens, gloves, scarves, and caps are often knitted or crocheted, as are a wide variety of garments for infants. In addition, knit or crocheted lace was long used to decorate women's undergarments.

Even garments of popular manufacture may be worn in a distinctive folk way. The man who wishes to identify himself with the folk end of the clothing continuum, for instance, will wear the appropriate head covering, whether a broad-brimmed hat, as in the 1850s, or a baseball cap, frequently called a "gimme cap" and decorated with different sayings or business names. Folk custom at different times has decreed that jeans be worn cuffless or with deep cuffs. Bandanas too have been used over the years as scarves, collars, halter tops, headbands, turbans, and belts. Cherokee lacrosse players have even worn them as breech cloths.

In the South both sectarian and ethnic groups have at times set themselves off from the larger community by wearing distinctive dress in their everyday lives. By the end of the 18th century the plain style had emerged among the Quakers, Methodists, and Baptists. A southern variation of this style was worn by the white Quakers of the Maryland Eastern Shore and the Piedmont.

The most distinctively southern sectarian dress emerged among the Holiness churches in the 20th century. These churches prescribe rules of modesty for women, forbidding slacks or trousers and requiring long sleeves, high necks, lower hemlines, and uncut hair. Women in these churches, like Quaker women before them, frequently found in the styles of an earlier period a way to meet their religious obligations. In the 1980s Holiness women frequently wear the shirtwaist dress that was an item of popular culture in the 1950s, and on dress occasions put up their long hair in a style suggestive of the bouffant hairdos of that same period.

Mennonite women in the South, cut off from the center of Mennonite culture in Pennsylvania, frequently wear a "plain" style that is much like that of Holiness women. They retain the Mennonite cap or "prayer covering," however, and their hairstyle is more severe. Old Regular Baptists likewise favor conservative dress. In this sect, as in some Mennonite groups, men do not wear neckties. Afro-American churches frequently have distinctive clothing for choirs, nurselike white uniforms for deaconesses, and white gowns for baptisms.

One of the most distinctive ethnic folk clothing traditions in the United States is found among the Five Civilized Tribes of the Southeast (Creek, Cherokee, Choctaw, Chickasaw, Seminole). These tribesmen very early abandoned aboriginal dress and made a distinctive adaptation of European dress. They took the hunting shirt, added to it the lace collar from the inner shirt, belted it with a colored sash, and wore it over leggings or trousers and moccasins or boots. Formal headgear was a turban, an item 18th-century gentlemen wore in place of a wig at home. Beads and gorgets (pieces of armor protecting the throat) completed the costume. This costume survives, much altered, especially among the Seminoles. Up until World War II Seminole men often wore brightly colored hunting shirts as their sole garment. The shirts are now made in two parts, a full top and a gathered skirt.

The Seminole women also developed a distinctive version of southern dress. They came to prefer a blouse with a long ruffle all around the yoke. In time this ruffle was lengthened to waist length, and the remainder of the blouse was no longer necessary, the upper garment becoming a full chiffon cape dropping to the waist and worn over a full skirt made of horizontal bands of materials. Patchwork began to show up early, and the treadle sewing machine, introduced to the Seminoles about 1890, made possible the elaborate patchwork bands out of which traditional Seminole garments are composed today.

After World War II most Seminole men exchanged the skirts of their shirts for jeans, but they still favored the patchwork tops. By the 1970s these tops were frequently worn as windbreaker jackets. Because construction of traditional patchwork garments is time consuming, Seminoles since World War II have tended to wear them only on dress occasions or when dealing with the public.

Dress for self-presentation on public occasions is another type of folk costume. Country music groups have frequently chosen cowboy clothes. Some, like the Coon Creek Girls, wore stylized versions of turn-of-the-century clothing, and some comic groups chose the hayseed or "hillbilly" image—bib overalls, plaid shirt, straw hat, and bandana handkerchief. The western image has faded from popularity among female singers, and many male singers now don sequined tuxedos along with stetsons and boots. Gospel groups, black and white, sometimes dress like country groups, sometimes wear choir robes, and sometimes dress in formal attire.

At festivals and craft fairs the presenters, especially women, often dress to suggest heritage. The typical costume for women is a long-sleeved blouse, long gathered skirt, apron, and sunbonnet. The "southern belle" outfit may also qualify as a folk costume, since it represents not a historical picture of antebellum women's clothing, but a folk sense of the period. Even unbecoming stereotypes provide inspiration in costuming for self-presentation. The Applachian county seat that is celebrating Hillbilly Days will be full of solid citizens wearing variations of the hayseed costume and drawing on corncob pipes or whiskey demijohns.

Mumming, or the wearing of a costume for disguise as part of a celebration or ritual, seems not to be widespread in the South. Costuming is a more recent development in the celebration of Halloween in this part of the country. But folk costume has long been a part of the Mardi Gras celebration all along the Gulf Coast from Mobile to southwest Louisiana. In New Orleans folk costume can be quite elaborate, especially in the feathered creations of the black "Mardi Gras Indians." East and west of New Orleans, the folk costumes tend to be more informal. On the Mardi Gras ride in Mamou, La., anything that will disguise or conceal the wearer can be worn. Similar informal costumes were also worn in the Christmas mumming known as Dry Setting once practiced in Alabama.

Disguises of the Ku Klux Klan are more serious. The typical costume is a long white robe and a tall pointed hood that conceals the face. But red and black are also used, and the robes are sometimes elaborately decorated with Klan symbols.

As elsewhere in the country, costumes are worn at Christmas, Easter, and Purim; for parties, plays, and pageants. In New Orleans, children dressed as Mary and Joseph or as angels have a role in the 19 March Saint Joseph's Day celebration. On this day, too, the Mardi Gras Indians don their costumes for a final march before destroying the finery so that it cannot be used the following year.

Folk clothing continues to mark the distinctiveness of subgroups. As not only functional objects but expressive ones, items of clothing highlight religious, family, social class, and community values and heritages throughout the South.

See also BLACK LIFE: / Mardi Gras Indians; ETHNIC LIFE: Indians

Bill McCarthy
College of the Ozarks

John Blay, *After the Civil War: A Pictorial Profile of America from 1865 to 1900* (1960); Joseph Doddridge, *Notes on the Settlement and Indian Wars of the Western Parts of Virginia and Pennsylvania from 1763 to 1783,*

Inclusive, Together with a Review of the State of Society and Manners of the First Settlers of the Western Country (1824); Ralph Henry Gabriel et al., ed., *The Pageant of America: A Pictorial History of the United States*, 15 vols. (1925–29); Leon H. Grandjean, *New Orleans Characters* (1949); Margaret Wood, *Native American Fashion: Modern Adaptations of Traditional Designs* (1981); Don Yoder, in *Folklore and Folklife: An Introduction*, ed. Richard M. Dorson (1972), in *Forms upon the Frontier: Folklife and Folk Arts in the United States*, ed. Austin Fife, Alta Fife, and Henry Glassie (1969). ☆

J. Frank Dobie, Texas folklore scholar, c. 1940s

Collectors

||||||||||||||||||||||||

When folklorists organized the American Folklore Society in the late 19th century, they intended to use the society to record and preserve the old ballads, songs, and beliefs that members thought would disappear in the face of rapid modernization. Among the subjects they felt should be preserved were "relics of old English folk lore" and "lore of negroes in the Southern states." Both subjects attracted numerous collectors who scoured the South for material. Many collectors romantically viewed the isolation of the mountain and river people of the South as nurturing folklore that had died in other areas. In the mountains, song collectors found a homogenous population of English descendants; along the rivers they found tightly knit communities resisting change; in the lowlands they looked for segregated black communities preserving vestiges of African and plantation lore. Although modern folklorists do not generally share the antiquarian outlook of the past, they are still drawn to the South as a particularly fertile ground for folklore collection.

The first collection of black folksongs, *Slave Songs of the United States*, was published in 1867 by a trio of non-southerners (William F. Allen, Charles P. Ware, and Lucy M. Garrison) collecting in the South. Following their work was the collection of black folktales by Joel Chandler Harris in the 1880s. He rewrote the texts and published them in a successful series of Uncle Remus books. His books sparked new interest in the folktales of the South. The *Journal of American Folklore*, for instance, founded in 1888, published over a hundred articles and notes on black folklore, most of them coming from the South. The zeal for collecting such material could still be felt generations later in the publication of *American Negro Folktales* (1967) by the dean of modern American folklorists, Richard M. Dorson (1916–81). His book was based largely on his work in the 1950s among Mississippi and Arkansas blacks.

Major collectors also staked their reputations on gathering relics of old English folklore, and especially folksong, in the South. Standing out was Cecil J. Sharp (1859–1924). Sharp was well known in the early years of the century for collecting folksongs in England. Traveling to America to assist with the staging of a New York play, he was visited by Olive Dame Campbell, the wife of John C. Campbell, the director of the Russell Sage Foundation's Southern Highland Division. She showed him songs she had collected from Appalachian residents. He recognized remnants of English folksongs and was determined to pursue the lead. In the summer of 1916 he traveled with a former student, Maud Karpeles (1886–1976), hunting folksongs. They returned for two more extended trips before 1918. Their pioneering efforts resulted in the publication of the monumental *English Folk songs from the Southern Appalachians* in two volumes. The first edition appeared in 1917 and was revised in 1932 and 1952.

Several southerners distinguished themselves with extensive collections of folksongs. Josiah H. Combs (1886–1960), for example, published his collection of southern folksongs in Paris, and in 1967 the collection was published as *Folk-Songs of the Southern United States* by the American Folklore Society. Combs hailed from Hazard, Ky. He came under the influence of another great collector of southern folksongs, John Harrington Cox (1863–1945) of West Virginia University, who published his *Folk-Songs of the South* in 1925 and *Traditional Ballads, Mainly from West Virginia* in 1939. Cox was a student of the famous ballad scholar

George Lyman Kittredge (1860–1941) of Harvard. In Virginia, Arthur Kyle Davis, Jr. (1897–1972), a professor of English at the University of Virginia, compiled the influential *Traditional Ballads of Virginia* in 1929. Mississippi native Arthur Palmer Hudson (1892–1978) added to the hefty bookshelf of southern folksong collections in 1936 with his well-received *Folksongs of Mississippi and Their Background*. Another Mississippi-born collector, John A. Lomax, had completed his comprehensive *Cowboy Songs and Other Frontier Ballads* by 1910, and he went on to gather and publish a wide range of American folksongs. His son, Alan Lomax, and daughter, Bess Lomax Hawes, continued the tradition. The efforts of these collectors and others resulted in the founding of the two longest-running regional folklore journals in America, *Southern Folklore Quarterly* (established 1937) and *Tennessee Folklore Society Bulletin* (established 1934).

The South also provided the setting for landmark collections of folk belief. Harry Middleton Hyatt (1896–1978) and Newbell Niles Puckett (1898–1967) independently put together volumes of material taken primarily from southern blacks. After compiling the folklore of Adams County, Ill., in the 1930s Harry Hyatt left his native Illinois for field trips up and down the southern coast and inland to New Orleans. Hyatt, an Episcopal minister, had a natural interest in religious and magical practices. He meticulously recorded encounters with root doctors, conjurers, and hoodoo men. Eventually his notes filled five volumes of *Hoodoo-Conjuration-Witchcraft-Rootwork* published from 1970 to 1978.

Newbell Niles Puckett was born in Columbus, Miss., and went on to teach sociology at Western Reserve University in Cleveland. His magnum opus was *Folk Beliefs of the Southern Negro* brought out by the University of North Carolina Press in 1926. To get his collection, he interviewed over 400 informants mostly from Mississippi, Alabama, and Georgia. Puckett took great pains to compare what he collected to other finds from around the world. He added photographs that documented the believers and their surroundings.

Frank C. Brown (1870–1943), a colorful teacher and administrator at Duke University, was an avid collector of North Carolina folklore who received most of his recognition after his death. He sought to record the range of folklore from games to songs, beliefs to legends, and proverbs to tales. After his death leading folklorists edited his collection into seven weighty volumes entitled the *Frank C. Brown Collection of North Carolina Folklore* (1952–64). The work is now a standard reference of folklore.

Perhaps the most indefatigable folklore collector in the South was writer Vance Randolph (1892–1980). Although originally from Kansas, he spent most of his years collecting and writing in the Ozarks. He marveled at the lively oral tradition he found there, and he devoted his career to reporting it. He began publishing articles on folk beliefs he found in the late 1920s. His first two books, *The Ozarks: An American Survival of Primitive Society* (1931) and *Ozark Mountain Folks* (1932), were general descriptions of Ozark mountain life, which included chapters on dialect, folksong, folk belief, and magic. Beginning in the 1940s, Randolph increased his folklore collecting and publishing. Among his notable contributions were *Ozark Folksongs* (4 vols., 1946–50), *Ozark Superstitions* (1947), *We Always*

Lie to Strangers: Tall Tales from the Ozarks (1951), *Who Blowed Up the Church House? and Other Ozark Folk Tales* (1952), *Down in the Holler: A Gallery of Ozark Folk Speech* (1953), *The Devil's Pretty Daughter* (1955), *Hot Springs and Hell, and Other Folk Jests and Anecdotes from the Ozarks* (1965), *Ozark Folklore: A Bibliography* (1972), and *Pissing in the Snow, and Other Ozark Folktales* (1976).

Collectors were also drawn to the distinctive handicrafts and housing of the South. A major work that brought attention to this trove was Allen Eaton's *Handicrafts of the Southern Highlands* (1937). Eaton (1878–1962) had erected craft exhibitions at major expositions and lectured on art appreciation in the North. The same Olive Dame Campbell who influenced Cecil J. Sharp invited Eaton to the Appalachians. Eaton then helped organize the Southern Highland Handicraft Guild and collected examples of native craftsworkers and their arts and architecture. In his book he chronicled the efforts to organize southern craftsworkers, and he carefully documented a wide range of artisanship from spinning to whittling, house construction to furniture making, and pottery to basketmaking. His book thus was partly a valuable record of Appalachian material folk culture and also a proposal for reviving and protecting the crafts economy.

Although today's motivation for collecting is different from that of the past, the fervor for collecting southern material remains strong among folklorists. Native southerners such as William Ferris of Mississippi, William Lynwood Montell of Kentucky, and Daniel Patterson of North Carolina have used their southern university bases to collect tales, songs, and material culture in their native states. In Tennessee, David Evans and Charles Wolfe are deeply involved in the collection of blues and old-time music, respectively. John Michael Vlach with his book *Charleston Blacksmith* (1981), about a black craftsman from South Carolina, and Michael Owen Jones with his *The Hand Made Object and Its Maker* (1975), about Chester Cornett, a Kentucky chair maker, have added greatly to the knowledge of personalities behind the folklore usually collected. Also concerned with material culture, Henry Glassie scrupulously documented southern folk architecture in "The Types of the Southern Mountain Cabin" (appearing in Jan Harold Brunvand's *The Study of American Folklore*, 1968) and *Folk Housing in Middle Virginia* (1975). In Kentucky and Georgia, Thomas A. Adler collects and studies regional foodways and music, and in Missouri Howard Wight Marshall reveals the southern influences on foodways and folk architecture in publications including *Folk Architecture in Little Dixie* (1981). Picking up from where Vance Randolph left off, W. K. McNeil, equally indefatigable, has continued collecting folklore in Arkansas and Missouri.

In addition to this mere sample of folklorists independently working in the South, centers of southern folklore collection and study encourage and carry out collecting at the University of Texas, Western Kentucky University, University of Kentucky, University of Alabama, University of North Carolina at Chapel Hill, University of South Carolina, Center for Southern Folklore in Memphis, and Center for the Study of Southern Culture at the University of Mississippi. Appalshop in Whitesburg, Ky., produces films and records about Appalachia, and Eliot Wigginton's Fox-

fire project in north Georgia collects and publishes Appalachian folklife materials. Journals featuring collections of southern folklore are published by state and regional folklore societies in North Carolina, Virginia, Mississippi, Tennessee, Kentucky, Arkansas, Missouri, and Florida. An Association of Folklorists in the South produces a newsletter to reach the many professional collectors and scholars working in the South. They are building on the proud legacy of earlier collectors, who often worked without the benefit of academic credentials or outside funding. They saw in the South a large and distinctive crop of folklore, and they harvested a copious amount of material for future generations to appreciate and study.

See also BLACK-LIFE: Folklore, Black; EDUCATION: / Campbell, John C.; *Foxfire*; LANGUAGE: / Randolph, Vance; LITERATURE: / Harris, Joel Chandler

Simon J. Bronner
Pennsylvania State University
Capitol Campus

W. Amos Abrams, *North Carolina Folklore* (1964); Simon J. Bronner, *American Folklore Studies: An Intellectual History* (1986); Bertrand H. Bronson, *Journal of American Folklore* (October–December 1977); Jan Harold Brunvand, *The Study of American Folklore: An Introduction* (2d ed., 1978); Richard M. Dorson, *American Folklore* (rev. ed., 1977), *Buying the Wind: Regional Folklore in the United States* (1964); Susan Dwyer-Shick, "The American Folklore Society and Folklore Research in America, 1888–1940" (Ph.D. dissertation, University of Pennsylvania, 1979); Herbert Halpert, *Journal of American Folklore* (July–September 1981); Ed Kahn, *Kentucky Folklore Record* (October–December 1960); W. K. McNeil, "A History of American Folklore Scholarship before 1908" (Ph.D. dissertation, Indiana University, 1980); D. K. Wilgus, *Anglo-American Folksong Scholarship since 1898* (1959). ☆

Family Folklore

||||||||||||||||||||||||||||||||||||||||||

Family folklore grows out of the shared experiences of family members and their shared view of a common past. These experiences are often given creative expression in such forms as stories, songs, sayings, pastimes, names, customs, photographs, and memorabilia. Often traditions are passed down through several generations of a family; other times they are created anew, shaped to meet the demands of the present. Quite often a successful party becomes an annual family event or a word mispronounced becomes a private family expression. Families frequently develop their own calendar of pastimes and celebrations, their own repertoire of stories and expressions, their own version of the family's past.

Southerners have long maintained a strong sense of the importance of family, not only the nuclear group but a broad family network that includes several branches, distant cousins, and persons who may not be blood kin. This is partly because many southern families have lived in the same area for several generations, developing strong ties with their relatives and their communities. Although many nuclear family groups also have a wealth of family traditions, families who have maintained continuity with relatives and community for generations often develop an especially rich store of folklore. Sociologists James Bossard and Eleanor Boll, who define

family rituals as the "ceremonial use of leisure," found in their study of American families that the "larger the family the more numerous and rich the rituals." This may be explained in part because the more time family members spend with their relatives, the more experiences they have to draw on in their folklore; and the more continuity there is between generations, the more likely it is that traditions will survive over time.

In large, extended family groups, traditions often serve an important role in defining family membership and in keeping separate the different branches of the family. Which relatives are invited to traditional family events and, of those invited, which ones regularly participate, can be a telling indication of who is a member. In communities with several large, interrelated families, an invitation to an annual picnic may be a more important sign of family membership than the same last name. Family membership and a sense of family identity may derive from shared traditions as much as from blood ties.

The South has often been called a region of storytellers, and quite often stories are a major genre of southern family folklore. Remarkable similarities show up in family stories throughout the United States. Studies suggest that American families tend to tell stories about major transitions, such as births, courtships, and migrations, and about the personalities of family members. These broad themes appear in southern family stories, shaped by the southern experience.

Historical events and periods, such as the Civil War and the Great Depression, which had a tremendous effect on southerners, provide material for many family stories. Legends of Civil War heroes and rogues, tragedies and triumphs, have kept that event alive for many families. A common American story-type first described by Stanley Brandes is the "lost fortune story." In it, a family describes how an ancestor lost what would have been a fortune for them through foolishness or a lack of entrepreneurial spirit. In the South this theme often appears in stories of a family member burying the family silver to prevent Yankee troops from finding it and then forgetting where it was buried or dying without telling relatives the location. In black families, stories are often told about the capture of ancestors by slave traders in Africa, the indignities of slavery, and ancestors who rebelled against their slave-masters.

Bossard and Boll, in their study of American families, argue that leisure is the key to family rituals, that the more time allowed for leisure in a family, the more rituals it will develop. In an area where leisure has long been held up as one of the virtues of the southern way of life, family pastimes not only become important in themselves but provide the shared experiences that give rise to other forms of folklore; they also provide the setting for sharing them. Stories are often told, as well as set, at family picnics, parties, vacations, and other leisure events.

Family relationships and the traits and personalities of family members are also dominant topics of southern family folklore. The legends that grow out of long-standing family feuds, especially common in the southern Appalachians but found in other parts of the South as well, tell of the violence and bitterness that sometimes erupt between, and within, clannish southern families. More often, however, family folklore celebrates the ties that bind. In communities with several large interrelated families, the relationships among kin become complex, and family members can use their folklore to reaffirm kinship connections that might otherwise be forgotten. Drawing on characteristic traits associated with family names, stories often connect a relative with different branches of the family by showing how he or she exhibits family traits. Such stories may begin with a statement such as, "You know how stubborn the Hardens are," and then follow with an example of how Amy Johnson, whose grandmother was a Harden, refused to change her position in a family argument. The folklore of family traits may be seen as part of a larger preoccupation in the South with genealogy and with "placing" persons in terms of their family background, social class, race, and geographical location.

Southern family stories and expressions also dwell frequently on the idiosyncracies of relatives, the traits that distinguish them from other members of the family. The eccentric uncle, the flamboyant aunt, the relative who is "set in his ways" are central figures in much family folklore and often are given a special status as "family characters." The folklore surrounding these "characters" may be one way in which large, closely knit family groups accept nonconformity among their relatives and thus maintain family harmony.

The emphasis on leisure time, the strong continuity between generations of many families, the interest in family background and genealogy, and the love of storytelling have contributed to a rich folklore among southern families.

See also BLACK LIFE: Family, Black; Genealogy, Black; MYTHIC SOUTH: Family;

WOMEN'S LIFE: Genealogy; Maiden Aunt; / Family Reunion

Amanda Dargan
Queens Council on the Arts
New York, New York

Mody Boatright et al., *The Family Saga and Other Phases of American Folklore* (1958); James Bossard and Eleanor Boll, *Ritual in Family Living: A Contemporary Study* (1950); Stanley H. Brandes, *Journal of the Folklore Institute* (No. 1, 1975); Deirdre LaPin, *Hogs in the Bottom: Family Folklore in Arkansas* (1982); Kathryn Morgan, *Children of Strangers: Stories of a Black Family* (1980); Steven J. Zeitlin et al., *A Celebration of American Family Folklore: Tales and Traditions from the Smithsonian Collection* (1982). ☆

Folk Medicine

||||||||||||||||||||||||||||||||||||||||||

Folk medicine can be defined as a cultural system using herbs, roots, over-the-counter drugs, and folk specialists to achieve health. It is based on the integration of scientific medicine with traditional knowledge. Although exact statistics on the distribution and frequency of folk medicine are unavailable, the practice has been, and remains, widespread, particularly among the poor in both rural and urban southern areas.

Folk medicine has been utilized for chronic health problems more frequently than acute ones, by both blacks and whites and by men and women. Women are most often sought out for help. Men, however, are also often folk healers. Blacks will use white healers and whites will use black ones. Hazel Weidman (1978) reports that in choosing a healer the power of the healer is more important than ethnic background to the client.

Illnesses treated through this system generally exhibit familiar symptoms that do not seriously incapacitate the victim. Most home remedies are easily available animal products (i.e., milk, fat, bones), chemical or mineral substances (i.e., sulphur, ashes, vinegar, sugar, turpentine), and plants (i.e., yellow root, tree bark, sassafras). A variety of these substances are kept in the home for use in treating colds, indigestion, burns, sores, sore throats, fevers, headaches, and general aches and pains. Plants are administered in the form of teas. Knowledge of these folk remedies is widespread, and although substances may change for particular health problems, confidence in them remains. Many substances used in the home are "over-the-counter" medicines and the repertoire keeps changing. There has been an increasing reliance on medicines advertised in the media. Some of them have been used for years but new ones advertised by drug companies continue to be incorporated into health beliefs and behaviors. Folk healers will often combine new remedies with more traditional roots or herbs in their treatment of illness. For example, a root doctor in North Carolina prescribes Pepto-Bismol mixed with whiskey for the "shakes."

Several types of traditional healers can be found in the rural and urban South. They are referred to by a variety of names such as hoodoo doctor, voodoo doctor, herb doctor, root doctor, and conjurer. The practice of voodoo medicine is concentrated on the coast of Georgia and South Carolina and in southern Louisiana, although its influence has survived in other areas with large numbers of blacks. Voodoo specialists have reputations that span several hundred miles, and people will travel considerable distances to see them for healing purposes.

Among many blacks in the South illnesses from natural causes are organized into a belief system based on the need to balance the blood in the body. Blood can become unbalanced by being either too sweet ("high blood") or too bitter ("low blood"). Imbalance can be caused from an improper diet (too many sweet or bitter foods), a lack of proper rest, or too much worry. The treatment involves diet modification, family counseling to deal with stress, and herbal remedies. Furthermore, when blood is not balanced, other bodily fluids also may be out of balance, resulting in an individual becoming more susceptible to illnesses. Thus, the individual must keep a balance between the good and evil forces.

Some healers are believed to be particularly competent to treat specific problems. There are specialists who "talk the fire out of burns," "stop bleeding," "cure the thrash," and "conjure warts." Root doctors are often used for "high blood" or "low blood" and for other ailments such as headaches, tiredness, or itching. They may heal either with herbal remedies (a natural condition) or with "rootworks" (an unnatural condition). They are frequently consulted by people who also participate in the scientific medical system. Others have the knowledge and ability to rid the body of general aches and pains and mental stress.

People use these specialists for symptoms such as headaches, backaches, occasional loss of memory, tiredness, thinking about a particular subject or person too much, and sexual impotency. The folk healer will diagnose such cases

as overwork, "nerves," or worry. They generally do not compartmentalize the problems of their clients into mental and physical problems. Healers seek knowledge of the social and religious life of their clients before making a diagnosis and recommending treatment. Clients are consequently treated on physical, psychological, and social levels simultaneously. Through the ritual use of roots and herbs, diets, popular medical cures, passages read from the Bible, and counseling, the healer attempts to restore a balance in the patient's life.

Health is seen as maintaining a balance between the good and bad forces in the universe. These forces are believed to be ever present and the individual is continually caught between them. The individual must maintain harmony with these forces through his or her own behavior. Illnesses are classified according to natural or unnatural causes. For example, a study of root doctors in North Carolina found that they determine whether an illness is the result of unnatural causes, such as spells, which are treated by counter rootwork, or natural causes generally treated by herbal or medicinal remedies. Furthermore, the root doctors decide if the illness is predominantly a problem of the body or of the mind. Most illnesses, though, are classified as both (such as nerves and hysterics) and the proper treatment prescribed. Indeed, in folk medicine the cause of the illness is more relevant than symptoms in diagnosis and treatment.

Southern folk beliefs about health are widely shared by people who practice folk medicine. Obviously, their concepts of disease and illness involve a broader conceptual framework than those of scientific medicine. It combines elements of African culture, European culture, Greek classical medicine, American Indian medicine, scientific medicine, and voodoo religion. These elements are synthesized within the framework of fundamentalist Christianity and provide the participants in the folk medical system with a broad belief system allowing them to explain illness and misfortunes.

See also ENVIRONMENT: Plant Uses; SCIENCE AND MEDICINE: Self-dosage; WOMEN'S LIFE: Healers, Women

Carole E. Hill
Georgia State University

Wayland Hand, ed., *American Folk Medicine* (1976), *Magical Medicine: The Folkloric Component of Medicine in the Folk Belief, Custom, and Ritual of the Peoples of Europe and America* (1980); Carole E. Hill, *Southern Medicine* (1976), *Journal of Popular Culture* (Spring 1973), with Holly Mathews, in *Perspectives on the American South*, vol. 1, ed. Merle Black and John Shelton Reed (1981); Harry Middleton Hyatt, *Hoodoo-Conjuration-Witchcraft-Rootwork*, 5 vols. (1970–78); Alice H. Murphree, *The Health of a Rural County: Perspectives and Problems* (1976); Newbell Niles Puckett, *Folk Beliefs of the Southern Negro* (1926; reprint ed., 1968). ☆

Folk Painting

||||||||||||||||||||||||||||||||||||

Southern folk painting cannot be understood apart from American folk art in general. Scholars, folk art collectors, museum curators, and others have hotly debated the nature of American folk painting, describing it with terms such as *primitive*, *visionary popular*, *provin-*

cial, amateur, schoolgirl, crude, naive, unsophisticated, grass roots, outsider, innocent, homemade, or *nonacademic.*

Art historians often view folk painting within the context of academic styles and movements, but some art historians argue that true folk painters derive their creative inspiration from isolation. Curators and collectors sometimes see these paintings as quaint artifacts of rural, preindustrial life. Folklorists view the folk painter within the context of the traditional ideas in a particular folk culture. They point out that folk paintings, like all folk artifacts, have utilitarian functions, are not limited to one historical era, and are not inevitably rural. Folklorists shy away from an all-inclusive definition of folk art that takes in all times and places, preferring to concentrate on the life history and biographical case study of a particular folk artist.

Popular interest in folk art began with 19th-century romantic nationalism, and efforts of American scholars and collectors to study folk painting increased in the 1930s. The egalitarian spirit of that decade promoted an interest in the art of the common people, expressed in Thomas Hart Benton's studies of folklife and in New Deal murals. Holger Cahill, art historian and museum director, assembled a pioneering folk painting exhibition at the Museum of Modern Art in 1932, and the catalog, *The Art of the Common Man in America, 1750–1900*, appeared the same year. Well-illustrated volumes from the 1940s to the 1970s portrayed folk painting as consisting mostly of 19th-century portraits, genre paintings, landscapes, seascapes, town views, house and farm views, history scenes, religious images, patriotic images, *fraktur*, and still lives. Portraiture, often executed by itinerant painters, has been seen as the major category of southern folk painting before the Civil War. Irish-born Virginia artist John Toole, for example, was perhaps the most prominent early 19th-century itinerant painter, traveling the Piedmont and Tidewater areas of Virginia and painting over 300 still-extant works. Joshua Johnston is the best-known black folk painter of the early 1800s. Southern women artists produced a large number of watercolors at female seminaries and elsewhere, and these are viewed as folk paintings by art historians. Many of these same works, styles, and artists also figure, however, in discussions of early American academic art.

The regional aspect of American folk painting has long been a category used by scholars and collectors, but until recently they have downplayed the importance of the South. Nina Fletcher Little, an early historian of folk art, wrote in 1957 that "New England was the richest center of folk art because it was richest in craftsmen," but "in the South there is less evidence of folk art." In fact, collections of American folk art have often included a disproportionately large number of works by southerners without acknowledging the region's dominance. The flowering of scholarship on black folk art since the 1960s has shown that most Afro-American folk painting is southern in origin.

Memory is at the core of the work of many southern folk painters. Older contemporary southerners have witnessed the change from preindustrial life to the space age. Folk painters in the region often reflect on what one of them calls "that long time behind and that short time ahead." Respect for elders is a constant theme among these folk artists. They regard the past with reverence and acknowledge older masters from whom

they learned skills. Many self-taught folk artists learned their skills at an early age but did not become active artists until late in life. North Carolina's Minnie Reinhardt liked to draw during her school years, but most of her life was spent engaged in, as she says, "more practical" tasks. Not until she was 77 years of age did she begin to chronicle from memory the folklife of the North Carolina Piedmont. Similarly, Queena Stovall of Virginia painted no pictures until she was 62, Jessie Du-Bose Rhoads of Alabama did not paint seriously until after an illness and her husband's retirement, and Theora Hamblett of Mississippi began her visionary works only after her mother's death.

Folk painters are conscious of the place and season in which they work. Theora Hamblett drew places from memory, and her paintings recapture the landscape, buildings, and family that shaped her childhood in Paris, Miss. Sam Doyle portrays local characters such as Dr. Buz, the voodoo doctor, from his home on Saint Helena Island in South Carolina. Clementine Hunter's scenes of everyday life are usually set at the Melrose plantation near Natchitoches, La., where she has long resided. Texas artist Fannie Lou Spelce painted works with evocative titles of rural life such as *Peach Season*, *County Memorial Fair*, *Roadside Fruit Stand*, and *Bennett's General Store*. Minnie Reinhardt similarly chronicles the everyday life of her "place" in North Carolina. Charles G. Zug III noted that she painted a dozen or so basic scenes, including homeplaces, the Hog Hill School, Possum John Rudisill's cabin, Wade Smith's pottery, plowing, the wheat harvest, cornhusking, cotton picking, molassesmaking, and flowers. A male artist such as Bill Traylor might paint scenes of coon hunting and drinking matches as well as of the routines of farm life.

Southern folk art often shows an affinity for animals and the natural world. The painter's eye portrays barnyard animals with affection or annoyance and wanders also to creatures such as crawfish, alligators, raccoons, bullfrogs, opossums, and snakes. Artists are curious about animal life and sometimes imagine themselves as the animals they portray.

Dream vision painting, in which literal and imaginary worlds often merge, is another major category of southern folk art. Revelations often appear while the artist is asleep or in a semiconscious state, haunting the painter until they are released through artistic creation. Theora Hamblett felt that her gift for visions was inherited from her grandmother who frequently dreamed of supernatural events. Hamblett had only to close her eyes to see visions. Literal and imaginary worlds often merge. Another Mississippian, Luster Willis, discovers characters as they run through his mind, and he puts these "made-up" people in his paintings. Minnie Evans of North Carolina portrays Oriental images, exotic floral patterns, and baroque designs with multiple sets of eyes.

Folk painters in the South draw heavily on religion as a source of images. Their works are filled with biblical characters, stories, and themes. Luster Willis illustrates parables such as the story of Lazarus. Minnie Reinhardt painted a dinner-on-the-grounds series to preserve the memory of the yearly homecoming ritual at her neighborhood's Corinth Baptist Church each August. Other folk artists have painted camp meetings and revivals, baptizings, Sacred Harp singings, funerals, and decoration days at church graveyards.

Southerners are also fond of painting apocalyptic visions. Sister Gertrude Morgan of New Orleans did a series of New Jerusalem paintings, and Minnie Evans was inspired by the book of Revelation to portray fantastic scenes, although her images are more gentle than biblical accounts. The Reverend Howard Finster's work portrays a vision of apocalypse that combines Old Testament prophecies, scenes from Revelation, and modern images of nuclear war. Finster's *Crossing Jordan* (1971) fills the canvas not only with visual images but with words as well. The river Jordan runs with biblical and biblical-sounding sayings: "The Lord Will Deliver His People across Jordan," "Enemies Wish to Destroy Me. They Despise My Prayers, and My Works," "My Only Escape Is Hope." The South's oral folk culture and its Bible Belt religion are appropriately transposed to a visual image in which prominently displayed words reflect a revelation rooted in evangelical religion.

Repetition, balance, and superimposition of materials and perspectives are characteristic features of southern folk painting. When artists repeat a visual idea, the repetitions are never precise, but all are variations on a general theme. Balance and symmetry cause the eye to focus on a central image. When materials are superimposed, the surface textures can affect responses from the viewer. Combining oil paint, stitches, cloth pieces, and other items on a primary surface deepens texure and creates a three-dimensional look. Savannah, Ga., native Ulysses Davis's *Farmhouse with Airplane* (1943) and Mississippi-born Elijah Pierce's *Monday Morning*

Velox Ward, Sunday Afternoon *(1966)*

Gossip (1935) employ both paint and carving on a wood surface.

Contemporary folk art often combines painting with other media to create distinctive environmental art. Georgia artist Nellie Mae Rowe covered her walls with photographs, her crayon drawings, gifts from friends, and plastic flowers. The Temple Compound of Saint Eom—an acronym for artist Eddie Owens Martin—in Buena Vista, Ga., features painted scenes with images from world religions, along with carved walls, dance platforms, totems, gods, and shiny tin roofs. In such creations the lines between painting and a broader conception of folk art as environment are blurred.

Film and video resources on southern folk painting include: *Fannie Lou Spelce: Folk Artist*, Sandra Mentz and Larry Cormier, producers, Institute for Texan Cultures, 1978; *Folk Artist of the Blue Ridge*, Colonial Williamsburg Foundation, producer and distributor, 1963; *Four Women Artists*, William Ferris, producer, Center for Southern Folklore, 1977; *Missing Pieces: Contemporary Georgia Folk Art*, Steve Heiser, producer, Georgia Council for the Arts, 1976; *Queena Stovall: Life's Narrow Space*, Jack Ofield, producer, Bowling Green Films, 1980; *Reverend Howard Finster: Man of Visions*, John F. Turner, producer and distributor, 1981; *Made in Mississippi: Black Folk Art and Crafts*, William Ferris, producer, Center for the Study of Southern Culture, 1975.

Charles Reagan Wilson
University of Mississippi

William Ferris
University of Mississippi

Jan Arnow, *By Southern Hands: A Celebration of Craft Traditions in the South* (1987); Robert Bishop, *Folk Painters of America* (1979); Patti C. Black, ed., *Made by Hand: Mississippi Folk Art* (1980); David C. Driskell, *Two Centuries of Black American Art* (1976); William Ferris, ed., *Afro-American Folk Art and Crafts* (1983), *Local Color: A*

Sense of Place in Folk Art (1982); Herbert W. Hemphill, Jr., and Julia Weissman, *Twentieth Century American Folk Art and Artists* (1974); Elinor Lander Horwitz, *Contemporary American Folk Artists* (1975); Sidney Janis, *They Taught Themselves: American Primitive Painters of the Twentieth Century* (1942); Jean Lipman, *American Primitive Paintings* (1942), with Alice Winchester, *The Flowering of American Folk Art, 1776–1876* (1974); Jane Livingston and John Beardsley, *Black Folk Art in America, 1930–1980* (1982); Cynthia E. Rubin, ed., *Southern Folk Art* (1985); Cecilia Steinfeldt, *Texas Folk Art: One Hundred Fifty Years of the Southwestern Tradition* (1981); John Michael Vlach and Simon J. Bronner, eds., *Folk Art and Art Worlds* (1986); Anna Wadsworth, ed., *Missing Pieces: Georgia Folk Art, 1770–1976* (1976); Charles G. Zug III, in *Five North Carolina Folk Artists*, ed. Charles G. Zug III, with Quincy Scarborough, Mary Anne McDonald, and W. Neal Conoley, Jr. (1986). ☆

Folk Sculpture
||||||||||||||||||||||||||||||||||||||

See ART AND ARCHITECTURE: Sculpture

Folksongs
||||||||||||||||||||||||||

A folksong is a song without an identifiable composer that survives in a community through oral tradition. Isolated, agrarian southern communities have fostered the survival of folksong traditions. Genres as diverse as Native American ballads, coal-mining songs, mountain love songs, Delta blues, coastal fishing songs, and camp-meeting spirituals, produced and perpetuated by traditional communities, form the core of the southern folksong repertoire.

Southern folksong developed largely from the musical resources of Great Britain and Africa. Both areas made important contributions to southern music, and aspects of those traditions became components of new forms created by southerners, particularly during the 19th century, a period of great innovation and synthesis. Unfortunately, attention to the many varieties of folksong inspired by these two great traditions has been uneven, and knowledge of the development of southern folksong has gaps. Especially prized in the 19th century and early 20th century were the venerable British ballads, and many American versions were collected and published, albeit collected at times from less accurate secondary sources and published without tunes. The most thorough early collecting effort was that of English folklorist Cecil J. Sharp, who embarked on a series of song-hunting trips in the southern highlands beginning in 1916 and uncovered firsthand the richness of southern balladry. The songs Sharp collected (published as *English Folk Songs from the Southern Appalachians*, 1932) echoed vividly their British origins but also displayed remarkable adaptations to the American context, as evidenced by altered place names, modified references, and the replacement of plain-spoken British bawdiness with a characteristically American sense of decorum and moral reserve.

Also common in the South were versions of songs of more recent British origin, including such broadside ballads as "Jackie Munroe" and "The Butcher Boy." There were also songs British in style but American in origin, among them ballads on various subjects of local and regional interest, modeled after not only the British ballads themselves but also the ballad-meter English hymns found everywhere in southern hymn-books. Popular ones were the railroad ballad "The Wreck of the Old 97," the cowboy ballad "The Streets of Laredo," and numerous murder ballads such as "Poor Omie" and "On the Banks of the Ohio." Other songs in the British mold included widely known lyric songs such as "Drowsy Sleeper," "The Cuckoo," and "The Wagoner's Lad."

A great many Anglo-American folk-songs from the South are religious, and although they were not as widely noticed by early collectors, their influence has been considerable. The oldest were un-harmonized hymns based on British models, sung to traditional tunes and often lined out. Traces of that tradition still survive among the more conservative of the Primitive Baptists and some black congregations. Surviving folk hymns in the old style include the tune "New Britain," usually sung today with John Newton's text "Amazing grace, how sweet the sound." The spirituals, unlike the hymns, were American creations, arising in the wake of religious revivals taking place on the 19th-century frontier. The great camp meetings of the Second Great Awakening, beginning in Kentucky around 1800, produced hundreds of these easily learned songs, which were based loosely on elements from British hymns in combination with local musical elements. Some of them, including "Wondrous Love" and "Pisgah," were harmonized and found their way into shape-note songbooks compiled by and for southerners in the 19th century and still in use today in the Deep South and parts of the highlands. The first gospel hymns arose after the Civil War. Based in part

on the old hymns and spirituals and blending traditional and popular musical elements, gospel singing has proved remarkably adaptable and has grown into a thriving commercial industry, national in scope but strongest in the southern states that have been its creative center.

While the sacred folksongs of white southerners tended at first to be under-documented, the religious songs of southern blacks were among the first Afro-American songs to attract attention. A by-product of the abolitionist movement in the 19th century was the great interest in black spirituals as symbols of the noble aspirations of the slave population. The first published collection of southern black folksong was William Francis Allen's *Slave Songs of the United States* (1867), which contained mostly sacred and a few secular songs. Numerous other collections of black spirituals followed. Many of the anthologies of black music that came to public attention, however, failed to reveal the energy and essence of the black musical tradition, both by ignoring secular song and by reshaping songs to fit European performance style. Black singing, nevertheless, has been an enormously creative force, ranging from game songs ("Little Sally Walker"), work songs ("Long John"), and field hollers, to later forms including the blues and black gospel, both of which were among the primary components of rhythm and blues and, later, rock and roll.

Although scholars have disagreed, occasionally acrimoniously, as to the relative dominance of black and white sources in southern folksong, the most accurate view seems to be that the two traditions have not been separate and parallel musical streams, but inter-locked components of a single tradition.

Only in a few regions, where the population was predominantly white (the southern uplands), or predominantly black (the Sea Islands of Georgia and South Carolina), did song traditions remain relatively close to British or African sources. In most of the South the creative exchange between black and white singing gave southern folksong its identity and strength. Because blacks and whites often worked side by side and participated in the same social events, there was ample opportunity for musical exchange. Black singers learned European instruments and adapted them to a black aesthetic, while white singers absorbed these products of the black synthesis. Blacks attended church with whites and learned the same hymns, while white singers used black musicians to entertain at social gatherings. The ballad was a European song form, but some of the best-known American ballads began in the black community, including "John Henry" and "Frankie and Johnnie." The spirituals represented a joint effort, bringing together the structure and rhythm of African music and the melodic and textual elements of British song. The banjo, best known as a staple of the white folk tradition since the late 19th century, was an African import, and blacks as well as whites contributed to the songs and performance style associated with it. The obvious differences between black and white folksong style have served to obscure this cultural interdependence.

Afro-American and Anglo-American sources are by far the dominant influences on southern folksong, but several smaller, more localized traditions have also survived. One of the best-known regional traditions is represented by the Cajun and Creole songs of southern Louisiana, the most culturally complex region in the South, bringing together elements of African, British, Spanish, and French traditions. Cajun music, the songs of the French-speaking Acadians, whose ancestors came to Louisiana from Nova Scotia in the 18th century, includes songs of 17th- and 18-century France as well as Cajun versions of familiar southern songs. Creole music contains both African and French elements and includes counterparts of black songs from other regions of the South, songs with strong African or Afro-Caribbean elements, and versions of Cajun songs. The Spanish-language songs of the Texas-Mexican border, particularly the balladlike *corrido*, have been well documented by collectors and on older commercial recordings. A number of smaller and more isolated song traditions in the South are associated with religious communities and include the hymns of the Dunkards (or German Baptist Brethren) of Virginia and Cherokee-language versions of Protestant hymns in western North Carolina.

Southern folksongs are more than the fossilized remnants of archaic art forms. In the lively American context, adapting to changing conditions has been as much a part of the folk process for local communities as passing along the old songs. Neighboring ethnic traditions, local songwriters, and even commercial popular culture have contributed new songs that have taken their place in the oral tradition alongside older ones. "Frog Went A-courtin' " is a folksong, but so, in a broader sense, are "Weave Room Blues," written and recorded by Dorsey Dixon, a member of a South Carolina textile mill community, and Louisville journalist William Shakespeare Hays's sentimental song "Little Old Log Cabin in the Lane." Since the advent of the commercial recording of traditional music in the 1920s, local artists have served not only to steer the course of local tradition but also to channel traditional songs into popular culture. The list of southern singers with traditional roots whose influence has spread well beyond their communities includes Tennessee's Uncle Dave Macon, for many years a performer on the Grand Ole Opry; Mississippi-born Jimmie Rodgers, an innovative blender of black and white traditions and a pivotal figure in the foundation of country music; and singer/guitarist Huddie Ledbetter, known as Leadbelly, who absorbed a large and varied repertoire of folk material and later in his life came to represent the southern black tradition for urban audiences who had no other access to the genre.

The richness and vitality of southern traditional song are due to no particular group or locality but to a creative exchange of musical ideas over 150 years. Southern music is a continuum, and there is no clear point at which southern folksong becomes southern song or American song. As traditional spirituals are arranged for choir and set down in denominational hymnbooks, as blues becomes rhythm and blues, as old-time mountain music is incorporated by bluegrass and country and western music, new kinds of songs arise, expressing changes in southern communities, yet without severing their nourishing traditional roots. Thus, age-old links between communities and their folksongs survive even as new musical forms evolve.

See also BLACK LIFE: Music, Black; MUSIC articles

Brett Sutton
Carrboro, North Carolina

Josiah H. Combs, *Folk-Songs of the Southern United States* (1967), ed. D. K. Wilgus; William Ferris and Mary L. Hart, eds., *Folk Music and Modern Sound* (1981); Henry Glassie, Edward D. Ives, and John F. Szwed, eds., *Folksongs and Their Makers* (1970); Charles Joyner, *Folk Song in South Carolina* (1971); Alan Lomax, *Folk Songs of North America* (1975); Newman I. White, ed., *Frank C. Brown Collection of North Carolina Folklore*, vols. 2–5 (1952); D. K. Wilgus, *Anglo-American Folksong Scholarship since 1898* (1959). ☆

Folktales

||||||||||||||||||||||||

Southern folktales existed long before the transatlantic migration of Europeans and Africans to the New World. The Cherokees, the Creeks, the Choctaws, and other Native American groups told stories of origins—of how the Great Sun, the earth, the clans, corn, bears, and fire came to be—as well as lighter etiological tales explaining such things as "Why the Possum Grins" and stories about the adventures of the fabulous rabbit trickster. Such narratives were common across the Southeast.

Beginning in the 16th century, the Spanish became the first to import European folktales into the South. Planting colonies in what is now South Carolina, Florida, and Louisiana, and exploring from Texas to California, the Spanish left a strong cultural imprint on these areas. Following the Spanish, French settlers in South Carolina and especially in Louisiana brought zestful versions of such Gallic narratives as "Beauty and the Beast." The English at the dawn of the 17th century settled the coastline between the Chesapeake Bay and Spanish Florida, accompanied by their storehouse of such folktales as "Jack the Giant Killer." The British folktale repertoire was enhanced in the 18th century with the coming of large numbers of Scotch-Irish, who pushed down from Pennsylvania into the backcountry and highlands of the South.

But Europeans were not the only transatlantic settlers of the South. From Senegal and Gambia, from Guinea and Angola came shiploads of enslaved African men, women, and children. They brought with them shared traditions of storytelling and a host of animal trickster tales.

In the crucible of a new physical, social, and cultural environment, the folk narrative traditions of all southerners—Native Americans, Euro-Americans, and Afro-Americans—were modified by one another. Tales of European origin have been collected from black southerners; tales of African origin have been collected from white southerners; and both African and European tales have been collected among the Natchez, the Creeks, and the Seminoles. Old World tales entered Native American tradition through both Euro-Americans and Afro-Americans. Although there has been considerable interchange among the folktales of black, white, and Indian southerners, there has been less syncretism of the narratives of such Asian southerners as the Mississippi Chinese, who came to the South in the 19th century.

The most characteristic Afro-American tales in the South are animal trickster tales, and the most characteristic Euro-American tales are narratives that are often called "fairy tales," such as "Cinderella," "Jack the Giant Killer," and "Rumpelstiltskin." Folktale scholars call them *Märchen* after the usage of the Brothers Grimm.

There are European animal tales told in the South (such as the widespread "Three Little Pigs"), but the Afro-American animal tales are preeminently stories of the fabulous trickster Brer Rabbit. Although these tales are widely published in authentic field-collected versions, they are best known in Joel Chandler Harris's Uncle Remus books. Numerous tale types in the Uncle Remus canon, once thought to be of European origin, are now confirmed as African.

Southern Indians also have a tradition of animal trickster stories, but the Afro-American rabbit trickster differs from the Native American rabbit trickster in important ways. Although he sometimes fails (and may be repaid for his trickery in kind), Brer Rabbit is neither a clown nor a self-devourer, as is the Indian trickster figure. The main attribute of the Brer Rabbit stories is their focus on small but sly animals who gain the advantage over more powerful adversaries by using their brains rather than their muscles. The central theme of these tales is the struggle for mastery between the trickster Rabbit and his adversaries—Brer Bear, Brer Fox, Brer Gator, and Brer Wolf. Other animal tales were told by black southerners, including their own versions of such tales as "The Tail Fisher," a humorous explanation of why Rabbit's tail is short and his ears are long.

There was also a cycle of human trickster tales among black southerners. On the slave plantations the trickster was usually called John, and he was a real slave, not a surrogate like Brer Rabbit. The continuing battle of wits as the master sought to avoid being duped by John's mischief and guile paralleled the central struggle of the Brer Rabbit tales. The slave trickster tales have had their post-Emancipation counterparts in similar tales of High John, John the Conqueror, John Henry, John Hardy, Railroad Bill, Stagolee, Dupree, Brady, DaddyMention, and Crooked-Foot John.

In the South, as in Europe, white folktales exhibit formulaic beginnings and endings ("Once upon a time . . ." and "They all lived happily ever after"); remote settings; casts including royalty, giants, dragons, and helpful animals; and triepisodic plots with such motifs as transformations and magical objects. The protagonist is typically a poor stepchild who gains wealth and power through pluck, luck, and supernatural assistance.

Southern white folktales derive largely from British tradition, but distinctive versions of some of them have developed in the South. One of the most famous stories, best known as "Cinderella," has been found in several forms in southern tradition. A story found in most European collections, called by the Grimms "Hansel and Gretel," survives in a traditional North Carolina version entitled "Mutsmag." Another story known throughout Europe as "Beauty and the Beast" still lives in Arkansas, North Carolina, and Virginia, as well as in a Kentucky version known as "The Girl Who Married the Flop-eared Hound Dog." Distinctive southern versions of "The Taming of the Shrew" have been collected in Virginia, Kentucky, Arkansas, and Texas. An Afro-American version of "Rumpelstiltskin" has been recorded in North Carolina, and an entire cycle of "Jack Tales" has been collected in the southern Appalachians.

Another characteristic form of southern folktale is the tall tale. It was developed for European audiences using the exaggerations of explorers' adventures in the New World as early as Peter Martyr's accounts of the Spanish exploration of Chicora on the South Carolina

coast in the 1520s. These accounts pandered to their readers' desire for strange and wondrous descriptions of savages and wild beasts in an exotic environment. One of the Chicora Indians, baptized Francisco when he was taken to Spain, regaled the royal court with his stories of Datha, the king who was born of normal size but was stretched to gigantic proportions during his childhood, and of a race of highly intelligent humans with long, inflexible tails who inhabited the South Carolina coast.

By the 19th century similar tall tales were told throughout the backwoods South, especially in Georgia, Alabama, and Mississippi—the Old Southwest. They were often told in competitive liars' contests in which frontier narrators outdid one another in spinning tales about "The Split Dog," "The Snakebit Hoehandle," mythical beasts, crops that grew overnight, and impossible weather.

Many of these tall tales—including fabulous narratives of Davy Crockett, the Tennessee congressman who was both storyteller and subject of tall tales—are known to posterity by having been printed in the newspapers and in a series of antebellum almanacs. Drawing their style and characters from such tall tales, a new kind of fiction known as Southwest humor emerged in Augustus Baldwin Longstreet's *Georgia Scenes* (1835), Johnson J. Hooper's *Adventures of Simon Suggs* (1845), Joseph Baldwin's *Flush Times in Alabama and Mississippi* (1853), and George W. Harris's *Sut Lovingood's Yarns* (1867). Southwest humor influenced the writings of Mark Twain, and it survives in the work of William Faulkner and Guy Owen.

Many examples of European *jestes* have also been collected in the South, such as versions of "The Deaf Peasant" in the Carolinas. The Texas version of "The Hat That Pays for Everything" and the South Carolina Sea Island version of "Clever Elsie" are examples of what folktale scholars call *Numskull Stories*, a subdivision of *jestes*. Stories about preachers—such as "Counting Souls," the Mississippi version of an English tale known as "The Sexton Carries the Parson"—are another subdivision, as are such stories about married couples as the "step-husband tales" of the southern Appalachians. There is even a South Carolina version of the famous European "shaggy dog" story, "The Farmer and His Ox."

Two kinds of formula tales remain widespread in southern oral tradition, the cumulative tale and the cante-fable. The cumulative "Yay! Boo!" cycle not only survives in tradition but has passed into popular culture. The cumulative tale known among folktale scholars as "The Troll Who Was Cut Open" survives in numerous versions in the southern Appalachians. Cante-fables (folktales in which songs are an integral part) have been collected across the South, including an Appalachian version of "Jack and the Beanstalk," the South Carolina Sea Island "Barney McCabe," and North Carolina, Kentucky, and Tennessee versions of "The Robber Bridegroom," or "Mr. Fox's Courtship."

These and other forms of folktales have been narrated in the South for centuries, enriching the lives of generations of southerners, whether their ancestors came from Europe or from Africa—or were already here.

See also BLACK LIFE: Folklore, Black; / Sea Islands; ETHNIC LIFE: Indian Cultural Contributions; HISTORY AND MANNERS: / Crockett, Davy; LITERATURE: Folklore in Literature; / Clemens, Samuel; Faulkner, William; Harris, George W.; Harris, Joel Chandler; Longstreet, Augustus Baldwin

Charles Joyner
University of South Carolina
Coastal Campus

J. Mason Brewer, *Worser Days and Better Times: The Folklore of the North Carolina Negro* (1965); Marie Campbell, *Tales from the Cloud-Walking Country* (1958); Richard Chase, *The Jack Tales* (1943), *The Grandfather Tales: American English Folk Tales* (1948); Richard M. Dorson, *American Negro Folk Tales* (1967); Joel Chandler Harris, *Uncle Remus* (1881); Charles Joyner, *Down by the Riverside: A South Carolina Slave Community* (1984); Elsie C. Parsons, *Folk-Lore of the Sea Islands* (1923); Vance Randolph, *The Devil's Pretty Daughter, and other Ozark Folktales* (1955), *Pissing in the Snow and other Ozark Folktales (1976)*, *Who Blowed Up the Church House, and other Ozark Folktales* (1952); Leonard Roberts, *South from Hell-fer-Sartin: Kentucky Mountain Folk Tales* (1955); South Carolina Writers' Program, *South Carolina Folk Tales: Stories of Animals and Supernatural Beings* (1941); William O. Tuggle, *Shem, Ham, and Japeth: The Papers of W. O. Tuggle* (1973); Newman I. White, ed., *Frank C. Brown Collection of North Carolina Folklore*, vol. 1 (1952). ☆

Foodways
||||||||||||||||||||||||

See HISTORY AND MANNERS: Foodways

Funerals
||||||||||||||||||||||||

Southern funerals have served sacred and social functions. As far back as the colonial era, a funeral was the occasion for the display of both grief and hospitality. Although the early Puritans in the North held simple funerals, Virginians made their death ceremonies into elaborate events. Southern settlement patterns made for rural isolation, but the funeral was a recognized time to overcome the separation. Mourners shared with the bereaved family the loss of a community member, as well as the need ritually to overcome it. The firing of guns, the consumption of liquor, and the funeral feast tradition brought from England were all characteristic of public funerals.

In the early 19th century southern funerals in general did not differ markedly from those in the rest of the country. Plantation funerals, however, were distinctive occasions. Slaves and slave-owning families shared the same burial grounds. When a slave died, the plantation community responded with an immediate burial and, later, an elaborate memorial service, usually on Sunday, the day of rest. When a slaveowner died, activity on the plantation stopped and a grand public funeral resulted, complete with both real and feigned grief among the planter's chattels.

In the late 19th and early 20th centuries, southern funerals came to differ from those in the rest of the nation. Funerals for public figures like Robert E. Lee and Jefferson Davis were true ceremonies of the southern identity. Symbols of Dixie were prominently displayed, while eulogies explained the contribution of the deceased to the South as a region. Funerals of the average person reinforced social and cultural characteristics associated with the South. They were among the region's chief ceremonies. Neighbors and friends played a major role in them, thus strengthening the bonds of community.

Funerals nurtured also the sense of family. Death resulted typically in a homecoming and a gathering of the extended kin.

Funerals reflected caste and class arrangements so important in the region. Whites and blacks at times attended funerals together, but they behaved in highly patterned ways reflecting racial segregation. Blacks at white funerals sat or stood in the back of the room, but whites at black funerals sat on the front row and viewed the body before others attending did so.

For the southern poor, death was an event to be dealt with in a memorable way. A proper funeral was deemed necessary by people who had so little in life. If he had no other recourse, the poor rural tenant farmer so common in the South might borrow money from the landowner or merchant, driving the tenant deeper into debt. Burial societies became especially prominent in the South as a cooperative way to set aside money for funerals.

The funeral industry transformed the way Americans handled death in the late 1800s, but southerners persisted in old-fashioned ways. The American way of death as it emerged in the Northeast and the Midwest included the embalming process, elaborate caskets, funeral homes, and a secular funeral service. Professional funeral directors set the tone for the funeral, and they tended to discourage emotional expressions. The development of the funeral industry lagged in the South because of the poverty, rurality, and religious outlook of southerners. Southern funerals have remained distinctive because of the level of their emotional displays of grief. Southerners in general have been more outgoing in their grief than northerners, with Pentecostal services, black funerals, and the death ceremonies of the rural poor the most visibly grief-ridden and emotional. While the American way of death downplayed such emotional grief, sentimental southerners typically nurtured it.

The traditional southern funeral went through a series of stages. It was a community affair throughout, with family, neighbors, and friends directing each stage, including laying out the body, constructing a coffin, visiting at the deceased's home, and shoveling dirt into the grave. A distinctive regional custom was the "sitting up" ceremony, between the death and the burial. Family and friends stayed with the body, even through the night, in a modified wake. A sad, solemn occasion for the bereaved family, it was a social event as well. Distinctive regional food and drink were usually in abundance during the wake. The funeral service was held at home or in church. A church funeral and the presence of a minister were especially important for a proper funeral. The most trying time was likely at the burial itself, as everyone stayed until neighbors, friends, and family had shoveled the last spade of dirt into the grave. Hysterical behavior was not uncommon at this point.

The southern funeral was shaped by the predominant evangelical, fundamentalist religious style and outlook. A central focus of the funeral was the evangelical sermon, which used the death to remind mourners of their own mortality and of the need to get right with God. Funeral hymns and prayers portrayed the peace of heaven, but they also kept southerners aware of the inevitability of death.

Southern funerals in the contemporary era increasingly reflect the standardization and secularization of death. Funeral directors now arrange the process, resulting in less community and

family involvement. Regional customs such as the sitting up ceremony and the open-casket funeral are on the decline, although they remain a common occurrence. Attitudes toward death and funerals show even greater continuity with the past. Religion and the churches continue to be so central to southern life that religious beliefs shape the predominant view of death. The churches continue to be popular locations for funerals, ministers are still regarded as necessary for proper services, and emotionalism is probably more common than elsewhere. Finally, the funeral remains a prime ceremonial occasion for eating southern food, hearing southern music, and nurturing the region's renowned sense of family and community.

See also BLACK LIFE: Funerary Customs, Black

Charles Reagan Wilson
University of Mississippi

Christopher Crocker, in *The Not So Solid South: Anthropological Studies in a Regional Subculture*, ed. J. Kenneth Morland (1971); James J. Farrell, *Inventing the American Way of Death, 1830–1920* (1980); Charles O. Jackson, *Passing: The American Vision of Death* (1977); William Lynwood Montell, *Ghosts along the Cumberlands: Deathlore in the Kentucky Foothills* (1975); James I. Robertson, Jr., *Georgia Review* (Spring 1959); Charles Reagan Wilson, *Georgia Historical Quarterly* (Spring 1983). ☆

Grave Markers

The southern grave markers most distinctive to the region are normally the work of vernacular craftsmen. Most monuments currently made in the South follow nationally popular design patterns, and their makers employ standard industrial tools and techniques. Even for most of the 19th century, when the local hand-cutting of stones remained a vigorous occupation, most carvers followed national fashions in their choice of stone, profile, lettering, and design motifs. Work peculiar to the South is the output of earlier stonecutters or of craftsmen working in geographic or ethnic or economic isolation from American popular culture. Their products are in fact "southern" chiefly in their extreme localism and diversity.

The earliest monuments erected were either locally carved wooden headboards and footboards (long since decayed) or stones imported from the British Isles and, in particular, from the northern colonies. The sandy Tidewater South provided no supply of stone and hence failed to support a stonecutting tradition among 17th- and 18th-century English settlers. The cemeteries of a Charleston or a Wilmington are therefore museums of early New England stone carving.

The rocky uplands, however, offered the German and Scotch-Irish immigrants of the 18th century a wide choice of workable material: sandstone, limestone, slate, granite, and especially soapstone. Their output is scattered in two kinds of sites—the churchyard and the family plot—marking the two institutions of greatest importance in the lives of the settlers. The churchyard stones have had the better chance of survival to the 20th century.

Many 18th-century churchyards show a few examples of early local amateur carving. Any significant output, however, is usually the work of a settler who arrived with prior training as a stonecutter. Because few localities had the density of population or wealth to support a full-time monument business, most such craftsmen cut stones as a sideline to farming and other activities. Like other master artisans settling in the southern backwoods, the stonecutter typically became a jack-of-all-trades.

A major exception was the Scotch-Irish workshop of the Bigham family— Samuel, Sr., his sons Samuel and William, and at least two others probably trained by them. Carvers from this workshop tradition had been active from about 1740 in Lancaster and Adams Counties, Penn., and in the 1760s they made their way to Mecklenburg County, N.C., where they settled near two major transportation arteries—the Great Wagon Road from Philadelphia to Charleston and the Catawba River. They were patronized by the wealthier Scotch-Irish settlers, and some 850 of their skillfully carved soapstone markers survive in early Presbyterian churchyards scattered across seven counties of North and South Carolina, the earliest artwork demonstrably the product of this Piedmont region. The Bigham stones illustrate clearly the transformation of the immigrant ethnic settler into the American patriot. The designs on the earliest stones were Scottish motifs (the thistle) or Scotch-Irish emblems (most typically, a sprig-bearing dove) or family armorial bearings. Across the decades the animal motifs of the coats of arms (lions, stags, horses, falcons, fish, two-headed eagles) came to be used as independent decorations. At the time of the Revolution the Bighams began to reinterpret the coat of arms as a national emblem, filling the shield with 13 stars, selecting eagles for the supporters, topping the design with a fist and sword, and for the motto choosing "Virtue, Liberty, Independence." The spread eagle became another of their favorite nationalistic designs. After the revolutionary era, they further filled the coat-of-arms form with symbols drawn from the Masonic repertory, showing another identity that their patrons were assuming. Late Bigham stones also show rear-face decoration and motifs such as the swastika, both traits suggestive of influence from neighboring German settlers.

Although no direct German-American models for these Bigham stones have as yet been located, several major German workshops did exist in the southern uplands. One active between 1800 and the 1840s in Davidson County, N.C., produced remarkable pierced or "open-work" soapstone markers with such symbols of resurrection as swastikas and trees of life. In their profiles and their use of molding, the stones also betray their cutters' knowledge of woodworking and cabinetry. Another major German workshop was that of Laurence Crone, who left work in Wythe, Roanoke, and Pulaski Counties, Va., between 1815 and 1836. His large, handsome sandstone markers typically bear a rear-face carving of a heart rising from the earth and flowering into roses.

The early southern stonecutting traditions normally ended abruptly in an area with the death of the carver (such as Laurence Crone or the South Carolina stonecutter Hugh Kelsey) or his westward migration (as in the case of Samuel Bigham, Jr., and his brother William, who moved to Tennessee, or the Davidson County carvers, some of whom left for Indiana, or Samuel Watson, who removed from South Carolina to Missouri). They were succeeded by carvers who simply followed national tastes, decorating white marble slabs with weeping willows, urns, figures in togas, and fat cherubs.

For both economic and cultural reasons many grave markers made by post-Civil War and 20th-century blacks are exceptions to the dominance of popular culture. Older black burial sites show graves decorated with seashells or household objects—practices interpreted as a survival of West African traditions. Beginning in the 1920s, Afro-Americans working in building trades that trained them in the use of concrete started to cast grave markers of that material, incising or painting them with designs, or decorating them with shells or pebbles or colored glass marbles. An occasional gifted craftsman like William Edmondson of Nashville, Tenn., worked in stone, impelled by religious inspiration to become a stonecutter and guided by it to his characteristic sculptural forms: doves, lambs, and angels. In the absence of any strong persisting vernacular tradition or any compelling economic necessity, only such a religious imperative is likely in the foreseeable future to inspire black or white craftsmen and their patrons to ignore popular commercial products that embody popularly accepted standards of taste and symbolize affluence attained. Only a religious vision is likely to cause them to dignify the resting places of their dead with monuments made locally to express the values of a local subculture shaped by the South.

See also ART AND ARCHITECTURE: Sculpture; BLACK LIFE: Funerary Customs, Black; ETHNIC LIFE: / Germans; Scotch-Irish

Daniel Patterson
University of North Carolina
at Chapel Hill

Ruth Little-Stokes, *Newsletter of the Association of Gravestone Studies* (Summer 1982); Bradford L. Rauschenberg, *Journal of Early Southern Decorative Arts* (November 1977); Klaus Wust, *Folk Art in Stone, Southwest Virginia* (1970). ☆

House Types

||||||||||||||||||||||||||||||||||

The initial spread of house types characteristic of the South was brief and decisive. It manifested aspects of the frontier experience that were less obvious in other dimensions of southern history and geography. Three major phases occurred in the diffusion of the typical folk and vernacular houses of the South—colonial (1604 to 1775), frontier (1775 to 1850), and modern (1880 to 1940). Each phase revealed distinct aspects of the southern experience.

Understanding southern house types requires knowing the people who immigrated to and migrated across the South, as well as the changing, shifting conditions that made possible expression of the ideals, preferences, and tastes of southerners. During the first century of colonial settlement, the houses built in the South reflected, in simplified rendering, the homes that had been built in Britain. In Virginia and the Carolinas, common houses had plans based upon the British bay, or pen, an oblong unit with a gable roof, a chimney on one gable end, and doors on the two eave sides. Commonly made of one or two such units, the earliest versions lacked the broad porches and the pier foundations so typical of later models. All along the Tidewater and into the valley of Virginia, these basi-cally British houses of brick, half-timber, and lumber sheltered the small class of white commoners. Somewhat later, and mainly through Charleston, new traits arrived from the Caribbean; these included galleries, external stairs, and pier foundations.

After about 1725 new settlers, arriving from northern Ireland and Rhineland Germany, settled lands in the backcountry in the western parts of Pennsylvania, Virginia, and the Carolinas. They entered the colonies principally through Philadelphia and Charleston, moving north and south along the then main road of the colonies, running between Philadelphia and Charleston by way of Roanoke. Commercial traffic, repeated moves, and flights from Indian attacks promoted a common awareness of a variety of building traits from both British and German sources. Gradually, during the span from 1725 to 1775, shared experience produced a frontier solution to building a house; that packet of ideas spread westward during the next two generations to nearly all places in the wooded eastern United States, south of the Great Lakes drainage. The very suddenness of the diffusion showed that the novel solution was destined to enter the new settlement zones of the Old West.

In the frontier South the British pen and German log-notching provided the basic plan and the most distinctive building techniques, although the record clearly shows that many of the earliest houses in any area were built of, in addition to logs, timber framing, lumber, brick, and even stone. The very first cabins in an area normally had dirt floors, crude log walls, and roofs of split boards held down by poles or stones. Such cabins were, however, universally regarded as temporary. The permanent structure was a house, a well-made, reasonably stylish home with a proper floor and a foundation of piers. Its walls were formed of shaped and dressed logs or of such materials as sawn lumber, brick, or stone. In any case, the house of the frontier, rather than being a crude invention fathered by necessity, was an expression of current fashion worked in available material. The main significance of notched logs lay in the southern acceptance of them as suitable for permanent houses and in the advantage that they gave southerners relative to others competing for the wooded eastern United States.

The theme of ethnic origins showed in the persistence of the dogtrot, double-pen, saddlebag, and I plans among the houses built by southerners in the frontier context and on into the 20th century. These two-room-wide models were worked in the available materials and adorned in the contemporary fashion. The dogtrot had an open central hall between two pens, whereas the saddlebag had a central chimney in that location. The double pen lacked both the hall and the central chimney. Chimneys normally, except for the saddlebag, appeared on the exterior ends of the houses. The I house is a two-story version of the other three, most typically, a two-story dogtrot or central-hall house.

Fashion, whether stylistic or technical, can gain dominance in the landscape only during periods of local prosperity. Periods of prosperity, such as the first and the last thirds of the 19th century, made possible the adoption of innovations in houses no less than in industry. The commercial dominance of contemporary fashion introduced the third phase in the spread of southern house types. Modernity in houses was a departure from the ethnic models, characterized by the acceptance of nationally distributed, expertly created, commercial models. Especially significant for the South was the California bungalow style of architecture. This once new-fangled, exotic fashion gained such wide acceptance during the flush times of the early southern lumber boom that it now, incorrectly, seems to be a southern creation.

From about 1900, then, such national styles as the bungalow increasingly displaced the old folk models of the frontier phase. By World War II the southern types had largely ceased to be built, and by the 1950s nearly all southern construction involved national models.

See also ART AND ARCHITECTURE: Vernacular Architecture

M. B. Newton, Jr.
Louisiana State University

Fred B. Kniffen, *Annals of the Association of American Geographers* (December 1965); Fred Kniffen and Henry Glassie, *Geographical Review* (January 1966); Dell Upton and John Michael Vlach, *Common Places: Readings in American Vernacular Architecture* (1986); H. J. Walker and W. G. Haag, *Geoscience and Man*, vol.5 (1974). ☆

Legends

No more fertile ground for legends exists than the South. The terrain, the climate, and the inhabitants have shaped unique legends, many of which are nationally known. Many folklorists define legends only in terms of oral lore, but legends are also part of the historiography of any region. Although the body of oral legends reflects the heritage of diverse subcultures in the South, the southern legends popular in literature and movies, like American legends in general, focus more on males than females, more on whites than nonwhites, and more on Protestants than non-Protestants.

Anglo-American southerners have worked diligently to keep the nation mindful of their roots in the region. Legends abound, for example, about the mysterious lost colony of Roanoke, site of the first attempted English colony in the New World and birthplace of Virginia Dare, the first English child born in this land. Paul Green's outdoor drama, *The Lost Colony*, has celebrated the tale for countless visitors to North Carolina.

Jamestown, Va., site of the first permanent English settlement in America and capital of colonial Virginia from 1607 to 1699, lives in legend partly because of Captain John Smith's purported rescue from execution by the Powhatan Indian princess Pocahontas. Romantic tales about the pair flourished in the mid-19th century, and the legend was immortalized through a bronze sculpture and a painting in the Capitol rotunda in Washington. When writers in the late 1800s tried to debunk the legend, southern authors leapt to its defense.

Southerners strove, too, to shape the legends surrounding Virginian George Washington, revered as the nation's quintessential statesman and public servant. Parson Mason Weems, a Maryland minister and author, concocted the most famous Washington stories such as the cherry tree tale. A more scholarly

effort was Chief Justice John Marshall's five-volume official biography of Washington. The state of Virginia in 1784 commissioned the French sculptor Antoine Houdon to create a bust of Washington, and the U.S. government eventually distributed plaster copies to public schools nationwide. A reflection of the white upper-class South's high esteem for Washington was the Confederates' selection of the general to appear on their great seal.

Virginians further nurtured the traditions of the antebellum planter class through special reverence for Thomas Jefferson, the South's and the nation's legendary Renaissance man. Up to the Civil War, however, it was not Jefferson but Francis Marion, dubbed "the Swamp Fox," who "ranked next to Washington as the idol of the South," according to Dixon Wecter. Marion's brilliant guerilla tactics against the British in the 1780s gave rise to biographies (Parson Weems produced one), folklore, paintings, and poems.

Other legendary southerners of the late 1700s and the early 1800s embodied a bold, adventuresome nature. The South could not lay full claim to Daniel Boone, a native of Pennsylvania who moved to Virginia at age 15. However, Boone's exploits throughout the Kentucky territory and his establishment of Fort Boonesborough garnered him a special place in southern folklore. The entire nation enjoyed and participated in the South's creation of its own outrageous, comic version of the frontiersman by weaving tall tales about Tennessean Davy Crockett. Dying in a blaze of glory at the Alamo, Crockett became a symbol of the country's bold expansionist goals. Legends of rough-hewn, firebrand southerners developed, too, around the exploits of General

Andrew Jackson, who led his Tennessee troops against the British in the Battle of New Orleans during the War of 1812. Known as "Old Hickory" or simply "the Hero," Jackson, a native of South Carolina and later a Tennessee resident, was once called "the most roaring, rollicking, game-cocking, horse-racing, card-playing, mischievous fellow that ever lived in Salisbury [N.C.]." The South's raw edge had begun to take shape in legend.

Southerners' brilliance, tenacity, and fearlessness in war certainly were central to legends of the Lost Cause. Legends of Confederate heroes and of pivotal battles carry in them a southern apologia, white southerners' answer to the question of whether one could be both a good Confederate and a good American. Cavalry expert J. E. B. "Jeb" Stuart with a bold stroke disarmed the federal army of the Potomac in 1862; Nathan Bedford "First with the Most" Forrest repeatedly disrupted federal campaigns with daring cavalry raids; and William C. Quantrill's raiders made a bloody, infamous raid on freestate guerillas in 1863. During the war Stonewall Jackson reigned as the Confederates' supreme hero. Belle Boyd, daughter of a prominent planter, disrupted numerous Union plans and gained notoriety as a spy.

After the war, however, the South's most revered warrior was Robert E. Lee, described by Marshall Fishwick as "the archetypal cavalier." The legends of Lee's military abilities, devotion to duty, nobility, deep religious faith, integrity, charity, self-denial, and wisdom abound. Says Dixon Wecter, Lee "reclaimed her [the antebellum South's] chivalry from bombast, and made into poetry the fact of her defeat. The South lost the war, but she still had Robert E.

Lee." White southerners launched innumerable efforts after Lee's death to immortalize him, and until the beginning of the 20th century, the Lee cult flourished almost exclusively in the South. Over time, though, the Lost Cause's saint has gained acceptance in national legends as the exemplar of grace in defeat.

The Civil War brought to a head the conflicting legends of black and white southerners. While whites exalted Lee, southern blacks—and Union supporters in general—heralded Kentucky-born Abraham Lincoln as the Great Emancipator. Eventually, southern whites who had offered Lee as an example to the nation came to accept Lincoln as legendary too. But black southerners' legends, shaped by the experience of slavery, had a long and rich history apart from the legends that grew in white culture.

Based on a rich oral tradition, black creation legends and trickster tales had clear roots in African culture. Lawrence W. Levine notes that "African trickster figures were more obsessed with manipulating the strong and reversing the normal structure of power and prestige." This emphasis on overcoming powerful forces through shrewdness persisted until well after emancipation, and only after that time did tales of grandiose individual exploits become common among blacks.

Among the individuals who became legendary among blacks were the conjurer Old Julie and voodoo queen Marie Laveau. Legendary slave insurrectionists included Denmark Vesey and his chief lieutenant, Gullah Jack (Jack Pritchard); Nat Turner, leader of the Southampton insurrection; and Bras Coupé, leader of a group of runaway slaves in New Orleans in 1830. Revered, too, was Harriet Tubman, a Maryland-born abolitionist and former slave who aided Union troops in South Carolina and led more than 300 slaves to freedom through the Underground Railroad.

Minority ethnic groups' legends have also flourished. Cajuns warned of the *loup-garous*, or werewolves, and preserved the tragic tale of Emmaline Labiche, or Evangeline, whom Henry Wadsworth Longfellow immortalized. American Indians emphasized legends of the mystery and power of nature, and the communal relationships between humans and nature. Through a strong oral tradition, American Indian tribes in the South passed on a variety of creation legends, such as the Cherokee's tales of the sun as a life-giving female. Legends from non-white cultures have had little place in white culture, although Anglo-Americans have lauded legendary Indians, such as Pocahontas and Sequoyah, who lived peaceably with whites.

After emancipation many of the best-known legendary figures were workers, and southerners celebrated their amazing occupational feats. Legendary figures immortalized in song include John Henry, the black railroad worker who died after outperforming a steam drill, and Casey Jones, the white railroad engineer who lost his life in a train crash. Tall-tale characters include Annie Christmas, a huge black female longshoreman who could outdrink, outwrestle, and outlift any man; riverboatmen and gamblers James Girty and George Devol; and riverboatman Mike Fink, so-called king of the keelboatmen, who was known for his skills on the river and his sadistic pranks. Some heroes worked outside the law, and few can rival in notoriety the pirates Blackbeard, Gas-

parilla, and Jean Lafitte, who patroled the southern coastline.

Women have seldom been the subject of southern legends, although they have been among the most ardent hero worshippers in the region. The characteristics most exalted in American legendary figures—tenacity, drive, independence, and bravery—have been culturally defined as antithetical to femininity. In the South the most concerted efforts to create heroines have centered around the mothers or wives of famous men. One notable exception is Helen Keller, who overcame limitations of deafness and blindness through the devotion of her teacher, Anne Sullivan.

Southern legends deal not only with illustrious individuals but with star-crossed lovers (the lovers of Dismal Swamp in Virginia), disastrous feuds (the Hatfields and McCoys), haunted locales (Metairie Cemetery in New Orleans), and buried treasures (Jean Lafitte's booty). Although many such legends grow out of superstition, a love of exaggeration, or a sense of fun, southerners also transmit legends to preserve traditions, solidify cultural images, and express beliefs.

Sharon A. Sharp
University of Mississippi

Benjamin A. Botkin, ed., *A Treasury of American Folklore* (1944), *A Treasury of Southern Folklore* (1949); Marshall Fishwick, *American Heroes: Myth and Reality* (1954), *The Hero, American Style* (1969); Zora Neale Hurston, *Mules and Men* (1935); Lawrence W. Levine, *Black Culture and Black Consciousness: Afro-American Folk Thought from Slavery to Freedom* (1977); *The Life Treasury of American Folklore* (1961); Lyle Saxon, Robert Tallant, and Edward Dreyer, *Gumbo Ya-Ya: A Collection of Lou-*

isiana Folk Tales (1945); Dixon Wecter, *The Hero in America: A Chronicle of Hero-Worship* (1941); Gary Wills, *American Heritage* (February–March 1981). ☆

Personal Experience Narratives

||||||||||||||||||||||||||||||||||||||||||||||||||||||

First-person stories are based on whatever an individual considers important or entertaining enough to relate. Southern regional identity will partially determine the aspects of a person's life that are worth telling stories about, but these narratives also relate to American culture and to universal human concerns.

Southern personal experience narratives reflect specific southern customs and patterns of behavior; for instance, courtship stories clearly indicate courtship and marriage traditions for the time and place in which they are set. Elderly couples in the Blue Ridge Mountains of Virginia and North Carolina tell personal narratives about their courting days, which show that 50 to 60 years ago courting took place in community and family contexts, at church socials and in homes. An idealized view of love relates the stories to the tradition of medieval courtly love; the woman is presented as an untouchable object of desire to be pursued from a distance until her heart has been won and the marriage takes place. Traditional sex roles are fulfilled; the man is the active pursuer and the woman is a passive object. Dual narration often occurs in which the husband and wife interrupt and correct each other; the mode of nar-

rating is a model for the marriage itself in that there are disagreements but cooperation overcomes these so that the relationship continues.

Personal experience narratives can occur in families or in larger contexts such as occupational groups. Commercial fishermen along southern coastlines tell stories about personal disasters or narrow escapes while at sea. Some of these have to do with men injured at sea who almost bleed to death before they make it back to land; others deal with men, often brothers or other close relatives, swept overboard during storms. The survivors recount these disasters as reminders to others about the dangers of their occupation, one of the most hazardous in the United States. These narratives are an important indication of the physical risk and uncertainty of their occupational environment; anxiety is a part of their work. This in turn helps to explain the dependency of commercial fishermen on magic and superstition. Their superstitious behavior is an attempt to get control of their environment, thus relieving some of the anxiety. Other hazardous occupations in the South, such as coal mining, also have traditions of personal disaster stories.

Another area of experience that is traditionally the subject of stories in the South is personal contact with local characters, individuals whose eccentric behavior is often noted in comic ways. Stories are still being told about two brothers who lived along the Gulf Coast of Texas in the 1930s and 1940s. People who knew them remember incidents of their abnormal behavior: they never took baths, they lived in a shack with a pack of dogs, and they never worked at regular jobs. They broke many of the norms of the society, such as personal hygiene, but they also had a freedom from societal restraint that was admired by other men in the community. Several of the stories about outsiders, especially from the North, who are brought into contact with the brothers as a prank. The people in the community knew that outsiders would be offended, thereby establishing boundaries between themselves and outsiders and also projecting a community identity that allows a wide range of acceptable behavior. The outdoorsmen of the Gulf Coast see these brothers as perennial Huck Finns who have permanently lit out for the territory and rejected societal restraints, especially those associated with women.

The great range of personal experience narrative is apparent when viewing the mundane comic antics of local characters on one side and the sacred spiritual quality of personal conversion stories on the other. The emphasis in southern Protestant fundamentalism on personal revelation, on being born again through a transcendent experience, results in a large body of traditional stories existing within this religious context. The stories are based on individual mystical experience, but they reflect traditional and communal patterns. Often people speak of visions and voices, of being in contact with angels, Christ, or God, of being outside of ordinary reality. These traits suggest a ritual process that is cross-cultural; there is a separation from everyday existence, an entering into a mystical state in which the person experiences oneness with God and all humanity, and then a return to structured society. The personal experience narrative acts as a means of reincorporating the mystical event into everyday reality, a structuring of an unstructured incident so that it can be shared with and perhaps inspire, others.

See also WOMEN'S LIFE: Marriage and Courtship

Patrick B. Mullen
Ohio State University

Roger D. Abrahams, in *Folklore Genres*, ed. Dan Ben-Amos (1976); Patrick B. Mullen, *Folklore and Folklife in Virginia* (1980–81), *I Heard the Old Fishermen Say: Folklore of the Texas Gulf Coast* (1978); John Robinson, *Journal of American Folklore* (January–March 1981). ☆

Pottery

||||||||||||||||||||

Pottery vessels for storing, processing, and handling food and drink were indispensable in American life before the availability of inexpensive glass, metal, and plastic containers. This was especially true for the South, where the mild climate made food preservation even more critical. Most colonial pottery was earthenware, composed of a reddish-brown clay and glazed with lead in the British and German manner. However, by the time the interior of the South was becoming extensively settled in the early 19th century, stoneware—a harder, more durable product made from a purer, higher-firing clay—emerged as the dominant medium for traditional utilitarian ceramics.

Throughout the North and Upper South, stoneware was glazed in the European way by throwing salt in the kiln at the height of firing to form a transparent coating of glass over the gray or tan clay, and it was decorated with cobalt-oxide paint that produced a deep blue color when fired. Salt-glazed stoneware was made sporadically in the Deep South, but rarely was it cobalt decorated. Instead it often displayed unintentional surface irregularities (brick drippings, melted fly ash blown from the fuel, puddled salt deposits, and fire-flashing) resulting largely from the regional rectangular kilns.

A second type of stoneware glaze, applied as a solution before firing, was unknown in the North but was widely used—especially in the second and third quarters of the 19th century—from the western Carolinas to east Texas. Using slaked wood ashes or lime to help melt the other ingredients (normally clay and sand), it produced colors in the green or brown range and sometimes a drippy texture. These distinctly regional alkaline glazes may have been developed in Edgefield District, S.C., about the second decade of the 19th century, possibly inspired by a published account of similar glazes in the Far East (the only other part of the world where they are well known). Some Edgefield potters in the 1840s and 1850s decorated their alkaline-glazed stoneware with white and dark brown slips (liquid clays), a technique adapted from European earthenware.

A characteristic southern vessel type is the large, two-handled syrup jug, whose prevalence is linked to the importance of molasses as a liquid sweetening in the regional diet. Novelty jugs with stylized or grotesque human faces, although occasionally made elsewhere, are concentrated in the Southeast, where they are still produced by folk potters. Ceramic grave markers, wheel-turned or molded to serve as headstones or planters, although scattered through the Midwest, are more focused in the region bounded by southwestern Pennsylvania and east Texas, where they date mainly from the 1870s through the 1920s.

Certain aspects of the production

technology are specific to the South. The most significant is the wood-burning rectangular kiln with its arched ceiling, firebox at one end, and chimney at the other. It sometimes was surrounded by earth, giving rise to the term *groundhog kiln*. Northern kilns, by contrast, were round. Rectangular kilns were used to fire stoneware in Germany and France, and, although rare, a 17th-century example is known for England. The earliest discovered for the South at Yorktown, Va., dates from the 1720s.

The frequency of the place name "Jugtown" testifies to the tendency of southeastern potters to cluster in communities, most of which are located in the Piedmont plateau near suitable clay. Georgia's folk potters (who typically were also farmers) were concentrated in eight centers, the most extensive being Mossy Creek in White County where over 70 have worked. These pottery centers were dominated by key families who shaped localized ceramic styles. The Browns, who trace their ancestry to an English immigrant potter, have been potting in the South for more than eight generations. Individuals not born into pottery families often became potters after marrying into them, and members of different "clay clans" tended to marry one another, thus consolidating the pottery dynasties. With some notable exceptions, access to the craft was limited to white males. This family control and transmission of the craft (as opposed to the formal apprenticeship more common elsewhere) may be tied to the centrality of the kin group, dispersed settlement, and agrarian life characteristic of the region.

Prohibition and the shift away from self-sufficiency lowered demand for folk pottery and led to its decline in the 20th century. Rather than abandon clay work, some traditionally trained potters changed to the production of unglazed flowerpots and other "garden" pottery or colorful artistic and table wares oriented to a more affluent urban market. A fair number of these transitional potters or their offspring continue to make a good living at the trade today. A smaller number of potters, including Georgia's Lanier Meaders, North Carolina's Burlon Craig, Alabama's Norman Smith, and Mississippi's Gerald Stewart, remain faithful to the older tradition, carrying on an essentially 19th-century approach to pottery making. As the last stronghold of American folk pottery, as in other realms of culture, the South can be seen as a region of survivals where old ways die hard.

See also ART AND ARCHITECTURE: Decorative Arts

John A. Burrison
Georgia State University

John A. Burrison, *Brothers in Clay: The Story of Georgia Folk Pottery* (1983), *Southern Folklore Quarterly* (December 1975); Stephen T. Ferrell and T. M. Ferrell, *Early Decorated Stoneware of the Edgefield District, South Carolina* (catalog, 1976); Georgeanna H. Greer, *Antiques* (April 1977), *Northeast Historical Archaeology* (Spring 1977); Ralph Rinzler and Robert Sayers, *The Meaders Family: North Georgia Potters* (1980); Nancy Sweezy, *Raised in Clay: The Southern Pottery Tradition* (1984); John Michael Vlach, *Ceramics Monthly* (September 1978). ☆

Pottery, North Carolina

||||||||||||||||||||||||||||||||||||||||||||||||||||||

North Carolina is the only state in the nation that possesses a balanced folk ceramic heritage of lead-glazed earthenware, salt-glazed stoneware, and alkaline-glazed stoneware. This unique combination of the three major types of traditional pottery results from North Carolina's position as a "border state" between the North and the South. From Virginia up into New England, earthenware and salt-glazed stoneware predominated: the former was produced in small, family-run shops; the latter, particularly after the mid-19th century, in very standardized, cobalt-decorated forms, most often in large factories. To the south and west of North Carolina, however, the picture was very different. Almost no earthenware existed, and the salt-glazed stoneware was normally unembellished and made in modest quantities in scattered communities. What best characterizes this southern region is the alkaline-glazed stoneware that was "turned" and "burned" by many generations of potters from North Carolina south to Florida and west into Texas.

The first pottery produced in North Carolina was lead-glazed earthenware. Although the earliest permanent settlement occurred in the 1650s in the Albemarle region in the northeast corner of the state, potters did not appear for another 100 years. The Coastal Plain lacks first-rate clays; more important, the early plantation economy and active commerce with England, the West Indies, and the Northeast seem to have discouraged potters from setting up shop. Thus, the bulk of the pottery was produced in the Piedmont, largely by British and German immigrants who began to flood the midsection of the state in the middle of the 18th century. Here an abundance of readily accessible sedimentary clays, a rapidly swelling population, an economy characterized by small, independent farms, and a relative isolation from outside markets all combined to create ideal conditions for the folk potter.

From the 1750s to about 1825 the most prominent craftsmen were the Moravians, who in 1753 commenced building a palisaded settlement called Bethabara on the north side of what is now Winston-Salem, in Forsyth County. For such a frontier community, their pottery was highly varied, and included "bottles, jugs, jars, drinking vessels, bowls, pans, pots, plates, lighting devices, miscellaneous forms, and pressed ware." No less remarkable was their emphasis on decoration—they "considered slip-decorated ware a standard item in their everyday production." Under German-born masters like Gottfried Aust and Rudolf Christ, the potters concentrated on lead-glazed earthenwares, but they also experimented with English creamware, stoneware, and even faience. Through the first quarter of the 19th century these potters worked within a small, closely controlled craft community in which the pottery was owned by the congregation, the potter was a full-time craftsman, and the craft was perpetuated by the guild system with its ranks of apprentice, journeyman, and master.

The thoroughly documented achievements of the Moravians tend to obscure the work of a far larger body of potters who were simultaneously producing earthenwares across the Piedmont from Orange County in the east to Lincoln in the west. Few of their wares were signed or decorated; thus, it is extremely difficult to attribute them to a particular potter, date, or place. The most common surviving forms are jars, dishes, bowls, jugs, and, less commonly, kegs, chamberpots, colanders, and grease lamps. Unlike the Moravian shops, these were family businesses run by farmer-potters,

men who worked at the craft as a sideline in order to generate the cash or barter to acquire the goods they could not make for themselves.

At some point during the first quarter of the 19th century, the potters began converting to stoneware, and by 1850 two highly concentrated centers of production had emerged. The larger one was located on the adjacent borders of Randolph, Chatham, and Moore counties in the eastern Piedmont, where at least 200 potters, most of British stock, made salt-glazed jars, jugs, milk crocks, churns, and pitchers. The gray-green jug in the accompanying photograph well illustrates their achivement. A sturdy, utilitarian container for molasses, vinegar, or "medicinal" liquors, it also exhibits a striking bulbous form, bold opposed handles, and a rich texture of brown spotting from the fly ash blowing through the kiln. Other than the incised rings and "sine waves" on the jug's shoulder, North Carolina pottery was rarely decorated in any self-conscious sense. The blue cobalt oxide so common on northern stoneware was

Salt-glazed stoneware jug, Randolph County, North Carolina, c. 1850

expensive and hard to obtain; at best, it was used to delineate the gallon capacity (as shown here), accent the handle terminals, or provide a bit of colorful trim. Pictorial designs such as trees, birds, and Masonic emblems are only rarely encountered. To the local potter this entailed extra time and labor and made the pot no more "useful." And, ultimately, his competition did not warrant such extra flourishes.

Although the salt glaze prevailed in the east, the alkaline glaze was used throughout the western Piedmont and also in the relatively small number of shops in the mountain region. The major concentration of potters occurred along the western border between Lincoln and Catawba counties; in a compact area once called "Jugtown," 150 potters, most of German descent, turned out thick, flowing alkaline glazes. The term *alkaline* designates the flux used to lower the melting temperature of this glaze. In North Carolina this was almost always wood ashes, which contain varying amounts of such alkaline substances as calcium, sodium, and potassium. Moreover, the potters designated two major glaze subtypes, based on the silica source: the typically brown and runny "cinder glaze," made from the slag collected from early iron furnaces in Lincoln County, and the smooth, greenish "glass glaze," which employed instead crushed glass from windowpanes and bottles. In all, the heavy use of the alkaline glaze—combined with the highly variable, unembellished forms in the salt glaze—firmly sets North Carolina in the southern ceramic tradition.

Because of a complex mix of social and economic forces, the folk tradition terminated in the eastern Piedmont about the time of World War I but continued in the west and the mountains until World War II. Many descendants of the old turners still flourish by selling a new line of domestic, artistic, and horticultural wares to a middle-class clientele, but today only a single folk potter remains at work. In Lincoln County Burlon Craig still digs his own clay out of the local river, "kicks" his treadle wheel, grinds his alkaline glazes by hand in a stone mill, and burns his wood-fired groundhog kiln half a dozen times a year. Behind him lies a tradition extending over two centuries and comprising 700 to 800 potters, who worked efficiently—and sometimes with stunning aesthetic force—to supply the essential needs of a rural, self-sufficient people.

Charles G. Zug III
University of North Carolina
at Chapel Hill

Dorothy Cole Auman and Charles G. Zug III, *Southern Exposure* (Summer-Fall 1977); John Bivins, Jr., *The Moravian Potters in North Carolina* (1972); Daisy Wade Bridges, ed., *Potters of the Catawba Valley, North Carolina* (1980); Jean Crawford, *Jugtown Pottery: History and Design* (1964); Stuart C. Schwartz, *North Carolina Pottery: A Bibliography* (1978); Charles G. Zug III, *Pioneer America Society Transactions* (1980), *The Traditional Pottery of North Carolina* (1981), *Turners and Burners: The Folk Potters of North Carolina* (1986). ☆

Pottery, Texas

||||||||||||||||||||||||||||||||||||||||

Pottery in the Southwest is a distinctive variant of the southern ceramics tradition. The area known as Texas entered the scene of American crafts at a late date, after the establishment of the Republic of Texas in 1835. During the 17th and 18th centuries, and the first quarter of the 19th, this area was governed by Spain and then Mexico. Even after Texas became a part of the Union in 1846, Native American and Spanish-influenced crafts were manufactured in the southern and western areas of the state, which had not yet become "Americanized."

The U.S. Census Population Schedule for 1860 listed five women in the Isleta township of El Paso County as "Potteress." Presumably, these were women producing traditional coil-formed American Indian pots for their local area. Cameron County population schedules for that same year list Severino Najare, born in Mexico, as an earthenware manufacturer. He was undoubtedly manufacturing simple, lead-glazed earthenwares based on the Spanish tradition. Ware of this same type has been used continually until the present day by Mexican Americans in the preparation of their traditional foods, but there is little evidence of manufacture here. Such earthenwares are freely available along the Mexican border and imported locally in most areas predominantly Mexican in population.

The population of Texas by emigrants from the United States took place very rapidly after the war with Mexico ended in 1848. Farmers, craftsmen of all types, and professional men poured in through the northeastern, eastern, and Gulf of Mexico entrances to the state. During the 19th century pioneering craftsmen were involved in farming and settling land as well as the pursuance of their craft. When they arrived in

Texas, they followed this established pattern. Most potters farmed a crop, potting at intervals in that work.

Coarse earthenwares were produced in Texas in very small amounts. The persistent manufacture of traditional American Indian vessels occurred in the western part of the state, and traditional Spanish earthenwares were noted along the Rio Grande in 1860. One pottery is known to have produced common earthenwares of the Anglo-American type near the city of Houston in 1847. There were possibly one or two other very early small earthenware potteries in that area. A pottery operating in Jackson County in 1860 was found to have been producing poor-quality salt-glazed stoneware and numerous lead-glazed earthenware milk bowls.

The stoneware produced by the majority of the potters in Texas during the second half of the 19th century was of the utilitarian or folk type. Most of the vessels were formed by wheel throwing and fired in simple updraft or rectangular groundhog kilns. The common stoneware glazes of the period were employed for the single firing process used by these potters. Salt glazes applied during firing by the vapor method, southern alkaline glazes prepared mainly from wood ash and clay, and slip glazes prepared from natural clays were all used. After 1875 the Albany and other commercially dug slip clay glazes of that type became available. During the last two decades of the 19th century, slip glazing of both the interior and exterior of pots became popular.

The vessel forms most commonly manufactured were large storage jars (3- to 10-gallon capacities), preserving jars (¼ to 2 gallons), churns (3 to 6 gallons), jugs (½ to 5 gallons), and milk pans (½ to 2 gallons). Pitchers of various sizes, chamber pots, spittoons, and serving bowls were made in smaller numbers. The pots were almost entirely undecorated and frequently unmarked. Decoration with trailed cobalt slip before 1900 was limited to a few pieces made in Denton County and having cobalt calligraphic design and numbers. A small amount of underglaze combing was done by J. C. Rushton in Rusk County, and mugs combed and decorated to resemble tree bark were popular in Bexar County around 1900. Ceramic tombstones or cemetery markers occur only in one small area in east Texas. Toys, whimseys, or other decorated pieces are exceedingly rare, and no anthropomorphic or grotesque jugs have so far been found that were made in Texas.

Potters of the southern tradition entered the state directly from the east and began to manufacture their traditional alkaline-glazed pots before 1850. Texas also received emigrant potters from the midwestern states and from foreign countries over the next several decades. The 1850 Census Population Schedules show that seven potters working in Texas were from families associated with the southern alkaline-glaze tradition, which moved westward out of South Carolina through Georgia, Alabama, and Mississippi into Texas. The eighth potter in that census was German born and undoubtedly used the salt glaze.

After the Civil War there was a continued influx of potters from other parts of the United States, England, and Germany. The majority of the shops were then located along outcroppings of the Wilcox geological formation that occur along a line diagonally from Texarkana in the northeast to near San Antonio in the southwest. This formation still supplies clays for the brick and tile industry.

By 1900 larger shops, semiindustrialized potteries, had developed and were beginning to produce large amounts of stoneware covered with a white Bristol form of glaze. A number of these shops continued to operate through the first quarter, and well into the second, of the 20th century. Today only the Marshall Pottery at Marshall in Harrison County continues to produce wheel-thrown ordinary stoneware pitchers, jars, churns, and water coolers. These represent only a small part of their output, the majority being pressed red clay flower pots.

Georgeanna H. Greer
San Antonio, Texas

Georgeanna H. Greer, *American Stonewares: The Art and Craft of Utilitarian Potters* (1981), with Harding Black, *The Meyer Family, Master Potters in Texas* (1971); Sherry B. Humphreys and Johnell H. Schmidt, *Texas Pottery, Caddo Indian to Contemporary* (1976); Cecelia Steinfeldt and Donald Stover, *Early Texas Furniture and Decorative Arts* (1973); U.S. Bureau of the Census, *Industry and Manufacture for Texas* (1850, 1860, 1870, 1880); U.S. Bureau of the Census, *Population Schedules for Texas* (1850, 1860, 1870, 1880). ☆

Storytelling

|||||||||||||||||||||||||||||||

A robust and vital storytelling tradition is part and parcel of the South's persona. "A storied region," folklorist Benjamin A. Botkin aptly called the South. Indeed, southern narrators boast extensive repertoires of folktales, legends, jests, and anecdotes. Attracted by the lure of this trove, early folklore collectors flocked to isolated pockets of the Appalachians, Ozarks, and bayous to find centuries-old tales of international circulation. But the romantic draw of pristine backsections aside, storytelling holds social significance throughout the South.

Verbal artistry dramatizes and gives meaning to mores, locales, and events. Even though communities acknowledge a particularly adept storyteller, each person knows narratives that he or she can occasionally relate. Nonetheless, of significance to many communities is how people cherish the styles and stories of that favorite yarnspinner. They easily remember those particular settings for the good story—the store, the porch, the courthouse, and the city street.

Despite the misleading homey image of southern storytelling as a quaint form of peripheral entertainment, narration continues to touch on central social roles in modern settings. The tale teaches values, develops communicative skills, binds people together, and imbues life with art. Storytelling can be described in terms of the narrator and the content, social context, and style of the expression.

Content. Although remnants of the European fairy tale (or *Märchen*) tradition seemed not to survive the growth of the new American nation, folklorists found in the South versions of numerous such tales, canonized in *The Types of the Folk-Tale* (1964) by Antti Aarne and Stith Thompson. The title story of Vance Randolph's collection *The Devil's Pretty Daughter and Other Ozark Folk Tales* (1955), for example, was proudly described as a version of Type 313, "The Girl as Helper in the Hero's Flight." The

narrator had localized the text by an unusual introduction of folk beliefs to reinforce obstacles in the hero's flight. To give credence to the South's claim for the highest order of preserving old traditions, Randolph reported variants collected in Virginia, South Carolina, Louisiana, Texas, and Missouri.

Many of the distinctive qualities of such Old-World folktales have also been uncovered in Kentucky by folklorists Kenneth and Mary Clarke. They report tales having familiar motifs of remarkable adventures or quests, magical objects or incantations, and giants or other fearsome creatures. Yet the variants found by collector Leonard Roberts of "Jack and the Beanstalk," "Jack the Giant Killer," and "The Devil's Pretty Daughter" have a decidedly Kentucky flavor to them. For the most part, the European *Märchen* types popularized by the Brothers Grimm lose their supernatural and fantastic elements in America. The tales reportedly become shorter; often the actions or characters are made humorous.

Although the early folklorists spotlighted the New World *Märchen*, this genre actually constituted a minor part of most narrators' repertoires. Vance Randolph, in fact, redressed his own preoccupation with reaping *Märchen* by publishing *Hot Springs and Hell* (1965), a collection of traditional jokes and anecdotes. Put down on paper, many of the local jests lose the cutting edge of humor. Still, doing so points out the abundance of comical situations made for the storyteller's interpretation. Take the story collected by Randolph and called "Fit to Sleep with the Hogs":

There was a fellow named Howard that had a pretty wife, but somebody says that Howard's wife ain't fit to sleep with the hogs. Howard got pretty mad when he heard that, and he says "She is too!" So then everybody laughed.

The themes of language misunderstood or maimed, marital relations ridiculed, and the fool made foolish give this story a familiar ring.

Folk humor frequently revolves around stereotypical, comical characters or "folktypes." Typically, southerners have sheafs of stories using either the mountaineer (or "hillbilly"), the poor white, the black, the preacher, or the city slicker as the butts of humor. Using the veil of laughter, the jests deal with the concerns and tensions of southern society. There is the caution against hypocrisy in fundamentalist southern religion and the fallibility of the clergy underlying the popular series of preacher jokes, for example. Racial tensions and rural-urban conflicts of values also find expression in the South's folk humor. The characters themselves establish categories in the minds of people, often based on the exaggeration of one or two traits, for people to confront the diversity of regional, occupational, and ethnic groups within the unity of the South.

Perhaps the most celebrated genre in the narrator's repertoire is the tall tale, also called "windies," "whoppers," or simply "lies." The tales can be brief exclamations, such as the following boast collected in Mississippi: "You think your tomatoes are big? Well, I had a tomato so big the picture of it weighed five pounds!" Typically though, tall tales are extended narratives, as in common stories like "The Lucky Shot" collected by folklorist Richard M. Dorson from Mississippi-raised J. D. Suggs:

Fellow went out hunting. He didn't have but one shell. And he happened to look up, and first thing he seed was ten ducks sitting on one limb. He looked over to one side before he shot, and saw a panther standing there. He looked over on his left—there was a big buck standing there. He looked behind, and there was a covey of partridge right behind him. He didn't know which one to shoot at. He looked straight in front of him and he seed a big bear coming towards him. He knowed he had to shoot the bear, for the bear would kill him—he knowed that. So he cocked both muzzles of a double-barreled muzzle loader, pulled both triggers the same time. The shot killed the bear. The ramrod shot out and hit the limb and caught the ducks' toes before they could fly away. And the hammer on the left, it flew off and killed the deer. The right hammer, it flew off and killed the panther. He kicked his overcoat off, and smothered the covey of partridges.

This tall tale, Type 1890 in Aarne and Thompson, is widely reported in the South, having been collected by Zora Neale Hurston from Florida's Larkins White and by Arthur Huff Fauset in Alabama—to name just two notable southern folklore collectors.

Another form of the tall tale is the embellished personal experience story. Folklorist Kay L. Cothran found many such stories in the Okefenokee Swamp Rim of Georgia, where narrators delighted in relating remarkable hunting and fishing exploits. The success of the tall tale, according to folklorist Jan Harold Brunvand, "does not depend on belief in the details of the story, but rather on a willingness to lie and be lied to while keeping a straight face. The humor of these tales consists of telling an outrageous falsehood in the sober accents of a truthful story." Depending therefore on common situations and themes, the storyteller creatively weaves his characters and remarkable exploits together and then stretches the tale to the tallest limits his audience will tolerate.

The South's particular folk heroes have a strong part to play in story and ballad. Yet the lines between folk and popular tradition often become blurred in accounts of Davy Crockett, Stonewall Jackson, Jesse James, and others. More common in today's oral tradition are local characters given notoriety by storytellers. In the Mississippi Delta, for instance, a local outlaw, "Bad Man Monroe," is the subject of many narratives told about his remarkable deeds, extraordinary size and strength, and difficult capture. Also in the Delta, moonshiner, outlaw, or lawman (depending on who you listen to) Perry Martin remains an important folk hero to the river people. In southern Kentucky, the guerilla actions of Beanie Short during the Civil War for the Confederate cause, or, some say, for his own gain, still circulate. Like other legendary figures, they give rise to not one but a series of stories. Beanie Short's legend includes accounts of buried treasure, ruthless activity, and tragic death. In the communities of the South, these legends compose the rich folk history of the locality and help give residents a sense of past and place.

Context. The occasion and the setting for people gathering influence the types of stories told. Folklorist Patrick Mullen, for example, contrasted the fishing spots, feed stores, and public festivals at which Texas storyteller Ed Bell performs. Mullen found that Ed told personal experience narratives at the feed store but related tall tales to festival audiences. In the studies of folklorists William Ferris and Kay Cothran, setting also played a crucial role, for storytelling was generally found to be dominated by men and thus recurred in sexually segregated activities like hunting or music making. In a Mississippi storytelling session documented for *Folklore Forum*, the men involved entertained themselves trading stories in a gamelike atmosphere. The presence of two recognized storytellers led to a competitive spirit in the session. At one point, though, a woman entered and disrupted the session. It became inappropriate to continue, because the context had changed.

Storytelling often occurs in "sessions." In social centers people gather to hear and tell stories. The session provides entertainment and passes time, but by drawing people together, it also reinforces shared values and binds a group together. In the Okefenokee Swamp, for example, the storytelling custom of "talking trash," says Kay Cothran, "comes from a time when men did not work by the time clock but by cycles of nature. Talking trash today is an act of identification with that older way of life, and whether one does it as a matter of course or as something of a rebellion, talking trash is a sneer at middle-class subservience to continuous gray work and a denial of that class's identification of the materially unproductive with the counterproductive." In other areas, the "liar's bench" at the courthouse, the hunting camp, or the general store may also serve as appropriate places for the activity. But storytelling sessions are not limited to rural areas, for city and industrial hangouts nurture narrative exchange also.

In encounters outside storytelling sessions, people use stories in bartering and conversation to make a rhetorical point. The context of dog and horse trading is a prime example. Folklorist Richard Bauman found hunters and traders using stories in the process of negotiating for a purchase or trade:

> Byers too has been taken in a trade. He comes back with his account of having traded once for two dogs that were supposed to be good fox dogs and then discovering that the "sumbitches wouldn't run a *rabbit.*" This story establishes that he has already been victimized at least once in a trade and, by implication, that he does not intend to let it happen again.

William Ferris found similar interaction with Mississippi horse trader Ray Lum, and also reported that, indeed, Lum's popular reputation was based in part on his stature as a renowned storyteller.

The ages of participants are also contextual factors. Although the popular image exists of the grandfather warmly relating a tale to a child on his knee, storytelling occurs from early childhood on. In early years, fantasy and fictional narratives dominate; in adolescence, legends and jokes about matters close to teenage concerns of sex, driving, morality, and education hold center stage. Later, personal experience narratives become prevalent parts of conversation and entertainment. The age of the storyteller's listeners and of the storyteller frequently dictate the type of material related. In fact, development of narrative skills is part of the aging process, for in early years formulaic tales, rhymes, and patterned narratives prevail, whereas later, when cognitive and social skills increase, more creative experiential narratives take precedence. Of course, other factors, like primary social contacts, also affect content. In

Mississippi, William Ferris found ghost stories limited largely to the repertoires of children and old people, whereas protest tales were found primarily among black adolescents and adult informants who encountered racial tension daily in their work.

Storytelling is a way of communicating ideas and concerns that may not be effectively articulated or desired in conversation. Often, putting feelings and ideas on the fictive plane of a story helps to clarify or act out personal and social concerns. Further, storytelling changes according to the needs and demands of the situation in which it occurs. The function of storytelling—be it entertainment, education, or social maintenance—depends on the intent of the narrator and the composition of the audience, as well as the place in which they interact and the nature of the material presented. As there are many contexts for people to gather, so there are many contexts for storytelling. Vance Randolph thought that the isolation of places like the Ozarks and the ample time on the hands of its residents explained the vitality of the region's storytelling, but the existence of storytelling in new urban and suburban areas and in other modern contexts challenges that notion. Given the proper time and setting wherever people interact, people need and demand the good story told well.

Style. A common hunting-camp story is told about an old hunter who would entertain his comrades by exclaiming "number three!" Sure enough, the fellas would respond with laughter. A novice hunter hearing this decided to try his hand by interjecting "number four." But to him they gave a harsh silence. Puzzled, he asked why he failed. One of the hunters came over, put his hand on the youngster's shoulder, and explained, *"Well, some can tell 'em and some can't."* What often distinguishes the storyteller and gives depth and meaning to texts, the youngster learned, are expressive qualities arranged and repeated as a *style*. In storytelling, style especially comes into play when presenting and delivering narratives.

Observers of southern styles usually note the relaxed, casual verbal performance, paced, Botkin claimed, "to the relaxed tempo of Southern living." Dorson agreed and also commented on the distinctive chants, mimicry, whiny dialogue, rhymes, and bits of song that punctuated narratives he collected from southern blacks. Imitations of animal sounds and even the preacher's rhythms mark many a tale's telling. Altering one's voice to identify different characters or to emphasize an action is another common stylistic technique. Of course, narrators try to distinguish themselves by adopting a personal style, but reports of southern storytelling refer often to the shared qualities of understatement and casualness.

Although formula openings and closings are not as common in southern storytelling as elsewhere, certain qualities still stand out. Zesty phrases and localized vocabularies spice up the content of stories. "He was busier than a one-armed paper hanger," Kentuckian Steve Poyser said during one story, and topped even that with "and making more noise than two skeletons in armor making love on a tin roof—with brass bras on!" One can also hear "lit out" for "left" or "lickety-split" for "at high speed." To the question "What are you doing?" Vance Randolph's informants would whimsically reply "fattenin' frogs for snakes," "makin' kitten-britches for

tomcats," and "punchin' peth out of elders." According to Dorson, "All these piquancies of speech do not constitute a primitive dialect, but a vivid and racy handling of the common tongue."

Southern storytellers share with other narrators general attributes of folk composition. The tale is given symmetry and order by use of *threes*, for example. One finds the recurrence of three episodes, three tasks, or three characters to structure the tale. The narrator also often uses oppositions like good and evil, north and south, city and country to underline that structure. Plots in folk narrative tend to be unified and single stranded; they typically begin calmly, work toward a climax, and close calmly. No more than two characters usually appear in a scene, and when they do, they commonly are stark contrasts to each other. Description and reflection take distant back seats to action. Dialogue commonly carries the action.

The cultivation of stylistic technique in oral deliveries is apparent when someone offers you the smooth flow of a "good one," or just slips it into conversation. Symbolizing this pride in vocal ability is Andy Griffith's gleeful comment in the play *No Time for Sergeants*. When asked if he could do Hamlet, he replied, "No, but I *tell it*." Indeed, the power of style is evidenced by humorist Jerry Clower's remark, "I don't tell funny stories, I tell stories funny."

Whereas manipulating the voice to produce a captivating, melodic tone is important to any sense of style, developing expressive gestures and motions is also crucial. Among many southern storytellers, the hands are powerful tools of persuasion. They express emotions, point out directions, and give dimensions in the tale. The hands work with the pliable face to give full expression to the narrator's words. Style, then, helps give the story form and feeling, and insures that listeners will remember the narrator, too.

Narrators. Even before recording equipment was available, writers used storytelling characters to give novels and short stories the ring of vernacular authenticity. Perhaps best known was Joel Chandler Harris's Uncle Remus, set in Georgia. Writing in the late 19th century, Harris inserted folktales into his literature by letting the story apparently develop from Remus's lips rather than from the author's pen. Similarly, Carolina-raised Charles Chesnutt introduced Uncle Julius; Tennessean George Washington Harris had Sut Lovingood; Kentuckian Jesse Stuart used Uncle Op Akers and Grandpa Tussie. Despite literary embellishment, the authors commonly base such characters on real people and thus give a glimpse of storytelling that otherwise would go unwitnessed.

Sometimes, storytellers gain renown through circulation of their stories in almanacs, pamphlets, and other forms of popular literature. Free use of dialect and vernacular mark these stories as oral narrative adapted to print. Davy Crockett's tall tale account of "Bear Hunting in Tennessee" is one widely circulated example; another is Colonel Charles Noland as "Pete Whetstone of Devil's Fork." Writing from his Arkansas home for the weekly *Spirit of the Times*, he re-created numerous tall tales, including the favorite "Bear Hunt."

With the introduction of cylinder recording the public could actually hear the tale being told whenever they wanted. The telling of "The Arkansas Traveler" was released by Edison at least three times prior to 1920. Rural-styled entertainers like Arthur Collins and Cal Stewart (popularly known as Uncle Josh) captured on disc numerous folk narratives, often in the guise of "rube sketches." The record, though, placed limitations on the storyteller's performance. The story had to conform to a certain time limit, and the teller had to strain to get a clear reproduction of his voice. More often the trained voice, rather than the authentic, relaxed raconteur, found its way onto the early recordings.

Radio shows, however, like the Grand Ole Opry, gave many genuine southern folk humorists a chance to ply their craft effectively before a wide listening audience. Benjamin Francis (Whitey) Ford, popularly known as the Duke of Paducah, and Archie Campbell were Opry humorists who combined theatrics and traditional texts in their performances. Campbell was especially adept at a tongue-twisting form of storytelling—the spoonerism. He built stories on the interchange of word sounds, such as "Rittle Led Hiding Rood."

Television spread southern storytelling further. *Hee Haw*, for instance, regularly featured genial John Henry Faulk storytelling against the backdrop of a country store and Archie Campbell holding court in a barber shop. Out on a porch another of the show's amiable raconteurs, the Reverend Grady Nutt, specialized in anecdotes and preacher jests.

Hosting his own show is Mississippi's ebullient Jerry Clower. He developed his narrating skill regaling customers with stories while working for a fertilizer company in Yazoo City. Clower has achieved national popularity, but many storytellers are recognized and occasionally celebrated only in their home localities. Near Banner Elk, N.C., Marshall Ward and Ray Hicks perform Jack tales that have attracted folklore collectors. Solsberry in southern Indiana annually holds a liar's contest featuring the Ray brothers, specialists in tall tales, from whom folklorist Brunhilde Biebuyck collected 200 tales. Some local storytellers, like Ed Bell of Luling, Tex., have gone beyond their hometowns to present personal experience stories and tall tales at an occasional regional or national folklife festival.

Despite the spotlights placed on the aforementioned storytellers, American folklorists have generally given more attention to the narrator's texts than to the narrator. Recently, though, some folklorists have explored the biography, repertoire, and creativity of several outstanding southern narrators.

James Douglas Suggs, for example, gave folklorist Richard M. Dorson almost 200 folktales. Born in Kosciusko, Miss., in 1887, the black Suggs worked the famed Rabbit Foot Minstrel Show throughout the South in 1907. He sang and played guitar, danced, and told jokes. The years after found him working as a professional baseball player, railroad brakeman, and cook. With his wife and many children he eventually settled in Calvin, Mich., an area populated largely by southern blacks. He absorbed many narratives in his various occupations and travels, recounting them to the workers at the next job and to friends at the tavern. In 1952, while searching for storytellers in the field, Dorson was directed by a local barkeep to Suggs, whom she knew as a "good talker." In Suggs's repertoire animal stories predominated, followed by equivalent numbers of ghost and hoodoo stories, tall tales, preacher jests, and

Ol' Marster tales. Dorson's visit was opportune, for Suggs died two years later. Suggs's life and narratives compose a major portion of Dorson's classic study *American Negro Folktales* (1967).

Eugene Powell is a comparable figure among Mississippi black narrators. Born in 1908, Powell was raised amidst song and story in the Mississippi Delta. After sharecropping for a time, he turned to operating a roadhouse and music making for a livelihood. Powell expanded his narrative repertoire and honed his storytelling ability in frequent sessions that took place at the roadhouse. When Powell moved to Greenville, he gave up the roadhouse but still hosted many a storytelling session among friends at his house. Powell had a remarkable memory for folk narratives and songs. He knew scores of animal stories, preacher jokes, and John and Ol' Marster tales—many of which he passed on to his storytelling son Ernest. In addition, Powell related a host of local historical legends and personal experience narratives.

Another notable narrator is Ray Lum, loquacious mule trader of Vicksburg, Miss. Lum's rapid-fire delivery unveils a quick wit and an impressive verbal ability, which serves to relax people in trades. Indeed, the trader as clever trickster and affable talker runs throughout Lum's many tales.

Storytellers do not hang out shingles or announce their wares. Storytelling is rather an informal part of their jobs or social life. In a traditional anecdote attributed to many raconteurs, the renowned Texas Munchausen, Gib Morgan, when asked for a good "lie" by fellow oilworkers, would tell them that he was too busy to lie right then, for his brother lay sick and Gib had to leave. Later the workers discovered that indeed they were told a good lie. Such informal, impromptu exchanges recur often today at work and at play. Less easily spotted than the European wonder-tale-telling counterpart, the American storyteller nonetheless thrives on informal opportunities for a joke or anecdote. The South's sociable, leisurely image and its strong oral tradition help foster the association of the region with storytelling.

See also BLACK LIFE: / Chesnutt, Charles; Hurston, Zora Neale; HISTORY AND MANNERS: / Crockett, Davy; Jackson, Stonewall; LITERATURE: Humor; / Harris, George Washington; Harris, Joel Chandler; MUSIC: / Grand Ole Opry; RECREATION: Roadhouses; VIOLENCE: Outlaw Heroes; / James Brothers

> Simon J. Bronner
> Pennsylvania State University
> Capitol Campus

Richard Bauman and Roger D. Abrahams, eds., *And Other Neighborly Names: Social Process and Cultural Image in Texas Folklore* (1981); Benjamin A. Botkin, *A Treasury of Southern Folklore* (1949); Simon J. Bronner, *Folklore Forum* (Fall 1981), *Mid-South Folklore* (Summer 1977); Richard Chase, ed., *The Grandfather Tales: American-English Folk Tales* (1948); Kenneth Clarke and Mary Clarke, *The Harvest and the Reapers: Oral Traditions of Kentucky* (1974); Hennig Cohen and William B. Dillingham, eds., *Humor of the Old Southwest* (1964); Kay L. Cothran, in *Readings in American Folklore*, ed. Jan Harold Brunvand (1979); Richard M. Dorson, *American Negro Folktales* (1967); Arthur Huff Fauset, *Journal of American Folklore* (July–September 1927); William Ferris, *Journal of American Folklore* (April–June 1972), *Ray Lum: Mule Trader* (1977); Zora Neale Hurston, *Mules and Men* (1935); *North Carolina Folklore Journal* (September 1978). ☆

Voodoo

||||||||||||||||

For the average American, the term *voodoo* suggests vague notions of black magic and practices found in isolated Caribbean Islands. In reality voodoo is an underground American religious sect that has often merged with or borrowed from Christianity in its use of the crucifix and saints as religious symbols. The religion is widespread in many areas of the United States and is by no means limited to blacks in its belief and practice.

Voodoo is also called "vodun" and "hoodoo" and derives from the religion of Dahomey in West Africa, where the term *vodu* designates gods worshipped by Dahomeans. The cult first entered the United States in the latter part of the 18th century when the French brought slaves from Haiti to Louisiana. Through strong leaders such as Sanite Dede and the two Marie Laveaus (mother and daughter), voodoo influenced New Orleans's black and white communities. Voodoo is still openly practiced in Haiti and has deep roots in New Orleans and southern Louisiana.

Though extensive research on voodoo by Zora Neale Hurston and Newbell Niles Puckett focuses on the New Orleans area, voodoo cults exist throughout the United States. Stores in Philadelphia, Penn., New Haven, Conn., and New York City specialize in the sale of candles, charms, and ointments used either to hex or to remove hexes. Urban "doctors" and "healers" solicit business through leaflets and are more open in their practice than are rural practitioners.

In the rural South those who have intimate knowledge of voodoo are called "doctors" and often combine voodoo spells and herbal remedies in their practice. Voodoo doctors have power of life and death over people regardless of whether they believe in voodoo. The "mojo" reaches the lives of all—white or black, believer or nonbeliever—and can curse or heal depending on the doctor's will.

The vehicle through which a spell is placed or removed is usually a "mojo hand," or in abbreviated form, a "hand" or "mojo." The mojo hand is a small cloth sack that is carried in a wallet or purse and may contain parts of dead insects, animals (especially lizards), birds, and items that have had intimate contact with the person being hexed (underclothing, feces, fingernails, and hair). Through "sympathetic" magic, objects closely associated with the person to be "hoodooed" are doctored to produce the desired effects, which range from influencing their love to death.

Hoodoo doctors are often older men or women who have apprenticed under earlier practitioners. Their skills are passed on orally, and there is an unspoken taboo against writing verbal wisdom on paper that might fall into the wrong hands. The hoodoo doctor is often marked from birth as exceptional and is likely to develop hoodoo skills. One born with a veil (with the placenta) over his face or the seventh son of a seventh son will have special powers.

Medical doctors are often unable to diagnose illnesses that are imposed through hoodoos because no physical signs of sickness exist. The medical doctor will find his patient in good health except for fatigue and depression. To the hoodoo doctor, however, these signs are clear evidence of a "jinx," and cures must be worked immediately to counteract a spell that might prove to be fatal to the patient.

The pervasiveness of voodoo, among blacks especially, is seen through its role in music. Blues recordings often speak of hoodoo and its importance in love. A classic blues verse on hoodoo says, "Going down to Louisiana, get me a mojo hand./ Gonner show all you womens how to love a good man."

Blues musicians have special power over women through their music, which is associated with the Devil. At times, they call on hoodoo doctors to enforce this power. In 1932 "Jelly Jaw" Short from Port Gibson, Miss., recorded the "Snake Doctor Blues":

I am a snake doctor man, gang of
   womens everywhere I go.
I am a snake doctor man, gang of
   womens everywhere I go.
And when I get to flying, sometimes I can see a gang of womens
   standing out in the door.

The hoodoo doctor, as the verse suggests, has the power to fly through space.

The snake, or "Damballah," is the chief god in Dahomean vodun cults and also plays a major role in hoodoo work. As a symbol of hoodoo, the snake assumes sexual meaning when used in the blues such as "Crawling King Snake Blues" by John Lee Hooker.

In 1953 Walter Davis of Grenada, Miss., recorded the "Root Doctor Blues" with the verses:

The root that I'm selling, from it
   you can get a lot of juice.
The root that I'm selling, from it
   you can get a lot of juice.
And when I'm giving it to you,
   Momma, you don't want to turn
   it loose.

I was doctoring a woman, she said
    I can't see how it can be.
I was doctoring a woman, she said
    I can't see how it can be.
She say go way from here, doctor,
    you got too much root for me.

The most popular root used in hoodoo is "John the Conqueror root," the most potent root used to conjure. It is also called "High John the Conqueror," and those who understand hoodoo tremble at the sight of its presence in the hands of others. The root is mentioned in several blues tunes, including "I'm a Man" by Bo Diddley. It is best known through the 1954 recording of "Hootchie Kootchie Man" by Muddy Waters:

I got a black cat bone. I got a mojo
    too.
I got the John the Conqueror Root.
    I'm gonner mess with you.
I'm gonner make you girls lead me
    by the hand.
Then the world will know the
    Hootchie Kootchie Man.

Voodoo clearly evolved from West African culture, but knowledge of it in the United States is by no means limited to blacks. Wherever the hoodoo doctor practices his mojo, both white and black follow him. Zora Neale Hurston worked with a Doctor Jenkins in New Orleans and commented that "most of his clients are white and upper-class people at that." And in *After Freedom*, a sociological study of Indianola, Miss., Hortense Powdermaker found one hoodoo doctor had 1,422 white clients, roughly one-third of his total. Both male and female white clients consulted him regularly.

Southern writers have been drawn to voodoo. Charles Chesnutt's *The Conjure Woman*, George Washington Cable's *The Grandissimes*, Ernest Gaines's *Bloodline*, and Alice Walker's *The Third Life of George Copeland* all devote major sections to voodoo. Southern schools of medicine and psychiatry are increasingly interested in the study of voodoo as a valid part of medical practice. The University of Mississippi Medical School has worked with voodoo doctors to heal patients who in traditional diagnoses would be considered paranoid schizophrenics. Although African in origin, voodoo has affected the lives of white and black southerners in many ways. Their religious beliefs, music, literature, and even medicine attest to the old and continuing influence of voodoo on the American South.

See also ENVIRONMENT: Plant uses; ETHNIC LIFE: Caribbean Influence; WOMEN'S LIFE: Healers, Women

William Ferris
University of Mississippi

Wayland D. Hand, ed., *American Folk Medicine* (1976); Zora Neale Hurston, *Mules and Men* (1970); Harry Middleton Hyatt, *Hoodoo-Conjuration-Witchcraft-Rootwork*, 5 vols. (1970–78); Newbell Niles Puckett, *Folk Beliefs of the Southern Negro* (1926; reprint ed., 1968); Robert Tallant, *Voodoo in New Orleans* (1967). ☆

Weddings
||||||||||||||||||||||||

Throughout the world, weddings are momentous events. In the South wedding ceremonies and celebrations have been shaped by traditional beliefs and practices that affirm marriage as an occasion for familial and communal celebration.

Weddings in the 18th- and 19th-century South were typically brief and plain. They were held in the home rather than a church (even in Catholic southern Louisiana), though they were presided over by a minister or priest. The courtship and nuptials of slaves constituted the simplest of southern wedding ceremonies, often being arranged by a master with a view toward an increased slave population. Slaves often had no ceremony at all, merely getting or being given a master's permission to move into a cabin together. Some slaves and poorer whites were pronounced husband and wife after "jumping the broomstick"— hopping over a broomstick together and afterward being feted at a gathering with food and drink. Most southern marriages, black and white, occurred in the morning or at noon to allow family and community to gather at the bride's house after the wedding for a meal and often dancing, music, and games.

"Racing for the bottle," the shivaree, the infare, and a pounding—18th- and 19th-century southern pre- and postnuptial traditions—were common marriage rituals extant throughout preindustrial, rural America. Occasionally, on the wedding morning the groom's friends would gather at his home as an escort and would ride on horseback to the bride's house or the scene of the ceremony, "racing for the bottle." The prize would be shared by the victor. More often the infare, pounding, and shivaree were postnuptial rituals, because most southern newlyweds, not enjoying the 20th-century opportunity for travel and thus for honeymoons, immediately joined a community. In some areas of the South a

bride and groom's association with a community was recognized with a celebration a few days after a wedding to help newlyweds set up housekeeping. The "pounding" was a gathering where furniture and food were brought to the new home by neighbors and family. The whole community was generally invited to the "infare" or "infaire"—a dinner at the bridegroom's parents' house held the day after the wedding or occasionally immediately following the wedding.

Particularly in the Upper South, newlyweds came to expect, even anticipate, a "shivaree" (derived from the Old World custom and word charivari). Friends of the bridal couple would surround their home, awakening them with rough music, shouting, and pestering until the couple invited them inside for refreshments. If the new couple failed to be hosts, the groom was "taken for a ride on a rail" or thrown into the nearest creek or pond regardless of the weather. In Kentucky and Tennessee it was traditional to kidnap the bride and groom on their wedding night until the abducted offered food, drink, or even money to their abductors. Although some couples looked forward to the test of the shivaree as proof that they were well liked in the community, the shivaree became less and less prevalent because of occasional violent and tragic results. In the South today the only remnants of the mischievous shivaree tradition are more harmless practical jokes and noisemaking—tying noisemakers to the getaway car or sabotaging the newlyweds' luggage.

In the South a rich corpus of folk beliefs and practices is associated with love, courtship, and marriage. The hoped-for future of many southern women was marriage and children; the supreme apprehension was spinsterhood. Because of the frequently passive role of southern women in mate selection, love potions, charms, divinations, and signs and practices to predict spouse selection or insure marital happiness were women's special prerogative. Certain signs foreboded a solitary life—falling up steps, taking the last piece of food on a serving dish, sitting on a table, or sneezing three times in a row. Omens promised or predicted marriage—if a grasshopper spit on you, you would marry within the year; if you caught a bridal bouquet, you would be the next female to marry. Love charms and potions having European and African parallels (a 10-fingered plant, a lodestone, sassafras, cherry pits, or soapstones worn secretly about the neck, or possession of some of one's lover's hair), often predicated on the principles of similarity or contact, were used to manipulate the future.

Signs of love were numerous—dropping a dishcloth, unintentionally making a rhyme, or having an untied shoelace. If you threw a love vine on a bush and it grew, your sweetheart loved you; if you could blow all the down from a thistle in one breath, your love was returned. Southern women made use of a number of methods to determine the character, fortunes, and physical characteristics of their future husbands. It was believed a girl could prophesy the precise identity of her mate by looking in pools of water on her birthday or May Day. Some southerners believed that to insure that the course of true love would run smoothly, the bride-to-be should walk backwards downstairs the first morning after she was engaged.

The precarious status of the bride reinforced many protective beliefs, customs, and taboos: the bride risked her happiness if she made her own wedding dress, tried on her complete bridal array prior to the wedding, or was seen in public between the time the wedding invitations were issued and the ceremony occurred. Auguries of the future included the bride's clothes: for luck the bride must wear something old, new, borrowed, and blue, and to insure financial success she should have an old coin in her shoe. Weather was also important. In the Ozarks and other parts of the South it was unlucky to marry when it was snowing or raining; in other locations a snowy wedding day assured great happiness. Special precautions were taken at the ceremony. Some couples were careful to stand so that the floor planks ran straight from the minister to the couple. Contemporary southern brides and grooms and their families still observe some of these practices that are believed to insure the success and happiness of their marriages.

Although distinctive and regulated by a conception of southern tradition, the structure and rituals of prenuptial and postnuptial southern wedding ceremonies and festivities today reflect many national trends. For example, in the South as elsewhere, there has been a return in the last several years to expensive, traditional wedding cermonies. Many contemporary southern weddings are notable for their distinctive style, although the style of wedding ceremonies and receptions varies to some extent according to personal preferences and economic, social, religious, and ethnic considerations. Southern weddings tend to be preceded by prenuptial showers, teas, and dinners. Registering for gift preferences at local stores is prevalent, as are church weddings with large numbers of guests. Many stores in larger cities target brides and grooms from wealthy "old" southern families, and in some weddings magnolias and antebellum-style dresses are used to evoke an Old South atmosphere. In most cases, though, southern traditions are incorporated into weddings in more modest ways. A bride may wear a brooch that her grandmother wore on her wedding day, or a groom may carry his great-grandfather's watch, for instance.

Southern individuality is proclaimed in wedding festivities more than in the celebration of any other rite of passage. Contemporary weddings in the South still clearly reflect a romanticization of womanhood. At its core, a southern wedding pays homage to the bride. It is usually the bride's picture alone that appears in the announcements of engagement and marriage; it is her dress, veil, and flowers that are described in detail in these announcements; it is she who is the center of attention. In addition to the emphasis on the bride, southern weddings reveal southerners' strongly developed sense of community and family and their commitment to hospitality. Some southerners strive in weddings to emulate a genteel image of the region, and some see the wedding as a commitment to religious ideas of marriage.

See also WOMEN's LIFE: Marriage and Courtship

Carolyn Lipson-Walker
Bloomington, Indiana

Frances Boshears, *Tennessee Folklore Society Bulletin* (September 1953); Jan Harold Brunvand, *The Study of American Folklore: An Introduction* (2d ed., 1978); Philip W. Conn, in *Glimpses of Southern Appalachian Folk Culture: Papers in Memory of Norbert F. Riedl*, ed. Charles H. Faulkner and Carol K. Buckles, Tennessee Anthropological Association, Miscellaneous Paper No. 3 (1978); Amanda Dargan, *Center for Southern Folklore Magazine* (Summer 1981); J. Hampden Porter, *Journal of American Folklore* (April–June 1894); Newbell Niles Puckett, *Folk Beliefs of the Southern Negro* (1926; reprint ed., 1968); Vance Randolph, *Ozark Superstitions* (1947); Joe Gray Taylor, *Eating, Drinking, and Visiting in the South: An Informal History* (1982); Newman I. White, ed., *Frank C. Brown Collection of North Carolina Folklore*, vol. 1 (1952); Henry Wiltse, *Journal of American Folklore* (July–September 1901). ☆

"ARKANSAS TRAVELER"

A classic, humorous dialogue, a tune, a play, and a patchwork quilt pattern are all known by the title "Arkansas Traveler." Most of the printed references to the "Arkansas Traveler" deal with the history of the dialogue, which is one of the most pervasive folk stories in the southern storytelling tradition. The basic story tells of a traveler on horseback who has become lost and confused and who approaches the log cabin of a fiddling squatter. The traveler ends up as a "straight man" in a comic contest of wits in which the squatter evades or pretends to misunderstand his questions. Finally, though, the traveler offers to play the balance or "turn of the tune" the squatter is playing on his fiddle, and in this manner he breaks down the other man's resistance and is heartily welcomed.

Such whimsical dialogues between a traveler and a local person are relatively common in the literature of the British Isles and frontier America, but none achieved the fame of the "Arkansas Traveler." A melody of the time, "Arkansas Traveler," originated sometime prior to the mid-1840s, but the first known printing occurred in 1847, when an arrangement by William Cumming was published at Louisville and Cincinnati as "The Arkansas Traveller and Rackinsac Waltz." The tune was certainly popular before the first printing of the dialogue and apparently predates it. Although three individuals are commonly cited as the composer, they most likely appropriated a melody that was thriving in oral tradition. By 1850 both the melody and the name had achieved widespread popularity.

The earliest known commercial recording of the "Arkansas Traveller" was by Len Spencer, a blackface minstrel popular during the first two decades of the 20th century. Certainly the most widely distributed recent recording is by the Stanley Brothers. The piece has been a very popular number for recording artists and, in fact, was one of the first two tunes put on record by country musicians. In June of 1922, Eck Robertson and Henry Gilliland, two old-time fiddlers, recorded "Sally Goodin" and "The Arkansas Traveller" for Victor Records. Fittingly, Robertson was a native of Arkansas.

During the late 19th century a five-act melodrama entitled *Kit, the Arkansas Traveler* (originally known as *Down the Mississippi*) was extremely popular, going through hundreds of performances between 1869 and 1899. Certainly the magazine the *Arkansas Traveler*, established in Little Rock in 1883 by humorists Opie Read and P. D. Benham, was inspired by the dialogue, and Texas composer David Guion's symphonic composition was based on the tune. The dialogue and tune also influenced the Arkansas Traveler patchwork quilt pattern, which apparently does not predate the 1850s. The design is of large squares consisting of four smaller squares pieced from seven still smaller scraps. Every unit is of a simple, straight-edged, geometrical shape allowing for the most economical use of various scraps of material. Similar designs were relatively common in frontier homes.

W. K. McNeil
Ozark Folk Center
Mountain View, Arkansas

Fred W. Allsopp, *Folklore of Romantic Arkansas* (1931). ☆

BOTTLE TREES

Bottle trees are a product of southern black culture with roots in the animistic spiritualism and totemism of several African tribal cultures. Glassblowing and bottlemaking existed as far back as the ninth century in Africa, and the practice of hanging found objects from trees or huts as talismans to ward off evil spirits also existed. The bottle tree was a Kongo-derived tradition that conveyed deep religious symbolism.

The bottle tree was once common throughout the rural Southeast. Trees were made by stripping the foliage from a living tree, with upward-pointing branches left intact. Bottles were then slipped over these branch ends. Cedars were a preferred species, because they were common, resisted decay, and were well-shaped with all branches pointing upward.

Folk custom dictated that spirits would enter the bottle because of the bright colors and become trapped. When the wind blew and shook the tree, the spirits would be heard moaning inside the bottles. In some cases, paint was poured into the bottles before hanging them on the trees. This was done ostensibly to help trap "spirits," but the addition of color to clear bottles may have been the true motivation.

Today bottle trees are scarce. Those that exist in northeast Mississippi, for example, are produced by rural whites as often as blacks. Like the hex signs of Pennsylvania Dutch barns, they are a vestige of the past, produced more for the sake of art than for protection from the supernatural. They can be beautiful and even the worst examples are still curiosities.

Southern authors, notably Eudora Welty, have commented on bottle trees, perhaps because they have a primal fascination. Sunlight on and through colored glass has charmed people for centuries; the bottle tree can be considered the poor person's stained glass window.

See also LITERATURE: / Welty, Eudora

Jim Martin
Yazoo City, Mississippi

Robert Farris Thompson, *Flash of the Spirit: African and Afro-American Art and Philosophy* (1983); John Michael Vlach, *The Afro-American Tradition in Decorative Arts* (1978); Eudora Welty, "Livvie" in *The Wide Net* (1943), *One Time, One Place* (1971). ☆

BRER RABBIT
||||||||||||||||||||||||||||||||||||||||||

The most widely known trickster figure associated with Afro-American folklore is Brer Rabbit (the word *Brer*, of course, is a contraction of *Brother*). The rabbit trickster was commonly known in those areas of Africa from which slaves came to America. Although several folktale

collectors have recorded Brer Rabbit texts, the tales are best known to the general public through their presentation in several volumes by Joel Chandler Harris (1848–1908), beginning with *Nights with Uncle Remus* (c. 1881). Harris's versions are edited and are closer to literature than folklore. The Georgian proclaimed himself both an accidental author and an unintentional folklorist. Harris was dogmatic on the matter of origins, proclaiming that the narratives were certainly of "remote African origin." Others, most notably folklorist Richard M. Dorson, have been less convinced, arguing that the Brer Rabbit and other animal narratives in the Afro-American repertoire came from a number of dispersal points including Europe.

In the 19th century there was also debate about the Afro-American–Native American exchange of rabbit trickster tales. Bureau of American Ethnology scholars like John Wesley Powell and James Mooney espoused the view that the Indian would be less likely to borrow black tales than the black would be to take over Indian narratives. Harris, of course, held the opposite view of an issue that has been debated off and on to the present. Folklorists Stith Thompson and Alan Dundes inclined toward Harris's view, whereas such books as Mary Alicia Owen's *Voodoo Tales* (1893) provide evidence for the Powell-Mooney view.

Most authorities have interpreted the Afro-American rabbit trickster hero narratives as protest tales in disguise. Thus, when the rabbit triumphed over a stronger animal because of his superior wits, it was really a tale of black slaves triumphing over their white oppressors. Certainly, such an interpretation is consistent with rabbit trickster tales, but those who insist that blacks totally identify with the rabbit trickster hero may be overstating their case.

See also LITERATURE: / Harris, Joel Chandler

W. K. McNeil
Ozark Folk Center
Mountain View, Arkansas

Richard M. Dorson, *American Negro Folktales* (1967); Alan Dundes, *Southern Folklore Quarterly* (September 1965); Maria Leach, ed., *Funk & Wagnalls Standard Dictionary of Folklore, Mythology, and Legend* (1949–50); Lawrence W. Levine, *Black Culture and Black Consciousness: Afro-American Folk Thought from Slavery to Freedom* (1977). ☆

BUNGALOW HOUSE

An enigmatic type of common house in the South, the bungalow played a minor role in the cultural landscape until the late 19th century. The word *bungalow* comes from a Hindustani word *Bangla*, meaning a low house with surrounding porches. An international house type, its antecedents include adobe dwellings in the Southwest, Japanese houses, the raised Creole cottages of Louisiana, the Swiss chalet, and barn and log cabin buildings. The plan of the bungalow is two rooms wide and three or more rooms long. Normally built of lumber, it has a foundation of piers and a gable roof with eaves to the sides (causing some confusion with the shotgun type). It often has a porch across the front and additional rooms on the rear or side. In some urban settings, it has been divided down the middle to form two apartments, giving rise to the mistaken notion that the form is usually a duplex.

The bungalow was normally the home owned by an independent family. During the early 20th century it became in many areas the standard tract house, filling in large areas of the early suburban cityscape. The California bungalow gained nearly complete dominance of southern domestic construction in the 1890–1920 period. As a consequence, many—perhaps most— southern bungalows also sport at least some elements of the California bungalow style.

In both rural and urban contexts, the flurry of bungalow building in the early 20th century reflected the increased prosperity of middle-income southerners. Brick bungalows proliferated after World War I, one of the first times brick was used extensively in popular domestic architecture. After World War II, however, the bungalow type ceased to be built, giving way to national styles and to mobile homes. The bungalow served as the transition from traditional to modern housing throughout the South.

M. B. Newton, Jr.
Louisiana State University

Anthony D. King, *The Bungalow: The Production of a Global Culture* (1984); Clay Lancaster, *The American Bungalow, 1880–1930* (1985); Leila Wilburn, *Southern Homes and Bungalows: A Collection of Choice Designs* (1914). ☆

CLOWER, JERRY

(b. 1926) Entertainer.

Clower is a modern humorist who uses the rustic settings of the South and the animated styles of the southern storyteller to entertain concert audiences across the country. He has recorded many albums that have reached the national charts; he appears on the renowned Grand Ole Opry; and he hosts a nationally syndicated television show. His stories have been published in two best-selling books, *Ain't God Good!* (1977) and *Let the Hammer Down!* (1978), and in a series of long-playing record albums.

His success as an entertainer sprang from his many years as a fertilizer salesman for the Mississippi Chemical Company in Yazoo City, Miss. In the best tradition of the salesman-talker, he accompanied his sales with humor grown from the homespun life of the Deep South. Born in Liberty, Miss. (on a dirt road, he reports) in 1926, he knew the land and its characters well. He drew laughter of affection and nostalgia for the region and its values.

Clower rose within the company and became a sought-after banquet speaker. At the urging of a friend, he recorded his banquet stories for a local label in 1971. "A Coon-Hunting Story," which used traditional tall-tale storytelling techniques spiced with Clower's distinctive style, caught the southern public by storm. Acclaim for the sincerity and directness of Clower brought him offers to record and perform nationally. Stories such as "Bully Has Done Flung a Cravin' on Me," "The Chauffeur and the Professor," "Sittin' Up with the Dead," "A New Bull," "Bird Huntin' at Uncle Versies," and "Marcel's Talkin' Chain Saw" have become nationally famous.

Clower's boisterous vocal delivery and exaggerated southern speech and gestures (saying "what" for "that," framing superlatives like "most hugestest rat," letting go whoops and hollers, and embellishing phrases with favored adjectives like "cottonpickin' ") raise the effect of his down-home humor. His colorful cast of characters, including Marcel, New-Gene, Aunt Pet, and Uncle Versie Ledbetter, endure, thanks to his yarnspinning, as favorite comic figures of the South. Yet Clower is serious about his storytelling and the cultural heritage, and Christian conviction, from which he springs. Clower continues to regale audiences outside the South, gaining fame as he does, but in performances he makes sure to show great pride in the life and people of the South. His stories serve to bring laughter and to preserve the color and spirit of the region.

Simon J. Bronner
Pennsylvania State University
Capitol Campus

Tom Chaffin, *Southern Exposure* (September–October 1983). ☆

COBB, NED (NATE SHAW)
||||||||||||||||||||||||||||||||||||||||||||||||||||||||||||||||||||
(1885–1973) Sharecropper.

Ned Cobb (alias Nate Shaw in Theodore Rosengarten's *All God's Dangers: The Life of Nate Shaw* [1974]), was a cotton farmer from Tallapoosa County, in east-central Alabama—gentle hill country, once extensively cultivated, now in pine woods and pastures. Cobb was born in 1885, the oldest son of Liza and Brown Cobb, former slaves and poor tenant farmers. He went to school for a total of two weeks, spending most of his childhood farming for his father and working for white people. At 21 he married Viola Bentley, an educated young woman whose parents owned land and were able to help the couple buy a mule and get a start. The Cobbs progressed rapidly from sharecropping to tenant farming; in the late 1920s, by which time nine children had arrived, they began buying a farm. In spite of the depression that struck agriculture right after World War I, the Cobbs prospered. But as cotton prices fell to six cents a pound, they, too, were pressed to meet their debts. When landlords and merchants cut off credit in their neighborhood in 1931, Cobb sought and received federal loans to buy fertilizer and see his family through the harvest.

In late fall 1932 the Sharecroppers Union, a voluntary organization of farmers founded the year before to defend the rights and interests of its members, formed a local near Reeltown. Ned Cobb was one of the first to join, moved by the idea of collective resistance to economic and social injustice. In December he assembled with other union men at the home of a neighbor to stop the sheriff from foreclosing on the man's livestock. A shootout ensued and several union men were killed or wounded. Cobb was shot in the back, but he managed to get away and evade arrest for one day. (The episode is the subject of John Beecher's epic poem *In Egypt Land*.) Along with a handful of other survivors, he was tried for attempted murder, convicted, and sent to prison for 12 years. Several times he refused a parole conditional on his never returning to Tallapoosa County. In 1945, at age 59, he went home and resumed farming. But he was a mule farmer in a tractor world, and he lacked the education and capital a man needed to get ahead. Toward the end of his life, he worked on shares with his son Wilbur, a successful cotton grower who had held the family together in his absence. Ned Cobb sold his last mule in 1970 and lived quietly, making white-oak baskets for which he was renowned,

until his death in 1974, just before his 88th birthday.

See also SOCIAL CLASS: / Sharecroppers Union

> Theodore Rosengarten
> McClellanville, South Carolina

CORNETT, CHESTER

(1912–1981) Chairmaker.

Chester Cornett was an eastern Kentucky craftsman who embodied in both his life and his work the tradition of folk craftsmanship. Born on King's Creek, Letcher County, Cornett learned the traditional design and construction of chairs from his maternal uncle, grandfather, and great uncle. Though he worked briefly in a commercial carpentry shop before his induction into the army in World War II, Cornett never owned or used power tools as an independent chairmaker until 1967, and even after that date he preferred to work "by hand."

A trying early life left its mark on Cornett. He was rejected and deserted by his parents, a girl he intended to marry, and his first and second wives. He emerged from his two years of military service in the Aleutian Islands with "a nervous condition," a skin disease, bad teeth, and eye troubles. He could not or would not tolerate the marginal life he lived in Hazard, Ky., where he worked as a handyman, stacked cases of Coca-Cola, and briefly worked in a coal mine. About 1947 he moved to the vicinity of Dwarf, Ky. In a secluded hollow on Main Lotts Creek he resumed making chairs, though against his wife's wishes, for his low income from the only work that gave him personal satisfaction insured their continued poverty. By 1950 he abandoned the use even of his foot-powered lathe and began to build his chairs with eight-sided pieces produced with axe and drawknife.

In 1953 Cornett built his first eight-legged chair, inspired in part by the geometric possibilities inherent in octagonal legs and posts, and in part by his belief that a novel design would enhance his ability to sell or barter his chairs. Over the next 15 years he developed a remarkable set of stylistic trademarks that blended novel and "antique" elements. The innovative design features, which began with octagonal rather than turned pieces, continued with Cornett's increasing emphasis on very large chairs with many deeply curved slats, his exaggerated use of pegs as decorative elements, his development of many variations in bark widths and weaving patterns used in chair seats, and his employment of contrasting species of wood. Though all his later, larger, chairs suggest a sense of protective enclosure that is lacking in traditional models, and though some of his chairs were, by his own designation, "strange," Cornett felt that most of the trademark elements he employed were antique features. The antique hallmarks of Cornett's work include emphatically decorative pegs, the large "knobs" (finials) of slat-back chairs, and the pronounced outward and backward bend on the rear posts of "mule-eared settin' chairs"; in Cornett's view, these features distinguished his "handmade" chairs from the "homemade" chairs of other eastern Kentucky chairmakers, as well as from "factory chairs" made with power tools and kiln-dried lumber.

Cornett became the subject of scholarly attention in 1965 when folklorist Michael Owen Jones met him and began to study his work, along with that of other traditional chairmakers from southeastern Kentucky. He received increased popular attention after April 1965, when Kentucky writer Gurney Norman published an article on him in the *Hazard Herald*. Subsequent articles in state, regional, and national periodicals brought Cornett orders for chairs from far beyond his locale. In 1981 he became the subject of a film entitled *Hand Carved*, in which he makes a chair of a type he had invented 20 years before, the eight-legged "two-in-one" rocker; he also describes the advantages and disadvantages of making chairs by hand for a living. Chester Cornett died in a Veterans' Administration nursing home in Ft. Thomas, Ky., soon after the film's release.

Thomas A. Adler
University of Kentucky

Hand Carved (Herb E. Smith and Elizabeth Barret, directors, Appalshop Films, Whitesburg, Ky., 1981); Michael Owen Jones, "Chairmaking in Appalachia: A Study in Style and Creative Imagination in American Folk Art" (Ph.D. dissertation, Indiana University, 1969), *The Hand Made Object and Its Maker* (1975); *The Mountain Eagle* (18 June 1981). ☆

DOGTROT HOUSE
|||||||||||||||||||||||||||||||||||||||||||||||||

A house with an open hallway separating two rooms under a roof that has its gables to the sides is a dogtrot house. Such a house may have been built of log, lumber, heavy timber, or other materials. In the popular mind, however, the dogtrot house is made of logs, and that manner of building seems to have been one of the determinants of the form.

Although there were European antecedents, with open passages between two rooms under the same roof, the American dogtrot drew only peripherally from that Old World tradition. At least as likely a source for the house was the Georgian Revival, which emphasized bilateral symmetry: two sides of the facade mirroring each other across the midline. When early settlers were entering the backcountry and preparing for the great sweep westward across the South, the Georgian style dominated.

The pioneers set about building British bay, or pen, houses, using German log-working methods, and in the Georgian style. The resulting ideas on enlarging a log house to embrace two rooms included, among others, the dogtrot plan. Two log pens, say 20 feet across the front and 18 feet from front to back, were built side by side and surmounted by a common roof. Under Georgian rules, they had to have like facades, placed so as to share a common hall. The result was a dogtrot (also known by many folk names: hallway house, possum trot, two pens and a passage). Limited by log construction, the building of a two-pen house with a central hall made the enclosing of that hall a special problem. When it was enclosed, it was with other material and usually at a later date.

Whatever the origin of the dogtrot in the eastern part of the South, it spread over the region from the Appalachians to the edge of the Great Plains and from just north of the Ohio to near the Gulf shores during the brief span from 1775 to 1835. In this diffusion, the dogtrot was one of the steady hallmarks of the Upland (as opposed to the Lowland or Tidewater) South.

The dogtrot has been a frequent image in southern literature. William Faulkner uses the dogtrot as home to both poor white and black families in his fictional Yoknapatawpha County. Examples in *The Reivers*, *The Mansion*, *Go Down, Moses*, and *As I Lay Dying* range from the classic dogtrot with its open hallway to those with enclosed hallways and second floors added. As dwellers become more affluent, they make predictable changes in their houses. In Eudora Welty's *Losing Battles* Granny Renfro and her dogtrot home are a link with life "a long time ago."

Dogtrot house, Hickory Flat, Mississippi, 1968

Although times have changed, Granny Renfro has neither painted her dogtrot nor "to this day closed in" its central hallway.

Photographers who worked with the Farm Security Administration, including Eudora Welty, Dorothea Lange, Arthur Rothstein, and Russell Lee, documented dogtrot homes in the 1930s South. In *Let Us Now Praise Famous Men*, Walker Evans and James Agee explored the dogtrot with painstaking detail through Evans's photographs and Agee's text. William Christenberry, who grew up in Hale County, Ala., the locale for the Agee and Evans book, now photographs dogtrots in his home county and has re-created a dogtrot house in his studio in Washington, D.C.

The dogtrot house has inspired folk artists in the South with its distinctive shape. Mississippi's Theora Hamblett, for example, painted the home she knew as a child, focusing the viewer's eye through its central hall. Architects such as Arnold Aho and William Turnball have been inspired by the aesthetic and functional aspects of this traditional southern home, and Aho has even designed a passive solar "neo-dogtrot" house utilizing cross ventilation.

M. B. Newton, Jr.
Baton Rouge, Louisiana

Walker Evans and James Agee, *Let Us Now Praise Famous Men* (1941); William Ferris, ed., *Afro-American Folk Art and Crafts* (1983); Richard H. Hulan and Douglas K. Meyer, *Pioneer America* (July 1975); Terry G. Jordan, *Texas Log Buildings: A Folk Architecture* (1978); Dianne Tebbetts, *Pioneer America* (June 1978); Eugene M. Wilson, *Pioneer America* (July 1971). ☆

FIRST MONDAY TRADES DAY

Known in most southern states, but most notably Texas and Alabama, the First Monday Trades Day harks back to an earlier, more neighborly time. On a regular basis, usually the first Monday of each month, the people of some southern counties held an open market for traders, commonly on the street surrounding the courthouse. During the monthly session of the county court, the town and country folk gathered to trade by cash or by barter all manner of goods: dogs, canned goods, horses, used tools, stitchery, notions, fresh produce, and indeed nearly anything of value. Itinerant peddlers often joined the trading, and impromptu fiddling, picking, storytelling, and gossiping added a carnival tone to the monthly gathering.

Among the best-known trades days are those at Scottsboro, Ala., and Canton, Tex. Even before the recent rise in popularity of "flea markets," these two had acquired wide repute and attendance numbering in the thousands. On Labor Day, the greatest First Monday of the year, Canton drew tens of thousands of visitors, all determined to enjoy bartering, food, yarns, friends, and animals. Where several nearby counties held trades days, some had to content themselves with second, third, or fourth Monday as their regular time for the event; such was the case in much of east Texas. Once the flea-market mania gained hold of the South, some of the First Mondays had to be moved to the outskirts of the county seats. Despite the "Monday" name, trading often began on the Saturday before the first Monday, resuming late Sunday and continuing until sundown Monday.

The origin of First Monday is ascribed to "hard times when folks had no money and had to barter." The question arises, however, as to why the same solution appeared—presumably spontaneously—at so many places across the South, why it is always associated with the sessions of the county court, and why it focused so much on dogs and horses. The practice seems more likely to have been an element of backcountry commerce carried westward with the frontier. Similar trades days are common in Ireland and Great Britian and suggest a historical reason for the tradition.

Names for the event differ somewhat. At Abingdon, Va., it is "Jockey Day," referring to the trading and racing of horses that accompany the trading. At several places, it is called "Court Day," referring to the concurrent county business. In most places, however, "First Monday" is the preferred term.

M. B. Newton, Jr.
Baton Rouge, Louisiana

FRAKTUR
||||||||||||||||||||||||||

The art of *fraktur*—illuminated manuscripts—was a German tradition brought to this country by emigrants coming from the Rhineland in the late 17th and 18th centuries. The art form entered the South as these Germans, who had settled primarily in Pennsylvania, began migrating down the wagon road into and through the Shenandoah Valley. As a result, pockets of Germanic settlement appeared in Maryland, Virginia, North Carolina, and South Carolina. From these regions, especially Virginia, numerous examples of *fraktur* have survived.

The German work *fraktur* referred originally to a 16th-century German typeface, which resembled the calligraphic script often used on medieval documents. Birth and baptismal certificates, *taufshein*, and other family documents and texts were lettered with this script and decorated with watercolor illustrations. Decorative writings, called *zierschrift*, were a type of *fraktur* common to Mennonites of Swiss ancestry who moved from Lancaster County, Penn., to the Shenandoah Valley in Virginia.

Fraktur produced in the South, where artists used both English and German script, was much the same as that drawn by northern artists. The watercolor embellishments were usually colorful borders incorporating stylized and symbolic figures. Popular motifs, such as hearts, tulips, and birds, were painted in bright reds, blues, greens, yellows, and oranges, and sometimes outlined in black ink.

Because producing *fraktur* required reading and writing skills, ministers and schoolmasters were the predominant *fraktur* artists. At different times a post rider, a cobbler, and a schoolmaster, Peter Bernhart sold *fraktur* forms prepared by a Pennsylvania artist before he began producing his own in Rockingham County, Va. Dated examples exist from the period 1789–1819. The 40 known works by the "Stony Creek" artist date from 1805 to 1824, with over half having been prepared for members of the Stony Creek Lutheran and Reformed Zion Congregation in Shenandoah County (now Page County), Va. Jacob Strickler, born in Shenandoah County in 1770, may have been a Mennonite preacher. Ten of his works have been identified and date from 1787 to 1815. Also from Shenandoah County was Barbara Becker Hamman (1774–1850), who produced *fraktur* as early as 1786. She developed her calligraphic skill through training at a German school in Strasburg, Va.

At least 28 works by the *"Ehre Vater"* artist, who produced *fraktur* in western North Carolina and South Carolina (as well as in Pennsylvania), are known. The *"Ehre Vater und Mutter"* (Honor Father and Mother) appears on much of the work by this artist, probably an itinerant schoolmaster in Lutheran or Reformed schools. There were other southern *fraktur* artists, many unidentified. Together, they continued a tradition begun by their European forebears, thus adding to the artistic culture of the South.

Jessica Foy
Cooperstown Graduate Programs
Cooperstown, New York

John Bivins, *Journal of Early Southern Decorative Arts* (November 1975); Nancy Goyne Evans, *Antiques* (February 1973); Cynthia Elyce Rubin, ed., *Southern Folk Art* (1985); Klaus Wust, *Virginia Fraktur: Penmanship as Folk Art* (1972). ☆

FURNITURE MAKING
||||||||||||||||||||||||||||||||||||||||||||||||||

In the 18th- and 19th-century South, furniture was made in both small towns and isolated farming communities. Craftsmen in both places used the same woods—oak, maple, ash, and hickory (rather than the mahogany popular in the fancy furniture of the city). The closer the craftsman lived to town the more tools he used, the more aware he and his clients were of fashion, and the more he mixed styles and used ornamentation to please his clients. The town craftsman was influenced by city styles and derived his status from his craft. The more isolated the craftsman, the fewer tools he used. A chairmaker used only a draw knife, pen knife, froe, axe, and pole lathe for a slat-back chair compared to the 75 to 100 tools the town craftsman employed for a chest. The rural craftsman worked at his craft only part-time, farming the remainder; although aware of style, he usually produced less ornamented furniture for a clientele who saw an object's principal attribute as its utility. His status was not dependent on the use and acceptance of popular fashion; rather, the rural craftsman maintained his reputation through his quiet skill.

In the late 19th century mass-produced urban furniture shipped by rail from centers like High Point, N.C., displaced the work of the town craftsman. In rural locales, though, cheap, handmade furniture—bedsteads, chests, cabinets, and chairs—continued to find a narrow market until mass merchandizing arrived there also.

At this point southern furniture became synonymous with concepts of folk "simplicity." The birth of southern handicraft publicized southern crafts nationwide and allowed the rural craftsman to continue his work within the furniture industry. His new customer base required that an object simply appear rustic and handmade.

Although the craftsman fashioned essentially the same types of furnishings as his urban counterpart, his awareness of the outsider's romantic conceptualization of "folk" and "natural" increased. The rustic object, once thought of negatively, became, within this century, positive. The rural southern furniture maker carefully began to preserve the appearance of country, while creating a technology that allowed him to increase his output. Rather than limit production to suit his neighbors' needs, he produced as much as his skills and resources would allow for an ever-widening market. Rather than building by hand and relying on notching and the calculated shrinkage of wood to hold his furniture together, he adopted more modern technology. Nails and power tools, for example, quickly achieved the same end. Rather than minimizing fashion's impact, he studied furniture catalogs for ideas that would fit the "country" image of his crafts.

Southern traditional furniture has evolved into a furniture produced for a mass audience frequently using modern techniques, and it owes much of its continuing existence to America's changing attitudes toward things country.

See also INDUSTRY: / Furniture Industry

Charles E. Martin
Alice Lloyd College

Antiques (March 1968); Michael Owen Jones, *The Hand Made Object and Its Maker* (1975); Charles E. Martin, *Appalachian Journal* (Fall 1981); Christine Ritter, *Early American Life* (December 1977); Warren E. Roberts, *Midwestern Journal of Language and Folklore* (Fall 1981). ☆

"GET RIGHT WITH GOD"
|||||||||||||||||||||||||||||||||||||||||||||||||||||||||||||||

Often done in a rough, hand-lettered style, numerous signs greet the traveler of southern back roads. They proclaim abrupt and straightforward messages of salvation: "Christ is the Answer," "Jesus Saves," "Get Right with God." These terse testimonies set forth the central tenet of fundamentalist Chris-

tianity, which is that, above all, good Christians must believe in God. From this belief flows the strict moral order that determines the proper conduct of a righteous life. Simple and direct, these signs allow no leeway in interpretation. Just as their message is uncompromisingly to-the-point, so too one's faith should be firm and unshakable.

Sophisticated observers smirk at the homemade plywood placard that, in dripping left-over paint, says: "Christ Died for Your Sins." The sophisticate does not share the painter's emotion and believes that surely such matters as religion, morality, and the afterlife are not to be summed up in four or five words. Given the aesthetic of southern Christianity, the roadside signs should not be so easily targeted for derision. Folk hymns have high, tight, restricted harmonies. Sunday meeting is a demanding all-day affair allowing little time for secular diversions. Country churches have almost no ornamentation and are noted

Roadside sign, Mississippi Delta, 1975

for their stark, solitary settings where their white clapboarded facades dominate the landscape. In this context a terse proclamation that "Jesus Saves" is not only consistent but appropriate. To say more would suggest a degree of uncertainty rarely encountered among devout believers. A roadside sign, although a minimal statement, is densely packed with significance. It is an icon of faith, a modest but meaningful symbol conveying the truths upon which a stable, reasonable life can be built.

John Michael Vlach
George Washington University

Samuel S. Hill, ed., *Encyclopedia of Religion in the South* (1984); *Southern Exposure* (Fall 1976). ☆

GHOST STORIES
||||||||||||||||||||||||||||||||||||||||||

The word *ghost* seems to be a straightforward term. Traditionally many terms —*ghost, revenant, wraith, specter, apparition*, and *spirit*, to name the most popular—have been used for essentially the same phenomenon. Complicating the matter of definition, the returning dead supposedly come back in several forms. First, they may come back in the same body they had while alive; second, they may appear in some sort of spectral form; third, they may be invisible and known only by their deeds, noises, or mischief. For simplicity's sake a ghost can be defined as a being returned from the dead in human or animal form or having some features of humans or animals.

The best bearers of ghost lore—or any type of folklore—are sometimes stereotyped as rustic illiterates. Like most stereotypes this one has an element of truth but is also misleading. Certainly unschooled rural people know and tell such stories, but by no means do they have an exclusive hold on them. Indeed, ghost narratives flourish as well if not better in cities because more people can hear and tell them. Suffice it to say that most southerners—in fact, most Americans—know or know of such tales, which they have heard related by friends and acquaintances, sometimes as firsthand experiences but more often as something that happened to a friend of a friend.

When one speaks of ghost stories, many people think of an old abandoned house with loose, banging shutters and doors that seem to be closed by some unseen hand. Such a thought is logical, for houses are the favorite hangouts of ghosts; but ghosts are also commonly found in battlefields, mines, highways, boats, graveyards, gallows, and wells. Most ghosts are bound to a single place, but some carry their haunting farther afield. Usually the wraiths move about by horseback or automobile rather than by supernatural means. This activity has a lengthy tradition throughout Russia and much of Europe. As early as the 1660s people were telling stories about these traveling ghosts, and they were undoubtedly being discussed prior to that time.

Most ghosts return for a specific reason, one of the most popular in the South, indeed in the United States, being to reveal the whereabouts of hidden treasure. Other reasons for ghostly hauntings include unjust execution, suicide, a restless soul, a need to complete business left unfinished at the time of death, and attempts to find some forgotten possession. Many ghosts are harmless to anyone with a clear conscience, but some are vengeful and malevolent and return to torture their victims eternally. Often the ghosts of dead lovers or husbands and wives return to haunt their faithless sweetheart or spouse. Sometimes a parent comes back to make life unpleasant for his or her children; on other occasions the ghost returns to slay a wicked person or take revenge on the person who murdered, injured, or cheated him or her. Frequently, the dead return to punish a person who has stolen part of the corpse or who has in some way disturbed the grave; at other times they punish someone who is mistreating a relative. A few southern ghosts have no specific motivation for their return, but these purposeless wraiths are rare.

W. K. McNeil
Ozark Folk Center
Mountain View, Arkansas

W. K. McNeil, ed., *Ghost Stories from the American South* (1985); Flo Hampton Scott, *Ghosts with Southern Accents and Evidence of Extra-Sensory Perception* (1969); Fred Siemon, *Ghost Story Index* (1967); Jack Solomon and Olivia Solomon, eds., *Ghosts and Goosebumps: Supernatural Tales from Alabama* (1981); Dean Faulkner Wells, ed., *The Ghosts of Rowan Oak: William Faulkner's Ghost Stories for Children* (1980); Kathryn Tucker Windham, *Thirteen Georgia Ghosts and Jeffrey* (1973). ☆

GUMBO

The heady, aromatic soup that goes by the name of gumbo is the product of varied cultures that produced this hybrid of southern cuisine. From Africa comes its name—*ngombo*, the Bantu word for okra. The herbs, spices, the carefully chopped and sautéed seasoning vegetables, the seafoods, meat, fowl, and the rice with which it is always served come together in a nourishing and enticing amalgam that is unique to the region.

In Louisiana, gumbo has several classifications. First, there is *Creole*. The word began as a description of offspring of European settlers (in Spanish, *criollo*) and then evolved into meaning homegrown (as in "Creole" tomatoes). Creole cooking, as a style, refers to that practiced in the areas in and around New Orleans by European and African immigrants and their descendants. Then there is *Cajun*: a shortening of the word *Acadian*, which refers to French settlers of the Nova Scotia region displaced by the English who finally settled in the Louisiana Southwest in the late 18th century.

As in any kitchen dispute, there are as many theories as there are cooks, but the usual difference between a Cajun and a Creole gumbo lies in the "roux." Browning flour in fat (slowly, slowly, stirring all the while) creates a roux and in Cajun gumbos this is a necessary thickener. Creole gumbos rely mainly on vegetable aids for thickening, with a much thinner roux if one is used. Cajun gumbos have more pepper and other spices.

In both Creole and Cajun gumbos one finds two families—okra and filé. Okra, when slowly sautéed over a low flame (not in a cast iron pot that would blacken it), loses its ropey consistency and forms a smooth thickening agent. Filé (powdered dry sassafras leaves) gets its name from the French because when improperly used it makes threads (*filé*), and green gummy blobs appear. Properly used (never added to a boiling liquid) it gives a lightly gelatinous texture to liquids. Filé, in the 19th century, was chiefly manufactured by the Choctaw Indians on the north shore of Lake Pont-chartrain. They came to the French Market, by the Mississippi River at the French Quarter, and sold their product to generations of New Orleans house-wives.

Gumbo always begins with what some chefs call the "holy trinity" of vegeta-bles—onion, celery, and bell pepper. These are seasoned and sautéed, and seasonings might include salt, black pepper, cayenne pepper, thyme, garlic, green onions, parsley, bay leaves, and basil. In okra gumbo, tomatoes are added. A typical filé gumbo contains the above seasonings, plus chicken or other fowl and its stock, oysters and oyster water, and a seasoning pork—ham, an-douille sausage, a smoked sausage, or tasso (dried and smoked meat, in this case, pork). A seafood gumbo contains okra, tomatoes, all the above season-ings, possibly a flavoring pork, and shrimp (with stock from boiling their shells) and hard shelled crabs (also with stock). Crabmeat may be added.

Any variations on the two above rec-ipes are possible: some people use both filé and okra. Rice always accompanies the dish, and some cooks sprinkle filé over each bowl rather than add it to the pot. Chefs have been known to add a serving of potato salad on top, but this is not recommended for novices.

Two other gumbo families exist. One uses meats, either beef or game, and this is usually an okra gumbo. The other is gumbo z'herbes, which is very similar to what is called greens and pot liquor in other southern kitchens. When sea-soning meat is left out, gumbo z'herbes becomes an ideal Lenten soup, and the number of greens in a Good Friday gumbo z'herbes can correspond to the number of apostles.

Gumbo does have other meanings. Gumbo mud is black, sticky, and is best created by the Mississippi River. Gumbo or "Gombo" French is a patois of French and African languages once spoken by New Orleans blacks. Gumbo, meaning a mixture of many ingredients, also is used in a Cajun saying: "Gumbo ya-ya," roughly translated as "Every-body talks at once."

Carolyn Kolb
New Orleans, Louisiana

Howard Mitcham, *Creole Gumbo and All That Jazz: A New Orleans Seafood Cookbook* (1978); *The Original Picayune Creole Cook Book* (1966); Paul Prudhomme, *Chef Paul Prudhomme's Louisiana Kitchen* (1984); Lyle Saxon, ed., *Gumbo Ya-Ya: A Collection of Louisiana Folk Tales* (1945). ☆

HAMBLETT, THEORA
(1895–1977) Painter.

Theora Hamblett was born 15 January 1895 in the small community of Paris, Miss. Hamblett lived the first half of her life on her family's modest farm in Paris. Her experience as a white woman growing up and living in the im-poverished rural South was typical of her times, with the exception that she never married or had children. From 1915 to 1936 Hamblett taught school intermittently in the counties near her family home. In 1939 she moved to the nearby town of Oxford, where she sup-ported herself as a professional seam-stress and converted her home into a boardinghouse.

Hamblett began painting in the early 1950s, fulfilling an interest in art that had begun in her youth. Although she enrolled in several informal art classes and a correspondence course during her later life, Hamblett was largely self-taught. Her first paintings depicted

*Theora Hamblett, painter, Oxford,
Mississippi, 1973*

memories of her childhood, and she
painted scenes of southern country life
for the next two decades, culminating
in a series of paintings about children's
games. Hamblett's most unusual works
are the over 300 religious paintings representing biblical subjects and Hamblett's own dreams and visions. These
paintings began in 1954 with *The
Golden Gate*, later renamed *The Vision*.
Today, this first painting is owned by
the Museum of Modern Art in New York;
most of Hamblett's religious paintings
and many memory paintings were never
available for sale, and were bequeathed
by the artist to the University Museums
in Oxford, Miss.

Hamblett's religious paintings and
interpretations of her dreams and visions were firmly rooted in her personal
religious history. The popular, trans-
denominational southern Protestantism
practiced in the churches, revival meetings, and hymn sings Hamblett attended
in and around Paris, Miss., all emphasized the possibility of unmediated

encounters between God and commu-
nicants, usually taking the form of visionary or dreamlike experiences.
Church services were often structured
around testimonies in which the worshippers described these experiences,
and hymn lyrics regularly referred to
them. Hamblett's vision and dream
paintings bear structural similarities to
traditional testimonies, and many of her
paintings employ images from the popular southern hymnody.

Hamblett's aesthetics and working
methods were also largely products of
her background. The needlework skills
she learned as a southern rural woman,
and with which she occasionally supported herself, are evident in her art.
Hamblett's characteristic tiny brush-
strokes of unmixed color resemble embroidery stitches, and many of her
images suggest lacework and tatting.
Hamblett's interest in painting was not
unusual, but the dedication with which
she pursued that interest and the role it
played in her life were exceptional. The
record her work provides of a vanishing
regional history and the complex associations of her religious paintings raise
Hamblett from the status of an amateur
to that of a significant artist of popular
southern traditions.

Ella King Torrey
Philadelphia, Pennsylvania

William Ferris, *Local Color: A Sense of Place
in Folk Art* (1983); *Four Women Artists* (William Ferris, director, Center for Southern
Folklore, Memphis, Tenn., 1977); Theora
Hamblett, in collaboration with Ed Meek
and William S. Haynie, *Theora Hamblett
Paintings* (1975); Ella King Torrey, "The
Religious Art of Theora Hamblett, Sources
of Attitude and Imagery" (M.A. thesis, University of Mississippi, 1984). ☆

HENRY, JOHN

The legend of John Henry, the "steel-driving man," had its beginnings in the building of the Chesapeake & Ohio Railroad in West Virginia in the early 1870s. Construction of tracks for the C & O line through the mountainous terrain required a series of tunnels, the most important of which was the 1¼-mile-long Big Bend Tunnel, which was completed in 1872. According to tradition, John Henry worked on the construction of this tunnel, which at the time was the longest in the United States. Although the song about John Henry is popular with both blacks and whites, he is generally thought of as an Afro-American folk hero, an example of the black hero who defeats white society on its own territory and by its own rules. He is also seen as a symbol of human strength prevailing over machines, an appropriate theme for southerners faced with industrialization of their region.

The first published report of a John Henry ballad was in a brief note in a 1909 issue of the *Journal of American Folklore*. The most extensive studies of the traditions came over two decades later with the publication of books by Guy B. Johnson and Louis W. Chappell. Johnson's *John Henry: Tracking Down a Negro Legend* (1929) and Chappell's *John Henry: A Folk-Lore Study* (1933) resolved the questions of John Henry's relationship to John Hardy, another black West Virginia hero, and the factual basis for the steam-drilling contest in which John Henry lost his life. The books, however, did not stop popular interest in the black hero, who appeared as a figure in a play, a popular book, and several children's books; in addition, there are now over 65 recordings

of the ballad. The ballad has also been anthologized in numerous folksong collections.

W. K. McNeil
Ozark Folk Center
Mountain View, Arkansas

Louis W. Chappell, *John Henry: A Folk-Lore Study* (1933); Guy Johnson, *John Henry: Tracking Down a Negro Legend* (1929); Lawrence W. Levine, *Black Culture and Black Consciousness: Afro-American Folk Thought from Slavery to Freedom* (1977); Alan Lomax, *The Folk Songs of North America* (1960). ☆

"HILLBILLY" IMAGE

Although the word *hillbilly* probably predates the 20th century, no known record of the word appeared in print until 23 April 1900. On that day the *New York Journal* referred to a hillbilly as "a free and untrammelled white citizen of Alabama, who lives in the hills, has no means to speak of, dresses as he can, talks as he pleases, drinks whiskey when he gets it, and fires off his revolver as the fancy takes him." Except that he is confined to Alabama, this is an accurate description of the major stereotypes of the hillbilly, who is now thought of as being any resident of the southern mountains.

The stereotyped hillbilly made his first widespread appearance in the comic dialogue-song the "Arkansas Traveler," first published in the 1840s. Although he was not specifically identified as a mountain resident, it was generally assumed that the Arkansan who supplied humorous retorts to the eastern traveler's questions was a mountaineer. The hillbilly was poverty stricken and apparently unconcerned with improving his lot in life, but those faults were somewhat compensated for by his wit and love of music. This figure was a far different personality from those mountain men encountered in Hot Springs, Ark., by the protagonist of the song "The State of Arkansaw." These hillmen had "misery depicted in their melancholy faces," and were lantern jawed with stringy, unkempt hair that hung in rattails down their faces. Without redeeming qualities, these personalities were akin to the hillbilly of 20th-century popular imagery, a stereotype that was spread by various forms of mass media as well as by scholarly sources.

Popular literature was one of the forces perpetrating and propagating the hillbilly image. In Charles S. Hibbler's *Down in Arkansas* (1902) the hillbilly is depicted as a conservative, almost regressive being, who "is proud in his poverty, contented with his environment, happy in his seclusion." Thomas W. Jackson's *On a Slow Train through Arkansaw* (1903) provided a more graphic account of the hillbilly, not so much in the text but in the illustrations accompanying the volume. Here the mountaineer was presented in the classic pose, as a person who is obviously stupid, uncouth, unkempt, and no stranger to poverty. This concept reappeared in a large number of later books such as Marion Hughes's *Three Years in Arkansaw* (1908). Other works of fiction, such as Mary N. Murfree's *In the Tennessee Mountains* (1884) and John Fox's *Trail of the Lonesome Pine* (1908), although not specifically negative, pictured the mountaineer as a person in conflict with the forces of the modern industrial age. In so doing they contributed to the common belief that the hillbilly was really a living anachronism, a contemporary

but one who temperamentally and intellectually belonged to an earlier era.

Movies also helped keep the hillbilly image alive. The so-called hick flicks such as the low-budget films of the Weaver Brothers and Elviry, Ma and Pa Kettle, and others presented a corny, hard-working, decent, poor but honest, uneducated hillbilly who was often unintentionally funny. In the 1960s this hillbilly was transferred to television most notably in the form of *The Beverly Hillbillies*, whose humor, like that of the earlier rural films, largely revolved around the conflict between the hillbilly's manners and philosophy of life and those of city folks. The characters in this and similar series had little touch with reality or modern civilization.

In 1934 two comic-strip figures who have had far-reaching effect in keeping the popular concept of the hillbilly alive first appeared. L'il Abner was, throughout the comic strip's long run, a noble and naive character possessed of little education, intelligence, pretension, or ambition, blissfully happy in his ignorance and poverty. The other figure, Snuffy Smith, eventually became the main character in the comic strip *Barney Google*, which ultimately was retitled to include both names. At first Snuffy was somewhat rambunctious and obnoxious but he later became a milder personality temperamentally akin to L'il Abner. Older than Abner, Snuffy was equally lazy, unambitious, uneducated, poverty stricken, and unfamiliar with modern conveniences. Unlike Abner, Smith was inclined to feuding and drinking moonshine. These were two of the most popular comic-strip heroes that kept a certain stereotyped view of the hillbilly before the American public, but there were others, such as Ozark Ike, a tall, thin, bumbling, and ignorant ball player, who helped perpetuate the image.

These various views of the hillbilly were not confined to mass media but also permeated scholarly thought and writing on the southern mountaineer. The popular writer John Fiske, in *Old Virginia and Her Neighbors* (1897), stated as fact something that, at best, can only be speculation when he declared that the southern mountaineer was descended from criminals and "degraded white humanity." Fiske observed, though, that the hill residents of his day were noted more for shiftlessness than for criminality. William Goodell Frost, long-time president of Berea College, thought of the mountaineer as a living anachronism, a "contemporary ancestor." The eminent British historian Arnold Toynbee found him little more than a barbarian. Harry M. Caudill, a mountain native, averred in *Night Comes to the Cumberlands* (1963) that Fiske's account of the mountaineer's origin was accurate, and that these people were shiftless and lazy, unskilled and illiterate, and had degenerated into wild and cruel beings. James Dickey's novel *Deliverance* (1970) offered a contemporary version of the cruel, forbidding hillbilly, an image of the "redneck."

Even those who were kindly disposed to the mountaineer and his problems often accepted the image as reality. Thus, organizations such as the Tennessee Valley Authority, the Office of Economic Opportunity, Council of the Southern Mountains, the Appalachian Regional Commission, and others generally failed in their expressed goals of improving the lot of the southern mountaineer, in part because they assumed unrealistically that he represented a "deviant subculture" whose problems were primarily due to physical isolation, depleted gene pools, pathological inbreeding, feuding, moonshining, and welfarism. These groups carefully avoided the word *hillbilly*, but they accepted the stereotype conjured up by the term.

See also MYTHIC SOUTH: / "Crackers"; Rednecks

W. K. McNeil
Ozark Folk Center
Mountain View, Arkansas

John C. Campbell, *The Southern Highlander and His Homeland* (1921; reprint 1969); Harry M. Caudill, *Night Comes to the Cumberlands: The Biography of a Depressed Area* (1963); James Masterson, *Tall Tales of Arkansaw* (1943; reprinted as *Arkansas Folklore*, 1974); Mitford Mathews, *A Dictionary of Americanisms on Historical Principles* (1951); Henry D. Shapiro, *Appalachia on Our Mind: The Southern Mountains and Mountaineers in the American Consciousness, 1870–1920* (1978); *Strangers and Kin: A History of the Hillbilly Image* (Herb E. Smith, director, Appalshop Films, Whitesburg, Ky., 1984); David E. Whisnant, *All That Is Native and Fine: The Politics of Culture in an American Region* (1983), *Modernizing the Mountaineer: People, Power, and Planning in Appalachia* (1979). ☆

HUNTER, CLEMENTINE
(1882–1988) Painter.

Born Clementine Rubin, the granddaughter of slaves, in 1882 at Hidden Hill Plantation, south of Natchitoches, La., Clementine Hunter late in life became a renowned primitive painter sometimes called "the black Grandma Moses."

At age 15 Hunter moved to Melrose Plantation, where she worked as a field hand picking cotton, gave birth to seven children, married twice, tended a garden, and became a cook and maid. Melrose was founded in the 1740s but was a 20th-century colony for artists, writers, photographers, and scholars. An artist left tubes of paint at the plantation house in 1940, and Hunter, who was nearing 60 then, discovered them in cleaning. When she expressed interest in painting, author François Mignon, who was also staying at Melrose, encouraged her, providing brushes, turpentine, and a window shade for a canvas. At first she sold her paintings along with watermelons in her front yard to help pay hospital bills for her husband Emmanuel (who died in 1942). Famous visitors to Melrose championed Hunter and promoted her popularity. She received a Rosenwald Foundation grant in the late 1940s, and *Look* magazine did a feature on her work. The New Orleans Museum of Art honored her with its first one-person exhibition of a black artist's work. The Smithsonian Institution in Washington, D.C., and the American Museum of Folk Art in New York City have also given major exhibitions of her work.

Clementine Hunter's first painting was of a baptism, and her more than 5,000 oil paintings in general closely reflect southern life. She records the rituals of daily living, painting weddings, funerals, laundry days, Saturday afternoons in town and Saturday nights in juke joints, Sunday dinners, and children decorating Christmas trees and hunting for Easter eggs. Her works feature farm animals and colorful flowers. Religious images are frequent, including angels in flight, a black Jesus on the cross, and nativity scenes with the manger set in a cotton field. Hunter's creativity was also expressed in baskets she

wove, dolls she made, and colorful quilts she crafted.

Charles Reagan Wilson
University of Mississippi

Herbert W. Hemphill, Jr., and Julia Weissman, *Twentieth-Century American Folk Art and Artists* (1974); Jackson *Clarion-Ledger* (24 August 1986); Jay Johnson and William C. Ketchum, Jr., *American Folk Art of the Twentieth Century* (1983). ☆

I HOUSE

Whenever and wherever southerners prospered during the late 18th and the 19th centuries, they built bigger, more commodious, stylish houses. The concept that governed their choice of a plan remained nameless throughout the time of its popularity. Later academic practice called the form the "I house." The reasons for the name lie in the vagaries of a gradually awakening scholarly awareness, inspired by the efforts of Fred B. Kniffen to make sense of the houses that he was seeing in Indiana, Illinois, and Iowa (hence, the *I*). Further study showed that the form was the most widespread customary type of house in the United States.

The minimum criterion of the I-house form was a plan two rooms wide, one room deep, and two rooms tall. This plan has been dubbed "two over two." The whole was surmounted by a gable roof with eaves to the front and rear. The house might have had a gallery on the front, shed (or pent-roofed) rooms on the rear, and pavilion rooms on the sides. The I house might have had chimneys on the ends, in the center, or even on the rear of the main rooms (pens). It might have had a central hall or even an open passage (dogtrot) on one or both stories. Earlier versions often had blind (windowless) end walls. I houses were built of log, timber, lumber, brick, and stone. All these elements are independent variables; they do not alter the basic classification.

Through the northern part of the South, the I house was usually of a plainer, leaner variety. Farther South, however, exterior chimneys, broad galleries, and central halls stressed horizontals for a feeling of repose. In one distinct version, the Carolina I house, these feelings are still more accentuated. In the Carolina I house, which appeared in the country back of Charleston and is everywhere connected with migrants from that region, the basic two-over-two plan had two standard additions: a one-story gallery, added to the front, and a one-story shed added to the rear.

Although not uniquely southern, the I houses of the South contributed to popular imagery of the region and illustrated the South's conversion of an architectural form to its own tastes.

M. B. Newton, Jr.
Baton Rouge, Louisiana

Fred Kniffen, *Annals of the Association of American Geographers* (December 1965); Fred Kniffen and Henry Glassie, *Geographical Review* (January 1966). ☆

JACK TALES

Jack tales are long, episodic, oral prose narratives that chronicle the fictional adventures of a poor, teenaged Appalachian farm boy named Jack as he journeys from his home on an eventually successful quest to eliminate poverty from his and his family's lives. As C. Paige Gutierrez has shown, Jack's success is usually due to the nature of his character: a clever, quick-thinking trickster, basically virtuous and kind (but capable of cruelty, violence, and deceit), who regularly displays skill, courage, industry, perseverance, imagination, independence, and a propensity for attracting good luck and supranormal assistance. The consistency and frequency of the association of these traits with Jack essentially define the subgenre.

Jack tales are derived ultimately from an international and widely distributed fund of traditional tale types and motifs, but correspond most closely to European (especially British) *Märchen* and African trickster stories. Appalachian storytellers have combined these inherited narrative elements with their creative imaginations and regional ethos into verbal art that both reflects and informs the Appalachian worldview. Although Jack tales have been collected throughout central Appalachia (the region to which the subgenre belongs)—eastern Kentucky, eastern Tennessee, southwestern Virginia—the center of Jack tale activity seems to be the Beech Mountain area of northwestern North Carolina, in which numerous storytellers such as Ray Hicks, Stanley Hicks, and Frank Proffitt, Jr., continue to keep the tradition alive.

The standard collection of Jack tales is Richard Chase's *The Jack Tales* (1943), which includes 18 texts that Chase recovered largely on or near Beech Mountain. Unfortunately, Chase printed composite texts that were pieced together from several different performances. A valuable feature of the book is folklorist Herbert Halpert's "Appendix," in which he discusses qualities of the tales and provides copious notes on their sources and parallels.

An indispensable work of scholarship on the subject is the "Jack Tales" issue of the *North Carolina Folklore Journal* (September 1978), in which editor Thomas McGowan has assembled transcriptions of four field-collected texts and essays by C. Paige Gutierrez, W. H. Ward, and Charles T. Davis that analyze the stories in terms of distinguishing characteristics, context, setting, narrative style, literary unity, and archetypal patterns.

Storyteller Ray Hicks may be heard and seen performing Jack tales on *Ray Hicks of Beech Mountain, North Carolina, Telling Four Traditional "Jack Tales"* (Folk-Legacy Records FTA-14) and in the Appalshop film *Fixin' to Tell about Jack*. Stanley Hicks tells a fine "Jack and the Giants" on *It Still Lives* (Foxfire Records 001). Several recordings of authentic performances are housed in both the Appalachian State University Oral History Collection and the East Tennessee State University Burton-Manning Folklore Collection.

William E. Lightfoot
Appalachian State University

Richard Chase, *The Jack Tales* (1943); *North Carolina Folklore Journal* (September 1978). ☆

JOHN AND OLD MARSTER
||||||||||||||||||||||||||||||||||||||||||||||||||||||||||||||||

John and Old Marster stories represent, along with animal trickster tales, the best-known cycle of Afro-American folk narratives. Joel Chandler Harris included one such story in his various publications but apparently was unaware that it was part of an independent cycle of tales. A direct expression of the plantation black character, John is a generic figure representing the antebellum slave who enjoyed some measure of favoritism and familiarity with his owner. The slave is always called John, and the white owner is known as Old Marster or Old Boss.

The John and Old Marster narratives are concerned with the physical circumstances of slave life and reflect the various ways in which slaves regarded those who held them in bondage. Both John and Old Marster know each other well and in many tales in the cycle engage in a good-humored battle in which John's petty thefts and duplicities are exposed. In others John outwits Old Marster. In several of the John–Old Marster narratives the slaveowner prizes his favorite hand's cunning and boasts about it to other planters. This bragging usually leads to a contest that John must win to avoid losing favor. The slave always wins, either by a ruse or luck. Some John–Old Marster texts suggest the brutal side of slavery and the harsh conflict that often existed between slaves and masters.

W. K. McNeil
Ozark Folk Center
Mountain View, Arkansas

John Q. Anderson, *Southern Folklore Quarterly* (September 1961); Richard M. Dorson, *American Negro Folktales* (1967); Lawrence W. Levine, *Black Culture and Black Consciousness: Afro-American Folk Thought from Slavery to Freedom* (1977). ☆

JOHN THE CONQUEROR
ROOT

IIIIIIIIIIIIIIIIIIIIIIIIIIIIIIIIIIIIIIIIIIIIIIIIIIIIIIIIIIIIIII

Centuries of superstitions surround John the Conqueror root, or High John the Conqueror, popular names for St. John's wort, a family of plants containing about 8 genera and 400 species. Considered one of the most potent herbs for warding off evil spirits and insuring good luck, the plant figures prominently in southern folk beliefs. *Hypericum perforatum*, the species on which European myths have been based, is not common in the southeastern United States, but the name John the Conqueror root has been loosely applied to the whole family. Species such as *H. punctatum* grow in fields, woods, and ditches throughout the Southeast.

In most species the leaves, and often the yellow petals, contain oil- and pigment-filled glands that appear as translucent reddish spots when held up to the light. These spots, according to legend, are the blood of the beheaded John the Baptist, and the herb's potency can supposedly be increased through rituals surrounding St. John's birthday, 24 June.

Voodoo conjurers and other folk medicine practitioners revere the herb, which may be used in root form, as an infusion from the leaves or stems, as an oil, or as a ground-up mixture one chews or mixes with other ingredients that go into a small pouch worn around the neck. Mail-order suppliers and drugstores that stock voodoo potions carry a range of John the Conqueror products. St. John's wort, which affects the central nervous system, has been used to treat everything from dysentery to pulmonary ailments. It is best known, however, for its supernatural applications.

Voodoo conjurers evoke awe and fear when they prescribe "John de Conker." Some practitioners distinguish varieties: for example, Low John de Conker to drive away evil spirits; High, or Big, John de Conker to insure good luck; White Man de Conker to insure that a black man will get a job from a potential employer who is white; Little John de Conker to insure gambling wins. In folklore the herb can also insure a favorable outcome in court, bring bad luck to one's enemies, and ward off ghosts, witches, and nightmares.

The plant's imagery figures prominently in many aspects of Afro-American folklore. Blues masters such as Muddy Waters sing of enticing women through voodoo conjuring with John the Conqueror root, and Zora Neale Hurston's folktales celebrate the exploits of the larger-than-life hero High John de Conquer, or in some stories Big John the Conqueror. The root's mystique is directly reflected, too, in the folktale character of Old John, described by B. A. Botkin as "the wizard and 'hope-bringer' of slave days." John the Conqueror root, says Botkin, is "a fitting symbol for a slave hero as the protector, healer, and prophetic eye of his people."

Sharon A. Sharp
University of Mississippi

Benjamin A. Botkin, ed., *A Treasury of Southern Folklore* (1949); David Conway, *The Magic of Herbs* (1973); William A. Emboden, *Bizarre Plants: Magical, Monstrous, Mythical* (1974); William Ferris, *Blues from the Delta* (1979); Zora Neale Hurston, *Mules and Men* (1935); Harry Middleton Hyatt, *Hoodoo - Conjuration - Witchcraft - Rootwork*, vol. 1 (1970); William Niering and Nancy Olmstead, *The Audubon Society Field Guide to North American Wildflowers: East-*

ern Region (1979); Newbell Niles Puckett, *Folk Beliefs of the Southern Negro* (1926; reprint ed., 1968); Harold W. Rickett, *Wild Flowers of the United States: The Southeastern States*, vol. 2 (1967). ☆

JONES, CASEY
||||||||||||||||||||||||||||||||||||||||
(1863–1900) Railroad engineer.

That John Luther "Casey" Jones lived at all surprises many people. Legend and song have embellished the life of this American folk hero, the railroad's version of a Davy Crockett or an Annie Oakley.

Born 14 March in the Missouri backwoods, Jones grew up in an age when railroads captured America's imagination. When Jones was a teenager, his family moved across the Mississippi River and into the tiny Kentucky town of Cayce. There, Jones watched steam locomotives draw water from tanks alongside the Mobile & Ohio tracks. The oldest of Frank and Ann Jones's five children, Casey Jones went into railroading, as did his three brothers. His boyhood home inspired the nickname "Casey" when he went to work for the Mobile & Ohio. When Jones told his mother of the newly invented, air-hose brakes for trains, she quoted him in her journal, saying that "riding on the train will be as safe as attending church."

In 1886 Jones married Jane Brady, the daughter of a boardinghouse proprietor in Jackson, Tenn., and there they made their home and brought up three children. By the time Jones was in his mid-20s, he worked for the Illinois Central, which promoted him to engineer. As he barreled through the countryside and cities along a line that ran through 13 states, his reputation grew as a man who liked to run his trains

fast. Those who lived near the tracks knew when Jones passed by: the whistle sounded like a whippoorwill call in the night.

Just before midnight on 29 April 1900, Jones pulled his train into Memphis. He had come from Canton, Miss., to the south and was told he would have to return to Canton with the Cannonball Express, a six-car train with passengers. The engineer scheduled to make the run was sick.

You could set your watch by Jones's trains. Considered the Illinois Central's fastest, the Cannonball on this night was 95 minutes behind schedule. Jones and his fireman, Sim T. Webb, worked hard to speed the 188 miles to Canton. In the foggy darkness at Vaughan, 12 miles north of Canton, Jones spotted the caboose lights of a train ahead. Jones told Webb to jump and he did. Jones stayed with the train. The Cannonball rammed into four cars of a freight laden with hay, corn, and lumber. The rest of the freight, stalled due to a broken air hose, was on a side track. Reports later said Jones perhaps did not see warning signals.

Jones was killed. He was the only fatality in an accident not noteworthy at a time of spectacular train wrecks. But a song, written by Wallace Saunders, soon made the crash the most celebrated of train wrecks. Saunders, a black railroad worker, was a friend and coworker of Jones, who was white.

In 1909, long after Jones was buried in Mt. Calvary Cemetery at Jackson, Tenn., the vaudeville team of T. Laurence Seibert and Eddie Newton revised Saunders's ballad. They set their story in the western United States, and it served as the basis for some 200 other versions, evoking train whistles and rumbling locomotives. Mississippi John

Hurt, the blues singer; the Grateful Dead, a rock group; and even a Boy Scout songbook commemorate Casey Jones. Yet most of these songs only remotely record what really happened in the early morning of 30 April 1900, on the edge of the Mississippi Delta.

Berkley Hudson
Providence, Rhode Island

Benjamin A. Botkin and Alvin F. Harlow, eds., *A Treasury of Railroad Folklore: The Stories, Tall Tales, Ballads, and Songs of the American Railroad Man* (1953); G. Malcolm Laws, *Native American Balladry* (rev. ed., 1964); Fred J. Lee, *Casey Jones* (1939). ☆

LUM, RAY

(1891–1976) Mule trader.

Lum was born on 25 June 1891 in Rocky Springs, Miss., a rural community of about 75 people located on the Natchez Trace. His grandmother reared him, and during childhood he milked cows, herded cattle and goats, and trained horses. At the age of 12 he moved to Vicksburg and was a delivery boy for two years in local stores. His trading career began at 14, when he bought a horse for $12.50 and sold it for $25.00. This trade launched him on a long and varied life during which he bought and sold livestock in every area of the United States. His base of operations was Vicksburg, where at one time he owned five stables and hundreds of horses and mules.

As a young man, Ray Lum traded with gypsies who were said to "hoodoo" horses because of their ability to make a plug look like a fine animal. From Vicksburg he traveled up the Sunflower River into the Mississippi Delta, where he sold horses and mules to farmers. Shortly thereafter he began regular trips to Texas to acquire the trainloads of stock that he auctioned at his three barns in Vicksburg.

Lum moved to Texas in 1922 and established a central sale barn in Fort Worth that was managed by his partner and ring man, Harry Barnett. Lum then set up throughout west Texas local sales run by "six Mississippians and thirty Texans." He shipped stock to every barn in the region and personally auctioned the animals on a partnership basis with his local managers. During this time he introduced night sales, where both buyers and stock could escape the Texas heat. After fifteen years of auctioning in Texas, Lum returned to live in Vicksburg. At this time (1937) he introduced registered Hereford cattle into the Deep South to upgrade the quality of beef.

As late as 1967 he auctioned uninterrupted for hours at large sales in Atlanta and Birmingham. Failing eyesight eventually forced him to withdraw from the extended auctions of his earlier years because he could no longer see bids. As recently as 1976, Lum traveled

Ray Lum, quintessential trader, Vicksburg, Mississippi, 1973

each week to sales in Mississippi at Lorman, Vicksburg, Port Gibson, Natchez, and Hazlehurst. He drove a large car filled with "everything pertaining to a horse." Bridles, bits, and curry combs were piled on the dashboard; boxes of hats and boots covered the back seat; saddles filled the trunk; and cans of ribbon cane syrup lined the back floor.

As a trader, Lum was adept at both humor and deception. At times he offered the customer veiled truth that only seasoned traders would understand. Ray Lum began as an "angel" (inexperienced buyer) when as a child he sold his wagon and team of goats in Port Gibson, Miss., for $20 after being promised $25. "That was one of the best lessons I ever got. That was the best five dollars ever I earned." He was beaten in this trade but afterwards was "awake." He learned from his mistakes and quickly became a shrewd judge of animals and people.

Ray Lum defined a trader as "a man that trades in everything. A real trader don't never find nothing that he can't use. If he is a trader—and you're looking at one right now—he will trade you for anything you have got. If he can't use it, he'll find someone else that can. There is lots of people that can take a pocket knife and run it into a barrel of money, and there are a lot of people that you can give a barrel of money and won't be long until they won't even have the pocket knife. It's all in who it is trading. Yes sir, I think traders are born." Ray Lum preserved his world through tales of men and animals he knew: "When you get 85 years old, you outlive all your friends. That's the bad part of being old; you can't find nobody to talk to about things that happened back there. They're all gone. You live

and learn. And then you die and forget it all."

William Ferris
University of Mississippi

William Ferris, *Ray Lum: Mule Trader* (1976); Ben Green, *Some More Horse Tradin'* (1972); Edward Mayhew, *Illustrated Horse Management, Containing Descriptive Remarks upon Anatomy, Medicine, Shoeing, Teeth, Food, Vices, Stables* (1864). ☆

MEADERS, LANIER
||||||||||||||||||||||||||||||||||||||||||||||||||
(b. 1917). Potter.

Quillian Lanier Meaders of Cleveland, White County, Ga., is identified with a domestic ceramics industry that flourished in parts of the rural South through the first quarter of the present century. Loosely organized in cottage-industry fashion, southern potters settled around their clay sources, combining craft work with farming. Technical skills were transferred rather informally through the male line, resulting in the formation of potter dynasties spanning several generations.

The Meaders family came to pottery making during the winter months of late 1892 through early 1893. Lanier's grandfather, John Milton Meaders (1850–1942), had earlier freighted ceramic ware, along with farm produce, for several artisans in clay-rich White County and evidently saw financial benefit in the work. He therefore directed his six sons (Wiley, Caulder, Cleater, Casey, Lewis Quillian, and Cheever) to build a ware shop and kiln on the family property where, with assistance from their neighbors, they commenced manufacturing stoneware preserve jars, dairy crocks, and sorghum syrup or whiskey jugs. A distinctive feature of the local product, one confined in the main to ware made in Georgia and contiguous parts of the Carolinas and Alabama, was the application of lime and wood-ash (alkaline) glazes. The family's "face jugs"—sometimes grotesque—are striking examples of how a simple jug can be molded to resemble a human face.

Though demand for ceramic vessels subsided after 1910, as glass and metal containers penetrated into local farm kitchens, the Meaders family sustained a limited market for their ware. Their persistence in this regard was first noted in Alan H. Eaton's *Handicrafts of the Southern Highlands* (1937). For three more decades, Cheever Meaders (1887–1967), the youngest of the original Meaders potters, derived a marginal livelihood from the production of alkaline-glazed stoneware, which he sold to local customers and to tourists.

Lanier Meaders, Cheever's bachelor son, continues today to manufacture the same traditional ware, employing a similar repertoire of tools and techniques as his forebears. His preservation efforts have won for him not only a devoted following of folk art collectors and crafts enthusiasts, but have encouraged a brother, Edwin, and a cousin, Cleater, Jr., to resume the work as well. In recognition of such efforts and the assistance he has provided folklife researchers in their attempts to reconstruct the history of southern industry, Lanier Meaders in 1983 was awarded a National Heritage Fellowship.

Robert Sayers
California Academy of Sciences

John A. Burrison, *Brothers in Clay: The Story of Georgia Folk Pottery* (1983); Ralph Rinzler and Robert Sayers, *The Meaders Family: North Georgia Potters*, Smithsonian Folklife Studies No. 1 (1980); Nancy Sweezy, *Raised in Clay: The Southern Pottery Tradition* (1984). ☆

MOBILE HOMES

Variously disparaged as tramps, Okies, and tin-can tourists, over 40,000 people took part in the Dust Bowl migration of the 1930s. Integral to their trek south and west was something akin to the ancient Hudson described in Steinbeck's *Grapes of Wrath*. "Half passenger car and half truck, high-sided and clumsy," it was the homegrown equivalent to the compact manufactured trailer first built in 1929 by the Covered Wagon Company of Detroit. Nine by six feet, complete with folding bunks and a coal-burning stove, early mobile homes met the need for mobility and inexpensive shelter for itinerant job seekers and tourists alike. By 1936 the industry was one of the fastest growing in the nation.

At first used interchangeably, the terms *trailer* and *mobile home* soon became distinct. World War II demonstrated the usefulness of mobile homes

Table 1. *Top 10 States in Manufactured Home Shipments in 1984*

State	Number of Homes
Texas	37,462
Florida	30,990
North Carolina	24,637
Georgia	17, 879
South Carolina	15,074
Louisiana	11,432
Alabama	11,318
California	10,425
Tennessee	6,834
Arizona	6,694

Source: Manufactured Housing Institute.

as low-cost housing on job sites. They became larger (10 feet wide was standard by 1955; 12 to 14 feet wide by the 1960s) and increasingly less mobile. In the rural South they often took the place of traditional folk or vernacular housing.

Like the tenant farmhouse of Alabama, described by James Agee as "an enlarged crate or box, scarcely modified to human use," the flat-roofed, metal-sided mobile home was basic, economical shelter, unconcerned with fashionable design or detail. Like the traditional shotgun house, it was linear in design—one room wide and two rooms deep—and could be placed short end to the road where lots were narrow or land expensive. A trailer often substituted for the small house out back or the additional rooms customarily added onto the family home when children married and families grew.

Mobile homes have increased dramatically in size; 16-foot-wide versions are now manufactured in Texas and multiple-section double wides are popular. Often "skirted" in sheet metal, brick, or wood to disguise wheels, with foundations, pitched and shingled roofs, cathedral ceilings, and "tip-outs" or bay window alcoves, many are all but indistinguishable from conventional site-built homes. Although still taxed as motor vehicles in some states, mobile homes gained a greater recognition as real estate through 1984 federal legislation allowing Veterans' Administration mortgage financing on the same basis as that provided for conventional housing. The relative immobility and appearance of permanence in modern mobile homes also improved the low-rent image of mobile homes and the transient stereotype of the people who live in them. In 1976 the industry officially adopted the term *manufactured housing*.

About 54 percent of today's manufactured homes are placed on individually owned property in rural or small-town locations. The majority of these homes end up in the South. Of the top 10 states in manufactured home shipments in 1984, 8 were southern, with the high growth states of Texas and Florida in the lead. Whether as unpretentious low-income rural housing, a temporary outbuilding, or part of a lushly landscaped retirement community, the mobile home has altered the topography of the southern landscape.

Elizabeth M. Makowski
University of Mississippi

Jean Hess Bergmark, *Kentucky Folklore Record* (January–December 1981); *Builder* (March 1984); Margaret J. Drury, *Mobile Homes: The Unrecognized Revolution in American Housing* (1972); John Brinckerhoff Jackson, *Discovering the Vernacular Landscape* (1984); Virginia McAlester and Lee McAlester, *A Field Guide to American Houses* (1984); *Manufactured Housing Quarterly* (Fall 1984); Charles W. Moore et al., eds., *Home Sweet Home: American Domestic Architecture* (1983); *New York Times* (20 April 1985); Michael Aaron Rockland, *Homes on Wheels* (1980). ☆

MULES

The South developed a regional culture of "mules and men" that spanned 200 years. The mule is a hybrid, born of a horse and an ass, and unable to reproduce. Southerners fervently endorsed the mule in preference to the horse, and defenders of the mule ranged from George Washington to thousands of small farmers throughout the South. The father of our country has also been called the "father" of American mule breeding, for Washington praised the animal and commented on the "great strength of mules, on their longevity, hardiness, and cheap support which gives them a preference over horses that is scarcely to be imagined." Washington bred mules on his farm, and when he died his will listed 57 mules. Other prominent mule owners in his period included Thomas Jefferson and John Skinner, editor of *American Farmer.*

Robert Lamb outlines three periods in which mules were widely used throughout the South: (1) antebellum (1850–60); (2) Civil War and westward expansion (1860–1900); and (3) southern rural economy (1900–25). As tractors were introduced (1925–50), mules declined in importance.

Travelers in the antebellum South often commented on the strength of mules and the diverse labors they performed. In Virginia, Frederick Law Olmsted noted, "Immense wagons drawn by six mules each, the teamster always riding on the back of the rear wheeler, are a characteristic feature of the streets." Olmsted marveled that mules that were roughly treated, poorly fed, and overworked continued to perform in good health. The animals pulled deep-running plows during both seeding and cultivation, and because of their speed and strength they were preferred to oxen.

In every period of southern history the roles of the mule and of black people were intimately linked. As slaves before the Civil War and as tenant farmers afterward, blacks worked with mules and both were essential to the southern economy. In 1925, for example, 84 percent of the mule farmers in the Mississippi Valley were black. During that period in Anderson, S.C., the money spent on mules each day exceeded the daily wages of blacks. The mule cost an

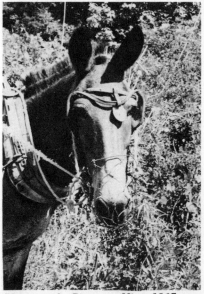

Plowing mule, Picayune, Miss., 1967

average of $1.32 per day to work and blacks were paid $1.25 per day. Blues singer Huddie "Leadbelly" Ledbetter sang a mule-skinner blues with the verse:

Honey, I'm down in the bottom, skinnin' for Johnny Ryan. Putting my initials, honey, on the mule's behind. With my line baby, with my line babe, with my line babe.

Blacks knew their mules so well that whites often felt they had a special gift to read the mule's thoughts.

Some white writers argued that only mules could endure the rough treatment accorded by black workers. This may sometimes have been the case during slavery, but accounts by blacks who owned their stock show that great care and love was shown for the animals. Nate Shaw (Ned Cobb), an Alabama sharecropper, stressed "my mules was more than slaves to me. . . . She'd make you a living if you plowed her right . . . you had to be careful with her." Shaw took such care of his mules that a neighbor once accused him of worshipping them. Shaw's mules worked to his voice commands. After picking up the lines and calling "All right, babies, let's get to it," says Shaw, "you'd see them big heifers fall out then. Oh, my mules just granted me all the pleasure I needed, to see what I had and how they moved." Shaw's mules were probably raised outside the South and shipped to his county by traders.

Most mules were raised in the border states and shipped to the "southern market." The prosperity of mule farms in the border states was directly proportional to that of southern farmers. When cotton and tobacco prices boomed, the mule business prospered. One of the biggest mule markets was Columbia, Tenn., where thousands of animals were raised and sold each year. Will Rogers called it "the biggest street mule market in the world. What the thoroughfare of Wall Street will do to you if you don't know what a stock is, Columbia will do to you if you don't know a mule. Maiden Lane, New York City, for diamonds, but Mule Street in Columbia for Mules." Mules were classed according to size and were sold for a wide variety of uses. Their major classes were (1) sugar mules (for southern sugar plantations), (2) rice and cotton mules, (3) levee mules (for Mississippi River levee work), (4) mine mules, (5) railroad mules, and (6) mountaineer pack mules. In addition to meeting these needs, Columbia supplied 5,000 mules purchased by the British army in 1916.

Mules reached their ascendancy in southern history during the first 25 years of this century. Their number doubled from 2½ million in 1900 to 4½ million in 1925, when almost four-fifths of the mules in the United States were in the South. During this period extensive re-search was done on the feeding and housing of mules and the relative merit of mules versus tractors, and as tractors began to replace them in 1931, writers argued that both were necessary for the successful farmer.

The number of horses and mules in the country peaked at almost 26 million in 1920 and declined to less than 4 million in 1958. As their numbers declined, those who remained were concentrated in the South. When tractors displaced horses and mules in the West, traders bought the animals and shipped them to southern farmers. During the period from 1937 to 1946 prices for horses and mules declined in every area of the country except in the South.

When southern farmers bought tractors this last mule market disappeared and the animals were slaughtered for animal food. During the 1950s half the horses and mules sold by farmers each year—more than 357,000 animals—were converted into cat and dog food. Their death signaled the end of an era; and one trader reflected, "I lived in a day when a man and a mule worked together. Now they've pensioned the man and eaten the mule."

In *The Reivers* (1962) William Faulkner wrote this eloquent tribute to the animal:

[A] mule is far too intelligent to break its heart for glory running around the rim of a mile-long saucer. In fact, I rate mules second only to rats in intelligence . . . assuming of course that you accept my definition of intelligence: which is the ability to cope with environment; which means to accept environment yet still retain at least something of personal liberty. . . . [The mule] will work for you patiently for ten years for the chance to kick you once. In a word, free of the obligations of ancestry and the responsibilities of posterity, he has conquered not only life but death too and hence is immortal; were he to vanish from the earth today, the same chanceful biological combination which produced him yesterday would produce him a thousand years hence, unaltered, unchanged, incorrigible still within the limitations which he himself had proved and tested; still free, still coping.

William Ferris
University of Mississippi

William Ferris, *North Carolina Folklore Journal* (September 1973); Robert Byron Lamb, *The Mule in Southern Agriculture* (1963); Frederick Law Olmsted, *A Journey in the Seaboard Slave States in the Years 1853–1854, with Remarks on Their Economy* (1904); U. B. Phillips, *Life and Labor in the Old South* (1957); B. D. Raskopf and M. T. Danner, *Public Horse and Mule Market at Nashville, Tennessee* (1947); Theodore Rosengarten, *All God's Dangers: The Life of Nate Shaw* (1974); James Westfall Thompson, *A History of Livestock Raising in the United States* (1942). ☆

MURDER LEGENDS
||||||||||||||||||||||||||||||||||||||||||||||

Legends are oral prose narratives about extraordinary persons, places, and events that are usually told in a conversational style. Acts of murder are, of course, unusual, and as they explode the most fundamental rule of social order, stories about them understandably persist in oral tradition.

Stories about murders are in all likelihood universal, and though they have a tendency to become localized, some become widely known through the media and the composition of narrative folksongs. In fact, most of the following murder legends also exist in ballad form.

Many prominent southern murder legends center upon the murderers, but in others the victims are dominant. Examples of the former include stories about such men and women as Alabama's Morris "Railroad Bill" Slater; Talt Hall, Doc "Red Rox" Taylor, and the Harpe brothers in Kentucky; Mississippi's Kinnie Wagner; Frankie Silvers and Tom Dula in North Carolina; Claud Allen of Virginia; and John Hardy in West Virginia. Legends in which the victims are central are those concerning Georgia's Mary Phagan; Kentucky's Pearl Bryan, Lulu Voyers, and Sammie Adams; Naomi Wise and Ella May Wiggins in North Carolina; South Carolina's Theodosia Burr Alston; and the Mormons killed at Cane Creek, Tenn. In legends about feuds (e.g., Kentucky's Jones-Wright, Martin-Tolliver, Hatfield-McCoy; Tennessee's Kelly-Turney), it is difficult to distinguish the aggressors from the victims.

A number of southern murder legends (like ones involving death by conjuring or voodoo, death by witchcraft as in Tennessee's "Bell Witch" stories, the ineradicable bloodstain, the corpse rising to accuse its murderer) contain supranormal themes that set them apart from the "historical" legends just cited.

See also VIOLENCE: / Hatfields and McCoys

William E. Lightfoot
Appalachian State University

Olive Wooley Burt, *American Murder Ballads and Their Stories* (1958); Richard M.

Dorson, *America in Legend: Folklore from the Colonial Period to the Present* (1973). ☆

NEEDLEWORK
|||||||||||||||||||||||||||||||||||||||

Through the years, women in the North and the South have created and produced needlework in many forms. Samplers, needlepoint (known as canvas work in the 18th century and as Berlin work in the 19th), crewelwork, drawnwork, beadwork, and lacework are examples of a craft practiced widely in the South. As early as 1766 a teacher in Virginia advertised instruction in "Petit Point in Flowers, Fruit, Landscape, . . . Embroidery in silk, Gold, Silver, Pearls or embossed, . . . Dresden Point Work, Lace." Of course, southern women have in the past been proficient also in sewing, usually providing clothing and other sewn items for their households.

Although often learning needlework skills from family members, many women learned the craft at female academies. There were several such institutions in the South, one of the best known being the Salem Female Academy, founded and operated by the Moravian community at Salem, N.C. Recognized for their needlework skills, the Pennsylvania Moravians were the first to teach silk embroidery in this country. The close interaction between the two groups of Moravians allowed the transfer of skills, techniques, and designs. One common motif frequently seen on Salem samplers, for example, is the covered well. The Moravian community produced many of the extant examples of early southern needlework and influenced its development and style throughout the South.

Though usually not easily distinguished from northern work, southern needlework can sometimes be identified by the prolonged presence of early designs and motifs. Southern samplers do not exist as abundantly as do northern ones. Early examples exist, however, such as the one made by Elizabeth Hext in 1743 in Charleston, S.C. She embroidered on her sampler "Elizabeth Hext is My Name Carolina is My Nation / Charles Town is My Dwelling Place and Christ is My / Salvation." Two samplers dated around 1865 carry distinctly southern scenes that depict the joy of freed slaves. Below four dancing blacks on a piece worked by Elizabeth Jane Hawkes in Salem, N.C., are the words "Hurrah Hurrah Hurrah / We come from Carolina and are all free now."

Southern scenes are found on needlework by other southern artists as well. On her needlework pictures, Ethel Wright Mohamed (b. 1907) of Belzoni,

Ethel Mohamed, needlework artist, Belzoni, Mississippi, 1976

Miss., embroiders scenes recalled from her own past. Sacred harp singing, other folk traditions, and experiences from her life and her family's life in Mississippi provide illustrations of a place and of a way of life. Thus, her work is uniquely southern. Other southern needleworkers have created motifs, scenes, and pieces that may not always be so readily identified with the South, but they have in great numbers participated in a craft, utilitarian and decorative, that has been widely popular and practiced throughout the region since its earliest years of settlement. The Mung people who have recently moved from Cambodia to Memphis have introduced detailed, colorful needlework, which they sell to supplement family income. Their designs are abstract and provide an interesting contrast to traditional southern examples.

See also RELIGION: / Moravians

> Jessica Foy
> Cooperstown Graduate Programs
> Cooperstown, New York

Elizabeth Donaghy Garret, *Antiques* (September 1978); Robert Morton, *Southern Antiques and Folk Art* (1976); Betty Ring, *Antiques* (October 1971, September 1974); Cynthia Elyce Rubin, ed., *Southern Folk Art* (1985). ☆

OKRA
||||||||||||||

If a southerner with a predilection for both ancestor worship and cooking decided to form a First Families of Vegetables society, okra would be a charter member. Thomas Jefferson recorded planting it and reported its cultivation in Virginia before 1781. It had reached Louisiana shortly after 1700.

Okra (*Hibiscus esculentus*) is a member of the mallow family (*Malvaceae*) as are cotton, hibiscus, and hollyhocks. The okra pod is a tapering, five-sided capsule containing numerous round seeds, and its best-known quality is its gummy, mucilaginous juice.

The word *okra* is *nkru* is the Ashanti language of West Africa; Accra, the name of the capital of Ghana, comes from the same root word. In Bantu, the language family of southern Africa, it is called *ngombo*, from which our word *gumbo* comes; *gumbo* and *okra* have been used interchangeably to refer to the vegetable.

Probably okra was first cultivated in Africa, and from there it spread to India (where it is called "lady fingers"). It was recorded in Egypt in the 13th century. Okra could have come to the South with Africans, either directly or via the West Indies, or it could have been brought in by European colonists who knew that it would grow in a warm climate. It is planted in early spring and matures in about eight weeks. Southern agricultural specialists tried to breed out okra's prickly outer surface with the Clemson Spineless variety.

Okra has vitamins A and C and a 3.5-ounce serving has about 29 calories. This, of course, does not apply to that favorite southern dish, fried okra, in which the cornmeal-salt-pepper coating and the bacon drippings in the frying pan add to the calorie count. Okra can be pickled, stewed with tomatoes, or— best of all—used as the thickening base for gumbo, a rich stew of seafood or meat.

Okra, like the peanut, has a myriad of uses: southerners have used it to staunch bleeding, substitute for plasma, make a coarse cloth or paper, adorn dried flower arrangements, produce seed necklaces, clean metal, unstop drains, increase milk yield of cows, and provide a poor coffee substitute from roasted and ground seeds. Raw okra will also adhere to the nose and forehead for a speedy Halloween mask.

Carolyn Kolb
New Orleans, Louisiana

Alphonse Pyramus de Candolle, *Origin of Cultivated Plants* (1884); Carroll Lane Fenton and Herminie B. Kitchen, *Plants We Live On: The Story of Grains and Vegetables* (1971); Thomas Jefferson, *Thomas Jefferson's Garden Book, 1766–1824* (1944); Sonia L. Nazario, *Wall Street Journal* (21 January 1983); Eileen Tighe, *Woman's Day Encyclopedia of Cookery* (1966). ☆

PLAY-PARTY
||||||||||||||||||||||||||||||||||

The play-party is a ritual event in which people gather to play singing games that feature dance movements; it is also a game played at such parties. These gatherings were known in other parts of the United States as "evening party," "flang party," "fuss," "frolic," "gin-around," "bounce around," and "bounce-about." Generally, the play-party is considered an activity for young people in rural settings, an assumption that is not altogether correct. Adults also attended play-parties and at one time they were common in urban as well as country surroundings. Religious prejudice against dancing was one reason for the popularity of play-parties, in contrast to true dances. Equally important was the flexible nature of the play-party, which required no musicians and thus could be arranged on short notice. It was not unique to the South but was popular there longer than elsewhere.

Typically, the play-party was organized by one or two young men looking for diversion and entertainment. In many rural communities homes were small, with rough native lumber floors and, more often than not, a bed in the front room that had to be removed to make space for the games. In good weather the play-party was held in the front yard. The games consisted of players swinging one another by the hand instead of by the waist, to the accompaniment of their own singing. Such devices as chasing and kissing as a means of choosing or stealing a partner were popular. Some games featured swinging or marching movements. "Skip to My Lou," which is derived from "Bull in the Park," was a popular accompaniment for these movements. Much of the song repertoire was borrowed from popular song ("Buffalo Gals," "Captain Jenks," "Old Dan Tucker") or, less often, religious song ("I Want To Be An Angel").

The activity itself is much older than the term *play-party*, which apparently came into widespread use only in the early years of the 20th century. A reference to the play-party in a 1902 Houston, Mo., newspaper is the earliest known printed use of the term. This traditional activity remained a vital form of amusement in the South until just prior to World War II when it went into decline, in large part because of the availability of other forms of inexpensive mass entertainment. Play-parties are seldom performed now, except by revival groups, but the songs are still remembered and sung.

W. K. McNeil
Ozark Folk Center
Mountain View, Arkansas

Benjamin A. Botkin, *The American Play-Party Song; with a Collection of Oklahoma Texts and Tunes* (1937); David S. McIntosh, *Folk Songs and Singing Games of the Illinois Ozarks* (1974); William A. Owens, *Swing and Turn: Texas Play-Party Games* (1936); Vance Randolph, *Journal of American Folklore* (July–September 1929). ☆

PORCHES
||||||||||||||||||||||||||

The distinction between southern porches and American porches is one both of kind and of degree. Although black and white southerners have traditionally used a variety of porch types in a variety of locations, the important "porch" for the student of southern culture is the public/private space across the front of a building.

Until the mid-19th century, only in the South were dwellings—"big houses" on the great plantations, slave cabins, and everything in between— routinely equipped with sitting porches, and since the decline of the bungalow, only in the South are new houses still equipped with front porches. The style of the porch and its supports has signaled the social status of those who use it. For example, two-story porches graced with Doric columns traditionally mean wealth and power; today imitations of such porches appear on banks, motels, and other establishments that wish to attract the would-be wealthy or powerful. Porches supported with incompletely trimmed posts, on the other hand, suggest working-class inhabitants.

These status delineations owe something to the history of the southern porch. While Thomas Jefferson, George Washington, and their contemporaries were searching for a truly American architecture, African slaves and less prominent white emigrants from the West Indies were adapting the architecture of their homelands to the American milieu. The porches on classic southern buildings may have borrowed from ancient Greek porticos, but the front porch as extended living space almost surely owes a great debt to the experience in dealing with an inhospitably hot and humid climate, experience that Africans and West Indians brought with them to the American South. Early aristocratic southern architecture (in Charleston, S.C., for instance), hid side galleries behind traditional European flush fronts; only after slaves and small farmers had demonstrated its usefulness for decades did influential southerners adopt the wide, columned-front porch. The development of screen porches, a bridge perhaps between the openness of the traditional front porch and the confinement of today's air-conditioned South, is unclear, but wire mesh itself can be traced to the looms of early 19th-century Shakers. Although southerners did adapt screen to their own needs for protection from insects and for increased privacy, the move indoors occasioned by widespread air-conditioning meant that the screen porch would remain, in modern times, more prevalent in non-southern America than in the South.

Southern porches have traditionally been transitional spaces between indoors and out where marginally welcomed guests could be entertained without violating the sanctity of the home. The races could comingle when necessary or desirable, and visitors on business could escape the elements while plying their trade. Much of the southern reputation for hospitality must emanate from the ubiquitous porch.

Even though pervasive air-conditioning makes the porch almost unnecessary today, new middle-class homes continue to sport vestigial porches with skinny imitations of grand columns, perhaps still to suggest affluence and power. And they continue to be furnished—albeit with antique wooden and wrought-iron benches useless for sitting but redolent of ancestry and hospitality. Spacious porches of older middle-class homes are also furnished—often with an abundance of rockers, gliders, and swings whose careful arrangement and spotless white paint imply that the furniture is for show rather than for sitting. These porches indicate not only concern with appearances but an unwillingness to relinquish bygone graciousness.

Southern porches have been used to entertain, to prepare food, to wash clothes and bodies, and to provide sheltered play space for children, but their most important ongoing use is to transmit folklore. Children continue to invent games designed around the architecture of a particular porch style, and fabled southern storytellers gather with family and friends on porches to benefit from any possible breeze and to regale each other with tales. Today's older southerners, unwilling to adjust to ubiquitous air-conditioning, pass family lore to children and grandchildren on ancestral porches, and folklorists as far back as Zora Neale Hurston in the 1930s have gathered the lore of the South on the porches of southerners.

Sue Bridwell Beckham
University of Wisconsin–Stout

Barrie B. Greenbie, *Spaces: Dimensions of the Human Landscape* (1981); Richard L. Perry, *Journal of American Culture* (Summer 1985); Davida Rochlin, *Home Sweet Home: American Domestic Architecture*, ed. Charles W. Moore et al. (1983); Ovid Vickers, *Mississippi Folklore Register* (Fall 1978); John Michael Vlach, *The Afro-American Tradition in Decorative Arts* (1978). ☆

POWERS, HARRIET

(1837–1911) Quilter.

Two quilts, beautifully crafted and historically significant, are the legacy of Harriet Powers, who was born a slave in Georgia on 29 October 1837. These quilts, classic examples of the appliqué technique, are also of interest because of Harriet Powers's use of the narrative folk tradition. One of the quilts, owned by the Smithsonian Institution, illustrates biblical stories; the second, at the Museum of Fine Arts in Boston, depicts biblical tales as well as local legends and astronomical occurences. Stories of the hog named Betts, who ran from Georgia to Virginia, and the man frozen at his jug of liquor are two of the illustrations in the Boston Powers quilt. The stories appear to be local, but each is actually the plot of a traditional folk narrative, which has been recorded in several versions. Legendary accounts of actual phenomena (eclipses, meteors, and comets) were intermingled with traditional motifs by Powers.

Central to Powers's religious symbols are the legends of biblical heroes such as Noah, Moses, Jonah, and Job, all of whom struggled successfully against overwhelming odds. The serpent of the Garden of Eden is portrayed with feet before it suffered God's curse; Adam's rib, from which Eve was made, is prominently featured. Harriet Powers's fascination with biblical animals and characters stemmed from her attendance at southern churches where vivid sermons, which she committed to memory, were the order of the day, according to Jennie Smith, a white woman who purchased the first Powers quilt.

Although narrative quilts are a distinctly American art form, the appliqué technique evident in Powers's quilts is traceable to Eastern and Middle Eastern civilizations with discernible roots in African culture. Harriet Powers's quilts form a link to the tapestries traditionally made by the Fon people of Abomey, the ancient capital of Dahomey in West Africa. Fon people brought to the South their knowledge of appliqué, which had been executed by men in Dahomey but was perpetuated by slave women in America.

Gladys-Marie Fry
University of Maryland

Marie J. Adams, in *Afro-American Folk Art and Crafts*, ed. William Ferris (1983); Gladys-Marie Fry, *Missing Pieces: Georgia Folk Art* (1976). ☆

PROVERBS

As metaphors of collective experience, southern proverbs embody the emphasis of the folk on generalized wisdom. The southern proverb repertoire seems to serve some southerners as a set of universal laws against which individual experience is measured. With their characteristic use of metaphor and their perceptions of similarity and difference, southern proverbs remain close to both poetry and philosophy. Proverbs have served several generations of southerners as guides to appropriate behavior and as informal channels of education. They are still in widespread use today.

Southern proverbs have their roots in the Old World, especially in Europe and Africa. Europeans and Africans alike adapted their traditions of proverb usage to a new natural and social environment in the South. The African preference for indirect and highly ambiguous speech, both as an aesthetic variation on drab everyday discourse and as a means of avoiding the sometimes painful effects and insults of direct commentary, had a counterpart in the South in the European proverb tradition. That tradition included British proverbs stretching from the 16th century's "Beggars cannot be choosers" and the 15th century's "Eat us out of house and home" to the 14th century's "Look before you leap" and the 12th century's "You can lead a horse to water, but you can't make him drink." That tradition also included such literary proverbs as St. Augustine's "When in Rome, do as the Romans do" and the classical Greek proverb "A rolling stone gathers no moss." Biblical proverbs, such as "Cast your bread upon the waters," "Pride goeth before a fall," and "Money is the root of all evil" were particularly widespread in the South. In the colonial period southern folk tradition also absorbed proverbs from Benjamin Franklin's *Poor Richard's Almanac*, such as "A word to the wise is sufficient" and "Early to bed and early to rise makes a man healthy, wealthy, and wise." Such proverbs are still used across the South.

Like all forms of folklore, proverb wording is subject to variation, but structural patterns of proverbs are relatively fixed. The most common structural forms in southern proverbs are simple positive or negative propositions, such as "Beauty is in the eye of the beholder" or "Nobody's perfect." But double propositions ("Everybody talks about the weather, but nobody does anything about it" or "Young folks, listen to what old folks say, when danger is near keep out of the way") are common in southern tradition, and triple propositions ("So I totes my powder and sulphur and I carries my stick in my hand and I puts my trust in God") are not unknown. Multiple propositions provide an apt structure for making invidious distinctions, as in the biblical "Man proposes, but God disposes."

In their proverbs, southerners make distinctions by comparison and contrast. They emphasize the equivalence of things ("Seeing is believing") or they deny it ("All that glitters is not gold"). Or they emphasize that one thing is bigger, or of greater value than another, as in "His eyes are bigger than his belly," "A bird in the hand is worth two in the bush," and "Half a loaf is better than none." Proverbs purport to explain how things come about ("Politics makes strange bedfellows" and "New brooms sweep clean") or to deny causation ("Barking dogs don't bite" and "Two wrongs don't make a right").

An important attribute of southern proverbs is their sense of authority, deriving partly from their detachment from common speech and partly from their allusive poetic nature. They are set off from ordinary discourse by such poetic devices as alliteration ("The proof of the pudding is in the eating" and "A miss is as good as a mile"), rhyme ("A friend in need is a friend indeed" and "Haste makes waste"), repetition ("All's well that ends well" and "No news is good news"), meter ("Nothing ventured, nothing gained" and "A word to the wise is sufficient"), and parallelism ("Like father, like son" and "The more he has, the more he wants").

Because of their poetic qualities

(their allusiveness and ambiguity), proverbs may be cited with equal authority in a broad range of situations. Their flexibility has sometimes made proverbs seem contradictory to modern readers. Are two heads better than one, or do too many cooks spoil the broth? Some proverbs used by southerners tout the virtues of cautious conservatism ("Look before you leap," "Rome wasn't built in a day," and "Haste makes waste"), whereas others, equally authentic, urge hearers to "Strike while the iron is hot" (similarly, "Time and tide wait for no man," "He who hesitates is lost"). But proverbs are not really contradictory. Just as a language gives its speakers words with which to praise or to criticize as necessary, the southern proverb repertoire enables southerners to offer whatever advice seems appropriate to a particular situation, to advise either action or inaction, and to do so through heightened poetic language.

In offering advice, a southern proverb might pursue either of two strategies. It might recommend acceptance of the situation or it might recommend action to relieve the situation. "Put up or shut up" and "Nothing ventured, nothing gained" are examples of the *action* strategy. Some proverbs counsel defensive action, such as "A stitch in time saves nine" and "An apple a day keeps the doctor away." Some *acceptance* strategy proverbs suggest that the situation is normal ("Accidents will happen" and "Boys will be boys"); thus, no action is called for. Some urge their hearers not to overreact ("Look before you leap" and "Barking dogs don't bite"). Others counsel patience, for troubles come and troubles go ("March comes in like a lion, but goes out like a lamb"). Some even suggest that the hearer is responsible for the situation and must accept the consequences ("You've made your bed, now you have to lie in it"). Yet other proverbs maintain that, no matter how hard the misfortune may seem, it can be borne ("Every back is fitted to the burden").

Though relatively simple in form, proverbs are perhaps the most complex of all folklore genres in their extreme sensitivity to context. The meaning and distinctiveness of the southern proverb does not lie in its form or content, but in the context of its use. And those contexts range as widely and deeply as southern life itself.

Charles Joyner
University of South Carolina
Coastal Campus

F. A. DeCaro and W. K. McNeil, *American Proverb Literature* (1970); Alan Dundes, *Analytic Essays in Folklore* (1975); Charles Joyner, *Down by the Riverside: A South Carolina Slave Community* (1984); P. Seitel, *Genre* (1969); Archer Taylor, *The Proverb* (1931); Archer Taylor and Bartlett J. Whiting, compilers, *A Dictionary of American Proverbs and Proverbial Phrases, 1820–1880* (1958); Newman I. White, ed., *Frank C. Brown Collection of North Carolina Folklore*, vol. 1 (1952). ☆

PYRAMIDAL HOUSE

Because of its popularity among upper-middle-class southerners, the pyramidal house symbolized economic security. Its distinctive feature is its high pyramidal roof, usually with two chimneys flanking its short ridge. Having two rooms on each side of a wide central hallway, the dwelling could house two families and was sometimes built in lumber-mill settlements to accomodate

workers. The form evolved from early gable-roofed, Georgian-style houses along the Carolina-Georgia coast. It was confined largely to the towns and rural areas of the Lowland South and was built from the mid-19th century to the early 20th century.

Jessica Foy
Cooperstown Graduate Programs
Cooperstown, New York

Henry Glassie, *Pattern in the Material Folk Culture of the Eastern United States* (1968); D. Gregory Jeane, ed., *The Architectural Legacy of the Lower Chattahoochee Valley in Alabama and Georgia* (1978). ☆

QUILTING, AFRO-AMERICAN

Afro-American quilts are characterized by strips, bright colors, large designs, multiple patterns, asymmetry, and improvisation, all design principles with roots in African textile techniques and cultural traditions. The antecedents of contemporary African textiles and Afro-American quilts developed in Africa over 1,000 years ago. The actual links between African and Afro-American textile traditions occurred from 1650 to 1850 when Africans were brought to the United States from areas that are now Senegal, Mali, Ivory Coast, Ghana, Republic of Benin Nigeria, Cameroon, Zaire, and Angola. When they came to the New World, African women combined their own textile traditions with American quilting traditions, creating a unique, creolized art—the Afro-American quilt. Their combined ideas were passed down from generation to generation, thus preserving many African textile traditions.

Like Anglo-American quilt tops, Afro-American quilt tops are made either by sewing pieces of cloth together (piecing) or by sewing cutout shapes onto a larger fabric (appliqué). Quilt tops are sewn to an inner padding and a bottom cloth (quilting). All these techniques (piecing, appliqué, and quilting) were known in Africa, Europe, and the United States, yet Afro-American quilts are profoundly different from European or Anglo-American quilts.

In West African textiles and in Afro-American quilts, strips are a dominant design element as well as a chief construction technique. For centuries in West Africa, most cloth has been constructed from strips woven on small, portable looms. Long narrow strips are sewn together into larger fabrics worn as clothing or displayed as wall hangings and banners. Strips are sometimes used in Euro-American quilts, but as only one of many geometric patterns.

The bold colors and large designs of the Afro-American textile aesthetic derive from the communicative function of textiles in Africa, where they are worn and displayed as an indicator of social status, wealth, occupation, and history. The strong contrasting colors characteristic of African textiles are necessary to insure a cloth's readability at a distance, in strong sunlight. Maintaining that aesthetic beyond its original function, Afro-American quilters think not in terms of pastel or coordinating colors, but speak of "colors hitting each other right." Their quilts are best seen from a distance, in contrast to New England quilts, which should be inspected in intimate settings.

Multiple patterning is another characteristic shared by African textiles and Afro-American quilts. Multiple patterns are important in African royal and priestly fabrics, for the number and complexity of patterns decorating a fabric increase in accordance with the owner's status. A cloth woven for a king or priest may include up to 30 patterns. Multiple-patterned cloth communicates the prestige, power, and wealth of the wearer. Contemporary Afro-American quilts do not communicate an owner's status, but they do retain this preference for mixing patterns as an aesthetic tradition.

In West Africa, when woven strips with many patterns are sewn together to make a larger fabric, the resulting cloth has asymmetrical and unpredictable designs. These characteristics are retained in Afro-American quilts, for lines, designs, and colors do not match up but vary with a persistence that goes beyond a possible lack of cloth in any color or pattern. Afro-American quilters have taken this tradition one step further, introducing improvisation. Black quilters often adapt traditional Euro-American quilt patterns, and "Afro-Americanize" them by establishing a pattern in one square and varying it in successive squares. Typical Afro-American quilt squares do not repeat but change in size, arrangement, and color. Although ostensibly reproducing Euro-American patterns, Afro-American quilters maintain through improvisation African principles of multiple patterning, asymmetry, and unpredictable rhythms and tensions similar to those found in other Afro-American arts, such as jazz, black English, and dance.

Whereas Euro-American appliquéd quilts are primarily decorative, Afro-American appliquéd quilts often tell stories and express ideas in the same manner as African appliquéd textiles. With bold appliquéd shapes, African cultures record court histories, religious values, and personal histories of famous individuals, using designs symbolizing power, skill, leadership, wisdom, courage, balance, composure, and other personal qualities. In contrast, with iconography drawn from their imaginations, from southern black rural culture, and from American popular culture (magazines, television, and cereal boxes), Afro-American appliquéd quilts mirror the diverse influences that shape the lives of black women in the southern United States.

Afro-American quilt making is inextricably linked to the thrift and industry that characterize rural black southern life, for Afro-American quilters grew up in a time when there was no social security and to survive was to keep constantly busy. Afro-American quilt making is unique in America, fusing two alternative textile traditions—the African and the Euro-American—to produce a third. Afro-American quilters maintaining this hybrid aesthetic demonstrate the strength of African cultural traditions in contemporary American society, affirming the extraordinary tenacity of African ideas over hundreds of years in the face of major historical obstacles. Practiced today mainly in the southern United States, this vital aspect of our nation's artistic and cultural heritage must be recognized and celebrated now so that it can be promoted and preserved in the future.

Maude Southwell Wahlman
Ella King Torrey
University of Mississippi

Jill Salmons, *Textile History* (No. 2, 1980); Robert Farris Thompson, in *Black Studies in the University: A Symposium*, ed. A. Robinson (1969), *Flash of the Spirit: African and Afro-American Art and Philosophy* (1983); John Michael Vlach, *The Afro-American Tradition in Decorative Arts* (1978); Maude Southwell Wahlman, *Contemporary African Arts* (1974), with Ella King Torrey, *Ten Afro-American Quilters* (1983). ☆

QUILTING, ANGLO-AMERICAN

Having a long history in Great Britain, quilted items such as bed coverings, curtains, and clothing came to America with the colonists. Quilting skills and a variety of patchwork patterns that flourished and changed with time were brought to the southern United States through the migration of settlers.

The typical quilt, constructed with three bound layers, including a top of appliquéd or pieced patchwork, a cotton or wool batting, and a lining, offered good insulation against the cold, damp winters of the South. Quilt types have varied with the socioeconomic status and aesthetic standards of the makers and the intended use of the quilt. With cotton for batting plentiful in the South, even on small subsistence farms, but fabric scarce and expensive, simple "everyday" quilts were common. However, more decorative "fancy" quilts with elaborate color-coordinated patterns and intricate quilting were also made, frequently by members of the wealthier classes, who often had slave help until the Civil War, and also in fewer numbers by members of the lower classes.

Although quilters have bought at least some of their fabric, quilt making has been mainly a salvage craft, employing in its early years homespun, worn clothing, muslin flour and sugar sacks, cotton print feed sacks, as well as sewing remnants collected from the home, family, friends, and neighbors, and, more recently, from garage sales and clothing and fabric factories. Today synthetic fabrics, polyester batting, and machine piecing are often accepted by traditional quilters, although some quilters, more affected by the popular quilt revival, buy only cottons or cotton blends in coordinated colors and insist on hand sewing.

Traditional quilters, who learn their craft informally from family or neighbors rather than from books and formal classes as the revivalists do, pass along community standards and preferences. Traditional southern Anglo-American quilts, often with bright or pastel printed fabrics and intricate patchwork patterns, contrast sharply with the bold dark solids and simple large scale patterns of the Amish quilts and the bright solid colors of the Pennsylvania German quilts. Although the southern quilters do strive for their ideal of precise piecing of complex patterns such as the "Double Wedding Ring" or "Flower Garden" and tiny close quilting stitches, they do not often employ the elaborate hearts, plumes, and floral quilting motifs so common in the Pennsylvania German quilts. Today, southern Anglo-American quilts are typically quilted in wooden frames suspended from the ceiling or placed on chairs or "horses." Quilting is generally done "by the piece," with stitching about one-fourth inch from the edge of each patchwork seam. Early quilts may have more quilting often done in "shells," or concentric half circles.

As in the past, quilts are still made as heirlooms or gifts to mark occasions such as weddings and baby showers. Traditional quilters usually work alone; however, in urban areas senior citizens centers and women's groups are reviving the once-popular quilting bee. These groups, as well as many individual quilters, also quilt "for the public" to earn extra income and to keep busy. The survival of the quilting tradition may be attributed not only to the prevalent Protestant work ethic, which abhors waste of materials and time, but also the to social and symbolic functions of quilting in maintaining community, family, and personal creativity.

Susan Roach
Ruston, Louisiana

Ruth E. Finley, *Old Patchwork Quilts and the Women Who Made Them* (1929); Jonathan Holstein, *American Pieced Quilts* (1972); Susan Roach and Lorre Weidlich, *Folklore Women's Communication* (Spring 1974). ☆

SADDLEBAG HOUSE

The saddlebag house has a rectangular shape, a central chimney, two front doors, and is one room deep. As a popular means of enlarging a single pen structure, a second room was added to the chimney end of the original, thus forming the saddlebag house. Originally an English and then a Pennsylvania house type, it became common in areas of the South, where it was usually of frame rather than log construction. This vernacular house form did not appear frequently in the South until the 19th century, and its use there extended from Kentucky to North Carolina to the eastern Gulf Coast region.

Jessica Foy
Cooperstown Graduate Programs
Cooperstown, New York

Henry Glassie, *Pattern in the Material Folk Culture of the Eastern United States* (1968); Dell Upton and John Michael Vlach, eds., *Common Places: Readings in American Vernacular Architecture* (1986). ☆

SHINE
||||||||||||||||||

Shine is the hero of a series of Afro-American toasts, which are epic narrative poems involving an extended battle between protagonists. A trickster, Shine is said to be the only survivor of the 1912 *Titanic* disaster. As a black stoker aboard the ship, he frequently warns the captain of impending danger only to find his warnings ignored because he is black. Then, heedless of a number of temptations and threats, he jumps overboard and with superhuman skill swims to shore, thereby becoming the only survivor. As the ship finally sinks, he is drinking toasts at a bar in Philadelphia. In reality, of course, there were many survivors of the tragedy.

Shine survives and triumphs over his enemies by actual deeds and in doing so provides an explicit black rejection of white middle-class values such as respect for the law, romantic love, pity and gratitude, chivalry, and special consideration for women. Shine is, in short, a hero but not a gentleman. He is an epic figure whose exploits are performed in the name of his race. He breaks precedents and stereotypes; against all odds he defies white society and triumphs. His name is a generic one derived from the term *shine*, a slang word used by both blacks and whites to describe a very dark-skinned person. The name possibly comes from the idea of a person being so black that he shines. Stories about Shine were first collected in Louisiana and Mississippi in the late 1930s and early 1940s, but, considering Shine's association with the *Titanic*, they are probably at least two decades older.

W. K. McNeil
Ozark Folk Center
Mountain View, Arkansas

Langston Hughes, *The Book of Negro Humor* (1966); Bruce Jackson, *Get Your Ass in the Water and Swim Like Me: Narrative Poetry from Black Oral Tradition* (1974); Lawrence W. Levine, *Black Culture and Black Consciousness: Afro-American Folk Thought from Slavery to Freedom* (1977). ☆

SHOTGUN HOUSE
||||||||||||||||||||||||||||||||||||||||||||||

The shotgun house is distinctive to the land along waterways and to plantations, mill towns, and poorer urban neighborhoods of the Deep South. One room wide and three rooms long, under a gable roof, with eaves to the sides, almost all surviving examples have walls of sawn lumber and pier foundations. Extra rooms and porches may have been added to the ends, and, in some areas, long galleries appear along the sides and T or L additions across one end, usually the rear. In rare cases, a second row of rooms was added to one side, producing a double shotgun, a form often confused with the bungalow.

In New Orleans, the shotgun appeared about 1800, and excellent, comfortable, stylish examples there date from the 19th and early 20th centuries. Elsewhere, however, the type occurred in lower social contexts, such as rental tracts, plantation quarters, company housing, and stream-front "camps" (temporary homes for holiday diversion or for seasonal fishing and trapping). Adding complexity to the story, lumber companies in the late 19th century began offering shotguns on a commercial basis. The shotgun house has generally been a house for dependent people and not privately owned.

The most striking aspect of the shotgun house (and the bungalow) is its roof, oriented in a direction opposite to those of nearly all other historic southern houses. Whereas the other southern folk and vernacular houses had their gables to the sides, the shotgun had them to the front and rear.

Theories, each having respectable advocates, variously envision the shotgun house originating with marsh dwellers or American Indians, with the rise of the Greek Revival style, with the arrival of black Creoles from the Caribbean (who brought African-derived influences), with the beginning of prefabricated housing, or even as an adaptation to narrow city lots. Of these, the last explanation is the most easily criticized because the shotgun house was a common, and perhaps the oldest, rural form. Even so, the existence of narrow lots in urban areas, combined with the other factors mentioned, may account for the popularity of these houses today.

M. B. Newton, Jr.
Baton Rouge, Louisiana

William Ferris, *Blues from the Delta* (1984); Henry Glassie, *Pattern in the Material Folk Culture of the Eastern United States* (1968); M. B. Newton, Jr., *Melanges* (No. 2, 1971); John Michael Vlach, *Pioneer America* (January 1976). ☆

SIMMONS, PHILIP

(b. 1912) Blacksmith.

Born on Daniel Island, S.C., Philip Simmons has become one of the South's most distinguished artisans. He first came to Charleston in 1919 and began blacksmithing as a 13-year-old apprentice in 1925. He took over the blacksmith shop around 1931 and completed his first decorative piece about 1939. By the mid-1960s, when he was commissioned to build his masterpiece, Simmons had already acquired almost 40 years of experience. He was a general blacksmith and thus understood the work of the wheelwright and wagon builder, a horseshoer, a tool maker, and an ornamental ironworker.

"That snake taught me a lesson," recounted Philip Simmons during an evening of reminiscence. But what did he mean? What connection could there be between a reptile and the dean of the Charleston blacksmiths? The snake to which Simmons referred is a fearsome rattler that he fashioned and perched in the driveway gates of the Gadsden house in Charleston, S.C. Although Simmons has designed many gates—well over 200 in the Charleston area—the "snake gate" is the one of which he is most proud. It is his masterpiece. The labor, both physical and mental, that this gate demanded turned out to be a rite of passage. When that ritual was completed, Simmons's sense of his work was forever changed.

After several attempts at shaping the snake, he had found that the animal just did not seem right. He recalled, "You just see something that looked like a dead snake." But after continually shifting the eye in its head, Simmons made the snake come to life. Simmons claims that it seemed suddenly to look back at him. He was then satisfied with his sculpture, as was his client.

He had brought vitality to metal by applying extra effort to the task before him. That was the lesson of the snake—diligent effort yields excellence. The experience of making the snake gate showed Simmons that perseverance allows a special quality of vigor to emerge from raw material. In subsequent commissions that featured either animals or elements of nature, he again struggled to make them appear natural and lifelike. To Simmons they are alive like the snake; like the snake they represent his best effort.

Philip Simmons was a competent artist decades before he made the snake gate. He proudly carried on a profession that had been practiced in Charleston since 1739 and for which he can trace a personal genealogy of blacksmiths back to the 18th century. But despite the comforting influence of a praiseworthy history and his own energetic displays of skill, Simmons felt that he had not fully matured as a blacksmith. His own creative talents were not crucially tested until the snake-gate commission, for only then did he have the opportunity to make a unique contribution to the decorative ironwork of Charleston with the first wrought-iron animal sculpture to be seen in that city. Once the gate was completed, he could add to the confidence that comes from a noble past a confidence that comes from within: a confidence based on his own imagination and creative power.

John Michael Vlach
George Washington University

John Michael Vlach, *Charleston Blacksmith: The Work of Philip Simmons* (1981). ☆

SMOKEHOUSE

Because southerners for at least two centuries have not been willing to live without pork, their farms commonly have included smokehouses. Although any kind of meat could be dried and smoked, it was the butchering of hogs that truly necessitated the construction of this particular outbuilding. Mid-19th-century reports on southern pork consumption indicate that a male field hand was fed between two and five pounds of hog meat per week. Each year between 1840 and 1860 no less than 2.2 hogs were raised for every man, woman, and child in the South. This pork craving gave rise to a problem in meat preservation that the smokehouse solved.

Because the meat-packing industry was not well developed in the southern states, every farmer was left to fend for himself. Thus, in a spirit of self-sufficiency and independence, southern farmers made the smokehouse a central artifact in the conduct of the annual agricultural round. Hogs slaughtered late in the fall, after they were well fattened from foraging on the mast that they found in the woodlands, could be kept after they were smoked until the following year's butchering. Once the carcasses were cut into manageable sections, each piece was packed in salt for about six weeks. The pieces of meat were then washed and hung in the smokehouse to acquire the distinctive flavor of the slow-drying fire. In the popular mind, hickory is considered the universal fuel, but many different woods were used. In fact, some farmers in "Little Dixie" Missouri preferred fresh corn cobs, what they still call "meat cobs." The quantity and kind of smoke varied considerably from locale to locale and from person to person, as the main arbiter in these matters was one's own taste buds.

There has also been considerable variation in the kinds of structures used as smokehouses. Large plantations used sizable buildings constructed to the same dimensions as dwelling houses, say 18 feet by 26 feet. In colonial Virginia the smokehouse could have a tall pyramidal roof. Along the shores of the Chesapeake a small brick house with diamond-shaped ventilators in the gables served as the meathouse, whereas in the Alabama highlands the smokehouse might feature a gable-end doorway with a roof cantilevered several feet over one end to protect the entrance. Some Missouri smokehouses are two-story affairs with a smoking chamber below and a meat preparation area above. Taken collectively, the look of these various buildings might suggest a lack of cultural coherency. The behavior enacted in all these structures is, however, consistent. Whatever their particular form, the cultural statement made is clear—"we will take care of our needs, we will have ham and bacon when we want it."

John Michael Vlach
George Washington University

Henry Chandlee Forman, *Tidewater Maryland Architecture and Gardens* (1956); Sam B. Hilliard, *Hog Meat and Hoecake: Food Supply in the Old South, 1840–1860* (1972); Howard Wight Marshall, *Journal of American Folklore* (October–December 1979). ☆

T HOUSE

One of the first styles of popular domestic architecture to become widespread in the South was the one-story T house, sometimes called a "cross-plan" or "gable-front-and-wing" house. The style, although not uncommon to the rest of the United States, was widely adopted in the South for historical, aesthetic, climatic, and cultural reasons. Built primarily between 1880 and 1910, the T house is significant as a "hybrid" house type that reflects the confluence of architectural styles prevalent in the last part of the 19th century. It also reflects changes that took place during the New South period. The T house met an urgent need for inexpensive housing to shelter the burgeoning working- and middle-class population in small towns that proliferated around cotton-processing centers throughout the South. Built for a rapidly advancing white working class, the T house may also be seen as a reflection of the Jim Crow years.

The basic T house was almost always frame and consisted of a gable or projecting wing two rooms deep, one behind the other, straddled by a side wing one room deep. Usually there were three or four rooms, but T houses were frequently altered and augmented so that they appeared to be much larger and the T configuration was disguised. Often there was a central hall between the two wings. Rooms were nearly always close to square and similar in size, with high ceilings and internal chimneys.

The southerner's pervasive concern with managing oppressive climatic conditions is expressed quite clearly in the T house, which incorporated a number of structural elements enabling its inhabitants to defend themselves against intense summer heat and seasonal wetness. T houses were commonly built on pillars about two feet off the ground, with roofs that were rather steeply pitched. High ceilings, front porches, and the dogtrot-style alignment of front door with back door or window permitted maximum air circulation and cooling.

Three distinct architectural influences are evident in the T house: the folk tradition, the classical or formal tradition, and the popular building fashions of the day. By featuring a projecting gable in the Gothic Revival cottage style popularized by A. J. Downing and A. J. Davis, the T house abandoned traditional symmetry and "frontality" in its facade but retained spatial configurations and elements that were common to both southern high-style and folk houses: square, almost cubic rooms to each side of a central passage, and front porches. The T house provided southerners with the traditional living spaces to which they were accustomed but at the same time afforded them a means of "modernizing" their houses and expressing individual taste with the profusion of mass-produced Victorian millwork embellishments that became easily accessible in the late 19th century.

Cultural messages were strong in the T house. The projecting gable wing protected the porch and entrance from the view of other houses built in a row, very close together. An elevated porch and a central hall created transitional buffer zones to provide the family with more protection and privacy—modern concerns in an increasingly "urban" environment. The hall and boxlike rooms provided more private spaces away not only from outsiders but from other family members. An indication of the success of the T house as a southern domestic structure is that not only were many built in the New South, but many still survive. They survive as ubiquitous features of the southern landscape and as living examples of a very popular style, which was so pleasing and flexible

to southerners that they still enjoy inhabiting T houses a century later.

Lisa N. Howorth
University of Mississippi

Lisa N. Howorth, "Popular Vernacular: The One-Story T House in the South" (M.A. thesis, University of Mississippi, 1984); Paula Jane Johnson, "T House in Texas: Suiting Plain People's Needs" (M.A. thesis, University of Texas at Austin, 1981); Virginia McAlester and Lee McAlester, *A Field Guide to American Houses* (1984). ☆

THOMAS, JAMES
|||||||||||||||||||||||||||||||||||||||||||||
(b. 1926) Blues musician and sculptor.

James "Son Ford" Thomas was born 14 October 1926 on a farm near Eden in Yazoo County, Miss. His life embodies a spectrum of black folklife including blues music, clay sculpture, and storytelling, all of which are rooted in Mississippi Delta cultural traditions.

James Thomas learned to play the guitar by watching his uncle play, after which he imitated the chords in his own tunes. As a teenager Thomas moved to Leland, Miss., where he began playing blues on weekends. He played juke joints and barrelhouses around Leland and Greenville, Miss., through the 1960s. Since the early 1970s he has performed at folk music and blues concerts for colleges and universities, including Jackson State University (1971–72), the University of Maine (1972), Tougaloo College (1973), and Yale University (1973–76). He has participated in the Smithsonian Festival of American Folklife and at festivals in Norway and Germany. He has made records produced in the United States, Holland, West Germany, and Italy.

James Thomas is also a sculptor. His sculpture is largely self-taught rather

James Thomas and sculpture, Leland, Mississippi, 1968

than being derived from other artists. As a child he began making clay imitations of animals, patterning his first work after similar figures made by his uncle. He later made clay models of Ford tractors and was nicknamed "Son Ford." Apart from his uncle, Thomas had no continuing contact with artists who work with clay. His work has been highly personal, and perhaps the most unusual figures in his repertoire are heads and skulls, which often have openings in their tops and serve as containers or ashtrays. Animals, water, and death are recurring motifs. His clay faces present an image of the black man as poised and proud.

Son Thomas's sculpture attracted national attention at the opening of the exhibition *Black Folk Art* at the Corcoran Gallery in Washington, D.C. Thomas has been featured in three films: *James "Son Ford" Thomas: Delta Blues Singer* (1970), *Mississippi Delta Blues* (1974), and *Give My Poor Heart Ease: Mississippi Delta Bluesmen* (1975).

William Ferris
University of Mississippi

William Ferris, ed., *Afro-American Folk Art and Crafts* (1983), *Blues from the Delta* (1984); *Highway 61 Blues: James "Son" Thomas*, Southern Culture Records, sc 1701 (1983). ☆

TOASTS AND DOZENS

In Greenville, Atlanta, Memphis, or other towns and cities in the South, you might hear preadolescent, lower-class black boys playfully hurling rhymed insults at each other. The language is rough and the themes are risqué, but the composition is creative. They are playing the "dozens," as they often call it. "I fucked your momma on the levee," a Greenville, Miss., youth told his playmate while others looked on. "She said, 'get up baby, your dick's getting too heavy.'" The onlookers roared with delight. After shouts of encouragement to the butt of the insult, he replied "I fucked your momma in New Orleans, her pussy started poppin' like a sewing machine." The challenge was put to the first boy to top the retort. He came back strongly with "I fucked your momma on a fence, selling her pussy for 15 cents; a bee come along and stung her on the ass, started selling her pussy for a dollar and a half."

The dozens are social entertainment, a game to be played, but they have also sparked considerable sociopsychological comment. Folklorist Roger D. Abrahams observed, for example, that the dozens represent a striving for masculine identity by black boys. They try symbolically to cast off the woman's world, indeed the black world they see as run by the mother of the family, in favor of the gang existence of the black man's world. In dozens playing, the black boy is honing the verbal and social skills he will need as an adult male. A form of dozens playing, usually called "ranking," has also been collected among white boys, but most collections have stressed the black dozens, also called "woofing," "sounding," and "joning."

Although Roger Abrahams did his classic study of black verbal contests and creativity in Philadelphia, his informants had deep roots in the South. Other southern connections to the dozens are found in a spate of southern blues songs popular from the 1920s on. "The Dirty Dozen" was first recorded by Georgia's Rufus Perryman, known as Speckled Red, in 1929. Other versions quickly followed by southern artists including Tampa Red, Little Hat Jones, Ben Curry, Lonnie Johnson, and Kokomo Arnold. The content of the dozens was apparently in circulation even prior to these recordings; folksong collectors Howard W. Odum and Newman I. White found references in the field to the dozens before World War I. Alan Dundes and Donald C. Simmons have suggested an older existence of the dozens in Africa.

Also collected from lower-class blacks has been a form of narrative poetry called by their reciters "toasts." Toasts use many of the rhyming and rhythmic schemes and the rough imagery of the dozens, but are performed by young men as extended poetic recitations rather than ritualized insult. Indeed, Abrahams called toasts the "greatest flowering of Negro verbal talent" (although similar recitations are also known among whites).

The performance of toasts is intended to be dramatic. The settings are placed in barrooms and jungles; the characters are badmen, pimps, and street people; and the props are often drugs, strong drink, and guns. Here is an excerpt, for example, from a common toast, "The Signifying Monkey."

Down in the jungle near a dried-
up creek,
The signifying monkey hadn't slept
for a week
Remembering the ass-kicking he
had got in the past
He had to find somebody to kick
the lion's ass.
Said the signifying monkey to the
lion that very same day,
"There's a bad motherfucker heading your way.
The way he talks about you it can't
be right,
And I know when you two meet
there going to be a fight.
He said he fucked your cousin,
your brother, and your niece,
And he had the nerve enough to
ask your grandmom for a piece."
The lion said, "Mr. Monkey, if
what you say isn't true about me,
Bitch, I'll run your ass up the highest tree."
The monkey said, "Now look, if
you don't believe what I say,
Go ask the elephant. He's resting
down the way."

Other popular toasts in oral tradition include "Stackolee," "The Titanic," "Joe the Grinder," and "The Freaks (or Junkers) Ball."

The origin of the term and the tradition of toasts is uncertain. Bruce Jackson suggested roots in prison and hobo life. Roger Abrahams looked to the influence of recitations common on the blackface minstrel stage and in subliterary comic forms. The name *toasts* may be derived from once-popular books of after-dinner speeches, jokes, and drinking toasts, or from underworld slang.

Several collections of toasts come from the South. In the North most texts come from the cities. Although some southern examples are reported in cities like New Orleans and Austin, southern texts often come from the rural and small-town South. In Mississippi, David Evans, William Ferris, and Simon J. Bronner collected them in small towns. Bruce Jackson's book on toasts, *Get Your Ass in the Water and Swim Like Me* (1974), had texts primarily collected from prisons in Texas and Missouri. The connection to southern life is usually passed up by interpreters of toasts in favor of links to the life of the underworld and the urban ghetto. Relations exist, however, between the themes and heroes of the toasts and those of southern black folksongs including "Stackolee" and "The Titanic." The blues also are influenced by the erotic and violent verses of the toasts. Other connections are found between southern black animal folktales featuring the monkey and the toast "Signifying Monkey." Indeed, Richard M. Dorson reported prose versions of "Signifying Monkey" in his classic collection *American Negro Folktales* (1967) taken from southern-born blacks.

Dozens and toasts stand out because they are framed as play or performance, and they contain strong themes and sounds. Dozens and toasts creatively manipulate imagery and metaphor to bring drama to words. The boy telling dozens may eventually tackle the more sophisticated toasts. Mastering the techniques in these traditional performances gives the teller an important sense of prestige and power that is reserved for the man of words in black society. Their dozens and toasts entertain friends and pass the time; they communicate values and feelings. The tellers of dozens and toasts are narrators of imagined scenes and cultural critics for the audiences to which they perform. The tellers also draw attention because they are themselves characters in the social drama of communication through folklore.

Simon J. Bronner
Pennsylvania State University
Capitol Campus

Roger D. Abrahams, *Deep Down in the Jungle: Negro Narrative Folklore from the Streets of Philadelphia* (1970), *Positively Black* (1970); Simon J. Bronner, *Western Folklore* (April 1978); Richard M. Dorson, *American Negro Folktales* (1967); William Ferris, *Jazzforschung* (1974/75); Bruce Jackson, *Get Your Ass in the Water and Swim Like Me: Narrative Poetry from Black Oral Tradition* (1974); William Labov, Paul Cohen, Clarence Robins, and John Lewis, in *Mother Wit From the Laughing Barrel: Readings in the Interpretation of Afro-American Folklore*, ed. Alan Dundes (1973); Lawrence W. Levine, *Black Culture and Black Consciousness: Afro-American Folk Thought from Slavery to Freedom* (1977); Paul Oliver, *Aspects of the Blues Tradition* (1970); Dennis Wepman, Ronald B. Newman, and Murray B. Binderman, *Journal of American Folklore* (July–September 1974). ☆

TOYS

Handmade folk toys now seen as oddities at crafts fairs once served as principal playthings for children throughout the South. Especially in poorer, rural regions, adults fashioned toys from such native materials as wood, corn shucks, cane, vines, apples, and gourds. Native Americans shared techniques for making corn-shuck dolls with white and black settlers and made miniatures of their own weapons and implements. Many settlers brought or re-created toys from Europe, among them the cup-and-ball game based on the French bilboquet. Minstrel shows provided the idea for the limber jack, a marionette-type doll also called dancin' man and stomper doll. Children spent hours rubbing their notched, propeller-ended whimmydiddle sticks—also called whammydiddle sticks, hooey sticks, or gee-haw whimmydiddles. Miniature furniture, puzzles, and carved figures abounded. Many ingenious, carved action toys depicted everyday activities; for example, two men take turns chopping wood or chickens peck for corn.

Poppets, dolls made of buckeye wood, and other dolls with heads of dried apples or painted hickory nuts and stuffed cloth bodies enthralled youngsters. Children endlessly shot peas or rocks at targets with homemade flips and slingshots. Other favorites were the noisemakers such as "the buzz saw" and "the bull." On Sundays in many communities children could play only with biblically based toys such as the puzzles Pillars of Solomon and Jacob's Ladder. Today craftspeople often sell such folk toys through crafts fairs or small local shops and occasionally contract with large department stores like Bloomingdale's.

Residents of Appalachia and the Ozarks continued using homemade toys long after others in the country had shifted to store-bought toys. Although toy manufacturers in the northeastern and northcentral states long dominated the markets, some southern toys, such as the dolls of Wolf Fletcher and Philip Goldsmith in Covington, Ky., in 1875, had a wide appeal. No other southern toy, though, has ever rocked the nation

like the Cabbage Patch Kids. In 1977 Georgia artist Xavier Roberts began producing handmade cloth dolls, "delivering" them at Babyland General Hospital in Cleveland, Ga. Roberts negotiated a licensing agreement with Coleco Industries, whose mass-produced versions became *the* toy craze from 1982 to 1984 and garnered unprecedented media attention. Although a renewed appreciation for southern folk toys is growing, today's southern children, tantalized by television ads, clamor for the latest crazes—not flips or whimmydiddles.

Sharon A. Sharp
University of Mississippi

Allen H. Eaton, *Handicrafts of the Southern Highlands* (1937; reprint 1973); *Foxfire Book of Toys and Games* (1985); Inez McClintock and Marshall McClintock, *Toys in America* (1961); *Newsweek* (12 December 1983); *Southern Living* (December 1983); *Time* (12 December 1983). ☆

TRADERS
||||||||||||||||||||||||||

Whereas England has been described as a nation of horsemen, the South is a land of horse traders. Southerners are attracted to the trade more than to the animal, and Joseph Baldwin argued that in the South "nearly every man was a speculator; at any rate, a trader."

Mules and horses were raised in the cooler climate of border states by "graziers." During "court days" in states like Kentucky, streets were filled with stock and traders who bought and shipped their animals to livery stables in the Deep South to supply local farmers. The animals arrived in the late winter and early spring, and farmers would visit the barns to look them over. Customers quickly learned the relative merits of each animal and began to visit the trader and discuss terms. For the next two or three months the horse and mule barn was a center of business and social activity, and the trader the most important man in town. Mules were usually sold on credit with nothing down and one year to pay. These terms suited the dealer because he sold unbroken three- and four-year-olds, and if farmers broke them and kept them in good shape they would be worth $50 to $100 more the next year.

The southern trader usually left school and began trading at an early age. A seasoned trader often traveled with a "hossler," who was a black assistant, and the two were a skillful team. Manuel Allen was a black trader in Mississippi who always "traded slow." Allen's philosophy was "never to seem anxious to sell or trade if I wanted to make a good deal." He was awake to tricks of the profession, and once, when a man said his wife wanted to keep a mare for her buggy horse, Allen recalled, "Right then I knew he was baiting me and wanted me to take the mare."

Both trader and customer knew their "limits" and presented their cases with courtroom seriousness. Both remembered their trades and, more importantly, were judged for them by the community for years to come. The southern trade was a pact among men, and one emerged with honor or ridicule depending on his judgment.

The southern trader is known for his wit and is a shrewd judge of both animals and men. He weaves humorous tales and anecdotes into his work with special skill. Deception in folk humor reaches its most eloquent form among southern traders who argue that they never lie to a customer. All agree with

Mississippi mule trader Ray Lum that "the truth always fits in better." Rather than lie to a customer, traders tell a veiled or embroidered truth, using word play and double entendre in describing an animal. For example, Lum recalls an animal sold to a hunter who was told he could "shoot off him." When he fired his gun, the mule bucked and he literally "shot off him." Southern traders like Ray Lum also developed a "singing" style in both auctioneering and trading using phrases such as "broke to a queen's taste," "kept like a hat in a band box," and "If a fly lit on her he would slip off and break his neck."

The southern trader dressed well to impress customers with the professional quality of his work. An important part of his dress was the western hat, a trademark of the profession. He carried a whip or cane and skillfully used it to assure that animals moved with spirit before a customer. The trader's eloquence and graceful manners set the customer at ease and guided his imagination, if not his eyes, in the trade.

Of all traders, gypsies are said to have the greatest knowledge of horses, and in the South it is said they "hoodoo" horses with their powers. Gypsies sometimes love a horse so much that they will buy the animal back at a loss rather than lose it. Such affection for an animal is a clear exception to the practice of other traders, who always love the trade more than the horse. Gypsies also practice ritual burial of horses and strictly forbid the eating of their flesh. Ironically, gypsies, like other traders, are usually very poor horsemen and use horses either as draft animals or for barter.

Gypsy men taught their sons how to bring out a horse's good points and disguise his weak ones. They were not content simply to buy and resell animals, for their greatest art lay in "putting right" a horse's defects. An old horse became a spirited animal through "gingering," the insertion of a piece of ginger into its anus.

Both Ray Lum and Ben Green, author of *Hoss Trades*, described Irish traders as even more formidable than gypsies. Irish tinkers immigrated to the United States in the early 1800s, and in Washington they established a communal livery stable. After the Civil War their leader, Pat O'Hara, led the group south to Atlanta. From this center, groups settled in Nashville and Fort Worth and began trading with farmers.

Irish traders traveled in two-family convoys consisting of three cars, each drawing a trailer bearing living equipment, and three trucks for the stock. Often four generations traveled together and camped in tents with two large carpeted rooms. As soon as the presence of the traders was known in a community, local farmers brought their worn-out mules to the camp to trade for young five-year-olds. The farmer always paid "boot" to cover the difference between the two animals. The old field mules could still be used for light hauling in cities, and one of the trucks shuttled between stockyards and the camp to supply fresh stock and haul the old mules back. While the men traded mules, their wives often sold hand-sewn lace to the women of the community.

During their trades the Irish protected themselves with a secret language, or cant, which was used to conceal their conversations from outsiders. Their language was derived from the Gaelic language of ancient Ireland, "Bearlangair na Saer." Once a high-caste language, it declined as the status of wandering smiths declined and became no more than an argot among tinkers. Its speakers today refer to their speech with phrases such as "Shelta," "Bog Latin," "Tinkers' Cant," and "The Ould Thing," whereas for outsiders it is "the gibberish of tinkers." Cant is passed on from generation to generation and effectively protects the Irish trader from outsiders.

William Faulkner was attracted to traders whose narrative skills in many ways paralleled his own as a writer. In *The Hamlet* he developed Pat Stomper, a trader who "played horses against horses as a gambler plays cards against cards, for the pleasure of beating a worthy opponent as much as for gain."

Traders prospered throughout the South until about 1955 when tractors replaced the mule. Many traders then became used-car dealers where they adapted their talents to new forms of transportation and "horsepower."

See also ETHNIC LIFE: / Gypsies; Travelers

William Ferris
University of Mississippi

Jean-Paul Clébert, *The Gypsies* (1969); J. Frank Dobie, *Guide to the Life and Literature of the Southwest* (1969); William Ferris, *Mississippi Folklore Register* (Spring 1978), *North Carolina Folklore Journal* (September 1973); Ben Green, *Horse Conformation and Hoss Traders of Yesteryear* (1963); T. V. Harper, "Irish Traveler Cant: An Historical, Structural, and Sociolinguistic Study of an Argot" (M.A. thesis, University of Georgia, 1969); Robert Byron Lamb, *The Mule in Southern Agriculture* (1963); Albert Thomas Sinclair, *American Gypsies* (1917); S. G. Thigpen, *A Boy in Rural Mississippi* (1966). ☆

WAGNER, KINNIE
(1903–1958) Outlaw.

Kinnie Wagner was a particularly good candidate for popular acclamation as an outlaw hero. During his lifetime he ran whiskey, robbed from the needy, killed at least five people (including three lawmen), escaped four times from jail or prison; he also won the admiration of a grass-roots constituency that made him its champion. While critics attacked him, his supporters sang ballads about him and retold for generations legendary yarns about his marksmanship, cunning, and bravery. Indeed, Kinnie Wagner is one of the modern South's most controversial outlaws.

William Kenneth Wagner was born 18 February 1903 on a farm outside Gate City, Va. He spent most of his youth in the region, but in 1919 he left home and joined the Richard Brothers Wild West and Concert Show, working as a roustabout. During a swing through the piney forests of southeastern Mississippi, Kinnie left the circus and found work in lumber camps as a mule skinner. In the circus, Kinnie had taken to wearing western attire, and he passed himself off to local folks as a Texan. He started wearing sidearms that on some occasions he brandished, demonstrating that he was a skilled marksman.

Logging did not long appeal to Kinnie, and he started running whiskey from Mobile and Gulfport to customers as far north as Meridian and Jackson. In the summer of 1924 Wagner robbed a poor box and stole a gold watch from a mill guard in George County. Sheriff McLeod arrested him, and shortly he was sentenced to four months in the Lucedale jail. On 11 November Wagner escaped in a daring daytime breakout. A month later the authorities located Wagner living in a cabin outside McLain, Greene County. When a posse tried to recapture the fugitive, on 24 December, a gunfight erupted and Wagner shot to death Deputy Sheriff McIntosh before making his escape.

On 13 April 1925 he again eluded capture, this time leaving two Kingsport, Tenn., officers dead and one seriously wounded. The following day, however, Kinnie surrendered, and in less than two weeks he was tried, convicted, and sentenced to death. While awaiting a retrial, he escaped and fled to Mexico.

Wagner was back in the headlines on 19 August 1926. This time he surrendered to Sheriff Lillian Barber in Texarkana, Ark., after he had killed two men in a fight. He was returned to Mississippi to stand trial for the McIntosh slaying, for which Kinnie was convicted on 30 October. The Meridian jury, unable to agree on a death penalty, granted a life sentence. Wagner accepted the sentence and was moved to the Parchman State Prison Farm. He tried to escape the following year, but failed.

Wagner escaped from Parchman in 1940 and was retaken in 1943 by the FBI. Wagner had spent most of his time hiding out in the hills of northeastern Mississippi and Alabama, running whiskey. Back again in Parchman, Wagner became a model prisoner and received Christmas furloughs. But these rewards were not enough, and on 15 March 1948 he walked again from prison while on trusty duty. This time the fugitive eluded the law until 30 January 1956, when a contingent of Highway Patrol officers, state identification experts, and local officials in true Hollywood style captured the now-ailing Wagner near Shuqualak, Miss.

He was sent to Parchman with Mississippi's Governor Coleman saying that this prisoner would receive no special treatment. Wagner's health grew worse, and on 9 March 1958 he suffered a fatal heart attack. His body was returned home for burial, where according to an Associated Press account, over 10,000 persons turned out to view the famous gunman.

Richard Sweterlitsch
University of Vermont

Claude Gentry, *The Guns of Kinnie Wagner* (1969); Richard Sweterlitsch, *Mississippi Folklore Register* (Spring 1978). ☆

WARNER, PECOLIA

|||||||||||||||||||||||||||||||||||||||||||||||||||

(1901–1983) Quilter.

Born 9 March 1901 near Bentonia, Miss., raised on plantations in the Mississippi Delta, and educated in Yazoo City, Pecolia Leola Deborah Jackson Warner was taught to sew at the age of seven by her mother, Katherine Brant Jackson. One of seven children, Pecolia Warner learned from her schoolteacher mother to cook, clean, wash and iron, sew, and make quilts. Her first quilt was made from little "strings" of rectangular cloth, sewn into long strips alternately pieced with solid strips to fashion a top quilt. The pattern, called Spider Leg by Pecolia Warner's mother, is the oldest one known for Afro-American quilters. It is similar to African textiles made by sewing woven strips together, and it is the one most often first taught to young children.

Pecolia Warner, quilter, Yazoo City, Mississippi, 1976

Warner considered her quilt-making skills a gift from God. Although inspired by memories of her mother's quilts, by dreams, by quilt-pattern books, by household objects, and by farming artifacts, Warner's quilts are in the mainstream of Afro-American textile traditions. Pecolia Warner was as articulate verbally as she was visually, and interviews with her clarified those features that distinguished Afro-American quilts from Euro-American textile traditions: organizational strips; bold, contrasting colors; large designs; asymmetrical arrangements; multiple patterns, and improvisation. Warner often commented on how important it was for colors to "hit each other right," how "stripping" a quilt brought out the designs, and how varying parts of a pattern made quilt designs more interesting.

Pecolia Warner lived in New Orleans, Washington, D.C., and Chicago, working as a domestic servant for whites. She first received attention as a folk artist in 1977 when she was "discovered" by folklorist William Ferris and featured in his film, *Four Women Artists.* Her quilts were featured in "Folk Art and Craft: The Deep South," a traveling exhibition organized by the Center for Southern Folklore for the Smithsonian Institution Traveling Exhibition Service, as well as numerous other exhibitions. She was a featured artist at folklife festivals in the late 1970s, but her health became progressively worse in 1982. She suffered a series of small strokes and died at age 82 in March 1983.

Maude Southwell Wahlman
University of Mississippi

Patti Carr Black, ed., *Made by Hand: Mississippi Folk Art* (1980); William Ferris, ed., *Afro-American Folk Art and Crafts* (1983);

Robert Farris Thompson, *Flash of the Spirit: African and Afro-American Art and Philosophy* (1983); John Michael Vlach, *The Afro-American Tradition in Decorative Arts* (1978); Maude Southwell Wahlman, in *Something to Keep You Warm*, ed. Patti Carr Black (1981), with John Scully, in *Afro-American Folk Art and Crafts*, ed. William Ferris (1983), with Ella King Torrey, *Ten Afro-American Quilters* (1983). ☆

GEOGRAPHY

RICHARD PILLSBURY

Georgia State University

CONSULTANT

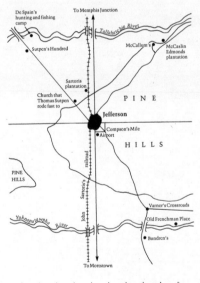

☆ ☆ ☆ ☆ ☆ ☆ ☆ ☆ ☆ ☆

*Overleaf: Yoknapatawpha County, Missis-
sippi*

LANDSCAPE, CULTURAL

||||||||||||||||||||||||||||||||||||||||||||||||||||||

The South is at once both the most visible and most ambiguous of all American cultural landscapes. The region's visibility stems largely from its strong sense of regional identity, its ambiguity from its lack of a definable geographic core. The vision of a unified southern cultural landscape is thus more myth than reality. A portrait of the region's landscape is possible only with the understanding that it is selective and synthetic.

Traditionally the South has been considered to extend northward from the Gulf of Mexico to the Potomac and Ohio rivers and westward from the Atlantic to eastern Texas. Transition zones, or spheres of influence, are found along the northern border, where the region intermixes with the Midwest, and on the western margins, where it mingles with the Hispanic Southwest. The western limits of the region are the most poorly defined today because of the recent explosive growth of eastern Texas. Dallas and Houston once were strongly influenced by southern themes and values, but today these roots are obscured.

Britain provided the basic cultural stamp of the human landscape throughout the colonial period, in spite of Spanish settlements in Florida and Texas and French settlement of southern Louisiana and the surrounding environs. The abiding significance of the initial Anglo role in the South is made clear by the Doctrine of First Effective Settlement, which suggests that new immigrants in previously settled areas live in houses already built and farm fields already cleared. The early settlers of the South may have initially desired houses like those of the old country, but local builders were unfamiliar with those designs and special materials were not available. Some New England–style houses were located in coastal South Carolina and Georgia and German houses near Winston-Salem, N.C., but these stand as anomalies in a greater landscape fabric.

The region's mixed racial heritage is only partially reflected in the visual cultural landscape of the contemporary South. Recognized black contributions to traditional southern landscape have been limited. Both the shotgun house form and swept-yard landscaping have African roots, but the racial origins of these elements were forgotten as they were amalgamated into the culture as a whole. Other landscape elements of black origin, such as the distinctive use of broken pottery in cemeteries, have continued to exist but mainly among blacks in isolated areas.

Maize and tobacco cultivation were the two most important aboriginal contributions to the regional landscape, but they are also largely unrecognized by the dominant culture. Other notable Indian contributions to the landscape were the raised-square corncrib, the use of multicropping techniques in house gardens, and the preference for small separated fields in the Upland and Gulf Coastal southern areas.

Defining the Traditional Southern Landscape. The South is the least urbanized culture area in the nation. Cities over a million in population are rare, and small towns are more common than the national standards. The county seat is the single most important type of community settlement in the region. The earliest county seats in Virginia were founded as linear collections of building lots mandated by the House of Burgesses. An enlarged central lot was designated as a courthouse square. Many of these and other southern county seats have never grown beyond a handful of buildings clustered around an isolated courthouse.

A typical mid-19th-century county seat was a planned community named for a prominent state or national figure, or the hometown of one of the development committee members. It was located on the highest vantage point near the geographic center of the county. The unpaved rectilinear streets gave form to about 25 building blocks with 80 to 100 one-quarter- to one-half-acre residential building lots, 30 or more narrow frontage commercial lots facing the square, and 20 or so larger commercial lots at the rear of the small commercial lots. The proceeds of the sale of these lots were used to pay for the development of the town and the construction of public buildings.

The central courthouse square was the focal point of the county seat. Early courthouses were of log or frame, but by the late 19th century most were two-story brick structures with a distinctive cross-hallway pattern. The courthouse was the most important building in town. Its rooms, halls, and steps were the stage for trials, sheriffs' sales, tax and permit payments, and gossip for the entire county. The jail occupied a separate building behind the courthouse, although many towns preferred to have it in a less conspicuous place. Town wells for public use and fire protection were located at one or more corners of the square. Confederate war memorial statues of a soldier in battle dress began to appear after about 1890. Many early towns allowed lawyers to have offices on the square.

The square, the courthouse, and the facing businesses formed the core of the town. The largest and most prestigious businesses included the hotel, four or five large general merchandise stores, a ladies' apparel shop or two, the bank, and a drugstore. Doctors', lawyers', and insurance offices were located on the second floors of these solid brick buildings. The post office, telegraph office, and livery and artisan shops were on the side streets. Churches were located off the square on a corner of a block touching the square.

Large residential building lots in southern towns encouraged the use of tall oaks, hickories, and magnolias to shade white painted houses. Large backyards and gardens furthered this bucolic look. The practice of utilizing widely differing sizes of lots in preplanned rectilinear towns is not found elsewhere in the nation.

Dispersed communities actually were the most common type of urban settlement in the region. These dispersed communities are not towns in the true sense of the word, but have the name, identity, and activities of such. They only lack traditional population density. Many are dying as rural out-migration continues and roads to larger communities with more comprehensive services improve. The church and the crossroads store often are the only functioning remnants today.

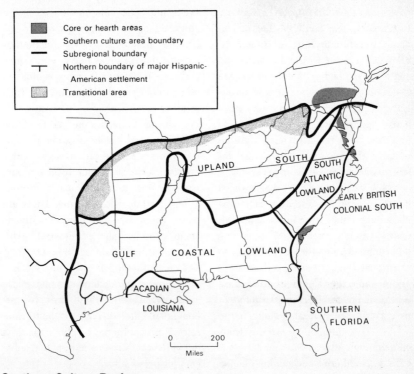

Core or hearth areas
Southern culture area boundary
Subregional boundary
Northern boundary of major Hispanic-
American settlement
Transitional area

UPLAND SOUTH

SOUTH ATLANTIC LOWLAND

EARLY BRITISH COLONIAL SOUTH

GULF COASTAL LOWLAND

ACADIAN LOUISIANA

SOUTHERN FLORIDA

0   200
Miles

Southern Culture Regions
Map by Richard Pillsbury

Land abandonment and piney woods are the overriding rural images for much of the region. Large commercial farms have replaced traditional farming in some areas, but these are mere pockets in the greater fabric of a rolling wooded landscape. Vast acreages of the Gulf Coastal Plains and Upland South are planted in tree farms of loblolly, slash, and other pines, or have been allowed to become wooded through land abandonment. Part of this wooded image, however, is illusory. The separation of fields by forest buffer zones creates impressions of wooded acreages that do not exist. These impressions are intensified for the casual traveler by the interstate highway system that frequently bypasses farmed areas in small towns.

Five diagnostic features of the South are particularly valuable in charting the cultural landscape of the region: vernacular house form, religion, individualistic attitudes, diet, and music. Vernacular house form is one of the clearest ways of determining the extent and subregionalization of a cultural landscape. Conceptually, house form refers to the arrangement, relative size, and function of a structure's rooms combined with its facade characteristics. These apparently superficial elements have proven to be amazingly effective indicators of cultural origins because they represent measures of a society's attitudes about family life and interaction within the home.

Residential construction preferences aid in the identification of regional forms. The classic southern vernacular house was raised 18 or more inches off the ground, rarely had a basement, had outside end chimneys, was of frame construction sheathed with clapboard, and usually possessed a porch or piazza stretching across the facade and possibly sides. Exterior walls of many rural houses appeared to be well aged, as paint has only recently been applied regularly. Fireplace chimneys are located inside the endwalls in several sections of Virginia. They disappeared altogether after the adoption of stoves for cooking and heating in the late 19th century. Stone construction was virtually unknown outside of the northern transitional zone. In scattered areas in Virginia and the Kentucky Bluegrass traditional houses were constructed of brick. Porches were least common in the Virginia Tidewater and northern transition zones.

Many southern vernacular house forms have existed, but only the southern hall-and-parlor house and the I house are found throughout the region. The hall-and-parlor house originated in Britain, and versions of it are found throughout the original colonies. It is a one-and-a-half story, one-room-deep house with two rooms across the facade. The southern hall-and-parlor house is found both with and without a central hallway separating the first-floor rooms. The I house developed as a two-story version of the earlier hall and parlor. It could be ornamented with elaborate piazzas, wings, and stylistic ornamentation, allowing its use both as a middle-class dwelling and as an elaborate plantation residence.

Religion is another factor that reveals the nature of the cultural landscape. Southern religion is distinguished by its conservative fundamentalist orientation, not its denominations. The South-

ern Baptist Convention is the largest single denominational body, and its distribution is often considered characteristic of the region. Church attendance and activities play a far more significant role in family and community life than in other parts of the United States.

A strong belief in the rights of the individual and the localization of political power is reflected in the South's political attitudes about local options, states' rights, and other manifestations of localized decision making. There are more counties, and each county is smaller and has more administrative duties than in any other region in America. The consolidation of school districts has been slower; state police units have less authority. These beliefs are also reflected in the region's violent-crime rate. Many southerners believe that it is the individual's right and duty to resolve conflict personally.

If regional attitudes can reveal southern distinctiveness, so can the distribution of regional and subregional foodways. The classic southern diet is distinguished by its wide use of quick breads (muffins and biscuits), corn products, grits, sweetened iced tea, and carbonated drinks. There is also greater dependence upon pork and chicken products for meat. Biscuits are so important to the southern breakfast that even McDonald's and Burger King have added biscuits to their breakfast menus. The consumption of grits is less evident than in the past but continues to be widespread. Consumption of carbonated drinks, especially colas, generally exceeds national averages. Fried foods and the overcooking (as judged by national tastes) of vegetables are two significant local preparation preferences.

Country music has long been recognized as a southern phenomenon but recently has lost much of its regional identity. Gospel music is less well known but is possibly more useful as a regional factor today. Thousands of gospel groups constantly perform throughout the South at revivals, churches, and concerts.

The Evolution of Subregions. The southern landscape began as a series of isolated settlement nodes along the Atlantic Coastal Plain that evolved independently throughout the 18th century. Three variables favored this situation: (1) the planters' desire to sell their products directly to British customers, rather than utilize American distribution centers; (2) the wide Atlantic Coastal Plain that allowed the unchallenged agricultural expansion into new lands; and (3) the presence of the Blue Ridge on the western frontier, which halted expansion of the agricultural frontier about the time that settlement overlap would have taken place.

The South thus has never possessed a homogeneous cultural landscape. The Atlantic Lowland is characterized by internal heterogeneity, which stems from its development prior to the Americanization of the landscape. The Gulf Coastal landscape primarily evolved from landscape features originating on the Atlantic Coast, with interregional differences stemming from its later development and the presence of large numbers of Upland South migrants and Caribbean immigrants. These two subregions form the Lowland South, but it is an uncomfortable unity. The Upland South developed more independently. Its original Pennsylvania culture was molded by a demanding physical environment and finally modified by transfusions of traditions from the Carolinas and Virginia. Some authorities

consider the Upland South a separate region.

The Lowland South: The Atlantic Lowland. The Atlantic Lowland was the first landscape created in the South and has the most internal variation. At least six subareas may be identified within its extent, as well as numerous pockets of two or three counties with less distinctive differences.

The urban landscape has the least consistency of character. A typical early Virginia Tidewater county seat has about 20 building lots on a single street. The two-story brick courthouse fronted by its aged Confederate war memorial and newer eternal flame is set on a central enlarged courthouse-square lot under a grove of sheltering oaks. A store covered with soft-drink signs faces it across the road; a nearby house or two completes the scene. In contrast, the later 19th-century county seats and rail centers were planned communities of substantial buildings looking much like those found throughout the remainder of the region.

The most important vernacular structures of the Atlantic Lowland are the southern hall-and-parlor house (Tidewater), the porched Tidewater house, the I house, and some special-function barns. Early regional houses were duplications of British houses with initial modifications, such as raised foundations for mildew control, primarily made to meet environmental problems. Houses were raised even higher in the Carolinas and southward to combat miasma. Kitchens were placed in a separate building to reduce house temperatures in summer.

Southern hall-and-parlor houses were built throughout the Atlantic Lowland, especially in Tidewater Virginia. The

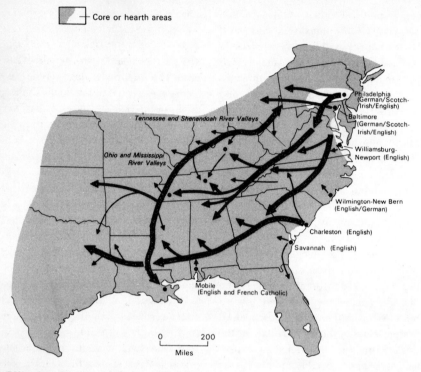

— Core or hearth areas

Philadelphia
(German/Scotch-
Irish/English)

Baltimore
(German/Scotch-
Irish/English)

Williamsburg-
Newport (English)

Tennessee and Shenandoah River Valleys

Ohio and Mississippi
River Valleys

Wilmington-New Bern
(English/German)

Charleston (English)

Savannah (English)

Mobile
(English and French Catholic)

0   200
Miles

Diffusion Routes of Cultural Patterns

Map by Richard Pillsbury

porched Tidewater is made distinctive with an incised front porch and frequent use of the catslide, or rear shed, kitchen. It was most common on the northern Piedmont and is found in scattered pockets in the Tidewater zone. Transitional versions of the house with attached porches are found in coastal Carolina and Georgia.

There is no standard I house in the Atlantic Lowland, although several distinct subtypes exist. Many early Chesapeake Bay examples are of brick, often with decorative glazed diaper brickwork. The later Piedmont Virginian version is a smaller frame three-bay structure with end chimneys. The typical Piedmont North Carolina version is squarer than those of Virginia, often with the chimneys placed inside the

endwalls. A South Carolina Tidewater and Savannah River version is larger and thinner and is distinguished by the centering of the fireplaces on the rear walls of the rooms.

Three distinctive barns are found in the region: the Chesapeake air-cured tobacco barn, the Carolina flue-cured tobacco barn, and the Carolina gable-opening barn. The Chesapeake air-cured tobacco barn is found on the western shore of Virginia and Maryland, in Lancaster County, Pa., and in the Bluegrass of Kentucky. It is an adaptation of the English flat barn modified for tobacco curing by placing the entries at the gable ends, adding racks for hanging the curing tobacco, and attaching movable siding to increase air flow through the structure.

Flue-cured tobacco barns are found in central North Carolina and in southeastern Georgia and adjacent Florida. The earliest Carolina flue-cured tobacco barns were saddle-notched log cubes with a small door in one side. Granny's apron porches wrap around two or more of the sides to shelter workers tying tobacco hands. Newer examples are of frame and clapboard construction. The entire structure is being phased out today by aluminum and galvanized metal garagelike buildings that can accommodate the tobacco wagons.

The Carolina gable-opening barn is found on the central Carolina Piedmont and environs with no obvious precursors. It is a large two-story structure with the upper floor used as a hay loft. The half-open center first floor may have been a threshing and unloading area for hay wagons. Two side aisles lead to a series of stalls for horses and cattle. This barn is related to the transverse crib barn of the southern Appalachians.

The cultural landscape has been shaped by many other factors as well. Baptist and Methodist denominations in the Atlantic Lowlands account for only 60 percent of the region's church membership. The Presbyterian Church of the United States, the Church of God, Disciples of Christ, the Pentecostal Holiness, and the Protestant Episcopal churches follow in order of importance. These denominations are found throughout the region as a whole, but several islands of atypical groups are also present. Central North Carolina, with its large population of the Society of Friends, Moravian, and United Church of Christ members, is the best known of these. Others are remnants of early settlements that have maintained their religious identities.

Regional dietary preferences reflect the Atlantic Lowland's prototypical relationship to the remainder of the South. Recipes for Brunswick stew, barbecue, and other regional favorites reflect these dishes at the earliest stages of their development. The standard regional menu also exhibits greater diversity than generally found farther west.

The Lowland South: the Gulf Coastal Lowland. The Gulf Coastal landscape begins near the Savannah River and extends westward into eastern Texas. The Federal Road, connecting Charleston, S.C., with Augusta, Ga., and thence along the fall line to Macon and Columbus, Ga., and Montgomery, Ala., and beyond, served as the single most important route for new settlers into the region. The Upper Federal Road connecting the Carolina and Virginia Piedmont with the Gulf Coast was nearly as significant. Moderate numbers of settlers from the Caribbean entered the region through Savannah, Mobile, and New Orleans. The northern section was strongly influenced by Appalachian settlers migrating through the valleys of the Tennessee River into northern Alabama and Mississippi.

Urban patterns in the region are essentially refinements of those established earlier on the Atlantic Seaboard. County-seat planners almost universally adopted the rectilinear street plan, the central courthouse square, large residential building lots, and standardized street names. The dispersed community continued to be the most common urban type, although railroad builders established hundreds of cotton gin and warehouse centers during the 19th century. Morphologically these towns follow national models: rectilinear street pattern; main business district facing the depot; relatively smaller residential lots; and streets numbered in one direction and in the other direction either lettered or named after plants, animals, or important people.

The rural scene is also an extension of the Atlantic Lowland landscape. Wooded sections are more frequent, and forest buffers between fields are more common. Southernmost areas are composed of seemingly endless tree farms, which often obscure the presence of the traditional agrarian landscape. The Gulf Coastal Lowland was once known as the cotton belt, but the boll weevil, competing agricultural areas, and polyester have changed that. Large acreages have reverted to forest, others have been converted to pasture, and the remainder have been used primarily for corn and soybeans. Cultivation of agricultural products including strawberries, pecans, peanuts, table vegetables, and catfish adds variety to the landscape.

The classic image of a Gulf Coastal tenant farm is of a small two-room frame hall-and-parlor house with rusting galvanized metal roof and unpainted clapboard walls. Two or three chairs sit on a drooping, attached porch that stretches across the front. The house stands in the midst of a hard-packed swept yard in the shade of a huge chinaberry tree. The attached rear kitchen is connected to the house with a wraparound porch on the inside of the "L." A frame single-crib barn with shed addition on one side sits behind the large family garden. Dried gourds for purple martin houses hang from a line stretching from a pole in the garden to the barn. The small, raised, square, log corncrib and smokehouse to one side are shaded by giant oaks. Three small cornfields behind the barn can barely be seen through the hazy white heat of summer. Gulf Coastal vernacular houses have

lower-pitched rooflines than those of the Atlantic Lowland because of the popularity of the Greek Revival in the early 19th century, when most were built. Summer heat also made the lofts difficult to use. Central hallways were often widened into breezeways to promote cross-ventilation. The dogtrot hall— meaning here a central hallway extending the length of the house—was used on all house forms in the region. True dogtrot houses—those with a covered, open-ended hallway between two wings of the house—were common as well. Gulf Coastal houses had taller foundation pillars than were found to the east. The detached kitchen was moved closer to the house so that only a few feet separated the two buildings, with an inside "L" rear porch tying them together.

The most important vernacular house forms during the early period were two versions of the hall-and-parlor house, the I house, and the dogtrot house; the southern pyramidal, shotgun, and frame saddlebag house types were popular in later periods. The southern (Louisiana) bungalow was widely used after World War I. National styles dominated the scene after 1930.

Tenant and small farmers were the most frequent occupants of the smaller hall-and-parlor house described previously. The larger hall-and-parlor house often served as the main house of small plantations. It was modified with a flattish roofline and enlarged returns on the eaves. A stylish Greek Revival portico stretched across the center third of the facade to give the house greater presence. The kitchen was a catslide (shed) extension across the rear of the house.

Gulf Coastal I houses tended to be larger and somewhat more pretentious than those of the Atlantic Lowland. The central hall was wider, often with double front doors; the rooms were larger; and the facade was built with five bays. It was a favorite house form to be modified for use as a plantation house with splashes of exterior ornamentation such as columns, porticos, friezes, and/or brackets.

Dogtrot houses began as two single-pen log units tied together with a floored breezeway, porch, and common roof. The origin of the house is unknown. Isolated examples may be found as far north as Maryland, although the upper Tennessee River basin was apparently the earliest center for their widespread use. Log versions of the houses are found on the northern Gulf Coastal Plain, but it is more widely seen as a frame-and-clapboard house in the southern half of the region.

The shotgun house originated in Africa, matured in the Caribbean, and first appeared in America in New Orleans and in other Caribbean settlement areas. Most Gulf Coastal shotgun houses probably were not an expression of the region's vernacular tradition. Thousands were sold in the late 19th and early 20th centuries as tenant and worker housing by lumber companies specializing in precut and prefabricated houses. Most are in the mill and lumber towns of the Mississippi drainage basin, where their narrow frontage was in demand.

Saddlebag houses were used as tenant and worker houses during this period in the eastern Gulf Coast. They are frame, central-chimney, two-front-door, two-room houses, which were occasionally used to shelter two families. A two-room, rear-kitchen-shed addition is typical. The form originated in Britain and was adapted for log construction in Pennsylvania. The frame version was developed by Appalachian settlers in

the 19th century. Most were built after the Civil War from precut or prefabricated house kits.

The southern pyramidal probably evolved during the mid-19th century from an earlier straight gable house in the Savannah River area of Georgia. The oldest version of this house has four rooms with a wide central hall. A high-peaked pyramidal roof with two chimneys placed a few feet on either side of its short roofridge distinguishes the house. This was a favorite town home of the upper middle class from Reconstruction to the Depression, although it is found in smaller numbers in rural areas as well. Prefabricated housing companies also marketed several other versions of this house for management and worker housing in company towns.

Frame single-crib barns with side-shed additions are the most visible outbuildings of the Gulf Coast. These structures evolved from the single-crib log barns of the Upland South. Some double-crib log barns are also found along the northern margins of the region, but they are not common. Several types of corncribs are found, although the most distinctive is of Cherokee (possibly Creek) origin and is a squarish log (or frame) crib raised a few feet off the ground.

Religious patterns helped to distinguish this subregion, as with other areas in the South. The Southern Baptist and United Methodist churches claim more than 80 percent of all church membership on the Gulf Coast. In some areas as much as 90 percent of the population tabulated by the United Council of Churches in a 1971 survey claimed membership in these two bodies. The region's dietary patterns are also a simplified version of those found on the Atlantic Coastal Plain. The dominance in foodways of pork, chicken, and corn products is almost complete, although yams are also popular. The high consumption of colas, sweetened iced tea, buttermilk, catfish, hush puppies, greens, and peas is also significant.

The Upland South. The evolution of the Upland South began with the southward migration of Pennsylvanian settlers along the limestone valleys of the Ridge and Valley physiographic province. They mixed with Piedmont Virginians moving up the Potomac and James rivers and Carolinian elements entering by way of the Wilderness Road and the Little Tennessee River. A cultural milieu soon evolved that was strikingly different from that of either hearth region. Complexity was added by the Cherokee nation, which stopped significant European expansion into their section of the southern Appalachians through 1838 and contributed many cultural elements to this milieu. The Mississippi and Ohio rivers and the Natchez Trace were significant commercial arteries serving the region, but they had little impact on the evolution of the cultural landscape.

Urban landscapes in the Upland South are dominated by three types of centers: industrial cities, county seats, and coal camps. The Industrial Revolution left its mark on the region's larger cities: grimy brick buildings, thriving chemical plants, abandoned factories, tortuous streets bent to match sites never meant for urban living, and aged housing. In contrast, the region's county seats are marked by their formal designs and relative cleanliness, as are those of the Gulf Coast.

Traditional coal and agrarian landscapes have always maintained an un-

easy coexistence in the Upland South, each almost unaware of the other. Miners rarely strayed from their camps, perched precariously overlooking the mine apparatus or squatting in a straggling line of matchbox houses along a narrow hollow leading to the overshadowing mine, tipple, and slag piles. There has always been a sense of impermanence about these places, although most are more than 50 years old. The recent rise of strip mining and decline of the fixed-site mining operations have spelled doom for many.

Land abandonment is the most pervasive phenomenon in the rural Upland South. Despite a widely scattered population, few people make their living from the land. The sense of having a homeplace and of being connected with distant forefathers is, nonetheless, strong here. Appalachia has the highest percentage of rural nonfarm population in the nation. Many have left, only to discover the depth of their attachment to home. It has taken more than 30 years of living and working in Pittsburgh, Detroit, and other industrial cities for many of the post–World War II expatriates to finally begin to set roots in their new homes.

The terrain of the Upland South favors the creation of many distinctive landscapes. A typical traditional farmstead of central West Virginia consists of a log saddlebag or small-frame I house, a single-crib log barn, a small house garden, a springhouse, a smokehouse, and several fields of corn or hay, all clustered in a small hollow. The hay is piled on poled haystacks in the fields, the fences are made of split rail, and the plowing is done with a horse—or more recently with a large rototiller. Transverse crib barns, double-crib log barns, log dogtrot houses, fewer outbuildings, and larger fields are more common in southern Appalachia.

Larger houses, mechanization, and commercial agriculture appear where the land is better—in the Ridge and Valley province, the Nashville Basin, and elsewhere. The rolling limestone pastures, thoroughbreds lolling behind their wooden fences, and mansions of the Kentucky Bluegrass certainly form yet another landscape. So, too, do the estates, orchards, and poultry farms of the Shenandoah Valley, the dairy farms of the Ridge and Valley province, and the horse farms of central Tennessee.

Log houses are still widespread in the region. Early builders favored central-European log construction featuring hewn logs, half dovetail corner timbering in the earlier and "V" corner notching in the later structures, and boards to cover the eaves. Group house raisings were one of the most important forces in the early evolution of standardized construction and housing styles. Construction techniques became simplified through time. Logs continued to be used in the house and outbuilding construction until the 1930s, and isolated examples were built as late as the 1970s.

Log single-pen houses, log and frame saddlebag houses, I houses, and single-

Cabin in eastern Kentucky mountains, 1940

and double-crib barns are the most common traditional structures in the region. Dogtrot houses frequently appear in southern Appalachia. Four- and six-crib transverse barns possibly originated in the southeastern section. Coal mining introduced company towns and several new house forms to the region: gable-facing I houses, a saltbox duplex, and a simple southern pyramidal house. The gable-facing I house is a common Industrial Age company house in America, created by turning a standard I house 90 degrees on its axis to reduce street frontage. Two-story duplexes with rear shed sections, much like the New England saltbox, were popular in the northern coal camps. The pyramidal house was most common in the South. It has four interconnected rooms and stove heating.

In regard to the other diagnostic features of southern regionalism, literal interpretation of the Bible is the most identifiable feature of the religion of the Upland South. The Baptist and Methodist churches dominate numerically, but the region's religious character stems from its unaffiliated churches and small denominations that stress fundamentalism. Most are untabulated in church membership surveys, but the larger denominations include the Church of God, Disciples of Christ, Assemblies of God, the Churches of Christ, and the Pentecostal and Holiness sects. The Presbyterian church is strong in many areas because of the numerous early Scotch-Irish settlers.

Country music has recently undergone a dramatic nationalization making it less clearly than before tied to the South. However, recording continues to be concentrated in Nashville, and performers continue to be predominantly southern in origin. Gospel music and general religious programming in the electronic media are far more distinctive to this area today than is country music.

Other Cultural Landscapes: Acadian Louisiana. The South also encompasses areas that are not a part of the mainstream regional landscape including Acadian Louisiana and, increasingly, southern Florida. Transition zones often become distinctive in their look as well. Acadia began to develop in southern Louisiana after the arrival of French settlers from maritime Canada in the 18th century. These Acadians, or Cajuns, formed a coherent community along the waterways of southern Louisiana and adjacent areas. Their isolation continued until the discovery of oil in the early 20th century brought outsiders, roads, a new Cajun self-awareness, and money. Recently, too, tourism has increased.

Acadian Louisiana illustrates well the role of culture in determining the look of a place. Inheritance laws required the equal division of estates among the children, so land lots are fairly uniform in size. The importance of water access for transportation and commerce, coupled with the character of the natural levee lands that the Acadians traditionally settled, virtually forced the division of the lands into narrow farms radiating away from the streams. Strassendorfs, or street villages, developed as landowners built their homes along the lot frontages. Today most commercial activities, and the Catholic churches, are located in the formal towns.

The Acadian house is a one-and-a-half-story, four-room house with an incised front porch. The rooms may be separated by a central hall. Fireplaces are located between the two rooms on each side of the hall. The rear kitchen addition looks like a smaller mirror image of the main house. Drainpipe systems and cisterns once collected rainwater for household use in low-lying areas. Houses with partial Acadian features are found, as well as greatly enlarged "plantation" houses.

Other significant elements of the Acadian cultural landscape include Roman Catholicism, place names, a variety of unique dietary preferences, and some retention of the French language. Almost 88 percent of the entire population of St. Martin Parish and more than 80 percent of all church adherents in Acadia belong to the Roman Catholic church. French alliterations and terminology, especially the names of saints, dominate the region's place names. The term *bayou* is commonly used and is believed to be French in origin, although, in fact, it is from the Choctaw word *bayuk*. The most striking dietary preferences include dark-roast and chicory coffee, rice, and seafood. Crawfish have almost become a fetish in recent years. The Cajun French language is rarely heard on the street today but is still used in the home by older citizens. Most residents have a distinct regional accent.

Other Cultural Landscapes: Southern Florida. Southern Florida was only sparsely settled prior to the 20th century, and little traditional cultural landscape remains. Population growth began with the construction of railroads in the 1890s and dramatically increased after World War II. This unfettered development created a unique melange of early tourist kitsch and 20th-century fads beneath a garish, land-promoter facade.

Most of Florida was originally subdivided by the township-and-range land-division system. The straight lines and square properties are often only obvious in the many straight segments of the secondary road system. This unique 20th-century landscape is dominated by the familiar. Most older towns have rigidly numbered street grids with endless modern, curved-street subdivisions. The 1920s are early history here, and the architectural styles and structures of that period, especially the Spanish stucco rococo, dominate the older sections of many towns. The 1950s brought the legitimization and widespread use of stucco-faced concrete block construction; brick is less common.

Florida's late-developing towns in many ways epitomize strip-development America. Strong central business districts are rare, as the commercial landscape is dominated by chaotic strips of white concrete suburban shopping centers, with pale yellow and green galvanized facades above plate-glass windows, interspersed among fast-food stores and motels at the edge of town. Endless walls of high-rise condominiums now separate the beaches from the public along the Florida coastlines.

The arrival of thousands of Cuban and other Caribbean immigrants since the late 1950s has had a revolutionary impact on the landscape. The addition of over 100,000 Cuban immigrants in the early 1980s further intensified the Cubanization of the Miami and southern Florida cultural milieu. Currently, over 40 percent of metropolitan Miami is of Hispanic descent, whereas only 6 percent of the state's overall population has a similar origin. Language and other cultural differences have tended to accentuate the Cuban presence, much as they did that of the Italian, Polish, and Czech immigrants in the Northeast. The

Cubans have built few distinctive edifices, but the rise of Cuban food specialties, the increase in the number of signs in Spanish, and the use of more vibrant colors have made the Hispanic residents a visible part of the landscape.

The greatest changes in Florida's landscape in recent years stem from the state's rapid industrialization. Small factories are springing up throughout the state as it is becoming an electronics, consumer-goods, and apparel-manufacturing center. Miami is replacing New Orleans as the gateway to the Caribbean and South America. Melbourne and Orlando have become major electronics centers. The last remnants of the regional landscape are disappearing as rapid growth covers the poorly preserved past.

Other Cultural Areas: Transition Zones. Transition zones between two dynamic areas are typified by cultural tension as residents adapt their lifestyles to fit the changing milieu. The term *Little Dixie* has been applied to a variety of southern border areas in Arkansas, Missouri, Oklahoma, and Illinois. These places are characterized by a mixture of the traits of the South and adjacent regions. Surviving southern traits generally include accent, the importance of the Baptist denomination, and the retention of some food preferences.

New Directions. Change is sweeping the traditional South and creating a new landscape. Saddlebag houses lie abandoned in overgrown fields, camp-meeting grounds are deserted, and boarded cotton-gin towns stand beside their railroad tracks. Landscapes are never static, but the nationalization of the southern landscape has been exceptionally rapid. The new era began with the exposure of thousands of young American soldiers to Europe and the migration of southerners to the labor-short northern factories during World War I. World War II sent another generation of young men away but also introduced many northern soldiers to snowless winters. The postwar period saw the death of traditional tenant farming and the virtual emptying by out-migration of vast sections of the agricultural South. These shifts in the region's population set the stage for the massive changes in culture and landscape that were to follow.

Television and the national print media have long been considered two of the most potent forces underlying the homogenization of contemporary American culture. They brought national fads, accents, and trends into southern living rooms. The impact of national retailers and franchisers has been recognized less frequently, but their insensitivity to regional tastes and their reliance on homogenized menus, central purchasing, and standardized inventories have been equally destructive of regional personality. There is little room here for men in overalls sitting at country stores, drinking R. C. Colas and eating Moon Pies.

The southern landscape has not been altered uniformly. Change has been most rapid in the cities, least rapid in rural areas. Traditional cuisine, regional vernacular housing, and southern values are increasingly difficult to find in Atlanta. The skylines and street scenes of Atlanta, Dallas, and Houston look much the same as those in other 20th-century American cities. Their landscapes are dominated by department stores, restaurants, specialty retailers, malls, and fast-food chains that

strive for national identities. Even southern and non-southern street signs are alike.

Simultaneously, small towns with such names as Union Point, Jackson, Haralson, and Magnolia are enduring slow deaths as stores close, buildings crumble, and weeds find their way through the cracks in the streets. Thousands of small towns are passing from the landscape because they no longer seem to have a role in modern society; paved roads, automobiles, and increased ties to national culture have seen to that. There has been some return to the small town, but mainly as a residential retreat within urban commuter zones.

Industry is thriving in the South. North Carolina has the third highest percentage of industrial workers in the nation. Small, labor-intensive factories increasingly are coming to the region's towns in search of cheap labor. These towns are transformed, too, as traditional courthouse-square business districts are bypassed by national retail and food chains that prefer suburban, automobile-oriented commercial strips. New subdivisions and houses fashioned from images in *House Beautiful* and *Family Circle* spring up helter-skelter around the towns' edges.

The rural scene has undergone even more radical change. Dispersed communities focused on country stores are changing as the rural residents increasingly seek nonfarm occupations and commute to jobs in town. Traditional housing is rapidly giving way to the new southern "vernacular" architecture of Jim Walters and mobile homes.

The South's contemporary experience is a reminder that landscapes are composed of overlays of new fashions and technologies, and the cultural elements of each new era compete with those of earlier times. The new thus pushes aside the old and continually creates a new landscape.

See also ART AND ARCHITECTURE: Farm Buildings; Vernacular Architecture (Upland South); ENVIRONMENT articles; ETHNIC LIFE: Caribbean Influence; Indian Cultural Contributions; Mountain Culture; / Cajuns; Cubans; FOLKLIFE: House Types; / Dogtrot; I House; Pyramidal House; Saddlebag House; Shotgun House; HISTORY AND MANNERS: Foodways; / Beverages; LANGUAGE: Names, Place; MUSIC: Country Music; Gospel Music, Black; Gospel Music, White

Richard Pillsbury
Georgia State University

Thomas R. Ford, ed., *The Southern Appalachian Region: A Survey* (1962); Raymond D. Gastil, *Cultural Regions of the United States* (1975); Henry Glassie, *Pattern in the Material Folk Culture of the Eastern United States* (1968); J. Fraser Hart, *The Southeastern United States* (1967); Sam B. Hilliard, *Hog Meat and Hoecake: Food Supply in the Old South, 1840–1860* (1972); John Brinckerhoff Jackson, *American Space: The Centennial Years, 1865–1876* (1972), *The Southern Landscape Tradition in Texas* (1980); Terry G. Jordan, *Annals of the Association of American Geographers* (No. 4, 1967), *Texas Graveyards* (1982); D. W. Meinig, *The Shaping of America: A Geographical Perspective on 500 Years of History: Atlantic America, 1492–1800*, vol. 1 (1986); Howard W. Odum, *Southern Regions of the United States* (1936); James R. Shortridge, *Journal for the Scientific Study of Religion* (June 1977); John R. Stilgoe, *Common Landscape of America, 1580–1845* (1984); Rupert B. Vance, *Human Geography of the South: A Study of Regional Resources and Human Adequacy* (1932); Wilbur Zelinsky, *The Cultural Geography of the United States* (1973), *Social Forces* (December 1951). ☆

Appalachia

||||||||||||||||||||||||||||

See ETHNIC LIFE: Mountain Culture

Ethnic Geography

||||||||||||||||||||||||||||||||||||||||||||

Many of the social systems and distinctive elements of culture that vary within the South and that collectively help distinguish the region can be explained on the basis of ethnicity. Ethnic geography explores the spatial aspects of ethnicity. Place is an important component of ethnicity, and ethnic groups exhibit territorial patterns of organization by clustering in defined areas. Ethnic groups in the South are distributed in spatial units that range from a few relatively large regional concentrations, including Mexican Americans along the borderlands of Texas, Cubans in south Florida, and Cajuns in southern Louisiana, to numerous small rural and urban enclaves scattered throughout the region.

The impact of ethnicity on the culture and landscape of the South, vis-à-vis other large regions of the country, depends to some extent upon the operational definition of *ethnic group*. Traditionally, ethnic groups have been defined strictly on the basis of common ancestry, national origins, and associated cultural traits. By this standard the South is comparatively lacking in ethnic diversity, considering that the region has attracted proportionately few foreign immigrants, especially foreign-born Caucasians, since the mid-19th century.

Many groups in the South, however,

can best be characterized by traits that are essentially ethnic in nature. One of the most significant identifying elements of an ethnic group is an internalized sense of distinctiveness and an external perception of that distinctiveness. Ethnic identity is not ascriptive; it is a matter of individual and group choice. The recognition of minority status tends to foster among members of an ethnic group an intense feeling of belonging to a community.

Examples of ethnic indicators might include race, religious affiliation, ancestral or mother language, common settlement and employment patterns, political philosophy, shared literature, folklore and music, cuisine preferences, and migratory status. By these indicators blacks, American Indian tribes, mixed-blood groups, various religious sects and groups, and perhaps even selected occupational enclaves in the South may be considered—and are most likely to consider themselves—ethnic groups.

The South has been called the most "native" region of the country because most southerners trace their ancestry in the United States back to settlers who arrived before 1850, and in many cases before 1800. The South's share of the nearly 50 million immigrants who have settled in America since the beginning of the 19th century is disproportionately small. The region's inability to attract foreign immigrants has been due to limited economic opportunities, a social climate many of them found unacceptable, and a xenophobia on the part of southerners. Although ostensibly more ethnically diverse through recent immigration, the South in 1980 had fewer than 5 million first- and second-generation Americans. Moreover, well over half of these were either of Mexican

or Cuban descent and resided on the geographical fringes of the region.

The relative lack of foreign immigration is coupled with the fact that the Anglo population of the South is derived overwhelmingly from one source area—northwest Europe, especially the British Isles. The black population, too, though diverse in its African ethnic origins, was rather quickly homogenized into an Afro-American mold.

The consequences of this pattern of settlement were profound, particularly in terms of the relatively uniform cultural milieu that evolved. The narrowed range of religions, for example, resulted in the South's becoming the most Protestant region of the country. This lack of ethnic diversity greatly influenced the shaping of the southern identity and southern attitudes toward both the region itself and the rest of the world. The relative cultural and social homogeneity of the South has even led some scholars to suggest that white and black southerners should be considered ethnic groups in their own right.

The lack of diversity has served to heighten ethnic groups' awareness of their minority status. This has encouraged such groups to settle in well-defined, often small-scale concentrations, thereby increasing their external visibility. Residential segregation likewise tends to increase social interaction and reinforces institutional differences between the group and the larger society, thus perpetuating distinctive ethnic identities. Although ethnic exclusiveness is a source of mutual support and cultural security, it may also lead to conflict through clannish suspicion and distrust of outsiders.

Ethnic groups are the keepers of distinctive cultural traditions. From the Germans of the Ozarks and the hill country of Texas to the Hungarians in Tangipahoa Parish, La., to the mixed-blood Lumbees of North Carolina, ethnic groups foster the continuity of culture and of social systems. These traditions are reinforced through friendships, family ties, business contacts, church affiliations, and social activities. Periodic celebrations and festivals, both secular and religious, also strengthen these ties.

The nonmaterial elements of culture, including language, religion, music, symbols, beliefs and values, along with cuisine preferences, are generally retained longer than most material elements of culture. Yet land-survey systems, settlement patterns, agricultural practices, and architectural preferences, among other material elements, may persist indefinitely among certain groups; they provide graphic imprints of an ethnic group's tenure in an area.

While ethnic groups persist in the South, they also change through the process of acculturation. The Scotch-Irish, for example, have been completely assimilated, existing only in the memories of their descendants. As migration continues to add new ethnic groups to the South, ethnicity continues to enrich the life and landscape of the region.

See also BLACK LIFE: Immigrants and Blacks; ETHNIC LIFE articles; RELIGION: Ethnic Protestantism

James R. Curtis
University of Miami

Russel L. Gerlach, *Immigrants in the Ozarks: A Study in Ethnic Geography* (1976); Terry G. Jordan, *German Seed in Texas Soil: Immigrant Farmers in Nineteenth-Century Texas* (1966); William Lynwood Montell, *Saga of Coe Ridge: A Study in Oral History*

(1970); Lauren C. Post, *Cajun Sketches: From the Prairies of Southwest Louisiana* (1962); George B. Tindall, *The Ethnic Southerners* (1976); Wilbur Zelinsky, *The Cultural Geography of the United States* (1973). ☆

Expatriates and Exiles

||||||||||||||||||||||||||||||||||||||||||||||||||||||||||||

Basil Ransome, a character in Henry James's *The Bostonians* (1886), left his native South after the Civil War and headed for New York City "with fifty dollars in his pocket and a gnawing hunger in his heart." He exemplified what Thomas Wolfe described as the southerner consumed by an "eternal wandering, moving, questing, loneliness, homesickness." The uprooted southerner, Wolfe's Ishmael, has been a culturally important figure since the Civil War. Despite the notable southern attachment to localism, mobility has also been a characteristic of 20th-century southerners, but perhaps because of the power of memory and of place, emigrant southerners have continued to ponder the region and its meaning.

"Exile" is used here in the *Webster's* definition of "voluntary absence from one's country or home." Many of the thousands of Confederates who left the region after the Civil War did so for political reasons, as did many blacks at that same time and since, who left to escape the South's racial system. These were political emigrés, of a sort, but they were part of the broader phenomenon of individuals who left the region for economic, intellectual, or social reasons, as well as political ones, and yet took their southern identity and customs with them. White working-class emigrants and black emigrants established communities in northern cities, but the focus here is on business leaders, professionals, writers, scholars, teachers, painters, sculptors, and other intellectual and gifted southerners who left the region, causing a "brain drain" of talent out of the South.

In the aftermath of the Civil War, prominent former Confederates headed in all directions, to all parts of the United States and to other areas of the world. Unhappy with postwar conditions and fearful of the Reconstruction future, they left the South seeking better opportunities for financial, social, and artistic success. Confederate cabinet member Judah P. Benjamin went to England and had a successful legal career there. Diplomat John Slidell moved to Paris and was in England when he died. Former vice president John C. Breckinridge and Confederate general Jubal Early moved to Canada. Three Confederate generals (C. W. Field, William C. Loring, and Henry W. Sibley) went to Egypt to help train that country's army, and a few Lost Cause refugees wound up in Japan and Australia.

Between 4,000 and 6,000 Confederates immigrated to Central America, with Mexico attracting the largest number. Several thousand southerners set up colonies in Mexico, mostly at Carlota and Cordova, between Mexico City and Vera Cruz. Matthew Fontaine Maury, Confederate admiral and an oceanographer, served as commissioner of immigration to Mexican Emperor Maximilian's government and helped to launch a group exodus from the South. At least 17 Confederate generals were part of this migration, including Edmund Kirby-Smith, Thomas C. Hindman, Sterling Price, and John B.

Magruder. Other Confederates sought refuge in Honduras and on Caribbean islands such as Jamaica and Cuba.

Between 2,500 and 4,000 southerners reached South America, most of them before 1870 and most in Brazilian agricultural colonies. The Brazilian government, like that of Mexico, encouraged the immigration, offering cheap land, advertising in southern periodicals, and providing agents to promote and facilitate the migration. The Reverend Ballard S. Dunn of New Orleans proved to be an especially effective lobbyist for migration, with his book *Brazil, The Home for Southerners* (1866). Four areas of Brazil attracted southerners: Santarem, on the Amazon River; Rio Doce; Iguape, or "Lizzieland," as Ballard Dunn named it in honor of a daughter; and a cluster of three colonies (Campo, Retiro, and Villa America) in the São Paulo region.

Most of the emigrants to Latin America had returned to the United States by the 1870s, but about 20 percent of southern emigrants to Brazil settled there permanently, a greater percentage than in other areas of Latin America. Many descendants of Confederate emigrants to Brazil have lost any sense of their southern ancestry, but some still retain southern identity. Americana, Brazil, has 400 or so surviving descendants, and 440 tombstones, marked with English inscriptions, which mark the graves of ex-Confederates. A Fraternity of American Descendants meets quarterly in the cemetery and holds a potluck dinner. The menu in 1984 included such down-home fare as fried chicken, biscuits, corn bread, pecan pie, watermelon, and soda pop. As well as speaking Portuguese, many of these Confederate descendants can still speak the southern English dialect of their ancestors. Their association sells Confederate-flag decals to raise money.

A larger number of southern Confederates went north and west within the United States, but until recently scholars have been less interested in studying their lives than those of the more exotic migrants to foreign lands. "Texas fever" hit the South in the 1870s, and thousands of freedmen and whites went there seeking anonymity and a fresh start. Many became cowboys and participated in the postwar cattle industry. California also proved a popular spot for southern emigrants, but northern cities such as New York City, Philadelphia, and Boston attracted even more southerners. Most of these migrants were young— mostly under 35 years of age—and well educated. Many had lived in the North at times before the war or had been frequent visitors there. The key years for emigration were 1865–68, with a sharp drop after 1871. According to the leading scholar of this movement, Daniel E. Sutherland, 57 percent of a group of 298 subjects who have left detailed records remained in the North after going there.

Southern landowners who had fallen on hard times went north, as did professional and business people who hoped to find a better market than the postwar South for goods and services. Fear of the future motivated many of them. Northern schools, especially medical colleges, attracted those wanting to further their education. War widows were frequent visitors, sometimes for extended periods. Painters, sculptors, and architects sought training and patrons. Some young southerners, like other restless rural Americans, went north to seek excitement in the region's bustling cities. Sutherland noted, however, that these emigrants "remained southern in mind and heart."

New York City held the greatest attraction of all northern cities for these southerners. It was traditionally a gathering spot for southern financiers and vacationers and a hotbed of pro-southern sentiment during the war. As a result of earlier contacts, friends, relatives, and business acquaintances in the city provided assistance to postwar exiles such as Thomas F. Ryan and John H. Inman, who became financial magnates, and Charles B. Rouss, a former Confederate private who by the 1880s had become a leading wholesale and retail merchant. Roger A. Pryor in law, John A. Wyeth in medicine, William R. O'Donovan in art, and George C. Eggleston in literature were all former Confederates who made their reputations in the North.

Southerners in the North were a self-conscious group. They associated with each other, organized societies, went to church together, and assisted each other in time of need. Proud of their heritage, they donated money to the construction of universities, churches, and public buildings in the South. Many expatriates were sensitive to northern slights and scornful of Yankees. Though some were eager to exploit northerners, they nonetheless played a role in sectional reconciliation. Northerners generally accepted southerners in their midst, and personal contact mitigated political prejudices. Northern businessmen also used southerners with old names and admirable war records as liaisons to win back the southern market for their products.

The New York Southern Society, founded in 1886 by southerners who had succeeded in the North, preserved relics of the Old South, worked toward sectional reconciliation, and helped normalize business relations between the regions. The society welcomed New Yorkers of southern birth or heritage. Southern businessmen were allowed to enjoy the benefits of the club while in town. The society was more a New South organization than an unreconstructed Old South group. It canonized Washington and Jefferson more than Lee and Davis. It typically commemorated Washington's birthday, for example, in a gaudy manner, appropriate to the era. Banjo players provided music, members dined on dishes including Old Dominion Fried Hominy, and they toasted sectional harmony with large amounts of Magnolia Punch.

Black southerners are another, larger group that has frequently been in exile from its land of birth. Black migration out of the South in the early 20th century had important meaning for the emergence of a mature and distinct black artistic and intellectual tradition. Writers such as Richard Wright (Mississippi), Zora Neale Hurston (Florida), and James Weldon Johnson (Florida); scholars such as Arna Bontemps (Louisiana) and Carter Woodson (Virginia); performers such as Ma Rainey (Georgia), Bessie Smith (Tennessee), Leontyne Price (Mississippi), Roland Hayes (Georgia), Fletcher Henderson (Georgia), and later, Dizzy Gillespie (South Carolina), Lester Young (Louisiana), and Thelonious Monk (North Carolina)—all were southern born yet made their cultural contributions outside the region. Each took advantage of opportunities in the North that were denied under the South's repressive racial system. Also, the South's paucity of cultural and intellectual resources did not provide support for many kinds of cultural achievements for either race.

The Harlem Renaissance of the 1920s was an outpouring of energy in black literature, music, dance, and entertainment. It followed the great wave of black migration to the North during and after World War I, and many of the leaders of this renaissance were southern born and utilized southern settings and themes. Sterling Brown's collection of poems was called *Southern Road* (1932); Arna Bontemps's *Black Thunder* (1936) was based on Gabriel Prosser's 1821 slave revolt in South Carolina; Zora Neale Hurston's play *Color Struck* (1925) was set in a segregated railroad coach in the South; and Jean Toomer's *Cane* (1923), a series of poems, short stories, and vignettes, captured the life of black people in Georgia lumber camps of the 1890s.

It was natural that black intellectuals, many of whom were born in the South, would turn to the region for material. Exile from the region gave them both perspective and the freedom to work realistically with this material. Earlier black writers, though, had employed genteel literary traditions, frequently writing stories of well-off northern blacks. In the aftermath of the wave of black migration during and after World War I, intellectuals "discovered" the culture of southern black folk. Ohio-born Langston Hughes recalled that his view of black culture was shaped by seeing migrants from the South coming into and through Ohio. Southern blacks in exile, then, gained an opportunity for cultural achievement, using as their raw material their own personal and group experiences from the South.

The maturation of 20th-century southern intellectual life in general has depended on the exile experience. Critic Louis D. Rubin, Jr., argues that the writers of the Southern Literary Renaissance were alienated from their communities, partly because of time spent out of the South. All of the contributors to *I'll Take My Stand* (1930), the preeminent statement of southern Agrarianism, had spent time out of the South; Robert Penn Warren's essay for that volume was written while he was in England. Their perspective gained on the region came from leaving it. Future novelists and poets grew up in the traditional South of the 1900s and 1910s, went off to college, but did not return home after graduation. Education and living away from their communities distanced them from their origins. Some left the country. William Faulkner took a walking tour through France and Italy in the summer of 1925. Katherine Anne Porter worked for the revolutionary government in Mexico in that decade. Thomas Wolfe traveled extensively in Europe, and especially Germany. These southern writers were not, however, a part of the lost-generation exile experience, which centered in France and rejected tradition and the general idea of regionalism.

More important than European exile, almost all the South's major writers in this period went north at some point. Thomas Wolfe, growing up in Asheville, N.C., dreamed of "the golden vision of the city," as he says in *The Web and the Rock* (1939). The city was a place of escape and of fulfillment. Southern literature is filled with descriptions of youthful southerners loose without moorings in the big city: Peyton Loftis in Styron's *Lie Down in Darkness*; Eugene McLain wandering through San Francisco in Welty's *The Golden Apples*; and Quentin Compson in Faulkner's *The Sound and the Fury*, who wanders to and eventually commits suicide in far-off Cambridge, Mass. All are southerners far from home, estranged from their region, and yet also alienated from the

city. Most of these southern writers, however, did not remain in northern cities. Only Wolfe, the great American poet of exile, remained away. But those who returned south did not return to their hometowns. They went to university towns or metropolitan areas. Those few who did return to their home communities, like Faulkner and Welty, were only physically there; they were spiritual exiles, living in what Rubin calls "the faraway country," the South of their imaginations.

Allen Tate stayed in the South in the 1930s, convinced that southerners who left the South "sacrifice some great part of their deepest heritage." Nevertheless, many of his Agrarian colleagues, those seemingly most convinced of the need to preserve the South as a bastion against modernism, did eventually leave the region and move north. Writing in 1950, Richard M. Weaver admitted "a fairly general exodus of Southern Agrarians to the North," to the big cities and the renowned universities. "The truth about the Agrarians is that they were becoming homeless," he said. "The South no longer had a place for them." A long process of alienation was completed with the move north. Intellectuals who moved north could at least pursue their work in freedom. As Weaver noted, they were "regional expatriates," but in their new home "their ideas are negotiable" and "their convictions did not clash with local immaturities." The Agrarians were engaged in a worldwide battle between humanism and materialism. Instead of a flight of Agrarians, it was a "strategic withdrawal." Weaver betrayed a certain bitterness because the South had been lost. He applied to the region Stephen Dedalus's phrase about Ireland—"an old sow that eats her farrow."

Willie Morris, who is Thomas Wolfe's successor as poet of the southern exile experience, testified to the existence of an "exile" mentality in more recent southerners living outside the South. He wrote in his 1967 memoir *North Toward Home* of "New York's burgeoning and implacable Southern expatriate community," and he suggested that Mississippi and a few other southern states were the only states in the nation that "had produced a genuine set of exiles, almost in the European sense: alienated from home yet forever drawn back to it." Morris recalled the importance of the exile experience to a growing understanding of a common background and interest with black southerners.

Sociologist John Shelton Reed has argued for the importance of exile in nurturing cultural nationalism among southerners. By standing at a distance from a culture, one achieves perspective on it. The experience of the provincial youth in the city reminds those away from their homeland that they are from a culture viewed as inferior. Cultural nationalists engage in "the politicization of homesickness," nurturing their memory of the homeland and forgetting the divisions and disagreements back home. Being aware of people with different ways makes one, at times, appreciate the ways left behind. Southerners have been frequently reminded of being southern. The accent has marked one as identifiably southern, and non-southerners reacted accordingly by treating those with an accent as different. Many southern whites have been assumed to be racially bigoted. Those non-southerners who themselves are prejudiced may treat all white southerners as kindred spirits, while northern liberals may force white southerners to assume the personal burden for all the sins of the region. Southern black in-

tellectuals living in the North have complained of being treated as "rubes" by northern blacks and of hypocritical whites who spoke of equality but distanced themselves from personal relations with blacks. Looking back on his own education in Cambridge, Mass., in the 1960s, Reed has written that northerners "would apparently believe anything at all about the South, provided only that it was weird." The result was that southerners "almost had to think about the South." Many southerners apparently have discovered or intensified their regional identity while living away from the region.

Educated, exiled southerners outside the region frequently, when meeting, discuss where they are from and whether they have common friends or even family. They may complain about the coldness of the North, and of northerners, and exaggerate the legendary southern hospitality. The ritual of food has always been important as a token of retaining and renewing the southern identity in exile. Morris has recalled gathering with two southern black couples, the Ralph Ellisons and Albert Murrays, for a traditional southern New Year's Day dinner in 1967 in Murray's Harlem apartment, feasting on bourbon, collard greens, black-eyed peas, hamhocks, and corn bread. Morris, like other southerners, discovered the importance of food as a shared ritual of a common regional identity with blacks. He observed within New York that only in Harlem could a "southern white boy greet the New Year with the good-luck food he had had as a child."

The South's economic backwardness has had a discernible effect on the intellectual life of the region by promoting the exile of its intellectuals and artists. The loss of scholars, artists, entertainers, and others with special talents has been an enormous "brain drain" from the region. A study of the 1932–33 edition of *Who's Who in America* showed that of the 6,015 persons listed there as born in the South, 2,229 were living in other sections. The depletion was largest among editors, authors, educators, lawyers, judges, businessmen, religious workers, medical doctors, politicians, diplomats, army and navy officers, and actors and actresses. The superior opportunities for employment outside the region were singled out as the main reason for the loss of talented personnel. Another study in 1949 found similar findings but concluded that the South was retaining more of its talented offspring. The categories of loss have remained the same over the years, although with improved graduate and professional education in the region, the number of those remaining has increased.

Charles Reagan Wilson
University of Mississippi

Wilson Gee, *Social Forces* (March 1937); Eugene C. Harter, *The Lost Colony of the Confederacy* (1985); Lewis M. Killian, *White Southerners* (1970); Willie Morris, *North Toward Home* (1967); John Shelton Reed, *One South: An Ethnic Approach to Regional Culture* (1982); Daniel E. Sutherland, *Journal of Southern History* (August 1981); Richard M. Weaver, *Sewanee Review* (Autumn 1950). ☆

Foodways, Geography of

||||||||||||||||||||||||||||||||||||||||||||||||||||||||

The mechanisms of the natural environment and the historical processes of culture link food to place. Together, ecology and culture account for the diversity of foodways in the South. Early settlers carried with them knowledge, practice, and predisposition concerning food. Those traditions were usually derived from Europe, but they were also filtered through other parts of the New World such as Acadian Canada. Native Americans provided new culinary inspiration and strategies. Afro-Americans, in slavery and freedom, blended African food preferences, techniques, and even vocabulary with those of the predominantly European agricultural and urban populations.

For settlers, the South's natural habitats, whether coastal or interior, mountain, piedmont, or delta, established certain ground rules of availability and feasibility that tempered food traditions. Virtually everywhere, for instance, seemed appropriate for raising hogs and corn, two common features of agriculture and diet throughout the South. On the other hand, certain foods are closely tied to particular parts of the South because of ecological factors unique to those areas. Conch salad and conch chowder are known only in south Florida precisely for that reason. In comparatively recent times, agribusiness, contemporary food-marketing techniques, and the general blurring of regional boundaries—which is sometimes counterbalanced by the rise of regional self-consciousness—have all had their effects on the southern geography of food.

Corn and pork, two staples of the southern diet, illustrate the ways in which food varies with locality. Ground into meal, corn is the source of a variety of breads. Spoonbread, a puddinglike corn bread, is common in Tidewater Virginia and not unknown in Kentucky, at least in the Bluegrass. In south central Kentucky and parts of Tennessee, cornmeal is mixed in a batter and fried on a griddle, where it becomes corncakes, hoecakes, or just plain corn bread, depending on whom you ask. Mixed with onion and other seasonings and fried, cornmeal is the main component of hush puppies, a ubiquitous accompaniment for fried fish, especially catfish, a creature whose culinary acceptance appears to be spreading steadily northward from its original Deep South base. Bourbon is, of course, a corn-based distillation. Only Kentucky produces whiskey by that name, although other well-known brands of corn-based sour-mash whiskeys are produced in Tennessee. Bourbon is most popular in the Upper South, although it is also the most commonly consumed hard liquor in virtually the entire South.

The preparation of pork, particularly hams and barbecue, is clearly related to place. If in the process of curing, hams are hung from six months to two or more years, the resulting country ham is likely to come from either the vicinity of Smithfield, Va., or central Kentucky. Barbecue, which refers both to cooking techniques and to ways of serving the result, is so closely tied to place that for many it seems to serve as an emblem of home. Wherever it is found, barbecue is generally meat cooked slowly over embers and basted with a sauce. In North Carolina it must be cooked so long that it falls apart, and it is supposed to be served in shreds in a sandwich on a hamburger bun. Many North Carolinians add coleslaw to the sandwich as a topping for the meat, illustrating that food traditions may also involve "grammars" or rules concerning appropriate food combinations. In south central Kentucky, barbecue may be slices of pork shoulder, bones-in, dipped in a peppery sauce and served on slices of white bread. In parts of Texas, sausage

links are barbecued. And, of course, there are parts of the South in which barbecue is not pork. Texans eat barbecued beef brisket; in western Kentucky, mutton is the preferred meat. The International Barbecue Festival, in Owensboro, Ky., features mutton and chicken.

The potent combination of ecology and culture has yielded a number of very distinctive regional cuisines in the South. The best known of these, and perhaps the most distinctive of all, is that of the southwest Louisiana Cajuns. Journalist Calvin Trillin, the chronicler of regional American food traditions, has written a number of essays on Cajun foodways covering the local crawfish festivals, the liberal use of various sorts of peppers, and the now celebrated and generally familiar repertoire of Cajun food traditions.

In south Florida, Cuban immigrants have created another strongly distinctive set of food traditions, a more contemporary example of the same sorts of historical circumstances and cultural processes that underlie Cajun food traditions. Cuban sandwiches—long, narrow loaves of bread stuffed with roast pork, pickles, and other ingredients— are commonly available in south Florida, as is thick, rich Cuban coffee and the black bean soup that merits those same adjectives. And one should also note the Tex-Mex cooking of south Texas, another Spanish- speaking cuisine with a distinct southern accent. In these parts of the South, food is clearly emblematic of the region's plural cultures.

Even when recipes remain the same from place to place, vocabulary may vary. In the Deep South, the term *battercakes* refers to what in the Upper South is generally called pancakes. Reportedly, *flitters* are pancakes in southern Kentucky. Vocabulary may reflect settlement patterns. The distribution of the terms *smearcase* and *kochcase* in Texas provide a link to the history of German settlements in Texas. Elsewhere in Texas the term *cottage cheese* suffices.

Some southern foods have spread far beyond their original localities. If the "grits belt" was once thought to have covered roughly the same southern territory as the Bible Belt, President Jimmy Carter from Plains, Ga., helped nationalize that southern breakfast food, at least temporarily. A number of fast-food chains have recently begun serving biscuits for breakfast, first in the South where the practice is well known, and now through much of the country. Population shifts have also helped bring southern food traditions to much of the nation. The large out-migration of Afro-Americans to the North and Midwest brought soul food, a combination of distinctly African-American and regional southern culinary practices and preferences, to most of the cities of the Snowbelt. The geography of southern cooking, then, extends far beyond the South.

See also ENVIRONMENT: / Catfish; Collards; Shellfish; FOLKLIFE: / Gumbo; Okra; HISTORY AND MANNERS: Cookbooks; Foodways; / Barbecue; Beverages; Chitlins; Country Ham; Fried Chicken; Goo Goo Clusters; Grits; Mint Julep; Moon Pies; Moonshine and Moonshining; Soul Food; Whiskey

Burt Feintuch
Western Kentucky University

Linda Keller Brown and Kay Mussell, eds., *Ethnic and Regional Foodways in the United States* (1984); Charles Camp, *American Quarterly* (No. 3, 1982), *Journal of American Culture* (Fall 1979); Floyd M. Henderson, in *This Remarkable Continent: An Atlas of United States and Canadian Society and Cultures*, ed. John F. Rooney, Jr., et al. (1982); Sam B. Hilliard, *Hog Meat and Hoecake: Food Supply in the Old South, 1840–1860* (1972); Calvin Trillin, *American Fried: Adventures of a Happy Eater* (1974); Eugene Walter, *American Cooking: Southern Style* (1971). ☆

Indians and the Landscape

The southern American Indians at the time of the Europeans' arrival represented a population of about 1 million. These Indians spoke distinct languages of the Algonkian, Iroquoian, Siouan, Yuchean, Muskogean, Tunican, and Caddoan stocks. A short list of the better documented tribes speaking those languages includes the Powhatan, Shawnee, Tuscarora, Cherokee, Catawba, Yuchi, Choctaw, Seminole, Natchez, Tunica, Chitimacha, and the Natchitoches. After decimation by European diseases and forced movement west by secretly arranged treaties and violent expulsions, the Indian population in most of the South vanished. Although today their numbers in the region have grown to almost 195,000, this is a mere shadow of their historic presence. Indeed, that number is but a small percentage of the modern southern population. More salient than their numbers has been the sustaining cultural impact upon the Europeans who settled in the South. Indian trails became traces and eventually highways, their wild and domesticated foods became staples in the southerner's diet, their place names enhanced the southern landscape, and their ancient earthen monuments are now preserved as parks. Rarely, if ever, has one race intruded into the kingdom of another without drawing upon a share of the native culture, and European settlers in the South were no exception.

Even if most non-Indian southerners do not personally encounter their Indian compatriots in daily activities, they do constantly hear Indian words. A number of characteristically southern words are, in reality, of Indian origin. A few of the more familiar examples would include the words *bayou*, *hammock*, *hominy*, *opposum*, and *persimmon*. The very names of half the southern states are of Indian derivation: Alabama, Arkansas, Kentucky, Mississippi, Tennessee, and Texas. The same is true of the names of countless cities and towns (e.g., Chattanooga and Tupelo), mountains (e.g., Appalachian), valleys (e.g., Shenandoah), rivers (e.g., Monongahela, Atchafalaya), lakes (e.g., Okeechobee), swamps (e.g., Okeefenokee), islands (e.g., Assateague), and bays (e.g., Chesapeake). Indian place names are of value for their characteristic euphony, and they lie at the root of much historic research. In innumerable instances the native place names are the most valuable descriptors of locations and landmarks as they existed before European settlers altered geographical characteristics. For example, few people think of the city name *Chattanooga* as meaning "a rock rising to a point," yet this Indian name clearly applies to Lookout Mountain nearby.

The attraction to nature is another intangible Indian contribution to southern culture. The traditional southern affection for the pleasures, adventures, and freedom of the outdoors or backwoods was learned from Native Americans. This was not a trait brought from Europe by the majority of the peasants who settled in the South in the 17th and 18th centuries. In fact, few of them could have experienced such freedom under the authoritative oligarchies that prevailed in their native countries. Southerners' love of the outdoors might well be seen as a legacy of the Indian prowess that the colonists learned from and developed. It is ironic that this legacy is so prominent in the South, a region that exerted much energy to rid itself of its Indian habitants.

In the realm of tangible items the innumerable wild and domesticated food plants known to the Indians aided the European explorers and settlers and then became staples in the diets of populations worldwide. Cardinal among the food plants was the Native American cultigen maize, or corn, which has proved to be the favorite food for both man and animal in the South and the most notable staple in the southern diet. While other regions of the nation consumed wheat bread, the mainstay of the southern diet was corn bread. Corn, ground into meal, is not only used to make bread; it is concocted into a myriad of recipes and served as pone, muffins, biscuits, corn dodgers, hoecake, hush puppies, mush, sourings, griddle cakes, and waffles. Corn is also converted to hominy and grits. Nor can one forget to honor the contribution of corn to the manufacture of two particularly southern beverages, sour-mash whiskey and "moonshine."

The traditional beliefs, languages, crafts, and lifeways of the South's Native Americans have broadly influenced and immeasurably enriched the culture of the South.

See also BLACK LIFE: Indians and Blacks; ETHNIC LIFE: Indian Cultural Contributions; HISTORY AND MANNERS: Foodways; LANGUAGE: Names, Place

Robert W. Neuman
Louisiana State University

Alexander P. Chamberlain, *Proceedings of the American Antiquarian Society* (1905); Felix S. Cohen, *The American Scholar* (Spring 1952); Sam B. Hilliard, *Hog Meat and Hoecake: Food Supply in the Old South, 1840–1860* (1972); George R. Steward, *Names on the Land* (1945). ☆

Land Division

||||||||||||||||||||||||||||||||||||

A number of different survey systems were used in the American South, including the "metes and bounds" system, the "state rectangular systems," the "French long lot system" and the "U.S. township and range" system. Each of these helped shape the distinctive physical and cultural landscape of the South.

The metes and bounds survey system was introduced from Europe. It utilized natural boundary markers such as trees, streams, rocks, and other features. Very few of the areas where it was employed were surveyed before settlement. It created a series of very irregular and unsystematic landholding patterns. Surveyors made every effort to lay out these lots in rectangular shapes, but these patterns generally failed to survive through time. The sizes of the holdings were heterogeneous on the landscape but were usually between 200 and 1,000 acres. The metes and bounds survey system was indiscriminate at best. The system created incalculable lawsuits and challenges concerning property boundaries as well as actual land ownership. This unsystematic survey was employed in the southern Atlantic Seaboard colonies as far south as Georgia, where massive land frauds occurred.

The metes and bounds survey system extended westward in Georgia to the Oconee River. It was also utilized in some river valleys of the lower Gulf South, notably in the alluvial Mississippi Valley as well as in east Texas. Other vestiges of this survey system can be found scattered throughout the region. The states of Tennessee and Kentucky also employed the metes and bounds survey system.

One of the most spectacular and successful state-controlled rectangular survey systems employed in the American South was implemented in the early 19th century. Between 1805 and 1832 a state-controlled land-lottery system was established in Georgia, and a series of six lotteries was held. By this method the western two-thirds of Georgia was made available to the public at little or no expense to settlers. Each of the lotteries consisted of land districts containing rectangular lots that were surveyed before settlement and then offered to the citizens by public lottery. Several town sites were selected and surveyed at strategic locations, and town lots offered at public auctions. The individual land-lot sizes varied in different lotteries, but an effort was made to maintain rectangular land districts and land lots. The land-lot sizes in Georgia included lots of 40, 160, 202½, 250 and 490 acres. The land district lines in Georgia were primarily surveyed north-south and east-west. A similar state rectangular survey system was later used in portions of central and west Texas as well.

An unusual and not so well known survey system found essentially in the Gulf South and concentrated in the state of Louisiana is the French long lot system. There is evidence, however, of the utilization of long lot surveys in Tennessee, North Carolina, and Texas. The major concentrations of long lots in Louisiana are found in the Mississippi alluvial valley and related bayous, the Atchafalaya basin, and the Red River Valley. The long lot survey lines were laid out perpendicular to stream channels and roads; in southern Louisiana most were surveyed perpendicular to water courses. Usually the depth of the lot was three or four times greater than the width. Most of the lots were roughly rectangular in shape; a few were true rectangles. By surveying at right angles to stream courses, landowners were given access to a variety of environmental zones. They had access to the water courses, the well-drained lands along the levee, pasture lands, and woodland swamp areas.

The fourth major survey system used in the South was the U.S. township and range survey, which was initiated in the later 18th century in northeastern Ohio. The basic unit of measurement was a township or an area of 36 square miles. The survey began with a zero base line and a zero north-south coordinate; principal meridian units six miles in distance were then measured north and south of the base line and east and west of the principal meridian. These units were then designated Township one north (T1N) and Township one south (T1S) from the zero base line. Ranges were designated Range one east (R1E) and Range one west (R1W) of the principal meridian. Each of these townships was then subdivided into 36 sections of 640 acres each. These sections were numbered 1 through 36. Section number 1 was always located in the northeast corner of the township and section 36 in the southeast corner of the township.

Because the range lines were in fact meridians that converge as they extend northward, adjustments were made to prevent reduction in township widths. There was a total of four base lines and seven principal meridians used in the South. This survey system was superimposed on earlier surveys in the states of Florida, Alabama, Mississippi, Louisiana, and Arkansas. However, in many instances prior survey lines were honored and maintained. This was especially true in the long lot regions of Louisiana. Essentially, the major advantages of the township and range survey system were that land records were more nearly correct and more easily accessible to the public.

Gerald L. Holder
Sam Houston State University

Vernon Carstensen, ed., *The Public Lands: Studies in the History of the Public Domain* (1963); Everett Dick, *The Dixie Frontier: A Social History of the Southern Frontier from the First Transmontane Beginnings to the Civil War* (1948); Edward M. Douglas, *Boundaries, Areas, Geographic Centers, and Altitudes of the United States and the Several States*, Geological Survey Bulletin 817 (1930); Sam B. Hilliard, *Geographical Review* (October 1982), *Studies in the Social Sciences*, vol. 12, (1973); Gerald L. Holder, *Pioneer America* (September 1982); Hildegard Binder Johnston, *Order upon the Land* (1976); Roy M. Robbins, *Our Landed Heritage, The Public Domain, 1776–1970* (2d ed., 1976); Norman J. G. Thrower, *Original Survey and Land Subdivision* (1966); Payson J. Treat, *The National Land System, 1785–1820* (1910). ☆

Land Use

IIIIIIIIIIIIIIIIIIIIII

In its most general form, land use in the South may be viewed from the perspective of an Upland South and a Lowland South. The Upland South includes much of the Appalachian Highland and the Ozark-Ouachita Highland. These hilly to mountainous areas with steep slopes and poor soils have rarely supported an intensive and profitable agriculture. The predominant land-use pattern has been that of small, independently owned and operated farms on which woodlands and pastures served as low-quality grazing space for small livestock herds. Such limited farming enterprises, even with their provisional crops, have provided a meager living. Often the owners of such farms have had to seek supplemental work in forestry, mining, or manufacturing firms.

The Lower South includes the Atlantic and Gulf Coastal Plain and the outer Piedmont. It possesses the best of the southern agricultural resources—especially on the inner Coastal Plain from southern Virginia to southeastern Alabama and Mississippi, the Tennessee Valley of northern Alabama, the Mississippi Delta, the black prairies of Texas, and the Gulf Coastal prairies of Louisiana and Texas. These regions have provided the resources for the traditional cotton and tobacco crops, and, to a lesser extent, the sugar and rice crops. Currently they support such diverse crops as corn, soybeans, peanuts, cotton, tobacco, and rice, and they provide excellent pastures.

Land-use patterns emerge from the interactions of a given culture system with a physical habitat. Changes in the physical-cultural milieu within which these interactions occur induce change in the organization and structuring of land use. Such has certainly been the case in the American South, where for the past half century changes in land-use patterns have reflected the economic, social, and technological changes that have engulfed the region. Two broad and encompassing events provide a perspective for understanding recent developments in southern land use.

The first is an agricultural revolution originating in the early decades of this century. Developments such as the boll weevil infestation; agricultural depressions; erosion problems; competition for labor; rising expectations; genetic, chemical, and mechanical advances in agricultural technology; federal agricultural programs; and market forces, all in their own persistent manner, have changed land-use patterns. The imprint of this revolution on the landscape was widely evident by the post–World War II years.

Substantial areas within the South have experienced declining use of agricultural land, particularly cleared land on farms. The entire Piedmont and adjacent segments of the Coastal Plain, the Appalachian Highland of eastern Kentucky, and the interior highlands of Arkansas and northern Louisiana all experienced this loss. The cropland losses can be attributed to modest physical resources, federal programs, and the loss of competitive ability with respect to particular crops. Where agriculture has retained vitality the cropland has often been converted to the production of alternate crops, such as soybeans, corn, peanuts, and winter wheat. Agriculture has become decidedly more diversified. Other cropland has given way to forest or pasture—with terraces the only visible evidence of former cropland use. Indeed, forestry has become the single most common component of southern land-use patterns.

Sixty-two percent of all land area in the South is forested. Nearly 75 percent of this land is privately owned as woodland on farms or simply forested tracts. Nineteen percent of the forest land is owned by the forest industry and the remainder by national and state agencies. Though large forested tracts are owned by private corporations and the federal government, most forest land remains under the control and ownership of small holders; the average parcel is 66 acres. The quality of forest land is highly variable because of differences in management practices. Paradoxically, however, even though vast areas are forested and have experienced woodland expansion, other areas such as the lower Mississippi Valley and southwest Georgia have witnessed forest clearing for expansion of agriculture. Adaptation of modern irrigation technology has made some southern lands more valuable for agriculture.

A second major influence on land-use change has been urbanization. The peripheries of most southern cities have experienced a shift from nonurban to urban land use. The "growth zone" surrounding the city shows a curious juxtaposition of old and new patterns of land use. The edges of southern cities now extend far into the countryside—blurring the once-distinct rural-urban boundary and rendering the terms virtually obsolete. Some southerners have chosen to retain a rural environment for residence, and this has increased not only the rural nonfarm population but also the growth of retailing and services in response to that market. Many nonmetropolitan residents commute to met-

ropolitan work sites. This pattern is an outgrowth of new settlement patterns and modern transportation, and it has become extensive throughout the South, reflecting and reinforcing the continued change in nonmetropolitan land use.

The use of land for nonagricultural and nonforestry purposes increasingly extends beyond the metropolitan areas. The economic revolution has focused upon small cities and towns throughout the South—in fact the nonmetropolitan location of much of southern manufacturing growth has been one of the notable features of the regional experience. Numerous towns and small cities have gained new employment opportunities as a result of major American firms locating branch plants nearby. These local employment opportunities have reversed a longstanding population loss in towns and cities where surrounding peripheries, 20 to 30 miles in extent, realize residential expansion and the growth of retailing and services.

Any attempt to envision the patterns of southern land use in the future must recognize the following forces: (1) the rate of population increase in the South will exceed the national average for the foreseeable future; (2) contemporary patterns of settlement, including urbanization and the spread of urban and quasi-urban land uses into the nonmetropolitan periphery, will continue; (3) the demand for recreational space will increase; (4) the economic growth of the past two decades will continue as part of national decentralization and southern regional development; (5) the demand for prime agricultural land will increase; and (6) the forest industry of the United States, indeed of the world, will increasingly look to the American South. The result of the foregoing can only be increased competition for use of the best southern land.

See also AGRICULTURE articles; ENVIRONMENT: Forests; Land Use; URBANIZATION: Urban Growth

James S. Fisher
University of Georgia

J. Fraser Hart, *Annals of the Association of American Geographers* (December 1978, December 1980), with Ennis L. Chestang, *Geographical Review* (October 1978); Robert G. Healy and James L. Short, *The Market for Rural Land: Trends, Issues, Policies* (1981); Merle C. Prunty and Charles S. Aiken, *Annals of the Association of American Geographers* (September 1968, June 1972). ☆

Log Housing

||||||||||||||||||||||||||||||||||

Until the arrival in the backcountry South of central Europeans after 1723, notched-log construction was not popular in the region. A few log houses may have survived from the Swedish settlement in the Delaware Valley, but the distinctive traits of that area did not become those of the southern log-building tradition. The log buildings of the South were of either British or central European plan and were executed with central European techniques.

Pioneer German and Scotch-Irish settlers in the backcountry built houses much like those in the Old World. Even today, a few directly transplanted German log houses dot the Virginia Valley and the Piedmont (for example, at Winston-Salem). By the eve of the American Revolution, however, a small set of distinctively New World models had emerged. These forms became characteristic of the broad expanse of the South, spreading out to cover a million square miles between 1775 and 1835.

The forms that spread so suddenly and so extensively were six variant arrangements of a British pen, or bay, made using German methods. The basic unit was the single-pen house, an oblong, one-room house having its gables to the side, its doors on the eave front and rear, its chimney against the outside of one gable end, a wooden floor, and a foundation of piers. If built to stand alone, such a house would have measured from 16 by 20 feet to 20 by 26 feet.

Two versions of this basic pen spread, in succession, across the South. The earlier one, built of logs joined by half-dovetail notches, usually had a loft supported by joists that had been let through the front and rear walls by means of mortises. At the same tier or the next up, wall logs extended about 12 feet to the front and rear as cantilevers that supported the roof. The extension of the continuous-pitch roof permitted the plan to include a gallery in front and a room in back, both half the depth of the pen. The facade of the oldest of these had only a door, centered on the wall.

The second version, which followed

Porch on dogtrot house, Hickory Flat, Mississippi, 1968

the first by about a generation, had walls formed by V-notched logs. Its loft, if present, was supported by joists that had merely been sharpened and wedged between logs at the front and rear. Any porch or rear room added to the V-notched pen was usually a lean-to addition, rather than space lying under a cantilever-supported roof. The front facade commonly had a single door off center, plus one window between the door and the end having the chimney.

In time these two forms blended so that later, and especially more western, versions were likely to have traits of each. The half-dovetail forms of the northern South often lacked galleries, whereas those emanating from the back-country west of Charleston, the entry point of Caribbean immigrants, almost always had broad galleries.

To form larger houses, two pens were joined in one of three set ways. The most favored enlarged house, the dogtrot, was formed by setting two pens together along a common, central, open hallway. The other two plans involved separating the two pens either by a chimney (saddlebag) or a common wall (double pen). Any of these three types of houses may have had a gallery, loft, shed rooms, separate kitchen, dormers, or any of a host of architectural additions.

Where the owner was more successful, these two-room plans may also have been built in two stories. Such houses, known academically as "I houses," may have had one or both stories built of logs. I houses existed both with and without open dogtrots, central halls, and central chimneys.

Log construction extended also to the outbuildings. Log barns were built of various arrangements of units, known in this case as "cribs." The single-crib barn was an ancient, central European form. Its gable roof extended out over the area in front, sheltering the step to the door. The single-crib barn usually held corn still on the cob; consequently, the structure was set upon piers made of rocks or blocks of wood. The walls were formed of horizontal logs notched at their ends to join the tiers. Although all kinds of notches were used in barns, the saddle and V notches were the most common. Crib sizes differed widely, ranging from 8 by 10 feet to 20 by 30 feet, the length lying along the ridge.

The single-crib barn was put to many uses and served many functions. Many had dirt floors and shed-roofed areas on one or more sides. In some, a crib and a dirt-floored side room shared the same roof. Single-crib forms also served as smokehouses, well houses, and root houses. Single cribs were also combined to form larger structures. Two cribs set facing each other across a common drive-through space formed a double-crib barn. Four cribs under a common roof and sharing two crossing driveways formed a four-crib barn. Two sets of three facing a common driveway formed a transverse-crib barn. Some double-crib specimens had large, cantilever-supported lofts.

The making of log walls required shaping the log, forming the notches, and finishing the walls. Traditionally, the logs were split to form one face, the other being hewed to a line with a broad-axe; otherwise, both faces would be shaped by the broadaxe or sawed into the shape required. During the heyday of the log house, notches were formed on logs that had been raised to the top of the finished part of the crib; axemen standing atop the walls cut the bottoms of notches as needed. Once notched, the logs were rocked into place and the tops of their notches cut to receive the next logs. The most common notches for houses were half-dovetail and square (for one variety); V and saddle (for the other). Log walls were finished either by chinking between the logs with wood or stone chips and mud or mortar or by "sealing" the inside with sawn lumber. Cribs generally lacked any finish siding, the cracks aiding in the drying of the corn.

Notched-log construction is a technique, not a type or a style. Nearly any kind of building made of logs also appears in other material. Southern log work is central European in origin; the buildings are mostly British New World in form. That American log construction is basically southern is seen in the near uniformity of frontier log buildings, their specific forms having developed in the backcountry between Lancaster and Augusta.

See also ART AND ARCHITECTURE: Vernacular Architecture (Upland South); FOLK-LIFE: House Types; / Dogtrot; I House; Saddlebag House

M. B. Newton, Jr.
Baton Rouge, Louisiana

Terry G. Jordan, *American Log Buildings: An Old World Heritage* (1985), *Texas Log Buildings: A Folk Architecture* (1978); Fred Kniffen, *Pioneer America* (No. 1, 1969); M. B. Newton, Jr., *Geoscience and Man*, vol. 5 (1974); Eugene Murphy Wilson, "Folk Houses of Northern Alabama" (Ph.D. dissertation, Louisiana State University, 1935). ☆

Migration Patterns

The historical and geographical dimensions of southern culture are partly the product of human migration. Migration streams have brought to the South a mix of peoples, spawning a unique cultural milieu. The variation of culture within the region is the product of an intricate pattern of migration streams within its boundaries. Migration has also influenced the diffusion of many aspects of southern culture to other parts of the United States.

By 1700 the most populous of the European settlements along the Atlantic shore of North America were in the Chesapeake region. During the next century additional footholds gained prominence, especially Charleston, and the English and black-slave populations were supplemented by a variety of other ethnic enclaves. In the mid-18th century, 200,000 Germans and 250,000 Scotch-Irish migrated to the colonies and spearheaded a movement from the Philadelphia area down the Great Valley of Virginia, then ultimately westward across the mountains. That new immigration wave, plus various changes in agricultural systems, eventually led to a multitude of additional migration pathways, which carried persons of European origin westward within the South.

Migration forced upon a group or impelled by circumstances also played an important role in the South. After 1750, Cajuns began arriving in Louisiana as refugees from Acadia. Their imprint on the cultural landscape of Louisiana remains today. European settlements encroached on American Indians, forcing them to relocate, and mass expulsion of Indians to the Indian Territory occurred between 1820 and 1840. At least 50,000 Cherokee, Chickasaw, Choctaw, Creek, and Seminole were driven from their home areas in several southern states. The mass exodus, with its resultant high mortality rate as the Indians journeyed from northern Georgia through Tennessee, western Kentucky, southern Illinois, and southern Missouri, became known as the Trail of Tears.

Numerically, the most significant forced migration affecting the South was one having worldwide impact—the importation of slaves from Africa and the West Indies. This resulted in what has been perhaps the most important juxtaposition within one location of large and nearly equal numbers of people of European and African descent anywhere in the world. In 1750 there were more than 200,000 slaves in the colonies, and from 1750 to 1800 as many as 1 million additional slaves were imported. Changes in agriculture on the Atlantic Coastal Plain led to a variety of internal slave trade routes that shifted the center of the black population from Virginia in the 18th century to northern Georgia in the 19th century.

During the 19th century a number of important new black migration streams developed: migration to the Liberian colony, which involved 15,000 emigrés; the underground railroad routes carrying about 90,000 blacks into the North before the Civil War; a postwar movement of thousands to Kansas, resulting in a series of all-black towns in that state; and steady post–Civil War migration streams to northern cities.

The truly great mass exodus of blacks from the South, however, occurred in the World War I era. Both the "pushes" by agricultural labor surpluses and heightened social conflicts and the "pulls" of industrial jobs in northern and western cities are well documented. The net migration of blacks out of the South totaled about 3 million between 1910 and 1960.

A parallel movement of whites from the Upland South sent hundreds of thousands of people to northern cities, especially in the 1940s and 1950s. In both black and white movements the dependence upon friends and relatives as sources of information, advice, and comfort led to "channelized" streams of migration that connected migrants from the South with acquaintances in northern cities and even particular neighborhoods within those cities. These channelized flows initially followed rail lines and created regional connections such as northern Louisiana to Los Angeles; Mississippi to Chicago; the Carolinas to New York City; eastern Kentucky to Hamilton, Ohio; and southern West Virginia to Cleveland. Today, the nonmetropolitan South can still be divided into a complex mosaic of small subregions that traditionally depended upon different cities in the North and West as migration destinations, such as St. Louis, Mo.; Gary and Muncie, Ind.; Youngstown, Ohio; and Wilmington, Del.

Two other major migration patterns of the post–World War II era had earlier roots. The first was the rapid population growth in southern regional centers such as Charlotte, Atlanta, Jackson, Memphis, and Houston. Each gradually exerted a powerful draw on surrounding nonmetropolitan populations. The second was the rapid growth of Florida, which continues unabated today. Florida attracted migrants via mechanisms such as land developments and promotion, and it rapidly became the most important destination for elderly interstate migrants in the United States. The elderly, plus significant numbers of other migrants, streamed from the Midwest to the Gulf shore of Florida and from the Northeast (New Yorkers who moved to Miami and Miami Beach) to the east coast of Florida.

Beginning in the late 1960s, two new

major population redistribution patterns affected the nation as a whole, and especially the South. First, the South became a part of a broad population growth area, the "Sunbelt." Decentralization of employment from the traditional northeastern "core," plus the emergence of a great variety of new amenity growth regions, including the Arkansas Ozarks and extensive areas in the southern Appalachians, fueled the broad Sunbelt migration movement. The balance of migration toward the Sunbelt was significant, because for every migrant headed for the "Frostbelt," two were directed toward the Sunbelt. Also, many fewer persons moved from the rural South to cities outside of the region in the 1960s and 1970s, contributing to this migration pattern. Because for many years people in their twenties had moved outside the South, and birthrates had fallen, there were simply fewer people prone to move away from the rural South by the 1960s. By 1970 the South was attracting overall net in-migration from the Midwest and Northeast but was still losing migrants to the West, a region that had a considerable pull on southern out-migrants in the 1940s, 1950s, and 1960s. By the end of the period 1975–80, the South had a net gain of 800,000 from the Northeast, 700,000 from the Midwest, and 160,000 from the West. Blacks, lagging behind the population as a whole in these migration trends, left the South for all regions through migration in 1965–70; yet by 1975–80 the South was gaining black migrants from each of the three other regions.

A second recent trend was more abrupt than the broadening of the Sunbelt migration. A nonmetropolitan population turnaround occurred, whereby for the first time in memory more people were moving away from metropolitan areas than toward them. This pattern has been seen both within the South and in the nation as a whole. However, compared to the North, a large number of metropolitan areas in the South are still growing rapidly, primarily because of the Sunbelt migration streams.

Migration made another contribution to southern culture in the 1970s. In the 19th and early 20th centuries the South was not a major destination for European or Asian immigrants (as were the West and the North), but in the 1970s immigration became much more important to the region. Primary examples include an expansion of the traditional Mexican immigration into Texas, significant additional numbers of Cuban refugees settling in south Florida, large numbers of Haitians moving to Miami, and a pattern of settlement of southeast Asian refugees in Houston and other cities, including some "remigration" from the Frostbelt. Partly as a result of these recent migration streams, the cultural mosaic of the South continues to change.

According to census data, between 1980 and 1984 the South's population grew by 7 percent, increasing from 74,139,633 in 1980 to an estimated 79,340,321 as of 1 July 1984 (these figures include the 11 Confederate states plus Kentucky, Missouri, Maryland, and Oklahoma). Florida's population grew by 12.6 percent, the most marked growth in the region. Texas followed, with an increase of 12.4 percent in its population. The growing population and increasing cultural diversity will affect many elements of lifestyles in the South.

See also BLACK LIFE: Migration, Black; Northern Cities, Blacks in; ETHNIC LIFE: Caribbean Influence; / Appalachians; Cajuns; Cherokees; Chickasaws; Choctaws; Creeks; Cubans; Haitians; Mexicans; Okies; Scotch-Irish; Seminoles; HISTORY AND MANNERS: / Trail of Tears; INDUSTRY: Sunbelt South; MYTHIC SOUTH: New South Myth; URBANIZATION: / Atlanta; Charlotte; Houston; Memphis

Curtis C. Roseman
University of Illinois

George A. Davis and O. Fred Donaldson, *Blacks in the United States: A Geographic Perspective* (1975); Martin Gilbert, *American History Atlas* (1968); Daniel M. Johnson and Rex R. Campbell, *Black Migration in America: A Social Demographic History* (1981); M. B. Newton, Jr., *Geoscience and Man*, vol. 5 (1974). ☆

Ozarks

||||||||||||||||||||

The Ozark region is perceived as a remote backwoods area, a trans-Mississippi Appalachia devoted primarily to general or subsistence farming, where traditional lifestyles and technologies persist. However, rapid economic and social changes in the region over the past half century have rendered this broadly held view less valid.

The Ozarks, together with the Ouachita Mountains just to the south, comprise the only extensive elevations between the Appalachians and the Rocky Mountains. The region extends over 50,000 square miles, including all or part of a total of 93 counties in Missouri, Arkansas, Oklahoma, and Kansas. Several geographical features distinguish the region. The boundaries are marked in a general way by major rivers: the Mississippi on the east, the

Missouri on the north, and the Arkansas on the south. These rivers and their tributaries have defined and shaped the Ozark region and its people. People first came via the rivers, and many stayed because of the access to those rivers and to large man-made lakes.

The natural and aesthetic qualities of Ozark streams are at the center of a rich ecological system. The Current, Jacks Fork, Eleven Point, and Buffalo are pro-rivers. Several rivers sustain stocked trout. The surrounding oak-hickory-pine woodlands support squirrel, rabbit, quail, wild turkey, and deer. A large fur harvest is sustained by mink, otter, raccoon, beaver, and coyote.

Dolomite, a calcium magnesium limestone, and chert (flint) are abundant. The resistant chert, when weathered from the dolomite in which it is imbedded, accumulates at the surface and must be cleared from the fields. Streambeds are filled with chert gravel washed from steep hillsides, and the dark red upland soils are often choked with residual chert. There is an abundance of karst landforms, including such spectacular features as Grand Gulf, a massive collapsed cavern near Koshkonong, Mo., and Big Spring, near Van Buren, Mo., the largest single-opening spring in the United States. There are hundreds of caves, some of which, like Meramec Caverns and Blanchard Springs Cavern, are quite large.

Culturally, the Ozark region is more difficult to define. First, the region is rural. Rural suggests open country and an agricultural lifestyle that contrasts with city life. To some it implies rudeness and lack of polish; to others, idealized simplicity, solitude, and independence. All these things may be found in the Ozarks. Although urban centers like St. Louis, Springfield, and

Joplin in Missouri and Fayetteville-Springdale in Arkansas exert a strong cultural influence on the Ozarks in many ways, the general character of day-to-day living is rural.

Second, the Ozark heritage stems from the Upper South hill country of Tennessee and Kentucky. The population of the Ozark region is 98 percent white, native-born American, and Protestant. The paucity of agricultural resources discouraged settlement by the southern planter class with slaves, so there is none of the black legacy one finds in the Deep South.

Third, the region is something of an arrested frontier distinguished by traditional lifestyles, a slowness to accept change, and a distinctive cultural landscape that retains much of the past. The rural nature of the Ozarks, its frontier-like character, its Upper South hill-country heritage, its history of poverty, and a wealth of tourist advertisements combine to produce the popular imagery of the Ozark hillbilly, with all his cultural idiosyncrasies.

Ozarkers have an uncommon sense of place. Moreover, this sense of place transcends state boundaries. The word *Ozark* appears everywhere and in various forms. Schools, churches, planning agencies, clubs, and businesses carry the name. The 1983 Springfield, Mo., telephone directory listed more than 100 names containing "Ozark." Rural-come-to-town people freely identify themselves as Ozarkers, and, only half-jestingly, they refer to nonresidents as "outsiders." Rural-on-the-farm people tend to identify more closely with specific valleys, rivers, or towns, identities historically derived from the time when a trip to another valley or town was a trip to another world, another culture.

The Ozarks were settled in three phases: the old Ozarks frontier, the "New South" Ozarks, and the cosmopolitan Ozarks. The old Ozarks frontier progressed from the eastern border to the lead mines in the eastern interior and finally, by 1860, spread over the whole region. Ozark pioneers were a diverse population. French fur traders, miners, and farmers settled in the environs of Ste. Genevieve and the Old Lead Belt beginning about 1735. Scotch-Irish settlers, mainly from Tennessee and Kentucky, penetrated the interior by way of small streams and old Osage Indian trails even before the Louisiana Purchase of 1803. Cherokees, driven from their southern Appalachian home, migrated to the Oklahoma Ozarks over the Trail of Tears in the winter of 1838–39. German immigrants settled on the eastern and northern Ozark borders, forming a cultural enclave called the Missouri Rhineland. Later, when railroads were built, Germans, Italians, and other immigrant groups added their ethnic legacies.

The Reconstruction period and the so-called New South brought railroads and the spread of modern civilization to the Ozarks. Corporate mining replaced the "poor man's operations" in the Old Lead Belt in the eastern Ozarks and in the Tri-State Lead-Zinc Mining District of Missouri, Kansas, and Oklahoma. Company towns were founded, and deep ore deposits were exploited. Today closely spaced towns, mountains of waste rock, and ruins of mills and smelters identify these two defunct mineral districts. Railroads were built to open up lead and iron mines, pine forests, and hardwood timber tracts. Farms producing fruit, grain, livestock, and dairy products were laid out along the railroads, forming corridors of the New South development cutting into and finally surrounding the old Ozarks frontier. Many of the new immigrants who were attracted by the rapid economic development were progressive, liberal, capitalistic, educated, and bourgeois in culture.

Large lumber companies established company towns and became the largest property owners and the chief employers in many interior Ozark counties. In two generations the lumber companies had cut out the timber, leaving behind a depleted resource base, eroded soils, gravel-choked streams, tax-delinquent lands, and a few ramshackle lumber towns destined to fall into decay. During this same era resorts were established near some of the larger springs that were served by railroads, and the Ozarks became a vacation spot. New wealth in midwestern cities and a yellow fever epidemic in the Mississippi Valley contributed to the growth of a score of health resorts.

The third settlement phase, the cosmopolitan Ozarks, began with events connected with World War I and continues to the present. The initial stimulus for change during World War I stemmed from factors such as the military draft, high agricultural prices, loans that brought marginal land into production, pay sent home by soldiers, and new war-stimulated industries.

In three more wars (World War II and the Korean and Vietnam wars) the same shock waves washed over the Ozarks, each time reaching farther onto ridgetops and back into isolated valleys, carried by the new power generated in the internal-combustion engine. During the Great Depression the New Deal agencies discovered the region's poverty, and through political propaganda the national stereotype of the Ozarks was born. Ozarkers received "relief com-

modities," discovered such new foods as grapefruit and oranges, and became familiar with the label "poor." The Works Progress Administration (WPA), Civilian Conservation Corps (CCC), and a host of other social agencies provided work, training, education, and sustenance beginning in the 1930s. National forests were established in the same decade. Fort Leonard Wood, Fort Chaffee, and Camp Crowder came later, as did the Corps of Engineers and its dozen reservoirs. Tourism, second-home development, skyrocketing land prices, and the population explosion of the 1960s, 1970s, and 1980s are all part of the settlement phase known as the cosmopolitan Ozarks.

Evidence of all three of these development phases persists not only in human attitudes, beliefs, and daily activities but also in the landscape of the region, its buildings, farms, and technologies.

Events that have shaped the Ozarks since World War II, particularly in the last two decades, include the following: (1) the shift from agriculture and extractive industries (mining and lumbering) to secondary and tertiary activities (manufacturing and services); (2) large investments in public and social services and delivery systems such as highways and rural electrification; (3) significant increases in transfer payments, including social security payments, survivors' benefits, veterans' benefits, relief and welfare payments, unemployment benefits, and food stamps; and (4) population growth.

There has been a striking shift from general farming to livestock and dairying. Mining has been rejuvenated by the discovery of a new lead belt in Iron and Reynolds counties, Missouri. Lumbering and wood-products manufacturing have declined from former years, but the number employed in lumbering has stabilized. Manufacturing has increased substantially, and tourism is now a booming industry.

Since about 1965 population has grown rapidly. While the largest increases have occurred in towns, the most rapid rates of growth are in counties around large reservoirs. New Ozarks migrants fall into three categories: returnees, escapists, and opportunity seekers. Included in these categories are the back-to-the-land people, retirees, those who have local family ties, those escaping the real and imagined ills of big-city life, and those who are simply looking for employment and a place to live.

Ozarkers are concerned about the effects of this new population growth. There is concern about the loss of the small family farm, which inevitably leads to the disintegration of the native culture. Small farms are being purchased by absentee owners and by newcomers who have no intention of wresting a living from the land. There is particular concern about the crowds of people who camp and float on Ozark rivers and the rapid growth of tourist attractions and second-home developments near the large lakes. Although the economy is supported by tourism and agriculture, zoning, subdivision ordinances, and enforced septic controls are lacking. The conflict between the region's traditional rugged individualism and the encroaching signs of the tourist industry—flashing signs, A-frames intruding on ridge and valley alike, curio shops—is especially perplexing to residents around the Lake of the Ozarks and Table Rock Lake.

For many years the Ozarks was a backwater area affected only marginally by growth and development in the rest of the country. Just as the hilly terrain once diverted glaciers on its northern border, the poverty of the region halted settlers from the North and the East. Today, as a more affluent and mobile population is attracted to regions possessing scenery, water, and recreational potential, the Ozarks is experiencing rapid growth and development.

See also ETHNIC LIFE: / Germans; Scotch-Irish; INDUSTRY: / Mining; Timber Industry; RECREATION: Tourism

Milton D. Rafferty
Southwest Missouri State University

Russel L. Gerlach, *Immigrants in the Ozarks: A Study in Ethnic Geography* (1976); Milton D. Rafferty, *Missouri: A Geography* (1983), *The Ozarks: Land and Life* (1980); Carl O. Sauer, *The Geography of the Ozark Highland of Missouri*, Geographical Society of Chicago Bulletin No. 7 (1920). ☆

Plantation Morphology

||||||||||||||||||||||||||||||||||||||||||||||||||||

The southern plantation symbolizes large-scale agricultural operations and landscapes and contrasts with the smaller family farm in the South. Whether the sites of sugarcane, cotton, rice, indigo, or tobacco production, southern plantations inscribed distinctive traits into the landscape.

For nearly two centuries traditional plantations included large level fields extending over hundreds, even thousands, of acres. They were located primarily in the flat terrain of the Atlantic and Gulf coasts and Mississippi floodplains or in the rolling fields in the Upland South. A latticework of ditches, canals, and field roads were etched into the landscape. Centrally located outbuilding complexes consisted of sugarhouses, cotton gins, rice mills, mule barns, tractor and implement sheds, storage tanks and sheds, blacksmith and mechanical repair shops, stores, and churches. Laborers' quarters of simple houses formed characteristic patterns. And at a distant site, set amid moss-draped oaks or in the shade of magnolias and pines, stood the plantation mansion—a symbol of power, opulence, and cultural achievement.

The architecture of plantation mansions reflected the ethnic traditions of their builders. Creole plantation mansions on sugar plantations in southern Louisiana showed the taste of French Creole planters. Anglo plantation mansions are associated with Anglo-American planters who used architects from the Tidewater region of the Atlantic Coast, from Virginia to Georgia. Furthermore, Anglo plantation mansions with Upland traits largely reflect the tastes of Anglo-American planters from western Virginia, Kentucky, Tennessee, the Carolinas, Georgia, Alabama, Mississippi, and northern Louisiana.

Creole plantation mansions are characterized by (1) interior central chimneys at the center of the roof line; never exterior chimneys on the outside gabled ends of the house; (2) multiple front doors that allow all front rooms to open onto the gallery or front porch; (3) floor plans several rooms wide and one or two rooms deep, without a central hall; (4) all stairs on the exterior; (5) hip roof; (6) galleries, a wide front porch, and often wide porches on all sides of the house; (7) one-and-a-half- to two-story height; and (8) half-timbered wall or all-wood construction.

The traits of Anglo-American plantation mansions include (1) exterior chimneys; (2) a single front door; (3) floor plans usually one to two rooms deep and no more than two rooms wide; (4) inside stairs; (5) a central hall or passage extending from front door to back; and (6) construction materials of all wood, brick, and plaster but never half-timbered construction.

Anglo houses of Tidewater origin further display a front-facing gable, two full stories, pediments, porticos, large white pillars, end chimneys (outside end or inside end), a single front door and hallway, and, in some cases, side pavilions or wings, common to the Georgian style. Other modest Anglo plantation structures of the Upland South have traits of the southern pen tradition—one to two rooms wide, deep, and tall; single front door; central hall; and exterior brick chimneys.

Settlement patterns based on the arrangement of quarter houses within the plantation complex also have distinctive traits. On modern sugar plantations in Louisiana, the quarters—a villagelike settlement that once housed slaves—contain the dwellings of field laborers, tractor operators, sugar mill workers, field overseers, and mill foremen. The arrangement of dwellings follows traditional 18th- and 19th-century linear settlement patterns marked by parallel rows of quarter houses divided by a road that bisects the long axis of the plantation landholding. Traditional land surveys from the French long lot system created long, narrow landholdings, which dictated the arrangement of structures into a linear settlement pattern that is characteristic of early French plantations.

On other present-day Louisiana sugar plantations, on early cotton, rice, indigo, and tobacco plantations of the

Tidewater, and on cotton plantations of the Upland South distinctive block-shaped or gridded quarters are associated with Anglo-American plantation origins.

Elsewhere on southern cotton plantations, the antebellum quarters disappeared in the post–Civil War era, to be replaced later by individual sharecropper and tenant houses widely scattered among cotton fields. Blacks often insisted that quarter houses near the plantation mansion be relocated as a symbol of their new status. Such a dispersed pattern remained until the 1940s, when agglomerated plantation settlements reappeared on cotton enterprises in the lower Mississippi Valley and other parts of the South.

See also AGRICULTURE: Plantations; MYTHIC SOUTH: Plantation Myth

John B. Rehder
University of Tennessee

Lewis C. Gray, *History of Agriculture in the Southern United States to 1860*, 2 vols. (1933); Merle C. Prunty, *Geographical Review* (45, 1955); Roger L. Ransom and E. Richard Sutch, *One Kind of Freedom: The Economic Consequences of Emancipation* (1978); John B. Rehder, *Geoscience and Man*, vol. 19 (1978), "Sugar Plantations in Southern Louisiana: A Cultural Geography," (Ph.D. dissertation, Louisiana State University, 1971); Edgar T. Thompson, *Plantation: A Bibliography* (1957). ☆

Population

||||||||||||||||||||||||||||||

In 1980, 61,287,000 persons lived in the 11 states of the old Confederacy, as shown in Table 1. This number is almost double that of 1940, when 31,832,000 people lived in the region, and a more than 40-fold increase from the 1,454,000 enumerated in the nation's first census in 1790. Despite this growth, the South's share of the nation's population has, until recently, steadily declined from the 37 percent of 1790. A low 23 percent was recorded in 1930; the current share is 27 percent.

After initial settlement, the South became less a destination than a point of origin for migrants. In the 100 years following the Civil War, Alabama, Georgia, Mississippi, North Carolina, and Tennessee each recorded over a million more out-migrants than in-migrants. Only Florida (4.3 million) and Texas (1.5 million) consistently gained population from migration over this period. By the late 1960s the general pattern of net out-migration had begun to reverse. For the period 1975 to 1980, *all* southern states had population gains from migration.

For 1970–80 the South grew by 22.5 percent, almost double the nation's growth rate of 11.4 percent. Increased migration to the South is primarily responsible for the region's dramatic growth in recent years, although a high birthrate also has contributed. The South has long had a birthrate above the national rate; even when out-migration was high in the 1940s and 1950s, large numbers of births enabled the South to grow. In 1960 the South recorded 25.0 births per 1,000 population, while the nation's rate was 23.7 per 1,000. Both rates declined over the next 20 years, so that by 1980 the South remained marginally higher: 16.5 as compared to 15.9 for the entire United States. Of the 10 states with the highest birthrates, three are in the South: Louisiana (sixth nationally with 19.5 births per 1,000

Table 1. *Population of the South, by State, 1790–1980*

	1790	1860	1900	1940	1980
		Population in Thousands			
Alabama	—	964	1,829	2,833	3,894
Arkansas	—	435	1,312	1,949	2,286
Florida	—	140	529	1,897	9,746
Georgia	83	1,057	2,216	3,124	5,463
Louisiana	—	708	1,382	2,364	4,206
Mississippi	—	791	1,551	2,184	2,521
North Carolina	394	993	1,894	3,572	5,882
South Carolina	249	704	1,340	1,900	3,122
Tennessee	36	1,110	2,021	2,916	4,591
Texas	—	604	3,049	6,415	14,229
Virginia	692	1,220	1,854	2,678	5,347
TOTAL	1,454	8,726	18,977	31,832	61,287

Source: *U.S. Bureau of the Census,* Population Reports *(1790, 1860, 1900, 1940, 1980).*

population); Texas (seventh; 19.2); and Mississippi (ninth; 19.0). Utah led all states at 28.6.

The population of the South is younger than the nation as a whole. The median age in 1980 was 29.1 years, compared to the country's 30.0 years. This gap would have been even greater were it not for Florida; deleting that state with its median age of 34.7 years results in a median age for the remaining 10 states of 28.3 years. The proportion of southerners who are aged 65 and over is exactly the same as for the entire country, 11.3 percent. In Florida one in six residents is at least 65 years old, the highest proportion in the country. Excluding Florida, the remaining 10 southern states have a combined proportion 65 and over of 10.2 percent. More women (31.5 million) than men (29.7 million) live in the South, resulting in a sex ratio of 94.4 men per 100 women. This ratio is almost identical to that for the entire country, 94.5.

In 1980 the South's net death rate was 8.70 deaths per 1,000 population, lower than the 8.80 per 1,000 recorded for the entire nation. This lower rate is misleading, however; because the South has a younger population than the nation as a whole, it has relatively more of its population at those ages where the fewest deaths occur. When rates are adjusted for age, mortality in the South is slightly higher than that for all of the United States, a pattern that has held since adequate death statistics became available in the 1930s. Life expectancy figures for the 1979–81 period confirm this higher mortality. Nationally, newborns could expect to live 73.9 years on average, but this figure was surpassed in only one southern state, Florida, at 74.0 years. The four states with the lowest life expectancies were all in the South: Georgia (72.2 years), Mississippi (72.0), South Carolina (71.8), and Louisiana (71.7). (The District of Columbia had the nation's lowest life expectancy—69.2 years.) Infant mortality has been relatively high in the South; in 1980 there were 13.6 deaths in the first year of life per 1,000 births, compared to the national rate of 12.5 such deaths per 1,000 births. Among individual states, the four with the highest rates were in the South: Mississippi (15.9 infant deaths per 1,000 births); Louisiana (15.4); South Carolina (15.4); and Alabama (15.1).

The South has a smaller proportion of its population in rural areas (67.5 percent) than the country as a whole (73.7 percent). While a majority of southerners now reside in places of at least 2,500 population, this level of urban residence is a new phenomenon: as recently as 1950, over half of all southerners lived in rural areas. Two states, Mississippi and North Carolina, remain predominantly rural, and only two states—Florida and Texas—have proportionately fewer residents in rural areas than the nation as a whole.

Similarly, the South has proportionately fewer metropolitan residents (67.6 percent) than the entire United States (74.8 percent). Arkansas and Mississippi have fewer than 40 percent of their residents living in metropolitan areas, whereas Texas and Florida both exceed 80 percent. A total of 12 of the 50 largest metropolitan areas in the country are in the South: three in Texas (Dallas–Fort Worth; Houston; San Antonio) and three in Florida (Fort Lauderdale; Miami; Tampa–Saint Petersburg). Dallas–Fort Worth (3.0 million; ninth largest nationally) and Houston (2.9 million; 10th nationally) are the region's largest metropolitan areas. Washington, D.C., the nation's eighth largest metropolitan area (3.1 million), is partly located in the South, occupying part of Virginia.

The South's population is concentrated in two states, Texas (14.2 million inhabitants) and Florida (9.7 million). Combined they contain just under 40 percent of the region's population. All southern states have at least 2 million residents; Arkansas (2.3 million) and Mississippi (2.5 million) have the fewest residents.

The population of the South is largely of African and European stock. In 1980 just under one in five southerners was black. These 12 million blacks comprised over 45 percent of the total black population in the United States. As recently as 1960, more than half the nation's black population lived in the 11 old Confederacy states, and until the early 1900s over 80 percent of all blacks lived in the South. Mississippi (35.2 percent) and South Carolina (30.4 percent) have the largest relative black populations, although in absolute numbers Texas (1.7 million) and Georgia (1.5 million) have the largest black populations. All 11 southern states have a higher proportion of blacks than the nation's 11.7 percent.

Over one-quarter of all southerners indicate English ancestry. Other northern and western European groups are well represented: Irish, 16 percent; German, 13 percent; Scottish, 5 percent. (Some persons claimed more than one ancestry group.) Almost one-third of all persons claiming English ancestry live in the South, as do 30 percent of those claiming Scottish ancestry. Southern and eastern European immigrant groups are underrepresented in the South; only 1.9 percent of southerners indicate any Italian ancestry and only 1.1 percent have Polish ancestry. Other ethnic groups, uncommon in much of the South, are locally concentrated. Over a fifth of all Louisianans claim French ancestry, for example, and over half of all United States residents who claim Cuban ancestry live in Florida. Persons of Spanish origin, principally of Mexican descent, constitute 21 percent of Texas's population; in 1980, 2.7 million Texans claimed Mexican ancestry.

The South's population has the lowest educational attainment of any region in the country. In 1980 just under 60 percent of southerners aged 25 and over had completed at least four years of high school; the national proportion is 66.4 percent. Only one southern state, Florida, exceeds the national share; its figure is 67.2 percent. Of the 10 states with the lowest educational attainment, 8 are in the South: Alabama, Arkansas, Georgia, Louisiana, Mississippi, North Carolina, South Carolina, and Tennessee; the two remaining states, Kentucky and West Virginia, border the old Confederacy. Kentucky has the lowest proportion of its population aged 25 and over with at least four years of high school, 51.9 percent; the Deep South state with the lowest proportion is South Carolina (54.0 percent).

The two poorest states in the nation are in the South—Mississippi (per capita money income, 1979, of $5,327) and Arkansas ($5,467). Only Florida ($7,593) and Virginia ($7,549) exceed the national average ($7,313). The South has a disproportionate share of its population living in poverty, 15.2 percent, compared to the nation's 12.5 percent. Mississippi has the nation's greatest proportion, 24.5 percent; no other state is above 20 percent. Only Virginia (11.5 percent) of the southern states has a proportion in poverty below the national share. A total of 8 of the 10 poorest counties in the nation are in the South: Greene, Lowndes, and Wilcox in Alabama; Lee in Arkansas; Holmes, Humphreys, and Tunica in Mississippi; and Starr in Texas.

The rapid growth in the South since the late 1960s is likely to continue in the near future, particularly in Florida and Texas. From 1980 to 1983, Census Bureau estimates indicate that Texas grew by 1.5 million inhabitants, Florida by over 900,000. Together, these two states accounted for almost two-thirds of the South's population growth since 1980. Still, all southern states grew from 1980 to 1983, and all except four (Alabama, Arkansas, Mississippi, and Tennessee) exceeded the national rate of 3.3 percent.

See also BLACK LIFE: Migration, Black; SOCIAL CLASS: Poverty

> John P. Marcum
> Max W. Williams
> University of Mississippi

Estimates of the Population of States: 1970 to 1983, Current Population Reports, Series P-25, No. 957 (1984); *Historical Statistics of the United States, Colonial Times to 1970*, Bicentennial Edition (1975); National Center for Health Statistics, *U.S. Decennial Life Tables for 1979–81*, vol. 2 (1985); Harry M. Rosenberg and Drusilla Burnham, in *The Population of the South: Structure and Change in Social Demographic Context*, ed. Dudley L. Poston, Jr., and Robert H. Weller (1981); David F. Sly, in *The Population of the South: Structure and Change in Social Demographic Context*, ed. Dudley L. Poston, Jr., and Robert H. Weller (1981); *State and Metropolitan Area Data Book, 1982* (1982); U.S. Department of Commerce, *Statistical Abstract of the United States: 1983* (1984). ✫

Religious Regions

||||||||||||||||||||||||||||||||||||||||||||||||||

Viewed from a national perspective the South is remarkably homogeneous in its religion. Protestantism predominates and, in the majority of counties, Baptists and Methodists together account for nearly all church affiliation. The South is further distinguished by high rates of church membership in comparison with other regions of the country. Within the general uniformity of southern religion, however, a degree of diversity exists that is worthy of attention.

The dominance of Baptist groups is perhaps the most striking feature of southern religion. They predominate in most counties, reaching maximum strength along a corridor extending from southern Appalachia through Georgia, Alabama, and Mississippi and into northern Louisiana and Texas and southern Arkansas and Oklahoma. Baptists came to the South during the Great Awakening in the mid-18th century. They were extremely successful evangelists, in part because of a reliance on farmer-preachers who settled among the people they served.

Methodists were the chief rivals of Baptists within the southern missionary field. The two groups grew at similar rates throughout the 19th century, but they employed differing strategies. Methodist expansion emphasized a well-organized system of circuit riders and regular camp meetings. In the last half century the growth of Methodists has lagged behind that of Baptists, possibly because of the latter's strong regional ties through the Southern Baptist Convention. Methodism remains tremendously important, however. Large Methodist minorities exist in most counties, and majorities are found frequently in the Carolinas, the Virginias, Maryland, and Tennessee.

Baptists and Methodists together constitute the core of southern conservative Protestantism. Other groups of similar orientation include Disciples of Christ, Presbyterians, and the larger Pentecostal and Holiness denominations. These denominations are widespread throughout the region but have special concentration in the Upper South, where several of them originated, and in the Carolinas.

Concentrations of Catholics form the most significant exceptions to the Baptist-Methodist domination of the South. Some Catholic groups existed in the region before the growth of evangelical Protestantism; others are relatively recent immigrants. Catholics frequently represent not only religious diversity in the South but ethnic diversity as well, and locations where they are concentrated are major cultural "islands" in the region.

Southern Catholicism is most firmly established in southern Louisiana and southern Texas. The Catholic presence in Louisiana dates from the early 18th century, and it became firmly established in the middle of that century when French-speaking Catholics deported from Nova Scotia arrived in large numbers. Catholicism in Texas is even older, beginning with Spanish missions in the late 17th century. Catholics now constitute nearly three-fifths of the total church membership in Louisiana and nearly one-third in Texas. The cultural identities of both Cajuns and Mexican Americans are strongly intertwined with their faiths.

Smaller regions of Catholic influence occur along the northern border of the South. The oldest of these has its core in Maryland, a colonial center of Catholicism and of general religious tolerance under Lord Baltimore. Immigration of Marylanders to north-central Kentucky created another Catholic concentration. Farther west,

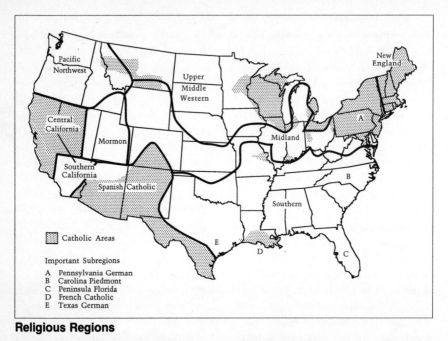

Religious Regions

Source: Raymond Gastil, **Cultural Regions of the United States** *(1975); modified from Wilbur Zelinsky, "An Approach to the Religious Geography of the United States,"* **Annals of the Association of American Geographers** *(1961).*

along the Ohio River in Illinois and Indiana and along the Missouri and Mississippi rivers in east central Missouri, Catholic clusters occurred through the migration of German and Swiss settlers. Recent migration is responsible for Catholicism in southern Florida—primarily the flow of retirees and other northerners. Cubans, Haitians, and other emigrants from the Caribbean region constitute another component of Florida Catholicism.

Subtle variations within Protestantism provide a second departure from the norm of southern religious geography. Areas best described as pluralistic, places where Baptist and Methodist strength is somewhat diluted, although rarely replaced, have a cultural or historical background different from the mainstream and are among the most religiously diverse places in the South.

Peninsular Florida has become a major area of pluralism during this century. The amenities of the Sunbelt have attracted Protestants of various persuasions, Jews, and Catholics alike. Episcopalians, Lutherans, the Reformed churches, and the United Church of Christ, as well as Disciples and Presbyterians, are all found in greater proportion here than throughout most of the region.

Another distinctively pluralistic religious subregion is the Carolina Piedmont, where Friends, Lutherans, Moravians, Presbyterians, and the United Church of Christ are all well represented. North Carolina's lack of restrictions on nonconformists attracted these groups to the area as early as the late 17th century, but the major immigration came during the 18th century. A scarcity of available good land in Pennsylvania prompted many people of varied religious backgrounds to migrate southeastward along the Appalachian front into the Carolinas. The Christian

Church, now part of the United Church of Christ, was founded in North Carolina and Virginia.

German, Scandinavian, and eastern European immigration to the hill country of central Texas during the mid-19th century created a distinctive religious and ethnic complex. Lutherans remain the most numerous group there, but Evangelical and Reformed adherents (now part of the United Church of Christ), Moravians, and Catholics are also important components of the hill-country religion.

Appalachia should also be considered a religious subregion within the South. Its distinctiveness came not from immigration but from the local emergence of numerous strongly fundamentalist denominations, mainly Pentecostal or Holiness in belief but sectarian in orientation. Religion here reflects the individualism, traditionalism, and localism of Appalachian society generally. In many ways this religion is a relic of the emotional, evangelical faith that characterized the interior South during the 19th-century frontier period.

A final zone of religious diversity lies along the northern border of the South, an area where northern and southern denominations intermix. Catholic concentrations here have already been noted, but one also finds Lutherans, Episcopalians, United Church of Christ congregations, Presbyterians, and other Protestant groups in occasional concentrations.

See also RELIGION articles

James R. Shortridge
University of Kansas

Roger W. Stump
State University of New York
at Albany

Sydney E. Ahlstrom, *A Religious History of the American People* (1972); Jackson W. Carroll, Douglas W. Johnson, and Martin E. Marty, *Religion in America: 1950 to the Present* (1979); Edwin Gaustad, *Historical Atlas of Religion in America* (rev. ed., 1976); Charles Heatwole, *Southeastern Geographer* (May 1986); Samuel S. Hill, ed., *Religion and the Solid South* (1972); Douglas W. Johnson, Paul R. Picard, and Bernard Quinn, *Churches and Church Membership in the United States: An Enumeration by Region, State, and County, 1971* (1974); James R. Shortridge, *Geographical Review* (October 1976); Wilbur Zelinsky, *Annals of the Association of American Geographers* (June 1961). ☆

Roadside

||||||||||||||||||||||||

Donald Davidson wrote in *The Attack on Leviathan* (1938) that southern cities reflecting "the finest flavor of the old regime" could not be reached except by passing "over brand-new roads where billboards, tourist camps, filling stations and factories broke out in a modernistic rash among the water oaks and Spanish moss." Davidson saw the roadside in the South as a prime symbol of the evils of modernization, which were destroying the best of the region's agrarian tradition.

The automobile has indeed reshaped the southern roadside in the 20th century, promoting Americanization and standardization through billboards, service stations, fast-food restaurants, trailer camps, motels, and other aspects of the car culture. But for travelers in motor vehicles the roadside also reflects and reinforces an awareness of southern history and culture and promotes the consciousness of being in a landscape different from that elsewhere. It has thereby promoted regional self-consciousness.

Historic sites, for example, especially Civil War battlefields, have become modern locales for pilgrimage. The war marked the southern roadside for generations. Most of the fighting during the conflict was on southern soil, and the countryside long after the war held tangible memories of the past. As Mary Winn, a traveler in the region, wrote in 1931, "At intervals on the road one passes a group of magnificent live-oaks, in the middle of which rises a tall chimney, all that is left of the 'great house' that was once the center of a feudal property." Virginia pioneered in erecting historical markers by the side of the road, and now the history of every state in the region is revealed in concise statements on signs, markers, and monuments on the roadside. Historian Thomas D. Clark suggested in 1961 that traffic congestion from automobile tourists made it more dangerous to pull off the road "to take a leisurely look at the scene of a Civil War battlefield than it was to have engaged in the battle itself."

Natural attractions have been roadside lures in the South. "See Rock City" and "Ruby Falls" were the most pervasive of signs painted on the side of southern barns, nailed to a tree as placards, or displayed on standard billboards. But there were also signs for Silver Springs, Natural Bridge, or even Dog Patch. "The southern landscape has been sacrificed in many places to this mad campaign to snatch the tourist dollar," wrote historian Clark. "Scarcely a roadside post, tree, fence, or barn has escaped the signmaker. On some of the main highways there is hardly a quarter of a mile left undefiled."

Engineers in the South, as elsewhere, generally adopted the utilitarian ap-proach to the countryside in roadbuilding, with aesthetics having little role. Wildflowers and trees, for example, were discouraged. Southern roadsides were, however, so naturally luxuriant, especially in the warm humid areas, that they could not be kept down, and the simple attraction of the region's plant life has always added a distinctive look to the roadside, one noted by outsiders looking for regional differences. In a 1938 book, native southerner Jonathan Daniels recalled the road north of Greenville, S.C., where "the dogwood, the mountain magnolia, the azalea and tiny nameless wild flowers bloomed in profusion on the May highway."

Tourist traps also grew up to give a distinctive ambience to the southern roadside. Billboards and handmade signs for miles announced what were sometimes rip-off businesses. "Pet baby alligators" would be a typical come-on. Reptile farms, bears on display, shetland ponies to ride—all were designed to lure tourists off the road and out of their cars to buy souvenirs, gasoline, or food. South of the Border, located on Interstate 95 near the North Carolina–South Carolina border, has a 220-foot-high Mexican sombrero, an artifact that automatically earns attention. Billboards from Virginia to Georgia announce its importance. Started in 1949, it has a gas station, campground, and volunteer fire department. Sometimes the artifacts at such places are a kind of folk-pop art. Mammy's Cupboard is at the top of a hill near Natchez, Miss. A 28-foot-tall black woman stands atop the rise, embodying the "mammy" image, down to her apron. Her "cupboard" lies beneath her crinoline skirt, which covers a 20-foot area. It was built in 1940, and its owners serve southern plate lunches inside and gasoline outside. The king of the southern roadside businesses is Stuckey's, whose spread nationwide represents an example of the "southernization of America." Gaudy red-and-yellow billboards dot the countryside advertising the place to buy pecans, candy, gifts and souvenirs, gasoline, and fast food. William Sylvester Stuckey from Eastman, Ga., founded his roadside business in 1932, in the middle of the Great Depression, with only a few sacks of peanuts and a $35 loan. He sold pecans to tourists passing through Eastman headed from New York to Florida, supplied candy to the military during World War II, and then expanded his roadside service nationwide after the war.

Souvenirs, artifacts of perceived "southernness," are part of the roadside in the South. They are localized, suggesting place. T-shirts, clothing, and ashtrays are common everywhere, but are marked with local references. There are country music references in Tennessee (hairbrushes in the form of guitars, Dolly Parton dolls); Confederate flags and miniature cotton bales are sold

in Mississippi; moccasins and other Indian goods are in North Carolina Cherokee country and in Florida Seminole land; hillbilly characters, outhouses, and scatological artifacts can be purchased on Appalachian roadsides; seashells and seashell art are common along the coasts. Natural products of the region are also popular souvenirs giving a sense of place—a packaged sack of oranges in Florida, grapefruit in south Texas, peaches in Georgia, boiled peanuts in south Alabama, and fresh honey all around. Folk and pop art, whether quilts, velvet paintings of Elvis, or ceramic animals for the yard, are common beside the road. Fireworks stands are pervasive in certain areas and increase before holidays. They sell Chinese fireworks that are repackaged to strike regional themes (as in the Robert E. Lee collection of firecrackers seen in one Kentucky stand).

Religious folk art has flourished on the southern roadside, especially in the Appalachians, Ozarks, and in rural areas. Both handmade primitive signs

Roadside store, near Savannah, c. 1940

and mass-produced ones are found. These provide among the most distinctive of regional touches to the roadside, because their messages are evangelistic, reflecting the region's predominant religious outlook and style. Statements include "Get Right With God," "Prepare To Meet Thy God," "Where Will You Spend Eternity," "Jesus Is The Answer," or simply "Jesus Saves." Scholar Samuel S. Hill has speculated they are most common in areas undergoing the trauma of modernization; they are most likely associated with Protestant sectarians. One rough drawing on wood in North Carolina had a stark picture of a hand with a nail through it, and blood spurting forth. "He Loved You So Much It Hurt," said the words under the drawing. Such signs are folk art reflecting the intense, passionate southern faith. Appropriately, Flannery O'Connor refers to them in *Wise Blood*. While driving along the road, Hazel Motes sees a gray boulder, emblazoned with white letters that say, "WOE TO THE BLASPHEMER AND THE WHOREMONGER! WILL HELL SWALLOW YOU UP?"

In the contemporary era the roadside along southern interstate highways is becoming more bland, although southerners in cities, in small towns, and on smaller roads maintain in places the colorful man-made landscape. The use of portable signs—the small, metal-framed and illuminated signs on wheels—is especially popular in the South. *New York Times* reporter William E. Schmidt noted in 1984 that they "seem to be crouched everywhere beside highways across the South these days." Since the mid-1970s over 100,000 of them have appeared throughout the nation, providing a useful message board to the small businesses who use them. They are most typically found along suburban commercial strips. Their garish flashing lights and arrows effectively catch the eye of the motorist; and garages, service stations, barber and beauty shops, bakeries, and nightclubs all use them. Marietta, Ga., attempted to restrict their use, but the Supreme Court ruled in 1984 that restrictions were unconstitutional limitations on businesses' First Amendment rights of expression. Churches have adopted them widely, delivering for the motorist not only evangelistic messages but also general moral precepts and homely proverbs.

See also ENVIRONMENT: Parks and Recreation Areas; FOLKLIFE: / "Get Right With God"; HISTORY AND MANNERS: Automobile; Historic Sites; RECREATION: Tourism, Automobile

Charles Reagan Wilson
University of Mississippi

John Baeder, *Gas, Food, and Lodging: A Postcard Odyssey through the Great American Roadside* (1982); Warren J. Belasco, *Americans on the Road: From Autocamps to Motel, 1910–1945* (1975); Thomas D. Clark, *The Emerging South* (1961); John Brinckerhoff Jackson, *The Southern Landscape Tradition in Texas* (1980); John A. Jakle, *The Tourist: Travel in Twentieth-Century North America* (1985); Chester H. Liebs, *Main Street to Miracle Mile: American Roadside Architecture* (1986); William E. Schmidt, *New York Times* (19 October 1984). ☆

Southwest
||||||||||||||||||||||||||||

The term *Southwest* has long been used popularly and by scholars to refer to a major subregion of the South. The Old Southwest of the early 19th century included lands recently opened to white settlement—Alabama, Mississippi, Tennessee, Kentucky, Arkansas, and Louisiana. By the 1840s the Southwest included Texas. With the acquisition and settlement of land reaching to southern California, the "Southwest" grew to the west, but the relationship of this land to the South was increasingly unclear.

The problems in defining the Southwest are important ones in understanding the complexities of southern culture and its cultural boundaries. Until recently, scholarly attempts to define regions have reflected physical and economic patterns rather than broader cultural ones. Some scholars have seen the American Southwest as a distinct region, altogether separate from the South. Sociologist Howard W. Odum in *Southern Regions of the United States* (1936) wrote that Texas, Oklahoma, New Mexico, and Arizona were the Southwest, one of six major American regions. Using over 200 indices of specific sociocultural characteristics, Odum concluded that "Texas and Oklahoma qualify as 'southern' in less than a third of the indices selected." He insisted that placing the Southwest with the Southeast was inaccurate and "detrimental to genuine regional analysis and planning." Ruth F. Hale identified the same four states as the Southwest in a more recently developed "Map of Vernacular Regions," based on a mail sample of people's identification with region. Cultural geographer D. W. Meinig identifies New Mexico and Arizona as the main focus of the Southwest, exploring the cultural contributions of Anglos, Indians, and Hispanics to its distinctiveness. Although not a part of the "South," Meinig's Southwest was formed partly through contributions of southern whites, particularly Texans, who, he wrote, were "a special regional type, differentiated by political and racial attitudes, religion, and social mores."

Political scientist Daniel Elazar in *Cities of the Prairies* (1970) defines the Southwest to include Louisiana, Arkansas, Missouri, Oklahoma, Texas, and New Mexico (with half of Texas and Oklahoma in what he calls the Greater South and half in the Greater West). Elazar's definition is based on "the expression of social, economic and political differences along geographic lines." Cultural geographer Wilbur Zelinsky divides the United States into five regions with Texas divided between the South and the West. In creating his division, Zelinsky uses such indicators as food habits, religion, language, and self-conscious identification with region.

Most of these definitions of the Southwest come from broader attempts to chart the nation's overall regional boundaries. From the viewpoint of southern history and culture, questions about the nature of a western *part* of the South center on Texas and Oklahoma. In one of the most recent efforts at defining regions, Raymond D. Gastil has placed most of Texas and Oklahoma in a "western" subregion of the South, based on secondary cultural factors "induced by differences in the origin of the people, the requirements of particular geographical situations, or subsequent creativity." Joel Garreau in *The Nine Nations of North America* (1981) does not use traditional regional terminology but carves up Texas and Oklahoma, placing the eastern portions of each in "Dixie" and the western parts in the "Breadbasket" (with southern and far western Texas in "MexAmerica").

The Southwest is clearly, then, a borderland area of the South, but it offers the opportunity to observe the cultural configuration of a subregion of Dixie, one that has a distinctive history and identity that is, nonetheless, closely related to that of other areas of the South. Texas is the core area of the South's Southwest, the centerpiece for any attempt to understand the line dividing the Southwest into "southern" and "western" spheres. Writer Willie Morris recalls the Texan who insisted the dividing line was Conroe, Tex., because west of there bar fights occur indoors and to the east they are outdoors. The "bar fight" line has never been formally charted, but environmental, demographic, historical, and cultural factors suggest an answer. For a study of the South, the Southwest is a most significant area for the clash of cultures, where a southern white-black tradition came into contact with a more pluralistic Hispanic-Indian-frontier culture.

Environmental and climatic factors suggest that much of Texas is southern. A fault line, the Balcones Escarpment, is a geological dividing line, marking in solid rock a physical separation between east Texas—the center of southern influences—and west Texas. In the middle of the state the land changes from piney woods in the east to grassy prairies to the west, with increasingly barren-looking plains and desert even farther west. Markedly decreased rainfall in west Texas reinforces the sense of a western physical landscape, nurturing different forms of animal and plant life. These physical differences were matched by differing settlement populations as well—blacks form a major population group in east Texas, gradually diminishing in numbers to the west, where Hispanics increase in numbers and cultural influence. Texas in general has been more ethnically diverse than the rest of the South, with Indians, Hispanics, Germans, Czechs, Danes, Swedes, and, more recently, Vietnamese significant populations in different areas of the state. The dividing line between southern and western parts of Texas based on these environmental and demographic facts, in any event, seems to be somewhere between the 98th meridian and the 103rd meridian. Walter Prescott Webb's *The Great Plains* (1931) was a landmark exploration of the response of frontier settlers to the challenges of a new environment in the West. Webb argued that the West began near the 98th meridian—or at that point where water becomes scarce.

In addition to environmental and demographic factors, history made Texas partly southern and partly western. The Anglo founder of Texas, Stephen Austin, was born in Virginia, and most early Anglo settlers were southern whites who brought their black slaves with them when they immigrated to Mexican soil. Cotton grew well in east Texas, and historian Frank Vandiver has noted that early Texans saw wealth in southern terms as "land, cotton, and slaves." The Republic of Texas (1836–45) was surely the creation of aggressive southern white Americans, symbolized by leaders such

Wheaton, **A Texas Rancher** *(date unknown)*

as Sam Houston, born in Virginia, and Davy Crockett, from Tennessee. The evangelical churches that dominated the rest of the antebellum South also dominated in Texas, among both whites and blacks, a situation that remains true in east and central Texas. Texas was a Confederate state, and with defeat in the Civil War Texans claimed the Lost Cause. The erection of Confederate monuments all the way west to El Paso established a southern landscape.

East and north Texas were dominated by sharecropping after the Civil War, with George Sessions Perry's *Hold Autumn in Your Hand* (1941) a major novel of southern social life under crop lien. These areas were among the centers of Populist agrarian discontent in the 1880s and 1890s, befitting their location between other areas of unrest in the Deep South and on the Great Plains. V. O. Key, Jr., discussed Texas as a southern state in *Southern Politics* (1949), showing that the state produced the kind of early 20th-century rural demagogues (James Ferguson, W. Lee "Pappy" O'Daniel) found elsewhere in the South, but they did not exploit the race issue to the same degree as elsewhere. Key noted that Texas was less concerned with race than "about money and how to make it."

The post–Civil War period had seen increasing southwestern divergence from southern patterns. The range cattle industry seemed by the end of the 1860s to be an economic substitute for the cotton economy. Cattle culture generated capital but, perhaps more importantly, a new mythology for the Southwest, one not shared with the rest of the South. The rancher became a southwestern hero and the longhorn a near mythic animal, but the prime new legendary figure was the cowboy, a symbol of west-

ern freedom. The cowboy, to be sure, had southern roots. Owen Wister's *The Virginian* created the model, a romantic figure who had much of the honorable cavalier in him. Black and white southerners after the war did go west seeking opportunity and some became cowboys, but they were seeking to escape the South. The cowboy's real life of hard work and loneliness made him more a working-class frontiersman than a cavalier. The cowboy has shown an enduring appeal for 20th-century Texans and other southerners, especially country music entertainers from Jimmie Rodgers to Charlie Daniels who have nurtured the cowboy legend. Cowboy hats and boots spread eastward to become common southern rural working-class badges of identification with the Southwest.

Discovery of oil at Spindletop near Beaumont on 10 January 1901 further differentiated the Texas economy from the southern, and oil and natural gas would provide a southwestern economic bond between Texas, Oklahoma, and Louisiana. Petroleum lore created another new mythology for the Southwest, as colorful wildcatters such as Dad Joiner became Texas legends. The massive amounts of money generated by petroleum would enable Texas culture and society to escape much of the enervating southern culture of poverty.

Twentieth-century southwestern culture has continued to reflect both southern and western influences. Before the 1920s, for example, Texas Anglo music came out of a southern heritage. Rural Texans played the same instruments and sang the same kinds of songs found elsewhere in the South. Western swing emerged in Texas and Oklahoma in the 1930s, showing the influence of ethnically diverse Texas and becoming a major genre of country music. Its creators, including Bob Wills and His Texas Playboys, dressed in western costume but played music drawing on blues and jazz as well as southern white fiddle music. The first country star, Jimmie Rodgers, lived his last few years in Texas and promoted a western, "singing cowboy" image. Later Texas country music performers such as Ernest Tubb and Gene Autry made "western" music a southwestern contribution to "southern" country music. Lightnin' Hopkins was similarly a major figure in a southwestern blues tradition centered in east and central Texas. Contemporary Tex-Mex music represents a blending of Mexican, German, and southern musical styles.

Southwestern writers have been, until recently, preoccupied with the frontier, which has been a source of the region's enduring mythology. Southwestern literature was traditionally peopled principally by hardy frontiersmen, gruff ranchers, romantic cowboys, and always-just Texas Rangers. The greatest literary achievements until the 1950s were in nonfiction. Folklorist-biographer J. Frank Dobie, historian Walter Prescott Webb, and naturalist Roy Bedichek were dominant forces. Novelist Larry McMurtry has noted that the "Big Three," as he calls them, "revered Nature, studied Nature, and hued to Nature." It was a literature celebrating western triumph rather than exploring the complex, tragic themes of modern southern literature. Since the 1950s writers such as William Humphrey, William Goyen, Bill Brammer, John Graves, and Larry King have created a southwestern fiction tradition that draws on themes earlier articulated by Faulkner and other southern writers. Larry McMurtry is perhaps the most ac-

complished and successful novelist, telling the story of the movement of Texans off the land and into a new urban Southwest.

Southwestern cooking illustrates the meeting of southern, western, and Mexican cultures. Southern dishes such as grits, biscuits, corn bread, turnip greens, fried chicken, country ham with redeye gravy, and pork sausage are all popular in Texas. Texan Elmore Tora was founder of the National Blackeyed Pea Association and marketed the pea in Asia. The chicken-fried steak is particularly popular fare in Texas truck stops and cafes; it applies a southern style of cooking to a piece of beef—battering and frying like cooking fried chicken. A cream gravy is the essential accompanying sauce. Larry McMurtry insists that "only a rank degenerate would drive 1,500 miles across Texas without eating a chicken-fried steak." Barbecue is the object of cult-like obsession, although southwestern barbecue is beef, not the pork found in the Deep South. Tex-Mex cooking is a particularly revealing product of a cultural borderland, combining ingredients and styles of cooking from Mexican, Indian, and Anglo traditions. Texas produces about 10 percent of the world's jalapeño pepper supply for its cuisine. Texans in 1951 formed the Chili Appreciation Society International in Dallas, launching a crusade for chili that has brought increasingly passionate identification of chili with the state. South, west, and central Texas are the centers of Tex-Mex cooking, but on the cultural borderland its popularity has spilled over into east Texas, Louisiana, and other parts of the South.

The 1970s saw the emergence of an energetic southwestern culture in central Texas. It was a youth culture, the

southwestern version of the countercul-
ture. Drinking beer (preferably the regional Lone Star Longnecks), smoking
marijuana, listening to "progressive
country" music (especially Willie Nelson), eating Tex-Mex food, admiring ar-
madillos—all were rituals of a lifestyle
that self-consciously identified with the
region. Periodicals such as the *Texas
Monthly* (begun in 1973), the *Texas Observer* (a reform journal that began publishing in 1954 and calls itself "a
window on the South"), and the *Southwestern Historical Quarterly* explore the
cultural dimensions of the Southwest,
including its southern ties. In a January
1977 feature entitled "How To Be
Southern," for example, *Texas Monthly*
noted that through the years "we Texans
have been the perfect fair-weather
friends of the South." Texans had "the
credentials to be Southern when we
wanted," but in trying times "we've
been able to step neatly aside into our
Southwestern identities." With Jimmy
Carter's inauguration the Southwest
seemed to reclaim a part of its southern
heritage. By the late 1970s, though, the
symbols and rituals of Texas culture had
come to predominate over either the
western or the southern identity.

See also ENVIRONMENT: / Armadillo; ETH-
NIC LIFE: / Mexicans; FOLKLIFE: Pottery,
Texas; INDUSTRY: / Oil Industry; LAW: /
Foreman, Percy; MUSIC: *Música Tejana*;
Western Swing; SOCIAL CLASS: / Oil Work-
ers; URBANIZATION: / Dallas; Houston;
VIOLENCE: Southwestern Violence

Charles Reagan Wilson
University of Mississippi

J. Frank Dobie, *A Guide to the Life and
Literature of the Southwest* (1943), *Some Part
of Myself* (1967); T. R. Fehrenbach, *Lone
Star: A History of Texas and the Texans*

(1983); Lawrence Goodwyn, *Texas Observer*
(27 December 1974); Ruth F. Hale, "A Map
of Vernacular Regions in America" (Ph.D.
dissertation, University of Minnesota,
1971); Jon Holmes, *Texas: A Self-Portrait*
(1983); Paul Horgan, *Southwest Review*
(Summer 1933); Terry G. Jordan, *Annals of
the Association of American Geographers* (De-
cember 1967, September 1970); Joseph
Leach, *The Typical Texan* (1952); Larry
McMurtry, *In a Narrow Grave: Essays on
Texas* (1968); D. W. Meinig, *Imperial Texas:
An Interpretive Essay in Cultural Geography*
(1969); Ben Proctor and Archie P. Mc-
Donald, eds., *The Texas Heritage* (1980);
Frank Vandiver, *The Southwest: South or
West* (1975); Walter Prescott Webb, ed.,
Handbook of Texas, 2 vols. (1952). ☆

Sports, Geography of

A trilogy of national games clearly dom-
inates the South. Football is the premier
sport, though baseball and basketball
are played, enjoyed, and in some places
avidly followed.

The best gauges of a sport's grip on
an area are per capita involvement and
the number of high quality performers
originating from the place. The per capita production of major college and
professional football (NFL) players has
been calculated for the period 1968–80
so as to identify regional differences.
The geographical origins of major league
baseball players and collegiate basketball players have been charted for the
same period.

The relative importance of baseball,
football, and basketball varies across
the South, as seen in Table 2. A value
of 1.00 in the table indicates that a
state's per capita talent output is equal

Table 2. *Southern Emphasis on Football, Basketball, and Baseball as Measured by Per Capita Production of Players*

State	Football Collegiate	Football Professional	Basketball	Baseball
Alabama	1.03	2.19	1.09	1.07
Arkansas	1.13	1.69	0.75	0.37
Florida	1.22	1.31	0.81	1.55
Georgia	1.21	1.92	0.80	0.73
Kentucky	0.88	0.57	1.37	0.60
Louisiana	2.20	2.26	1.19	0.87
Mississippi	1.63	3.40	0.81	0.71
North Carolina	1.00	1.43	0.88	0.69
South Carolina	0.83	1.43	0.70	0.95
Tennessee	0.99	1.15	1.46	0.54
Texas	1.60	2.18	0.73	0.97
Virginia	1.16	0.75	1.15	0.83

Source: John F. Rooney, Jr., American Demographics (September 1986).
Note: A value of 1.00 indicates that a state's per capita talent output is equal to the national average.

to the national average. Values in excess of 1.00 indicate that a state produces more players than would be expected, and values of less than 1.00 suggest that the state is placing less emphasis on the sport than the nation as a whole. The majority of southern states are near or above the national norm for America's three major sports. Among southern states Louisiana, Mississippi, and Texas stand out as producers of football talent; Kentucky and Tennessee are the basketball leaders; Florida is the dominant baseball producer. The majority of the southern states (unlike most northern ones) are above the national football norm.

Though football is a national game, the ability to play it well is inordinately concentrated in the South. As the figures in Tables 3 and 4 reveal, southern cities and rural areas lead the nation in producing football players on the major college level. The South adopted a northern game, absorbed it fully into its culture, and gradually outdid the innovators. Based on the basketball evidence for the period 1970 to the present, the same pattern has been repeated with that sport. Football mania peaks each autumn in towns like Knoxville, Tuscaloosa, Auburn, Oxford, Gainesville, Baton Rouge, Grambling, Athens, Clemson, and Columbia. In February the recruiting saga now overshadows basketball and other ongoing sporting activities. In high schools the level of community pride associated with football is unparalleled.

Football mania is still intensifying throughout the South. Young players with football promise are frequently held back, "redshirted in the eighth grade," so that they will be physically capable of meeting the challenges of high school and college ball. Blacks now have access to the southern university of their choice, and they select big-name foot-

Table 3. *Leading Metropolitan Areas in Production of Major College Football Talent, 1968–1980*

Metropolitan Area	Total Players	Per Capita Rate
1. Lake Charles, La.	125	5.20
2. Monroe, La.	91	4.55
3. Beaumont–Port Arthur, Tex.	214	3.81
4. Shreveport, La.	184	3.34
5. Midland-Odessa, Tex.	88	3.24
6. Longview, Tex.	62	3.06
7. Youngstown-Warren, Ohio	238	2.85
8. Boise, Idaho	59	2.62
9. Biloxi-Gulfport, Miss.	116	2.61
10. Baton Rouge, La.	175	2.60
11. Jackson, Miss.	117	2.56
12. Tallahassee, Fla.	49	2.29
13. Great Falls, Mont.	29	2.23
14. Tyler, Tex.	38	2.21
15. Gainesville, Fla.	39	1.99

Source: John F. Rooney, Jr., American Demographics (September 1986).
Note: A value of 1.00 indicates that a metropolitan area's per capita talent output is equal to the national average.

Table 4. *Leading Nonmetropolitan Counties in Production of Major College Football Talent, 1968–1980*

County	Total Players	Per Capita Rate
1. St. James, La.	20	6.66
2. Warren, Miss.	38	4.93
3. Wharton, Tex.	24	4.17
4. Natchitoches, La.	23	4.07
5. Acadia, La.	33	3.94
6. Lincoln, La.	21	3.67
7. St. Martin, La.	19	3.50
8. Iberia, La.	30	3.05
9. Clarke, Ga.	33	3.03
10. Washington, La.	19	2.89

Source: John F. Rooney, Jr., American Demographics (September 1986).
Note: A value of 1.00 indicates that a county's per capita talent output is equal to the national average.

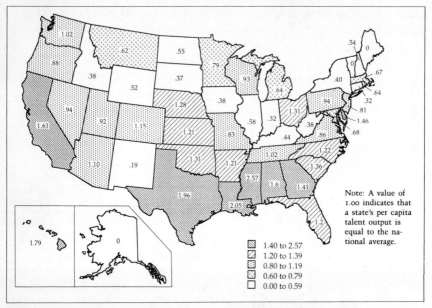

Index of Professional Football Players Produced by State, 1981

Source: John F. Rooney, Jr., "The Pigskin Cult and Other Sunbelt Sports," American Demographics (September 1986).

ball schools with increasing regularity. In fact, much of the growth in southern player production can be attributed to the rise of the black athlete.

As a result of the emphasis on football, most high school sports programs in the South are lacking in breadth. High school boys throughout the region have very limited access to competitive swimming, gymnastics, wrestling, and soccer. Georgia and Florida are the only states above the national norm in soccer participation. Track-and-field and cross-country programs are relatively scarce, and Texas is the lone state above the national average. Golf and tennis are absent from a sizable portion of the high schools.

Women's sports receive little support in the South. Federal legislation requiring equal opportunity for women in sports has thus far failed to bring the South up to national standards. Texas

and Oklahoma, possessing long-term basketball traditions, are exceptions to the southern void.

The South is heavily involved in a variety of other sports. Stock car racing is indigenous to the region, and even today the majority of the great drivers are of southern origin. Thoroughbred racing and breeding are concentrated in Kentucky and Virginia. Fox hunting and horse shows are common throughout the Upland South. Tennessee walkers are a distinct southern breed, and the quarter horse continues to grow in popularity throughout the Southwest. Florida is the shuffleboard capital of the world.

Though most southern states are below the national average in number of golf courses per capita, new course construction is proceeding at a rapid pace. Golf-oriented communities and golf resorts are highly concentrated within the region, creating the ultimate in luxury sports landscapes. Despite its lack of facilities, the South leads the nation in the output of professional golfers.

Lacrosse, rugby, and crew are largely absent from the southern sports scene, and for obvious reasons most activities requiring ice and snow are poorly developed.

See also BLACK LIFE: Sports, Blacks in; RECREATION articles

John F. Rooney, Jr.
Oklahoma State University

John F. Rooney, Jr., *American Demographics* (September 1986), *Geography of American Sport* (1974), *Geographical Review* (October 1969). ☆

Towns and Villages
||||||||||||||||||||||||||||||||||||||||||||||||||||||||

Early urban communities in the South were not founded by investors or entrepreneurs as they had been in New England and New York, nor were they created by government-subsidized railroads as in much of the Midwest and West. Rather, towns and villages that formed across much of the frontier South as service centers for a primarily agrarian clientele evolved out of transplanted European tradition and law. The plantations of the Tidewater colonies produced cotton, tobacco, and other commodities on a commercial scale, but their proprietors preferred to trade directly with Caribbean or European markets. Consequently, the market town did not develop early in eastern Virginia or the Carolinas as it did in the North, where farmers sold their surplus produce in village markets. Inland from the coast, the first hamlets were established by English, Scotch-Irish, and German settlers moving south from Pennsylvania along the Great Valley and Piedmont. At mill sites or where open country roads met, a farmstead or two, a church, school, and store would eventually coalesce into a loosely ordered crossroads hamlet.

The tradition of English law as established in the South was administered through a system of counties. County government was conducted at the county seat, usually the largest and often the only real town in the county. Government attracted professionals who served it and were served by it, and the county seat became the home of politicians, lawyers, bankers, enforcement officers, surveyors and engineers, and merchants—in short, the economic and social elite of the county. Their offices often faced a central town square on which stood the courthouse and jail, a county seat pattern that has diffused widely through the South from its origin in Pennsylvania. Few farmers lived in the county seat. If they lived in an urban place at all, it would be the crossroads hamlet. As the South grew, towns built around the central square appeared in adjacent territory and newly formed counties.

Variations on this urban scheme appeared as early as the 1760s when French Acadian migrants from Nova Scotia moved into Louisiana's Mississippi River Delta marshlands. There they built small line villages atop the natural levees of major streams according to a system of community organization and land division that had begun to mature in French Canada.

Before the Civil War, the economy of the South remained largely agricultural, and its urban settlements were small and parochial. The largest towns were coastal cotton shipping ports: Galveston, New Orleans, Mobile, Charleston, and Savannah. Inland, a string of river or fall line towns grew up at mill sites and navigational breaks: Richmond, Petersburg, Raleigh, Columbia, Augusta, and Macon.

After the Civil War, fundamental changes in regional and national culture and economy began to lay a foundation for dramatic alteration of the urban system. Freed slaves created a new type of settlement in some areas. Freedmen on many cotton plantations settled on dispersed parcels of plantation land in an initial stage of the sharecropping system. On sugar plantations in Louisiana and the livestock estates of the Kentucky Bluegrass, a somewhat different pattern of black resettlement occurred. In Louisiana, sugar plantations had large labor requirements during harvesting and refining. Consequently, freedmen working on plantations were housed in small linear hamlets, often located near sugar mills. In Kentucky, large Bluegrass estates required workers to handle livestock and produce hemp and tobacco cash crops. Slave quarters were eliminated and freedmen were given, or were allowed to rent or buy, housing in small hamlets, which were often subdivided out of a portion of estate property.

The end of the Civil War marked the rebuilding and extension of the southern rail system and the establishment of reliable trade links with the North. Rail lines focused at coastal harbors, river bridging points, and mountain gaps; when a new rail line was built into an existing town there was often a small boom in development as local entrepreneurs built lumberyards, tanneries, furniture plants, textile mills, and cotton gins. Towns on the Piedmont near streams that could provide small-scale hydroelectric power, or those near the hardwood stands of the Appalachian uplands, tended to benefit most from this transportation revolution. In peninsular Florida the effect of rail building was substantially different. Inhospitable marshlands became accessible for the first time, allowing rail companies to establish a number of new towns and resorts along the coasts.

The extension of railroads into the South also brought entrepreneurs seeking resources to fuel northern industry. Pennsylvania coal, for example, was used in local iron furnaces until high-strength steel rails and rolling stock made mining in the central Appalachians a profitable alternative. After 1870 northern industrialists sent representatives into the southern mountains to buy mineral rights over broad areas. As coal mines were established in eastern Kentucky, Tennessee, western Virginia, and West Virginia, company towns were built to house the men that the companies hoped to employ. Some towns, constructed by poorly financed companies, were small and pitifully built. Others, such as Lynch and Wheelwright, Ky., were extensive, planned communities housing populations of a thousand or more within a year of completion. Southern blacks, European immigrants, and local hill farmers were hired to mine coal and were settled in socially stratified towns. Small miners' houses were often crowded together in a valley bottom. More substantial mine managers' homes were usually placed upslope, away from dust, noise, and the miners. About 1870 several small company towns grew amidst the ridges and hardscrabble farms of north-central Alabama where local coal, iron ore, and limestone were used to produce iron. Gradually, the town of Birmingham grew from several such towns.

By the 1880s and 1890s the textile milling industry, so strongly entrenched in New England before 1860, was beginning to migrate to the Carolina and Georgia Piedmont. Mill owners, as they had done in England a century before and in New England after about 1790, built small towns at their mill sites to house workers. Many Piedmont farmers, burdened by debt and constrained by poor farming practices that produced little more than eroded fields, sent their wives and children to work in nearby mills. Mill homes clustered around a central company store, where workers purchased food and dry goods or used the post office or barber shops. Pay was often in scrip negotiable only at the company businesses.

Recreational towns began to appear at Virginia's thermal springs in the ridge and valley country west of Roanoke by the turn of the 19th century. Their growth was paralleled by high-altitude resort towns in the southern Blue Ridge Mountains such as Asheville and Highlands, N.C., which attracted wealthy Coastal Plain planters and merchants seeking relief from oppressive summer heat and miasma.

The broad pattern of small market towns interspersed with large numbers of crossroads hamlets and clusters of specialized company towns changed little until about 1930 when improved roads and automobiles allowed greater residential flexibility. Since World War II the population of many small towns has stagnated or even declined, and a new urban form, the linear roadside housing strip, has evolved. People purchase road-front lots from farmers, build

homes, and commute to work in nearby towns. Consequently, town population may not change noticeably, but rural nonfarm density increases substantially. This process is especially evident in the Carolina Piedmont.

See also BLACK LIFE: Towns, Black; INDUSTRY: Industrialization in Appalachia; Industrialization in Piedmont; SOCIAL CLASS: / Company Towns; URBANIZATION articles

Karl B. Raitz
University of Kentucky

Conrad M. Arensberg, *American Anthropologist* (December 1955); Dwight B. Billings, *Planters and the Making of a "New South": Class, Politics, and Development in North Carolina, 1865–1900* (1979); John C. Campbell, *The Southern Highlander and His Homeland* (1921); Robert D. Mitchell, *Commercialism and Frontier: Perspectives on the Early Shenandoah Valley* (1977); M. B. Newton, Jr., *Geoscience and Man*, vol. 5 (1974); Peter Smith and Karl Raitz, *Geographical Review* (April 1974). ☆

BLACK BELT

The Black Belt region, also called the Black Prairie, extends 300 miles across central Alabama and northeast Mississippi and into Tennessee. It is flat land, 20 to 25 miles wide, and lies from 200 to 300 feet below the uplands that are north and south of the region. The dark soil for which the Black Belt was named was once famous for its richness and the abundant cotton produced in it. Cotton was, in fact, the main cash crop from the 1820s until early in the 20th century, when losses from the boll weevil forced agricultural diversification. Some geographers speculate that the region, drained by the Alabama and Tombigbee river systems, was originally a grass-land.

Social scientists sometimes use the term *black belt* to refer to that part of the South dominated by cotton planta-tions and having a high proportion of blacks in the population. Howard W. Odum, for example, in *Southern Regions of the United States* (1936), defined the Black Belt as extending into Georgia, the Carolinas, and western Mississippi. The culture of the poor who live in these areas has been the topic of several major studies, beginning with Odum's and in-cluding Charles S. Johnson's *Growing Up in the Black Belt* (1941) and Arthur F. Raper's *Tenants of the Almighty* (1943). These accounts give an insight into the lives of tenant-farm families and portray the changes that they experi-enced as tenancy collapsed. Johnson's description of the lives of rural black youths in several southern counties, based largely on interviews, gives de-tails of their home life, education, as-pirations, and attitudes toward whites. The Black Belt has been the incubator for much black culture, probably be-cause of the concentration of popula-tion. Raper's study of Greene County, Ga., examines the benefits brought to the area by New Deal programs de-signed to alleviate the poverty of ten-ancy and to improve living conditions in the area. Other observers have noted the insularity of the region.

The region's white tenant-farm fam-ilies were the subjects of James Agee and Walker Evans's *Let Us Now Praise Famous Men* (1936). Their blend of compassion and objectivity in photo-graphs and text gives an intimate por-trait of the lives of poor whites in Hale County, Ala., and includes vivid details of clothing, education, housing, and work. The book inspired William Chris-tenberry, a Hale County native, to pho-tograph the rural southern landscape, preserving the icons of that culture. Christenberry's artwork has attracted further attention to the unique Black Belt area and its people. The Black Belt Folk Roots Festival in Eutaw, Ala., celebrates the culture of western Alabama and eastern Mississippi each August.

Karen M. McDearman
University of Mississippi

William Christenberry, *Southern Photo-graphs* (1983); Nevin M. Fenneman, *Phys-iography of Eastern United States* (1938); William D. Thornbury, *Regional Geomor-phology of the United States* (1965). ☆

CHEROKEE SETTLEMENT

The Cherokee nation, located in eastern Tennessee, the western Carolinas, northeastern Alabama, and northern Georgia, was one of the last important American Indian strongholds in the eastern United States in the early 19th century. The direct impact of their his-torical presence is confined to a few his-toric sites and buildings scattered throughout their home region and the small Qualla Reservation in North Carolina. Their influence on contem-porary rural Appalachian settlement landscape, however, continues. Cher-okee settlement patterns represent a case study of Indian influence on the South.

The Cherokee were divided into four

culturally distinct communities on both sides of the Great Smoky Mountains at the time of European contact in the 18th century: the Valley, Overhill, Middle, and Lower Towns. The core of Cherokee settlement was in the Middle Towns along the upper reaches of the Little Tennessee River in the western Carolinas. This period's settlement landscape featured large palisaded villages of 350 to 600 persons located in the major stream valleys of the region.

On his visit to the Cherokee country during the 1770s, William Bartram found clustered villages focusing upon roundish council houses located on an artificial hill or rise, as well as some scattered dwellings. The palisades around the villages disappeared during the relatively peaceful mid-18th century, and a more dispersed settlement pattern soon followed.

The four most common Cherokee building types during the 18th century were the council house, the summer and winter residential houses, and storage buildings. The council house was a large domed post-and-beam structure designed so that each of the Cherokee clans present in the village would have equal access to the center during community meetings. Its size varied depending upon the population of the village. The summer house was a three-roomed, raised, rectangular, post-and-beam house with woven reed or wicker walls. A long porch was built across the facade for use during the muggy summers. The adjacent winter house was often occupied by more than one family. It was built of poles in a domed shape with heavy walls, no windows, a small door, and an upper air hole for a chimney. A fire burned continually during the winter. Beds were located around the sides of the single room. The corn storage sheds were small post-and-beam structures raised four to five feet off the ground.

The Cherokee settlement landscape was massively altered after the incursion of white influences in the region. Population pressures and conflict along the eastern and northern borders moved the focal point of power from the western Carolinas first to Tennessee and later to northern Georgia. The Cherokee settlement pattern at the time of removal was also almost totally transformed. Clustered village settlements were replaced by isolated farmsteads. The traditional domed council house vanished. The summer and winter houses were replaced by small, single-pen, hewn-log, one-story, puncheon-floored, wooden-end chimney cottages. These log houses were occasionally enlarged to dogtrot, saddlebag, and I-house forms, but more often a second or third structure was built when additional space was needed. The outbuildings were also patterned on the white frontiersman's buildings and included, in declining order of frequency, corncribs, smokehouses, potato houses, and stables. The remainder of the farmstead consisted of a small truck garden near the house and one or more 5- to 20-acre cornfields.

The impact of Cherokee settlement upon both initial white settlement and the current landscape has been greater than generally believed. The Cherokee were removed from their traditional lands in the 1830s, and the vacated areas were distributed among white settlers. White settlement of the region, therefore, was essentially a continuation of the previous Indian patterns of field and house-site selections. The recently vacated Cherokee housing generally was occupied by new white owners; many such houses are still used today. Indian agricultural methods, especially in the house gardens, crop complexes, and philosophies of field selection, also continued to be important in the white landscape. Indian paths and roads became white wagon roads and were eventually preserved in the state and county highway systems.

The principal differences between the two landscapes have been in the growth of towns. There were no true European-style Cherokee towns in northern Georgia at the time of removal. The Cherokee capital of New Echota, for example, never had more than a handful of houses occupied at one time, most of those by whites. At the time of removal, Cherokee towns were social and economic communities, whose residents were widely dispersed. Thus, at the time of removal the Indian "town" of Hightower had more than 100 residents scattered along 30 miles of the Ellijay River Valley, whereas the white town of Ellijay founded in the same location had only about 50 residents clustered around the courthouse within three years of its occupation.

See also ETHNIC LIFE: / Cherokees

Richard Pillsbury
Georgia State University

Gary C. Goodwin, *Cherokees in Transition: A Study of Changing Culture and Environment prior to 1775* (1977); Henry T. Malone, *Cherokees of the Old South* (1956); Richard Pillsbury, *Geoscience and Man*, vol. 23 (1983). ☆

COTTON GINS

Cotton gins once were common features on the landscape across much of the Lowland South. The demise of cotton in areas where it was king and the replacement of many small gin plants by a few large ones in areas where cotton continues to be an important crop have resulted in the dramatic decrease in the number of cotton gins in the South. The number declined from 30,000 in 1900 to less than 10,000 in 1945. In 1981 only 1,819 active cotton gins remained in the southern states. However, the average number of bales processed per cotton gin increased from less than 500 in 1900 to more than 5,000 in 1981.

During the early part of the 20th century larger, centrally located plants employing what was termed a "ginning system" replaced small, labor-intensive antebellum-type ginning facilities. The type of ginning facility that developed prior to the Civil War consisted of a ginhouse in which the removal of seed from the lint, or ginning, took place. In the ginhouse the seed cotton was fed into a gin stand powered by horses or mules. The lint cotton was carried in baskets from the ginhouse to a horse- or mule-powered press. Most of the cotton plantations had such a facility, and it could process three or four bales of cotton in a day.

The ginning system was developed during the 1880s. A steam-powered plant integrated the ginning with the baling and automated the movement of cotton through the facility. A ginning system contained several gin stands and could process three or four bales of cotton per hour. The term *cotton gin* came to refer to such plants, whereas in its original usage the term had referred to just the gin stand.

The introduction of mechanical harvesters following World War II initiated another period of dramatic change in cotton ginning. Because mechanically harvested cotton contains more trash and moisture than cotton picked by hand, seed-cotton dryers and lint-cleaning devices had to be added to gin plants, and whereas hand picking commenced in late summer and frequently continued into December, mechanical pickers compressed the harvest season into a period of approximately six weeks. High-capacity gin plants with larger gin stands were introduced to handle the increased flow of cotton from the fields. Recent innovations include module storage of cotton prior to ginning and the use of universal density presses that produce bales ready for shipment to distant markets without further compressing.

A modern cotton gin represents a substantial capital investment and is capable of ginning 10 or more bales of machine-harvested cotton per hour. Antebellum-type ginning facilities were within 2 to 4 miles of one another, and plants employing ginning systems were 3 to 12 miles apart. Modern cotton gins may draw cotton from a 30-mile radius.

See also AGRICULTURE: / Cotton Culture

Charles S. Aiken
University of Tennessee

Cotton gin, Mississippi, no date

Charles S. Aiken, *Geographical Review* (April 1973); Charles A. Bennett, *Cotton Ginning Systems in the United States and Auxiliary Development* (1962), *Saw and Toothed Ginning Developments* (1960). ☆

COURTHOUSE SQUARE

The county seat was the South's most traditional urban form. The courthouse and its square were the scene of the vital governmental activities, as well as the focal point of the town's commercial life. Four basic courthouse-square designs have been found in the South. The oldest is the widened-street design dating from 17th-century Virginia. It consists of an enlarged courthouse lot on one side of the main street. The plan is most common in Tidewater Virginia, although examples are occasionally found in earlier settled areas throughout the South. The widened street, an extension of the medieval European market-street concept modified to meet the needs of a courthouse site, is rarely found outside of Virginia.

The second design, called the secant square, is a subform of the widened-street plan. It was created by cutting back the four corners of the main intersection to leave an open square in the street. In America the design was first used in 1681 to create space for the Philadelphia city hall. This geometric adaptation of the widened street plan was most common in county seats founded after 1790 in the Upland South, especially in the southern Appalachians.

The third design, the central square, is considered to be the regional archetype. It consists of a full-city-block square at the intersection of the two main through roads. This is the most common courthouse square pattern in county seats founded after 1800, and its distribution parallels the founding of new counties in the South after that date.

A fourth design is the off-set central-square subform created when the courthouse block is astride the main through road. This design, with obvious ancillary antecedents in the secanted design, has the advantage of placing the courthouse in a position of physical, visual, and psychological dominance within the town plan. Used primarily after 1800, the off-set square design appeared occasionally in the later settled South.

The courthouse square is significant because of its centralizing influence within a community. The square was for decades the center of governmental, economic, and social life in the surrounding area. Nineteenth-century county courthouses almost always were located on the square. Other typical structures on the early-19th-century square included wells, cisterns, and occasionally the jail and lawyers' offices. County officials in later periods tended to move the jail off the square to a less prominent location.

Examples from Georgia illustrate the range of activities common on late-19th-century courthouse squares. The most common retail activities on the blocks facing the square in Georgia county seats at this time, in declining order of frequency, were general-merchandise stores, offices, grocery stores, dry-goods stores, millineries, drugstores, hotels, lodge halls, and saloons. The second most common land use on the blocks facing the square was residential: typically about 20 percent of this space was devoted to dwellings located along one side and at the back of other blocks.

The courthouse square of the late 20th century has undergone a metamorphosis since the halcyon days of a century before. The original courthouse has frequently been replaced with a new building on a different site. The automobile has often forced competitive retailers to new locations on the commercial strip at the edge of towns. The remaining commercial establishments often have a sagging air of knowing that their time has passed. The smallest of the county seats have lost their viable commercial functions to larger towns. A few attempts at historic preservation and downtown revival impede this process, but even these activities often do little more than highlight the decline of this urban form.

Nonetheless, the courthouse has long been identified as the geographical center of southern communities. In *Requiem for a Nun*, William Faulkner wrote of Jefferson, Miss.: "But above all, the courthouse: the center, the focus, the hub . . . looming in the center of the county's circumference . . . laying its vast shadow to the uttermost rim of the horizon . . . ; dominating all: protector of the weak, judicate and curb of the passions and lust. . . ."

Courthouse in Monticello, Florida, 1939

Richard Pillsbury
Suzanne Andres
Georgia State University

Richard Francaviglia, *The Geographical Survey* (1973); Richard Pillsbury, *Southeastern Geographer*, vol. 18 (1978); Edward T. Price, *Geographical Review* (January 1968). ☆

CUBAN SETTLEMENT
||||||||||||||||||||||||||||||||||||||||||||||||||||

Cuban Americans represent the third largest group of Latin American origin living in the United States, being exceeded in number only by Mexican Americans and Puerto Ricans. Currently, about 1 million Cubans live in the United States, approximately 70 percent of whom are in the state of Florida. Very few Cubans live in other southern states (even in Florida they account for only about 6 percent of the state's population), but their importance is magnified because they are heavily concentrated in the metropolitan area of Miami, where over 600,000 persons of Cuban descent live. They have made a distinctive mark on a southern subregion. In Dade County (Metropolitan Miami) about 41 percent of the population consists of persons of Hispanic origin, and about 80 percent of these people are either first- or second-generation Cubans. The Cubans have had a major impact on the cultural landscape and economy of Miami, so much so that their major area of concentration is called "Little Havana."

Cubans came as permanent settlers to Key West as far back as 1831. Immigration to Florida, and especially to Tampa, increased in the 1870s. These early Cuban Americans came to the United States for a variety of reasons; many were simply unemployed or looking for better jobs, while others in the 20th century were politically alienated from right-wing Cuban regimes. The number of emigrants from Cuba rose sharply after the 1959 Castro Revolution. The Cubans who have moved to the United States have not, until recently, been representative of the population left behind in Cuba. The earliest significant wave of immigrants after 1959 was especially selective of professionals and entrepreneurs and thus created a serious "brain drain" in Cuba. As a result of this selection, a social and economic base was established in Miami that would help ease the adjustments of future immigrants. Today, Cuban Americans generally enjoy high levels of socioeconomic status compared to most other groups of Latin American descent.

Without warning, in April 1980, Fidel Castro suddenly allowed a massive exodus to the United States through the Cuban port of Mariel. Over the next six months approximately 125,000 Cubans immigrated to this country, with about 80 percent settling in south Florida. The "Marielitos" come closest as a group to representing the population in Cuba. Although the Cuban government included in their number about 5,000 prisoners from Cuban jails and patients from mental institutions, the vast majority (perhaps 95 percent) were not criminals or misfits. The collective wisdom of most who have studied them is that the Mariel immigrants will quickly and effectively accommodate themselves to life in the United States.

Cuban Americans attempted to preserve parts of their island culture after moving to Florida. The refugees from the 1959 revolution especially worked at this goal. The widespread use in south Florida of Spanish in shops, restaurants, banks, churches, and government offices is the most visible evidence of their success in maintaining cultural forms. Spanish-language bookstores stock writings of Cuban expatriates, Cuban-born artists perform in ethnic theater and dance groups, and neighborhood grocery stores in Miami stock fruits and vegetables traditional to the Cuban diet. Spanish-language television and radio stations broadcast programs for Cuban Americans, and a daily newspaper—owned, like the broadcast facilities, by Cuban Americans—publishes stories of interest to the community. Latin rhythms are heard in the nightclubs in Little Havana.

See also ETHNIC LIFE: / Cubans

Thomas D. Boswell
University of Miami

Thomas D. Boswell, in *Ethnic Minorities in the United States*, ed. Jesse O. McKee (1983), with James R. Curtis, *The Cuban-American Experience: Culture, Images, and Perspectives* (1983); Sergio Diza-Briquets and Lisandro Perez, *Cuba: The Demography of Revolution*, Population Reference Bureau, vol. 36, no. 1 (April 1981). ☆

DELTA
||||||||||||||||

The Yazoo–Mississippi Delta is not the true delta of the Mississippi River, but the fertile alluvial plain shared by the Mississippi and Yazoo rivers. One hundred sixty miles long and 50 miles wide at its widest, the Delta encompasses all of 10 Mississippi counties and parts of 8 more. Distinguished by its flatness and its fertility, the Delta was even better defined by its late-developing plantation economy and the distinctive society that economy nurtured.

Destined to become the richest agricultural region in the South, the Delta was only sparsely settled in 1860 and still not far removed from the frontier in 1880. During the next two decades a new network of levees and a modern railway system opened the plantation South's last frontier for full-scale settlement and development.

The fertile Delta drew not only ambitious whites, but blacks who saw it as the best place to test their newly won freedom and climb the agricultural ladder to become independent landowners. For many whites the Delta became a land of wildest fantasies fulfilled, but for thousands of blacks the Delta that had promised them the rural South's best chance for upward mobility became the burial ground for hopes and dreams. In reality the Delta proved to be little more than a stopover for many southern blacks on their way (via the conveniently located Illinois Central Railroad that bisected the area) to the North. The Delta experienced a massive out-migration of blacks in the years after World War I. During the same period the region was emerging as a spawning ground for the blues. This new musical idiom explored the shared experiences of southern blacks who had tested the economic, social, and political parameters of their freedom, as defined by a rigidly enforced system of caste, and discovered that, for them, the American Dream was little more than a cruel myth.

Meanwhile, despite their constant fears over labor shortages, Delta planters thrived on the annual gamble on the price of cotton, living lavishly and laughing at debts. Even the onslaught of the boll weevil did the Delta relatively little harm. Meanwhile, the Agricultural Adjustment Administration (AAA) confirmed the dominance of the large landholder in the region by channeling all of its acreage reduction and related payments through planters and looking the other way as these same planters illegally evicted now-superfluous sharecroppers. In 1934, 44 percent of all AAA payments in excess of $10,000 nationwide went to 10 counties in the Delta. This largesse facilitated the mechanization and consolidation of agriculture, and as federal farm programs continued, the money kept rolling in. In 1967 Delta planter and U.S. Senator James Eastland received $167,000 in federal payments. The Delta's poor blacks were not nearly so fortunate, as a power structure dominated by lavishly subsidized planters declared war on the War on Poverty.

Many Delta planters finally met their day of reckoning in the farm crisis of the 1980s and, although the Delta was the birthplace of the Citizens' Council and a citadel of white resistance to racial equality, the black-majority area finally elected a black congressman, Mike Espy, in 1986. The region's history had been one of tension and struggle—between the races, against the poorer hill counties, against the impenetrable swampy wilderness and the ravages of flood, pestilence, and disease, and, finally, against the intrusions of civil rights activists and federal civil rights policies.

Out of this tangle of tension and paradox came a remarkable outpouring of creativity, one that made the Delta's artistic climate arguably as rich as its agricultural one. Greenville alone produced writers William Alexander Percy, Walker Percy, Shelby Foote, Ellen Douglas, Hodding Carter II, Hodding Carter III, David Cohn, and Beverly Lowry. Classical composer Kenneth Haxton is from the Greenville area, as are sculptor Leon Koury and artist Valerie Jaudon. The Delta has produced a host of entertainers including Jim Henson, creator of the Muppets, country singers Charley Pride and Conway Twitty, and an especially large number of blues singers past and present, from the legendary Charley Patton to contemporary artists like B. B. King and James "Son" Thomas. Sometimes appalling, always fascinating, the Delta's historical and cultural experience often seemed that of an entire region in microcosm. It richly deserved the title, accorded it by writer Richard Ford, "the South's South."

See also BLACK LIFE: / Citizens' Council; FOLKLIFE: / Thomas, James; LITERATURE: / Foote, Shelby; Percy, Walker; MEDIA: / Carter, Hodding; MUSIC: / King, B. B.

James C. Cobb
University of Alabama

Robert L. Brandfon, *Cotton Kingdom of the New South: A History of the Yazoo Mississippi Delta from Reconstruction to the Twentieth Century* (1967); David L. Cohn, *Where I Was Born and Raised* (1967). ☆

FAULKNER'S GEOGRAPHY

Most of William Faulkner's works are set in Yoknapatawpha County. Yoknapatawpha is a fictional place inhabited by fictional persons, but Faulkner integrated it into a geographical setting that included prominent actual places. Yoknapatawpha County is in north central Mississippi, 70 miles south of Memphis, Tenn. Faulkner thought of

Yoknapatawpha as having the same geographical position as the real Lafayette County, Miss., and the geography of the fictional place is based heavily on the geography of that county. Like Lafayette, Yoknapatawpha County is drained in the north by the Tallahatchie River and in the south by the Yoknapatawpha, the fictional name of the Yocona River. Jefferson, the political seat of Yoknapatawpha County, has many geographical similarities to Oxford, the political seat of Lafayette County.

Despite similarities between Yoknapatawpha County and Lafayette County, many differences exist. Faulkner created Yoknapatawpha by combining the real, the modified, and the imaginary. The geography of Lafayette County and Oxford was changed in four principal ways—locations were shifted, place names were changed, components were omitted, and reality was blended with fabrication. Shifts in locations of objects, places, and events were sometimes intercounty and involved temporal as well as geographical changes. In addition to Lafayette County, Faulkner also drew from Marshall, Tippah, and Panola counties, Miss., in creating Yoknapatawpha.

In developing his model for Yoknapatawpha County, Faulkner intended it neither as Lafayette County thinly disguised nor, at the other extreme, as the entire South in microcosm. Rather he viewed it as a place that, though located in the South, was one in which he could describe the universal experience of humankind.

See also LITERATURE: / Faulkner, William; MYTHIC SOUTH: / Yoknapatawpha County

Charles S. Aiken
University of Tennessee

Charles S. Aiken, *Geographical Review* (January 1977, July 1979); Calvin S. Brown, *A Glossary of Faulkner's South* (1976). ☆

GEORGIA LAND LOTTERY
||||||||||||||||||||||||||||||||||||||||||||||||||||||||||||||||||

The land-lottery system used to distribute Georgia public lands to citizens of the state after 1803 was unique, and, although little known outside the state, it brought about a considerable change in the method of land occupation and settlement. Instead of pioneers moving into former Indian territories and claiming vacant land almost at random, orderly land acquisition was achieved after 1803. The new lands were systematically surveyed and mapped by the state prior to their occupation by settlers.

The Headright Land Act of 1783 proved to be a reasonable method of dispensing public lands to Georgia's citizens until 1789. From 1789 to 1802, however, the state became entangled in a series of land frauds concerning land within the present state limits as well as a vast territory extending west from the Chattahoochee River to the Mississippi River.

The radical new system of distribution adopted in response to this situation was a public land lottery controlled and conducted by state officials. Six lotteries were held between 1805 and 1836. Each area of the public land to be opened for settlement was created as a county unit and then divided by survey into large numbered land districts. Each district was then subdivided into numbered land lots. The size and area of both land districts and individual land lots in each lottery were determined by the specific legislative acts authorizing each of the six lotteries. Land-district and land-lot lines were generally aligned with the four principal compass points—north, south, east, and west—with the exception of the lotteries of 1805 and 1807 and a portion of the 1820 lottery. Fragments of land lots in the various lotteries were retained by the state and, after each lottery, sold at public auction.

After the lottery was authorized, qualified citizens of the state registered for it in their respective counties. The list of registrants was then sent to the capital, where each name was placed on an individual lottery ticket and put in a drum. Each land lot offered in the lottery was identified by county, land district, and land-lot number on another ticket (for example, "District 2, Lot 27, Baldwin County"), and each of these was placed in a second drum. Winners were required to pay a small grant fee. Upon payment the land won became theirs. Lots that were not claimed reverted to the state and were sold later. Once a person received land by lottery draw, there were no requirements for improvements or even residence on the land in order to maintain possession. Essentially, all of the territory west of the Oconee and Altamaha rivers was distributed by means of public lottery.

Gerald L. Holder
Sam Houston State University

James E. Callaway, *The Early Settlement of Georgia* (1948); Georgia Secretary of State, Surveyor General Department, *Land Lotteries* (1966); S. G. McLendon, *History of the Public Domain of Georgia* (1924). ☆

LITTLE DIXIE
||||||||||||||||||||||||||||||||||||||

The establishment of "dixies" beyond the boundaries of the Confederacy itself in the 19th century was a phenomenon rich with meaning. The idea of a "Little Dixie" located outside the geophysical South echoes important themes in cultural history. Although there are "dixies" in Utah, Wyoming, Oklahoma, southern Illinois and Indiana, and probably elsewhere, the best-known of these islands of southern culture is Missouri's "Little Dixie" folk region.

Little Dixie is a cultural region in northern Missouri (significantly not in the widely publicized Ozarks of the southern part of the state) composed of eight counties and a vague zone of transition in surrounding counties. The principal counties are Howard, Boone, Callaway, Audrain, Randolph, Monroe, Pike, and Ralls. The main towns are Fayette, Keytesville, Salisbury, Marshall, Columbia, Fulton, Mexico, Huntsville, Moberly, Paris, Monroe City, Bowling Green, New London, Hannibal, and Palmyra. The region was settled in the early 19th century by emigrants from the Tidewater and Piedmont areas of Virginia, Maryland, the Carolinas, Kentucky, and Tennessee, with Virginia and Kentucky the most important sources. The settlers were largely of British Protestant stock and transplanted their cultural traditions alongside their valuable crops of burley tobacco and hemp. These pioneers were well suited to the new environment, and many chose this area because it so closely resembled their home territories.

The region, which comprises forest, prairie, and rich bottomland, is bounded by major rivers—the Missouri on the south and the Mississippi on the east. The northern border of Little Dixie coincides with later settlement by northerners and easterners, while the western border is vague and lingers along the Missouri River toward Kansas City. The region lies culturally and physiographically between the Ozark Highlands and the corn belt.

Upland southern traditions of fiddle playing, social dance, basketmaking, the preservation of meat, religious practices, dialect and speech, attitudes toward social organization, and most eloquently, perhaps, architectural patterns and political behavior demonstrate the linkages between the people of Little Dixie and the home regions of the Piedmont, the Tidewater, and the Bluegrass. The "old southern mansions" that mark the rural landscape and the persistent devotion to "the Democratic party" are reminders of a way of life now nearly lost because of the Civil War (and particularly the memory of Reconstruction), settlement by "Yankees," and simply the passage of time. Material culture—architecture, diet, farmstead site arrangement, craft traditions, agricultural economic practices—can still, however, provide a tangible nexus for regional feeling. The region's most famous son, Samuel Langhorne Clemens (Mark Twain), born to a slaveholding family in Monroe County, first learned about life and human behavior at his Uncle John Quarles's farm in Missouri's Little Dixie.

Disenfranchised by Reconstruction "carpetbag" administrators and left with a meager remnant of the prewar way of life, white southerners after the Civil War began to create a psychological space for themselves, a region thought of as Little Dixie, in which old ways and old things retained meaning in the face of change and loss. For older white southerners, the postwar events that upset the economy and altered hierarchical social patterns, and the coming of northerners and Germans able to purchase the lands of the impoverished settlers, represented the close of an era that

would later be thought of as a golden age of prewar Missouri.

The idea of Little Dixie evolved in the 1870s and 1880s in response to the malaise and loss experienced by those who had originally created much of Missouri society. A feeling of continuity and order was achieved through evolution of a memory culture that respected and lauded past ways of life and work. The vision of Little Dixie's residents is largely based on a "southern" past (which some call "the old slave days") of log houses, tobacco fields, country hams, fox hunts, rail fences, and what they imagine to have been a more genteel lifestyle, and on the dominance of the Democratic party in political life.

Today media attention keeps the vision of Little Dixie alive in Missouri and in other areas. Such visions operate with the tacit approval of the local population who created a microregion and a safe harbor beyond the geographic South.

Howard W. Marshall
Missouri Cultural Heritage Center
University of Missouri at Columbia

Robert M. Crisler, *Journal of Geography* (November 1950), *Missouri Historical Review* (October 1947, July 1948); Howard W. Marshall, *Folk Architecture in Little Dixie: A Regional Culture in Missouri* (1981), *Journal of American Folklore* (October–December 1979), in *Readings in American Folklore*, ed. Jan Harold Brunvand (1979). ☆

MASON-DIXON LINE

"An artificial line . . . and yet more unalterable than if nature had made it for it limits the sovereignty of four states, each of whom is tenacious of its particular systems of law as of its soil. It is the boundary of empire."

Writing his history of the Mason-Dixon line in 1857, James Veech reflected the well-founded anxieties of the day: the fear that the horizontal fault between slave and free territory was about to become an open breach. Although the Mason-Dixon line was long associated with the division between free and slave states, slavery existed on both its sides when it was first drawn. To settle a long-standing boundary dispute arising from ambiguous colonial charters, the Calvert and Penn families chose English astronomers Charles Mason and Jeremiah Dixon to survey the territory. After four years of work (1763–67) they fixed the common boundaries of Maryland and Pennsylvania at 39° 43'17.6" north latitude, marking their line at every fifth mile with stones bearing the arms of the Penn family on one side and the Calvert crest on the other. Mason and Dixon were halted in their westward survey by the presence of hostile Indians, but their work was concluded in 1784 by a new team that included David Rittenhouse, Andrew Ellicott, and Benjamin Banneker.

In 1820 the Missouri Compromise temporarily readjusted the fragile tacit balance between slave and free territory and extended the Mason-Dixon line to include the 36th parallel. By that date, all states north of the line had abolished slavery, and the acceptance of the line as the symbolic division both politically and socially between North and South was firmly established.

The Mason-Dixon line has been a source of many idiomatic expressions and popular images. Slogans ("Hang your wash to dry on the Mason-Dixon line") originated with early antislavery agitation; variations on the theme (Smith and Wesson line) and novel applications (the logo for a cross-country trucking firm) are contemporary phenomena. A popular shorthand for a sometimes mythic, sometimes very real regional distinction, the term *Mason-Dixon line* continues to be used and its meaning is immediately comprehended.

Elizabeth M. Makowski
University of Mississippi

Journals of Charles Mason and Jeremiah Dixon (1969); John H. B. Latrobe, *History of Mason and Dixon's Line* (1855); James Veech, ed., *Mason and Dixon's Line: A History* (1857). ☆

MILLS AND MILLING

Southern gristmills were generally small, custom-grinding operations that were scattered profusely across the landscape. Their service area was small, and frequently they were built where water could power a waterwheel.

The southern mill (as distinct from that of the Mid-Atlantic, Midwest, or New England) was usually a frame structure of one or two stories. The earliest mills were occasionally log and closely resembled the Norse mill of central and northern Europe. Water was directed against the vanes of a horizontal wheel attached to a vertical shaft. The shaft passed through a stationary bedder stone and balanced a runner stone that turned at the same speed as the wheel. Found mostly in mountainous areas of the South, this horizontal mill quickly gave way to the vertical mill.

Southern mills were neither as sophisticated nor as structurally well built as those encountered in the North or in

Grist mill, on the way to Skyline Drive, Virginia, 1938

Europe. They also differed as a regional feature in that they persisted in the use of vertical waterwheels long after the turbine was commonly accepted in other parts of the eastern United States. Rather than changing from waterwheels to turbines as rapidly as possible for the sake of efficiency, the change and requisite regearing occurred when the old wooden or iron wheels required replacement. As a result, larger northern mills modernized more rapidly and outstripped southern grinding capacity.

In addition, southern gristmills focused almost exclusively upon the production of cornmeal. Wheat was a secondary crop, especially in the Deep South, and other cereals were even more rare. Wheat milling, or merchant milling, was restricted to urban areas, where there was a demand for sifted flour and where capitalization for the necessary additional equipment was more readily available. Thus, the smaller frame mill served primarily for private use by local farmers.

Milling was one of the earliest economic activities in the South. Although European, technological antecedents are undisputed, the southern miller and millwright were quite flexible in adapting mills to meet local demands. No evidence exists to support the generally held view that mills acted as magnets drawing settlers to the frontier, either within or without the South, nor did mill sites often serve as centers for town development. Merchant milling, changes in dietary preference, and the blacktop road and automobile all had an impact on the decline of milling in the South. This decline was evident in the 1930s and accelerated by the end of World War II to the point that southern gristmilling ceased to be a viable economic activity. *Waterground* (Appalshop Film, Frances Morton, director, 1977) is a film study of one of the last waterpowered gristmills.

D. Gregory Jeane
Auburn University

Charles Howell and Allan Keller, *The Mill of Philipsburg Manor, Upper Mills and a Brief History of Milling* (1977); Charles Bryon Kuhlman, *The Development of the Flour-Milling Industry in the United States* (1929); John Storck and Walter Dorwin Teague, *Flour for Man's Bread* (1952). ☆

NORTHERN CITIES, WHITES IN

The most visible southern culture found in northern cities is black culture, but millions of white southerners have also migrated, taking their southern culture with them. Like most migrants they have been a varied lot, including professional people, artists, and intellectuals. The largest segment has been poor people seeking work. They have concentrated in low-rent areas accessible to factories or transportation lines, developing neighborhood institutions and informal networks.

In these places both "southern culture" and stereotypes of southerners as "hillbillies," "rednecks," or "crackers" have been most evident. Clannishness, a proclivity to violence, love of hillbilly music, and low standards of sexual morality, household cleanliness, and personal hygiene have been part of the stereotype. White southerners have also been accused of diffusing attitudes of white supremacy to other regions.

Although appearing to be ethnically distinct because of differences in language, music, and food preferences, such culture is ethnic only by coincidence. The overlay of southern ethnic features on working-class culture is seen most clearly in the "hillbilly taverns" found in sections of some northern cities. The language is English, but it is spoken with a southern accent. The music is country or western, the ambience small-town.

The distinctive accent and regional food preferences constitute enduring traits of southern culture. The most pervasive and persistent feature of regional culture retained by these southerners living outside the South is religion, evangelical Protestant Christianity. Storefront churches of southern Pentecostal sects are most noticeable, but Baptist, Methodist, and Presbyterian churches have found their customs influenced by the presence of southerners.

Lewis M. Killian
University of Massachusetts
at Amherst

Lewis M. Killian, *Social Forces* (October 1953), *White Southerners* (1970); William W. Philliber, *Appalachian Migrants in Urban America: Cultural Conflict or Ethnic Group Formation?* (1981). ☆

PIEDMONT

The Piedmont region extends from the Hudson River to central Alabama, bordering on the Blue Ridge and Appalachian mountains, and ranges from 10 to 125 miles in width. While it is part of the Appalachian highlands, the Piedmont landscape is not mountainous but rolling. Its relatively infertile soil discouraged settlers until the late 18th and early 19th centuries. The region has been known predominantly as an agricultural region, although it developed industries such as textiles and furniture making in the 19th century. The development of the southern Piedmont (extending to Birmingham, Ala.) has been shaped by the iron and coal industries.

The term *Piedmont* refers to the Piedmont "crescent," of North and South Carolina, continuing into parts of Georgia and Alabama. The Carolina Piedmont has been characterized in the mid- to late-20th century by urban growth. Its cities are headquarters for various large business enterprises, including R. J. Reynolds tobacco company in Winston-Salem, N.C., and Burlington Industries in Greensboro, N.C.

The textile industry was the first industry to develop in the Piedmont. Numerous small streams attracted power spinning (built on waterwheels) as early as 1790 in several South Carolina communities. The first mill was built in North Carolina in 1813, and, after the Civil War and Reconstruction, abundant cheap labor gave the area's textile industry an enormous boost. The low humidity of the region was originally thought to be an obstacle to the operation of the mills, but artificial humidity was developed to create the necessary atmosphere.

Tobacco is one of the most important crops in the northern Piedmont area. The attendant tobacco industry, the manufacture of cigarettes and chewing and smoking tobacco, is concentrated in a few centers in Virginia, Kentucky, and Tennessee, but is centered in North Carolina. James B. Duke's use of the first cigarette-rolling machine in the 1880s catapulted the region into its prominent (and, at one point, dominant) role in the industry.

The Piedmont region has been the source of and the setting for some important southern literature. *The Mind of the South* (1941) was written by W. J. Cash from Gaffney, S.C., whose father was an employee of a textile mill. His interpretation of the nature of southerners rests largely on his treatment of his native Carolina Piedmont region. Cash focused much of his study on the rise of the upland cotton planter in the early 19th century and the later growth of the textile mill and mill village. The fiction of Reynolds Price, from Macon, N.C., is set in the rural Piedmont South. His works, such as *A Long and Happy Life*, his first novel, and *The Names and Faces of Heroes*, a collection of stories, use regional syntax and colorful description to evoke an understanding of the setting. Other writers who were influenced by their roots and study in the Piedmont region are Thomas Wolfe, born in Asheville, N.C., and Erskine Caldwell, whose *Tobacco Road* (1932) is set in Wrens County, Ga.

Karen M. McDearman
University of Mississippi

Neal R. Peirce and Jerry Hagstrom, *The Book of America: Inside 50 States Today* (1983); Louis D. Rubin, Jr., *William Elliott Shoots a Bear: Essays on the Southern Lit-* *erary Imagination* (1975); Anthony M. Tang, *Economic Development in the Southern Piedmont, 1860–1950: Its Impact on Agriculture* (1958); William D. Thornbury, *Regional Geomorphology of the United States* (1965); Rupert B. Vance, *Human Geography of the South: A Study in Regional Resources and Human Adequacy* (1932). ☆

PINEY WOODS

The piney woods, or pine belt, of the Southeast is a vast region of forestland stretching through nine southern states from the Carolinas through Georgia and into Texas. The land of the "pine barrens" is not particularly well suited for agriculture, but the heavy rainfall and long, warm, sunny summers provide ideal conditions for the rapid growth of pines. The most important species of pine found in the region are the shortleaf, longleaf, loblolly, and slash pine. The heaviest and strongest of these, the southern longleaf yellow pine, is the most popular among timber growers.

The piney woods has been the victim of human settlement and exploitation. Pioneers used burning techniques they learned from the Indians to clear the land for cultivation and building. Industries later developed markets for pine products and methods for extracting resins and producing turpentine. Beginning in the 20th century, pine was used for a variety of timber products including pulpwood for paper. The free grazing of livestock also took its toll on the piney woods region.

During the antebellum period the national government first attempted to preserve and protect forests. At the turn of the century the government began the development of policies that recognized that forests are not only commodities to be exploited but are renewable resources. During the New Deal era, state and national conservation efforts were given a boost by the Civilian Conservation Corps, which planted acres of worn-out farmland with trees.

Geographers and historians have studied the way people have adapted to the southern forests. The region has been characterized by poverty and relatively sparse population because of the dense woods. Frank L. Owsley showed in the early 1950s that classification of antebellum pine-belt inhabitants as agricultural poor whites was misleading. Actually, the primary occupation of the people of the piney woods was grazing cattle and hogs. They also hunted and trapped for food—true to their character as frontiersmen, according to Owsley.

Developments in the south Mississippi area drained by the Pearl River are indicative of 20th-century trends in the piney woods region. The Pearl River, positioned halfway between the Mississippi River and the Alabama and Tombigbee river systems, runs through the heart of the pine belt. The Pearl River bottomlands were uncharacteristically fertile for the pine lands, and some cotton plantations were developed there. Migrants eventually set up communities along the river and cleared the land, using the river to transport pine and cypress logs to the sawmills downriver. Railroads eventually changed the landscape further, and the timber industry flourished. By the 1930s, however, the pine supply had been devastated and the cutover soil depleted of nutrients, forcing the region to turn to alternate sources of income. Initially the lower Pearl River residents planted the Chinese tung tree for its nuts, from which oils were extracted for sale to varnish and paint companies. Hurricane

Camille in 1969 destroyed the troubled tung industry. At the same time, a National Aeronautics and Space Administration (NASA) rocket test facility in the area also gave economic hope to the piney-woods people, but the NASA program fell short of expectations and once again the region was left in poverty.

Karen M. McDearman
University of Mississippi

John Hawkins Napier III, *Lower Pearl River's Piney Woods* (1986); Howard W. Odum, *Southern Regions of the United States* (1936); Frank L. Owsley, *Plain Folk of the Old South* (1949); Rupert B. Vance, *Human Geography of the South: A Study in Regional Resources and Human Adequacy* (1932). ☆

PRIMOGENITURE
|||||||||||||||||||||||||||||||||||||||||||||||||||

Legally defined, *primogeniture* is the right of the eldest son to inherit to the exclusion of younger sons the estate of his family because of his seniority of birth. In Europe the practice was long included in so-called entail laws, which limit the inheritance of property. These ancient European practices had virtually no impact on the landholding patterns that emerged in the South. Although southern colonial history dates back to Jamestown, the medieval concept of one great landed aristocracy in the southern colonies passing down vast domains to their eldest sons is false. In fact, ambitious sons interested in land, agriculture, and profit moved south into the Carolinas and Georgia and later westward as far as coastal Texas. These locations offered an abundance of land superior in quality to much of that found in Tidewater Virginia.

Primogeniture had a formidable and

unrelenting foe in the person of Thomas Jefferson of Virginia. For him these practices represented an evil that must not be allowed to exist in the American colonies. Through the efforts of Jefferson and many other southern patriots, primogeniture was abolished and legally prohibited throughout the South by 1791.

Therefore, if primogeniture was ever important in the South, it was short-lived and was implemented in a rather restricted geographical region. Although the concept appeared in regional folklore and in earlier historical accounts, in fact the law did not shape the landholding systems of the early South.

Gerald L. Holder
Sam Houston State University

John R. Alden, *The South in the Revolution, 1763–1789* (1957); Julian P. Boyd, *William and Mary Quarterly* (October 1955); Walter Clark, ed., *The State Records of North Carolina (1895–1905)*; Thomas Jefferson, *Notes on the State of Virginia*, ed. William Peden (1955); C. Ray Keim, "Primogeniture and Entail" (Ph.D. dissertation, University of Chicago, 1926), *William and Mary Quarterly* (October 1968); Richard B. Morris, *Columbia Law Review* (1927). ☆

SUGAR PLANTATIONS

Sugar plantations are traditionally large agricultural enterprises with landholdings ranging from 200 to 8,000 acres. Primary functions of a sugar plantation are planting, cultivation, and harvesting of sugarcane and processing of cane juice into brown sugar and molasses.

Sugar plantations have been a distinctive part of the southern landscape since the mid-18th century. They orig-inated in New Orleans, La., in 1742. By 1806, 75 enterprises were dispersed along the Mississippi River to Baton Rouge. By 1844 some 464 French- and Anglo-American-owned sugar plantations of 200 acres or more each had made their appearance along the Mississippi River and westward into south central Louisiana along the alluvial natural levees of Bayou Lafourche, Bayou Teche, and the bayous of Terebonne Parish.

Although sugar mills numbered 1,240 in 1845, their zenith was reached in 1849 with 1,536 sugar mills on the Louisiana landscape. The Civil War, cane diseases, and the incorporation and consolidation of enterprises brought the number of mills to 50 on 190 plantations by 1970. Recently, depressed sugar prices, rising fuel and machinery costs, environmental regulations, and the urbanization and industrialization of cane lands have reduced the Louisiana sugar industry to 21 mills.

Elsewhere in the South, small numbers of antebellum sugar plantations once occupied parts of coastal South Carolina, Georgia, Florida, and southeastern Texas. Louisiana, however, dominated the sugar industry with 95 percent of the total antebellum production and continued to hold dominion over the southern sugar industry until 1973. Today a modern sugar industry in Florida leads the South with 54 percent of the cane acreage and 65 percent of production from seven high-capacity mills. By comparison, Louisiana now has 39 percent of the acreage and 29 percent of the production from 21 mills. In the lower Rio Grande Valley of Texas, a single new mill accounts for the remaining 6 percent of the southern sugar crop.

Eighteenth- and 19th-century source

areas for sugar plantation traits in Louisiana were principally the French Caribbean and Anglo-American areas of the Upland and Tidewater South. The French Caribbean contributed (1) the initial sugarcane plants and cultivation techniques of Jesuits in 1742 from Santo Domingo (Haiti); (2) an early but specialized sugar technology brought by skilled Caribbean sugar makers; (3) a cultural mix of French Caribbean settlers, planters, and slaves; (4) architectural traits, most notably the hip roof and *galeries* (wide porches) for plantation mansions, half-timbered construction (a trait also directly from France), and quite possibly the shotgun house type initially used for slave quarters. Furthermore, from France, the arpent survey system of linear measure (192 feet per arpent) produced long, narrow landholdings 40 arpents deep, which led to linear settlement patterns among French plantations.

The Anglo-American source areas of the Upland South and the Atlantic Tidewater region supplied the sugar plantation system with: (1) landscape traits of block-shaped or gridded settlement patterns; (2) Tidewater architectural traits in plantation mansions with front-facing gables, porticos, pediments, and Georgian symmetry in floor plans; (3) architectural traits from the Upland South's houses of the pen tradition with paired rooms, central hallways, and exterior chimneys; and (4) a significant cultural mix of culture-bearing planters and settlers from the English-speaking South.

See also AGRICULTURE: / Sugar Industry; FOLKLIFE: / Shotgun House

John B. Rehder
University of Tennessee

Bob Angers, *Acadian Profile* (April 1982); John B. Rehder, "Sugar Plantations in Southern Louisiana: A Cultural Geography" (Ph.D. dissertation, Louisiana State University, 1971); J. Carlyle Sitterson, *Sugar Country* (1953); U.S. Department of Agriculture, *Sugar and Sweetener Report*, vol. 5 (February 1980). ☆

TIDEWATER
||||||||||||||||||||||||||||||||

The Tidewater coastal region extends from Delaware to northeastern Florida and from northwestern Florida to the Mississippi Delta. It is a low, flat, sandy or swampy area that enjoys abundant rainfall and a long, warm growing season. The Tidewater is known particularly for its agriculture, forest industries, commercial fishing and oystering, and military installations. It is also attractive to millions of tourists. The Outer Banks, a chain of islands off the North Carolina coast, is the site of a rapidly developing tourist industry that features the Wright Brothers National Memorial and many public recreational areas.

The term *Tidewater* is often used to refer only to the coastal area of Virginia, stretching some 100 miles inland from the sea and southward to the North Carolina border. Tidewater Virginia has been called "a blend of romance and fact." It is in the Virginia area that historic preservation efforts have successfully restored and promoted the region's history as tourist attractions. Beachfront tourist sites and recreational facilities have been developed, and each year thousands of people visit the Tidewater's historic areas, including Jamestown, Williamsburg, and the Yorktown battlefield. The popular Assateague Island nature preserve and the seashore town at Chincoteague testify to the natural beauty of the region. The southern Tidewater in Virginia contains the important seaport of Hampton Roads and the center of the region's sea industry. The densely populated area is the headquarters for the U.S. Navy's Atlantic fleet, as well as one of the biggest shipyards in the world. Norfolk, Va., the largest city in this branch of the Tidewater, was renewed during the mid-20th century and today boasts new downtown and waterfront developments, as well as a convention center and the Eastern Virginia Medical School.

Some of the swampy areas of the Tidewater have recently been drained in an effort to reclaim the rich soil for agriculture. New crops, such as soybeans, have proved successful on some of this reclaimed land. Two of the area's famed swamps are protected as wildlife refuges and state park areas. Okefenokee Swamp, which lies mostly in Georgia, is the third largest swamp in the South. Legendary Dismal Swamp in Virginia is the home of a variety of unique wildlife and species of plants, and since the 1960s it has been the focus of concerted preservation efforts.

Karen M. McDearman
University of Mississippi

Neal R. Peirce and Jerry Hagstrom, *The Book of America: Inside 50 States Today* (1983); Paul Wilstach, *Tidewater Virginia* (1929). ☆

HISTORY
AND MANNERS

CHARLES REAGAN WILSON

University of Mississippi

CONSULTANT

☆ ☆ ☆ ☆ ☆ ☆ ☆ ☆ ☆ ☆

Overleaf: Ruins of Windsor, antebellum mansion, in Mississippi

HISTORY

|||||||||||||||||||||||||||||||||||||||||

Anthropologist Clifford Geertz argues that culture is a "historically transmitted" pattern of meaning, suggesting the central importance of historical experience and the collective memory of it in providing a sense of identity and purpose to a culture. Two points are central in exploring the relationship between southern history and culture. The first is the connection between history and the sense of identity among southerners as a distinct people. The southern people have had characteristic assumptions, values, and attitudes apart from other Americans. When did that identity arise and how was it transmitted to future generations? How did historical events and forces create a sense of common purpose among people in the South and how was that purpose passed on from generation to generation, adapting to new circumstances? How did a sense of history in itself contribute to the identity? The second broad point to explore is the way of life at the heart of southern culture, the complex pattern of institutions, rituals, myths, material objects, and other aspects of a functioning culture. This pattern reveals how the region differed from other areas of the United States in behavior as well as attitude. It also shows the degree to which cultural integration occurred over time, despite formal attempts to maintain racial separation between whites, blacks, and Native Americans.

Origins. The English first attempted a colony in North America in 1587 when settlers arrived in Roanoke Island off the coast of present-day North Carolina, but Jamestown in Virginia was the first successful English colony, established in 1607. Other southern colonies would follow, but they had separate identities, leading historian Wesley Frank Craven to note that historians of the colonial South have "to write about the South when there was no South." When southern self-consciousness emerged, it grew out of concrete differences in institutions and attitudes that had appeared earlier.

The early South differed from the northern colonies in physical environment and motives for settlement. The first settlers in Virginia were charmed by the sights and smells of the new land. Observers focused on the climate as a key factor in the region. The climate favored a long growing season, which promoted an agricultural economy based on tobacco, rice, and indigo, and later cotton and sugar. The climate and environment affected architecture, clothing, and seemingly even the very pace of life and speech. Geography, however, unified neither the early nor later South. The region is divided by mountain ranges and rivers, and its plains and valleys run north and south, connecting with land in other regions. Partly because of geography different societies developed in the colonial South: an aristocratic society along the Chesapeake Bay; a second elite-dominated society in the Carolina Low Country; a frontier land to the west of the Tidewater; and perhaps another, loosely formed society in central North Carolina.

The motives of early Virginia settlers and of later southern colonists differed significantly from those of the North. Although both groups were predominantly middle-class English, the southern colonists came primarily for economic reasons, seeking opportunities not available in England. If the Puritans established New England to be a City on a Hill, the early southerners portrayed their area as a new Garden of Eden. The first signs of an emerging southern self-consciousness appeared couched in this mythic outlook. But ease of environment seemed to promote a decline in the moral character of the people. Residents south of Chesapeake Bay compared themselves with northern settlers, sometimes to their own disadvantage. William Byrd II, for example, saw New Englanders as "Frugal and Industrious," whereas those in the southern colonies had "very loose and Profligate Morals." Blessed with a beneficent land, southerners seemed to give in to the environment, and failed to live up to another part of their cultural legacy—the demands of a Christianity heavily tinged with Calvinism.

The colonial South had already begun to develop in distinctive ways. New England made a partial commitment to public education as early as the 1640s, but the South did so only much later. Eight colleges existed in the North by 1776, compared to only one (the College of William and Mary) in the South. The colonial South lacked not only schools and colleges, but libraries, books, and periodicals as well. Religion was also institutionally weak, lacking the intensity, idealism, and organization of that in the North.

At the top of the social structure was a small class of large planters who dominated society through control of land, wealth, and political power. Prominent southern colonial planter families included the Byrds, Randolphs, Carters, Burwells, Pages, Beverleys, Lees, Masons, Fitzhughs, and Wormsleys in Virginia, and the Rutledges, Pringles, and Draytons in South Carolina. Their names have reappeared throughout the ages of southern history as symbols of social prestige, southern style. The life of the English country gentry was their model, and their mansions are symbolic of southern gentility. The planters dominated the imagination of the region, symbolizing social success.

Members of the middle class were sometimes related by blood or marriage to the wealthiest planters. They enjoyed a degree of social mobility themselves and aspired to be seen as gentry. Beneath the middle class were the poorer whites. This group included landless farmers, farm workers, unskilled laborers, indentured servants (who agreed to work a period of time for a colonial employer in exchange for passage to America), and craftsmen who were not self-supporting. A separate, peculiar group known already in the 1700s as the "poor whites" also existed. They appear in colonial writings as a defeated people, subject to disease, beset by illiteracy, given to laziness (in middle-class eyes), and living in physical isolation on the worst lands.

Afro-southerners were at the bottom of the social structure. A system of white racial dominance developed as soon as Europeans, Indians, and blacks encountered each other in the early days of Virginia. A Dutch ship brought 20 Africans to Jamestown in 1619, the same year that Virginia established the House of Burgesses, embodying the

Artist unknown, **The Plantation** *(c. 1825)*

hope of political liberty. The slave population expanded throughout the late 1600s and early 1700s, creating economic prosperity but fueling whites' fear of blacks. Southern whites saw slavery as a method of racial control as well as an economic system. Although powerless, blacks became one of the central factors in early southern society, both passively and actively.

Scholars have only recently begun a serious study of the cultural integration that began in the South in the colonial era. The history of the South begins, in fact, with the role of the American Indians as pioneers of cultural patterns in the southern part of North America, although until recently histories of the American South hardly mentioned the Indians and studies of Indian history ignored the relationship between early Indian history and later southern developments. Anthropologists such as Charles Hudson, historians such as J. Leitch Wright, and archaeologists have recently shown, though, that early In-

dian cultures established many of the patterns involving use of natural resources and location of settlements and transportation routes that Europeans later exploited. Indians introduced Europeans and Africans to New World ways of living, and many white and black southerners have Indian ancestry. The Indians named rivers and states. They influenced the agricultural and dietary habits of later southerners, and folk medicine used by southerners consists of Indian herbal knowledge mixed with European and African elements. Many of the folk tales in southern oral tradition are influenced by Native American lore.

English colonists adapted their institutions and customs to the American environment and combined them with native ways. British social hierarchy, European musical and literary forms, Christian institutional forms and worldview, European agricultural methods— all of these became a part of early southern culture. Upper-class, elite culture from the colonial period to contemporary times has been based on values and behavior of the English gentry. In exploring the cultural contributions of previously overlooked groups in the South, recent scholars have shown little interest in English cultural contributions, but these contributions were surely crucial. Later generations of influential southerners often acted as though English culture was the South's culture.

By the beginning of the 18th century African slaves mediated between Indian and European cultures. West Africans and Indians, who were more familiar with the South's kind of environment than the English, shared a similar body of customs and knowledge. As Indians declined in power and numbers, blacks helped preserve traditional Indian lore and passed it on to Europeans. Africans also brought useful knowledge with them from their homelands. They were familiar with techniques of herding livestock and cultivating rice and indigo, which became key early crops in the early Carolina Low Country. Some crops may even have been introduced from Africa and plants such as okra surely were. Europeans realized the economic advantages of slaves with such knowledge and made use of them. Despite the rigid legal boundaries of an emerging caste system, cultural integration was beginning through the transfer of knowledge, customs, and ways of separate peoples.

While cultural integration of a sort was occurring among white Europeans, African blacks, and Native Americans, a distinctive Afro-southern culture was also appearing. Before 1700, black cultural life was restricted by the relatively small numbers of slaves in North America and by their wide geographical distribution. The 18th century saw the

forging of a rigid racial caste system and the creation of a separate black culture by slaves. South Carolina was the center of this emerging black culture because it contained a critical mass of Africans concentrated in a relatively narrow, coastal, rice-growing area.

About 60 percent of all slaves brought to what would be the United States came between 1720 and 1780, and these years represent the cultural watershed for black southerners. Africans from different areas and tribal backgrounds learned in the New World to communicate through pidgin languages and found a common identity in the South. The common factor brought from Africa was an intellectual outlook, a worldview, with definite attitudes about the deity, time, social relations, and rituals of life. Slaves preserved African notions about kinship, the individual's place in the cosmos, musical forms, and concrete skills such as metalworking and wood carving, herding, boat making and navigation, and rice cultivation. Where slaves were concentrated in significant numbers, blacks created distinctive southern cultural traditions involving everything from music and dance to customs of child raising, crafting, and even speaking. The planter's mansion was recognized from the colonial era on as a symbol for one aspect of southern culture; the slave quarters deserve recognition as the hearthstone for another central aspect of that culture.

The frontier experience was also crucial to the formation of a southern character. In the late 1600s and early 1700s settlers flocked west, and sectional tensions appeared between Tidewater aristocrats and backcountry farmers. These were class conflicts, reflecting the social divisions between frontier and Tidewater. The upcountry Piedmont frontier was the scene of Bacon's Rebellion in Virginia in 1676 and the Regulator movement in western North Carolina in 1766–71 on the eve of revolution.

Some disputes on the frontier were also ethnic conflicts. Land-hungry Scotch-Irish and German settlers migrated from western Pennsylvania into the Piedmont and later crossed the Appalachian Mountains. The Scotch-Irish represented the other large ethnic tradition introduced into southern life in the colonial era, one that became closely associated with the frontier. If the Tidewater aristocracy was English in style and outlook, the frontier was predominantly Scotch-Irish. Like the Africans, this group brought distinctive institutions and customs, which were Celtic in origin, reflecting long-held attitudes about kinship, work, religion, music, and herding and farming skills. By the end of the colonial era, the Scotch-Irish had established communities in what would become Tennessee and Kentucky. This was the "dark and bloody ground" of legend, with brutal warfare between white settlers and Indians and a struggle for survival in the lush wilderness of the Great Meadow. Daniel Boone was the romantic symbol of this phase of southern life.

The frontier experience promoted both individualism and communal neighborliness, impatience with formal institutions, and allegiance to family; it encouraged hard work; it promoted violence, and yet evangelical religion flourished there. Most southerners lived in frontier conditions up to the time of the Civil War. Recent migrants to the areas they lived in, they engaged in subsistence or small-scale commodity farming, used rivers and streams for transportation, and vividly remembered the Indian wars that preceded settlement. They lived in simple log cabins, which became another major symbol of southern culture. Many of the traits now called "southern" were nurtured in these isolated outposts. The frontier experience was common in America, but perhaps nowhere else in the nation did frontier attitudes and ways persist over so many generations through the preservation of a rural folk culture permeated by the effects of the frontier.

Historians do not agree as to when a self-conscious southern identity appeared. The American revolutionary era (1775–89) was, though, one landmark in its definition. John Alden referred to it as the time of the "First South," which was at that time geographically defined toward the west by the Mississippi River with major settlements along the Atlantic Coast. The phrase "southern states" was frequently used in those years. At the beginning of the period, though, the term *southern* was used to describe all the colonies except those in New England, from New York to Georgia. When Charles Mason and Jeremiah Dixon drew a surveyor's line between Pennsylvania and Maryland in the 1760s to settle a boundary disagreement, there was no understanding that a "North" and a "South" were being divided. But *southern* soon acquired a more restrictive meaning, as *middle states* was increasingly used to describe New York, New Jersey, Pennsylvania, and Delaware. There was the abiding problem of definition, with some observers including Maryland as southern and others excluding it. By the end of the Revolution the common view was that the northern boundary of the South was the Ohio River and the Mason-Dixon line. The southern population in the first census of 1790 showed approximately 1.9 million people (over a third of whom were black) below that line and 2 million above it.

The Revolutionary War gave the colonists a common enemy and served to draw northern and southern colonists together. Many unifying forces existed: a common language, a predominantly British and Western European background among colonists (except for the politically powerless slaves), a clear cultural and political heritage, and transportation, communication, and trade ties among the colonies. The term *American* was increasingly used both in the colonies and outside of them to describe the residents of the 13 colonies.

Nationalism surely triumphed in the revolutionary era. White southerners played a crucial role in events from the First Continental Congress in 1774 to George Washington's Administration as president in the 1790s. Yet nationalism was a necessary precondition for the appearance of sectionalist concerns. The Revolution, for example, created heroes who were national but also local and regional. Disagreements between the North and South appeared as early as the conflict over the embargo sponsored by the First Continental Congress, and as John Alden has written, "that body during the years 1781–1787 was often rived by strife between South and North. Southern fears of Northern domination appeared in the Philadelphia Convention of 1787, and were frequently and forcefully asserted in the contests over ratification of the Constitution which took place below the Mason-Dixon line."

Economic conflicts emerged over regional interests, especially those related to trade and to the protection of slavery. The revolutionary ideology expressed in words such as *liberty* and *equality*, in documents such as the Declaration of Independence, and in emerging antislavery sentiment made southerners aware of their dilemma as slaveowners in a democratic republic and thereby helped to promote regional self-consciousness. Events that dramatized the South's racial situation included the debate over slavery during the Philadelphia Convention in 1787, the slave uprising in Santo Domingo in the early 1790s, and Gabriel Prosser's slave conspiracy near Richmond in 1800. These events connected southern identity to peculiar racial concerns and promoted racial fears. They helped to crystallize the South's commitment to slavery as a system of race control. By 1800 southerners felt threatened by outsiders, generating the siege mentality that would later characterize the evolving southern identity.

Thomas Jefferson, with his party and supporters, was the central political and intellectual force in the South during the years from the Revolution to the 1820s, and he is crucial to understanding southern developments. The South in this era, according to Clement Eaton and others, appeared to be a liberal, humane society. Southern leaders such as Jefferson and Madison reflected the intellectual influence of the Enlightenment, expressing belief in the natural rights of human beings and confidence in human reason. Freedom of thought and expression was respected, and the rhetoric of liberty and equality was articulated not only by Jefferson but by many other southerners.

Racial fears did not disappear, though, nor did the commitment to the maintenance of white supremacy. Slavery was not dying out, contrary to the hopes of some earlier southern leaders. Most southerners saw it as a profitable system when well managed; the planter's lifestyle depended upon it; social success—the southern version of the American dream—was defined within its parameters; and the fear of black equality without slavery remained. Racism was the dark underside of the luminous Jeffersonian dream of a chosen agrarian people.

The Jeffersonian era experienced an economic transformation that contributed to southern identity. The invention of the cotton gin in 1793, the emergence of sugar growing in Louisiana in the mid-1790s, and the rising prices for frontier lands in the early 1800s brought an increased commitment to an agriculture of staple crops. Outlandish profits could be made by a few people, further strengthening the power of the elite planters. Cotton became the prime symbol of the South's expansive development into the Old Southwest in this era. Like Faulkner's Thomas Sutpen in *Absalom, Absalom!*, the pioneer planters of the Deep South carved slave plantations out of frontier forests. The mentality of the planter was thus transferred to the frontier; in the Southwest a rough-hewn character such as Andrew Jackson could become a self-made man and take on the trappings of an elite planter. The raw materialism of the frontier challenged the paternalism of the Tidewater planters as a cultural ideal.

Old South to New South. The Civil War has generally been seen as the crucial watershed in southern history. For the cultural historian, though, the period from 1830 to 1910 is a single era. After 1830 the self-conscious identification with "the South" notably increased, and a distinctive pattern of institutions, values, myths, and rituals took shape, reflecting a southern worldview that developed but never fully matured before the Civil War. The war and Reconstruction stand as the crystallizing events that promoted the postbellum development of a peculiar regional culture.

The years 1830 to 1832 were particularly important in the growth of a southern regional consciousness. Sectionalism dramatically appeared in politics during the preceding decade with the Missouri Compromise of 1819–20. After a bitter debate, Congress admitted Missouri as a slave state and Maine as a free state, and drew a 36° 30′ line of latitude, prohibiting slavery above the line. The Missouri Controversy awakened southern fears over the region's position as a minority section in the Union and pointed the way to an emerging regional consciousness that took form after 1830.

A minority psychology developed as the northern population outgrew that of the South. North-South conflict developed over control of the national government and the direction of national policy. A southern states' rights philosophy and the fears underlying it were seen in the nullification crisis of the late 1820s and early 1830s. South Carolina challenged the national government, specifically over the issue of the national government's power to pass a tariff, but more generally over the rights of the majority to legislate over a minority—defined as a regional population. John C. Calhoun emerged as the premier figure of antebellum southern politics, a defender of southern rights, one of the nation's greatest political philosophers, and a symbol of the southern consciousness.

The driving force propelling southern identity was racial fear. Rumors of slave unrest periodically appeared, reinforcing white uneasiness. The Nat Turner rebellion in 1831, a slave uprising led by a visionary slave preacher, killed 60 whites in Southampton County, Va., and became a symbol thereafter for the potential of slave rebellion. It solidified white fears and led to new restrictions on the activities of slaves and free blacks. William Lloyd Garrison, one of the chief Devil figures to southern whites, also stirred racial fears in 1832 when he began publishing the *Liberator*, a Boston antislavery newspaper that called for immediate, uncompensated emancipation of the slaves. He led a strident new antislavery movement that stressed the immorality of slavery. The southern reaction was an equally strident intellectual defense of the "peculiar institution"—a proslavery argument that justified the institution as a positive good, using religious, scientific, and historical arguments.

By the 1840s southern attitudes toward history were beginning to change with the growing sense of regional self-consciousness. More and more southerners after 1830 began questioning the national republican tradition as the proper framework for telling the regional story. The conflict with the North caused southern whites to stress their belief in a common historical experience and to play down differences within the South. The Virginia Historical Society appeared in 1831, the first such organization in the South, and other historical societies proliferated in the region during the next two decades of growing North-South tensions. By the 1850s southern histories had shifted from focusing on the national contributions of southern states to documenting the differences in the historical experiences of the South and the North. Southerners believed, moreover, that only they could be trusted to write their history. Dates

of historic events in the South were ritually honored with celebration that praised the South's noble history. National revolutionary heroes such as Patrick Henry and Francis Marion were seen after 1830 as state or regional heroes. The refocusing of American history into southern history was a factor in forging a self-conscious regional identity.

The 1830s also witnessed the emergence of a new mythic center for the southern identity: the Cavalier image, which embodied the belief that southerners were descendants of aristocratic Royalist exiles from Cromwell's England in the 1600s. Northern colonists, according to the legend, were Puritans by origin. Many Americans came to believe that these two "types" generated northerners and southerners with differing temperaments, psychologies, and concerns.

John Pendleton Kennedy's *Swallow Barn* appeared in 1832 and became a prototype for the romantic plantation legend. Kennedy and other writers portrayed the southern plantation as an orderly, feudal world of harmonious, static, hierarchical relationships between master and slave. The southern planter was a noble, honorable figure, and the southern lady, a vital part of the myth, was chaste, saintly, sacrificial, and spiritual. Slaves were childlike and loyal. The contrast between the Cavalier planter and the grasping Yankee was popular among conservative northerners and had remarkable power among southern whites.

Northerners and southerners still shared much in this era, but belief in the differences between northerners and southerners had some basis in reality. The slave-based plantation system was uniquely southern, and its crops were distinctive to the region. The nature of the southern population was different from that elsewhere, with English, African, and Scotch-Irish elements remaining dominant at a time when the northern population was being transformed through immigration. Southerners remained rural, while industry, immigration, urbanization, and reform were changing the North.

The southern way of life reflected not only the region's central theme of racial obsession, but positive features as well. There was a strong attachment to local communities and to the family, which offered both blacks and whites a refuge, a measure of security and warmth. Both races shared an intense religious faith that promised ultimate salvation after time served in this vale of tears. For whites the rural, daily monotony was broken by rituals such as visiting neighbors and relatives, attending political gatherings and camp meetings, observing the activities of county court days, participating in community militia days, and wagering on sports such as horse racing and cockfighting. These events provided entertainment and pageantry, but they also displayed the symbols of power in this society and reinforced the hierarchical social structure and the paternalistic bonds between wealthy and plain folk.

This southern social structure was the background against which a distinctive culture appeared. Planter hegemony over society was based partly on control of the South's wealth. Wealthy planters owned the best farming land, and the productivity of these lands was greater than that of smaller farms. The planter elite included two groups: those traditional southern families whose wealth extended back several generations or more, taking on the refinements and

prestige of "old money," and a larger group of self-made men, humble in origins, who had seized opportunities and luck to amass fortunes from cotton. Eugene D. Genovese has portrayed the planter elite as paternalist and precapitalist, but other historians point out their essentially bourgeois outlook. Their cultural significance was in their control of cultural and social values in the South. The "big house" was the tangible symbol of their power over the southern imagination.

The yeoman farmer, the independent landowner, was the Jeffersonian ideal and W. J. Cash's "man at the center." Historians overlooked the importance of the "plain folk" until Frank L. Owsley in the 1930s showed they were the largest class in the Old South. White racism brought a shared racial solidarity between the wealthy planters and the yeoman farmers. The commitment of the South was to both slavery and democracy. The term *herrenvolk democracy* describes the southern system of democracy for the master class and repression for a subordinate group. The region's political rhetoric said that all white men were created equal with inalienable rights, which depended, though, on black subjugation. Seeing slaves around them led whites to value their own freedom and to celebrate their bond with whites in other classes. This ideal triumphed in the period of Jacksonian democracy in the 1830s and promoted a sense of internal southern white solidarity in facing the North.

North-South tensions became an urgent national issue during the 1850s. The debate over slavery in the western territories, which were gained as a result of the Mexican War, stirred sectionalism to a new pitch in the late 1840s. The Nashville Convention, an expression of southern consciousness during this debate, met in 1850, but moderates controlled it, and the situation was diffused by the Compromise of 1850. A litany of laws and events polarized the nation throughout the decade: the publication of *Uncle Tom's Cabin* (1851), the Kansas-Nebraska Act (1854), the civil war in Kansas (late 1850s), South Carolina Congressman Preston Brooks's beating of Massachusetts Senator Charles Sumner in Congress (1856), the death of the Whig party and emergence of a northern-based Republican party, the Supreme Court's Dred Scott decision (1857), John Brown's raid on Harper's Ferry, Va. (1859), and the election of Abraham Lincoln (1860).

The Civil War was the crucial event cementing the southern white identity. The experience of fighting and losing a war would isolate the region's people. As C. Vann Woodward has written, losing the Civil War became a central burden of southern history.

The Confederate States of America stands as the supreme statement of the southern desire for self-determination. The Confederacy aimed at preserving a traditional life that seemed threatened by outside intervention. It did not attempt any utopian transformation for the future but represented instead a conservative political revolution aimed at preventing social and economic changes in its fundamental institutions. White southerners did not simply justify the war as a crusade for slavery. Orators emphasized not race but the issues of self-determination, localism, righteous holiness, and constitutional rights. Nonetheless, there is no escaping the racial dimension of a war fought by a slave society; the conflict was a logical culmination of the proslavery argument. Historians generally agree that south-

Confederate soldiers from Georgia

erners during the Civil War developed only a limited sense of political nationalism and that a romantic cultural nationalism may have been more a product of the war than a cause for it. As David M. Potter noted in *The Impending Crisis, 1848–1861* (1976), "The Civil War did far more to produce a southern nationalism which flourished in the cult of the Lost Cause than southern nationalism did to produce the war." Novelist Robert Penn Warren has written in *The Legacy of the Civil War: Meditations on the Centennial* (1961) that the Confederacy became immortal, a "City of the Soul," when it expired, and the memory of it has had a tenacious hold on the southern imagination. No southern *War and Peace*, *Guernica*, or "Gettysburg Address" came out of it. Its tragedy, however, surely shaped postwar southern life. Southerners learned the lessons of defeat, the lessons of human limitation and mortality, and the virtues of upholding the basic human values of family, community, and economic survival. The war was a tremendous bonding experience for southern whites who had tried and failed at independence; that separate history would forever differentiate the region from others in the nation.

The economic base of southern culture had been transformed by the end of the war. A $2 billion investment in land had been destroyed, a $3 million cotton crop confiscated, factories dismantled, banks closed, public buildings damaged, and cities leveled. The physical landscape had changed. Throughout the South there were damaged bridges, roads, railroad tracks, and burned cotton gins, factories, fences, and barns. Chimneys stood without houses. Few horses, mules, sheep, cattle, or hogs could be found. Items necessary for daily living had vanished, and no replacements could be found. Lack of tools, livestock, and seed made even good land useless.

The human toll was even more awesome. There were 258,000 dead and 150,000 disabled. Every third household saw one of its members dead, a rate that was four times that of the North. Lingering wounds and illnesses plagued the surviving soldiers; the number of widows and orphaned children was uncounted. A spiritual depression settled on the region, as its people tried to understand how they could lose a war they had been told was a holy one. The South was cast back into subsistence living, into frontier life, "the frontier the Yankee made," said W. J. Cash. The North moved into a new modern era after the war while the South reverted to a primitive, violent, individualistic, provincial life. A culture of poverty appeared that would haunt the region.

The Reconstruction era from 1865 to 1877 was nearly equal to the Civil War in forging a self-conscious white southern identity. It marked white southern-

ers against northerners on the one hand and against southern blacks on the other. Fear, grievance, defensiveness, and the memory of hardship and bitterness—all were central to cementing this identity. The southern white view of Reconstruction was preserved and passed on for generations by the South's official history books, by literature such as Thomas Dixon's *The Clansman* (1905), and by family stories told generation after generation. Eventually the southern white legend of Reconstruction was nationally reinforced by D. W. Griffith's film *Birth of a Nation* and academic histories produced by William A. Dunning and his students at Columbia University.

Journalist Hodding Carter called Reconstruction "the angry scar," and it was a major setback for black-white cultural integration in the South. Under slavery there had been much social interaction because of the intimate role blacks played in the lives of southern whites. Blacks helped in the birthing, nursing, and raising of white children; they tended to white men and women throughout their lives and were there at high moments of marrying and dying. Blacks continued that intimate role, but under very different circumstances. There was less paternalism and less institutional, public contact.

Developments in religion were revealing. Blacks had once worshipped as members of the same churches as whites. To be sure, slaves had their "invisible institution," the religion they practiced in their slave quarters, outside the bounds of Christian institutions. Nonetheless, their Christian worship was a shared communion, where baptism, the ritual of church worship, and the ecstasy of revivalism were shared with whites. During Reconstruction blacks withdrew from white churches and set up independent congregations. They joined the northern-based African Methodist Episcopal church or the African Methodist Episcopal Zion church in large numbers. Others joined the Colored Methodist Episcopal church, an organization created with the assistance of southern white Methodists. Thousands of independent black Baptist churches emerged logically from the Baptist heritage of local church autonomy. These churches were often established with the encouragement and active support of white congregations, and fraternal ties remained. This development was one of the most significant results of Reconstruction and was vital for the emergence of a distinct black culture. It was a peaceable separation; the violence seen in politics was not reproduced here. But in terms of a culturally integrated southern life, it was a setback. Ironically, white and black southerners shared many beliefs, but the region's spiritual life was now segregated.

The southern legend of Reconstruction drove a psychological wedge between blacks and whites. Southern black legends of nightriders reflected the opposite side of a Reconstruction myth, also centered on fear, but fear of the awesome brutality southern whites would tolerate to preserve their racial purity. The memory of Reconstruction's failure and of an era of violent racial conflict was, thus, the same for both races, although the substance of the fears and the meaning of the failure differed in each case.

The mind of the white South after the Civil War was dominated by myths—the romantic legend of the Old South, the tragic Lost Cause, and the pragmatic creed of a New South. The myth of the "moonlight-and-magnolias" Old South

originated in the antebellum era, but the idealization of the plantation world received its most influential expression in the 1880s and after in the local color stories of Thomas Nelson Page and others. The myth of the Lost Cause described heroic men from plantations and farms crusading for the Confederacy against invading forces of evil. Ministers and religious groups created a civil religion that tied regional patriotism and religion together so that the remembered Confederate cause took on spiritual significance.

After the Civil War southerners worked hard to preserve the memory of their regional historical experience. The sense of history was given a tangible meaning through memorial celebrations, the erection of monuments, and the expansion of historical societies. Paintings of Robert E. Lee and Jefferson Davis were hung in schoolrooms across the region. Folk ballads, poems, and storytelling by the old passed on to the young the region's memory of the Civil War. Patriotic societies such as the United Confederate Veterans and the United Daughters of the Confederacy campaigned for the teaching of southern history in schools and for the preservation of historical records. The Southern Historical Society was organized in 1873 and soon accumulated an archive of Confederate history. Southerners complained of the bias against the South in textbooks written by northerners and began writing their own histories and lobbying for southern school boards to adopt them. In all these efforts white southerners wanted to explain their view of the past, especially the Confederate and antebellum eras, confident of their ultimate vindication. "Lest ye forget," which appeared on countless Confederate monuments, was an apt motto for southerners of that era. The intense cultivation of an interest in history surely helped preserve the self-conscious southern identity. The history was more a cultivation of myth than a critical examination of the past. The historical record, though, became a prime foundation for the preservation of southern ways.

If the myth and history of the Lost Cause looked to the past, the story of the New South embodied the hope of change. The key word was progress. The central historiographical issue of the period was continuity versus change. C. Vann Woodward in *The Origins of the New South, 1877–1914* (1951) made the case for the significance of the Civil War as a profound break in southern history; Carl N. Degler in *Place over Time: The Continuity of Southern Distinctiveness* (1977) makes the case for continuity. Recent historians focus on the planter and the sharecropper as the main symbols for the issue. Agriculture after the Civil War seemed very different from before, but new institutions simply emerged to accomplish aims similar to those before the war. The plantation survived, albeit transformed, and blacks were held in near peonage as sharecroppers. During Reconstruction the crop-lien system emerged, providing a way for landowners with little cash or credit and laborers without land or money to restart the economy. Sharecroppers and tenants made the crop and shared the harvest with the landowner. Credit for food, tools, livestock, seed, and living necessities was based on the tenant's mortgaging a crop that had not yet been planted. This credit system involved great risk for all concerned and it opened the way for severe exploitation of the poor.

The postwar planter remained a cru-

cial southern character, and recent studies by Dwight B. Billings, Jonathan Wiener, and others suggest the antebellum planter class continued to exercise considerable power in the New South. But other cultural figures also emerged. The planter himself had to rely frequently on the storekeeper. Thomas A. Stribling wrote of the merchant in *The Store* (1932), and William Faulkner created a portrait of a mercenary family of merchants in his Snopes trilogy. Newspaper editors such as Henry W. Grady of the Atlanta *Constitution*, Henry Watterson of the Louisville *Courier-Journal*, Richard H. Edmonds of the *Manufacturer's Record* in Baltimore, and Francis W. Dawson of the Charleston *News and Courier* became especially prominent supporters of a New South. The businessman as hero became a new part of the folklore of the South in this era. Businessmen were typically self-made men from the middle class. The lumber, tobacco, textile, furniture, iron and steel, and mining industries expanded in the 1880s, generating wealth and a new privileged class. Lawyer-politicians were powerful figures in the New South, dominating courthouse rings, monopolizing public offices, and supervising public expenditures.

If the nature of the New South can be conveyed through these social types, its meaning can also be seen through the appearance of newly important institutions on the landscape. Textile mills had existed before the Civil War, but in the 1880s southerners went on a veritable crusade for industry, which focused mainly on the mills. W. J. Cash called it "a mighty folk movement," the "dream of virtually the whole southern people." The cotton mills were to be the salvation for the South's poor whites, providing employment opportunities for them but not for blacks. By 1915 the South produced more textiles than the rest of the nation combined, but this production was achieved at a great cost in human misery, in the form of desperately low wages, 72-hour work weeks, and the exploitation of women and children. The mills exacerbated the culture of poverty rather than ending it.

Railroads became as important a symbol in the southern psyche as they had been in the North generations earlier. They nurtured ties with the regional past by hiring Confederate generals such as Jubal Early as representatives. In fact, though, northerners controlled the South's expanding rail system after the Civil War, with southerners usually involved only in support positions. Ambitious young southerners were now allied with Yankee businessmen, not fighting them as their fathers had. Railroads helped bring the development of cities such as Atlanta, Birmingham, and Durham, which emerged as New South industrial and commercial centers.

Despite these changes, race in the late 19th century was still the central theme of southern identity. The New South was achieved at the expense of blacks. Life for southern blacks reached its lowest point between the end of Reconstruction and the beginning of World War I. Economically, they were prisoners of a sharecropping system that kept them in near bondage to the land. They lost political power as disfranchisement was achieved through poll taxes, residency requirements, literacy tests, "understanding the Constitution" tests, grandfather clauses basing the right to vote on ancestors having voted, and whites-only primaries. Segregation of the races became an accepted part of New South life. In the decades after the

Civil War a period of experimentation in race relations had occurred. Although custom had prevented extensive social mixing between the races, both blacks and whites had commonly used the same public facilities. This changed in the 1890s; Jim Crow laws sought to establish a rigid caste system. A torrent of legislation was passed in the 1890s, setting up a comprehensive legal framework for a biracial society. Unwritten customs of racial etiquette also hardened. The economy segregated black jobs and white jobs. The Supreme Court case of *Plessy* v. *Ferguson* (1896) gave federal approval to southern actions by declaring "separate-but-equal" facilities to be legal. Railroads, schools, theaters, hotels, restaurants, rest rooms, water fountains, parks, public offices, and even cemeteries were segregated by the early 20th century. The landscape itself reflected this aspect of the New South—"colored" and "white" signs were soon pervasive. In spite of this terrible setback for black-white cultural interaction, daily occasions often arose for contact between blacks and whites, especially in the region's small towns and rural communities.

The late 19th century was perhaps the age of the most cohesive regional culture and an identifiable, distinctive southern way of life. In addition to the peculiar racial system, a host of customs and cultural ways were associated with southern blacks and whites. Poverty and rural isolation promoted the persistence of attitudes and customs. Blacks and whites placed a high value on family and kinship. People dined, entertained, lived, and visited, all within the boundaries of the family. The family sheltered maiden aunts, distant cousins, and respected grandparents. Household matters were central concerns. Distinctive culinary styles of the typical family were noted by southerners and others as well. On a less positive note, violence was common in the South, which had a high homicide rate, lynchings, public executions, and in general a visible culture of accepted violent behavior.

Churches became even more important institutions in southern culture after the war. Whites joined evangelical churches, and separate black churches emerged. Religious institutions were racially segregated, yet black and white worshipers shared a Protestant, predominantly Baptist and Methodist, orientation. Southern Baptists, Methodists, and Presbyterians did not reunite with their northern brethren after the Civil War but instead worshiped in regionally organized churches. Southern whites remained evangelical and fundamentalist at a time when northern religion was becoming pluralistic in denominations and liberal in theology. Churches extended a pervasive moralism into southern culture through crusades for prohibition of alcohol, for blue laws honoring the Sabbath, and for restrictions on gambling.

Southern culture was also transmitted through distinctive regional rituals such as Confederate Memorial Day, Sunday dinners on the church grounds, political campaign barbecues celebrating the Democratic party, religious camp meetings, and revivals. On such ritual occasions one heard storytelling and swapping of folk sayings, proverbs, and superstitions; ballad singings; and the formal oratory of the political rabble-rouser and the fiery itinerant evangelist. Sports were a central part of living for southerners. Hunting and fishing had long been regional favorites and remained so for a people who were predominantly rural.

The emergence of agrarian political and economic protest in the 1890s marked the beginning of nearly 30 years of efforts at reform and represented the most serious challenge to southern orthodoxy. Efforts for change began in the Grange, and then the Farmers' Alliance spread over the South, gaining 3 million white members by 1890–91 with over a million more in the Colored Alliance. The Alliance was significant in southern history in trying to forge a class coalition by overcoming racial divisions. Its reformers called for structural changes in the economy to give the federal government a greater role in regulating and controlling an economy increasingly dominated by corporate power. Agrarian protesters attempted to substitute economic issues for racial issues as the dominant concerns in public policy. Historian Lawrence Goodwyn in *Democratic Promise: The Populist Moment in America* (1976) argues that the agrarian movement represented the last chance for true structural reform in American society. It was a direct class appeal to the poor, articulating the profound grievances of farmers and forging a democratic political culture. Other historians see the movement as backward looking, parochial, and conspiratorial. They think agrarian reformers sought a black-white coalition out of convenience, not principle, and only a minority of reformers used a rhetoric of class appeal across racial lines. In their view, agrarian radicals were not entirely alienated, in other words, from the southern way of life. Radicals accepted the color line, used the words and teachings of evangelical Protestantism in demanding reform, and did not challenge the sharecropping system.

The existence of agrarian protest suggests also that the southern way of life was not monolithically conservative. Southern reformers developed a political culture that reflected the abiding democratic and religious style of the South. Southern culture has periodically produced charismatic spokesmen demanding reform for an oppressed people. Rural protesters such as Pitchfork Ben Tillman in South Carolina and James H. "Cyclone" Davis and H. S. P. "Stump" Ashby in Texas used the incendiary language of itinerant democratic ministers and politicians. With the failure of serious reform by the turn of the 20th century, racial extremism appeared. Political demagogues blamed blacks for the failure and exploited the emotions of poor whites.

The Progressive era presented a social type seldom seen in the earlier South—the middle-class, liberal reformer. Like Progressives in other regions, southern Progressives favored reform to deal with political corruption and irregularities, to rationalize society along more businesslike and scientific lines, to limit business monopoly and the abuse of society, and to restore traditional moral values. They accepted racial segregation and disfranchisement, regarding them as forms peculiar to the South. Southern Progressives thus attempted to achieve reform at the expense of blacks. Lynchings and race riots were ironically at a peak in this era of reform. The appearance of biracial groups such as the National Association for the Advancement of Colored People and the Commission on Interracial Cooperation did lay the basis for future change.

Black cultural attitudes in this period were symbolized by two leaders—Booker T. Washington and W. E. B. Du Bois. Born a slave, educated at Hampton Institute in Virginia, and ap-pointed director of Tuskegee Institute in Alabama in 1881, Washington expressed the predominant black view favoring economic self-help. Rather than directly challenge segregation, Washington proposed that blacks work toward building community strength. Washington was one of the most influential southerners in the nation. He communicated with blacks and whites, northerners and southerners, and advocated postponement of political and civil rights and concentration on individual self-improvement. Washington secretly challenged features of the southern system, but publicly he strongly supported black economic development through jobs, landownership, training in business leadership, and vocational skills. Du Bois came to maturity in the early 20th century and reflected the outlook of the Progressive era. He helped found the NAACP and urged concentration of black efforts on gaining political and civil rights. His book *The Souls of Black Folk* (1903) was an evocative description of turn-of-the-century black southern life.

Americanization. The major theme of the years from 1910 to 1985 was the Americanization of the South. Woodrow Wilson was a southerner by heritage and training, and his election as president in 1912 (along with the election of a Democratic party-controlled Congress) marked the reappearance of southern political influence on the national scene.

While Wilson was president, World War I promoted patriotic nationalism in the South. The Spanish-American War (1898–99) had been an earlier landmark reincorporating southerners into the nation, and by 1917 memories of the Lost Cause and Reconstruction had diminished enough to make southerners enthusiastic about the nation at war. Soon southerners were honoring fallen warriors for the nation rather than the region.

The outbreak of war in 1914 led to economic advancement for the South, because of a rising demand for agricultural goods. The employment picture in the region improved and cash incomes rose. The war-related changes also promoted mobility. Southerners had been a relatively static people in the late 19th century, but they now flocked to southern and northern cities seeking jobs. The South was the setting for the training of American troops after the United States entered the war in 1917. Northerners came south, and almost a million southerners served in the army and naval forces, helping to diminish the isolation characteristic for generations of southern life. Blacks in particular began leaving the plantations to seek work elsewhere.

Change in the post–World War I South became apparent with the decline in the price of cotton in 1921. On top of that, the boll weevil entered the southern landscape and psyche, devastating cotton in the 1920s and thereafter. The specter of starvation was especially significant in further spurring black migration from the land to northern cities. The southern economy, in general, made some improvement in the 1920s, with an increase in the number of textile mills, a growing chemical industry that had been stimulated during the war, expansion of coal and iron production, and advancement of hydroelectric power. Nonetheless, the southern economy as a whole was in decline well before the stock-market crash of 1929 set off the Great Depression.

The Depression was more devastating to the South than to any other region. A federal government report referred to the region as "the Nation's no. 1 economic problem." Franklin D. Roosevelt's New Deal directed a disproportionate share of programs to the region, as symbolized best perhaps by the TVA, relief and public-works projects, and farm and crop-control efforts. The southern populace generally supported the New Deal, although many regional political leaders became critical of it as an experiment in socialism. They especially feared the effects of social experimentation on the region's racial caste system. Overall, New Deal farm programs and farm mechanization combined to promote a revolutionary exodus of sharecroppers and tenants from the land.

The Americanization of the South brought a crisis in the southern identity. The years from 1920 to 1945 were creative ones for southern culture, but the creativity came out of a period of transition. The identity crisis especially affected the region's intellectuals and artists who felt the impact of the region's transition from a traditional society to a modern one. What did the regional identity—being southern—mean in the context of world wars and international, modernist intellectual currents? During the 1920s the region appeared to the nation as, in George B. Tindall's phrase, the "Benighted South" symbolized by the Ku Klux Klan, hookworm and pellagra, chain gangs, lynchings, the Scopes Trial, and the Fundamentalist movement in religion. The leadership of the South was in the hands of those of the booster mentality. Intellectuals realized they could no longer take the southern identity for granted. Literary critic Louis D. Rubin, Jr., called the 1930 Agrarian manifesto *I'll Take My Stand* "an assertion of identity."

The South to the Agrarians represented the last hope of the Western world to tame industrialization and the forces of modernization and dehumanization. Generations of material deprivation had given a spiritual strength that should be used. Intellectuals began questioning and rejecting the romantic and sentimental view of southern culture.

From this period of transition came the Southern Literary Renaissance and a flowering of studies in the social sciences. Journalism, literary criticism, history, fiction, and poetry were all affected by the new spirit of self-criticism, which set the stage for changes after World War II in the southern identity and way of life. Daniel J. Singal, Michael O'Brien, and others have analyzed this watershed southern intellectual period from 1920 to 1945. Scholars are just beginning to place southern achievements in music, art, architecture, and other fields into this framework.

These changes also affected the South's folk culture. Small-town, rural folk culture had survived longer in the South than in other regions of the nation. It nurtured distinctive musical, painting, and craft traditions. In the years from 1920 to 1945 the folk culture provided materials for the expansive achievements in popular culture that would flourish in the era after World War II. Authentic, traditional folklife has survived in the South despite the commercialization of mass culture. That the folk culture combined black and white contributions became increasingly clear after World War II. Southern ideology had never sanctioned such cultural miscegenation, yet two races living for 300 years on the same soil, often isolated in rural areas from outsiders, had exchanged much specific knowl-edge and skill and had developed shared attitudes on such matters as religion, the family, recreation, and the importance of land and community.

The South since World War II has experienced a revolution. World War II itself was central to change in the region; it may prove to be even more significant for the region than the Civil War. The pace of economic development stepped up as the federal government poured defense-related investment into the South. The region's lingering isolation was broken as the war encouraged mobility. Many blacks and whites left the South to serve in the military, and civilian workers left rural areas to work in southern cities or left the region to work in northern and western defense industries. Millions of non-southerners came into the region, exposing southerners to new influences. The war turned the South's interests outward.

The war laid the basis for postwar economic development and the emergence of the Sunbelt. The decade of the 1960s was the key period, an era of extraordinary growth. Incomes and the standard of living rose. There was still a gap with the rest of the nation, but the once-pervasive poverty was broken. Agriculture was transformed. There has been a drastic decline in the number of farms and the farm population. Cotton no longer is king. Mechanization has helped to displace rural tenant farmers and sharecroppers. Farming has become agribusiness, a commercial enterprise, not the activity promoting the agrarian life urged by the contributors to *I'll Take My Stand*. The southern economy has diversified, and industry is now more economically important than agriculture, even in the most predominantly rural state, Mississippi. To be sure, problems remain. Southern economic development has been based on exploiting extractive resources, such as coal or oil, or on low-wage industries such as textiles. Tax and wage policies have left fewer economic benefits than advocates of those policies earlier claimed. Much of the growth has been through branch plants controlled by national firms. Moreover, the growth has been uneven, with Texas, Florida, Georgia, and North Carolina the major beneficiaries. Pockets of poverty remain in states such as Mississippi, Alabama, and Arkansas, and among Appalachians and rural blacks. The Sunbelt image of regional prosperity has become, though, a new myth of southern success.

The southern landscape has changed as a result of the dramatic economic developments. Gangs of cotton pickers are gone, and tenant shacks are torn down or covered with kudzu. In the 1980s soybeans and peanuts, as well as cotton, grow in southern fields, and rural homes have television satellite dishes. Southern cities look much like those elsewhere, and the modern highway strip, mobile home parks, and shopping malls are more typical of the region's urban areas than the once powerful symbol of the county courthouse. The nation's communications and transportation systems have drawn the South in and ended its isolation. If one had to pick a symbol of the modern South, it might be the sight of the bulldozer on a construction crew where once the mule or later the tractor worked.

The average contemporary southerner has more money, lives in a larger urban area, goes to better schools, and goes to church in bigger buildings than his or her ancestors. Sunbelt wealth has dramatically affected traditional southern culture. Material advances have promoted cultural achievements—more art galleries, symphonies, universities, and libraries. But the evolving southern culture shows continuities with the past as well. In religion, for example, many southerners use their newfound incomes to contribute to their denominations, which build bigger church centers. The church remains a dominant symbol on the southern landscape. Sports have become a new secular religion, combining recreational, military, and religious features of the traditional South.

Another major development since World War II is the decline of race as the central theme—and obsession—of the South. In the 1950s black activists entered a new stage of the struggle to end the region's caste system. The NAACP's traditional strategy of working through the judicial system led to a legal victory over segregation in *Brown* v. *Board of Education* (1954), which overturned the *Plessy* decision of the 1890s legalizing racial segregation. Southern white conservatives responded with a strategy of massive resistance, and legalists such as journalist James J. Kilpatrick revived interposition theories from the 19th century. The 1950s witnessed a resurrection of Confederate symbolism and die-hard racism. Groups such as the Ku Klux Klan and the White Citizens' Councils led the opposition to change. They proposed once again associating southern identity with race alone. Moderate whites stood on the sideline and offered little constructive leadership, with a few notable, brave exceptions.

Black civil rights activists, led by the eloquent Martin Luther King, Jr., took the offensive, with a campaign of nonviolent resistance based partly in regional religious tradition. Civil rights leaders faced economic and physical intimidation, mean spiritedness, and outright violence. The height of violence was 1963–68, when 97 people were killed in racial conflict in the South, according to figures compiled by the Southern Regional Council. Through television the world witnessed sit-ins, freedom rides, boycotts, marches, and freedom summers. Little Rock, Selma, Oxford, Montgomery, Birmingham, Neshoba County, and Greensboro may one day rank as great battlefields in the southern imagination, along with Shiloh, Manassas, Antietam, and Gettysburg. The Southern Christian Leadership Conference may take its place beside the Army of Northern Virginia in the southern mind.

External pressure from the federal government, along with the internal pressure of civil rights reformers, led to the passage of the Civil Rights Acts of 1964 and 1965 and the Voting Rights Act of 1965. These laws destroyed the legal basis of caste, overturning the segregation laws and promoting the return of blacks to southern politics. Belief in white supremacy was surely not destroyed, but the South's racial picture by the 1980s resembled the nation's pattern more than its own once-distinctive system. An emerging myth of the Redemptive Biracial South even suggested the region would achieve true integration before the rest of the nation.

The modern South has experienced dramatic change—the end of the one-crop cotton economy, the growth of industrialization and the end of its culture of poverty, the rise of the Republican party and the end of the one-party Solid South, the draining of the rural countryside and the growth of cities, the end of isolation and the incorporation of the region's peoples into the national culture, and the end of the peculiar racial caste system embodied in Jim Crow laws. Despite the changes, a degree of continuity with the region's past remains—religion, as distinct as ever, is expressed in the overwhelming dominance of evangelical Protestant denominations; regional traditions in literature, music, sports, eating, and the appreciation of leisure time, outdoor life, family activities, and community life remain vital; and the willingness to use violence and force in certain situations is still a regional trait. Studies by sociologist John Shelton Reed suggest that a profile of the future southerner has already appeared—he or she is well educated, well traveled, middle class, attuned to the nation's communications systems, lives in a suburb, and has the strongest sense of regional identity of anyone living in the South. The locus of southern identity has thus shifted from the rural plantation and small farm of a century ago to the most modern form of residential living, the suburb.

Despite these changes in the contemporary South, the sense of history thrives and continues to provide a foundation for the idea of southern distinctiveness. C. Vann Woodward's seminal volume *The Burden of Southern History* (1961) argues that the South's military defeat, poverty, guilt over slavery, and strong attachment to localism were distinctive experiences in U.S. history and would continue to nourish a sense of southern identity. Woodward's argument was an outgrowth of the stress on research and published scholarship in the increasingly sophisticated field of southern history after World War II. The founding of the Southern Historical Association in 1934 and the publication of the *Journal of Southern History* the following year were turning points in the emergence of a critical view of the southern past that finally replaced the mythic view. Revisionist views of slavery, the Civil War, and Reconstruction, along with the growth of black history in the 1960s, offered southerners a revolutionary new vision of their past.

Interest in the South's history was also seen in improvements in university, state, and local libraries. Historical societies took on new life, and institutions such as the Institute for Early American History and Culture at Williamsburg and the American Association for State and Local History in Nashville appeared. Southern university presses came to specialize, in many cases, in publishing regional history. The publication of the collaborative 10-volume *History of the South* by the Louisiana State University Press and the Littlefield Fund for Southern History at the University of Texas introduces important new scholarship on the region.

Southern interest in history transcended the academic context as genealogical and patriotic societies and museum and archaeological collections thrived. History was learned from parents and grandparents, school teachers, local storytellers in small towns, from letters, diaries, journals, photographs, and other family artifacts. Historic preservation groups maintained the image of the past through restoration of mansions and older public buildings. The South is full of Civil War battlefields, which continue to fascinate and instill a sense of history. Modern southerners in the short stories of Bobbie Ann Mason may watch television and frequent the shopping malls, but they also still visit Shiloh.

In the 1974 Jefferson Lecture in the Humanities, Robert Penn Warren said that "a society with no sense of the past, with no sense of the human role as sig-

nificant not merely in experiencing history, but in creating it can have no sense of destiny." The South's destiny is now an American destiny, but its historical experience provides a distinctive perspective to draw on in charting the future.

Charles Reagan Wilson
University of Mississippi

Thomas P. Abernathy, *The South in the New Nation, 1789–1819* (1961); John Alden, *The First South* (1961), *The South in the Revolution, 1763–1789* (1957); Kenneth K. Bailey, *Southern White Protestantism in the Twentieth Century* (1964); Numan Bartley, *Rise of Massive Resistance: Race and Politics in the South during the 1950s* (1969); Ray Allen Billington, *Westward Expansion: A History of the American Frontier* (1949); John W. Blassingame, *The Slave Community: Plantation Life in the Antebellum South* (1972); John B. Boles, *Black Southerners, 1619–1869* (1983), *The Great Revival, 1787–1805: The Origins of the Southern Evangelical Mind* (1972); Carl Bridenbaugh, *Myths and Realities of the Colonial South* (1952); Edward D. C. Campbell, Jr., *Celluloid South: Hollywood and the Southern Myth* (1981); Clayborne Carson, *In Struggle: SNCC and the Black Awakening of the 1960s* (1981); W. J. Cash, *The Mind of the South* (1941); William H. Chafe, *Civilities and Civil Rights: Greensboro, North Carolina, and the Black Struggle for Freedom* (1980); Thomas D. Clark, *The Emerging South* (1961), with Albert D. Billington, *American South: A Brief History* (1971); James C. Cobb, *Industrialization and Southern Society, 1877–1984* (1984), with Michael V. Namorato, eds., *New Deal and the South* (1984), *The Selling of the South: The Southern Crusade for Industrial Development, 1936–1980* (1982); Wesley F. Craven, *The Southern Colonies in the Seventeenth Century, 1607–1689* (1949); James McBride Dabbs, *Who Speaks for the South?* (1964); Pete Daniel, *Breaking the Land: The Trans-*

formation of Cotton, Tobacco, and Rice Cultures since 1880 (1985), Standing at the Crossroads: Southern Life in the Twentieth Century (1986); F. Garvin Davenport, Jr., The Myth of Southern History: Historical Consciousness in Twentieth-Century Southern Literature (1967); Richard Beale Davis, Intellectual Life in Jefferson's Virginia, 1790–1830 (1964); Carl N. Degler, in The Development of an American Culture, ed. Stanley Coben and Lorman Ratner (1983), The Other South: Southern Dissenters in the Nineteenth Century (1974), Place over Time: The Continuity of Southern Distinctiveness (1977); Clement Eaton, Growth of a Southern Civilization, 1790–1860 (1960), The Waning of the Old South Civilization, 1860–1880s (1968); John S. Ezell, The South since 1865 (1963); Gilbert C. Fite, Cotton Fields No More: Southern Agriculture, 1865–1980 (1984); J. Wayne Flynt, Dixie's Forgotten People: The South's Poor Whites (1979); Paul M. Gaston, New South Creed: A Study in Southern Myth-making (1970); Eugene D. Genovese, The Political Economy of Slavery: Studies in Economy and Society of the Slave South (1966), Roll, Jordan, Roll: The World the Slaves Made (1972); Patrick Gerster and Nicholas Cords, eds., Myth and Southern History (1974); Henry Glassie, Pattern in the Material Folk Culture of the Eastern United States (1968); David R. Goldfield, Cotton Fields and Skyscrapers: Southern City and Region, 1607–1980 (1982), Promised Land: The South since 1945 (1987); Dewey W. Grantham, Southern Progressivism: The Reconciliation of Progress and Tradition (1983); Joanne V. Hawks and Sheila Skemp, eds., Sex, Race, and the Role of Women in the South (1983); William R. Hesseltine and David L. Smiley, The South in American History (2d ed., 1960); Samuel S. Hill, ed., Encyclopedia of Religion in the South (1984), Southern Churches in Crisis (1966); Fred Hobson, Tell about the South: The Southern Rage to Explain (1983); C. Hugh Holman, The Immoderate Past: The Southern Writer and History (1977); Arthur Palmer Hudson, Folklore Keeps the Past Alive (1962); Charles Hudson, Southeastern Indians (1976); Rhys Isaac, The Transformation of Virginia, 1740–1790 (1982); Winthrop D. Jordan, White over Black: American Attitudes toward the Negro, 1530–1812 (1968); Charles Joyner, Down by the Riverside: A South Carolina Slave Community (1984); Benjamin B. Kendrick and Alex M. Arnett, The South Looks at Its Past (1935); V. O. Key, Jr., Southern Politics in State and Nation (1949); Jack Temple Kirby, Media-Made Dixie: The South in the American Imagination (1978), Rural Worlds Lost: The American South 1920–1980 (1987); Lawrence W. Levine, Black Culture and Black Consciousness: Afro-American Folk Thought from Slavery to Freedom (1977); Leon F. Litwack, Been in the Storm So Long: The Aftermath of Slavery (1979); Bill C. Malone, Southern Music / American Music (1979); John McCardell, Idea of a Southern Nation: Southern Nationalists and Southern Nationalism, 1830–1860 (1979); Forrest McDonald and Grady McWhiney, American Historical Review (December 1980); D. W. Meinig, The Shaping of America: A Geographical Perspective on 500 Years of History: Atlantic America, 1492–1800, vol. 1 (1986); Edmund S. Morgan, American Slavery, American Freedom: The Ordeal of Colonial Virginia (1975); George Mowry, Another Look at the Twentieth-Century South (1973); I. A. Newby, The South: A History (1978); Michael O'Brien, Idea of the American South, 1920–1941 (1979); Howard W. Odum, The Way of the South (1947); Frank L. Owsley, Plain Folk of the Old South (1949); U. B. Phillips, Life and Labor in the Old South (1929); David M. Potter, The Impending Crisis, 1848–1861 (1976), The South and the Sectional Conflict (1968); Albert J. Raboteau, Slave Religion: The "Invisible Institution" in the Antebellum South (1978); James G. Randall and David Donald, The Civil War and Reconstruction (1969); Charles P. Roland, The Improbable Era: The South since 1945 (1976); Louis D. Rubin, Jr., et al., The History of Southern Literature (1986); Henry Savage, Jr., Seeds of Time: The Background of Southern Thinking (1959); Anne Firor Scott, The Southern Lady: From Pedestal to

Politics, 1830–1930 (1970); Charles G. Sellers, Jr., ed., *The Southerner as American* (1960); Henry D. Shapiro, *Appalachia on Our Mind: The Southern Mountains and Mountaineers in the American Consciousness, 1890–1920* (1978); Frances Butler Simkins, *The Everlasting South* (1963), with Charles P. Roland, *A History of the South* (1972); Daniel J. Singal, *The War Within: From Victorian to Modernist Thought in the South, 1919–1945* (1984); Charles S. Sydnor, *The Development of Southern Sectionalism, 1819–1848* (1948); William R. Taylor, *Cavalier and Yankee: The Old South and American National Character* (1961); Emory Thomas, *The Confederate Nation, 1861–1865* (1979); George Tindall, *Emergence of the New South, 1913–1945* (1967), *Ethnic Southerners* (1977); Kerry Trask, *Southern Studies* (Summer 1983); Joel Williamson, *Crucible of Race: Black-White Relations in the American South since Emancipation* (1984); Peter H. Wood, *Black Majority: Negroes in Colonial South Carolina from 1670 through the Stono Rebellion* (1973); C. Vann Woodward, *The Burden of Southern History* (1960), *Origins of the New South, 1877–1913* (1951), *Strange Career of Jim Crow* (1955); J. Leitch Wright, Jr., *The Only Land They Knew: The Tragic Story of the American Indians in the Old South* (1981). ☆

Anglo-American Antebellum Culture

||||||||||||||||||||||||||||||||||||||||||||||||||

The Old South's high culture was marked by two strong currents: it began and remained an Anglo-American culture in its tastes and loyalties, and it was sustained by an agrarian economic system partially supported by black slave labor. The first was seen in a strong taste for goods from abroad, and the second created tensions and anxieties about man's relation to man.

White colonial settlers in the South were northern European, predominantly from the British Isles, who were not always seeking the same religious and political freedoms as their Puritan contemporaries in the North. The cultural evolution of the Old South proceeded as a logical extension of the English squirearchy, the Whig mentality wherein communal political authority was held in less regard than the customs of the local aristocracy. This aristocracy respected men of ability who became men of means, the type of "natural aristocrat" Thomas Jefferson espoused. Save in Virginia, the most English of the southern states, a hereditary aristocracy did not develop. Indeed, as Clement Eaton has written, "With few exceptions, the ruling families were developed on the native soil from middle class origins."

Affiliation with the Church of England through the colonial period in the South resulted in a consensus code of behavior. Abstract codes of honor and decency coalesced into an Anglo-Saxon common law of human behavior. Unlike the Puritans who felt they were living in a time of declension from the virtues of a distant past, southern whites, according to Bertram Wyatt-Brown, "believed that they had made peace with God's natural order." By and large southern culture was at odds with the national culture and was inclined to regard property and local option as the most important aspects of a democratic society and disinclined to respect external elective authority. These attitudes led inevitably to theories of nullification, actual secession, and war.

The southern antebellum economy was agrarian, stratified into large and small farms, many of which were called, in the archaic fashion of the 17th century, *plantations*. One lingering colonial trait within the culture was a factor system of exchanging agricultural produce for manufactured commodities from abroad or the North. This exchange system had a significant effect upon the market for local commodities and may have retarded the growth of the southern plastic arts.

Any understanding of southern plastic arts prior to 1861 must involve the integration of architecture, furnishings, and the exotic within the home. Coastal colonial architecture was by and large built of brick in the English manner of the 18th century, broadly fenestrated and preferring rear or side galleries to frontal porticoes. As the South moved west, builders used timber available from the virgin forests being cleared for farm lands and developed the first high-style frame architecture in the West. The rage for Greek Revival architecture, which seized most of the Western world in the first 50 years of the 19th century, was especially strong in the South.

The English gentry were fascinated with the classical age, as were southerners of a comparable class. Southern states were also dotted with towns named Troy, Athens, and Rome, and southern children were called Lucius, Cassius, Marcus—even Valerius Publicola in several Tennessee families. Collegiate education emphasized classical studies, not mechanical arts. Clearly, in the midst of an awesome controversy over slavery and its moral ramifications, some southerners thought of themselves as living in an ancient agrarian utopia, enshrined in white-columned temples.

Initially excellent and recently neglected traditions emerged in the plastic arts of the South. Superior cabinetmaking developed in the Coastal Plains, especially in Baltimore and Charleston. Baltimore remained through the period an important source for crafted and imported goods, though later in the period rivaled by New Orleans in influence and significance as a source for manufactured goods. Equally strong rural cabinetmaking traditions emerged in North Carolina and Kentucky, using cherry and hickory woods. Southern cabinetmakers tended to favor existing English styles, notably those to be seen in the pattern books of Thomas Sheraton, Thomas Shearer, and George Hepplewhite. An exception to the English taste was found in New Orleans, which introduced the French Empire and Rococo Revival styles to the Lower South.

Silversmiths excelled in the South, especially Samuel Kirk & Sons in Baltimore, Frederick Marquand in Savannah, James Conning in Mobile, and the Hyde and Goodrich firm of New Orleans. Many local craftsmen rendered silver coins into a variety of cups, pitchers, and spoons, but the works of Kentucky silversmiths, such as Asa Blanchard, were particularly prized.

In keeping with the tastes of England, portraiture was more esteemed than landscape painting, although a few painters, such as Granville Perkins (1830–95) and George Cooke (1793–1846), attempted to depict the scenic splendors of the region. George Caleb Bingham's (1811–79) river and political paintings are vivid documents of southern life and work.

Much of the portraiture of the Old South was rendered by itinerants, who established seasonal studios in favored urban areas like Natchez or Richmond. Some traveled from plantation house to plantation house, entertaining and depicting several members of a family at once. Under the influence of Gilbert Stuart (1755–1828) and Thomas Sully (1783–1872), a strong neoclassical portrait tradition emerged in Lexington, Ky., represented by William Edward West (1788–1857), Matthew Harris Jouett (1788–1827), Joseph Henry Bush (1794–1865), and Oliver Frazer (1808–64). New Orleans was a major center for portrait activity, especially by French academicians working there between 1820 and 1850. These artists, including Jean Joseph Vaudechamp (1790–1866) and Jacques Amans (1801–88), influenced several generations of southern itinerant painters, most notably C. R. Parker, who painted in Alabama, Mississippi, Georgia, and Louisiana.

Oratory was esteemed and well attended, favorites being the fire-eating secessionist speeches of William Lowndes Yancey (1814–63) and Robert Barnwell Rhett (1800–76). Chautauquas were held on the subjects of natural science, historical curiosities, and female education. "Camp meetings" by religious fundamentalists were particularly popular in the Upper South and were attended by as many as 15 to 20 thousand people at a time. Although a certain amount of speaking in tongues and writhing in the Holy Ghost took place at these gatherings, Clement Eaton felt that "beneath the tumult and excitement of the camp meetings can be discerned the craving of lonely frontier people for human companionship."

The literary tastes of affluent southerners mingled English influences with more homespun products. Romances of the medieval period, especially those of Sir Walter Scott, were wildly popular. So too were the humorous sketches of frontier southern life written by Augus-tus Baldwin Longstreet (1790–1870) and William Tappan Thompson (1812–82). Historical fiction by William Gilmore Simms (1806–70) assuaged the southern desire for a cavalier past, while the morbid Gothic musings of Edgar Allan Poe made little impact. Literary journals, such as *De Bow's Review* and the *Southern Literary Messenger*, combined humor, political speculations, and natural history articles.

The 40 years following the Missouri Compromise of 1820 saw the southern mind become increasingly paranoid, hysterical, and preoccupied with the slavery issue. Paternalism "accepted by both masters and slaves," says historian Eugene D. Genovese, "afforded a fragile bridge across the intolerable contradictions inherent in a society based on racism." Southern culture was conservative and deeply suspicious of the Industrial Revolution, an attitude it shared with the English intelligentsia of the same period, several of whom, including Thomas Carlyle and Charles Darwin, supported the South in secession.

The material culture that evolved from English influences on the antebellum South reflected the tastes of local aristocrats. The ruling families, most of whom came from middle-class backgrounds, sought tangible expressions of their good fortune and their aspirations. A strong cultural belief in the sanctity of private property prevailed, obscuring for many southerners the moral issue of keeping other human beings in bondage.

See also ART AND ARCHITECTURE: Decorative Arts; Greek Revival Architecture; Painting and Painters; Sculpture; BLACK LIFE: Slave Culture; EDUCATION: Classical Tradition; FOLKLIFE: Aesthetics, Anglo-American; LANGUAGE: Conversation; Oratory; MYTHIC SOUTH: Romanticism; / Anglo-Saxon South; Cavalier Myth; Celtic South; SOCIAL CLASS: Aristocracy

Estill Curtis Pennington
Lauren Rogers Museum of Art

Frances Gaither Blake, ed., *Mary Savage Conner of Adams County, Mississippi: A Young Girl's Journal, 1839* (1982); Clement Eaton, *The Freedom of Thought Struggle in the Old South* (1964), *A History of the Old South* (1964); Eugene D. Genovese, *Roll, Jordan, Roll: The World the Slaves Made* (1974); Robert Manson Myers, ed., *The Children of Pride: A True Story of Georgia and the Civil War* (1972); Estill Curtis Pennington, *Southern Quarterly* (Fall 1985); Jessie Poesch, *The Art of the Old South: Painting, Sculpture, Architecture and the Products of Craftsmen, 1560–1860* (1983); William R. Taylor, *Cavalier and Yankee: The Old South and American National Character* (1961); Bertram Wyatt-Brown, *Southern Honor: Ethics and Behavior in the Old South* (1982). ☆

Automobile

‖‖‖‖‖‖‖‖‖‖‖‖‖‖‖‖‖‖‖‖‖‖‖‖‖‖‖‖

"**N**obody with a good car needs to be justified," said Hazel Motes in Flannery O'Connor's *Wise Blood*. She was satirizing the idea, but the suggestion that the automobile can be the source of salvation has not been far off for many southerners in the 20th century. The automobile has had a profound impact on changing the region. It has affected class relationships, economic development, geographical mobility, and physical and psychological landscapes. "Such names as Ford, Chrysler, Olds, Willis, Nash, Shakespeare, Reo, Studebaker, and Dodge had more long-range economic meaning for the South

than all the Civil War generals combined," writes historian Thomas D. Clark. "The established way of life in the South was shaken to its very foundation by this new Yankee machine."

The South was the scene of occasional early automotive activity. In 1906, for example, at a mile run at Ormond Beach, Fla., a Stanley Steamer averaged the unheard-of speed of 127.66 miles per hour. Long-distance road races stressing speed were started in the late 1890s, and many were held over closed routes on southern public highways. The American Automotive Association sponsored the Vanderbilt Cup races in Georgia and Florida, the nationwide Glidden tours came into the South for the first time in 1910 and 1911, and the National Association of Automobile Manufacturers held the first official showing of 1910 model cars in Atlanta, the first time the show had been held outside of New York or Chicago. All this promoted a new attitude toward the South in the industry.

Despite such activity, motor vehicles at first made less impact in the South than elsewhere. The region's poverty made the automobile a luxury for most, and its dispersed rural population meant no concentrated urban market. In 1910 statistics on the ratio of automobiles registered to persons aged 18 or over showed the highest-ranking southern state to be Louisiana, but it ranked only 33d. All the southern states were well below the national average. In the geographic distribution of registered automobiles by state, Texas was the highest ranking of the former Confederate states in 1900 at 12th, with only 180 cars. But change was coming. "Southerners have finally awakened to the importance of the automobile," said a writer in *Motor* magazine in 1909.

The key decade of the automobile's

introduction into the region was the 1920s. Historian Blaine A. Brownell has argued that the southern attitude toward the automobile in that decade was one of "ambiguity and uncertainty" that "cut across class and racial lines." People in the region bought cars and adopted the car culture, but this involved dramatic changes, which were part of the general rural-urban conflict of the times. Newspapers promoted the automobile through special advertising and travel sections. Annual automobile shows promoted awareness of the car, and roads improved dramatically. In 1921 a writer in *Motor* praised "the tendency of the automobile to bring into intimate and helpful contact sections of our population which normally would never meet." Automobile outings and vacations became national institutions in the 1920s, as the car became a middle-class possession, and it fostered a new mobility of the labor force as well. Buses soon crisscrossed the region, facilitating the movement of people and freight. A few motor-vehicle assembly plants were brought to such southern states as Georgia, and raw materials needed for automobile manufacturing were processed in the South. The development of wholesale and retail businesses related to some aspect of the car was especially significant in the regional economy. In a typical case car dealerships represented 14.4 percent of Birmingham's 1929 retail trade, and businesses listed in the U.S. census as automobile related accounted for 20.5 percent of retail trade that year in Nashville and 16.5 percent in Atlanta.

Although southerners adopted the automobile, some of them criticized its effect on living patterns. Jonathan Daniels referred to the salesmen of Chevrolets as the "most profoundly disturbing agitators" in the region. Ministers blamed the automobile for leading to a decline in sexual morality by loosening courtship habits, and they said it nurtured crime, desecrated the Sabbath, hurt family bonds, and reinforced materialistic instincts. One of the most frequent complaints was of traffic congestion. As Faulkner noted in his 1927 novel *Mosquitoes*, traffic in New Orleans "inched forward, stopped, inched forward again." The lack of parking space was a continual concern of businesses seeking customers downtown. The rising number of deaths and injuries from automobile accidents also was a concern. The country music song "Wreck on the Highway," with its graphic images of shattered glass, screams, and whiskey and blood running together, conveyed the negative side of the automobile's impact in the region.

The automobile led to the reshaping of the southern land through road building. Organized southern efforts toward good roads began in the 1890s. By the second decade of the 20th century, writes historian Thomas D. Clark, "surfaced roads were still so much a novelty that pictures of them appeared in southern elementary textbooks as modern wonders." By this time, though, "the southern campaign for good roads had almost achieved the fervor of a religious revival." By 1920 all the southern states had established state highway commissions, which acquired tremendous amounts of money and power In 1918 North Carolina voters, for example, approved a $50 million bond issue to build improved road systems, and in 1956 they took on $76 million in debt for 1,771 miles of new roads. Governors and county public officials have found this a major source of patronage.

The automobile helped to revolutionize the southern relationship to the federal government. The passage of the

Federal Highway Act of 1921 led to a massive involvement of the federal government in the southern states. It has pumped billions of dollars into the region for road building, and the Federal Bureau of Highways has standardized requirements for bridges, roadbeds, and road markings and has employed inspectors to administer the guidelines. Despite recurrent talk of states' rights by southern congressmen, they have not opposed federal support for interstate highways.

Southerners are supposedly not attuned to technology, but this has not been so with automobiles. In Faulkner's *The Reivers*, a character has a vision of the nation's future "in which the basic unit of its economy and prosperity would be a small mass-produced cubicle containing four wheels and an engine." Despite this fear, the image of the mechanic as a rather romantic working-class hero has been common, "the romance of the backyard mechanic with grease up to his elbows," says Sylvia Wilkinson. The good old boy image is closely tied to the automobile. Like the cowboy and his horse, the good old boy needs his car. A good man knows cars and takes care of them.

The current image of the automobile man in the South is the clean professionalism of a stock-car driver and crew. To be sure, the driver may have wild tales to tell of his youth. Robert Mitchum symbolized this as a moonshine runner in the film *Thunder Road*, and Burt Reynolds's series of *Smokey and the Bandit* movies has taken it to its extremes. It is a male world in its imagery; women are not allowed in the pits and are considered to be bad luck. It is a sometimes violent world, where violence is direct and graphic. Junior Johnson recalled that in his early days

driving on dirt tracks in the South the drivers "liked to fight about as good as race." He remembered arming himself with a cola bottle for a fight with a competitor on the infield. The "rambling man" is another romantic southern figure associated with the automobile. He is a common figure in country music as far back as Jimmie Rodgers. Merle Haggard's 1977 song "Rambling Fever" expressed this theme, as did Kris Kristofferson's "Me and Bobby McGee." Even the automobile factory worker has made it into regional folklore. A Johnny Cash song tells of an assembly-line automobile worker who sneaks car parts out of the factory, one piece at a time, until he has a new automobile at home. The plight of southerners working in northern automobile plants is poignantly explored in "Detroit City." A great number of blues and rock-and-roll songs—such as "Mabelline"—celebrate the automobile.

The automobile has affected modern southern recreation. Hank Williams wrote that "a hot-rod Ford and a two dollar bill" was all that was required in the 1950s for a southern good time, while Lefty Frizzel in "If You've Got the Money, I've Got the Time" sang of good times in Cadillacs. In stock car racing, the South produces the majority of the tracks, races, and participants, as well as a massive turnout of spectators. Dirt-track racing is an important participant form of southern sport in local communities throughout the region. Recreational vehicles are pressed into service on weekends for camping, promoting the traditional southern pastimes of fishing and hunting.

One should not forget the recreational significance of the drive-in movie, a good example of a new recreational institution based on the automobile. The first drive-in opened on 6 June 1933 in Camden, N.J. It helped to structure recreation for a generation of Americans. The drive-in was at its peak in the 1950s, serving as a source of family entertainment and a central locale for teenage courtship. The number of drive-ins was greatest in 1958, when 4,000 were in operation. The "passion pits" have continued that role, although the number is on the decline, with 3,178 drive-ins nationwide in September of 1982. Most now are located in suburban areas, on the edge of cities, or in rural areas and small towns. Drive-in movies were surely not uniquely southern, yet the southern climate and the pervasiveness of small towns and rural communities have given them special recreational significance in the region. They are open later in the year than elsewhere and are a larger component of entertainment in small towns and rural communities.

The automobile had a particularly important effect on the southern poor. Mobility liberated impoverished sharecroppers from their chains to the land. In their automobiles they found "both dignity and independence," says historian Thomas D. Clark. Rich and poor, black and white, all rode in the same kind of vehicle, which proved to be a leveling device. W. J. Cash pointed out that the mill worker as well gained status from the car.

Mobility and speed were the keys to understanding the special appeal of the automobile to a southern populace suffering geographic and social stagnation. In Flannery O'Connor's short story "The Life You Save May Be Your Own," Mr. Shiflet notes that "the body, lady, is like a house: it don't go anywhere: but the spirit, lady, is like a automobile: always on the move, always." "Sugar-Boy

Young people and the automobile, Florida, 1930s

couldn't talk," said Jack Burden while riding with Willie Stark's driver in Robert Penn Warren's *All the King's Men,* "but he could express himself when he got his foot on the accelerator." The automobile meant escape from the farm or the mill village. It was a way out of poverty. It represented an escape from the negative side of the strong southern sense of place, the static rootedness. Thanks to the car, says the hitchhiker in Warren's novel, "a man could just get up and git, if'n a notion came on him."

Some scholars argue that southerners have shaped the very character of the car culture. Landscape historian John Brinckerhoff Jackson has written that "the rest of the United States sees the highway and car culture as essentially a Southern phenomenon." He outlines the southern roots of the contemporary car culture:

Our interstate highways are extensions of the Southern landscape: truck stops as far west as Utah or Colorado provide Southern breakfasts and Southern music on the jukeboxes, Southern banter with the waitresses. Small (and I must say) uninviting roadside nightclubs advertise the music of young Southerners with names like Clyde and Jesse and Leroy and Floyd. The Southern accent is widely adopted by used car salesmen all over America.

Other scholars, however, would see some of his examples as more national than regional.

The contemporary era has seen the increasing impact of motor vehicles on southern cities, furthering suburban growth, close rural-urban ties, and interregional connections. The problems of the automobile have been recognized in the South, as in the nation. The sheer number of cars is a key concern, especially because of air pollution. Heavy traffic leads to congestion equal to the California freeways, on streets sometimes not even built for automobiles. The lack of planning and zoning has created a cluttered jungle of businesses serving the automobile and its inhabitants. Moreover, automobiles are violent killers in the South. As historian Clark has written, "They take an annual toll of life that approaches that of the old regional diseases." The poverty of the South's people has made the accident and death problems worse, because poor tires and poorly maintained cars hamper safety.

See also AGRICULTURE: Good Roads Movement; MYTHIC SOUTH: / Good Old Boys and Girls; RECREATION: Stock Car Racing; URBANIZATION: Urban Transportation

Charles Reagan Wilson
University of Mississippi

Blaine A. Brownell, *American Quarterly* (March 1972); Thomas D. Clark, *The Emerging South* (1961); Cynthia G. Dettle-bach, *In the Driver's Seat: The Automobile in American Literature and Popular Culture* (1976); William E. Geist, *New York Times* (7 June 1983); John Brinckerhoff Jackson, *The Southern Landscape Tradition in Texas* (1980); Howard L. Preston, *Automobile Age Atlanta: The Making of a Southern Metropolis, 1900–1935* (1979); Sylvia Wilkinson, in *The American South: Portrait of a Culture*, ed. Louis D. Rubin, Jr. (1980). ☆

Battlefields

||||||||||||||||||||||||||||||

Southerners honored those who fought in the Civil War, but they had a markedly different response to hallowing the fields on which nearly 1 in every 19 white southern males died. A monument erected in the county seat or state capital was an immediate and local recognition of "our heroes," a very personal expression of the community's grief and affection. Battlefields were another story. They had been all too infrequently the sites of southern victories, and for the vast majority of southerners major battlefields were remote places. The courthouse monument or local marker gave southerners the opportunity to honor the men and women of the Confederacy and their cause at home.

The earliest battlefield parks set aside—Gettysburg and Shiloh—began as adjuncts to national military cemeteries. Their supporters, like the memorial associations, wished to honor those brave men who had fallen in battle. All six of the major battle sites that became military shrines in the 19th century became so because of Union veterans' initiatives, congressional action, or both. Two of these sites, Gettysburg and Antietam, were outside the boundaries of the Confederacy. Founded on 30 April 1864, the Gettysburg Battlefield Memorial Association was the first organization of its type—North or South. The association maintained the site until 1895, when it deeded some 600 acres to the federal government. This land was the nucleus of the battlefield park that today contains more than 3,400 acres. Dotted with state and unit monuments, Gettysburg is one of the most heavily visited Civil War battlefields in the country.

While Union groups were actively working at Gettysburg, Kennesaw Mountain, and other battlefields, southerners were noticeably inactive. Historic preservation really came into its own in the South during this period, but preservation focused on buildings and, for the most part, the 18th century.

Southerners did not create battlefield shrines until after World War I. Appropriately, Manassas was one of the first sites set aside. In 1922 the Manassas Battlefield Confederate Park, Inc., and the Sons of Confederate Veterans purchased the 128-acre Henry Farm. In 1938 they deeded the land to the federal government as an "everlasting memorial to the soldiers of the Blue and Gray." Significant additions were made to the original property during the 1940s so that today both the Stone House and Dogan House are within the nearly 3,000 acres of Manassas National Battlefield Park.

The nation's military showed considerable interest in Civil War sites. In 1920 the Historic Section of the U.S. Army War College conducted a historical survey of battlefields in the United States. The War Department operated all national military cemeteries, parks, and sites until 1933 when President Franklin Roosevelt ordered them placed under the Department of the Interior.

Shiloh, Vicksburg, Antietam, Petersburg, Gettysburg, Manassas, and Chickamauga and Chattanooga are among those currently operated by the Department of the Interior as military or battlefield parks. In addition to these, important fortifications such as Fort Sumter in Charleston are national monuments.

Southern state governments have created a number of Civil War battlefield parks. Some are of peculiarly local interest, such as Rivers' Bridge (near Ehrhardt, S.C.), Natural Bridge (near Woodville, Fla.), and Poison Spring (Ark.). Others, such as Fort Morgan (Ala.), Fort Pickens (Pensacola, Fla.), and Bennett Place (Durham, N.C.), are of regional or national interest.

The creation of Rivers' Bridge State Park in South Carolina displayed the typical evolution from cemetery to battlefield park that occurred elsewhere in the South. In the spring of 1876 men of the Rivers' Bridge community gathered the remains of Confederate soldiers who had been killed during Sherman's advance into South Carolina and reinterred them at Rivers' Bridge. A monument and a pavilion were erected, and the site became the location of an annual Confederate Memorial Association observance. In 1938 the Rivers' Bridge Memorial Association was given 90 acres, which included the breastworks thrown up in a vain attempt to halt the Union advance into the state. The association, in turn, deeded the site to the state. Rivers' Bridge State Park is the *only* state park in South Carolina honoring the Confederacy.

In southern state parks history certainly takes a back seat to fishing, boating, hiking, or just about anything else. The parks are there and the Civil War themes are loudly proclaimed, but for the most part there does not seem to be a great deal of interest in preserving Civil War battle sites. There is far more interest in creating antebellum plantation parks.

A visit to some state parks will confirm this not-so-benign neglect. Fort Gaines, at the entrance to Mobile Bay, scene of one of the more important naval/land battles of the war, is in a sad state of disrepair. Those tourists bored with history can view a live alligator in a tank created out of a Spanish-American War powder magazine! The significance of the site would suggest a better fate, but at least it survives.

Given the importance of the Civil War in southern history, the relatively small number of state parks identified with Civil War battles is surprising. The colonial, frontier, and antebellum eras have far more attraction as themes than does the war itself. One obvious reason for this is that the battlefields often were the scenes of Confederate defeats. This was particularly true in the coastal areas of the lower South. No amount of promotional literature can erase the cold facts of history. It is no wonder that the initial efforts to preserve Civil War battlefields as battlefields per se came from the victors.

Walter Edgar
University of South Carolina

Charles B. Hosmer, Jr., *Presence of the Past: A History of the Preservation Movement in the United States before Williamsburg* (1965), *Preservation Comes of Age: From Williamsburg to the National Trust, 1926–1949*, 2 vols. (1981); Emory Thomas, *Travels to Hallowed Ground: A Historian's Journey to the American Civil War* (1987). ☆

Beauty, Cult of

||||||||||||||||||||||||||||||||||||||||

"**T**he modern Southern belle has, of course, long been the Pageant ideal," writes Frank Deford of the Miss America contest, "so that—even in those years when a Southerner does not win—the likely winner is still probably patterned after that type." The "fundamental Southern-belle personality" that has become the nation's beauty ideal is "vivacious, sparkle-eyed, full of fun, capable of laughing at herself, and incapable of speaking either (a) briefly, or (b) without using the hands to illustrate all points." She has poise and personality beneath the outward physical attractiveness.

Beauty pageants such as the Miss America competition suggest the influence of southern ideas in shaping national ideals of beauty. Within the specifically southern context, beauty pageants are part of a cult of beauty, with certain definite ideas on what beauty is and why it is significant to be beautiful. The South's cult of beauty reflects southern attitudes on race, social class, and especially gender and sexuality, and these attitudes have changed significantly over time.

Beauty has long been related in the South to color. English colonists in North America brought European concepts of beauty, which became a factor justifying the enslavement of black Africans. Historian Winthrop D. Jordan has noted that "the English discovery of black Africa came at a time when the accepted standard of ideal beauty was a fair complexion of rose and white. Negroes not only failed to fit this ideal but seemed the very picture of perverse negation." Judged on this standard, blacks were seen as "pronouncedly less beautiful than whites." In his age, Thomas Jefferson asked whether skin color is not "the foundation of a greater or less share of beauty in the two races?" He insisted that "the fine mixtures of red and white" were "preferable to that eternal monotony" of black skin. Jefferson's concept of beauty included "flowing hair" and an "elegant symmetry of form," both of which he attributed to whites more than to other races. "The circumstance of superior beauty," he wrote, "is thought worthy of attention in the propagation of our horses, dogs, and other domestic animals; why not in that of man?" The idea of beauty was tied in for southern whites with ideas of sexuality and morality. Southern whites used the dark skin color of slaves as an outward indicator of the immorality of blacks, attributing to them impurities, lasciviousness, and evil.

The myth of the Old South included a prominent role for the beautiful white lady. Indeed, as W. J. Cash noted in *The Mind of the South* (1941), she became identified "with the very notion of the South itself." Physical beauty was a part of the definition of southern womanhood. The 19th-century conception of woman's appearance emphasized her fragility, purity, and spirituality, rather than her physical nature. The southern lady, according to Anne Firor Scott, was to be "timid and modest, beautiful and graceful." Anne Goodwin Jones has pointed out that white women in the Old South "became not only the perfect embodiments of beauty" but also "the appropriate vehicles for the expression of beauty in language." Beauty itself, like the lovely woman who best represented that quality, "was fragile and ethereal, or sensuous and pleasurable, but it was finally irrelevant to the serious business

of life." Beauty was a culturally admired trait, but it was also a limiting one for women.

The identification of whiteness and women with beauty has survived in the 20th century. Cash wrote that the southern woman was "the South's Palladium," "the shield-bearing Athena gleaming whitely in the clouds," "the lily-pure maid of Astolat." Carl Carmer wrote in *Stars Fell on Alabama* (1934) of the University of Alabama fraternity dance that included a toast: "To Woman, lovely woman of the Southland, as pure and chaste as this sparkling water, as cold as this gleaming ice, we lift this cup, and we pledge our hearts and our lives to the protection of her virtue and chastity."

The southern ideal of the beautiful woman has evolved, though, in this century. The Scarlett O'Hara type, who is associated with the Old South, is beautiful but somewhat artificial. Sexuality is much more openly associated with beautiful women in the modern South. Victoria O'Donnell's typology of images of southern women in film points out that one dominant type is the "Sexual Woman": "She is beautiful, voluptuous, only partially clothed, and openly erotic. She is able to give sexual fulfillment, but she does so in order to impart strength to her man." Sometimes the beautiful southern woman becomes the "Rich, Spoiled Woman," who has "beauty, money, men, and friends" but is "spoiled and wild." Another film image of the modern southern woman portrays her as "earthier, gaudier" than women of the past, embodying open "carnal qualities, for she has lost her purity and chastity and is glad of it." The "Unfulfilled Sexual Woman" wants to be sexually appealing, but she is frustrated because "she has little to offer in terms of physical beauty." For all of these social types in the southern imagination, beauty remains an important ingredient of culturally determined happiness, which now includes sexual satisfaction.

Changing attitudes toward the sun have affected the southern ideal of beauty. In Western civilization white, pallid skin was traditionally a sign of upper-class status, and such makeup as face powder and rouge highlighted whiteness. With industrialization, upper-class Europeans and white Americans, including eventually southerners, developed an interest in outdoor life. The laboring class now worked indoors so the upper class sought suntans and outdoor recreation as an indicator of social-class status. "The lithe, sun-tanned, tennis-playing, outdoor woman," writes Marvin Harris, "became a respectable alternative to the cloistered, snow-and-alabaster ideal of the old regimes." Soon the middle class adopted this ideal of a physically healthy, athletic, sun-tanned woman.

This cultural change had special significance in the South, where the sun is intensely felt and "whiteness" has its most deeply rooted racial-cultural meaning. The sun has long helped determine southern social status—rednecks were laborers, and their women were said to be less beautiful because they were less pallidly white than the plantation wife. By the 1920s the South, according to historians Francis Butler Simkins and Charles Roland, had "learned to regard its very hot and very bright sun as a beneficent friend instead of as a cruel tyrant." Sunbonnets and long, tight-fitting clothes were abandoned for lighter garments, and the sun was soon regarded as a source of health. Sun bathing gradually became common,

and "the acme of Southern comeliness became blue eyes, blond hair, and brown skin."

Black attitudes toward beauty have gone through their own changes. Illustrations of Afro-Americans up to the 1880s show a predominance of natural hair and little cosmetic beautification of the face. By the turn of the 20th century, though, black males were beginning to use hot combs to straighten hair, while black women used oils and pomades. Evidence suggests that many blacks internalized white ideals of beauty. They used cosmetics to lighten the skin color and hair straighteners to "conk" the hair in attempting to approach the white ideal. This probably reached a peak during the 1940s. Beauty parlors became important institutions of the black community, and cosmetic manufacturers were among the wealthiest of black Americans.

Skin color has been a symbol of social class status *within* the black community. John Dollard noted in *Caste and Class in a Southern Town*, his 1937 study of Indianola, Miss., that "consciousness of color and accurate discrimination between shades is a well-developed caste mark in Southerntown; whites, of course, are not nearly so skilful [*sic*] in distinguishing and naming various shades." Toni Morrison's *The Bluest Eye* (1970) portrays the tragic results of a black family's self-hatred because of a "white skin" ideal of beauty. Lawrence Levine cautions, however, against overemphasizing the effect of a cultural ideal of white beauty on blacks. For many blacks a light skin did not suggest social status within the black community, but rather a corruption of the race. If some black people have admired white skin, others have viewed black skin as natural, and many cosmetics have existed not to cloak that color but to highlight it. Moreover, when color preference has been seen in black cultural expressions such as blues lyrics, it has most often been brown, rather than either black or white-yellow. Paul Oliver's study of blues lyrics, *Blues Fell This Morning: The Meaning of the Blues* (1960), found that rural folk expressed an ideal of beauty somewhat different from the urban black and white ideal of "the streamlined woman." Bluesmen admired the "big, fat woman with the meat shaking on her bone." They also celebrated certain physical features, such as teeth that "shine like pearls" as a natural and attractive contrast with dark skin.

The civil rights movement of the 1950s and 1960s surely strengthened pride in a black ideal of beauty. "Black Is Beautiful" reflected a new appreciation of dark skin specifically as well as a more general pride in black culture. Magazines such as *Beauty Trade* and *Essence* are now published by blacks outside of the South, but their ideas influence the southern beauty industry and black ideals of beauty. Black beauty pageants have become a fixture on black campuses and in black communities across the South.

The beauty pageant is the ritual event that best displays modern national and regional attitudes about beauty. Predecessors of American beauty pageants were European festivals that crowned queens. European May Day activities have included selection of beautiful women as symbols of fertility. In the colonial era this custom took root more in the South than among the Puritans. Schools for young southern white women throughout the 19th century included contests for selection of attractive, popular queens. Southern romanticism

expressed itself in antebellum tournaments, re-creating medieval pageants, and these festive occasions included queens selected for their beauty. Postbellum festivals also included selection of beauties. Mardi Gras chose its first queen in 1871, despite the protest of some moralists who objected to any public display of women. These May Day, tournament, and festival queens were upper-class figures, and these contests reinforced, as historian Lois Banner has written, "the centrality of physical beauty in women's lives and made of beauty a matter of competition and elitism and not of democratic cooperation among women."

Commercial beauty pageants appeared first in the late 19th century. P. T. Barnum sponsored a female beauty pageant in 1854, but it involved only the display of daguerreotypes of women, with observers voting on winners. Carnivals in the South, often attached to agricultural fairs, helped pave the way

Young competitor in a children's beauty pageant, Atlanta, 1986

for beauty contests displaying beautiful women in native costumes from around the world. The Atlanta International Cotton Exposition of 1895 had a beauty show on its midway, and this part of the exposition was described as "the Mecca of the show." By 1900 chambers of commerce and fraternal groups in the South sponsored carnival beauty shows at fairs, but it was still not considered appropriate for middle-class women to be on display in competitive contests. The first true competitive beauty contest was the Miss United States contest at Rehoboth Beach, Dela., in 1880, but the South's beach resorts did not follow suit generally until after the turn of the century.

The Miss America pageant began in 1921, but the judges did not select a southerner until Texan Jo-Carrol Dennison was chosen in 1942. With the Americanization of the South—and the southernization of the United States—in recent decades, southerners have become identified with love of beauty pageants. *Newsweek* magazine (17 September 1984) estimated that 750,000 beauty contests are held each year in the United States, ranging from pageants for school homecoming queens, county- and state-fair queens, and festival representatives to the Miss America contest. "The phenomenon is strongly regional," said *Newsweek.* "The 'Pageant belt' stretches from Texas (where there are men who will date only titleholders) throughout the South, overlapping the Bible belt with odd precision."

Beauty pageants in the South are part of a regional cult of beauty. Young southern white ladies have long been encouraged in the feminine arts, and aspects of beauty have been taught in female academies, charm schools, and modern modeling salons. Cosmetologists, beauticians, and hairdressers are well-known figures in small and large southern towns, where concern for "looks" is endemic. Eudora Welty reproduced the ambience and conversational sound of the southern beauty parlor in her short story "Petrified Man."

Cosmetics were slow to take root in the poor rural South of the early 20th century. Even today, some Pentecostal-Holiness groups stress an ascetic ideal of outward plainness and inner beauty. Nevertheless, most women in small southern towns and cities have long accepted national views on cosmetics. Mary Kay Ash, founder of the successful Mary Kay Cosmetics, is from Texas; a key figure in the black cosmetic industry in this century, Madame C. J. Walker, came from Louisiana. Changes in contemporary southern religion's attitude toward beauty are evinced by Tammy Faye Bakker, the television celebrity formerly on the Pentecostal-oriented show, the *PTL Club.* Bakker flaunted her makeup by using a great deal of it. She even launched her own line of cosmetics.

Beauty pageants are central to small-town, middle-class life in the South and the nation. In 1970, for example, only 8 of 50 contestants in the Miss America pageant were from the nation's 25 largest cities. Few large urban areas sponsor contests, and even statewide beauty pageants tend to take place in smaller cities and towns. James Rucker, a former executive director of the Miss Mississippi contest, notes that whereas big-city northern girls enter the contest for the scholarship money or a chance at show-business success, "in Mississippi, it's tradition for the best girls to come out for the Pageant. In Mississippi, the best girls just want to be Miss America."

Beauty contests are community events in towns and small cities. Beauty-contest winners are contemporary regional celebrities—the female equivalents of football stars. Beauty queens, whether Miss America or Miss Gum Spirits (representing the southern timber industry), make personal appearances, travel extensively, earn scholarship money, and have their photos on calendars. Meridian, Miss., rewarded Susan Akin, Miss America in 1985, with an enthusiastic hometown parade. She rode through town before a cheering crowd that included young girls who had won their own honors as Deep South Beauty Queen, Cameo Girl, Mini Queen, and Miss Cinderella Queen. This ritual event showed an intense American middle-class patriotism. The band played "This Is My Country" and "God Bless America." State representative Sonny Meredith was there to praise her, and Meridian's mayor named the day in her honor. Religion was a central feature. The pastor of the First Baptist Church gave an invocation, thanking God for "letting us live in a country where a neighborhood girl could be selected Miss America." The Baptist kindergarten students had penned portraits of the queen. A friend from childhood told the crowd that Susan Akin was "the one of us who earned immortality."

Participants in the Miss America pageant and those who have studied it believe that southerners who compete have an advantage. After Tennessee's Kellye Cash won in 1986, another contestant claimed that Cash had won because judges desired a "sweet kind of nonaggressive Southern belle." Cash revealed her regional consciousness, when she said she was "basically a con-

Florida bathing beauties, 1920s

servative Southern gal." The contestant representing Mississippi that year insisted southerners had no special advantage, except that "they just work harder." Eight of the 10 finalists, in any event, were from former Confederate states. Miss Montana, Kamala Compton, gave no evidence of knowing about John C. Calhoun's concept of the concurrent majority, which proposed presidents from the North and the South, but she suggested a variation of it. Southerners were "just a lot more prepared than us Western girls who try once for a title," she told a reporter. "I mean, they should have a Southern Miss America and a Western Miss America."

Southerners clearly devote considerable time and resources to doing well in the Miss America pageant. University of Southern Mississippi sociologists Don Smith, Jim Trent, and Gary Hansen have theorized in unpublished research reported in the Jackson, Miss., *Clarion-Ledger* (15 October 1986) that southern contestants likely do better in the national contest because of three factors: (1) pageant officials, judges, and contestants assume, based on past experience, that southerners will do well; (2) the southern states encourage beauty contestants; (3) and southern states have strong pageant systems. Twenty-five states have never won the contest, whereas Texas, Alabama, and Arkansas have won twice, and Mississippi has won four times. Texas spends on contestants' clothes more than twice as much as Vermont spends for its entire pageant. Vermont has never placed a contestant in the top 10 at Miss America, but Texas obviously values its success. From 1945 to 1970 California led the nation in scholarship prize money ($47,300) awarded to contestants. Mississippi was second ($43,000), but Mississippi's commitment was much greater, given that the state had a tenth of California's population. Four of the top seven states in awarding scholarship money up to 1970 were Arkansas, Alabama, South Carolina, and Mississippi.

The Miss America contest and beauty pageants in general earn the condemnation of many men and women. "The whole gimmick is one commercial shell game to sell the sponsors' products," said critic Robin Morgan in 1968. "Where else could one find such a perfect combination of American values? Racism, militarism, and capitalism— all packaged in one 'ideal' symbol: *a woman.*" Spokesmen for the Miss America pageant defend it, noting it is the largest provider of scholarships for women in the United States. Women themselves are, of course, actively involved as participants and, behind the scenes, as trainers and managers, but men run the Miss America contest and other beauty contests. In September 1986, for example, no women served on the 12-member commission that represented the state pageants. The Jaycees are sponsors of most local Miss America contests, and men's service clubs are involved in other beauty contests. Pageants are hobbies for many men, a time

for having fun and for theatrical displays. The head of the Miss Arkansas contest wears a hog suit and cheers for his choice each year; the state chairman in Mississippi dresses in a tuxedo made from Confederate flags. Miss America pageant director Albert Marks, Jr., notes that "watching pretty girls" is "the greatest spectator sport in America." Southerners have been unusually involved in this sport as both participants and spectators.

Charles Reagan Wilson
University of Mississippi

Lois Banner, *American Beauty* (1983); Frank Deford, *There She Is: The Life and Times of Miss America* (1971); Lisa DePaulo, *TV Guide* (6 September 1986); *Ebony* (May 1983); Marvin Harris, *Natural History* (August-September 1973); Shelby Hearon, *Texas Monthly* (October 1974); Anne Goodwyn Jones, *Tomorrow Is Another Day: The Woman Writer in the South, 1859–1936* (1981); Winthrop D. Jordan, *White over Black: American Attitudes toward the Negro, 1550–1812* (1968); Robin T. Lakoff and Raquel L. Scherr, *Face Value: The Politics of Beauty* (1984); Lawrence W. Levine, *Black Culture and Black Consciousness: Afro-American Folk Thought from Slavery to Freedom* (1977); Victoria O'Donnell, in *The South and Film*, ed. Warren French (1981); Kathrin Perutz, *Beyond the Looking Glass: America's Beauty Culture* (1970); Anne Firor Scott, *The Southern Lady: From Pedestal to Politics, 1830–1930* (1970); Francis Butler Simkins and Charles P. Roland, *A History of the South* (1972). ☆

Civil War
||||||||||||||||||||||||

The South was once a small corner of an American Indian civilization that covered two continents. Then the South was in the middle of the western fringe of the British Empire. Next the South was one section within a union of former colonies. In that union the South became a self-conscious minority section, later a collection of "conquered provinces," and still later "Uncle Sam's other province." Whether the site of "the Nation's No. 1 economic problem" or the potential recipient of Sunbelt prosperity, the South has been a peculiar region within the American nation. And southerners have defined themselves within the context of a civilization, empire, union, or nation in which they have been a minority. The single exception to this was that four-year "moment" during which the South was itself a de facto nation, the Confederate States of America.

In theory, Confederate southerners should have been able to shape their corporate identity and define themselves as a separate people. In fact, a war for their survival as people and nation severely circumscribed the inclinations and efforts of southerners to create a recognizable Confederate culture. Some historians have even contended that the Confederate South never quite became a nation and thus never developed a national life worthy of the name. To be sure, the Confederacy lived only briefly, and then only in the midst of a devastating, modern war. But within limits, the Confederate experience led (and drove) southerners into novel cultural expressions and relationships, some of which outlived the abortive southern nation.

Discovering Confederate southern culture is a challenge. Examinations of some traditional forms of cultural expression—art, music, literature, and the like—are disappointing. During the war southerners sang and listened to music that was all but identical to that of their enemies. Both northern and southern armies marched to the strains of "Dixie," and soldiers on both sides sang romantic ballads like "Lorena." Paintings, such as William D. Washington's *The Burial of Latané*, enjoyed brief fame but have since served as examples of "sentimentalism," "exaggeration," and "historical anecdote" in 19th-century art. Confederate southerners produced little in the realm of belles lettres and less of any lasting value. And the trench networks at Vicksburg, Petersburg, and elsewhere were but sad architectural expressions that fortunately did not endure in southern life. None of this should be very surprising; wartime is seldom conducive to contemplative pursuits, especially when the war is going badly. Southerners, like most people at war, preferred escape and diversion to challenge and creativity in their theater, books, and songs.

Nevertheless, Confederates did make significant contributions to southern culture; the challenge in discovering these contributions lies in knowing where to look for them. Augusta Jane Evans's *Macaria or Altars of Sacrifice*, which was the most popular novel produced in the Confederacy, was not the best example of southern literature during the war. Southerners who responded immediately and directly to wartime experience in letters, diaries, magazines, and newspapers did, however, generate a body of literature that was lively and lasting. John M. Daniel and Edward A. Pollard in the Richmond *Examiner*, to cite only one newspaper, offered vigorous (often vicious) editorials as well as vivid coverage from the South's battlefields. The family papers of the Fleets in Virginia and the Joneses in Georgia have become classics a century after their composition, as *Greenmount, a*

Virginia Plantation Family during the Civil War and *The Children of Pride: A True Story of Georgia and the Civil War.* Likewise, the diaries of Mary Chesnut and Phoebe Pember continue, with reason, to charm readers. Confederate southerners generated a "literature of immediacy," which generally surpassed the leisured efforts of southern writers in the rest of the 19th century.

The Confederate experience affected southerners in myriad ways; the creation of an informal wartime literature is only one example. "Rebel ingenuity" is another. The agricultural southern people involved in an industrial war developed a remarkable resourcefulness. Esteemed oceanographer Matthew Fontaine Maury developed "torpedoes" (mines) for the Confederate navy, and officers in the niter and mining bureau learned how to use urine in the manufacture of gunpowder. On the homefront southerners experimented with substitutes for coffee and adjusted to the scarity of imported items.

Among Confederate institutions the church proved to be the most steadfastly patriotic. Most southerners recognized the authority of some Protestant evangelical denomination, whether or not they took an active part in organized religion, and southern churches were overwhelmingly supporters of the Cause. Quakers, Universalists, and the like who did not share the enthusiasm of their fellow Protestants were few in number compared to the evangelical majority, and other southern religious minorities, Jews and Roman Catholics, actively backed the Confederacy. In the early months of the war, sermons likened southerners to God's chosen people and northerners to Philistines. Later, when southern armies seemed to be losing, the church offered an expla-

nation: God was testing and chastening the southern people; in renewed righteousness lay God's favor and victory. Churches not only preached national salvation, they sent chaplains, and countless tracts, into Confederate camps for the sake of individual souls. Revivals swept through the ranks of the Confederate armies, especially during 1864, and religion offered spiritual comfort to many in the midst of death and defeat. Southern churches, too, developed a stronger social consciousness in response to wartime. Congregations donated their bells to be recast as cannon, offered their buildings as hospitals, and organized knitting and sewing sessions to fashion items of clothing for the troops. As the Confederacy collapsed, southern churches offered the consolation that religion transcends temporal circumstance and that righteousness would ultimately prevail.

Certainly the Civil War contributed to the southern "cult of the soldier"— the conviction that the military was an ultimate expression of manhood. Even when the dirt, disease, and death of war's reality contradicted this conviction, many southerners clung to the fantasy. For families of those who died in camp and combat and for thousands of wounded men, the association of military service with manhood somehow justified the sacrifice.

That the administration of Jefferson Davis and the Confederate Congress should have authorized the participation of black southerners in the "cult of the soldier" is some index of the war's impact upon the South. In 1861 Confederate Vice President Alexander H. Stephens proclaimed slavery to be the "cornerstone" of the southern nation. By 1864 the southern government was advocating the use of black troops in the war, and Robert E. Lee went on record as welcoming black men into his armies. When the Congress finally acted to arm the slaves, the Davis Administration made sure that black soldiers would serve as free men. These efforts occurred too late to save the Cause, but their very occurrence is significant.

The idea of woman as southern belle, ornament and object, did not fare well in wartime. Women often became heads of households when men went off to fight. Confederate women also became nurses, refugees, and factory workers. The variety of experience was novel, and to the degree that it became more than an emergency irregularity in the lives of southern women, it revised roles and expectations among these women.

However much wartime influenced southern life, the most profound effect of the Civil War upon southern culture occurred only after the war was lost. It is supreme irony that southern culture since 1865 has been more the product of Lost Cause mythology than Confederate realities. The southern response to defeat, reunion, and Reconstruction inspired a myth-history that ennobled the destruction of the southern nation. The Lost Cause mythology held that the southern cause was not only undefiled by defeat but that the bloodbath of war actually sanctified the values and mores of the Old South. High priests of this message were beaten warriors. Southerners enshrined the politicians and especially those military officers who had presided over failure and defeat. The influence of the unreconstructed proved to be pervasive.

The Lost Cause inspired a romantic literature perhaps best exemplified by Margaret Mitchell's *Gone with the Wind.* If literary critics are correct, the myth helped to spawn the Southern Literary Renaissance and fueled the intellectual movement known as the Nashville Agrarians. Indeed, the Lost Cause became a civil religion south of the Potomac, and it continues in various ways and degrees to influence southern thought and action.

The Civil War offered southerners the opportunity to win their independence and mold for themselves a national, as opposed to sectional, culture. As Confederates, southerners did respond creatively to the stress of wartime. But the most significant impact of the Civil War upon southern culture lay not in its reality but in its memory. The memory may have been myth; but for many southerners the Lost Cause has been myth believed and acted upon.

See also LITERATURE: Civil War in Literature; MYTHIC SOUTH: / Lost Cause Myth

Emory Thomas
University of Georgia

Henry Putney Beers, *Guide to the Archives of the Government of the Confederate States of America* (1968); Clement Eaton, *A History of the Southern Confederacy* (1954); Shelby Foote, *The Civil War: A Narrative,* 3 vols. (1958–75); Douglas Southall Freeman, *The South to Posterity: An Introduction to the Writings of Confederate History* (1939); Clarence L. Mohr, *On the Threshold of Freedom: Masters and Slaves in Civil War Georgia* (1985); Allan Nevins, James I. Robertson, Jr., and Bell I. Wiley, eds., *Civil War Books: A Critical Bibliography* (1967); James G. Randall and David Donald, *The Civil War and Reconstruction* (2d rev. ed., 1969); Charles P. Roland, *The Confederacy* (1960); James W. Silver, *Confederate Morale and Church Propaganda* (1957); Emory Thomas, *Confederacy as a Revolutionary Experience* (1971), *The Confederate Nation, 1861–1865* (1979); Frank E. Vandiver, *Their Tattered Flags: The Epic of the Confederacy* (1970);

Bell I. Wiley, *Confederate Women* (1975), *The Plain People of the Confederacy* (1943). ☆

Colonial Heritage

||||||||||||||||||||||||||||||||||||||||||||

Judged by a conception of culture as the pursuit and patronage of arts and letters, the early South has conventionally been found wanting. No more in the North than in the South, however, did early American poets, painters, or philosophers achieve a golden age of the mind, the spirit, or the imagination. No more in Boston or Philadelphia than in Williamsburg or Charleston did drama or divinity, song, story, or scholarship rise above provincial consequence.

By another standard the planters of the southern colonies were, in fact, highly significant. On the ethnographic level—culture as the integrated lifeways of an entire people—students of the outposts south of the Delaware need not be defensive at all. The southern provinces prefigured the American way of life more clearly than even the Middle Atlantic did. From the sunrise of settlement, at Roanoke and Jamestown, southern colonists manifested the norms and values that ultimately mastered the continent.

The colonial South was quintessentially American. Colonists were settled on the Chesapeake for almost a quarter of a century before the *Arbella* eased into Massachusetts Bay, and the priority of the plantations of the South was more than merely chronological. The men who established England's first successful stronghold in the New World were engaged in such decidedly American enterprises as racial exploitation, representative self-government, and market-oriented economic endeavor for a decade and more before the Puritans dreamed of departing their mother country. The men and women who succeeded them consolidated their initiatives and fused them into a coherent course of life.

That course appalled the few who clung to conventional European categories. Would-be reformers condemned again and again the immoderate acquisitiveness that dispersed southerners over the countryside and the importunate self-interest that left them indifferent to the common good. But the criticisms fell on deaf ears. Planters set out from the first to advance their own affairs. At Roanoke they abandoned the fort for their farms. From Jamestown they fanned out along the river rather than remain in the town. And ever after, they continued heedless of calls to congregate for the sake of religion, the common defense, or civility itself.

Southerners simply would not subordinate their unruly ambition to any public concern or sense of social responsibility. In the words of the 18th-century planter Robert Beverley, "the chief design of all . . . was to fetch away the treasure . . . aiming more at sudden gain than to form a regular colony." Exactly on account of such worldly priorities, southern colonial social institutions were always unable to control southern settlers.

Virginians and Carolinians, Marylanders and Georgians alike had crossed the ocean as adventurers and evolved virtues appropriate to their situation. They esteemed independence and prized personal liberty. They resented discipline, spurned spirituality, and often indulged themselves with hedonistic abandon. They cultivated a taste for proud display. As they did, they disdained civic consciousness and forfeited social cohesion. They committed little to the community. They valued their own private pursuits above all, and they measured them primarily by criteria of material accumulation.

None of this inattention to the common good was unique to the South or in any way exceptional in a wider prospect of English outposts in the New World. If there was a peculiar institution in early America, it was not southern slavery and the extravagant avarice it embodied. It was the New England town and the anachronistic restraint of greed it attempted. If southern ways were distinctive at all, they were distinctive only in their intensity. Lust for the good life—a heedless, headlong scramble after personal gratification—was already at the center of an emerging American dream. Such lust was simply less impeded in the southern provinces.

In their pell-mell pursuit of that dream southerners developed a recognizably American readiness for slavery, refusal of deference to their designated superiors, and attachment to a rough-hewn democracy of hustlers, speculators, and salesmen. In their devotion to the subtropical monocultures that afforded them their opportunities for aggrandizement, southerners enmeshed themselves more elaborately than any other mainland Americans in market relations and market values. And in doing so, southerners immediately encountered the enduring American dilemmas of labor and laziness.

When southern pioneers and publicists extolled their region, they exalted above all the indolent ease that the land allowed. In their New World as in Adam's, "everything seemed to come up by nature." Husbandmen lived "almost void of care and free from . . . fatigues." By the bounty of a benign providence, the earth brought forth "all things in abundance, as in the first creation, without toil or labor."

In every precinct colonists were content to "sponge upon the blessings of a warm sun and a fruitful soil." Domestic stock cost them "nothing to keep or feed" because animals grazed freely in winter as well as summer, sparing settlers the drudgery of fencing and the tedium of foddering. Cattle, swine, and sheep could all be left to themselves to feed on the rich and self-renewing grasses of the new continent. Fish and fowl too presented themselves for the settlers' effortless enjoyment. Marylanders met "rich bosoms" of marine creatures in their bays, all "easily taken." Carolinians could "easily gather" more oysters in a day than they could "well eat in a year." And all the planters encountered birds "so numerous . . . that you might see millions in a flock."

Everywhere men echoed the enthusiasm of the initial English endeavor in the New World, that the land lavished its largesse upon them without their exertion. The husbandman as much as the herder and the hunter lived on the "benevolent breast" of nature. Crops that others elsewhere had to cultivate with unremitting diligence simply "thrust . . . forth" in the South "as easily as the weeds." American grains were "so grateful to the planter" that they returned him "his entrusted seed" with a treble growth; and they were "so facilely planted that one man in 48 hours may prepare as much ground and set such a quantity of corn that he may be secure from want of bread all the year following." Men managed "very easily" though unwilling to work "above two or three hours a day" or more than "three days in seven." Indeed, under such circumstances, it was difficult to distinguish work from leisure. Planting presented itself as a pastime of "pleasure," hunting as an "exercise" of "delight," and fishing as a "pretty sport" for profit, in a land in which everything grew plentifully "to supply the wants or wantonness of man."

Yet such celebration of hedonic ease was a perilous ploy. Even as it stimulated real estate sales, it stirred specters of corruption, inciting castigation of the colonists as degenerate outcasts of the Old World. The exaggeration of effortlessness that enticed also offended. The emphasis on immunity from harsh labor that enthralled also appalled. Southerners uncertain of their own civility were sensitive to suggestions that they might be overwhelmed by the wilderness and lapse into self-indulgence.

Virginians therefore feared the felicity they flaunted, that so "little labor" was "required to fill their bellies." Carolinians bemoaned the blessing they boasted, that their paradise was "apt to make people incline to sloth." And Georgians trembled that their prolific province might be "deformed by its own

Payne Limner, Alexander Spotswood Payne and His Brother, John Robert Dandridge Payne, with Their Nurse *(c. 1790–1800)*

fertility." The same settlers who proclaimed their tracts gardens of earthly delight insisted that they would not welcome people who wished to live there in a "state of idleness and dependence." They declared that men "were appointed to cultivate the earth," not to bask in its bounty.

Exactly as they careened from one extreme to the other, colonial southerners enunciated the dilemma in economic ethics that would occupy the nation ever after. Just as they gloated over their effortless indolence in one breath and gloried in their exemplary industry in the next, so they anticipated the tension between the imperative to work and the compulsion to consume that would set the shape of aspiration for centuries in America.

Suspended between those demands for exertion and those dark desires for exemption from exertion, the planters of the southern provinces were also driven to develop an incipiently American temporal horizon. Because they disdained methodical economic endeavor yet sought the splendid display that rewarded such steadiness, they could only envision attainment of their ends by sudden strokes of fortune. Because they scorned unremitting application to a calling, they could only imagine success by slipping the constraints of history itself.

The past, then, held little fascination for southerners of the 17th and 18th centuries. It provided them no notable local heroes, memorialized for them no vivifying regional myths, and engendered in them no discernible curiosity. It certainly entailed no burdens. Indeed, it was rarely invoked even to validate prevailing social arrangements or to legitimate specific institutional establishments.

Early southerners simply ceded their patrimonies. The fragility of their attachment to traditions was evident in the unraveling of the religious and familial threads that webbed men and women in the mother country. The permanence of their ties to the land on which they lived was legible in the flimsy houses in which they encamped upon the country, far into the 18th century. And the transiency of their interests was apparent in the ease with which they departed their estates and operations for others elsewhere. As George Washington noted, the great fortunes of the Tidewater were not made by a steadfast cultivation of the southern staples. They were the result of shrewd speculation in frontier lands, and they reflected the readiness of the planters to relinquish established assets for the sake of visionary futures.

Colonial New Englanders might revere ancestors and look to the past for legitimate authority. Colonial southerners were impatient of inheritance and eager for futurity. Thomas Jefferson declared their sense of time in his insistence that "the earth belongs in usufruct to the living." He articulated the logic of their lives in affirming that he liked "dreams of the future better than the history of the past." And increasingly his countrymen, north as well as south, came to concur. That early southern sensibility came to color a national culture sublimely indifferent to history and uncommonly attracted to New Freedoms, New Deals, and New Frontiers.

Ironically, as the nation came to the colonial South's sense of time, the South itself came to take history seriously. First in the declining economies of the Tidewater, then across a region ravaged by civil war, southerners created legends of cavaliers and cherished memories of gallant warriors and galling defeat. But in their initial period of settlement their experiences embodied a quite different heritage.

Michael Zuckerman
University of Pennsylvania

David Bertelson, *The Lazy South* (1967); Timothy H. Breen, *Puritans and Adventurers: Change and Persistence in Early America* (1980); Carl Bridenbaugh, *Myths and Realities: Societies of the Colonial South* (1952); Richard Beale Davis, *Intellectual Life in the Colonial South, 1585–1763* (1978); Rhys Isaac, *The Transformation of Virginia, 1740–1790* (1982); Edmund S. Morgan, *American Slavery, American Freedom: The Ordeal of Colonial Virginia* (1975); Bertram Wyatt-Brown, *Southern Honor: Ethics and Behavior in the Old South* (1982). ☆

Confederate States of America

||||||||||||||||||||||||||||||||||||||||||||||||||

After Abraham Lincoln's election in November 1860, South Carolina called a convention, which unanimously adopted the Ordinance of Secession on 20 December 1860. A Declaration of the Immediate Causes of Secession justified the action, and the convention urged other southern states to follow this lead. Six other states promptly responded in early 1861: Mississippi, 9 January; Florida, 10 January; Alabama, 11 January; Georgia, 19 January; Louisiana, 26 January; and Texas, 1 February. There was considerable opposition to secession in many of these states. Georgia, a geographically crucial state for any southern resistance, seceded 4 March. The four border states were slow and cautious in approving secession, but after the Confederate attack on Fort Sumter, S.C., in April of 1861, Virginia (17 April), Arkansas (6 May), North Carolina (20 May), and Tennessee (8 June) left the Union. The slave states of Missouri, Kentucky, and Maryland remained in the Union, and the western counties of Virginia formed a new state, West Virginia. Divided in sentiment, the people in the border South were the source of the most frequent brother-against-brother warfare. The border South had economic and patriotic ties to the North, but slavery and social customs made it a southern area, too. Missouri was the scene of bloody fighting during the war, and 30,000 in that Unionist state fought for the Confederacy.

Delegates from the seceding states met at Montgomery, Ala., 4 February 1861 to organize a provisional government for the Confederate States of America. The delegates saw themselves following in the steps of the American revolutionaries fighting for self-determination against a distant, oppressive government. The Confederate Constitution was modeled on the federal document and contained few innovations. It did recognize and guarantee slavery in all territory belonging to the new government, and it prohibited protective tariffs, appropriations for internal improvements, and the payment of bounties. It overtly asked for the "favor and guidance of Almighty God." The new constitution was officially adopted 11 March 1861. Jefferson Davis of Mississippi was chosen president of the new government, and Alexander H. Stephens became vice president. The Stars and Bars became the official flag.

In proclaiming their political independence, southern leaders seemed willing to compromise on earlier principles.

Delegates to the convention created a stronger central government than secession rhetoric seemed to support. The concept of states' rights was not explicitly affirmed in the document. Leaders of the new government were generally moderates and conservatives, not the fire-eating revolutionary secessionists. The tension between centralization and localism would be a continual headache for those leaders.

At the start of the war, a serious discrepancy existed in the resources of the two combatants. The Union had a population of 22.7 million, compared to the 9 million (including 3.5 million slaves) in the Confederate states. In addition to its growing industrial capacity and an extended rail system for transportation, the Union had an established national government, navy, and regular army of 12,000. The Union strategy was a naval blockade of the southern coast and an invasion of the region from the North and Midwest. When Lincoln issued the Emancipation Proclamation on 23 September 1862 and declared slaves under Confederate control to be free after 1 January 1863, the goals of the Union war effort became not only nationalism but also human liberty. The North thus attempted to isolate the South economically, politically, and morally.

Southerners made war with great hopes of victory. The Confederacy raised and equipped a formidable fighting force. Josiah Gorgas, the chief of ordnance for the Confederate forces, resourcefully supplied the armies with needed weapons and munitions, and the Tredegar Iron Works produced innovative weaponry in the form of torpedoes, submarines, and plates for ironclads. Southerners had the enthusiasm of fighting for a cause, for tribal defense, and what seemed like basic

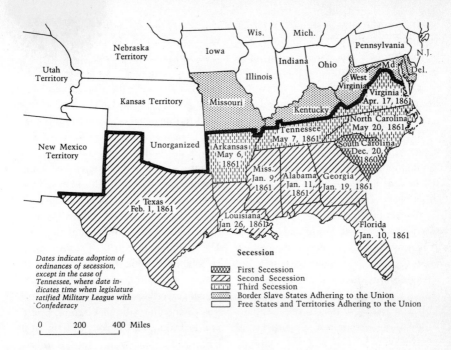

Secession

Source: Bernard Bailyn et al., **The Great Republic, 3d ed. (1985).**

human concerns—freedom, home, family, the land, and racial solidarity. They feared fundamental change in their way of life.

As the war progressed, though, divisions appeared in the social solidarity and cultural unity. Banking resources were inadequate, inflation rose, citizens refused to submit willingly to heavy taxes, and food shortages and protests about them occurred. Conscription became necessary, and desertion became a major problem for the military. Social-class conflicts appeared, as the burdens seemed to grow heavier for the humble as time went on, while some plantation families not near the fighting managed to do well and speculators clearly profited. Jefferson Davis proved to be an uninspiring leader and could not make an eloquent case for national unity. Advocates of states' rights, such as Governor Joseph E. Brown of Georgia and Zebulon B. Vance of North Carolina, hounded him, and by war's end Davis was unpopular.

Southern institutions and people in them generally rallied around the Confederacy, and they felt the disruptions of war. Churches, schools, colleges and universities, businesses, social groups, ethnic groups—all were affected by war. Colleges contributed soldiers and civilian leaders, while businesses reoriented their facilities to war work. Religion was particularly important in supporting political and military activities. Southern ministers and religious organizations supported the Confederacy and proved to be essential in maintaining morale. Leading ministers such as James Henley Thornwell and Stephen Elliot preached on the home front that the Confederacy was a holy crusade against the atheistic North, and revivals occurred periodically within the ranks of the Confederate armies. Episcopal Bishop Leonidas Polk and Baptist minister Mark P. Lowrey were only two of the many ministers who became Confederate generals.

The myth of the southern lady had appeared in the antebellum era, but the war challenged the image. Women were left to run the plantations and to raise the crops on small farms. They cared for the wounded under deplorable hospital conditions and found and shipped necessary supplies to men at the battle-front. The South's women experienced physical deprivation and the psychological trauma of the absence loved ones and grief over the dead. The Confederate experience surely provided the context for new roles and expectations for women in southern culture and perhaps represented one stage in their liberation from gender stereotyping.

War also led to the more dramatic emancipation of southern slaves from the peculiar institution. Although the Emancipation Proclamation issued in 1862 did not immediately free slaves in the Confederate-controlled areas, it was a symbolic landmark for southern blacks—the Day of Jubilee. The Thirteenth Amendment to the federal Constitution became law on 18 December 1865, providing a constitutional prohibition against slavery. Most slaves stayed on the plantations during the Civil War, but evidence of slave conspiracies and plots in Virginia, Alabama, and Arkansas has been discovered. Thousands of blacks fought for the Union against slavery. The legend of the faithful wartime slave became, nonetheless, a key part of a romanticized myth of the Old South plantation.

Despite defeat in the war, the southern military made its greatest impact on the southern imagination while fighting for the Confederacy. Confederate military leaders were the true cultural heroes of the period—Robert E. Lee was the Virginia cavalier, Thomas J. "Stonewall" Jackson the holy warrior, Jeb Stuart the gallant horseman, P. G. T. Beauregard the hot-tempered Louisiana Creole, and Nathan Bedford Forrest the Tennessee guerrilla fighter. The names of battles had a lyrical, biblical ring to them: Manassas (Bull Run) in July 1861; Shiloh in April 1862; Antietam in September 1862 (the bloodiest day of the war); and the crucial Confederate defeat at Gettysburg in July 1863. There was Chancellorsville in Virginia, where Lee lost Stonewall Jackson, victim of a bullet from one of his own soldiers; Vicksburg, where the Confederates lost the West; Chickamauga and Chattanooga, which had been the key to the Confederate heartland; the fiery battle of Atlanta; Sherman's march to the sea; and the melancholic Appomattox, where Lee surrendered his 26,000 troops and refused to approve a guerrilla war against the North.

Each battle contained its own folklore and legends, gave birth to its songs, jokes, stories, heroes. Writers, singers, painters, sculptors, storytellers, and others have attested to the Confederacy's continuing cultural appeal by producing artifacts that explore the war's memory. "For every Southern boy fourteen years old," wrote William Faulkner of the memory of the decisive Gettysburg in *Intruder in the Dust* (1948), "not once but whenever he wants it, there is the instant when it's still not yet two o'clock on that July afternoon in 1863, the brigades are in position behind the rail fence, the guns are laid and ready in the woods . . . and Pickett himself with . . . his hat in one hand . . . and his sword in the other looking up the hill waiting for Longstreet to give the word and it's all in the balance, it hasn't happened yet, it hasn't even begun yet, it not only hasn't begun yet but there is still time for it not to begin."

Charles Reagan Wilson
University of Mississippi

E. Merton Coulter, *The Confederate States of America, 1861–1865* (1950); Clifford Dowdey, *The Land They Fought For: The Story of the South as the Confederacy, 1832–1865* (1955); Clement Eaton, *A History of the Southern Confederacy* (1954); Paul Escott, *After Secession: Jefferson Davis and the Failure of Confederate Nationalism* (1978); Douglas Southall Freeman, *The South to Posterity: An Introduction to the Writing of Confederate History* (1939); Charles P. Roland, *The Confederacy* (1960); Emory Thomas, *Confederacy as a Revolutionary Experience* (1971), *The Confederate Nation, 1861–1865* (1975); Frank E. Vandiver, *Their Tattered Flags: The Epic of the Confederacy* (1970); Bell I. Wiley, *Plain People of the Confederacy* (1943), *The Road to Appomattox* (1956). ☆

Cookbooks

|||||||||||||||||||||||||||||

The first cookbooks in the South were brought from England by the early colonists. Until near the end of the 18th century cookbooks in the United States were simply manuscript collections or printed editions of English recipes. The first cookbook published in the colonies appears to have been *The Compleat Housewife; or, Accomplish'd Gentlewoman's Companion* (1742), by E. (Eliza) Smith, printed in Williamsburg. Hannah Glasse's *The Art of Cookery, Made Plain and Easy* (1747) was the most popular volume in Virginia, but others, such as *The English Huswife* (1623), by Gervase Markham, also were found throughout the South.

The Virginia House-wife (1824), by Mary Randolph, has been called by Karen Hess "the most influential American cookbook of the nineteenth century." Randolph was a member of a prominent family, and her cookbook reflected a knowledge of regional produce, cooking practices, and overall social context. In addition to showing the dominant English influence, Randolph's cookbook reflected Indian contributions to southern food, through recipes that included Native American foods such as maize, sweet potatoes, squash, beans, fruits, and nuts. An African influence came through recipes learned from servants who prepared food using such ingredients as field peas, eggplant, yams, and tomatoes (which possibly were of African background). Randolph's recipes used 40 vegetables and 17 herbs, but did not specify the extended cooking for meats and vegetables that later became a trademark of southern cooking.

The ritual of setting a good table has been a veritable religion in the South since Mary Randolph's time. Cookbooks have been guides to southern ways of eating and have reinforced the southerner's belief that the food eaten and the manner of eating it have social significance. In antebellum times the great distance between homes (especially plantations) meant that any social gathering was a real occasion. The food was the entertainment. The Civil War had a profound effect on the way southerners were able to carry out this ritual of eating. Polly Alice Masten Körner (Mrs. Jule Gilmer Körner) wrote in her memoirs as recorded in the *Körner's Folly Cookbook* of the "troublous times toward the end of the War and for some time thereafter" when her father buried things of value, including her mother's "brown flowered china and tea set to protect them from the Yankee soldiers." Emma S. Layton in *I Remember When* recalled that "during the Civil War the Yankees came through taking everything they could get." Her grandmother "hid a peck of meal in the cradle with the baby" and had one of her boys "hide a ham in a big oak tree. . . . Grandmother hid her silver in a barrel of hogfeed."

Setting a good table began with the table covering. The standard "snow-white cover, damask or home-made" reflected the character of the housewife as well as her table, according to *Mrs. Elliot's Housewife* by Sarah A. Elliot (1870). Elliot admonished her house-

Display of canned food, Greene County, Ga., 1941

wife to keep "her castors bright and well-filled."

The food available in the South prior to the modern supermarket was primarily grown "on the place." Spring or young chickens were available only in the spring; new potatoes were the first potatoes to mature; and green peas (called English peas) were fresh from the vines for only a few days each year.

Before World War II most recipes, called receipts, were not written down. They were instead carried around in the cook's head. Some of these cooks, possessed of great intuitive skill, still exist and will explain in detail the art of preparing pinto beans or stewed potatoes. What they cannot explain is the special knack they bring to any cooking enterprise, which makes such a difference in the finished product.

Often when a recipe was recorded, it was preserved simply as a list of ingredients on a piece of paper. There were no accompanying directions. It was assumed that once the cook knew the ingredients and their amounts, she could figure out the rest for herself. The following recipe by Mrs. Jed Giddings of Maryland was contributed to S. R. Rhodes's *The Economy Administration Cook Book* (1913):

TWO POUND CAKE BY MEASURE

The whites of twenty-four eggs, seven teacups of flour, four and one-half teacups of granulated sugar, two teacups of butter, one of sweet milk, a heaping teaspoon of cream of tartar. Have the pan warm and bake as quickly as possible.

When bound cookbooks started to appear in great numbers, they were put out by people like Henrietta Stanley Dull. She edited the weekly food page in the Atlanta *Journal*, which appeared under the slogan "It covers Dixie like the dew." Dull's name was a household word when her book *Southern Cooking* was published in 1928.

Another popular compilation of recipes in booklet form was by Sara Spano, food editor in Columbus, Ga. Her recipe for deep chocolate cake called for eight plain 5-cent chocolate bars and two 10-cent cans of chocolate—an indication of staple grocery prices in the 1920s and 1930s.

An early example of the many popular cookbooks put out by food companies is *The Rumford Complete Cookbook* by Lily Haxworth Wallace, published in 1934. Cookbooks published by churches, clubs, schools, and Junior Leagues also began to appear, bearing a wealth of excellent recipes. One of the most successful of these was *River Road Recipes* published by the Junior League of Baton Rouge, La. Its first printing was in 1959. By the 25th printing in 1971 at least 310,000 copies were in circulation.

Afro-American cooking styles and recipes are rooted in the South, and they are preserved in Sue Bailey Thurman, *Historical Cookbook of the American Negro* (1958), Jim Harwood and Ed Callahan, *Soul Food Cookbook* (1969), and Bob Jeffries, *Soul Food Cookbook* (1970). Norma Jean and Carole Darden assembled *Spoonbread and Strawberry Wine* (1978) through visiting relatives in Alabama, North Carolina, Virginia, and Ohio. Included are recipes for sweet potato biscuits, Cousin Johnnie K's macaroni and shrimp salad, Aunt Marjorie Palmer's every-kind-of-cookie-dough, and syllabub (a drink made from cream, sugar, nutmeg, and rum or brandy). Ernest M. Mickler's *White Trash Cooking* (1986) offers recipes from the southern rural poor. Like many recent cookbooks, *White Trash Cooking* contains numerous anecdotes and stories as well as 240 recipes stressing the use of salt meat, corn meal, and molasses.

Chef Paul Prudhomme's *Louisiana Kitchen* (1984) helped usher in a national fad for a southern subregional type of cooking. Another volume, Marjorie Kinnan Rawlings's *Cross Creek Cookery* (1942), assembled recipes from rural north-central Florida. Eudora Welty wrote the introduction to the Jackson Symphony League's *Jackson Cookbook* (1971), which includes a recipe for squash Eudora. The recipes of other southern writers appear in Dean Faulkner Wells's *Great American Writers' Cookbook*, published by Mississippi's Yoknapatawpha Press in 1981. It includes Harry Crews's snake steak, Roy Blount, Jr.'s garlic grits (and an "ode to grits"), and Willie Morris's John Birch Society beans (which cause a violent internal reaction).

Of course, southern cookbooks have their idiosyncracies. In 1969, when Albert Brewer was governor of Alabama, his wife, Martha Farmer Brewer, helped produce the *Alabama First Lady's Cookbook* as part of the celebration of the 150th birthday of the state. The book offered 41 recipes for preparing chicken, but not one for preparing fried chicken. The assumption was that everyone already knew how to fry chicken.

Among many things, the 1960s brought popular cooking programs on television, hundreds of new cookbooks, and a magazine named *Southern Living* based in Birmingham, Ala. A 23 November 1981 *Wall Street Journal* article described the magazine's formula for success as simply giving the readers what they wanted to read. The article mentioned a recipe for a nutmeg feather cake, which had appeared in an issue of the magazine, and predicted that "it would be safe to wager that nutmeg feather cakes will shortly appear on tables from Biloxi to Kannapolis."

In 1970 a cookbook named *Our Best Recipes* was published by *Southern Living*—the beginning of a series of cookbooks that is still tremendously popular. Their annual cookbook sells in excess of one and one-half million copies. In February 1985 Ann H. Harvey, managing editor of Oxmoor House, *Southern Living*'s book division, said that the division has approximately 35 titles. It began publishing an Antique American Cookbooks series in the 1980s, including historic southern volumes.

The library at the University of North Carolina in Greensboro, N.C., has an extensive collection of southern cookbooks. James H. Thompson, director of the library, describes it as one of the "strongest collections in the state and the South." Southern cookbooks reinforce a regional appreciation for tradition and encourage southerners to continue to enjoy the old favorites. People may not live by squash casseroles alone, but a southern cookbook without a recipe for at least one is rare.

Beth Tartan
Kernersville, North Carolina

Alabama First Lady's Cook Book (1969); John Egerton, *Southern Food: At Home, on the Road, in History* (1987); Sarah A. Elliott, *Mrs. Elliott's Housewife* (1870); Margaret Husted, *Virginia Calvacade* (Autumn 1980); Mary Randolph, *The Virginia House-wife* (1984 facsimile of 1824); Blanche S. Rhett, *Two Hundred Years of Charleston Cooking* (1984); Sarah Rutledge, *The Carolinian Housewife* (1984 facsimile of 1847); Lena E. Sturges, *Southern Living: Our Best Recipes* (1970); Beth Tartan, *Körner's Folly Cook-*book (1977); Hazel Valentine, ed., *I Remember When* (1978); Lily Haxworth Wallace, *The Rumford Complete Cook Book* (1908); Eugene Walter, *American Cooking, Southern Style* (1971). ☆

Debutantes
||||||||||||||||||||||||||||

The social institution known as the debutante season is certainly not a peculiarly southern (nor even American) phenomenon, but in the face of the turbulent 1960s and 1970s, it has exhibited more tenacity and vitality in Dixie than elsewhere in the United States or in Great Britain, where the custom began. A number of factors help explain the custom's popularity: the South's pride in its womanhood, a tendency to keep women on a pedestal, a conservative clinging to venerable institutions, social distinctions by status, and belief in a cavalier heritage.

Although many societies, both primitive and advanced, have had their own rituals to signal the coming of age of men and women, England's Queen Elizabeth I supposedly began the custom of formal presentations of eligible young women at court. However, nearly three centuries later, Great Britain's young Queen Victoria, shortly after she married Prince Albert, gave the ritual much of its present form, when the daughters of the rising *haute bourgeoisie* of the Industrial Revolution began to be included in court presentations, along with those of nobility and gentry. A century later, yet another British queen, Elizabeth II, ended such events after the last presentations in March of 1958.

The custom of debutante presentations spread across the Atlantic when America began to prosper during the late 19th-century Gilded Age. In New York, according to social historian Cleveland Amory, public presentations began in 1870 at Delmonico's. Dixon Wecter wrote 50 years ago how the costly rituals of debutante presentations symbolized the wealth of fathers. On the other hand, in the impoverished postwar South the custom displayed another dimension—emphasizing who had been well born before all was "gone with the wind." The criterion was necessarily not that of wealth but of the family's antebellum status and lineage.

At the turn of the 20th century the most exclusive of the southern debutante seasons was held in Charleston. The St. Cecilia Society began in 1737 as America's first concert society but abandoned that function by 1822 and became a purely social organization. This elite all-male society began to sponsor what has been termed "the ultimate debutante presentation in the South, if not the whole United States." It is so proper and exclusive that any local publicity about either the society or its ball is taboo.

In Montgomery, Ala., Lila Matthews was presented to society with a dance and collation at her parents' house in 1884. The 1900 *Social Directory of Montgomery, Alabama* listed 33 debutantes, and the Montgomery Debutante Club began in the depths of the Depression in 1931. Today, young women of Montgomery society are presented at junior, senior, and debutante assemblies and at mystic society balls. Most notable of these are the New Year's Eve Ball given by the men of the Mystic Order of Revelry, the Mardi Gras Ball of the male Krewe of the Phantom Host and the ball of the female Mystic Order

of Minerva, where debutantes are presented in pastel Victorian court dress with plumes, trains, 18-button gloves, and fan bouquets. There are also presentations of military officers' daughters at Maxwell Air Force Base, and since 1970 Montgomery's black debutantes have been sponsored by the local chapter of the national black teachers' sorority of Phi Delta Kappa, founded in 1923.

In Mobile, where mystic societies in America began, the season's leading debutante is queen of Mardi Gras, and she and King Felix III salute merrymakers from the Athelstan Club. Each season's debutantes are presented first at the Camellia Ball at Thanksgiving time. In New Orleans, which is synonymous with Mardi Gras, debutantes reign over the predominantly all-male Krewe festivities and are presented at the Debutante Club and Les Débuts des Jeunes Filles de la Nouvelle Orléans and many private debut parties.

Space permits only a limited listing of the debutante balls in other southern cities. Moving down the Atlantic Seaboard, Baltimore has its Bachelors' Cotillion; Washington, D.C., has its Debutante Cotillion and Thanksgiving Ball; Richmond has the Bal du Bois in June at the Country Club of Virginia; and the all-male Norfolk German Society selects those who will come out in that city. Raleigh's Terpsichorean Club stages the North Carolina Debutante Cotillion, Savannah features the Cotillion and Parents' Debutante Ball, Atlanta has its Halloween Ball at the Piedmont Driving Club, and Jacksonville has its Presentation Ball at the Florida Yacht Club.

In Birmingham the Redstone Club Christmas Ball is at the Birmingham Country Club and the Beaux Arts Ball at the Mountain Brook Club. The Mississippi Debutante Ball is in Jackson, while the Delta Debutante Ball is at the Greenville Country Club. In Memphis the Queen of Cotton Carnival reigns, and there is the ball at the Hunt and Polo Club. West of the Mississippi River at Texarkana there is the Cotillion Club Ball, at San Antonio the German Club Ball, and at Austin the Bachelors Cotillion. Dallas has its Idlewild Ball, where debutantes bow to the floor in all white at the beginning of the season and make their final bow at the Terpsichorean Ball in pastels.

See also RECREATION: Mardi Gras; / St. Cecilia Ball

Cameron Freeman Napier
Montgomery, Alabama

D. Susan Barron, *Sunday New York Times Magazine* (15 January 1984); Stephen Birmingham, *The Right People: A Portrait of the American Social Establishment* (1968); Lisa Birnbach, ed., *The Official Preppy Handbook* (1980); Bethany Bultman, *Town and Country* (November 1977); *Montgomery Advertiser* (6 February 1884, 4 November 1931, 15 April 1984); Mary Ann Neeley, *Alabama Review* (April 1979); *New York Times* (19 March 1958, 21 March 1958); Dixon Wecter, *The Saga of American Society: A Record of Social Aspiration, 1607–1937* (1937). ☆

Fashion

||||||||||||||||||||||

Fashion in the South, as in the rest of the nation, serves a variety of functions. People pursue fashion because they seek meaning in their existence or a sense of personal identity. They may use fashion to enhance their social status or to demonstrate their affluence. Fashion also expresses the nature of society— its ideas, values, and roles. In a rapidly changing society, fashion is a form of control, offering people a particular direction out of the myriad possibilities. Fashion can also be used by people to facilitate change, as when women adopt a style that clearly rejects a traditional female role.

During much of the 18th and 19th centuries, fashion both reflected and helped maintain the white southern way of life with its dominant planter class and its dependence upon England. The lavish, extravagant fashions of the upper class, in contrast to the homespun apparel of slaves and the white lower classes, reinforced the stratification of society. Inventories of clothing from the period reveal costly wardrobes of silk, satins, and laces for both males and females. Clothing and materials were imported from England and followed the latest London fashions. Most of the fashions, particularly those of women, were impractical, nonfunctional, and mainly decorative—the ideal apparel of an upper class that wanted to display its wealth and secure its status. For example, the 18th century hoopskirts of upper-class women reached as much as six feet in diameter. They were both inconvenient and costly, requiring yards of material. Shoes, available in bright colors and rich materials, were also useless for work or exercise. Perhaps the greatest impracticality and frivolousness was the fashion in hairstyles. The tower or commode arrangement had the hair piled high in rigid curls and puffs on a wire frame. The whole was intertwined with various ornaments. The elaborate hairstyles required a professional hairdresser and consumed extensive amounts of time. Consequently, arrangements were often made to last for weeks or even months, an unsanitary condition to say the least.

In the antebellum years fashion became an even greater factor in maintaining southern society. In response to rapid change, fragmentation, and challenge, the white South clung tenaciously to what it saw as the essence of its society—the planter's cavalier tradition with its emphasis on aristocracy, stability, gentility, and honor. Women played a central role in this tradition. The southern woman, viewed as inferior by nature and thus subject to the domination of her husband, was nonetheless idealized as the possessor of higher morals and purity. As she kept her place and her purity, she played an important stabilizing force in a threatened society. And her fashions provided guidelines for what was acceptable behavior. The restricted functions and ornamental nature of upper-class women were accentuated: waistlines became smaller as corsets became tighter, petticoats became heavier, and skirts became longer and more cumbersome. Indeed, the symbol of the cavalier tradition and southern chivalry was the pure, white female with her ever-present parasol to protect her pale complexion from the hot sun.

The decades following the Civil War witnessed a growing democratization in southern fashion. The hardships of war, to be sure, contributed to this. One traveler noted the decline in fashions and said that South Carolina was an excellent place to live for one forced to wear old clothes. The war also militated against the presumed uniqueness of the southern way of life and with it the system of rigid stratification. The realities of war, the impact of industrialization, the increased availability of ready-mades, sewing machines, inexpensive patterns, and dry goods, all combined to eradicate the sharp class distinctions in fashion.

In the final decades of the 19th century and increasingly throughout the 20th century, the South has experienced trends in fashion that have characterized the entire nation. Hemlines have risen and fallen; waistlines have shifted, disappeared, and reappeared; areas of focus in women's fashions have moved from head to bosom to leg and back again; the model type has moved from the "Gibson girl" to the "flapper" to the "New Look" and, ultimately, the "American Look." The American Look is characterized by egalitarianism, freedom, comfort, casualness, and action. These varied fashion trends have reflected and facilitated change toward an increasingly homogenized national lifestyle.

Although the American Look reigns supreme, local and sectional variations still exist. In part, variations are a practical response to differences in climate (differences that central heating and air-conditioning have minimized though not eliminated). The clothing needs, and hence the fashion choices, of a Georgia farmer's wife are very different from those of a female lawyer in Atlanta. But a good part of the variation arises from the more conservative traditions of the South.

Southern blacks have their own fashion traditions, based in a visual style emphasizing bright colors and sometimes bold designs. Although often poor, black people tried to dress well for Sunday church services and for special occasions. Urban clothing stores such as Lansky's in Memphis catered to distinctive black fashion tastes. Zoot suits in the 1940s and dashikis in the 1960s did not originate in the South, but many southern blacks adapted the styles. Black southern women helped make such African-derived ceremonial items as capes, turbans, caftans, and even braided hair into modern fashion wear.

The 19th-century view of woman and her role lingers on. Consequently, many of the more radical fashion changes, which seem to threaten the virtue and place of women, have met with resistance. Religious leaders, newspaper editors, and public officials have openly denounced radical fashions, whether the slit skirt of 1913 or the miniskirt of the 1960s. Fashions of this sort have been more slowly, and sometimes less widely, adopted in the South. The conservative tradition means that styles that are perfectly acceptable in most other parts of the nation may not be acceptable in areas of the South. For example, in some small-town and rural areas neither the local minister nor his wife may appear publicly in shorts with impunity. Nevertheless, with the exception of some women's fashions, and with due consideration for climatic differences and local moral codes, department stores in the South, especially the urban South, offer customers the same styles available in stores throughout the rest of the nation. Fashion serves the same functions for southerners as for the rest of Americans. For that reason, southerners are as fashion conscious as other Americans, though they are more cautious and a bit more discriminating.

See also FOLKLIFE: Clothing

> Jeanette C. Lauer
> Robert H. Lauer
> U.S. International University
> San Diego, California

Michael Batterberry and Ariane Batterberry, *Mirror, Mirror, A Social History of Fashion: 1900 to the Present* (1977); Ernestine Carter, *The Changing World of Fashion* (1977); Clement Eaton, *The Growth of Southern Civilization, 1790–1860* (1961); Prudence Glynn, *In Fashion: Dress in the Twentieth Century* (1978); Jeanette C. Lauer and Robert H. Lauer, *Fashion Power: The Meaning of Fashion in American Society* (1981); Naomi Sims, *All about Health and Beauty for the Black Woman* (1976); Julia Cherry Spruill, *Women's Life and Work in the Southern Colonies* (1938). ☆

Foodways
||||||||||||||||||||||||||||

The first white men to come into the South ate what the American Indians ate. From the southern Indians the Europeans had much to learn about cultivated plants, wild fruits and nuts, the animals of the forest, and the fish in ocean, rivers, and lakes. They had to learn these lessons to survive and later push their way westward.

The Indian diet included much game, and Indians near the coast ate large quantities of fish and shellfish. In their fields they grew corn, beans, squash, and other vegetables. They harvested wild plums, hickory nuts, chestnuts, blackberries, and other forest foods. Indians elsewhere on the continent domesticated the turkey and had developed the potato, tomatoes, eggplant, all peppers except black pepper, probably sweet potatoes, and possibly cowpeas. Both the Indians and the European settlers drew from other cultures, too. Originating in Brazil, the peanut was carried to Africa and later, bearing the African name "goober," was brought to Virginia aboard the slave ships.

As settlers reached the frontier, they planted corn and other food plants as soon as possible but relied at first on game or fish, although fish played a large role only along the coasts of the Atlantic and the Gulf of Mexico. The pioneer in the interior was happy to have a catfish, especially a large one, but he trusted his rifle more than his rod, net, or fish trap.

Buffalo provided the best meat, but they were quickly exterminated east of the Mississippi River. The pioneer also relished the meat of the black bear; he even salted it and cured it like pork. If killed in the autumn, the bear provided fat for shortening or other uses. Some southerners ate bear more or less regularly throughout the 19th century, but in most areas the animal disappeared as settlers multiplied. That left as big game the white-tailed deer, and venison was a frequent dish on southern tables until, and in some areas long after, the Civil War. Wild turkey were astonishingly abundant and unbelievably unwary in the pioneer South, and they played a large role in the pioneer diet. So did smaller game, especially rabbits, squirrels, raccoons, and opossums.

One should not think of the pioneer as baking a bear ham, roasting an opossum, or turning a haunch of venison on a spit. As often as not the southern frontiersman had only one cooking pot, and whatever was available went into that pot to mix with the previous day's leftovers.

The Indians lived in a feast-or-famine condition much of the year, and when food was abundant, they stuffed themselves. In the England that the earliest settlers called home, a host took as much pride in the quantity of the food he served his guests as in its quality. This background, combined with the abundance of food in the South as compared to the diets of German, English, Scotch, or Scotch-Irish peasants in the Old World, carried the concept of "big eating" over to the southern frontier and from the frontier forward to the Old South and eventually to the modern South.

As soon as he could, the pioneer farmer planted corn and established a herd of swine. Thus, the primary items in the diet of most southerners when the frontier had passed were corn bread and pork. Wild hogs were already in the forests, and those that the settlers brought with them were little tamer than their wild kinsmen. High in the shoulder, low in the rear, thin, with a long head and snout, and very swift of foot, they were often killed in the woods. More often, however, the owner carried out a "roundup" each fall, castrated excess boars, marked the ears of pigs born since the last roundup, and took those destined for killing home to be fattened on corn. Gradually, better-quality boars were brought in, and the quality of southern swine improved.

Hog killing usually took place during the first spell of cold weather that seemed likely to last for several days. Chitterlings (small intestines), livers, knuckles (ankles), brains, and other edible parts that could not be preserved had to be eaten quickly, and an orgy of pork eating followed hog-killing day. During those hectic days the fat was boiled in a large pot and rendered into lard. Cracklings, the crisp remnant of this process, were delicious baked into a pone of corn bread, called cracklin' bread. Scraps of leaner meat were pounded or ground into sausage.

Hams, shoulders, jowls, and sides of bacon could be cured to last indefinitely. After being trimmed, these pieces were buried in salt for four to six weeks. Then in the smokehouse they were smoked, preferably with smoke from hickory wood. Farmers differed as to the use of sugar, spices, and the like to flavor hams and shoulders, but almost all rubbed red pepper into exposed areas to prevent contamination by skipper flies, whose larvae would burrow through the meat.

So long as he had pork, the southerner ate it every day and at nearly every meal. Fried ham, shoulder, bacon, or sausage was almost an essential part of breakfast. The main meal, in the middle of the day, usually included pork, and unless it was Sunday or some special occasion, fried pork. Vegetables were normally either fried or, most often, boiled with a piece of fat-cured pork. A dish of green beans, for example, was not good unless it had enough grease in it to "wink back" when one lifted the lid and looked at it. This is the way vegetables were cooked in most southern households well into this century.

Southerners did eat meat other than fish, game, and pork from time to time. Once the frontier stage had passed and predatory animals had begun to follow the Indians into oblivion, it was possible to raise poultry; and chicken, duck, goose, and turkey became fare for Sundays and holidays. Fried chicken became the delicacy that it has remained ever since, and hen eggs and, occasionally, duck eggs became table items. Southerners sometimes ate beef, but it appeared on the table far more often in Texas and on the prairies of Louisiana than elsewhere in the South. Technically, what southerners ate was not really beef but veal, or "baby beef." Animals that had reached maturity were too tough for chewing.

Milk cows, on the other hand, were prized possessions. Compared to the dairy cows of today, they were inferior creatures that produced little milk, an important food for the antebellum southern family as well as for families in later eras. In general, mutton was not a favorite southern meat, but Virginians seem to have been fond of it, and it was certainly not unknown in Tennessee, Kentucky, and Louisiana.

Corn bread was the primary bread of nearly all antebellum southerners. Most southern mills ground corn well but could not handle glutinous wheat, though there were flour mills in the Upper South. Moreover, rust reduced the yield of wheat in most of the South. The more prosperous did eat yeast bread; beaten biscuits were a common item on plantation tables, but this was not true of the ordinary farmer's or townsman's table.

Corn bread took many forms, from the elementary hoecake baked on a hoe blade or board in front of the fireplace to various sophisticated mixtures of cornmeal with milk, buttermilk, eggs, shortening, and even sometimes flour or sugar. Cracklin' bread has already been noted. Hushpuppies were balls of corn bread and additives, such as onion, fried in the grease where fish were, or had been, frying. Corn bread did not keep well, and this led to the expectation of hot bread with meals, a fact that delayed and infuriated many a Yankee or foreign traveler.

Corn itself was an important vegetable, and for breakfast or supper many a living southerner has eaten cornmeal mush, which in modern parlance is a cereal. Green corn, "roasting ears," could be roasted in the shuck, boiled as corn on the cob, or sliced off the ear and cooked in various ways. Ripe corn, treated with lye obtained from an ash hopper, became hominy; and hominy, dried and broken into small bits, became hominy grits. Hominy grits, next to corn bread, was the most nearly universal southern food. It was, and still is, delightfully good served with butter or gravy—or even solidified, sliced, and fried.

In one or another part of the South almost all vegetables eaten anywhere else were served. Southerners were especially fond of green beans, butter beans (a variety of lima bean), okra, eggplant, red beans, and white or navy beans. Carrots, parsnips, squash, cabbage, and even green peas (usually called English peas) were eaten, but with less enthusiasm. Southerners enjoyed Irish potatoes, but they could not be kept over the winter for seed, and the necessity for imported seed limited their popularity.

The great triumvirate of southern vegetables was made up of turnips, cowpeas, and sweet potatoes, and it would be difficult to say that one was more important than the others. Turnips were often planted in an open space near a pioneer's house site before he had built the house, because they could be planted in late summer and would produce turnips and greens before a freeze ruined them. The greens were more valued than the turnips themselves, and in the spring they met the residents' almost desperate need for a green vegetable.

Cowpeas were of many varieties. Today, black-eyed peas, crowder peas, and "blue hulled peas" are almost the only variations known, but many others have flourished, including whippoorwills, britches and jackets, cuckold's increase, and tiny lady peas. Better green but good dry, peas were boiled with a piece of fat salt pork. With corn bread they provided enough calories and enough protein to sustain a hard day's work, and that was what the southern

farmer needed. The liquid in which any vegetable had been cooked—the "pot liquor"—could be eaten with corn bread, but the pot liquor of cowpeas was especially delicious. Local custom and preference determined whether the corn bread was dunked or crumbled.

It would be difficult to exaggerate the role of the sweet potato. From the harvest in late summer until as long as they lasted into the winter, sweet potatoes were a major item in the antebellum southern diet. Like the turnip, they could be preserved in a "hill" of earth and decaying vegetable matter, but some farmers had a "potato house," partly or wholly underground, in which the potatoes were stored for protection. Sweet potatoes could be boiled, baked, candied, fried, or made into pudding or pie. Most often they were baked in the coals of the fireplace, and a hot sweet potato with butter was an especially delectable dish.

On the great plantations the food in the mansion's dining room was far more elaborate and abundant than in the house of the ordinary southerner. Travelers and Yankee tutors have left accounts of gargantuan meals. Turtle, venison, ham, turkey, and chicken might grace the same meal, with fruits and vegetables in equal abundance. These plantation meals were often accompanied by good wines, whereas in the farmhouse or the townsman's home, milk, coffee, or whiskey was more likely to serve as the drink. Indeed, once the Scotch-Irish had learned to make whiskey from corn, tremendous quantities of that beverage were drunk on the frontier and in the antebellum South.

The food of the slaves, though sufficient, was as modest as the food of the great planter was abundant. In most of the South the basic slave ration was two to three pounds of cured pork and a peck of cornmeal a week per adult. In coastal areas fish might be substituted for pork much of the time, and in southwest Louisiana and Texas slaves got much beef, but these were exceptions. The basic ration was supplemented by vegetables in season, and especially by turnip greens, cowpeas, and sweet potatoes. On large plantations the slaves' meals might be prepared in a common kitchen, but in most instances they were cooked in the cabin. This meant primarily in a pot in the fireplace, and southern blacks became accustomed to boiled foods; until recently, and probably to this day, black people of the South tend to eat more boiled foods than do southern whites.

The Civil War left the South impoverished, and the lowest economic classes of society bore the hardest burden. The vast majority of former slaves became sharecroppers, and they were soon joined by millions of southern whites. Sharecroppers got their food and other necessities from a plantation commissary or from a general store. It was still cornmeal and pork, but the cornmeal now came from the corn belt, and in the milling much of the nutrition had been removed. The pork was no longer homegrown and killed on the plantation; it too came from the Middle West, but rather than bacon it was fatback, the layer of meat between the skin and the ribs, containing little protein. The basic diet of corn bread and fatback was not supplemented by fruits and vegetables nearly to the extent of antebellum days. Diseases associated with malnutrition, especially pellagra, which had seldom been observed before the Civil War, began to take a heavy annual toll. Nor was malnutrition confined to sharecroppers; cotton-mill workers, poor

townsmen, and the slum dwellers of the developing southern cities also suffered.

Some of the poorer yeoman farmers who managed to hold on to their land were malnourished also. In general, however, they ate pork that they had raised and killed themselves, and they took their own corn to the mill. They may have had to buy fatback from the general store part of the year, but most had milk from a scrub cow or two. Also, they planted a vegetable garden, and the old triad of turnips, cowpeas, and sweet potatoes helped them survive. Yeoman farmers were much more likely than tenants to have a fruit orchard.

Two very significant changes, one in food itself and the other in preparing food, took place during the later 19th century. As the result of increased wheat production and new milling methods, the great flour mills of the Middle West brought the price of flour down so low that even relatively poor southerners could afford it. Even the comparatively prosperous farmer or townsman had seldom eaten wheat bread before the Civil War, but by 1900 wheat-flour biscuits had become as common as corn bread. People ate huge quantities of biscuits. Many farmers bought one or more barrels of flour before the winter almost isolated them

Dinner after the corn shucking, Granville County, North Carolina, 1939

from the store. The smallest amount available for sale was twenty-four pounds in a cloth sack.

Food patterns formed on the southern frontier persisted well into the 20th century, until after World War II in many small-town and rural areas. Canned goods, commercial bread, and the refrigerator joined the cook stove and cheap flour in making a difference, albeit a small one. However, urbanization, the dislocation and travel brought on by two world wars, the ease of travel in the age of automobiles and interstate highways, and the homogenizing effect of radio and television eventually brought major changes in southern eating habits.

Probably the most basic change was the growth in "eating out," a trend spurred by the availability of reasonably good restaurants in the cities (superb ones in some cities) and, especially, by the advent of so-called fast foods. The hamburger emporium, the fried-catfish stand, and the fried-chicken establishment provide meals for a tremendous number of southerners every day. It is noteworthy that two of these foods, chicken and catfish, have been a part of the southern diet for two hundred years. Furthermore, they are still fried!

See also AGRICULTURE: Garden Patch; Livestock; Poultry; ENVIRONMENT: Plant Life; Plant Uses; / Catfish; Collards; ETHNIC LIFE: Indian Cultural Contributions; FOLK- LIFE: / Gumbo; Okra; GEOGRAPHY: Foodways, Geography of; MYTHIC SOUTH: / Watermelon; RECREATION: Fishing; Hunting

Joe Gray Taylor
McNeese State University

John Egerton, *Southern Food: At Home, on the Road, in History* (1987); Sam B. Hilliard,

Hog Meat and Hoecake: Food Supply in the Old South (1972); "Our Food, Our Common Ground," *Southern Exposure* (November-December 1983); Stephen A. Smith, in *American Material Culture*, ed. Edith Mayo (1985); Joe Gray Taylor, *Eating, Drinking, and Visiting in the South: An Informal History* (1982); Gertrude I. Thomas, *Foods of Our Forefathers* (1941); Rupert P. Vance, *Human Geography of the South: A Study of Regional Resources and Human Adequacy* (1935); Eugene Walter, *American Cooking, Southern Style* (1971). ☆

Foreign Policy

The southern experience in world affairs reflects variations on a set of ideas common to much of the American experience, indeed of Western civilization. At certain points in the 20th century, southerners have exhibited an intense belief in internationalism: belief in multilateral organizations, especially for European matters and Anglo-American cooperation. On several occasions since the Civil War, southerners also have shown signs of isolationism: a "nonentangling" outlook usually aimed at Europe and Britain but sometimes at Latin America, Africa, or the Pacific. Finally, a strong strain of expansionism persisted through much of the South's antebellum as well as postbellum experience. This belief in the justice of southerners' increasing their influence over foreign places has often appeared in conjunction with territorial growth and colonialism but, in other instances, it has surfaced in a nonterritorial form—expansion for trade and investment as well as for religious reasons. A review of the major episodes of the South's history in world affairs reveals internationalism, isolationism, and expansionism at work in particularly southern ways and places the South's experience in world affairs within the broader context of ideals and self-interest in American history.

Like most American viewpoints, southern ideas about the world began with the activism and assertiveness spawned by the Renaissance, Reformation, and Enlightenment. With these movements Western people increasingly perceived the improvement of their condition on earth as a matter of religious mandate. This concept of progress is a well-established part of New England's history, but the people of the southern colonies had much the same cultural background and reflected a similar optimism and fervor. Abundant natural resources, removal from the "decadent" Old World, a Puritan zeal even in the predominant Anglican churches, a liberal belief that "property" was a matter of "right" and the key to "individual freedom"—here were cornerstones of a powerful sense of Manifest Destiny and progressive idealism in the developing culture of the colonial South. Southern colonials also were subject to less idealistic forces. An unending frontier and brutal Indian fighting, plus more fighting and diplomatic intrigue against Spanish and French colonials, were all part of the unavoidable realities of living in a Western society and competing for empire in the new world. Because of these experiences, Anglos in the southern colonies developed a high tolerance for violence (though they rarely enjoyed, much less excelled at, soldiering) and became effective users of economic and political self-interest. By the end of the colonial era, two key ingredients of the South's

future foreign policy outlook had begun to surface: a faith in its mission (idealism) and a pursuit of realpolitick (materialism and self-interest).

During the American Revolution and the early national period, most views articulated in the South reflected these two strains of expansionism in equal, balanced proportions. A powerful array of southern expansionists—George Washington, Thomas Jefferson, James Madison, James Monroe, and Henry Clay—helped guide the nation through the first and second wars with Britain and onto a course of continental and foreign expansionism seen in the acquisition of Louisiana, Florida, and Missouri and also in the development of the Monroe Doctrine. The vast majority of southerners thrived in the mainstream of Jeffersonian expansionism. Sensitive to what soon would jell as "the Southern interests," that is, slavery and export economics, a subsidiary group of southern congressmen dissented, however, from the goal of a neighborly reciprocity with Latin America. This sectional self-interest would soon broaden and carry considerable weight.

Indeed, the transition from the Jeffersonian to the Jacksonian era brought major changes. Those southerners uninvolved with slavery continued to reflect the old balance of ideals and self-interest. Some slaveowners did, too, but for other Jacksonian planters, ideals quickly became subordinate to self-interest as abolitionists began to attack their "peculiar" labor institution. When the West realigned with the Northeast on the tariff issue, the already defensive planters became even more fearful. A new congressional alliance might ban slavery from the territories and weaken the South's role in national affairs. Thus, in the three decades before the

Civil War many planters who feared social and economic ruin showed little enthusiasm for the altruistic mission of expansionism. With a steely, defensive tone, they advocated territorial growth for their own sectional self-interest. If President James K. Polk was chiefly a commercialist with national goals, he still made good use of the South's practical and materialistic political focus—as well as the missionary idealism among other elements of the South—as he maneuvered the nation through its final transcontinental thrust to the Pacific. Ironically, the planters' realpolitick was a far less effective force in policy when it was channeled by its own sectional leaders. The southern dream of a Caribbean empire remained just that—a dream. And when secession and war finally came, the southern strategy of a supposedly hardnosed realpolitick lacked the deft diplomacy to translate this approach into the foreign negotiations essential to a Confederate victory.

After the war many white southerners became so embittered that they rejected the expansionist ideology of the conquering Yankees. Southern views of the late 19th century reflected severe misgivings about American expansion into Hawaii, Cuba, Puerto Rico, and the Philippines. Most southerners ultimately surrendered, though, to the patriotism generated by the 1898 action against Spain, showing cautious interest in the anticipated opening of Caribbean and Pacific markets. Yet they still talked incessantly about the pain and dislocation a similar surge of Yankee imperialism had brought to their own region just half a century earlier and characterized that type of expansionism as contrary to key American principles of self-determination. They also focused

on contemporary problems spawned by the new foreign expansionism: the annexation of nonwhites could cause further conflict in their already strained race relations. More than half the southern senators voted with the antiimperialist opposition to the treaty of Paris. In short, more than party politics was involved. Isolationism—generated out of antiimperialist principles and racism—grew to consensual proportions in the postbellum period. Such a tormented reversal made many southerners appear ambivalent, and many downright insular, as they reacted to America's rise to world power.

A small, vocal, and powerful group within the emerging middle class showed signs of being anything but isolationists. To publicists such as Alabama politicians John Tyler Morgan and Joseph H. Wheeler, both highly acclaimed veterans of the Confederacy, the American mission of the late 19th century remained as justified as it had been in the days of Jefferson, and the national mission could hardly hinder the blueprint for a revived, industrial South. On racial objections to world power they blithely responded that the problem could be solved with segregation. With ideals and self-interest harmonized in classic Gilded Age liberalism, these "new southerners" would simply export the emerging institutions of their own region.

In the 20th century Morgan's form of expansionism, an outlook intensely ethnocentric but nevertheless balanced in terms of mission and realpolitick, gradually prevailed as the dominant view in the South. The ascendancy of Woodrow Wilson spurred southern expansionism to rapid and full recovery. Most white southerners, even some of the lower classes, perceived President Wilson's crusade for a moral and legal world order receptive to American influence as clear indication of "the return of the South" to international prominence. In fact, with the exception of a few isolated cases like Mississippi's James K. Vardaman, southerners worshiped Wilson's notion of international order as something brought back to life from the presidency of another great southerner, Thomas Jefferson. That historical connection had serious flaws. Although born a southerner, Wilson derived his internationalism primarily from experiences with highly idealistic liberals of the Northeast, some with abolitionist roots and most with far less pragmatism than the sage of Monticello. Yet as Civil War memories dimmed and sectional reconciliation offered industry and profits as well as psychological security, southerners grasped at Wilsonian internationalism as "a Southern idea" reunited with American patriotism. Southern Wilsonians actually were motivated as much by the practicalities of New South economics and politics as by a renewed enthusiasm for the American mission. Still, they followed Wilson straight through the crusade of World War I and then down the unpragmatic, dead-end road of the League of Nations.

This ironic and contradictory outlook—balanced, Jeffersonian expansionism advanced through the medium of relatively strong idealism—did not die with Wilson. During the 1920s and 1930s the League of Nations Association and the Carnegie Endowment for International Peace, two organizational bridges between the Wilsonianism of World Wars I and II, recruited far more effectively in the South than in any areas beyond a few urban centers in the Northeast where they were based. Indeed, between the wars southern voices dis-

senting from Wilson's internationalism were uniquely few. And when war reopened in Europe in 1939, a regional arm of the Carnegie Endowment, the Southern Council on International Relations, worked to convert this regional sentiment into political support for President Franklin D. Roosevelt's developing war policies. As might be expected, when the war ended Southern Council members and other southerners urged the second chance at realizing the dream of Wilsonian internationalism—the United Nations. Nevertheless, in the early 1950s, shortly after the creation of the UN, most southerners turned against the organization because it seemed ineffective in achieving the Wilsonian goal of blocking the growth of socialist and communist power. They also feared Joseph McCarthy's attacks on supporters of organized internationalism. Such a waning interest in internationalism did not place southern leaders at odds with others associated with the general goals of Wilsonianism; on the contrary, it brought them closer together. The Cold War caused most Americans once committed to internationalism to move to the right and to espouse American rescue of the world through collective security agreements, economic expansionism, and interventionism. Considering this trend, the South's interventionist sentiment in the Korean War and in the initial stages of the Vietnam War appeared synchronized to late 20th-century American expansionism.

Other than a few antiexpansionist mavericks like Florida's Claude Pepper, there have been only two major exceptions in this recent harmony between southern and national attitudes. In the 1950s and 1960s Richard B. Russell of Georgia and many other southern leaders balked at sending economic aid to the nonwhites of Africa, Latin America, and the Mideast, whereas many expansionists and the few enduring internationalists from other sections generally supported these measures. Southerners feared that competing low-technology products might be developed in these lands with the assistance of American funds. More important, southerners exhibited a racial reaction to nonwhites that was triggered by the civil rights movement at home. In some ways this attitude resembled the isolationism reflected by southerners in the years following the Civil War. On the other hand, just as stabilization of southern internal affairs gradually eased southern insecurities after the turn of the century and resulted in a new interest in expansionism, so did the slackening of the civil rights movement a century later contribute to increased southern political support for numerous foreign aid projects.

At roughly the same time, the late 1960s and early 1970s, another peculiarly southern attitude emerged. At this time most southerners in Washington— and their constituencies—followed Mississippi's James Eastland in opposing withdrawal of American troops from Vietnam long after most other Americans had accepted the limits of interventionism. At least as early as World War I, southerners had seemed excited about formal military activity abroad because of investments and jobs it provided within the generally poor southern population: economic opportunities in home-front war industries and military bases, plus "jobs" abroad through actual military service. These same considerations, coupled no doubt with the southerners' relatively high tolerance for violence, encouraged what was char-

acterized as a prolonged southern militarism in the Vietnam episode. In time this attitude too gave way to internal forces.

As increased black voting power raised issues of human rights in southern politics and elevated Andrew Young and other advocates of economic aid to national prominence, the interventionist strain of southern expansionism lost out. Simultaneously, the economic development of the Sunbelt created more jobs and a slightly larger middle class of whites and blacks. These upwardly mobile businessmen and professionals lived off corporate profits and often looked to reports from the local chapter of the Council on Foreign Relations for appropriate responses to world problems. They advocated whatever moderation in American policy was necessary for American capitalism to reverse its energy shortages and trade imbalances and to establish more influential relations with developing nations.

Finally, out of this moderated expansionist consensus, in which ideals were increasingly harmonized with self-interest, there emerged Georgia's Jimmy Carter. President Carter's approach to foreign policy has been criticized for its lack of cohesiveness and its ineffectiveness. His approach to foreign policy included commitment to expanding American trade—a crusade foreshadowed by New South booster trips to Latin America while he was still a governor—complemented by an equal emphasis on human rights, reduction of nuclear arms, and other progressive internationalist goals. Indeed, despite occasional overzealous rhetoric, he usually advanced the human rights program with a policy well attuned— though not always effectively—to the influence the United States might expect to have in a given area of the world. Hence the Carter years suggest the possibilities of an ironic trend. In the minds of most educated Americans, and certainly many historians, Woodrow Wilson provided the ideological foundation for the predominant foreign policy sentiment of the 20th-century South. Yet the viewpoint that helped recent southerners reclaim some of their once-powerful role in world affairs and find new economic growth was not so much Wilsonian idealistic internationalism but the formula that had given the South its first period of prominence. It was the more basic Jeffersonian approach—minus the agrarian rhetoric—that harnessed ideals and self-interest to the cause of pragmatic influence abroad and assisted the emergence of a less distinctive but increasingly confident southern culture in the late 20th century.

Tennant S. McWilliams
University of Alabama at Birmingham

Henry Blumenthal, *Journal of Southern History* (May 1966); Wayne S. Cole, *An Interpretive History of American Foreign Relations* (1974); Alexander DeConde, *Journal of Southern History* (August 1958); George L. Grassmuck, *Sectional Biases in Congress on Foreign Policy* (1951); Alfred O. Hero, Jr., *The Southerner and World Affairs* (1965); Marian Irish, *Journal of Politics* (May 1948); Warren F. Kuehl, *Seeking World Order: The United States and International Organization to 1920* (1969); Charles O. Lerche, Jr., *The Uncertain South: Its Changing Patterns of Politics in Foreign Policy* (1964); James M. McPherson, *Civil War History* (1983); Tennant S. McWilliams, *The New South Faces the World: Foreign Affairs and the Southern Sense of Self, 1877–1950* (1988); Frederick Merk, *The Monroe Doctrine and Expansionism, 1843–1849* (1966); Robert E. Osgood, *Ideals and Self-Interest in American Foreign Relations* (1953); Paul Seabury, *The Waning of Southern "Internationalism"* (1957). ☆

Fraternal Groups

Fraternal organizations have long been an important part of the social life of southern communities large and small. Beginning with the introduction of Freemasonry in the colonial era, the spirit of fraternalism grew after the Civil War to support the Sons of Temperance, Good Templars, Red Men, Woodmen of the World, Knights of Pythias, Odd Fellows, Grangers, Masons, and others. Blacks in the region had separate, distinctive fraternal groups that were nonetheless closely related to white groups in style and significance. Patriotic societies such as the United Daughters of the Confederacy, the United Confederate Veterans, the Sons and Daughters of the American Revolution, and others were based on race and ancestry and thrived in the tradition-oriented South. The region had fewer immigrant societies, such as the Ancient Order of Hibernians and Sons of Italy, because of the proportionately smaller number of immigrants in the region. The Knights of Columbus was popular among southern Catholics. The Ku Klux Klan represented many things, and narrowly defined secretive fraternalism was one of them. "The elaborate ceremonies and rituals, colorful costumes, and mysterious titles helped members escape the humdrum aspects of their daily lives," concluded historian John S. Ezell. In the 20th century, service organizations such as the Kiwanis, Rotary, Lions, and

Service International clubs emerged as middle-class, business-oriented versions of fraternalism.

The Masonic order is the oldest and most extensive fraternal society in the Western world. Coming mainly from Britain and to a lesser degree from France, Freemasonry makes use of symbols and allegories derived from the craft guilds of the Middle Ages. It preaches the universal virtues of friendship, morality, truth, charity, and prudence. It does not permit discussions of religion and politics within its temples. Consequently it has surmounted many difficulties associated with those topics, even during the period of American fratricidal strife in the 1860s.

The Masonic order has two rites, commonly called York and Scottish, which allow for advancement in their particular teachings. The individual local lodge is governed by a Grand Lodge, which generally follows state lines and is sovereign within its jurisdiction. Although the two rites are international, they remain subordinate to their respective Grand Lodges. Masonry is secret only in certain salutations and dramatic rituals. Otherwise its membership, times and places of meeting, and organization are well known. As an organization, the Masonic order seldom, however, appears in public, except at the laying of the cornerstone of a building or at graveside ceremonies for its deceased members.

Attached to the lodge and its rites are bodies like the Shrine, Order of the Demolay (for boys), Order of the Rainbow (for girls), and the Order of the Eastern Star (largely female). An adopted southerner, Rob Morris, originally from Massachusetts, founded the Eastern Star in the 1850s at the "Little Red Schoolhouse"—now known around the world as a sacred spot to members of the group—at Richland in Holmes County, Miss. He wrote many of the manuals and originated the rituals still in use in the group.

In most states the Masonic lodges maintain homes for care of orphans, the aged, and the infirm. The Shrine has hospitals that specialize in treatment of crippled children and burn victims. Knights Templar, the peak of the York Rite, offers funds for treatment of correctable eye maladies; the Scottish Rite provides funds for the treatment of aphasia and also scholarships for students of political science.

The term *lodge* is also applied to the structure where Masons meet. Often in the past such a building was owned jointly by the Masons and a church, a school, or a business firm. More recently, however, the building typically is owned and used only by the order. The architecture varies from a simple, unobtrusive frame or brick structure to a pretentious edifice adorned with columns and exotic representations. But regardless of size or ornamentation, the lodge has been a center of unity for vast segments of the southern male population, Jew and Gentile alike.

The Masonic order that came to the South during the colonial era was derived mostly from the York Rite. Operating in the three basic degrees of "Blue Lodge" Masonry, these early York Rite lodges received their charters mainly from the Grand Lodges of either England or Scotland. The other primary Masonic movement in the colonial South was the Scottish Rite, which was introduced from either France or the West Indies.

Among the first of the early colonial lodges comprising the Provincial Grand Lodge of Virginia (where Masonry was introduced as early as 1729) were the Royal Exchange Lodge 172, established at Norfolk under an English charter in 1733, and Kilwinning Port Royal Cross Lodge, formed under a Scottish Charter in 1730. Elsewhere in the colonial South, first lodges were chartered in North Carolina at Wilmington (1755), in South Carolina at Charleston (1760), and in Georgia (through Solomons Lodge, organized by the founder of Georgia, James Oglethorpe, under an English Charter in 1734 and now the oldest of the English lodges in the United States).

After the Revolutionary War, the Provincial Grand Lodges became independent from their mother lodges in England and Scotland, and enunciated the doctrine of "exclusive jurisdiction"—only the Grand Lodge of any state had authority over the lodges within that state's borders. However, in the newly created states to the west of the Atlantic seaboard, the several Grand Lodges were free to charter and establish daughter lodges. In that way, the Grand Lodges of Virginia, North Carolina, South Carolina, and Georgia were largely responsible for the spread and diffusion of Freemasonry across the South. By 1800 Kentucky, Tennessee, and Louisiana had new York Rite lodges as well as those derived from the colonial period. By 1820 additional Grand Lodges had been established in Alabama, Mississippi, and Louisiana. The next three decades added Arkansas, Texas, and Florida. In the case of Florida, Freemasonry had been introduced during the British colonial period in the form of military lodges chartered in Scotland. The story of Louisiana Freemasonry was a particularly complex one of struggle between French and Spanish colonists and their descendants, the

early York and Scottish rites, and American and Spanish authorities in West Florida. In 1812, 12 Masonic lodges were chartered in Louisiana. From the five French-speaking lodges, the Grand Lodge of Louisiana was formed in 1812; 14 years later they were joined by the English-speaking York Rite lodges.

Masonry spread widely after the American Revolution and was a conspicuous feature of southern life. Virginian George Washington used a Masonic Bible during his first inauguration and a Masonic trowel in ceremonies laying the cornerstone for the Capitol building in Washington, giving the Masonic order new prominence. This prominence eventually resulted in suspicions of the secret order and a wave of anti-Masonic hysteria that affected the South, as well as the rest of the nation, in the late 1820s and 1830s. This was one of the few periods of Masonic involvement in national affairs.

Prominent southern Masons from the 19th century included U.S. Supreme Court Chief Justice John Marshall (Virginia), Senator John C. Breckinridge (Kentucky), John Blair (Virginia), Confederate General Albert Sidney Johnston (Texas), and Governor Robert Toombs (Georgia). Former Confederate General Albert Pike from Arkansas edited and rewrote the rituals of the Scottish Rite in the late 19th century.

Masonry is typical of other fraternal groups in being far more than a strictly regional association, yet it has been an important institution for southerners and has taken on peculiar features at times in adapting to the regional context. In the 1890s, for example, a controversy appeared in Freemasonry over whether it should go beyond its traditions and become more explicitly religious, specifically acknowledging Christianity.

Southerners and midwesterners, according to historian Lynn Dumenil, tended to link the health of Masonry to orthodox interpretation of the Bible. They were especially prone to "Masonic Biblicism." A few trials were even held in the South with the purpose of expelling nonbelieving Masons. At times, also, southerners showed a greater interest than other Masons in becoming involved in politics. The Southern Jurisdiction of Scottish Rite Masons, for example, enthusiastically supported political involvement in the 1920s. Leaders of Masonry in the region did, however, speak out against any Ku Klux Klan–Masonry connection in that period. Masonic magazines have supported good citizenship, public education, and "True Americanism," the latter a favorite phrase.

See also BLACK LIFE: Fraternal Orders, Black

Allen Cabaniss
Oxford, Mississippi

Ernest Easterly III
Baton Rouge, Louisiana

Allen Cabaniss, *Freemasonry in Mississippi* (1976); George B. Clark, *From Whence Came We: Masonic Ancestry and Antecedents of the Grand Lodges of the United States* (1953); Henry W. Coil, *Freemasonry through Six Centuries*, 2 vols. (1967); Lynn Dumenil, *Freemasonry and American Culture, 1880–1930* (1984); Glen L. Greene, *Masonry in Louisiana* (1962); Ray B. Harris, *Eleven Gentlemen of Charleston: Founders of the Supreme Council, Mother Council of the World* (1959); William J. Hughan, G. P. Jones, and Ray B. Harris, *Freemasonry* (1958). ✰

Frontier Heritage

In 1893 a Wisconsin-born historian, Frederick Jackson Turner, read a paper entitled "The Significance of the Frontier in American History" at the annual meeting of the American Historical Association. He launched a new hypothesis in which the American frontier was viewed as the dominant factor in the development of American civilization. "The existence of an area of free land, its continuous recession, and the advance of American settlement westward," he stated in his first paragraph, "explain American development."

Even today, more than 90 years after Turner read his paper, historians cannot ignore his thesis. A generation of graduate students at Wisconsin and later at Harvard studied under him. In time they wrote hundreds of monographs with Turner's thesis as their basic premise. Many of his students went on to become successful history professors. They in turn passed Turner's ideas on to more historians; they also produced a number of American history texts from elementary to college level. All of them were imbued with Turnerian ideas even if Turner was not mentioned by name. Although the frontier hypothesis has suffered considerably in the past 50 years, it must still bear consideration when American history is being interpreted.

In his essay Turner gave proper attention to the southern frontier. Land hunger, he noted, drove the Scotch-Irish, Germans, and many other colonials into the transmontane South. Discovery of salt springs along the Kanawha, Holston, and Kentucky rivers freed them from dependence for that commodity on the Atlantic Coast. These men of Kentucky and Tennessee were so fiercely independent that the new nation almost lost them. They demanded free navigation of the Mississippi and initially profited most from the Louisiana Purchase. As for the institution of slavery, Turner did not consider it of prime importance in the history of American development.

Finally, for all the American people, Turner found in the frontier experience "intellectual traits of profound importance." He perceived a "coarseness and strength combined with acuteness and inquisitiveness: that masterful grasp of material things, lacking in the artistic but powerful to effect great ends; that restless, nervous energy; that dominant individualism, working for good and for evil, and withal that buoyancy and exuberance which comes with freedom."

Davy Crockett, a southerner born along the Nolichucky River in east Tennessee in 1786, exemplifies just such a man. Restless yet ambitious, he moved first to middle Tennessee, served in military campaigns against the Creek Indians, and next settled for several years in west Tennessee. From there he was elected to the state legislature and later to Congress, where he served three terms. Still restless and not yet 50, he headed for Texas and achieved immortality by dying at the Alamo. Another exemplar was Sam Houston who possessed those same traits of intelligence, restlessness, a practical turn of mind, a dominant individualism, and an ability to effect great ends that Turner identified as frontier attributes.

Certainly the most successful southern frontiersman was Andrew Jackson. He was a leader of the rough-and-tumble society that constituted the businessmen's and planters' world of the Tennessee frontier. He had fought duels, lost and won horse races, speculated in land, purchased slaves, married a beautiful frontier woman, and entered into the turbulent politics of his adopted state. A natural leader of men, he climbed the frontier political ladder as the representative of a people who possessed a fierce belief in a rustic democracy that left no place for Indians and accepted the institution of slavery. The spirit of the frontier spoke through him when Jackson stated in his bank veto message that the benefits of government should, "as Heaven does its rains, shower its favors alike on the high and the low, the rich and the poor."

Turner's great essay embraced all frontiers, north and south (but always west), and a chronology from colonial times until the end of the frontier as defined by the Bureau of the Census in 1890. He did not differentiate regional frontiers.

Subsequent critics did, pointing out certain frontier characteristics that were not so admirable. The frontier, they said, demonstrably fostered violence, lawbreaking, discrimination against minorities, antiintellectualism, and individualism so fierce that it worked against the common good. Such unpleasant characteristics were self-evident in the lives of southern frontiersmen like Crockett, Houston, and Jackson.

The word *frontier* does not appear in the indexes of several of the principal texts and surveys of southern history. Emphasis has instead been placed on the antebellum South as a *rural* area— a dynamic but raw agrarian society advancing into a wilderness that indeed was the southern frontier, but which in the South was not always looked upon as such. A description of a southern frontier heritage may sound to some like an essay on the rural aspects of the South.

The southern frontier began with Jamestown and the beginnings of Virginia and spread northward into Maryland and southward along the coast eventually to embrace North and South Carolina, Georgia, and north Florida. Pioneers from the southern coastal colonies spilled over the Appalachians into Tennessee and Kentucky. After the War of 1812, the practical application of the cotton gin, and the rapid elimination of the Five Civilized Tribes, the Old Southwest filled in. This included the Black Belt, so named for its deep, black loam, which, with the warm, humid climate, made the cultivation of short-staple cotton economically profitable. Besides Georgia (1788) and Louisiana (1812), Alabama (1819) and Mississippi (1817) had achieved statehood by 1819. Within another generation Arkansas (1836) and Texas (1845) were added as states with a southern outlook. Florida, very much a frontier although south, not west, of the other states, entered the Union in 1845. W. J. Cash in *The Mind of the South* (1941) emphasized the persistence of frontier conditions in the South: "It is impossible to conceive the Great South as being, on the whole, more than a few steps removed from the frontier stage at the beginning of the Civil War."

In every sense the South's progression was along an advancing frontier. Crushing the Indians, buying the land, breaking it to the plow, and building cabins, outbuildings, and fences were common tasks. Roads had to be constructed leading to new villages where trade, religion, education, business, litigation, and government flourished. The steamboat, a practical conveyance by the 1820s, made water highways of the sluggish southern rivers. As with other frontiers, the southern one produced a raw, heavy-drinking, vulgar, speculative, turbulent society. Augustus Baldwin Longstreet in *Georgia Scenes* (1835) and Joseph Glover Baldwin in *Flush Times of Alabama and Mississippi* (1853) well portrayed the southern frontier society at the time of land booms and rapid settlement. In addition, there was the southern cattlemen's frontier. It included the red-clay hill regions of northern Georgia and Alabama, the pine barrens of the Carolinas, and central Florida's prairies; to a degree, the cattle industry thrived in every southern state in the antebellum period. However, the barefooted, floppy-hatted "cracker" with his long whip never struck the romantic vein of the national psyche as did his later counterpart, mounted and gazing out over the Great Plains.

All of this was a part of the frontier experience and was similar to the societies of the same period in the Old Northwest and trans-Mississippi West. Yet the South's frontier experience differed from the common frontier experience in a number of ways. One-crop agriculture, especially the raising of tobacco and cotton, both of which enervated the soil, made it absolutely necessary for southerners to advance to new lands. Soil depletion forced Virginians and Carolinians to pack up and leave their old fields for the Black Belt. Once there, they again depleted the soil. They practiced the negative frontier characteristic of waste. The land was abused because of the belief that more free land always lay to the west— even as far west as Texas's Brazos River bottoms. So too were the pine and live oak forests logged and left as wasteland to catch on fire or become a malarial morass. Such practices occurred on other frontiers, but in the South the damage was greater. This was not because the southern frontiersman was any more rapacious of the land than his northern or western fellow pioneers, but because the single-crop system, the southern climate with heavy rainfall, and the nature of the southern soil resulted in greater, longer-lasting damage. Soil erosion was an early problem resulting in the end of one frontier and the beginning of another.

These differences also created or made more inevitable a social system that is usually considered harmful to southern progress. Some have called the southern social system, based upon one-crop agriculture, which was callous to the maintenance of good soil and extremely detrimental to all but the most successful of southern planter-businessmen, a "hot-house" society. A yeomanry existed that was more likely to lapse downward into "po' white" status than rise to plantation aristocracy, and once the social status was set, it was very difficult for a white person to rise out of it. Beyond attaining manumission, blacks were relegated to lowest status, of course, as slaves. This social stratification was notably a southern frontier characteristic, not a national one. Yet the system was unstable, and southern literature is filled with narrations of aristocratic families who fell upon hard times and tried desperately to retain their status. William Faulkner's fictitious Yoknapatawpha County, with its Compson family, is of this genre. Eudora Welty's stories of southern families in rustic settings likewise harken back to frontier times.

Individualism, a trait common to all frontiers, was a fine-tuned tradition on the southern frontier. It manifested itself in a dislike of government—any government—that proposed to control a man's life—how he ran his plantation or his business, how he managed his slaves, or where he fired the woods or chose to go hunting. To the proud white southern agrarian, the Bill of Rights was the most important part of the Constitution.

This individualism did not extend to religion or political opinions. The frontier South worshiped God through many sects, but nearly all were fundamentalist and emotional in their attraction. Their religious spectrum did not include atheists, Deists, Unitarians, or other groups who questioned in any way the accepted emotional, fundamental appeal of religion by Bible, and Bible alone.

Slavery, as the solution to racial problems, broached no opposition, and although Turner was not bothered by slavery on the frontier, certainly it contributed to the South's distinctiveness. Similarly, on matters of the tariff, internal improvements, and interpretation of the Constitution, the white southern frontiersman accepted a common attitude and stuck to it. He was not, as men were on other frontiers, an equalitarian. He accepted the concept of class, beginning with the black slave, working upward past the free black, the poor white, the yeoman farmer, and the plantation owner; in towns, the merchant, banker, and gin operator (often one and the same person) adhered to many of the same ideas, though for a few years prior to the Civil War he may have voted Whig instead of Democratic.

The southern rural frontier allowed a white man to carry a gun, use profanity, break the Sabbath, participate in a lynching, drink heavily, or fight a duel, and have it all considered normal. Such a person, if he was capable of accepting discipline, made an excellent soldier. He served well in all the nation's wars (although he was on the Confederate side in the 1860s).

The southern frontier heritage, then, includes fundamentalist religion, perhaps the strongest rugged individualism in the modern nation, and a love of the outdoors stemming from frontier ruralism including hunting and fishing. A strain of violence may still be discerned. For many decades into the 20th century, to be a white southerner was also to be a Democrat, for the society demanded that everyone adhere to the majority political opinion. Loyalty to family, honor, love of the land, and devotion to country, all inherited from the frontier-rural traditions of their pioneering past, remain strong among southern whites today.

See also ENVIRONMENT: Indians and the Environment; RELIGION: Frontier Religion

Richard A. Bartlett
Florida State University

Ray Allen Billington, *America's Frontier Heritage* (1966); Thomas D. Clark, *The Rampaging Frontier: Manners and Humors of Pioneer Days in the Southern Middle West* (1939); Avery O. Craven, *Journal of Southern History* (August 1939); Gene M. Gressley, *Agricultural History* (October 1958); Todd M. Lieber, *Mississippi Quarterly* (Fall 1969); Frank L. Owsley, *Journal of Southern History* (May 1945); Malcolm J. Rohrbough, *The Trans-Appalachian Frontier: People, Societies, and Institutions, 1775–1850* (1978). ☆

Great Depression

||||||||||||||||||||||||||||||||||||||||||||||||

The Great Depression began with the collapse of the stock market in late 1929, and it devastated the American South more than any other region during the 1930s. The calamity's paralyzing severity and dismaying persistence enveloped the whole republic: nationwide statistics reveal fully a third of the work force unemployed, and by 1933 the nation's business activity had plunged to half that of 1929. But the American South suffered even greater harm as yearly per capita income plummeted from a national low of $372 in 1929 to just $203 in 1932.

Southern agriculture, in decline since the end of World War I and scarred by tenancy, sank deeper into stagnation; even nature seemed hostile as the 1930–31 drought, the most severe on record, staggered the failing southern farm economy. Southern industry, still in its infancy, with only 15 percent of the nation's factory workers, fell even farther behind that of the North. Partners in misfortune, both rural and urban southerners shared the bitter trials of the times as the Depression exacerbated long-standing problems of poverty, race, and class.

Some starved to death in the depths of the Depression; thousands scavenged through garbage dumps; many of the homeless took revenge in city parks; evicted families lived in packing crates, junked automobiles, or anything else that might provide shelter. Because a physician's fee was an easily cut expense, illnesses went untreated in a society hesitant to ask charity from physicians sometimes reluctant to give it. Fear and insecurity overwhelmed some, but for most there was an implacable determination to survive.

Southern Americans, dazed by the hard times, initially received little aid from government. The Depression's unprecedented demands quickly exhausted private charity sources, and welfare apparatuses of local and state governments collapsed almost as rapidly. The multiplying poor could turn only to their national government.

The baffled and lethargic Hoover Administration tried to stabilize agricultural prices by limiting foreign imports (Hawley-Smoot tariff, 1930) and offered limited federal aid for relief (Reconstruction Finance Corporation, 1932), but its actions were ineffective. The New Deal of Franklin D. Roosevelt took shape early in 1933 with times at their worst. Responding to a people now willing to accept unique solutions, FDR's government was well intentioned but never adequately funded. In spite of such imaginative programs as the Tennessee Valley Authority (1933) and the Rural Electrification Administration (1935), the New Deal remained an essentially conservative reaction to the nation's ills. Government aid, when it was sent, came in smaller quantities to the South; with some 28 percent of the nation's population, the South received only 15.4 percent of the aid disbursed by the federal government in a typical Depression year such as 1937.

Most blacks lived in the South, and the racist policies of all levels of government meant that southern blacks fared worst of all. The meager government subsidies directed south invariably ended in white hands for distribution. Following the inviolable patterns of a systematically segregated society, southern bureaucrats did not ignore all blacks' needs, but inevitably gave whites' problems first attention. And in some instances welfare agents simply refused to accept blacks' applications for aid. Washington made no serious efforts at correction; blacks had perhaps even fewer friends in the capital than at home.

Factory hands fared as badly as farmers. As a primarily agricultural region,

in 1929 the South had employed only 1,338,000 workers in industrial production. This newness to industry had produced 72-hour weeks, and wages lagged 40 percent behind those of the rest of the nation even before the Depression struck. The textile industry was the dominant industrial competitor. Virtually all factory workers were white, with blacks denied access to fledgling southern industry except in the most menial capacities.

The basic skills required in the textile mills meant that easily replaced workers enjoyed little success in organizing to improve wages, hours, and working conditions. And the industry's evolution had produced the company town where management owned or controlled housing, schools, churches, and government. Management generally responded to the Depression with wage reductions, increases in production quotas, and work stretch-outs. Workers' resistance to these cruel measures provoked immediate discharge underscored by institutionalized violence.

Resignation born of stunted expectations typified the industrial South. Even the company town's selective paternalism furnished support only so long as the worker kept his peace—and his job. Religion, family, or the close-knit society of a southern mill town provided what little enduring comfort employees gained. For the southern industrial worker the Depression was thus a lost decade; not until 1939 would the number of industrial jobs regain the 1929 level.

Southern farmers faced even worse circumstances. In the South's distinctive agricultural system, tenancy had replaced slavery as the "peculiar institution" after the Civil War. Most southern farmers were tenants; over 60 percent plowed land they did not own in the cotton states of Arkansas, Louisiana, Mississippi, Alabama, and Georgia. For blacks the figure ballooned to over 80 percent.

Cotton served as tenancy's dynamic. Half of all southern farms raised cotton, and tenants worked three-quarters of these; production had totaled 14,096,000 bales in 1929. The owner demanded cotton, for which a market always existed, but the Depression drove cotton prices to a record low of 4.6¢ per pound and production to only 10,613,000 bales. In addition, cotton neatly fitted a stringent pattern of controls over the life of the southern sharecropper, strictures the landowner tightened during the Depression.

Essential to the pattern was the country store, often owned by the landholder. Since the tenant usually began the crop year without cash, the owner guaranteed his credit at the nearby store where he was obligated to buy—at inflated prices and exorbitant interest rates. Attempting to insure steady purchases during the Depression, some landowners even forbade tenants to plant gardens or keep food animals. Although some did manage to flee to such comparative havens as Cleveland, Detroit, or California, many sharecroppers, black and white, lived in a state of outright peonage, ensnared by the South's skewed legal system.

The domination of the whole of southern society by the landowning class made all this possible. Political control insured complaisant lawmakers and enforcers who cowed the tenants. Denied access to public education, tenants had little comprehension of alternatives to their pattern of life. In the religious South even churches served planter interests by preaching to tenants the

need for hard work and debt payment and neglecting to urge upon landowners biblical injunctions concerning masters' duties to laborers. By 1935, in the peasant society that was the South, 1,831,475 farms were tenant operated.

In the cotton country of northeastern Arkansas, hard-pressed sharecroppers sought relief by forming the Southern Tenant Farmers' Union (STFU). The nonviolent and racially integrated STFU called for nothing more radical than fair treatment and adherence to established laws. But a planter-led reign of terror smashed this stirring of tenant assertiveness with shootings, beatings, kidnappings, and kangaroo justice.

Black and white alike bore the weight of this malignant system, which extracted from them the last measure of both labor and dignity, but the realities of a rigidly segregated society handicapped blacks even further. The most remarkable aspect of southern tenancy during the Depression is the striking triumph of human spirit over the inhumane environment. Caught in an economic and cultural trap in some respects fiercer than slavery, tenants displayed a luminous courage and an inexorable determination.

Only sweeping changes could restructure southern society after the Depression. The coming of World War II, with its military draft and insatiable demands for war-industry workers, drew the next generation of potential sharecroppers from the farm; seeing a better world, they would never return.

Many landowners, envisioning greater profits in operating mechanized and larger single units with governmental subsidies, had begun to encourage an exodus of sharecroppers as the Depression lingered. The New Deal's Agricultural Adjustment Administration (1933) paid landowners, not the tenants who did the work, 50 percent more for plowing under cotton than for producing it. At the same time, improved farm machinery and the availability of capital helped make mechanization more attractive; in 1930 southern farmers used only 134,000 tractors; this number climbed to 255,000 in 1940 and to 468,000 in 1945. These factors helped speed tenancy's demise, as the number of white tenants declined a remarkable 25 percent during World War II.

The South's Depression story is not, however, one of unrelieved misery. Normal work persisted to a degree; while perhaps a third of the labor force sat idle, the remainder still held jobs and often shared their meager bounty with impoverished friends, as traditional southern neighborliness proved more compassionate than Washington's geographically and racially distorted policies. Many crafts workers, although finding fewer tasks, did remain relatively busy. A favorably located merchant with a long-established clientele often maintained an acceptable trade. Not surprisingly, professionals in the legal and health fields, the planters' close allies, suffered perhaps least of all. Depression then, as always, was a matter of relative decline.

Most southerners, however, struggled through these years with wounds healed only slightly by a government more interested in relief and recovery than in real reform. The impersonal numbers on unemployment lists and graphs of falling income meant empty stomachs, sinking spirits, and desolate confusion. Although despair existed, the survival of an open-hearted and optimistic spirit may be the most remarkable legacy of these impoverished southerners.

See also AGRICULTURE: Country Store; Sharecropping and Tenancy; / Cotton Culture; Rural Electrification Administration; ENVIRONMENT: Tennessee Valley Authority; INDUSTRY: / Textile Industry; SOCIAL CLASS: Politics and Social Class; Poverty; / Company Town; Southern Tenant Farmers' Union; Textile Workers

John L. Robinson
Abilene Christian University

James C. Cobb and Michael V. Namorato, eds., *The New Deal and the South* (1984); David E. Conrad, *The Forgotten Farmers: The Story of Sharecroppers in the New Deal* (1965); Pete Daniel, *The Shadow of Slavery: Peonage in the South, 1901–1969* (1972); Federal Writers' Project, *These Are Our Lives* (1939); Donald H. Grubbs, *Cry from the Cotton: The Southern Tenant Farmers' Union and the New Deal* (1971); Robert S. McElvaine, *The Great Depression, 1929–1941* (1984); Arthur F. Raper, *Preface to Peasantry: A Tale of Two Black Belt Counties* (1936); Roger W. Shugg, *Origins of Class Struggle in Louisiana: A Social History of White Farmers and Laborers during Slavery and after, 1840–1875* (1939); Gavin Wright, *The Political Economy of the Cotton South* (1978). ☆

Historians

|||||||||||||||||||||||||||||

The oldest tradition of historical literature in the South is that of state descriptions and history. This tradition began before the settlement of Virginia with the pamphlets and books that promoted and inflated the virtues of colonization. It continued through the studies of Robert Beverley (*History and Present State of Virginia*, 1705), William Stith (*History of the First Discovery and Settlement of Virginia*, 1747), and Thomas Jefferson (*Notes on the State of Virginia*, 1785). By the 19th century a considerable body of such writings existed, among them, David Ramsay's *History of South Carolina* (1808), which celebrated the American Revolution; Charles Gayarré's *Histoire de la Louisiane* (1846), which domesticated European historicism; and William Gilmore Simms's *History of South Carolina* (1840), which anticipated the Confederacy.

Such history was an amateur and gentlemanly undertaking, local in focus and patriotic in tone, though later useful for the gathering of documents and the establishment of state historical societies. Before 1861 such societies existed in 10 southern states: Virginia (1831), North Carolina (1833), Louisiana (1836), Kentucky (1838), Georgia (1839), Tennessee (1849), Alabama (1850), South Carolina (1855), Florida (1856), and Mississippi (1858).

Notable before the Civil War, however, was an absence of regional historiography, which had to wait until the late 19th century brought a generation of southerners schooled in sectional thought by the experiences of war and Reconstruction. The first regional historical organization was the Southern Historical Society, founded in New Orleans in 1869 by ex-Confederates and dedicated to the vindication of the Lost Cause. Its successor, the Southern History Association founded in Washington in 1896, was both more New South in persuasion and less bitter in tone; its *Publications* appeared between 1896 and 1907. Insofar as professional historiography is an offshoot of industrialization, it is no surprise that the southern historical and educational industry should have commenced outside

and on the borders of the South before moving into the region in the 1920s.

The earliest centers of academic southern history were the Johns Hopkins University, where Herbert Baxter Adams taught Woodrow Wilson and William P. Trent; Columbia University, where William A. Dunning instructed students of Reconstruction such as Walter L. Fleming and J. G. de Roulhac Hamilton; and the University of Chicago, where William Dodd directed Frank L. Owsley's studies. The first course in southern history was taught by James C. Ballagh at Johns Hopkins in 1896 and the first within the South by William K. Boyd at Trinity College (later Duke University) in 1907.

Usually under the direction of northern graduates born in the South, an infrastructure of graduate programs, journals, archives, presses, and professional organizations was fashioned indigenously after 1920. About a hundred doctorates in history were granted by southern universities between the world wars, mostly on southern topics. In 1930 the Southern Historical Collection, the largest archive of regional documents, was founded at Chapel Hill. In 1934 the Southern Historical Association was organized, and publication of its *Journal of Southern History* commenced in 1935. In the 1920s the University of North Carolina Press began to publish books on regional history and culture, and in 1937 the Louisiana State University press began a multivolume *History of the South*.

Southern history, as both a professional and an amateur pursuit, is largely written in the South by southerners for southerners and is published by southern journals and presses; occasionally non-southern publishers issue works on southern history, but these are usually by non-southerners or southerners living outside the region. The study of southern history thus forms an important subculture in American social discourse, possessed of many private symbols and rituals. There is a healthy amateur industry, flourishing as tourism, cheerfully anecdotal political journalism, and military and genealogical antiquarianism; all are characterized by a warmth of nostalgia: hooped skirts, Earl Long's penchant for strip-tease artists, grandfather's exploits at Shiloh.

Professional historians in the South are notable for being an accepted part of their society, often partisan toward the South, formerly bitter against the North but recently—as a function of growing relative affluence—more amiable. Their specialities are social history (particularly of slavery and race relations), biography, and political history. Military history, once popular as a function of bitterness, is now in decline. Economic history has been a weaker tradition, and intellectual history, save as literary history, has been almost nonexistent. Southern historians divide by social persuasion (usually conservative, often liberal, rarely radical), by place of birth (Virginians, Tennesseans), by ancestry (yeoman, planter, Tidewater, Piedmont), rather than by theoretical persuasion (Marxist, Hegelian, structuralist). However, the youngest generation of southern historians shows a growing interest in social theory.

Southern history is implicitly comparative history, because scholars of southern history assume a distinction from "northern" culture and occasionally offer comparisons with non-American cultures, as in the writings of Eugene D. Genovese (Japan and Sicily), Forrest McDonald and Grady Mc-

Whiney (the Celtic fringe), Carl N. Degler (Brazil), or C. Vann Woodward (Europe). More usually—and this is necessary to its function as social discourse—southern history is inward looking. The old tradition of state history continues and constitutes the bulk of southern historical literature, chiefly because archives and higher education are organized largely by states. Because the region is not merely a collection of states but a gestalt, however, the subject matter of a broad regional history is unclear. At present southern history thus tends to be either the aggregate of state histories or an impressionistic synthesis of unevenly gathered particularities, in which a specific state or social group is made to do service for the whole.

There is no known analysis of the social origins, recruitment patterns, or social habits of southern historians. As a category within the broad scheme of Western historical literature, southern history is an optional, rather than an inevitable, classification, imposed by author or reader, and strongest as social discourse when imposed by both.

See also MYTHIC SOUTH: History, Central Themes

Michael O'Brien
University of Arkansas

George H. Calcott, *History in the United States, 1800–1860* (1970); E. Merton Coulter, *Journal of Southern History* (February 1936); Arthur S. Link and Rembert W. Patrick, eds., *Writing Southern History: Essays in Historiography in Honor of Fletcher M. Green* (1965); Wendell H. Stephenson, *The South Lives in History: Southern Historians and Their Legacy* (1955), *Southern History in the Making: Pioneer Historians of the South* (1964); George B. Tindall, ed., *The*

Pursuit of Southern History: Presidential Addresses of the Southern Historical Association, 1935–1963 (1964). ☆

Historic Preservation

||||||||||||||||||||||||||||||||||||||||||||||||||

In the South, the past is more than learned; it is remembered. It is an integral part of present lives and gives meaning and character to future prospects. As William Faulkner wrote in *Intruder in the Dust* (1948), in the South "yesterday today and tomorrow are Is: Indivisible: One." So historic preservation in the region is more than merely a movement to preserve old structures; it seeks to preserve a part of the southern people as well. For the structures themselves are more than brick and mortar replications of a past style or fashion; they are the stories of the communities and generations that have resided there. So the historic preservation movement in the South, primarily a phenomenon of the last half century, was not so much a sudden awakening to a historical heritage, as a formal, organized response to a feeling and a culture most southerners had internalized.

Actually, organized historic preservation in the South predates this century. Since the 1850s the work of the Mount Vernon Ladies' Association in restoring and maintaining the home of the nation's first president has served as a model of privately funded preservation. But the major efforts in the region have occurred since the 1920s when Williamsburg, Va., Charleston's historic district, and the Vieux Carré in New Orleans received their initial support. The appearance and acceleration

of historic preservation efforts in the 1920s resulted from the modest prosperity experienced by cities in the region at the time. Poverty and stagnation had been excellent natural preservers. Relieved of the pressures of growth, ancient districts and structures survived in the twilight of indifference, secure that no wrecker's ball would penetrate their murky confines. As the booster mentality conquered southern cities, however, the prospect, if not fact, of growth became a great obsession. Thomas Wolfe lamented of his native Asheville that "a spirit of drunken waste and wild destructiveness was everywhere apparent. The fairest places in town were being mutilated at untold cost."

A survey of residential buildings conducted in Charleston in 1917 concluded, "May it . . . be hoped that what has accidentally been preserved may be long retained." The survey surprised Charlestonians by documenting an extensive collection of historic structures, many of which were suffering from neglect. When, a few years later, the Manigault house, constructed in 1790, was threatened with demolition, the women who had commissioned the survey sprang into action and organized a permanent watchdog committee, the Society for the Preservation of Old Dwellings, which effectively lobbied for a comprehensive Historic District Zoning Law that passed in 1931. City planner Charles Henry Cheney termed the ordinance "one of the most forward advances in city planning work and architectural control that we have ever yet had in the country." Six years later in New Orleans after a similar lobbying effort to save the historic Vieux Carré, the Louisiana Legislature established a commission, the first such publicly supported body in the United States, with broad powers ranging from the protection of structures within the French Quarter to the exempting of historic properties from local taxation.

These projects, together with the Rockefeller-funded Williamsburg restoration and the Natchez Garden Club, which in 1931 began using the techniques of annual pilgrimages to stimulate interest in preserving Natchez's unique collection of antebellum homes, thrust the South into the lead of a nascent national historic preservation movement. After World War II the movement regained and surpassed its prewar level, most dramatically in Savannah but also in the less notable towns and cities throughout the region, encompassing not only dwellings and public buildings but shops and factories as well. Most significantly, there was a drawing together of two former antagonists—the boosters and the preservationists—as the latter demonstrated that history was good business. In Savannah, for example, the preservation movement was largely responsible for developing a tourist industry that generated $60 million in revenue for the city by 1980. Also, by the 1960s there was increased participation by the federal government, and, especially after the 1974 Community Development Act, even those structures and districts not so obviously "historical" received funding support. "History" now inhabited not only the structures of the famous but the quarters of everyman as well.

By the 1970s, however, two clouds appeared on the otherwise-clear horizon of historic preservation. First, there was the question of equity. Southern cities and towns have not, historically, been particularly solicitous of their black residents, and the individuals attracted by the preservation movement—overwhelmingly white, typically professional, and often with family connections—have generally ignored the social consequences of the preservation movement, which have included the gentrification of neighborhoods and displacement of people, the difficulties of relocation, and the burdens of higher taxes for those remaining. Preservation and social equity can, of course, coexist nicely, as Lee Adler has demonstrated with his Savannah Landmark group, a project that has successfully preserved the city's Victorian District, by purchasing homes in the district and leasing them back at reasonable rents to the black tenants who have resided in the neighborhood for decades.

Second, there is a growing concern that historic preservation may be too successful in the region; that vast areas of towns and cities may become untouchable museums for the wealthy and the tourists. The depredations of developers notwithstanding, each generation, according to this view, should be allowed to add its own legacy to the rich historical traditions of the South. A fixed backward gaze could only degenerate into a self-centered antiquarianism that would belie the dynamic and comprehensive quality of historic structures and districts in the region.

The search for new methods and flexibility in interpreting and preserving historic structures to make them more usable for more of the people will likely continue: adaptive reuse of old textile mills into condominiums as in Greensboro, N.C., or the transformation of a graceful turn-of-the-century mansion in uptown New Orleans into a public library are increasingly seen not as desecrations of the past, but rather as paeans to that heritage, reinforcing that resilience and relevance of southern history and culture for all.

See also ENVIRONMENT: Gardens and Gardening; RECREATION: Tourism; / Colonial Williamsburg; URBANIZATION: / Charleston; Savannah

David R. Goldfield
University of North Carolina
at Charlotte

James Deetz, *In Small Things Forgotten: The Archaeology of Early American Life* (1977); Frank Gilbert, ed., *Readings in Historic Preservation* (1983); Charles B. Hosmer, Jr., *Preservation Comes of Age: From Williamsburg to the National Trust, 1926–1949*, 2 vols. (1981); David Kyvig and Myron Marty, *Nearby History: Exploring the Past Around You* (1983); Kevin Lynch, *What Time Is This Place?* (1972); Nathan Weinberg, *Preservation in American Towns and Cities* (1979). ☆

Historic Sites
||||||||||||||||||||||||||||||||||||||

With the founding of the Mount Vernon Ladies' Association of the Union in 1856, the South became an early leader in the historic preservation movement in the United States. The association, chartered by the Commonwealth of Virginia, was organized with the sole purpose of purchasing and preserving George Washington's home and its surrounding grounds. Also in 1856, Tennessee provided funds to purchase and preserve Andrew Jackson's estate, the Hermitage. Like so many early preservation efforts, these mansions were selected for restoration and perpetual care largely because of their association with important figures in American history. A few other sites and structures were saved because of their role in significant events.

The Civil War interrupted historic preservation efforts throughout the South and also provided scores of potential sites with which to memorialize the Lost Cause. By the end of the century several Civil War battlefields had been set aside as national military parks. Tennessee's Chickamauga and Chattanooga park, formed in 1890, was one of the first. By the early 1900s the South seemed intent on preserving almost any Civil War site of even moderate significance. Although the region was often forced to rely on federal aid to finance these preservation efforts, state and local activities continued. The Association for the Preservation of Virginia Antiquities, a private organization founded in 1888, concentrated its early efforts on preserving colonial sites in the Jamestown area. Other state and local organizations gradually emerged to tackle specific preservation projects. In Virginia, for example, Richmond's Confederate Literary Society was founded in 1890 to preserve the Confederate White House, and the Thomas Jefferson Memorial Foundation purchased Monticello in 1923. Both were typical of the local organizations that collectively have played a crucial and continuing role in southern preservation efforts.

During the 1920s John D. Rockefeller became interested in preserving and restoring Williamsburg, Va., and his interest and financial assistance in the project demonstrated the potential of private preservation efforts. Several other communities, including Charleston, S.C., and St. Augustine, Fla., drew on the experience, techniques, and spirit of the Colonial Williamsburg project to develop historic districts of their own. For the first time historic preservation in the South began to reflect larger cultural and historic concerns. While Williamsburg and similar sites were usually related to major historic events and personalities, the preservationists and historians associated with these projects also attempted to interpret patterns of everyday life. As the 1900s wore on, this impulse became ever more significant, but the portrayal of southern society at historic sites has nevertheless largely focused on the white elite.

Several major federal initiatives had enormous impact on the development of southern sites. The establishment of the National Park Service to administer federally funded sites (1916) and the Historic Preservation Act of 1935, which finally provided focus to the national preservation movement, were especially noteworthy. Although state and local organizations would continue to preserve and interpret the past throughout the region, southern reliance on federal leadership and funding for major projects, particularly in the area of military sites and parks, became increasingly important. At Civil War parks the significance of this national support has been seen in the tendency of federally funded areas to play down the Lost Cause myth in favor of a more straightforward interpretation of events. Still, southern organizations have often been able to contribute monuments and exhibits to national battlefield parks, which continue to emphasize, however subtly, the romance and glamor of the Confederacy. At other sites, particularly those related to the colonial period, federal leadership has tended to favor a portrayal of colonial life that emphasizes an emerging *national* character,

whereas those colonial sites administered by southern organizations often seek to demonstrate the uniqueness of the southern identity.

A number of culturally significant patterns emerge from an examination of the South's preservation activities. First, the sheer number of such areas in the South suggests that the region indeed *does* tend to be more enamored with its history than other portions of the United States. The 11 states of the Confederacy together with Maryland, Kentucky, and Missouri account for 45 percent of eastern historic sites listed in the *National Register of Historic Places* and over 36 percent of *all* listings. State and local sites, which sometimes are not included in the *Register*, are also a bit more common in the South than in other areas. Southern preservationists have the advantage, particularly in the Atlantic Seaboard areas, of an unusually lengthy history. Moreover, much of the Revolutionary War and virtually all of the Civil War were fought on southern battlefields. Nevertheless, the region's early leadership of the preservation movement and the continued high level of state, local, and individual enthusiasm for preserving the past have enabled the South to outstrip the level of commitment in most other regions.

The nature of the sites preserved and exhibited is also revealing. One important theme in the southern preservation movement always has been the memorializing of southern leadership during the colonial and revolutionary periods. Numerous sites, from the reconstructed House of Burgesses at Williamsburg, to the homes of Washington and Jefferson, through the Yorktown and Jamestown areas, demonstrate the crucial role played by southerners in shaping the early history of the United States. Although Virginia tends to dominate in this category, North Carolina, South Carolina, and Georgia have also preserved significant sites.

The southern insistence on its own uniqueness of identity and aristocratic origins is suggested by the dominance of plantation architecture among historic restorations. The life of the colonial and antebellum white elite is interpreted at literally scores of sites, and from George Mason's Gunston Hall in Virginia southward to Louisiana's Oak Alley the South seems to be one great plantation. The romance of the antebellum years and the heroic struggle for the Lost Cause are clearly central themes in historic preservation in the South. This was especially true of work carried out during the period from 1890 to 1930, but even in more recent periods this impulse has carried considerable weight.

Perhaps the best example of this movement to memorialize the plantation South is found at Stone Mountain Park near Atlanta, Ga. This state-owned recreation area includes the "Ante-Bellum Plantation" exhibit, a romantic reconstruction of a "typical" 1850s plantation. This plantation never existed, however, but has been assembled on the spot from period buildings that were moved to Stone Mountain from throughout the state. That the scene is drastically glamorized is confirmed by the use of the Kingston House to represent the home of the overseer and his family, for the structure was actually the *main* house at Allen Plantation near Kingston, Ga. Such portrayals, even those that are not so exaggerated, have played a significant role in shaping popular conceptions of southern history.

Other segments of southern society often have been slighted by this em-

phasis on the plantation South. Indeed, it might be argued that those elements that are missing from historic sites are as significant as those that are present. For example, many plantations have been preserved with little or no reference to slave life and culture. Although some sites have begun to exhibit slave quarters (Gunston Hall and the Stone Mountain Plantation, for example), many others have none at all. Some slave quarters that *are* preserved or reconstructed—for example, those at Mount Vernon—are not typical and are sometimes far more commodious and well furnished than would have been the case. The southern middle class, the southern merchant, and the southern poor white are similarly slighted, at least in terms of the number of sites preserved. Even when merchants and artisans are represented, as at Williamsburg, the overall effect often suggests that this portion of society merely provided support and service for the more important planter class. Another curious weakness in the portrayal of the region's history is found in the comparatively limited number of sites related to Native Americans. In terms of numbers of sites, only in Mississippi does the interpretation of the Native American impact on the South approach realistic proportions. Native Americans in Mississippi have pressed for recognition of their forebears' contributions, and one result has been a change in many historic plaques.

The record of southern history as preserved in historic sites is, then, both an illustration of the South's desire to maintain a sense of identity and a reinforcement of popular images of the region held generally throughout the nation. That the historic South as it is preserved never existed is not the point. The preserved past is a record of regional pride and identity that seeks to highlight and help preserve southern distinctiveness in the face of forces that would "Americanize" the region. As many scholars have suggested, the use of the past, particularly the preserved past, is an ideological exercise. Nowhere is this more clear than in the South.

See also MYTHIC SOUTH: / Lost Cause Myth; RECREATION: / Colonial Williamsburg

Christopher D. Geist
Bowling Green State University

Edward D. C. Campbell, Jr., *Journal of Regional Cultures* (Fall-Winter 1982); Alvar W. Carlson, *Journal of American Culture* (Summer 1980); Beverley Da Costa, *Historic Houses of America Open to the Public* (1971); Larry Ford, *Growth and Change* (April 1974); Christopher D. Geist, in *Icons of America*, ed. Ray B. Browne and Marshall Fishwick (1978); Charles B. Hosmer, Jr., *Presence of the Past: A History of the Preservation Movement in the United States before Williamsburg* (1965); U.S. Department of the Interior, National Park Service, *The National Register of Historic Places* (1974); Walter Muir Whitehill, *Interdependent Historical Societies* (1962). ☆

Holidays

||||||||||||||||||||||||

Sunday has been the most frequently commemorated holiday in the South. Originally kept with some solemnity, it has now become largely a celebration of the cessation of work, although it is still a *dies non* in law. Once there was also a weekly half holiday, usually Wednesday or Thursday, but a tendency to slacken work on Saturday has recently appeared. Banks have generally transferred most of their holidays to a Monday.

The only total holiday is Christmas and perhaps the day following. New Year's Day shares in some of the Christmas festivities, but it has become mainly an occasion for viewing football bowl games. The popular meaning of Memorial Day is that it is the beginning of summer and vacation season. Early in the 20th century the South observed it as a memorial to veterans of the Spanish-American War. In many southern states 26 April is the special Confederate Memorial Day; in others it is 3 June; still others combine it with the national Memorial Day. The Fourth of July Independence Day was observed by southern blacks, but whites mainly viewed it as a nonworking day or picnic day. The 1976 bicentennial commemoration revived its significance, and it has grown in popularity. Labor Day used to be marked by a parade and baseball game, but now it generally marks the end of summer and vacation time. Thanksgiving in the South never had quite the importance it held outside the region. It is a time of hunting and feasting, and also the date for special football games.

The preceding holidays are of primary regional importance, but southerners, like other Americans, celebrate a variety of additional special occasions as well. St. Valentine's Day (14 February) is an occasion promoted by gift and stationery shops. The George Washington observance is a bank and post office holiday. Mardi Gras (Shrove Tuesday) is a major festival in New Orleans, Mobile, and Pensacola, the culmination of a season of Carnival preceding Lent. St. Patrick's Day (17 March) has grown from an ethnic Irish commemoration to a more extensive observance, once again promoted by gift and stationery shops. Easter Sunday is a high religious festival but, being a Sunday, is somewhat less commercialized than Christmas. Both Easter and Christmas celebrations tend to be only day-long rather than season-long events. The Jewish days of Rosh Hashanah, Yom Kippur, and Hanukkah are quietly recognized by the news media and stationery shops. Halloween (31 October), especially the night, is a party festival and a time of pranks by children and some adults.

A third group of holidays are, as yet, minor days to be noted. The birthdays of Robert E. Lee (21 January), Stonewall Jackson (22 January), and Matthew Fontaine Maury (24 January) are observed by organizations of descendants of Confederate veterans. Groundhog Day (2 February) is noted by news media and schools. St. Joseph Day (19 March) attracts major attention in New Orleans and some other Roman Catholic communities, and Good Friday is a legal holiday in Louisiana. May Day evokes some school attention. Flag Day (14 June) is a legal holiday. The days of St. John (the baptizer, 24 June, and the evangelist, 27 December) are occasions for Masonic lodges (picnics in summer, banquets in winter). There is a sentimental Francophile notice of Bastille Day (14 July) and a school recognition of Columbus Day. All Saints' Day (1 November) is a legal holiday in Louisiana. In nearby states it is an occasion for decorating cemeteries, although the latter practice belongs more aptly to the following day, All Souls' Day. Armistice Day (11 November) used to be a widespread observance, but under the designation of Veterans' Day it has become a day noted by veterans' organizations of all wars from World War II onward.

Four holidays—Christmas, New Year's, the Fourth of July, and Thanksgiving—are times when most institutions of a community are closed. Memorial Day and Labor Day are also nonworkdays for many; they serve to signal the opening and closing respectively of resort areas and vacation spots. Other holidays attract less attention (except for Easter), but they are nonetheless generally commemorated. The Jewish high holy days have gradually become more significant, especially because of the prominence of Jewish merchants and Jewish academics, many of whom celebrate Rosh Hashanah and Yom Kippur.

Among blacks there used to be extensive, if informal, commemoration of Emancipation Day (variously 8 May, 19 June, and perhaps others); businesses did not close, but blacks frequently did not report for work. Blacks in Texas celebrated the distinctive Juneteenth holiday. More recently other events, as, for instance, those of the civil rights activities of the 1960s, as well as disillusionment with the progress of emancipation, have pushed it into the background. The late Martin Luther King, Jr's birthday (15 January) won approval in 1983 as a federal holiday.

See also BLACK LIFE: / Juneteenth

Allen Cabaniss
University of Mississippi

Hennig Cohen and Tristram P. Coffin, eds., *The Folklore of American Holidays* (1987); Jane M. Hatch, *The American Book of Days* (3d. ed., 1978); Robert Lee, *National Forum* (Summer 1982); Robert J. Myers, *Celebrations: The Complete Book of American Hol-*

idays (1972); William E. Woodward, *The Way Our People Lived: An Intimate American History* (1944). ☆

Jacksonian Democracy

‖‖‖

The source of the political division of antebellum America into Jacksonian and Whig parties lay in the expansion of the market economy in the years between the War of 1812 and the Civil War. Acceptance of the values of the marketplace and resistance to those values each implied a conception of the meaning of freedom. For Jacksonians—dedicated to defending the ideal of economic and social self-sufficiency and fearful of being exploited by centers of power in the society—freedom was something the citizenry had by right, although evil, antidemocratic forces were attempting to take it away. A man was free when he was dependent on no one else for his livelihood and welfare. Movements and institutions whose success would diminish the existing autonomy of the individual were thus by definition aristocratic and inimical to the American experiment. For Whigs freedom was not something Americans already had but something for which they perpetually strived. A man became free by fulfilling his potential, by becoming all that he could be. The shackles of ignorance and poverty were his greatest enemies; the expansion of knowledge and opportunity was his principal security. Morality and justice required that citizens cooperate in order to build a better social order for all.

These differing definitions of freedom carried with them differing notions of the proper role of government. Whigs sought the enactment of programs intended to break the bonds that they felt held the mass of Americans in economic, social, or moral bondage: governmental aid for the construction of railroads, roads, and canals; protective tariffs; central regulation of the currency supply and the banking system; the establishment of public schools; the prohibition of the sale of liquor; and the creation of hospitals to cure the insane, institutions to train the deaf and blind, and penitentiaries to redeem criminals. Jacksonians generally regarded all such programs as the products of paternalistic elitism. They thought it intolerable that the ordinary citizen should be taxed to benefit railroads, factories, and banks; that his private conduct should be regulated; that his children should be forcibly indoctrinated with alien, urban ideals.

The Jacksonians campaigned for the abolition of all property qualifications for voting and officeholding, hoping that a broadened electorate could use the government not to assist the growth of corporations but to restrict and ultimately to destroy them. But beyond such activities, which they considered defensive, Jacksonians sought limited government, states' rights, and strict construction of federal and state constitutions. They viewed their political party as a trade union of the electorate through which ordinary citizens, individually weak, could band together and use their numbers to counterbalance the power of the wealthy. Whigs, on the other hand, were often doubtful that poverty-stricken, ill-educated citizens were capable of appreciating what was actually in their own best interest. Whigs conceived of their party as a sort of religious denomination, an organization of believers seeking to convert and to save the society at large. Though practical political considerations quickly led Whig politicians to abandon their early defense of restrictions on voting and officeholding, the Whigs continued to insist upon examinations for admission to such professions as law and medicine—examinations that Jacksonians frequently opposed.

In the Lower South the origins of Whiggery lay in the use of nullificationist doctrines to insist upon the right of each state to expel the Indians within its boundaries. The ease with which these nullifiers embraced the broad-constructionist program of the national Whig party in the later 1830s is an index of the degree to which ideology in the region was an extension of interest. Those merchants and planters who had eagerly sought the opening of Indian lands for speculation and commercial exploitation also eagerly awaited roads, railroads, and the easy credit promised by a national banking system. Although the majority of planters supported the Whigs, planters were not the cutting edge of the party; the intellectual leaders of Whiggery were the urban merchants and factors, whom the planters envied and emulated. The strength of the Jacksonians, in contrast, was usually to be found concentrated in those areas of the region most isolated from large-scale market agriculture.

In the Jacksonian period the attitudes and programs at issue between the parties in the South were essentially the same as those at issue throughout the nation. The expansion of the market economy and its values was a national phenomenon, and the response to it was national, embodying fears and hopes as real in the South as in the North. However, states' views toward one institution—slavery—differed. Slavery was an integral assumption in the ideology of each party. Jacksonians conceived of it protecting communities of self-reliant small farmers from the marketplace; as they saw it, with slaves to supply plantation labor, the white, independent yeomanry could not be converted into a proletariat, subservient to planters and capitalists. Whigs thought slavery a mechanism of social mobility, another of the many happy institutions facilitating the efforts of the industrious to achieve economic success. Both regarded it as essentially American, a bulwark of the freedom and democracy that were the Republic's distinguishing characteristics. Therefore, when proposals to exclude slavery from the western territories gained popularity in the North, both Jacksonians and Whigs in the South concluded that the absence of slavery from the territories would lead to the establishment in them of a hierarchical, un-American society, on the northern model.

Just before the advent of the party period in the early 1830s, Lower South factions that would become Jacksonians and Whigs were united in desiring the expulsion of the Indians—the Jacksonians so that settlers could establish independent farms on the Indians' lands and the Whigs so that the territory could be brought into the expanding American economy. The end of the party period in the mid-1850s found Jacksonians and Whigs throughout most of the region equally united in desiring slavery in the West—the Jacksonians because it would permit the yeomanry to be secure from the exploitation of the rich and the Whigs because it would promote the settlers' material advancement. In the intervening decades, however, the issues dominant on the national scene—banking, tariffs, and aid to internal improvements—revealed the sharply differing conceptions of freedom held by the more upwardly mobile and by those less willing to take risks in both the South and the nation at large. The salience for a time of this set of issues permitted the definition of the two parties in the southern states.

With the collapse of the Whig party in the 1850s the Democrats lost their social and ideological coherence. A group of ambitious younger Democratic politicians, who generally accepted the label "Young America," began to use aspects of Jacksonianism, especially its devotion to laissez-faire and strict-constructionist doctrines, in ways that defended rather than attacked commercial and industrial interests. Adopted in most instances as well by the leaders of the Republican party during the 1850s, these ideas became the ideology of American's dominant culture after the Civil War; they have often been called, though misleadingly, "social Darwinism."

Reconstruction in the southern states led to virtually all whites in the region becoming Democrats and had the effect in the later 19th century of depriving the yeoman constituencies—to which southern Jacksonianism had most strongly appealed—of a political party dedicated to defending them from rival sectors of society. And the heretical "social Darwinist" formulation of the Jacksonian creed deprived them, in some measure, of their familiar ideology upon which to ground a protest against their evident marginalization, in the South as elsewhere. The elimination of the public domain, and with it the squatter who had lived upon it, as well as the

end of the open range for the grazing of livestock with the passage of fencing laws, left the yeomanry's economic and social position increasingly precarious. Yet important elements of the Jacksonian tradition persisted, particularly in the most isolated, small-farming areas of the South. Its influence is to be seen in the Independent movement of the late 1870s, in the Farmers' Alliance of the 1880s, in the Populist movement of the early and mid-1890s, and, indeed, in the appeals of popular political leaders well into the 20th century.

J. Mills Thornton III
University of Michigan,
Ann Arbor

Lacy K. Ford, Jr., "Social Origins of a New South Carolina: The Upcountry in the Nineteenth Century" (Ph.D. dissertation, University of South Carolina, 1983); Steven Hahn, *The Roots of Southern Populism: Yeoman Farmers and the Transformation of the Georgia Upcountry, 1850–1890* (1983); Lawrence F. Kohl, "The Politics of Individualism: Social Character and Political Parties in the Age of Jackson" (Ph.D. dissertation, University of Michigan, 1980); J. Mills Thornton III, *Politics and Power in a Slave Society: Alabama, 1800–1860* (1978); Harry L. Watson, *Jacksonian Politics and Community Conflict: The Emergence of the Second American Party System in Cumberland County, North Carolina* (1981); Rush Welter, *The Mind of America, 1820–1860* (1975). ☆

Jeffersonian Tradition

|||||||||||||||||||||||||||||||||||||||||||||||||||||||||

Thomas Jefferson is invariably linked in the American mind with such concepts as liberty, freedom, and democracy. Indeed, the Jeffersonian tradition, as a general pattern of recognizable beliefs and behavior, provides much of the basis for America's liberal tradition. Through Jefferson, Charles M. Wiltse writes in *The Jeffersonian Tradition in American Democracy* (1960), "the political liberalism of accumulated centuries passed into the American democratic tradition, where it helped to mold the American way of life." To basic liberal tenets Jefferson added his own strain of agrarian thought, which praised the superiority of a self-sufficient, agricultural lifestyle. The independent yeoman farmer became a symbol for American democracy, and the image persisted, particularly in the South, into the 20th century.

Southerners have invoked Jefferson's precepts on numerous occasions in the 160 years since his death. For much of America's history the South has served as "a kind of sanctuary of the American democratic tradition," according to David M. Potter. Until comparatively recently the region was still a bastion of Jeffersonian ideals, at least for liberal critics of American society. There, Jefferson's agrarian descendants carried on resistance to the crass commercialism

Monticello, Thomas Jefferson's home

and capitalism of the Northeast and Midwest.

Following themes elaborated by Frederick Jackson Turner in the late 19th century, Americans easily linked the frontier with the development of democratic institutions and economic opportunity. Turner's "frontier thesis" exalted the role of the West, yet agrarian democracy and frontier democracy share obvious similarities, as William E. Dodd later noted in *Statesmen of the Old South* (1911). One of the first historians to realize the implications of agrarian democracy, Dodd asserted that the "real South" was precisely the South of Thomas Jefferson. Any conservative, hierarchical developments, as opposed to progress along democratic, equalitarian lines, were mere aberrations from true southernism. Dodd subjected his thesis to little critical evaluation, and later writers have disputed his findings. But his version was not entirely lacking in historical foundation. Jefferson and the Jeffersonian tradition originated in the South, and for much of American political history the region has supported men who shared such ideas.

Southerners have invoked, in addition to Jefferson's agrarian philosophy, a number of other principles that can be traced to the intellectual and political heritage of the third president. His name is often associated with arguments sustaining states' rights, and southerners cite his authorship of the Kentucky Resolution of 1799 as evidence of his opposition to the extension of federal power. Inhabitants of the region recall his arguments against Alexander Hamilton's plans for industrialization, national banks, and tariffs, and much of America's antiurban tradition can be traced to Jeffersonian origins as well. Ironically, for all his praise of yeoman farmers as God's "Chosen People," Jefferson eventually admitted the need for commerce and manufacturing, and his immediate successors in the White House acquiesced in the chartering of a Second Bank of the United States and the development of a tariff policy. Slavery also received considerable attention in Jefferson's writings, but his recommendations for abolition did not endear him in the South. Few southerners would admit that such ideas represented Jefferson's settled policy.

Jefferson's commitment to liberalism, grounded in the 18th century Enlightenment, provided the intellectual foundation for his writings on agrarianism, states' rights, and restricted governmental power, as well as his opposition to slavery. The most widely known examples of his ideas on liberal political theory appear in the Declaration of Independence and in other sources, including his *Notes on the State of Virginia*. His liberalism contributed to the practical reforms that connected his administration with those of Andrew Jackson, Woodrow Wilson, and Franklin D. Roosevelt. Both Jeffersonian agrarianism and idealism surfaced in the programs advocated by the Populists in the 1890s and in the writings of the Nashville Agrarians in the 1930s.

Jefferson's influence in the South remains difficult to assess precisely. The region unquestionably cherished his agrarianism and his defense of states' rights, but his more liberal, equalitarian doctrines languished there in the years after independence. By the "era of good feelings" Jefferson was viewed as the defender of states' rights in his native Virginia, where his principles coincided with powerful economic and political interests. The nullification movement in South Carolina contributed to the trans-

formation of his image in the South. The patriot who was eulogized in 1826 as the "Apostle of Liberty" in 1826 became the "Father of States' Rights."

Jefferson's Kentucky Resolution enhanced his position among nullifiers, because his words in that document implied that nullification of an unconstitutional federal law was a legitimate procedure. Nullification, Merrill D. Peterson asserts in *The Jefferson Image in the American Mind* (1960), "was the pivot upon which many states' rights Jeffersonians swung toward the policies of sectionalism, slavery, and secession." At the very least, the Jeffersonian tradition was linked to the South's cause, and the episode also demonstrated that Jefferson's ideas could be appropriated for purposes alien to the original intent.

The nullifiers were not the only faction in Jacksonian society to rely on the Jeffersonian tradition. Jacksonian democracy itself revived essential Jeffersonian themes that were modified and strengthened by new influences in the 1830s and 1840s. In the *Age of Jackson* (1945) Arthur M. Schlesinger, Jr., defines Jacksonian democracy as a "more hard-headed and determined version of Jeffersonian democracy," adding that democrats had to accept that new era's industrialism, factories, mills, labor, banks, and capital—all distasteful to orthodox Jeffersonians. The latter's view of independent yeomen as the nation's unique class of producers had to be enlarged to accommodate urban wage earners.

In the meantime, defenders of slavery still invoked Jefferson, noting that the Virginian had owned extensive property in slaves throughout his life. At the same time, the Wilmot Proviso linked the Jeffersonian heritage with the growing opposition to the extension of slavery into the western territories. The proviso revived the language and intent of the old Northwest Ordinance of 1787, which banned slavery in the states of the Old Northwest. Jefferson made no contribution to that legislation, although he had proposed a similar ban on slavery in congress's 1784 land ordinance. Congress had rejected that restriction, only to add its own to the Northwest Ordinance. Southerners viewed Jefferson's alleged authorship of the antislavery provision as one of his "fatal legacies," but most doubted that he ever favored outright abolition. Later, southerners advocated the concept of popular sovereignty in Jefferson's name, for it implied frontier individualism, self-government, and local control. Even Stephen A. Douglas described his brainchild, popular sovereignty, as "the Jeffersonian plan for government in the territories."

As the South's leaders gradually retreated from the democratic idealism of the Jeffersonian tradition, the Democratic party lost a degree of its identity, and its spokesmen seemed opposed to the doctrines that many Americans typically defined as being Jeffersonian or liberal. In the 1850s the new Republican party easily incorporated the Jeffersonian commitment to human rights, antislavery, and agrarian democracy. The powerful rhetoric of free men and free soil composed an idealistic image for the new Republican party. And in the political upheaval that flowed logically from the compromises of 1850, the Republican platform corresponded to what most Americans imagined to be Jeffersonian and "in essentials," Merrill D. Peterson adds, "with what had in fact been Jeffersonian."

After the Civil War, Democratic leaders called for a return to Jeffersonian principles, but Jefferson's influence in the party remained limited until the 1880s and 1890s. Only in 1892, for example, did the party's platform openly reaffirm allegiance to the principles formulated by the third president. As for the New South of the postwar era, its dynamic leaders preached industry, business, and progress. By the 1880s such tendencies in the region stimulated the rise of a vocal group of Jeffersonian critics. The oratory of such men as Robert L. Dabney and Charles C. Jones conjured up the polemics of John Taylor of Caroline and reflected more clearly the influence of Thomas Jefferson than Jefferson Davis. These critics saw the growing cities of the South much as Jefferson and John Taylor had earlier described urban centers—"sores on the body politic."

By the 1890s some southern Jeffersonians had drifted toward the Populist party, and in that era of agrarian revolt they emphasized the radical side of the Jeffersonian tradition. Although men like George G. Vest of Missouri and John Sharp Williams of Mississippi remained within the Democratic party, Tom Watson's disillusionment led him to the Populist party where he worked to revive the agrarian alliance of earlier years. The Populist-Democratic fusion and the ensuing defeat of William Jennings Bryan in 1896 destroyed Watson's hopes and those of most agrarians in the South.

When Populists invoked Jefferson's philosophy in the 1890s, they harked back to the lost world of independent cultivators, doing so at a time when the South yearned to advertise its new, modern outlook. At the same time, agriculture had become more of a business and less of a way of life. Still, Populists evaded their critics by appealing to the body of native southern tradition and doctrine that dated back to the writings of the revolutionary period. Moreover, southerners recalled the ideas upon which their ancestors relied when they provided the leadership against Hamilton's Federalists and later against the Whigs. The Texas Populist "Cyclone" Davis campaigned with volumes of Jefferson's collected works tucked under his arm, and in response to questions responded: "We will now look through the volumes of Jefferson's works and see what Mr. Jefferson said on this matter." Professor Dodd is likely correct in his contention that Jefferson would have been a Populist in 1892.

With the Populist defeat the Jeffersonian tradition entered a period of quiescence, although Woodrow Wilson invoked his name and praised his philosophy in the years before World War I. By the 1920s the Jeffersonian tradition was of limited value in America; clearly its agrarianism was of little worth in the Jazz Age, and liberal reform found few successful advocates. Yet in the next decade, Franklin D. Roosevelt's Administration was keenly aware of its intellectual and political roots in the liberal tradition of Jefferson, and such measures as the Civilian Conservation Corps reflected the president's personal commitment to the land. Roosevelt, too, shared a Jeffersonian suspicion of the crowded atmosphere of large cities and feared their detrimental impact on people. As a result of the New Deal's response to the Great Depression, the Democratic party of Thomas Jefferson became the Democratic party of Franklin D. Roosevelt.

Jeffersonian ideals flourished in the 1930s, according to a newspaper columnist who declared, "Everyone has a kind word for him. Nearly everyone writes a book about him." Jeffersonian agrarianism enjoyed a special resurg-

ence in some parts of the South, following publication of *I'll Take My Stand: The South and the Agrarian Tradition* (1930). The essays by the Twelve Southerners, or Nashville Agrarians, praised the agrarian way of life while damning the modern, industrial New South. The book stimulated a vigorous debate in southern intellectual circles, but this last agrarian revival ran its course before the end of the decade. Still, the movement testified to the tenacity and vitality of the Jeffersonian tradition. For southerners, Jefferson's writings served as a bulwark against unwanted change and as a defense for the southern way of life. If the Jeffersonian heritage could not exclude the forces of progress or defuse the power of an ever-expanding federal government, those concepts always offered a calm, self-sufficient alternative to the exigencies of modern life.

George M. Lubick
Northern Arizona University

Daniel J. Boorstin, *The Lost World of Thomas Jefferson* (1948); Merrill D. Peterson, *The Jefferson Image in the American Mind* (1960), ed., *Thomas Jefferson: A Profile* (1968); David M. Potter, in *Myth and Southern History*, ed. Patrick Gerster and Nicholas Cords (1974); Twelve Southerners, *I'll Take My Stand: The South and the Agrarian Tradition* (1930); Charles M. Wiltse, *The Jeffersonian Tradition in American Democracy* (1960); C. Vann Woodward, *Origins of the New South, 1877–1913* (1951). ☆

Korean War

Historians have found few distinctively regional aspects to the Korean War. In fact, neither southern historians nor American military historians have even sought systematically to explore either the role the South played in the war or the role the war played in the South.

The economic effect of the Korean War was similar in the South and the rest of the nation. Inflation appeared in 1950, leading to rising prices, including the historic end of the nickel Coca-Cola. The position of the region's farmers did not improve, despite the rising demand for food; costs of production rose to offset rising farm prices. The federal government's freeze on wages and prices in January 1951 helped control inflation in the South, and increased prosperity and lowered unemployment marked the final two years of the war. Defense spending for the Cold War as well as the Korean War was especially important in promoting southern economic improvement in the early 1950s. As in World War II, southern bases were key mobilization points for American soldiers.

A few prominent southerners symbolized various aspects of southern attitudes toward the war. Georgian Dean Rusk was one of Secretary of State Dean Acheson's closest advisors; Senator Tom Connally of Texas, chairman of the Senate Foreign Relations Committee, was an unquestioning supporter of President Harry Truman's policies; Congressmen L. Mendel Rivers of South Carolina endorsed Douglas MacArthur's request to use atomic weapons during the war against North Korea and China; Lieutenant General Walton H. Walker of Texas, Commander of the Eighth Army, was a high ranking military figure; Virginia Durr opposed the war and her husband, Clifford, lost his job with the Farmers Union after she signed a petition opposing American involvement. The Korean War was the first occasion testing Truman's policy, established by executive order in July 1948, of desegregating the military.

Southern public opinion generally supported the Korean War enthusiastically. Americans were convinced the conflict was a just one, caused at the height of the Cold War by communist aggression. When Herbert Hoover suggested in December 1950 a new isolationist policy and abandonment of Korea, Ralph McGill of the Atlanta *Constitution* wrote that this would be national suicide, and he seemed to reflect regional attitudes. Conservative southerners were uncomfortable with a national policy aimed not at total military victory, but limited war for strategic purposes.

Charles Reagan Wilson
University of Mississippi

Bernard C. Nalty, *Strength for the Fight: A History of Black Americans in the Military* (1986); John Edward Wiltz, in *The Korean War: A Twenty-five Year Perspective* (1977). ☆

Manners
||||||||||||||||||||||||

Manners are a formal code of proper behavior. The South has stressed etiquette and has attributed much significance to the form of verbal expression and behavior in a group. Stark Young wrote in *I'll Take My Stand* (1930) that "manners are the mask of decency that we employ at need, the currency of fair communication," and William Alexander Percy insisted in his memoir *Lanterns on the Levee* (1941) that "manners are essential and are essentially morals." Southerners have, in fact, traditionally equated manners—the appropriate, customary, or proper way of doing things—with morals, so that unmannerly behavior has been viewed as immoral behavior. Thus, in the South moral codes, laws, and manners have been intertwined, with the aim of curbing individual aggressiveness and maintaining social order through a combination of external community pressures and internalized individual motivation.

"He did everything correctly, but with the faintest smile, as though to say he knew what he was doing and could do it another way if necessary," wrote James McBride Dabbs in *The Southern Heritage* (1958) about his bachelor uncle who embodied the ideal of manners many southern mothers taught their children. "He was a balance of reserve and openness, of formality and informality, which the South aimed at but often failed to attain." Southerners such as Dabbs who have written about manners mention words such as polite, courteous, kind, gentle, hospitable, friendly yet dignified. Rigidity in following the rules is not prized as much as the flexibility and resiliency that enable the well mannered to handle any situation graciously. There are, to be sure, rules: one must respect one's parents ("Yes, sir," "No, ma'am"), honor obligations to kin, welcome neighbors, and protect the weak and helpless; a gentleman must open doors for a woman and stand when she enters a room; one must not dive into the food before grace is said and everyone served. In the colonial era, particularly, manners were of a prescriptive nature, defining for the upper classes the standards for behavior indicative of refinement, good breeding, and sophistication. Among the wealthy, manners served in general as parameters for social class relations.

The concern for manners goes far back in southern history. The ideal of the English country gentleman provided the basis for proper manners among the colonial planters. European, particularly English, books on manners were commonly found in plantation libraries: Richard Brathwaite's *The English Gentleman*, Harry Peacham's *The Compleat Gentleman*, Count Baldesar Castiglione's *The Book of the Courtier*, and the most influential of all for the southern elite—*The Whole Duty of Man* (usually attributed to Richard Allestree), one of the first books printed in Virginia and the popular source for guidelines on behavior until the mid-19th century. Estates with English names, such as Drayton, Berkeley Hundred, and Exeter Lodge, became famous centers of the best formal colonial manners. William Byrd II chronicled in his diary the etiquette of the people in that society, suggesting their power, the respect they received when displaying their manners, and their aspirations to noblesse oblige. A code of honor appeared that provided strict rules for proper conduct in all situations.

The frontier was a very different force that affected the development of manners among early southerners. Observers characterized plain folk on the frontier and in settled areas as generous, hospitable, and polite. Everyone also agreed their behavior was deplorably crude. Travelers from abroad saw little refinement or sophistication among them and were sometimes dismayed at southeners' disregard for the proper rules of behavior. The formal manners of the Virginia and Carolina Tidewater, to be sure, were transferred to the southwestern frontier. Andrew Jackson was a frontiersman, but in social circles he displayed the courteous manners expected of the planter he became. On the frontier, manners could help an ambitious person create a persona with a well-bred background. Manners among the nouveau planters were, nonetheless, simpler and less formal than among the Tidewater elite. The veneer came off easily on the frontier. Disagreements were often settled with an angrily drawn pistol instead of through the honorable code duello. W. J. Cash insisted, though, that an enduring and basically admirable ideal of manners developed among the antebellum frontier plain folk, an ideal that promoted, he wrote, "a kindly courtesy, a level-eyed pride, an easy quietness, a barely perceptible flourish of bearing."

Between 1830 and 1850 the southern cult of chivalry became a major expression of southern romanticism, and the cult had significance for manners. Southern whites believed they were descended from aristocratic English noblemen, from Cavaliers, who were the ultimate embodiment of proper manners. The key was in ritual. After a trip to Richmond in 1853, Frederick Law Olmsted noted that "more ceremony and form is sustained" among southerners than "well-bred people commonly use at the North." A regional fondness for the splendid gesture, theatrical behavior, and extravagant pageantry had appeared.

Women in the antebellum era were central to the southern code of manners. The cult of chivalry taught that the mythic lady was the essence of manners. A white woman's social role was highly restricted by "proper" conduct, and the men around her had to be on their best behavior as well. The myth of the lady was not unique to the South, but, as Anne Firor Scott stresses in *The Southern Lady* (1970), southern regional culture was distinctive in the intensity and tenacity of the ideal. Southern courtship

and marriage had clear expectations of correct behavior stressing male agressiveness and female coyness. This romanticized ideal of mannerly behavior between the sexes was reinforced in the late 19th and early 20th centuries by Victorian sentimentalism and Protestant moralism. Those attitudes are no longer predominant in the late 20th century South, but the code of southern courtship manners retains vestiges from the past. Florence King's *Southern Ladies and Gentlemen* (1975) is a near-definitive account of southern sexual manners practiced by regional types such as the Self-Rejuvenating Virgin, Dear Old Thing, Good Old Boy, Bad Good Old Boy, and Gay Confederate. She explores such central southern concepts as "trashy" behavior, "passing the time of day," the "freeze" (a blood-curdling look of disapproval), the "pert plague" among women, and the "deliverance syndrome" among men.

Southern culture has much lore on the effort to teach manners to the young. Manners have been encouraged by schools and churches and sometimes by the legal systems. Folklore from the region's blacks and whites tries to link crude manners with unpleasant results. Singing while eating will bring bad luck, taking the last bit of bread on a plate means a young man will never find a wife, and eating too rapidly leads to marriage before one is ready. Such sayings are apparently intended to scare the young into respectability.

Accounts of teaching manners in the South frequently focus on meals. In *Black Boy* (1945) Richard Wright told of the preacher coming to Sunday dinner, finishing his soup early, and then eating piece after piece of fried chicken before young Wright could even finish his soup. He finally stood up and said, "that preacher's going to eat *all* the chicken!" His mother, he wrote, gave him "no dinner because of my bad manners." In *To Kill a Mockingbird* (1960) young Scout is reprimanded when she comments on her classmate Walter's habit of putting syrup on all his food. The young man had come to lunch, and Scout's father had made him feel at home until her breach of manners. Her father pours syrup on his own bread to put the guest at ease—another gesture of good manners. The black housekeeper Calpurnia lectures Scout for poor behavior. All of these examples suggest the crucial role of women, black and white, in nurturing southern manners. Sometimes manners are enforced with the harsh discipline of Calvinistic patriarchs, but more commonly women teach proper behavior.

An emphasis on manners reflects the South's stress on community. As Stark Young wrote in *I'll Take My Stand*, manners are only understood in regard to "a state of society that assumes a group welfare and point of view." Southerners have valued their individualism, but their regard for manners has been the counterbalance to individualism. In the large industrial cities of the North from the 19th century on, people have moved among strangers, creating little pressure for observing the niceties of behavior in a pressurized world. In contrast, in the South's characteristic smaller communities and rural areas one conducted business and daily living among people one saw all too frequently. "Manners are to be seen," wrote James McBride Dabbs, suggesting that manners are a public matter of image among a group of people well known to each other. The upper-class elite, in particular, set the tone for etiquette in society. "The aristocrat was to reveal," observed Dabbs, "to make public, what life could, and should, be."

Southern manners were not only a community binding force, an agreed upon code for groups to aspire to; they were also divisive, separating those with manners from those without. The Tidewater planter looked down on the manners of the backcountry folk. Virginians looked down on the manners of those in early North Carolina (William Byrd II referred to them as lazy, ignorant, and filthy). Southerners by the antebellum era looked down on northern manners. South Carolina Congressman Preston Brooks cane-whipped Massachusetts Senator Charles Sumner in 1856 over alleged poor manners, an insult to honor, contained in a Sumner speech. Such violence has often been ascribed to violations of the code of honor, and mannerly behavior has cloaked violent instincts. A southerner is courteous and friendly, goes an old saying, until he is mad enough to kill. Southerners ironically viewed manners and decorum as so vital to the maintenance of social order that defense of such codes warranted violence.

This double-edged emphasis on manners has been apparent in other ways, too. In many cases manners have been a veneer that masked social inequities while institutionalizing them. Manners have been seen as one aspect of upper-class ideology and power. The southern elite used manners to soften tendencies toward social class conflict. At public gatherings, wrote W. J. Cash of a typical plain farmer, "there would nearly always be a fine gentleman to lay a familiar hand on his shoulders, to inquire by name after the members of his family, maybe to buy him a drink." The result was to patronize the yeoman farmer, but in such a smooth way that he went home "not sullen and vindictive" at all over the planter's wealth and prestige. Manners were an aspect of a paternalistic style. The personal kindness and thoughtfulness of the landowner and later the millowner, moreover, bound whites together. Mannerly behavior between whites of different social groups helped cement Cash's "Proto-Dorian" bond.

A deeply rooted code of etiquette is found among black families in the South. Frederick Douglass suggested black etiquette derived from similar African codes and noted, "there is not to be found, among any people, a more rigid enforcement of the law of respect to elders, than they maintain. . . . There is no better material in the world for making a gentleman, than is furnished in the African."

Melville Herskovits in *The Myth of the Negro Past* (1942) argued that "outstanding among the intangible values of Negro life in the United States is strict adherence to codes of polite behavior." Newbell Niles Puckett in *Folk Beliefs of the Southern Negro* (1926) also stressed the importance of etiquette in black life, which links "unpleasant results with uncouth manners in an attempt to frighten the young into a quicker acquisition of American good-breeding." Herskovits noted a number of practices of etiquette that have important African roots. Respect for elders among southern blacks can be also found among Africans who feel that "old folks" are "almost ghosts." An ancestral cult thus developed with the understanding that ancestors have the power to help or harm their descendants.

Herskovits also observed African etiquette in "the matter of turning the head when laughing (sometimes with the hand over the mouth), or in speaking to elders or other respected persons of averting the eyes and perhaps the face." In the *Etiquette of Race Relations* (1939) Bertram Doyle showed how such polite-

ness was adopted in dealing with whites. Gestures of respect reserved in Africa for elders were a defense against white aggression in the South. Black writers such as Ralph Ellison have preserved this racial etiquette in their fiction. Ellison's protagonist in *The Invisible Man* remembers his father's advice: to survive in the white man's world, you must "yes'em to death." Politeness is the ultimate weapon the old man bestowed on his son.

Black etiquette is thus a double-edged tradition. Its African roots, like those of whites in Europe, were formed in Old World cultures to regulate relationships within families and communities. Faced with slavery and later with segregation, southern blacks adopted etiquette as a means of survival. They developed a racial etiquette as a foil to the racism of southern whites.

Racial etiquette also revealed a southern stress on personal relationships. Post–Civil War southerners developed a complex and elaborate ritual to govern interracial behavior. William Alexander Percy argued that only their good manners enabled the two different races to live together in an orderly, single way of life: "The Southern Negro has the most beautiful manners in the world, and the Southern white, learning from him, I suspect, is a close second." But, in addition to this, a distinctive caste etiquette worked to maintain racial separation. The etiquette required whites to behave in certain ways toward blacks, ways seemingly at odds with their normal code of good manners. One should use first names, not "Mr." or "Mrs.," in addressing blacks; one did not shake hands with a black person or tip a hat. Blacks should address all whites with respect, should not crowd whites on sidewalks, should enter the home of a white person through the back door, should sit at the back of a bus, and should stand or wait at the end of a line for service until all whites had been served. Segregation laws enforced some racial behavior, but "manners" were enforced by individual and collective white intimidation of blacks. "Uppity" blacks were a constant worry of southern whites. A breech of racial manners by a black man could lead to a tongue-lashing, humiliation, and sometimes violence. When black teenager Emmett Till violated ultimate sexual-racial manners in Mississippi in the 1950s by whistling at a white woman, he was lynched.

Racial manners were justified by the "best" people as a way to maintain social distance between the races and thus prevent overt aggression. Interracial etiquette did at times ease tensions between blacks and whites. Kindly manners between persons who happened to be of different races helped to soften the rigidity of the segregated society. Many southern whites treated blacks with respect and were concerned not to hurt their feelings. Kindly manners did not, however, ease the injustice of that society, but rather nurtured a ritualized, daily sense of inferiority among blacks. Outsiders were expected to follow southern racial manners, and there are legendary stories of northerners moving south and adopting them more enthusiastically than southern whites. The requirements of racial manners in the South meant that blacks lived in an atmosphere of daily intimidation and frequent anxiety. Blacks were polite because they were dealing with a life-and-death matter—an ultimate expression of southern regard for manners.

With the end of racial segregation laws in the 1960s an accompanying change in southern racial manners has taken place. The decline in the formal code of polite and honorable behavior that both black and white southerners have proclaimed seems to be a by-product of long-term social changes in the region. W. J. Cash saw a decline in southern manners dating back to the New South era of the late 19th century. A grafting of northern back-slapping heartiness onto southern geniality, he wrote, created "the Rotary ideal," which represented "an unfortunate decline in the dignity of the southern manner." The Agrarians of *I'll Take My Stand* saw threats to the survival of formal manners in any industrial, business-oriented society. Robert B. Heilman, in an essay entitled "The Southern Temper," warned of a decline of manners in the contemporary South because southern whites had "popularized and made the object of public self-congratulation" their tradition of manners. "Promotional facisimilies" of manners, involving the exploitation of hoop-skirted ladies dressed for tourists, marks, he said, a decline in the real thing.

Sociologist John Shelton Reed's studies of contemporary North-South attitudes have shown that both northerners and southerners continue to see southerners as more mannerly than persons from north of the Mason-Dixon line. Respondents to a North Carolina opinion poll in the early 1970s described southerners by using words such as *considerate, polite, friendly, courteous, hospitable, genteel, cordial,* and *nice*— terms synonymous with the manners that southern mothers, black and white, have tried to teach their children.

Southerners have not written any widely known etiquette books despite the continued fascination of the gentry and the upwardly mobile with manners. One theory for this is that southerners prefer to learn proper behavior from mothers rather than from books. Southerners are rarely mentioned in etiquette books nowadays. Judith Martin, better known as Miss Manners, has chastized southerners for wearing white shoes after Easter rather than at the proper time, after Memorial Day. The often-hot southern spring is perhaps responsible for this abiding regional faux pas, but her criticism is a reminder that northerners not those from the South, have traditionally set national standards of manners.

The southern fascination with manners, though, has been expressed in literature. Peter Taylor's short stories, Reynolds Price's and Hamilton Basso's novels, and all of Eudora Welty's works are among the most subtle explorations of southern manners. Three of Welty's best-known works show how the southerner's sense of ritual led to an appreciation of form: *Delta Wedding* explores a happy ceremony of marriage, *Optimists' Daughter* a sad one of death, and *Losing Battles* a joyous yet melancholy family reunion. Southern concern with family and kin, the proper clothing, food, courtesy in daily living, talking and visiting—all are expressed in the region's best writing.

See also BLACK LIFE: Race Relations; LANGUAGE: Conversation; MYTHIC SOUTH: Racial Attitudes; / Hospitality; WOMEN'S LIFE: Child-raising Customs

Charles Reagan Wilson
University of Mississippi

W. J. Cash, *The Mind of the South* (1941); Thomas D. Clark, *The Rampaging Frontier: Manners and Humors of Pioneer Days in the Southern Middle West* (1939), *Travelers in the New South*, 2 vols. (1962), *Travelers in the Old South*, 2 vols. (1959); James McBride Dabbs, *The Southern Heritage* (1958), *Who Speaks for the South?* (1964); John Dollard, *Caste and Class in a Southern Town* (1937); Bertram Doyle, *The Etiquette of Race Relations in the South* (1937); Clement Eaton, *The Mind of the Old South* (1967); Melville Herskovits, *The Myth of the Negro Past* (1941); Florence King, *Southern Ladies and Gentlemen* (1975); Rollin G. Osterweis, *Romanticism and Nationalism in the Old South* (1949); Newbell Niles Puckett, *Folk Beliefs of the Southern Negro* (1926; reprint ed. 1969); John Shelton Reed, *The Enduring South: Subcultural Persistence in Mass Society* (1972), *Southerners: The Social Psychology of Sectionalism* (1983); Anne Firor Scott, *The Southern Lady: From Pedestal to Politics, 1830–1930* (1970); Bertram Wyatt-Brown, *Southern Honor: Ethics and Behavior in the Old South* (1982). ☆

Maritime Tradition
||||||||||||||||||||!||||||||||||||||||||||||||||||||

American experience began on the water and steadily moved inland. The various peoples who discovered, explored, and settled this country depended on bodies and arteries of water. Of necessity they were conscious of matters marine and riverine. The writings of the colonists who settled along the Atlantic Seaboard, the Gulf region, and even the interior abound with references to the importance of the waters and their existence. This was equally true of both southerners and those who lived north of the Chesapeake Bay. Yet few historians, including southerners, recognize that the southern states have a maritime heritage. For example, in 1954 Clement Eaton characterized southerners as "agricultural and unskilled in the ways of ships."

This was certainly not true in the colonial period. In 1769 exports from the southern colonies to Great Britain were four times more valuable than the products sent there from the colonies above Chesapeake Bay. In the English colonies, Norfolk and Savannah, along with a number of small ports such as Edenton and New Bern, N.C., and Georgetown, S.C., were established by the crown as official ports. Charles Town (Charleston) was the most important port of the colonial South. In 1769 two hundred vessels carried Charleston's exports to market in Europe, the West Indies, and the other American colonies. In that year more ships entered Virginia and Maryland ports than those of all other colonies combined.

The majority of ships engaged in maritime trade with the southern colonies were built outside of those provinces. Nevertheless, a substantial shipbuilding industry did develop in the South. This was inevitable considering the section's dependence upon water transportation as well as the availability of abundant timber. Between 1740 and 1773 there were at least five shipyards in South Carolina that built a total of 24 square-rigged ships as well as a large number of sloops and schooners. During the decades preceding the Revolutionary War, nearly a hundred ships engaged in the coastal and foreign trade were built in North Carolina.

Fishing was primarily for subsistence in the colonial period. Salted fish in barrels were sold to ships trading with the southern colonies, and occasional cargoes were carried to the West Indies. Weirs and fishpots were employed, and large seines were introduced in the 1760s. Fishing was not done in the ocean but rather in the rivers and sounds.

The American Revolutionary War was as much a maritime as a land war in the southern colonies. The British blockade extended as far south as Savannah, and privateers from Charleston, New Bern, Norfolk, and other ports along the South Atlantic Seaboard ranged as far as the West Indies seeking prizes. Lord Cornwallis's surrender at Yorktown in October 1781 was at least partially a result of naval action in the Chesapeake Bay and the subsequent siege of British forces on land and water.

The War of 1812 was primarily a maritime war in the southern states, occasioned by blockade and privateering, and concluded by the British combined attack against New Orleans in January 1815.

The early decades of the 19th century witnessed the expansion of the United States to include the Gulf region from Florida to Texas. The rapid growth of sugar and cotton production along with exports from the Midwest made New Orleans by 1820 the second most important port in the country. New Orleans had been founded as a port by the French early in the 18th century, but it was the development of steam transportation on the Mississippi River and its tributaries that crystalized the port's rapid rise in importance. Mobile, another Gulf port with French origins, also developed rapidly and by the Civil War was the third largest exporting city in the country.

The first half of the 19th century saw the appearance of dozens of small ports throughout the region. The expansion of steam navigation on inland waters along the seaboard and the interior states was a major factor in the development of the southern economy. Steamboats became feeders, carrying cargoes to coastal ports and later to rail centers.

Shipbuilding expanded as shipping expanded. In the United States as a whole, over 8,000 vessels of wood or iron were constructed between 1849 and 1858. Of this number, southern shipyards built approximately 1,600. One writer in 1850 estimated that the South, including Maryland and Kentucky, had 145 shipyards.

In the middle of the 19th century, commercial fishing began to emerge as an industry of importance in the South. This was partly a result of improved transportation, which enabled fish and shellfish to reach inland markets, and partly the result of seasonal trips to southern waters by New England fishermen. In the 1830s Connecticut fishermen were using gill nets off Savannah, and smack fishermen were reaching as far south as Florida. By 1860 North Carolina had 33 commercial fisheries, and its herring fishery concentrated in the Albemarle Sound area was among the largest in the world.

The Civil War was devastating to southern fishermen, as it was to others engaged in maritime activities. The Union blockade, although never totally effective, was tight enough severely to limit maritime trade. Union combined operations gradually gained control of the navigable waters in the Confederacy. Maritime activities in the southern states, however, achieved some success. Several hundred vessels ran the blockade, bringing into southern ports badly needed supplies and other goods. An impressive number of warships, including more than 20 armored vessels, were built for the Confederate navy. Many of these ships contributed to the defense of southern ports, including Mobile, Savannah, Charleston, and Richmond.

The postwar years saw a revival and expansion of maritime activities in the South. Shipping along the coast, linking the Gulf and South Atlantic ports with the Northeast, revived but with some important changes. Wooden schooners continued to carry certain low-grade cargoes, particularly lumber and naval stores. With the expansion of railroads into coastal areas, steamship traffic declined. Local river steamers prospered, however, carrying passengers and cargo to railheads.

While the construction of wooden vessels declined nationwide after the Civil War, it gradually revived in the South late in the 19th century. Nearly 3,000 wooden vessels were built in the southern states in the period between 1865 and 1900. Various factors contributed to this: local needs, the development of a wooden barge-building industry for inland waterways, and the rapidly expanding commercial fishing industry in the South.

Improved rail transportation resulted in the introduction of the iced-fish trade in the mid-1870s. First introduced in North Carolina, it spread farther south in the 1880s. By 1880 Charleston had an important offshore fishery with the catch of blackfish, flounder, and red snapper being shipped to northern markets. Of the 17 schooners and 49 sloops built in Charleston from 1870 to 1880, two-thirds were engaged in commercial fishing. In the 1880s the oyster industry became important in the North Carolina sounds, but it was not until the 20th century that shrimp would become commercially important.

Although the fishing industry would continue to expand in the 20th century, only in the shellfisheries (oyster, crab, shrimp), particularly shrimp, did the southern states gain a position of prominence. Louisiana would take the lead in shrimp harvesting, followed by Texas and Florida. The introduction of the outboard motor and the otter trawl early in the century, the development of refrigeration in the 1920s, and the continued improvement in transportation in the coastal areas were the major factors that stimulated the shrimp industry. By the middle of the century, southern shrimping had overtaken in value all rival shrimp or shellfish catches from Maine to Alaska. In 1956 the national shrimp catch (more than 90% from southern waters) paid fishermen $70 million, followed in order by salmon ($46 million), tuna ($43 million), and oysters ($30 million). In 1950, the New England states had approximately 10,500 fishermen while the southern states claimed more than 23,000. Today nearly 38 percent of the total poundage of fish and shellfish caught in the United States comes from the southern states.

The shipping industry in the southern states went through a transition in the latter years of the 19th and early years of the 20th centuries. Developments in road and rail transportation resulted in a significant decline in river and coastwise traffic. This in turn gradually ended the maritime commerce for most of the small southern ports. Only the ports with deep-water harbors capable of holding the large ocean-going vessels survived and actually expanded. New Orleans continued to lead southern ports and today is the third largest port in the United States. The Hampton Roads area, comprising the ports of Norfolk, Newport News, and Hampton, Va., grew into the largest exporter (in volume) in the country and today handles 90 percent of coal exports. Charleston is 13th, and Houston and Galveston, Tex., Wilmington, N.C., Savannah, Ga., and Tampa and Jacksonville, Fla.,

also rank among the country's important ports.

Shipbuilding has also gone through a transition. The decline in inland and coastwise shipping resulted in a parallel decline in shipbuilding in the southern states. At the turn of the century only a few southern yards had built iron or steel ships; the overwhelming majority concentrated on wooden ship construction. Only Newport News Shipyard in Virginia was building metal vessels on a large scale. World War I witnessed a revival of the ship-building industry in the South with the construction of steel, concrete, and wooden vessels. This boom ended shortly after the war was over. The pattern recurred in World War II. Today a large number of shipyards in addition to Newport News build steel merchant and naval vessels in the South.

Wooden vessels continued to be built in southern yards, but by the second decade of the 20th century nearly all of them were small fishing vessels. In the last two decades, steel and fiberglass fishing vessels have challenged the wooden boat-building industry.

Finally, the U.S. Navy has long been a major presence in the coastal South. Southern naval bases have been the training and embarkation points for soldiers and sailors in overseas conflicts since the Spanish-American War. Pensacola's Naval Air Station has been the home of the navy's air training program since 1914. Bases such as the Norfolk Navy Yard and the Charleston Navy Yard are major economic forces in their communities and beyond. Charleston, for example, has a Polaris submarine base, a Sixth Fleet supply and ammunition depot, and a mine warfare program, as well as nearby Air Force and Marine facilities. Maritime activities of many sorts, then, continue to be important in the region's economic life.

See also ENVIRONMENT: / Chesapeake Bay; Shellfish; RECREATION: Fishing; URBANIZATION: / Charleston; Houston; Mobile; New Orleans; Savannah; Tampa

William N. Still, Jr.
East Carolina University

Charles C. Crittenden, *The Commerce of North Carolina, 1763–1789* (1936); Rusty Fleetwood, *Tidecraft: The Boats of Lower South Carolina and Georgia* (1982); Joseph A. Goldenberg, *Shipbuilding in Colonial America* (1976); Herbert Ryals Padgett, "The Marine Shellfisheries of Louisiana" (Ph.D. dissertation, Louisiana State University, 1960); William N. Still, Jr., *Confederate Shipbuilding* (1969); George Rogers Taylor, *The Transportation Revolution, 1815–1860* (1951); Emory Thomas, *Georgia Historical Quarterly* (Summer 1983). ☆

Mexican War

||||||||||||||||||||||||||||||||||||

The War with Mexico (1846–48) was a significant episode in the cultural life of mid-19th-century America. Widely perceived as the country's first foreign war, the conflict embodied many elements of romanticism. Fought in a strange and exotic land against an unfamiliar foe at a time when Americans were reaching out to distant places, the war provided a window on a civilization and a people that differed markedly from their own. At the same time, it assumed all the rhetorical trappings of a romantic nationalism that preached a unique mission and destiny for the Republic. The war was viewed as an opportunity to recall Americans to the idealism of the American Revolution at a time when the revolutionary generation was passing from the scene and to advance the republican form of government the Revolution had sired. Stung by the taunts of Europeans against their "experiment in democracy," many Americans saw the war as a test of republican vitality. In fighting against a country dominated by military leadership, Americans regarded the war as a measure of the ability of a republic, lacking a strong professional military force and relying on untrained citizen-soldiers, to fight a successful foreign conflict. The Mexican War was an exercise in national self-identity, as Americans looked more closely at themselves and their place in the sweep of history.

Although the imaginative response of the South to the war did not differ significantly from the national norm in its general manifestation, southerners did perhaps react to the war with greater homogeneity and less equivocation. The tension between republican simplicity and the rise of what was called the "commercial spirit," with which northerners were grappling, was largely absent in the agrarian South. The elements of romanticism, fostered by a concern for the past, a reverence for heroes, and an allegiance to a code that emphasized honor, had a stronger grip on the southern than on the northern mind. Opposition to the war, seated in the North in such reform activities as the abolition and peace movements as well as in certain constituencies of the Whig party, was less evident in the southern states. And finally, the militant tradition, so widely identified with the South, made southerners more receptive to the romance of the war. There is, however, danger in exaggerating the difference between the South and the rest of the United States, for Americans in all parts of the nation shared essentially the same imaginative outlook.

When President James K. Polk issued his first call for volunteers following the outbreak of the war, southerners were among the first to enlist. In some states, like Tennessee, the numbers so far exceeded the quotas levied by the president that large numbers had to be turned away. Many of the volunteers were motivated by a spirit of adventure and a curiosity to visit a land they had only read about in storybooks. Mexico, with its ruins of a destroyed civilization and its stirring tales of the heroic struggle between Montezuma and Cortez, held the aura of romance for which so many Americans yearned. To a generation nurtured on Sir Walter Scott, the Mexican War seemed to be a step into a romantic past. Volunteers were likened to young knights, and there was much talk of chivalry. Many were the soldiers who fancied themselves marching off to meet the foe on some medieval field. The mountains and villages of Mexico and the Mexican soldiers themselves, especially the colorful, armorclad mounted lancers, seemed straight out of the books. To the *Southern Quarterly Review*, an "age of chivalry" had returned, every soldier fighting "as if he were striving to pluck from the 'dangerous precipice,' the glittering flowers of immortality."

Because of its geographic proximity to the Mexican battlefields, the South played an important part in the logistics of the war. New Orleans became the principal supply depot and embarkation point for the army in Mexico. Volunteers from the western states traveled down the Ohio and Mississippi rivers to a staging area on the site of Jackson's triumph over the British south of the city. New Orleans newspapers dispatched the first war correspondents to the scenes of action; their reports, first printed in the New Orleans press, were speeded to newspapers throughout the country. The first perceptions of the conflict to be circulated were those of southern newspapermen. When the volunteers returned to the United States, they sailed to New Orleans (and to a lesser extent, Mobile), where they were accorded their first triumphant homecoming celebrations. Southern orators, poets, and politicians vied with one another in their colorful rhetoric as they welcomed the returning heroes. The veterans were compared with the "sainted fathers of our land," carrying on the analogy between the Mexican War and the American Revolution that was so large a part of the imaginative response. Lighting anew the "fires of freedom," they had unfurled the "standard of the stars above those lofty palaces where once floated the golden gonfalon of Cortez." Jefferson Davis's Mississippi Rifles, fresh from their triumph on the field at Buena Vista, were received with a wild enthusiasm; their feats, it was said, would live on in the "enduring records" of the Republic. Future Civil War heroes such as Davis and Robert E. Lee first made their military reputations in Mexico.

The war penetrated the American (and hence, the southern) imagination in many different ways, in literature, poetry, art, music, and drama. Soldiers kept diaries and journals and published accounts of their campaigns soon after their return home. Historians began writing histories of the war almost as soon as the war began. New Orleans newspaperman Thomas Bangs Thorpe, with a reputation already established as a writer of southwestern humor, not only followed the army as a correspondent but wrote the first accounts of the campaigns on the Rio Grande and against Monterrey. Albert Pike, an Arkansas volunteer, wrote a poetic description of the Battle of Buena Vista on the field before the guns had hardly cooled, and his work was widely reprinted throughout the country. In South Carolina, Marcus Claudius Marcellus Hammond, younger brother of the prominent planter-politician, penned the first complete analysis of the war's military operations, serialized in the *Southern Quarterly Review*.

In a class by himself was William C. Falkner, of Ripley, Miss., great-grand-father of the 20th-century novelist, who was turned back at the first call for volunteers. He later served in Mississippi's Second Regiment but to his disappointment was too late to take part in any of the fighting. Nonetheless, Falkner commemorated his service in a 493-stanza, 4,000-line poem, *The Siege of Monterey*, in which he portrayed the war's leaders as Homeric heroes. Undaunted by the failure of his poem, Falkner turned to fiction in *The Spanish Heroine: A Tale of War and Love*, a stock romance dealing in part with the battle of Buena Vista.

The South's greatest antebellum literary figure, William Gilmore Simms of South Carolina, was among those American writers who helped create the mood in which the war was viewed. From his early poem *The Vision of Cortes* (1829) to his biography of the Chevalier Bayard, published during the war, Simms wove a romantic net that captured the southern responses to the conflict. His work on Bayard held up to the wartime generation the ideal of a soldier in whom

heroic valor was blended with the gentle virtues of knightly honor and chivalry. When South Carolina's Palmetto Regiment returned home after winning distinction in the battles around Mexico City, Simms celebrated the event with a collection of verses, *Lays of the Palmetto: A Tribute to the South Carolina Regiment, in the War with Mexico*, the "outpourings of a full heart, exulting in the valor and worth, and lamenting the misfortunes and losses, of the gallant regiment."

The Mexican War was marked by bitter conflict between North and South over the explosive question of the expansion of slavery into the western territories. The clash of northern and southern interests seemed to polarize popular sentiment. At the same time, however, there were those in the South who perceived the war as a force for national unity, symbolized by the volunteers from both North and South who marched, camped, and fought side by side. It was symbolic, for example, that a New York Regiment and South Carolina's Palmetto Regiment fought together in the Valley of Mexico in a brigade commanded by an Illinoisan.

Southerners (and northerners) saw something in the war that transcended sectional conflict. It was put into words by President James K. Polk, North Carolina born and Tennessee reared. The war gave meaning to the American Republic. "Who can calculate the value of our glorious Union?" Polk asked. "It is a model and example of free government to all the world, and is the star of hope and haven of rest to the oppressed of every clime." The war, in the imaginations of countless Americans, had demonstrated the strength of the Republic and had legitimized its mission. "We may congratulate ourselves," said

Polk, "that we are the most favored people on the face of the earth."

See also MYTHIC SOUTH: Militant South; Romanticism

Robert W. Johannsen
University of Illinois

Marcus Cunliffe, *Soldiers and Civilians: The Martial Spirit in America, 1775–1865* (1973); Clement Eaton, *The Mind of the Old South* (rev. ed., 1967); Robert W. Johannsen, *To the Halls of the Montezumas: The Mexican War in the American Imagination* (1985); Ernest M. Lander, Jr., *Reluctant Imperialists: Calhoun, the South Carolinians, and the Mexican War* (1980); Rollin G. Osterweis, *Romanticism and Nationalism in the Old South* (1949); Fred Somkin, *Unquiet Eagle: Memory and Desire in the Idea of American Freedom, 1815–1860* (1967); Ronnie C. Tyler, *The Mexican War: A Lithographic Record* (1973). ☆

Military Bases

||||||||||||||||||||||||||||||||||||||||||||

Observers of the southern scene have long remarked upon Dixie's distinctively martial spirit. One highly visible evidence of this is the presence of so many military, naval, and air installations in the South. They range in time from the Castillo de San Marcos in the South's oldest city, St. Augustine, to the futuristic George C. Marshall Space Flight Center in Huntsville, Ala. They range in size from Williamsburg's restored Powder Magazine, which supplied Virginia Frontier Rangers, to the 465,000 acres of sprawling Eglin Air Force Base in Florida, where both the Tokyo raiders of 1942 and the Son Tay raiders of 1970 secretly trained. They range in climate and terrain from the green live oaks and manicured lawns of Fort Myer in humid Tidewater Virginia to the sunbaked parade-ground plaza of Fort Bliss in the desert of El Paso, Tex.

During the colonial wars three European powers—Spain, France, and England—established forts in the South. Spanish soldiers and monks were probing northwards from Spanish Florida, cavaliers and *voyageurs* established French Louisiana on the Gulf Coast and were moving up the Alabama River, while English traders and trappers were pressing inland from Charles Towne in Carolina down around the tag end of the Appalachians. There were military posts at Saint Elena, on the site of today's Parris Island Marine Corps Base; at Fort Frederica, near the present Glynco Naval Air Station near Brunswick, Ga.; and at Fort Maurepas on Biloxi Bay, close to the modern Keesler Air Force Base. Within 80 miles of the site of Montgomery, later to be the Cradle of the Confederacy, were the short-lived Spanish Fort Apalachicola on the Chattahoochee, the French Fort Toulouse commanding the Alabama, and the British post at Okfuski on the Tallapoosa. The key to the strategy of all the contenders was control of southern coasts and rivers.

The British eventually won the prize of North American hegemony, only to be displaced in turn by their American colonial cousins in the War for Independence, the outcome of which was finally decided at the fortifications around Yorktown, Va. Then the infant United States had to fortify its seaboard against foreign invasion and to garrison inland posts against the perceived threats posed by American Indians, the British still in Canada, and the Spanish still in the Floridas. One southern stronghold gave us our national anthem—Fort McHenry in Baltimore Harbor during the War of 1812. Defense of two other forts created rallying cries for war—the Alamo in 1836 in the Texas War for Independence and Fort Sumter in 1861, site of the opening battle of the Civil War.

As the United States became a world power in the 20th century, climate influenced the choice of the South for military installations To raise mass armies to fight abroad in two world wars, America needed good weather to train its forces, especially its new air arm. In World War I, 13 out of the total of 16 National Guard cantonments were in the South, as were 6 of the 15 national army camps. There arose camps (later forts) Lee, Gordon, and Benning, not to mention the inappropriately named camps McClellan and Sheridan in Alabama, while aviation cadets learned to fly at Langley, Carlstrom, Brooks, and Kelly fields.

Surviving military posts represent a history of military architecture. There are the wooden stockades from the colonial wars, restored at James Towne and Fort Toulouse. Brick coastal defense forts built after the British seaboard invasions during the War of 1812 are strung around the southeastern littoral. Among these are Fortress Monroe, Va., where Confederate President Jefferson Davis was later held by Union authorities, and Fort Massachusetts on Ship Island in Mississippi Sound, site of "Beast" Butler's advance in occupying New Orleans. Rifled artillery rendered all these masonry forts obsolete before they were finished. Some of these forts were overlaid with the low-level concrete-and-steel coast artillery batteries of the Spanish-American War period, batteries that never fired a shot in anger, much like those twin forts Washington and Hunt guarding the Potomac River approach to Washington, D.C., and forts Morgan and Gaines protecting Mobile Bay, past which, earlier in 1864, Admiral Farragut had damned the torpedoes and ordered full speed ahead.

After World War I some of the sprawling temporary cantonments were kept. Tar-paper and fiberboard huts were replaced by brick, stucco, and tile barracks, many of Spanish-inspired architecture, at such bases as Quantico, Pensacola, Maxwell, and Randolph Fields, and forts Knox and Sam Houston. Then during World War II they were swamped with inducted men and women. "Tent cities" mushroomed alongside well-groomed peacetime garrisons. New temporary installations arose, only to be activated again for the Korean War, made permanent in the Cold War, and used again to train men for the Vietnam War. The first special warfare groups to go to Vietnam in 1961 were the army's Green Berets from Fort Bragg, the navy's SEAL Teams from Little Creek, Va., and the Air Commandos from Hurlburt Field, Fla.

Local citizens were both attracted to and repulsed by military bases. On the one hand, they appreciated the dollars the bases brought to local economies, not just as extra monies during wartime booms but as cushions against depressions and recessions. On the other hand, the honky-tonk atmosphere surrounding many bases repelled local citizens—never mind that local businessmen often foisted land "on the wrong side of town" on the services. One recalls Jacksonville, N.C., in 1944. Southern townspeople often disliked northern servicemen, whom they viewed as loud-talking Yankees with brusque manners; some northern servicemen felt a reciprocal dislike. Nevertheless, many non-southerners fell in love with the South, met and married southern women, and stayed. Many non-southern servicemen who experienced the discomforts of preparing for war at camps Lejune, Blanding, Shelby, or Polk were glad to get home to Waukegan or Walla Walla. If the servicemen were black, and especially if they were from the North, assignment to a post in the still rigidly segregated South was painful. There was racial trouble, for instance, at Camp Van Dorn, Miss. At Tuskegee Army Air Field, however, black men proved they could fly and became combat pilots over Europe in the thrice-decorated 99th Fighter Squadron.

Military bases are the centers for a distinctive sense of community among active and former service personnel. Today, retired military officers and noncommissioned officers congregate in Norfolk, Charleston, Southern Pines, Montgomery, and San Antonio. Military amenities abound because such senior southern congressmen as Georgia's Carl Vinson, South Carolina's L. Mendel Rivers, and Mississippi's John Stennis have so packed military installations into their districts that they have been accused of sinking their states under the weight.

The military tradition continues to attract southerners. Sociologist Morris Janowitz found in 1950 and 1971 that officers with southern affiliations of birth, schooling, or marriage continued to be represented disproportionately in America's military. During the Vietnam War, when there was a national backlash against the military, ROTC continued to thrive on southern college campuses, and the Virginia Military Institute and South Carolina's Citadel maintained their traditions of military service. Currently, the 101st Airborne Division easily meets its recruiting quotas in the area around its Kentucky

home, Alabama's National Guard is the largest in the nation, and southern small-town armories and American Legion posts remain social clubs for good old boys.

See also EDUCATION: Military Schools; INDUSTRY: Military and Economy; MYTHIC SOUTH: Fighting South

> John Hawkins Napier III
> Montgomery, Alabama

Army-Navy-Air Force Times Magazine (28 June 1978); Irvin Hass, *Citadels, Ramparts and Stockades: America's Historic Forts* (1979); Morris Janowitz, *The Professional Soldier* (1960, 1971); Theo Lippmann, Jr., Baltimore *Sun* (20 April 1969); David McFarland, *Montgomery Advertiser and Alabama Journal* (20 June 1982); John H. Napier III, *Alabama Review* (October 1980); Duncan Spencer, Washington *Star-News* (1 May 1974). ☆

Military Tradition

For a century and a half commentators have written about the bellicosity and martial spirit of the southerner. Other observers have analyzed Dixie's military proclivities to determine the reasons for their enduring tenacity. More recently, some writers have sought to deny the existence of a peculiarly southern military tradition.

Back in 1835 Alexis de Tocqueville reported that the white southerner was "passionately fond of hunting and war." During World War II D. W. Brogan, in explaining to his fellow Britishers their wartime American Allies, stated that "in the South, the heroes were nearly all soldiers." In 1943 Alabama editor John Temple Graves II devoted a book to *The Fighting South*. Later the distinguished black historian John Hope Franklin examined the antebellum South and saw there a distinctive military spirit, as did fellow historian Avery O. Craven and political scientist Samuel P. Huntington.

However, the British historian Marcus Cunliffe has denied that before the Civil War the South was any more martial than was the North. He held that Dixie's martial prowess was a post-Appomattox myth fostered for the benefit of northerners to rationalize why it took them four bloody years to win the Civil War, despite the overwhelming odds in their favor, and as solace to southerners for their crushing defeat. The South's earlier enthusiasm for fighting the War of 1812 and the Mexican War, in contrast to northern tepidity and even civil disobedience in both conflicts, has been explained away as a drive to extend chattel slavery into new lands. Yet the South *did* rally behind the national war effort in 1812 and 1846 and went down fighting to the last in 1865.

Some writers think that the South's enthusiasm for the military ethos was even more marked after Appomattox than before Fort Sumter, and much evidence supports this idea. Military schools and colleges continued to attract public support and students. After Reconstruction volunteer military companies proliferated in the South. For instance, in 1885 Montgomery, with a population of less than 25,000, had five military companies, and later a black unit appeared. W. J. Cash noted in *The Mind of the South* (1941) that in 1898 young southerners rushed to don *blue* uniforms for the Spanish-American War. They had also been drawn back to West Point and Annapolis, so that by 1910, 93 percent of U.S. Army general officers had southern affiliations—by birth, family, residence, schooling, or marriage. In World War I two of the three top commanders in the American Expeditionary Force (AEF) in France were General John J. Pershing from the border state of Missouri and Lieutenant General Robert E. Lee Bullard from Alabama. All four commanders of the first outfit to fight on the Western Front, the 1st Division ("The Big Red One"), were southerners.

Before Pearl Harbor, Texans bragged that the federal government introduced the draft to keep them from filling up the ranks of the armed forces. Professor Brogan explained that southerners early favored American intervention on the Allied side in World War II more than other citizens because from experience they "knew that war could settle a lot." When the Korean War broke out, 46 percent of the American military elite still had southern affiliations, although the South's population was then only 27 percent of the country's total. When the U.S. armed forces intervened actively in Vietnam the top army and air force commanders were southerners, and later antiwar activism was almost nonexistent on the campuses of Dixie.

More recently, indications are that southern over-representation in the officer corps may have ended, perhaps because of declining southern distinctiveness along with increasing urbanization and affluence. Other factors may include changes in the military profession itself, with the military manager nearly replacing the heroic warrior, and a lingering racist perception that the services are filling up with blacks. The democratization of the career military force has resulted in a decline in participation by the southern upper and upper-middle classes, following the pattern set earlier by their northern peers.

Various explanations have been offered for the traditional military bent of the white southerner. One was southern upper-class affinity for the ideal of the English country gentleman, with its concept of *noblesse oblige* and the pattern of the oldest son's farming and the others' choosing the church, the law, and the army. More recently F. N. Boney has denied the reality of this ideal and asserted that the plain folk, the "rednecks," were the uniquely belligerent warriors of the South. However, he also denies the reality of a distinctive planter elite, holding that most of them were "at heart rednecks on the make." Grady McWhiney and Forrest McDonald claim, despite the demographic evidence to the contrary, that southerners were of Celtic descent and more ferocious than northerners who, they argue, were all "Anglo-Saxon."

Contradictory explanations would have it that Johnny Reb was particularly amenable to hierarchy and discipline coming as he did from a deferential so-

Texan Audie Murphy, World War II battlefield hero and movie star, a modern embodiment of the military tradition

ciety, or on the contrary that he was an unregenerate individualist standing up for his rights. A favorite explanation is that he was rural, an outdoorsman expert at camp life, hunting, and shooting, but today's largely urbanized South still provides more than its share of recruits for the forces. Preoccupation with honor supposedly predisposed the young of the past to the profession of arms, but that concept is virtually extinct today with the "me generation" and probably was 30 years ago with the "silent generation." Yet another construal is that the southerner is militant because he is a violent white racist, Cash's "proto-Dorian," who just lives to shoot "gooks," but the southern black man also has made a fine soldier. During the Civil War 186,000 blacks served in the Union army and 29,000 were in the Union navy. The Department of War created four Afro-American units after the war, and many black southerners served in them in the western Indian Wars. Blacks fought in World War I and II, although in segregated outfits. President Harry Truman opened new opportunities for black southerners in 1948 when his executive order ended military segregation.

A mystique of the southern martial spirit and tradition does remain, however, curiously immune to analysis or debunking. The southern military tradition may have become self-reinforcing, as with other elements of southern distinctiveness, persisting in an age that threatens to smother and level differences. The South struggles to maintain its own *Gemeinschaft* against homogenization, and the rest of the nation will not allow the idea of the South to perish. "The consensus remains that a separate quality of myth, tradition, and values characterizes the South despite the compelling forces of modernization," write

Thomas L. Connelly and Barbara L. Bellows. A key element of this lingering regional quality is the tradition of "the Fighting South."

John Hawkins Napier III
Montgomery, Alabama

F. N. Boney, *Midwest Quarterly* (1980), *Southerners All* (1984); D. W. Brogan, *The American Character* (1944); Thomas L. Connelly and Barbara L. Bellows, *God and General Longstreet: The Lost Cause and the Southern Mind* (1982); Avery O. Craven, *The Growth of Southern Nationalism, 1848–1861* (1953); Marcus Cunliffe, *Soldiers and Civilians: The Martial Spirit in America, 1775–1865* (1968); John Hope Franklin, *The Militant South, 1800–1861* (1956); John Temple Graves II, *The Fighting South* (1943); Samuel P. Huntington, *The Soldier and the State: The Theory and Politics of Civil–Military Relations* (1957); Morris Janowitz, *The Professional Soldier* (1960, 1971); Grady McWhiney and Forrest McDonald, *American Historical Review* (December 1980); John Hawkins Napier III, *Alabama Review* (October 1980); Bertram Wyatt-Brown, *Southern Honor: Ethics and Behavior in the Old South* (1982). ☆

Modernism

||||||||||||||||||||||||||||||

To the popular mind "modern" is simply that which is up to the moment, but modernism was a specific cultural movement that was both reactionary and radical, conservative and revolutionary, packaging its puritanism in the latest fashions. The modernists were simultaneously the avant-garde and the guards of the derriere. The modern movement was part of a conservative effort that used revolutionary techniques. Everything about the movement implied tension, mediation, paradox. To many observers, modernism was mainly a matter of technique: new styles and structures; new and startling juxtapositions of language; new strategies of form in painting, sculpture, poetry, and fiction; fresh use of mythology and ritual in providing a literary framework; new stress upon personality and motivation in characterization and a new vocabulary to express the workings of the mind; new applications of time and memory. These techniques represented a new view of existence, a view corroborated by the sciences. By the early 20th century science had begun to uncover the discontinuities and uncertainties that existed beneath the surface of commonsense reality. Daniel Singal summarized the movement as an attempt "to reintegrate the human consciousness and thus to liberate man from the restrictive culture of enforced innocence with which the century began."

Scholars disagree as to the precise years of the modernist movement. Monroe Spears, in *Dionysus and the City* (1970), a study of modernism in poetry, suggests 1870 as a rough beginning for "modernism as an epoch in the cultural history of the West." Evidence of early modernism included the work of the French and Russian novelists, symbolist poets, and impressionist painters, plus a range of other styles and attitudes that appeared before, during, and after the fin de siècle. Spears chooses 1909 as "the beginning of modernism as a specific movement in the arts," as seen in the beginnings of cubist painting and sculpture; the emergence of Schönberg and Stravinsky's music; Hulme, Pound, and Eliot's poetry, Stein and Joyce's fiction; and the increasing popularization of Freud's psychology, Frazer's mythology, and Bergson's philosophy. Walker Percy argues that the age that began three centuries ago with the dawn of science came to an end with modernism in the early 20th century and along with it the lessons science offered for human self-understanding. Those who realized this and took it seriously suffered the symptoms of alienation, either wordlessly because they did not know the cause of their problem or, like Percy, by looking for new meanings. The modernist generation felt these discontinuities and was engaged in a search for new meaning.

The Southern Literary Renaissance of the 20th century has usually been seen as the prime expression of modernism in the South. Some scholars see the Renaissance as unique, because the region's writers did not, as Richard James Calhoun has written, fully feel "the historical and metaphysical discontinuities of the most modern writers." They were not "completely modern." But the southern movement, according to another critic, Lewis Simpson, was "fully joined in the wider literary and artistic opposition to *modernity*." Southern experience during the years in question was similar to that of the rest of the Western world, and the Renaissance should, therefore, not be seen as a unique regional experience but as part of modernism. Louis D. Rubin, Jr., has observed that this was the first generation of southerners since the antebellum era to confront directly "the vanguard of the most advanced thought and feeling of their times," but nevertheless they were part of a national literary generation, all of whom had grown up under certain cultural and familial pieties, whether they were raised in Oak Park, St. Paul, Reading, Cambridge, or a

southern community. They were all part of what Simpson called a general "culture of alienation."

The attempt to isolate the so-called Southern Literary Renaissance from the modernist movement has given a false sense of distinctly regional achievement to southern writing. To be sure, the regional historical experience has provided the southern writer with paradoxical advantages in exploring the uncertainties that modernism has typically been interested in. The southern modernists were preoccupied with the myth of the fall of traditional southern society, an excellent regional metaphor for a world condition. The serpent was not only in the southern garden; he whispered his knowledge of the discontinuities all around.

Harry Levin has identified the experience of expatriation as one of the chief preconditions of becoming a modernist. The most acclaimed southern literary figures—Glasgow, Welty, Faulkner, Warren—traveled widely outside the South, thus experiencing changes that were transforming the traditional world of their childhood into the modern world of their maturity. But they returned to be "underfoot locally," having seen that the country of the mind is a far country indeed, to most people, and one might as well live where one finds the material. Indeed, by staying at home, engaging in an "inner expatriation," one is perhaps in a better position to monitor the discontinuities of the modern age.

The study of modernism's influence in the South has mainly focused on literary concerns. Recently, however, scholars have suggested broadening the scope of the inquiry to include music and painting. Musical contributions have been among the South's most important in the 20th century. Jazz, in particular, bears on the issue of modernism. Jazz was southern by origin, and regional expatriates have been its prime practitioners. It represents an authentically new form of music, and its existential qualities and its stress on the individual, on spontaneity, and on the present moment seem appropriate modernist concerns. However, much work remains to be done exploring the relationship of music, and particularly jazz, to the broader cultural context within the South.

The idea of a Southern Renaissance should also be applied to 20th-century painting in the region. "For painting in the South," writes art historian Rick Stewart, "the period between the two world wars was marked by the problematical relationship between a romantic sectionalism and a modernist internationalism." To be sure, southern painters generally followed Thomas Hart Benton's direction in combining modernist forms with the idea that art had a moral obligation to instruct. But Black Mountain College in North Carolina was the institutional center of more experimental modernist painting in the region, especially through the influence of Charles Olson and Josef Albers. One can date the beginnings of modernist painting in the region from 1933, when Albers came to Black Mountain. However, the full impact of the movement was not felt until the 1960s. George Bireline's painting *Malcolm's Last Address*, for example, was an influential abstract painting exhibited in 1965. It seriously challenged the dominance of realism in regional work and has led to the increased prominence of abstract forms. By 1976 critic Elizabeth C. Baker could write that contemporary southern art "bespeaks an almost uni-

versal acceptance of the modern vernacular."

The failure to relate modernism adequately to 20th-century southern cultural development, and especially to the Southern Literary Renaissance, has fostered the belief that the Renaissance is over. Postwar southern writing can be characterized as postmodern, but that should not imply a radical break with what went before. The gnosticism that is supposed to characterize postmodernism existed in the work of Eliot and Faulkner from the beginning, and it existed in the writing of Melville, Hawthorne, and Poe much earlier. Modernism found deep significance in the real, linked the contradictions, fused the ambiguities, made the mirror and the lamp into a single tool, mediated between past and present, and tried to bridge the supposed chasm between reason and intuition. This modernist impulse is still present in the Western world—including the South. The literary, musical, and artistic achievements of the South will likely continue to exist because the South will continue to "go modern"—that is, it will still be forced to confront the discontinuities of life and be able to name them.

See also ART AND ARCHITECTURE: Painting and Painters; BLACK LIFE: Art, Black; GEOGRAPHY: Expatriates and Exiles

Thomas L. McHaney
Georgia State University

Richard H. King, *A Southern Renaissance: The Cultural Awakening of the American South, 1930–1955* (1980); Thomas L. McHaney, in *Southern Culture in Transition: Heritage and Promise*, ed. Philip Castile and William Osborne (1983), *William Faulkner: Materials, Studies and Criticism*, vol. 3 (1980); Michael O'Brien, *The Idea of the*

American South, 1920–1941 (1979), *Perspectives on the American South*, vol. 4, ed. James C. Cobb and Charles Reagan Wilson (1986); Darden Asbury Pyron, *Perspectives on the America South*, vol. 2, ed. Merle Black and John Shelton Reed (1984); Lewis Simpson, in *Southern Literary Study: Problems and Possibilities*, ed. Louis D. Rubin, Jr., and C. Hugh Holman (1975); Daniel J. Singal, *The War Within: From Victorian to Modernist Thought in the South, 1919–1945* (1982); Rick Stewart, in *Painting in the South, 1564–1980*, Virginia Museum of Fine Arts (1984). ☆

Monuments

||||||||||||||||||||||||||||||||

Before 1860 Americans, including southerners, erected very few monuments other than grave markers. Some, like the statue of George III in Charleston, S.C., were holdovers from the colonial period; others, such as the Baron de Kalb Monument in Camden, S.C., honored heroes who had fallen fighting for American independence. The still-young country had not yet acquired a pantheon of gods to be immortalized in stone and bronze. The American Civil War, however, provided ample subject matter, North and South, for sculptors and memorial committees.

It is not unusual to honor those who fought for a victorious cause, but it is unusual to memorialize those who supported a lost cause. In remembering its military men, the South stood apart from the rest of the triumphant United States. In 1865 there were no victory parades, no laurel wreaths, no congratulatory speeches for a job well done. The shock of the collapse of the Confederacy precluded such a homecoming, but the South did remember her heroes and within a few decades inscribed their names and faces in stone on monuments throughout the region.

In 1866 Henry Timrod composed a stirring "Ode" that was "sung on the occasion of decorating the graves of the Confederate Dead, at Magnolia Cemetery, Charleston, S.C." Given what transpired during the next 50 years, Timrod's words were prophetic. The ravages of war and economic dislocation had left precious little money available for permanent markers. The scene in Charleston could have been repeated in scores of cemeteries across the South:

Sleep sweetly in your humble
  graves,
Sleep, martyrs of a fallen cause!—
Though yet no marble column
  craves
The pilgrim here to pause.

Southerners, particularly southern women, mourned their lost menfolk. "Humble graves" would simply not do. In town after town, memorial associations sprang up. At first, they busied themselves with decorating graves on Confederate Memorial Day; then they turned to working for suitable monuments honoring the men who had fought for the Lost Cause. One of the earliest markers was a simple marble shaft erected at Fort Gordon, Ga., in 1866.

The earlier monuments tended to be shafts or obelisks. Their designs were similar to cemetery markers of the day, but also bore a striking resemblence to the triumphant monuments designed decades earlier by Robert Mills.

Reconstruction and occupation did nothing to stimulate economic growth. And, in some states, it was not politically expedient to publicly espouse much enthusiasm for the Confederacy. It is estimated that only 5 percent of the Confederate monuments standing today were dedicated prior to the end of Reconstruction in 1877.

Although the end of Reconstruction did not bring prosperity, it restored the old elites that had led the South into war. The changed political climate and the mythology of the Lost Cause led to public veneration of the men who had participated in the war. This veneration took many turns: pensions, Confederate homes, and monuments.

In state capitals, county seats, and towns, committees organized for the sole purpose of raising funds to construct Confederate monuments. Public as well as private funds were used, and women usually took the initiative. In the half century after the Civil War, 60 percent of the existing monuments were dedicated.

These monuments appeared in a variety of forms. The shaft was still popular, but in larger towns it tended to be truncated and topped with a life-sized stone likeness of a Confederate soldier. The figure, in virtually all cases, was "at ease," not on the attack. Inscriptions on the base usually included some statement about the cause. These words from the monument in Manning, S.C., were typical: "Hope like the eastern sun rose bright in the heart of the Southerner for home, covenant and the Confederate States of America. Contending against armies overwhelming in numbers and with resources inexhaustible he fought with patriotism undaunted, and love of country unexcelled in history. Unawed by fear of defeat, he defended the sacredness of home and the sovereignty of his state."

The phrase "OUR HEROES" or "OUR CONFEDERATE SOLDIERS" generally appeared in outsized lettering. Occasionally, there was a list of the men from the locality who made the supreme sacrifice.

Toward the end of the century, the sacrifices of southern womanhood began to be recognized with monuments. Sometimes female figures were included in larger monuments along with soldiers' memorials and at other times southern womanhood was honored by a monument of its own. The sacrifices of the home front became as much a part of southern lore as those of the battlefield.

The various organizations responsible for honoring the Confederacy were local in nature and sprang up spontaneously in communities all across the South. News of their activities was reported in the pages of the *Confederate Veteran* and other publications such as those of the United Daughters of the Confederacy and the Confederated Memorial Associations of the South.

By the 1930s the war was not even a memory for most southerners, yet monuments continued to rise. The Civil War Centennial in the 1960s saw a number dedicated, particularly on battlefields. Even with the onset of the civil rights

Lloyd Tilghman monument, Vicksburg, Mississippi, battlefield

movement and a downplaying of the Confederacy by public officials, groups of determined southerners have seen to it that no spot has gone unmarked.

The largest monument of all, at Stone Mountain, Ga., was finally completed in the 1970s. Its larger-than-life-sized carved figures of Davis, Jackson, and Lee dominate the north Georgia plain. Two allegorical monuments unveiled at Stone Mountain in 1978 continue the main themes appearing in southern monuments for over a century. "Valor" is depicted by a youth with upraised arms; he clasps in his right hand a sword broken off just above the hilt. "Sacrifice" is a tribute to southern womanhood and shows a female figure carrying an infant on her shoulder.

Defeated Valor and Noble Sacrifice, the twin themes that run through the creed of the Lost Cause, are evident in monument after monument across the South, in metropolis and in rural crossroads: in Mobile, New Orleans, Nashville, Charleston, and Richmond; and in Camden, Ala.; Tallulah, La.; Lebanon, Tenn.; Cheraw, S.C.; and Dinwiddie, Va. The size of the community might dictate the intricacy of the monument, but not the decision to erect one. Fading memories have not stopped the process. Since the Civil War Centennial, at least three dozen more have been added to the lists.

Other public monuments in the South honor local citizens, veterans of later wars, and industry and agriculture, but these are not uniquely southern. Anytown, USA, could have a Doughboy Monument for World War I or a statue of the local boy who became governor. Only southern towns have monuments commemorating a Lost Cause and honoring the men who fought it and the women who supported them.

In 1866 Timrod wrote:

In seeds of laurel in the earth
The garlands of your fame are
   sown;
And, somewhere, waiting for its
   birth,
The shaft is in the stone.

Over the years, the poet was proven a prophet.

See also ART AND ARCHITECTURE: Sculpture

Walter Edgar
University of South Carolina

Confederated Southern Memorial Association, *History of the Confederated Memorial Associations of the South* (1904); Stephen Davis, *Journal of Popular Culture* (Winter 1982); Mrs. B. A. C. Emerson, compiler, *Historic Southern Monuments: Representative Memorials of the Heroic Dead of the Southern Confederacy* (1911); W. Stuart Towns, *Florida Historical Quarterly* (October 1978); Charles Reagan Wilson, *Baptized in Blood: The Religion of the Lost Cause, 1865–1920* (1980). ☆

Museums

The South's approximately 1,500 museums represent almost 25 percent of the 6,000-plus institutions recognized by the American Association of Museums. By the AAM definition a museum is "an organized and permanent nonprofit institution, essentially educational or aesthetic in purpose, with professional staff, which owns and utilizes tangible objects, cares for them, and exhibits them to the public on some regular schedule." The AAM recognizes 13 major categories of museums: art, children's and junior, college and university, company, general, history, science, and specialized museums; exhibit areas; libraries with collections in additions to books; national and state agencies, councils, and commissions; nature centers; and park museums and visitor centers. Within these categories are such diverse settings as archaeological sites, zoos, planetariums, and wildlife refuges. Many museums span several classifications, and certain museum types predominate in the South, as is true in other regions. The tremendous variation in museums is well represented in the South.

The growth of all types of museums in the South accelerated in the 20th century, although more slowly in the Deep South than in states such as Virginia, Maryland, and the Carolinas, all of which stand out in the history of American museums. The Charleston Museum, founded in 1772, was the first permanent museum in the American English colonies and began as a natural history museum containing such objects as an Indian hatchet, human skeletal remains, and minerals. One of the nation's oldest and most renowned historic house museums is Mount Vernon, George Washington's Virginia plantation. Ann Pamela Cunningham of South Carolina spearheaded the campaign to restore Mount Vernon, and she ranks as one of the country's first and most noted historic preservationists. Arlington, home of Robert E. and Mary Ann Custis Lee, became the first federally owned historic home following a 21-year controversy. Federal troops occupied the house in 1861, and the federal government auctioned off and illegally bought Arlington and established a national cemetery on its grounds in 1864. In 1882, however, George W. C. Lee, Robert and Mary's son, won his case before the U.S. Supreme Court regarding ownership of the estate but stuck by an earlier offer to convey the property to Congress in return for a fair monetary settlement.

The South has led the way in other aspects of museum history. Colonial Williamsburg, the beautifully restored capital of 18th-century Virginia, opened in 1926 as the nation's first major outdoor museum and is still considered by many to be second to none. Preservation of historic districts began in the South: Charleston, S.C., and New Orleans, La., both of which were developed in the 1930s, were the first such projects in the United States. In historic districts selected buildings are designated as museums, but the architecture serves as the setting for modern-day activities. Outdoor museums of other sorts also have roots in the South. The zoos in St. Louis, Mo. (1913), and Fort Worth, Tex. (1923), were two of the first major zoos in the United States; and the nation's first safari zoo, Lion Country Safari, opened near West Palm Beach, Fla., in 1966.

Other landmarks in the nation's museum history exist in the South. Two of the country's battle galleries, a museum type uncommon in the United States, are in the South. In Battle Abbey of the Virginia Historical Society, Richmond, Va., stand four large murals of Confederate heroes and battles painted by Charles Hoffbauer; and at Stone Mountain, Ga., loom Gutzon Borglum's gigantic sculptures of the Confederate leaders Lee, Davis, and Jackson. Somewhat similar in concept and popular in the 1800s were panoramas, or cycloramas, which surrounded the viewer with a huge circular painting of a battle or other scene. One of only two panoramas of the 1880s still being shown in the United States is the *Battle of Atlanta* at the Cyclorama in Atlanta. The battle galleries and panoramas effectively represent the post–Civil War South's penchant for memorializing Confederate heroes and their war efforts.

History museums are the most prevalent museum type in the South and include, among other things, historic structures and sites, preservation projects, and military museums, many of which are overseen by national and state agencies, councils, and commissions. Many of the South's historic museums grew from the burgeoning efforts in the 1890s and early 1900s to establish memorials, museums, and monuments and to preserve historic buildings associated with the Civil War. Economic difficulties of the Reconstruction period severely limited efforts at historic preservation in the South, but in the 1890s countless preservation organizations—primarily women's societies—were created. Monuments were erected in courthouse squares throughout the South, and numerous local museums preserving Civil War relics were established. The preservation societies' efforts drew much popular support, even though funds garnered from the scattered, rural, largely poor populace of the South were often limited. In undertaking large-scale restoration projects southern preservationists usually relied heavily on state or federal monies and fundraising activities rather than on the support of wealthy individuals. Such was true, for instance, of the Ladies' Hermitage Association's efforts to preserve Andrew Jackson's home in Nashville. For many years the preservation of buildings and relics associated with the Civil War far outstripped museum efforts of other types in the South. The South's homage to military sacrifice is further seen not only in the battlefields of the Civil War,

such as Shiloh National Military Park and Cemetery, Shiloh, Tenn., but also in battlefields of the American Revolution, such as Cowpens National Battlefield, Chesnee, S.C., and in battleship museums commemorating World War II combat, such as the USS *Alabama* at Mobile, Ala.

The heritage of the South is evident in a wide variety of other historic museums. The struggles and triumphs of the South's Afro-American citizens are commemorated in such institutions as the Old Slave Market Museum and the Avery Institute of Afro-American History and Culture, both in Charleston, S.C. Numerous sites and museums preserve the heritage of the South's Native Americans. Examples include the Natchez, Miss., Grand Village of the Natchez Indians, site of the capital village of the Natchez Indians from 1700 to 1730; New Echota, Calhoun, Ga., where the Cherokee Indians constructed a capital in 1825; Marksville State Commemorative Area, Marksville, La., site of a prehistoric Indian ceremonial center from A.D. 1 to 400; and the Native American Museum at Pembroke State University, Pembroke, N.C., an institution preserving relics and images of tribes throughout the South. Ethnic diversity of the region is further celebrated in museums ranging from the Bayou Folk Museum in Cloutierville, La., and the Acadian House Museum in St. Martinsville, La., to the Mexican American Cultural Heritage Center in Dallas, Tex.

The South's religious background is evident in numerous historic churches, religious museums, and settlements established by religious groups. Examples include not only the World Methodist Building at Lake Junaluska, N.C., and the Baptist Museum of the Southern Baptist Historical Commission at Nashville, Tenn., but also the Archives Museum, Temple Mickve Israel at Savannah, Ga., and the Immaculate Conception Catholic Church, Natchitoches, La. Other fascinating examples of the South's religious heritage include Old Salem in Winston-Salem, N.C., and Shakertown at Pleasant Hill, Ky. Old Salem, a town founded in 1766 by Moravian settlers from Pennsylvania, has well-restored homes, shops, taverns, and a church plus the Museum of Early Southern Decorative Arts. At Shakertown the restored buildings and exhibits of tools, weaving looms, and other implements reflect the lifestyle of the Shakers, a religious group whose adherents lived communally at the site from 1805 to 1910.

Homes or birthplaces of countless famous individuals have been preserved in the South. Some statesmen whose homes or birthplaces have become museums include John C. Calhoun, Henry Clay, Jefferson Davis, Andrew Jackson, Thomas Jefferson, Abraham Lincoln, James K. Polk, and George Washington. Numerous writers with southern links have been commemorated, including Pearl S. Buck, William Faulkner, Ernest Hemmingway, O. Henry, Edgar Allan Poe, Marjorie Rawlings, Carl Sandburg, Mark Twain, and Thomas Wolfe. In addition to female writers, several other famous southern women honored by historic sites include Clara Barton, Helen Keller, Mary Todd Lincoln, Annie Riggs, and Lurleen Wallace. Booker T. Washington and Martin Luther King, Jr., two of the nation's most prominent black leaders, have been recognized through southern museums. Commemorated, too, have been scientists such as George Washington Carver and John James Audubon, military leaders such as Francis Marion

and Douglas MacArthur, and musicians such as W. C. Handy, Stephen Foster, and Elvis Presley.

Vestiges of the antebellum South are preserved at numerous plantations and historic homes, ranging from Boone Hall Plantation, Mount Pleasant, S.C. (one setting for the movie *Gone with the Wind*) to Madewood in Napoleonville, La., and Melrose in Natchez, Miss. The plantation homes represent many architectural styles, and numerous historic home museums and other historic buildings interest both the general public and preservationists primarily because of their design. For example, the Sarasota, Fla., residence of circus owner John Ringling represents the ornate architecture of the Gilded Age. Palatial Biltmore House in Asheville, N.C., designed for George Vanderbilt, dazzles visitors with its opulent French Renaissance features. The elaborate, eclectic Victorian-style Bishop's Palace, Galveston, Tex., has been cited by the American Institute of Architects as one of the most outstanding buildings in the United States. These are but a few of the historic home museums in the South that represent architectural trends and reflect lifestyles of earlier eras.

An overview of other museum types in the South provides a picture of the region's diverse institutions. Art museums include such long-standing institutions as the Telfair Academy in Savannah and the Gibbes in Charleston plus city-owned art museums in most major southern cities. Various museums, libraries, monuments, and historic sites are classified as libraries with collections in addition to books. A historical focus is important in these and many other southern museums, although there is increasing emphasis on experiential learning in museum settings. Children explore the collections of such institutions as the Cobb County Youth Museum in Marietta, Ga., the Estelle Carmack Bandy Children's Museum in Kingsport, Tenn., the Junior Museum of Bay County in Panama City, Fla., and the Youth Cultural Center of Waco, Tex. Many southern college and university museums exhibit outstanding art collections. Other college and university collections take the form of planetariums, arboretums, historical exhibits, herbariums, marine science exhibits, and even zoos. The George Washington Carver Museum at Tuskegee Institute and the Tuskegee Institute National Historic Site are examples of college-based museums honoring renowned southerners, in this case both Carver and Booker T. Washington. Obviously, southern college and university collections are not restricted to large institutions. The Berea College Museums at Berea, Ky., are an excellent example of small museums that effectively display the region's culture. Three museums at Berea College focus on the folk culture of the southern Appalachian highlands through exhibits of native arts and crafts, demonstrations by craftsmen, photographs, and oral history tapes.

Other examples of museums exhibiting southern folkways are the Blue Ridge Institute, Ferrum, Va.; the Mississippi Crafts Center, Ridgeland, Miss; the Museum of Appalachia, Norris, Tenn.; the Ozark Folk Life Center, Mountain View, Ark.; and the Rural Life Museum, Baton Rouge, La. On display at these museums are such items as folk artwork, crafts, farm tools, and household furnishings and implements. Several notable folk art museums focus on musical and literary contributions, such as the Stephen Foster State Folk

Culture Center, White Springs, Fla., and Wren's Nest, the Joel Chandler Harris Memorial, Atlanta, Ga.

The South has a limited number of company museums, but two related to textiles are located in North Carolina: Biltmore Industries' Biltmore Homespun Shops in Asheville and the Cannon Mills Company's Cannon Visitor Center in Kannapolis. Other company museums include the U.S. Tobacco Company's Museum of Tobacco Art and History in Nashville, Tenn., and the Coca-Cola Company's Schmidt Museum of Coca-Cola Memorabilia in Elizabethtown, Ky. Other museums commemorate particular industries; for example, the Fort Worth, Tex., Western Company Museum, which highlights the history of the petroleum industry, and the McCalla, Ala., Iron & Steel Museum of Alabama at Tannehill Historical State Park.

Exhibit areas vary widely and include such examples as the Branchville Railroad Shrine and Museum, Inc., Branchville, S.C.; the Morehead Planetarium at Chapel Hill, N.C.; and the Barnwell Garden and Art Center at Shreveport, La. At Dry Tortugas Island off of Key West, Fla., visitors to the Fort Jefferson National Monument examine the largest masonry fort in the United States and see Brown Noddies and frigate birds in their natural habitat. Similar sights exist at such nature centers as the Seashore State Park Natural Area Visitor Center, Virginia Beach, Va.; the Audubon Park and Zoological Garden, New Orleans, La.; and the Big Bend National Park, Big Bend, Tex. Many nature areas are also classified as park museums, a designation that applies as well to many historical sites.

In the category of general museums are institutions such as the Kiah Museum, Savannah, Ga., which exhibits African, folk, 15th-century, and contemporary art, among other things. The Cottonlandia Museum in Greenwood, Miss., and the Daughters of the Republic of Texas Museum in Austin, Tex., are but two of the many other general museums. The former exhibits regional agricultural implements and household furnishings plus artifacts of the Mississippian-period Indians. The latter, housed in an 1857 land-office building, contains Indian artifacts, archives, and objects relating to early Texas history, coins, stamps, and artwork.

Southern science museums encompass varied collections, including the following: the Huntsville, Ala., Alabama Space and Rocket Center; the Salisbury, N.C., Catawba Museum of Anthropology; the Winter Park, Fla., Beal-Maltbie Shell Museum; the Dallas, Tex., Dallas Arboretum and Botanical Garden and the Dallas Zoo; the Birmingham, Ala., Red Mountain Museum; the Murrells Inlet, S.C., Brookgreen Gardens, society for southeastern flora and fauna; the Asheville, N.C., Colburn Memorial Mineral Museum; the Bailey, N.C., Country Doctor Museum; the Charleston, S.C., Macauley Museum of Dental History; and the Memphis, Tenn., Mississippi River Museum at Mud Island. Specialized museums include such sites as the Tifton, Ga., Georgia Agrirama, the State Museum of Agriculture; the Fort Smith, Ark., Patent Model Museum; the Pine Ridge, Ark., Lum and Abner Museum and Jot 'em Down Store; the Nashville, Tenn., Country Music Hall of Fame and Museum; the Front Royal, Va., Warren Rifles Confederate Museum; the Louisville, Ky., Kentucky Derby Museum; and the Murray, Ky., National Museum of the Boy Scouts of America.

Clearly, the South's museums preserve and promote countless national, regional, and local treasures, and the growth of museums in the South parallels a national trend toward heightened appreciation for such institutions.

See also ART AND ARCHITECTURE: / Art Museums; RECREATION: / Colonial Williamsburg; SCIENCE AND MEDICINE: Charleston Museum

Sharon A. Sharp
University of Mississippi

Edward P. Alexander, *Museums in Motion* (1979); American Association of Museums, *The Official Museum Directory, 1984* (1983); American Heritage Publishing Co., *Historic Houses of America* (1980); Edward D. C. Campbell, Jr., *Journal of Regional Cultures* (Fall/Winter 1981); Charles B. Hosmer, Jr., *Presence of the Past: A History of the Preservation Movement in the United States before Williamsburg* (1965); Reader's Digest Association, *Treasures of America* (1974). ☆

New Deal
||||||||||||||||||||||||

Agriculture in the 1930s was the South's major economic activity; and New Deal farm programs—such as the Agricultural Adjustment Act (1933), the Resettlement Administration (1935), and the Bankhead-Jones Farm Tenancy Act (1937)—by cutting production, raising farm income, and pushing southerners from farm poverty to southern and non-southern cities created the basis for the sweeping change soon to come to the largely rural South. Along with the agricultural revolution the New Deal infusion of federal money disrupted the

verty, and the region's econ-
i to merge with that of the
nation. New Deal labor legislation such
as the National Labor Relations Act
(1933), the Social Security Act (1935),
and the Fair Labor Standards Act (1935)
helped to spur the first significant unionization of the country (one of every four
workers by the end of the 1940s). The
South, with its major industry, textiles,
overwhelmingly nonunionized, was the
most underunionized region of the country, with all the attendant cultural and
economic impact of nonunionization. In
the nation's poorest region, the Federal
Emergency Relief Administration provided limited but badly needed amounts
of money to fund welfare programs;
and the Public Works Administration
(1933), Civilian Conservation Corps
(1933), and the Works Progress Administration (1935) offered public service
work to the unemployed.

At first the personal popularity of
Franklin D. Roosevelt and his Depres-
sion-fighting New Deal programs meant
rocklike support among southern politicians and southern voters. But New
Deal politics and programs threatened
white supremacy and lessened the
power of local oligarchies. The centralizing tendencies of the New Deal men-
aced the basic institutions of southern
life. The subsequent slow defection of
southern Democrats from the New Deal
created a new conservative southern political culture.

The role of the New Deal in creating
the modern political economy of southern society remains controversial. Statistical study indicates that the Dixie
economic miracle dates from the 1940s.
Ambiguity surrounds the New Deal
years in the South. In many ways the
New Deal nationalized southern culture,
and the South became by the 1940s

not the nation's number one economic
problem but its ever-growing, ever-
Americanizing region. The persistence,
however, of such cultural patterns as
racial segregation, dire poverty, and
rural and small-town control kept the
South looking more old than new. The
New Deal, with its host of centralizing
agencies and its nationalized political
ideology, changed the Old South but did
not destroy it. Only the war years, the
racial revolution of the 1950s and
1960s, emigration, and the postwar
prosperity of industrialization and urbanization would do that.

See also ENVIRONMENT: Tennessee Valley
Authority; INDUSTRY: / Textile Industry;
POLITICS: National Politics; SOCIAL
CLASS: Politics and Social Class; Poverty

James A. Hodges
College of Wooster

James C. Cobb and Michael V. Namorato,
eds., *The New Deal and the South* (1984);
Pete Daniel, *Agricultural History* (July
1981), *Breaking the Land: The Transfor-
mation of Cotton, Tobacco, and Rice Cultures
since 1880* (1985); Gary Fink and Merl
Reed, eds., *Essays in Southern Labor History: Selected Papers, Southern Labor History
Conference, 1976* (1976); Frank Freidel,
FDR and the South (1965); Donald H.
Grubbs, *Cry from the Cotton: The Southern
Tenant Farmers' Union and the New Deal*
(1971); Michael Holmes, *The New Deal in
Georgia: An Administrative History* (1975);
John B. Kirby, *Black Americans in the Roo-
sevelt Era: Liberalism and Race* (1980); Rob-
ert S. McElvaine, *The Great Depression,
1929–1941* (1984); Paul E. Mertz, *New Deal
Policy and Southern Rural Poverty* (1978);
John Dean Minton, *The New Deal in Ten-
nessee, 1932–38* (1959); Harvard Sitkoff, *A
New Deal for Blacks: The Emergence of Civil
Rights as a National Issue*, vol. 1 (1978);
George B. Tindall, *The Emergence of the
New South, 1913–1945* (1967). ☆

New Deal Cultural Programs

||||||||||||||||||||||||||||||||||||||||||||||||

The Great Depression had a substantial impact on many parts of southern life. The region's economy, its relationship with the federal government and the Democratic party, and social relations between the races were all profoundly and lastingly changed by the New Deal. Franklin D. Roosevelt's policies also had repercussions on the culture of the South. The New Deal legacy may be less apparent here than in other areas, but that legacy continues to have perceptible consequences for modern southern culture.

FDR and his relief administrator, Harry Hopkins, shared a desire to use the opportunity provided by the Depression to begin an experiment in federal patronage of the arts. Attempts were made to give "appropriate" employment to writers and artists during the short-lived Civil Works Administration in the winter of 1933 to 1934, and the Treasury Department's Section of Painting and Sculpture began commissioning works of art (usually murals) for public buildings (most often post offices) in 1934. The principal effort of the New Deal to encourage culture through providing suitable work relief for people involved in the arts began with the launching of the Works Progress Administration in 1935.

Included under WPA Federal Project One were the Federal Writers' Project, Federal Music Project, Federal Theater Project, Federal Art Project, and the Historical Records Survey. The dream behind the WPA arts projects was nothing less than the democratization of American culture. Stimulated by the Depression era's revival of interest in uncovering and building a distinctively American culture, the Federal One projects set out with great expectations. One of the basic problems that they confronted from the start was that the national culture they sought to shape had distinctive demarcations. Regionalism was a major movement in the 1930s, and it was strongest in the South, where it was inspired by such intellectuals as the Nashville Agrarians who published *I'll Take My Stand* in 1930 and, in a quite different way, by University of North Carolina sociologist Howard W. Odum. The regional traits peculiar to the South led to the development of unique characteristics in the New Deal arts projects in that region. At the same time the federal supervision of its projects carried forward a slow process of homogenization of the South with the rest of the nation.

The Federal Writers' Project had a greater impact upon the South than did any of the other WPA arts projects. The FWP's most publicized accomplishment was the publication of a guidebook for each state. Their quality varied, of course, but on the whole they were a remarkable achievement. The compilers of guides in the southern states faced considerable difficulty in their treatment of blacks. Many of the white writers employed by the FWP shared the white South's stereotypical perceptions of blacks and wrote those views into the state guides. The Louisiana guide portrayed "the Negro" as "imitative." FWP editors strove to reduce such references, but sometimes they failed. They did manage to delete from the Mississippi guide the statement that "the passing of public hanging was, in the eyes of the Negro, a sad mistake," but the published version took what has been described as a tone of "amused condescension" toward blacks. For example, the authors claimed that "the Mississippi folk Negro" is "credulous," yet "he has never been known to take anyone's advice about anything."

One of the Writers' Project's most important contributions was the conducting of more than 2,000 interviews with former slaves. These slave narratives constitute an invaluable historical resource, although most of the interviewers were white and thus may have elicited less than complete candor on the part of some of the former slaves. FWP writers employed these slave narratives in writing the path-breaking *The Negro in Virginia*, published in 1940. This book and the treatment of blacks in several other FWP publications played a small role in the building of a more realistic picture of black life, history, and values. Accordingly, the FWP was one of the New Deal agencies that helped sow the seeds for the later civil rights movement.

Another important FWP contribution to southern culture was the collection of "life histories" of southern workers and farmers. These interviews, some of which were edited by W. T. Couch and published in 1939 under the title *These Are Our Lives*, marked a truly pioneering effort in social history at the same time that they turned the storied of "ordinary" people into a genuine literature. Under the direction of Benjamin F. Botkin, the FWP also collected folklore in the South. Many of these tales reached print under such names as *Bundle of Troubles, and Other Tales*, *God Bless the Devil! Liar's Bench Tales*, and *Gumbo Ya-ya: A Collection of Louisiana Folk Tales*.

The Federal Writers' Project's single most significant contribution to modern southern culture was the nurturing of several leading writers in the region whose talents might never have been developed had it not been for their FWP employment. Notable among these was Richard Wright, who won a $500 prize for four stories he wrote in 1939 while employed on the project. They were published as *Uncle Tom's Children*, and Wright applied the prize money toward completion of his masterpiece, *Native Son*. Eudora Welty traveled and wrote for the project in Mississippi. Her photographs are included in the Mississippi guidebook.

The Federal Music Project sought to bring first-class orchestral music to a wider audience while providing work for unemployed musicians. Its major impact on the culture of the South, however, fell into a quite different realm. It was a collaborative effort by Charles Seeger of the FMP and Alan Lomax of the FWP to collect the region's folksongs. This effort made a lasting contribution by helping to preserve a most important aspect of regional life.

The Federal Theater Project was the largest and most controversial of the WPA arts projects, but its activities in the South were not as extensive as they were in some other parts of the nation. The FTP did have some notable success stories in the region, particularly in North Carolina, where its actors put on the historical pageant *The Lost Colony*. Also, FTP directors assisted amateur groups throughout North Carolina and in Jacksonville, Fla., which became the center of a small drama revival in northern Florida.

The Theater Project in the South was not free from the political controversy that swirled about it elsewhere. FTP companies in Birmingham, Tampa, and Miami were among 22 nationwide that produced Sinclair Lewis's *It Can't Happen Here* in the fall of 1936, but officials in Louisiana refused to allow the play about the potential for dictatorship in America to be performed in New Orleans a year after the assassination of Huey Long. Thomas Hall-Rogers's *Altars of Steel*, which portrayed labor-management strife in the southern steel industry, set off an uproar when it premiered in Atlanta.

The FTP's success in bringing live theater and new ideas to the South was limited. Black FTP units were set up in Atlanta and Birmingham. The latter produced *Great Day*, a musical depicting early African history. Traveling companies existed briefly in the region, but by the fall of 1937 the FTP was operational in only three states in the South.

The contribution of the Federal Art Project in the South was principally through its sponsorship in six states of Community Arts Centers, some of which became permanent museums, as in Mobile in conjunction with its art education programs. More persuasive were the murals of the Treasury Department's Section of Painting and Sculpture. This was not a relief program but one with the sole aim of public beautification. Post office murals were painted in many cities and towns across the region. They offer a revealing view of southern culture in the 1930s and early 1940s, because the artists were, at least in theory, required to consult local public opinion in determining what to paint. Most southern communities seemed to prefer historical themes—themes that provided a sense of stability in the midst of the uncertainty of the Depression.

One other aspect of the New Deal played an important part in southern culture. The photography project begun under the Resettlement Administration and carried forward by the Farm Security Administration brought together many of the nation's leading photographers. Most of them spent some time working in the South. The FSA photographers, especially Walker Evans, left indelible images of southern life in the Depression years.

See also MYTHIC SOUTH: Regionalism; / Agrarians, Nashville

Robert S. McElvaine
Millsaps College

F. Jack Hurley, *Portrait of a Decade: Roy Stryker and the Development of Documentary Photography in the Thirties* (1972); Alan Lomax, Woody Guthrie, and Pete Seeger, eds., *Hard-Hitting Songs for Hard-Hit People* (1967); Robert S. McElvaine, *The Great Depression, 1929–1941* (1984); Richard D. McKinzie, *The New Deal for Artists* (1973); Jerre Mangione, *The Dream and the Deal: The Federal Writers' Project, 1935–1943* (1972); Karal Ann Marling, *Wall-to-Wall America: A Cultural History of Post-Office Murals in the Great Depression* (1982); Jane DeHart Mathews, *The Federal Theatre, 1935–1939* (1967); Monty Noam Penkower, *The Federal Writers' Project: A Study in Government Patronage of the Arts* (1977); William Stott, *Documentary Expression and Thirties America* (1973). ☆

Philanthropy, Northern

Northern philanthropy emerged as a significant social, economic, and political force in the South following the Civil War. At a time when the region was suffering from the effects of defeat, desolation, and social confusion, northerners, as individuals and through corporate bodies, sought by means of philanthropic gifts to influence the current and future direction of southern life. Generally, the philanthropists were attempting in a variety of ways to assist in "bringing racial order, political stability, and material prosperity to the American South." These goals were perceived as supportive of two crucial ends: insuring that the South's restoration enhanced rather than weakened the United States and promoting the "reformation and elevation" of the southern people, their institutions, and their politics by bringing them into greater conformity with the North.

Between the closing years of the Civil War and the middle decades of the 20th century, northerners of means invested millions of philanthropic dollars in the South. Although this giving had several phases, most donations fell into a number of clearly identifiable categories: (1) support of segregated public and private education for southern blacks and whites; (2) aid to individuals, programs, and governmental agencies endeavoring to increase the skills and productivity of southern farmers; (3) creation and support of programs designed to raise the quality of southern rural life through educational and medical programs to eliminate social diseases, increase public knowledge in regard to hygiene and health, and provide adequate medical services; (4) direct grants and matching funds to southern schools, colleges, and universities to build endowments, raise salaries, and erect new buildings; (5) studies and grants to assess and upgrade medical education and incorporate it into the major universities of the region; (6) improvement of library services and the erection of new libraries; and (7) aid to theological education.

Beginning in the 1920s some philanthropic agencies also began to support programs designed to facilitate the exchange of ideas and information between black and white leaders of the South. Although all of these programs made contributions to southern life, some had a widespread positive effect throughout the region, particularly those that sought to develop an adequate system of public and private education for whites; to increase southern farmers' productivity and improve the quality of rural life; and to professionalize and elevate the quality of medical education.

The earliest group of northern philanthropists to have an impact on the South was the Protestant missionary societies, which began during the Civil War to send money and workers into the region. Although a significant number of large and small church-related organizations engaged in this activity, the most important, in terms of money expended, schools and other institutions established, as well as constancy of interest, were the American Missionary Association (nominally nonsectarian, but primarily Congregational), the Freedmen's Aid Society of the Methodist Episcopal Church, the American Baptist Home Missionary Society, and the Presbyterian Church's Board of Missions for the Freedmen. Fueled by missionary energy and the abolitionist desire to uplift the freedmen, these organizations increased their efforts after the Civil War and, in conjunction with the federal government's Bureau of Refugees, Freedmen, and Abandoned Lands, became the major forces for "uplift" and education among blacks.

When the "Freedmen's Bureau" went out of existence in 1870, these organizations remained actively involved in this work, becoming even more important to blacks and more controversial among southern whites. Whites accurately perceived them as subverters of traditional southern racial mores because of their support of black education based on northern models, espousal of character reform that sought to transform Afro-Americans into black Yankees, and support of black political rights. The northern missionary societies strengthened the hostility of white southerners by an almost exclusive interest in the southern black community and its welfare. From the post–Civil War period to the first decade of the 20th century, the northern church agencies, as the largest contributors to black education, were a major philanthropic force in the South. Although the denominations that supported these groups would maintain an interest in southern blacks throughout the first half of the 20th century, after 1900 the secular philanthropic agencies began to make a greater impact.

Between 1867 and 1902 a small number of secular philanthropic foundations established by wealthy white northerners joined the missionary societies in the work of reforming and elevating the South. By 1910 these foundations, because of their focused goals and numerous connections with white business and political leaders in both the North and the South, were more visible and influential than the missionary societies. The most important of the foundations active in the South were the General Education Board of the Rockefeller Foundation, the Southern Education Board, the Julius Rosenwald Fund, the Phelps-Stokes Fund, and the Carnegie Foundation. All these agencies were established between 1866 and 1918 in direct response to two parallel developments in United States history—the growth of large personal fortunes derived from business and the presence of a powerful movement to promote more efficient philanthropy through organization.

The intersection of these two movements with the interest of secular philanthropists in the South is reflected in the individual histories of these foundations. Often considered the first modern American foundation, the Peabody Fund was established in 1867 by George Peabody, a wealthy banker who lived in England. This fund, using its $2 million endowment, promoted public and private black and white education in the South until it was liquidated in 1914. In 1881 a Connecticut merchant named John F. Slater, impelled by his belief that the education of the former slaves would promote black welfare and ensure "the safety of our common country," placed $1 million in the hands of a board of trustees for this purpose.

John D. Rockefeller's lifelong concern to distribute a portion of his earnings to charity led to the creation of the General Education Board in 1902. Because of its immense resources, creative programs, and capable administrators and trustees, it would become the most important of the foundations involved in southern life. Organized as a discretionary perpetuity with an endowment of over $153 million, it sought, according to its stated goals, to promote "education within the United States, without discrimination of race, sex, or creed."

Between 1885 and 1920 public concern about America's educational, medical, and social problems increased. The South, burdened with poverty, low standards of public education, health problems, and peculiar racial problems, was a special focus of these concerns. The philanthropic possibilities created by the multiplication of great private fortunes and by Andrew Carnegie's influential argument that the rich were obligated to serve others increased public esteem for the agencies established by Peabody, Slater, and Rockefeller. At the same time, they caused many wealthy Americans to view the foundation as an excellent means for stimulating efforts to solve a wide variety of problems. This belief was reflected in the increasing rate with which foundations were established after 1900. To the Progressive era, such organizations seemed the embodiment of the new "scientific philanthropy," which sought not simply to concern itself with the symptoms of social disorder but, through research and careful application of insights, to eliminate the root causes of social problems.

During the second decade of the 20th century the Phelps-Stokes Fund and the Julius Rosenwald Fund were established. Before her death in 1910, Caroline Phelps-Stokes of New York City made provision in her will for a charitable endowment to support the efforts of black Americans to improve their conditions, especially through education. Accordingly, a foundation bearing her name was established and incorporated in 1911. This fund provided occasional direct grants to individual black schools and colleges, but its major support of black education was through a series of surveys and studies for which it provided money and other forms of assistance.

As early as 1910 Julius Rosenwald had begun a regular program of gifts to support educational and social-service institutions in the South and to provide direct aid to "talented individuals." In all instances, southern blacks were beneficiaries of his largesse. After 1917

Rosenwald's giving was institutionalized in the Julius Rosenwald Fund. Disliking the restrictive nature of perpetual endowments, Rosenwald included provisions for the termination of the fund within 25 years of his death. Sixteen years after his death in 1932 it was liquidated, having provided roughly $63 million to improve rural education, racial relations, and black health education.

The wealth of these northern philanthropic agencies gave them the power to influence greatly the lives and futures of black and white southerners. In their dealings with whites the agencies pursued specific goals but in most cases exercised a cautious and diplomatic approach designed to secure the cooperation and support of white southern leaders. By 1910 this had produced strong and, in some quarters, enthusiastic white southern endorsement of the foundations as "friends."

Initially, though, white southerners greeted the secular philanthropic agencies with the same suspicion and distrust the missionary societies received. Their public and financial support of black education and character reform at first seemed another variant on the familiar Yankee reformer, plotting to elevate blacks at the expense of southern whites. However, after 1902, as the General Education Board began to dominate the field of southern philanthropy, directly influencing the work of most other northern secular philanthropies and much of what was done by the missionary societies, the policies and programs of the secular philanthropic agencies began to convince white southerners that their welfare was uppermost in the minds of the individuals directing these organizations. This was an accurate assessment, because from 1902 to the early 1920s the major programs of the secular northern philanthropists included (1) the development of a comprehensive educational system for southern whites justified by the belief that the southern white community would neither tolerate nor fund a comprehensive educational system for blacks until they first had a good system of public and private schools for themselves; (2) a commitment to the development and maintenance of a working relationship between northern philanthropy and the dominant forces in southern society; and (3) a strong espousal of industrial rather than collegiate and professional training for blacks, based on the judgment that they needed basic skills and training that inculcated the dignity and worth of labor.

To promote racial order, political stability, and material prosperity in the South, the secular philanthropic agencies, the most important forces in northern philanthropy, accepted and made their peace with white supremacy in the South. Consequently, from 1902 to 1960, when the General Education Board exhausted its funds, the bulk of the monies expended by northern secular agencies in the South went for programs that benefited southern whites solely. Frequently, the relations of the philanthropic agencies with blacks contrasted sharply with the treatment accorded their white counterparts. With blacks, these organizations were often more directive and far less flexible in pursuing policies and programs they saw as suitable. At times, some foundation officials deemed it part of their work to directly influence the conduct of black institutions, in some instances effecting removal of persons heading them and the selection of others considered more suitable.

From the mid-1920s until the U.S. Supreme Court's 1954 decision in *Brown* v. *Board of Education* outlawing segregation, the major northern philanthropic agencies manifested a growing concern over the weakness of black institutions and a disenchantment with industrial education as the major tool for black development. This led to an increase in the number and amount of their grants to southern black institutions of higher education, efforts to make southern governments less discriminatory towards blacks in their distribution of public funds, and support of interracial conferences. Little was done directly, however, to attack or publicize black poverty, segregation, and political powerlessness—the root causes of the problems that plagued the southern black community. Instead, northern philanthropic agencies sought to aid blacks primarily by grants and programs designed to create a strong separate southern black community, an impossible goal given the foundations' limited resources, the size of the black community, the impact of black poverty, and the scant interest of powerful southern whites in supporting such a goal. After 1954, with the emergence of the civil rights movement, northern philanthropists began to reevaluate their programs and goals. However, the increased involvement of the federal government in all aspects of southern life steadily reduced the importance of these organizations.

Although southern blacks were the major direct beneficiaries of the northern missionary societies, the investments and programs of these groups, by providing blacks with skills and education, as well as by strengthening their will to work for a genuinely democratic and biracial society, benefited all southerners. In contrast, the second phase of northern philanthropic activity in the South, signaled by the dominance of the secular philanthropic agencies, was more conservative. These organizations gave lip service to the missionary societies' goals with regard to black education, development, and political rights, but the chief beneficiaries of their money and programs were southern whites, with whom they collaborated until 1954 in the subordination and segregation of the southern black community.

See also BLACK LIFE: Education, Black; EDUCATION: / General Education Board

Alfred Moss
University of Maryland
College Park

Henry A. Bullock, *A History of Negro Education in the South: From 1619 to the Present* (1967); Edwin R. Embree and Julian Waxman, *Investment in the People: The Story of the Julius Rosenwald Fund* (1949); Abraham Flexner, *Funds and Foundations: Their Policies, Past and Present* (1952); Louis R. Harlan, *Separate and Unequal: Public School Campaigns and Racism in the Southern Seaboard States, 1901–1915* (1968); Elizabeth Jacoway, *Yankee Missionaries in the South: The Penn School Experiment* (1980); Jacqueline Jones, *Soldiers of Light and Love: Northern Teachers and Georgia Blacks, 1865–1873* (1980); Ullin Whitney Leavell, *Philanthropy in Negro Education* (1930); James M. McPherson, *The Abolitionist Legacy: From Reconstruction to the* NAACP (1976); Joe M. Richardson, *Christian Reconstruction: The American Missionary Association and Southern Blacks, 1861–1890* (1985); Morris R. Werner, *Julius Rosenwald: The Life of a Practical Humanitarian* (1939). ☆

Populism

||||||||||||||||||||||||||

Adherents of the People's party, launched formally in 1892, were commonly known as Populists. The nucleus of the third party was the combined strength of the southern and northern branches of the Farmers' Alliance, which had grown from a local organization of Texas cattlemen and farmers in the 1880s into a formidable national body. Local, county, state, and national alliances developed coordinated programs designed to achieve economic reform and benefit the agricultural classes. Southern Alliance warehouses, exchanges, and stores engaged in numerous ventures in cooperative buying and selling. Even as its lecturers and newspapers denounced the impoverished condition of the agrarians, the Farmers' Alliance promoted social and educational activities for farmers and their families.

The South produced a number of Alliance leaders, such as Leonidas L. Polk of North Carolina. Dr. Charles W. Macune, an itinerant reformer, edited the *National Economist* from the Alliance's headquarters in Washington, D.C. Macune championed the subtreasury plan, which would have enabled farmers to store perishable products in local warehouses and receive loans on their goods while waiting for better prices. The subtreasury plan became the basic economic demand of the Southern Alliance. It was denounced as socialistic heresy by the ruling Democrats, a group of conservative politicians often called Bourbons. The alliance was both specific and general in its program that decried the results of one-crop agriculture and tenant farming: soil depletion, rising costs and falling prices, and the loss of a sense of worth and dignity.

In the South members of the Farmers' Alliance backed Bourbon Democrats who pledged themselves to enact the subtreasury plan and other measures (fertilizer inspection laws, railroad regulation, reform of the tax laws on land). The alliance leaders' plan was to gain control of the Democratic party and pursue their program from within the power structure. It went awry when the Bourbons reneged on campaign promises. It seemed logical that southern alliancemen, like their counterparts in the Midwest, would break away and form a third party. Yet a similar defection in the South was more difficult. There the Democrats had gained control of state government at the end of Reconstruction. Since the mid-1870s the region had been controlled by the Bourbons who pledged themselves to honesty in government, fiscal conservatism, and, most importantly, white supremacy. Any divisive issue that threatened a return to Reconstruction and Republican rule was stifled. Reconstruction was blown out of proportion as an era of corrupt dominance by dishonest carpetbaggers, traitorous scalawags, and ignorant blacks.

Most white southerners wanted to maintain white supremacy and looked to the Democratic party as the sacrosanct instrument of that preservation. Yet as the alliance program faltered, desperate white farmers turned to the People's party. Their sense of solidarity led them to abandon the "party of the fathers," which was no longer sensitive to their needs.

Populism had many facets, but when viewed as the sum of its parts, it was a class movement. The southern experience was distinct and unique. Southern

Populism drew its foot soldiers from the ranks of the farmers, many of whom were bedrock alliancemen. This was so even though some Alliance leaders (for example, Benjamin R. Tillman in South Carolina, James S. Hogg in Texas) refused to leave the Democrats and branded the Populists dangerous radicals.

Realizing the need for additional support, southern agrarians broadened their party's appeal. The Populists favored direct election of U.S. senators and other plans to secure political democracy. They sought the regulation of monopolies and carriers and a revision of the nation's monetary policy. Campaigning in urban areas, the Populists depicted the Bourbons as a selfish elite opposed to the common people whether they lived in the city or the countryside.

Workers in textile mills and mines were outside the mainstream of southern life. The embryonic labor movement had different goals from those of Populism, but workers and farmers had many miseries in common. Although national labor unions remained neutral, in Alabama union leaders supported reform, and a majority of the coal miners marked their ballots for Populist candidates.

Populist tenets and those of the Republicans were widely dissimilar. Yet the two parties "fused" in some elections, particularly in North Carolina, and achieved victory. The fusion occurred because of their mutual antipathy to the Democrats who controlled the election machinery, manipulated the votes of blacks, and defied legal attempts to challenge their tactics. Whatever the differences between Republicans and Populists, political cooperation was a small price to pay to unseat the Democrats.

Blacks continued to vote after Reconstruction, and their votes were crucial in the 1890s. Large landholders in cotton-producing counties, in the area known as the Black Belt because of the large black population and the color of the soil, held economic mastery over the sharecroppers. They also controlled the blacks politically. The conservative planters aligned with the industrialists in the cities to dominate various states.

Challenging this arrangement, Populists openly sought black support. If their appeals fell short of promoting social equality, such a program was not credible in the 1890s. Even so, numerous Populists declared that skin color bore no relation to political freedom and economic opportunity. If part of the Populists' courtship was based on political expediency, their commitment to improved race relations was greater than that of the Democrats. The brief political alliance between whites and blacks was aborted when Democrats resorted to flagrant election abuses. This fleeting racial liaison was shattered by the Populist defeat in 1896 and destroyed in the decades of racism that followed. Yet the interlude was a significant phenomenon.

Various Populists were middle-class farmers and businessmen who simply opposed Bourbon arrogance and self-aggrandizement. Yet impassioned leaders—Hardy Brian in Louisiana, Thomas E. Watson in Georgia, and Joseph C. Manning in Alabama—were philosophers as well as politicians, theorists as well as power seekers. They viewed Populism as a movement, an upheaval spawned by the lower classes and directed against their self-proclaimed betters. Theirs was a native radicalism that wished not to destroy democracy but to reform it so that the poor could share in its promise.

See also RELIGION: Politics and Religion; SOCIAL CLASS: Politics and Social Class; Religion and Social Class; / Bourbon / Redeemer South; Farmers' Alliance

William Warren Rogers
Florida State University

Robert F. Durden, *The Climax of Populism: The Election of 1896* (1965); Helen G. Edmonds, *The Negro and Fusion Politics in North Carolina, 1894–1901* (1951); Lawrence Goodwyn, *Democratic Promise: The Populist Moment in America* (1976); Sheldon Hackney, *Populism to Progressivism in Alabama* (1969); William I. Hair, *Bourbonism and Agrarian Protest Louisiana Politics, 1877–1900* (1969); Robert L. Hart, *Redeemers, Bourbons, & Populists: Tennessee, 1870–1896* (1975); Robert C. McMath, *Populist Vanguard: A History of the Southern Farmers' Alliance* (1975); Theodore Saloutos, *Farmer Movements in the South, 1865–1933* (1960); C. Vann Woodward, *Tom Watson: Agrarian Rebel* (1938). ☆

Progressivism

IIIIIIIIIIIIIIIIIIIIIIIIIIIIIIIIIIII

During the early years of the 20th century the South experienced an extraordinary wave of political and social reform. Unlike Radical Reconstruction, this reform was largely an indigenous phenomenon, and, in contrast to the Populist movement, it was both less disruptive and more successful in achieving its objectives. Progressivism embodied a series of movements for public education, railroad regulation, more efficient agricultural methods, and a more adequate welfare system. Although the South's distinctive institutions, one-party politics, and perennial concern with the "race question" no doubt shaped its social reforms, the region shared in the national progressive ethos and interacted with other parts of the country in developing its own brand of progressivism.

Southern progressivism was a wide-ranging but loosely coordinated attempt to modernize the South and to humanize its institutions without abandoning its most prized values and traditions. Its origins can be found in a confluence of internal and external developments in the late 19th century: the growth in industry, urbanization, and the importance of business and professional classes; the restructuring of southern politics in the 1890s and early 1900s; the emergence of a stronger and more pervasive sense of social needs; and the belief in southern progress, an idea encouraged not only by the concept of economic development but also by a group of critics who wanted to reform various institutions and practices in the South. Improving economic prospects, the easing of political turmoil in the late 1890s, the apparent success of the new racial settlement, and the intersectional harmony displayed in the patriotic response to the Spanish-American War combined to provide a favorable setting for southern progressivism. Although rural influences were important in many of the reform movements, southern progressives were, characteristically, middle-class men and women, inhabitants of the urban South, and representatives of the new commercial and professional groups. They were moderate, eclectic, and resourceful in their approach to social problems. In general they sought to impose a greater measure of social order, to foster economic opportunity and efficiency, and to promote the well-being and morality of children, women, and other dependent persons.

One group of reforms was primarily concerned with establishing social controls and state regulation in troublesome areas such as race relations. The white consensus on race that evolved during this period reflected a widespread conviction that disfranchisement, segregation, and black proscription constituted a workable system of racial control and that these measures promised less corruption in politics, more consideration of "real" political issues, and a greater degree of social stability and public calm. Another example of the regulatory impulse was the movement to control railroads, insurance companies, and other large corporations. Given impetus by insurgent factions in the Democratic party, "reform governors," and coalition campaigns involving freight bureaus, farm organizations, and other interests, the effort to restrict the corporation induced most southern states to reorganize and strengthen their railroad commissions, to enact laws against corrupt practices and lobbying, and to try in various ways to protect consumers and to make government honest, efficient, and publicly responsive. State legislatures passed pure food and drug legislations, conservation measures, penal reforms, and other regulatory statutes. Almost all the southern states eventually adopted statewide laws prohibiting the manufacture and sale of alcoholic beverages.

A second significant class of reforms revolved around the theme of social justice. Social reforms of this kind included the movement to curb child labor, a series of spirited campaigns to establish public schools in the southern states, and an organized charity movement. Efforts to promote social justice in the South were closely related to the woman's movement, which emerged more distinctly in the region early in the 20th century. As time passed, this feminist reformism tended to find greater focus in the drive for suffrage. There was also an embryonic movement, spearheaded by black leaders and black organizations, to provide public services for Afro-Americans and to strengthen the black community.

Social efficiency, especially as it applied to economic development, was a discernible motif in another category of progressive endeavors. Among these concerns were a multifaceted attack on the ills of southern agriculture, a succession of civic improvements and municipal reforms, and an array of laws pertaining to railroad employees and other industrial workers. Efficiency was also an objective in the movements for public education, good roads, and public health. The success of these campaigns demonstrated that the state had become the source of vital new services.

By the time Woodrow Wilson assumed the presidency in March 1913, a new stage had arrived in the evolution of southern progressivism. Reform movements in the southern states, as in other sections, were increasingly influenced by national organizations, standards, and solutions. This tendency was evident in the formation of the Southern Sociological Congress, a regional civic association established in 1912; in the antitrust movement and the prohibition crusade; and in the South's greater involvement in the debate over national issues and elections. The region took a long step during the Wilson years in the direction of a more positive role in national politics. World War I also enlarged the presence of the federal government in the South and provided additional opportunities for the mobilization of the section's resources for social improvement as well as for military preparedness. Although the end of the war and the collapse of the Wilson administration in 1919 and 1920 weakened southern progressivism and disrupted its unity, reform continued to manifest itself in the form of "business progressivism" at the state level, in the work of the Commission on Interracial Cooperation, and in the struggle to preserve traditional morality.

Southern progressives espoused a complex of ideas that included material progress, efficiency, ethical standards, social order, a more vigorous regulatory state, social justice, public services, and especially the vision of a revitalized regional community. Even though the social balance they had nourished lost much of its vitality in the 1920s, the synthesis that resulted from their efforts to reconcile progress and tradition survived for half a century as an important influence in the politics and social thought of the South.

See also POLITICS articles

Dewey W. Grantham
Vanderbilt University

Hugh C. Bailey, *Liberalism in the New South: Southern Social Reformers and the Progressive Movement* (1969); Dewey W. Grantham, *Southern Progressivism: The Reconciliation of Progress and Tradition* (1983); Sheldon Hackney, *Populism to Progressivism in Alabama* (1969); Jack Temple Kirby, *Darkness at the Dawning: Race and Reform in the Progressive South* (1972); Raymond H. Pulley, *Old Virginia Restored: An Interpretation of the Progressive Impulse, 1870–1930* (1968); George B. Tindall, *The Emergence of the New South, 1913–1945* (1967); C. Vann Woodward, *Origins of the New South, 1877–1913* (1951). ☆

Railroads

||||||||||||||||||||||||||

Even before the steam engine arrived in America, southerners considered the possibility of rail travel. In the late 1820s the Charleston & Hamburg tried sail-cars (which overturned or knocked the passengers out of their seats as the winds shifted) and cars drawn by a brace of dogs. For all their deficiencies—the sparks they showered on passengers, the jolting ride given by the stagecoaches used as cars, the high rate of accidents—the early steam engines worked much better. By 1830 the Baltimore & Ohio had introduced steam power to the South. That same year, Kentucky chartered the Lexington & Ohio, and Louisiana approved the Pontchartrain line from New Orleans to its nearby lake. As late as 1840 Georgia had only 185 miles of track, South Carolina 137—and they were better provided than most other southern states.

But in the next two decades railroads spread. During the 1850s mileage increased 244 percent in Virginia, 158 percent in North Carolina, and 1,062 percent in Mississippi. Visionaries of the Confederacy could not have wished them to grow faster. Until the late 1850s New Orleans had no rail link to Richmond; on the eve of the Civil War Arkansas had a mere 38 miles of track. During the conflict the North could depend on railroads to bring in supplies far more than could the South; and while the former expanded its network in wartime, the latter diminished it. War brought havoc, worst of all in South Carolina, where Union troops lifted rails from the roadbed, heated them, and twisted them around trees as "Sherman's hairpins." With American military aid in 1865 and public aid thereafter, a new railroad boom began. By 1900, 10 southern states had some 35,000 miles of track and Arkansas over 3,000.

Not all southerners appreciated railroads. Many suspected them as an alien invader of the plantation world they cherished. Thus, in eastern Kentucky the Louisville & Nashville found locals so unhelpful where one station was being planned that it finally named the place Uz, after the land in which Job had suffered. Two generations earlier, the same railroad's president was so offended by rudeness and squalor in Danville, Ky., that he ordered surveyors to build the track beyond earshot of the town; from then on, townsfolk could catch the train only by chartering taxis for a three-mile trip outside the city limits. In the 1830s a leading Barnwell landholder forced a projected railroad to pass through a town 10 miles distant by refusing a right-of-way across his land. To such folk, the railroad was, as a farmer once called it, "hell in harness."

But to most southerners railroads were welcome. Believers in a New South in the 1870s saw the lines as an essential beginning: without them, no immigrants could be brought in, mineral resources exploited, or factories built. Atlanta owed its growth to railroads, just as Milledgeville owed its decline and the loss of the state capital to its refusal to fund lines in the 1850s. Where Birmingham stood in 1900 there had been only farms in 1865; the crossing of two railroads had made a city known for its coal and steel production. Those who wanted a South economically independent of the North pressed for a transcontinental line from the Gulf to southern California and sought federal subsidies for it; so eager were they that a few Republican politicians in 1877 hoped to resolve the disputed presidential election by promises of aid. Southern Democrats denounced national aid to railroads, but they backed bills helping southern railroads, took land grants for the Mobile & Ohio and the Cairo & Fulton, and used state legislatures to provide still more aid.

Few doubted that railroads would make any town prosper. In the 1890s the Missouri & Northern Arkansas showed its influence, as construction created 33 new towns. The line fostered zinc mining and turned Harrison into a major Ozark trading center whose population increased by 117 percent in the second decade of the 20th century. Bypassing Carrollton, Duff, and Old Mount Pisgah, the road doomed them all. But for this reason, competition for railroads set southern state against state, town against town, as each tried to obtain special connections and prevent any rival from sharing in the benefits. Irritated by the lack of rail connections, Florida's panhandle threatened secession; annoyed by central Alabama's relationship with Pensacola, Mobile merchants hinted that they would join their city to Mississippi unless railroad aid was forthcoming. Louisville directors dreamed of an empire reaching the Gulf; Gilded Age Atlanta businessmen strove to dominate the Atlantic Seaboard and vied with Richmond interlopers. Often, fights dubbed "the Railroads against the People" turned out to be no more than the fight of one southern railroad's backers against another. Thus, the South became less united through railroad quarrels.

It also became less southern. From 1870 on, northern capital was crucial to southern lines, and with it northern control intruded. Of 311 directors on south-

ern major roads (those with 100 or more miles of track) in 1900, 193 were northerners, including 121 New Yorkers. Northern railroads, eager to exploit Appalachian coal and timber, set the pace of development there, denuded the hillsides, and left slag and stumps where forests had been. Nor did railroads end the cash-crop economy. Rather, railroads opened new lands to cotton growers. Thus, Raymond, Miss., shipped 1,100 bales in 1851 and 7,000 bales in 1853.

Even so, railroads were welcomed with subsidies, land grants, and liberal charters. A line's completion became a holiday. When the Baltimore & Ohio commenced building, its ceremonies featured national politicians, Baltimore's mayor and city council, and surviving veterans of the American Revolution. To break ground, the company chose Charles Carroll of Carrollton, the last surviving signer of the Declaration of Independence. In 1896 the railroad even made a catastrophe an occasion by inviting visitors to Crush, Tex., to watch a railroad collision— which, when a boiler exploded, killed two onlookers and injured several more.

The railroads also took on a special, if dubious, mystique in popular culture. They became a part of the landscape, described by writers such as William Faulkner, Eudora Welty, and Thomas Wolfe. They symbolized mobility, escape from the confinements of rural life. Southern musicians frequently sang of the rails, partly because so many of them had personal connections to railroad life. Bluesman Sleepy John Estes was a caller on track gangs in west Tennessee; Jimmie Rodgers ("the Singing Brakeman") grew up the son of a section foreman for the Gulf, Mobile & Ohio Railroad; A. P. Carter worked on a railroad crew; and Peg Leg Sam lost a leg while riding a freight train.

Two of the most popular railroad songs enshrined southern figures. As an engineer on the Illinois Central, Casey Jones saved his passengers at the cost of his own life in 1900; in 1950 the postal service issued a special stamp with the Missourian's likeness on it. John Henry, the black steel driver, who probably worked on the Big Bend Tunnel in West Virginia around 1870, actually did challenge the steam drill and win, and he may actually have driven a 14-foot hole when his rival could only do a 9-foot one. Other southern railroad ballads have a tragic flavor: classics like "The Wreck of Old 97," based on a 1903 Virginia smash-up, and "The Wreck of the C & O," based on a catastrophe some years later. Other blues and country songs take a melancholy tone from their recollection of that "lonesome whistle" sound.

Other expressions of popular culture humorously noted the inefficiency of southern lines. Playing on initials, observers christened the Georgia & Flor-

Louisville & Nashville railroad in mountains

ida the God-Forgotten; the Carolina & Northwestern was the Can't and Never-Will; and the Houston, East & West Texas was the Hell Either Way You Take It. In 1903 Thomas W. Jackson published a best-selling joke book, *On a Slow Train through Arkansas,* mocking that state's transportation. One story told how a train halted. "There are some cattle on the track," the conductor explained. Soon the train was moving again, but not for long. "We have caught up with those cattle again," passengers were told. The lines' unprofitability may even have made the roads safer from robbery, though in the 1880s Rube Barrow robbed at least seven trains in the Old Southwest and even held up the same train three days apart, once on the northbound and once on the southbound journey. After the Civil War a bandit stopped the Cotton Belt, and the company president got off to chide him. "Aren't you ashamed of yourself to . . . try to rob a road as poor as this one?" he is said to have complained. "Why don't you go over and hold up the Iron Mountain?" The bandit slunk away—and took the advice.

But such joking never concealed the real need the railroads answered, nor the petty favors they could do. Southbound trains entering Florida would toot to warn farmers of a coming freeze; the branch line into Lebanon, Tenn., would blast its whistle to announce an important news story or spread the fire alarm. In Kentucky a thoughtful engineer reportedly broke into church services to play "Oh, How I Love Jesus" on his whistle, but he blasted his reputation with the ministers the next week by playing "How Dry I Am." In the early 1900s railroads ran special trains to bring city folks to lynchings in outlying counties. More substantially, the Illinois Central encouraged Mississippians to go into commercial vegetable farming by sponsoring practical demonstrations of new methods and carrying in agricultural exhibits. Thanks to railroad encouragement, Lebanon, Tenn., cedar served in the building of Pittsburgh and adorned the lounge of Chicago's Palmer House.

Southern railroads continued to grow until the 1920s. Then, under increasing competition with automobiles and trucks, the rail lines cut back service, merged, or closed down operations altogether. Between 1916 and 1960 mileage fell over 20 percent in Arkansas, Louisiana, and North Carolina. After the Depression the roads never fully recovered. The Pontchartrain was sold, and its roadbed became a boulevard, Elysian Fields Avenue. The Middle Tennessee & Alabama shared a similar ignominious fate. With the railroads' decline the towns that had been built around them either adapted to highways or died out. As engines switched to diesel power, towns that had provided coal, wood, and water vanished as quickly as they had come. Today most southern towns have at best a boarded-up depot, a mute monument to the New South that was.

See also FOLKLIFE: / Jones, Casey; Henry, John; INDUSTRY: / Railroad Industry; MYTHIC SOUTH: New South Myth; SOCIAL CLASS: / Railroad Workers

Mark W. Summers
University of Kentucky

Eugene Alvarez, *Travel on Southern Antebellum Railroads, 1828–1860* (1974); Benjamin F. Botkin and Alvin F. Harlow, eds., *A Treasury of Railroad Folklore: The Stories, Tall Tales, Traditions, Ballads and Songs of the American Railroad Man* (1953); Norm Cohen, *Long Steel Rail: The Railroad in American Folksong* (1980); Lee A. Dew, *Arkansas Historical Quarterly* (November 1970); Lawrence R. Handley, *Arkansas Historical Quarterly* (Winter 1974); Steve Hoffus, *Southern Exposure* (Spring 1977); Richard D. Lawlor, *Tennessee Historical Quarterly* (Winter 1972); James L. McCorkle, Jr., *Journal of Mississippi History* (May 1977); John Hebron Moore, *Journal of Mississippi History* (February 1979); John F. Stover, *The Railroads of the South, 1865–1900: A Study of Finance and Control* (1955); Mark W. Summers, *Railroads, Reconstruction, and the Gospel of Prosperity: Aid under the Radical Republicans, 1865–1877* (1984). ☆

Reconstruction

||||||||||||||||||||||||||||||||||||||||||

Reconstruction was the period from 1865 to 1877, when national efforts were concentrated after the Civil War on incorporating the South back into the Union. The period involved important constitutional and political issues, but from the viewpoint of cultural history Reconstruction's underlying significance was its effort to remake southern culture. Neither before nor since have northerners had the opportunity to refashion a peculiar region. Some northerners approached this in a spirit of vengeance, seeking to punish southerners for the war; others had political motives for wanting to reduce southern influence and insure Republican party dominance and patronage for themselves; others were adventurers out to earn their fortune; still others were idealistic reformers hoping to aid freedmen adjust to their new status. Organizations such as the Freedmen's Bureau, the American Missionary Association, the northern Protestant denominations, the Republican party, and the Union League represented the forces of the North. The image of the Yankee schoolmarm in the South was a prime example of this effort at cultural transformation. The Union soldier was another symbol of the effort: under the Reconstruction Act of 1867 the South was divided into five military districts and troops enforced government decisions. The cast of characters also included rapacious carpetbaggers, traitorous native scalawags, and ignorant freedmen.

This at least was the mythic view of Reconstruction. According to the myth of Reconstruction, for a decade after 1867 carpetbaggers, scalawags, and freedmen ran the governments of the southern states, looting their financial resources, passing high taxes, denying whites a role in government, and spreading terror throughout the region. Only with the withdrawal of federal troops in 1877 did the terror end. Claude Bowers spoke for a generation of historians when he called Reconstruction "the tragic era."

Beginning in the 1950s modern historians such as Kenneth Stampp, C. Vann Woodward, and others challenged and revised this mythic view. Reconstruction, for example, did not last as long in most states as the myth suggests. Southern conservative, white-dominated governments took power in Virginia and North Carolina in 1870, in Georgia in 1871, in Arkansas, Texas, and Alabama in 1874, and in Mississippi in 1876. Federal troops were not withdrawn in South Carolina, Louisiana, and Florida until 1877. Moreover, actual military rule ended in 1868 in all the states except Virginia, Mississippi, and Texas, where in each case it ended in either 1869 or 1870. Civil state governments were in charge after that, except for brief periods of reliance on the militia or federal troops. No more than 20,000 federal troops were involved in the process.

Fraud surely occurred in elections, but the same was true of elections elsewhere in that period and under the conservative regimes that followed the Reconstruction governments. Only 150,000 whites were disfranchised under the initial military phase of Reconstruction, out of an 1868 white registration of approximately 630,000. Few whites voted and many blacks did, and more than disfranchisement, this explains the character of the participants in the governments. Blacks held offices during Reconstruction, mostly at the local level, but only in South Carolina was there a black on the Supreme Court and only the South Carolina and Louisiana legislatures had a majority of blacks. And no black served as a southern governor.

"The tragedy of Reconstruction is that it failed," wrote Carl N. Degler in *Out of Our Past: Forces That Made Modern America* (1970). Degler points out that modern historical scholarship rejects the idea of Reconstruction as a unique period of bad government and oppression, but one should remember that generations of southerners believed the myth, which nurtured in them the belief in regional differences and a consciousness of past abuse at the hands of northerners and their own former slaves. At the end of the war southern whites had accepted the end of slavery, but Reconstruction showed their real commitment to a racial color line. This, not slavery, was a life-and-death matter. The thought of black social and political equality was unacceptable to whites. Southern whites united in the 1870s in resisting northern-imposed radical change designed to end white supremacy. After the war, in fact, the defense of white supremacy became more clearly a southern position than before. In the proslavery argument the defense of white supremacy was couched in the broader defense of slavery, but race itself became the key issue in the postbellum era.

Reconstruction was a struggle fought on many fronts. The same conflicts and issues seen in political life were also present in other areas of the culture. The Protestant denominations, for example, experienced troubles between blacks and whites, northerners and southerners. The spirit of Christian brotherhood did temper religious disputes more often than political conflicts. The northern missionary was an important symbol of Reconstruction. Missionaries came south to convert the freedmen and succeeded as blacks joined several northern-based, predominantly black denominations. They also came expecting that southern whites would reunite with the northern churches, but southern whites exercised their spiritual self-determination during Reconstruction by preserving their regionally organized churches—the Southern Baptist Convention, the Protestant Methodist Episcopal Church, South, and the Presbyterian Church in the United States of America.

Education also reflected issues of Reconstruction. Northern teachers believed education would end the ignorance and brutality that abolitionists said existed in the South. Schools would promote democracy and class equality in good American idealistic fashion. Blacks responded enthusiastically to the opportunities, but faced the opposition of southern whites, who ostracized the northern teachers. Sometimes blacks also faced condescension of northern teachers who had their own racist preconceptions about southern blacks. Ultimately, though, the Radical Reconstruction program for public education was accepted. The southern white-controlled governments that came after Reconstruction did not reject black education, although insisting on racially segregated systems of instruction.

In the development of southern black culture, the Reconstruction period should not be seen as a failure. Much progress occurred in the development of vital institutions: in education and landowning, in particular, and in community development. New leadership was tested for the future. Scholars have shown that the family survived slavery and in Reconstruction became a typically southern focus for individual endeavors. There was, to be sure, a debate on approaches toward the future. Was the best strategy racial self-help or interracial cooperation? Some black leaders worked for civil and political rights, while others—and probably the majority of the freedmen themselves—favored land and education.

Efforts by southern whites to end Reconstruction began almost as soon as the radical state governments took power. Not until northern weariness with enforcing Reconstruction took hold could much be done. Virginia was the first state "redeemed," a term southern whites used. Redemption was the process of replacing the radical governments with conservative southern white governments. It was a well-organized political effort that also involved economic intimidation, community ostracism, political fraud, and violence. The

Ku Klux Klan was the most common group involved in the violence. The Klan was a terrorist group that used violence against blacks and white Republicans in the name of preserving the morality and virtue of white civilization. Conservative whites eventually favored disbanding the Klan, which Nathan Bedford Forrest, its grand wizard, did in 1869, charging that outlaws had diverted it from its once high mission. Groups such as the Knights of the White Camellia and the White Brotherhood carried on the Klan's tradition, and Congress passed three Enforcement Acts in 1870–71 to deal with their violence. Nonetheless, the use of violence and other tactics led to the election of white southern conservatives, who maintained power thereafter, ending the threat to white supremacy. These methods of regaining power were called the Mississippi plan, because they were perfected in that state in 1875–76. The Compromise of 1877, an informal, extralegal arrangement between southern Democrats and northern Republicans, brought the removal of federal troops from the South and the official end of Reconstruction.

Reconstruction had a positive legacy for the South. New state constitutions were written, many of which are still in effect as the basic documents of the states. It brought reforms in judicial systems, in codes of government procedure, in operation of county governments, in procedures for taxation, and in methods of electing governmental officials. Education was advanced, laying the basis for free public education. And constitutional amendments passed in that era supported the 20th-century civil rights movement's use of federal force to change the South's system of legal segregation.

See also MYTHIC SOUTH: Reconstruction Myth

Charles Reagan Wilson
University of Mississippi

Dan T. Carter, *When the War Was Over: The Failure of Self-Reconstruction in the South, 1865–67* (1984); LaWanda Cox and J. H. Cox, *Reconstruction, the Negro, and the New South* (1973); Avery O. Craven, *Reconstruction: The Ending of the Civil War* (1969); Robert Cruden, *The Negro in Reconstruction* (1969); John Hope Franklin, *Reconstruction: After the Civil War* (1961); Michael Perman, *The Road to Redemption: Southern Politics, 1869–1879* (1984); Howard N. Rabinowitz, ed., *Southern Black Leaders of the Reconstruction Era* (1982); George C. Rable, *The Role of Violence in the Politics of Reconstruction* (1984); James G. Randall and David Donald, *The Civil War and Reconstruction* (1961); Kenneth M. Stampp, *Era of Reconstruction, 1865–1877* (1965); Mark W. Summers, *Railroads, Reconstruction, and the Gospel of Prosperity: Aid under the Radical Republicans, 1865–1877* (1984); C. Vann Woodward, *Reunion and Reaction: The Compromise of 1877 and the End of Reconstruction* (1951). ☆

Revolutionary Era

The revolutionary era did not create the southern states, but it did help to create the South as a section. The efforts of national leaders during the period failed to bring the region fully and comfortably into the new national framework at the same time that events turned the South into a more distinct, uniform region. The resulting conflicts marked and marred the antebellum period and ultimately led to civil war.

Prior to 1774 southerners unquestionably thought of themselves as distinct from "eastern" or northern residents, but they thought in provincial rather than in sectional terms. When Patrick Henry in 1774 told the members of the First Continental Congress that he was "not a Virginian, but an American," the alternatives he chose were state and nation, not North and South. Fifteen years later he had changed both his outlook and his choice of terms. Fighting adoption of the Constitution, he was to argue that "southern" interests would be overpowered by the demands of "northern" states.

This is not, of course, to suggest that there was no thought of regional characteristics before the American Revolution. George Washington, arriving in Boston to take command of the Continental army, found New Englanders impossibly democratic. Abigail Adams blamed the institution of slavery for the cruelty and selfishness she found in southerners. Thomas Jefferson had clearly given some thought to sectional characteristics long before 1785, when he reported to the Marquis de Chastellux that northerners were hypocritical in religion, cool, sober, independent, and conniving, while southerners were fiery, voluptuary, indolent, generous, candid, and unsteady. Even after the adoption of the Constitution some South Carolina leaders found New York City a more acceptable location for the national capital than Annapolis because the former was more accessible.

At the beginning of the revolutionary era at least three distinct regions existed within the South. The Chesapeake, with its tobacco culture, differed significantly from the South Carolina Low Country with its rice, indigo, and majority-slave population. Even more distinct was a third region, the vast southern upcountry, which stretched from Virginia into Georgia and was characterized by the absence of a full-scale slavery system, smaller land holdings, and a significant population of Native Americans. The revolutionary era helped to erase many of the distinctions between these regions and contributed to a sense of sectional solidarity.

The South was ultimately defined, though, by slavery and the plantation system. The rise of the great planter families, the reduced flow of emigration from Europe, the fear of slave revolts, the desperate efforts to replicate English society, and the failure to develop a strong commercial or industrial economy were all tied to the institution of slavery. Edmund S. Morgan has suggested that even the commitment of Virginians to freedom during the Revolution was made possible by the establishment of an enslaved, and therefore powerless, working class.

The Revolution and the creation of a new nation intensified the distinction between North and South. At first the contradiction between fighting for freedom and holding slaves bothered many prominent southerners, just as it did leaders in the northern states. Pauline Maier, in a provocative essay on Richard Henry Lee, has argued that for at least one prominent Virginian, slavery was only one in a series of problems that made the South feel inferior, at least in theory, to New England. Virginia's colonial government had been inferior, the College of William and Mary was unsuitable, the economy was backward, and the climate was unhealthy. It seems unlikely that many prominent southerners gazed enviously at the "New England Way," but certainly many considered the effects of slavery unhealthy for both the enslaved and the enslavers.

With the formation of the new nation and the elimination of slavery in the colonies north of Maryland, the sense of southern isolation intensified. The Constitution marked the effort of a group of major leaders from Virginia and South Carolina to bring their states fully into the new national framework on acceptable terms. Compromises on slavery and restrictions on regulating trade marked that effort. Both northerners and southerners gave ground in a sincere attempt, temporarily successful, to bring the diverse interests of the two sections into harmony. In the long run this effort would fail, in large part because slavery became more firmly entrenched in the South.

The development of political parties in the new nation illustrates the growing sense of common economic and political interests among the southern states. James Madison's unsuccessful attempt to remain supportive of the emerging Federalist party is illustrative. Men like Madison and Jefferson opposed the Federalists not simply because the Washington Administration was increasing the power of the new central government but, more importantly, because they feared the influences that seemed to dominate the policies of the Federalists. Alexander Hamilton's financial plans regarding the nation's and the states' debts and the Bank of the United States seemed to favor commercial interests, and the South appeared destined to remain agricultural and rural. The French Revolution and the ensuing conflict between England and France further divided the nation along sectional lines. The importance of trade brought the northern states to the support of England, while southerners were moved by

the struggle of the French revolutionaries. Along with this hardening of sectional lines, the development of the cotton gin in 1791 was to reduce further the differences between the coastal areas and the upcountry, as the extension of slaveholding and the rise of an upcountry planter class in South Carolina would illustrate.

By the time John Adams took office, the so-called Virginia-Massachusetts alliance, which had so often dominated the revolutionary movement, was clearly broken, and at least some Federalists seemed determined to crush the southern dissidents once and for all. The Alien and Sedition Acts and the machinations of Alexander Hamilton drove the new nation close to disruption, and the refusal of Adams and Jefferson to communicate for years after the election of 1800 further illustrates the divisions between the two sections.

The Virginia presidents after 1800 seemed to unite the nation again and bring the South not only back into the mainstream but into a position of dominance. Benjamine W. Labaree, among others, has noted that it was the merchants of the North who screamed for disunion by the second decade of the 19th century. Below the surface, however, the peculiar needs of the South, which had presumably been guaranteed by constitutional compromises—the three-fifths clause, the prohibition of export duties, the limits on restricting the slave trade—were still at odds with the rest of the nation. The tendency of southerners to look to England and Europe for culture was to continue, and regional dialects flourished.

Although it is important to remember that the South was not monolithic—the area that produced John C. Calhoun also brought forth Andrew Jackson—the dominant influences binding the South made it distinct from the North and, ultimately, from the West. South Carolinians from the Charleston area who for a time supported the Federalist party and even the protective tariff were to be disappointed in their hopes of creating a commercial center. In the end they would lead the movement to secession and become the most rabid southerners of all.

Many contradictions existed in the revolutionary South. Those who accused New Englanders of being levelers became the firm supporters of the French Revolution; southerners who cherished their English heritage gave up their established church, while New Englanders clung to theirs; plantation owners who condemned slavery and constantly worried over the issue in their private correspondence refused to free their own slaves. Southerners were open, hospitable advocates of the ideals of freedom and virtue, fiercely loyal to their region, and confused by the seemingly insoluble problems of slavery.

The enthusiasms of the revolutionary movement of 1774 to 1776, which bound the colonists together and brought Patrick Henry to declare himself "an American," soon faded as a variety of sections—and individuals— began to pursue their own interests. The South was different, and that difference could not be masked. In agriculture, in political institutions, in culture, and— most importantly—in the development of slavery and the plantation system, there were differences that set the region solidly apart from the rest of the nation. The Revolution did not create those differences and, for a time, the development of a new nation seemed to reduce their importance. But for good or for bad the South was a distinct region in 1776

and despite many variations on the theme has remained so.

David Ammerman
Florida State University

John R. Alden, *The First South* (1961), *The South in the Revolution, 1763–1789* (1957); Carl Bridenbaugh, *Myths and Realities: Societies of the Colonial South* (1952); Jack P. Greene, *The Quest for Power: The Lower Houses of Assembly in the Southern Royal Colonies, 1689–1776* (1963); Rhys Isaac, *The Transformation of Virginia, 1740–1790* (1982); Benjamin W. Labaree, *Patriots and Partisans: The Merchants of Newburyport, 1764–1815* (1975); Pauline Maier, *The Old Revolutionaries: Political Lives in the Age of Samuel Adams* (1980); Edmund S. Morgan, *American Slavery, American Freedom: The Ordeal of Colonial Virginia* (1975); Charles Royster, *A Revolutionary People at War: The Continental Army and American Character, 1775–1783* (1979); Robert M. Weir, *"The Last of American Freemen": Studies in the Political Culture of the Colonial and Revolutionary South* (1986). ☆

Sexuality

||||||||||||||||||||||||

The South is often portrayed as a subculture obsessed with sexual repression yet charged with undercurrents of sexual tension. Little concrete evidence exists, however, for evaluating the uniqueness of sexual attitudes and behaviors among southerners, despite widespread attention to the study of human sexuality in the 20th century. Many social-science researchers either do not control for or do not consider regional differences in analyzing their data. In addition to the limited data from social science, however, many insights about southerners and sexuality can be found in the region's literature, music, and oral folklore.

Probably the best-known images of southern sexual relations are the portrayals of steamy antebellum-era trysts in the vein of Kyle Onstott's *Mandingo*, emphasizing miscegenation and brutal control and use of sexuality. Historians generally agree that certain codes of behavior did in fact dominate the antebellum South: white men had the greatest latitude in fulfilling their sexual desires; black women were expected to be sexually accessible and more sexually expressive than white women; black men's sexuality was viewed as threatening and was tightly controlled; and white women were expected not to have sexual desires and to stand as asexual paragons of virtue. Sociological studies such as John Dollard's *Caste and Class in a Southern Town* (1937) confirmed the persistence of some of these attitudinal and behavioral patterns during the early 20th century.

Aspects of the striking gender and race-based double standards were not endemic to the South but represented national trends as well. Nineteenth-century physicians, moralists, and social commentators were obsessed with appropriate channeling of men's sexual urges and with suppression of women's sexuality. Physicians writing in the *New Orleans Medical and Surgical Journal* in the mid-1850s, for example, recognized men's strong sex drives but warned against masturbation because it drained men of the will for self-sufficiency. Women were exhorted to be virtuous, chaste, and pious—to keep their minds above sexuality. Married women, though, were also duty-bound to be available sexually to their husbands.

Historian Barbara Welter refers to this view as "the cult of true womanhood," which flourished nationwide between 1820 and 1860. Although historian Carl N. Degler and others question the extent of actual acceptance of such exhortations, a strong double standard prevailed and was probably intensified by the chivalric code in the South.

Some examples of brutal repression of sexuality in the South exist. During the 18th and 19th centuries the nationwide trend was toward disapproval of the use of castration as a legal punishment. However, notes Eugene D. Genovese, "scattered evidence suggests that some masters continued to apply it [castration] especially to slaves who had become their rivals for coveted black women." Female castration became common throughout the country after 1872, when Georgia physician Robert Battey developed the surgical techniques for "normal ovariotomy," a procedure he enthusiastically endorsed for "problems" ranging from "erotic tendencies" to "troublesomeness." As G. J. Barker-Benfield notes, this technique remained popular until about 1921, and numerous female circumcisions and clitoridectomies were also performed.

Scientific studies of sexual behaviors and attitudes began in the late 1800s. Unfortunately, no regionally specific data are available from such early studies as those of Dr. Clelia Mosher and Katherine Davis. Even Alfred Kinsey and associates employed no regional identifiers in analysis of the data from their landmark 1948 study, *Sexual Behavior in the Human Male*. Other demographic variables such as religion, education, and urban-rural residence that are confounded with region of residence were the primary bases for analyses. According to Kinsey and associates' *Sexual Behavior in the Human Female* (1953), approximately 3,600 of their total male and female samples of 16,392 cases were southerners. Nevertheless, the researchers commented in the 1953 volume that despite widespread assumptions about regional differences in sexual behavior, "we have an impression, as yet unsubstantiated by specific calculations, that there are actually few differences in sex patterns between similar communities in different portions of the United States." This impression seems to have guided much subsequent research.

As the so-called sexual revolution gained momentum, interest grew in the changing rates of premarital intercourse, and regional comparisons became more common. One important early investigation was Winston Ehrmann's 1959 study of premarital sexuality among students at the University of Florida. Sixty-five percent of the 576 males and 13 percent of the 265 females in the sample reported having had premarital intercourse. In a major 1964 study, Ira Reiss concluded that there was a nationwide trend toward acceptance of premarital intercourse on the basis of affection but not necessarily commitment to marriage, though in behavior the double standard still prevailed. Sixteen percent of the high-school and college students in Reiss's Virginia sample accepted the "permissiveness with affection" standard compared to 72 percent of the respondents in New York.

Attention to regional differences heightened with publication in 1968 of Vance Packard's *The Sexual Wilderness*. Packard reported results of a study of college juniors and seniors nationwide, with a total of 185 respondents from

3 southern institutions represented. Among the southern respondents about 69 percent of the males and 32 percent of the females reported having had premarital intercourse. This rate for males was the highest in the country; the rate for southern females was next to the lowest. Furthermore, southern males were the most likely to have taken part in a one-night affair with someone they never dated again. "The South has the nation's strongest reputation for a double standard in regard to sexual behavior," said Packard. "That reputation receives support in the survey results." Regarding attitudes, Packard found the strongest support of the double standard among females from the South and the Midwest. Commented Packard, "A major surprise (to us) was that next to the Easterners the males most untroubled by the idea of courting a nonvirginal girl were the Southerners (36 percent responding 'no')." More recent investigations have shown that southerners are now following the trend toward "permissiveness with affection." For example, researchers who compared data from 1965, 1970, and 1975 samples of students at one major state university in the South found trends congruent with national ones, particularly in the "dramatic liberalization in both premarital sexual behavior and attitudes for college females."

Beyond the information on premarital sexual standards, especially among the college educated, however, little reliable information exists about regional variations in sexual behavior and attitude, whether normative (e.g., sexual relations among married couples) or nonnormative (e.g., extramarital sexual relations, homosexual or lesbian relations). Most recent large-scale studies of sexuality have not dealt with regional patterns. Laws in the South regarding sexual activities, however, provide valuable insights about the mixture of attitudes regarding sexuality.

For a brief period during the Civil War, Nashville registered and periodically inspected prostitutes, the first such system in the nation. As of 1885 Louisiana, Arkansas, and New Mexico were the only three states in which "red light" districts for prostitution were legal. New Orleans's notorious district, Storyville, was such an accepted institution in the late 1800s that guide books were distributed at restaurants, taverns, and other tourist attractions. As of 1975 Mississippi was the only state that allowed conjugal visits for married prisoners and provided cottages for such meetings. When the streaking craze hit the country and many locales prosecuted the participants for indecent exposure, the Louisiana Legislature "excluded from prosecution streakers who did not attempt to arouse the sexual desires of their viewers." Also, southern states legalized use of birth control by married couples and interracial marriage before some other states.

On the other hand, although many states in the 1960s and 1970s revised their penal codes to allow adults to engage in any sexual acts in private, Georgia doubled its penalties for consensual sodomy. Georgia, Kentucky, South Carolina, and Wisconsin stood out for years as the few states specifically penalizing both female and male homosexual practices (most states overlooked lesbian activities). In 1986 national attention focused on the Georgia sodomy statutes when the U.S. Supreme Court heard the case of a homosexual man from Georgia and upheld the state's right to define sodomy (oral or anal sex) as a felony punishable by 20 years in prison. As of 1986, 12 of the 24 states that had criminal penalties for sodomy were southern, with maximum penalties in the South ranging from a $200 fine in Texas to Georgia's 20-year term. Southern laws gained further attention in 1986 when a federal appeals court panel upheld Virginia's laws against fornication and cohabitation, enacted in 1829 and 1860 respectively.

Impressionistic information about southern sexuality abounds in anecdotal accounts, literary images, and representations in television, movies, and popular music. According to historian Thomas L. Connelly, southern folklore contains a variety of sexual stereotypes, such as "the high school bad girl," who dresses provocatively and undulates rather than walks, and the "good old boy tribal shouter," who hangs out of his pickup truck to "deliver ancient Celtic tribal shouts such as 'who-oo-wee' " when an attractive girl passes by. Southerners have not been reticent about examining sexuality's role in their lives. Writers such as Florence King, author of *Southern Ladies and Gentlemen* (1976), and Rayna Green, a contributor to *Speaking for Ourselves: Women of the South* (1984), provide lively personal observations on southern morals, sex roles, and sexual behaviors. For decades southern poets and novelists have grappled with "sin, sex, and segregation," according to Richard H. King, and examples of southern writers' struggles with the theme of sexuality are innumerable. Southern newspaper columnists write openly about sex and social relationships in the region; country music and blues lyricists incorporate many frank sexual themes; "common folk" readily swap sexual tales and advice; and such "sex symbols" as Burt Reynolds, Cybill Shepard, George

Hamilton, and Lauren Hutton cast images of southern sexuality. Nevertheless, strong community, family, and religious norms remain important influences on southerners' views about sexuality; and a majority of southerners maintain that these influences are the keys to addressing such problems as the region's alarmingly high teenage pregnancy rates. Much remains to be discovered about sexual behaviors and attitudes in the South and their integral ties to religion, race relations, social class, and gender stratification.

Sharon A. Sharp
University of Mississippi

Edward G. Armstrong, *Journal of Sex Research* (August 1986); G. J. Barker-Benfield, in *The American Family in Social-Historical Perspective*, ed. Michael Gordon (2d ed., 1978); Thomas L. Connelly, *Columbia Record* (30 August 1985); Carl N. Degler, in *The American Family in Socio-Historical Perspective*, ed. Michael Gordon (2d ed., 1978); John R. Earle and Philip J. Perricone, *Journal of Sex Research* (August 1986); Winston Ehrmann, *Premarital Dating Behavior* (1959); Paul H. Gebhard, *Sexual Behavior in the Human Female* (1953); Eugene D. Genovese, *Roll, Jordan, Roll: The World the Slaves Made* (1972); Rayna Green, in *Speaking for Ourselves: Women of the South*, ed. Maxine Alexander (1984); Herant A. Katchadourian and Donald T. Lunde, *Fundamentals of Human Sexuality* (2d ed., 1975); Karl King, Jack O. Balswick, and Ira E. Robinson, *Journal of Marriage and the Family* (August 1977); Richard H. King, *A Southern Renaissance: The Cultural Awakening of the American South, 1930–1955* (1980); Alfred C. Kinsey, Wardell B. Pomeroy, and Clyde E. Martin, *Sexual Behavior in the Human Male* (1948); *Newsweek* (14 July 1986); Vance Packard, *The Sexual Wilderness* (1968); Ira L. Reiss, *Journal of Marriage and the Family* (May 1964), *The Social Context of Premarital Sexual Permissiveness* (1967); Bradley Smith,

The American Way of Sex (1978); Barbara Welter, in *The American Family in Socio-Historical Perspective*, ed. Michael Gordon (2d ed., 1978); John Wheeler and Peter Kilman, *Archives of Sexual Behavior* (June 1983). ☆

Spanish-American War

Congress declared war against Spain on 11 April 1898. The conflict grew out of the general imperialist sentiment of the age, the desire of the American business community for overseas trade, the frustrations accompanying economic depression in the early 1890s, the growth in American military power, and humanitarian interest in the supposed Spanish repression of the Cuban people. The war was short and decisive, lasting 113 days, costing 5,500 American lives (most of those died from disease or accident rather than in battle), and resulting in American control of Cuba, Puerto Rico, Guam, and the Philippines.

Southerners supported the war enthusiastically, reflecting longtime regional interests in the Caribbean. Southerners had dreamed of controlling Cuba—the "Pearl of the Antilles"—before the Civil War. Mississippian John Quitman had helped plan a filibustering expedition to seize the island in the mid-1850s. Southerners saw Cuba as the target for sectional Manifest Destiny, which would extend plantation slavery to Cuba and promote southern political strength. This hope for a southern empire in the Caribbean was the "purple dream" immortalized by Stephen Vincent Benét in *John Brown's Body.*

In the 1890s the Spanish-American

War brought prosperity to parts of the South. New South boosters saw the war as a boon to regional economic growth. Chickamauga, Tenn., Mobile, Ala., and New Orleans were assembly points for American troops, while Tampa, Fla., was the chief training and embarkation site for the invasion of Cuba. South Florida had become before the war the center of Cuban settlement in the United States, as refugees from the island worked in cigar factories and planned the overthrow of Spanish rule. José Martí, the chief Cuban revolutionary figure, had visited in Tampa in 1891.

Racial attitudes were important in creating southern reactions to the war. The nation had accepted the "white man's burden" in this era of Anglo-Saxon racism. Southerners saw this national attitude as a confirmation of regional segregation. Over 10,000 black troops—known as "smoked Yankees"—served in the volunteer army that waged war. The four regular-army regiments of black troops, who had served in Indian campaigns in the West, moved to the South in preparation for a Cuban invasion. They endured segregated restaurants, hotels, waiting rooms, saloons, and other public facilities, and violence resulted. About 4,000 black soldiers were stationed in Tampa and Lakeland, Fla., and tensions there led to rioting between white and black soldiers and civilians. Shortly after this, black troops played a key role in the Cuban invasion, especially at San Juan Hill.

The Spanish-American War was a landmark of North-South, post–Civil War reconciliation. Young men from Dixie eagerly volunteered for the fighting. Methodist Bishop Warren Candler spoke for many other southerners when he said that the military tradition, the memory of the Confederate past, and

belief in fighting for princ[...] spired the patriotism of [...] South. "Visions of heroic [...] the courage of gallant sons," he said in a speech. Southern newspapers pronounced the Spanish-American War the real end of the Civil War. Some of the unreconstructed, to be sure, proposed that southern troops be allowed to wear gray uniforms while fighting for the Union, but that was not taken seriously. Two veterans of the Confederate cause, Fitzhugh Lee and "Fighting Joe" Wheeler, were appointed as major generals, and Wheeler was credited with the best line of the war. As the Spaniards retreated during the battle, Wheeler yelled, "We've got the damn Yankees on the run." The saying was widely retold, and the humorous appreciation of it by all sides contributed to the feeling of reconciliation. The spilling of northern and southern blood in a common cause, fighting for liberty, represented a new national bond. Southerners now honored young heroes of nationalism. "These dead, at least, belong to us all," said a Confederate veteran's meeting in 1899. President William McKinley promoted this spirit, pledging in Atlanta in 1898 that the national government would now care for Confederate graves. The memory of the Spanish-American War was preserved in the stories of, and tributes to, the veterans of the struggle and by the regional folksongs such as "Manila Bay."

Charles Reagan Wilson
University of Mississippi

Paul Buck, *The Road to Reunion, 1865–1900* (1938); Frank Freidel, *The Splendid Little War* (1958); Willard B. Gatewood, Jr., *"Smoked Yankees" and the Struggle for Empire: Letters from Negro Soldiers, 1898–1902* (1971); Gerald Linderman, *The Mirror of*

War: American Society and the Spanish-American War (1974); H. Wayne Morgan, *America's Road to Empire: The War with Spain and Overseas Expansion* (1965); David F. Trask, *The War with Spain in 1898* (1981). ☆

Stoicism

||||||||||||||||||||||||

This philosophy entered the South through the influence of the Enlightenment, when there was renewed appreciation of the classical tradition. Cosmopolitan southerners of the revolutionary era were familiar with Greek and Roman writings. One of the most influential of southerners, Thomas Jefferson, read avidly at an early age the classical moral philosophers, although no comprehensive philosophy emerged from his study and he was never a true disciple of them. Jefferson was attracted to both stoicism, with its emotional restraint, and epicureanism, with its hedonistic ethics. He saw moral advantages in each position and tried to hold them in balance. Stoicism seemed especially strong in his youth. In one of Jefferson's earliest letters he wrote that human beings must "consider that whatever does happen, must happen," and they must "bear up with a tolerable degree of patience under this burden of life." Jefferson surely admired the discipline of the will he saw in stoicism. Like many Enlightenment thinkers, Jefferson saw both stoicism and epicureanism as systems of practical morality, separate from any church or governmental connection. He used the classical Stoics to prove that an adequate moral philosophy could exist without any supernatural justification. In general, for Jefferson and early southern students of classical thought, epicureanism provided the goal of a good life, and stoicism, with its control of the will, offered the means of attaining it.

A few intellectuals like Jefferson had been attracted to stoicism in the 18th century, but the philosophy took on a broader social significance in the antebellum period of the 19th century. The southern cult of honor became deeply rooted in the region under the influence of Enlightenment rationalism. The southern model of honorable behavior conformed to the classical heritage. One had to face public examination for a moral failure rather than experience private alienation from God. James McBride Dabbs once wrote that the "basic flaw at the heart of the South" was "the unresolved conflict between Christianity and Stoicism." Walker Percy, another analyst of regional stoicism, has agreed, arguing that the South was always more stoic than Christian. When a southerner named a city Corinth, Percy wrote, "he did not mean Paul's community." Whatever degree of nobility and graciousness has existed in the South, according to Percy, "was the nobility and graciousness of the Old Stoa."

Stoicism took root in the Old South partly because of its stress on individualism, which seemed to suit the planter elite. Human freedom was all important to the early Stoics, and living surrounded by slaves apparently made the same concern a central one of southern planters. But freedom was not unrestrained. In its social role stoicism in the South was based on paternalism, reflecting a hierarchical social structure, as had the earlier Greek version. It taught the southern elite to behave with noblesse oblige. Not to behave honorably would be, again in Percy's words, "to defile the inner fortress which was oneself."

From another direction, a pronounced moralistic tendency among some southerners also provided fertile ground for stoic thought. Religious moralism set forth clear guidelines for life, and southern Protestants could use stoic moralism to reinforce their views. The religion of the Old South was predominantly evangelical, concerned primarily with individual sin, guilt, and private redemption. Evangelical Protestantism, with Calvinistic theology one of its sources, promoted a fatalistic view of the world, an outlook that fit comfortably with practical stoicism. Dabbs claimed that stoicism enabled southerners to be both Cavaliers and Puritans, nurturing both a romantic outlook toward the social world and a moralistic outlook toward individual religious experience, combining outward grace and inner sternness.

The Civil War provided a crucial stage in the development of stoicism in the South. Rather than destroying the philosophy of the prewar elite, the conflict and its aftermath confirmed a fatalistic, even tragic outlook on life. The collapse of the outer world confirmed the southern stoic's original decision to invest everything in the sanctity of the inner self. Just as evangelical Christianity took stronger hold of the South as a result of defeat, so did stoicism. Stoicism has generally been most influential in societies undergoing social decay and collapse, and this seems true of the postbellum South. Robert E. Lee exemplifies this postwar stoicism. An admirer of Marcus Aurelius, a fanatic in his dedication to such stoic virtues as duty, honor, patriotism, loyalty, and humility, Lee combined with these qualities the

moralism and Christian piety that in the South could even rub off on an Episcopalian. Lee was notably ambivalent—confident in the material world, yet brooding and guilt ridden in in his religious outlook. Lee embodied the southern tendency toward stoic reserve. Honor, which in many times and places has been related to pride, in Lee was tied in with humility. He was the supreme example of the South's attempt to balance Stoic and Christian virtues. Dabbs saw two religions in the late-19th-century South—"the social religion of this world and the individualistic religion of another." The result of the first, which was a reflection of stoic influences, was to equate God with the southern way of life and to provide a philosophical basis for what would emerge after the war as a southern civil religion.

Stoicism in the late 19th century became tied in with, and hard to separate from, Victorianism. James Branch Cabell, Ellen Glasgow, and other transitional writers of the turn-of-the-century South were skeptics. They saw decline in the region and tried to face it with the dignity and courage that Victorians valued. Sometimes, to be sure, they seemed detached from their society and from pondering man's fate, but at other times they preached of enduring the tragedies of life with fortitude. Glasgow, who came from a Presbyterian background, wrote of the "vein of iron" that was necessary for survival in her era. She came to believe that the universe was governed by blind chance and her society was coming apart. Renewed moral fiber was the only hope. Her novel *Barren Ground*, with its good stoic title, came out of her inner turmoil. The central character, Dorinda Oakley, learns to live a joyless existence and to suppress her natural instincts. As Daniel Singal argues, *Barren Ground* illustrates "nineteenth century theology got up in stoic dress." However, southern stoicism was not complete in Glasgow; Dorinda cannot stop longing for something more than the "agnostic realism" that seemed to be Glasgow's position. Her stoicism was different in origins, then, from that of earlier southerners. Hers was an attempt to reconcile her Calvinistic legacy with the realities of late-19th-century naturalistic science, with its belief in the evolution of an unstable universe. The result was what can be called her "stoic realism," a position that saw little meaning in human events.

The Agrarian writers of the 1920s and 1930s also reflected stoic influences. John Crowe Ransom, for example, struck a pose of stoic detachment in dealing with conflicts in his own mind between the modern demands of balancing rationality and spontaneity. He hid his inner conflicts behind a front of stoic reserve—self-control, mannerly behavior, and ironic humor. Ransom believed that artists should tap and express their emotions but his stoicism made this difficult for him to do in practice. William Alexander Percy shared many of the literary concerns of the Agrarians, and he achieved perhaps the South's greatest literary expression of the stoic philosophy. *Lanterns on the Levee* (1940) reflected a profound debt to the *Meditations of Marcus Aurelius* in both the form of the work and its content. Percy, the descendent of a distinguished family and himself both a planter and a poet, believed that the good do not triumph, and he chronicled the decline of the southern elite, as seen in his own history and that of his family. The Agrarians believed the old order could be restored, but Percy did not.

He strove in his personal life and his writing to embody the stoic virtue of graceful acceptance of defeat. As Richard King says, "he was the melancholy Roman to the end" and found only temporary relief from his prophecies of southern decline. He did affirm the ability of the individual to effect at least limited change through individual actions in a limited area. Percy was a respected leader of his local community (Greenville, Miss.), and he believed that in such a place a person could do good. In any event, the important point was individual integrity and courage in making the effort. No one better exemplified what Walker Percy calls the spirit of "a poetic pessimism" at the heart of modern southern stoicism.

William Faulkner portrayed southern stoicism through numerous characters. Quentin Compson's father speaks of "fate, destiny, retribution, irony" and of the "stage manager" behind it all. Rosa Coldfield calls her region a "land primed for fatality" and "cursed with it." But stoicism by Faulkner's time was difficult to separate from a generalized Calvinism, a predestinarian, mechanistic philosophy that was also a 20th-century southern legacy. Faulkner did not draw directly on the ancient or modern Stoic philosophers. Cleanth Brooks suggests that Faulkner's stoicism cannot be understood apart from its close connection with Christianity, in both of which the essence of human living is freedom. The Christian concept that God grants freedom through grace, though, is weak in Faulkner, who seems closer to Epictitus's belief that man achieves freedom through self-discipline.

Faulkner, then, saw the human problem in Christian terms—the world is a fallen world—yet he did not advocate the Christian solution of redemption through God's grace. He was willing to rely on individual virtue, as embodied by a Sartoris during the Civil War, to gain a modicum of dignity, if not redemption. Man must rescue himself through stoic virtues such as courage, honor, justice, duty, endurance, and reason. Stoicism was transmuted in Faulkner into the generalized trait of endurance. Dilsey in *The Sound and the Fury* and other black literary characters in the modern South embody the ancient wisdom best of all. Theirs is no grim stoicism but a cheerful one of overcoming. As Isaac McCaslin says of blacks in "The Bear," "they will endure. They will outlast us." Poor whites also are blessed with endurance, for example in *The Mansion*, where Mink Snopes waits 40 years to carry out an act of vengeance. Faulkner's appreciation of endurance reflects the stoic attitude toward time. The Stoics believed one could transcend time through detachment and patience. Characters such as Quentin Compson and Gail Hightower in *Light in August* seem almost primitive in their belief in re-creating the past, so that the normal historical boundaries are overcome.

Writing in the 1950s in the midst of the conflicts over racial desegregation, Walker Percy argued that the South could no longer afford stoicism alongside Christianity. In a democratic society, he said, stoicism cannot exist as the social philosophy of any social class. "What the Stoic sees as the insolence of his former charge— and this is what he can't tolerate, the Negro's demanding his rights instead of being thankful for the squire's generosity—is in the Christian scheme the sacred right which must be accorded the individual, whether deemed insolent or not."

Stoicism, then, since the early 19th century has been a philosophy of the educated southern elite, held alongside of and sometimes in contradiction to evangelical Protestantism. The philosophy has been less influential on society as a whole in the 20th century, but is probably still held by some southerners as a guide to individual behavior.

See also MYTHIC SOUTH: / Agrarians, Vanderbilt; RELIGION: / Fatalism

Charles Reagan Wilson
University of Mississippi

Cleanth Brooks, *William Faulkner: The Yoknapatawpha Country* (1963); James McBride Dabbs, *Who Speaks for the South?* (1964); Richard H. King, *A Southern Renaissance: The Cultural Awakening of the American South, 1930–1955* (1980); Adrienne Koch, *The Philosophy of Thomas Jefferson* (1943); Walker Percy, *Commonweal* (6 July 1956); Daniel J. Singal, *The War Within: From Victorian to Modernist Thought in the South, 1919–1945* (1982); Bertram Wyatt-Brown, *Southern Honor: Ethics and Behavior in the Old South* (1982). ☆

Tobacco

Tobacco was the most important herb among the American Indians and later became closely associated with the South. The Indians used it as snuff, chewed it, smoked it as cigars, smoked it as cigarettes wrapped in corn husks, and made poultices of snake fat wrapped in tobacco leaves. They sometimes also swallowed tobacco pellets as a tranquilizer. But pipe smoking was the near universal method of use in North America. Tobacco in the sacred calumet was the ritual way to seal peace. American Indians smoked "ancient tobacco" (*Nicotiana rustica*), which dated to pre-Columbian times. They used it in medicine and religion, two realms that were believed to be connected. Sickness was believed to stem from spiritual imbalance, and Native Americans used tobacco to nurture their spirituality before sacred rituals.

European colonists in the South thought of tobacco mainly in medical terms and discounted its religious significance. It was seen as a panacea that would cure cancer, asthma, headaches, coughs, cramps, gout, worms, female troubles, and any other ailment. Physicians supported this belief, disagreeing only on the best way to use the weed. The medieval theory of the humors—which taught that sickness came from an imbalance in the body's four humours (blood, yellow bile, black bile, and phlegm)—still had its adherents, who saw tobacco consumption as a way to keep balance in the body and thus maintain good health. In early America, including the South, tobacco was used to cure respiratory, head, internal, and skin diseases.

Tobacco growing and its use became the bases for early Virginia's prosperity. North American Indians had long smoked *Nicotiana rustica*, but it proved too bitter for many European colonists. John Rolfe in 1612 introduced into Virginia a sweet-scented tobacco developed by the Spanish in the West Indies. Sir Walter Raleigh is credited with making tobacco use a fad among the elite in London. The tobacco market expanded, and soon the people of Jamestown were growing it in the streets. By 1624 the Jamestown colony was exporting 60,000 pounds of tobacco a year, and in the colonial era it also became the major crop in Maryland and North Carolina. The English Navigation Acts of the 1660s made tobacco one of the "enumerated goods" that were regulated by shipment from the colonies through English ports.

The dominant form of tobacco consumption in the colonial era was pipe smoking. Snuffing became popular, though, among the colonial elite by the mid-1700s. They used the snuffbox and its required gestures, a ritual that came from France, through London, to the colonies. In the second third of the 19th century the way of using snuff changed: instead of sniffing it through the nose, people began dipping it, placing a pinch in the mouth.

In the first half of the 19th century chewing became the main method of consumption. It was popular after the American Revolution and was seen as an American way to use tobacco, a variation from the European styles. Appropriately, the use of chewing tobacco seems to have peaked in the Jacksonian era, the age of the common man. The frontier now seemed to be setting the tone for society. English traveler Charles Mackay thought the national symbol for the United States should not be the eagle but the spittoon.

From the Civil War to World War I the annual consumption of tobacco in the United States rose dramatically. The cigar became something of a fad in the South after the Mexican War and was certainly popular among, and associated with, the upper classes in the Gilded Age. In fact, the cigar has been an accessory of power for important southern politicos throughout the 20th century as well.

A sudden shift to smoking tobacco occurred during and after the Civil War.

This was the era of cigarettes, both hand rolled and machine made. Bright-leaf tobacco was developed beginning in the 1850s in North Carolina, and by 1880 it was grown from Virginia south to Georgia. In this age of the New South the tobacco industry grew and expanded. Durham and Winston-Salem, N.C., Louisville, Ky., and Richmond, Va., became the centers of the cigarette industry, bringing economic prosperity to North Carolina, Virginia, and Kentucky, in particular, and promoting the use and consumption of the weed by southerners. A southerner, James A. Bonsack of Virginia, invented the cigarette-rolling machine in 1880, and this led to a steady increase in demand. Annual national per capita consumption rose from 1.5 pounds in 1860 to 5.5 pounds in 1900, a 267 percent rise. The Duke and Reynolds families became new power brokers in the South and symbols of success. The landscape reflected the new importance of tobacco. Tobacco barns became pervasive, and by the 1880s the towering, stolid tobacco factories producing cigarettes were new symbols on the landscape. In 1929 the South produced 60 percent of all tobacco in the United States and 84 percent of the cigarettes.

This success story has a dark side, though. Opposition to tobacco use goes back to the colonial era. By the late 1600s debunkers of tobacco smoking were dismissing it as a nasty, ungodly, dangerous habit. King James I opposed smoking tobacco, calling it a "stinking weed." It was, he said, "a custome Lothsome to the eye, hatefull to the Nose, harmfull to the braine, dangerous to the Lungs, and in the blacke stinking fume thereof, nearest resembling the horrible Stigian smoke of the pit that is bottomeless." Others charged that smoking actually upset the balance of the body instead of maintaining it. The American Anti-Tobacco League led opposition to tobacco in the 19th century. The anti-tobacco crusade of 1830–60 was led by northerners, but Virginian John Hartwell Cocke was one southerner actively involved in the movement. Cole Blease of South Carolina and Dr. Alton Ochsner of New Orleans later were prominent southern opponents of "Demon Nicotine." Religious groups, even in North Carolina, have periodically been vocal in opposition to the sinfulness of tobacco use.

Tobacco advertising has long enlivened the southern countryside and provided some of the region's most notable material artifacts. James B. Duke used promotion of his tobacco products as one way to consolidate his dominance of the tobacco industry. Tobacco vendors used wooden Indians in front of shops selling cigars and tobacco goods. A landmark of advertising was when John Ruffin Green adopted the symbol of the bull after the revival of the tobacco business in Durham at the end of the Civil War. He saw a bull's head on a jar of Colman's mustard, which came from Durham, England. A neighbor had a breeding bull, which became the model for the trademark Durham Bull. It caught the imagination of rural southerners and others as well. His company later fought hard in courts and elsewhere for control of the bull as a trademark and won. The company blanketed the southern rural countryside with testimonials from prominent people, including ministers. The greatest sign painter of the bull symbol was J. Gilmer Koerner, who was known as Reuben Rink.

By the 1890s the industry was more sophisticated in marketing, and more artifacts began to appear. Chewing plugs now had tin or paper tags with the name of the maker and the brand name of the product. Colorful lithographs were pasted on wooden boxes of chewing tobacco. This was a regionally produced and identified pop art that used a variety of images: flowers, historical events and people, animals; nude girls sometimes appeared. The sides of barns became the canvas for painters such as Koerner. Whereas the cigar salesman and advertising, with strong ethnic overtones, had become identified with the North's urban areas by the early 20th century, advertising for smoking and chewing tobacco stressed rural themes appropriate to the South.

In the 20th century several tobacco products have been especially identified with the South. Snuff is one. Margaret J. Hagood reported in 1939 that half of the North Carolina Piedmont tenant women she studied used snuff. In Erskine Caldwell's *Tobacco Road* the Lester family's landlord, Captain John, stops giving rations and snuff at the store, and the grandmother in the story is desperate for restoration of her snuff. "There were times when she would have been willing to die, if she could only have for once all the snuff she wanted." Even after World War II sales of snuff in the region did not drastically decline. Black women, farm women, and mountain women all had reputations as snuff dippers.

The South is also still identified as the home of tobacco chewing. In 1947, 100 million pounds of chewing tobacco were still produced, most being consumed in the rural South, and cuspidors were common until the 1950s. Texas author John Graves has written of the virtues of chewing tobacco, which he calls "a great solacer." Unlike the "fury of a tense cigarette smoker's puffing,"

chewing is a laid-back method of use that calms and offers perspective.

Chewing tobacco has made a comeback in the 1970s and 1980s, appealing now to the young and the middle class, as well as to bluecollar and farm workers, who never abandoned it. Chewing tobacco now takes three forms. The first is the *plug*, which is a compressed brick of tobacco wrapped in a light brown leaf. A variation of the plug is the "twist," which has become rare except in rural parts of the South. A second form of chewing tobacco used to be called "scrape." It is coarse, sweet shreds, packed in foil pouches. Legendary brand names include Beech Nut, Red Man, and Mail Pouch. The third form of chewing tobacco in the modern South is "smokeless tobacco," or "snoose" as it is known in the Midwest (that name probably comes from *snus*, the Swedish-Danish name for snuff). Smokeless tobacco is a wet, grainy tobacco, flavored with mint, wintergreen, and the unlikely raspberry packed in cylindrical boxes with tin lids. It has brand names such as Skoal, Copenhagen, and Levi Garrett. A communal symbol of the regional importance of chewing tobacco is the tobacco spitting contest, which has become a staple of several southern communities. Jeff Barber won the National Tobacco Spitting Contest in Raleigh, Miss., in 1981 with a heave of 33 feet, 7¼ inches, a record that the *Guinness Book of World Records* has noted as a landmark.

See also INDUSTRY: / Tobacco Industry; SOCIAL CLASS: / Tobacco Workers

Charles Reagan Wilson
University of Mississippi

John Graves, *Texas Monthly* (November 1978); Charles Hudson, *The Southeastern*

Indians (1976); Katherine T. Kell, *Journal of American Folklore* (April–June 1965); Joseph C. Robert, *The Story of Tobacco in America* (1949); Robert Sobel, *They Satisfy: The Cigarette in American Life* (1978). ☆

Victorianism

||||||||||||||||||||||||||||||||||

When in 1953 the Armstrong Browning Library at Baylor University acquired a first edition of Robert Browning's *Pauline*, its collection of the poet's first editions was complete. Housed in a magnificent building of Texas stone, Italian marble, bronze doors, and stained-glass windows, this library today is a surprising conglomeration of memorabilia, first editions, manuscripts, and scholarly works dealing with the Brownings and their Victorian world. In Browning's day scholars and critics of the poet would not have imagined traveling to Waco, in the central plains of Texas, to pursue their research. This splendid collection of Victoriana in a seemingly unlikely place is partly the result of Texas wealth, regional pride, and especially the indefatigable work of A. Joseph Armstrong at Baylor. But the Browning Library is also a reflection of the profound and persisting influence of Victorian ideas, ideals, and personalities on the culture of the South, even as it extends itself westward into Texas.

In the imagination of the Southerner, Browning epitomizes many of the Victorian qualities particularly appealing to a people whose lives and history bristled with losses, spiritual and material. In his robust optimism, Browning represents the profound belief that, despite the disillusionment of lost causes, the law of history is one of development and progress. One who "marched breast forward," and "never doubted clouds would break," incarnated in his person and his work an optimism that refused in a benighted world of crass materialism to give up the notion that human beings are more than biological organisms or economic animals devoid of a higher destiny and significance. His influence in the South was assured by hundreds of Browning Societies that developed in communities throughout the region in the 20th century. And Pippa Passes, Ky., was named for one of his more sentimental poems.

In good Victorian fashion the South has always been given to heroes and hero worship. "You can know a man by his heroes" has the force of a southern proverb. For southerners, as for Matthew Arnold, the ancient heroes were Hellenic and Hebraic, captured in the personalities of Socrates and Jesus and in the ideas and myths associated with these seminal figures. In a narrower vein, the South idealized with great imaginative power the Founding Fathers, particularly Jefferson and Washington. After the tragedy of the Civil War, southern healing was promoted by the nostalgic romanticization of Robert E. Lee, who became an incarnation of the Victorian ideal of the complete gentleman: patriot and statesman, military genius, scholar, educator, philanthropist, and Christian family man. Only slowly, through several decades, did Lincoln take his place in the pantheon of southern heroes. Even Texas's own particular frontier heroes, Houston, Travis, and Crockett, became Victorian heroes.

To such heroic status southern imagination also elevated the eminent Victorian literary geniuses: Arnold, Carlyle, Tennyson, Sir Walter Scott, and Browning. But the typically Victorian anti-Catholic feeling in the South made John Henry Newman suspect despite his literary and religious genius. Southerners, like their English counterparts, could never fully forgive a man of Newman's brilliance and stature for having given up his Oxford heritage to join forces with that most un-English of traditions, the church of Rome. On the other hand, despite his secular humanist assumptions, John Stuart Mill has enjoyed heroic status among that intellectual elite in the South who are jealous of individual liberty. In declaring "eternal freedom from the dual tyranny of priest and sword," early Texas heroes, for example, sought to establish constitutionally the personal freedoms that later found classic formulation in Mill's *On Liberty*.

But among the eminent Victorians, Browning seems most to have epitomized the southern ideal of the heroic. Himself a commoner, he nevertheless enjoyed status and favor with the nobility, including Queen Victoria herself. Not personally identified with the ancient centers of learning and authority at Oxford and Cambridge, he yet was acclaimed a poet of the intellect. Many southern intellectuals could admire that. Without allegiance to any particular dogma or institutional tradition, Browning was still deeply religious—a classic example of that muscular Christianity fully at home in the world, a temporal existence ennobled and idealized by the confident assumption that "God's in his heaven, all's right with the world." Like Matthew Arnold, Browning represented and espoused that sweetness and light which combined the humane intelligence of Socrates with the

reverence for life and passion for social justice of Jesus.

The higher criticism of the Bible emanating from the German universities touched Christianity in the South even less than it affected the Christianity of Victorian England. Southerners were, like their English ancestors, a people of the book—and that book was the Bible. Despite isolated struggles over the implications of Darwin and the new geology—and some momentary debates dealing with Strauss and the historical Jesus—popular biblicism in the South went fundamentally unchallenged well into the middle of the 20th century.

As in Victorian England, a hallmark of southern culture has been its profound commitment to Protestant Christianity. Puritan influences, also at work in Victorian England, have left their indelible mark, not only on the role of the Bible in popular culture but also on the most basic human institutions and daily activities: the understanding of family life and sexuality; attitudes toward work and leisure; the significance of education and learning; and ultimately the very meaning of human life.

Southern life has been dominated by the Victorian notion of the primacy of the patriarchal family, centered around a deference to the father and idealization of the mother, extended in concern and caring to children, cousins, and other kin. This family ideal captures that most basic of southern convictions, biblical in origin, that human beings are above all relational creatures. Rooted in an unacknowledged sexism, the cultural ideal of the family elevated women to a special status and role. Women represented the altruistic virtues of nurturing, compassion, morality, and religious piety. Their place was in running the home, in educating the young, and in caring for the sick. They were far removed from the areas of finance and commerce, the manufacture and distribution of goods, the military service, the law, or politics and public policy. Men were, therefore, in the ideal, thrust into positions and roles of power and responsibility for the common good. Such roles demanded knowledge, a high level of intelligence and rationality, emotional toughness, and a sense of justice. Not surprisingly, higher education in the South, as in Victorian England, was therefore dominated by classic Christian models designed for a male intellectual elite.

Southern sexual attitudes and mores reflected the deep ambivalence also found in English Victorian responses to sexuality. Tenaciously holding to the biblical and Christian view that all God's creation is essentially good, southern culture managed to affirm sexuality as a part of God's good intention. Hence celibacy was strongly suspect, both as a religious ideal and as a personal way of life. Unmarried males were peculiarly problematical, smacking of the unnatural. Although, like the "other Victorians" among their English counterparts, southerners allowed a certain unspoken sexual license in private, the cultural norm has always been an idealized version of erotic love, buttressed by the Christian notions of monogamy and lifelong fidelity. This made it possible to glorify the virtue and purity of wives and mothers while allowing certain concessions to the animal nature of males. Sexual expression before and outside of marriage for males, although never fully accepted as a norm, was nonetheless tacitly tolerated.

It is impossible to understand the sexual values of the South without recognizing their deep, indeed symbiotic, relationship to the racial values. Here again, English Victorian notions gave southerners categories of thought that explained existing social arrangements and sensibilities. Victorian England often justified to its Christian conscience its expansive colonialism and imperialism as a way of bringing civilization to the heathen. "Darkest Africa" symbolized the aboriginal savages' life before the impact of the humanizing influences of Christianity and culture. Much of this Victorian attitude is found in southern conceptions of blacks after emancipation. Blacks at best were children, to be tolerated and patronized; at their worst they were savages, to be controlled and kept in their place. Never fully citizens nor quite finally human, blacks evoked a complex set of symbols in the white southern imagination. It is no surprise that such elemental racist symbols should form a symbiosis with elemental sexist symbols to produce cultural mores and sensibilities defying rational explanation or rational redress. In this sense, southern racism has been and is deeply sexual in nature and origin.

In its grand outlines southern culture has been formed and informed by staple Victorian certainties: an idealized anthropology; a confidence that history reveals an inevitable progress in human affairs; the conviction that the universe is ordered and its laws are discoverable by human reason. Such confident views of epistemology and morality were grounded in a nondogmatic, personalistic biblical Christianity. Darwin, Freud, and Marx were long ignored or resisted by southerners, who viewed humankind as rational, free, and responsible. The nether regions of the psyche, the animalistic dimensions of the self, fundamental economic instincts and interests—all these were covered up or ignored by the emphasis on freedom and dignity of man. History, in its inevitable progress, reflects the rationality of humankind and the order of the cosmos, energized and directed ultimately by the providential intentionality of God.

Hence the moral certainty. Hence the anxiety before change, and the emphasis upon personal, social, and political peace and equanimity. Hence the genteel insistence upon courtesy and propriety of conduct, and the disfavor toward critical temperaments and unconventional ideas and behaviors. Above all, uncertainty, open conflict, and overt criticism are to be kept in check and resisted. Victorian cultural traits represented a restraint on contrary, paradoxical southern tendencies toward extreme individualism and brutal violence. When Victorian restraints dropped, the result was what W. J. Cash called the "savage ideal." Only in the 20th century has a fusion of ideological elements been forced to yield to modern circumstances and intellectual categories. And even in the New South the forces of Victorianism have not been fully spent.

> W. D. White
> St. Andrews Presbyterian College

William L. Burn, *The Age of Equipoise: A Study of the Mid-Victorian Generation* (1964); Walter E. Houghton, *The Victorian Frame of Mind* (1957); Gertrude Himmelfarb, *Ideas and Beliefs of the Victorians: An Historic Revaluation of the Victorian Age* (1966); Richard H. King, *A Southern Renaissance: The Cultural Awakening of the American South, 1930–1955* (1980); Richard A. Levine, ed., *Backgrounds to Victorian Literature* (1967); Daniel J. Singal, *The War Within: From Victorian to Modernist Thought in the South, 1919–1945* (1982). ☆

Vietnam War

IIIIIIIIIIIIIIIIIIIIIIIIIIIIIIIIIIII

The American South, whose people were the only group of Americans to suffer a military defeat prior to the Vietnam conflict, assumed an important role in leading the United States out of the malaise that followed the collapse of American efforts in South Vietnam. The southern way of handling defeat has been to persist in the idea that the cause is never lost, that defeat is beyond belief, so deeply are the roots of honor sunk into a land dearly loved.

The key to understanding the South's regional contribution to the Vietnam War is its rhetoric of belligerence, rhetoric backed by action-out of necessity— to serve a cause with honor. To a southerner, all of this follows naturally from an ingrained sense of duty. As the Vietnam War ground to its perplexing conclusion, people in many parts of the nation wavered in their sense of purpose, but the South's fundamental conservatism held fast. Every president since Richard Nixon has needed a "southern" strategy, and the core of that strategy rests in an appeal to patriotism—to a reverence for American ideals, which for southerners includes a readiness to defend democracy aggressively and the essential right of self-determination, no matter how cloudy and uncertain the specific case may be.

Texan Lyndon Johnson believed in the power of this rhetoric, but he lost faith in it with the sweep of nightmarish television images and week-by-week statistics of American casualties, which led to his surrender of the presidency. Beginning with the 1968 election and continuing through the 1970s, George C. Wallace—operating sometimes as a candidate of the American Independent party and sometimes as a Democratic party nominee—championed the rhetoric of belligerence, thus giving Richard Nixon, Jimmy Carter, and Ronald Reagan a clear signal on how to win the heart of the South in the post-Vietnam era. Ironically, the southerner Carter did not catch the signal; he became the next president after Johnson to see his ambitions fall to ruin in the wake of perceived American military weakness during the Iranian hostage crisis. Carter's pardon of Vietnam draft resisters—his first major act as president—had led southerners much earlier to conclude that he was not zealous enough on the matter of patriotism.

During the major escalation of an American military presence in Vietnam, the war had distinctly southern overtones. A Texan's administration sent the marines ashore. Bill Moyers, another Texan, had to field the early hard questions about combat activity involving U.S. troops, although when the questions loomed larger than the answers, Moyers departed, a foreshadowing of what would happen later to his president.

For Dean Rusk, a native of Cherokee County, Ga., Vietnam became the dark center of his tenure as secretary of state. And heading the order of battle in Vietnam was William C. Westmoreland, of Beaufort County, S.C. When Westmoreland first left the South for West Point at the outset of his military career, he was reminded by his great-uncle (a veteran of Gettysburg who had also been with Lee at Appomattox) that Lee and Jackson, not just Grant and Sherman, had gone off to the academy in their time. Westmoreland brought to the Vietnam War a clear image of the honorable warrior, an image inherited directly

from Robert E. Lee. The image, of course, was not sufficient to win the war.

The southern quality of the war reached far beyond Westmoreland himself. In the early 1970s, four out of five army generals were from southern towns. The disproportionate overrepresentation of southerners in the army and marines reached all the way down to the lowest ranks; many southern blacks were brought into the army through Robert McNamara's three-year Project 100,000. This infamous scheme opened up military service to "marginally qualified" youths as an escape from impoverished backgrounds. All too frequently, however, the exit led only to Vietnam—or to desertion. Largely because of the southerners placed in the service through Project 100,000 (which eventually involved more than 240,000 men), the South is overrepresented in the cases of military desertion.

Another blemish on the honor of southerners came through the court-martial of William Calley, a Floridian. Nevertheless, many southerners were quick to defend Calley, angrily denouncing the hypocrisy of those who would punish Calley while at the same time forgiving draft resisters. Senator Strom Thurmond of South Carolina made this point frequently, though he was hard-pressed to reconcile his harsh views on Vietnam protesters with the historical precedent in the pardon extended to southerners in the aftermath of the Civil War.

The South had only 22 percent of the nation's population, but it produced 29 percent of the Medal of Honor recipients for Vietnam service, reaffirming its claim to honor. These figures confirm the enduring nature of an outlandish rage to valor in the region, sometimes manifesting itself in nonsensical ways, which have been well documented in war scenes from William Faulkner's fiction of an earlier time. Moreover, on the home front the protest movement against the war never reached the cataclysmic proportions in the South that it did in the North and far West. Despite a few major incidents on southern campuses—particularly the shooting death of two blacks by policemen during the 1970 confrontation at Jackson State—and student-led marches and demonstrations throughout the South, protest activities tended to be more moderate there than elsewhere.

Nevertheless, some voices of protest sounded. An important protest movement within the military developed at Fort Bliss in El Paso, Tex., where the GI's for Peace staged public rallies and published a newsletter, *Gigline*. Also, at the University of North Carolina at Chapel Hill, after a series of student-administration standoffs in the late 1960s, the war resistance movement evolved to a weekly silent vigil in front of the post office on East Franklin Street. Yet even as quiet as this protest was, it drew the ire and contempt of Jesse Helms, then a radio commentator for WRAL in Raleigh. At one point, when the North Carolina legislature was considering creation of a state zoo, Helms responded that there was no need to create a zoo—all the legislators needed to do was put a fence around the university in Chapel Hill. Such a response typified the stance taken by southern practitioners of the rhetoric of belligerence. L. Mendel Rivers of South Carolina, chairman of the Armed Services Committee, asserted during the war that Americans protesting the government's war policy were "filthy buzzards and vermin," a viewpoint more recently revived by Senator Helms of

North Carolina to fit anyone who questions the use of American military capabilities wherever and whenever the need arises.

Backing for such a determined position on the American role in Vietnam came readily and regularly from the churches in the South, particularly those represented at the Southern Baptist General Convention. The military itself had a formidable presence in the South as well. In 1967, a typical war year, 42 percent of the stateside payroll for military personnel went to the 11 states of the Confederacy. Two outcomes merit special attention. First, this particular infusion of federal dollars resulted in dependence on the military by an extended network of people and proliferation of sprawling ghettos of seamy nightclubs and other clip joints around military bases. These situations continued after the Vietnam conflict ended; thus, the South's economic status was tied closely to war. Second, large numbers of soldiers who went to Vietnam passed through training at southern bases: Fort Benning and Fort Gordon in Georgia; Fort Bragg in North Carolina; Parris Island in South Carolina; and Fort Polk in Louisiana.

Many southern bases built mock Vietnamese bases for training soldiers in the ways of war, Vietnam style. In this endeavor the climate of the South contributed significantly, giving trainees a feel for the heat, humidity, and other discomforts to be encountered in combat. Anyone entering the main gate at Fort Polk, La., was greeted by an unabashed declaration of southern pride in preparing soldiers for battle in Vietnam: "Welcome to Ft. Polk, Birthplace of Combat Infantrymen for Vietnam."

Occasionally, people of southern origin found themselves at odds with the

American role in Vietnam—and hence at odds with their own background. Two such southerners, Dan Rather of Texas and Tom Wicker of North Carolina, often seemed to be in the vanguard of critics of the war in the national press; Wicker eventually landed on President Nixon's "enemies list" for his denunciation of several military strategies in Vietnam. Rather and Wicker had both left the South, and perhaps this distance, coupled with their journalistic preoccupation with facts instead of rhetoric, contributed to their individual variation from the southern norm.

The case of the southern veteran after the war also shows some cracks in the rhetoric of belligerence. The proportion of Vietnam veterans to total population in the 1980 census is the same for the South as for the nation generally, about 22 percent. The South was disproportionately represented in enlistees, so it appears that many southern soldiers chose to remain in the military rather than return to civilian life. For the veterans who returned ravaged by the horrors of their combat experience, coping with the mood at home has not always been easy. Southern veterans interviewed in Myra McPherson's *Long Time Passing: Vietnam and the Haunted Generation* reflect some of the same sense of dislocation suffered by veterans across the nation. As elsewhere, veterans in the South suffer quietly.

One exception to this pattern is James Webb, a decorated marine veteran and author of *Fields of Fire*, perhaps the most widely read novel of the Vietnam War, with over a million copies in print. Webb's southern heritage is reflected in one of the novel's main characters, a lieutenant named Robert E. Lee Hodges. Three members of the Hodges family died at Gettysburg, all full of the glory of fields of fire; his grandfather died in battle under Pershing; and his father fell in the Battle of the Bulge. Hodges himself dies in Vietnam, yet the express purpose of Webb's fiction is to reassert the honor of fighting for one's country.

Thus do fiction and fact converge, with the South seemingly less traumatized than other regions and undaunted by the failure to preserve some semblance of democracy in Southeast Asia. In an ironic twist of fate, the Vietnamese refugees who have found Gulf Coast weather to their liking are living proof of an American military defeat. Still, the South seems to repeat the rhetoric of belligerence. After sending the 82nd Airborne from Fort Bragg, N.C., to the tiny island of Grenada, Ronald Reagan gained a good measure of southern allegiance in his 1984 reelection campaign. An understanding of presidential politics in the 1970s and 1980s must thus include recognition of the South's steadfast role in the Vietnam War.

Owen W. Gilman, Jr.
St. Joseph's University

Kent B. Blevins, *Foundations* (July–September 1980); Marion A. Bressler and Leo A. Bressler, *Country, Conscience, and Conscription: Can They Be Reconciled?* (1970); G. David Curry, *Sunshine Patriots: Punishment and the Vietnam Offender* (1985); Melton A. McLaurin, in *Perspectives on the American South*, vol. 3, ed. James C. Cobb and Charles Reagan Wilson (1985); Myra McPherson, *Long Time Passing: Vietnam and the Haunted Generation* (1984); James Reston, Jr., *Sherman's March and Vietnam* (1985); Charles P. Roland, *The Improbable Era: The South since World War II* (1976); James Webb, *Fields of Fire* (1978); William C. Westmoreland, *A Soldier Reports* (1976). ☆

War of 1812

|||||||||||||||||||||||||||||||||

The people in the southern states generally supported the War of 1812, reflecting the strong spirit of American nationalism in the region in that era. Southern presidents Jefferson and Madison steered the nation's course in the events leading to war, and southern congressmen endorsed efforts to gain respect for American neutral rights—the main cause of war. A majority of congressmen representing the farming areas of the South and West voted for war, whereas the members from the maritime regions of the Northeast voted against the declaration of war. British interference with American trade had damaged southern farm exports in cotton and tobacco, hurting the region economically and making it eager to stand up to the British.

In addition, Americans on the frontier, in both the South and the Northwest, saw war with the British as a way to end Indian attacks on pioneer settlers and gain land in Canada and Florida. The "War Hawks" were congressmen eager for war, and many of them were southerners—Henry Clay from Kentucky, John C. Calhoun and William Lowndes from South Carolina, and Felix Grundy from Tennessee. Virginian John Randolph tagged them "War Hawks" because of their belligerent nationalism that sought a fight.

The nation was unprepared for war, though, when it came. The earliest fighting in the South included a Native American uprising on the frontier. The Creeks won a victory at Fort Mims, north of Mobile, in August 1913, but Andrew Jackson then led a volunteer militia campaign that crushed Indian resist-

ance. The key battle was at Horseshoe Bend, on the Tallapoosa River, in March 1814. The Creeks surrendered about 60 percent of their territory as a result of the Treaty of Fort Jackson in August of that year. The British campaign in the South concentrated on blockading the coastline and raiding coastal settlements. The Chesapeake Bay area was especially hard hit, including the invasion of Washington, D.C., on 24 August 1814. The British moved on to Baltimore but did not launch a major attack on the well-fortified U.S. forces.

The battle of New Orleans was the culminating event of the War of 1812 and a major contribution to both the national and regional imaginations. The British hoped to seize the port city and gain control of the Mississippi River. Andrew Jackson organized efforts to strengthen the Gulf Coast defenses in the fall of 1814 and led an unauthorized raid into Pensacola, in Spanish Florida, where the British had been planning attacks. In November, Americans put up new fortifications on various approaches to New Orleans. The Treaty of Ghent was signed in Europe on 24 December 1814, officially ending the war, but this news did not reach the combatants in North America until after the battle of New Orleans. On 8 January 1815 British commander Sir Edwin Pakenham, who was contemptuous of the Americans, launched a frontal attack on Jackson's forces, who included an eclectic combination of frontier riflemen, upper-class Creole volunteers, free blacks, and pirates. Pakenham and about 2,000 British died in the assault.

The peace treaty ending the war settled few of the trade problems that had led to war, but the conflict itself became a major symbol of early American nationalism. The South was particularly proud of the victory over the British at New Orleans. The republican form of government now seemed safer than before. After the war, southern congressmen such as John C. Calhoun, who later would be the greatest sectionally oriented politician in the South, supported nationalistic legislation.

The legend of the battle of New Orleans was an especially important cultural legacy. From it General Jackson augmented his enormous popularity on the southern frontier and gained a reputation as one of the great national heroes. Folksongs about "The Hunters of Kentucky" and their sharpshooting communicated pride in southern fighting abilities and popularized the phrase "half horse, half alligator" as a description of the bigger-than-life frontiersmen in the region. (The free blacks, pirates, Creoles, and other defenders did not, however, receive similar cultural immortality for their roles in the battle.) In the 1950s the highly popular tune "The Battle of New Orleans," by country singer Johnny Horton, reminded listeners of this heroic event in the southern past.

Charles Reagan Wilson
University of Mississippi

Roger H. Brown, *The Republic in Peril: 1812* (1964); Gilbert Byron, *The War of 1812 on the Chesapeake Bay* (1964); Reginald Horsman, *The War of 1812* (1969); John K. Mahon, *The War of 1812* (1972); Bradford Perkins, *Prologue of War: England and the United States, 1805–1812* (1961); Robert Remini, *Andrew Jackson and the Course of American Empire, 1767–1821* (1977); John William Ward, *Andrew Jackson: Symbol for an Age* (1955). ☆

World War I

The onset of a seemingly remote war in Europe set in motion forces that would have great consequences for southern life. The most immediate impact was a sharp economic downturn caused when the British blockade of the Central Powers denied cotton producers access to the continental market. Abruptly punctuating a period of modest prosperity for southern agriculture, the collapse initially stirred considerable hostility toward the Allies. Even as the United States moved closer to its own declaration of war, many prominent southerners urged President Woodrow Wilson to maintain American neutrality. This attitude stemmed partly from parochialism as well as economic concerns, but southern opposition also drew on the region's strong anticorporate impulse. Spokesmen such as Congressman Claude Kitchin and Senator James Vardaman believed that business interests were eager to turn a profit on a war the United States did not need to enter. Several southern legislators opposed the president's preparedness program, and a few even voted against his declaration of war. Senator Vardaman's criticism of the war ultimately cost him his political career.

Skeptical though southerners might have been of a foreign conflict, the region nevertheless threw itself into the war effort. Both culturally and ethnically the white South had strong ties to Great Britain, a link the British shrewdly stressed by purchasing huge amounts of cotton. Moreover, the military tradition has always been strong in the South, and the patriotic call to arms in 1917 stirred a tide of popular sentiment. Perhaps typical of the attitudes of his fellow southerners was Tennessee draftee Alvin C. York, who initially requested deferment on religious grounds but later became America's most decorated combat soldier.

Although individual southerners were eager to seize arms, the region's traditional distrust of centralized federal power and the economic giantism of major corporations sparked opposition to many aspects of the political economy of the war years. Led by Kitchin, southern legislators worked for a revenue policy that fell most heavily on upper-income groups. Others such as Secretary of the Navy Josephus Daniels criticized the growing partnership between big business and big government and alleged that industry was exploiting the crisis to enhance its profits. Whatever their criticisms of the corporate state, however, southern leaders were determined to see that their region got a substantial share of wartime profits. The army placed a majority of its training camps in southern states, and naval contracts stirred new life in the shipbuilding industry. At a time when the government was imposing price controls on many commodities, southern political clout exempted cotton from this list, allowing its price to soar, thereby fueling a burst of regional prosperity.

The war also accelerated important changes in the structure of the southern economy. The federal government began construction of explosives and wood chemical plants, which helped to spur the growth of hydroelectric power and chemical manufacturing after the war. Most important was the nitrate plant and dam at Muscle Shoals, Ala., which represented the idea of cheap, federally sponsored power and later served as the model for the Tennessee Valley Authority projects of the 1930s.

Moreover, the war years saw a general rise in regional prosperity, a prosperity that bred optimism about the future for a section long marked as the poorest in the nation.

World War I had enormous human consequences for the South as well. Military service diminished the region's provincialism as thousands of native southerners left Dixie for assignments elsewhere while thousands of nonsoutherners came to the area for training. These masses of people in transit created considerable stress, especially in race relations. The number of lynchings increased markedly during the war years, and blacks occasionally retaliated in kind, as in Houston, Tex., where a black army unit responded to racial harassment by killing 17 civilians. Simultaneously, the war years saw the beginning of the Great Migration, the massive shift of blacks from the rural South to the urban North. With immigration disrupted and the draft under way, industry needed a source of cheap labor, and by 1920 roughly a million blacks had moved north, the beginning of one of the most important demographic shifts in American history. Southern women also saw important changes in their lives as the women's suffrage amendment moved closer to ratification, although only a few state legislatures in the South supported the proposal. Another longtime political goal of many southern women, prohibition, also won ratification shortly after the war.

The Great War left the South an important cultural legacy. The years after the Armistice saw a great flowering of letters known as the Southern Renaissance. "With the war of 1914–1918," Allen Tate wrote in 1945, "the South re-entered the world—but gave a backward glance as it stepped over the border: that backward glance gave us the Southern renascence, a literature conscious of the past in the present." Led by William Faulkner, Thomas Wolfe, the Nashville Agrarians, and many others, for the next two decades the South stood at the forefront of American literature. Indeed the sense of a changing perspective was a hallmark of southern life during the Great War. After a half century of material poverty and political impotence, the South returned to influence in Washington and embraced some of the idealism and internationalism of its native son, Woodrow Wilson, by supporting both his great crusade and his League of Nations.

See also BLACK LIFE: Migration, Black; GEOGRAPHY: Migration Patterns

David D. Lee
Western Kentucky University

Richard M. Abrams, *Journal of Southern History* (November 1956); Howard Allen, *Journal of Southern History* (May 1961); Dewey W. Grantham, *North Carolina Historical Review* (April 1949), *Southern Progressivism: The Reconciliation of Progress and Tradition* (1983); Arthur S. Link, *American Scholar* (Summer 1951), in *Studies in Southern History in Memory of Albert Ray Newsome, 1894–1951*, ed. J. Carlyle Sitterson (1957), *Wilson*, 5 vols. (1947–1965); George B. Tindall, *The Emergence of the New South, 1913–1945* (1967); Richard Watson, *Journal of Southern History* (February 1978). ☆

World War II

||||||||||||||||||||||||||||||||||

The South has probably undergone more change since World War II than at any other time in its history. Given the Civil War, this claim may seem astounding; yet the region in 1940 was more like the antebellum South than like the South of today. Nowhere is the discrepancy more apparent than in the realm of economic development. In 1938 President Franklin D. Roosevelt characterized the South as "the Nation's No. 1 economic problem." In 1980, on the other hand, one of President Jimmy Carter's commissions classified the South as part of the booming "Sunbelt" in contrast to the economically declining "Frostbelt" of the North.

Although the change occurred over several decades, World War II brought a decisive shift away from the South's economic backwardness, its distinctive rural life, and its poverty. For better or worse, it finally started becoming more like other sections, with roughly the same standard of living. Some agrarians bemoaned this transition, but the great majority of southern whites and blacks have, with good reason, welcomed it.

To appreciate the impact that wartime spending had on the South, one has to keep in mind that World War II produced the biggest boom in American economic history. The figures are startling. Between 1940 and 1944 the 10 largest recipients of government war contracts alone received about the same amount of money as the federal government spent on *everything* from 1932 to 1939. During the war the volume of American industrial output increased at an average rate of 15 percent a year; the average rate of increase for the period 1896 to 1939 had been 4 percent. By 1945 the direct investment by the government in new plants and equipment had increased the productive capacity of the economy by about 50 percent.

With the South receiving its full share of this spending, the regional impact was immediate. Between 1939 and 1943 approximately 1.2 million new industrial jobs were created. "For the first time since the War between the States," according to *Fortune* magazine, "almost any native of the Deep South who wants a job can get one." The combination of military installations and defense plants altered the lives of southerners in ways that would have been inconceivable only a few years earlier. Economically marginal persons, displaced since the 1920s by the collapse of the South's traditional cotton economy, now had an alternative to migration to leaving the South. Many found employment in the booming shipyards along the Atlantic and Gulf coasts, others in the aircraft, metals, machinery, petroleum, and chemical industries that began to dot the region. Relatively minor regional cities, such as Houston and Tampa, began a process of growth that would eventually make them national urban centers.

Persons caught up in these changes found them profound. Some complained that only old men, women, and children were left in the countryside. "Them that ain't gone in the army," one Alabamian told a visiting reporter, "have gone to the shipyards." Not all who moved necessarily wanted to abandon rural life, but the economic incentive to do so was irresistible. Migrants to rapidly urbanizing areas found them dirty, overcrowded, and unpleasant, but wages of a hundred dollars or more per week represented small fortunes to people accustomed to hardscrabble lives.

The South was, in fact, booming. According to the U.S. Bureau of the Census, Mobile County, Ala., was the fastest-growing metropolitan area of the entire country. The bureau estimated that during the war more than 15 million persons (i.e., 12 percent of the entire

United States population) moved to counties different from those in which they had been living at the time of Pearl Harbor. Along with West Coast cities, those in the South were the biggest gainers. Together with Mobile, the Norfolk, Va., and Charleston, S.C., areas comprised three of the four fastest growing areas of the nation. Like Mobile, Norfolk attracted thousands to its shipyards. In the case of Charleston, its busy industries and proximity to Fort Benning, Ga., the army's largest basic training center, prompted the following advice to prospective travelers: "You'll drive blocks looking for a place to park, and just about the time you begin wondering where all the people came from you bump into a new housing development, or run into a squadron of navy uniforms, or if the wind is right, get a whiff of Charleston's pulp mill."

Not all parts of the South would be affected so dramatically, but repercussions were nonetheless widespread. When compared to the sharecropper's endless cycle of indebtedness or the meager wages of the typical prewar southern textile worker, war-related jobs represented a step forward for large

Soldier home on furlough with his family outside a service station in Brown Summit, North Carolina, 1944

numbers of southerners. These jobs not only gave them their first taste of prosperity but began to tear apart the paternalistic patterns to which many southern whites as well as the great majority of blacks had been subjected. All the highly publicized talk among middle- and upper-class southerners about "how difficult it was to get good help any more" reflected not only their racism and paternalism but also the economic transformation that was taking place. Most of its beneficiaries were white, but the overall rise in the South's economic situation was such that some blacks were also included. Perhaps the most telling trend was that the South's industrial growth was slowest in what up to World War II had been its most important industry, textiles. In effect, a structural transformation was occurring in the very nature of southern industry.

Both the intensification of southern economic change and its implications for the future were exemplified by the region's most famous wartime industrialist, Andrew Jackson Higgins. In 1939 Higgins Industries in New Orleans consisted of one plant, which employed about 400 workers manufacturing shallow-draught boats for use in the swampy bayous of southern Louisiana and Mississippi. Higgins's gross sales amounted to $850,000, and rumor had it that his best customers were bootleggers. In 1941, however, his designs for landing craft and patrol torpedo boats were accepted by the U.S. Navy, and Higgins's prominence skyrocketed. By 1944 his operations in New Orleans consisted of eight plants that employed over 20,000 workers; his gross sales were estimated at $120 million. Higgins became a local folk hero who disregarded many southern traditions. He was willing to work with labor unions and also willing, in-

deed eager, to hire blacks and pay them on the same basis as whites. To be sure, he maintained segregation, but his shipyards were relatively free of the racial tensions that periodically erupted into violence elsewhere, most notably in 1943 at the Alabama Drydock Company in Mobile.

Although the impact of the war on southern agriculture was less dramatic, the developments were hardly insignificant. The prices of traditional commodities such as cotton and tobacco rose sharply, as did the production of new ones like peanuts and livestock. Booming war plants and military mobilization led to severe labor shortages—a sharp reversal of what until recently had been a longstanding problem of surplus agricultural labor. Increasingly, the region's planters and commercial farmers resorted to mechanization or to novel solutions such as importing migrant laborers from Mexico and the West Indies, or, more novel still, leasing Axis prisoners of war to do fieldwork. (Over 400,000 enemy prisoners were interred in the United States during the war, most of them in the South.) Occasionally, planters even resorted to paying native workers reasonable wages and providing them with better living conditions.

The very nature of American mobilization during the war altered what C. Vann Woodward has called the "counterpoint" of "North-South dialogue." Twelve million Americans entered the armed services during the year, and at least half of them spent some time at southern military bases, which accounted for more than half the nation's military installations. A substantial number of outsiders experienced their first direct contact with the region during the war, and the impressions and attitudes that they carried away with them had an indelible impact upon postwar sectional issues, particularly civil rights. However much these northern GIs may have been impervious to racial injustices in their own areas, or were themselves prejudiced against blacks, given the time and place, not to mention the circumstances of war, most did not find the white South's highly visible efforts to enforce segregation compatible with the democratic ideals they were ostensibly defending.

At the same time that large numbers of northerners were discovering the South, southern whites and blacks were also exposed to new locales, ideas, and influences outside the region. The impact of wartime experience on southern blacks is significant. Over 1 million saw military service, which for many was a prelude to subsequent civil rights involvements. Medgar Evers of Decatur, Miss., served with U.S. Army forces in Normandy and received his college education on the GI Bill; Harry Briggs, the plaintiff in the 1949 Clarendon County, S.C., case that launched into the courts the issue of public school desegregation, had spent all of his 34 years in the county, except for the three he spent in the South Pacific with the navy; and Oliver Brown of Topeka, Kan., whose daughter was the focus of the suit that led to the *Brown* v. *Board of Education* decision, was a veteran. During the war black Americans argued that the discrepancy between the democratic values for which the United States was fighting overseas and the realities of racially discriminatory practices at home had become intolerable. This attitude particularly affected blacks who experienced these discriminations firsthand while in their country's uniform.

The war disturbed the South's economic, social, and moral isolation and had a demonstrable impact on one of the region's greatest natural resources—its literary imagination. Flannery O'Connor's masterful story "The Displaced Person" conveyed the full sense of World War II's impact on the South. In it, O'Connor evoked a powerful image of the traditional world of the rural South—a world of white landowners and their poor white and black tenants—about to be torn asunder by the arrival of a Displaced Person, literally a DP, a refugee from Poland who with his family had somehow managed to survive Hitler's death camps and who had come to the South to work as a hired farmhand. To the farm's white tenants the displaced person, whose name is Guizac, brings home all the recent horrors of Europe—"the devil's experiment station"—of which they had been only dimly aware. Guizac is most efficient, a much better farmer than the resident white and black tenants, who fear that his industriousness makes them expendable. With his lack of understanding of the social conventions of the Jim Crow South, though, Guizac might as well have been from Mars. His ultimate transgression is to promise in marriage to one of the farm's black males his 16-year-old female cousin, whom Guizac wanted to bring to the United States from Poland. This is too much for the social world of a southern tenant farm, and the story ends with Guizac's being crushed to death by a runaway tractor as the landlady and her tenants, who could have warned the Pole to move out of the way, stand by mutely. Guizac's death, however, only hastens the breakdown of the farm, which is sold at a loss while its inhabitants disperse—an appropriate ending for a story conveying the social, economic, and moral impact of World War II on the South.

William Faulkner, the South's foremost literary chronicler, captured the totality of the changes in the region. In his first postwar novel, *Intruder in the Dust* (1948), Faulkner vividly portrayed the economic transformation reaching into Jefferson, the seat of his mythic Yoknapatawpha County. He contrasted Jefferson's "old big decaying wooden houses," which had known several generations of the town's residents and the South's anguished history, with the decidedly Sunbeltish image of "neat, small, new, one-story houses designed in Florida and California set with matching garages in their neat plots of clipped grass and tedious flowerbeds, three and four of them now, a subdivision now in what twenty-five years ago had been considered a little small for one decent front lawn, where the prosperous young married couples live with two children each and (as soon as they could afford it) an automobile each and memberships in the country club and the bridge clubs." For Faulkner, tawdriness was a by-product of the South's new prosperity. Yet few, including Faulkner, mourned the passing of the endemic poverty that had shackled the region for so long.

Morton Sosna
Stanford University

Carl Abbott, *The New Urban America: Growth and Politics in Sunbelt Cities* (1981); James C. Cobb, *The Selling of the South: The Southern Crusade for Industrial Development, 1936–1980* (1982); Pete Daniel, *Breaking the Land: The Transformation of Cotton, Tobacco, and Rice Cultures since 1880* (1985), *Standing at the Crossroads: Southern Life in the Twentieth Century* (1986); William Faulkner, *The Mansion* (1955), *Requiem for a Nun* (1950); David R. Goldfield, *Cottonfields and Skyscrapers: Southern City and Region, 1607–1980* (1982); Calvin B. Hoover and B. U. Ratch-

ford, *Economic Resources and Policies of the South* (1951); Bernice Reagon, *Southern Exposure* (Nos. 3 and 4, 1974); George B. Tindall, *The Emergence of the New South, 1913–1945* (1967). ☆

BARCECUE

Three topics upon which southerners never agree are religion, politics, and barbecue. Depending upon where they live, from the coast of the Carolinas to the plains of Texas, southerners will argue that barbecue is beef or pork, mutton or goat, ribs or chicken, or even link sausage. Universally loved in the South, barbecue is a menu of meats, sauces, and side dishes that changes from state to state, and even from one town to the next. And in each locale, residents claim their style of barbecue is the best.

Barbecue begins in the eastern Carolinas either as a whole hog or shoulders cooked over hardwood coals. The meat is then chopped finely, sprinkled with a sauce of apple-cider vinegar, salt, and pepper, and usually served with cole slaw, hush puppies, and Brunswick stew.

As one moves westward through the Deep South, sauces thicken and turn redder from a tomato or catsup base. West of the Mississippi River, beef and pork share the bill of fare in Louisiana, Arkansas, and Oklahoma, but Texans normally acknowledge barbecue only in the form of beef, usually a four- to eight-pound slab of boneless brisket. Traditionally, beef was wrapped in burlap and smoked underground, but it is now usually cooked in pits over hickory, oak, or mesquite wood. It is served with potato salad, baked beans, cole slaw, and two slices of white loaf bread, with spareribs as a side delicacy. The sauce is a dark-brown brew, consisting of butter, catsup, Worcestershire sauce, chili powder, vinegar, lemon juice, salt, pepper, and sugar.

Other meats that dominate certain locales include goat in south and west Texas; link sausage in central Texas; mutton in Owensboro, Ky.; and ribs in Memphis, Tenn.

Once, barbecue was prepared primarily for special occasions; in the antebellum South, many of the cooks who prepared it were black. When numerous barbecue restaurants opened in the middle of the 20th century, many were black establishments, to which whites, in a strange reversal of Jim Crow traditions, made stealthy excursions for take-out orders. Now, whites sit down for service in such black businesses as Cromwell's Barbecue in Phenix City, Ala., Archibald's Drive-In in Northport, Ala., and The Spare Rib in Greeneville, Tex.

Buildings that house barbecue restaurants fall mainly into two architectural classifications. One might be called barbecue primitive style—the older, usually rural eateries, identified by torn screen doors, fire-sale furniture, jukeboxes, cough-syrup calendars, and always the counter and stools, all producing an ambience strikingly similar to a county-line beer joint. Establishments in more urban areas decorate with old tin signs and farm equipment and dress their help in cute calicos and denims, all in an attempt to look country. These facilities can be categorized as the neoprimitive revival barbecue style.

The barbecue "addict" who is also a seasoned traveler looks only at the parking lot to prejudge a restaurant's product. If he notices pickup trucks parked next to expensive imports, he knows the barbecue is good because everyone in town eats there. More than any other cuisine, barbecue draws the whole of southern society, from down the street and from miles around. Many will drive miles to a revered barbecue shrine that serves what its customers claim as the best barbecue in the world.

Gary D. Ford
Southern Living

John Egerton, *Southern Food: At Home, on the Road, in History* (1987); Gary D. Ford, *Southern Living* (May 1982); John Marshall, "Barbecue in Western Kentucky: An Ethnographic Study" (M.A. thesis, Western Kentucky University, 1981); Jerry Simpson, *Southern World* (May–June 1980); Stephen A. Smith, *Studies in Popular Culture* (No. 1, 1985); Kathleen Zobel, *Southern Exposure* (1977). ☆

BEVERAGES

The first mechanical refrigeration plant for the manufacture of ice was built in New Orleans in 1865, but long before that inventive southerners found ways to slake the thirst of long hot summers in the region. In springhouses, cellars, and underground icehouses, 19th-century housekeepers cooled sweet milk, buttermilk, cider, and other liquids. Using winter ice insulated with straw, they made special-occasion pitchers of lemonade and iced tea. In winter they drank hot coffee, tea, and cocoa, imported beverages used widely in the South before the Civil War. Later, orange juice and other juices from Florida-grown citrus fruits became universally popular. Mineral water from the hot springs of Arkansas was first bottled in 1871.

Southerners also drank homemade beer, wine, and whiskey. In the late

1700s Kentucky became a mecca for whiskey makers, and the sour-mash bourbon that originated there is now world renowned; in fact almost all the whiskey made from corn and limestone water comes from Kentucky and Tennessee.

Besides the generic liquids just mentioned, a number of brand-name beverages originated in the South and now enjoy wide popularity. Ten of the better-known drinks, listed in the order of their origination, are as follows: (1) Dr Pepper, created in 1885 by Charles Alderton in Waco, Tex., and named for Dr. Charles K. Pepper of Rural Retreat, Va., in 1885; (2) Coca-Cola, created by John S. Pemberton, a pharmacist in Atlanta, Ga., in 1886; (3) Maxwell House coffee, roasted and blended by Joel O. Cheek in Nashville, Tenn., about 1880; (4) Pepsi-Cola, created in 1896 by Caleb D. Bradham, a pharmacist in New Bern, N.C.; (5) Barq's root beer, developed by Edward A. Barq in Biloxi, Miss., in 1898; (6) Buffalo Rock ginger ale, developed by Sidney Lee of Birmingham, Ala., about 1901; (7) Blenheim ginger ale, created by Dr. John May of Blenheim, S.C., in 1904; (8) Dixie beer, brewed in 1907 by Valentine Merz in New Orleans, La.; (9) RC Cola, developed in Columbus, Ga., in 1933 by successors to Claud A. Hatcher, a pharmacist whose first commercial soft drink in about 1902 was a ginger ale he called Royal Crown; and (10) Gatorade, developed by Dr. Robert Cade, a University of Florida kidney specialist, at Gainesville, Fla., in 1965.

John Egerton
Nashville, Tennessee

Harry E. Ellis, *Dr Pepper: King of Beverages* (1979); Sam B. Hilliard, *Hog Meat and Hoe-*cake: Food Supply in the Old South (1972); E. J. Kahn, Jr., *The Big Drink: The Story of Coca-Cola* (1950); Martha McCulloch-Williams, *Dishes and Beverages of the Old South* (1913); John J. Riley, *A History of the American Soft Drink Industry: Bottled Carbonated Beverages, 1807–1957* (1958); Joe Gray Taylor, *Eating, Drinking, and Visiting in the South: An Informal History* (1982); Rupert B. Vance, *Human Geography of the South: A Study in Regional Resources and Human Adequacy* (1935). ☆

BEVERLEY, ROBERT
|||||||||||||||||||||||||||||||||||||||||||||||||||||
(c. 1673–1722) Virginia gentleman and planter.

Beverley was the first native-born American to write a history of the Virginia colony—*The History and Present State of Virginia* (1705). Educated in England, he returned to Virginia at 19 when he inherited from his father a large estate. In 1697 he married Ursula Byrd, the 16-year-old daughter of Colonel William Byrd I. She died less than a year later in childbirth, and Beverley never remarried. He held various governmental clerkships and was elected to the House of Burgesses in 1699, but his political career ended about 1703 after he criticized Governor Nicholson and his administration for subverting the rights of Virginians. Settled at Beverley Park in King and Queen County, he pursued his studies and speculated in land. He identified strongly with the New World, proclaiming "I am an Indian," and in spite of his great wealth lived a deliberately simple life, using furniture made on his own plantation and producing wine from his own grapes He went on Colonel Alexander Spotswood's 1716 expedition over the Blue Ridge Mountains with the group later known as the "Knights of the Golden Horseshoe." Shortly before his death, he prepared a revised version of the *History* (1722) and *An Abridgement of the Public Laws of Virginia.*

His history was characteristically colonial southern in its approach. Although Puritan histories explained events in terms of divine providence, Beverley's was secular and rationalistic; the nearest he came to any supernatural wonders was in a story of Indian rainmaking, which he handled with the skeptical amusement of later front-porch, rocking-chair tellers of folktales. Nature he viewed not as a wilderness but as a paradise of natural abundance; his descriptions ranged from scientific observation to rhapsodic wonder. He gave extended, sympathetic treatment of Native Americans and indicted white society for the tragic injustice it inflicted on them. Ironically, however, he referred to black slavery in the briefest terms, merely remarking that slaves generally were not overworked. Demonstrating pride in being an American, he was sharply critical of oppressive English economic policies and of mismanagement by royal governors. But he also lamented the indolence and luxury of the colonists themselves and urged them to work to improve the natural garden of Virginia, to diversify their agriculture and develop manufactures, and to live moderately. He thus held forth a pastoral ideal for the American South.

Judy Jo Small
University of North Carolina
at Chapel Hill

Robert D. Arner, *Southern Literary Journal* (Spring 1976); Robert Beverley, *The History and Present State of Virginia*, ed. Louis B. Wright (1947); Judy Jo Small, *American Literature* (December 1983). ☆

BOONE, DANIEL

(1734–1820) Frontiersman.

The idea of the frontier serves as one of the main themes in the American and southern self-images, and it is impossible to discuss the frontier without discussing Daniel Boone. In fact and in myth perhaps no single individual is more central to the frontier experience.

Nearly 70 of his 86 years were involved with the exploration and settlement of the frontier. On 2 November 1734 Boone was born on the western perimeter of European settlement in Berks County, Penn. At the age of 31 he ventured as far south as Pensacola, Fla., in search of a new home. Four years later, on 7 June 1769, after a 37-day trek that he called "a long and fatiguing journey through a mountainous wilderness," he first "saw with pleasure the beautiful level of Kentucke." When he died on 26 September 1820, he was living on the western boundary of frontier settlement in St. Charles County, Mo., one of the outposts for fitting out expeditions to explore the Rocky Mountains. Boone constantly placed himself upon the advancing edge of settlement and did so with evident relish.

In the popular imagination Daniel Boone is the prototype of the frontier hero. His life formed a general pattern that was reenacted with certain variations by the next three major heroes of the westward frontier of the 19th century—Davy Crockett, Kit Carson (a distant relative of Boone), and Buffalo Bill Cody—and as well as by Natty Bumppo, the protagonist in James Fenimore Cooper's *Leatherstocking Tales.* Boone and Crockett most clearly symbolize the southern phase of the frontier. Like the physical frontier, Boone progressively moved to the west. Indeed, he and others like him were largely responsible for the retreat of the frontier toward the setting sun. Like the frontier, he remained an invaluable spiritual constant. Daniel Boone exemplified both the American way of life and the ideals of frontier independence and virtue, which were embodied in the expanding 19th-century South of yeoman farmers. In a country whose history has been dominated by continuing migration, the majority of early Americans believed themselves to be pioneers to some extent and, as such, identified with Boone as their hero.

Boone also mirrored the conflict between civilization and the wilderness: which was the ideal state? Boone was the pioneer, a man happy to do his part to help civilize the frontier and to praise these improvements, but, equally the hunter and man of nature, he was appalled at the encroachments of civilization and retreated before its corrupting influence to insure his own happiness. His achievements and fame live on for Americans in this dual role of pioneer and preserver because this is the dual role—imagined, desired, or enacted—of the American people, as well.

Significantly, Boone still functions as a model worthy of emulation. Dan Beard, the founder of the Boy Scouts of America, a group that influences the lives of millions of young Americans, based his conception of this organization upon the following premise: "A society of scouts to be identified with the greatest of all Scouts, Daniel Boone, and to be known as the Sons of Daniel Boone."

Michael A. Lofaro
University of Tennessee

John E. Bakeless, *Daniel Boone: Master of the Wilderness* (1939; 1965); Michael A. Lofaro, *The Life and Adventures of Daniel Boone* (1978); Richard Slotkin, *Regeneration through Violence: The Mythology of the American Frontier, 1600–1860* (1973). ☆

BURMA SHAVE SIGNS

In 1930 travelers on southern roads joined in a rapidly spreading national pastime—reading Burma Shave signs. Set 100 paces apart along the roadside, a series of six signs contained a catchy jingle promoting Burma Shave, a new brushless shaving cream. A typical gem was the jingle "Water Heater/ Out of Kilter/ Try the Brushless/ Whisker/ Wilter/ Burma Shave." The humorous, often public-spirited advertising tickled the nation's fancy for almost 40 years, providing a focal point for travelers throughout the country.

In Minneapolis in 1925 Clinton Odell and his sons, Allan and Leonard, introduced Burma Shave, the key product of their Burma-Vita Company. A year later Allan proposed the use of sets of roadside signs with catchy jingles to plug the new product. The soaring popularity of the signs was matched by impressive sales records throughout the Midwest in 1926 and 1927, on the Pacific and Atlantic coasts in 1929, and in the South and New England in 1930.

Though lacking the population density—and therefore the potential market—of more urbanized regions, the South offered many locations suitable for the Burma Shave signs. Having found a good spot, the company agent contacted the owner of the land and offered him a jar of Burma Shave and a small fee for a year's lease of the site.

Many of the farmers purportedly became very attached to the signs, repairing them when damaged and willingly renewing the leases. This facet of the automobile age changed southern landscapes, and a new product became part of changing lifestyles.

None of the 600 jingles used between 1926 and 1963 had a specifically regional theme, but one jingle referred to a southern locale: "From Saskatoon/ to Alabam'/ You Hear Men Praise/ The Shave/ What Am/ Burma Shave." Regional marketing campaigns and contests for new jingles were used, and the contests sparked a tremendous response. One Alabama woman, for example, contributed the safe-driving jingle, "A Girl/ Should Hold On/ To Her Youth/ But Not/ When He's Driving." Another example is the 1952 series used in the South, "Missin'/ Kissin'?/ Perhaps Your Thrush/ Can't Get Thru/ The Underbrush—Try/ Burma Shave."

By the mid-1950s the Burma-Vita Company faced decline, and in 1963 Philip Morris, Inc., bought the company and abandoned the signs. The demise of Burma Shave signs caught the public's attention, and one set of signs was eventually placed in the Smithsonian Institution. A national marketing phenomenon had incorporated the South and tapped the rich folk humor of the nation. The television show *Hee Haw* used the signs in the 1970s in evoking its image of the South.

Sharon A. Sharp
University of Mississippi

Frank Rowsome, Jr., *The Verse by the Side of the Road* (1965). ☆

BYRD, WILLIAM, II

||||||||||||||||||||||||||||||||||||||||||||||||||

(1674–1744) Virginia aristocrat, lawyer, politician, planter, writer, and amateur scientist.

Born 28 March 1674, Byrd inherited a large plantation on the James River and the family home, called Westover, from his father, Colonel William Byrd I (1652–1704). Son of a London goldsmith, Colonel Byrd had risen to prominence by inheriting the estate from his uncle and acquiring vast wealth through land speculation, fur trading, and importation of indentured servants and black slaves. Like other wealthy southern colonials, the young Byrd was educated in England, where he developed many of his talents and tastes. He went to grammar school in Essex, studied law at the Middle Temple, was elected to the Royal Society, attended the theater frequently, and moved in London's elite social and literary circles. He lived in England in the years 1681 to 1696, 1697 to 1705, and 1715 to 1726. He married Lucy Parke in 1706, and after her death in 1716 he courted several wealthy women and carried on intrigues with various others before finally marrying Maria Taylor in 1724.

In Virginia, Byrd devoted his time to managing his plantations. He enlarged Westover into a splendid Palladian mansion with luxurious furnishings, improved its gardens, and entertained friends with generous hospitality. He collected one of the best and largest libraries in colonial America and read nearly every day in Latin, Greek, or Hebrew as well as in modern literature. He also took an active role in public affairs, as a man of his station was expected to, serving in the House of Burgesses briefly and in the Executive Council from 1708 until his death. He was the chief member of the joint commission that traveled in 1728 from the coast to the mountains surveying the disputed boundary line between Virginia and North Carolina. The manner of his life was in some ways modeled after the ideal of the English country gentleman, and the cosmopolitan Byrd sometimes described his world in pastoral terms. In continually buying and selling land, though, he represented a new southern type divergent from the English. Though he was a slaveholder, Byrd disapproved of the institution of slavery because of its inhumanity and its fostering of severity in slaveholders, laziness among whites, and the danger of bloody insurrections. His attitude toward New England Puritans blended admiration for their industriousness with contempt for their hypocritical traffic in rum and slaves.

Byrd's writings, marked by urbane good humor, were diverse. He was author of a scientific treatise for the Royal Society, gallant and witty verses, and *A Discourse Concerning the Plague* (1721), an anonymous pamphlet recommending tobacco as a preventive for plague. He seems to have written part of *The Careless Husband*, a play he also directed at a private house in Virginia, and he contributed to a promotional tract in German, *Newgefundenes Eden* (1737). His letters and three portions of his shorthand diaries have been found and published. Most important are the accounts of his travels—*A Progress to the Mines* (1841), *A Journey to the Land of Eden* (1928), and two versions of the dividing-line expedition. Of these, *The Secret History of the Dividing Line*, a travel journal circulated privately among friends and not published until 1929, is rich in racy humor and satirical caricatures of the commissioners; the much longer *History of the Dividing Line* (1866), evidently intended for London publication, diminishes the personal elements and includes political and natural history. Both versions, from the vantage point of a Tidewater Virginian, ridicule the vulgarities of shiftless backwoods Carolinians. Byrd thus inaugurated the southern tradition of literary humor dealing with poor whites.

Judy Jo Small
University of North Carolina
at Chapel Hill

Richard Beale Davis, in *Major Writers of Early American Literature*, ed. Everett Emerson (1972); Pierre Marambaud, *William Byrd of Westover, 1674–1744* (1971); Louis B. Wright, ed., *The Prose Works of William Byrd of Westover* (1966). ☆

CHITTERLINGS

Many aspects of Afro-American and southern white cuisine have their roots in the eating habits of the Old South. Many of the principal foods and dishes use pork products. These dishes include fatback, pigs' ears, pigs' feet, pork chops, and chitterlings. Chitterlings, or chitlins, are the small intestines of hogs, cooked in batter. Studies of early Afro-American eating habits suggest that such foods as chitlins came into the "soul food" diet because of the necessity for rural, poverty-ridden southerners to use every bit of food available. When a hog was slaughtered, no edible part was wasted.

To prevent spoilage, chitlins were prepared and eaten soon after the hog was killed. The common method of preparation was to clean the intestines carefully, soak them in water for a day, parboil them, and only then to fry them in batter. Viscera have been part of the staple diets of other cultures, including the Eskimos and people in Central Europe and the Balkans. They have been found to be nutritious and a good source of iron.

Southerners have disdained the eating of viscera at times, and those eating chitlins attempted to hide them behind names such as "Kentucky oysters." Not all southerners are ashamed of the uncommon food, however. Each fall in Salley, S.C., as many as 20,000 people gather to celebrate chitlins at the Chitlin' Strut festival. The one-day event features the crowning of Miss Chitlin' Strut, the frying and eating of 5 tons of chitlins, and the Chitlin' Strut contest itself. The "Chitlin' Strut" is a dance with twisting gyrations reflecting, some participants say, "the way chitlins make you feel."

Karen M. McDearman
University of Mississippi

William Price Fox, *Chitlin Strut and Other Madrigals* (1983); Bob Jeffries, Soul Food Cookbook (1970); Julian H. Lewis, *Negro Digest* (April 1950); *Southern Living* (November 1979). ☆

CHRISTMAS
|||||||||||||||||||||||||||||||||||

The first celebration of Christmas in North America was likely by the Spanish in the 1500s, and it certainly took place in the South, although whether in Florida or the Southwest is unknown. The first recorded commemoration of Christmas in the British colonies on the mainland was in Jamestown, Va., in 1607. About 40 of the original 100 colonists, unsure of their survival, gathered in a primitive wooden chapel for a somber day. Until well into the 19th century, the Protestants of New England looked with suspicion upon Christmas as a "popish" day, but southerners generally encouraged a joyous celebration.

Gentleman-farmers, in particular, regarded the day more as a time of relaxation and social activity than as a religious holiday. They preserved such European customs as caroling, burning the Yule log, and decorating with greenery. But the environment worked to make a distinctive festival. Native seafood and turkey replaced the traditional European dishes of beef and goose. Southerners added regional touches such as eating fried oysters, drinking eggnog with rum, and going on a Christmas-morning hunt for foxes or other small game. Pines replaced European firs and cedars for the Christmas tree, and Spanish moss was used as a primitive "angel hair" for decorating in the Deep South. The poinsettia became a custom in 1825 when a Charleston man with that name brought a red flower back from Mexico as a gift, and others were soon decorating with poinsettias.

The French in Louisiana introduced the tradition of Christmas fireworks, setting off firecrackers and firing rifles. Until the World War I era southerners rarely used fireworks on the Fourth of July but did punctuate the Christmas holiday with them. A long-standing Cajun custom is the Christmas Eve bonfires, known as *feux de joie* (fires of joy), burning all night along the Mississippi River from Baton Rouge to New Orleans.

Three southern states were the first in the nation to make Christmas a legal holiday—Louisiana and Arkansas in 1831 and Alabama in 1836. The plantation was the center for the most elaborate and distinctive antebellum southern celebration of Christmas. In back-country rural areas plantation houses became the scene of sometimes extravagant Christmas partying, eating, and playing, including the morning hunt. For slaves, Christmas had special meaning. December was a slow work month on the typical plantation, and it became the social season for them. The slaves' holiday lasted until the Yule log burned, which sometimes took over a week. The setting off of fireworks became a noted custom among the slaves as well as the whites.

Christmas as currently celebrated, in broad outline, was an invention of the 19th-century Victorians, who sentimentalized the day and made it the focus for new traditions. By the 1930s the celebration of Christmas had become even more secular than before, with the exchange of gifts for adults and Santa Claus for children. The religious aspects of Christmas were played down by the Victorians, but in the mid-20th century this dimension has become stronger. Some Protestant churches even imitate, in modified manner, the Catholic midnight Eucharist. In Jewish communities the festival of Hanukkah has expanded and absorbed many of the characteristics of Christmas.

Christmas has become the holiday par excellence in the South as elsewhere in the United States. Merchants begin to prepare for it and to advertise their offerings long before Halloween. The Santa Claus parades come early in December, if not sooner, and parties are given throughout the month. Fireworks, the antebellum custom, are still seen. Christmas trees adorn the streets, and one southern state, North Carolina, is the nation's largest producer of Christmas trees. Christmas programs and music are the fare on television and radio. Cards and presents flood the post offices. Charities set up stalls on street corners and with ringing of bells summon passersby to make contributions. Churches, of course, have special services. A few southern families make some effort to celebrate the 12 days culminating on 6 January, a day sometimes called "Old Christmas" (which is perhaps a faint recollection of when Britain adopted the Gregorian calendar in 1752, changing the celebration of Christmas from the 6 January date on the Julian calendar). In New Orleans the season of Carnival officially begins with Twelfth Night parties on the eve of Old Christmas. Many communities now sponsor candlelight tours of historic places at Christmas, reinforcing the holiday's ties to the idea of tradition itself.

Allen Cabaniss
University of Mississippi

William M. Auld, *Christmas Traditions* (1968); John E. Baur, *Christmas on the American Frontier* (1961); Harnett T. Kane, *The Southern Christmas Book: The Full Story from the Earliest Times to the Present: People, Customs, Conviviality, Carols, Cooking* (1958); Joanne B. Young, *Christmas in Williamsburg* (1970). ☆

CLAIBORNE, CRAIG

(b. 1920) Food critic.

Born in Sunflower, Miss. (population 500), Craig Claiborne cherishes childhood memories of beaten biscuits, churn clabber, hot corn bread, and chicken barbecues tended by his father. Another memory, that of his mother's monogrammed silver spoon, used to stir so many sauces that "the lip once a perfect oval [was] worn down by an inch," had special significance. Forced by financial setbacks to move to Indianola and open a boardinghouse in 1924, his mother used her ability to "divine" ingredients, reproducing countless dishes from Creole snapper to Brunswick stew, to keep the family solvent and make "Miss Kathleen's" one of the most "genteel" and well-regarded establishments in the Mississippi Delta. John Dollard rented a room in her home while researching his classic study of southern race relations, *Caste and Class in a Southern Town*.

Shortly after graduating from the University of Missouri in journalism (June 1942), Claiborne enlisted in the navy, having "never sampled a glass of wine" nor eaten anything more exotic than jellied consommé. By the end of his tour of duty, however, he had tasted Moroccan lamb couscous and French pastries in Casablanca and had visited cafés and bistros throughout Europe. Following a brief stint in advertising and publicity in Chicago, another year in Europe and reenlistment in the navy at the outbreak of the Korean War, he finally decided to fuse his interests in food and writing and enrolled in the Lausanne Professional School of the Swiss Hotel Keepers Association.

Claiborne settled in Manhattan and after a series of part-time jobs, including freelance work for *Gourmet* magazine and bartending in upstate New York, met and was interviewed by Jane Nickerson of the *New York Times*; upon her resignation in 1957 he became the paper's food editor, a job he held with only brief interruption for more than 25 years.

Shortly before the publication of his now-classic *New York Times Cook Book* in 1961, Claiborne began to test and prepare recipes with Pierre Franey, former chef of Manhattan's *Le Pavillon* restaurant. Working together in Claiborne's East Hampton home, the two concocted recipes that enriched the food pages of the *Times* and served as the basis for a series of cookbooks.

In addition to his regular column, cookbooks, and a dining guide to Manhattan, Claiborne published *A Feast Made for Laughter* (1983), a memoir complete with 100 favorite recipes. Listed next to the *oeufs á la chimay* is, of course, a recipe for cheese grits.

Elizabeth M. Makowski
University of Mississippi

CONFEDERATE MEMORIAL DAY

Honoring the graves of warriors is an ancient custom, and southern whites after the Civil War made the custom a central ritual of southern life. Vicksburg, Miss., Petersburg, Va., Columbus, Miss., Charleston, S.C., and Columbus, Ga., have all claimed the first observance honoring the Confederate dead after the war. The early observances were spontaneous efforts by individuals or small groups.

Southern states could not agree among themselves which day would serve as the official Memorial Day, but by 1916, 10 states had designated 3 June, Jefferson Davis's birthdate. Other dates set aside have included the fourth Monday in April (Alabama and Mississippi); 10 May, the date of the capture by Union troops of Jefferson Davis in 1865 (North Carolina and South Carolina); and 26 April, the anniversary of the final surrender in 1865 of Confederate General Joseph E. Johnston in

Durham, N.C., (Florida and Georgia). The choice of a date has sometimes been tied to an event of local importance, such as the death of a Confederate leader or anniversary of a nearby battle.

Whenever celebrated, Confederate Memorial Day was a time of solemn ritual. There were speeches, sermons, prayers, the decoration of graves with flowers and Confederate flags, the singing of religious and wartime anthems like "Dixie," and the playing of Taps. A military honor guard usually fired a salute to end the ceremonies. The day's rhetoric reminded southerners of their regional identity, based on the Confederate experience. Women played a key role in this ritual, with the United Daughters of the Confederacy particularly prominent in organizing activities. Groups like the United Confederate Veterans, the Sons of Confederate Veterans, and the Children of the Confederacy also assisted. Various states— Georgia, Florida, Arkansas, Alabama, and Mississippi—soon adopted state flags based partially or fully on the design of Confederate banners. They also proclaimed state holidays commemorating Robert E. Lee's birthday (19 January), Jefferson Davis's birthday, or a separate Confederate Memorial Day. Ministers were actively involved in this holy day. As one would expect, black southerners were not prominently involved in the day's events, although former slaves regarded as "loyal" occasionally were encouraged to speak. After World War II, Confederate Memorial Day declined as a vital holiday in the South. In states where it still exists, Confederate Memorial Day is observed on Mondays to give state employees long weekends. Many small towns continue to have popular ceremonies, but even in these places the

Fourth of July has emerged as a more notable community event.

Charles Reagan Wilson
University of Mississippi

Wallace Evan Davies, *Patriotism on Parade: The Story of Veterans' and Hereditary Organizations in America, 1783–1900* (1955); Lucille C. Lowry, *Origin of Memorial Day in Dixie* (1937); Charles Reagan Wilson, *Baptized in Blood: The Religion of the Lost Cause, 1865–1920* (1980). ☆

CONFEDERATE VETERANS
||||||||||||||||||||||||||||||||||||||||||||

To the white southerners who fought it, the Civil War remained forever poignant; and even after many years had passed, it dominated their thinking. To be sure, a few veterans regarded the war and all its trappings as having been too horrible; their greatest desire was to forget. But for most of them the memory refused to fade.

Reverence for the Lost Cause, it has been argued, grew into a new civil religion after the war. As long as any of them remained, the actual veterans were

Aged Confederate veterans, at Soldiers' Home in Richmond, 1930s

that religion's living apostles. And, just as is the case with a religion, the veterans tended to nurture their identity institutionally through various organizations—especially the United Confederate Veterans (UCV).

Initially, Confederate veterans, impelled by emotional pressures of living with defeat, associated informally. The basic psychological impetus was an intense belief that the world misunderstood both the history and the people of the South. As time passed, the relationships and organizations they engendered grew more symbolically meaningful. The great episode had "sanctified" its participants, and that sanctification spilled into the UCV's ancillary groups—the United Daughters of the Confederacy, the Sons of Veterans, the Children of the Confederacy, the Confederated Southern Memorial Association, the Order of the Stars and Bars, and the Confederate Choirs of America.

The UCV officially prohibited "the discussion of political or religious subjects" at meetings and forbade taking "any political action." What they meant to avoid was internal controversy. Their activities had considerable religious aspects: prayers, inspirational lectures, memorial ceremonies, even a special funeral service. Although they showed certain clear and strong political preferences, they rationalized such attitudes as not actually being political: any Confederate veteran obviously was more qualified for public office than a nonveteran; and benefits such as state pensions, soldiers' homes, and relief for needy veterans or their families, as well as the financing of hundreds of Civil War monuments, were humanitarian issues transcending politics.

The Confederate veteran wanted his name mentioned in historical writings, and he desired vindication as well as status and deference within his own society. He certainly managed to get all of that; it might well have come to him even without his efforts. During his more contemplative moments he wished for a "just treatment" in historical interpretation of himself and of his region. He was a powerful force, both a subject of, and a contributor to, the Lost Cause.

See also MYTHIC SOUTH: / Lost Cause Myth; Reb, Johnny

> Herman Hattaway
> University of Missouri
> Kansas City

Herman Hattaway, *Louisiana History* (Summer 1971; Winter 1975); William W. White, *The Confederate Veteran* (1962); Charles Reagan Wilson, *Baptized in Blood: The Religion of the Lost Cause, 1865–1920* (1980). ☆

COUNTRY HAM
||||||||||||||||||||||||||||||||||||||||||

Country ham is a 19th-century southern term for a pork delicacy that has been known and loved in Asia and Europe for more than 2,000 years. It is the hind quarter of a hog that has been cured with salt, colored and flavored with wood smoke, and hung up to age through a summer or longer.

The first British colonists who came to Virginia brought pigs with them, and they also brought a knowledge of the ancient technique of preserving meat by covering it with salt. The necessary combination of winter cold for slaughtering and summer heat for curing was ideally found in the colonies of Virginia, Maryland, and North Carolina, and ever since, country hams have remained popular in those states and their westward extensions, particularly Kentucky and Tennessee. Virginia's renowned Smithfield hams and the prime products of western Kentucky and other places in the region are unsurpassed by the best that France, Italy, and other nations have to offer.

Modern food technology has developed short-cut methods of duplicating the appearance of genuine country ham, but not its taste. As a result, most commercial "country" hams on the market today have been artificially cured, smoked, and aged and do not have the rich aroma and flavor of hams produced by traditional processes. Diligent inquiries in rural areas of the Upper South can still turn up hams that are in every way equal to those that came from the smokehouses of the region more than 300 years ago.

Ideal country hams are produced from year-old hogs that weigh at least 300 pounds and have been fattened on corn or peanuts. Such hams will weigh 20 to 25 pounds when properly cured and aged. As soon as a hog has been butchered in cold weather, the hams are rubbed down with a dry mixture of salt and other additives, usually sugar and saltpeter. Next, they are completely covered for four to six weeks in a bed of salt, then washed off and trimmed, and finally hung by their hocks in a dark smokehouse, there to take on a deep nut-brown appearance and a distinctive flavor from the enveloping hickory smoke. The hams must remain suspended to sweat through the hot summer months. A bare minimum of nine months is needed to complete the entire curing, smoking, and aging process; a full year, or even two years, is considered more nearly ideal.

Many variations on this basic method are favored from one ham maker to the next. Some mix a large amount of sugar with the salt and call their hams "sugar cured" (though sugar is not a preservative); some make smoke with oak or sassafras; some skip the smoking stage altogether, claiming it has no effect on flavor. But for salt and the summer sweats, there are no substitutes and no alternatives, modern technology notwithstanding.

When a ham is ready to eat, it may be baked in the oven, boiled on top of the stove, or sliced and fried. The latter method yields a rich bonus in the form of red-eye gravy, produced by adding a little water to the frying skillet. In whatever form it is prepared, country ham is as old as the South itself.

John Egerton
Nashville, Tennessee

John Egerton, *Southern Food: At Home, on the Road, in History* (1987); Sam B. Hilliard, *Hog Meat and Hoecake: Food Supply in the Old South* (1972); Stephen A. Smith, in *American Material Culture*, ed. Edith Mayo (1985). ☆

CROCKETT, DAVY

(1786–1836) Frontiersman, politician, humorist.

The life of the historical David Crockett is interesting but in no way as remarkable as the legendary lives of *Davy* Crockett. Born on 17 August 1786 in Greene County, Tenn., Crockett was a first-rate but relatively obscure backwoods hunter and Indian fighter with a knack for storytelling. He parlayed his local reputation into a state, and then national, political career. He was elected to the Tennessee Legislature in 1821 and 1823 and won congressional elections in 1827, 1829, and 1833. In Congress he promoted sale of public land at low prices but was frequently at odds with President Andrew Jackson. Crockett became perhaps the representative symbol of both the noble and savage aspects of frontier life in Jacksonian America. His death at the Alamo on 6 March 1836 assured him a prominent place in the history of the South and the nation and, more importantly, opened the cultural floodgates to the boundless expansion of his legendary image in the popular media of his day and ours.

Crockett promoted himself as a simple, down-home country boy whose extraordinary marksmanship was a metaphor for his character: he was a straight shooter. By the early 1830s his image had achieved a life of its own, so much so that in 1834 he published his autobiography (*A Narrative of the Life of David Crockett*) to counteract the compilation of tall tales printed under his name a year earlier by Matthew St. Clair Clarke as the *Sketches and Eccentricities of Col. Crockett*.

David was becoming Davy, the screamer and "ring-tailed roarer" who could "run faster, jump higher, squat lower, dive deeper, stay under longer, and come out drier, than any man in the whole country." Davy was not the first to give vent to the backwoods brag, but in the hands of the Boston literary hacks who produced the tall tales for the *Crockett Almanacs* (1835–56), he became its finest practitioner. This fictional Davy was both the Promethean figure who saved the earth by unfreezing the sun from its axis and the "humanitarian" who killed and boiled an Indian to help cure his pet bear's stomach dis-

Davy Crockett, frontier humorist and politician

order. He was also an ardent advocate of expansionism, with Mexico and Oregon but two of his targets.

The violent, racist, and jingoistic Davy of the almanacs competed with and was eventually subsumed by over 150 years of romantic melodrama. From Nimrod Wilfire, James Kirke Paulding's Crockettesque character in his play *The Lion of the West* (1831), to the Davys played by Fess Parker and John Wayne, 19th-century drama and 20th-century film always presented the hero in the kindest light. Courageous, dashing, and true blue, this nature's nobleman protected his country and those who were helpless with equal fervor.

Both the outrageous and the idealized Davy were firmly grounded in a southern sense of place. Whether as the purveyor of southern or southwestern humor over the full spectrum of good and bad taste or as the gallant southern gentleman, the knight errant of the backwoods, Davy reflected the range of the region whose hero he became and, in the larger context, the diversity and individuality of the entire nation.

Michael A. Lofaro
University of Tennessee

Richard Boyd Hauck, *Crockett: A Bio-Bibliography* (1982); Michael A. Lofaro, ed., *Davy Crockett: The Man, the Legend, the Legacy, 1786-1986* (1985); James A. Shackford, *David Crockett: The Man and the Legend* (1956). ☆

DAVIS, JEFFERSON
|||||||||||||||||||||||||||||||||||||||||||||||||
(1808–1889) Politician.

"The man and the hour have met," a distinguished secessionist proclaimed when Jefferson Davis became president of the Confederate States of America. In most ways Davis seemed ideally suited to directing the South's struggle for independence. Born in Fairview, Ky., in 1808, Davis and his family moved to Wilkinson County, Miss., when he was still a boy. Experienced in warfare and politics, he had attended the U.S. Military Academy (graduating in 1828), participated in the Black Hawk War, commanded a regiment of Mississippi volunteers and been wounded in the Mexican War, served as President Franklin Pierce's secretary of war, and headed the U.S. Senate's Military Affairs Committee. A brave, bold, erudite agrarian who believed in slavery and the right of secession, Davis worked tirelessly for the Confederacy.

Against the localism of certain governors and congressmen, he advocated measures for the Confederacy such as a military draft, conscription of blacks into the army, impressment of private property, government management of railroads and blockade runners, and an income tax.

But his inability to maintain the support of the Confederate Congress and his unwillingness to delegate authority except in certain areas created problems; so did his direction of military strategy and tactics. Ironically, it may have been in military affairs, where so much was expected of him, that Davis failed. He picked only one outstanding army commander, Robert E. Lee; other commanders proved to be unsuccessful, distrusted by Davis, or both. Squabbles among generals and over military politics hampered the Confederate war effort, and, as Union armies advanced, Confederate morale deteriorated. Davis hoped that his defensive-offensive strategy would save the South, but in practice it became little more than a series of courageous but costly attacks on enemy forces until dwindling manpower forced the Confederates on the defensive after 1863.

Davis may have been "perverse and obstinate" and "an indifferent judge of men," as his critics claimed, but he maintained during the last months of the war an unfailing will to win and even tried to continue the war as the Confederacy collapsed. Captured in May 1865 and imprisoned for two years without a trial, he became in the North the symbol of the South's treasonable sins. In the *Rise and Fall of the Confederate Government*, which he wrote after release from prison, Davis shared much of the blame for Confederate defeat with others. Throughout the remainder of his life

Jefferson Davis, Confederate president, 1861–65

he neither repented nor asked forgiveness for himself or for the cause he led.

Grady McWhiney
Texas Christian University

James T. McIntosh, ed., *The Papers of Jefferson Davis* (1971–); Dunbar Rowland, ed., *Jefferson Davis* (10 vols.; 1923); Allen Tate, *Jefferson Davis* (1929); Robert Penn Warren, *Jefferson Davis Gets His Citizenship Back* (1980). ☆

FLAG, REBEL

The so-called rebel flag is a well-known *oblong* red banner on which is a blue cross of St. Andrew (saltire) edged with white and bearing 13 white five-pointed stars. It is a modification of the Confederate battle-flag, which was *square*, reputedly designed by General P. G. T. Beauregard, and erroneously, but popularly, called "the Stars and Bars." The battle-flag, however, was never adopted by the Confederate Congress and never officially flew over government offices of the Confederate states. It was not employed officially by Confederate veterans organizations and seldom by any of the later societies of descendants of Confederate veterans.

Yet out of that limbo emerged the modern imitation generally called a "rebel flag." This imitative innovation owed its origin to the simplicity of the battle flag's design as well as to ignorance about authorized flags of the Confederacy. It did not reach its great popularity until the 1950s, possibly owing to widespread southern white dissatisfaction with the federal government during that period. Several extremist groups, such as the Ku Klux Klan, have made notorious use of the *oblong* cloth. It has now more or less been confined in conventional use to sporting events in the South, especially football games. Black students at the University of Mississippi protested the school's use of the flag in 1983 and forced the administration to discourage use of the flag as an official symbol. Predictably, emotions associated with the flag run deep among both white and black southerners.

Allen Cabaniss
University of Mississippi

Whitney Smith, *The Great Flags of America* (1974). ☆

FORREST, NATHAN BEDFORD

(1821–1877) Confederate general.

A man of little formal education and no prior military experience, Nathan Bedford Forrest became one of three Confederate soldiers with no military training to rise to the rank of lieutenant general. Born in Bedford County, Tenn., Forrest struggled from poverty to a position of considerable wealth as a planter and slave dealer. Soon after the outbreak of the Civil War he raised and equipped a battalion of cavalry, of which he was elected lieutenant colonel. Forrest performed brilliantly at the battles of Fort Donelson and Shiloh and as an independent cavalry commander behind enemy lines through the summer of 1863, rising to the rank of brigadier general.

In command of the cavalry on the right wing of General Braxton Bragg's Army of Tennessee during the battle of Chickamauga, Forrest led his troops, fighting as mounted infantry, through some of the most severe fighting of the war. Afterward he quarreled bitterly with Bragg, was relieved of his corps, but was granted an independent command in west Tennessee and north Mississippi and promoted to major general.

Operating out of northern Mississippi, Forrest staged several intrepid and damaging raids against federal supply links and depots in Tennessee while

Nathan Bedford Forrest, Confederate hero

successfully defending his base against numerous incursions by greatly superior Union forces. Forrest was reassigned to the Army of Tennessee as commander of all cavalry during John Bell Hood's abortive Tennessee campaign, and only his bold and skillful rear-guard actions saved that army from utter annihilation following the Confederate disasters at Franklin and Nashville. Although elevated to the rank of lieutenant general for his heroic efforts on the retreat from Nashville, Forrest was at last overwhelmed by vastly superior federal numbers at Selma, Ala., in April 1865.

Following the collapse of the Confederacy, Forrest served for some years as president of the Selma, Marion, & Memphis Railroad and was reportedly the principal organizer and first Imperial Wizard of the Ku Klux Klan. To many military historians, though, Nathan Bedford Forrest remains significant as the preeminent American cavalry leader.

Because he was the only unvaryingly successful Confederate commander in the western theater and because of the relative poverty of his origins, Forrest quickly became the darling of the plain people of the Old Southwest. Unlike the Virginia aristocrats, Lee and Stuart, or the Louisiana Creole, Beauregard, Forrest was a product of the South's hardscrabble frontier and an archetypal example of Jefferson's yeoman class. Writers in the 20th-century South, most notably William Faulkner and the Nashville Agrarians, seized upon Forrest as a symbol of the best that the South's frontier culture produced. Andrew Lytle's biography, *Bedford Forrest and His Critter Company* (1931), Caroline Gordon's novel *None Shall Look Back* (1937), and Jesse Hill Ford's *The Raider* (1975) are full-length interpretations of Forrest's character and military career, and the Confederate "Wizard of the Saddle" also provided material for George Washington Cable, who served under him in the war's final year; Stark Young, whose father rode with Forrest; Robert Penn Warren, whose grandfather was one of his captains; and Donald Davidson, who attempted but failed to complete an epic poem based on the great cavalryman's campaigns. To each of these writers Forrest represents the highest emanation of Anglo-Saxon, agrarian democracy on the Old Southwest frontier, an unlettered man of the soil hurling back in confusion the minions of modern industrial, materialistic society. Of the legend of Forrest and his men, William Faulkner wrote that "even seventy-five years afterwards, [it was] still powerful, still dangerous, still coming!"

Thomas W. Cutrer
Texas State Historical
Association

R. S. Henry, *"First with the Most" Forrest* (1944); James H. Mathes, *General Forrest* (1902); John A. Wyeth, *That Devil Forrest* (1959). ☆

FRIED CHICKEN
||||||||||||||||||||||||||||||||||||||||||||

Columbus brought chickens to America in 1493, and they have graced American tables—particularly in the South—ever since. Southern fried chicken is probably the single most popular and universally consumed food ever to come from this region of the country. It appeared in the earliest cookbooks; Mary Randolph's *The Virginia House-wife* (1824) recommended a method strikingly similar to that commonly used today: cut-up pieces of chicken dredged in flour, sprinkled with salt and pepper, and fried in hot fat.

There are, of course, numerous variations on the basic technique. Some cooks insist on frying chicken in lard, but others prefer vegetable oil; some say pan frying in an inch or so of fat is best, and others choose deep frying instead; some use flour alone as the dusting substance, but others add cornmeal or milk or egg; some restrict seasoning to salt and pepper, while others go for spicier or more pungent tastes, such as hot sauce, garlic, red pepper, or lemon; some seek a dry, crisp, crunchy exterior, and others pour gravy or cream sauce over the finished product.

Virtually the only aspect of southern fried chicken that no one debates is the best way to eat it: with the fingers, the only practical means of separating the crisp skin and tender meat from the bone. "Finger lickin' good" became a motto of Colonel Harland Sander's Kentucky Fried Chicken when the Corbin, Ky., entrepreneur launched a fast-food chicken business in 1956.

With Kentucky Fried Chicken still in the lead, numerous fast-food franchise outlets now dispense the popular finger food in cities and towns throughout the nation and the world. The volume of fried chicken sales is such that the raising of chickens has become a major agricultural industry in the South. Purists note that mass production yields an inferior fowl, one that lacks the leanness, tenderness, and taste that young pullets had when they scratched in southern yards and received ample rations of cracked corn as they approached frying size. Nonetheless, southern fried chicken has truly become a universal food, even as the delectable taste of lean and tender young pullets has faded into memory.

Chicken gravy remains one of the classic examples of southern food, its qualities undiminished by changes in the chickens themselves. Gravy is made from the dregs in the frying skillet, supplemented by a mixture of flour and either milk or water and seasoned with salt and pepper. Spooned onto potatoes or rice or biscuits, chicken gravy offers a savory flavor that southerners have known and loved for generations.

See also INDUSTRY: / Sanders, Colonel Harlan

John Egerton
Nashville, Tennessee

John Egerton, *Southern Food: At Home, on the Road, in History* (1987); Page Smith and Charles Daniel, *The Chicken Book* (1975); Stephen A. Smith, in *American Material Culture*, ed. Edith Mayo (1975); *Southern Living* (July 1982). ☆

GARDNER, DAVE
|||||||||||||||||||||||||||||||||||||||||||
(1926–1983) Entertainer.

Gardner, stand-up entertainer, comedy recording star, and shrewd observer of southern manners in the 1950s and 1960s, was born in Jackson, Tenn., on 11 June 1926. Christened David Milburn Gardner, he grew up in and near Jackson, where he attended junior high school—the last he would see of school until his brief enrollment in a Baptist college. His brother, Kent, recalls that "Dave was always a quiet kid, rather puny, and never much of an outgoing person. His comedy did not show up until he was in his twenties, and then it evolved as an off-the-top-of-his-head thing. He never had writers."

In fact, Gardner, who was playing the drums professionally when he was 13, began his career in the late 1940s as a drummer and singer. Then he struck out on his own as a comedian. It

was 1957 before opportunity knocked, and he made the first of a number of appearances on NBC-TV's *Tonight Show*, then hosted by Jack Paar. Almost overnight "Brother Dave," as he liked to be called, found himself with a national following; but nowhere was he more warmly received than on the college campuses of the South where, cigarette in one hand, microphone in the other, he ad-libbed his way through performances.

Brother Dave's routines were a crazy mixture of one-liners, stories that enabled him to make use of his amazing ear for regional speech, jive talk, and sly profundity. He picked no particular target but poked fun at them all: black civil rights leaders, bikers, good old boys, preachers, presidents. "Dear hearts," he would say in the midst of the protest of the 1960s, "I'm for the minorities—the Armed Forces and the Po-leece." Though he was accused by some of racism, he may have been closer to the truth when he told one interviewer toward the end of his life, "I was *left* when the world was *right.*"

At the peak of his success he made several comedy albums for RCA and later for Capitol. His popularity faded in the social and political turmoil of the Vietnam years, but after a writer for the Atlanta *Constitution* found him living in obscurity in Dallas in 1981 and wrote a Sunday magazine article about him, Gardner made a comeback in Atlanta. While doing a film in 1983, he suffered a heart attack and died in Myrtle Beach, S.C.

Charles East
Baton Rouge, Louisiana

Larry L. King, *Harper's* (September 1970); Robert Lamb, *Atlanta Weekly* (22 November 1981). ☆

GAYS
||||||||||||||

Poverty and religion, both so prevalent in southern life, have molded homosexuality and society's reaction to it. The sexual attitudes of the poorer classes result both in widespread bisexual experimentation and in a violent reaction against such behavior. Often nominally justified by religion, this reaction is actually based on paranoia over the threat that effeminacy poses to the masculinity cult of the poorer classes. Thus, in the South some teenage boys go through a phase as amateur prostitutes with homosexual customers, yet the region has had more than its share of witch-hunts against homosexuals. Florida's homosexual witch-hunts since 1945 include the notable Anita Bryant "crusade" of 1977.

Religion, however, has been a comfort to southern homosexuals, who originated the "gay church" movement. The concept of homosexuality as a "sexual orientation" or a "sickness" tends to be replaced in the South by an attitude that the basic division is not between homosexuals and heterosexuals but between those who are active/masculine and those who are passive/effeminate (an idea widespread among the poorer classes throughout the world, whereas "sexual orientation" tends to be a middle-class concept). The southern attitude is that homosexuality is not a condition or a sickness but a sin of which (according to evangelical doctrine) anyone is capable. The idea of orientation suggests that homosexuality is limited to a small group of unusual people, but if it is seen (as it is in the South) as a sin, it will be seen more as habit than as condition, and by no means limited to a small in-group. The evangelical idea that "all men are sinners" can be used to suggest that all men are able to practice homosexuality. Universal sin is translated into universal bisexuality.

Half of the 24 states that have not decriminalized sodomy are in the South. The sodomy laws in Arkansas and Texas apply to homosexuals only, and the laws in the remaining southern states apply to both homosexuals and heterosexuals. Sodomy is a misdemeanor in Florida, Texas, and Arkansas, but is a felony in nine other southern states. Lesbian acts are specifically included as a felony in Georgia. In the South the punishment for sodomy ranges from a $200 fine in Texas or a maximum 60-day jail term in Florida to a maximum 15-year jail term in Tennessee or a 20-year term in Georgia. In July 1986 the Georgia sodomy law came to national attention when it was upheld by the U.S. Supreme Court in a case involving homosexual partners. Although the Georgia statute applies to any sodomy, the court's majority opinion addressed only the state's right to prohibit homosexual acts, a move seen as a direct threat by gay rights activists.

Many homosexual men move from small towns to cities, such as Atlanta, New Orleans, and Key West, which have large homosexual subcultures. However, many small towns have a "town queer" who is the focus of the covert bisexuality of the local youths. Many of these youths know only the word *queer* without ever having heard the words *gay* or *homosexual*. On the other hand, the homosexual subculture is so developed in the cities, especially in New Orleans, that homosexuality tends to be associated with the artistic and literary elements in the South more than in other sections. There is a long tradition of homosexual transvestism associated with Mardi Gras. But even middle-sized towns such as Pensacola, Fla., and Jackson, Miss., have well-organized homosexual subcultures. When interracial homosexual relations have taken place, it has been traditional for the black partner to play the active/masculine role and the white partner to play the passive/effeminate role. This role playing derives from social class, as well as racial factors. American concepts of masculinity are associated with the proletariat, and most concepts of effeminacy are associated with the middle classes. Sexual role playing involves imitating the behavior of one class or the other, so that it is really class role-playing rather than anything sexual, and yet is linked with sexual relationships.

The literature on homosexuality in the South is rather meager. Negative views include the interviews with policemen in *The Puritan Jungle: America's Sexual Underground* by Sara Harris (1969), and the official pamphlet *Homosexuality and Citizenship in Florida* (1964). Sociologists can read *Sex in Prison: The Mississippi Experiment with Conjugal Visiting* by Columbus B. Hopper (1969), *Scottsboro Boy* by Haywood Patterson and Earl Conrad (1950), and "The Social Integration of Peers and Queers" by Albert J. Reiss in Hendrik Ruitenbeek's *The Problem of Homosexuality in Modern Society* (1963).

James Kirkwood's *American Grotesque: An Account of the Clay Shaw-Jim Garrison Affair in the City of New Orleans* (1970) deals with political persecution of homosexuals, while Mississippi writer Jere Real's cover article, "Gay Rights & Conservative Politics" (*National Review*, 17 March 1978) urged political restraint on sexual issues. Southern writers such as Tennes-

see Williams (in *Cat on a Hot Tin Roof*; *Suddenly Last Summer*; and *Small Craft Warnings*), Truman Capote (in *Other Voices, Other Rooms*), Carson McCullers (in *Reflections in a Golden Eye* and *Ballad of the Sad Cafe*), Charles Henri Ford, and Erskine Lane, have discussed homosexuality, as have some biographies and autobiographies (Craig Claiborne's autobiography *Feast Made for Laughter* is one such work). Mississippi playwright Mart Crowley studies a homosexual Mississippian living in Manhattan in his drama *The Boys in the Band* (1968) and that same character's adolescence in his later *Breeze from the Gulf* (1973) and in his *Remote Asylum* (1970). Edward Swift's 1978 novel, *Splendora*, is a comic tale of sexual confusion in a small Texas town. Florence King's *Southern Ladies and Gentlemen* (1975) has a satiric chapter on southern homosexuals. The national gay news magazine *Advocate* has done extensive reportorial accounts of gay life in various southern cities and states.

Stephen Wayne Foster
Coral Gables, Florida

Jonathan Katz, *Gay American History: Lesbians and Gay Men in the U.S.A.: A Documentary Anthology* (1976); *Newsweek* (14 July 1986); William Parker, *Homosexuality: A Selective Bibliography of over 3,000 Items* (1971), *Homosexuality Bibliography: Supplement, 1970–1975* (1977); Troy Perry, *The Lord Is My Shepherd and He Knows I'm Gay* (1972); *Southern Exposure* (September–October 1985). ☆

GOO GOO CLUSTERS

"A Good Ole Southern Treat," announces the six-pack box of Standard

Candy Company's Goo Goo Clusters. Often advertised as "the South's favorite candy" and "the Goodest Bar in town," the Goo Goo Cluster has been a candy staple in the Nashville, Tenn., area and throughout the South for over 70 years.

First created by William H. Campbell in Nashville in 1912, the Goo Goo Cluster is a combination of caramel, marshmallow, peanuts, and pure milk chocolate. (Recently the company has been making Goo Goo Supremes, which substitute pecans for peanuts.) Though the packaging and distribution techniques have changed with modernization and company expansion, the ingredients, cooking methods, and essential southern identity have remained the same.

The Goo Goo Cluster has been a curiosity since its origin. One account says that Campbell settled on the name because his son, only a few months old at the time, uttered those words when first introduced to the new candy. Another version suggests that Campbell was struck with his son's first utterance and decided it was an appropriate name. Whatever the true version, Standard Candy Company has contended for years that a Goo Goo is the first thing a southern baby requests.

Along with the Goo Goo, the company, founded in 1901, produces the ever-popular King Leo stick candy, a staple in many southern homes and a common Christmas treat and gift. Since 1968 the Grand Ole Opry has been singing the praises of the Goo Goo, sharing the wise culinary advice with those in attendance and reaching thousands more over WSM radio. So closely associated is the candy with the Opry, some have suggested that "Goo" stands for Grand Ole Opry. Grant Turner continues to let listeners know how to order the candy by mail, encouraging them further with the familiar slogan: "Go Get a Goo Goo. . . . It's Good."

Tom Rankin
Southern Arts Federation
Atlanta, Georgia

Margaret Loelo, *Wall Street Journal* (8 December 1982); John F. Persinos, *Inc.* (May 1984). ☆

GRITS

Grits are—or is, as the case may be—a by-product of corn kernels. Dried, hulled corn kernels are commonly called hominy; grits are made of finely ground hominy. Old-fashioned grits may also be produced from hard corn kernels that are coarsely ground and bolted (sifted) to remove the hulls.

Writing in the *New York Times* on 31 January 1982, Turner Catledge of New Orleans provided a succinct history of grits in the South:

Grits is the first truly American food. On a day in the spring of 1607 when sea-weary members of the London Company came ashore at Jamestown, Va., they were greeted by a band of friendly Indians offering bowls of a steaming hot substance consisting of softened maize seasoned with salt and some kind of animal fat, probably bear grease. The welcomers called it "rockahominie."

The settlers liked it so much they adopted it as part of their own diet. They anglicized the name to "hominy" and set about devising a milling process by which the large corn grains could be ground into smaller particles without losing any nutriments. The experiment was a success, and grits became a gastronomic mainstay of the South and symbol of Southern culinary pride.

Thus, throughout its history, and in pre-Columbian times as well, the South has relished grits and made them a symbol of its diet, its customs, its humor, and its good-spirited hospitality. From Captain John Smith to General Andrew Jackson to President Jimmy Carter, southerners rich and poor, young and old, black and white have eaten grits regularly. So common has the food been that it has been called a universal staple, a household companion, even an institution.

Grits cooked into a thick porridge are so common in some parts of the South that they are routinely served for breakfast, whether asked for or not. They are often flavored with butter or gravy, served with sausage or ham, accompanied by bacon and eggs, baked with cheese, or sliced cold and fried in bacon grease. Mississippi-born Craig Claiborne loves grits and has published elegant recipes for their preparation.

Some historians assert that neither hominy nor grits were universally eaten in the South prior to the Civil War, but most food scholars conclude that Indian corn in all its myriad forms—grits, hominy, roasting ears, succotash (usually a combination of corn kernels and lima beans), and various kinds of corn bread—sustained the pioneers and their succeeding generations from the beginning of European settlement on the Virginia coast.

Curiously, grits have seldom caught on in the North or spread to other countries, although expatriate southerners do

often eat them and serve them to company. Stan Woodward's film *It's Grits* (Weston Woods, 1978) chronicled national and regional attitudes toward the dish. Grits enjoyed a surge of popularity during the early part of the Carter Administration but have since returned to their status as a distinctly regional food. One noted foreign visitor who took a liking to grits was the Marquis de Lafayette, hero of the American Revolution. So much did he enjoy eating the dish during his return visit to the United States in 1824 to 1825 that he took a substantial supply back to France for himself and his friends.

John Egerton
Nashville, Tennessee

Arkansas Gazette (14 August 1983); Gorham Kindem, *Southern Quarterly* (Spring–Summer 1981); Stephen A. Smith, in *American Material Culture*, ed. Edith Mayo (1985). ☆

HAMMOND, JAMES HENRY

(1807–1864) Planter and politician.

Hammond was born in 1807 in upcountry South Carolina. Son of an impecunious schoolmaster who had moved South at the turn of the century, young Hammond graduated from South Carolina College in 1825. After several years of teaching while he prepared for the bar, he began the practice of law in Columbia. The excitement of the nullification controversy gave Hammond his initial prominence as a strongly sectionalist newspaper editor. After a fortunate marriage to a Charleston heiress, Hammond left public life to manage the Savannah River plantation and 147 slaves he had acquired as a result of the union. Elected to Congress, Hammond moved to Washington in 1835, but after a dramatic debut attacking the reception of abolition petitions by the House of Representatives, he was stricken with a nervous ailment and resigned his seat in Congress to travel in Europe.

In 1842 Hammond reentered politics as governor of his native state and gained attention during the next few years with an extreme sectionalist position more radical than that of John C. Calhoun. At the end of his term a scandal over charges of improprieties in his relationship with his four nieces, the daughters of the powerful Wade Hampton II, returned Hammond once again to his plantation, where he continued to write on agricultural and political topics and to experiment with agricultural innovations until he was chosen for the U.S. Senate in 1857. More sanguine about the possibilities for the South in the Union than at any previous time of his life, Hammond had profound doubts about its readiness for secession. Upon Lincoln's election, he resigned and privately differed sharply and vociferously with the Davis Administration on Confederate policy. His health declined throughout the war years, and he died in November of 1864, just before Sherman began his march through South Carolina.

One of the South's leading intellects, Hammond is perhaps best remembered for his widely distributed tracts defending slavery as a positive good, *Two Letters on Slavery in the United States, Addressed to Thomas Clarkson, Esq.* (1845) and *Letter of His Excellency Governor Hammond to the Free Church of Glasgow on the Subject of Slavery* (1844), as well as for his oft-quoted proslavery "mud-sill" speech to the U.S. Senate in 1858. His extraordinar-

ily rich personal, political, and plantation papers have been extensively used by 20th-century historians of slavery and the South.

Drew Gilpin Faust
University of Pennsylvania

Carol K. Bleser, ed., *The Hammonds of Radcliffe* (1981); Drew Gilpin Faust, *James Henry Hammond and the Old South: A Design for Mastery* (1982); James Henry Hammond Papers, Library of Congress; James Henry Hammond Papers, South Carolinian Library, University of South Carolina, Columbia. ☆

JACK DANIEL DISTILLERY

Lynchburg, Tenn. (pop. 361), the seat of a dry (Moore) county in the Cumberland foothills, is the home of the nation's oldest registered distillery.

In the 1860s, Jack Newton Daniel chose Lynchburg's Cave Spring Hollow as the site for his whiskey-making business. Using cold spring water stabilized at a year-round 56 degrees and all but free of iron and other trace minerals, a "yeasting back" process (retaining some of the mash from previous runs to use as a starter), charcoal leaching, and oaken-cask warehousing, Daniel produced a distinctive Tennessee whiskey that by the turn of the century was winning international acclaim.

Inheriting the business from his uncle in 1907, Lem Motlow was forced to turn to the mule and harness trade (he opened Lynchburg Hardware in 1912) during Prohibition, but he resumed distillery operations soon after repeal. When Motlow died in 1947, the prosperous distillery passed on to his four sons.

Continuity, an unshakable commitment to traditional brewing standards and methods, marks the history of Jack Daniel Distillery. In 1946 when the war-effort ban on whiskey production was lifted on condition that processors use inferior grades of grain, Daniel's preferred to reopen a year later rather than compromise quality. Today, burning rick yards producing the hard sugar-maple charcoal through which the whiskey is slowly mellowed still dot the hollow; white oak barrels continue to be used for aging. Although twist caps have replaced cork stoppers, the "square shooter" bottle chosen by Jack Daniel

in 1895 continues to be the company trademark.

Owned now by Brown-Forman, Inc., the Jack Daniel Distillery avoids a corporate image and stresses in its advertising the timeless character of its small-town operations. Ad copy has immortalized the Lynchburg General Store (where Coke still costs a dime), Miss Mary Bobo's Boarding House (where Mr. Jack took his noonday meals), and the Moore County Court House, built in 1884.

Although consumer profiles note that the average Jack Daniel drinker is an upwardly mobile, college-educated, urban male, it is clear that he still finds a place in his heart for a little southern town that has not changed much, and for a whiskey that "hasn't changed at all."

See also INDUSTRY: / Liquor Industry

Elizabeth M. Makowski
University of Mississippi

Jeannie R. Bigger, *Tennessee Historical Quarterly* (Spring 1972); Ben A. Green, *Jack Daniel's Legacy* (1967). ☆

The "Black Jack" bottle—a southern icon

JACKSON, STONEWALL

(1824–1863) Confederate general.

Born in far western Virginia, at Clarksburg, on 21 January 1824, Thomas Jonathan "Stonewall" Jackson was raised by an uncle after his parents died when he was a child. He graduated from the U.S. Military Academy in 1846, gained renown in the Mexican War, and in 1851 accepted a professional appointment at Virginia Military Institute. He commanded his institution's cadet corps, which was involved in the public hanging of John Brown on 2 December 1859. He served as a field officer in the Confederate army, first as colonel and then, on 17 July 1861, as brigadier general. As commander of a brigade at the first battle of Bull Run (21 July 1861), he and his troops earned everlasting fame when Confederate General Barnard E. Bee praised them for standing "like a stone wall" in battle.

Promoted to major general on 7 October 1861, Jackson assumed command in the Shenandoah Valley on 5 November and led the Shenandoah Valley Campaign from March to June 1862. One of the most praised and studied of all American military displays of tactics and strategy, the Valley Campaign showed Jackson's ability to use speed, mobility, secrecy, and sheer willpower to distract a larger force. With fewer than 20,000 soldiers, Lieutenant General and Corps Commander Jackson frustrated the movements of over 125,000 Union troops. Jackson was less successful in the Seven Days Campaign, but he regained his dominance of northern commanders at Harper's Ferry (15 September 1862), Antietam (17 September 1862), Fredericksburg (13 December 1862), and Chancellorsville (1–2 May 1863). During the night of the Chancellorsville victory, Jackson was wounded by one of his own troops, and he died of pneumonia on 10 May. He was only 39 years old, but Jackson, a lieutenant general when he died, had already become Robert E. Lee's most trusted subordinate.

Jackson was an eccentric personality. Untidy in appearance, rigidly moral and devoutly religious, shy and quiet, Jackson nonetheless was a charismatic figure to the Virginia soldiers he drove relentlessly. His success in the Shenandoah Valley made Jackson's name well known to southerners, most of whom apparently regarded him less as Lee's subordinate than as a coinstrument with Lee of God's destiny for the South.

Jackson was a military genius. English biographer George F. R. Henderson claimed in his 1898 study that Jackson's few written maxims "are almost a complete summary of the art of war." But Jackson's importance to southern culture transcended his military significance. He was a stern Calvinist, a spiritual descendant of Cromwell. Southern ministers during and after the war pointed to Jackson as a prophet-warrior on the Old Testament model. They admired his unbending righteousness. The moralistic, hardscrabble South identified with Jackson, the puritanical teetotaler. Henry A. White even included Jackson as an exemplar of his denomination's faith in *Southern Presbyterian Leaders* (1911). Allen Tate's search for the southern heritage in the 1920s led him to write a narrative biography of Jackson, published in 1928. More recently, Bob McDill's country-western song "Good Old Boys" refers to the songwriter's childhood, when a picture of Stonewall Jackson hung on the wall, quietly teaching southern lessons.

Jackson was, along with Lee and Jefferson Davis, one of the Confederate trinity of saints. A group of English admirers raised the money to erect a statue of him in Richmond in October of 1875, and another one was later dedicated on that city's Monument Boulevard. A bronze monument marks his grave in Lexington, Va., and a statue by Moses Ezekiel guards the parade grounds at the Virginia Military Institute. VMI's Preston Library displays items from Jackson's life. Elected to the Hall of Fame for Great Americans in 1955,

Jackson now has a monument in New York City as well. His image has been carved into the Stone Mountain Memorial in Georgia. The third Monday in January is a Virginia holiday honoring Jackson and Lee.

Charles Reagan Wilson
University of Mississippi

Robert Lewis Dabney, *Life and Campaigns of Lieut. General Thomas J. Jackson* (1866); Allen Tate, *Stonewall Jackson: The Good Soldier* (1928); Frank E. Vandiver, *Mighty Stonewall* (1957). ☆

JAMESTOWN
||||||||||||||||||||||||||||||||||||

The founders of Jamestown, Va., had an unrealistic vision of the South's promise. They imagined a lush, naturally abundant, semitropical paradise replete with exotic fruits ripe for the picking, peopled by friendly natives who would shower them with precious jewels and metals. They hoped to find, as well, the illusory Passage to India, which continued to draw scores of Europeans to America's shores.

By the 19th century generations of Americans had devised their own myths about the first English settlement to survive in the New World. Some talked of a race of noble Englishmen who carried Christianity and civilization to America and, with the creation of the hallowed House of Burgesses in 1619, provided the country with democratic self-government. Others, not so generous, noted that the first slave ship also arrived on Virginia's shores in 1619, creating an institution that would tear the nation apart in less than two centuries. Finally, everyone loved the romantic tale of Pocahontas, the Indian princess who fell in love with Captain John Smith, saving him from certain death at the hands of Chief Powhatan and fostering an era of friendly relations between Native Americans and the European interlopers.

The actual story of Jamestown's settlement was neither romantic nor inspiring. Financed as a short-term joint stock company under the auspices of Sir Thomas Smith's Virginia Company, the odd mix of gentlemen, servants, and ne'er-do-wells who sailed into Chesapeake Bay in the spring of 1607 were looking for profit for the company and reward and adventure for themselves. They would work for the company seven years. Then, their obligations at an end, they would be free to make their own fortunes in a bountiful new land.

But no one got rich in Virginia. The company did not send adequate supplies to its New World servants, and the men living in America either would not or could not procure sufficient food for themselves. Consequently, they suffered a "starving time." Well over half the population died the first year, and by 1611 only 60 of the 500 adventurers who came to America were still alive.

Successive charters in 1609, 1612, and 1619, authorized by Sir Edwin Sandys, introduced two important innovations—the headright system and the House of Burgesses. The headright system gave the settlers a stake in the country by promising land to anyone who came to America on his own or who paid for someone else's transportation. The House of Burgesses had very limited powers. Its laws, mere recommendations, became valid only when approved by the company in London. Never particularly democratic, it quickly became a means by which the most ambitious and ruthless adventurers could exploit their less fortunate counterparts. Still, it was the first representative legislative assembly in English America.

In 1619 the first slave ship arrived in Jamestown. Slavery did not take root in Virginia, though, until the end of the century. The mortality rate for new settlers was so high that white servants, often provided gratis by the company, were more economical than chattel slaves.

With the introduction of tobacco into the colony, Virginia found itself a money-making crop. But though the "noxious weed" brought riches to a few, it caused the development of what Edmund Morgan has described as "boom town" mentality in Jamestown and its environs. Settlers refused to grow anything but tobacco. Sharp dealing and outright thievery abounded; the streets were filled with men who whored, drank, and gambled away their fortunes in a single night. While some Americans became rich in Jamestown, the company's English investors failed to realize any profits on their investments. Lack of communication, loss of control over its servants, and the self-interest of its settlers combined to destroy the Virginia Company. An Indian massacre in 1622 demolished any remaining hopes for success that the company's investors may have harbored. In 1624 the crown assumed control of the settlement, and Virginia became the first royal colony in America.

A short-term company designed for quick profit had evolved into a permanent society. It was not a society characterized by the close-knit communities that dominated New England. Rather it was highly individualistic, some would say almost anarchistic. It had few churches and fewer cities; its members lived on widely dispersed farms and consequently developed a distrust of outsiders that would to some extent translate to hostility toward royal interference in the next century. A disappointment to its founders, it nevertheless successfully survived penury, greed, and mismanagement to become England's oldest enduring New World possession.

Sheila Skemp
University of Mississippi

Philip L. Barbour, *Pocahontas and Her World: A Chronicle of America's First Settlement in Which is Related the Story of the Indians and the Englishmen, Particularly Captain John Smith, Captain Samuel Argall, and Major John Rolfe* (1969), *The Three Worlds of Captain John Smith* (1964); Carl Bridenbaugh, *Jamestown, 1544–1699* (1980); Edmund S. Morgan, *American Slavery, American Freedom: The Ordeal of Colonial Virginia* (1975); Alden T. Vaughan, *American Genesis: Captain John Smith and the Founding of Virginia* (1975). ☆

JEFFERSON, THOMAS

(1743–1826) Politician, writer, planter, scientist, architect.

Thomas Jefferson was born 17 April 1743 on the edge of the frontier in colonial Virginia. He went on to acquire as fine an education as America offered, graduating from the College of William and Mary in 1762. He studied law under George Wythe and practiced at the bar until the Revolution. He was elected to the Virginia House of Burgesses in 1769. Already the inheritor of large landholdings, he increased his property greatly through the dowry of his wife, Martha Wayles Skelton, whom he married in 1772. They had two daughters who survived to maturity.

In 1774 Jefferson drew political attention with his pamphlet *A Summary View of the Rights of British America*, the best remonstrance against the king and defense of colonial rights that had yet been seen. He carefully controlled his writing style so that any literate reader might follow his argument. Then, in 1776, Jefferson—now a member of the Continental Congress—was chosen to write the Declaration of Independence. It is his masterpiece and America's fundamental political document. In succeeding years he was elected governor of the state of Virginia and member of Congress and was appointed minister to France. From 1790 to 1793 he served under Washington as the first secretary of state.

Jefferson's only book, *Notes on the State of Virginia*, was published in 1785. In it he recorded the milieu of early America. Jefferson was an advocate of the scientific method, and his book included efforts to classify botan-

Rembrandt Peale, Thomas Jefferson *(1805)*

ical, geological, and paleontological specimens. He showed the confident Enlightenment belief that science could promote progress. His collection and classification of items reflected the practical need of a farmer to know the environment, as well as simply the desire to satisfy his curiosity. He agonized over the question of slavery (he held many slaves), echoing most of the persistent stereotyping of blacks so noticeably American. Yet he was a true Enlightenment man, also voicing—as in the Declaration—the finest of ideals concerning justice, religious freedom, and equality.

He was paternalistic, not only at home but in his attitudes toward Indians, blacks, women, and commoners. Thus, his long political service was noblesse oblige. He was elected third president of the United States in 1801 (a second term followed). While president he arranged the Louisiana Purchase (1803), doubling the size of the nation.

Always busy, he designed his mansion, Monticello, the Virginia capitol at Richmond, and, late in life, the University of Virginia. He designed an Episcopal chapel in Charlottesville, dozens of Virginia country homes, simple and functional courthouses, and even jails in Cumberland and Nelson counties. He accumulated an architectural library of 50 titles in French, Italian, German, and English. His architectural achievement was to adapt classical forms to Virginian and southern needs.

Jefferson personified character, vision, grace, scholarship, and leadership—the qualities of the early southern gentleman that are part of his legacy. Students of southern culture look to him as the exemplar of major themes, ideals, and achievements of the region as well as the nation.

William K. Bottorff
University of Toledo

Julian P. Boyd et al., eds., *The Papers of Thomas Jefferson* (1950–); Fiske Kimball, ed., *Thomas Jefferson, Architect: Original Designs in the Coolidge Collection of the Massachusetts Historical Society, with an Essay and Notes* (1968); Dumas Malone, *Jefferson and His Time*, 6 vols. (1948–81). ☆

LEE, ROBERT E.

(1797–1870) Confederate general.

Robert Edward Lee was born at Stratford, Va., the son of Revolutionary War hero "Light Horse Harry" Lee and Anne Hill Carter. He graduated from West Point in 1829, became an officer in the engineer corps, served with distinction in the Mexican War, was appointed superintendent of West Point in 1852, commanded the marines who captured John Brown in 1859, and became one of the South's preeminent military figures during the Civil War and its most famous hero afterwards.

Lee's hero status benefited from the adulation of three seemingly disparate groups: Virginians, other southerners, and other Americans. Each group lauded and idealized many of the same features when viewing Lee. The devoted son of an ailing mother, Lee was a young man of abstemious habits and a model student at West Point. He was the loving, devoted husband of ailing Mary Custis, the "child of Arlington." In his life before the Civil War and thereafter, Lee displayed elements of a gentlemanly, Christian character shared by few others. His life was the epitome of humility, self-sacrifice, and reserve.

Even Robert E. Lee's involvement in the Civil War was viewed as different. Lee was the reluctant rebel who disliked slavery and secession, one whose love for the Union transcended that of other southern officers in 1860 and 1861.

After the Civil War, Lee the Confederate became Lee the American. He refused to prolong conflict by guerilla warfare; Lee declined as well to flee the South or to keep alive the embers of sectional bitterness. Instead, the Virginian shunned lucrative business offers and accepted the modest post as president of Washington College. There he counseled moderation and acceptance of defeat. By his postwar example, Robert E. Lee thus helped to restore the Union. The consistent repetition of these images is evident first in southern writings and then in general American literature from 1865 until World War I.

The rapid development of the Lee mystique is one of the most remarkable developments in the genre of American heroic symbolism. Evidence from con-

Robert E. Lee, April 1865

temporary accounts indicates that Lee's status as a hero did not evolve until after his death in 1870. In wartime he shared popularity with such Confederate notables as generals Thomas "Stonewall" Jackson, Joseph E. Johnston, and P. G. T. Beauregard. A number of writers criticized Lee's military leadership, particularly his direction of the Gettysburg campaign.

By the 1870s, after the general's death, the tone of Lee historiography changed markedly. A high degree of organization was evident in the commemoration of Lee's exploits, as groups such as the Lee Memorial Association, Lee Monument Association, and Ladies' Lee Monument Association labored to improve his image. They were aided by the Southern Historical Society, whose *Papers* became the most respected southern outlet of Civil War history in the late 19th century. The society and its *Papers* were dominated totally by Lee devotees such as former generals Jubal Early and Fitzhugh Lee and exrebel chaplain John William Jones. For them and scores of others, mainly Virginians, the depiction of the stainless Robert E. Lee became a crusade for the Lost Cause.

The literary dominance of Virginia authors continued in a second generation of writers whose main literary impact was felt in the period between the 1880s and World War I. Although the postwar generation had written mainly for a southern audience, the new authors wrote for the northern public. Virginia authors seemed to dominate the topic of the Civil War in both fiction and nonfiction. For several decades, beginning in the 1880s, the national reading public was fed a version of the war by Virginia writers such as Thomas Nelson Page, Francis Hopkinson Smith, Constance Cary Harrison, Robert Stiles, Philip A. Bruce, Robert E. Lee, Jr., Sara Pryor, and many others.

The new generation was attuned to new ideas in American thought, such as social Darwinism and the influence of environmental forces in shaping social values. The environmental argument was a keystone of late 19th-century southern authors. For them the South possessed a two-edged sword of triumph and tragedy. For apologists Lee was the supreme example of the alchemy of the noble and tragic. He was the man of superior virtues entrapped in a civilization beset by environmental faults such as human bondage.

The second generation of southern apologists stressed the postwar Lee— an emphasis that meshed well with the elements of both social Darwinism and New South imagery. Lee the war chieftain was now Lee the nationalist, who stressed reunion, shunned the old issues, and emphasized practical mechanical skills for Washington College students.

Lee, then, was the central focus of two generations of southern authors who used his heroic status for different reasons. The earlier generation coped with a theological dilemma. Defeat had gone against the Calvinistic ideal that success is a sign of God's grace. To replace this, the Lost Cause artists fashioned a complicated image whereby the southern cause became a knightly quest in which the righteous may lose but ultimately endure. Lee, the supreme image of this argument, became almost a Christ symbol, evidence that good men do not always prevail at first.

Henceforth the Lee image would change little, except to be altered in succeeding generations as the national mood demanded. In the 1930s an America faced with economic defeat in the Depression era identified with the imagery of Lee and the defeated South.

Later, in the 1950s a nation approaching the Civil War Centennial and reflecting a new post–World War II nationalism would concentrate more upon the qualities of the post–Civil War Lee.

Thomas L. Connelly
University of South Carolina

Thomas L. Connelly, *The Marble Man: Robert E. Lee and His Image in American Society* (1977), *Civil War History* (March 1973), with Barbara L. Bellows, *God and General Longstreet: The Lost Cause and the Southern Mind* (1982); Marshall Fishwick, *Lee after the War* (1963); Douglas Southall Freeman, *R. E. Lee*, 4 vols. (1934–35); Dixon Wecter, *The Hero in America: A Chronicle of Hero-Worship* (1941). ☆

L. Q. C. LAMAR SOCIETY

Founded in 1969 outside Durham, N.C., the Lamar Society brought together middle- and upper-middle-class professionals to share information and ideas about the future of the South. The group named itself after L. Q. C. Lamar, an ardent Mississippi secessionist in the 1860s who became a champion of conciliation after the Civil War.

From the states of the old Confederacy plus Kentucky the Lamar Society accepted members who shared the vision of a South that preserves its regional distinctiveness while overcoming its perennial problems of racism and poverty. The members were particularly concerned with how the South and its way of life would fare in a rapidly growing technological and industrial society. They hoped to point the way for the South to avoid some of the problems that plagued the North after rapid urbanization, such as decay of the cities, destruction of the land, and a government removed from the people.

While the Lamar Society has been compared with the Nashville Agrarians of the 1930s because of the similar structure of the two groups and because each offered a vision of a future South, the agendas of the two are very different. H. Brandt Ayers, one of the Lamar Society's founders, wrote that although this comparison would inevitably be made, the Lamar Society would provide "a new definition of the South, by a new generation of southerners, just as deeply devoted to their region as the Agrarians but more democratic and realistic." The Agrarians felt that the traditional southern culture they applauded was threatened by a modernizing, urbanizing society and called for a return to the values of the agrarian, preindustrial South. The Lamar Society, on the other hand, sought to stress the advantage of a modernizing South in alleviating poverty and overcoming backwardness. Rather than attempting to retard urbanization, the members of the group called for new ideas to help the southern leaders create a "humane urban civilization." This concept involved retaining what the members saw as the best of traditional small-town southern life and incorporating these characteristics (such as responsive, direct-participation government) into new cities.

In 1972 the Lamar Society published a volume of essays called *You Can't Eat Magnolias*, which presented their vision of the South in much the same way as did the Agrarians' *I'll Take My Stand* (1930). During the 1970s the society issued the *Southern Journal*, which served as a forum for the ideas of its members. Inspired by the activities of the Lamar Society, the Southern Growth

Policies Board was formed in late 1971 to coordinate regional growth strategies. Now located in Washington, D.C., the Lamar Society has focused on the desegregation of school systems. The society's leadership in defining the southern challenge of adapting regional myths in an urban setting has been successful in its aim of provoking discussion thoroughout the region.

Karen M. McDearman
University of Mississippi

H. Brandt Ayers and Thomas H. Naylor, eds., *You Can't Eat Magnolias* (1972); Stephen A. Smith, *Myth, Media, and the Southern Mind* (1985). ☆

MADISON, JAMES

(1751–1836) Politician and political philosopher.

Madison defended the interests of Virginia and the South within the framework of the federal government that he helped create. Educated by private tutors at plantation schools in Orange County, Va., and at the College of New Jersey (now Princeton University), he became an effective spokesman for his state and region. In the Continental Congress, 1780–83 and 1787–88, he worked to ensure Virginia's cession of western lands to the Confederation government on conditions favorable to his state. He urged that the United States secure navigation rights to the Mississippi River—then controlled by Spain—which he recognized as crucial for the South's economic development.

At the 1787 Constitutional Convention Madison urged that the federal government be strengthened with delegated powers while the states retained re-

served powers. As a congressman he worked to establish the new government while opposing efforts by the Federalist administration for further consolidation of national powers. His 1798 Virginia Resolutions defended civil liberties and asserted the right of states to interpose their authority to declare unconstitutional the Federalist-sponsored Alien and Sedition Acts. Those resolutions became the foundation of states' rights doctrine for early 19th-century Republicans.

Sectional divisions and his own Republican scruples over legislative supremacy impeded Madison as fourth president of the United States, 1809 to 1817. Long-standing disputes with Great Britain finally erupted in the War of 1812, which was supported in the South but unpopular in the North. In retirement, Madison was embarrassed when—during the 1828–33 South Carolina nullification controversy—states' righters invoked his Virginia Resolutions. He objected that his proposals for interposition meant only cooperation

James Madison, fourth president of the United States

among the states to repeal federal laws or amend the Constitution. He advised President Andrew Jackson and cabinet officers on responding to the nullifiers.

Madison deplored slavery but remained economically dependent on the slave labor of his plantation. He was a founder and president of the American Colonization Society, which worked to return free blacks to Africa. His interests ranged beyond political theory and practice to architecture, the visual arts, and education. Madison supervised additions to Montpelier, his Orange County house, which he filled with his collection of books and paintings. He worked with his lifelong friend and political confidant, Thomas Jefferson, to establish the University of Virginia, which he served as visitor and second rector. Throughout an extraordinarily long career, Madison advanced the political and cultural life of his state, region, and nation.

Thomas A. Mason
University of Virginia

Irving Brant, *James Madison*, 6 vols. (1941–61); William T. Hutchinson et al., eds., *The Papers of James Madison*, 16 vols. (1962–); Ralph Ketcham, *James Madison: A Biography* (1971). ☆

MINT JULEP
||||||||||||||||||||||||||||||||

The mint julep, along with white columns, moonlight, jasmine, and magnolias, is of the very fabric of the southern myth. The only volume devoted solely to its history asserts: "Wherever there is a mint julep, there is a bit of the Old South. For the julep is part ceremony, tradition, and regional nostalgia; and only by definition liquor,

simple syrup, mint, and ice. It is all delight. It is nectar to the Virginian, mother's milk to the Kentuckian, and ambrosia to southerners anywhere."

The origin of the South's most famous drink—excepting only Coca-Cola—has as many claimants as Homer's birthplace: Virginia, Maryland, New England, Georgia, Kentucky, and Louisiana. It may be all of these locales, for wherever whiskey was drunk in the Federal period (and it was drunk enthusiastically almost everywhere), it was natural that it should be drunk with the local plant that imparted a most delectable flavor to the rough distillation of those days.

Actually, credit for the julep belongs to Virginia. Its first recorded use was there. In 1797 the *American Museum* described the Virginian who upon rising "drinks a julep made of rum, water, and sugar, but very strong." The mint was added a few years later. Describing life on a James River plantation in his *Travels in the United States* (1803), John Davis noted the early morning mint julep.

Mint was as widespread as alcohol in America, and the drink spread to Maryland (made, as in Virginia, with rye whiskey), to New England (made with rum), to Kentucky (made with the corn whiskey that was ancestor to bourbon), to New York (made with anything, even gin), and to Louisiana (made with brandy). Recipes for the drink were wildly varied, sometimes full of fruit to the point of resembling a salad, often with rum ladled on top of other liquors, sometimes with bourbon lending additional flavor to apricot or peach brandy.

As tastes changed in post-Prohibition America the drink became simpler but no less ceremonial. It has been praised by historians—C. J. Latrobe, Frederick

Marryatt, and W. H. Russell—and used for atmosphere by O. Henry, Margaret Mitchell, and a thousand other writers of fiction. It has truly passed into the realm of cliché, but this concoction of bourbon whiskey, sugar, mint, and ice retains both its charm and its good taste.

Richard B. Harwell
Athens, Georgia

Richard B. Harwell, *The Mint Julep* (1975); Soule Smith, *The Mint Julep: The Very Dream of Drinks* (1949); Jerry Thomas, *How To Mix Drinks* (1962). ☆

MOON PIES

The Moon Pie, long marketed as "the original marshmallow sandwich," had humble beginnings at the Chattanooga Bakery in Chattanooga, Tenn. Although its precise origin is not known, the Moon Pie is believed to have been created in 1918 or 1919. Legend has it that a traveling salesman stopped by the bakery and suggested that a snack consisting of two cookies with marshmallow in between and covered with chocolate would sell. At that time, reports one version, the bakery produced over 200 different items; so successful was this one suggestion that it now is the only snack produced by the company.

Since their invention Moon Pies have had broad appeal throughout the South and have been a favorite snack food for both children and adults. Consisting of one quarter inch of marshmallow sandwiched between two cookies about four inches in diameter, Moon Pies have been coated with chocolate, banana, coconut, or vanilla frosting. Many companies have attempted to imitate the

Moon Pie and capitalize on the snack's popularity, but any discerning southern palate can distinguish the real taste.

In 1969 the bakery introduced a "Double Decker" pie, featuring two layers of marshmallow sandwiched between three cookies and then covered with flavored frosting. This version can be found primarily in convenience stores. With increased interest and new distribution techniques, the Moon Pie has moved beyond its traditional southern territory and is now available in nearly all parts of the country. The Moon Pie Cultural Club is a Charlotte, N.C., group dedicated to spreading "the story of the Moon Pie" and establishing "club chapters throughout the civilized world."

Thomas Rankin
Southern Arts Federation
Atlanta, Georgia

Ron Dickson, *Moon Pie Handbook* (1985); William E. Schmidt, *New York Times* (30 April 1986). ☆

MOONSHINE AND MOONSHINING

Blockade whiskey, corn liquor, corn "squeezins," panther's breath, rotgut, ruckus juice, tiger's sweat, and white lightning are all names for moonshine. Comic-strip character Snuffy Smith, a Kentucky moonshiner, is one of its most ardent defenders, sometimes outwitting the "revenooers," but not always. The same is true for many actual moonshiners in the rural South, where the illegal making of corn whiskey has been carried on since the 18th century.

Moonshine looks clear, tastes raw,

and sells fast. It usually runs close to 100 proof or more. To make it, sugar, water, yeast, cornmeal, and malt (cornmeal made from sprouted kernels) are variously combined and processed in three stages: fermentation, distillation, and condensation. Bootleggers today, frequently unconcerned about quality, have been known to add such substances as lye and embalming fluid to the product to give it a sharper flavor.

The moonshining factory is the still. There are several types, but the most prevalent is the simple pot still. It consists of an airtight kettle with a "worm," or copper coil, running from its cap through a barrel filled with cool water. Hiding the stills is essential, and methods of concealment range from bending saplings over them to setting them up in dug-out underground rooms. Nighttime is the safest time for working a still, with the moon providing enough light by which to see—hence, the name moonshine.

Many Scotch-Irish immigrants settled in the southern Appalachian mountains, bringing with them the practice of making whiskey. The beginnings of moonshining can be traced back to 1791 when the government, trying to pay Revolutionary War debts, imposed an excise tax on whiskey. Unwilling to pay the tax, distillers operated secretly. Illicit distilling persisted and flourished in the South largely for economic reasons: corn liquor brought higher prices than did the unprocessed vegetable; it was readily marketable; it assured a steady income in the poorly developed, economically unstable region; and, because of the bad road conditions, it could more easily and efficiently be transported to the distant marketplaces than could bulky bushels of corn.

Moonshining is a tax violation, so tax agents and other law enforcement officers seek offenders. Garland Bunting, an Alcoholic Beverage Control officer in Halifax County, N.C., has seized and destroyed hundreds of stills and is the subject of Alec Wilkinson's *Moonshine: A Life in Pursuit of White Liquor* (1985). Selling fish and preaching sermons are two of the many, diverse tactics he has used to accomplish his purpose. There are moonshiners enough in his territory to keep him busy, and they still operate in large numbers elsewhere in the South—carefully selling their goods.

Corn is a major southern cash crop. The production of "corn juice" has proved economically advantageous to many a southerner. Land has represented the basis of a way of life for many mountain people. Moonshine has also been a popular beverage. During the Depression, consumers bought it when they could buy no other alcoholic beverage. Through the years, moonshine has become significant in the popular culture of the region, frequently appearing in literature and in country songs like George Jones's "White Lightnin'." *Raw Mash* (Blaine Dunlap and Sol Korine, directors; Center for Southern Folklore, 1978) and *Tradition* (Bill Hatton and Anthony Slone, directors; Appalshop, 1973) chronicle aspects of mountain moonshining.

See also INDUSTRY: Liquor Industry

Jessica Foy
Cooperstown Graduate Program
Cooperstown, New York

John C. Campbell, *The Southern Highlander and His Homeland* (1921); Esther Kellner, *Moonshine: Its History and Folklore* (1971); Horace Kephart, *Our Southern Highlanders* (1913); Robert A. Pace and Jeffrey W. Gard-

Revenue agents with captured still, Kentucky, date unknown

ner, *Tennessee Anthropologist* (Spring 1985); Eliot Wigginton, ed. *The Foxfire Book* (1972). ✩

OLMSTED, FREDERICK LAW

||||||||||||||||||||||||||||||||||||||||||

(1822–1903) Travel writer and architect.

Olmsted, born in Hartford, Conn., was nurtured by a tolerant father who encouraged him to explore his various talents, a background that prepared him to be a cultural observer. Like many of his New England generation, Olmsted sought to assist his fellowman, and his opportunity to write about the South proved to be beneficial for his subsequent work. Olmsted left farming to make a tour of England, a trip that became the basis for his book *Walks and Talks of an American Farmer in England* (1852) and the paradigm for much of his travel and cultural observation.

Because of that book's success Olmsted was asked to tour the South and do a series of articles for the New York *Daily Times*, a project that began modestly but led to many articles, three books, and the 1861 compilation, *Journeys and Explorations in the Cotton Kingdom*, an abridgment of his books about the South.

The process of the development of Olmsted's writings from newspaper accounts to books and rearrangement into *The Cotton Kingdom* is a complicated textual story. It reveals much about the era when Olmsted sought to become a member of what he described as "the republic of letters." In 1855 he purchased an interest in the company that published his first southern book, *Journey in the Seaboard Slave States* (1856); yet its financial collapse and the sudden death of his brother, John (who had written a considerable portion of Frederick's *A Journey through Texas* [1857] from Olmsted's notes), complicated his life sufficiently to make desirable a shift in 1857 toward landscape architecture.

The urgency of abolition and his free-state interests were reflected in Olmsted's writing. An apparent sympathy for slaveholding dwindled as his articles were rewritten for books, then abridged. He gradually became convinced that a slave economy could not be profitable. Even though predisposed to find the South backward, one of his valuable accomplishments was to reveal that southern states were remarkably more complex than might have been assumed in the North. A desire for objectivity allowed him to provide a documentation of antebellum conditions that present-day historians corroborate.

Olmsted sought to be factual. His two long trips (from 1852 to the spring of 1854) yielded a cumulative record of farms and villages, a way of life that did not support stereotyped views. He showed the real South as culturally diverse; in the German settlements of Texas, for example, he reported the good results of democracy, freedom, and efficiency. *A Journey in the Back Country* (1860) documented many types of living conditions. The artistic design of Olmsted's writing should also be noted.

His southern writings have proven beneficial for over a century. As source material for various studies, as demonstrated in *Olmsted South* (1979), his writings remain valuable. As a landscape architect Olmsted returned South in the 1890s and imprinted his vision at places as diverse as Biltmore, the Vanderbilt estate, near Asheville, N.C., and the Druid Hills area of Atlanta, which together are his most important living southern legacies.

Victor A. Kramer
Georgia State University

Albert Fein, *Frederick Law Olmsted and the American Environmental Tradition* (1972); Victor A. Kramer and Dana F. White, eds., *Olmsted South: Old South Critic, New South Planner* (1979); Elizabeth Stevenson, *Park Maker: A Life of Frederick Law Olmsted* (1977). ☆

PATRIOTIC SOCIETIES

Southern reporter Pat Watters once wrote about "all the complex stratifications (clubs and circles and hierarchies of elitism) of high society that the South continued to take more seriously than the rest of the country." He had in mind that web of clubs of all kinds—town, country, yacht, debutante, literary, garden, bridge, luncheon and service, junior leagues and auxiliaries, ball societies, fraternities and sororities, and, not least, hereditary patriotic societies, all of them with their own pecking orders. Patriotic societies, based upon descent from an ancestor's services to colony or nation, received their greatest impetus in the Northeast during the wave of late 19th-century immigration. Nonetheless, they also had southern roots and particularly southern flavors.

The first society in the 13 colonies, named for Scotland's patron saint, was the St. Andrew's Society of Charleston, S.C., founded in 1729 and followed there in 1733 by the St. George's Society. The Society of the Cincinnati, composed of Continental army officers and their eldest male descendants, was founded 10 May 1783, with Virginian George Washington as its first president general. The Society of the War of 1812 was founded in 1814 by the defenders of Fort McHenry after the British withdrawal, and its first commander was

Maryland's Revolutionary War hero, Major General Samuel Smith of Baltimore, who had led the defense. In Mexico City on 13 October 1847 United States military officers organized the Aztec Club on primogenitive lines, and its first president was John A. Quitman of Mississippi, who had led the successful attack upon "the Halls of Montezuma." However, the greatest impetus to the organization of patriotic societies in the South came after the Civil War and during Reconstruction, with southern women in the lead.

One year to the day after General Joseph E. Johnston surrendered the last large Confederate field army, southern women began organizing to care for Confederate soldiers' graves, and April 26, "the South's All Souls' Day," became the most popular Confederate Memorial Day. Ladies' Memorial Associations appeared across Dixie, with Columbus, Ga., and Columbus and Jackson, Miss., each claiming the "first." Later, as the South revived in its fortunes and as urbanization increased, came formation of the United Confederate Veterans in New Orleans in June 1889, the United Daughters of the Confederacy in Nashville in September 1894, the Sons of Confederate Veterans in Richmond on 1 July 1896, and the Children of the Confederacy under U D C auspices in Alexandria, Va., also in 1896. Much later came the Military Order of the Stars and Bars for the male descendants of Confederate officers, in July 1938 in Columbia, S.C. Robert E. Lee's and Jefferson Davis's birthdays, January 19 and June 3, also became southern holidays.

Meanwhile, spurred by the centennial celebration of the American Revolution and in reaction to emigration from outside northern Europe, heredi-

tary societies arose to memorialize the Revolutionary War: the Sons of the Revolution in 1883, the rival Sons of the American Revolution in 1889 (both organized in New York City), and the Daughters of the American Revolution in 1890 in Washington, D.C. Two of the founders of these three groups were southern women. Others reached farther back in time to found the rival Societies of Colonial Dames in 1890 and 1891 and their male counterpart, the Society of Colonial Wars, in 1893. As a rule of thumb, except for the sui generis Cincinnati, the more remote the ancestor, the greater is the society's exclusiveness and prestige and the higher its members' social status. As one Alabama matron put it, "Heaven on earth in the Black Belt is to be a Kappa Delta, a Colonial Dame and an Episcopalian." By the time of the Spanish-American War, these colonial and revolutionary hereditary organizations were established in the Deep South.

Also concerned with remembrance of the past, but not organized on hereditary lines, were the societies founded to save historic houses. First came the Mount Vernon Ladies' Association, which Charlestonian Ann Pamela Cunningham organized in 1853 to rescue George Washington's home. Others of note were the Ladies' Hermitage Association, founded in Nashville in 1889 to preserve Andrew Jackson's mansion, the Confederate Memorial Literary Society in Richmond in 1890 to maintain the second White House of the Confederacy there, and the White House Association of Alabama in Montgomery in 1900 to enshrine the First White House of the Confederacy.

More recent arrivals on the southern scene are such state or family-oriented organizations as the Daughters (1891) and Sons (1893) of the Republic of Texas, Maryland's Society of the Ark and Dove (1910), Louisiana Colonials (1917), Jamestown Society (1936), National Huguenot Society (1951), Southern Dames of America (1962), Order of First Families of Mississippi (1967), Society of the Lees of Virginia (1921), Washington Family Descendants (1954), and the Davis Family Association (1973). Standing at the head of these is that apotheosis of the FFV, the Order of First Families of Virginia (1912).

Each of these organizations has its place in the social scheme of things for certain southerners. The gentlemen's hereditary societies seem to be important status indicators in the more mobile societies of the New South, in newer industrial cities such as Birmingham, rather than in Old South cities such as Montgomery, where primacy goes to the local Society of Pioneers of Montgomery (1955), the membership of which is limited to 100 gentlemen with ancestors living there before 1855. Historian Francis Butler Simkins once admitted that, "in the aristocratic aspiration of Southerners are elements of snobbery" but he added that "ancestor hunting is an important activity" because a "consciousness of illustrious forebears gives satisfactions not unlike those of religion to old people without material assets."

John Hawkins Napier III
Montgomery, Alabama

Cleveland Amory, *Who Killed Society?* (1960); Jerome Francis Beattie, ed., *The Hereditary Register of the United States of America* (1978); Bethany Bultman, *Town and Country* (November 1977); Sophy Burnham, *The Landed Gentry* (1978); Wallace Evan Davies, *Patriotism on Parade: The Story of Veterans' and Hereditary Organi-* zations in America, 1783–1900 (1955); Lucy Kavaler, *The Private World of High Society* (1960); Marie Bankhead Owen, *The Blue Book*, Montgomery, Alabama 1909–1910 (1909). ☆

PICKUP TRUCK

The pickup truck in the South has a variety of uses, most of which do not involve hauling cargo. In fact, the pickup is next to worthless for anything but light hauling on paved roads. Being front-end heavy, it bogs down on wet grass, spins out in its own shadow, and can even flip on a straight, dry stretch of roadway. The cab offers little storage space, and anything carried in the bed is open to theft.

Beginning in the second decade of this century the pickup (essentially a car with the back seat and trunk removed and replaced with a wooden or metal platform) proliferated on the farms. In the last 30 years, despite its limited hauling potential, the pickup's popularity has grown. About half the new vehicles sold in the South are pickups. Often constituting a second family vehicle, the pickup has become a status symbol for many. In a historical and literary context, a "good old boy" without a pickup is like a cowboy without a horse. "Work" (or "rat" or "bad") trucks, battered and rimmed with rust from long-standing farm or construction work, carry lock boxes full of tools and materials of the owners' trades.

In a more modern vein, the rising number of fancy pickups, the "showboats," in suburban driveways represents a curious phenomenon in America's love affair with motorized vehicles. New models, unburdened with dents and scratches, offer the means of escape for the suburban family. Various attachments (from simple bed covers to fancy camper tops) allow the entire family to go "camping" on the weekends. Whether for work or for pleasure, the pickup truck represents ties to the bygone rural aspects of American life. And, because of its rural ties, the pickup is associated with the South.

More particularly, the pickup is associated with the male southerner. Usually, the second vehicle in a family, the pickup most often is the man's to drive and to care for. Men drive them to work, whether that work occurs in a factory, medical center, or courtroom. For the younger man not tied to a family, the pickup becomes his chariot, in which he cruises around looking for women. Apparently, the higher riding the pickup (jacked up with large frame-extending shock absorbers and bouyant on oversized mud tires), the more likely the southern boy will land a date with a cheerleader. Of course, the ever-present gun rack (with rifle or shotgun prominently displayed, or, in more urban settings, simply an umbrella) reflects ties to the rural mystique of southern culture.

Underscoring both its lack of utility and its importance as a status symbol, the pickup has changed drastically in the last 30 years. In 1950 Ford introduced a handsome pickup with styling of its own, the F-100. Ford still uses the F-series designation on trucks, but the company turned pickup sales around with the slogan "Where men are men, trucks are Ford V8s." Ford dominated pickup sales for several decades until Chevy countered with its "built tough" trucks with cowboy names. The Scottsdale, Silverado, Bonanza, and GMC confirmed their position, as did the Sierra Classic. Styling and male imagery

are key appeals; Power Wagon brought Dodge trucks out of the doldrums, and Ram Chargers and The Little Red Express keep them out.

Trucks imported from Europe never caught on in America. The Volkswagon suffers from having the truck bed preloaded with its own engine and transmission. The British Morris Minor was good, but faded over 25 years ago. There was country-boy resistance to the first small trucks from Japan. Chevy called one Luv, and Ford's was the Courier, avoiding Oriental-sounding names. But as American pickups grew more larger and more expensive, Toyota, Datsun-Nissan, Mazda, and Isuzu earned respect with their pickups, as they had with their cars. To counter this market invasion Ford introduced the smaller Ranger, Dodge a smaller Ram, and Chevy the S-10, all of which are slightly larger than Japanese trucks and increasingly popular.

From the basic platform wagon on four wheels the pickup now embraces a multitude of styles and options. Deluxe models (with more chrome trim than found on 1950s automobiles) include passenger seats in the rear of an extended cab, long wheel bases, dual rear wheels, fourwheel drive, magnesium wheels, long-range fuel tanks, and lights similar to those found on the 18 wheelers, not to mention quadraphonic stereos and elegant CBs. Such extraneous options, again, reflect southern values, especially that of individuality. An owner reveals his character with his choice of options.

If the pickup reflects southern culture, its very popularity may tend to whittle away at the "southernness" of its heritage. As with the trucking culture in general, the pickup truck is becoming subsumed in a more general American culture, becoming a common sight in urban areas far removed from the South.

Gordon Baxter
Car and Driver

Floyd Clymer, *Henry's Wonderful Model T (1955).* ☆

PILGRIMAGE
||||||||||||||||||||||||||||||||||

In the spring of 1931 the Mississippi State Federation of Garden Clubs held its annual meeting in Natchez, Miss. For a combination of reasons, including a blighting freeze in late spring and the depressing state of the economy, the ordinarily ornate gardens of Natchez were not in peak condition. As an alternative to garden tours, the Garden Club of Natchez prevailed upon the owners of the city's antebellum mansions to open their homes for two daily tours during the two-day convention. The response to the mansion tours was so enthusiastic

that Mrs. J. Balfour Miller organized another tour of Natchez antebellum homes the next year. She publicized the week-long pilgrimage throughout the South and in other parts of the country where she had friends or connections with the media.

The response to the first Natchez Pilgrimage in 1932 exceeded all Miller's expectations, and, following her slide presentation explaining the pilgrimage to the National Convention of Garden Clubs in 1933, the movement spread quickly throughout the South. In many southern towns these annual pilgrimages now provide a significant boost to the community's economy. Most southern pilgrimages are accompanied by Confederate pageants or balls commemorating life in the Old South, and southern belles who show the visitors through the mansions are dressed in Old South styles, which include long, swaying hoop skirts, layers of petticoats, and bonnets. In recent years some southern communities have demphasized the Confederate connection and have re-

Elms, Natchez, Mississippi, one of the South's most visited homes

styled such a tour, calling it a "Parade of Homes." The new designation allows other homes in the community that are not antebellum to be included on the tours.

See also URBANIZATION: / Natchez

David Sansing
University of Mississippi

James T. Black, *Southern Living* (March 1983); Les Thomas, *Southern Living* (March 1978). ☆

RANDOLPH, JOHN
(1773–1833) Politician.

John Randolph of Roanoke represented the interests of traditional slaveholding Virginians in Congress and expressed the aristocratic style of the Virginia past in American public life from the early Republic through the Jacksonian period. Randolph entered public life as part of the Jeffersonian opposition to the Adams Administration and was a prominent member of the congressional leadership in Jefferson's first administration. He broke with Jefferson and, along with purist Republicans, formed an extreme group called the "tertium quids" within the party.

Beginning with an uncompromising assertion of states' rights, in time they became suspicious of democracy as well as American nationalism, detecting in the growth of the federal government an ultimate threat to slavery and the plantation way of life. Randolph's career was largely one of opposition, although he sometimes found allies on particular issues. He was probably the first important American statesman to stake out the positions that came to characterize the secessionist southern view of the Union. Although he dismissed Calhoun's metaphysics, he influenced the South Carolinian's development as a sectional leader.

Randolph's notorious, exciting, and eccentric public persona, his witticisms and verbal challenges, and his stinging contempt for the barbarities of American democratic public life contributed to the mythology of southern bluebloods and hot bloods. Randolph seized the American imagination, North and South, in a pattern that would come to characterize the southern hold on the American imagination.

In his antidemocratic and anticommercial conservatism, his states' rights consistency and republican purity, and his prophetic sense of where southern slaveholding interests must lie, Randolph earned his place in the pantheon of southern activists. In his extravagant and dramatic eccentricity, his keen eye for the appetites of the democratic electorate, and his attempt to embody the Virginia heritage, Randolph earned a lasting place as a mythic southerner.

Robert Dawidoff
Claremont Graduate School
Claremont, California

William Cabell Bruce, *Randolph of Roanoke: A Biography Based Largely on New Material*, 2 vols. (1922); Robert Dawidoff, *The Education of John Randolph* (1979); William R. Taylor, *Cavalier and Yankee: The Old South and American National Character* (1961). ☆

SOUL FOOD

Popularized in the 1960s, the term *soul food* refers to a distinctive, traditional southern style of cooking. Use of the term implies that this cuisine is limited in popularity to blacks, but it is in fact the native fare of both black and white southerners of all economic and social strata.

The distinctive ingredients of southern cuisine, as well as the distinctive styles of cooking them, have been common for centuries in Africa but not in Europe. Sweet potatoes, okra, chicken and fish rolled in meal or batter and deep fried, greens and cowpeas boiled with pork and served with pot liquor, and corn bread in many varieties form the basis of a regional cuisine whose roots may be more African than European. Maize and sweet potatoes were taken from America to Africa by Portuguese traders in the 16th century, and peas of the black-eyed type have been eaten in Africa for some 400 years. Even specialized local cuisines with identifiable European roots, such as French cooking in Louisiana, have been heavily influenced by Afro-American taste in such things as the heavy use of red pepper and the creation of dishes like gumbo based on ingredients, such as okra, that came from Africa. In fact, the black presence may explain why foods like maize and cowpeas, which will grow anywhere in America and were eaten in other parts of the country while the frontiers lasted, remain staple foods only in the South, aside from those areas of the Southwest where they were staple foods of Native Americans. Some scholars see Native American influences on soul food as well.

Margaret Jones Bolsterli
University of Arkansas

Eugene D. Genovese, *Roll, Jordan, Roll: The World the Slaves Made* (1976); Bob Jef-fries, *Soul Food Cookbook* (1970); Bruce F. Johnston, *The Staple Food Economies of Western Tropical Africa* (1958); Helen Mendes, *The African Heritage Cookbook* (1971). ☆

SOUTHERN HISTORICAL ASSOCIATION

In November 1934, 18 historians from throughout the South met in Atlanta to form the Southern Historical Association, a group focusing on "the promotion of interest and research in southern history, the collection and preservation of the South's historical records, and the encouragement of state and local historical societies in that section to vigorous activity." To address this objective, the founders launched the *Journal of Southern History*, a quarterly publication. Historians from the South, such as Charles Knapp of the University of Kentucky, Philip Hamer of the University of Tennessee, Thomas Abernethy of the University of Virginia, and Benjamin Kendrick of the Women's College of the University of North Carolina, led the group's early efforts but encouraged participation by historians throughout the country.

Changes over the years in leadership and focus in the association reflect in large part the fluctuations in parochialism and sectionalist fervor among historians throughout the South. E. Merton Coulter, the association's first president, avoided controversial sectional sentiment, but Frank L. Owsley in a 1940 presidential address indicted the North for an egocentric sectionalism, which he viewed as a principal cause of the Civil War. A South-versus-North focus, rooted partly, too, in disagreements with President Franklin Roosevelt's policies, flourished for several years in the association. Historian Robert Durden notes that "[Albert B.] Moore's diatribe of 1942 signalled the high-water mark of polemical bitterness in the presidential addresses . . . and such sectionalist sentiments virtually disappeared from the succeeding addresses."

Among the other outstanding historians who have headed the group are Fletcher M. Green, who in 1945 delivered an influential address on political democracy in the Old South; Ella Lonn, the first female president, who in 1946 examined 20th-century reconciliation between the North and South; C. Vann Woodward, who in 1952 delivered a widely respected address entitled "The Irony of Southern History"; Francis Butler Simkins, who "in 1954 sounded what may have been the last bugle call . . . for the old-time sectional verities and attitudes" with his address entitled "Tolerating the South's Past"; James W. Silver, who in his 1963 address on "Mississippi: The Closed Society" scrutinized the South's white-supremacist policies; Robert Durden, who examined "A Half Century of Change in Southern History" during the association's 50th annual meeting in November 1984; and Carl N. Degler, who in 1986 dialectically assessed the evolving relationship of the South, the North, and the nation. The various leaders have not only mirrored prevailing sentiments of their times regarding sectionalism but also shaped new frameworks for gaining perspective on southern history.

Articles in the *Journal of Southern History* pinpoint the South, but the association's annual meeting includes sessions on American, European, and Latin American history as well as special-interest sessions. The organization

gives various awards for outstanding books and articles on southern history, and it maintains an editorial office at Rice University and administrative offices at the University of Georgia.

Sharon A. Sharp
University of Mississippi

Robert F. Durden, *Journal of Southern History* (February 1985); Arthur S. Link and Rembert W. Patrick, eds., *Writing Southern History: Essays in Historiography in Honor of Fletcher M. Green* (1965); George B. Tindall, ed., *The Pursuit of Southern History: Presidential Addresses of the Southern Historical Association, 1935–1963* (1964). ✩

SOUTHERN HISTORICAL SOCIETY

In May 1869 a group of Confederate veterans met in New Orleans to establish an organization to collect, preserve, and publish records of the Confederacy. General Braxton Bragg chaired the newly formed group, which planned to establish an affiliate in every southern state. The new group floundered in its first few years, but supporters convened in August 1873 at White Sulphur Springs in Virginia to reorganize the Southern Historical Society. Headquarters for the group were moved from New Orleans to Richmond, Va., where an archive of Civil War documents was established at the state capitol.

General Jubal A. Early, first president of the reorganized society, served with a group of vice-presidents, one from each southern state. Historian Merton Coulter noted that the group might well have been called the Confederate Historical Society, because the leaders were "erstwhile warriors turned historians and conservers of history," determined to garner evidence for the tribunal of history. Racing to collect Confederate materials before the federal government completed its congressionally mandated gathering and publication of official records of the Civil War, the Southern Historical Society members rekindled the flames of Confederate patriotism by exhorting good southerners to contribute to their cause—the assembly of the archives of the covenant. Materials collected included wartime correspondence, memoirs, unit rosters, books, newspaper articles, manuscripts, military reports, maps, charts, speeches, ballads, and poetry. Initially the society published materials regularly in the *Southern Magazine* of Baltimore. In 1875 the Reverend J. William Jones, who had been the society's temporary secretary, became the permanent secretary-treasurer and served until 1887. Jones, described by historian Charles Reagan Wilson as "the most influential and well-known clergyman in the cult of the Lost Cause," shaped what became the preeminent publication institutionalizing the preservation of Confederate history, the *Southern Historical Society Papers*. Launched in 1876 as a monthly publication, the papers were published quarterly from 1880 until 1888, when they became annual volumes, then occasional publications until 1959. Jones edited 14 of the total 52 volumes of the *Southern Historical Society Papers*, and in so doing shaped and disseminated one of the most valuable and complete bodies of information available on Confederate military history—and its interpretation from a Confederate viewpoint. Some of the state organizations, such as North Carolina's and Kentucky's, separately published materials, too.

After 1900 membership in the society

waned, and only a few members in the Richmond area remained by the 1950s. Among the last members was noted journalist and historian Douglas Southall Freeman, whose death in 1953 marked the demise of the society. In its heyday, however, the Southern Historical Society had organized the documentation and galvanized the core of ideas upon which the vision of the South as a defeated "redeemer nation" flourished for decades.

Sharon A. Sharp
University of Mississippi

E. Merton Coulter, *Journal of Southern History* (February 1936); Gaines Foster, *Ghosts of the Confederacy: Defeat, the Lost Cause, and the Emergence of the New South, 1865–1913* (1987); Arthur S. Link and Rembert W. Patrick, eds., *Writing Southern History: Essays in Historiography in Honor of Fletcher M. Green* (1965). ☆

STONE MOUNTAIN

Stone Mountain is a natural landmark, a historic site, and a recreational area located 16 miles east of Atlanta, Ga. The world's largest mass of exposed granite, the 825-foot dome rises 1,683 feet above sea level on a path once used by Creek Indians. The mountain is 285 to 294 million years old. Carved on its side is the world's largest piece of sculpture, a memorial to the Confederacy composed of the mounted figures of Robert E. Lee, Jefferson Davis, and Thomas J. "Stonewall" Jackson. The United Daughters of the Confederacy (UDC) leased the land in 1915 and commissioned Gutzon Borglum, an Idaho sculptor who would later carve Mount Rushmore, to design and execute a carving of Lee. Borglum conceived a grandiose plan—a gigantic model of Confederate leaders riding around the mountain. Little progress on the memorial occurred before the end of World War I. In November of 1915 Colonel William Simmons, a former Methodist circuit rider and salesman, used Stone Mountain as the location for a fiery ritual resurrecting the Ku Klux Klan. The locale thereafter was periodically the scene of Klan rallies.

In May of 1916, with a huge Confederate flag, 30 by 50 feet, draped across the face of the cliff, southerners dedicated the unfinished Stone Mountain as a memorial to the Lost Cause. Still in need of financing though, Borglum traveled throughout the South promoting the project. In 1923 Atlanta businessmen took charge of the project, forming the Stone Mountain Monumental Association. Borglum began work on the carving in June of 1923 and unveiled the partially carved head of Lee on 19 January 1924, the general's birthday, before an estimated crowd of 20,000. After a rift developed between Borglum and the UDC, Augustus Lukeman began work on the project but was unable to finish the carving before the UDC lease ran out in 1928.

For more than 30 years the memorial remained unfinished, with the property owned by the Venable family. In 1958 the state of Georgia decided to develop Stone Mountain as a tourist attraction. The state commissioned Walter Hancock to complete the memorial and to develop the park around it. George Weiblin was hired to direct completion of the carving, with Roy Faulkner as chief carver. Using a thermo-jet torch and working at times in the face of 70-mile-per-hour winds on the side of the mountain, the crew finished the project between 1964 and 1970, when the memorial was dedicated.

The carving, which is 90 feet high by 190 feet wide, in a frame 360 feet square, depicts Lee, Davis, and Jackson—the Lost Cause trinity—on horseback; Lee's horse, Traveller, stretches across 145 feet. Stone Mountain became a major tourist attraction at the heart of a 3,200-acre park. More than 5 million people a year come to the park, which is geared, according to promoters, to family recreation. The park features a 90-room inn and a 500-site campground. Inside the park, visitors can see a 19th-century plantation and a gristmill, drive across a covered bridge, fish, circle the mountain on a train or scale it on a skylift, ride the side-wheeler riverboat the *Scarlett O'Hara*, play tennis or golf, or stroll through the grounds, which contain flowers such as the now-rare Confederate daisy (*viguiera porteri*). Guides costumed in hoop skirts or Confederate army uniforms provide assistance. In Confederate Hall a light-and-sound performance shows Sherman's "March to the Sea." The Georgia Heritage Museum contains artifacts and documents from the state's history. An Antique Auto and Music Museum contains antique toys, cars, trains, musical instruments, gas pumps, and other items. Indigenous animals roam the 60-acre Stone Mountain Animal Forest.

In the summer, tourists now come to see "A Night on Stone Mountain," which is said to be the world's largest outdoor laser show. Laser beams flash onto the carving such images as spiders, spaceships, and animals, accompanied by fireworks. In the finale, the Confederate heroes gallop off the mountain, courtesy of the laser lighting, all to the familiar tune of "Dixie."

Charles Reagan Wilson
University of Mississippi

Robert J. Casey and Mary Borglum, *Give the Man Room: The Story of Gutzon Borglum* (1952); Gerald W. Johnson, *The Undefeated* (1927); Bari R. Love, *Southern Living* (June 1984). ☆

STUART, JEB
||||||||||||||||||||||||||||||
(1833–1864) Confederate general.

During his short life, James Ewell Brown "Jeb" Stuart accomplished much. Born in Patrick County, Va., in 1833, "Jeb" Stuart graduated from West Point (1854) and served on the western frontier in the United States Army until 1861. He resigned to serve Virginia and the Confederacy as commander of a regiment of cavalry. Stuart was conspicuous at First Manassas (Bull Run) and tireless in his employment of mounted troops as scouts and pickets between rival armies. Promoted to brigadier general in September 1861, Stuart expanded his command and his fame. In June 1862 Stuart rode completely around George B. McClellan's Union army and was able to supply Robert E. Lee with the intelligence upon which Lee based his Seven Days Campaign. In July 1862 Stuart became a major general and assumed command of the cavalry component of the Army of Northern Virginia. He led other cavalry raids— Catlett's Station in August 1862, Chambersburg in October 1862, and Dumfries in December 1862—which embarrassed his enemies and enhanced his fame. At Chancellorsville (May 1863) Stuart succeeded Stonewall Jackson in command of an infantry corps and played a key role in the Confederate victory.

The cavalry battle at Brandy Station (June 1863) opened Stuart to criticism because he allowed the federals to surprise him. His protracted raid during the Gettysburg campaign deprived Lee of his "eyes and ears" and contributed to the Confederate defeat. But when Stuart suffered a mortal wound at Yellow Tavern in May of 1864, he died a southern hero. He had worn a plume in his hat, collected a retinue that included a banjo player, and flirted with women wherever he went. He had sung and danced and laughed; but he had avoided alcohol, remained faithful to his wife, and set an example of Christian piety.

Stuart made himself a legend while he lived, and later his legend grew larger than life. Stuart has stood for southerner as cavalier and knight in the American mind. As symbol he is eternally dashing, romantic, and gallant. Stuart's life may have been brief, but his legacy yet lives.

Emory Thomas
University of Georgia

Burke Davis, *Jeb Stuart: The Last Cavalier* (1957); Henry Brainerd McClellan, *I Rode with Jeb Stuart: The Life and Campaigns of Major General J. E. B. Stuart* (1885, 1958); Emory Thomas, *Bold Dragoon: The Life of J. E. B. Stuart* (1986). ☆

TAYLOR, JOHN
|||||||||||||||||||||||||||||||||||||||||
(1753–1824) Political philosopher.

Taylor, born in December 1753 in Caroline County, Va., is referred to as "John Taylor of Caroline"; he was one of the fathers of southern politics. He was more famous in his own time than later; his prestige was such that he was several times elected U.S. senator from what was then the most powerful state in the Union without campaigning and against his wishes. He was a soldier in the American Revolution who died regretting that the Revolution had ended in the construction of a federal government more dangerous to the colonies than that of Great Britain. He retired from a lucrative law practice to become not only a highly successful planter and agricultural reformer but the foremost political defender and philosopher that American agriculture ever had. He was an eloquent advocate of economic, political, and religious freedom for the citizen, and an unbending defender of slavery.

Taylor may even be said to have been a pioneer figure in southern literature. His books and pamphlets are not only full of keen political and economic analysis but are written in a colloquial style—full of satire, hyperbole, and front-porch digressions—highly suggestive of the oral tradition evident in later southern writers.

Taylor embodied many persistent and recurrent tendencies and themes of southern politics. He represented both a conservative allegiance to local community and inherited ways and a radical-populist suspicion of capitalism, "progress," government, and routine logrolling politics. He was at the same time more radical and more conservative than his friend, admirer, and fellow Virginia planter Thomas Jefferson. Taylor was Jefferson's down-home side—exactly what Jefferson would have been had he been less cosmopolitan and less of a practical politician. In many respects Taylor was a more authentic voice of Jeffersonianism than was Jefferson himself. Taylor's Old Republican defense of states' rights, strict construction, and intelligent farming and his opposition to federal power, judicial oligarchy, paper money, stock jobbing,

taxation, and expenditure were reflexive, reluctant defenses of native soil and were based upon the unyielding conviction that an unoppressed and predominantly agricultural population was the only possible basis for free government.

At the core of Taylor's thinking was a belief that the world is divided between producers and parasites. The producers are decent folk who labor in the earth for their daily bread and produce everything of real economic and moral value in society. They are subject to endless depredations from those that Taylor referred to as "aristocrats." By "aristocrats" he meant not people of good birth but people, mostly northerners, whose main business was manipulating the government for artificial advantages for themselves. This view of the world, as much a folk attitude as a philosophical position, is a recurrent theme in much southern behavior.

Taylor's more important works are *Definition of Parties, or the Political Effects of the Paper System* (1794); *An Enquiry into the Principles and Tendency of Certain Public Measures* (1794); *A Defense of the Measures of the Administration of Thomas Jefferson* (1804); *Arator, Being a Series of Agricultural Essays, Practical and Political: In Sixty-Four Numbers* (1814); *An Inquiry into the Principles and Policy of the Government of the United States* (1814); *Construction Construed, and Constitutions Vindicated* (1820); *Tyranny Unmasked* (1822); and *New Views of the Constitution of the United States* (1823).

Clyde N. Wilson
University of South Carolina

M. E. Bradford, introduction to John Taylor, *Arator* (1977 reprint); Eugene T. Mudge, *The*

Social Philosophy of John Taylor of Caroline (1939); Robert E. Shalhope, *John Taylor of Caroline: Pastoral Republican* (1980). ☆

TRAIL OF TEARS
|||||||||||||||||||||||||||||||||||||||||||||

In 1838 the U.S. government uprooted some 13,000 Cherokee Indians from their land east of the Mississippi River and forced them westward into the Oklahoma territory. The 1,000-mile route they took to Oklahoma is called the Trail of Tears because of the hardships of weather, disease, and starvation that accompanied the Native Americans.

The forced migration along the Trail of Tears was a dismal journey, much of which took place in the middle of a harsh winter. Eyewitness accounts by missionaries, soldiers, government officials, and the uprooted Indians themselves describe how natives marched and suffered for hundreds of miles before reaching Oklahoma. Thousands of Native Americans died on the trip, which took them from north Georgia through middle Tennessee, southern Kentucky, and Missouri, and into present-day Oklahoma. The trip itself was only part of the harrowing experience the Indians endured in this stage of the removal. Federal troops held as many as 15,000 Cherokees in detention camps prior to the trip. Many of the detainees died of starvation or disease while in the camps.

The Trail of Tears has become a symbol for the historic oppression of Native Americans by whites, of which the forced removal of Indians to the west between 1820 and 1840 is only a part. Many southern Indians were tricked with unfamiliar legal practices or intimidated into giving up their land. The federal government demoralized the Native Americans by reducing the supply of game and negotiating separate treaties with certain tribesmen who were willing to accept white civilization. The Removal Acts of 1830 proposed the "final solution"—the exile of the southeastern Indians to the territories west of the Mississippi. At the time of the Indian removal, some Cherokees, like John Ross, advocated the move as the natives' only hope of survival; others, like John Ridge, argued for remaining in the Southeast and preserving traditional ways.

Today, the Trail of Tears has become a historic route developed by the Tennessee Department of Conservation in conjunction with the Department of Tourist Development. Along the route the tourist can see the final capitol of the Cherokee nation near Cleveland, Tenn., the only remaining stockade where the Indians were imprisoned before removal, and Andrew Jackson's home outside Nashville. The inclusion of Jackson's home, the Hermitage, is ironic because as president, Jackson was a staunch advocate of many of the brutal policies against the Indians, and he was instrumental in implementing the forced migration policy. Sixty thousand Indians were relocated west of the Mississippi under Jackson's direction.

Karen M. McDearman
University of Mississippi

Gloria Jahoda, *The Trail of Tears: The Story of the Indian Removal, 1813–1850* (1975); *Southern Exposure* (November–December 1985). ☆

TRUCKING
|||||||||||||||||||||||||||||||

Trucking culture materialized as the business of trucking transformed the way that goods were transported in the

United States. Trucking as a business began in the 1920s, after World War I had proven the commercial value of the new motorized wagons. Veterans of the European conflict and farm boys familiar with steam machinery entered the new business of trucking. Lured by travel to exotic places such as New York City, enticed by the money to be made, and drawn by the opportunity to escape the routine of farm life, many midwestern and southern young men became truckers. Although trucking as a business appeared first in the Midwest and East, trucking as a culture quickly took on southern elements, particularly in language, food, music, and religion.

The essential loneliness of trucking—one man, one truck; driving many hours at night—kept the culture out of view of mainstream America until the popularization of the Citizens Band radio during the oil embargo of 1974. National news personalities featured the cowboy loneliness and the rich, unique language of the truckers on strike.

The Confederate flag—an icon of the trucking culture

Whether from Montana or Maine, Oregon or Ohio, truckers talked to one another with southern inflections and syntax. Accurately described as a cross between an Arkansas and a west Texas dialect, this "good old boy" style captured the faddish fancy of the American public. Millions of nontruckers purchased a CB and joined in the southern subculture that promoted evasion of highway patrol radar, as well as simple camaraderie during long and lonely drives along the nation's highways. Truckers and automobile drivers alike became "good buddies," many of them attempting to copy the southern dialects. Thus, in the 1970s the American public discovered a distinctly southern subculture that had been in the making since the 1920s.

Trucking culture reflected not only southern language but also other attributes that tended to rest on a peculiarly southern base. Southern fried food appeared in truck stops across the nation. Country songs climbed the popular music charts, and Hollywood movies drew in customers as the mass media exploited the emerging southern image of trucking. New lyrics (set to old cowboy and blues melodies) extolled the virtues of truckers, while detailing the evils and stupidity of governmental regulations and the state and local police who enforced them. Movies featured good old boys breaking speed laws and easily evading potbellied, cigar-chomping southern sheriffs.

Meanwhile, another aspect of southern culture, religion, influenced trucking. Evangelical ministers, such as the Reverend Jimmy Snow, son of country-and-western singer Hank Snow, used the CB to reach lonely drivers on the road. Other ministers established mobile churches and traveled from truck stop to truck stop looking for converts.

The very media that exposed the southern influence in the trucking culture, alas, have also led to a dilution of that regional influence. Certainly truckers continue to wear traditional western clothes (jeans, cowboy boots and hats, and western shirts) and many continue to operate their rigs just the other side of the law (much as southern moonshiners have done). Yet organization of trucking associations, more efficient trucks, and massive truck stops catering to the entire traveling public have muted the rebellious and unique spirit of trucking and, by extension, the southern culture supporting it.

See also INDUSTRY: / Trucking Industry

James H. Thomas
Wichita State University

Frederick E. Danker, *Journal of Country Music* (January 1978); Jane Stern and Michael Stern, *Trucker: Portrait of the Last American Cowboy* (1975); James H. Thomas, *The Long Haul: Truckers, Truck Stops, and Trucking* (1979); D. Daryl Wyckoff, *Truck Drivers in America* (1979). ☆

UNITED DAUGHTERS OF THE CONFEDERACY (UDC)

Southern fiction frequently portrays indomitable southern women in the Civil War. Given the late 19th century's predilection for organizations, it was perhaps inevitable that real-life die-hard women who saw themselves as guardians of the Lost Cause would create the United Daughters of the Confederacy (UDC) in Nashville in September 1894. The roots of the UDC may be traced back to the wartime Ladies' Aid Societies that sprang up spontaneously throughout the South in 1861 to assist Confederate soldiers. Perhaps the earliest organized voluntarism among Victorian southern women, these societies began as sewing groups, many of them in the churches, to prepare socks, mufflers, gloves, balaclava helmets, uniforms, and blankets for Confederate soldiers. As war took its human toll, some societies changed into Women's Hospital Associations, which set up hospitals and convalescent homes for Confederate sick and wounded soldiers.

During the spring of 1866 many of these organizations reorganized as Ladies' Memorial Associations to insure proper interments for hastily buried Confederate dead, to honor their graves on 26 April (Confederate Memorial Day), and then to raise funds for monuments and statues commemorating the Lost Cause in settings ranging from courthouse squares to battlefields.

Many members of the Ladies' Memorial Associations joined the UDC when it was organized, with its founders' declared goal of obtaining an accurate history of the Confederacy. The UDC was and is a social, literary, historical, monumental, and benevolent association made up of widows, wives, mothers, sisters, and other lineal descendants of men who rendered military, civil, or other personal service to the Confederate cause.

Organized 10 September 1894, the UDC was incorporated in the District of Columbia on 18 July 1919. It has erected numerous memorials, it presents Crosses of Military Service to lineal Confederate descendants who themselves have served in later American wars, and it presents awards to outstanding service academy cadets and midshipmen. At its height in the early 20th century, the UDC totaled some 100,000 members and was a political force to be reckoned with. As the years took their toll and memories faded, its membership dwindled to about 20,000 in the 1950s; but since the Civil War Centennial a quarter of a century ago, interest has revived. Today there are about 27,000 members, including those in chapters in northern and western states, as well as in Paris and Mexico City. Associated organizations include the Sons of Confederate Veterans (SCV), founded in 1896; the Children of the Confederacy, organized in 1899; and the Military Order of the Stars and Bars, (MOSB), begun in 1938 and made up of male descendants of Confederate officers.

Cameron Freeman Napier
Montgomery, Alabama

Jerome Francis Beattie, ed., *The Hereditary Register of the United States of America* (1972); Wallace Evan Davies, *Patriotism on Parade: The Story of Veterans' and Hereditary Organizations in America, 1783–1900* (1955); Mary B. Poppenheim et al., *The History of the United Daughters of the Confederacy* (1925; reprint 1956). ☆

WASHINGTON, GEORGE

(1732–1799) U.S. president.

Washington was born into a well-established and prosperous Virginia family in 1732. By his own efforts and by his marriage to Martha Dandridge Custis he entered the ranks of the First Families of Virginia. In youth his loyalties were to Virginia and the British empire. Convinced that it was wrong for one people to have power to tax and to dominate another, he came to the forefront of the Virginia patriots.

As commander in chief of the Continental army he was one of the first to indicate that he desired independence from Britain. In the fall of 1775 he referred to America as "my country" and "my bleeding country." He gave utter allegiance thereafter to the American Republic. In the 1780s he referred to Virginia as a "middle" state rather than a southern one. He condemned the Articles of Confederation because they gave the central government insufficient power, and he was the most influential champion of the Constitution. As president he steadily and effectively toiled to assure the safety and growth of the nation. He denounced sectionalism of every sort, in particular condemning all efforts to set the emerging sections, North and South, against each other. It is fair to say that he was an ardent Federalist in his last years.

Washington was a land speculator and a farmer rather than a planter, for he turned away well before 1775 from emphasis upon tobacco growing to general husbandry. With the years he became increasingly hostile to black slavery. He declared that it ought gradually to be abolished, said that he would vote for emancipation, and arranged in his will to free his slaves and those of his wife.

John R. Alden
Duke University

John R. Alden, *George Washington: A Biography* (1984); James Thomas Flexner, *George Washington*, 4 vols. (1965–72); Douglas Southall Freeman, John A. Carroll, and Mary W. Ashworth, *George Washington: A Biography*, 7 vols. (1948–57). ☆

WHISKEY

From the throat-searing drop of moonshine fresh from the copper worm of a still to the dark amber waves of Kentucky's mellow bourbon in a silver julep cup, the quencher for a southern thirst through the years has been whiskey.

The first southern whiskey produced from corn was probably made on the James River in Virginia in a still run by Captain George Thorpe, who was killed by Indians 27 March 1622. Later Scotch-Irish settlers brought with them pot stills. Those who practiced their trade using such devices in early Pennsylvania revolted at the institution of excise taxes on their product. The crushing of the Whiskey Rebellion in 1794 proved the strength of the new government, but some hardy souls intent on the least possible government interference in their trade removed themselves to the lands that would become Kentucky and Tennessee. The rye they had used in Pennsylvania was in large part replaced by corn. And, taxed or not, the whiskey flowed. Already Kentucky had seen nearly a generation of whiskey makers.

The process of whiskey making was simple enough for an energetic small farmer. It would also bring him greater economic yield per bushel of corn than other uses, perhaps a 300 percent price increase. Besides, whiskey was easier to get to market, and age improved it.

Whiskey fueled the riverboat men, gave courage to pioneers going over the Appalachians, provided the perfect repentable sin for saved souls in the Great Awakening—in short, whiskey, its making and its drinking, its rampant enjoyment and its aftermath of misery, seemed particularly suited to the complex southern temperament from an early point. With that peculiarly southern trait of both embracing and rejecting at one time, the South both intemperately imbibed and then as vigorously espoused temperance.

Early southern seaboard residents were at first accustomed to rum or peach brandy as their hard liquor of choice. Whiskey changed this, being readily available, less expensive, and produc-

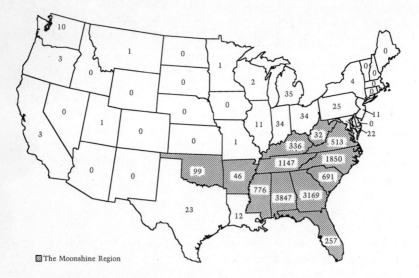

▨ The Moonshine Region

Number of Illegal Stills Seized, 1968

Source: Licensed Beverage Industries, Inc., Moonshine: The Poison Business (1971). Reprinted with permission of Distilled Spirits Council of the U.S.

ing like results. "You see no persons besotting themselves with imported spirits, wines, liquors, cordials, &c. Whisky claims to itself alone the exclusive office of sot-making," wrote Thomas Jefferson in 1823.

Nineteenth-century southerners drank enormous quantities of whiskey, both homemade and store-bought. Journal writers bragged on their capacity. Malcolm Bedford in Stark Young's Civil War novel *So Red the Rose* (1934) sips his toddy while he composes florid obituaries for his still-living friends. Other southerners seemed to reflect the dictum expressed well by singer Willie Nelson. "Whiskey," observed Willie, "makes you want to fight." Whiskey is the topic of countless popular songs in the South, such as "Whiskey River," "Whiskey and Gin Blues," "Rye Whiskey, Rye Whiskey," and "Whiskey Heaven," where "Jack Daniel's falls like rain."

It also made others wish to stop all drinking. The South experienced early periodic local temperance crusades, but it was after the Civil War (when the stigma of the organized temperance movement's ties to abolitionism was removed) that the effort began in earnest. Part of this could have been the middle-class wish to impose higher standards on those they saw as less fortunate. There was also genuine religious fervor as the Baptists, Methodists, and other evangelical sects came out strongly against drink. The result was not only the passage of the Eighteenth Amendment but years of skirmishes both before and after repeal. Will Rogers once said that Mississippians will "vote dry as long as they can stagger to the polls." All southern legislatures regularly faced the "wet or dry" issue, producing a mass of conflicting, confusing, and still-changing laws. One result was the flour-

ishing of an illegal liquor industry that exists today: the making and distributing of whiskey without government taxation.

Whiskey, to the South, is more than a drink. It is at once the problem and the solution. It adds fire not only to the orator who imbibes but also to the preacher who inveighs against it. Its production and consumption—legal or not—provide an income to thousands. It is the topic of countless songs, from hymns to ballads to country music's latest hits.

See also INDUSTRY: / Liquor Industry

Carolyn Goldsby Kolb
New Orleans, Louisiana

Gerald Carson, *The Social History of Bourbon: An Unhurried Account of Our Star-Spangled American Drink* (1963); Kim Chapin, *Fast as White Lightning: The Story of Stock Car Racing* (1981); J. C. Furnas, *The Americans: A Social History of the United States, 1587–1914* (1969); Joseph R. Gusfield, *Symbolic Crusade: Status Politics and the American Temperance Movement* (1963); Harry Kroll, *Bluegrass, Belles and Bourbon: A Pictorial History of Whisky in Kentucky* (1967); Joe Gray Taylor, *Eating, Drinking, and Visiting in the South: An Informal History* (1982). ☆

WILSON, WOODROW

(1856–1924) U.S. president.

Born in Virginia and raised in Georgia, South Carolina, and North Carolina, Woodrow Wilson was one of the South's most influential leaders in American history. His first memories, he once said, were of the news of Lincoln's election and the outbreak of the Civil War. The most important influence on his early life was his father, Joseph R. Wilson, a prominent Presbyterian minister who helped form the Presbyterian Church in the United States and ardently defended slavery. Woodrow Wilson later declared that "the only place in the country, the only place in the world, where nothing has to be explained to me is the South."

He began his education at Davidson College in North Carolina, completed his undergraduate work at Princeton, and pursued his legal training at the University of Virginia under John B. Minor. For a brief time in Atlanta he practiced law, which he found at odds with to his primary interests—history and literature. During this period he met his first wife, Ellen Axson Wilson, herself the daughter of a distinguished family of southern Presbyterian ministers. He left Atlanta to do doctoral work at the Johns Hopkins University, where he received his Ph.D. for his work *Congressional Government*.

Southern observers watched with pride as Wilson steadily achieved fame and influence as an educator, historian, man of letters, and political commentator, and Wilson's successful campaign for the White House in 1912 was due in great measure to his ability to portray himself paradoxically as both a southerner and a national figure.

In fact, he was both. He retained southern attitudes toward women throughout his life but insisted on a college education for his own daughters. He shared the racist values of American society of his day and as president (1913–21) presided over the segregation of federal agencies yet never trafficked in blatant racism. In his historical writing he lauded the South for its adherence to principle in fighting the Civil War but described both the

institution of slavery and the South's understanding of the Constitution as doomed by the progressive forces of history. He disciplined himself and his wife to drop their southern accents, although his southern political alliances brought him to national power.

Wilson's political achievements include breaking the Republican hold on the White House in the post–Civil War period and bringing the South into national politics. But perhaps the greatest irony is that this son of a region known for its parochialism should have laid the foundations for America's self-understanding in world affairs. Ellen Axson Wilson praised him for being "an infinitely better, more helpful son to her [the South] than any of those who cling so desperately to the past and the old prejudices." "I believe," she said, "you are her *greatest* son in this generation and also the one who will have the greatest claim on her gratitude."

John M. Mulder
Louisville Presbyterian
Theological Seminary

Arthur S. Link, *Journal of Southern History* (February 1970), *Wilson: The Road to the White House* (1947); John M. Mulder, *Woodrow Wilson: The Years of Preparation* (1978). ☆

YORK, ALVIN C.

(1887–1964) Soldier.

In the last days of World War I, Alvin C. York came marching out of the Argonne Forest with 132 German prisoners and a tale of individual daring unsurpassed in the nation's military annals. One of the least likely heroes in history, the Tennessee-born York was initially a conscientious objector who was drafted only after his pleas for a deferment on religious grounds were rejected. However, his army superiors persuaded him that America was fighting God's battle in the war, an argument that transformed the pacifist from the Appalachian Mountains into a veritable soldier of the Lord.

During the final Allied offensive of the conflict, York single-handedly outshot an entire German machine-gun battalion, killing 25 men in the process. His explanation that God had been with him during the fight meshed neatly with the popular attitude that American involvement in the war was truly a holy crusade, and he returned to the United States in the spring of 1919 amid a tumultuous public welcome and a flood of business offers from people eager to capitalize on the soldier's reputation. In spite of these lucrative opportunities, York decided to return to his native hamlet of Pall Mall, where he spent the rest of his life working to bring schools and other public services to his mountain neighbors.

York's Appalachian heritage was central to his popularity, because the media portrayed him as the archetypal mountain man. At a time of domestic upheaval and international uncertainty, York's pioneerlike skill with a rifle, his homespun manner, and his fundamentalist piety endeared him to millions of Americans as a kind of "contemporary ancestor" fresh from the backwoods of the southern mountains. As such, he seemed to affirm that the traditional virtues of agrarian America still had meaning in the new era. In short, York represented not what Americans were but what they wanted to think they were. He lived in one of the most rural parts of the country at a time when a majority of Americans lived in cities; he rejected riches at a time when the tenor of the nation was crassly commercial; he was pious at a time when secularism was on the rise.

For millions of people, York was the incarnation of their romanticized understanding of the nation's past when men and women supposedly lived plainer, sterner, and more virtuous lives. Ironically, although York endured as a symbol of an older America, he spent most of his adult life working to bring roads, schools, and industrial development to the mountains, changes that irrevocably altered the society he had come to represent.

David D. Lee
Western Kentucky University

Samuel K. Cowen, *Sergeant York and His People* (1922); David D. Lee, *Sergeant York: An American Hero* (1985); Thomas Skeyhill, ed., *Sergeant York: His Own Life Story and War Diary* (1928), *Sergeant York: Last of the Long Hunters* (1930). ☆

INDUSTRY

JAMES C. COBB

University of Mississippi

CONSULTANT

☆ ☆ ☆ ☆ ☆ ☆ ☆ ☆ ☆ ☆

Overleaf: Birmingham steel mill and workers' houses, 1930s

INDUSTRY AND COMMERCE

|||||||||||||||||||||||||||||||||||||||||||||||||||||||||||

The perception of the antebellum South as a plantation society and southerners as "an agricultural people" is rooted in both myth and reality. The belief that a large number of southerners were "agrarians" who shunned all industrial investments and commercial pursuits is largely rooted in myth. Prominent southerners have voiced their fears or their disdain of industrialization, but the primary influences that held back southern commerce and industry were economic, rather than cultural or political.

The traditional wisdom has been that slavery stunted the South's economy, particularly its commercial and industrial growth, by tying up the region's already scarce capital and discouraging immigration by free labor, all the while stigmatizing labor as an activity unbefitting a white person, regardless of social status. The result was a society obsessed with land and slaves and lacking in the labor, markets, money, and human energy needed to stimulate industry and commerce.

In recent years economic historians have questioned this theory. They have shown that cotton planting was a reasonably profitable endeavor. If only whites are considered, on the eve of the Civil War average wealth was almost twice as great among southerners as among their northern counterparts. Moreover, despite the planter's dominant position in the socioeconomic and political hierarchy, overall distribution of the wealth was not significantly more unbalanced south than north of the Mason-Dixon line.

Antebellum Industrialization. The antebellum South was capable of supporting considerably more industrial and commercial activity than it ever generated. In fact, annual returns from investments in southern manufacturing were often higher than the national average and as much as twice as high as those from investments in planting. Such evidence suggests either that southerners were too naive to realize they were missing a good bet by not investing in a mill or a business or that they simply succumbed to social pressures by pursuing wealth in cotton and slaves rather than in textiles, lumber, or general merchandise. Certainly, planters had no desire to surrender even a particle of their preeminence to industrialists, and they seldom forfeited an opportunity to lionize themselves as the noblest of southerners and their profession as the highest calling known to man. They were obviously nervous about a challenge to their social or political status from members of the industrial or commercial classes. Such a challenge, after all, might divide southern society and undermine the institution of slavery.

State and local policymakers rarely translated their anxieties into legislation that forbade or hindered the expansion of industry and commerce. Consequently, there were few legal impediments to the growth of the nonagricultural sector in the antebellum South's economy. Did most southerners simply fail to recognize the opportunities for profit they were forfeiting by clinging to agriculture? If not, why did they settle for returns so much lower than those they might have gained from investing in industry? The answer lies not in ignorance but in conservative investment behavior premised on the notion that the more dependable profits (in the neighborhood of 10 percent) offered by planting involved considerably less risk than the much higher profits possible in a still-uncertain manufacturing sector. Such behavior was certainly cautious but hardly irrational or abnormal.

It is unlikely that the antebellum South would ever have been industrialized on a scale comparable to the North even if its investors had been more venturesome. Climate, topography, and the slave-labor system gave the region a comparative advantage in agriculture that shaped its economic destiny. In the antebellum era most southern industry involved the processing of agricultural products and raw materials. Flour and corn milling accounted for much of this processing activity across the South, and the tobacco industry was crucial to the industrial economy of Virginia and the Carolinas. Cotton mills took advantage of the South's abundant cotton, water power, and cheap labor. Richmond's Tredegar Iron Works was the major heavy industry in a region whose entire industrial output was less than that of Pennsylvania in 1860.

So long as cotton prices were good, the South was in a position to overindulge its advantage in agriculture, but the end of the antebellum cotton boom and the slowing of the rate of growth in demand for cotton after the Civil War put the southern states well behind the vibrant northeastern and central states, which were experiencing an economic revolution in the late 19th century. With technology, labor, capital, and resources all in their favor, the northern states attracted the overwhelming majority of investments in the dynamic industries and businesses needed to sustain rapid economic growth in that period. The South, on the other hand, had little to offer industries but abundant labor, certain raw materials (particularly cotton and wood), and a fervent desire for industry.

A New South. The postbellum South's most prominent advocate of industrialization was Henry W. Grady, an Atlanta newspaperman who became famous as the orator of the New South movement. Grady preached industrialism and economic independence and stressed sectional reconciliation as a means of creating a happy marriage of northern capital with southern labor and raw materials. Although Grady promised a "New" South, he also took great pains to assuage the concerns of southern planters that industrial development would not drain off the cheap, controllable labor that was essential to the preservation of the plantation system of agriculture. Critics charged Grady with "selling out" to the planters as well as to the northern investors who sought to perpetuate an exploitive colonial relationship with the South. Although Grady and his disciples could not be exonerated on this count, he and his followers had few options. Planters remained influential enough to block or severely impede the industrial development effort if it promised to reduce their supply of cheap labor or undermine their dominance of the South's socioeconomic hierarchy. As for facilitating the further "colonization" of the South's economy, New South leaders may have had little choice given the region's resemblance to other underdeveloped regions of the world that have experienced economic growth only by offering their labor and raw materials to absentee investors at bargain rates. The South's economic destiny was less in the hands of its own leaders than at the mercy of the external resource, labor, and market factors that were at the heart of national and international growth patterns in the late 19th century.

The structure and the administration of the South's railroad system helped to shape its economic development. With nearly all the region's railroad mileage controlled by northerners by the turn of the century, highly discriminatory freight rates were the rule when shipping goods within the South. It was much cheaper, for example, to ship Arkansas cotton to Massachusetts than to South Carolina. Also, as the railroads penetrated the countryside, small crossroads towns sprang up as mercantile, processing, and marketing centers. With such excellent connections outside the region, the products of these towns of approximately 10,000 people went directly to northern cities without passing through major southern cities (with the probable exception of the regional hub city of Atlanta). As a result, the configuration of the South's railroads played a major role in retarding urban growth in the region. Meanwhile, the country store and small-town merchant occupied the pivotal position in a capital-scarce economy where cotton often served as currency. Prosperous merchants supplied everything from farm implements to face powder and often provided banking, postal, and other services, all the while serving, as David R. Goldfield noted, "as the middleman in the link between plantation and northern market."

In the South of 1900 only 18 percent of the work force was employed in pursuits unrelated to agriculture, and per capita income stood at 51 percent of the national average, exactly where it had been 20 years earlier. Industry remained largely confined to the extraction of raw materials and the elementary processing of agricultural products. Absentee owners drew away much of the income from these activities, and wages were meager. In 1910 the manufacturing payroll for the entire state of Georgia was smaller than that for the city of Cincinnati. Moreover, much of the South's nonagricultural economy was devoted to commerce rather than manufacturing. Even in a relatively industrialized city like Memphis the value of annual trade in 1900 was 10 times that for manufacturing.

The structure of the post-Reconstruction South's economy was directly related to its ultraconservative social and political climate. The region's commitment to low-wage, labor- and resource-exploitive industries required a parallel commitment to maintaining social and political stability and an austere, rigidly conservative government disinclined to regulate or tax too heavily or to see any side but management's in a labor-management dispute.

Late-19th- and early-20th-century economic development helped to shape southern society and culture. The commercial classes dominated policymaking in southern cities, and their ties to the agricultural and processing activities of the countryside made them wary of any alterations of the status quo likely to create instability in an economy based on labor control, low taxes, and minimal government interference. Tensions were always present, but during the late 19th and much of the 20th century the urban South accommodated itself to the politics of the countryside.

Atop the South's agriculturally oriented system of commerce sat a sinister nabob described by Ralph McGill as the "small-town rich man" who "according to his geographic location," owned the gin, the cotton warehouse, the tobacco warehouse, or the turpentine works. He also owned the town's largest store, selling feeds, fertilizer, and other farm supplies. Often, he served as a director of the local bank. He controlled local credit and was on a first-name basis with his governor, his legislator, his senators, and his congressman. Paranoid about maintaining a large pool of cheap labor loyal only to him, he hated New Deal relief programs and union organizers with equal passion. Because he dominated the South's rurally biased state political systems, the small-town rich man was an agent of inertia representing a large segment of the region's business and industrial capitalists.

The Crusade for Economic Development. Despite the region's social and political stagnation, the South's efforts to industrialize continued unabated as the 20th century unfolded. The almost religious fervor of the crusade for economic growth revealed itself in the "Atlanta Spirit," an urban booster ethos that rallied the leaders of southern cities to intense, competitive crusading for growth during the 1920s. Commercial and civic leaders, black spokesmen, and even the Ku Klux Klan joined the hunt for more smokestacks. Any industry was better than no industry to these zealots, but not so to the Vanderbilt

Agrarians, a group of 12 conservative writers whose views were published in 1930 in *I'll Take My Stand*, a spirited critique of industrialism typified by John Crowe Ransom's assertion that "the dignity of personality is gone as soon as the man from the farm enters the factory door." The Agrarians offered a Depression-ridden South a stout defense of southern traditionalism but no real alternative to the impoverished, benighted society that dependence on agriculture had bequeathed to the region. Most southerners who knew about the Agrarians at all probably would have, for once, agreed with H. L. Mencken, who ridiculed them for "spinning lavender fancies under a fig tree."

The Depression era saw the campaign for growth intensify and expand. The Atlanta Spirit spread from the cities to the small towns in response to a series of shocks beginning with the boll weevil invasion of the 1920s. Plummeting cotton yields drove both landowners and sharecroppers from the land and posed a serious threat to the agriculturally oriented commerce and industry that was the mainstay of the southern economy. As Georgia's cotton belt played unhappy host to the boll weevil at its hungriest, the state amended its constitution to allow tax exemptions for new industries. Coming on the heels of the boll weevil, the Depression intensified the insect's impact, forcing both planter and sharecropper off the land. Ironically, the New Deal's Agricultural Adjustment Act, which paid farmers to produce less, further reinforced the trend toward farm consolidation and reduced farm labor requirements. The dwindling farm population posed a serious threat to the merchants, lawyers, bankers, and other professionals who comprised the small-town middle class because demand for goods and services was certain to shrink proportionally. Out-migration of displaced farm labor might lead ultimately to a similar fate for many members of the small-town middle class if a means could not be found to provide alternative employment (and income) to a burgeoning surplus labor force. Industrialization seemed the most likely solution to the problem, especially since concerns over any potential shortage of agricultural labor had been greatly reduced.

In its zeal for payrolls the small-town South prostrated itself at the feet of any and all industrialists who looked its way. The enterprising employer who required no more than a building and a work force could usually get the former for nothing and the latter for not much more. Subsidies for buildings were raised by public subscription or mandatory deductions from already meager employee paychecks. Tax exemptions, legal or not, were seldom difficult to secure, and local law enforcement officials were prepared to discourage any union organizers who might come to town. Not surprisingly, some companies exploited an already advantageous situation by hiring unpaid or barely paid trainees, or moving almost overnight to any industry-hungry community ready to raise the ante. Out of this chaotic scramble for payrolls came more organized, state-sanctioned programs to attract industry, most notably Mississippi's "Balance Agriculture with Industry" (BAWI) program (1936–58), which used tax-free municipal bonds to finance plant construction, and Louisiana's organized tax-exemption plan for new industries. Both approaches spread across the South and ultimately much of the nation. Although designed to make southern communities more attractive to industry, subsidy programs only confirmed the existing pattern of industrial development based on low-wage industries because such operations, attracted to the South initially by their need to save on labor costs, were also the ones most likely to be swayed by an opportunity to save on construction and tax costs. Although the old agricultural system was yielding to mechanization and consolidation, the traditional pattern of industrial development remained fundamentally unchanged.

The concentration of southern manufacturing in small-town and rural locations helped to minimize the cultural and demographic impact of industrialization in the region. As Dixie's most industrialized state, North Carolina showed a population in 1900 that was less than 10 percent urban. As technological advances slowed, the southern textile industry became less likely to spawn the rapid urbanization that had accompanied industrialization in the North. Moreover, after 1900 the proliferation of electric power and the automobile allowed even greater dispersal of manufacturing facilities. Industrialists chose locations where they could draw on a large-scale surplus of underemployed agricultural workers eager to

Inside a Cherryville, N.C., textile mill, 1908

work for steady, if meager, wages. Such workers were also prepared to commute long distances in order to continue to work their farms. Because they were not forced to relocate in industrial communities, they could maintain the cultural ties and lifestyles associated with life on the farm.

Worker-farmers sacrificed much of the independence and periodic leisure they had known when they were only farmers. Many of them took night-shift jobs so that their days would be free to work their fields, the result being that they actually held two jobs. Ironically, employers justified the substandard wages they paid such workers on the ground that these employees were supplementing their paychecks with their farm incomes and therefore needed less than their counterparts elsewhere in the country. The same was true for farm wives who were actively recruited for work in small "sewing" (apparel) plants. Not only did they live on a farm that supplied much of their food, but they were merely working to supplement their husband's farm, or farm and industrial, income and should be willing to accept even lower wages than those paid farm-based male workers. At the same time she was being underpaid, the wage-earning farm wife was being overworked. She not only performed her eight-hour job at "the plant" but kept up with her cooking, cleaning, and canning just as she had when she was "only" a farm wife. As the profitability of farming declined and government subsidies of the New Deal and post–New Deal era encouraged farmers to farm less, or not at all, the former head of the household was often reduced to the status of "a go-getter" whose principal duty each day was to take his wife to work and "go get 'er."

Effects of World War II. Although much of the South's new industry continued to choose rural and small-town locations, World War II did more to alter the course and pace of southern economic development than any other event since the Civil War. The war's greatest contribution consisted of a large helping of federal money for a traditionally capital-starved region. More than $4 billion went into military facilities and perhaps as much as $5 billion into defense plants. The result was a 40 percent increase in the South's industrial capacity. Per capita income tripled during the 1940s, leaving southerners with enough disposable income to make them attractive potential consumers for a number of market-oriented industries that had previously found the South's consuming capacity too puny to justify the location of a production or distribution facility in the region. Automobile assembly and parts plants, for example, began to spring up in the Atlanta vicinity as executives realized the growing potential of the southeastern market.

With its rapidly mechanizing agricultural sector and its consumer markets expanded by World War II, the South became a region even more firmly committed to industry. The terrible memories of the 1930s spurred a renewed commitment to industrialization and a determination not to surrender wartime gains. All the southern states strengthened and extended their development programs, and more state and local leaders became involved. The governor became the state's supersalesman, and no gubernatorial aspirant dared to neglect economic development as a campaign pledge. Growth indicators suggested that this vigorous development effort was paying off, but the more rapid expansion of the post–World War

II era was primarily the result of basic economic considerations related to costs, markets, and demographic shifts.

The stunted neocolonial economy of the South had preserved lower labor and general operating costs even as the war-born boom stimulated consumer buying power. Meanwhile, the traditional pattern of out-migration gradually reversed itself in the 1950s, augmenting the South's traditionally high birthrate and enhancing the region's market attraction.

As the South was experiencing its long-awaited economic boom, the industrial North was beginning to show definite signs of decay. Mounting labor and tax costs, technological obsolescence, labor agitation, rising crime, and an increased government regulatory role were among the considerations that led industrialists to forego expansion or new investments in the North in favor of a new plant in the South. As investment capital moved out, so did a number of residents, many of whom found new homes and jobs below the Mason-Dixon line.

By 1960 the trends set in motion by World War II were readily apparent. Between 1940 and 1960 the South's population had shifted from 65 percent rural to 58 percent urban. In the latter year only 10 percent of the population still worked in agriculture, while 21 percent worked in manufacturing. Average per capita income stood at 76 percent of the national average.

The Sunbelt Era. Although World War II marked the beginning of the South's economic takeoff, not until the end of the 1960s did the region begin to bask in the glow of "Sunbelt" prosperity. Between 1970 and 1976 the South enjoyed a net population gain of nearly 3 million. In contrast to the past, by the mid-1970s

those moving into the region were significantly younger and better educated than the national average. The South's climate and relatively uncomplicated lifestyle were also pulling in retirees whose fixed incomes made lower living costs important. The South finally had its all-important nucleus of middle-class consumers. Industrial output and employment skyrocketed. Houston alone accounted for 79,000 new jobs in 1979. Much of Houston's growth was energy related, but the bulk of the region's expansion in the 1970s came in services such as retail trade, real estate, and banking.

Much of the industrial and commercial capital invested in the South had traditionally come from outside the region, and in the Sunbelt era an increasing amount came from outside the nation as well. Foreign investors moved in to take advantage of expanded markets and all of the region's traditional enticements—cheap, nonunion labor; low taxes; cooperative government; and a generally lower cost of living. By the end of the decade, the Carolina Piedmont was spotted with plants from Germany, France, and Japan, to name but a few. The Nissan truck plant at Smyrna, Tenn., attracted considerable attention as a prime example of the way in which Japanese management styles could be transferred to an American plant. Ironically, the "one big happy family" approach used by the Japanese bore a striking resemblance to the paternalism practiced in the cotton mills of the late-19th- and early-20th-century South.

Like many of their domestic predecessors, the foreign employers hoped to avoid unionization of their workers, and toward that end they provided wages and benefits that were better than the local and regional average, although generally still below national norms. The foreign executive and managerial personnel who moved into southern communities often regarded the local populace with curiosity and friendly amusement, but the culture gap appeared to narrow quickly as the loyalty of the work force and the hospitality of the community turned "foreigners" into southerners whose accents simply happened to be more distinctive than those of the natives. The Spartanburg, S.C., area attracted such a diverse mixture of foreign plants that Swiss rolls with Viennese jam soon became as much of a local delicacy as biscuits and redeye gravy.

The Sunbelt, however, was not always aglow. The Sunbelt could be more accurately described as an area splotched by "sun spots" with large areas of shade in between. High unemployment remained the rule in states like Mississippi with large concentrations of rural blacks. Such areas had little attraction for many industries, which appeared to shun locations with significant black populations.

Meanwhile, even in fast-growing areas, Sunbelt growth left many of the region's old problems unsolved. In cities like Atlanta, skyscrapers and an intimidating futuristic airport created the impression of prosperity, but the developed downtown had little to offer low-income blacks except custodial employment. In the meantime, rapid commercial growth and the mania for taller, more ostentatious buildings left no room for an adequate supply of low-cost housing in the downtown area. Although blacks shared but little in the expansion of Atlanta's commerce, by 1980 the city's population was two-thirds black. Across the South, cities continued to

attract blacks who opted for a disproportionately small share of the urban boom rather than struggle for subsistence in rural areas where the boom had yet to be felt.

Meanwhile, middle-class whites continued to flee the urban South, leaving the unemployed and underemployed of both races to inhabit cities that were commercial meccas during the day and hotbeds of crime at night. Houston, the acknowledged growth leader, was also the Sunbelt's homicide capital, and Atlanta became known as a wonderful place to visit if one could do so without having to venture out onto the streets.

Economic Development and Southern Culture. In 1973 country songwriter Bobby Braddock proudly reported his observations of "wooded parks and big skyscrapers where once stood red clay hills and cotton fields" and "sons and daughters of sharecroppers drinking scotch and making business deals." Not everyone shared Braddock's enthusiasm for a "risen" South. Along with the concern of some southerners that Sunbelt progress had not touched many areas sufficiently to solve their problems came the fear that this progress was creating cultural problems of its own. Many of those who were once critical of the South for its backwardness now lamented its rapid growth, expressing the belief that a more prosperous South would soon cease to be the South at all. Marshall Frady feared a "cultural lobotomy" as fast-food restaurants, discount stores, and industrial parks spread over the landscape.

Frady's concern was, of course, not a new one. The Agrarians had already expressed the same fear by the end of the 1920s. Post-Reconstruction literature had celebrated the South's "pastoral" tradition, as opposed to the New South creed espoused by Henry W. Grady and others. In the face of the boosterism that enveloped the South after World War I, writers like Thomas Wolfe and William Faulkner decried the materialism of the booster ethos and expressed particular regret at the conquest of the South's wilderness areas. Erskine Caldwell had the lowly Jeeter Lester in *Tobacco Road* express his preference for farming, even sharecropping, over work in a cotton mill. After World War II had accelerated the South's economic growth and spurred industrialization and the mechanization of agriculture, Flannery O'Connor wrote a short story about a "displaced person" who brings mechanical, but impersonal, Yankee-like precision and skill to a rundown Georgia farm only to have his contribution rejected by the inhabitants, who allow him to be flattened by a runaway tractor.

The same concern was reflected in country music, where examples of a fear and loathing of the alien, "northernizing" influences of the city and the factory and a preference for the idyllic agrarian lifestyle abounded. Songs like "Cotton Mill Colic" and "Weave Room Blues" depicted the dreariness of industrial life, while "Detroit City" and "Streets of Baltimore" presented the northern city as a heartless and foreboding place.

The proliferation of shopping centers and chain stores had a homogenizing effect on the small-town South, where restaurant cuisine soon featured corn dogs and tacos instead of corn bread and turnip greens. Unknown and impersonal salesclerks and two pieces of identification to pay by check were other seemingly inevitable concomitants to progress. Many observers insisted that southerners had managed to some extent

to humanize the technological and commercial advances that had bred anonymity and alienation elsewhere, but such contentions were usually more impressionistic than objective. It was difficult to identify what part, if any, of the region's response to economic modernization was clearly southern instead of the predictable reaction of any traditional rural and small-town society to dramatic changes in its means of production and exchange.

On the other hand, opinion surveys of better-educated, more affluent southerners showed economic progress was finally eroding the racism, traditionalism, and authoritarianism that constituted some of the darker elements of the South's traditional value structure. Still, the young beneficiaries of the region's economic progress were the most likely of all southerners to prize their identities as southerners and to express a preference for foods, friends, and an overall lifestyle identifiable as southern. Paradoxically, while economic progress appeared to be undermining certain traditional values, it was also reinforcing the southernness of those whose imminent baptism in the economic mainstream posed the threat of a rootless, anonymous existence.

Although it was clearly true that in fast-growing areas young southerners were being drawn into mainstream mass culture and even their parents and grandparents were being affected to a lesser extent, the notion that factories, skyscrapers, and interstate highways had "northernized" the South rested on the assumption that there were distinct value differences between industrial and agrarian societies and that, as industrialization proceeded, industrial values were bound to triumph.

For many years liberal social scientists and journalists had seen agrarian traditionalism and economic progress as arch enemies, the former being the villain in the ongoing saga of southern backwardness, with the latter cast in the role of oft-thwarted would-be savior. In the widely accepted scenario, if southern traditionalism could be weakened sufficiently to allow economic modernization to gain a foothold, its benevolent and progressive influences would then overwhelm the vestiges of racism and reactionary politics and transform Dixie into an enlightened liberal society like the industrial Northeast. Ironically, however, the South's economic emergence not only failed to follow this widely accepted model, it practically turned it on its head. The "favorable business climate" so vital to the Sunbelt South's fabled economic success story was actually rooted in the historically conservative social and political atmosphere long condemned as the nemesis of southern progress. Cheap, intimidated labor, low taxes, and a cooperative rather than meddlesome government—all of these were both trademarks of the traditionalist, plantation South and keys to the Sunbelt South's appeal to business and industrial investors. The South's belated economic emergence demonstrated that the "value gap" between agrarian and industrial-commercial societies had been greatly exaggerated. The experience of the Sunbelt South also had profound implications for those who prescribed economic modernization as a panacea for the problems of underdeveloped nations, particularly those who continued to expect American investors to sponsor progressive reform and the overall democratization of these societies.

Businessmen and industrialists fleeing northern locations were actually running away from labor activism, government supervision, and mounting tax and living costs. They were, therefore, generally opposed to any changes likely to introduce such conditions in their new southern locations. But what of the long-awaited middle class swelled by the migration of executives and managers? Would not this new "white-collar" class become a force for innovation and improvement in government and public services and facilities?

In the post–World War II years the South's business and professional middle class, fed by more rapid commercial and industrial expansion, played an increasingly active role in promoting social and political change in the region. Immediately after the war, young veterans returning to the South's business and professional ranks led a series of "GI Revolts" that overthrew local political rings in urban areas and small towns across the South. These political uprisings represented the first wave of a long-awaited assault on a political structure built around an agricultural system rooted in the rural, small-town South and presided over by the small-town rich man.

Urban businessmen pushed for slum clearance, mass transit, and expansion of public facilities and services. In cities like Atlanta, Dallas, and Charlotte, business leaders became the reluctant advocates of racial moderation, and although their efforts seldom extended beyond the promotion of tokenism, the importance of their intervention was underscored by the ugly events in the 1950s and 1960s in Birmingham and New Orleans where the business elite failed to act vigorously enough, soon enough. The growth of the business and professional classes also paralleled the emergence of a viable Republican political alternative in the traditionally Democratic South.

Middle-class expansion clearly did bring some major changes to the South in the post–World War II period, but the impact of this expansion was not as far-reaching as had once been predicted. Business-inspired political reforms tried to create conditions favorable to efficient operation and rapid expansion of industrial and commercial enterprises. Government became more efficient and generally less corrupt but remained fiscally conservative and especially frugal in the social welfare arena. In Atlanta and elsewhere business boosters patted themselves on the back for urban renewal, freeway, and mass-transit projects, but their enthusiasm for low-cost public housing was lukewarm at best. Tax structures remained quite favorable to business and industry. The effective business tax rate stood below 60 percent of the national average, while the regressive sales tax was grossly overworked. The underutilization of tax potential left high-growth areas facing the dilemma of keeping taxes low enough to please business and industry without sacrificing the expanded services that a burgeoning population and revived economy seemed to demand.

The rise of two-party politics had been seen as a genuine plus for southern blacks because they seemed likely to represent the balance of power between the Democratic and Republican camps. As it emerged in the wake of the Goldwater campaign of 1964, however, southern Republicanism fused a business-oriented fiscal conservatism with an appeal to discontented white Democrats based on opposition to social programs and government intervention in behalf of blacks. The result was a virtual write-off of black voters by the GOP in the South and a reciprocal response that compelled southern blacks to work within a Democratic party whose white leaders regarded them with unease and whose white voters declined to support them when they appeared on the ballot. With the white middle class flocking to the GOP banner and working-class whites still unenthusiastic about a biracial political coalition, blacks failed to reap the anticipated benefits of two-party politics in the South.

In sum, the expansion of the business and commercial middle class fed many of the changes that marked the post–World War II years, but the growth of the middle class failed to spark the rapid social and political transformation many had predicted. The failure of the southern bourgeoisie to sponsor more dramatic change was due in large part to the region's lack of a unified, upwardly mobile working class capable of forcing the middle class to support more far-reaching reforms in the interest of maintaining overall stability in southern society. The South's working class remained largely unorganized and hesitant about class-oriented political action. Significant intergenerational progress left southern workers reluctant to challenge a system that they seemed to feel had rewarded them reasonably well. In the absence of pressure from below, the South's middle class was left to use its influence to create and maintain the economic and living conditions it preferred. Many social scientists had predicted that a bona fide middle class would demand drastic improvement in education and other public services, but white-collar southerners declined to sponsor such improvements, opting instead for the short-run enjoyment of the lighter demands placed on them by the

South's conservative tax climate and minimal service and social welfare commitments.

The story of the development of commerce and industry in the South suggests the difficulty of predicting the outcome of one society's economic development on the basis of another's. For many years the Marxian perspective drew on the experience of Western Europe to identify certain inevitable social, cultural, and political concomitants of economic progress. American scholars buttressed this notion with the experience of the industrial Northeast, which they viewed as the epitome of the modern, enlightened liberal capitalist society.

Fascinated with the North's "success story," many American scholars underestimated the technological, demographic, and resource factors that accounted for the economic, social, and cultural differences that separated the North and the South. The South's persistence as a distinctive region was surprising largely because so many scholars and other observers had assumed that economic modernization had certain universal results. In reality, the South's experience with economic transformation, though distinctive, was hardly remarkable. No society has ever modernized economically in precisely the same fashion as another because the same set of social, cultural, historical, and economic circumstances is never in place in two truly distinct societies. The South of industrial parks, skyscrapers, and fast-food emporiums bore scant resemblance to the South of planters, slaves, or sharecroppers, but its elusive identity still reflected the influences of an intense and complex history and a cultural heritage that had not only withstood but had shaped its economic development.

See also AGRICULTURE: Country Store; / Boll Weevil; BLACK LIFE: Migration, Black; Workers, Black; HISTORY AND MANNERS: Great Depression; New Deal; World War II; LITERATURE: Agrarianism in Literature; / Caldwell, Erskine; Faulkner, William; O'Connor, Flannery; Wolfe, Thomas; MYTHIC SOUTH: New South Myth; / Agrarians, Vanderbilt; Mencken's South; POLITICS: County Politics; Ideology, Political; Partisan Politics; Taxing and Spending; RECREATION: Tourism; SCIENCE AND MEDICINE: Aerospace; URBANIZATION articles; WOMEN'S LIFE: Workers' Wives; Working Women

James C. Cobb
University of Mississippi

Fred Bateman and Thomas Weiss, *A Deplorable Scarcity: The Failure of Industrialization in the Slave Economy* (1981); Reinhard Bendix, *Comparative Studies in Society and History* (April 1967); Dwight B. Billings, *Planters and the Making of a "New South": Class, Politics, and Development in North Carolina, 1865–1900* (1979); James C. Cobb, *Industrialization and Southern Society, 1877–1984* (1984), *The Selling of the South: The Southern Crusade for Industrial Development, 1936–1980* (1982); Pete Daniel, *Agricultural History* (July 1981), *Standing at the Crossroads: Southern Life in the Twentieth Century* (1986); Ronald D. Eller, *Miners, Millhands and Mountaineers: The Modernization of the Appalachian South* (1982); Paul M. Gaston, *The New South Creed: A Study in Southern Mythmaking* (1970); David R. Goldfield, *Cotton Fields and Skyscrapers: Southern City and Region, 1607–1980* (1982); Emory Q. Hawk, *Economic History of the South* (1934); Broadus Mitchell and George S. Mitchell, *The Industrial Revolution in the New South* (1930); Wayne Mixon, *Southern Writers and the New South Movement, 1865–1913* (1980); Gerald D. Nash, *Journal of Southern History* (August 1966); William H. Nicholls, *Southern Tradition and Regional Progress* (1960); William N. Parker, *Southern Economic Jour-*

nal (April 1980); Roger L. Ransom and Richard Sutch, *One Kind of Freedom: The Economic Consequences of Emancipation (1977)*; Robert S. Starobin, *Industrial Slavery in the Old South* (1970); Jonathan M. Wiener, *American Historical Review* (October 1979), *Social Origins of the New South: Alabama, 1860–1885* (1978). ☆

Antebellum Industry

||||||||||||||||||||||||||||||||||||||||||||||||||||

The distinctive qualities of business and industry in the Old South have been obscured by the pervasive shadow of the plantation. The roar of a blast furnace or the din of a cotton factory were more likely to jar the southern imagination than to capture it, given the South's traditional idealization of itself as a pastoral paradise. Much less specialized than their northern peers, southern factory owners often blended their careers with those of planter and politician. Because they owned a disproportionate share of the region's surplus wealth, planters who themselves did not become businessmen often invested capital in the industrial expansion that did occur. If planters and businessmen managed and financed this expansion, the established social and economic imperatives predetermined that slaves would turn the wheels of industry just as surely as they picked the South's cotton. In fact, the use of slave labor was the most distinctive characteristic of southern industry.

Tobacco factories relied on slave labor almost exclusively. Two centers of production dominated the market, the eastern district of Virginia and North Carolina and the western district of Kentucky. In the eastern district many tobacco-factory slaves were hired hands; however, the employers also owned a sizable proportion of their workers. The number of slave workers—either owned or hired—at tobacco factories in the district was always large, totaling 12,843 by 1860.

Hemp production represented another leading industry of the Old South. During the 18th century Virginia hemp became a major staple from which osnaburg, linsey woolsey, linen, rope, and sail were manufactured. Many Virginia planters, such as Robert Carter of Nomini Hall, erected small establishments for the commercial production of cloth and, even in these first small transitionary shops between the homespun and the factory stages, slaves spun and wove the finished products. During the Revolutionary War numerous slaves worked at Virginia's public ropewalk and similar establishments. By the turn of the 19th century, however, the center of the American hemp industry had shifted westward to Kentucky, where the fiber became a staple of major importance. In fact, without hemp slavery might not have flourished in Kentucky. By the Civil War nearly 200 Kentucky hemp factories utilized 5,000 bondsmen. At the same time, another 2,500 slave operatives toiled in the hemp factories of Missouri.

Southern salt production was centered primarily in the Kanawha River Valley of western Virginia. The constant demand for this vital food preservative led to a steadily increasing capital investment in its manufacture. Between 1810 and 1850 the industry grew dramatically; and as production increased, the slave population grew to 3,140 in 1850. Because so few bondsmen resided in the district, surplus hands from eastern Virginia and Kentucky formed the backbone of the labor force at the Kanawha saltworks.

The South possessed an abundance of forest resources. Out of the Mississippi and Louisiana swamps black bondsmen chopped, trimmed, and rafted cypress to New Orleans and Natchez, where still other slaves operated the steam-powered sawmills that could be found in most southern cities. These mills became sizable operations, frequently employing more than 100 slaves. Many black slaves disappeared into southern swamps for months at a time to cut wooden shingles and barrel staves. On the eve of the Civil War most of the 16,000 men who labored in the region's lumbering operations were slaves. Similarly, the naval-stores industry relied on blacks almost entirely. The industry was centered in the Carolinas, an area that produced over 90 percent of the nation's tar and turpentine in 1850. Large turpentiners such as Daniel W. Jordan of North Carolina utilized slave work forces totaling 200 or more in 1850. By 1860 the South's turpentiners worked 15,000 bondsmen.

Southern fisheries yielded a very important protein supplement to the diet of slaves and masters alike, and exports of the product reached significant, if yet undetermined, proportions. The famous traveler Frederick Law Olmsted observed that the fishing industry constituted a "source of considerable wealth." Like most industries, fisheries also employed "mainly negroes, slave and free." By 1861 upwards of 20,000 slaves operated fisheries in the region.

Although the South lagged far behind the North in internal improvements, the region's turnpikes, bridges, canals, levees, railroads, city sewers, and water-lines were all built by slave labor. Probably a total of 20,000 slaves toiled on the southern railroads during the antebellum period. Blacks also frequently worked in shipyards (Frederick Douglass being the most famous) and labored by the hundreds in southern brickyards and by the thousands in the small local gristmills that ground flour throughout the South. Commercial mills, such as the Gallego and Haxall mills (the world's largest) of Richmond, Va., operated with slave manpower. Throughout the South Carolina and Georgia Tidewater, hundreds of slaves toiled at the rice mills concentrated in that area. Likewise, Louisiana and Texas sugar mills worked bonded labor exclusively.

Few nonagricultural occupations in the Old South utilized slaves so universally and over such an extended period of time as the production of iron and the mining of coal. For a half century prior to the American Revolution, Maryland and Virginia iron dominated the colonial export market. Although the Chesapeake region lost its national preeminence after the Revolution, within the South it remained the most important single center for the production of iron. At least 65 Maryland and Virginia ironworks during the colonial era and about 80 during the antebellum period utilized thousands of slave laborers. Similarly, the eastern Virginia coalfield yielded the major supply of coal for homes and industries along the Atlantic Coast, from the development of the first commercial mine in the 1760s until the 1840s, when railroads made it economically feasible to develop the enormous reserves of bituminous coal in western Virginia and Pennsylvania. Until the late 1850s, however, when the Alabama and Tennessee fields assumed a minor importance, commercial coal mining in the South was confined almost exclusively to Virginia. A minimum of 40 coal companies in the Richmond Coal Basin employed several thousand slave workers.

With the growth of southern industry, slaveowners found themselves caught on the horns of a dilemma: which was the best form of labor, black slave or free white? More than simply a question of labor allocation, the ensuing debate reflected a mixture of economic, political, and social anxieties about the nature of southern society. Extensive industrialization threatened the planters' way of life. There was a relative loss of control over blacks in the more fluid industrial setting, but planters had even less control over a free white industrial proletariat. In practice, however, the perennial labor shortage forced southern manufacturers to employ any kind of available labor, and frequently that meant a "mixed" labor force of free whites, slaves, and free blacks.

See also AGRICULTURE: / Naval Stores; Tobacco Culture; SOCIAL CLASS: / Coal Miners; Timber Workers; Tobacco Workers

Ronald L. Lewis
University of Delaware

Ronald L. Lewis, *Coal, Iron, and Slaves: Industrial Slavery in Maryland and Virginia, 1715–1865* (1979); James E. Newton and Ronald L. Lewis, eds., *The Other Slaves: Mechanics, Artisans, and Craftsmen* (1978); Frederick Law Olmsted, *A Journey in the Seaboard Slave States, with Remarks on Their Economy* (1859); Robert S. Starobin, *Industrial Slavery in the Old South* (1970). ☆

Black Business
|||||||||||||||||||||||||||||||||||||||||

See BLACK LIFE: Business, Black

Civil Rights and Business
|||||||||||||||||||||||||||||||||||||||||||||||||||||||||||||||||||

The civil rights movement of the 1950s and 1960s represented a major departure in southern history. In accommodating itself to that movement's assaults on white supremacy, the South took a giant step toward moving into the mainstream of American society and culture. That step was possible because of an erosion in traditional values that had been under way in the South for three-quarters of a century.

Out of the trauma of defeat in the Civil War, southern businessmen and publicists forged a new ideology to guide the South in its quest to rejoin the national family. Promising to build a New South from the ashes of defeat, the sponsors of this program proposed an end to southern hostility toward the North, antipathy to industrialization, and the more virulent expressions of racism in the region. Although by no means a dominant mode of thought at the time of its formulation in the 1870s and 1880s, the New South ethic steadily gained adherents in succeeding decades. It blossomed into the business progressivism of the 1920–50 period, laying a foundation for the triumph of commercial and industrial values that was a major by-product of the civil rights movement.

W. J. Cash argued eloquently in *The Mind of the South* in 1941 that the Old South did not die with the Civil

War; indeed, Old South values were strengthened and confirmed by that most tragic of American conflicts. Nor did these values succumb under the concerted assaults of the New South prophets, or even at the hands of those prophets' heirs, the business progressives. When Harry Ashmore proclaimed their demise in 1958 with his *Epitaph for Dixie*, many skeptics took a quick look across the South and declared it was not true.

The civil rights movement heralded the triumph of a new set of values in the South, values that had been stirring beneath the surface and growing imperceptibly for years, values that finally emerged dominant—to the surprise of many southerners—in the heat of the civil rights struggle. Simply stated, the desire for white supremacy at last yielded primacy in southern thought to the desire for progress.

The South's cities were the battlegrounds for most of the region's civil rights struggles, and the cities were dominated, as always, by small groups of economic or business elites. The degree to which these elites had accepted commercial and industrial values, or, in other words, the degree to which they were willing to place the goal of economic progress above the goal of maintaining white supremacy, determined the nature of their cities' responses to the civil rights assault on traditional southern race relations. From the quintessential New South city of Atlanta—the city that was "too busy to hate"—to the fine old southern community of St. Augustine—where violence and extremism abounded—the South's cities ranged across the spectrum from progressive to traditional. In most of these cities, after the dust had settled from the initial shock of disbelief and the occasional abdication of power to the extremists, the businessmen regained control of their communities and worked with varying degrees of enthusiasm to preserve their cities' progressive images. In city after city, from Norfolk to Tampa to Birmingham to Dallas, as the economic impact of yielding to extremism and violence in Little Rock and New Orleans became clear, the business elites threw their influence behind the desegregation efforts in an attempt to shield their cities from this very real threat to economic growth and progress. This is not to say that the businessmen became advocates of the civil rights cause or champions of racial equality; in most cases, in fact, the businessmen worked to yield a minimum of change and to maintain control in their own hands. They did, however, become public advocates of the dreaded changes in southern race relations, and they used their influence to guarantee acceptance of the changes in their communities.

Social scientists often note that the city has traditionally functioned as an agent of change and as a catalyst for reform, and the South's cities clearly performed these functions for the region in the 1950s and 1960s. Social scientists also argue that change must always be preceded by establishing the respectability of the proposed new ideas, and this was the function of the South's businessmen; in becoming reluctant advocates of the fundamental alteration of southern racial patterns that the civil rights movement demanded, the southern business elites led the way toward acceptance of a new pattern of thought in the South. Southern leaders would never have capitulated to such fundamental changes in their "way of life" if they had not believed—because of unremitting federal and activist pressures—that the changes were inevitable.

For a brief time, southern business leaders allowed themselves to believe they could maintain the traditional pattern of the South's race relations at the same time they pursued industrialization and progress; the civil rights movement made them realize they had to choose. In choosing, they consciously accepted a new ordering of their values and priorities, placing economic imperatives above racial ones. At last, the "common resolve indomitably maintained" that the South should preserve white supremacy yielded to a new resolve to share in the nation's prosperity. In short, the civil rights movement brought to fruition a revolution in the southern businessman's values.

See also BLACK LIFE: Freedom Movement, Black; LAW: Civil Rights Movement; MEDIA: Civil Rights and Media; URBANIZATION articles on cities

Elizabeth Jacoway
University of Arkansas
at Little Rock

Harry Ashmore, *Epitaph for Dixie* (1958); Numan Bartley, *The Rise of Massive Resistance: Race and Politics in the South during the 1950s* (1969); Blaine A. Brownell and David R. Goldfield, *The City in Southern History: The Growth of Urban Civilization in the South* (1977); William Chafe, *Civilities and Civil Rights: Greensboro, North Carolina, and the Black Struggle for Freedom* (1980); Paul M. Gaston, *The New South Creed: A Study in Southern Mythmaking* (1970); Elizabeth Jacoway and David R. Colburn, eds., *Southern Businessmen and Desegregation* (1982). ☆

"Colony," South as

|||||||||||||||||||||||||||||||||||||||||||||||||||||

From Jamestown to Fort Sumter there was a three-way conflict over exactly who would control the output of southern labor, white and black. The British crown attempted, sporadically, to gain control of the southern surplus of goods for itself or at least for its merchant friends. The commercial interests of the northern colonies, later states, wanted to control the surplus, whereas the southern planters thought it would be appropriate to keep it close to home. As long as the institution of slavery existed, the southern planters could explore strategies to maintain high prices partly through low labor costs. Once slavery and its political power were destroyed, it was hardly to be expected that a new system of high wages would replace it.

In this view, then, the colonial position of the South was first defined in the explicit establishment of the slave system. As in many "settler colonies" the planters of the South attempted to avoid the losses of unequal exchange with other areas and to keep the surplus of produced goods at home. In these efforts the planters were extremely sensitive to the pitfalls of a colonial status, they advanced the cause of the American Revolution, and they subsequently propounded an ideology of southern nationalism. Their ultimate failure left the South in the late 19th and early 20th centuries in its most clearly colonial situation.

The treatment thus far of the South as a colony helps to reconcile conflicting views of the colonial status of the region. On the one hand, those historians who have tended to label the South a colony have emphasized the striking sensitivity of southern leadership to symptoms of colonial status, e.g., low levels of urbanization, specialization in agriculture, and a poor system of transportation. On the other hand, those who have denied the colonial position of the South have pointed to the high levels of productivity and per capita income achieved in the mid-19th century. In the present approach to defining a colony, the relatively high per capita income of the South represented the remarkable success of the planter class in injecting itself between slave and market. The sensitivity of that class to symptoms of dependency underscored their awareness of the precarious role they were playing. Surely the most dramatic change in the distribution of the national income in the United States occurred between 1860 and 1880. The planters' success in the antebellum period represented a prodigious juggling act, and the Civil War seemed to expose their weakness.

It would be surprising if the southern worldview did not reflect the region's experience with colonial status. Indeed, some would argue that white southerners are far too engrossed in the colonial analogy. At least in part this is the result of the white southerner's direct observation of slavery. The awareness of slave dependency gave a uniquely southern meaning first to the revolutionary protest and subsequently to a broad spectrum of political-economic initiatives. The assertion of the South's colonial status explained, even if it did not justify, the origin and persistence of slavery for many southerners. At the same time, the denunciation of the colonial status created a way for white southerners to prove that they, unlike the slaves around them, would not tolerate a condition of dependency. In the late 19th century and the early 20th these themes, only

slightly modified, became stock components of southern politics. As a result, even those most closely allied to northern interests were likely to use the colonial analogy. And, of course, this analogy lies behind the entire history of the states' rights debate, both its serious content and its cliché rhetoric. The idea of economic and political dependency has been continually present in both the formal and popular thought of the South.

In the 20th century the South has experienced a strong and surprisingly steady economic growth. This record has often been used to question the colonial designation. But the issue is not so much whether the South was dependent on the North circa 1900, which would be difficult to deny, but rather why its subsequent development was so different from a colonial area such as Latin America. Quite simply, some colonies are more favored than others. The South, because of location, political security, and political integration, was a logical first choice for capital seeking low wages. The process was anything but speedy. Nevertheless, it did occur, and the post–World War II economic development has resulted in a substantial rise in southern wages. Indeed, the difference in development between the now-advanced southern United States and the Third World economies of Mexico or Argentina tends to reveal just how essential geographic, political, and other noneconomic factors are in making the classical convergence of labor and capital to build a growing economy work.

For years the colonial analogy cited by southerners has been sustained by an awareness of their differentness from other Americans and a sense of being abused. With the ongoing homogenization of the regions of the United States, there is the temptation to consider this matter closed. But southern writers who have considered the South's role in the nation have always insisted that the desirable alternative to overly specialized regional economies is not a characterless collection of interchangeable parts. For all of their reactionary leanings and racist psychology, intellectuals like George Fitzhugh in the 19th century and the Vanderbilt Agrarians in the 20th century understood that parity in income between the regions is not the same as self-determination for all of them in the national context. Although unequal wages between North and South may have long been the cause of the colonial condition, equal wages now still may not establish full southern economic independence. The degree of independence possible in the modern technocratic society remains in question.

Joseph Persky
University of Illinois at
Chicago

David Bertelson, *The Lazy South* (1967); Clarence Danhof, in *Essays in Southern Economic Development*, ed. Melvin Greenhut and W. Tate Whitman (1964); Arghiri Emmanuel, *Unequal Exchange: A Study of the Imperialism of Trade* (1972); George Fitzhugh, *Sociology for the South* (1854); John McCardell, *The Idea of a Southern Nation: Southern Nationalists and Southern Nationalism, 1830–1860* (1979). ☆

Industrialization, Resistance to

||||||||||||||||||||||||||||||||||||||||||||

In the South before the Civil War the prevailing philosophy held that a culture rooted in an agricultural economy and agrarian values was superior to any other. Although manufacturing, largely of the household variety, existed in the region on a level comparable to that of New England early in the 19th century, sectional differences soon began to emerge. Aided by the disruption of overseas commerce surrounding the War of 1812, the factory system began to expand in the North. By mid-century, northerners who 50 years before had harbored grave doubts about extensive industrialization viewed it as a positive good.

By and large, southerners underwent no such conversion. Here and there, a manufacturer such as William Gregg or an editor such as J. D. B. De Bow heralded the benefits of industrial progress. Yet economic factors seemed to offer no compelling reason to promote industrialization. If one might earn a high return on an investment in manufacturing, it was also possible to make good money in the more customary manner of investing in land and slaves. To many cautious and conservative southerners the proper study was still the improvement of agriculture.

Broad social concerns were more important than narrow economic considerations in the antebellum South's resistance to industrialization: the popular belief that a factory system might rely on the labor of black slaves and the accompanying fear that discipline would be diminished and the chance of rebellion enhanced; the suspicion that if white people were employed, their attachment to slavery might be weakened by adopting an industrial outlook; the conviction that industrial labor robbed a person of humanity and rendered him or her a wage slave of little social worth.

In the good society that antebellum southerners believed was theirs, the

the beau ideal. Rare indeed [...] [pl]antation master who left the [...] [h]ome an industrialist. Among the plain folk, or yeomen, there were many who believed with Thomas Jefferson that "those who labour in the earth are the chosen people of God . . . his peculiar deposit for substantial and genuine virtue."

The Civil War worked a fundamental change in the attitude of many southerners. One of the region's most notable casualties was the agrarian ideal, severely wounded in the conflict. Union armies had hardly sealed the fate of the Old South before southerners began proclaiming a New South. For many of its leaders a New South meant above all else an industrialized South with an economy modeled on that of the victorious North.

As the ranks of industrial promoters swelled, recruited largely by urban editors such as Henry W. Grady, Henry Watterson, and Richard H. Edmonds, those southerners who resisted industrialization increasingly found themselves a besieged garrison, heavily outnumbered. Still, they fought hard, from the end of the war to the end of the century. Whether opposing industrialization in general as contrary to the best in southern tradition or denouncing the form of regional industrialization as wantonly exploitative, the critics often upheld the ideal of the South as an Arcadian alternative to a materialistic national culture. Yet, despite the best efforts of an orator such as Charles C. Jones, Jr., of editors such as Albert T. Bledsoe and D. H. Hill, of churchmen like Robert L. Dabney, J. C. C. Newton, and Benjamin M. Palmer, and of writers like Sidney Lanier, Mark Twain, George W. Cable, and Joel Chandler Harris, those who resisted industrialization

were seldom able to effect action. Even the Populists of the 1890s, the strongest challengers of Gilded Age capitalism, could not reverse those policies of the New South establishment that encouraged reckless industrialism from which, the Populists argued, most southerners received little benefit.

As of 1900 the New South movement toward industrialization had failed to change the South's economic position relative to that of other parts of the nation. Notwithstanding a considerable increase in the number of factories, the South remained predominantly agricultural, with only a little more than 6 percent of its labor force working in manufacturing.

Undaunted, southern leaders early in the 20th century continued to pursue industry. Convinced that poverty, illiteracy, and disease were the result in great measure of the region's agricultural economy, many southern Progressives believed that industrialization would deliver the region from those evils.

A few southerners were not so sure. Here and there, voices were raised in dissent. In the pages of *Uncle Remus's Magazine* Joel Chandler Harris warned that the liabilities of industrialization might overbalance the assets. The historian William E. Dodd wondered what effect the educational philanthropy of northern industrialists would have upon the independence of southern academicians. The Reverend Alexander J. McKelway, a leader in the movement to prohibit labor by children in southern factories, became disgusted with what he called the mercenary New South.

The objections of the skeptics notwithstanding, the industrial tide continued to roll in, cresting in the boosterism of the 1920s. During the "dollar decade" resistance again came largely from bookish people whom practical men either ridiculed or ignored, although the work of some of those intellectuals would provide a telling critique of industrialism.

Many of the 12 men who contributed essays to *I'll Take My Stand: The South and the Agrarian Tradition* (1930) celebrated the yeoman ideal; all of them lamented the coming of an industrial society that massed individuals physically as it atomized them spiritually, reducing them to pawns of the marketplace. In more than 200 essays written throughout the 1930s, some of these Vanderbilt Agrarians continued to defend the South's agricultural society, charging that large-scale industrialization, by allowing too few people to own too much wealth and by creating a large, insecure proletariat, would rend the social fabric and encourage a politics dominated by either plutocrats or socialists. The Agrarians proposed that the pernicious influence of industrialism be contained by distributing land widely among the American people, by encouraging subsistence farming, and by establishing regional governments to insure that the South remain free of northern domination.

For a brief season in the 1930s some of the Agrarians' proposals received a hearing from public officials, but glimmerings of economic recovery rekindled the desire of southerners for more industry. Even before the Great Depression had ended, the booster spirit of the 1920s had reappeared in full force.

Propelled by World War II, manufacturing accelerated throughout the South. The region was becoming more industrial than agricultural, with only one-third of its population still on the farm in 1945. After the war the attempts of promoters to "sell" the advantages of the South to industrialists elsewhere reached unprecedented proportions. Public efforts to attract industry were many and varied: local governments financed plant construction, sometimes in violation of state constitutions; tax levies were either abnormally low or nonexistent; advertising expenditures far exceeded the rest of the nation's; labor was kept cheap, docile, and unorganized; and state governments implemented "start-up" programs for new businesses. By 1960 southern cultural thought had come full circle. What distinguished the South from the rest of the nation was not the fervor of the region's resistance to industrialization but rather the intensity of its yearning for more of it. And the desire grew ever more ardent, as many southerners felt that, at long last, it was their turn to enjoy a fair share of American affluence.

Opposition either to the idea of further industrialization or to the form that it took in the South came largely from literary men, a tradition that had emerged with Lanier and Harris, continued through the Agrarians, Thomas Wolfe, and William Faulkner, and found contemporary expression in writers such as Wendell Berry, Harry M. Caudill, and James Dickey. Opposition came occasionally from scholars: a distinguished southern historian warned that if the region's past were any guide, the South would fail to profit from mistakes made by the North during the course of its industrialization and would suffer many of the same problems. Organized opposition also came from those directly victimized by the excesses of industrialism: residents of Appalachia and other parts of the South suffering displacement by the strip mining of coal; miners suffering from black lung;

textile workers suffering from brown lung. Southerners generally became aware of a major cost of extensive industrialization—pollution. As industrial waste fouled the streams, coastline, and air of the South, state governments responded by creating agencies to control that refuse; each southern state had such a body by 1971. Moreover, chambers of commerce and development boards sometimes recruited industries more selectively. Occasionally, industrial projects were abandoned because it was feared that they would irreparably damage an area's ecology.

Critics of industrialization charged that all too often the regulators failed to enforce the inadequate restrictions that did exist, particularly against powerful offenders, and that a clean environment took second place to economic growth in the South's scale of values. Critics contended that the spillover from urban sprawl caused by industrialization was resulting in the overdevelopment of areas of great natural beauty such as the southern mountains. They questioned the promoters' claims that higher incomes and an unprecedented abundance of material goods meant perforce that life was better for most southerners. They pointed to data that suggested that the quality of life in the South had not been improved at all by industrialization and to other data that showed that for all the impressive gains the South had made, it remained, even in strictly economic terms, at the bottom of the nation, despite a hundred years of industrial promotion. Critics feared that if industrialization continued apace, the atomistic mass culture that characterized much of the rest of the country would overwhelm the organic folk culture that had long distinguished the South. Nevertheless, as the region entered the 1980s, those articulate southerners who resisted industrialization appeared to be the distinct minority.

See also HISTORY AND MANNERS: Jeffersonian Tradition; Populism; Progressivism; World War II; LITERATURE: Agrarianism in Literature; / Cable, George W.; Clemens, Samuel; Dickey, James; Faulkner, William; Harris, Joel Chandler; Wolfe, Thomas; MYTHIC SOUTH: New South Myth; / Agrarians, Vanderbilt

Wayne Mixon
Mercer University

Fred Bateman and Thomas Weiss, *A Deplorable Scarcity: The Failure of Industrialization in the Slave Economy* (1981); James C. Cobb, *The Selling of the South: The Southern Crusade for Industrial Development, 1936–1980* (1982); Paul M. Gaston, *The New South Creed: A Study in Southern Mythmaking* (1970); Wayne Mixon, *Southern Writers and the New South Movement, 1865–1913* (1980); Norris W. Preyer, *Georgia Historical Quarterly* (Fall 1971); Twelve Southerners, *I'll Take My Stand: The South and the Agrarian Tradition* (1930); Mary Ann Wimsatt, *Mississippi Quarterly* (Fall 1980). ☆

Industrialization and Change

||||||||||||||||||||||||||||||||||||||||||||||||||||||

It is a persistent myth, running through popular and academic writing, that industry in the South is of recent origin. Some views attribute the birth of industrialism to the New South movement at the end of the 19th century, others to the notable rise of the Sunbelt South since World War II. Such truncated accounts of economic modernization ignore the deep roots and persistent patterns of southern industrial development. For at least 100 years, from the antebellum origins of the factory system to the collapse of the plantation system during the Great Depression, the shape and pace of industrial growth and social change in the region developed in relation to southern agriculture.

Slaveholding and the plantation system set limits on industrial and urban growth in the antebellum South. Antebellum cities developed as marketing and transportation centers for plantation products. Slaveholding inhibited the growth of domestic markets for manufactured goods, although some mass-produced items such as cheap clothing and farm implements were in demand. A limited number of antebellum industrial establishments developed in response to this market. Also, a significant number of factories, especially in the cotton textile industry beginning in the 1830s, were established to process plantation products. Many early factories were built by planters, some experimenting with the use of slave labor in manufacturing. In general, however, southern planters feared all-out industrialization, arguing that industry would compete with the labor needs of agriculture and threaten social control. Prior to the Civil War most agricultural profits were reinvested in land and slaves.

Perhaps the most rapid phase of industrial expansion in the South occurred from 1860 to 1864. Southern planters sponsored a thoroughgoing, nondemocratic, and state-controlled form of industrialization through confiscation and government investment in order to build a war machine. Under the auspices of the Confederate States of America, the South rapidly built ironworks, shipyards, textile mills, coal and iron mines, machine shops, clothing and food-processing plants, and munitions factories. The South lost the war but acquired significant industrial experience.

The extent and rapidity of industrial expansion after the Civil War, especially in the Piedmont states, led many observers to view the New South in an entirely different way. Despite stress on the demise of the planter class and the plantation system that characterized New South promotional literature, recent studies show that planters remained economically and politically dominant in many southern states at the end of the 19th century. Former slaveholders retained their land and reasserted labor control through sharecropping and the debt peonage system that effectively bound tenants to the soil. A culture of paternalism persisted well into the 20th century, influencing industrial patterns. In the Deep South, where cotton growing remained profitable and white labor was relatively scarce, planters continued to oppose all but minimal industrial growth. In contrast, planter-industrialists in the Upper South, who were faced with declining agricultural returns and drew on labor reserves of impoverished white farmers, accommodated industry to the postbellum agrarian social order.

Traditionally, the most important sector of southern industry has been cotton textile manufacturing. Here the influence of plantation agriculture was greatest as the ethos of the cotton plantation was extended into rural mill villages. The South's forced labor system of plantation agriculture was transferred to the industrial-capitalist sector at first primarily through all-white wage labor in the textile mills, but this was done with great strain, requiring immense measures of social control. The old culture of paternalism and the new logic of capitalist industrialism were tensely interwoven. Despite industrial expansion, individual textile plants remained small and personal. Southern workers were far more dependent on mill-village services than were northern workers. Mechanization permitted heavy reliance on unskilled labor, including children; isolation, paternalism, and racial exclusivity blunted occupational militancy. Low wages and long workdays enabled southern millowners to compete with northern manufacturers and eventually to draw northern textile firms and capital into the region.

The textile industry set the pattern for southern industrial culture, though work relations outside the planter-dominated textile industry developed contrasting characteristics. This was most notably true in tobacco manufacturing and coal mining. As proclaimed for the whole of postbellum industry, the tobacco industry was built by "new men" in North Carolina after the Civil War. By 1900 the Dukes and their associates in Durham had transformed a small craft industry into the South's largest industrial enterprise, the American Tobacco Company. Outside the sphere of planter interests, tobacco manufacturers employed large numbers of black workers. Realizing greater profits than the textile industry, they paid significantly higher wages and accepted unionization. The coal industry in Alabama and the southern Appalachians also employed black workers and, faced with an extraordinarily militant work force, was forced to accept unionization. Some of America's bloodiest labor struggles occurred in the mining communities of the southern highlands where,

unlike the textile villages, corporate paternalism and wage pressures did not accord with the mountain heritage of agricultural self-sufficiency and with underground worker autonomy.

By the time of the New Deal, the plantation system was giving way in southern cotton fields to crop subsidies, mechanization, and federal welfare payments just sufficient to keep an unemployed labor supply on the land. Southern agriculture became increasingly capital intensive. Institutionalized paternalism lingered in the textile industry; but consolidation, rationalization, and, more rarely, industrial conflict became the rule. Demise of the nonwage system in agriculture intensified the drive for further industrialization. Southern towns competed to lure industrial plants to their localities by offering tax incentives, subsidies, and nonunion labor to corporate employers.

Since 1950 the South's rate of economic expansion has been greater than the national average. New growth sectors include agribusiness, defense industries, energy resources (oil and nuclear as well as coal, gas, and water), and "high-tech" research and development complexes such as North Carolina's Research Triangle Park. Educational and public services, along with race relations, have improved dramatically; but much industrial expansion is still dependent on a repressive, nonunion labor environment. (Research complexes such as North Carolina's Research Triangle Park encourage highly paid managerial and research personnel to migrate south without their unionized blue-collar work forces.) Average industrial wages in the region remain substandard. North Carolina and South Carolina, in the heart of the textile industry, rank as the two most heavily industrialized states in the United States. At the same time, however, they rank 49th and 50th in wage and unionization levels. Both the accomplishments and the failures of southern industrialization are evident in such statistics.

See also AGRICULTURE: Plantations; BLACK LIFE: Workers, Black; HISTORY AND MANNERS: Confederate States of America; MYTHIC SOUTH: New South Myth; SOCIAL CLASS: / Coal Miners; Company Towns; Textile Workers; Tobacco Workers

Dwight B. Billings
University of Kentucky

Dwight B. Billings, *Planters and the Making of a "New South": Class, Politics, and Development in North Carolina, 1865–1900* (1979); James C. Cobb, *The Selling of the South: The Southern Crusade for Industrial Development, 1936–1980* (1982); Ronald D. Eller, *Miners, Millhands, and Mountaineers: The Modernization of the Appalachian South* (1982); Eugene D. Genovese, *The Political Economy of Slavery: Studies in Economy and Society of the Slave South* (1967); Jay Mandle, *The Roots of Black Poverty: The Southern Plantation Economy after the Civil War* (1978); Jonathan M. Wiener, *Social Origins of the New South: Alabama, 1860–1885* (1978); C. Vann Woodward, *Origins of the New South, 1877–1913* (1951). ☆

Industrialization in Appalachia

||||||||||||||||||||||||||||||||||||||||||||||||||

Although the southern mountain region has sometimes been said to be predominantly agricultural in its economy and rural in its culture, industrial development occurred there much as it did elsewhere in the United States and at the same times. During the antebellum period extractive and manufacturing activities developed as decentralized, locally capitalized, and locally managed enterprises, serving a local or regional market. During the late 1860s, in Appalachia as elsewhere in the nation, these same activities became increasingly centralized through the emergence of large-scale enterprises serving a national or international market and developed with nonlocal capital by nonlocal entrepreneurs. The impact of these changes on all aspects of American life was substantial, not least because they completed the transformation, begun by the transportation revolution of the 1820s, of the mixed American landscape into the characteristic American cityscape of our own time.

As early as the 1840s visitors to the southern mountains had noted the region's untapped resources in minerals, timber, and waterpower; its human resources of a hardworking, healthy population free of the taint of slavocracy and its ideology of leisure; the potential of its rivers to serve as arteries of commerce; and a landscape and climate conducive to the development of tourism. During the 1860s the list of apparent economic advantages of Appalachia came to include the availability of a rail system and the proximity of the region to major national markets. The list has remained intact, except that concrete roads and air transportation have been added. The persistence of these factors has made Appalachia seem an underdeveloped region of the nation even at times when economic development was most vigorous and the resources of the region—both natural and human—were being depleted most rapidly.

During the 1870s the first systematic cutting of the Appalachian hardwood forests was begun under the same impulse that spurred timbering in Wisconsin and Minnesota and then along the Pacific Coast when the eastern forests were exhausted. During the 1880s the first systematic extraction of Appalachian coal, iron, and nonferrous metals was begun under the same impetus that promoted the growth of mining in Pennsylvania, Minnesota, and the Rocky Mountain states. Beginning in the late 1880s a variety of manufacturing centers were established in Appalachia through the same drive that yielded the great industrial cities on the Great Lakes from Buffalo to Duluth. These manufacturing activities included steel production in Birmingham and Bessemer, Ala., and Middlesboro, Ky.; wood finishing and furniture production, most notably around Asheville, N.C.; glass production at several sites in West Virginia; and textile milling throughout the Piedmont.

These developments in Appalachian timbering, mining, and manufacturing

Lumber mill, Tappahannock, Va., 1941

during the late 19th and early 20th centuries replicated the general pattern already evident in the American economy of a movement from small-unit production and local capitalization and control toward large-unit production and external capitalization and control. In these "new" industries, however, the conventional growth pattern with its normal impact on society and culture was compressed into a decade or less rather than spread over half a century or more. The social dislocations consequent to these developments in Appalachia, moreover, seem to have been more severe than the analogous dislocations felt in similar growth sites elsewhere in the nation.

Western timbering, for example, occurred largely on land acquired as part of the public domain. Much of the Appalachian timberland was owned, or at least claimed, by individuals who used portions of their holdings for agriculture. Many of these persons were displaced by the large timber companies, especially after the beginning of the 20th century, when large-scale forest preserves were established to ensure the profitability of future operations. Much of Pennsylvania coal mining, like most of western mining of all sorts, required deep-shaft mining and therefore yielded the establishment of permanent facilities for the industry and its workers, and a more or less permanent work force at a particular site. Most of the Appalachian coal mining around the turn of the century could be carried on as surface mining or by tunneling in short-term operations. When the mine played out, equipment, and often the buildings of a company town, were loaded on flat cars and moved to a new site. Appalachian coal mining thus tended to be a transient industry, worked by transients, many of whom had themselves been displaced by timber- or coal-company land purchases, who followed the job from place to place. The emergence of large-scale timbering and coal mining displaced those persons who had engaged in the same industries on a small scale, either by squeezing them out of the market or by denying them access to the natural resources they had previously exploited for their own profit, frequently as a complement to farming or some other activity. With no other source of income, these persons either were forced into subsistence farming or entered the labor market as transients.

With the notable exception of such "model" town developments as Pullman, Ill., most of the Great Lakes manufacturing of the late 19th century occurred in or near already established population centers. By contrast, almost all large-scale manufacturing in Appalachia developed on new sites and required a skilled labor force of inmigrants to the site, if not to the region. Although the real impact of massive immigration on the character of the Great Lakes cities cannot be denied, in Appalachia the development of manufacturing affected the rapid urbanization of a "rural" area previously dominated by small towns rather than cities, without displacing the system of social and political elites that dominated in courthouse and statehouse. At the same time, it brought to the region hundreds of thousands of new workers who were outsiders to the structure of local politics and society and who rapidly became either its victims, its rebels, or its exiles. That most of the manufacturing centers in Appalachia, as well as the short-lived timber towns and almost all the coal towns, were company owned and controlled exacerbated this situation by making impossible the local mediation of labor and social conflict that occurred in other urban areas during the Progressive era.

Turn-of-the-century tendencies toward vertical consolidation within industries, exemplified by the establishment of the Standard Oil Company, were extended horizontally across industries in Appalachia, yielding a pattern in which single corporations routinely controlled several industries at once—land development, timber and coal operations, transportation and marketing, and frequently all services needed to support the several sectors of their economic activity as well as those needed by their workers. Finally, although industrial development elsewhere in the nation generally has enriched all strata of the local economies by generating markets for additional goods and services, industrial development in Appalachia has often enriched only the local elites and has left the local economies highly vulnerable to the vagaries of market conditions.

See also BLACK LIFE: Appalachians, Black; ENVIRONMENT: / Appalachian Coal Region; Appalachian Mountains; ETHNIC LIFE: Mountain Culture; / Appalachians; FOLKLIFE: "Hillbilly" Image; MYTHIC SOUTH: Appalachian Culture; / Appalachian Myth; SOCIAL CLASS: Appalachia, Exploitation of; / Coal Miners; Company Towns; URBANIZATION: / Birmingham

Henry D. Shapiro
University of Cincinnati

Harry Caudill, *Night Comes to the Cumberlands: A Biography of a Depressed Area* (1962); Ronald D. Eller, *Miners, Millhands, and Mountaineers: The Modernization of the Appalachian South* (1982); Helen Lewis et al., *Colonialism in Modern America: The Appalachian Case* (1978); Gordon B. Mc-Kinney, *Southern Mountain Republicans, 1865–1900: Politics and the Appalachian Community* (1978); Henry D. Shapiro, *Appalachia on Our Mind: The Southern Mountains and Mountaineers in the American Consciousness, 1870–1920* (1978); David E. Whisnant, *Modernizing the Mountaineer: People, Power and Planning in Appalachia* (1979); John Alexander Williams, *West Virginia and the Captains of Industry* (1976). ☆

Industrialization in Piedmont

||||||||||||||||||||||||||||||||||||||||||||||||||||

Before 1830 the Piedmont region had a small but relatively diverse manufacturing sector, including woolen mills, foundries, and nail and rifle plants. But such promising industry dwindled with the expansion of the slave economy and concentration on the lucrative cash crop, cotton. By 1860 significant production was limited to a small number of cotton textile mills in towns such as Graniteville, S.C. The Civil War destroyed most of these modest gains, and manufacturing did not demonstrate any real momentum until the 1880s. But from that time forward cotton textile expansion and Piedmont industrialization became virtually synonymous. By the 1950s regional control of the textile industry had been wrested from New England and has continued since, with three-fourths of current output produced in the Piedmont states. Although northern competition was met successfully, that from foreign producers, especially

Japan, growing since before World War II, has presented an increasingly serious challenge to Piedmont mills.

One interesting difference between Piedmont and New England textile development is the wholehearted community support that marked early southern efforts to establish local industry. Religious leaders as well as state and local officials joined farm populations in what has been termed a "crusade" in the 1880s to urge entrepreneurs to open mills. The collective hope was that heavy investment in cotton textiles would not only provide desperately needed jobs for local workers and effectively use the region's main crop, but would also draw producers in related manufacturing and service industries to locate in the region. In turn, rapid urbanization would create demand for locally made goods as well as for meat, dairy, and other food items, leading to a healthier local agriculture, less dependent on the fortunes of the cotton crop.

By the time investment in Piedmont manufacturing began on a broad scale, machinery, power, and transport technologies were far more advanced than they had been at the inception of northern and midwestern industrialization earlier in the 19th century. Of particular importance was the critical impetus given Piedmont progress by the widespread availability of cheap hydroelectric power after 1900. Investment by power companies in the region was stimulated initially by demand from cotton mills, but other labor-intensive light industry located there in part to benefit from its prevalence. Textile-finishing plants; wood, paper, and furniture factories; knit-goods, apparel, and later synthetic-fiber factories all became numerous.

Even the presence of excellent water and wood supplies, however, could not compensate for a relative regional scarcity of heavy mineral deposits such as coal and iron, which laid the foundation for investment in capital-intensive industry elsewhere. Although the chemical industry is strongly represented through artificial-textile production, the location of this component of the industry in the Piedmont may be viewed as a function of the ease with which cotton mills and equipment could be converted for artificial-fiber manufacture. Its introduction into the Piedmont was thus linked more to the presence of the older cotton manufacture than to the region's supply of skilled labor and natural resources. Traditionally, the region has not attracted heavy industry, although textile- and electrical-machinery producers have long clustered near cotton-mill centers. Nontextile manufacture has tended to resemble cotton manufacturing in demanding a large supply of cheap unskilled labor and by having few economies of scale in production.

The social environment of the rural Piedmont contributed also to the distinctive character of its industrialization experience. Because mills were constructed in rural areas, housing had to be provided for workers and their families. In early New England textile towns, company-owned boardinghouses served an unmarried female work force but disappeared with the advent of immigrant labor. The concentration of New England mills in a few locations contributed to the growth of large cities. Piedmont mill villages did not undergo such an evolution for the most part. The agrarian tradition so often noted by students of southern culture was reflected in mill dispersion over a wide geograph-

ical area. The relative isolation of mills strengthened a comprehensive paternalism on the part of owners that, in contrast to New England, persisted, assisting owners in effectively thwarting unionization efforts by keeping workers dependent and suspicious of outside organizers. In addition, a perennial threat facing white workers in this labor-surplus agricultural region was that black labor, heretofore excluded from cotton mills, would be hired to replace union sympathizers. Thus, mill villagers remained remarkably homogeneous in cultural and religious heritage, race, and ethnic origin. Although they have been described as a transient group, they usually migrated only to another mill village, similar to the last in social structure and economic opportunity. One outcome of textile dominance in Piedmont industrialization has been that alternatives to farm work for the large black population of the region have historically been few. Only in recent years have cotton mills opened all job categories to blacks.

By the time of Piedmont industrial expansion, textile technology, particularly in spinning, allowed extensive use of child labor. This practice characterized Piedmont mills long after it had been eliminated in New England. When states introduced age-and-hour legislation more widely after 1912, Piedmont standards were distinguished by their inadequacy. The laws were rarely enforced, so the employment of entire families continued, entrenching the mill villages in the southern landscape and delaying the development of a skilled and literate nonfarm labor force, an essential resource for the attraction of high-wage, capital-intensive industry.

Although the very rapid rate of growth

of Piedmont cotton mills was a critical feature of its industrialization, it should not obscure the enduring rural character of the region. For example, although South Carolina was the preeminent southern textile state in 1900, fewer than 4 percent of its people were employed in manufacturing industry of any kind. The Piedmont's industrial pattern incorporated features of its rural heritage, and in this it contrasts with other regions where urbanization occurred relatively quickly as manufacturing expanded. Urban development in the Piedmont, on the other hand, has been more typically expressed through the rise of small towns than the growth of large cities. Scholars sometimes emphasize a tension between the agricultural and manufacturing sectors because the progress of one could threaten the labor supply of the other. But the development of Piedmont industry was accomplished by recruiting unemployed and underemployed white labor from local farms. The farm population increased for many decades at a rate more than sufficient to meet the demands of both farms and mills, so industrialization had a positive effect on the productivity of local farm labor.

As truck and automobile transportation became accessible in the 1920s, many Piedmont workers commuted to factories from farms. Such retention of a predominantly agricultural character in the long run helps to explain the slow progress of the Piedmont toward industrial diversification. The lack of skilled labor continued to dictate the type of manufacture located in the region. When considered with the related absence of essential large-scale economies, one can understand more fully the persistence of the region's low per capita income relative to other sections of the United States.

While certain distinguishing marks continue to characterize the industrial organization of the Piedmont today, there have been important economic changes in the region. World wars, larger and more sophisticated markets for southern goods, and foreign competition have lured more complex industry and have evoked a broader social and political awareness in the region. In small towns as well as in more urban areas, a middle class has developed with ambitions and lifestyles more American than regional. The peculiar industrialization experience of the Piedmont has had, nevertheless, a lasting impact on the cultural path of its society. The region's industrial structure has been molded not only by circumstances of time, technology, and resource utilization, but also by the character and social values of its populace.

See also SOCIAL CLASS: / Company Towns; Textile Workers

Mary J. Oates
Regis College

Fred Bateman and Thomas Weiss, *A Deplorable Scarcity: The Failure of Industrialization in the Slave Economy* (1981); Victor S. Clark, *History of Manufactures in the United States*, vols. 2 and 3 (1929); Victor R. Fuchs, *Changes in the Location of Manufacturing in the United States since 1929* (1962); Patrick J. Hearden, *Independence and Empire: The New South's Cotton Mill Campaign, 1865–1901* (1982); William N. Parker, *Southern Economic Journal* (April 1980); Anthony M. Tang, *Economic Development in the Southern Piedmont, 1860–1950* (1958); George B. Tindall, *The Emergence of the New South, 1913–1945* (1967). ☆

Military and Economy

|||||||||||||||||||||||||||||||||||||||||||||||||||||||||

Since the Civil War, and especially following World War II, the South has become the most powerful base of support for the continued American military buildup that has resulted in the rise of the *Military-Industrial Complex*, a term coined by Malcolm Moss and popularized by Dwight D. Eisenhower. More accurately, the complex should be styled the Military-Industrial-Technological - Labor - Academic - Managerial - Political Complex (MITLAMP). All sectors of modern technological society are involved in its functioning. Within the MITLAMP Complex are military and industrial beneficiaries, technical specialists, labor recipients of defense funds, academic elites, managerial elements, and political opportunists. These groups, especially in the South and in California, are reaping financial rewards and causing, particularly in the South, extraordinary cultural changes because of their continued support for the complex.

The origins of this regional military-economic relationship can be traced far back in southern history. Antebellum southern life and culture were conducive in many ways to an excessive spirit of militancy and extreme martial behavior. As the frontier moved westward in the 18th and early 19th centuries, southerners, like the frontiersmen of the Midwest, felt vulnerable to Indian uprisings. More importantly, as a slave-holding population, southern whites lived in constant fear of slave revolts, so the constabulary forces they organized patrolled the rural roads nightly. Many southerners, weaned on the novels of Sir Walter Scott, were obsessed with

a sense of honor. John Hope Franklin, W. J. Cash, and others have suggested this martial spirit of the South helped it face the consequences of secession with confidence, if not eagerness.

Following the Civil War southern males were even more obsessed with proving their manhood and, above all, regaining their lost sense of honor. Combine this fact with the existence of poverty and extreme racism in the region and it is small wonder that southerners, white and black, have been attracted in large numbers to the military establishment, in times of both peace and war. The South has more enlistees serving in the armed forces than any other region. No other section of the country has a greater percentage of personnel in the armed forces on a per capita basis. The report of the Secretary of Defense for Manpower Reserve Affairs and Logistics (1981) showed that in 1980, 35.7 percent of the enlistees in the professional armed forces were natives of the South, while southerners constituted 33.7 percent of the nation's population.

The subsequent economic benefits for the region are obvious. Southerners in the armed forces throughout the world are fueling the southern economy with allotment checks deposited in local banks. Moreover, although military personnel serve in many places during their careers, seldom do they escape service at some southern camp or station. This is especially true in the case of the army. Twenty-four of 46 major posts are located in the South. In 1980, 48 percent of all service people were located in southern states and the District of Columbia. Moreover, colonies of military retirees exist along the Florida coastline and in San Antonio and El Paso, Tex.

The impact of military expenditures on the southern economy is immense.

A total of 39.5 percent of all Department of Defense dollars ($50,091,677,000 of a total budget of $127,135,626,000) was spent in the South in fiscal year 1980. The one-party system combined with the rule of seniority enabled southerners to dominate the House and Senate Armed Services Committees and direct this heavy expenditure of defense funds to the South.

In addition, of the $10,696,556,000 allocated to the Department of Energy, $554,350,000 was expended in the South in conducting nuclear weapons activities for the Department of Defense. Further, National Aeronautics and Space Agency funds, closely linked to defense needs, are primarily allocated to southern states and the District of Columbia. The total NASA budget in 1980 was $5,365,761,000; $2,169,012,000 of this was spent in the South. Finally, Veterans Administration expenditures in the South amounted to $8,635,108,000 of an agency total of $22,106,822,000. Thus, the entire amount of military money spent in southern states and the District of Columbia in 1980 was $61,450,147,000. If one employs a conservative multiplier effect in order to determine the number

World War II naval vessel, the USS **Charleston**

of *real* dollars spent in the South by the military in 1980, the amount equals $122,999,822,000.

The vast wealth of the MITLAMP Complex is a significant, if not the significant, factor in explaining the economic boom that has taken place in the South since the 1950s. Military money constitutes close to 10 percent of the total income of the South ($667,400,000,000) and 33 percent of all federal expenditures in the South ($183,000,000,000). However, the money is not equitably distributed. While $2,752,509,000 is spent in Alabama and $12,066,000,000 is prorated to Texas, only $500,116,000 is expended in West Virginia, the least rewarded of the southern states.

Cultural changes are wrought by such vast military expenditures. In cities and towns where industries and military installations traditionally reflected racist views, employment and personnel policies have become more equitable. The white South has been forced to reconsider its racial attitudes as a consequence of the Supreme Court decisions and the civil rights legislation of the 1950s and 1960s enforcing equal employment opportunities for blacks in southern industries under contract to the federal government.

In addition, many northerners, including unskilled workers and skilled managers, technologists, engineers, and scientists, have moved South in search of the economic opportunities provided in the Sunbelt, further changing the character of life, especially in cities like Dallas and Houston. Thus, large military expenditures, producing social as well as economic results, must be considered important factors in the recent growth and development of the South.

See also HISTORY AND MANNERS: Military
Bases; Military Tradition; MYTHIC SOUTH:
Militant South; SCIENCE AND MEDICINE:
Aerospace; VIOLENCE: Honor

Alvin R. Sunseri
University of Northern Iowa

W. J. Cash, *The Mind of the South* (1941);
John Hope Franklin, *The Militant South*
(1956); *Geographical Distribution of Federal
Funds in Summary, Fiscal Year, 1980*; Alvin
R. Sunseri, in *War, Business and American
Society: Historical Perspectives on the Mili-
tary-Industrial Complex*, ed. Benjamin
Franklin Cooling (1977); U.S. Department
of Commerce, *Statistical Abstract of the
United States: 1981* (1982); *U.S. Government
Selected Manpower Statistics, Fiscal Year
1981*. ☆

New South

||||||||||||||||||||||||||

See MYTHIC SOUTH: New South Myth

Sunbelt South

|||||||||||||||||||||||||||||||||||

"**S**unbelt South" and, more generally,
the "American Sunbelt" are media creations designed to give coherence and
meaning to the dramatic population
growth and political upheavals that have
occurred in the South and Southwest
since 1940. Coined by political analyst
Kevin P. Phillips in his book *The
Emerging Republican Majority* (1969),
the concept of "Sun Belt" (or "Sunbelt")
lay dormant and ill-defined until the
mid-1970s, when a combination of census reports on migration, the growing

Republican potential in the South and
West, and the presidential candidacy of
Georgian Jimmy Carter brought the
lower tier of states to public attention.
Although he did not use the term *Sunbelt*, journalist Kirkpatrick Sale, in
*Power Shift: The Rise of the Southern
Rim and Its Challenge to the Eastern
Establishment* (1975), alerted northern
intellectuals to the emergence of the nation's "Southern Rim" as a new center
of power. Soon the *New York Times*, the
Wall Street Journal, *Fortune*, and news
weeklies discovered the region. *Time*,
prompted by Carter's nomination, devoted a special issue (27 September
1976) to "The South Today." Yet definitions remained unclear. Nearly all observers included in the Sunbelt the area
below the 37th parallel, along the northern borders of North Carolina, Tennessee, Arkansas, Oklahoma, New Mexico,
and Arizona and that in California below
Fresno. Some added Virginia, Kentucky, southern Nevada, and northern
California, while others cautiously included the slow-growing Mississippi
Delta. All agreed, however, on the general concept of an expanding southern
and southwestern region with a casual
and inviting lifestyle, a favorable business climate, and conservative politics
increasingly inclined to Republicanism.

For roughly five years the press showered the nation with promotional reports
of "the good life" in the Sunbelt that
was seemingly unattainable elsewhere.
By the early 1980s, however, the northern-based national media became less
enchanted and focused reports on crime
in Miami, the lack of services in Houston, and the high cost of living in southern California. By 1982 *Newsweek* saw
a "Dark Side of the Sunbelt," and the
New York Times began a follow-up on
its glowing 1976 series under the head-

line: "Sun Belt Having Difficulty Living Up to Its Promise." As a media creation, the concept of the Sunbelt faced severe editing.

If the Sunbelt South was partly a mythic image, it did reflect real demographic and economic trends. Between 1940 and 1980 the number of Americans living below the 37th parallel increased by 112 percent, whereas the combined populations of the Northeast and Midwest rose by only 42 percent. Southern California, Florida, and Texas each gained over 7.5 million new residents. By 1980 the populations of the Los Angeles–Long Beach, Dallas–Fort Worth, Houston, and Atlanta metropolitan areas had grown to more than 2 million each, and 18 Sunbelt metropolises (including 11 from the former Confederate states) had joined the nation's 50 most populous metro regions. This growth was especially strong during World War II, the 1960s, and the early 1970s.

Most commentators attributed this increase to economic development fostered by federal and state aid to business, and to changing American lifestyles. Beginning with World War II, Washington poured enormous sums into the South and West for the construction and maintenance of military installations and the production of modern weaponry. From Miami to Mobile to Monterey, these defense bases and plants lured wartime migrants who came and stayed. Cold War and Vietnam expenditures, protected by powerful congressional leaders such as L. Mendel Rivers (S.C.), John Stennis (Miss.), Edward Hebert (La.), and John Tower (Tex.), have guaranteed millions of Sunbelt jobs. Nondefense spending, shared more equally with the other states, also boosted Sunbelt growth through funding

for items ranging from construction projects to transfer payments. State governments scrambled for these federal dollars but also for new industries and their private payrolls. Beginning with Mississippi's plan to "Balance Agriculture with Industry" (1936), southern and southwestern government and civil officials attracted branch plants and encouraged new operations with promises of low costs for land, buildings, equipment, labor, and taxes, plus expanding markets. Packaged as, in the Texas vernacular, a "good bidness climate," these appeals emphasized tax concessions and weak labor unions—by-products of southern prejudice and right-to-work laws. "Business Loves the Sunbelt (and Vice Versa)," proclaimed a 1977 *Fortune* article.

A warm and inviting climate encouraged this mutual attraction and convinced many businessmen to move South. Winter temperatures in the 1960s and 250 to 350 days of sunshine annually made for an informal, outdoor-oriented lifestyle, equally appealing to retirees in Fort Lauderdale, top executives in Atlanta, and oil-field workers in western Oklahoma. Postwar affluence gave many northerners the wherewithal to relocate, and many moved to improve their quality of life.

This mighty demographic shift has triggered significant economic and political realignments. Economic power is drifting south and west, where Miami, New Orleans, Houston, and Los Angeles are now international trade centers, and Atlanta and Dallas service substantial regional markets. The Sunbelt is becoming dominant in energy development, technical innovation, tourism, and many categories of agribusiness. In national politics the region is already flexing its new muscles. The

1970 census was the first to give the South and West a majority in the electoral college, but every elected president since 1964 has come from the southern rim. In 1964 and 1980 voters chose among or between Sunbelt candidates. In 1940 only 121 congressmen came from below the 37th parallel, but the 1980 census awarded the region 145 seats, a gain of 12 since 1970. Drawing support from newcomers and old-line Democrats upset over civil rights and federal spending priorities, Republicans won many of the seats. Some were conservative ideologues, but most were pragmatic business types. Republicans swept west to east, from coastal areas to the inland and into the suburbs to win national and statewide offices barred to them a generation earlier. Blacks and Hispanics, encouraged by the civil rights movement and federal support, integrated the Democratic party and won local races. In the cities, once-entrenched commercial elites began to share power with young business promoters, suburbanites, and neighborhood and minority groups. The degree of sharing has varied, from almost none in Dallas—Fort Worth to an almost total power shift in Atlanta, where a black majority now rules.

The probusiness, laissez-faire attitude of the region has allowed problems, especially those related to density, to multiply unchecked; but so far crime, poor schools and services, and low wages have not destroyed the Sunbelt's appeal. Eventually, Sunbelt governments will have to expand their activities, but their constituents are in no hurry. As one observer claimed of archetypical Houston, it has a 19th-century outlook with 20th-century technology. In the meantime, migrants continue to stamp their approval on the region, for although lessening economic advantages and higher relocation costs have slowed Sunbelt growth in the early 1980s, the march is still southward.

See also HISTORY AND MANNERS: Military Bases; Military Tradition; MYTHIC SOUTH: New South Myth; POLITICS: National Politics; URBANIZATION: Urban Growth; / Atlanta; Dallas; Houston; Miami; New Orleans

Richard M. Bernard
Marquette University

Carl Abbott, *The New Urban America: Growth and Politics in Sunbelt Cities* (1981); Richard M. Bernard and Bradley R. Rice, eds., *Sunbelt Cities: Politics and Growth since World War II* (1983); James C. Cobb, *The Selling of the South: The Southern Crusade for Industrial Development, 1936–1980* (1982); David C. Perry and Alfred J. Watkins, eds., *The Rise of the Sunbelt Cities* (1977); Kevin P. Phillips, *The Emerging Republican Majority* (1969); Kirkpatrick Sale, *Power Shift: The Rise of the Southern Rim and Its Challenge to the Eastern Establishment* (1975); Bernard L. Weinstein and Robert E. Firestone, *Regional Growth and Decline in the United States: The Rise of the Sunbelt and the Decline of the Northeast* (1978). ☆

ATLANTA AS COMMERCIAL CENTER

Atlanta's role as the commercial center of the Southeast began in the late 1830s when the Georgia Legislature decided to build a railroad from the Chattahoochee River northwesterly to Chattanooga, Tenn. Atlanta grew around the terminus of this Western & Atlantic line. By the mid-1840s two private lines had arrived, and Atlanta had connections to Augusta and Savannah. Eventually, 15 rail lines would converge on the "Gate City" as she far surpassed her state rivals.

During the Civil War Atlanta served as a major manufacturing and supply point for Confederate forces until General William Sherman's troops destroyed it in 1864. Atlanta's location, railroads, and spirit guaranteed its phoenix-like revival from the ashes of war. In 1869 the city became the state capital, and in 1871 the chamber of commerce was formed. Boosters organized international trade expositions in 1881, 1887, and 1895. The Cotton States and International Exposition of 1895 drew 800,000 visitors to the ambitious city of 75,000. Atlanta had become the principal distribution center for the country-store economy of the South.

The city passed the 100,000 threshold shortly after the turn of the century. In the 1920s the chamber of commerce sponsored the "Forward Atlanta" movement, which attracted nearly 800 new businesses with over 20,000 employees. This was also the take-off decade for Coca-Cola, Atlanta's most famous business. Although the city had some important factories, manufacturing always lagged behind the trade and services sectors in a diversified employment picture.

As World War II began, Atlanta fell behind New Orleans and ranked close to Memphis and Birmingham in size. By 1980, however, metropolitan Atlanta had 2 million residents and far outstripped these regional competitors. The prewar base had been built on railroads, distribution, and state government. In the postwar era, Atlanta built on that foundation and became the preeminent southeastern center for air transportation, trucking, corporate offices, and federal government activities. The local power structure believed that a moderate approach to race relations would be good for the business climate, and Atlanta forged its image as the "City Too Busy To Hate." In the 1960s boosters launched another "Forward Atlanta" campaign. This one brought urban renewal, a gleaming skyline, and the Southeast's first major-league sports team, the Braves in baseball. Georgia could not match the phenomenal population growth of Florida, but none of the Florida cities could challenge Atlanta's commercial dominance of the eastern third of the Sunbelt. As the executive secretary of the chamber of commerce noted in 1976, "We found out that while Atlanta was trying to be a regional city, it had become one of a handful of national cities."

See also URBANIZATION: / Atlanta

Bradley R. Rice
Clayton Junior College

Franklin Garrett, *Atlanta and Environs: A Chronicle of Its People and Events* (1969); Truman A. Hartshorn, *Metropolis in Georgia: Atlanta's Rise as a Major Transaction Center* (1976). ☆

BANKING

During the colonial period banking and financial intermediaries, except for general fire and life insurance companies, were almost nonexistent. By 1781 the situation was beginning to change with the establishment by Robert Morris of the Bank of North America and the later creation of the First Bank of the United States.

Under Alexander Hamilton's guidance, Congress chartered the First Bank of the United States (1791–1811) to provide a uniform currency and enhance the stability of the economy. Although the First Bank was not completely successful in achieving these objectives, it did provide financial services to the South through its branches in Baltimore, Charleston, New Orleans, Norfolk, Savannah, and Washington, D.C. In 1811, with political opposition growing, Congress refused to renew the bank's charter. The financial difficulties that resulted from the War of 1812 convinced Congress, however, to create another central bank, the Second Bank of the United States (1816–36). Under the leadership of Nicholas Biddle, the Second Bank operated more consciously as a central bank in its attempts to provide for economic stability and as a way of controlling state banks. However, the Second Bank also encountered opposition, especially from President Andrew Jackson, who convinced Congress not to renew the bank's charter.

Centralized banking was a highly important, if short-lived, development for the growing American economy. Another state-supported form of banking developed thereafter. With the demise of the Bank of North America in 1784, both New York and Massachusetts incorporated banks, thereby setting a precedent other states followed.

In the South the development of banking largely paralleled the financial development of the North. Southern states chartered a large number of private commercial banks and a smaller number of state banks. However, there were differences. Savings banks did not become important in the South because the region did not possess the large middle class that provided the necessary funds for such banks in the East. In the

South "property banks" were unique in that their purpose was to attract foreign capital for agriculture and internal improvements, using real estate as collateral for notes. The liquidity of southern banks was low and bank runs were disastrous, causing southern state legislatures to be the mainstay of these banks.

The 1830s was a critical decade for southern banking. President Jackson's attack on the Second Bank in the early 1830s reduced its influence over other financial institutions, leading to a rapid expansion of banks throughout the nation. However, the southern agricultural depression from 1837 to 1843 retarded this growth and even forced many southern banks to close.

In the aftermath of these financial failures most states adopted regulations, especially stricter reserve requirements, to promote sounder banking practices. The most famous such action was Louisiana's Bank Act of 1842 providing for a specie-backed currency. By providing specie reserves as a percentage of bank notes issued and thereby limiting the amount of notes, Louisiana successfully stabilized its banking system. Several other southern states during the 1840s and 1850s adopted the free-banking system outlined in the Free Banking Act of New York. In some cases, like Louisiana, the free-banking system worked well.

The turbulence of the 1830s and the political hostility toward banks in the 1840s were replaced by cautious expansion of southern banking in the 1850s. Reflecting the growth of the southern economy, a period of sustained prosperity appeared imminent, until the outbreak of the Civil War. In 1861 many southern banks began to suspend the convertibility of their notes into gold. In the same year, southern banks subscribed heavily to the first Confederate loan, thereby losing much of their specie. During the Civil War the specie that the Confederate States of America was able to obtain came largely from Britain and the continent. With limited ability to tax and to borrow, the CSA used the printing presses to pay for the war effort.

Between January 1861 and January 1864 the South's money supply increased over 11 times. Bank notes and deposits increased less than threefold, because southern commercial banks drastically raised their reserve ratios in anticipation of mass withdrawals triggered by the approach of Union troops. Although this behavior moderated the increase of the money supply somewhat and provided some protection for individual banks, many southern banks did not survive the Civil War. And the aftermath of the war was even worse.

The major feature of the years 1865 to 1913 was the South's financial underdevelopment; banking services were severely limited relative to those in other regions. The South, in fact, was the last region to be integrated into a national capital market. Most economic historians attribute this situation to the banking structure that resulted from the National Banking Acts of the Civil War years. This legislation limited national banks in the South by restricting agricultural loans and imposing relatively large capital requirements. Its tax on state bank notes, moreover, hindered the development of state banks. The result was that many banks operated in a noncompetitive market, a situation that limited the amount of bank credit available and raising interest rates. Because of local bank monopolies, country stores began channeling credit to borrowers, with serious long-run ramifications for the structure of southern agriculture.

After 1880 interest-rate differentials declined as such institutional changes as the spread of commercial paper and a reduction of the money power of local banks took place. Local monopoly power of southern banks declined, in part because of the 1900 Gold Standard Act, which formally put the nation on a gold standard and reduced minimum capital requirements for national banks, thereby making it easier for small banks to become national banks.

The next major change in the nation's banking system was the establishment of the Federal Reserve System (FRS) in 1913. The FRS was designed to prevent financial panics by acting as a lender of last resort or, in other words, by operating as a central bank. However, the original legislation also attempted to diffuse power geographically by establishing 12 regional or district banks, which were to play a role in formation of monetary policy. Federal Reserve Banks in the South were located in Atlanta, Dallas, and Richmond. The framers of the legislation hoped that the regional banks would be more aware of and concerned with the problems of banks within their region than would one central bank in New York or Washington, D.C.

The establishment of the Federal Reserve System did not solve southern banking problems, as witnessed by the difficult experiences of southern banks in the 1920s. Indeed, the Roaring Twenties saw the South experience a disproportionate number of bank failures when measured either by the number of bank closings or by deposits. The high rate of bank failure was probably caused by the long agricultural depression beginning in the early 1920s, the large number of small state banks, lax supervision, and incompetent management.

The Depression of the 1930s was extremely traumatic for the southern banking industry, as it was for the nation's banking industry generally. From 1929 to 1934 assets of southern banks fell from $7 billion to $4.7 billion, a decline of about 33 percent, compared with 21 percent in the rest of the country. Southern assets reached the 1929 levels only a decade later.

Although after World War II the South's banking structure grew to more closely resemble the national system, a larger percentage of southern banks were, in 1945, still small, nonmember state banks. They were also nonpar, not paying the full value of checks but deducting a service charge from the face value of each check. More importantly, southern banks still held large net deposits in banks outside the region. After 1945 the substantial economic growth that the South experienced caused rapid expansion in southern banking as well.

During the 1950s all southern states except the unit bank states experienced a reduction in the number of banks and a rapid expansion of branch banks. This was due to the increased urbanization of the South and the concurrent growth of suburbs. In the 1960s and 1970s bank expansion was fostered in such states as Georgia, Texas, and Virginia through the device of bank holding companies. Major financial centers developed in Atlanta, Dallas, Houston, and Miami, while North Carolina National Bank Corporation and Wachovia Corporation became important regional banks.

During the 1960s the major southern banks rapidly expanded by following the national trend of increased utilization of liability management techniques. Rather than only managing assets within a given liability structure, southern banks began aggressively to pursue additional deposits in order to obtain a target asset growth. The period of rapid and often reckless expansion ended abruptly in 1974 when the real estate market collapsed. Because so much construction was going on in the South, southern banks were more affected by this collapse than were northern banks. Banks such as North Carolina National, Atlanta's Citizen and Southern, and Florida's Flagship Banks wrote off millions of dollars of bad loans. Since then, cautious growth on the long-term pattern of Wachovia has been the dominant trend. Although such stringent credit practices curtail asset growth, they do provide banks with an increased ability to survive economic difficulties.

Not all modern southern bankers are cautious, however. Bert Lance was forced to resign as President Jimmy Carter's budget director because of repercussions from his loose, small-town Georgia credit practices. Tennessee banking magnate Jake Butcher, a Democratic candidate for governor in 1978 and the driving force behind the 1982 Knoxville World's Fair, used to claim that he rose from southern rural poverty to financial and political power the honest way—by borrowing. In 1983, however, his financial empire began to unravel when the Tennessee Banking Commission shut down Butcher's flagship, the United American Bank of Knoxville, a $760 million institution. This fourth largest U.S. commercial bank failure since the 1930s resulted from what the commission cited as "large and unusual loan losses," many of them to Democratic politicians and the bank's directors.

The emphasis on international banking will likely continue in the near future, and the specter of interstate banking looms over all banks. Some southern bankers are urging an interim step of regional banking in order to allow southern banks to acquire the time and resources needed before having to compete with external money-center banks. Although this proposal has not yet been enacted and implemented, it does indicate the desire of southerners to avoid increased control by nonsouthern banks. No matter what the outcome of these structural changes, the 1980s will not be a decade in which a lack of financial resources will hinder economic development. Instead, southern financial institutions have progressed to the point where they can now provide the funds necessary for further economic expansion.

Michael V. Namorato
University of Mississippi

R. Stanley Herren
North Dakota State University

Lance E. Davis, *Journal of Economic History* (September 1965); Thomas P. Gavan, *Banking and the Credit System in Georgia, 1810–1860* (1978); George D. Green, *Finance and Economic Development in the Old South: Louisiana Banking, 1804–1861* (1972); Bray Hammond, *Banks and Politics in America: From the Revolution to the Civil War* (1957); Emory Q. Hawk, *Economic History of the South* (1934); Calvin B. Hoover and B. U. Ratchford, *Economic Resources and Policies of the South* (1951); John A. James, *Journal of Interdisciplinary History* (Winter 1981); George Macesich, *Commercial Banking and Regional Development in the United States, 1950–1960* (1965); Fritz Redlich, *The Molding of American Banking: Men and Ideas* (1951); Richard Sylla, *Journal of Economic History* (December 1969); Elmus Wicker, *Journal of Economic History* (September 1980). ☆

BULLDOZER REVOLUTION

Historian C. Vann Woodward has suggested that the most apt "symbol of innovation" in the modern South is the bulldozer. "The roar and groan and dust of it greet one on the outskirts of every Southern city," he wrote in a 1958 essay on "The Search for Southern Identity." The mule had been the popular symbol of the South's traditional agricultural economy, but the giant earthmoving machine in the post–World War II period had become central to the industrial revolution in the region. The bulldozer symbolized the revolution "in its favorite area of operation, the area where city meets country; in its relentless speed; in its supreme disregard for obstacles, its heedless methods; in what it demolishes and in what it moves."

The bulldozer made possible the rapid and concentrated urbanization of the South in the 1940s and 1950s, and it facilitated the clearing of land for suburban development in the same period. Southerners and others traveling through the region became familiar with the giant machine on the landscape. It made possible the transforming work of the Tennessee Valley Authority, the Corps of Engineers, and the construction crews building interstate highways. The bulldozer swept away sharecroppers' shacks to make way for Sunbelt shopping malls.

Robert G. LeTourneau was perhaps the most notable bulldozer businessman in the South. Born in Vermont and raised in Minnesota, LeTourneau spent his young adulthood in California, working as an automobile repairman. A natural inventor, he developed tools for sale to contractors and opened a small factory in Stockton, Calif., in 1935 and another one later in Peoria, Ill. His southern operations were at Toccoa, Ga., Longview, Tex., and Vicksburg, Miss. In the latter case, the Warren County Chamber of Commerce purchased much of the land LeTourneau needed in order to encourage him to come to the site eight miles south of Vicksburg. LeTourneau's factories made much of the earthmoving equipment used by the armed services during World War II. By 1952 the Mississippi plant alone produced 22 types of heavy machinery used in 44 states and many foreign nations.

LeTourneau sold his earthmoving business in 1953 for $31 million to Westinghouse Air Brake Company. He retained, however, his factories in the South and converted them to the production of offshore oil rigs and missile-loading transport machinery. LeTourneau reentered the bulldozer business in 1958. Born out of the region, LeTourneau came to live in the South and "adopted" it. He was an evangelical who found the region a congenial spot. Known as "God's businessman," he once observed that his life had "three planks—speed, the welding torch, and the Bible." This southern earthmover provided financial support for the Billy Graham revivals in the early 1950s, and Graham helped dedicate and bless LeTourneau's work.

Charles Reagan Wilson
University of Mississippi

Longview, Tex., *News-Journal* (1 January 1953); Vicksburg, Miss., *Evening Post* (26 November 1942); *Wall Street Journal* (28 January 1957); C. Vann Woodward, *The Burden of Southern History* (1960). ☆

CHAIN AND SPECIALTY STORES

After the Civil War the rural South witnessed the development of country or general stores. Mail-order houses such as Sears, Roebuck and Company caused socioeconomic rumblings, but the real merchandising revolution was the advent of specialty stores—which sold one product (such as shoes) rather than a variety of products—and their spread as chains under common ownership. These new stores grew in number during the early 20th century until by the 1920s they held a sufficiently large share of the market to feed the growing cult of consumerism through the promise of standardized goods and lower prices made possible by economies of scale. But if there was the prospect of a better standard of living, there was also the threat—or so it seemed to some—of the destruction of local proprietorship and community involvement in states held by absentee owners from the North. The issue of regional versus national culture was expressed in populist rhetoric in the context of an urban-industrial progressive spirit.

By the 1930s—in the face of the Great Depression—numerous attempts were made across the nation to regulate chain stores by means of municipal and state taxation and fair-trade laws. Many of these measures originated in the South, and some of the most significant Supreme Court cases concerning chain-store regulation involved southern states (*Stewart Dry Goods* v. *Lewis* [Kentucky]; *Liggett* v. *Lee* [Florida]; *A&P* v. *Grosjean* [Louisiana]). Among the more prominent antichain figures were southerners such as Congressman Wright Patman of Texas—who sought national chain-store regulation—and W. K. "Old Man" Henderson, who broadcast nationwide tirades against the chains over radio station KWKH, Shreveport.

Even in the face of such opposition chain stores prospered as the South's urban areas joined in the creation of innovative merchandising. Clarence Saunders of Memphis pioneered many self-service techniques in his Piggly Wiggly stores; the Florida-based Winn-Dixie stores became leaders in the food field. The growth of national and regional chains within the South reflected its increasing urbanization and transformation from a region characterized by Franklin D. Roosevelt as "the Nation's No. 1 economic problem" to a part of the developing Sunbelt. As it changed from exploited to exploiter, the South altered its characteristic forms of marketing. In a nation where merchandising is a key to culture, the results have been startling.

Carl Ryant
University of Louisville

Thomas D. Clark, *Pills, Petticoats and Plows: The Southern Country Store* (1944); Godfrey M. Lebhar, *Chain Stores in America*, 1859–1959 (3d ed., 1963); Carl Ryant, *Journal of Southern History* (May 1973). ☆

COCA-COLA
||||||||||||||||||||||||||||||||

William Allen White once called it "the sublimated essence of all that America stands for," and an anonymous but no less fervent admirer called it "the holy water of the American South." The "it," as the latest in a long line of slogans proclaims, is, of course, Coca-Cola.

John S. Pemberton, known as "Doc" like most pharmacists of his era, concocted Coca-Cola in 1886 primarily as a hangover cure. It has subsequently been many things to many people—to Robert Winship Woodruff, its high priest for nearly 60 years, "a religion as well as a business." Pemberton first made Coke, its nickname from early on, in Atlanta, and Coca-Cola men have bestrode that city ever since. Pemberton was pleased soon after his invention to sell the rights to it for $1,750 to another Atlanta pharmacist, Asa Candler. Candler was even more pleased in 1919 to sell the Coca-Cola Company for $25 million. It was the biggest financial deal, until then, in the history of the American South. (Candler sold only part of his bounty; earlier, in 1899, thinking that consumption of the drink would be limited largely to soda fountains, he had disposed of practically all the bottling rights to it for one dollar. The drink had first been bottled back in 1894 by Joseph Biedenharn in Vicksburg, Miss.) The prime mover in the 1919 transaction was the banker Ernest Woodruff. His son Robert (1889–1985) took over the company in 1923. "Asa Candler put us on our feet," one Coca-Cola executive would say years afterward, "and Bob Woodruff gave us wings."

Dwight D. Eisenhower once speculated that his good friend Bob Woodruff might be the richest man in the United States. Atlanta's Emory University, on whose predecessor campus Woodruff had spent less than a year as an undergraduate before being invited to leave, would over the ensuing years be endowed, by him and his family, with some $150 million of Coca-Cola largess.

Until World War II, when the Coca-Cola Company construed it to be its patriotic duty to get Coke to every thirsty American serviceman abroad, the drink was chiefly marketed in the United

States. Soon it was universal. Asa Candler briefly flirted with the idea of Coca-Cola cigars and Coca-Cola chewing gum at the turn of the century, but until the 1950s the company was strictly a one-product enterprise. Then it began to diversify. Orange juice, other soft drinks, eventually even wines, and most recently films (Columbia Pictures) were merchandised around the world. The placid liquid that Doc Pemberton had first mixed in a backyard, three-legged iron pot (stirring it with an oar) had become the foundation of a multibillion-dollar industry.

In 1985 Coca-Cola chairman Roberto Guizueta announced that, for the first time in 99 years, the drink's taste formula would be changed, leading to much hoopla and to criticism from some for yet another change in a southern tradition. The company relented in the face of public pressure and continued marketing "classic" Coke.

See also HISTORY AND MANNERS: / Beverages

E. J. Kahn, Jr.
The New Yorker

Bob Hall, *Southern Exposure* (Fall 1976); E. J. Kahn, Jr., *The Big Drink: The Story of Coca-Cola* (1951). ☆

DE BOW'S REVIEW
⁣

Established in New Orleans in 1846 by James Dunwoody Brownson De Bow, *De Bow's Review* was the preeminent southern antebellum journal of business, economics, and public opinion. Modeled on *Hunt's Merchant's Magazine* of New York, the *Commercial Review*, as it was

often called, was initially devoted to "the diversities and ramifications of commercial action." Always a partisan of the South, De Bow increasingly advocated southern nationalism and the defense of slavery after 1850, and he opened the journal's pages to supporters of secession, including Edmund Ruffin and George Fitzhugh.

Despite the *Review*'s importance, De Bow always had difficulty keeping the journal in print. Southerners refused to subscribe in sufficient numbers, and De Bow was forced to suspend publication in 1847 and 1849. Circulation never exceeded 5,000. Slow to realize the possibility of revenue from advertising, De Bow on the eve of the Civil War found the advertisements of northern firms to be his best source of income. He was also forced, after repeated failures with southern printers, to have the *Review* printed in the North, a fact he kept hidden from his readers. De Bow managed to keep the publication alive during the Civil War until April 1862, when financial problems, scarcities of printing supplies, and the fall of New Orleans forced suspension. One issue was published in 1864; the journal then lay dormant until war's end. De Bow resumed publication in January 1866 with the *Review* now devoted to the restoration of national unity and the development of the nation's wealth and resources. Some of the familiar contributors returned, for instance George Fitzhugh, but De Bow was unable to restore the magazine to its prewar eminence. De Bow's death in February 1867 brought a quick end to his journal. Sold in March 1868, the *Review* soon ceased publication.

Influential beyond its limited circulation, *De Bow's Review* reflected both southern opinion and the somewhat idiosyncratic views of its editor. Always advocating southern interests, De Bow's contributors ardently defended slavery, argued the superiority of southern civilization, promoted the improvement of southern agriculture, and after 1850 championed southern nationalism. De Bow, however, also firmly believed in promoting southern commercial, mercantile, and industrial interests. His frank advocacy of the urgent need to achieve commercial and industrial independence for the coming contest with the North set De Bow apart from the reigning planter ethos and probably limited the *Review*'s appeal to the planter elite. De Bow astutely recognized the economic and industrial weaknesses of the South, yet his untiring campaign to build a solid commercial and industrial economy failed. Not wholly typical of antebellum southern thinking, then, *De Bow's Review* still provides a superb window into the southern mind during the 15 years before secession and civil war.

See also MYTHIC SOUTH: / Fitzhugh, George; SCIENCE AND MEDICINE: / Ruffin, Edmund

Daniel J. Wilson
Muhlenberg College

De Bow's Review, vols. 1–34 (1846–64), After the War Series, vols. 1–8 (1866–70), New Series, After the War Series, vol. 1 (1879–80); Paul F. Paskoff and Daniel J. Wilson, *The Cause of the South: Selections from De Bow's Review, 1846–1867* (1982); Ottis Clark Skipper, *J. D. B. De Bow: Magazinist of the Old South* (1958); Diffee William Standard, *"De Bow's Review, 1846–1880: A Magazine of Southern Opinion"* (Ph.D. dissertation, University of North Carolina, 1970). ☆

DELTA AIRLINES

Beginning in 1924 as Huff Daland Dusters and specializing primarily in crop spraying in the southern United States and Latin America, Delta adopted its enduring name in 1928 from the Mississippi Delta region. Guided by Collett Everman ("C.E.") Woolman, a former county agricultural agent who ultimately became its patriarch and longtime chief executive, it began passenger operations in 1929 from its Monroe, La., base on a route eventually extending from Fort Worth to Atlanta. Forced to abandon this service in 1930 when it failed to win an essential federal government airmail contract, it survived precariously on meager earnings from crop dusting and fixed-base activities.

In 1934 congressional probing of irregularities in the awarding of previous airmail contracts led to cancellation of

Delta Airlines stewardess with portable Coca-Cola cooler, c. 1945

most existing contracts and fresh opportunity for Delta, which in June of that year won an airmail route from Fort Worth to Charleston via Atlanta and other cities. Resuming airline operations, the company became a vigorous regional carrier. Increasing capital requirements, partly connected with acquisition of Douglas DC-2 and DC-3 aircraft, led in 1941 to a transfer of Delta's headquarters to Atlanta.

Delta's intensive use of a restricted fleet in World War II produced earnings that, coupled with a Chicago-to-Miami route award granted by the Civil Aeronautics Board (CAB) in 1945, laid the basis for postwar expansion. Inflation, mounting costs, and other industrywide problems produced spotty earnings in the late 1940s; but thereafter Delta enjoyed steady profits, enlarging its system by absorbing another regional carrier, Chicago and Southern, in a 1953 merger and winning a route the following year from Atlanta to Washington and New York.

Delta was a pioneer of the jet age, the first line to inaugurate DC-8, DC-9, and Convair 880 service. It also won new routes to such key destinations as Los Angeles and in 1971 absorbed Northeast Airlines in another merger. Woolman's ability to project the company as a southern-style extended family promoted loyalty among Delta's mainly nonunion employees. After his death in 1966 a management team trained under his tutelage continued to emphasize this "family feeling" and retained his conservative financial policies. Such strategies, coupled with rigorous fleet standardization and new routes to such places as London, made Delta the most consistently profitable firm in the airline industry, a position it continued to hold in the 1970s and

early 1980s despite rising fuel costs, periodic recessions, and the onset of federal deregulation.

W. David Lewis
Wesley P. Newton
Auburn University

W. David Lewis and Wesley P. Newton, *Delta: The History of an Airline* (1979). ☆

DUKE, JAMES B.

(1856–1925) Businessman and philanthropist.

Youngest of three children of Washington Duke and Artelia Roney Duke, James Buchanan Duke was born in what was then Orange (now Durham) County, N.C., on 23 December 1856. Although his mother died in 1858 and his father was later drafted into Confederate service, "Buck" Duke, as he was known in the family, spent most of his childhood on his father's modest farm about three miles from the new village of Durham. He received some schooling at an academy in Durham and, after a brief stay at New Garden School (later Guilford College), attended the Eastman Business College in Poughkeepsie, N.Y.

Washington Duke began the home manufacture of brightleaf smoking tobacco after the Civil War, and James B. Duke grew up with a firsthand knowledge of every phase of the tobacco business. In 1874 Washington Duke sold his farm and moved his family into Durham to launch a more ambitious manufacturing operation. Displaying a rare talent for business and an appetite for hard work, James B. Duke became a full partner in W. Duke Sons and Company when it was incorporated in 1878.

James B. Duke, North Carolina business-man, c. 1900

Though the company prospered, it was overshadowed by the older, larger W. T. Blackwell Company, which produced the famed Bull Durham brand of tobacco. After bringing in handrollers from New York to produce the newfangled cigarette, the Dukes, apparently inspired largely by James B. Duke, gambled in the mid-1880s on a machine-made cigarette and entered into an important, secret contract for the machine invented by James A. Bonsack of Virginia.

The gamble paid off handsomely, for by 1890 W. Duke Sons and Company was the leading manufacturer of cigarettes in the nation, and James B. Duke, who moved permanently to New York in 1884 to manage the branch factory there, had played a key role in organizing the leading cigarette manufacturers into a combination or "trust," the American Tobacco Company. Within a decade, that company, with Duke as its president, controlled the major portion of the nation's entire tobacco industry—save for cigars—and with operations in Britain, Japan, and elsewhere in the

world became a pioneer multinational corporation.

Even before the U.S. Supreme Court called for the dissolution of the American Tobacco Company in 1911, James B. Duke, along with his older brother Benjamin N. Duke and others, had invested heavily in textile manufacturing in Durham and elsewhere in North Carolina. Partly as a result of that activity, the Dukes early became interested in the new electric-power industry and specifically in hydroelectric power. In 1905 they launched the Southern Power Company with headquarters in Charlotte, N.C., and, largely under the leadership of James B. Duke and a brilliant engineer with whom Duke worked closely, William S. Lee, the business eventually grew into the giant Duke Power Company serving the Piedmont regions of North and South Carolina.

Starting in the late 19th century, Washington Duke and his family began regularly to give substantial support to various philanthropic causes, especially, but not exclusively, Methodist-related ones. The Dukes were instrumental in bringing the Methodist-sponsored Trinity College to Durham in 1892, and Benjamin N. Duke became the family's main link with the college as well as its chief patron. In December 1924 James B. Duke, after several years of careful planning, established the Duke Endowment as a perpetual trust for certain philanthropic purposes in the Carolinas. Systematizing on a perpetual basis a long-standing pattern of family giving, James B. Duke specified that a prime beneficiary of the endowment was to be a new university organized around Trinity College, which, at the suggestion of Trinity's president William P. Few, was to be named Duke University. Annual support from the endowment went also to nonprofit hospitals for both races in the Carolinas, three other colleges (Davidson, Furman, and Johnson C. Smith), child-care institutions in the Carolinas for blacks and whites, and rural Methodist churches and retired Methodist preachers in North Carolina.

After a first marriage that ended in a much-publicized divorce in 1906, James B. Duke in 1907 married a Georgia-born widow, Mrs. Walker P. Inman (née Nanaline Holt), and in 1912 a daughter, Doris Duke, was born to the couple. James B. Duke died in his mansion on New York's Fifth Avenue on 10 October 1925 and is buried alongside Washington and Benjamin N. Duke in the Memorial Chapel on the campus of Duke University.

See also EDUCATION: / Duke University

Robert F. Durden
Duke University

Robert F. Durden, *The Dukes of Durham, 1865–1929* (1975); John K. Winkler, *Tobacco Tycoon: The Story of James B. Duke* (1942). ☆

FLAGLER, HENRY
(1830–1913) Businessman and promoter.

From the beginning of his Florida enterprises in 1885 until his death in 1913, Henry Morrison Flagler led the development of the east coast of Florida. Starting with the luxury resort hotel Ponce de Leon in St. Augustine, he opened a chain of hotels that stretched from Jacksonville Beach to Key West and across the Gulf Stream to Nassau. His Florida East Coast Railroad linked Jacksonville and Miami and ultimately

extended over the sea to Key West. The Model Land Company constituted the third division of Flagler's empire in Florida.

Born into modest circumstances in rural western New York in 1830, Flagler rose in the business world through force of will, tireless work, and entrepreneurial skill. He became one of the original partners with John D. Rockefeller in Standard Oil Corporation and was a multimillionaire when he arrived in Florida at the age of 55 to begin a second career as the builder of the Florida east coast. During his years in Florida he was praised for opening the frontier to settlement and providing employment through his enterprises, as well as for his philanthropic contributions to local communities. He was also condemned by populist-spirited individuals who opposed the plutocratic economic and political power he personified.

Florida's character was altered by the activities of men like Flagler and his west-coast Florida contemporary Henry B. Plant, the developer of Tampa. Departing from the typical Deep South cotton-state mold, Florida began to assume a new character based on tourism, citrus, and specialized agriculture. This was most true in the lower east coast area, which had been only very sparsely populated prior to the time when Flagler's railroad made it possible to transport northern tourists in and winter vegetables out. While panhandle and north Florida retained much of the ambiance of neighboring Alabama and Georgia, the newly settled parts of the peninsula showed the influence of large-scale immigration from northern states. Palm Beach, West Palm Beach, and Miami owe their existence to Flagler. A small tourist industry had existed since early in the century based on the infirm and the aged who sought relief from the northern winter. This changed in Flagler's day. The completion of the national rail network made it possible for larger numbers of tourists to come to Florida, and the tubercular invalid was displaced as the typical visitor by the pleasure-seeking, newly affluent class created by the urban-industrial revolution.

Flagler's use of Spanish Renaissance architecture in his St. Augustine hotels (but not elsewhere) foreshadowed the extensive employment of "Mediterranean" styles in the state in the present century.

Henry M. Flagler epitomizes such features of Florida's culture as the spirit of "development," the prominent role of the wealthy in society, and the injection of external influences, which have made Florida different from other Deep South states.

Thomas Graham
Flagler College

David L. Chandler, *Henry Flagler: The Astonishing Life and Times of the Visionary Robber Baron Who Founded Florida* (1986); Sidney Walter Martin, *Florida's Flagler* (1949). ☆

FOREIGN INDUSTRY
||||||||||||||||||||||||||||||||||||||||||||||||||

Foreign industry, or commercial enterprises owned by residents outside the United States, has been a part of America and the South from the beginning of American history. Food, tobacco, and forest-products industries were among the first sectors of foreign investments, followed by textiles and numerous other industries. Much of the early railroad and canal construction in the United States was also done or financed by for-

eign investors. However, the major influx of foreign industry occurred during the 20th century and became particularly significant for the South as late as the 1960s and 1970s. For example, only 10 percent of the foreign industry in South Carolina existing in 1983 was established before 1970. Much of the increase in foreign investments in the South during the 1970s can be attributed to increased awareness of foreign investors about the South—in both cultural and economic terms—caused in large part by the worldwide media coverage of the presidential campaign and subsequent presidency of Jimmy Carter.

While the South is not the dominant region of foreign investment in the United States, it does have a disproportionately high percentage of foreign industry, based on comparative population and industrialization. Since 1970 it has been the fastest-growing region in terms of attracting foreign investment. In several southern states, such as South Carolina, foreign investment accounts for more than 25 percent of all new manufacturing investments. In addition, southern employment in foreign industry is at levels generally four to five times higher than the national average.

The Dutch, English, Germans, French, and Canadians are the primary investors in the South, but Japanese investments have also become significant. In addition, more than a dozen other nations have invested in the region. Although the textile industry brought many early foreign investors to the South, other industries now attract more foreign backing, including rubber and plastics, petrochemicals, electronics, chemicals and pharmaceuticals, metalworking, machinery, scientific equipment, and stone, clay, glass, and cement. Still other foreign investments have occurred in retailing, commercial real estate, agriculture, and banking. In short, as the South's economy has diversified, so too has its foreign industry. In fact, much of the South's diversification occurred as a result of foreign investment.

No two states have equal amounts or varieties of foreign industry, making generalizations difficult. In value terms, South Carolina is the leader, but in employment North Carolina is the leader. Georgia is the leader in terms of Japanese investments, South Carolina in terms of German ones. Foreign industry in Florida is concentrated in banking and real estate; but in Louisiana it is in petrochemicals, in South Carolina in chemicals and tires, and in Georgia in sales offices and warehousing/distribution. In the Mississippi Delta a large tract of land is owned by the Queen of England.

Major similarities in all these include the motivations of the investors and the high degree of state promotional activity and investment incentives. Overall, the major investor attractions of the South appear to be labor, land, and lifestyle considerations. Labor is still relatively abundant, inexpensive, and nonunionized, and the labor force has an excellent track record of high productivity, low absenteeism, and stability of employment. Land is also comparatively abundant, inexpensive, and generally well connected through transportation to other areas of the nation and the world. The lifestyle of the South is perhaps the most similar of all American regions to that of Europe and Japan—more tradition- and family-oriented and hospitable, with numerous recreational opportunities.

Virtually all the southern states have become active and aggressive in state investment promotion activities and incentives. Numerous trade and investment missions are conducted to promote the states to foreign business interests, and packages of free worker training, site selection, tax credits, and industrial revenue bonds are also offered to potential investors. Numerous southern governors have played active roles in these promotional activities, underscoring the states' interest in and commitment to foreign investment in the minds of potential foreign investors.

Foreign industry has had an increasing impact on the South, economically and socially. The development of new industries, the expansion and modernization of existing industries, the upgrading of worker skills and wages, and the broadening of tax bases are only a few of the direct economic impacts. In turn, income generated directly by foreign investments creates additional income for suppliers, retailers, and other parts of the community. Foreign industry also has brought foreign people to the South, largely management and technical employees and their families, resulting in an internationalization of the communities in which they locate.

Neither the social impact of foreign industry nor its economic impact can yet be determined precisely, and some effects on existing firms have been negative. In both economic and cultural terms, foreign investments are still too new and, as a percentage of all activity, too small to have had any major impact. However, foreign industry will likely play a larger role in the future economic development of the South and, in the process, begin to have a larger impact on the culture of the South.

Jeffrey S. Arpan
University of South Carolina

Jeffrey S. Arpan and David Ricks, *Directory of Foreign Manufacturers in the United States* (1975); Jeffrey S. Arpan, Edmond Flowers, and David Ricks, *Journal of International Business Studies* (Summer 1981); Cedric Suzman, ed., *The Costs and Benefits of Foreign Direct Investments from a State Perspective* (1982); U.S. Department of Commerce, *Foreign Direct Investment in the United States*, vols. 1–9 (1976); Mira Wilkins, ed., *Foreign Investment in the United States* (1977), *Foreign Enterprise in Florida: The Impact of Non-United States Direct Investment* (1979), *New Foreign Enterprise in Florida* (1980). ☆

FURNITURE INDUSTRY

Most of the fine furniture used in the South during the colonial period was imported from England. As towns and cities grew in size and wealth, however, skilled craftsmen from England, Scotland, Ireland, Germany, and France and from northern cities in America made their way in increasing numbers into lucrative southern markets such as Williamsburg, Charleston, New Bern, and Savannah. Some of the early craftsmen were itinerants, some were employed on large plantations, and some established shops in the larger towns and cities. The common folk made most of their own furniture or used the products of local carpenters.

Woods used by early southern furniture makers were largely walnut, cherry, and pine. Mahogany became increasingly popular after 1750, but pine, oak, and poplar continued to be used for framing and as the base for mahogany veneers. Maple and birch were not used extensively until 1800.

Although a few small factories had been established in Nashville, Tenn., and Danville, Va., somewhat earlier, the South's entrance into modern furniture manufacturing occurred in 1888 when local businessmen built a factory in High Point, N.C. The abundance and low cost of both wood and labor gave High Point a cost advantage over northern competition, and the industry spread from there into nearby centers in North Carolina and Virginia. As worker skills improved, so did the quality of High Point furniture. The industry grew rapidly after World War I, and following World War II North Carolina moved ahead of New York to become the leading furniture-manufacturing state. By that time High Point and southwestern Virginia had established reputations for producing furniture of high quality, with cheaper grades coming from newer centers to the south and west. Besides North Carolina and Virginia, important centers of furniture manufacturing are found in Tennessee, Texas, Arkansas, Georgia, and Mississippi.

The southern furniture industry began, and remains, a largely craft-oriented, family-owned business. During recent years a number of small companies have been purchased by larger competitors, and other corporate structures have shown increasing interest in the high return on capital investments that has characterized the southern furniture industry. Whatever ownership structure may develop in the future, however, the South's abundant wood supplies and high-quality labor should continue to provide the competitive edges needed for substantial growth.

See also FOLKLIFE: / Furniture Making

Sidney R. Jumper
University of Tennessee

Paul H. Burroughs, *Southern Antiques* (1931); B. F. Lemert, *Economic Geography* (April 1934); *New York Times* (25 October 1984); Lonn Taylor and David B. Warren, *Texas Furniture: The Cabinetmakers and Their Work, 1840–1880* (1975); U.S. Department of Commerce, Bureau of the Census, *Census of Manufacturers: 1958* (1961). ☆

GRADY, HENRY W.
||||||||||||||||||||||||||||||||||||||||||||
(1850–1889) Newspaper editor.

Born 24 May 1850, in Athens, Ga., to William Sammons and Ann Gartrell Grady, Henry Woodfin Grady enjoyed a comfortable upbringing. The wise management of his father, a substantial merchant who died in 1864 from wounds received serving in the Confederate army, enabled Henry to enroll at the University of Georgia in 1866. Following graduation in 1868, he attended the University of Virginia for a year, excelling in oratory and displaying journalistic talent as a contributor to the Atlanta *Constitution*. Returning to Georgia in 1869, Grady located in Rome, edited various newspapers there, and married Julia King, his childhood sweetheart, in 1871. The next year, he purchased an interest in the Atlanta *Daily Herald* and moved to that bustling city to join the *Herald*'s editorial staff. When the *Herald* ceased publication in 1876, Grady, while serving as special correspondent to a number of papers outside of Georgia, joined the staff of the *Constitution*, the journal with which he would be associated until his death on 23 December 1889.

Part owner and managing editor after 1880, Grady helped build the *Constitution* into the region's most popular newspaper as he himself emerged as the leading spokesman of the New South movement, the attempt to revive the region largely through industrialization. For economic progress to occur, he said, the South must cultivate the goodwill of northern investors. Reconciliation between the sections depended, he believed, upon the social stability that would result from an amicable resolution of the race issue in the South. Given northern restraint and trust, white southerners would respect the civil and political rights conferred upon black southerners during Reconstruction but would maintain white supremacy and segregation—an arrangement, he argued, that merely reflected the instinct of both races.

Not only in the pages of the *Constitution* but before audiences from Boston to Dallas, Grady spread the gospel of southern progress. In his celebrated "New South" address of 1886, he assured New York's New England Society that southerners, while cherishing the memory of the Old South and the Confederacy, had accepted the verdict of war and bore the North no ill will. Hard at work rebuilding, the South, he contended, treated blacks equitably, desired intersectional harmony, and wished to promote further economic development.

Grady's vision of a South of "sunshine everywhere and all the time" gave hope to many of his contemporaries, yet at his death it remained still a vision.

See also MEDIA: / Atlanta *Constitution*

Wayne Mixon
Mercer University

Paul M. Gaston, *The New South Creed: A Study in Southern Mythmaking* (1970); Mills Lane, *The New South: Writings and Speeches of Henry Grady* (1971); Raymond B. Nixon,

Henry W. Grady, Spokesman of the New South (1943). ☆

GREGG, WILLIAM
|||||||||||||||||||||||||||||||||||||||||
(1800–1867) Businessman.

Gregg was born 2 February 1800 in Monongalia County, [West] Va., and died 13 September 1867 in Graniteville, S.C. His outspoken advocacy of manufacturing and his entrepreneurship of the Graniteville Manufacturing Company (1846–67) fixed his reputation as "the father" of the southern textile industry, an image enhanced by Broadus Mitchell's laudatory biography (1928). Initially, Gregg amassed a fortune as a jeweler and silversmith in Columbia (1824) and Charleston (1838). Introduced to cotton manufacturing at his uncle's small mill (circa 1810) near Madison, Ga., Gregg in 1837 purchased stock in the Vaucluse Mill (1833) in the Horse Creek Valley of Edgefield District, S.C.

In 1844 he retired as a merchant and devoted his energies and financial resources to industrialization. After touring New England mills, Gregg authored a series of newspaper articles, later published as *Essays on Domestic Industry* (1845), admonishing southerners to build more textile factories. By the late 1840s most South Carolina newspaper editors supported Gregg's crusade. In 1846 Gregg launched his own mill at Graniteville in the Horse Creek Valley. For the next 20 years he planned and directed every detail of the large-scale (initially 9,245 spindles and 500 looms), two-story granite factory and its surrounding village. Although only one of several pioneer southern entrepreneurs, Gregg was the region's best-known industrial publicist. In a cultural context his ideas and policies at Graniteville played a major role in creating the stereotypical image of the rural, paternalistic southern mill village. Antiurban in his writings, Gregg refused to invest in the nearby Augusta mills being erected during the 1840s. He advocated the model of an isolated, self-contained community. His company controlled the lives of the rural poor white families who moved into his picturesque wooden cottages. Such control over white operatives was possible in the South, Gregg suggested, because of the presence of potential black workers. His rhetoric punctuated the central tenet of the South's cotton-mill ideology: social as well as economic dividends flowed from industrialization. Mill villages would "uplift" the poor whites. Although his social ideas persisted and his mill paid reasonable dividends, the antebellum South, in general, failed to adopt Gregg's industrial philosophy.

See also SOCIAL CLASS: / Company Towns

John S. Lupold
Columbus College

Ernest M. Lander, Jr., *The Textile Industry in Antebellum South Carolina* (1969); Thomas P. Martin, *Journal of Southern History* (August 1945); Broadus Mitchell, *William Gregg: Factory Master of the Old South* (1928); Tom E. Terrill, *Journal of Economic History* (March 1976). ☆

INSURANCE
|||||||||||||||||||||||||||||||||

The persistence of deep-rooted facets of southern socioeconomic life and culture—limited financial assets, African-bred burial practices, rural lifestyles long retained by urban dwellers, insecurities derived in the painful adjustment from plantation paternalism to semifreedom—go far to explain the seeming paradox of the region's high personal-security consciousness linked with its below-average insurance coverage. In 1982 southern states accounted for 9 of the top 17 states in the number of life insurance policies in force, but only 5 states were above the national average in per family life insurance in force. No southern-headquartered insurer ranked among the top 30 in terms of assets.

In the antebellum period limited southern commercial expansion failed to lure scarce capital into the casualty business. The region also failed to share in the northern surge of life insurance activities induced by the extensive breakdown of rural-bred kinship ties. High mortality rates for poor white southern males discouraged sales, although plantation owners paid high premiums to northern insurers on the lives of their skilled slaves, especially those hired out for railroad construction and industrial work. As early as the 1790s free southern blacks organized mutual benefit societies to fulfill their obligations to the deceased in the "sweet sorrow" of passage to the netherworld, as well as to assure their own avoidance of a pauper's burial or, worse, disposal of their body to a medical school.

In the postbellum era southern white mortality rates improved, enhancing the market for large northern-based insurers, whereas black death rates rose dramatically, especially in the urban South. Black churches and lodges established a plethora of benevolent, often secret and ritualistic self-help societies. Over time, poor business practices and occasional peculation led to rising contempt for "coffin clubs." Between 1890 and 1910, as discriminatory hiring practices eroded employment opportunities for black males and denied them the franchise in state after state, black-owned-and-managed health and life insurance companies were organized, primarily to provide sickness and burial insurance coverage to all family members. The small weekly premiums were paid primarily by black women, who had an employment rate more than double that of white women.

Joining altruism with capitalistic incentives and motivated by black pride, such black entrepreneurs as Alonzo Herndon and John Merrick—both barbers with white clienteles—created well-managed companies that provided employment opportunities for college-educated black youth faced with restricted regional opportunities. (Thus, Walter White agonized over the decision to give up his job with Standard Life of Atlanta in 1917 in order to accept an administrative post in New York City with the National Association for the Advancement of Colored People.) Over the years successful black insurance companies, often associated with funeral homes and banks to which they channeled premium income, emerged as one of the most significant sources of wealth and high status in the southern black community.

Although they viewed the southern black population as their legitimate preserve, black insurers faced vigorous competition from white-owned regional stock companies offering the same coverage, usually at similar rates. Both white- and black-managed insurance enterprises in many instances achieved excellent records for solidity and financial reliability, provided mortgages for home buyers, and generated funds that flowed into regional utilities and state and municipal bonds. The failure rate for smaller and weaker insurers, however, was considerable, and when so dynamic and hitherto successful an enterprise as black-owned Standard Life collapsed in the mid-1920s, even a stalwart exponent of racial self-help like policyholder W. E. B. Du Bois was plunged into despair. Convinced that white-managed firms were safer institutions and that holding one of their contracts conveyed a measure of prestige, blacks in large numbers continued to favor white insurers. Successful white-owned enterprises provided a powerful vehicle for wealth accumulation in the region, and they afforded extensive employment to a legion of high-school-educated home service agents. Increasingly, large home-office operations stimulated the growth of Richmond, Nashville, Jacksonville, Atlanta, and Dallas as regional financial centers.

The burgeoning southern economy of the post–World War II period, with its expanding white middle class, led many larger insurers to phase out home service to the lower-income groups. A proliferation of small concerns, primarily white-owned, were organized to serve the still-large traditional market. A number of region-based, white-owned firms attempted to cultivate the biracial market, with its wide income disparities. They relied for a time on "sociological underwriting" to justify rate differentials between black and white policyholders.

With the passage of civil rights legislation in the mid-1960s, the top management of white-owned insurers began to take steps to integrate their sales and home-office staffs. The pace of compliance varied widely as many insurers experienced difficulty in overcoming the opposition of white employees and de-centralized sales staffs. The conventional belief was that black agents could not possibly sell white prospects, and widespread apprehension appeared regarding the ramifications of integrated staffs at social functions and company conventions. Nonetheless, a Wharton study in 1970 found that some southern white-owned insurers exhibited a greater willingness than those elsewhere to actively pursue nondiscriminatory hiring practices. By the early 1980s black-owned insurers found themselves outbid for black sales and technical specialists. Complaints of a "black brain drain" were voiced and stress was placed on the necessity for cooperative training programs and shared infrastructure in order to compete effectively.

During the 1970s a major merger-and-acquisition movement took place among white-owned insurers in the region, altering the structure of the industry. In the acquisition of Nashville-based National Life and Accident Insurance Company by American General Life Insurance Company of Houston, Tex., competition was considerably reduced. In 1979 Nationale-Nederlanden NV, the Netherlands' largest insurance company, acquired the Life Insurance Company of Georgia (organized in 1891 with negligible funds), for $360 million. The declining role of small and medium-sized regional insurers and the probable impact of this change upon the socioeconomic and cultural life of the South has thus far aroused little interest.

See also URBANIZATION: / Atlanta; Dallas; Nashville; Richmond

Jack Blicksilver
Georgia State University

Charles S. Johnson, *The Negro in American Civilization* (1930); Armand J. Thieblot, Jr., and Linda P. Fletcher, *Negro Employment in Finance: A Study of Racial Policies in Banking and Insurance*, vol. 2—*Studies in Negro Employment* (1970); Walter B. Weare, *Black Business in the New South: A Social History of the North Carolina Mutual Life Insurance Company* (1973); Viviana A. Rotman Zelizer, *Morals and Markets: The Development of Life Insurance in the United States* (1979). ☆

LIQUOR INDUSTRY

||||||||||||||||||||||||||||||||||||||||||||||||||

The distillation of southern liquor dates from the early colonial period. Efforts to reproduce European wines and beers generally failed, but colonists quickly learned to distill local fruits and grains. They made corn whiskey in Jamestown, for example, while Georgians distilled peach brandy. By the late 1600s cheaply imported rum had further confirmed colonial preferences for hard liquor, and Scotch-Irish immigration in the mid-1700s widely popularized whiskey making, particularly on the frontiers. Rye and barley distilling consequently flourished in Maryland and parts of Virginia, where even George Washington made rye liquor.

Whiskey production soared after the Revolution (which had disrupted the rum trade) as new western harvests increased grain supplies. Farmers routinely distilled surpluses, as whiskey kept better and brought higher prices than grains. By 1810 good water and abundant corn centered American distilling in Kentucky, where 2,000 stills annually produced over 2 million gallons of liquor. Some of these early Kentucky ventures became companies of considerable reputation (e.g., the James

Beam Distilling Company), and important enterprises also grew in Tennessee, Virginia, Maryland, and North Carolina. By mid-century, liquor was one of the South's most important products and had a firm place in sectional heritage. Southern producers, however, competed among themselves and with northern distillers, and by 1850 overproduction and falling prices increasingly forced them to view their operations in a national perspective.

Commercial whiskeys were chiefly corn blended with varied amounts of rye and other grains. Bourbon, aged in charred oak barrels, was the most distinctive. First distilled in Kentucky as early as 1789, production centered in Bourbon County until the 1840s and then spread regionally. Bourbon won national acclaim, while other blends, such as Tennessee Whiskey, were also popular. Rye remained important in Maryland. The industry standardized most blends by the turn of the 20th century, a process formalized in federal regulations by the 1930s.

By 1900 large distilling concerns (e.g., the Kentucky Distilleries and Warehouse Company) emerged as smaller producers merged in the face of competition and temperance agitation. National prohibition accelerated this trend as investors, anticipating repeal, acquired many southern distilleries. Thus, with exceptions such as Jack Daniel and Beam, many brand names steeped in southern tradition are now products of a few national beverage corporations.

Moonshining, never exclusively southern, also secured an important place in sectional history. As early as 1794, the Whiskey Rebellion, although centered in western Pennsylvania, engendered considerable sympathy in the

South, where many distillers ignored federal excises on their product. Over time, Kentucky probably was the largest single source of illegal whiskey, although Georgia, the Carolinas, Virginia, and sections of other states also boasted significant production, and moonshiners often enjoyed considerable local prestige. Moonshine was essentially corn and frequently was of higher proof than legal whiskeys. Production peaked in the 1950s but then dropped off as quality fell, law enforcement suffered, and drinking preferences shifted away from distilled beverages.

Despite the prominence of southern distilling, beer and wine did maintain a regional presence. Early attempts to establish European grapes, including efforts by Washington and Jefferson, failed as commercial ventures, but some small southern vineyards survived generally using local vines. The most important of these was the Catawba grape, native to North Carolina, which became the basis of a viticulture that spread beyond the South. Commercial brewing—never a significant part of the antebellum South—expanded with growing southern urban populations around the turn of the 20th century. Northern capital helped establish such regional companies as Lone Star Brewing (San Antonio) as early as 1883; and as the century advanced, Anheuser-Busch, Carling, Schaefer, and other national concerns opened brewing and distribution facilities in many southern cities. (Richmond, for instance, saw the nation's first sales of canned beer in the early 1930s). The border South was the center of regional beer production, notably in St. Louis and Louisville. New Orleans's Dixie Brewing Corporation has utilized regional imagery in marketing. Compared to distilling—legal

and illegal—however, brewing and viticulture remain lesser aspects of southern tradition.

See also HISTORY AND MANNERS: / Jack Daniel Distillery; Moonshine and Moonshining; Whiskey

Mark Edward Lender
Kean College of New Jersey

Stanley Baron, *Brewed in America: A History of Beer and Ale in the United States* (1962); Gerald Carson, *The Social History of Bourbon: An Unhurried Account of Our Star-Spangled American Drink* (1963); William L. Downard, *Dictionary of the History of the American Brewing and Distilling Industries* (1980); Mark Edward Lender and James Kirby Martin, *Drinking in America: A History* (1982). ☆

MINING
||||||||||||||||||||

Although coal was discovered in Virginia in the early 1700s, southern coal mining remained a small-scale enterprise until the late 19th century because of the lack of transportation. Following the Civil War the increased demand for coal as a fuel for the Industrial Revolution, the development of the steam-driven plow, which tunneled out the Appalachian Mountains, and the appearance of railroads in the mountains promoted the emergence of coal as a significant southern product.

The rise of the coal industry consumed farm land and life, as well as mountain culture, as the industrial transformation tied the previously rural, isolated regions to the international economy. In 1890 McDowell County, W.Va., produced 245,000 tons of coal a year; two decades later it was producing 13 million tons annually. In 1910 Harlan County, Ky., did not produce a single ton of coal; by 1926 the county yielded over 13 million tons of coal annually. By 1940 southern coalfields produced over 40 percent of the coal mined in the United States, and over half the nation's coal by 1960. West Virginia and Kentucky in that year accounted for 80 percent of southern coal production.

To house, feed, and shelter a work force in the isolated coalfields the coal companies established company towns in which the company built and retained control over every aspect of community life including houses, stores, churches, and schools. Miners in the northern coalfields struggled to unionize for higher wages, but southern miners sought to unionize for social, political, and economic reasons. To preserve their feudalistic controls and capitalistic profits the coal companies fought back tenaciously. The result was bitter and bloody labor-management conflicts; the "Armed March on Logan," the Mingo County Strike of the 1920s, and the Harlan County strikes of the 1930s are extreme, but good, examples of how far each side would go in pursuit of its objectives.

The southern coalfields were unionized in the 1930s, a combined accomplishment of John L. Lewis, the legendary chief of the United Mine Workers of America, President Franklin Roosevelt and his New Deal, and, most importantly, a massive uprising of miners. The union, however, failed as a counterbalance to the power of the coal companies as it became bogged down in internal corruption and autocracy. The coal companies established cultural and political hegemonies over the states of West Virginia and Kentucky and con-

tinued to exercise considerable political clout in other southern coal-producing states.

Mine disasters, labor-management strife, slag dams (such as the one that killed 175 people in February 1972 at Buffalo Creek, W.Va.), and strip mining (in 1970 strip mining accounted for about 35 percent of southern coal mining) have been the coal industry's legacy to southern culture.

By their control of the land, the coal companies have prevented the economic diversification of the coal regions. Underdeveloped and bound to a single industry, the economies of the southern coalfield regions fluctuate with the boom-and-bust cycle of the coal industry. A protracted and disastrous bust began in the 1920s with the rise of competing fuels, mainly oil and gas, and an overabundance of coal mines. In the late 1940s the southern coal industry mechanized, mainly in the form of the Continuous Miner, a machine that did the work of many miners. Automation may have saved the southern coal industry, but it prompted massive unemployment and poverty throughout the coal regions and resulted in thousands of miners migrating to the midwestern urban-industrial areas in search of employment.

The energy crisis and oil embargo of the 1970s produced another boom in the industry as the nation, especially under President Jimmy Carter's Administration, turned to coal as the means of achieving national energy security. The 111-day 1977–78 coal strike, a worldwide oil glut, and Reaganomics, which wiped out federal energy programs, led the nation away from coal and produced another bust in the southern coalfields.

In the 1960s oil companies began purchasing the southern coal companies. Occidental bought Island Creek,

Continental Oil took over Consolidation Coal, and more were to come. The impact of these takeovers remains to be seen, but with more capital and a greater emphasis on technology, especially strip mining, the oil companies' takeover of the southern coal industry does not promise a bright future for the land or the people.

See also ENVIRONMENT: / Appalachian Coal Region; SOCIAL CLASS: / Coal Miners; Company Towns; VIOLENCE: Harlan County, Kentucky

David A. Corbin
Arlington, Virginia

Appalachian Land Owner Task Force, *Who Owns Appalachia?: Landownership and Its Impact* (1983); David A. Corbin, *Life, Work, and Rebellion in the Coal Fields: Southern West Virginia Coal Miners, 1880–1922* (1981); Ronald D. Eller, *Miners, Millhands, and Mountaineers: The Modernization of the Appalachian South* (1982); William Graebner, *Coal-Mining Safety in the Progressive Period* (1976). ☆

MUSIC INDUSTRY

The development of commercial popular music in the South has paralleled trends in other industries. The region has served as a source of musical raw materials—styles, performers, and creative talents—for the nation as a whole. Until World War II, however, non-southerners controlled most of the institutions vital to marketing popular music, including publishing houses, recording companies, and theater chains. Professional musicians in the South pursued the American goal of material advancement, but profits tended to flow

toward New York, Chicago, or Hollywood, the three major music centers of the United States before World War II. Of course, there were exceptions to this generalization, chiefly in the form of southern publishers who were beginning to tap a market for spiritual music by the mid-19th century. Between the Civil War and World War I minstrelsy and ragtime music offered opportunities for both black and white southern musicians.

Northern executives also held sway in the pop market, the mainstream of American commercial music centering on Broadway shows, New York's "Tin Pan Alley" music-publishing district, and, later, Hollywood film musicals. This pattern continued as the music industry turned to country music (then called "hillbilly") and jazz in the 1920s. Both genres were southern based, but their markets were not strictly regional. In that decade the phenomenal growth of commercial radio frightened many recording executives, who saw radio as a competing source of popular entertainment. Northern record companies, eager to reach new markets, had ready access to the southern-born jazz musicians of both races who had left their native region for the thriving jazz centers of Chicago and New York. Record firms also brought white hillbilly singers north, or sent agents to Atlanta, New Orleans, Memphis, Charlotte, and other southern cities to record dozens of local musicians in the hillbilly and jazz fields. These musicians frequently received only flat fees (as opposed to long-term royalties) for their work. Northern businessmen and their southern allies (typically retailers in some other line who carried recordings as an adjunct product) often secured control of musical copyrights or stole them outright from relatively unsophisticated performers.

Some southerners were more industry wise, and they began to sell their own songbooks. A handful moved north and set up publishing houses. The most successful southern entrepreneurs in music-related endeavors prior to World War II were those who organized radio stations, in many cases companion operations to insurance companies, newspapers, or retail stores. Stations like Nashville's WSM originated programs for network broadcast and served as proving grounds for pop singers and big bands.

The modern southern music industry took shape during the two decades after 1940. Prosperity revived popular music markets that had been blighted by a decade of economic depression. Urbanization and interregional migration advanced the nationalization of country music, rhythm and blues, and rock and roll, all styles with solid southern foundations. The formation of the performance-rights society Broadcast Music, Incorporated (BMI) in 1940 paved the way for a decentralization of music institutions. Set up by radio networks to rival the older, exclusive, and pop-oriented American Society of Composers, Authors, and Publishers (ASCAP), BMI allowed songwriters and publishers in all fields to join, and it monitored local as well as network programming. By collecting and distributing performance royalties on a wide range of music, it assisted fledgling publishing operations that sprang up across the South and Midwest, including firms that soon captured significant shares of the pop, country, and rhythm-and-blues markets. After 1945 record manufacturers and recording studios complemented broadcasting and publishing in emerging music centers like Nashville, Atlanta, and Dallas. Southern music entrepreneurs extended a long tradition of urban boosterism through shrewd promotion and publicity, formed national trade organizations like the Country Music Association, and enhanced urban growth by investing in banking, real estate, and other ventures. Southern businessmen now sit on the boards of most national music organizations.

In the processes of commercialization and nationalization, southern music entrepreneurs have helped to transform the social settings that originally spawned folk-derived styles like country music and jazz and to dilute these music forms to the point that they have lost many of their qualities as southern-based idioms. To be sure, southern executives, after the fashion of their northern counterparts, have helped to perpetuate images of the region as a land of folksy and sometimes backwards characters, such as the unlettered white hillbilly or the exotic, sensual black. More often, southern businessmen have prompted the adoption of the cowboy or western image, a non-southern image more palatable to a national audience. All of these images have furthered the purposes of southern entrepreneurs and musicians, who have increasingly asserted their own interests within the world of commercial music.

See also MUSIC articles; URBANIZATION: / Nashville

John W. Rumble
Nashville, Tennessee

Bill C. Malone, *Southern Music/American Music* (1979); John W. Rumble, "Fred Rose and the Development of the Nashville Music Industry, 1942–1954" (Ph.D. dissertation,

Vanderbilt University, 1980); D. K. Wilgus, *Journal of American Folklore* (April–June 1970). ☆

NUCLEAR INDUSTRY
||||||||||||||||||||||||||||||||||||||||||||||||||||

During the 1950s and early 1960s the development of nuclear energy for peaceful purposes was widely regarded as a glamorous technological breakthrough that could offer dramatic benefits in industry, agriculture, medicine, and the generation of electrical power. The southern states acted with particular enthusiasm to promote the use of nuclear energy as a part of their effort to encourage economic growth. They also played a leading role in increasing the authority of state governments to safeguard public health and safety from radiation hazards, a reflection of their determination to protect traditional state responsibilities from federal infringement.

When Congress passed the Atomic Energy Act of 1954, it ended exclusive government control over nuclear technology and opened it to commercial enterprise for civilian applications. The South moved promptly to investigate the opportunities the measure presented. Responding to the appeals of Florida Governor LeRoy Collins, who argued that "nuclear energy for the South can mean economic emancipation," the Southern Governors' Conference sponsored a series of studies and meetings on the advantages that the technology could provide for the region. In February 1957, after concluding that exploitation of atomic energy promised substantial economic benefits, the governors created the Regional Advisory Council on Nuclear Energy. The council

embarked on an ambitious program to foster the growth of atomic technology in the South, not only through construction of nuclear power reactors but also through expansion in the use of radioactive isotopes and increased private investment in atomic energy-related industries.

At the same time, the advisory council and other southern spokesmen were lobbying to extend to the states regulatory authority over atomic energy, which had been largely delegated to the U.S. Atomic Energy Commission (AEC) by the 1954 act. Many state leaders protested federal "usurpation" of the states' traditionally dominant role in public health and safety. The South played an important part in persuading Congress in 1959 to amend the 1954 act to explicitly acknowledge state authority to regulate radiation hazards arising from certain atomic energy operations, not including those from power reactors. Under the amendment, a state with demonstrated technical competence could sign an agreement with the AEC to assume specified functions.

The Regional Advisory Council on Nuclear Energy achieved another of its major goals in 1962 by the creation of a regional compact for nuclear energy, administered by the Southern Interstate Nuclear Board. The board boasted the same year that "the states of the South have achieved a national lead in preparing for the nuclear age" and cited several significant "firsts" for the region: the first regional compact for nuclear energy, the first state to assume atomic regulatory duties formerly exercised by the federal government (Kentucky), the first state nuclear-development program (Texas), and the first college reactor (North Carolina State University). The board also expressed pride that regional efforts since 1955 had made nuclear energy "a substantial factor in the South's total economy."

In the early period of peaceful atomic development, the promotional and regulatory activities of the South were not unique. Other states also acted to obtain economic benefits by encouraging atomic growth and state participation in regulating against the hazards of atomic energy. Yet southern efforts were exceptional in degree, if not in manner and motivation. As a region, the South established broader programs more promptly than other sections and most individual states. The South's economic status relative to other parts of the country made atomic technology especially appealing and gave southerners greater incentive to move quickly. Southern leaders heeded LeRoy Collins's 1955 warning that unless they took immediate measures, "nuclear energy for industrial use will gravitate to the existing industrial areas, mostly in the North." The South's particular sensitivity on the matter of states' rights, especially at a time when the growing civil rights struggle made the issue increasingly controversial, intensified its commitment to preventing exclusive federal authority over nuclear regulation. Sooner and in greater numbers than states in other sections, southern states signed agreements with the AEC to undertake the regulatory responsibilities permitted them. In these respects, the response of the South to the opening of atomic technology to private enterprise was distinctive.

In the last decade the nation's nuclear industry has faced increasing challenge, especially after the dramatic 1979 accident at the Three Mile Island plant in Pennsylvania. Plants have been abandoned in the South as elsewhere, with the Clinch River Breeder Reactor in Tennessee being one of the most famous. Several southern states were considered as possible locations for the storage of nuclear waste, although none had been so designated by mid-1985.

See also ENVIRONMENT: / Nuclear Pollution; POLITICS: / Southern Governors' Association

> J. Samuel Walker
> United States Nuclear
> Regulatory Commission

Redding S. Sugg, Jr., ed., *Nuclear Energy in the South* (1957); J. Samuel Walker, *Prologue* (Fall 1981). ☆

OIL INDUSTRY

Within a year after E. L. Drake brought in the nation's first oil well outside Titusville, Penn., the South entered the petroleum picture. In the spring of 1860 a well in Wirt County, Va. (about 12 miles southeast of Parkersburg), began producing 37 to 50 barrels per day. After the creation of West Virginia, all the oil activity was in the new state. As important as oil was in West Virginia (well into the 20th century), significant numbers of West Virginia and Pennsylvania oil field workers migrated to the nascent Texas industry. The 1894 discovery in Corsicana signaled the beginning of commercial production in Texas, but the strike at Spindletop, near Beaumont, on 10 January 1901 immediately made the South a major force in the industry. The Texas Gulf Coast fields in the next few years produced quantities of oil that transformed the national, as well as the regional, economy. This new

Workers at a Queen of Waco Oil Company derrick, Wortham, Texas, c. 1925

industry attracted much northern capital, mainly from Pennsylvania, and it created thousands of jobs to which farm boys flocked, thus beginning to shift the balance from a rural to an industrial economy. Once farmers went into the oil field, they usually stayed, following the booms from one new field to another.

Although Spindletop caught the national spotlight, other southern states quickly contributed significant quantities of oil. Louisiana's first important field, just outside Jennings, opened in September 1901, to be followed by the Caddo field in 1906 and Haynesville in 1921. Since World War II southern Louisiana has continued prolific production. Arkansas had two banner fields in the early 1920s—El Dorado (where H. L. Hunt entered the business) and Smackover. Oil wrought tremendous changes in the lives of farm folk in Texas, Louisiana, and Arkansas, but it had much more impact on the Indians of Oklahoma. Even before statehood in 1907, Oklahoma had experienced several notable strikes—at Bartlesville

(1897), Red Fork (1901), Cleveland (1904), and Glenn Pool (1905). The last occurred on Creek land south of Tulsa, making the Creeks wealthy and Tulsa the "Oil Capital of the World." The Burbank field (1920) tapped the Osage pool, and members of that tribe experienced far more affluence than most could prudently manage. Developing that field was E. W. Marland, who in 1935 became governor of Oklahoma. That oilmen were influential in politics was also attested to when Ross Sterling, onetime president of Humble, was elected governor of Texas in 1930.

Refineries have been important, along with oil fields, in the urbanization and industrialization of the South. The region's first sizable refinery, the Standard Oil (now Exxon) plant in Baton Rouge, opened in 1909. From the 1920s onward, the Texas Gulf Coast has boasted such giants as the Magnolia (now Mobil) in Beaumont, the Gulf and Texaco in Port Arthur, and the Humble (now Exxon) in Baytown. Offshore drilling symbolizes the technological sophistication of the 1980s, but the South's first wells in water were in the Goose Creek, Tex., field in 1908. Subsequent drilling in the Red River between Texas and Oklahoma helped develop the techniques that now enable behemoth rigs to drill in the deep Gulf waters off Texas and Louisiana.

See also SOCIAL CLASS: / Oil Workers

Walter Rundell, Jr.
University of Maryland

Kenny A. Franks, *The Oklahoma Petroleum Industry* (1980); Carl C. Rister, *Oil! Titan of the Southwest* (1949); Walter Rundell, Jr., *Early Texas Oil: A Photographic History, 1866–1936* (1977). ☆

RAILROAD INDUSTRY

Even though the South possessed many navigable rivers and had basically an agricultural rather than an industrial economy, it was active in the promotion of railroads in the early 19th century. Baltimore businessmen obtained a charter for the Baltimore & Ohio in 1827, and Charleston interests built a 136-mile railroad to Hamburg, S.C., between 1830 and 1833. In 1860 the 15 slave states had more than 10,000 miles of railway, or about one third of the national total. Virginia, Georgia, and Tennessee led the South in rail mileage. On the eve of the Civil War southern railroads lagged well behind northern lines in the quality of original construction, equipment, the number of employees, traffic volume, and maintenance facilities. Long before Appomattox the southern lines were suffering from a growing deterioration of service due to general neglect, poor track repair, lack of equipment, and the war itself. By early 1865 Confederate railways were in a crippled condition.

In the late 1860s and early 1870s the South suffered from railroad carpetbaggers, men more interested in personal profit than in building new railroads. The greatest corruption was in North Carolina, South Carolina, Georgia, and Alabama. After the Panic of 1873 nearly half of the southern lines faced the sequence of default, receivership, and foreclosure. Southern rail mileage expanded with the appearance of the New South, though, and by 1900 the former slave states possessed a network of about 60,000 miles, nearly a third of the national total. In the last years of the 19th century many southern lines were merged into larger systems, con-solidations generally dominated by northern men and money.

By the turn of the century the major lines serving the South included the Baltimore & Ohio, Chesapeake & Ohio, Norfolk & Western, Southern, Atlantic Coast Line, Seaboard Air Line, Louisville & Nashville, Mobile & Ohio, Illinois Central, Southern Pacific, and Missouri Pacific railroads. Both in World War I and World War II the contributions to victory made by southern railroads were unique because so many military installations were located in the South. By the 1920s southern railroads, like those of the entire nation, were being hurt by the growing competition from highways, airlines, pipelines, and improved river and canal barge service. During World War II southern railroads prospered even more than northern or western lines. This prosperity continued after the war as southern rail freight expanded with the economic surge toward the Sunbelt. By the 1980s such giant rail networks as the Family Lines, csx, and Norfolk Southern were among the most prosperous and efficient of American railroads.

John F. Stover
Purdue University

Robert C. Black III, *The Railroads of the Confederacy* (1952); U. B. Phillips, *A History of Transportation in the Eastern Cotton Belt to 1860* (1908); John F. Stover, *The Life and Decline of the American Railroad* (1970). ☆

RESEARCH TRIANGLE PARK

Research Triangle Park is a planned industrial research park in the Raleigh-

Durham area of North Carolina including more than 5,000 acres near three research universities: Duke University, North Carolina State University, and the University of North Carolina at Chapel Hill. Developed by the nonprofit Research Triangle Foundation, it includes 40 research organizations with 20,000 employees, an annual payroll of $400 million, and an investment of $1.6 billion in construction and equipment.

The park contains industrial laboratories and trade associations, federal and state government laboratories, nonprofit research institutes, and university-related research activities. Areas of concentration include environmental sciences, pharmaceuticals and agricultural chemicals, microelectronics, and computer technology.

Governor Luther Hodges initiated the program in 1955 with the appointment of the Governor's Research Triangle Committee of corporate and university leaders. With private funding, the Governor's Committee was incorporated in 1956, and sociologist George Lee Simpson, Jr., from the Chapel Hill faculty, was appointed director. The plan was to promote the region for industrial research, and faculty members were employed initially to promote the idea. The objectives were to improve the state's low per-capita income by attracting industrial laboratories and high-technology industry to North Carolina; to diversify the industrial base from the traditional tobacco, textiles, and furniture; to reverse out-migration of North Carolina youth trained in science and engineering; and to help the universities attract and retain science and engineering faculty members by expanded consulting opportunities.

In 1957 private venture capital, with public stock offerings, was invested in 4,000 acres of scrub pinelands as "Pinelands, Inc.," but by fall 1958, the committee recognized the advantages of nonprofit ownership of the research park. With the theme of "an investment in North Carolina," banker Archie K. Davis raised $1.5 million in gifts from corporations and citizens of North Carolina to purchase Pinelands. In December the Committee became the Research Triangle Foundation, Inc., and the Research Triangle Institute was established. The institute has a staff of 1,000 with research contracts exceeding $40 million annually.

Educational support activities in the park include the North Carolina Board of Science and Technology, the Triangle Universities Computation Center, and the Triangle Universities Center for Advanced Studies, Inc. (TUCASI), which holds 120 acres in the park for joint activities of the three universities. On the campus of TUCASI are the National Humanities Center and the Microelectronics Center of North Carolina.

Although the park was developed without state appropriations, the state provided leadership, cooperation, and the support of its educational base. The success of the Triangle is a notable example of effective cooperation among state government, higher education, and the corporate community.

See also EDUCATION: / Duke University; North Carolina, University of; National Humanities Center

> William F. Little
> University of North Carolina
> at Chapel Hill

Victor J. Danilov, *Industrial Research* (May 1971); W. B. Hamilton, *South Atlantic Quarterly* (Spring 1966); Luther H. Hodges,

Businessman in the Statehouse (1962); Ruth Walker, *Christian Science Monitor* (15 June 1982); Louis Round Wilson, *Louis Round Wilson's Historical Sketches* (1976). ☆

SANDERS, COLONEL HARLAND

(1890–1980) Businessman.

To people all over the world the words "It's finger lickin' good" evoke the image of a quintessential southerner, the Kentucky colonel, personified by Harland David Sanders. Neither a native southerner nor an army colonel, Sanders built a chicken franchise empire that began in the back room of a filling station in Corbin, Ky., and grew to revenues totaling $3.5 billion by 1986, with 6,500 stores in 56 countries.

Harland David Sanders was born 9 September 1890 in Henryville, Ind., to Wilbert D. and Margaret Ann Sanders. Wilbert D. Sanders died when his son was young, and Sanders left home when he was only 12. He enlisted in the army at 16; then worked on the railroad; and after taking correspondence courses in law, began representing clients in court. What by some accounts was a promising legal career ended with a courtroom incident in which Sanders was charged with assault and battery by his own client.

Sanders began selling—first insurance, then Michelin tires. Realizing that he had a knack for business, Sanders in 1930 bought a Shell Oil service station in Corbin, Ky., on old U.S. Route 25, which went south to Atlanta and east to Asheville. At the foot of the eastern Kentucky mountains, Corbin lay in an area known locally as "Hell's Half Acre." Sanders soon moved his dining-room table and six chairs into a storage room and began cooking and serving boardinghouse-style meals for truckers and travelers. He then expanded his operation from Sanders Cafe to Sanders Court, a motel with seven rooms, and began experimenting with pressure cookers and a fried chicken recipe given to him by a neighbor.

By 1949 Sanders had received from Governor Lawrence Wetherby his second Kentucky colonel's commission, an honor typically bestowed for outstanding community service or as a political favor. Although Sanders himself said "It don't mean a daggone thing" when he received the first commission from Governor Ruby Laffoon in 1935, he apparently took the second commission more seriously. He began signing his name "Colonel Harland Sanders," grew a moustache and a goatee, and allowed his nearly white hair to lengthen. Later he added the white suit and string tie to complete the Kentucky colonel image traditionally caricatured in popular films and literature: an aristocratic and chivalrous Dixie gentleman with a fondness for good horses and good bourbon. (The Colonel, though, never touched a drop.)

By 1950 the Colonel had settled on the cooking method and the 11 herbs and spices that would make his chicken world famous. In 1953 the first franchised Colonel Sanders' Kentucky Fried Chicken was sold at the Dew Drop Inn in Salt Lake City, Utah. To accommodate his daughter's distaste for dishwashing in her Florida restaurant, the Colonel came up with the notion of a "take-home" store. The prototype KFC franchise was erected in Jacksonville, Fla., and the fast-food industry was revolutionized.

By 1960 there were more than 200 franchises in the United States and

Canada. The Colonel sold KFC, Inc., to John Y. Brown, Jr., and Nashville entrepreneur Jack Massey for $2 million. The Colonel was to continue in the services of the corporation as a goodwill ambassador. At times, he was more of an embarrassment than an asset, commenting publicly that the gravy he had worked so hard to perfect "tasted like wallpaper paste."

In 1971 KFC Corporation merged with Heublein, Inc., in a $288 million deal. The tireless colonel, now in his 80s and in failing health, continued his promotional work for charities and KFC, and he attended the dedication of the Colonel Sanders Museum in Louisville in 1978. In 1980 he was hospitalized with pneumonia and died on 16 December. Colonel Harland D. Sanders, the man who personified an American dream and a southern myth, lay in state in both the Kentucky capitol and the corporate offices of KFC before interment in Louisville's Cave Hill Cemetery. Governor John Y. Brown, Jr., eulogized the colonel, quoting from *Hamlet*: "He was a man. Take him for all and all. We shall not look upon his like again."

In 1982 R. J. Reynolds (now RJR Nabisco, Inc.) acquired KFC, and in July 1986, Pepsico, Inc., agreed to buy the company for a book value of $850 million.

Lisa Howorth
University of Mississippi

John Pearce, ed., *The Colonel: The Captivating Biography of the Dynamic Founder of a Fast-food Empire* (1982); Harland D. Sanders, *Life as I Have Known It Has Been Finger Lickin' Good* (1974); Lawrence S. Thompson, *Georgia Review* (Spring 1953). ☆

SOUTHERN GROWTH POLICIES BOARD

The Southern Growth Policies Board was established through an interstate compact in December 1971 by nine southern governors who saw that the region was undergoing rapid growth in its population and economy. Terry Sanford, former governor of North Carolina and president of Duke University, proposed the idea for a regional planning agency in a speech to a reform group, the L. Q. C. Lamar Society. Sanford suggested that interstate planning and cooperation would be the keys to helping the South "win the awesome race with time to save the cities and preserve the countryside. Now is the time, and the South can lead the way."

The member states now include Alabama, Arkansas, Florida, Georgia, Kentucky, Louisiana, Mississippi, North Carolina, Oklahoma, South Carolina, Tennessee, and Virginia, as well as the Commonwealth of Puerto Rico. Texas, Maryland, West Virginia, Missouri, Delaware, and the Virgin Islands are also eligible to join.

The agreement specifies that the board shall consist of five members from each participating state—the governor, a state senator, and a state representative appointed by their respective presiding officers, and two leading citizens appointed by the governor. A governor serves as chairman of the board for a one-year term. The work of the staff is reviewed quarterly by an executive committee of approximately 15 board members, and the staff is headed by an executive director.

Article III of the Interstate Agreement directs the board to prepare and maintain a "Statement of Regional Objectives," including recommended approaches to regional problems. The statement may also identify projects deemed to be of regional significance. It is amended or revised at least once every six years.

The first "Statement of Regional Objectives" was prepared in 1974 by a distinguished panel of civic leaders appointed by the governors. The mission of this panel, known as the Commission on the Future of the South, was to recommend policies to foster continued economic growth, while at the same time mitigating adverse sociological and environmental effects. The commissioners concluded that a policy of "no growth" for the South was neither feasible nor desirable and suggested that the staff consider policies to influence the distribution of growth in the region.

Within this framework the board strengthened its research and information capabilities, emphasizing region-wide economic-development activities. The board also developed a significant role in representing the interests of the southern states in Washington in the so-called Sunbelt-Frostbelt conflict. As the board became more deeply involved in federal issues, a second office was staffed in Washington in 1977 to monitor federal actions that could result in negative consequences for the region.

In 1980 the second Commission on the Future of the South framed a new report to guide the board's program activities. Their recommendations focused on four areas of regional development: the economy, cities, children, and energy. Utilizing this basic planning document, the board began to assess and redefine its mission.

In 1982 the board relinquished its Washington office, maintaining a reduced presence in a new office to be supported by the Southern Governors' Association. At its Tenth Anniversary Conference, the board rededicated itself to regional economic development—specifically, "to provide an early alert system for our states as to intermediate-range policy options of regional importance which will maximize opportunities for and minimize impediments to economic growth and development."

The board today represents a unique vehicle for regional coordination and public-private cooperation. The availability of opportunities in the region, the positive attitudes regarding future growth potential, and the healthy confluence of business and government interests provide a strong framework for future progress.

See also HISTORY AND MANNERS: / L. Q. C. Lamar Society; POLITICS: / Southern Governors' Association

William Winter
David Crews
Jackson, Mississippi

James C. Cobb, *The Selling of the South: The Southern Crusade for Industrial Development, 1936–1980* (1982); *New York Times* (9 January 1977); Southern Growth Policies Board, *Annual Report* (1977). ☆

STEVENS, J. P., AND COMPANY
||||||||||||||||||||||||||||||||||||||

J. P. Stevens and Company traces its beginnings to a Massachusetts woolen mill founded in 1813 by Nathaniel Stevens. In 1899 John P. Stevens, Nathaniel's grandson, established the New York commission house from which the present firm takes its name. Stevens came to serve as selling agent for a number of southern cotton textile firms, eight of which merged with the Stevens family interests in 1946 to form the modern corporation. In succeeding years, Stevens transferred its woolen operations to the South, in part to counter unionization efforts. It also expanded its holdings of southern mills, becoming the second largest publicly held American textile corporation.

In 1963 the Textile Workers' Union of America (TWUA) launched a campaign to organize Stevens's southern plants. Company management, notably Board Chairman James D. Finley, a native Georgian, responded aggressively, being found guilty repeatedly of illegal harassment of organizers and prounion workers. The TWUA was unable to win a representation election at any Stevens mill until workers at the firm's Roanoke Rapids, N.C., plants gave the union a small majority in August 1974. Despite its victory, however, the union was unable to negotiate a contract. Complaining of company delaying tactics, the newly created Amalgamated Clothing and Textile Workers' Union (ACTWU) launched a boycott in June 1976 against Stevens products. The boycott proved ineffective, but it successfully focused national attention on Stevens as a symbol of southern antiunion obduracy. Numerous church groups endorsed the boycott, and demonstrators besieged stockholders' meetings; the Roanoke Rapids saga became the basis for a critically acclaimed motion picture, *Norma Rae* (1978).

More telling than the boycott was ACTWU's innovative "corporate campaign," which mobilized the investment power of unions and their sympathizers to press Stevens's lenders and "outside" directors to sever their links to the company. Pressure of this sort, along with

growing internal problems, began to sap the company's strength, while the retirement of Finley in January 1980 permitted it to take a more flexible stance. In October 1980 Stevens and ACTWU reached an accord, the company agreeing to contracts at unionized mills, the union to calling off its anti-Stevens campaign. Although unionization has made little progress at Stevens since 1980, contests have been largely free of irregularities, and collective bargaining has proceeded routinely. All outstanding legal disputes between the company and the union were settled in October 1983.

See also SOCIAL CLASS: / Textile Workers

David L. Carlton
Vanderbilt University

Mimi Conway, *Rise Gonna Rise: A Portrait of Southern Textile Workers* (1979); Lloyd C. Ferguson, *From Family Firm to Corporate Giant: J. P. Stevens and Company, 1813–1963* (1970); Jim Overton et al., *Southern Exposure* (Spring 1978). ☆

TEXTILE INDUSTRY

Small-scale textile mills could be found in the South as far back as the American Revolution, and the textile industry gained a firm foothold in the Piedmont area of Virginia, North Carolina, South Carolina, and Georgia during the antebellum era. By 1850 more than 200 textile mills operated in the South. Leaders of the industry included William Gregg and Daniel Pratt, both of South Carolina. The textile mill has made its greatest impact on the region in the past hundred years. Developing rapidly after 1880, the industry soon rivaled the enormous New England center in plants, equipment, and personnel. The number of spindles in operation more than doubled in the 1890s, and the amount of capital invested in the southern textile industry rose from $22.8 million in 1880 to $132.4 million in 1900. It remains today the region's major industrial employer.

The pattern of mill expansion in the South differed in important ways from that which marked the older textile region chiefly because of distinctive physical and labor conditions of the area. Hydroelectric power, developed extensively because of the geographic advantages of the Piedmont, enabled mill entrepreneurs to locate their factories in rural areas where labor was relatively more plentiful. Textile technology required comparatively large numbers of unskilled workers. Cheap labor was to be found in the Southeast and this, more than any other single factor, stimulated indigenous textile expansion and, in time, lured northern capital to the region.

Although the pool of surplus white farm labor in the Piedmont has varied over time with changing agricultural and industrial conditions, it has generally been large. Unlike those in other southern industries, textile-mill jobs were long reserved for these white workers. The virtual certainty of widespread social protest long discouraged mill managers from employing black operatives. Only in recent years have black workers been welcomed in the mills, where they now account for approximately one-fourth of southern textile employees.

Remote mill sites encouraged the construction of owner-controlled mill villages to house workers and their families. The pattern developed in the antebellum era from the factory and mill village built by William Gregg at Gran-

iteville, S.C. Mill villages traditionally contained housing for workers, as well as schools, general stores, churches, and sometimes medical centers and recreational areas, all owned and operated by the manufacturing company. Although mill housing has been worker owned since the 1950s, this strong community orientation continues to distinguish the industry in the South. The Southeast remains a region with good transportation facilities and few large cities. Its rate of urbanization has been slower than that of other industrial centers, a fact related to its established dependence on the textile industry. The organizational structure adopted by the industry in the South was dictated by unique qualities in the factors of production in the region. In turn, the textile industry has powerfully influenced the culture and socioeconomic position of the modern South.

See also SOCIAL CLASS: / Company Towns; Textile Workers

Mary J. Oates
Regis College

Jack Blicksilver, *Cotton Manufacturing in the Southeast: An Historical Analysis* (1959); Glenn Gilman, *Human Relations in the Industrial Southeast: A Study of the Textile Industry* (1956); Broadus Mitchell, *The Rise of Cotton Mills in the South* (1921). ☆

TIMBER INDUSTRY

Beginning with a concentration on naval stores (turpentine and pitch), the southern timber industry has come to include a diversity of products related primarily to southern yellow pine but including cypress and other hardwoods as well.

The 17th- and 18th-century timber industry was located in the Carolinas and characterized by small, low-capital establishments with low annual production. Sawmills and distilleries for turpentine were located in the woods. Those industries used slave labor organized on a task system. The smaller, less-developed but still-important business of searching for live oak timbers used in shipbuilding often involved migrant crews who searched the coastal islands for appropriate timber.

Lumbering in western North Carolina, postcard, early 20th century

By the middle of the 19th century the entire industry was both shifting its location and broadening its scope. During the years immediately after the Civil War, naval stores and sawmilling operations moved into Georgia, Florida, and the Gulf Coast South. In the 1880s Georgia led the South in naval stores and timber production, and in the 20th century Florida and Gulf Coast states have come to dominate. That shift was accompanied by the increasing use of southern pine not only for naval stores but also for other timber products including crossties, building materials, and, increasingly, pulpwood for paper manufacturing.

Changing labor patterns accompanied expansion. Slave labor gave way to free labor at the end of the Civil War. Many of the early postwar laborers were migrants from the Carolinas who followed the timber industry into other states. Later timber workers included both contract migrant workers and seasonal workers who retained ties to the agricultural economies of the Southeast. In some areas of the timber belt, labor came from the often-harsh convict lease system. Lumber camps and lumber towns similar to textile towns appeared throughout the South and particularly the Gulf Coast South as the industry expanded. Regardless of the source of the labor, the laborers were a colorful but transient population. Not as radical as their Pacific Northwest counterparts, southern timber workers nevertheless participated in the activities of the Knights of Labor and the Industrial Workers of the World.

In the 20th century small-scale industries gave way to large concerns owning substantial tracts of land throughout the South. Although originally exploitive and unscientific, southern timber companies have built on the turpentine and conservation experiments of Charles Holmes Herty to provide an important example of scientifically inspired diversity of products and management of renewable resources. Led by trade associations such as the Southern Pine Association, timber operators have standardized the product and often controlled the price. A diverse product line, large-scale operations, and the control of land continue to make the timber industry an important part of the southern economic landscape. For many southern laborers and cities such operations are crucial to survival.

See also AGRICULTURE: / Naval Stores; ENVIRONMENT: Trees; / Cypress; SCIENCE

AND MEDICINE: / Herty, Charles Holmes;
SOCIAL CLASS: / Timber Workers

Thomas F. Armstrong
Georgia College

Thomas D. Clark, *The Greening of the South:
The Recovery of Land and Forest* (1984), *Mis-
sissippi Quarterly* (Spring 1972); James
Defebaugh, *History of the Lumber Industry
of America* (1906); Percival Perry, "The
Naval Stores Industry in the Ante-Bellum
South" (Ph.D. dissertation, Duke Univer-
sity, 1947). ☆

TOBACCO INDUSTRY

Tobacco is the fifth most important cash
crop in the United States. It has occupied an important position among crops
grown in the southeastern United States
since the days of Sir Walter Raleigh.
North Carolina and Kentucky are the
principal tobacco-producing states in
the country, but Virginia, South Carolina, Georgia, Tennessee, and Florida
all contain significant areas where tobacco is grown. In recent years tobacco
has meant $1 billion annually for the
farmers of North Carolina and approximately half that amount for their counterparts in Kentucky. All five major
tobacco regions of the United States are
in the South: the Burley Belt, the Old
Belt, the New Bright Belt, the Border
Belt, and the Georgia-Florida Belt.

Towns in tobacco regions are dotted
with large warehouses, some as big as
a football field, where the crop is sold
at auction. From 2 to 12 such structures
may be concentrated in a single town,
giving it a distinctive character. A typical tobacco town of 40,000 people has,
for example, 3,000,000 square feet of
floor space under the roofs of specialized

*Scene at a Kentucky tobacco auction, c.
1960*

structures designed for selling tobacco,
a process that lasts for only three and a
half months.

The processing of tobacco (redrying,
cleaning, and stemming) is carried on
in the same towns where the sales warehouses are located; thus, the processing
normally takes place within the borders
of producing regions. Tobacco products,
such as cigarettes, pipe and chewing
tobacco, and snuff, are manufactured in
large cities—near, but not necessarily
in, the areas where the crop is grown.
Notable among tobacco-manufacturing
centers are Richmond, Va.; Durham
and Winston-Salem, N.C.; and Louisville, Ky. Partially processed tobacco
and tobacco products are important
American agricultural exports. The two
outstanding tobacco ports of the United
States are Norfolk, Va., and Wilmington, N.C.

Tobacco was the last important cash
crop in the United States to be mechanized. Within the past quarter century
that process has replaced thousands of
workers in all the flue-cured tobacco

producing areas. The shift to machinery has freed a large labor force from agriculture. Unlike the mechanization of other cash crops, tobacco mechanization has not resulted in massive out-migration of recently emancipated farm workers; they have remained at home and become a powerful force in attracting many new factories into the old tobacco districts. In fact, the "eastern" or "New Bright Belt" of North Carolina has shifted from a predominantly rural economy to a mixed economy in a single generation.

One of the oldest agricultural products of the United States, and an indigenous crop, tobacco is still a cornerstone of the agricultural economy of no less than five southern states. It is a controlled substance in the sense that growth of the crop is strictly regulated by an elaborate federal acreage-poundage crop-allotment and price-support system. As a revenue source, tobacco is a crop of national significance. When additional money is needed, tobacco products are always on the list for a tax increase. Though a warning from the surgeon general about cigarette smoking being dangerous to one's health appears on every cigarette pack, and religious groups, including the Southern Baptist Convention, have discouraged use of tobacco, the multibillion-dollar tobacco industry appears to be alive, well, and growing.

See also AGRICULTURE: / Tobacco Culture; SOCIAL CLASS: / Tobacco Workers

Ennis L. Chestang
East Carolina University

W. W. Garner, E. G. Moss et al., U.S. Department of Agriculture, _Yearbook of Agriculature_ (1922); J. Fraser Hart and Ennis L. Chestang, _Geographical Review_ (October 1978); Tobacco Institute, _Tobaccco Industry Profile_ (1982); U.S. Department of Commerce Bureau of the Census, _Census of Agriculture_ (1978). ☆

TRUCKING INDUSTRY

Though trucking appeared in the Northeast and Midwest soon after World War I, the industry's southern beginnings were slow. Initially, trucks connected rural locales and serviced metropolitan areas, but no large cities on the scale of those in the North existed in the South of the 1920s. Early southern trucking, moreover, met with hostile actions from its natural competitor, the railroads. Suffering revenue losses, particularly to cotton-hauling trucks, rail executives pressured legislators in Texas, Louisiana, Kentucky, and Tennessee to enact restrictive motor-carrier laws in the late 1920s and early 1930s. Ad hoc truck associations challenged these laws, but Texas successfully defended its statutes before the U.S. Supreme Court in 1932. The state's right to protect and conserve its highways emerged as the controlling issue in these cases.

Southern truckers remained undeterred, however, and, in a somewhat unsouthern manner, joined forces with executives from other sections of the country in the fall of 1933 and established the American Trucking Association, Inc. (ATA). As part of the National Recovery Administration of the New Deal, southern officials in the ATA offices in Washington, D.C., and in the state associations worked hard to stabilize the disparate industry. In a few instances intimidation forced white and black truckers alike to join the state organizations and to register their vehicles

Trucking on U.S. Route 29 in Georgia, 1943

with the federal agency. The subject of regional wage scales elicited some concern for the welfare of black truckers. One business manager urged the North Carolina Truck Owners Association to keep "the wage scale sufficiently low," for "[w]ith conditions being the same the great majority of employers of labor will hire white men to the total exclusion of negro men." With the advent of federal regulation in 1935, the trucking industry nationwide began a protected existence under which it has since flourished.

The growth of trucking in the South paralleled the rise of the Sunbelt phenomenon. By the 1970s every southern state except Arkansas, Mississippi, and South Carolina received over $1 billion in salaries from the industry each year (Texas received over $5 billion). In fact, the South as a region leads the nation in trucking salaries. Further, if pickups and vans are included, the South contains over one-third of all trucks registered in the United States. From a slow beginning, trucking has become an integral aspect of the southern economy.

See also HISTORY AND MANNERS: Automobile; / Pickup Truck

William R. Childs
Ohio State University

William R. Childs, *Trucking and the Public Interest: The Emergence of Federal Regulation, 1914–1940* (1985); Milton S. Heath, *Southern Economics Journal* (August 1934); Motor Vehicle Manufacturers Association of the United States, Inc., *Motor Truck Facts* (1974). ☆

WALTON, SAM M.

(b. 1918) Businessman.

U.S. News & World Report magazine in 1986 proclaimed Sam Moore Walton of Bentonville in northeastern Arkansas the wealthiest man in the United States. He had, at that point, made $4.3 billion from his 900 Wal-Mart discount stores that operated in 22 states, mainly in the South and Southwest. Walton and his family own 39 percent of Wal-Mart, which had fiscal 1985 sales of $6.5 billion.

Walton began in retailing working for J. C. Penney, and then in 1945 he and his brother J. L. raised $25,000 to open a variety store in Newport, Ark., and

Sam Walton, founder of Wal-Mart Stores, Inc., 1980s

later bought a five-and-dime store on the town square. By 1962 the Waltons operated 15 dime stores, and the number had grown to 30 by 1970, when the business went public. Walton targets small towns especially for his stores, and they have been vital economic forces in many southern states. Walton, through Wal-Mart and a new business, Sam's Wholesale Club, created more employment in Mississippi in the 1980s than any other person.

Despite his success Walton remains an almost stereotypical traditional southerner in many ways. He continues to live in a modest house on a shady street in his small hometown in Arkansas; he drives a 1979 Ford pickup truck, hunts quail, and has his hair cut at a traditonal, three-chair, no-waiting barbershop. He encourages a family feeling among his Wal-Mart employees, and his store openings are southern theater—combining the emotionalism of revivalism, fiddling contests, and school pep rallies.

Charles Reagan Wilson
University of Mississippi

Forbes (28 October 1985); *U.S. News & World Report* (21 July 1986). ☆

LANGUAGE

MICHAEL MONTGOMERY

University of South Carolina

CONSULTANT

☆ ☆ ☆ ☆ ☆ ☆ ☆ ☆ ☆ ☆

Overleaf: Sequoyah, inventor of the Cherokee alphabet

ENGLISH
LANGUAGE
||||||||||||||||||||||||||||||||||||||||||||||||

Few traits identify southerners as readily as their speech. For better or for worse, the way that southerners use the language is often noticed first by non-southerners and draws the most comment from them. When Lyndon Johnson and Jimmy Carter ran for president, the country and the media gave extraordinary attention to their accents. Frequently the way southerners talk also draws admiration. When Sam Ervin chaired the Watergate hearings, the nation was spellbound by this North Carolinian's adroit manipulation of the English language. Southerners are well known for their ability to stump, to preach, and to tell stories.

For many southerners, speech is a badge that signifies much about them: their upbringing, their loyalties, their education, and their roots. Speech is as much a part of their heritage as grits, football, and barbecue. Speech is inseparable from local and regional pride and cultural traditions. Yet southerners are acutely aware of how conspicuous their speech is to non-southerners (Tennessee Williams was given his nickname by his fraternity brothers in the Midwest because of his thick southern accent) and that their speech is often caricatured elsewhere in the country. They are thus often schizophrenic about their speech, unsure whether they want to be set off from the rest of the country. This makes some southerners insecure, and over the past two generations many middle-class southern parents have tried to eradicate the more distinctive regional features of their children's speech.

Most southerners, however, defy the notion that they have any reason to change the way they talk. A typical way for a southerner to put his feelings is "I don't want my speech to be viewed as nonstandard, but I don't want to change my speech, either." When an urban university in the South recently offered a course for southerners wanting to change their accents, particularly those aspiring to traffic with non-southerners, the instructor of the course was publicly vilified and harassed.

Although the South is the most distinctive speech region in the United States, it is hardly more uniform than the nation as a whole. Most discussions have obscured the diversity within the region by unfortunately contrasting a generalized "southern English" with "General American English" or "Standard English," the latter two being abstract, even mythical entities never described and certainly not uniform. Neither the Mason-Dixon line nor any other demarcation has ever set the region off from the rest of the country by its speech. Early immigrants to the South were as heterogeneous as those in any other region, and the South was no more isolated as a whole than other regions. Yet all Americans, southerners and non-southerners alike, tend to perceive the South as a speech region. Linguistic research cannot, however, identify any common denominator that can safely be termed a "southern accent" or a "southern dialect."

Explaining the discrepancy between linguistic facts and folk perceptions and beliefs is not easy. Take the putative "southern drawl," for instance. Linguists have hardly begun to describe it and are now relying on spectrographic analyses to do so; to them *drawl* refers to the lengthening and raising of accented vowels, normally accompanied by a change in voice pitch. It involves the addition of a second or even a third vowel but does not necessarily entail a slower overall speech tempo. What non-linguists mean when they say "drawl," however, is different. To the general public a drawl is a very broad and inclusive term for the speech cadence, voice quality, and general language patterns most often associated with southerners. These speech qualities (rhythm, cadence, intonation, and vowel qualities) are noticed by non-southerners, and this is why the term *drawl* is so widely and loosely applied.

The persistent folk notions alleging a distinctive speech in the region usually refer to a "drawl" and mention the influence of the hot climate and the slow pace of life. The heart of why the region's speech is distinctive, though, lies in the mundane realms of demography and social factors on the one hand and, on the other, in the realm of psychology, in the consciousness of the region's people.

The South is more diverse in speech than any other region of the country, with the most distinctive varieties of southern speech found in isolated areas such as the mountains and the coastal areas of the Outer Banks, the Chesapeake Islands, and the Sea Islands. Speech patterns vary immensely within the region, so that even the well-worn

stereotypes (e.g., the lack of *r* after a vowel, or the use of *y'all*) do not characterize speakers throughout the territory. Moreover, nearly all features usually ascribed to the South can be found, usually among old-fashioned speakers, elsewhere in the country. The usual admonitions against stereotypes apply here not only because of the vast range of speakers within the region, but also because many linguistic features considered southern often differentiate citizens within the region sociologically. One can see, for example, several features that characterize most speakers of the region and that also characterize most black speakers outside the South, whose language is a "transported English" one or two generations removed from the rural South.

Among the representative grammatical features that are southern, some of which do not have exact equivalents in other varieties of American English, are the following: (1) *y'all* and *you all* (the second being the somewhat more formal variant) as second-person plural pronouns; (2) "double-modal" or "multiple-modal" constructions such as *might could, may can,* and *might should*; (3) "perfective" *done* used for emphasis, as in *I done told you that*; (4) *liked to,* meaning "almost," as in *I liked to died*; (5) frequent use of the *a-* prefix with verbs ending in *-ing,* as *a-walking* and *a-talking*.

Among representative phonological features of southern English are the following: (1) the tendency to pronounce as a diphthong [ai] the monothong [i] in words like *tide* and *time*; (2) *r*-lessness, for blacks, upper-class whites, and many middle-class whites, in words like *beer* and *bear*; (3) drawling of vowels (discussed previously), especially common in the Lower South, in words like *bid*, *bed*, and *bad*; (4) "breaking" of some vowels, especially common in the Upper South, so that *steel* is pronounced like *stale*, and *stale* like *stile*; (5) similar pronunciation of front vowels before nasal consonants, so that pairs of words like *pen* and *pin* and *ten* and *tin* are pronounced alike; and (6) nasalization of vowels, as in words like *pumpkin*.

If no unique linguistic features distinguish the South as a speech region, then on what basis do linguists identify it as a speech region? Three characteristics differentiate the region linguistically: (1) a unique combination of linguistic features; (2) the use of these linguistic features more often and by a wider range of the population than in other regions of the country; and (3) the consciousness of the people in the South that they form a region with characteristic southern speech. These three qualities are clearly interrelated; a person's use of "southern features" can best be correlated with his or her attachment to the region. Because the South is so large and diverse and because linguistic research is so painstaking, only a few comprehensive descriptions of the speech of the region exist, among these being Gordon Wood's *Vocabulary Change* (1971) and the *Linguistic Atlas* volumes on the South Atlantic states (Kurath, 1949, and Kurath and McDavid, 1961) completed by material on the remaining southern states (Pederson et al., 1981 and Pederson et al., 1986).

From the beginning, scholarly study and popular curiosity have focused on two general issues: (1) When and how did the distinctiveness of southern speech develop? What is its extent? How distinctive is it, and how is it changing? and (2) What is the relationship between white speech and black speech in the South? In exploring its distinctiveness one must detail the history of southern speech and its geographical dimensions by outlining the principal speech areas within the region. The history of the study of southern English is another aspect of the story, as is the consciousness of the speakers of the region. Finally, one must outline the relevant issues surrounding the question of how white speech and black speech are related. There is not yet a consensus on these general issues, but present-day linguistic research in the South is very active and promises to bring a fuller understanding.

The subregional designations based primarily on Linguistic Atlas research will be used here. These are, namely, the Coastal Southern (also known as Lower Southern or Lowland Southern, covering the Atlantic Coastal Plain from Virginia to Texas), and the South Midland (sometimes known as Upland Southern or Upper Southern, covering the Piedmont and the southern Appalachians from Virginia through South Carolina and the hill areas above the Piedmont in Georgia and Alabama).

Historical Derivation. What historical factors account for the development of a distinctive southern speech? Several have been proposed. Theories about the impact of climate and personality are widely adhered to, but they must be dismissed as invalid.

1. Climate and pace of life. The notion that weather is responsible for habits of southern speech is widely prevalent but easily refuted. The nasality of South Midland speech is often attributed to rainfall and humidity, and the "drawl" of the Coastal and Lower South to the long, hot summers, which supposedly retard the pace of life and

consequently the pace of speech. Put forth by several early social scientists and journalists (such as Clarence Cason in his *90° in the Shade*) and still widely believed by the general public, this theory is clearly inaccurate. Natives of Charleston and the South Carolina Low Country, among the hottest areas of the region, normally speak with abbreviated vowels rather than the elongated ones of the "drawl"; besides, southerners are not known to talk more rapidly in the winter.

2. Personality of the people. The notion that southerners and their speech are distinctive out of politeness and gentility is a sentimental folk notion. While such qualities may be encoded in speech (such as in the traditional use of *ma'am* and *sir* as modes of address in the South) and in other social behavior, the case for any close connection between southern hospitality and typical language behavior can hardly be carried far.

3. Demographic factors. These are the most valid suggestions, particularly regarding original settlement patterns, migration, and the influence of topography.

A firm understanding of the exact area(s) of the British Isles from which the speech of the South's early settlers derives continues to be an elusive quest because of three factors: the diversity of the early settlers; the uncertain social dynamics of the 17th, 18th, and 19th centuries; and the intrinsic problems of "proving" dissemination of a linguistic feature. Even though a majority of the early white settlers in the Lower South, for instance, were from London and the southern counties of Britain, scholars know little about their speech patterns of more than 200 years ago. No doubt the competition of languages and dia-

lects in the early days of settlement in the South involved a leveling and an amalgamation, producing a sort of middle ground between dialects; this differed from region to region of the country. The speech of the coastal areas of the South seems to resemble the speech of the eastern counties of Britain, the speech of the Lower South in general resembles that of London and the southern counties of Britain in many respects, and the speech of the southern hill country is akin to the speech of the north of Britain, of Scotland and Northern Ireland.

Such gross connections with British speech patterns can be made because far fewer non-English-speaking immigrants from continental Europe settled in the South than in the northern colonies. But the influx of millions of Africans, speaking many dozens of languages and brought against their will, has multiplied the complexity of the situation manyfold, and their social disparity with the white population compounds it as well. The cauldron of competing speech varieties and languages brought by different speakers was the norm throughout the region, even in remote locations. But widely encountered statements about isolated areas of the South—whether the Outer Banks, the Chesapeake Islands, or the southern Appalachian Mountains—preserving "pure Scotch-Irish" or "pure Elizabethan" are exaggerations, however powerful or appealing these myths may be and however ardently they may be held by the local population or by the early linguistic literature on the region.

South Midland speech derives ultimately from the colonial settlements in the Delaware Valley of Pennsylvania. It was carried southwestward down into Virginia and North Carolina and then in the 19th century across the northern parts of Georgia, Alabama, and Mississippi and also across Tennessee, Kentucky, Arkansas, and into east Texas. Coastal Southern speech was also carried southwestward from the colonial settlements in Virginia and the Carolinas into southern Georgia, Alabama, and Mississippi and then northward into Arkansas, western Tennessee, and Kentucky, into Louisiana and east Texas, and into Florida. Crossing migration patterns have blended these two general varieties of speech in the interior South, so that the more clear-cut distinctions found in the Atlantic states diminish. Language contact with non-English speakers—French, Mexican, American Indian—also distinguishes the English one finds in the interior South.

When the speech of the South became distinctive is unclear, although the first half of the 19th century, the period when the region achieved its fullest expression of regional consciousness, would make the most sense. Brief statements of Noah Webster and the Reverend John Witherspoon in the late 18th century noted (and condemned) characteristic southern usages as contrary to the national ideal. In the early 19th century one can find extended published comments about speech in the South, such as Fanny Kemble's comments (see Mathews 1931).

Although the vocabulary of American English began to differ from that of British English almost immediately, because of borrowing from the American Indians and from African and continental European settlers, the grammar and the pronunciation throughout the colonies remained close to the mother country until their separation; a large proportion of colonists were either born in Britain or were one generation re-

moved. The comments of British travelers and journalists both before and after the American Revolution focused on a few peculiarities of American speech (usually to condemn them, even though they were with rare exception terms derived from regional British speech), but more often they expressed wonder at the relative uniformity of American dialects, even those of the backwoods. After the Revolution all aspects of American English increasingly diverged from British English, either by diminishing contact or by deliberate choice (e.g., spellings and pronunciations attributed to Noah Webster's Anglophobia). (This does not mean, however, that American English was usually the innovator; American English, especially in the South, exhibits a kind of colonial lag in retaining many words and pronunciations prevalent in Britain in the 17th and 18th centuries.)

Just as the South has been conservative in its cultural institutions and agrarian habits, so too southern speech in general (not just the isolated relic areas) has been more conservative than other regional varieties of American English, preserving many usages common to 19th-century British speech that today are rarely found either in Great Britain or in any other area of the United States. Most of the salient older forms preserved in southern speech are lexical (e.g., *poke*, *tote*, these features usually being considered "quaint"), and grammatical (e.g., the past tense verb forms *holp*, *clum*, *knowed*), but several of the region's distinctive pronunciations are in fact preserved from the 18th century. The pronunciations of *get* as *git*, the alveolar pronunciation of the suffix *-ing* as *in* in words like *singing* and *dancing*, and the absence of *r* after vowels were all fashionable British usage 200 years ago, for example, even though many such pronunciations today are ignorantly stigmatized as "nonstandard" and discouraged in the 20th-century schoolroom. Cleanth Brooks (1937) claims these pronunciations survived in southern English, as opposed to New England speech, because of a strong oral tradition that has resisted admonitions of schoolteachers to pronounce words as they are spelled. Thus, if they wish, southerners can with some justice claim that their speech is closer to the "King's English" than that of most other Americans, although it is certainly not "Elizabethan."

The southern interest in determining roots applies to language no less than to bloodlines, so efforts to establish cross-Atlantic ties continue to be undertaken, by both linguists and nonlinguists. Hans Kurath, the founder and longtime director of the Linguistic Atlas project, designed the Atlas questionnaire to collect linguistic items that could be compared to regional British dialects, and several scholars have made comparisons of this kind. The odds against establishing clear relationships are staggering, but the quest continues. The matter of time span is not as problematic as the means of establishing proof. Cleanth Brooks has contended for over 50 years that southern speech, including such general features as the drawl and specific archaic pronunciations such as *gyarden* (for *garden*) and *bile* (for *boil*), derives primarily from the southwestern counties of Britain. In his efforts to hear the rhythm and record the echoes of the southern idiom in the old country, Brooks tried to compare the intonation of British speech with that of southern speech, a quest far more elusive than pinning down individual words.

For over a century researchers in the South, often nonlinguists, have published studies detailing analogs of southern features in British English. Most often these have been lists comparing words in the speech of relic groups such as mountaineers, blacks, islanders, or southerners in general to forms found in Chaucer, Shakespeare, and even Old English. A combination of regional and local pride and defensiveness about southern English has motivated such efforts.

Change in Southern Speech. Southern speech has undergone major changes in the latter half of the 20th century, as have all regional varieties of English in our highly mobile and increasingly urbanized and industrialized society. Yet this does not mean, as linguistic research reveals, that southern English is necessarily converging with other varieties of American English or losing its distinctiveness. Changes in vocabulary are the most dramatic and are primarily in the direction of homogeneity with the rest of the country, but grammar and especially phonology, while evolving, are by no means moving in the direction of the rest of the country. One recent study has shown, for instance, that young men in a small Alabama city use the "drawl" more than older women, an important indication of the desire of southerners to preserve their speech, since grammar and pronunciation carry more social weight and tend to be stigmatized more than vocabulary.

The sentimental often bewail linguistic change, especially in vocabulary, as the demise of a language that had more color, expressiveness, and charm. Their assumption is that the standardized, nondescript speech of the national media, and of newscasters in particular, is responsible for homogenizing Americans' speech in our television-addicted society. This assumption has little foundation in empirical evidence, and it presupposes conditions unlikely to be true for most individuals: that the newscasters themselves possess sufficient prestige to be mimicked and that Americans talk back to their televisions and radios (linguists believe people usually pattern their speech after real-life models). Television is not standardizing American speech, nor is homogeneity developing.

The principal forces of change in contemporary American English are social ones—mobility (especially the upward kind), mass education, and urbanization (the massive shift of the population to urban areas since World War II). In the South these forces have blurred the traditional distinctions in speech lingering from the days of greater social stratification. The speech, even of natives, in the urban South of Atlanta or Memphis today is very different from that of a generation ago. The speech of successive generations just down the road in the small-town South of Milledgeville, Ga., or Henning, Tenn., is not nearly so divergent. Today young, middle-class speakers of the urban and suburban South are often closer to their counterparts in the urban North and West than to their peers in the rural South living just a county or two away. One doubts that urbanites watch more television than their country cousins. The extent to which the speech of modern-day, middle-class citizens in the urban and suburban South, and in a few respects the speech throughout the country, is converging reflects common social forces, not the influence of television.

The influence of these social forces has meant two things: (1) the variety of regional dialects in the South is being replaced by social dialects, and (2) regional dialect boundaries are shifting in the South, as the South Midland region expands at the expense of the Lower Southern region. Whereas urban centers such as Charleston, Savannah, and Richmond exercised prestige in the days of the colonies, the newer metropolises in the Upper South, such as Charlotte, Nashville, and Atlanta, are now the dynamic centers for linguistic change and development of regional standards of speech.

McDavid (1957) claims the older type of "elegant" Lower Southern speech found in the former plantation belt, from Virginia southward and then westward to west Texas and northward into Kentucky and dominated by such focal areas as Charleston and Richmond, has been losing its prestige. The influence of Charleston is also receding, even though it was still strong and spreading in the 1920s (see McDavid, 1948). McDavid attributes this not to the influence of a national standard but rather to the increasing dominance of both the Upper Southern speakers and the former lower- and middle-class speakers who have ascended the social ladder. Other studies, in Georgia and Alabama, confirm the expansion of the Upper South or South Midland dialect's influence at the expense of the Lower South.

There is, however, scant evidence that the recent settlement of northern migrants and retirees in the region is making southerners speak more like these new arrivals. Most southerners are rather strongly attached to their way of talking, and one of the last things they would want is to talk "like a Yankee." Recent research suggests that the accents of some younger southerners are becoming more distinctive and less like those of either their parents or non-southerners.

The Scholarly Study of Southern Speech. There is more commentary on the speech of the American South (including the southern Appalachian areas) than on that of any other region of the country. Much of this has been written by nonacademics, suggesting that the people of the region are curious about and proud of their own speech. Their work is motivated by a fascination with local language patterns and an antiquarian interest in exotic and picturesque localisms found in such isolated relic areas as southern Appalachia, the Outer Banks, and the Sea Islands. Localisms are used most often by older, less-educated, and less-traveled speakers. The frequent discussion of such expressions has in some respects exaggerated the exoticism of the region's speech, particularly the speech of blacks in the South.

The South is the only region to have a book-length bibliography devoted to its speech. The *Annotated Bibliography of Southern American English* (1971) has been recently updated to include over 3,000 items. The early literature on southern speech, until roughly 1930, was predominantly word lists, collections of picturesque and unusual localisms. These collections, rarely rigorous or based on surveys of any kind, dealt mostly with vocabulary but occasionally commented on phonology and grammar. With few exceptions, they discussed speech impressionistically, without relating the use of language to social variables such as age, social status, education, occupation, or gender. Neglecting these variables has led to a presentation of southern speech as more uniform and more different from the rest of the country than has ever been the case.

The collection of phonological information on southern English from local surveys, especially in Louisiana, predominated through the 1930s and 1940s. The systematic study of language patterns in the region began in earnest with the completion of fieldwork for the *Linguistic Atlas of the Middle and South Atlantic States* (*LAMSAS*) in the late 1930s. Details on the age, education, occupation, and social habits and contacts of each informant for the project were noted. Summary volumes covering this territory, which includes Maryland, Virginia, North Carolina, South Carolina, eastern Georgia, and the northernmost part of Georgia, are by Kurath (1949), Atwood (1953), and Kurath and McDavid (1961). The data from well over 2,000 informants reported in the *LAMSAS* and the *Linguistic Atlas of the Gulf States* (*LAGS*) (begun in 1968 and published in microtext in 1981) roughly equal the data from all the individual studies that have been conducted. Atlas methodology, investigating hundreds of specific items using a standardized questionnaire for features of grammar as well as vocabulary and phonetics, has been highly influential in the region and has spawned a number of small-scale studies.

Central to the Linguistic Atlas and other regionwide projects has been determining the number and the designation of subregions of southern English. This major effort has generated considerable controversy over methodology and the designations of specific speech areas. The lines for dialect areas are drawn closer to principal migration routes than to topographical features, but the lines are hardly exact and can vary according to the supporting data one adduces. They also become less and less clear as one moves west across the region.

Early subjective studies divided

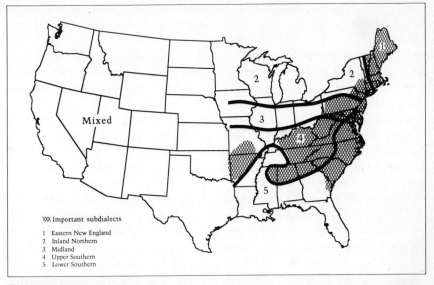

XXX Important subdialects
1 Eastern New England
2 Inland Northern
3 Midland
4 Upper Southern
5 Lower Southern

Dialects

Source: Raymond Gastil, **Cultural Regions of the United States** *(1975); modified from Jean Malmstrom and Annabel Ashley,* **Dialects-USA** *(1963), and other sources*

American speech into three areas— New England, Southern, and General American (Western)—but it was Hans Kurath in 1949 who first made the systematic case, on the basis of vocabulary, that the eastern states have three general dialect areas—Northern, Midland, and Southern. In dividing the Midland area into two subareas, the North Midland (from Pennsylvania southwestward into West Virginia) and the South Midland (extending southward into South Carolina, Georgia, and Alabama), Kurath made the proposal that the speech of the southern mountains and hills had more affinities to Pennsylvania speech than to that of the Lower South.

Also using vocabulary, Wood (1971) identified three principal subregions, the first two of which correspond generally to Kurath's major division: Coastal Southern, extending from southern Maryland through the Atlantic states south to Florida; Mid-Southern, extending from West Virginia south through the hill country of Alabama and Georgia

and, in another belt, from southern Missouri southwesterly through Arkansas and Oklahoma into Texas; and Gulf Southern, a region of mixed vocabulary extending from the Alabama-Georgia border west along the Gulf states and northward through the Mississippi Valley.

In a 1986 formulation based on grammar and pronunciation as well as vocabulary, Pederson and associates identified at least 11 major subregional dialects of southern speech and as many as 14 urban dialects.

The Consciousness of Southern Speakers. The regional consciousness of southerners accounts in part for the region's distinctive speech patterns. One's speech, as well as much of the rest of one's social behavior, expresses one's identity—local, regional, and national—and indicates the speakers with whom one prefers to be identified. The attachments of most southerners to their home, community, and region tend to be strong and are expressed through choice of speech features. These attachments are perhaps the strongest buffer against the disappearance of southern English; as long as there is regional consciousness in the South, a discernible variety of speech will likely express and embody it.

The native southern dialect usually commands regional, but rarely national, prestige, and this often means that southerners acquire one or more varieties of speech in addition to the one they already have and thus develop a repertoire of two or more different styles of speaking (depending on the audience or situation). Many southerners have long had this ability to shift styles. A Tennesseean who has moved to New York City may alter his speech for New Yorkers, but with other Tennesseeans who have migrated to the city, he will shift his speech quickly and naturally. Because of the class and ethnic structure of the region, many southerners command more than one variety of southern English; this ability to shift language styles makes it more difficult to identify their typical speech.

The self-consciousness that southerners have about their speech is perhaps most acute when a southern politician is in the national limelight or when they hear southern speech in the movies and on television shows such as *The Beverly Hillbillies*, the *Dukes of Hazzard*, or *Hee Haw*. Southerners are embarrassed by the stereotypes of mountain people, hayseed bumpkins, and stock car addicts, even though such programs frequently portray southerners using their country wisdom to thoroughly outwit their city counterparts. Southern speech and behavior are often caricatured in a fashion consistent with northern stereotypes of southern speakers. Southerners frequently find themselves striving to overcome these stereotypes. This does not mean, however, that southerners are slow to capitalize on them. The tourist-shop exaggerations of southern speech in popular booklets found throughout the region are vastly overpriced but sell well, expressing pride in the local speech and profiting from Yankees at the same time.

The national media's consuming attention to southern speech whenever a southern politician gets his due alternately pleases and pains southerners. Jimmy Carter's presidential campaign in 1976 sparked countless newspaper stories by Washington feature writers who feared they would have to learn a second dialect and also produced a rash of cocktail-circuit primers on the region's speech. In 1984 the populace was presented with such a caricature of the speech of South Carolina's Ernest Hollings during the presidential campaign that few knew his positions on any issue or took him seriously as a candidate (one national columnist claimed that Hollings's "lockjaw Southern drawl is almost unintelligible"). Southern politicos are also often recognized as having superior linguistic and rhetorical skills. Sam Ervin of North Carolina captured the imagination of the country with his down-home quips and anecdotes when chairing the special Watergate investigating committee in 1973. And Jesse Jackson of South Carolina thoroughly enlivened the Democratic presidential primaries with his powerful rhetoric in 1984.

The Speech of Whites and Blacks. The question of how speech differs between blacks and whites in the South is as sensitive as the general issue of the social relations between the races. It is a question that has inspired countless researchers and commentators, many of them antiquarians trying to record unusual speech forms before they disappear, to offer their evidence and proposals. Popular notions on the subjects of the extent and origin of differences between white and black speech lack all perspective, but scholarly views have and still do run the entire gamut and have rarely been dispassionate. Uninitiated readers of the principal commentators on the issue are easily confused by the attendant politics of the various scholarly camps—linguistic geographers, sociolinguists, and creolists—and there is little, if anything, on which the specialists agree. (For a survey of recent research and an attempt at an evenhanded explication of the scholarly issues, see Montgomery and Bailey [1986].)

The question of how the speech of blacks and whites differs has two principle subquestions—one historical, the other pedagogical. Most research on and discussion of black-white speech differences has centered on the pedagogical issue: How teachers can handle a diversity of dialects in the teaching of literacy skills? The answer to this question, however, inevitably hinges on the answer to the historical question: What are the origins of speech patterns and the relative influences of African, Caribbean, and British Isles linguistic heritages?

Here the views run the gamut. At one extreme is the view that the speech of blacks (except for Gullah, the creole language spoken on the offshore Sea Islands of South Carolina and Georgia) retains only a small handful of nouns (e.g., *goober*, *gumbo*, *juke*, *zombie*) and names from African languages and that the otherwise distinctive features of

black speech derive from older (17th- and 18th-century) or regional British speech, these features having been acquired from whites on plantations and perpetuated by segregation.

At the other extreme is the view that present-day black speech represents a superficial English derivative of a plantation creole language (one similar to present-day Gullah or a Sea Island creole). This plantation creole is said to have been heavily influenced, lexically and to some extent gramatically, by African languages and Caribbean creoles and was ultimately derived from a pidgin language spoken in West Africa.

The charged social tensions and the close connection that speech has with racial identity have made both blacks and whites reluctant to discuss the connection between black speech and white speech and to give any credence to the notion that there is such a thing as "black English." Whites have historically been uneasy about inferences that their speech resembles that of black southerners, resisting the notion that their speech has been influenced by the speech of blacks. White scholars have tried to trace southern English (both white speech and black speech) to regional British dialects in part in an effort to show that white speech does not de-

Language and humor among friends in Franklin, Ga., 1941

rive from black speech. Whites are upset when northerners say they sound like blacks and when, as has often happened, non-southern linguists label features found in speech throughout the South as features of black speech. Blacks are aware of how frequently the differences between white speech and black speech have been exaggerated and that their distinctive speech patterns have often been isolated and exploited to brand them easy targets for discrimination. Thus, they usually minimize the differences (and insist, often correctly, that the differences are merely older white English) and are often suspicious that modern-day descriptions of "black English" are disguised paternalism.

In point of fact, the case for "racial dialects" is far more difficult to substantiate in the South than in the urban North. Social differences are often more significant than racial ones, and a key problem with much of the research comparing white and black speech is that whites and blacks of comparable education and social status have not been contrasted. Few, if any, specific linguistic forms are now used exclusively by either blacks or whites. The differences that do exist are probably greatest in intonation and rhythm, the parts of language structure most difficult to describe and to generalize about.

See also BLACK LIFE: Creolization; Preacher, Black; Speech, Black; / Jackson, Jesse; FOLKLIFE: Storytelling; GEOGRAPHY: Expatriates and Exiles; LAW: / Ervin, Sam; LITERATURE: / Brooks, Cleanth; MYTHIC SOUTH: Stereotypes; / Carter Era

Michael Montgomery
University of South Carolina

E. Bagby Atwood, *A Survey of Verb Forms in the Eastern States* (1953); Cleanth Brooks, in *A Southern Treasury of Life and Literature*, ed. Stark Young (1937), *The Language of the American South* (1985); William A. Kretzschmar, Jr., ed., *Dialects in Culture: Essays in General Dialectology by Raven I. McDavid, Jr.* (1979); Hans Kurath, *Word Geography of the Eastern United States* (1949), with Raven I. McDavid, Jr., *Pronunciation of English in the Atlantic States* (1961); Raven I. McDavid, Jr., *American Speech* (April 1948), in *The Structure of American English*, by Winthrop Nelson Francis (1957); James B. McMillan, ed., *Annotated Bibliography of Southern American English* (1971), with Michael Montgomery, eds., *Annotated Bibliography of Southern American English* (2d ed., 1986); Mitford M. Mathews, ed., *The Beginnings of American English* (1931); Michael Montgomery and Guy Bailey, eds., *Language Variety in the South: Perspectives in Black and White* (1986); Lee A. Pederson et al., eds., LAGS: *The Basic Materials* (1981) et al., eds., *Handbook of the Linguistic Atlas of the Gulf States* (1986); Gordon R. Wood, *Vocabulary Change: A Study of Variation in Regional Words in Eight of the Southern States* (1971). ☆

Black Language
||||||||||||||||||||||||||||||||||||||

See BLACK LIFE: Speech, Black

Conversation
||||||||||||||||||||||||||||||||||||||

Sometimes referred to as talking, chatting, visiting, jawing, small talk, or repartee, conversation involves the oral exchange of ideas, opinions, and sentiments. Unstructured, it flows along according to whims and inclinations with little purpose beyond visiting or "passing the time of day." Allen Tate, in an essay entitled "A Southern Mode of the Imagination," argued that northern conversation was about ideas, whereas "the typical southern conversation is not going anywhere; it is not about anything. *It is about the people who are talking.*" An aspect of regional manners, Tate wrote, southern conversation is a way "to make everybody happy." Ellen Glasgow in *The Woman Within* (1954) insisted that in the South "conversation, not literature, is the pursuit of all classes."

In the frontier South with dwellings miles apart and life lonely and often harsh, lengthy visits were common, and hospitality was extended even to strangers. Church meetings, court days, political rallies, funerals, and even hangings became occasions to socialize, to hear the news, and to discuss mutual concerns. At the country store loafers congregated, and in cold weather they clustered around the warm stove to play checkers or cards and swap yarns.

Southerners took pride in being, and listening to, great talkers, making folk heroes of preachers, lawyers, politicians, and storytellers. Whether conversing in a lowly cabin, a white framed house, or a mansion, they reveled in loquaciousness. Young ladies mastered the art of "small talk"; matrons loved to gossip about household matters, child rearing, and sensational happenings. Thomas Nelson Page commends "the master of the plantation" as a "wonderful talker" who "discoursed of philosophy, politics, and religion." When discussing hospitality Page reports, "The conversation was surprising: it was

of crops, the roads, politics, mutual friends, including the entire field of neighborhood matters, related not as gossip, but as affairs of common interest which everyone knew or was expected and entitled to know."

In Charleston, New Orleans, Natchez, and other cities, planters and professionals met in their social and literary clubs, welcomed distinguished guests, and engaged in enlightened repartee, sometimes over dinner or while sipping old wines.

Blacks, meanwhile, developed distinctive conversational skills. Zora Neale Hurston, in *Mules and Men* (1935), recalled from her childhood in Eatonville, Fla., the men who gathered at the country store or on the front porch to exchange tales, and her works are filled with examples of black conversation, including the "lying" sessions when stories were swapped. Writers such as Ralph Ellison and Alice Walker structure their works around conversational lore.

In more recent times the front porch (the "gallerie" to Cajuns) attracted the

Swapping stories, Vicksburg, Miss., 1974

family and their friends. Shaded perhaps by tall trees and equipped with rocking chairs and sometimes palm-leaf fans or ceiling fans, it was a place to relax, to watch passersby, and to welcome relatives, neighbors, the postman, a salesman, the minister, whoever happened to stop and "sit a spell." In French Louisiana the visitor might be offered dark-roast coffee, in other areas iced tea or lemonade; the mint julep sometimes encouraged joviality on plantation verandas. With the advent of radio, television, and air-conditioning, the front porches were enclosed or gave way to cooler interiors out of the heat and dust, and no longer were people as likely to pass the time with simple conversation. Nonetheless, Hobson Pittman's late 1940s painting *The Conversation* conveys the traditional importance of conversation in the South, portraying a dreamlike setting of two women talking while sitting in chairs, both dwarfed by a high-ceilinged interior—a remembered scene from the artist's childhood.

See also BLACK LIFE: Folklore, Black; HISTORY AND MANNERS: Manners

Waldo W. Braden
Louisiana State University

Roger D. Abrahams, *Southern Folklore Quarterly* (March 1968); Waldo W. Braden, *The Oral Tradition in the South* (1983); Merrill G. Christophersen, *Southern Speech Journal* (Winter 1954); Everett Dick, *The Dixie Frontier: A Comprehensive Picture of Southern Frontier Life before the Civil War* (1948); Frank L. Owsley, *Plain Folk of the Old South* (1949); Allen Tate, *Essays of Four Decades* (1968). ☆

Folk Speech

Southern folk speech refers to the variations in speech from the standard, formal language taught in the schools. It is a simple form of verbal folklore—the expressions, place names, and ways of speaking commonly accepted by people in the South. Most southerners value their region's folk speech highly because it preserves and keeps alive a wealth of traditions, sometimes through slang, proverbs, and euphemisms. The southern dialect, in general, includes variations in grammar, pronunciation, and vocabulary. There is often, for example, the use of the past tense of verbs ("I seen him"). Linguistic atlases profusely document the differences in pronunciation of words in different American regions ("greasy" or "greazy"). Linguists verify the popular perception as well that southerners' vocabulary often differs from that of other Americans. The southerner's use of "y'all" is perhaps the best example of folk speech in the region.

The American Dialect Society, which started in 1889, is an institutional focus for the study of southern folk speech, and its journal, *American Speech*, published since 1925, is a chief organ for publication in the field. The study of folk speech in the region has often focused on the legacy of, or deviations from, British speech patterns in Appalachian or rural southern areas. The nature of black English, the influence of other languages, and the relationship between speech and social class have also been central concerns. A variety of linguistic atlas projects—including Frederic G. Cassidy's *Dictionary of American Regional English* (1985–),

Hans Kurath and associates' *Linguistic Atlas of the Middle and South Atlantic States*, and Lee A. Pederson's *Linguistic Atlas of the Gulf States*—precisely shows the distribution of speechways across the region.

Folk speech uses language that calls attention to itself. *Raining like an old cow pissing on a flat rock in Arkansas* gets much more immediate notice than *It's pouring rain.* This immediacy of reaction is precisely what allows southern folk speech to make its double contribution. Hans Kurath, director of the Linguistic Atlas project, used the label "folk-speech" to identify nonurban, uneducated performance in American dialects, and folklorists incorporated this definition into their work. But a community's folk speech is better defined not in terms of its users but of its uses, its style, and its saliency. When speech is based in and uniquely valued by its own community, it is *internal* folk speech; when it is everyday talk found anywhere, it is not folk speech. A southerner who says *He's so high he couldn't hit the floor with his hat* ("drunk") will be understood by his or her own community as using folk speech; one who says *I'll carry you to Greenville* ("give you a lift"), will not. Non-southerners overlook such distinctions and tend to see any talk by southerners as folk speech.

A review of southern speech sources would duplicate the region's settlement history, and the relations of groups to specific items would be speculative. A better approach is an admittedly cross-classifiable taxonomy of types and an indication of how they have fared in past scholarship.

Below the word. Folk noises and morphemes have hardly been studied, though chants, calls, and imitations have figured in a few works, and the "rebel yell" is a famous folk cry.

The word. The numerous publications of the *American Dialect Society, Dialect Notes, American Speech,* and regional publications might have contributed to a regional slang dictionary, but they rarely distinguish between words that are limited socially and geographically and those that are especially valued and recur throughout the region—folk speech. Regional words that may qualify have been extensively collected and appear in dictionaries of slang and of American language usage.

Phrases. In the area of phrases and proverbial sentences southern folk speech (and the study of it) shines. Proverbial comparisons are the subject of much study. *As X as a Y* (or *X-er than a Y* and other obviously related forms) is the target of Preston (1975)—*busy as a one-armed paperhanger. So X that Y* is studied by Halpert (1951)—*so tight* [that] *he wouldn't give a dime to see the Statue of Liberty piss across New York Bay.* Most collections combine the grammatical forms cited above with the others—*X enough to Y* and *too X to Y* (both related to *so X that Y*); *to X like a Y* (often interchangeable with some forms of *as X as a Y*); and other minor comparative forms. Boshears (1954) is the largest individual collection—*look like a sheep-killing dog, run around like a chicken with its head cut off, make more noise than 99 cows and a bob-tailed bull.*

Though comparisons dominate, a few other forms based on nouns (*the straw that broke the camel's back*), verbs (*come a cropper*), and prepositional phrases (*in hot water*) are included in most studies along with other expressions not so easily classified grammatically. Some might be identified as threats (*I'm going to jerk a knot in your tail*), wisecracks and comebacks (*your feet don't fit no limb*—said to one who asks *who?*), exclamations and warnings (*Katy bar the door!*), insults (somebody doesn't *amount to a hill of beans*), taunts (*redhead, cabbage-head, 10 cents a pound* directed to a redheaded person), boasts (*Hooo-eee! I'm half horse and half alligator!*), and miscellaneous sentential items (*hope in one hand and shit in the other and see which fills up first*), though such a classification is practical rather than theoretically exhaustive.

Randolph and Wilson (1953) and Whiting (1952) are noteworthy collections. Taylor and Whiting (1958), although not exclusively concerned with southern speech, provide important references as do the dictionaries and periodicals already mentioned. Proverbs, mentioned in many of these collections, are excluded from folk speech, although borderline examples of items that may be fully integrated in conversations exist.

Beyond the sentence. Least studied are aspects of folk speech having to do with so-called stylistic tendencies. For example, the classical tradition in southern education left behind names and references. This, combined with a traditional knowledge of the Bible, produced a genre known as "fancy talk" in black speech and influenced southern pulpit styles in general. Rosenberg (1970) and Kochman (1972) have studied these and other aspects, though the focus has been primarily on black genres.

McMillan (1971) shows that local language has always been an important aspect of southern culture. Though every American reader will sense the "southernness" of these contributions, comparable studies from the North are sparse, and comparisons are limited (but see Preston, 1975). Although content analyses of southern folk speech reveal preoccupation with rural, traditional matters, newer items display changing attitudes and concerns. Growing evidence suggests that southerners more than any other Americans may assign particular importance to folk speech. Such speech is important to the region, has a distinct local flavor, and will likely be around as long as the culture exists.

See also **BLACK LIFE**: Speech, Black

Dennis R. Preston
State University of New York
at Fredonia

Lester V. Berrey and Melvin Van den Bark, *The American Thesaurus of Slang, with Supplement: A Complete Reference Book of Colloquial Speech* (1947); Frederic G. Cassidy, *Dictionary of American Regional English* (1985); Sir William A. Craigie and James R. Hulbert, *A Dictionary of American English on Historical Principles* (1938–44); Herbert Halpert, *Midwest Folklore* (1975); Thomas Kochman, *Rappin' and Stylin' Out: Communication in Urban Black America* (1972); James B. McMillan, *Annotated Bibliography of Southern American English* (1971); Mitford M. Mathews, ed., *Dictionary of Americanisms on Historical Principles* (1951); Dennis R. Preston, *Orbis* (1975); Vance Randolph and George P. Wilson, *Down in the Holler: A Gallery of Ozark Folk Speech* (1953); Bruce A. Rosenberg, *The Art of the American Folk Preacher* (1970); Archer Taylor and Bartlett J. Whiting, *A Dictionary of American Proverbs and Proverbial Phrases, 1820–1880* (1958); Richard H. Thornton, *An American Glossary: Being an Attempt to Illustrate Certain Americanisms upon Historical Principles* (1962); Harold Wentworth and Stuart Berg Flexner, eds., *Dictionary of American Slang* (1958); Norman I. White, ed., *The Frank C. Brown Collection of North Carolina Folklore* (1952). ☆

French Language

IIIIIIIIIIIIIIIIIIIIIIIIIIIIIIIIIIIIIIIIIIIII

There was a time when the French language could have been heard throughout the vast area of the North American continent west of the Appalachian divide. Along the Mississippi River, place names from Baton Rouge to St. Louis recall the French presence, and the pronunciation of Indian names such as Arkansas (note the silent final consonant) indicates that they were transmitted to English through French. But the early French speakers were explorers and traders, and permanent settlements were few. Except for a small enclave at Old Mines, near Ste. Geneviève, Mo., where the oldest people still remember the language, French survives today only in southern Louisiana and adjacent parts of Texas.

Groups of Huguenots (French Protestant refugees) settled in some of the eastern colonies, especially South Carolina, where the French language was used in church services until the mid-18th century. This group appears, in the main, to have been linguistically assimilated by the time of the Revolution. An enclave of Provençal-speaking Waldensians is found in the town of Valdese, N.C.

Three varieties of French were formerly spoken in Louisiana. Colonial French, the language of the Creoles (here meaning white settlers coming directly from Europe and their descendants—of German and Spanish origin as well as French), was close to standard (educated) French. Many Creole children received a good education; some went to school in Europe. Obviously, spoken usage differed from that of France, particularly in the vocabulary for local customs, fauna, flora, and foods. The pronunciation had a regional flavor, but the grammar was basically standard.

The second type of French was brought to the southern and southwestern parishes of Louisiana by the Acadian, or Cajun, refugees from the Alantic provinces of Canada. Deported by the British from a place where, after over a hundred years, they had created a unique culture and way of life, these people spoke a type of French whose roots lay in 17th-century western France, particularly the provinces of Poitou and Aunis. It differed from standard French in its preservation of archaic and regional vocabulary, pronunciation, and grammar. For some time after its introduction into Louisiana in the mid-18th century, it maintained its special characteristics through relative isolation.

Finally, most black people spoke what linguists call Louisiana Creole—the word Creole used here in a technical linguistic sense, meaning a language with a largely French-derived stock of words, but restructured in grammar, pronunciation, and semantics. So, for example, the definite article follows the noun instead of preceding it: "the book" is *liv-la*, not *le livre*. Verbs are conjugated by prefixed participles instead of endings: "I shall see" is *mo va oua* or *m'a oua*, not *je verrai*.

Much controversy surrounds the origin of Creole, of which several types are found in the Caribbean and the Indian Ocean. Current research suggests that it resulted in part from a deliberate policy among slave traders and plantation owners of teaching their African captives a simplified version of French or English, for which a precedent existed in the Portuguese-derived trading jargon of the West African Coast. Another factor was the social isolation and incomplete acculturation of the plantation slaves, who had no single African language to use as a common tongue and so had to create an emergency communication device from whatever bits and pieces of French they had learned. Inevitably, some African ways of saying things were included in the new language, although it continued to contain few specific words of African origin (and these have often spread to white dialects, and even English: e.g., *gombo*, "gumbo"). In any case, Louisiana Creole is too similar to other forms of Caribbean Creole to be altogether independent of them. By the time the first

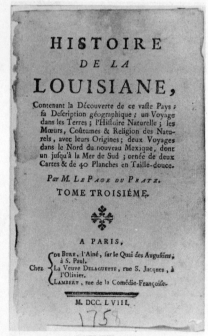

French book circulated in Louisiana

slaves arrived in Louisiana about 1719, planters and traders must have had some knowledge of existing Creole dialects, and they tried to teach them to newly arrived Africans. Later, emigration from Santo Domingo (Haiti), following the slave revolts at the end of the 18th century, left its imprint on the language through Haitian imports (although there are certain fundamental differences: e.g., "his book" is *so live*, instead of the Haitian *liv-li*—literally, "book him").

Today, the boundaries between the three varieties of Louisiana French have been blurred. Many descendants of Creoles now speak only English. In the rural areas Cajun has survived but has lost some of its uniqueness. Louisiana Creole, mixed with Cajun, is still spoken in some black families, particularly in St. Martin Parish, and by many whites (an inheritance from the days when white children learned their first language as much from their black servants as from their parents). Louisiana French today, then, is a blend, showing much variation in vocabulary, grammar, and pronunciation. English borrowings and expressions are pervasive.

A whole generation of children received no education in French and were discouraged from speaking it. Recent attempts to revive the use of French by teaching it in the schools have encountered a dilemma: should the standard language or the local dialect(s) be used? For many, there can be no question: only standard French is worth teaching, because the ultimate goal must be to give young Louisianans a useful second language. This approach, sponsored by CODOFIL (the Council for the Development of French in Louisiana), has been challenged by Cajuns who point out that children of French-speaking families often find their grandparents cannot understand the words they are learning in school. Recently, a textbook was created to teach Cajun French in an English-based spelling system easier to learn than the irrational standard French orthography. This would give Cajun children a pride in their heritage but would make it more difficult for them to continue with French later if they wished. The future of French in Louisiana, already endangered, will depend on finding a solution to this problem.

See also BLACK LIFE: African Influences; Creolization; Speech, Black; ETHNIC LIFE: Caribbean Influence; / Cajuns; Creoles; French

Alexander Hull
Duke University

James F. Broussard, *Louisiana Creole Dialect* (1942); James Donald Faulk, *Cajun French I* (1977); John Francis McDermott, *A Glossary of Mississippi Valley French, 1673–1850* (1941); Raleigh Morgan, Jr., in *Texas Studies in Bilingualism*, ed. Glenn G. Gilbert (1970); Larbi Oukada, *Louisiana French: An Annotated Linguistic Bibliography* (1979); William A. Read, *Louisiana French* (1931; rev. ed., 1963); Dorice Tentchoff, in *The Culture of Acadiana: Tradition and Change in South Louisiana*, ed. Steven L. Del Sesto and Jon L. Gibson (1975). ☆

German Language

||||||||||||||||||||||||||||||||||||||||||||||

German immigrants arrived in America as early as 1683. They formed self-sufficient farm communities and small rural towns, where they maintained their German language and customs. In the

South, varieties of German survive in two areas: (1) Virginia, in the western parts of Shenandoah County (Jerome) and Rockingham County (Criders and Dayton) and in neighboring Pendleton County, W. Va. (Sugar Grove and Propst Gap); and (2) Texas, in the city triangle San Antonio-Austin-Houston, particularly in the counties of Gillespie, Kendall, Comal, Guadalupe, Lee, Washington, Austin, Fayette, DeWitt, and Medina. The German immigrants did not speak a single, homogeneous variety of German, and the German dialects still spoken in Virginia and Texas differ from each other and from Pennsylvania German, with which they are often compared.

The Germans began to settle Virginia in the 18th century via Pennsylvania, but they were, for the most part, native Germans or their children, who had come from Switzerland, Alsace, and the Palatinate. The Dayton area of Rockingham County became a stronghold of the plain sects, especially of Mennonites, who are known for their German-language loyalty, which helps them maintain their isolation from mainstream American society. In addition to specific lexical items and phonological features that are peculiar to Virginia German varieties, such as the loss of *r* and word-initial *sch*, Dayton German retains the front rounded (or umlauted) vowels of standard German. (These vowels are not found in dialects of Pennsylvania German.) Virginia German is not one single dialect but a cluster of similar dialects, each one exhibiting independent developments.

German settlements in Texas were first established in 1831, and, as in Virginia, Texas German developed independently of other varieties of German in the United States. The German settlers in Texas came predominantly from north and middle Germany, and linguistic studies of Texas German reveal a loss of southern German dialect features found in Pennsylvania and Virginia. Texas German is a dialect more closely approaching the middle-northern-based standard German. However, the influence of English has been pervasive. The German of Fredericksburg in Gillespie County, for example, shows a loss of front rounded vowels and the adoption of the American English vowel sound found in *cat*. American English influence on Texas German is also found in the pronunciation of *l* and *r* and in the merger of the German dative and accusative noun cases.

In spite of the great numbers of German immigrants who settled in America, the language never achieved an official status. Its communicative functions are being increasingly fulfilled by English, and German as a spoken language in Virginia and Texas may be expected to die out within the next two generations.

See also ETHNIC LIFE: / Germans

Marion Lois Huffines
Bucknell University

Glenn G. Gilbert, *Texas Studies in Bilingualism* (1970), *The German Language in America: A Symposium* (1971); Elmer Lewis Smith, John G. Stewart, and M. Ellsworth Kyger, *The Pennsylvania Germans of the Shenandoah Valley* (1964). ☆

Gullah

||||||||||||||||

Gullah is the most conservative form of "black English" spoken in the United States today. It preserves features of vocabulary, grammar, and idiom that other kinds of black English have lost, or never had. It is a true "creole" language, the only creole English still alive in the United States and a close cousin to the flourishing creoles of the Caribbean: Jamaican, Guyanese, Trinidadian, Barbadian, and others. Like these, Gullah preserves features of African languages brought in by plantation slaves as far back as three hundred years ago.

Gullah is spoken chiefly on the coastal islands—the so-called rice islands—that stretch for 160 miles along the seaboard of South Carolina and Georgia, but it is also heard on parts of the adjacent mainland. Until recent years these settlements were isolated, as some still are, so that the black inhabitants, who worked in rice fields, had little contact with the English of the white and black communities ashore. Gullah was thus sheltered from the process of "decreolization," by which creole speech gradually changes under the influence of the prevailing language. Gullah, with its mixture of English and African features, is quite adequate for the daily life of its speakers. But outsiders do not readily understand it, and as the Gullah communities become less isolated, linguistic features differing most from the surrounding American English are bound to yield.

The word *Gullah* may come from *Gola*, the name of a people from Liberia and Sierra Leone (West Africa), whence some slaves were brought to the Carolina colony. This group, however, was relatively small, whereas a very large number of slaves were brought earlier and over a longer period from Angola. The latter, therefore, seems the more plausible source for the word. The Gullah people and their language, however, are far more mixed, as both the history of slave importations and the surviving African language features show.

The Charleston colony, founded in 1670, is the geographical center of Gullah. Planters from Barbados started it, bringing their slaves who in the early years were from the Gold Coast (now Ghana) and Nigeria. Others came later from the entire coast of West Africa, which stretches over 3,000 miles from Senegal to Angola, bringing various languages and dialects. Thus, the creole English of these first slaves was constantly affected by new importations. The African features that have survived best in Gullah must have arrived early and have been reinforced by the continuing influx of Africans. Creole blacks—those born in America—looked down on the African-born as savages and made little or no attempt to keep African languages alive. But it is striking that a large number of African features in Gullah are like those flourishing in the Caribbean today, in French-, Dutch-, and Spanish-based, as well as English-based, creoles. This implies either a similar origin or else convergence so that for linguistic or other reasons the same basic features emerged as the dominant ones. These and other possibilities are now being debated by scholars in the field. In many fundamental ways at least, Gullah is strikingly like its Caribbean cousins already mentioned.

The main features that set Gullah apart from the rest of American English, black or white, are sound, word form, and syntax. Vocabulary, being a superficial feature (words come and go more easily than any other part of language), will be treated briefly. In records made about 1940, Lorenzo Turner, the first

linguist to study Gullah closely, found African words and phrases still in use or at least remembered, though in many cases they were being replaced by English words. Such foodstuff names as *okra, yam, benne, cush, goober,* and *cala* were at least locally known; others included *buckra,* "white man," *hoodoo,* "sorcery," and *cooter,* "tortoise or turtle." Turner also collected hundreds of the personal names that the Gullah give their children at birth—all of African derivation. Though the meaning and origin of these names are forgotten, the names continue to be used out of tradition.

More significant, however, are features of syntax, such as the plural pronoun *una* meaning *you all,* which is prevalent in southern speech. *Una,* however, is not a translation of *you all;* it comes from one or more West African languages, and its cognates are widespread in the Caribbean, from the Bahamas to Jamaica, Belize, Tobago, the Nicaraguan shore, and Guyana. Similarly, the little word *da* (or *duh*) is used to indicate continuing verbal action. *We go* does not specify the time or status of the action, but *we da go* or *we da goin* shows progressive action. The latter is a feature of several West African languages, which survives also in the creole speech of the Caribbean colonies. Apart from use of *-ing,* verbs have a single form, usually taken from the English infinitive or else from the past: *mek* and *tek* (make, take), in common with most other English-based creoles, betray north-of-England origin. One other such feature is the use of *dem* (and them) added to a noun, especially a person's name, to mean that person and those associated with him or her (usually family members). This explains a Gullah expression such as *Sancho dem,* "Sancho and his bunch," as reported by Ambrose E. Gonzales. This Gullah feature was also reported from white speech in Memphis, Tenn., in the 1920s.

The greatest number of Gullah words are not African but English, though many are disguised by phonetic changes, most of which are, or were, also found in general black speech: the lack of *th-* sounds, so that *this* is *dis* and *through* is *tru*; use of *b* for English *v*, so that *very* is *bery* and *vexed* is *bexed*; and the loss of final consonants especially from clusters, so that *past*, *wasp*, *blind*, and *salt* become, respectively, *pas*, *wass*, *bline*, and *saal*. Gullah has special pronunciations of its own, however: *put* is regularly *pit*, *see'em* is *shum*, *ain't it* becomes *enti*, and *young* is *nyoung*. Sometimes, under influence of African word endings, a vowel is added in Gullah: *wikiti*, "wicked"; *nekiti*, "naked." And a goodly number of African turns of speech are translated in Gullah: *hard-ears*, "stubborn," *peel-head*, "bald," and so on.

The famous Uncle Remus stories of Brer Rabbit (Joel Chandler Harris) are told in the language of middle Georgia, not Gullah. But the corresponding tales in Gullah may be found in two good sources, *Negro Myths from the Georgia Coast* (1888), by Charles Colcock Jones, and *The Black Border* (1922), by Ambrose Gonzales. In *Africanisms* (1949) Lorenzo Dow Turner included phonetic transcriptions and translations into standard English of 14 texts that he had recorded on phonograph records. Much study has been done since, but little of it has been published. Gullah especially interests scholars of creole languages because it is the most distinctive and archaic type of American black English. But the attention is almost too late, for with the exploitation of the rice islands

for tourist development the process of decreolization has accelerated. Gullah, especially in its more traditional form kept alive by isolation, is now fading fast. Dialects, however, are surprisingly vital; Gullah may survive as the intimate, home talk of rice island natives for generations.

See also BLACK LIFE: African Influences; Creolization; Speech, Black; ETHNIC LIFE: Caribbean Influence; FOLKLIFE: / Brer Rabbit; LITERATURE: / Harris, Joel Chandler

Frederic G. Cassidy
University of Wisconsin

Ambrose E. Gonzales, *The Black Border: Gullah Stories of the Carolina Coast* (with a glossary) (1922), *With Aesop along the Black Border* (1924, 1969); Guy B. Johnson, *Folk Culture on St. Helena Island, South Carolina* (1930); Raven I. McDavid, Jr., and Virginia G. McDavid, *American Speech* (1951); Julia Peterkin, *Scarlet Sister Mary* (1928); John E. Reinecke et al., *A Bibliography of Pidgin and Creole Languages* (1975); Lorenzo Dow Turner, *Africanisms in the Gullah Dialect* (1949, 1968); Norman E. Whitten, Jr., and John Szwed, *Trans-Action* (1968). ☆

Indian Languages

Like the more familiar languages of Europe, the aboriginal languages of the Americas fall into families, each traceable to a single parent or protolanguage in the past, much the way the modern Romance languages are traceable to, and descended from, Latin. Of the 11 or so major linguistic families or stocks of North America, seven were represented in the South. There were also numerous language isolates whose affiliations cannot be determined. All told, probably upwards of 75 different Indian languages were once spoken in the South.

Languages of the Algonkian family were spoken primarily in the North and Northeast, but there were intrusions into the Southeast, notably the Pamlicos of North Carolina, the Powhatans of Virginia, and the widely traveled Shawnees. Most of the tribes of coastal Virginia were Algonkian speaking, but their languages became extinct at an early date. Shawnee is still spoken by some tribal members (those over 40 years of age) in Oklahoma.

Iroquoian languages are also spoken primarily in the Northeast. Southern offshoots fall into two groups: (1) Meherrin and Nottoway in Virginia and Tuscarora in North Carolina, and (2) Cherokee, still spoken by approximately 10,000 Cherokees whose families were deported to Oklahoma in the 1830s and 1,000 or so who remain in North Carolina. Sequoyah developed the justly famous Cherokee Table of Syllables in the early 1800s. The system served the tribe well for many decades, and for a period of time there was considerable publication in the language. Many Cherokees still learn the syllabic writing, although several recent grammars and dictionaries have added or substituted a romanized script.

In historical times most of the languages of the Siouan family were found spread across the prairies and plains from Missouri to Alberta, but there were pockets of Siouan speakers in the Southeast as well, and it is still unclear whether these represent an intrusion or a remnant. The Ofo and Biloxi tribes of Mississippi spoke Siouan languages, as

did the Tutelos, Occaneechis, and Saponis of Virginia. All of these languages are apparently now extinct. Also Siouan speaking were the Quapaws of Arkansas and the Osages and Missourias of Missouri, all of whom were closely affiliated with the more westerly Siouan groups. Of their languages only Osage is still spoken.

The Catawbas and Woccons of the Carolina Coastal Plain and Piedmont spoke languages that were apparently distantly related to the Siouan. Both were documented but are now extinct. A number of other tribes are mentioned on early maps of the Carolinas and are assumed to have spoken languages related to Catawba, although these were never recorded. This group included the Cheraw, Eno, Congaree, Pedee, Santee, Sewee, Wateree, Waxhaw, Yadkin, and other tribes.

Yuchi (or Uchee) was spoken by the tribe of the same name in Georgia and adjacent portions of Tennessee and Alabama. It may be distantly related to the Siouan and Catawban language families. Yuchi is still spoken by about 30 people in the Sapulpa, Okla., area.

Two major areas of the South were inhabited by tribes that spoke languages of unknown affiliation—the Florida peninsula before the arrival of the Muskogean-speaking Seminoles and the lower Mississippi Valley and adjacent areas of eastern Texas. The Florida languages included Timucua, Calusa, and Tawasa, all now extinct. In Mississippi, Louisiana, and Texas the isolates included Chitimacha, Atakapa and Akokisa, Tonkawa, Karankawa, Tunica, and Natchez. The last two may be distantly related to Muskogean. Again, all are now extinct.

Arkansas, Louisiana, and eastern Texas were probably the original home of the Caddoan-speaking peoples. The Caddo language proper is well documented in the historical period and is still spoken in Caddo County, Okla. The related tribes, the Wichitas, Pawnees, and Arikaras, migrated northward, some all the way to North Dakota.

Although the South has become home to a number of tribes speaking languages of diverse affiliations, only the languages of the Muskogean family were spoken entirely within the confines of the area at the time of first contact with Europeans. Those Muskogean-speaking tribes were the politically and socially dominant groups, and their languages have been selected to illustrate grammatical structure.

The Muskogean family consists of four separate languages, each with two mutually intelligible dialects corresponding to tribal groupings. All except Hitchiti are still spoken in Oklahoma (Choctaw, Chickasaw, Creek, and Seminole), in Florida (Miccosukee, Seminole), in Mississippi (Choctaw), in Louisiana (Choctaw, Coushatta), and in Texas (Alabama, Coushatta). Choctaw-Chickasaw represents the western branch of the family, and the other languages the eastern branch. The speech sounds of the Muskogean languages are relatively simple, containing few of the "exotic" sounds found in some Indian tongues. Each language contains certain linguistic features such as the plosives *p*, *t*, *ch*, *k*, and all but Creek-Seminole have an asymmetrical *b*. Fricatives include a voiceless *l* (written *thl* here) along with *f*, *s*, and *h*; Choctaw-Chickasaw has an *sh* in addition. Resonants *m*, *n*, *l*, *y*, *w*; three vowels—*i*, *a*, *o*—with contrasting length; and a pitch or tonal accent complete the system.

Grammatically, the Muskogean lan-guages share certain characteristic features. In all, the subject (S) precedes the object (O), and the verb (V) comes at the end of the sentence. The Miccosukee equivalent of the English sentence "The girl drinks water" is *Taykot okon iskom*, literally, "Girl water drinks." Although nouns do not normally distinguish singulars from plurals, many verbs signal the number of their accompanying nouns. Totally different verb roots are used for a single concept depending on whether the subject (for intransitive verbs) or the object (for transitive verbs) is singular, dual, or plural. Thus, there are three different Creek roots for "run" to agree with the number of the implied subject: *Litká-haanís*, "He's going to run," *Tokothlká-haanís*, "They (two) are going to run," *Pifaatkáhaanís*, "They (three or more) are going to run." A transitive verb like "take" has two distinct forms to agree with the number of the implied direct object: *Isáhaanís*, "He's going to take it (one)," *Chawáhaanís*, "He's going to take them (two or more)."

Although the Cherokee, Creek, and Choctaw nations adopted written words in the 19th century, most of the other indigenous languages of the South remained unwritten. Each tribe has a rich oral literature consisting of folktales passed from generation to generation. Some myths explain the existence of natural phenomena or recount the exploits of native folk heroes, but the vast majority of the traditional tales deal with encounters among animals, with Rabbit playing the role of trickster. Many of the Uncle Remus stories have parallels in the Indian tradition.

Since the 1960s there has been renewed interest among Indians in their native languages, and many Indian schools and colleges in communities where Choctaw, Creek, Seminole, Miccosukee, or Cherokee is spoken now offer course work aimed at teaching reading, writing, and fluency in the spoken languages.

See also ETHNIC LIFE: Indian Cultural Contributions; FOLKLIFE: / Brer Rabbit; GEOGRAPHY: Indians and the Landscape

Karen M. Booker
Robert L. Rankin
University of Kansas

Lyle Campbell and Marianne Mithun, *The Languages of Native America: Historical and Comparative Assessment* (1979); Wallace Chafe, *International Journal of American Linguistics* (1962); James M. Crawford, in *Studies in Southeastern Indian Languages*, ed. James M. Crawford (1975); Mary R. Haas, *The Prehistory of Languages* (1969); T. Dale Nicklas, "The Elements of Choctaw" (Ph.D. dissertation, University of Michigan, 1974); John R. Swanton, *The Indians of the Southeastern United States* (1946). ☆

Linguists

||||||||||||||||||||||||

A southern "school" of linguists has never been formed, but southerners have pioneered in language study, ranging widely and energetically over the discipline. Perhaps because of the diversity of the region, southerners usually understand variation as a fundamental linguistic fact, and they seldom conceive of language in monolithic terms. For this reason, southerners tend to view language as a changing cultural artifact rather than an innate, quasi-mathematical product of mechanically operating grammatical rules. Further-more, many southern linguists react negatively to academic orthodoxy, a fact that helps explain their theoretical and methodological innovations.

Thomas Pyles is characteristic. Through 17 years of teaching at the University of Florida, Pyles led a generation of educated Americans to see language in evolutionary perspective. In *The Origins and Development of the English Language*, Pyles assembled an opulent collection of facts, invited the reader to form opinions, and demonstrated sound methods of critical evaluation. Instead of teaching a narrow doctrine, *Origins* continues to show us how "our language is inextricably bound up with our humanity." It also helps us to see that to understand ourselves, "the best place to start . . . is with our own language, the one that has nurtured our minds and formed our view of the world."

And more than other Americans, southerners have assiduously studied their own speech. James B. McMillan's *Annotated Bibliography of Southern American English* lists literally hundreds who have given some part of their lives to this task. A short list of worthies, concentrated in the first part of this century but extending back well into the last, might include Cleanth Brooks, Robley Dunglison, Norman Eliason, Bennett Wood Green, Archibald A. Hill, Atcheson L. Hench, Sumner Ives, Vance Randolph, Maximilian von Schele de Vere, Edward A. Stephenson, James Sledd, William R. Van Riper, Floyd C. Watkins, Gordon Wilson, and Gordon R. Wood.

This random selection could be updated and expanded indefinitely, but the acknowledged dean of the congregation since the 1940s has been Raven I. McDavid, Jr. McDavid's abridged version of H. L. Mencken's *The American*

Language summarized two centuries of scholarship in a bold, readable idiom, and, with Hans Kurath, McDavid wrote the first full-dress treatment of English below the Potomac. In dozens of original studies that clarify the relations between southern language and culture, McDavid characteristically focused on the impact of postwar industrialization, urbanization, and mass education while reveling in "the flux, the competing forms and styles, the endless possibilities for innovation that a language must possess if it is to be alive."

In spite of McDavid's preeminence, if a school of southern linguists were to form today, it would necessarily gather around the *Linguistic Atlas of the Gulf States*, the work of McDavid's student Lee A. Pederson, of Emory University. The LAGS project, in 5,000 tape-recorded hours, exhibits the southern tongue from the Savannah River to the Rio Grande and from the TVA lakes to Key West. It surpasses even its great European and American models in scope, methodological innovation, and usefulness for orienting further work. Properly interpreted, LAGS and its parent, the Linguistic Atlas of the Middle and South Atlantic States project, will yield new insight into southern American English and, in turn, into southern population movements, the development of trade areas and transportation systems, the growth of cultural centers and institutions, and the stratification of society.

By applying traditional methods of linguistic analysis to southern cultural institutions and freely inventing or adapting new techniques as needed, southern linguists have generated other remarkable innovations. David W. Maurer, for example, used scholarly, lexicological methods to study criminal argots, for which Louisville, Ky., pro-

vided a unique laboratory. Robert A. Hall, Jr., pioneered in the study of creole languages. E. Bagby Atwood was the first linguist to use data-processing equipment to attempt a comprehensive description of American morphology and syntax, and to study the effects of urbanization over a wide area.

Meanwhile, the impact of African language contact, apparent in loans like *juke* and *goober*, has been carefully studied by Lorenzo Dow Turner and Juanita V. Williamson. Linguists elsewhere concentrated on syntactic patterns in the speech of isolated black groups, but Williamson succeeded in a thorough phonological and grammatical analysis of an adequately representative sample, and thus uncovered the profound-structural identity of black and white speech.

Southern linguists enjoy the support of a half-dozen forums for the exchange of ideas, where lively discussions range over the topics that interest linguists everywhere, not excluding Japanese syntax and the verb forms of Old Church Slavonic. But the title of a recent collection edited by David L. Shores and Carole P. Hines, *Papers in Language Variation*, reveals an enduring concern. When in 1829 Robley Dunglison noticed that "the population of our country is of a motley character" and its language is therefore "modified by admixture," he expressed the common southern view. So perhaps what appears to *auslander* as fiercely independent thought is, to the thinkers themselves, just obvious common sense. If so, it is common sense laced with creative scholarship.

See also BLACK LIFE: Speech, Black

Michael I. Miller
Virginia Commonwealth University

E. Bagby Atwood, *A Survey of Verb Forms in the Eastern United States* (1953), *The Regional Vocabulary of Texas* (1963); Cleanth Brooks, *The Language of the American South* (1985); William A. Kretzschmar, ed., *Dialects in Culture: Essays in General Dialectology by Raven I. McDavid* (1979); Hans Kurath, *A Word Geography of the Eastern United States* (1949), with Raven I. McDavid, Jr., *The Pronunciation of English in the Atlantic States* (1961); David W. Maurer, *Language of the Underworld* (1981); Raven I. McDavid, Jr., *Varieties of American English* (1980), with Raymond K. O'Cain and George T. Dorrill, eds., *Linguistic Atlas of the Middle and South Atlantic States* (1979, volumes forthcoming); James B. McMillan, *Annotated Bibliography of Southern American English* (1971); H. L. Mencken, *The American Language: The Fourth Edition and the Two Supplements*, ed. Raven I. McDavid, Jr. (1963); Lee A. Pederson et al., eds., LACS: *The Basic Materials*, part 4 (1981); Thomas Pyles and John Algeo, *The Origins and Development of the English Language* (3d ed., 1982); David L. Shores and Carole P. Hines, eds., *Papers in Language Variation: Samla-Ads Collection* (1977); Juanita V. Williamson, "A Phonological and Morphological Study of the Speech of the Negro of Memphis, Tennessee" (Ph.D. dissertation, University of Michigan, 1961). ☆

Literary Dialect

||||||||||||||||||||||||||||||||||||||||||

The South has produced a large number of writers sufficiently interested in regional language variations to render many of them in literature. Among the earliest examples are the works of the mid-19th-century frontier humorists like George Washington Harris of Tennessee, creator of the comic character Sut Lovingood. But in a sentence like the following, from "Sut Lovingood's Daddy, Acting Horse" (1854), the language variation is more apparent than real: "Look out, mam, . . . better sen' fur sum strong man body tu keep him frum huggin' yu tu deth." Words like *fur* "for," *tu* "to," *frum* "from," and *deth* "death" are simply examples of the convention of "eye dialect," or nonstandard spellings that represent perfectly standard pronunciations. The aim is not to convey exact regional or social variation but to give a broad comic impression. Yet such eye dialect should not be scorned; for its purpose, it is an effective device.

In general, however, those who are considered genuine practitioners of literary dialect are writers like Joel Chandler Harris, who, while occasionally using eye dialect—go beyond it and attempt to represent precise regional and/or social departures from a standard, not only in pronunciation but in grammar and vocabulary as well. And though there were early exemplars of literary dialect like William Gilmore Simms of South Carolina, whose novel *The Yemassee* appeared in 1835, the heyday of the art in southern literature, and in American literature in general, is usually conceded to be the latter part of the century—especially the 1870s and 1880s. In addition to Joel Chandler Harris in Georgia, the roster for these two decades would include at least George Washington Cable in Louisiana, Mary Noailles Murphree—alias Charles Egbert Craddock—in Tennessee, Thomas Nelson Page in Virginia, and Irwin Russell in Mississippi. For the last decade of the century, Ruth McEnery Stuart in Arkansas and Louisiana and Charles W. Chesnutt in North Carolina would probably be added.

Moreover, literary dialect is not confined to minor writers but appears also in works of major authors like Mark Twain in Missouri and Edgar Allan Poe in Virginia. Nor is literary dialect just a curious artifact from the last century. Its use continues in works of major contemporary authors like William Faulkner in Mississippi, Flannery O'Connor in Georgia, and Jesse Stuart in Kentucky and Tennessee, as well as in the writings of non-southerners like Marjorie Kinnan Rawlings, who lived in and wrote about Florida, and children's writer Lois Lenski, who has captured dialects in Texas, South Louisiana, North Carolina, and Florida with the sure touch of a native.

The most widely known literary dialect is probably that of Joel Chandler Harris's Uncle Remus stories, exemplified in the following passage from *Uncle Remus: His Songs and Sayings* (1880):

> "Atter Brer Fox hear 'bout how Brer Rabbit done Brer Wolf," said Uncle Remus, scratching his head with the point of his awl, "he 'low, he did, dat he better not be so brash, en he sorter let Brer Rabbit 'lone. Dey wuz all time seein' one nudder, en 'bunnunce er times Brer Fox could er nab Brer Rabbit, but eve'y time he got de chance, his mine 'ud sorter rezume 'bout Brer Wolf, en he let Brer Rabbit 'lone."

The Uncle Remus stories were not written primarily as children's books. With their unique blend of black folklore and folk speech, they have—like most good children's books—an appeal that is well-nigh universal.

A lesser known, yet equally perceptive, dialect writer who worked at the same time as Joel Chandler Harris but with a quite different kind of literary dialect was George Washington Cable. His special combination of French and English, the speech of the fashionable, French-speaking upper-class society in and around New Orleans, is reflected in this passage from his best-known novel, *The Grandissimes* (1880):

> "Doze Creole' is lezzy," said Aurora. . . . " 'Sieur Frowenfel,' " said Aurora, leaning her head on one side, "some pipple thing it is doze climade; 'ow you lag doze climade? . . . I thing Louisiana is a paradize—me! . . . W'ere you goin' fin' sudge a h-air?" She respired a sample of it. "W'ere you goin' fin' sudge a so rich groun'? De weed' in my bag yard is twenny-five feet 'igh . . . twenty-six! . . . W'ere you fin' sudge a reever lag dad Mississippi?"

In spite of the enthusiastic reactions of writers like Mark Twain, the appeal of this dialect has been something less than universal. Yet the speech of Aurora is as probable as that of Uncle Remus; and both would pose few problems of comprehension if read aloud—particularly by a speaker from the same area. This was dramatically demonstrated by the warm reception Cable received when reading his dialect works on the lecture circuit with Mark Twain.

Implicit in this audience reaction are two points of some importance about literary dialects. The first is that there is a significant difference between a spoken dialect—standard, as well as nonstandard—and a written one. The quasi-phonetic spelling and the grammatical restructuring that the dialect writer may be obliged to adopt often make the dialect look more exotic, and thus more difficult to decipher, than it really is. Harris works primarily with sound in the Uncle Remus passage, changing consonants, as in *dat* "that," and especially omitting initial and final elements, as in *'ud* "would," *'bout* "about," and *en* "and"—the latter a frequent characteristic of relaxed speech.

The Cable passage, however, seems more difficult because Cable alters not only consonants, as in *sudge* "such," but also vowels, as in *pipple* "people" and *reever* "river," and transforms the grammar as well—often by deletion— as in *W'ere you goin' fin' sudge a h-air?* "Where are you going to find such air?" Considering the obvious influence of French, the variation here is real, but much of the difficulty is only apparent and can be largely eliminated by reading the passage aloud.

The second thing to remember about literary dialect is that it is useful—at times crucial—to know something about the speech of the writer and the area. For example, in the Georgia speech of Uncle Remus, a form like *sorter* "sort of" is not meant to rhyme with the word *porter*, as pronounced by most non-southerners, but rather with a word like *aorta*. In other words, both Uncle Remus and his creator, lacking a final *r* sound like so many other southern speakers, would have said what many dialect writers would spell *sorta*. But Harris, quite naturally taking his own usage as a norm, wrote *sorter* since a final *-er* spelling represented for him the same sound as a final *-a*. The question lurking behind all this, of course, is how far to go in accuracy of detail without losing the reader. This is the dialect writer's perpetual dilemma.

One thing is clear, however: A reader of literary dialect in the 1980s has a distinct advantage over a reader of the 1880s, for a great deal—and not just in reference to *r* sounds—has been recorded about southern dialects in the ensuing century. In a wide variety of dialect studies—many of them part of the Linguistic Atlas of the United States project—readers near and far now have extensive resources for understanding a literary dialect and for gauging a writer's accuracy. As a number of language/literature scholars have shown, some writers—Joel Chandler Harris, for instance—are very accurate indeed, while still maintaining a balance between linguistic authenticity and literary artistry.

At its best, southern literary dialect—like the southern local color writing that it so often helps to enhance— transcends its local origins and becomes an invaluable part of the cultural heritage of the South and of the English-speaking world.

See also FOLKLIFE: / Brer Rabbit; LITER-ATURE: Folklore in Literature; / Cable, George Washington; Harris, Joel Chandler

William W. Evans
Louisiana State University

Harold B. Allen and Gary N. Underwood, eds., *Readings in American Dialectology* (1971); William W. Evans, *American Speech* (Fall–Winter 1971); Charles W. Foster, "The Representation of Negro Dialect in Charles W. Chesnutt's *The Conjure Woman*" (Ph.D. dissertation, University of Alabama, 1968); James B. McMillan, *Annotated Bibliography of Southern American English* (1971); Lee A. Pederson et al., eds., LAGS: *The Basic Materials*, part 4 (1981); Juanita V. Williamson and Virginia M. Burke, eds., *A Various Language: Perspectives on American Dialects* (1971). ☆

Mountain Language

|||||||||||||||||||||||||||||||||||||||||||||||||||||

*M*ountain English is a broad term covering the varieties of English spoken in two geographically separate mountainous areas of the United States—the Ozark region of northwestern Arkansas and southern Missouri, and the southern Appalachian Mountains of eastern Kentucky and Tennessee, mid-to-southern West Virginia, western Virginia and North Carolina, and northern Georgia. The separate terms *Ozark English* and *Appalachian English* denote the language of the two regions.

Mountain English has long been the object of much curiosity. Outsiders often comment on its old-fashioned flavor and its colorful figures of speech. Early study of it was limited to the search for relic usages and pronunciations. Mountain speech has often been romanticized and stereotyped as *Elizabethan* or *Shakespearean*, terms that connote a language frozen in time from the late 17th and early 18th centuries, when emigrants from the British Isles first settled in southern Appalachia.

Some speakers of Mountain English still use the pronouns *hit* and *we'uns*. But Mountain English is, in fact, no more frozen than any other variety of American English; all varieties retain archaisms, as well as exhibit features in various stages of change. Speakers of Mountain English tend to use certain linguistic features—some archaic and some innovative—to provide social and regional identity and the cultural cohesion to bind them as a group. This is the way dialects work. The specific features are not absolute; it is their frequency of use that characterizes the group. In other words, an old-time resident of Hazard, Ky., may not use the archaic form *done* to emphasize a completed action every time it might "fit" into her speech, but she probably says *They done got married* or *He done made me forget*, or some such phrase, more often than a native-born resident of, say, New Harmony, Ind. The higher frequency of use of features like *done* distinguishes Mountain English from other varieties of American English.

Another archaism that occurs with a degree of regularity in Mountain English is the *a-* prefix, which intensifies a continuous action, as in *He was a-tellin' the truth*. Both the *a-* prefix and completive *done* were used in the early history of English and still survive in mountain speech. Interestingly, both forms seem to be dying out in the Ozarks, with little evidence of their use by younger generations. The *a-* prefix occurs with less frequency among younger speakers of Appalachian English as well, but completive *done* is holding its own.

Innovation, or language change, seems to be occurring in two specific grammatical areas of Mountain English: subject-verb concord and the marking of principal parts of verbs. Whereas American English in general distinguishes between *was* and *were* for grammatically singular and plural subjects (having historically lost this distinction with all other past tense verbs), Mountain English speakers often eliminate the distinction, using *was* with plural or singular subjects. In both Appalachian English and Ozark English, the change is almost complete in constructions with the expletive *there*, as in *There was many flowers on the grave*. The same type of grammatical simplification is evident in the use of *don't* with third-person singular subjects, as in *She don't know the truth*. In present tense affirmative constructions, however, there is less evidence of simplification, with utterances like *I have a teacher that explain things* occurring rarely. This low frequency of *-s* deletion marks Ozark English and Appalachian English as distinct from other nonmainstream varieties of English that are otherwise much like them in their simplified use of *was* and *don't*.

Mountain English speakers tend to regularize the principal parts of verbs that other American speakers of English keep irregular. (Irregular verbs are those like *grow [grew/grown]* as distinct from those like *own [owned/owned]* that form the past forms with *-ed*.) In Mountain English, some regularized forms, such as *knowed*, are used for both the past tense and past participle; some irregular past tenses are also used for the past participle, as in *go (went/went)*; and some bare root forms are generalized to both the past tense and past participle, as in *give (give/give)*. Although other varieties of American English also show wide variation in their verb principal parts, the combination of linguistic forms within patterns of variation— forms like completive *done*, *a-* prefix, simplified subject-verb concord, and regularized verbs—work together to characterize Mountain English.

Before recent studies (such as Christian et al., 1984) documented the similarities between language patterns of the Ozarks and southern Appalachians, a sameness of language and culture was assumed. Although geographically separate, the two regions share, after all, a common cultural heritage. Many of the descendants of the Scotch-Irish who settled in southern Appalachia in the 1700s moved on to northwestern Arkansas in the 1800s, when incentives in the form of free or cheap land were offered by the state to those who would homestead it. Characterized by a strong sense of place, their rural isolation, a stable social system bordering on clannishness, and a common heritage, the people of the Ozarks and southern Appalachia have maintained a singular ethnic and linguistic identity.

See also ETHNIC LIFE: Mountain Culture; / Appalachians; GEOGRAPHY: Ozarks

Linda Blanton
University of New Orleans

Lester V. Berrey, *American Speech* (February 1940); Linda Blanton, in *Toward a Social History of American English*, ed. J. L. Dillard (1985); Donna Christian, Walter Wolfram, and J. Duke, *Variation and Change in Geographically Isolated Communities: Appalachian English and Ozark English* (Final Report to the National Science Foundation, Grant No. BNS 8208916, 1984); Walter Wolfram and Donna Christian, *Appalachian Speech* (1976), *Sociolinguistic Variables in Appalachian Dialects* (Final Report to the National Institute of Education, Grant No. NIE-G-740026, 1975). ☆

Names, Personal

||||||||||||||||||||||||||||||||||||||||||||||

Personal names can document the settlement history of the South. The names of the English and the Celts (the most numerous colonists), the Spanish, French, Germans, Sephardic Jews, and others are linked to the cities or states they built. But names do more than substantiate historical facts; they convey the southern ethos.

Commemorative given names have been popular in the South. Surnames of the first families of the South—Byrd, Carroll, Clay, Jefferson, Pinckney, Taylor, and Washington—are bestowed on yeoman and patrician alike, as witnessed by any southern telephone book. In particular, the first and third presidents have had great influence on names. George Washington Cable was the novelist of the Creoles, and George Washington Carver was an accomplished black botanist and inventor. (The surname was adopted by many blacks after emancipation.) Jefferson Davis, the president of the Confederate States of America, was named for the famous Virginia president, as was Thomas Jefferson Wertenbacker, the historian.

The South has consistently honored military heroes. Andrew Jackson Hamilton was a governor of Texas and Andrew Jackson Montague a governor of Virginia. Francis Marion Cockrell, a Confederate general and Missouri governor, pays tribute to the Swamp Fox. Robert E. Lee's name is perpetuated by many southern lads with the surname Lee. (Robert E. Lee Prewitt, the protagonist of James Jones's *From Here to Eternity*, possessed the heroism if not the gallantry of his namesake.) French and Hispanic heroes are also honored. The names of Florida governor Napoleon Bonaparte Broward and the distinguished Confederate hero Simon Bolivar Buckner illustrate the process.

Some southern magnificoes have been remembered ironically. The Gowrie Twins—Bilbo and Vardaman—in Faulkner's *Intruder in the Dust* are shiftless and nocturnal and satirize the two Mississippi politicians for whom the boys are named. The most common type of commemorative naming, however, does not invoke the heroic or illustrious. Rather, it passes on a family name, like an heirloom, from generation to generation. Often a surname is given as a first or middle name, e.g., Davis Smith, Bobby Brown Travis, or James Strom Thurmond, the Dixiecrat-turned-Republican, who is called by his mother's maiden name.

In naming, as in southern architecture, the classics have been influential. Many southerners bear a first or middle name of Greco-Roman origin, Augustus being among the most popular. This naming practice reveals the South's respect for antiquity as well as its hope that Herculean feats would be replicated in Dixie. Without rival, onomastically speaking, was Lucius Quintus Cincinnatus Lamar, the South's "Redeemer Politician" and later Supreme Court justice. Although abating in the last 50 years, the custom has flourished for centuries. Caesar Rodney represented Delaware in the Continental Congress; Cadmus Marcellus Wilcox distinguished himself on the battlefields of Virginia; Cassius Marcellus Clay, like the pugilist now known as Muhammad Ali, was a famous Kentuckian; Augustus Baldwin Longstreet portrayed the South movingly in fiction; Virginius Dabney is an award-winning journalist; Cleanth Brooks is a respected literary critic; and Thomas Dionysus Clark an eminent historian. In southern literature, characters with classical names perpetuate a noble tradition (Atticus Finch in Harper Lee's *To Kill a Mockingbird*) or suggest mythic models (Phoenix Jackson in Eudora Welty's "A Worn Path"). In the popular arts, Homer and his biblically christened partner, Jethro, offered bardic entertainment, mountain style.

Although known as the Bible Belt, the South does not surpass the North in using biblical first names. Still, the practice is strong. Biblical names are borne by distinguished senators from North Carolina (Jesse Helms), Alabama (Jeremiah Denton), and Tennessee (James Sasser), among others. Some southerners have been named for religious figures. Texas outlaw John Wesley Hardin carried the name of the early Methodist leader; his father was a circuit-riding preacher in that church. Martin Luther King, Jr., was named for the Protestant reformer, and other young southerners later carried King's name.

If southern names reflect the grandeur and formality of tradition, they also embody the folksy congeniality cherished by the region. More than in other parts of the nation, names in the South are diminutives, ending in *y* or *ie*, making them friendlier and less pretentious. The Carter brothers Jimmy and Billy typify in name and character an affection for this sentiment. Other similarly named southern dignitaries in the U.S. House of Representatives as of 1984 included Ronnie Flippo (Alabama); Andy Ireland (Florida); Larry Hopkins (Kentucky); Lindy Boggs, Billy Tauzin, Jerry Huckaby, and Cathy Long (Louisiana); and Jamie Whitten (Mississippi). Few in America would recognize William Franklin Graham, although Billy Graham is a household name. Nor are these folksy names considered inappropriate for someone of status. Diminutives such as Bubba (which approximates a young southerner's pronunciation of "brother"), Buddy, Lonnie, Sissy, Sonny, and Stoney are recorded legal names.

Many southerners have a double given name, one or both parts often a diminutive or shortened form. Such names suggest the southern ideals of youthful vigor and inviting informality. Among males, characteristic doublets are Billy Bob, Danny Lee, Eddie Ray, and Larry Gene. For belles, popular names are Bonnie Jean, Connie Ann, Ellie Mae (Jed Clampett's daughter in *The Beverly Hillbillies*), Suzy Kay, or Tammy Jo. A subpattern for females combines a male and a female name— Billy Sue, Johnnie Mae, Tommy Ruth, Willie Jean. By a reverse process, some men in the South have female names, thus making the popular song "A Boy Named Sue" less bizarre. Beryl, Doris, Emma Gene, Lynn, and Zelma Kay are given to southern men *and* women. The explanation for these bisexual names may be in commemorative patterns (boys named for mothers or aunts) or simply idiosyncratic independence. The gender of the tragic lovers implied in the song title "Frankie and Johnnie" is less disconcerting below than above the Mason-Dixon line.

An extreme example of unpretentious names is the use of initials in place of first names in the South. Sometimes these initials stand for first names (J. R. of *Dallas* fame), but the initials are also given as legal first names—B. J., B. W., J. T., and T. W. Initial names discomfit the U.S. government, especially the military, which adds "only" after such initial first names for easier processing of recruits.

Perhaps more than any other section of the country, the South is distinguished by picturesque names, including nicknames. From politics come William "Fishbait" Miller, the longtime doorkeeper of the House of Representatives; Goat Harris, an official in Durham, N.C.; Foxy Robinson, the water commissioner of Laurel, Miss.; and Shag Pyron, a former Mississippi football star and highway commissioner. The world of sports, too, glitters with the names of southern luminaries—

Bear Bryant, Dizzy Dean, Mudcat Grant, Catfish Hunter, Bum Phillips, Vinegar Bend Mizell, and Oil Can Boyd.

Philip C. Kolin
University of Southern Mississippi

Adele Algeo and John Algeo, *Names* (June 1983); Philip C. Kolin, *Names* (September 1977); Forrest McDonald and Ellen Shapiro McDonald, *William and Mary Quarterly* (April 1980); Grady McWhiney and Forrest McDonald, *Names* (June 1983); Thomas Pyles, *American Speech* (December 1947), *Names* (June 1959). ☆

Names, Place

||||||||||||||||||||||||||||||||||||||||

Place-names in the South, as elsewhere, reflect the concerns and interests of the early inhabitants of the region. Not all of the most informative ones have yet been collected and explained, however. Although book-length studies of the best-known names in 9 of the 11 states of the Confederacy have been made, only those appearing on maps have been included because of space and time limitations. William S. Powell's *The North Carolina Gazetteer: A Dictionary of Tar Heel Places* and Bertha E. Bloodworth and Alton C. Morris's *Places in the Sun: The History and Romance of Florida Place-Names* are among the best of this kind of study, but each book contains only a few thousand of an estimated 50,000 or more names per state.

As Raven I. McDavid, Jr., says in his article "Names *Not* on the Map," the Place Name Survey of the United States,

now under way, should include not only the kinds of names in the books already published but also those of features too small to be on maps and the informal designations used by the local residents for the well-known places. A large number of names not on maps have been collected by the field workers for the *Linguistic Atlas of the Middle and South Atlantic States* (fascicles 1 and 2, 1980) and the *Linguistic Atlas of the Gulf States* (1986), whose data are also on microfilm, but much work remains to be done to identify and explain many of them. Meanwhile, it is possible, by consulting the best of the state and national studies and those dealing with the periods and processes of place naming like George R. Stewart's *Names on the Land* and Mary R. Miller's "Place-Names of the Northern Neck of Virginia: A Proposal for a Theory of Place-Naming," to discover some of the main characteristics of southern geographical names.

The first inhabitants of the region, the Indians, gave names like *Sooktaloosa*, "black bluff," for a prominent landmark; *Cotahaga*, "locust-tree-there-standing," for a noticeable plant or animal of the area; or *Quilby*, "panther-there-killed," for an event occurring at the place. Because the Indians had little use for mountains, they rarely gave them distinct names. Often the mountains simply acquired the one already given to a certain area. *Appalachian*, recorded in 1528 as *Apalachen*, the Indian name of a province, was applied by the English to the southern part of the mountain system included in this area.

When settlers from Europe arrived, they retained a number of the Indian names for places and gave others to some of the settlements they founded. For example, *Tallahassee* and *Miami* both are Creek names, the former meaning "old town" and the latter, first applied to the river, then to the settlement, meaning "very large." Sometimes in attempting to pronounce and spell these names, the European settlers changed the form, as with the Choctaw term *bok*, "creek," which the French made *bayou*, and with *Arkansea*, the name of a tribe and village, which the French changed to *Arkansas*. At other places, they translated the Indian names. *Baton Rouge* is the French translation of the Indian term for a red stick or post used to mark the boundary between the hunting grounds of two tribes. The many *Cedar* and *Bear* creeks are likely examples of translations made by the English settlers. Not only did the English translate many of the Indian names, but they also sometimes translated the names earlier given by the French. *Little Rock* is a translation of *Petite Roche*, a designation used to distinguish this location from a larger area farther upstream on the Arkansas River, which the French had called *Grande Roche*.

In the South the English established tobacco and rice plantations rather than towns, as the settlers of New England did, and gave many of them and the colonies where they were located names in honor of their kings or queens, such as *Virginia*, a designation for Elizabeth I; *Carolina* for Charles I; and *Georgia* for George II. A number of plantations, which grew into towns, and counties were given names borrowed from England. Richmond on the James River, which honored James I, was named in 1733 for the town in Surrey located on the Thames River; the seaport of Norfolk in 1691 received the same designation as the Virginia county, which earlier had been named for the county in England; and Birmingham, Ala., because of its steel industry was named in 1871

for the city in Warwickshire famed for its manufacturing of steel. The English settlers also remembered the early explorers and colonizers of their new land. For example, the names of Columbia, S.C., and Raleigh, N.C., honored, respectively, Christopher Columbus in 1786 and Sir Walter Raleigh in 1792.

The French, like the English, named places for their kings or members of their nobility. Louisiana honored Louis XIV in 1681, and La Nouvelle (New) Orleans was named in 1718 for the regent of France, the Duc d'Orleans. The Spaniards, on the other hand, frequently chose the names of saints for their settlements. *St. Augustine* was the one given in 1665 to the fort founded in Florida (whose Spanish name means "flowerlike") because land was sighted on that saint's day; and *San Antonio*, the Spanish form of the name of the saint who helps persons find lost articles, was given first to the small river, then the mission, and finally the city in Texas, the territory whose name was derived from an Indian term meaning "friends."

Sometimes the settlers gave regions, particularly Mississippi, Alabama, and Tennessee, the name of an important river. *Mississippi* is Algonquian for "great water," and *Alabama* is "river of the Alibamons" (the Choctaw name, meaning "thicket clearers," for an Upper Creek people). *Tennessee* was named for the Tennessee River, which got its name from that of an ancient Cherokee town, recorded by the Spanish in 1567 as *Tanasqui* and by the English in 1707 as *Tinnase*, no longer having any literal meaning.

After the Revolution few names were borrowed from England. New settlements and counties honored national heroes, statesmen, and events. Greene County in Alabama, Mississippi, Georgia, Tennessee, and Virginia, and Greenville in North Carolina, South Carolina, Georgia, and Mississippi were all named for Nathanael Greene, a general of the Revolution. Knoxville and Nashville, Tenn., honored two other generals of the Revolution, Henry Knox and Francis Nash. Eutaw, Ala., commemorated a battle of that war occurring at Eutaw Springs in South Carolina. Austin and Houston, Tex., honored two of that territory's important early settlers and statesmen, Stephen F. Austin and Samuel Houston.

As the growing of cotton became important in the early 1800s, many new plantations came into being. By this time the planters' wives were doing some of the naming. Having through their study of music become familiar with Italian, they recommended such designations as *Belmonte*, "beautiful mountain," and *Monte Sano*, "healthful mountain." They also liked names containing "hall," such as *Stanton Hall*, because of the associations this word had with English country life. Literature provided plantation or town names like *Melrose* (mentioned in Scott's novels) and *Auburn* (in Goldsmith's poem "The Deserted Village"). During this period, exotic names like *Memphis* for the city in Egypt and *Carthage* for the ancient city in northern Africa were also popular. A few years later, in 1845, because what were thought to be feminine forms were considered appropriate for city names, *Atlanta* was derived from *Atlantic*.

Few names in the South are directly related to the days of slavery. Cities with "quarters" may reveal some trace of this period, and an all-black community with a name like *Freedman's Village* commemorates the emancipation of the slaves. The name *Pinder*, a town in

South Carolina, comes from an African word for the peanut. The name was probably given by the white residents after this word had attained general currency in the region.

See also ETHNIC LIFE: Indian Cultural Contributions

Virginia Foscue
University of Alabama

Bertha E. Bloodworth and Alton C. Morris, *Places in the Sun: The History and Romance of Florida Place-Names* (1978); Kelsie B. Harder, ed., *Illustrated Dictionary of Place Names, United States and Canada* (1976); Raven I. McDavid, Jr., et al., *Names* (December 1985); H. L. Mencken, *The American Language: The Fourth Edition and the Two Supplements*, ed. Raven I. McDavid, Jr. (1963); William S. Powell, *The North Carolina Gazetteer: A Dictionary of Tar Heel Places* (1968); George R. Stewart, *American Place Names: A Concise and Selective Dictionary for the Continental United States of America* (1970), *Names on the Land* (3d ed., 1967); Fred A. Tarpley, *From Blinky to Blue-John: A Word Atlas of Northeast Texas* (1970), *1001 Texas Place Names* (1980). ☆

New Orleans English

Greater metropolitan New Orleans—where precincts, wards, major streets, levees, bridges, and bayous are natural boundaries linguistically dividing a populace—includes seven parishes: Orleans, Jefferson, St. Bernard, Plaquemines, St. Tammany, St. Charles, and St. John the Baptist. The terms *city* and *country*, in the greater metropolitan area, no longer conveniently describe the geographic or demographic landscape or lifestyle of the parishes.

It is imprecise to speak of "white" or "black" English as discrete varieties of American English in the South, and the lack of precise rubrics is even more noticeable in referring to the English of the New Orleans areas. For example, in rural New Orleans and outside of Orleans Parish there are black speakers of Louisiana Creole and white speakers of Louisiana Cajun as well as whites who know Creole and blacks who perceive themselves as being culturally more Cajun than Creole. These groups are also native speakers of English. Commingling has always been the key to the cultural and linguistic development of New Orleans. In southern Louisiana spoken English has been greatly enriched by the penetration of vernacular French. Many ethnic groups, in fact, have created the public culture of New Orleans—not only the Europeans from Ireland, Germany, Yugoslavia, Hungary, Italy, France, and Spain, but also blacks from West Africa, Haiti, Belize, Virginia, and South Carolina. The creation continues today in the city's Honduran restaurants, Vietnamese restaurants and shops, Greek festivals, Filipino social organizations, and spiritualist churches of Mississippi blacks.

Though there are linguistic differences among speakers of New Orleans English, common elements do exist. Certain idiomatic expressions, for example, are characteristic. Idioms with *make* abound: *make groceries* "shop for groceries," *make menage* "clean house," *make dodo* "take a nap." The term *save* also appears as a frequent verb form, meaning "to put away," as in *save the groceries, save the dishes, save the clothes, save the jewelry.* Just as *ya' hear* can be used in many varieties of southern English as a tag at the end of a sentence, the terms *hear, yeah,* and *no* or an objective pronoun are often used as sentence tags in New Orleans English, as in *I'm gonna have another cup of coffee, hear?*, or *I don't like that, no,* or *She's smart, her.*

Some phrases in the English of New Orleanians show a division in usage according to gender. Some terms are known by both male and female but are more often used by males because they describe activities in which men more frequently participate—for example, *to shine*, meaning "to hunt with lanterns at night" during duck season, or *chunk*, meaning "to throw a ball extremely hard."

A double subject is frequently encountered in southern speech, as in *My brother, he went to the store*; however, among speakers of New Orleans English one will hear, for emphasis, a triple subject with three pronouns, as, for instance, in *Me myself I don't like to drive over that bridge.* Also, in a double-subject form characteristic of New Orleans speakers, where another person can be the second subject named, the pronoun precedes the second subject (*Me and my daddy*, or *Myself and Mr. Frank*, or *I and Helen*). Doublets also occur in expressions such as *Yet and still* for "however" or *feel to believe* for "I believe beyond all doubt," as in *I feel to believe that she'll get better.*

Various semantic changes seem to be taking place in New Orleans English. For example, *still* has taken on the implied meaning of "all the same" or "nonetheless," as in *I thought I was picking up the white wine instead of this red. It's still good (though).* As for verb forms, *had* + the past participle of a verb is replacing the simple past tense form. Teachers not originally from New Orleans report its frequent appearance in the essays of university students. Thus, the following kind of narrative is not uncommon: *Yesterday afternoon I had run into Sylvia. I had told her we're thinking about going to Dauphin Island for the weekend. And she had said that she'd get in touch with us tonight.* One way to interpret this usage is to say that *had* + the past participle conveys a notion of past + present (i.e., when the speaker is narrating the events). In these and other ways the rich heritage of New Orleans English continues to evolve.

Mackie J V Blanton
University of New Orleans

Madeline Aubert-Gex, "A Lexical Study of the English of New Orleans Creoles" (M.A. thesis, University of New Orleans, 1983); Mackie J V Blanton and John Cooke, eds., *Perspectives on Ethnicity in New Orleans* (1981); Joseph Logsdon, in *Perspectives on Ethnicity in New Orleans*, ed. John Cooke (1979); Margaret M. Marshall, *Anthropological Linguistics* (Winter 1982); Dorice Tentchoff, *The Culture of Acadiana: Tradition and Change in South Louisiana*, ed. Steven L. Del Sesto and Jon L. Gibson (1975). ☆

Oratory

The mythical southern orator is a white male said to possess qualities that distinguish him from speakers heard in other regions. This regional persona speaks emotionally, in ornate symbolic language with expansive gestures and a thunderous voice, about sacred themes. General John B. Gordon speaking against Reconstruction policies embodied this mythical presence. Exhibiting a "rare physical vigor," this scar-faced Confederate veteran dramatically trumpeted "Dixie," "our soil," "sacrifice," "our fathers," and the "spirit of Lee." Prideful public performance became the hallmark of the southern orator, no matter that John C. Calhoun talked "impersonally" with "few gestures" and that Joseph Brown rejected "sickly sentimentality" for unadorned speech about financial prosperity.

Conceived in Old South culture and created in suffering and defeat, this ostentatious persona helped shield the region from federal encroachment, economic exploitation, social change, and outside criticism, while maintaining traditional thought and policies at home. Even as veterans of the Confederacy died and their children and grandchildren forgot the war, this fictive image of the raging public warrior persisted, providing speakers with stock rhetorical forms of delivery, argument, and language as well as topics for their oratory.

A second type of southern oratory consists of the real-life performances of whites, blacks, males, and females of different postures and persuasions from the 1800s to the 1980s. White males held communicative dominance in the region, developing the authoritative strategies of white superiority, southern manhood, and southern ladyhood. Some women spoke effectively in public, but always in a manner considered suitable to their low social status. More recently, although women had won the vote and a wider voice in society, defeat of the Equal Rights Amendment in the South demonstrated that many persons still preferred traditional social and rhetorical roles for women and men in the region.

Until the 1960s black men and

women experienced few safe and meaningful opportunities to speak in the general cultural institutions. As slaves, blacks confronted coercive sanctions with both a defensive posture of accommodation and an aggressive assertion of exploitation. Former slaves from the South did become influential orators in the northern antislavery movement. Drawing on their southern experiences, they offered dramatic testimonials about slavery. Frederick Douglass, a former slave from Maryland, became one of the 19th century's greatest orators. With the physical gifts of a great orator—tall in stature, melodious in voice—Douglass won converts to abolition throughout the North and in England. During Reconstruction some blacks spoke a new rhetoric that rejected racist stereotypes and called for equal opportunities. The black church became the most significant forum for black public speaking, although the style was more one of folk speech than oratory. Audience interaction with the preacher and the use of biblical language, musical rhythms, and sometimes even chanted sermons—all in a passionate religious setting— characterized speaking in the black church. After the judicial and legislative decisions of the 1950s and 1960s, blacks had increased opportunities for open communication. They marched in streets and talked in churches, on campuses, and over television of constitutional rights, basic freedoms, human dignity, economic opportunities, and cruel discrimination.

Prior to the Civil War, white leaders saw the threat to their slave society and responded with a "rhetoric of desperation." They differed on the nature and future of the Union, and a new sectional awareness emerged. Confronting social and economic change, orators perfected defensive rhetorical forms dealing with the recurring themes of constitutionality, states' rights, regional pride, Old South culture, white superiority, agrarianism, and God. Equally important was the omission from public discourse of the topic of civil rights for blacks.

During Reconstruction most white speakers supported the restoration of white rule in state government. Initially, some leaders refused to participate in Reconstruction politics and thereby legitimize the political role of former slaves. A few whites called for submission to northern conquerors as a means of reclaiming economic security and political control and, as a consequence, were ostracized from public office for a number of years. To resist Reconstruction laws and to restore white authority, the majority of white orators constructed regionally appealing arguments from mythic themes of the Old South, white superiority, threats to southern womanhood, regional pride, states' rights, constitutional claims, violence, economic prosperity, and regional security. Supplementing these stock southern appeals were emotional references to God, sacred principles, and past loyalties, as well as to Civil War experiences, including heroic acts by soldiers, sacrifices of women left behind, regional suffering, and economic ruin.

From 1800 to 1954 whites relied on racial authority, hoping to hold blacks in their rhetorically impotent status as obedient listeners. At the same time, to communicate with northerners, white orators practiced a "rhetoric of accommodation," a stance opposite to their Reconstruction discourse of resistance. This conciliatory posture combined a regional loyalty oath with an emphasis on sectional prosperity. Listeners heard the same orators talk of Old South themes of "southern honor" and New South appeals of "practical progress" for the "new age." Between 1880 and 1946 a number of southern demagogues, noted for their fiery delivery, belligerence, magnetism, assumed infallibility, and monopolizing strategies, governed the region. During the 1940s, when courts ruled that blacks could participate in white primaries, these demagogues and other less dogmatic whites began a new round of intimidating bribes and threats.

The most dramatic change in southern oratory occurred from 1954 to the 1980s, when the Supreme Court ruled against racially segregated public schools and the Congress passed civil rights legislation. Blacks challenged the dominant rhetorical status of whites. A pluralistic public speaking emerged, with a variety of views being stated on questions of race, economy, political parties, crime, national defense, ecology, industry, and education. Blacks were able publicly to communicate feelings, convictions, and aspirations previously kept private. Blacks and some whites directly confronted the morality, expediency, economy, and legality of racial discrimination. Many blacks abandoned their former accommodating posture and developed more candid and assertive language, strategies, topics, and arguments appropriate for newly won freedom.

Martin Luther King, Jr., used oratory as a key weapon in the civil rights movement. He drew from the communications style of the black folk church and combined biblical themes with national egalitarian ideals. His "I Have a Dream" speech at the 1963 March on Washington echoed Lincoln's language in the Gettysburg Address, portraying the South as the locale of a hoped-for racial reconciliation.

To oppose social changes resulting from legal and judicial decisions, many whites escalated their defensive rhetoric of white superiority, black inferiority, constitutional interpretations, states' rights, God, free enterprise, and racial segregation. Increasingly, however, whites were forced to share the public forum with blacks. As more blacks registered to vote and campaigned for office, whites for the first time since Reconstruction were required to communicate directly and respectfully with the new minority audience. Although awkward intially, white orators experimented with rhetoric appropriate to their new, less-powerful status. In the 1970s a few governors actually called for an end to racial discrimination. Some writers have called this new white male speech an "oratory of optimism," but a more accurate characterization would be a public admission of the expediency of social change and shared authority.

See also BLACK LIFE: Preacher, Black; / Douglass, Frederick; King, Martin Luther, Jr.; POLITICS: Demagogues

Cal M. Logue
University of Georgia

Waldo W. Braden, ed., *Oratory in the Old South, 1828–1860* (1970), *Oratory in the New South* (1979), *Southern Speech Journal* (Summer 1964); Kevin E. Kearney, *Southern Speech Journal* (Fall 1966); Cal M. Logue, *Quarterly Journal of Speech* (February 1981); Cal M. Logue and Howard Dorgan, eds., *The Oratory of Southern Demagogues* (1981); John D. Saxon, *Southern Speech Communication Journal* (Spring 1975). ☆

Spanish Language

Ethnic Hispanics who habitually speak Spanish are rare or almost nonexistent throughout much of the South. Yet in three southern states—Louisiana, Texas, and Florida—the Hispanic presence historically antedates English settlement and incorporation into the United States. And in two of those states (Texas and Florida), the 1970s and 1980s have witnessed dramatic increases in foreign-born Spanish speakers. Thus, Spanish in the American South is widespread in a few states but almost totally absent in others.

Although New Orleans and its suburbs are not without a certain Hispanic presence, chiefly the product of contemporary immigration, only in the eastern reaches of St. Bernard Parish (lying southeast of New Orleans between the Mississippi and Lake Borgne) does one find a concentrated Hispanic population historically linked with pre-American Louisiana and the Spanish language. They are the *isleños*, "islanders," so named after their 18th-century place of origin, Spain's Canary Islands. The *isleños'* ancestors were brought to Louisiana from 1778 through the 1790s by Bernardo de Gálvez, governor of the province. Settling in small communities (today Shell Beach, Yscloskey, Delacroix, and Reggio), the *isleños* led a largely isolated fishing-trapping-farming existence throughout the 19th century and into the 20th, thereby retaining Spanish in the face of only moderate pressures to acquire French and later English.

Isleño Spanish was spoken by the several thousand *isleños* in the 1940s, when it was investigated by Raymond R. MacCurdy, but that is no longer the case. At present, only the oldest residents are Spanish-dominant and use the language regularly. Middle-aged *isleños* typically understand it well but speak it haltingly, and the younger generations range from poor speaking ability and middling comprehension to no knowledge of Spanish at all. (Reputedly, however, there are differences between the two main settlements: Shell Beach/Hopedale, where Spanish loss is most advanced, and Delacroix, where Spanish retention is somewhat higher.) Language loss can be attributed to the usual factors: longer attendance at consolidated schools where English is the sole medium of instruction, improved transportation, expanded contacts with the outside world, marriages outside the group, and increased economic opportunities. Today, while *isleño* culture and sense of Hispanic identity are undergoing a revival, local Spanish is effectively moribund.

The Spanish spoken by *isleños* is Canary Island dialect with numerous lexical borrowings from French and to a lesser extent English. Linguistically, the Canary Islands have always formed a bridge between the Andalucía region of southern Spain and the New World. Andalusian Spanish (together with Canary Island, Caribbean, and, in general, "coastal" Spanish throughout much of the Western Hemisphere) can be characterized by weakened, altered, or eliminated consonants at the ends of syllables or words, by occasionally nasalized vowels (as in French), by a rather lax manner of producing voiced consonants, and, of course, by the absence of the Castilian voiceless "th" sound. The overall acoustic effect of *isleño* Spanish is not unlike that of the rural dialects of Cuba and the Dominican Republic.

In recent years, Dallas and especially Houston have become home to increasing numbers of Central and South Americans, but when Hispanics in Texas come to mind, one first thinks of Mexicans. This is inevitable, given the status of Mexican Americans as Texas's largest minority group (22 percent of the state's population of more than 12 million).

Whereas small though significant numbers of Spanish-speaking families have lived in what is now Texas from the 17th through the 19th centuries, the majority of Mexican Americans/Chicanos in the state today are descendants of 20th-century immigrants or are immigrants themselves. According to figures from the 1980 U.S. census, 29 of Texas's 254 counties now have Mexican-American majorities, in several cases well in excess of 66.7 percent. Mexican Americans form the majority population in two of Texas's five biggest cities— San Antonio and El Paso. Mexican-American settlement patterns reveal, however, an uneven distribution throughout the state, with the greatest numbers concentrated in a 150- to 200-mile-wide strip along the international border. Save for the Dallas and Houston areas, north and east Texas are home to relatively few Mexican Americans.

In Texas, is "Mexican American" coextensive with "Spanish speaking"? According to a study by Calvin J. Veltman, based on the 1976 National Survey of Income and Education, Hispanic Americans in general are more conservative of their ethnic language than are other major American ethnolinguistic groups. For example, although slightly over 60 percent of Americans of Italian descent born in the United States switch over to English monolingualism, only about 30 percent of Hispanics do so. However, the rate of Hispanic linguistic anglicization varies from region to region, with the highest Spanish loss being found in the Rocky Mountain states and the lowest in Texas. So the report provides some statistical confirmation of what the unaided ear can hear:

that a lot of Spanish is spoken in Texas. Yet the size and great diversity of Texas almost guarantee that for Spanish, degrees of usage and levels of proficiency will vary widely too. Socioeconomic standing, place of residence, generation of removal from Mexico, sex, profession, family ties, education, degrees of local Anglo/Chicano ethnic tension, sociopolitical attitudes, and many other factors influence how much Spanish one speaks, to whom and how well one speaks it, what type(s) of Spanish one uses, and whether one will pass Spanish on to the next generation. For example, it is popularly known that a larger number of Mexican Americans speak Spanish more often and with greater proficiency in border cities like El Paso, Laredo, and Brownsville than in Fort Worth, Lubbock, or Port Arthur. But even on the border, variability takes its toll (though in cities like El Paso it is almost impossible to find a native Mexican American who does not at least *comprehend* Spanish).

In Texas the Spanish of Mexican Americans is the Spanish that they or their ancestors brought north and altered through increased contact with English and decreased contact with a society that is exclusively Spanish speaking. Allowing for the impossibility of generalizing about *the* language and language behavior of a population as diverse as are the Mexican Americans of Texas, it is still useful to describe the Spanish of a hypothetically typical speaker with the following composite picture. As compared to an *isleño* or a Cuban American, his consonant system is strong. His grammar is probably that of the rural Mexican with the concomitant regularizations, archaisms, hypercorrections, and forms of respect. The years in Texas will have brought about a diminution in the use of the subjunctive mood and an expansion of English-parallel patterns such as the present progressive tense. His lexicon will show on the one hand an increasing adaptation of English words and phrases and on the other hand a decrease in learned Spanish terminology, especially of the technical sort.

There are certain historical parallels between Texas and Florida, but not many. Thus, while Florida was steadily claimed by the Spanish crown from 1513 until 1763, colonization was not extensive, and nearly all Spanish subjects abandoned San Agustín (the only settlement of any substance) in 1764 with the onset of British occupation. Twenty years later, Spain again took formal possession of the peninsula, but the period between then and 1819 (when the United States added Florida to its domains) was chaotic, unstable, and unmarked by any serious success in Hispanicization. Ironically, the only Hispanic or, more properly, Iberian settlers' group to survive the English-speaking onslaught well into the 19th century were the descendants of the 1,100 Minorcans who were brought to what is now the New Smyrna Beach area in 1768 by Andrew Turnbull during the two-decade period of British colonization. In 1777 Turnbull's plantation venture collapsed, and the Minorcans migrated northward to settle in San Agustín (modern-day St. Augustine). Although half the Minorcans departed Florida in 1784, the remainder stayed on. The language indigenous to the Mediterranean island of Minorca is a dialect of Catalan, not Spanish, and it is thus not possible to speak of the Minorcan's permanence as representing a Spanish-speaking presence in Florida. It is probable that Spanish (and English)

were added to their linguistic repertoire during the first five decades of their settlement in Florida. In any event, studies such as that by Rasico (1983) point to a growing loss of the Minorcan language by the end of the 1800s save for several dozen words and expressions retained by some of the settlers' descendants well into the 20th century.

With the exception of the famous 1868 migration of large numbers of Cuban cigar makers to Key West, and a similar movement in 1886 to the Ybor City neighborhood of Tampa, the bulk of Florida developed into a southern state not unlike the others until 1 January 1959, a date that marked the beginning of the Cuban exodus from the regime of Fidel Castro. Since then, well over a million Cubans have left Cuba, with the majority of them settling in southeastern Florida. At present, Dade County's population of 1,750,000 contains around 450,000 persons of Cuban descent, who, together with smaller colonies of Puerto Ricans, Central Americans, and others, constitute between 55 and 60 percent of the population of the city of Miami proper.

Periodically, Cuban mass arrivals make international headlines, and these "wave" immigrants give rise to local Anglo fears of inundation. These fears culminated in 1981 in the passage of a law voiding a generalized 1973 proclamation of official bilingualism. In light of this, it may be surprising (and to nervous Anglos, reassuring) to learn from Carlos A. Solé, a professor at the University of Texas, that "language shift [to English] seems to have already begun among young Cuban-Americans in spite of the recency of the Cuban arrival and settlement." But for an unpredictable number of years to come, Miami will continue to impress the visitor as "Spanish speaking," given the steady stream of new arrivals from the Caribbean basin and beyond.

For the moment, though, the Spanish of the Miami area can still be equated with Cuban, so to describe Cuban Spanish is to describe the varieties of Dade County: weak consonants, vowel nasalization, and an intonation rhythm that gives out a somewhat machine-gun effect. Inevitably, English borrowings will enter Miami Spanish as they have the Spanish of Texas, though perhaps not to the same degree, because the average Cuban political exile typically enjoyed a level of education that the average Mexican economic refugee did not.

See also ETHNIC LIFE: / Cubans; Mexicans; Spanish; URBANIZATION: / Dallas; Houston; Miami; New Orleans; Tampa

Richard V. Teschner
University of Texas at El Paso

Raymond R. MacCurdy, *The Spanish Dialect in St. Bernard Parish, Louisiana* (1950); Philip D. Rasico, *El Escribano* (1983); Carlos A. Solé, *A Festschrift for Jacob Ornstein: Studies in General Linguistics and Sociolinguistics,* ed. Edward L. Blansitt, Jr., and Richard V. Teschner (1980); Calvin J. Veltman, *The Assimilation of American Language Minorities: Structure, Pace and Extent* (1979); U.S. Bureau of Census, *Population and Housing; Advance Reports, Texas, Final Population and Housing Counts* (1981). ☆

Urban Speech

The Linguistic Atlas of the Gulf States project consists of interviews with informants in eight southern states (Tennessee, Georgia, Florida, Alabama, Mississippi, Arkansas, Louisiana, and Texas), with a lexical Urban Supplement added to the basic work sheets of 164 of the 1,121 interviews. These 164 urban records cover the speech patterns of 100 white and 64 black informants, 79 of whom are age 30 or younger. The majority of the records represent natives of the larger cities in the area—Knoxville, Chattanooga, Atlanta, Jacksonville, Tampa, Miami, Nashville, Birmingham, Montgomery, Mobile, Memphis, Jackson, New Orleans, Shreveport, Little Rock, Dallas, Houston, and San Antonio. The remainder report the speech of primarily younger informants from smaller cities and towns, included for comparison with their urban counterparts.

LAGS evidence shows that urban speech in the South retains distinct regional characteristics, particularly among older and more insular informants. For example, although *dragonfly* is preferred by a large majority of urban informants, the South Midland form *snake doctor* is strong in Tennessee, Arkansas, and the upper portions of Georgia, Alabama, and Mississippi; and among residents of the lower South *mosquito hawk* prevails in Florida, Louisiana, Gulf Alabama, Gulf Mississippi, and the lower portion of Georgia. Likewise, *chigger* is the dominant term among informants in Tennessee, Arkansas, and upper Georgia, while *red bug* occurs more frequently elsewhere in the territory.

Younger urban informants, however, preserve fewer of the regionalisms usually noted in dialect surveys. Most of these southerners, for instance, offer no variant for *peanuts*, though some recognize *goobers* as an old-fashioned or rural form. Such choices as *ground peas, goober peas*, and *pinders* are rare. To many urban informants, there are no valid distinctions among types of peaches: *cling* is recognized only as a descriptor on the label of a can. Thus, such regional patterns as *press* versus *plum peach* are lost in the cities.

In some sections of the urban South, regionalisms have developed for items covered in the Urban Supplement. A coin-operated self-service laundry, known by the trade name *Laundromat* in most places, tends to be a *washateria* in east Texas, a *washhouse* in Miami, and a *wishy-washy* in Nashville. A *hero sandwich* is usually a *submarine* in the eastern and east-central zones of the LAGS territory and a *poor boy* in the west-central and western zones, probably reflecting the influence of the New Orleans focal area where the *poor boy* was reputedly invented. Exceptions occur in Florida, where *Cuban* is common, and in the east-central zone, from middle Tennessee to Gulf Alabama, where the sandwich is often called a *Dagwood*, after the comic-strip character.

Other items investigated by the Urban Supplement show no such regional variation. *Water fountain* prevails over *drinking fountain* throughout the LAGS territory, and an informal room in the house is usually a *den* everywhere, with *family room* a distant second. In Florida, it may be called a *Florida room*, but even there, *den* occurs more often. The speech of urban informants, particularly the younger and more sophisticated, contains a variety of synonyms for the LAGS words associated with crime, street life, and illegal activities, among them synonyms for marijuana and other drugs, colloquial names for money such as *bread* and *cabbage*, and derogatory names for policemen.

Urban speech in the South, while retaining some of the old regionalisms, has developed various new regionalisms, while other items evoke a common response from city to city. Regional distinctions are more likely to appear in the speech of southerners over age 30. Younger urban southerners, both black and white, are more likely to share the vocabularies of their peers in other parts of the country.

Susan Leas McDaniel
Emory University

Charles E. Billiard, Susan E. Leas, and Marvin W. Bassett, eds., *A Manual for Dialect Research in the Southern States*. 3d ed., *The Protocols*. LAGS: *The Basic Materials*, Part 1 (1981); Charles E. Billiard and Lee A. Pederson, *Orbis* (1979); Susan E. Leas, LAGS Working Papers (First Series), no. 7 (1981); Lee A. Pederson, *American Speech* (Spring–Summer 1971, Fall 1980). ☆

CHESAPEAKE BAY DIALECT

The South is more diversified in speech than other major geographical areas of the United States. In such coastal regions as the Chesapeake area, one finds particularly pronounced language differences. The most linguistic diversity in the Chesapeake is found among those who live in the southern island communities (Tilghman, Deal, and Smith in Maryland; Saxis, Chincoteague, and Tangier in Virginia) and make their living by fishing, crabbing, clamming, and oystering.

At times, outsiders, especially journalists, grossly exaggerate the speech they hear in these areas as "pure dialect," "fossilized language," and "Elizabethan English"—labels that are nonsense but hard to dispel. All American English derived, of course, from 17th-century British English, which at the time was itself quite diverse. What one finds throughout the United States—especially on the Atlantic Seaboard, the region of original settlement—are survivals of British English. The dialects of the islands (relic areas, to dialectologists), however, seem quite different, and they are; but to look at them as old-fashioned and preservers of Chaucerian and Elizabethan speech is incorrect.

Nevertheless, the islanders and their language are very special. Tangier Island, which is the best known and has received the most attention, is 3.5 miles long and 1.5 miles wide and is roughly at sea level. It lies in the middle of the Chesapeake Bay, a part of Accomac County on the Eastern Shore of Virginia. The closest neighbors are on Smith Island, just across the Virginia line in Maryland. Tangiermen think that their own language is different from the Smith Islanders'. Except for daily necessities, the islanders have relatively little contact with the mainland. The approximately 800 residents, persuaded by the authority of a national historical marker and some imaginative brochures and newspaper stories, believe that their history goes back to 1686, the year a certain John Crockett settled the island, although "facts" have not been substantiated by the records. A more likely date for settlement would be somewhere around 1790 to 1800.

A homogeneous community of working-class whites of English descent (called watermen), Tangier reflects very few social differences. Lives are simple and hard, and inhabitants are independent, deeply religious, and patriotic.

Tangiermen are essentially single-style speakers, but when encountering strangers they occasionally correct toward what they believe to be standard speech. Their speech is distinctive in grammar, word forms, and vocabulary, but most striking are the unusual tenseness and emphasis that characterize pronunciation. These traits, plus the Tangierman's curious mixture of double negatives, stated opposites, clipped phrases, nicknames, and nautical terms can be both amusing and baffling to an outsider.

The Tangier dialect does not share the commonly cited distinctive features of eastern Virginia speech still heard in the Piedmont and Tidewater areas: the broad *a* of *aunt*; the loss of *r* in words like *car*, *corn*, *year*, and *dinner*; or the pronunciation of *afraid* and *naked* as *afred* and *neked*. Some of the rustic pronunciations heard along the coastal localities of the Chesapeake are not heard on Tangier; for example, *can't* with the vowel of *paint*, *push* with the vowel of *pooh*, *dog* with the vowel of *hoe*, *fish* with the vowel of *fee*, and *poor* with the vowel of *Poe*. The Islanders do not distinguish *hoarse* and *horse*, *mourning* and *morning*, and *poor* and *pour*, as many southerners do. *Mary* and *merry* are pronounced as many pronounce *Murray*. They pronounce *tire*, *tired*, *wire*, and *fire* with the vowel of *lard*. *Chair*, *care*, and *scared* are pronounced with the vowel of *curd*, as are *year*, *hear*, *here*, and *ear*. *Paul* and *ball* are pronounced like *pull*. All words that rhyme with *trash* invariably have the vowel of *bay*. *Creek* has the Pennsylvanian sound, that of the vowel of *tick*. *Bomb* and *bum* are pronounced the same. *Calm*, in reference to slatelike water, is *cam*. *Zinc* is used for *sink* (kitchen), and *spider* and *frying pan* are used interchangeably, but at times show age distribution. *Coal oil* is more prevalent than *kerosene, curtains* is used for *roller shades,* and *bateau* is the common term for *small boat.*

The most prominent aspect of Tangier speech is the phonetic diversity of the vowels, which are pronounced in such a way that one seems to be hearing several vowels in a continuum and Cockney-like drawling and whining. Tangier speech then seems to be a mixture, sharing features with the speech of the Middle Atlantic states to the north, the southern mountain area, the southern Coastal Plain, and the outermost Atlantic communities.

See also ENVIRONMENT: / Chesapeake Bay

David L. Shores
Old Dominion University

William Cabell Greet, *American Speech* (December 1933); David L. Shores, *Journal of English Linguistics* (1984); William W. Warner, *Beautiful Swimmers: Watermen, Crabs, and the Chesapeake Bay* (1976). ☆

CONCH
||||||||||||||||||

The term *Conch* refers both to a subset of the population of the Florida Keys and to the distinctive speech of this group. Unlike many other groups in the United States, the Conchs are characterized not by ethnicity or the use of a non-English language, but by settlement history and regional and social insularity. The Conchs originated with the formation in 1649 of a company of Cockney Englishmen, the Eleuthian Adventurers, who migrated to Bermuda seeking religious and political freedom. During the next century the group migrated again, this time to the Bahamas.

From there, many of them settled in Key West after its acquisition by the United States from Spain in 1819, and by the middle of the century they had moved into the upper Keys as well. The absence of direct transportation routes and the economic activities of the Conchs served to isolate them from the United States mainland and to favor continued cultural and commercial relations with the Bahamas, which provided a steady stream of new settlers, and later with Cuba. Initially, their economic activity revolved around the ocean, with salvaging, sponging, and fishing (the conch was a major source of food as well as the source of the name for the people) the primary commercial activities.

During the last quarter of the 19th century, however, Key West became the world's most important center for manufacturing cigars. In spite of the infusion of new people from the United States mainland and Cuba, the Conchs associated primarily with their own people and often educated their children separately. The demise of the cigar industry and subsequent decline in population after 1910 reinforced their isolation. Although tourism and military installations brought a new flow of people from the mainland after World War II, the Conchs continue to maintain a strong sense of their distinctiveness as a group.

The linguistic consequence of their history is a dialect that is clearly different from any other spoken on the U.S. mainland. To outsiders it sounds much like the speech of the Bahamas, and as linguist Frank K. LeBan shows, it shares some features with British English. Although the Conch vocabulary includes a number of unique words, such as *locker* for *closet, grits box* for *stove,* and *natural sponge* for *dishcloth,* the dialect is more remarkable for its distinct pronunciation. Like British and southern American speech, Conch speakers do not pronounce the *r* after vowels. More importantly, the vowels in words like *coat* and *hot* are closer to the British than the American pronunciation. The combination of these features, along with others, provides a speech that is unique, as is the social history of the Conchs.

Guy Bailey
Texas A&M University

Frank K. LeBan, in *A Various Language: Perspectives on American Dialects*, ed. Juanita V. Williamson and Virginia M. Burke (1971), "A Phonological Study of the Speech of Conchs, Early Inhabitants of the Florida Keys, at Three Age Levels" (Ph.D. dissertation, Louisiana State University, 1965); Lee A. Pederson et al., eds., *LACS: The Basic Materials* (1981). ☆

DRAWL

The southern drawl is a slow speech heard in the South and distinguished in part from the more general American drawl. Myth associates the southern drawl with the prestige of first families whose ancestors owned antebellum plantations. Observation shows that among the best families there are those who drawl and those who do not, and within the same family a grandmother may drawl markedly while her grandsons may not do so at all. Furthermore, the poor white cousins living on farms and in mill towns probably have entirely different characteristic speech patterns. The range and complexity of black southern speech have yet to be explored systematically throughout the entire South.

If the southern drawl has identified speakers as socially prominent, it has also served as a vehicle for public amusement in the way that any regional speech amuses. The Missourian Mark Twain regularly entertained his audiences by reading from Joel Chandler Harris's Tar Baby story; its black dialect let Twain give a virtuoso display of the range of his southern drawl.

The American drawl has often been noted as a defect—witness Noah Webster's *Dissertations* (1798), which urged New England workers to correct their "drawling, nasal manner of speaking." The southern drawl cannot be traced to the influence of personal laziness, a hot climate, or the presence of a black mammy rearing planters' children during infancy. (How any given mammy spoke, incidentally, is lost in the past. Using diaries and similar evidence, Norman Eliason stated in *Tar Heel Talk* [1956] that in North Carolina slaves learned to speak English from "largely illiterate or semi-literate overseers." Little other evidence on the point has been assembled.)

A distinguishing feature of the southern drawl is that it differs from the southern mountaineer's pronunciation of *thing* as *thaing*, notably by using an added *y* sound and by losing an *r* in particular settings: *dyuty*, *tyube*, and for some Virginians *cyah*, and *gyahden* sound more drawn out than do *duty*, *tube*, *car*, and *garden*. These pronunciations arose among 18th-century British aristocrats and were adopted by well-to-do southern colonial planters and their social equals. The effect of the lost *r* on the pronunciation of preceding stressed vowels or diphthongs is shown in the graphic tables of Kurath and McDavid, *The Pronunciation of English in the Atlantic States* (1961); no comparable graphs exist for the states formed after the American Revolution.

See also BLACK LIFE: Speech, Black

Gordon R. Wood
Southern Illinois University

James B. McMillan, *Annotated Bibliography of Southern American English* (1971); Thomas Pyles, *Words and Ways of American English* (1952). ☆

INDIAN TRADE LANGUAGES

Because the North American Indians spoke a great variety of languages, they developed several ways of communicating among themselves or with the European settlers regarding preparations for travel or war, peacemaking, and, chiefly, trade. Though the sign language of the Plains Indians is well known, Native Americans generally used second verbal languages, like the Chinook jargon of the Northwest. A number of such jargons, lingua francas, or trade languages developed in the Southeast.

Robert Beverley, at the beginning of the 18th century, cited Ocaneeche (perhaps actually Tutelo) of eastern Virginia as a trade language. John Lawson, writing at the beginning of the 1700s, found Tuscarora, the language of the Iroquois tribe of the same name, widely used by smaller tribes in eastern North Carolina. Not long after Lawson's publication, the Tuscaroras went to war with the settlers, and, after being defeated, slowly migrated to New York and Ontario, thus ending use of their tongue as a trade language. According to James Adair (1775), the Catawba language was used

in South Carolina much as was the Tuscarora farther north. Francis Le Jau in 1706 remarked that, according to hearsay, the Savanna (Shawnee) language was similarly in use in Georgia. Evidence exists that the Shawnee used Muskogee (Creek) as a trade language, so Le Jau was likely making a first reference to Creek as a lingua franca.

The Muskogee spoken by the Creeks of Alabama and Georgia was closely allied to the languages spoken by the Chickasaws and Choctaws and by several smaller southeastern tribes. The Creek political confederacy included the Alabama, Chickasaw, Koasati, Hitchiti, Natchez, Shawnee, and Yuchi tribes, all of whom probably spoke Muskogee (Creek) until about 1840, when the last of the southeastern Indians were forcibly moved west. Some scholars suggest, however, that the common language was, in fact, Mobilian, and clear evidence exists that the Alabamas, Chickasaws, Natchez, and Koasati did use Mobilian.

Mobilian, doubtless the most widespread and long-lasting of the southeastern intertribal languages, was also at first called the Chickasaw trade language. The term *Mobilian* was first used by the French founders of Louisiana, who encountered it among Indians in the vicinity of their original Gulf settlements near Mobile, Ala. Other French travelers in the lower Mississippi Valley first encountered it among the Chickasaws in present-day Tennessee. Le Page du Pratz (1758) states that "Tchicacha" and "Langue Mobilienne" were the same and comprised a jargon used by tribes of both Muskogean and non-Muskogean linguistic stocks to communicate with the French. Le Page du Pratz spoke of Mobilian as "a corrupted Chickasaw," meaning that it had pidgin qualities—lexical, grammatical, or both. The Indian agent John Sibley, writing in the period just after the Louisiana Purchase, stated that the Biloxi, Alabama, Taensa, and Pascagoula (all by then in central Louisiana) were among the dozen tribes still relying on Mobilian. Some black and white inhabitants knew it as well. Caddoan, according to Sibley, was used by a number of northwest Louisiana tribes.

In the 1960s Mary R. Haas learned that Mobilian speakers could still be found among the remnants of Kosati and Alabama bands in western Louisiana and central Texas, and in 1970 James Crawford undertook their scientific study. Crawford published his data chiefly in *The Mobilian Trade Language* (1978), which provided a substantial glossary, with comparisons to Choctaw and Alabama usages. Unlike most of his predecessors, Crawford thought Mobilian developed as a result of French settlement. Emanuel Drechsel, whose dissertation followed Crawford's book, did further fieldwork and archival research and increased the glossary to more than a thousand words. He rejected Crawford's theory of the origins of Mobilian as a reaction to European presence. As a whole, the research of Haas, Crawford, and Drechsel has provided invaluable insights about the complexities and extensive usage of the primary southeastern intertribal language.

Viron L. Barnhill
George F. Reinecke
University of New Orleans

James M. Crawford, in *Studies in Southeastern Indian Languages*, ed. James M. Crawford (1975), *The Mobilian Trade Language* (1978); Emanuel Johannes Drechsel, "Mobilian Jargon: Linguistic, Sociocultural and Historical Aspects of an American Indian Lingua Franca" (Ph.D. dissertation, University of Wisconsin, 1979), *Ethnohistory* (Summer 1983); Mary R. Haas, in *Studies in Southeastern Indian Languages*, ed. James M. Crawford (1975); John Lawson, *A New Voyage to Carolina*, ed. Hugh Talmage Lefler (1967); John Sibley, *American State Papers*, Class II, Indian Affairs, vol. 1 (1805). ☆

LINGUISTIC ATLAS OF THE GULF STATES PROJECT
||||||||||||||||||||||||||||||||||||||||||||||

Directed by Lee A. Pederson of Emory University, the Linguistic Atlas of the Gulf States (LAGS) project is an extensive survey of regional and social dialects in eight southern states: Tennessee, Georgia, Florida, Alabama, Mississippi, Louisiana, Arkansas, and Texas (as far west as the Balcones Escarpment). As the largest and most inclusive research project on southern speech, LAGS provides basic texts for the study of speech in the region and a description of the sociohistorical and sociolinguistic contexts necessary for their interpretation. Ultimately, the project seeks to achieve four additional, interrelated goals: (1) an inventory of the dominant and recessive patterns of usage in the Gulf states; (2) a global description of regional and social varieties of southern speech; (3) an abstract of regional phonology, grammar, and lexicon; and (4) an identification of areas of linguistic complexity that require further study.

From its inception in 1968, LAGS has been an extension of the direct method of dialect geography initiated by Gilliéron in France and refined by Kurath in the United States. These methods involve the following: selection of a network of communities, including focal, relic, and transitional communities, on the basis of the social history of the region; conversational interviews with natives of these communities conducted with a questionnaire of selected items; and recording of the responses in finely graded phonetics. LAGS regards the county or parish as the community. The LAGS territory includes 665 of these, but they are grouped into a grid of 168 units on the basis of their social history. Although only one county in each grid is an obligatory target, the sample includes interviews with 1,118 informants in 451 counties. The informants are of three types: Type I, folk informants with a grade school education or less (40 percent); Type II, common informants with a high school education (35 percent); and Type III, cultivated informants with a college education (25 percent). Blacks comprise 22 percent of the sample, which also contains a number of informants whose first language is Spanish, French, or German. Both the questionnaire and the system of phonetic notation are adaptations of those used by Kurath.

The LAGS corpus includes two basic components, with three projected interpretive components. The primary corpus, the field records, consists of some 5,300 hours of tape-recorded speech stored at Emory University. The protocols are the principal analogues of these field records. They contain phonetic transcriptions of questionnaire items and of other phonological, grammatical, and lexical data and serve as guides to the field records. The 1,118 protocols, along with the questionnaire and a guide to phonetics and protocol composition, were published in micro-

text by University Microfilms in 1981. A concordance to the protocols is forthcoming. The three interpretive components will include a handbook, summarizing LAGS methodology and the social history of the region, published by the University of Georgia Press; a series of maps, summarizing the distribution of data; and a legendry, providing descriptions of the data on maps.

Guy Bailey
Texas A&M University

Lee A. Pederson, *American Speech* (Winter 1981), *Papers in Language Variation*, ed. David L. Shores and Carole P. Hines (1977), et al., eds., LAGS: *The Basic Materials* (1981). ☆

LINGUISTIC ATLAS OF THE MIDDLE AND SOUTH ATLANTIC STATES

The *Linguistic Atlas of the Middle and South Atlantic States* (*LAMSAS*), together with the *Linguistic Atlas of New England* (*LANE*), is the record of a dialect survey of the area of American colonial settlement. This survey was proposed in 1929 by Hans Kurath. Fieldwork in New England was carried out from 1931 to 1933 under Kurath's direction and *LANE* was published in three two-part volumes from 1939 to 1943. Meanwhile, a preliminary survey of the South Atlantic states was carried out by the principal field-worker of *LANE*, Guy Lowman, during 1933 and 1934. Lowman completed 68 interviews, primarily in the states of Maryland, Virginia, North Carolina, South Carolina, and Georgia, using a modified version of the New England questionnaire with about 700 items designed to elicit variations in pronunciation, usage, and vocabulary.

In 1935 Lowman began a systematic survey of the South Atlantic states. He had completed the fieldwork in Maryland, Virginia, and North Carolina and the survey of the Middle Atlantic states except for upper New York state by the time of his death in 1941. Kurath hired Raven I. McDavid, Jr., to complete the fieldwork, but McDavid was able to complete only a few field records in South Carolina before World War II interrupted the survey. After the war, McDavid resumed fieldwork and completed the survey in New York, South Carolina, and Georgia by 1949.

Publishing the findings of the two surveys (now combined into *LAMSAS*) was not possible; rather, Kurath published an important analysis of the data, *The Word Geography of the Eastern United States*, in 1949. Two other summary volumes followed—E. Bagby Atwood's, *A Survey of Verb Forms in the Eastern United States* (1953) and Kurath and McDavid's *The Pronunciation of English in the Atlantic States* (1961). Upon Kurath's retirement in 1964, McDavid became editor-in-chief of *LAMSAS* and continued editorial work on it, hoping eventually to achieve full publication. At the time of his death in 1984, two fascicles of a proposed 60 of *LAMSAS* had been published by the University of Chicago Press (1980), and nearly all the basic materials were available on microfilm from the Regenstein Library of the University of Chicago. William A. Kretzschmar, Jr., succeeded McDavid as editor-in-chief, and the atlas materials are now on deposit at the University of Georgia.

LAMSAS is an invaluable repository of cultural and linguistic information on the vocabulary of a rural society that is in the process of disappearing. The study of the language of a community can provide an important means of interpreting the culture of that community.

George T. Dorrill
University of South Carolina

William A. Kretzschmar, Jr., ed., *Dialects in Culture: Essays in General Dialectology by Raven I. McDavid, Jr.* (1979); Raven I. McDavid, Jr., *Orbis*, vol. 5 (1956); Michael Montgomery and Guy Bailey, eds., *Language Variety in the South: Perspectives in Black and White* (1986). ☆

McDAVID, RAVEN I., JR.
(1911–1984) Linguist.

Raven Ioor McDavid, Jr., was born and raised in Greenville, S.C. He graduated from Furman University in 1931 and received his Ph.D. in English in 1935 from Duke University, with a dissertation on the political thought of John Milton. In 1937 he attended a summer linguistic institute at the urging of his commandant at The Citadel (his first teaching position), who wanted McDavid to get remedial training in elocution. He was selected as a model informant for a dialectology class at the institute, was intrigued with what he heard there, and proceeded to become the foremost student of southern speech—and of American English more generally—of his time.

McDavid entered the field of linguistics just at the point of its rapid development as a modern academic discipline. After his initial spark and further institute training, he embarked on a survey of South Carolina for Hans Kurath's American Linguistic Atlas project. World War II intervened, but after working in the Army Language Section during the war, McDavid became Kurath's chief field-worker. During the next 15 years he spent a great deal of his time in the field with informants from Ontario south to Florida; he eventually completed over 500 interviews (averaging six to eight hours each), a record unmatched by any other American dialectologist. At the same time McDavid wrote prolifically, including landmark articles, his abridgement of H. L. Mencken's *The American Language* (1963), and, with Hans Kurath, a volume that still serves as a standard reference, *The Pronunciation of English in the Atlantic States* (1961). His first major academic appointment was at Case Western Reserve University in 1952. In 1957 he moved to the University of Chicago, the institution with which he was most closely identified. In 1964 McDavid succeeded Kurath as editor-in-chief of the *Linguistic Atlas of the Middle and South Atlantic States* (McDavid et al., fascicles 1 and 2, 1980, 1982), and in 1975 accepted responsibility for the *Linguistic Atlas of the North-Central States* (McDavid et al., 1976–80). He directed editorial work on both projects until his death. Recognition came late for McDavid, but in time he won major funding for his atlas projects from the National Endowment for the Humanities and received honorary degrees from Furman, Duke, and the Sorbonne. The *Linguistic Atlas of the Middle and South Atlantic States* began appearing in print in 1980 from the University of Chicago Press. The university's Joseph Regenstein Library contains microfilm copies of the *Basic Materials* volumes from the two atlas projects.

McDavid's experience in the field shaped his thought: he always insisted on the importance for linguistics of primary data, of real speech by real people, as opposed to rarified theory. He believed that contemporary speech was a product of the cultural circumstances of its speakers, of their social and economic life, and of the historical development of that life, and that an accurate understanding of our speechways could have a positive effect on the well-being of all members of society.

These ideas made McDavid a primary force in the development of sociolinguistics. His first landmark article, "Postvocalic /-r/ in South Carolina: A Social Analysis" (1948), shows a mature handling of the complex correlations between South Carolina culture and speakers' pronunciation of *r* after vowels. Another benchmark, "The Relationship of the Speech of American Negroes to the Speech of Whites" (1951, written with Virginia G. McDavid), provided a corrective to common misapprehensions about the speech of blacks long before black English became a sociolinguistic industry. McDavid was in the vanguard of those examining the effects of population movements and urbanization upon our speech, and, in an effort to carry benefits from dialectology to a wide audience, McDavid also promoted applications of his research, especially for the schools. McDavid studied the speech of all regions of the United States but never forgot his roots in the South: his extensive bibliography is studded with both technical and popular essays such as "The Position of the Charleston Dialect" (1955), "Changing Patterns of Southern Dialects" (1970), and "Prejudice and Pride: Linguistic Acceptability in South Carolina" (1977, written with Raymond K. O'Cain).

William A. Kretzschmar, Jr.
University of Wisconsin—
Whitewater

McDavid's articles cited above are reprinted in one or both of two collections of his essays: William A. Kretzschmar, Jr., ed., *Dialects in Culture: Essays in General Dialectology by Raven I. McDavid, Jr.* (1979); and Anwar Dil, ed., with a bibliography by William A. Kretzschmar, Jr., *Varieties of American English: Essays by Raven I. McDavid, Jr.* (1980) ☆

OUTER BANKS DIALECT

Early settlement, separation from the mainland, and cultural isolation shaped the distinctive speech patterns of the Outer Banks in North Carolina. The relic dialect spoken by Outer Banks residents has, through cultural and geographic isolation, preserved some archaisms and linguistic divergences.

Settlement of the Outer Banks started in the first quarter of the 18th century and was relatively complete by midcentury. Most of the settlers were originally of English descent and came to the Outer Banks from Tidewater Virginia and the Albemarle Sound region and from other settlements to the south and west. Until the introduction of highways, vehicles, mailboats, ferries, and modern conveniences such as improved fishing rigs and refrigeration, the people had little to do with outsiders, or "strangers," as they tended to call them. Just when others began to think of them—or they, of themselves—as "Bankers" or "different" is hard to tell, but their cultural habits and speechways probably began to take on a distinctive color early in the 19th century. Even though Outer Banks residents live in an area stretching over 150 miles along the Carolina coastline, they are somewhat homogeneous socially; whether their language is homogeneous is a different

matter. Exact statements about the diversity of speech among the villagers need more detailed study.

The distinctiveness of Outer Banks speech has been long recognized by laymen and specialists alike. Lay observers mislead others when they characterize the Outer Banks speech as Old English or Elizabethan English. They notice the unfamiliar, but the tenacious use of *pint* for *point*, *bile* for *boil*, *holp* for *help*, *tard* for *tired*, *cam* for *calm*, and *hit* for *it* makes no particular claim for antiquity or distinctiveness. Outer Banks speech is not, therefore, Elizabethan—or, for that matter, 18th-century English—but clearly it is different and may be accurately called a "relic dialect." As a rule, the speech follows that of the coastal South, but it differs significantly in some respects. The dialect of the Bankers derived from 17th-century British English, which at the time reflected much regional and social diversity, but since then it has taken on a character that deserves such labels as "Outer Banks speech" or the "Outer Banks brogue."

Like other relic dialects, the Outer Banks dialect is most distinctive in pronunciation, not in word forms, grammar, and vocabulary. In vocabulary, as one would expect, the Outer Banks is southern and eastern, but not exclusively so. With reference to the hour, *quarter to*, a southern expression, stands alongside *quarter of* and *quarter till*, northern and midland expressions respectively. Outer Banks residents use *breezing up*, *squall*, *gutters*, and *kerosene*, the last of which shows some influence from the North. *Coal oil*, a midland term used frequently by Chesapeake Bay fishermen, rarely, if ever, occurs on the Outer Banks. *Spider*, a New England feature, is heard, but *skillet*, primarily a midland term, is the normal word. *Armful* (of wood), distinctively a midland term, is used over *turn-of-wood*, the usual southern form. *Lightwood* and *curtains*, basically southern forms, are heard in some villages rather than *kindling* and *window shades*. Sometimes *coal hod* and *corn husks*, typically northern forms, are found beside *coal skuttle* and *corn shucks*. *Comforter*, the northern form, is more common than the usual southern form, *comfort*. *Throw-up* is used more than *vomiting*, but *spew* and *puke* are also heard. A local word rarely heard elsewhere is *mammock*, "tear in shreds," which some dictionaries list as obsolete or "dialectal."

As they do among fishermen everywhere along the coast, certain nautical terms persist. Among them are *nor'east* or *no'theast*, *sou'west*, *windward*, and *leeward* (the last two respectively pronounced as "win'erd" and "loo'erd"), and for rising and falling tides, *flood tide* and *ebb tide*. For a grove of trees on certain parts of the islands *hammock* is used; and for menhaden, the oily fish used for fertilizer and cosmetics, *fatback*, which seems to be limited to the Outer Banks. Two other interesting usages are *abreast*, "across from," and *to* as in "he's to the marina."

There are few, if any, words and expressions that are exclusively and characteristically Banker ones. But what is important is that the language of Outer Banks residents, like that common to the islanders of the Chesapeake, shows northern and midland, as well as southern, influences.

Their pronunciation is quite another thing, often described as a "strange accent" or "brogue." But even in pronunciation, the language poses few problems once an outsider gets attuned to the intonation patterns. There is a strong pronunciation of *r* after vowels and in the final position of words in examples like *farm*, *thirty*, *door*, *car*, and *dinner*. This feature stands against the mixed pattern of *r*-lessness historically found on the coastal mainland of the Atlantic Seaboard. The most distinctive feature is the quality of the vowel in words like *eyes*, *tie*, *tide*, *light*, and *time*, which many journalists and other visitors erroneously report as rhyming with *toy*. They, for example, distort the Bankers' pronunciation of *high tide* as "hoy toyde." The sound is highly recognizable and clearly identified, but its precise quality cannot accurately be indicated without phonetic notation.

Another feature long recognized by mainland North Carolinians, but also difficult to describe, is what linguists refer to as the centralization of onsets of the vowels in words like *east*, *beach*, and *three* and in *great*, *age*, and *eight*. In these words the vowels have the "uh" sound as if the first syllable of "about" occurs before them, giving the impression of hearing several vowels. Moreover, the vowels in some words are fronted, for example: *musty* and *rusty* are pronounced with the vowel sound of "rest," and *boat* with the vowel sound of "boot." Words like *dish*, *fish*, and *wish* have their vowels fronted and raised to the vowel sound in "be." One also hears *year*, *hear*, and *ear* pronounced with the vowel sound in "fur." These features are benchmarks of a single dialect, even though they crop up in widely separated areas. They represent important linguistic traditions associated with the Outer Banks.

See also ENVIRONMENT: / Outer Banks

David L. Shores
Old Dominion University

Robert Howren, *American Speech* (October 1962); Hilda Jaffee, *Publication of the American Dialect Society* (November 1973); David Stick, *The Outer Banks of North Carolina* (1958). ☆

RANDOLPH, VANCE
IIIIIIIIIIIIIIIIIIIIIIIIIIIIIIIIIIIIIIIIIIIIIIIII
(1892–1980) Folklorist.

Vance Randolph's academic training was in psychology (M.A., Clark University, 1915) and Randolph described himself most often as a "hack writer." The shelf of books resulting from his long lifetime's work in the Arkansas and Missouri Ozarks, however, is responsible for Vance Randolph's continuing reputation as one of the nation's premier regional folklorists.

Randolph was born in Pittsburg, Kan., just west of the Ozarks, but he lived his adult life in small Missouri (Pineville, Galena) and Arkansas (Eureka Springs, Fayetteville) towns, where he assiduously sought out and perpetuated in print and on recordings the sayings, doings, singings, and believings

Vance Randolph, linguist and folklorist, 1930s

of his Ozark neighbors. His first books, *The Ozarks* (1931) and *Ozark Mountain Folks* (1932), are long out of print but remain notable as excellent examples of what later were called folklife studies. Randolph's methods and definitions were often in advance of their time; he included, for example, discographical references to "hillbilly" records in his four-volume folksong collection *Ozark Folksongs* (1946–50) at a time when many scholars found such recordings unworthy of notice. As early as 1956 he was urging the notion of folklife museums upon Arkansans, suggesting that they "imitate, in a small way, the work of the State Historical Association at Cooperstown, New York."

Randolph first achieved renown as a student of dialect when his article-length studies were lavishly praised by H. L. Mencken. His major work in this area, *Down in the Holler: A Gallery of Ozark Folk Speech*, did not appear until 1953. Along with his massive folksong collection, the 1940s saw the publication of Randolph's major study of folk belief, *Ozark Superstitions*, in 1947. In the 1950s Randolph published five volumes of folktales, including *We Always Lie to Strangers: Tall Tales from the Ozarks*. A collection of jokes, *Hot Springs and Hell*, appeared in 1965, and Randolph's huge bibliographic work, *Ozark Folklore: A Bibliography*, was published in 1972. His classic collection of bawdy humor, *Pissing in the Snow*, was finally published in 1976. Taken together, Randolph's many books provide a detailed and sympathetic portrait of Ozark traditional life. Academic folklorists honored Randolph in 1978 by electing him a Fellow of the American Folklore Society.

Robert Cochran
University of Arkansas

Robert Cochran, *Vance Randolph: An Ozark Life* (1985). ☆

SCHELE DE VERE, MAXIMILIAN VON
||||||||||||||||||||||||||||||||||||||||||||||||
(1820–1898) Linguist.

Schele was Professor of Modern Languages at the University of Virginia from 1844 to 1895. He taught French, Spanish, German, Anglo-Saxon, Latin, and modern history and participated actively in university governance. His publications include *Stray Leaves from the Book of Nature* (1855), *Studies in English* (1867), and *The Great Empress* (1870), a novel. Schele (pronounced shay-lee) also translated German romances, wrote grammars of Spanish and French (which Robert E. Lee thought too complicated), and contributed to periodicals like *Harper's New Monthly Magazine*.

A native Swede, Schele had studied at Bonn, Berlin (Ph.D., 1841), and Greifswald and had served in the Prussian army—a family tradition—before immigrating to Boston in 1843 and then to Virginia. During the Civil War of 1861–65, he functioned as drillmaster to the university's faculty defense squad, and in 1863 he prepared for a secret diplomatic mission to Napoleon III. But he never saw action or left Virginia during the war.

Students liked Schele, and William Dwight Whitney recognized his *Outlines of Comparative Philology* (1853) as a groundbreaking popularization. However, Schele's ignorance of articulatory phonetics encouraged absurd etymologizing, as, for example, that English *more* and *most* derived from *to mow* because "what was mown made a little heap." Schele's acquaintance with Bopp, Humboldt, and Grimm nevertheless placed him one step ahead of Noah Webster.

And in spite of phonological innocence, Schele was the first Virginia professor, perhaps the first in the United States, to teach spoken along with written language, a revolutionary feature of Jefferson's original plan. Working at a leading southern university, Schele frequently studied southern words and became, in effect, an early student of language in the region as well as the nation.

Schele considered language "a faculty, planted in the inmost nature of man," but his professorship required him to teach both language and the ethnological history of modern Europe, a circumstance that led to repeated theorizing about the bonds between language and culture. In this field, his most enduring work was *Americanisms: The English of the New World* (1871), a precursor of Mencken's *The American Language. Americanisms* achieved a novel effect by discussing American English topically (e.g., the influence of the Indian, the railroad, cant, and slang) rather than in dictionary form. And 50 years after its publication, Sir William Craigie still considered *Americanisms* "a treasure trove."

The *Dictionary of American English* credits Schele with having discovered the earliest uses of *bob*, "sled," *bound*, "resolved," *hike up*, "rise," among others. Furthermore, he contributed useful material on *benzene, buckra, yam, tar heel, lynch, saloon, bar-tender, sleeper, derail, ditch* (verb), *be* (as finite verb), *hired man, casket, pew*, and many others. On the negative side, Schele was capable of explaining *papoose* as a corruption of *babies*. Such nonsense aside, his generous enthusiasm for everything American added new illustrative material, new definitions, and even a few successful etymologies to the record. *Americanisms* remains, moreover, an entertaining treatment of how "we still speak English, but we talk American."

Michael I. Miller
Virginia Commonwealth University

Michael Crowell, "The Lexicography of Americanisms to 1900" (Ph.D. dissertation, Northwestern University, 1966); Atcheson L. Hench, *Publication of the American Dialect Society* (1966); David W. Maurer and Atcheson L. Hench, *Studies in Linguistics in Honor of Raven I. McDavid, Jr.* (1972). ☆

LAW

MAXWELL BLOOMFIELD

The Catholic University of America

CONSULTANT

☆ ☆ ☆ ☆ ☆ ☆ ☆ ☆ ☆ ☆

*Overleaf: Outside a courtroom, Decatur
County, Georgia.*

LAW AND SOUTH-ERN SOCIETY

IIIIIIIIIIIIIIIIIIIIIIIIIIIIIIIIIIIIIIIIIIIIIIIIIIIIIIIIIIIIIIIIIIIII

The legal history of the South, apart from the topic of slavery, has not yet been explored in a systematic way, although pioneering essays and monographs on specialized subjects have begun to appear in recent years. Until scholars know more about regional patterns of legislative and judicial policy-making—the selective borrowing of one state's institutions by another—they can only sketch the possible contours of a distinctively southern legal culture. At the outset, moreover, it must be emphasized that southern lawyers and statesmen have always shared the core values of the Anglo-American legal tradition and have never tried to create an alternative system, even in antebellum times. Although Louisiana did adopt the civil law of France as the basis of its legal system, it modified the Napoleonic Code in many ways to reflect the more liberal mores of a republican society. The revised constitutions adopted by the South Atlantic states before the Civil War displayed the same democratizing trends in voting and officeholding requirements that characterized the constitutions of northern and midwestern states. Southerners who framed the Confederate Constitution included specific guarantees for the protection of slavery, but otherwise carried over verbatim most of the provisions of the U.S. Constitution.

Antebellum South. The peculiar legal needs of a developing plantation economy caused the jurisprudence of the Old South to diverge from national norms in some major ways. Historians have described antebellum southern society as partriarchal and particularistic, rooted in a class structure and in the traditional folkways of a scattered rural population. Unlike the modernizing commercial and industrial elites of the North, southern planters favored a nonbureaucratic legal system that left important public powers in the hands of private individuals. A personal and discretionary approach to the settlement of disputes suited the temper of the English and Scotch-Irish settlers who predominated throughout the South. Preindustrial attitudes and behavior—clan loyalties, submission to community standards, an unwritten code of masculine honor—remained strong in the Cotton Kingdom long after they had been displaced elsewhere by the more impersonal mores of a market-centered legal order. Without the presence of slavery, however, these factors would have produced only minor legal differences between the South and the rest of the nation. Every state, after all, possessed some idiosyncratic laws and institutions that grew out of diverse settlement patterns, geographic conditions, and socioeconomic needs. Slavery alone unified the South and shaped a unique regional mentality that found expression in every aspect of antebellum southern culture, including the law.

The slave codes established an oppressive system of social control that denied basic common-law and republican values. Common-law doctrines protected a person's natural rights of life, liberty, and property; republican ideology encouraged enterprising individuals to share in the risks and profits of a developing capitalist economy. But market individualism and personal autonomy had no place in slave law. The master-slave relation, unlike the employer-employee relation, rested not upon voluntary agreement, but upon force. Confronted with the impossible task of reconciling two antithetical labor systems within a single body of law, southern lawmakers tried to create a separate category of paternalistic regulations that defied the laissez-faire thrust of modern property law. Slave issues could not be completely divorced from the rest of American law, however, nor could masters always claim exclusive control over their slaves. Personal injuries, contracts, and crimes often involved nonslaveholding whites, and southern judges in such situations looked for guidance to the leading decisions of northern jurists. As the Civil War approached, capitalistic values made increasing inroads into the law of slavery and threatened to undermine even the status slaves had as "chattels personal."

In mortgage cases involving slaves, for example, some southern courts at first fashioned equitable remedies to preserve slave families and to give hard-pressed masters additional time to redeem their slaves. By the 1850s, however, judges had become more responsive to the legal claims of creditors and tended to treat slaves no differently from other forms of property subject to forced sale. (Harriet Beecher Stowe did not exaggerate the cruelty of slave auctions in her classic *Uncle Tom's Cabin*.) The treatment of slave victims

and defendants in criminal cases followed a similar pattern. Although a few judges made common-law protections available to slaves through statutory construction, most agreed that slaves had no enforceable legal rights. The slave codes did prohibit the worst kinds of white abuse, such as maiming and killing, but penalties varied greatly, depending on whether the offender was a master, a lessee, an overseer, or a total stranger. Such a classification scheme strongly resembled that used to compensate any property owner for the loss or impairment of a valuable commodity.

Did a paternalistic or anticommercial ethic significantly influence other areas of law in the antebellum South? Preliminary inquiries by historians indicate that southern lawmakers espoused some policies that may actually have impeded the region's economic development. Despite the emergence elsewhere of a modern contract law based upon objective market values, southern judges adhered for decades to the older standard of a "just price" and protected individuals from the consequences of one-sided bargains. In insolvency cases, courts displayed unusual sympathy for debtors, and attachment laws exempted from seizure much property that would have been available to creditors in many northern states. Although legislatures throughout the South chartered banks, railroads, and other corporations, judges often resisted the principle of limited liability for stockholders and refused to apply other procorporate doctrines, such as the fellow servant rule, that had become standard in the industrial Northeast. The pervasive localism of the Old South further insured that small railroads, built to serve the limited needs of inland farmers and merchants, would not be consolidated into efficient trunk lines.

For the enforcement of their laws and customs, southerners relied much more than other Americans upon informal agencies of social control. In every southern state, the judicial and police systems were rudimentary and weak, compared to the bureaucratic structures that existed in the North; and southerners sought extralegal solutions to many problems that would have been resolved elsewhere through litigation. The gentlemanly elite—large planters, merchants, and professionals—demanded reparation for personal insults on the dueling ground; slaveholders dispensed discretionary justice on their plantations, which resembled slave prisons in some ways, and convened special courts to settle neighborhood slave disputes; and slave patrols, made up in large part of nonslaveholders, served as a private police force to apprehend runaway slaves and prevent insurrections. As the antislavery movement intensified after 1830, local vigilance committees incited mobs to assault (and sometimes kill) abolitionist critics, while other vigilante groups meted out summary punishment to those who violated a community's moral standards, such as gamblers and prostitutes.

States' Rights. To defend their slave society against political interference from the more numerous free states of the Union, southern theorists developed a states' rights argument based upon a compact model of constitutionalism. In the Virginia and Kentucky resolutions of 1798 and 1799, Thomas Jefferson and James Madison contended that the states had delegated only limited powers to the national government and could interpose their authority to prevent the

implementation of unwarranted federal policies within their borders. Antebellum law students, most of whom were self-taught, learned strict constructionist and states' rights principles from the appendix to St. George Tucker's edition of *Blackstone's Commentaries* (1803), the most widely read legal text in the nation prior to 1852. Southern law schools, such as the University of Virginia Law School, combined Tucker's *Blackstone's Commentaries* with later states' rights commentaries on the Constitution to train generations of elite practitioners and judges in the ways of "true republicanism." The proslavery argument culminated in the *Dred Scott* decision of 1857, in which Chief Justice Roger B. Taney held that Congress had an affirmative duty under the Fifth Amendment to protect slave property in all federal territories. When antislavery forces captured the presidency in the election of 1860, 11 southern states declared the constitutional compact broken and seceded from the Union to form a new government, the Confederate States of America.

Although founded as the expression of a distinct regional subculture, the Confederacy had little time to establish its separatist claims. Four years of bloody fighting and military defeat left the South devastated, slavery abolished, and the national government in apparently firm control of the reconstruction process. Legal differences between the South and other regions thereafter diminished perceptibly, as improved transportation and communication networks brought southerners into ever-closer contact with modern corporate America. The transition from patriarchy to mass society was slow and painful, however, and antebellum folkways continued to influence the developing law of labor relations, family relations, and civil rights.

The Law and Postwar Economic Adjustment. Since emancipation made the law of master and slave irrelevant, southern planters sought new legal means to control a work force of "free" blacks. At first they insisted that the freedmen sign long-term written contracts that tied them to the land for a full year in return for share wages. Military commanders and officials of the Freedmen's Bureau approved such arrangements, which promised to stabilize agricultural production and enable landless exslaves to become property owners in time. But the planters and their legal allies soon managed to circumvent the rights of tenants under existing law by constructing a novel system of sharecropping that was peculiar to the South. The cropper, unlike the tenant, had no possessory rights in the land he farmed but was merely a wage worker, subject in practice to whatever conditions his employer imposed. Farm credit legislation further contributed to a vicious debt cycle that impoverished many white yeoman farmers and brought croppers and tenants alike under the permanent control of a new business class of landlords and merchants.

The Redeemer legislatures of the post-Reconstruction 1870s enacted crop-lien laws that greatly increased the power of rural creditors. Landlord-tenant law had long recognized a landlord's right to seize the crop of a tenant who had not paid his rent; the new legislation extended the rental lien to cover all advances made by a landlord or merchant and exempted little or none of a debtor's personal property from attachment. If the sale of a particular crop did not repay all advances, southern courts ruled that the remaining indebtedness would operate as a preferred lien on future crops. The only way a poor farmer could escape from a mounting burden of debt was to move away and find a new landlord, but lawmakers foreclosed this possibility by using the criminal law to enforce contractual duties. Antienticement statutes made it a criminal offense for anyone to hire a laborer already under contract; other laws imposed criminal penalties upon those who failed to fulfill a contract after receiving money or other advances from an employer. Despite the doubtful constitutionality of such measures, they remained in effect in many southern states well into the 20th century.

Black tenant farmers and sharecroppers suffered most from the neopaternalism of postwar labor relations. Just as the black codes of 1865–66 had attempted to compel freedmen to work, the contract-labor laws and analogous vagrancy statutes established a modern system of peonage in the South. A defaulting black farm worker might be arrested and returned to his workplace; an unemployed stranger in town might be charged with vagrancy and put to work on a road gang or sent to a backwoods plantation until he earned enough money to pay his fine. Although the Thirteenth Amendment clearly prohibited such "involuntary servitude," peonage persisted in some southern areas for decades and may not be completely eradicated today. By appealing to customary bonds of deference and personal loyalty as well as to comprehensive laws, southern landlords achieved a degree of control over their work force unmatched by employers elsewhere in the nation. Local power structures did not begin to collapse until the emergence of

New Deal farm policies in the 1930s. As federal agencies, such as the Agricultural Adjustment Administration and the Farm Security Administration, set production quotas and regulated farm credit, southern agriculture lost its distinctive legal characteristics and entered the age of mechanization and standardization in earnest.

Did regional values play as important a role in shaping the industrial policies of the New South? On the basis of available historical research, it seems doubtful that they did. From the beginning of industrialization in the late 19th century, southern workers engaged in proportionally as many strikes as their northern counterparts and maintained a consistently high level of union organizing activity. Although southern mill-owners and manufacturers treated their employees in a paternalistic and arbitrary fashion, northern industrialists, such as George Pullman and Henry Ford, behaved in much the same way.

Southern legislatures were slow to enact workmen's compensation statutes—Mississippi, the last holdout in the nation, capitulated only in 1948— while right-to-work laws and other union-busting measures proliferated. Without comparative studies of regional labor practices, however, the distinc-

A jury section in a courtroom, Franklin, Georgia, 1941

tiveness of the southern experience remains unclear. The changes in class relations introduced by the factory system may well have evoked similar responses from employers and lawmakers everywhere. By the 1930s, in any event, the passage of the National Labor Relations Act, the Fair Labor Standards Act, and other congressional measures effectively ended any lingering claims of regional autonomy, as the federal government began to regulate labor conditions throughout the country.

Family and Religion. Ongoing research in family law suggests that the late 19th century also witnessed the reconstruction of domestic relations in the South. Prior to the Civil War, southern judges tended to uphold patriarchal authority in the household and seldom intervened in family matters except to protect wives and children from physical abuse. Although Mississippi inaugurated a nationwide movement toward married women's property acts in 1839, such laws gave wives only limited control of their separate estates. Rather, they served, especially in the South, to protect a woman's blood relatives by shielding family assets from the creditors of an improvident husband. Liberalized divorce laws, which opened the courts to women of the middle and lower classes in the North, received restrictive interpretations from many southern jurists and benefited primarily the wives of the propertied elite. In child custody cases, southern appellate judges lagged behind their northern counterparts in acknowledging the separate interests of wives and children and almost invariably denied challenges to parental authority from relatives or other third parties.

The defeat of the Confederacy marked

the end of a patriarchal slaveholding society and left many southern widows in charge of one-parent households. Courts responded to these realities by playing a more active supervisory role in family disputes and by scrutinizing more rigorously the behavior of husbands and fathers. In an increasing number of cases judges awarded custody rights to mothers and third parties, while narrowing the scope of other common-law doctrines of paternal power. Although patriarchal values continued to influence many areas of jurisprudence (as they did, to a lesser extent, in other regions), the modernization of southern family law was virtually complete by the turn of the century. Jurists now embraced a more psychological and contractual view of domestic relations and used their power to reshape conditions within the home. Instead of relying on a network of patriarchs to preserve social order, they linked family members directly to the state through new forms of public control. By doing so, they entered the mainstream of American legal history.

Law and religion have long influenced each other in the South. The fundamentalist outlook so noticeable in the region's spiritual life has also been present in attitudes toward the law. Southerners have had great respect for the U.S. Constitution of 1787, for example, as shown in a literal-minded adherence to its supposed original meaning. They made few changes in the federal Constitution in adapting it as the Constitution of the Confederate States of America. Before and after the Civil War the South has reiterated the belief in the supremacy of an unchanging, literally interpreted constitution and has looked upon itself, in historian Charles S. Sydnor's words, "as the special custodian

and defender" of this near sacred legal document.

Southerners have often used the legal system to maintain the moral code of the Protestant churches. To be sure, the Baptist tradition includes belief in the separation of church and state, and the southern Presbyterian doctrine of "the spirituality of the church" taught that the church was a strictly religious, not secular, institution. Southerner Thomas Jefferson's "Bill for Establishing Religious Freedom" in 1786 disestablished religion in Virginia and contributed to the federal government's guarantees of religious freedom as expressed in the First Amendment.

Most religious southerners have, nevertheless, seen strict obedience to the moral law as prime evidence of a Christian society and have suppressed doubts they might have had about using the legal system to achieve that society. Gerald Johnson saw southerners committing "the heresy that equates legality with morality." When antislavery advocates attacked slavery, the southern defense was a typical one, citing chapter and verse of a literal reading of selected biblical passages suggesting God's sanctioning of the institution. Before the Civil War southern believers, moreover, campaigned for strict enforcement of blue laws promoting Sabbath observance and, after 1839, for state legislation enforcing prohibition in the sale of alcoholic beverages. The Methodists and Presbyterians led the antebellum temperance campaign, but southern reformers were less successful than those in the North. After Reconstruction, the southern temperance movement gained strength, as Methodists and Baptists, the relative latecomers to the issue, led the call for nationwide prohibition. Religious leaders and institutions crusaded also for still stricter enforcement of Sabbath observance, control of gambling, and the limitation or prohibition of dancing, card playing, and professional sports activities. The churches favored rigorous enforcement of the Eighteenth Amendment when it established national prohibition and, after repeal of the amendment in 1933, they continued to support legal prohibition at state and local levels.

The late 1970s and 1980s have witnessed a resurgence of conservative legal moralism in the South, as in the nation. The Moral Majority, a Virginia-based organization associated with Jerry Falwell, has established a *legal* agenda, especially centering on the constitutional amendment, as a way of achieving such moral goals as opposition to abortion and the promotion of school prayer.

Civil Rights. In the field of civil rights law southern resistance to change was particularly intense and unyielding. Although Congress intended to place the civil rights of freedmen and other Americans under comprehensive federal protection through the Thirteenth, Fourteenth, and Fifteenth Amendments, the U.S. Supreme Court blocked the nationalizing potential of these measures by construing their provisions narrowly. In the *Civil Rights Cases* (1883), for example, the Court ruled that the Fourteenth Amendment prohibited only state violations of individual rights; acts of private discrimination remained subject to state, not federal, control.

Encouraged by judicial adherence to antebellum principles of federalism, southern states proceeded to construct an elaborate caste system that prescribed racial segregation in restaurants, schools, housing, theaters, public conveyances, and other facilities. The Supreme Court approved such Jim Crow laws as reasonable exercise of a state's police power in *Plessy* v. *Ferguson* (1896). Reflecting the social Darwinist temper of the time, Justice Henry Billings Brown noted: "In determining the question of reasonableness [a state legislature] is at liberty to act with reference to the established usages, customs, and traditions of the people, and with a view to the promotion of their comfort, and the preservation of the public peace and good order." Customary racial practices in the South thus gained new legitimacy at the hands of the nation's highest court. With the further imposition of poll taxes, literacy tests, and other electoral "reforms" in the 1890s, southern lawmakers completed a modern structure of racial suppression. Its victims—the mass of poor southern blacks as well as poor whites—found themselves effectively disfranchised and unable even to protest their degradation through normal political channels.

As in antebellum days, a mix of public and private law enforcement agencies policed the social order and used terror as a major weapon against blacks and other suspect groups. Professional police forces, whose capabilities varied greatly from place to place, tended on the whole to be politicized and often corrupt. Nor could black defendants in criminal cases expect impartial treatment from southern trial judges, who usually shared the racial outlook of their local white electorates. At times, indeed, the official system of criminal justice openly flouted the requirements of due process. In the notorious Scottsboro case of the 1930s, successive all-white juries found a group of young blacks guilty on rape charges, despite the absence of any meaningful evidence against them. Such flagrant miscarriages of justice were uncommon, however. With all their faults, southern courts and other public agencies at least professed respect for individual rights and operated according to fixed procedures. The same could not be said of vigilantes, who also flourished in the New South as the self-appointed defenders of a crumbling agrarian culture.

The Ku Klux Klan, the most celebrated vigilante organization, arose during Reconstruction to preserve white supremacy by intimidating black voters and their Republican allies. In the 1920s and the 1950s a revived Klan resorted to further acts of violence and terrorism in defense of white Anglo-Saxon Protestant hegemony and the folkways of a vanishing rural society. Such planned violence formed part of a larger pattern of regional lawlessness that included an alarming increase in lynchings between the 1880s and World War II. Most lynch victims in the South were blacks and most lynchings went unpunished because of the obvious collusion that existed between law officers and local mobs. Antilynching organizations, including the Atlanta-based Commission on Interracial Cooperation and its affiliate, the Association of Southern Women for the Prevention of Lynching, called repeatedly for strong federal legislation to remedy the problem. But southern senators filibustered all proposed antilynching bills to death, invoking states' rights and racist arguments that might have been lifted from the congressional slavery debates of the 1850s. Like their antebellum counterparts, the statesmen of the New South took an inflexible stand on racial issues and refused to bow to changing circumstances.

Civil libertarians, on the other hand, had never accepted the caste laws of the late 19th century. From the beginning many black communities, often inspired by charismatic black ministers, engaged in economic boycotts and other forms of protest against local segregationist measures. The pioneer black lawyers of Galveston, Tex., sought to mobilize black voters by establishing a Poll Tax Club and also challenged Jim Crow laws in the local courts. Some of their arguments anticipated those found in successful Supreme Court briefs of the 1930s. Further research in the records of southern trial courts—a source hitherto neglected by most historians—should uncover other patterns of early civil rights litigation.

With the founding of the National Association for the Advancement of Colored People (NAACP) in 1909, civil rights strategy began to be formulated on an interstate basis. By the 1930s black NAACP attorneys launched a carefully orchestrated legal campaign that culminated in *Brown* v. *Board of Education* (1954). The *Brown* decision—handed down by a unanimous Warren Court—rejected *Plessy* v. *Ferguson* and held that segregated schools violated the equal protection clause of the Fourteenth Amendment. Because of the long-standing and complex nature of the segregation issue, however, the Court granted state school boards a reasonable time in which to submit desegregation plans to federal district judges for their approval.

Southern authorities responded to *Brown* by vowing noncompliance. White Citizens' Councils called for a return to antebellum policies of interposition and nullification; police assaulted peaceful black demonstrators; and some state legislatures replaced their public schools with "private" institutions. Despite the rise of "massive resistance," however, southern whites remained deeply divided over civil rights. The economic boom that accompanied World War II had accelerated the urban and industrial development of the South and created a large middle class of businessmen, professionals, and white-collar employees. These groups feared economic instability more than integration and helped to mediate tense racial confrontations, as in the Little Rock crisis of 1957. The Warren Court's reapportionment decisions strengthened urban liberalism by curbing the power of entrenched rural white minorities; both *Baker* v. *Carr* (1962) and *Reynolds* v. *Sims* (1964) struck down unrepresentative political structures in southern states. Yet the Second Reconstruction stalled until Congress belatedly passed a comprehensive Civil Rights Act in 1964 and the supplementary Voting Rights Act the following year. Vigorous federal enforcement of these measures brought a recalcitrant South under control at last. By the early 1970s every southern state had made substantial progress toward the integration of public facilities.

Southern legal culture today displays no striking deviations from national norms. Even professional training has become standardized and homogenized through the accreditation requirements imposed upon law schools across the country. The legal props supporting white hegemony could not survive the collapse of the traditional rural society that had fostered their development. In the fast-paced and ultracompetitive world of the contemporary Sunbelt, the idea of a hierarchical and paternalistic legal order evokes only smiles—nostalgic in some cases, derisive or incredulous in others.

See also AGRICULTURE: Sharecropping and Tenancy; BLACK LIFE: Commission on Interracial Cooperation; POLITICS: Ideology, Political; Segregation, Defense of; RELIGION: Fundamentalism; VIOLENCE: Crime, Attitudes toward; Honor; / Ku Klux Klan, Culture of; Ku Klux Klan, History of; Mob Violence; Peonage

Maxwell Bloomfield
The Catholic University of America

Elizabeth K. Bauer, *Commentaries on the Constitution, 1790–1860* (1952); Maxwell Bloomfield, *American Lawyers in a Changing Society, 1776–1876* (1980), *Vanderbilt Law Review* (January 1979); David J. Bodenhamer and James W. Ely, Jr., eds., *Ambivalent Legacy: A Legal History of the South* (1984); W. Hamilton Bryson, ed., *Legal Education in Virginia, 1779–1979: A Biographical Approach* (1982); Harvey C. Couch, *A History of the Fifth Circuit, 1891–1981* (1984); Pete Daniel, *The Shadow of Slavery: Peonage in the South, 1901–1969* (1972); George Dargo, *Jefferson's Louisiana: Politics and the Clash of Legal Traditions* (1975); Fletcher M. Green, *Constitutional Development in the South Atlantic States, 1776–1860: A Study in the Evolution of Democracy* (1930); Steven Hahn, *Radical History Review* (September 1982); A. Leon Higginbotham, *In the Matter of Color: Race and the American Legal Process: The Colonial Period (1978)*; Michael S. Hindus, *Prison and Plantation: Crime, Justice, and Authority in Massachusetts and South Carolina, 1767–1878* (1980); Herbert A. Johnson, ed., *South Carolina Legal History* (1980); Richard Kluger, *Simple Justice: The History of Brown v. Board of Education and Black America's Struggle for Equality* (1976); Steven F. Lawson, *Black Ballots: Voting Rights in the South, 1944–1969* (1976); Suzanne D. Lebsock, *Journal of*

Southern History (May 1977); Gail W. O'Brien, *The Legal Fraternity and the Making of a New South Community, 1848–1882* (1986); William M. Robinson, Jr., *Justice in Grey: A History of the Judicial System of the Confederate States of America* (1941); A. G. Roeber, *Faithful Magistrates and Republican Lawyers: Creators of Virginia Legal Culture, 1680–1810* (1981); Charles S. Sydnor, *Journal of Southern History* (February 1940); "Symposium on the Legal History of the South," *Vanderbilt Law Review* (January 1979); Mark V. Tushnet, *The American Law of Slavery, 1810–1860: Considerations of Humanity and Interest* (1981); Harold D. Woodman, *Agricultural History* (January 1979). ☆

Civil Rights Movement

||||||||||||||||||||||||||||||||||||||||||||||||||||||||||||

After the Civil War many black leaders worked for equal status between blacks and whites. The most prominent spokesman for this aspiration in the early 20th century was W. E. B. Du Bois. The National Association for the Advancement of Colored People was founded in 1909, and a year later the National Urban League was organized. Nonetheless, the nation made little progress in the field of civil rights until the end of World War II.

The emergence of New Deal social programs and the egalitarian rhetoric of World War II produced a change in American thought and helped to undermine the intellectual justification for racial segregation in the South. In turn, this development produced a gradual but significant shift in the role of the federal government. President Harry S. Truman identified his administration with the movement for equal rights. In

1948 Truman issued an executive order eliminating segregation in the armed forces. He also called for a Fair Employment Practices Commission and a ban on poll taxes. Although Congress rejected Truman's legislative program, he established civil rights as a national issue. Moreover, the federal courts began to adopt a broader reading of the equal protection clause of the Fourteenth Amendment. During the late 1940s several Supreme Court decisions outlawed segregation in interstate transportation and higher education. This trend culminated with the historic 1954 decision in *Brown* v. *Board of Education*, which proscribed compulsory segregation in public schools as a violation of the equal protection clause.

Important new developments also took place at the state level and in the private sector. Several northern states passed laws against racial discrimination. In 1946 Jackie Robinson became the first black to play major league baseball. Four years later diplomat Ralph Bunche became the first black to win the Nobel Peace Prize.

The NAACP led the legal battle against segregation, working for civil rights legislation and instituting litigation to compel desegregation of public schools in the South. Despite the *Brown* ruling and pressure from the NAACP, only a limited amount of racial integration occurred in southern schools between 1954 and 1964. Most southern states rallied to the banner of "massive resistance" and sought to obstruct implementation of racial desegregation. President Dwight D. Eisenhower did not envision an active role for the federal government in promoting school desegregation. Nonetheless, he did send federal troops to Little Rock in 1957 when state authorities attempted to block implementation of a court-ordered desegregation plan.

Other organizations also struggled for equal rights. Foremost among these was the Southern Christian Leadership Conference, headed by Dr. Martin Luther King, Jr. Late in 1955 blacks in Montgomery, Ala., under King's guidance, began nonviolent protest by instituting a successful boycott of the city's segregated bus system.

During the early 1960s the civil rights movement underwent several important changes. After a period of hesitation, President John F. Kennedy placed the executive branch of the federal government squarely behind desegregation efforts. In 1963 Kennedy endorsed a broad civil rights proposal to outlaw segregation in public accommodations. At the same time, many blacks grew impatient with the slow progress in achieving desegregation. Blacks increasingly resorted to direct forms of protest. There were sit-ins at segregated lunch counters and Freedom Rides that challenged segregation in transportation facilities. Defenders of segregation often employed violence against blacks or civil right workers in an attempt to halt their activities.

The civil rights movement may have reached its climax in August of 1963 when more than 200,000 persons took part in the March on Washington. King, who had emerged as the leading spokesman for the civil rights movement, delivered an impassioned plea for racial equality. President Lyndon B. Johnson responded to this initiative by calling upon Congress to enact sweeping civil rights legislation. The resulting Civil Rights Act of 1964 required equal access to public accommodations and outlawed discrimination in employment. The Voting Rights Act of 1965 suspended literacy tests in several states and strengthened federal protection of the right to vote. The Twenty-fourth Amendment, ratified in 1964, barred poll tax requirements for participation in federal elections. Subsequently the Supreme Court declared unconstitutional the poll tax in state elections. Thus, by the mid-1960s the civil rights movement had attained most of its original objectives, which concerned conditions in the South.

The late 1960s saw a marked shift in the goals of civil rights leaders. The large-scale migration of blacks to northern cities, which had begun by World War I, produced recurrent ethnic conflict in urban neighborhoods. Accordingly, the movement increasingly focused upon racial discrimination in the North. In particular, black leaders challenged residential segregation, poor schooling, high unemployment among members of racial minorities, and alleged police brutality. Given the heavy concentration of impoverished blacks in the inner-city areas, resolution of these problems proved extremely difficult. Indeed, civil rights gains hardly affected the living conditions of many northern blacks. A wave of urban riots across the North highlighted racial tensions and also served to alienate white opinion.

In addition, by promoting new remedies for discrimination, civil rights activists moved well beyond the national consensus in favor of equality. The busing of pupils from one neighborhood to another in an effort to integrate schools, although endorsed by the Supreme Court in 1971, threatened traditional neighborhood schools and was opposed by the vast majority of whites. Congress debated numerous proposals to restrict this practice. In 1974 the Supreme Court ruled against busing across school district lines to achieve integration between suburban areas and the inner city. Affirmative action policies in employment and university admissions were widely perceived as favoritism to members of minority groups. In 1978 the Supreme Court outlawed the use of quotas to aid racial minorities in the university admissions process.

As a consequence of these trends during the 1970s the civil rights movement became increasingly fragmented and isolated from the opinions of a majority of whites. Civil rights supporters did win an extension of the Voting Rights Act in 1982.

See also BLACK LIFE: Freedom Movement, Black; / King, Martin Luther, Jr.; National Association for the Advancement of Colored People; Southern Christian Leadership Conference; MEDIA: Civil Rights and Media

James W. Ely, Jr.
Vanderbilt University

James W. Ely, Jr., *The Crisis of Conservative Virginia: The Byrd Organization and the Politics of Massive Resistance* (1976); Richard Kluger, *Simple Justice: The History of Brown v. Board of Education and Black America's Struggle for Equality* (1976); Anthony Lewis and the *New York Times*, *Portrait of a Decade: The Second American Revolution* (1964); Harvard Sitkoff, *A New Deal For Blacks: The Emergence of Civil Rights as a National Issue* (1978); J. Harvie Wilkinson III, *From Brown to Bakke: The Supreme Court and School Integration, 1954–1978* (1979). ☆

Common Law

||||||||||||||||||||||||||||||||||

The reception of English common law by the American colonies along the southern Atlantic Seaboard was largely a consequence of the shared cultural heritage of the dominant English-speaking folk. The continued growth and development of the common law in the South, however, was principally determined by external influences: (1) availability of case reports and law treatises, (2) legal training of the bar, and (3) a common English language. These factors not only resulted in the preservation of the common-law inheritance of the settlers but promoted resistance to Benthamite codification efforts surfacing in New England. These influences also encouraged the transplanting of the English-based common law to the South's western frontier.

To the colonists, legal tradition was embodied in the common law, which was in essence a set of personal rights in the form of procedures that governed and restricted the exercise of sovereign power. The view of common law as tradition and custom, the inherent birthright of the English settlers, became preserved in the form of judicial decisions and statutes. This enshrinement of the common-law heritage would have perhaps succumbed to external political movements favoring codification, however, but for the conservative influences of the entrenched professional bar of the South and a body of legal literature that enunciated the common-law tradition.

Early colonial America had no regular school of law. Unless American lawyers were so fortunate as to study in England with its Inns of Court, professors of law at Oxford and Cambridge, and learned judges, they entered practice with little formal law education, i.e., they only "read" law. For their instruction, postrevolutionary lawyers depended upon such literary sources as William Blackstone's *Commentaries on the Laws of England.* One cannot over-estimate the influence of Blackstone's *Commentaries* on the early bar of the American South. From this work, American lawyers acquired knowledge of natural law, common law, equity, and "the charter rights of Englishmen." Indeed, the *Commentaries* were probably more influential in the American South than in the British Isles. Blackstone's treatises remained the standard manual for the South's lawyers until the publication in 1826 to 1830 of Chancellor James Kent's *Commentaries on American Law.* These early sources of case law and commentary were at once highly traditional, grounded in precedents of actual experience, and capable of growth and adaptation. Thus, no perceived need existed for a comprehensive written code. Even though there were repeated attempts at codification in New England, all failed in the southern states (except, of course, in Louisiana, where a previous legal heritage prevailed before the entry of the common law).

As Americans settled west of the original 13 states of the young Republic, not only did they carry with them the common law, but often they found that it preceded their arrival. The governor and the judges of the Northwest Territory, for example, adopted the Virginia Act of Ratification (1788), which put into force in the area the common law of England and all English statutes of general application. Similarly, when the Mississippi Territory was established in 1798, its law embraced most of the provisions of the Northwest Ordinance and Virginia Act of Ratification as regarded the common law.

Generally being bookish people, the early frontier lawyers and judges brought the common law with them rather than making their own law, especially in the Old Southwest. As Judge Thomas Rodney of the Mississippi Territory wrote: "Special Pleading is adhered to in our Courts with as much strictness, elegance and propriety as many of the States, so that even the young lawyers are obliged to read their books and be very attentive to their business or want bread."

In addition to the treatises and doctrinal writings of Blackstone, Kent, and Joseph Story, frontier lawyers had access to an abundance of both English and American case reports, evident in their frequent citation of English and early American case precedents. In that way, the English common law was transmitted westward across the American South.

Ernest S. Easterly III
Baton Rouge, Louisiana

Interior of law library, City Hall, Memphis, Tennessee, date unknown

William Blackstone, *Commentaries on the Laws of England* (1765); Melvin E. Bradford, *A Better Guide Than Reason: Studies in the American Revolution* (1979); René David & J. E. C. Brierley, *Major Legal Systems of the World Today: An Introduction to the Comparative Study of Law* (1978); Ernest S. Easterly III, *Geojurisprudence: Studies in Law, Liberty and Landscapes* (1980); W. B. Hamilton, *South Atlantic Quarterly* (Spring 1968); Russell Kirk, *The Roots of American Order* (1974); A. Kocourek, *American Bar Association Journal*

(October 1932); Roscoe Pound, *The Spirit of Common Law* (1921). ☆

Criminal Justice

||||||||||||||||||||||||||||||||||||||||||||||

The South has a long-standing reputation for violence and criminal disorder. It also has an image as a region where violent white men went unpunished and where, until recently, citizens frequently resorted to vigilantism to maintain order. Recent scholars have blamed the region's poverty, its racism, its pessimistic view of human nature, and even its debatable Celtic heritage for this crime and violence. Historians have suggested that an ineffective legal system intensified the combativeness of southern society.

Two themes from the Old South—frontier individualism and the plantation system—have served most frequently to explain the legal system's inability to deal with crime. No one has advanced these ideas with more assurance than W. J. Cash in his book *The Mind of the South* (1941). To Cash, an intense individualism, buttressed by a belief in white supremacy, blunted the development of law and government, while the growth of the plantation system kept the police power decentralized. An effective legal system was neither expected nor desired.

Historians have done little to rebut Cash's interpretation. Charles S. Sydnor, for example, declared that just as geographical distance isolated the westerner from legal restraints, so "the social order diminished the force of law in the South." For other scholars the private discipline enforced by masters over their slaves found its counterpart in extralegal or illegal means of resolving disputes between whites.

Although an ineffective legal response to crime may be yet another burden of southern history, there are reasons to doubt traditional interpretations of its causes. Students of the westward movement are no longer so certain that the frontier experience was abnormally violent or excessively individualistic. Much of the frontier, including the South, was a peaceful place where settlers tried to maintain order and recreate community. The urban disorder of the 19th and 20th centuries, especially in the North, also makes it difficult to conclude that lawlessness was uniquely western or southern. Moreover, the idea that informal punishment of slaves diminished respect for legal process finds little support in recent scholarship. Several studies reveal a surprisingly high regard for due process in slave trials in the lower courts and upon appellate review. Thus, slavery may not have dulled the region's legal sensibilities, as many scholars have supposed.

Two other problems remain with older interpretations of southern criminal justice. Historians have rarely compared the southern experience with that of other states, even though such comparisons are essential to the argument that an inefficient criminal process was peculiarly southern. A more fundamental weakness is that the literature on southern justice often has not examined the best evidence of the region's legal behavior, local court records.

Recent efforts to gauge the response of local courts to crime suggest the need to revise significantly—but not to abandon completely—standard themes advanced by historians, especially as they apply to the colonial and antebellum South. There is considerable evidence, for example, of the inability of local southern courts to complete prosecution in a large percentage of criminal cases. An examination of colonial courts in North Carolina found that only half of all bills of indictment brought before the General Court reached trial; almost one criminal action in three simply disappeared from the system. More dismal figures surfaced in a study of four counties in antebellum Georgia, where just one case in four reached a decision on the merits of the accusation. But in neither instance was the southern experience unique. Comparisons with local courts in colonial New York and antebellum Indiana revealed strikingly similar patterns of ineffective prosecution. Southern law enforcement, in other words, was not atypical in its inability to secure judgments in criminal cases; the problem was endemic to rural, prebureaucratic communities in both the North and the South.

Many of the patterns of prosecution in southern jurisdictions parallel those found elsewhere. Most criminal actions involved petty offenses, although prosecutions for felonies consumed much of the time courts devoted to criminal matters. Of the more serious crimes, theft and other property offenses appeared regularly on criminal dockets, with urbanizing areas devoting considerable prosecutorial energy to these cases. The available data suggest, moreover, that southern grand juries and prosecutors, like their northern counterparts, identified those without property as offenders in such cases.

Crimes against morality also occupied the attention of local authorities. Although the incidence of prosecution was less than in the colonies and states of Puritan New England, gaming, liquor-related offenses, and sexual immorality were frequent crimes before southern trial courts. These findings not only suggest a modification in traditional interpretations that emphasize southern laxity in crimes against morality but also in recent arguments that 19th- and 20th-century criminal process ignored such crimes in its attempt to protect the economic order. Perhaps crime as theft replaced crime as sin in the criminal codes of other states, but southern courts continued the effort to maintain a common morality.

Of course, violent crime rather than theft or moral disorder gave the South its image as a lawless region. Tales of duels, murder, and assault were stock items in scores of travel accounts, newspapers stories, and grand jury presentments. Historians also have credited southerners with a readiness to settle private disputes with fists, dirks, or pistols. Examinations of felony indictments appear to confirm this conclusion. Crimes against persons were constant items on court dockets; some studies have discovered that almost 4 of every 10 indictments involved either petty or serious acts of personal violence. This circumstance, present in the earliest records, continues to exist. In the mid-1970s the southern states led the nation in these crimes. Forty-two percent of all murders in 1975 were committed in the South, and the region's fastest-growing urban area, Houston, had earned the name "Murder City" for its large number of capital crimes.

While the rate of indictments for violent behavior surpasses the standards for other regions, it is inaccurate to claim that grand juries and circuit solicitors ignored violent crime or treated it casually. Instead, the figures suggest that prosecution of violent crime was a central concern of the legal system. In cases tried to a verdict, moreover, the violent offender stood little chance of acquittal, especially in jurisdictions with urbanizing areas. The degree of success enjoyed by courts in securing convictions in cases of violent crime underscores the social agreement that law and not private vengeance provided the most acceptable method of resolving personal conflicts. For most southerners, criminal justice remained a matter for the courts.

See also VIOLENCE: Crime, Attitudes toward

David J. Bodenhamer
University of Southern Mississippi

Edward L. Ayers, *Vengeance and Justice: Crime and Punishment in the 19th Century South* (1984); David J. Bodenhamer, *Criminal Justice History* (1983); Bradley Chapin, *Criminal Justice in Colonial America, 1606–1660* (1983); Daniel Flanigan, *Journal of Southern History* (November 1974); Michael S. Hindus, *Prison and Plantation: Crime, Justice, and Authority in Massachusetts and South Carolina, 1767–1878* (1980); Kathryn Preyer, *Law and History Review* (Spring 1983); Philip J. Schwarz, *Ambivalent Legacy: A Legal History of the South*, ed. David J. Bodenhamer and James W. Ely, Jr. (1984); Donna J. Spindel and Stuart W. Thomas, Jr., *Journal of Southern History* (May 1983). ☆

Criminal Law

||||||||||||||||||||||||||||||||||||

Criminal law outlines standards of conduct for every member of the community and sets the punishment for violation of those rules. Its substance proscribes behavior that might variously be described as immoral, violent, disruptive of public order, or destructive of property rights and relationships. Its procedures seek to ensure that accused persons receive a fair hearing on the merits of charges against them. Yet, as sociologists, criminologists, and legal scholars have demonstrated in numerous studies, the law in operation at times bears little resemblance to its formal codes, maintaining a close, supportive relationship to the dominant class in society.

Historians have generally failed to study the South's criminal process. Nowhere is this neglect more pronounced than in the written and common law that defined criminal behavior. Available scholarship, however, tends to refute the traditional view of the South as a region with primitive, unenlightened penal codes. From the colonial period to the Civil War, southern legislators and jurists joined with reformers elsewhere to rid the law of the vast number of crimes and harsh punishments of 16th- and 17th-century England. Although the South moved to prescriptive or legislative law somewhat later than did New England, criminal law in the colonial South relied more heavily on English precedent. It was strongly affected by local interpretation and less reliant on biblical injunction than was true in the northern, especially Puritan, colonies.

The tenets of revolutionary republicanism demanded a limitation on the power of the state, thus stimulating reform of the criminal law throughout the new nation, including the South. Heavily influenced by 18th-century rationalism, the writings of Montesquieu and Cesare Beccaria, and the codification efforts of Edward Livingston, southern legislators by the 1820s had drafted criminal codes that rivaled those of northern jurisdictions. In fact, some scholars have labeled Georgia's code of 1816 the first successful codification of criminal law in the new Republic. Reforms included a sharp reduction in the number of statutory crimes and in the punishments prescribed for their commission. Capital crimes for whites were limited to treason (rarely enforced), murder, arson, and rape of a minor; and imprisonment in a state penitentiary—originally created as a place for the reformation of the individual miscreant—became the norm for most other serious crimes. Criminal procedures conformed closely to the due process requirements of state and federal bills of rights, at least as interpreted by 19th-century judges and commentators. Recent studies of local trial courts, moreover, reveal that patterns of prosecution, conviction, and sentencing paralleled those found in non-southern jurisdictions with similar demographic and economic characteristics.

These reforms in the written criminal law did not, however, apply to slaves, and in practice their application to free blacks was uncertain and idiosyncratic. Separate laws for slaves, often called black codes, prescribed different courts, fewer procedural safeguards for defendants, and harsher punishment upon conviction. In addition, enforcement of punishment for misdemeanors and even some felonies was often left to owners or overseers.

It would not be accurate to claim that trial and punishment of criminal slaves fell outside the legal system or that their treatment was totally at the whim of the master. Undoubtedly, justice at the local level varied widely, depending upon the locale, the ratio of blacks to whites, and the nature of the crime. But historians have probably overestimated the degree of discretionary justice attendant upon slave trials. Several studies reveal a surprisingly high regard for due process in the lower courts and upon appellate review. This result should not suggest that the white South was wedded to the concept of equal rights before the law for slaves, but rather that the application of due process in these cases satisfied the formal requirements of a legal culture without jeopardizing white control over blacks. Procedural safeguards for slaves and free blacks were, for example, at risk whenever black violence threatened the status quo.

In one area of criminal law, namely, statutory prohibitions of immorality, the South differed from the North. Laws against crimes such as adultery, fornication, intemperance, and gambling remained prominent in southern codes long after northern legislatures had shifted attention to property and economic crimes. Crime as theft may have replaced crime as sin elsewhere, but official regulation of immoral conduct continued to be a feature of the criminal law in southern states. It was no accident that prohibition and other moral crusades found ready reception in the South; the region's legal system had a long history of attempting to regulate morality.

The abolition of slavery and an increased level of violence that followed the Civil War caused dramatic changes in southern criminal law. Separate courts and codes for blacks disappeared, but the law did not suddenly become color-blind. A breakdown of the traditions that, together with the plantation system, had kept the races separate led to late 19th-century revisions in criminal law designed to punish violations of racial separation, although most of the infractions were properly classed as misdemeanors rather than felonies. Extralegal actions, especially lynching and vigilante actions, were used for more serious violations of racial and moral order.

Except for the area of race, southern criminal laws in the 20th century resembled those in other regions of the country. Codes became more complex and defined more possible criminal actions as the South became more urban and industrial. But there remained some differences between South and North. Although details are sketchy, southern lawmakers and prosecutors appeared less willing to use criminal statutes to prosecute corporate offenders but did increase considerably the severity of punishment for individuals convicted of economic crimes, especially those involving racial violence. For example, some southern states by the 1930s had enacted laws that allowed the death sentence for convictions of armed robbery, a clear reversal of a two-centuries-long trend to limit the number of capital crimes.

Criminal law in the modern South is virtually indistinguishable from codes elsewhere. At least three reasons account for this: pressures from the federal judiciary and the U.S. Justice Department, especially in the area of civil rights; the growth of a professional bar in the southern states; and the incorporation of southern states into a national economy. In the interpretation and enforcement of these laws, however, regional differences remain because of the force of precedent in the Anglo-American legal tradition and because of the unique influence each community exercises in decisions to prosecute criminal violations and, through the jury, in decisions on individuals charged with crimes.

See also VIOLENCE: Crime, Attitudes toward

David J. Bodenhamer
University of Southern Mississippi

Edward L. Ayers, *Vengeance and Justice: Crime and Punishment in the 19th Century South* (1984); Bradley Chapin, *Criminal Justice in Colonial America, 1606–1660* (1983); Daniel Flanigan, *Journal of Southern History* (November 1974); Michael S. Hindus, *Prison and Plantation: Crime, Justice, and Authority in Massachusetts and South Carolina, 1767–1878* (1980); A. E. Nash, *Virginia Law Review* (February 1970); Kathryn Preyer, *Law and History Review* (Spring 1983); Charles S. Sydnor, *Journal of Southern History* (February 1940). ☆

Family Law
||||||||||||||||||||||||||||||

The rules of family law have varied significantly from one southern state to another since the 17th century. From the beginning of English colonization of the southern area of North America, the family law that prevailed there was *English* in the sense that marriage was monogamous and indissoluble, and rules of succession were similar to prevailing English rules. Few disputes, however, turned on familial status, and, unlike in England, no system of ecclesiastical courts adjudicated them. Significant French and Spanish colonization in the southwestern region did not occur until the 18th century. In the Spanish settlements the law of Castile prevailed along with special rules promulgated for the Indies, and these principles replaced the custom of Paris in the formerly French territory of Louisiana in 1769. For a decade in the mid-18th century a Spanish auxiliary bishop resided in Florida, and from the end of the 18th century a Roman Catholic bishop was in New Orleans. But episcopal jurisdiction was never exerted in a way that had any permanent effect on the development of familial legal institutions.

Marriage. In Virginia until 1794 marriages were by law performed by an Anglican clergyman, but thereafter civil marriages by a magistrate were allowed. Elsewhere in the English South, civil marriage and marriage by the rules of various nonconformist sects had been tolerated from the 17th century. The governor's license to marry could generally be substituted for the premarital ecclesiastical publication of banns throughout the English South.

In the Spanish region marriages were entered into in accordance with the formalities required by the Roman Catholic church. In the absence of a priest, the Spanish military commandant acted as a notary with two witnesses and supervised written contracts to marry, contracts that were solemnized by a priest at the first opportunity. In the case of unions of non-Roman Catholics this formality was frequently not followed by a later religious ceremony.

As a consequence of the early lack of available religious officiants, in some areas during the 18th century informal (or common-law) marriage defined by agreement, cohabitation, and public notoriety was recognized or went uncontested. In the 19th century this institution was particularly well rooted in the Lower South and Texas. Else-where in the South other legal doctrines accomplished the same results as the informal marriage, though without giving the marriage validity for all purposes. Today 4 of the 13 states recognizing informal marriages include Georgia, Alabama, South Carolina, and Texas; and where entered into by citizens of those states, the marriage can be dissolved only by divorce and not by agreement.

Some legal requirements for marriage, such as waiting periods before marriage, vary widely nationwide as well as within the South. Other requirements, such as the age for marriage without consent of a parent or guardian and/or the court, are fairly uniform nationwide. Only four states' minimum ages for marriage without consent vary from 18 for both parties; two of the four exceptions are in the South. In Mississippi both parties must be 21, and in Louisiana the minimum age is 16 for the woman and 18 for the man. The requirements for marriage with consent, however, vary widely regionally and nationally. Kentucky, like three non-southern states, requires parental and/or court consent for either party if under 18, but specifies no minimum age. The age for marriage with consent is 14 in Alabama and Texas for both males and females and in South Carolina for females (16 for males). These are the lowest specified ages in the South, though not in the nation.

Marital Property. As under Spanish law, equal sharing of the gains of marriage (community property) between spouses continued to prevail in Louisiana and Texas and is still maintained there. In other former dominions of Spain, the English law of marital property quickly supplanted the Spanish law as those territories were incorporated into the United States. Whereas under Spanish law the personality of both spouses was distinctly recognized in law, under English law the married woman's legal capacity was largely merged into that of her husband. All of her movable property became her husband's on marriage, he had the power of management of her lands, and he owned the income derived from them.

The married woman was given significant control over her lands and slaves first in Mississippi in 1839 and later elsewhere (Alabama, in 1848; North Carolina, in 1849; Tennessee, in 1850). In Alabama a judicial means was provided as early as 1872 for a married woman to have her disabilities removed so that she might enter into business transactions. Similar legislation was enacted elsewhere. But unless complying with such requirements, married women in most of the South lacked general contractual power. Spanish principles that recognized a married woman's capacity to enter into contracts survived only in Louisiana. In order to protect the creditors who supplied a married woman with goods necessary for her subsistence and that of her children, the law generally recognized the wife as her husband's *agent of necessity*, so that he was liable on such contracts that she made. Married women did not acquire full contractual capacity throughout the South until the mid-20th century.

Though all the southern states protected such necessary movable property as household furniture and tools of trade from the claims of creditors, Texas extended this protection to the family home in 1839. The concept of the homestead was rapidly adopted throughout the Lower South but not in Virginia or the Carolinas until the late 1860s. From the early 19th century a number of states also gave the surviving spouse occupancy of the homestead during widowhood.

Children. In the social and economic conventions of the 17th through the 19th centuries, the husband-father was the head of the family and was responsible for its support. All family members, including the wife, were identified by his surname. This legal requirement no longer exists, although the practice is still widespread. Though the law traditionally has not imposed a duty on children to support needy parents, such support generally has been provided.

Divorce. As in the states to the North, legislative divorce had been available in some southern states from the late 18th century (in Virginia and North Carolina as early as 1789 and 1794, respectively), and some legislative divorces were granted in almost every southern state. For a time Georgia, Mississippi, Alabama, and Louisiana required a prior judicial divorce before a legislative divorce could be granted, but during the first half of the 19th century over 300 legislative divorces were, nevertheless, granted in Georgia alone. From the mid-19th century onward, legislative divorce disappeared in the South, as elsewhere in the United States.

Although judicial marital dissolution for a cause arising during marriage was introduced in Connecticut in 1667 and some other northern states followed this example, it was not available in the South until Tennessee so provided in 1798. Judicial divorce followed rapidly in the Mississippi Territory, Louisiana, Georgia, and the Missouri Territory. In the Upper South it was somewhat delayed (North Carolina, 1827; Virginia, 1850), and divorce was finally provided in South Carolina in 1872. But almost as soon as it was adopted in South Carolina, judicial divorce was abolished there, and it was not reinstituted until 1949. A single act of adultery of the wife and persistent adultery of the husband were generally recognized as grounds for divorce, and North Carolina and Virginia recognized no other grounds than marital infidelity until the early 20th century. Elsewhere cruel treatment and incompatibility of disposition were recognized as additional grounds and, where recognized, these causes were relied on in most cases.

When faced with the need to provide for the wife on divorce, the laws of most southern states restored her lands to her and ordered the exhusband to pay her support (alimony) until her remarriage or death, rather than making a division of property (which usually meant the husband's property). Louisiana and Texas divided the community property on divorce, and in Louisiana, but not in Texas, alimony might also be granted. From 1872 alimony after divorce was not available in North Carolina but it was restored to a limited extent in 1919. As a substitute for granting support to an exspouse, by the late 20th century all southern states had shifted to allowing a division of property associated with the marriage.

Divorce occurred infrequently in the 19th century, but there was no question that the father had a continuing liability for the support of his minor children after a divorce. Though many statutes of southern states spoke in terms of "nullification" of a marriage by divorce, they specifically provided that the children of the marriage were nonetheless legitimate. There seem to be few disputes as to parental fitness for custody of children, and on the divorce of their parents children of tender years were typically put in the custody of their mothers as a matter of course.

Existing patterns of family law remained largely intact in the South until after World War II. In the 1940s divorce became more widely sought, but local standards were strictly maintained in some states, as in Virginia and North Carolina, or divorces were simply not made available, as in South Carolina. For some years Alabama courts tended to open their doors to outsiders by applying very lax standards of proving local residence, and some southerners also sought divorces in non-southern locations with lax residence standards. By 1985 divorce for marital incompatibility or breakdown of the marriage, so-called no-fault grounds, was possible in Alabama, Florida, Georgia, Kentucky, Mississippi, Tennessee, Texas, and West Virginia. Arkansas, Louisiana, North Carolina, South Carolina, and Virginia were among the 12 states nationwide that did not have no-fault or modified no-fault grounds for divorce. By the mid-1980s the custody of minor children was commonly awarded to fathers as well as to mothers. Mothers as well as fathers were also required to support minor children after divorce. Although reciprocal legislation was passed as interstate compacts to achieve enforcement of postdivorce support of exspouses and minor children, the system was too cumbersome to have much practical effect, and with greater population mobility, support orders became increasingly difficult to enforce.

During the 1970s and 1980s the states have enacted uniform laws to govern jurisdiction in the modification of child-custody orders when parents and children move from one state to another. At the same time the federal government has attempted to assist in the enforcement of child-support orders and to prevent abduction of minor children contrary to child-custody decrees. But the success of these efforts is, thus far, difficult to measure.

Legitimation and Adoption. Where English legal traditions were maintained, a child's rights of intestate inheritance rested on its being the legitimate offspring of its parents. Most southern states followed the model of the Virginia succession statute of 1785 in making children born out of wedlock legitimate as to their mothers, and legitimate as to both parents if they later married. Legitimacy as to the father who did not marry the mother required legitimation on the part of the father by administrative or legislative act.

In the legislative records of southern states from about 1810 there are increasing instances of changes of children's names. Many name changes are unrelated to legitimation, but some clearly have intestate succession as their object. In the early 19th century, however, many legislative acts for legitimation began to be identified as such, and some legislative acts mix the terminology of legitimation and adoption. Most southern states also provided for bastardy proceedings by which a father was required to support his illegitimate minor offspring; these proceedings, however, did not legitimate the children.

As a further consequence of concern for illegitimate birth and orphanage of minor children, instances of *legislative* adoption in the South increased after 1820. First in Mississippi (1846) a *judicial* means of adoption was also pro-

vided, while Texas (1850) and Alabama (1851) provided for adoption by formal, administrative process. Both of these patterns were followed in other states and became the standard modes of adoption after the new state constitutions of the 1860s and 1870s made private legislative acts of adoption unavailable. Virginia, however, did not provide for judicial adoption until 1892.

Succession. By the end of the 18th century the rule of intestate succession in the English South in favor of the eldest male had been everywhere replaced by intestate inheritance in favor of all children equally, and parents were forbidden to create entails. Apart from the right of the surviving widow, however, a married man had the right to dispose of his property as he pleased and to disinherit children with or without cause, except in Louisiana and Texas. In 1856 forced inheritance of children was abandoned in Texas, but the right of descendants to inherit a portion of a parent's estate has been maintained in Louisiana except for certain specified reasons for which they may be disinherited. Until 1981 only Louisiana also assured ancestors a share of a child's estate, though the ancestor could have been disinherited for certain specified causes.

In most of the South married women were not allowed to make an effective will as long as their husbands lived. But the law was otherwise in the former Spanish provinces and has so remained in Louisiana, Florida, and Texas. Married women did not obtain the power to make wills elsewhere in the South until the late 19th century. Because in most of the South so much of a wife's property and its control passed to her husband at marriage, the married woman was provided (as under English law) with a dower interest in one-third of her husband's land if she survived him. During the late 19th century this principle was expanded in most of the South to a statutory right in both lands and movable property in favor of either spouse in the property of the other, in spite of any provisions made by will. In Louisiana and Texas, however, the surviving spouse was entitled to his or her half-share of the community property as well as a share of the separate property of the deceased spouse.

In this century no significant changes have been made in the law of succession except with respect to illegitimates who have attained the right of intestate inheritance in Louisiana and have been accorded the status of legitimation when paternity is proved during the father's lifetime in Texas.

Slave Families. In the era prior to the end of the Civil War a sizable part of the population—the black slaves—was outside the legal scheme of familial relations, and that fact had a significant impact on social mores and legal institutions of the region for some time to come. In the subculture of slavery, which prevailed in all of the South until the fall of the Confederate government, the family was not a recognized legal entity. Marriage between free whites and blacks (free or slave) was generally prohibited (as it was in many other states at that time), and criminal sanctions were provided for breach of the rule. Legitimization of illegitimate children of color was also generally forbidden. After the Civil War former slave unions were recognized as marriages, but legislation prohibiting and punishing interracial marriages persisted in most areas of the South well into the 20th century. With

the repeal of antimiscegenation laws, interracial marriages are now permitted, and the prohibition of them in the Mississippi Constitution until 1987 was a relic of past times.

See also BLACK LIFE: Family, Black; Miscegenation; Slave Culture; HISTORY AND MANNERS: Sexuality; MYTHIC SOUTH: Family; Fatherhood; Motherhood; WOMEN'S LIFE: Child-raising Customs; Elderly; Family, Modernization of Marriage and Divorce Laws

Joseph W. McKnight
Southern Methodist University

Jane T. Censer, *American Journal of Legal History* (January 1981); Carl N. Degler, *At Odds: Women and the Family in America from the Revolution to the Present* (1980); Joseph W. McKnight, *Southwestern Historical Quarterly* (January 1983). ☆

Labor Relations and Law

No other area in the United States has been so affected by labor shortages as the South, and problems stemming from this situation have been reflected in southern law. The early European colonists in the New World discovered the need for labor, a need partially satisfied through Indian acculturation, Indian slavery, European indentured servitude, and finally African slavery. Contact between Europeans and Indians resulted in cultural interaction, but it did not solve the labor shortage problems of the white settlers. By the end of the 17th century British traders in the Carolinas had resorted to an extensive Indian slave trade, particularly in the deerskin trade network, but wars and diseases would terminate this experiment with forced Indian labor.

Indentured servitude was legally sanctioned, and it enjoyed longer existence. Indentured servants were at least declared "persons" within the meaning of the law, but the right to their labor was distinctly the property of their masters. Indentured servants did have the right to contract, and this contract was negotiated to secure passage to the New World and to work to pay out this debt. The labor contract could be modified once the servant arrived in the colonies. Conflicts soon arose between free whites, indentured whites, and slaves; the poor whites had only their labor to sell, and blacks in slavery eventually precluded this sale in the South. This led to the appearance of rudimentary guilds and unions, whose members adamantly refused to train either slaves or, often, free blacks.

In North America slavery was centered in the South. Some scholars believe that the southern plantation had labor needs that could not have been met in any other way. These economic needs spawned legislation designed to augment and preserve the labor system that evolved. Other historians posit that the structure of law did not reflect the evolution of slavery but promoted it, aiming at industry and production. They contend that slavery could not have existed but for "positive legislation."

Laws, however, were not designed to guide the system, but to correct it. Regulation was not imposed until problems had already become evident. Much of the early legislation was directly borrowed from Barbados, where the English had vast legal experience in the control and marketing of slaves. South Carolina adopted the 1688 Barbados Slave Code

in 1712; Georgia, which originally forbade slavery, followed, and Florida adopted the Georgia Code in 1822. Most of the laws were not aimed at particulars of slave existence but at the preservation of the institution itself.

By 1755 most of the southern colonies had adopted slave codes that included under their jurisdiction most blacks and persons of mixed blood, excluding most Indians. The lineage of a black was also a factor because the child's status followed that of the mother. Any free black who remained in slave territory for 12 months or more might be enslaved and a freedman could be reenslaved. A free black in the South was merely a paroled inmate. In fact, Georgia and Florida required all free blacks to have a guardian appointed; there were criminal sanctions for an omission.

Still there were few actual *labor* laws in the colonial South. Not until after the colonial period did extensive labor legislation and litigation occur. The masters seemed to make up the rules as they went along, and only changes in the economy and political pressures eventually forced sophisticated labor legislation.

Labor legislation in the South after the American Revolution began to reflect more clearly certain applicable concepts of property. The ownership of a slave was the ownership of equipment capable of labor. Most of the laws governing slaves and slave trade came to be based upon existing principles of property and, later, tort law. Most labor law was enforced on the plantation itself or in a local municipal court. Often punishments for slaves were quite harsh. Particularly stringent punishments such as lashings or mutilations were imposed for brawling and drinking. As the black population grew, southern states required identification papers and travel cards for slaves leaving their master's land for any reason.

Because the slave was property (as later defined in *Dred Scott* v. *Sanford*), the masters were taxed accordingly. Some states required an importation tax and also a yearly tax for keeping slaves. The use and sale of slaves became an important business; labor brokers were jealously protected. The slave trade was second only to the production of cotton as a mainstay of the southern economy; labor was big business. Importation costs were great for slave traders, and they preferred a domestic trade. Hence, the market was reduced by forbidding the importation of new slaves. This stabilized the market and kept the demand for labor high. Statutes were passed making it illegal to buy, use, possess, or sell any illegally imported slaves.

With the taxation of slaves and the reduction of the importation of slaves, a new business arose to meet the labor demand: slave renting. Most renting contracts were for 50 weeks with two weeks off near the Christmas holidays. The lessor held title to the slave, but the lessee assumed all responsibility for the slave. If the slave ran away, the lessee paid; if the slave committed a crime or tort, the lessee had the responsibility for making it right. The lessee was also responsible for food, clothing, and medical care of the slave as well as paying the annual taxes for "owning" a slave.

Southern courts heard a number of contract disputes concerning the rights of lessees and lessors in slave-rental relationships. The Georgia Supreme Court ruled, for example, in *Latimer* v. *Alexander* (1853), that the lessee of a slave was to be held responsible for reasonable medical costs, adding that any other ruling would undermine the labor system.

Clearly any master could hire out a slave for any period of time, but a slave or former slave was not allowed to offer his own services for hire. If the temporary master allowed any harm to befall a slave, the lessor could demand compensation for loss of value. Sometimes the lessee found it easier and cheaper to purchase the slave rather than pay compensation. In later years slave insurance became available and many rental masters required the lessee to purchase a policy before allowing the slave to leave.

The actual regulation of labor was left to the plantation owner, slaveowner, or overseer. Any law enforcement was carried out as a private matter upon private land. Almost every aspect of the slave's life was dependent upon the needs or the whims of the master. Few laws existed to control the time or type of his labor. Slaves were not allowed to work for themselves or on Sundays, and they were not to be kept in the fields more than 14 to 16 hours per day. Certainly by the advent of the Civil War, the master could determine with minimal interference the kind, degree, and time of labor to which the slave was subjected. Such was the state of southern labor law.

Immediately after the Civil War, most white southerners still thought of "labor" as black. Widespread fears were that labor would leave the South or that it would be unstable. This prompted efforts to restrain the newly freed blacks in their exercise of what are generally perceived as traditional rights of labor. A highly restrictive crop-lien system, which led to pervasive sharecropping, was devised that featured exorbitant rents and one-sided contracts. When blacks tried to leave the South, white

...acted by imprisoning the ...rs" for debt or by using vio-... Black codes were passed by southern legislatures, forcing many blacks to labor against their wishes. These took the form of work contracts, peonage, convict labor, and surety agreements.

During the late 19th century economic developments placed even greater stress upon a labor-short southern society. The Industrial Revolution spread to the South, and it was particularly evident in the southeastern states with their abundant water. The industrialization of the Piedmont occurred with labor that was white and youthful. Much of the labor demand was for work in cotton, textile, tobacco, or lumber mills.

Child labor was especially prominent in southern manufacturing, in part because poorer whites and blacks stayed on the farm, sending their children to work in the plants. By 1889 Louisiana was the only southern state to limit child labor in manufacturing to certain ages (between 12 and 14, depending upon the industry), and by 1900 only Tennessee had any further age restriction.

The end of the 19th century brought with it a young, exuberant breed of politicians who wanted to fight the nation's social problems. They wanted to use law to reform society, and in the South this fervor took the form of fighting for child-labor legislation. North Carolina was a leader in southern progressivism, beginning with the election of Governor Charles Brantley Aycock in 1900. In 1903, during Aycock's term, the first child-labor law in North Carolina was passed. This culminated a campaign begun by southern ministers such as Alexander J. McKelway and by northern textile manufacturers. Many ministers reflected the public indignation at the maiming of young children by machinery. The states of the Northeast had enacted child labor laws; and manufacturers there saw the South as operating at an unfair advantage, particularly in textiles.

North Carolina industrialists fought the child-labor laws with vigor. The first major child-labor court test came one year before the North Carolina Legislature acted. In *Fitzgerald* v. *Alma Furniture* (1902) the North Carolina Supreme Court ruled in favor of a nine-year-old boy who had suffered a smashed hand while working. The case sent a message to the North Carolina Legislature, which adopted child-labor legislation the next year. That legislation would be tested and upheld in North Carolina's courts in *Rolins* v. *R. J. Reynolds Tobacco Co.* (1906) and *Gaines Leathers* v. *Blackwell Durham Tobacco Company* (1907). By 1909 all the southern states had adopted child-labor laws.

The federal government also passed child-labor legislation. In 1916 Congress approved, and President Woodrow Wilson signed into law, the Owen-Keating Act, which prohibited passage in interstate commerce of any goods produced by child labor. This all-encompassing legislation was strongly opposed by southern industrialists who supported a test case in the U.S. Supreme Court. In *Hammer* v. *Dagenhart* (1918) the Court held the Owen-Keating Act to be unconstitutional because it exceeded the commerce powers of Congress and preempted powers reserved to the states. The Charlotte, N.C., cotton mill involved in the case could continue to hire children and to have its products shipped interstate. The states were now left to regulate the age at which minors could work, and for the South it remained at 12 to 14.

Eventually the *Hammer* precedent

was struck down. Under the New Deal, the Fair Labor Standards Act of 1938 incorporated virtually the same language as the Owen-Keating Act. This was tested in 1941 in *United States* v. *Darby*. Although Darby violated portions of the Fair Labor Standards Act that did not apply to child labor, the full act was held as constitutional. The fight for child-labor regulation at the national level was over, and southern employers, such as Darby of Georgia, had to adjust accordingly.

The shortage of labor and the attitude toward labor relations as a private rather than public affair created in the 20th-century South a climate hostile to unionization. Membership in unions was protected by the Erdman Act, enacted in 1898 in the aftermath of a national railroad strike. Section 10 of that act prohibited any employer from requiring an employee not to become a member of a labor organization. The prohibition of "yellow dog" contracts was challenged by the Louisville and Nashville Railroad when it fired William Adair, a master mechanic, because he had joined a union. The U.S. Supreme Court decision in *Adair* v. *United States* (1908) validated "yellow dog" contracts. Conditions of employment were not deemed the proper sphere of national regulation, and the Erdman Act became illegal.

The *Adair* case and a particularly vicious longshoreman's strike in Galveston, Tex., in 1920 encouraged southern states to pass antistrike legislation, termed right-to-work laws. Texas implemented five right-to-work laws. The first was instituted by Governor W. Lee O'Daniel. The O'Daniel Act made violence in the course of a labor dispute a penal offense. In 1943 the Manford Act was passed regulating unions. A 1947 law contained three sections that gave all workers the right to bargain individ-

ually without discrimination, and it outlawed contract clauses providing for union security. The Parkhouse Act of 1951 placed contracts containing union-security clauses under the antitrust laws of the state of Texas, and an act of 1955 made it illegal to strike or picket in order to force an employer to bargain with any except a majority union. By 1947 every southern state except Alabama and Louisiana had right-to-work laws, and in 1954 Alabama adopted one. Today only Louisiana is without right-to-work legislation in manufacturing.

Challenges to southern right-to-work legislation by labor have been fruitless. Exemplary was the Tennessee case of Joe Mascari, who questioned a union contract providing for a closed shop. In *Mascari et al.* v. *International Brotherhood of Teamsters et al.* (1948) the Tennessee Supreme Court upheld the Tennessee Open Shop Law and, furthermore, made the act retroactive to those contracts of a closed-shop nature signed prior to the act.

See also AGRICULTURE: Sharecropping and Tenancy; SOCIAL CLASS: Labor, Organized; Tenant Farmers

John R. Wunder
Clemson University

David Brion Davis, *The Problem of Slavery in Western Culture* (1966); J. R. Dempsey, *The Operation of the Right-to-Work Laws* (1961); Eugene D. Genovese, *From Rebellion to Revolution: Afro-American Slave Revolts in the Making of the Modern World* (1979); Herbert Gutman, *The Black Family in Slavery and Freedom, 1750–1925* (1976); Sarah S. Hughes, *William and Mary Quarterly* (April 1978); Gary B. Nash, *Red, White, and Black: The Peoples of Early America* (1974); William F. Ogburn, *Progress and Uniformity in Child-Labor Legislation* (1968); Nell Irvin Painter, *F*

Migration to Kansas after Reconstruction (1976); William M. Wieck, *William and Mary Quarterly* (April 1977); Peter H. Wood, *Black Majority: Negroes in Colonial South Carolina from 1670 through the Stono Rebellion* (1974). ☆

Law Schools

|||||||||||||||||||||||||||||||||||||

For most of the 19th century studying in a law school was not the predominant method of preparing for admission to the bar in this country. Although law schools had existed in the South since the founding of William and Mary Law School in 1779, most candidates for admission to the bar prepared by studying in a law office as required in many states by the rules of the local courts. If no such preparation was required, then self-study was the usual method. Study in a law school, however, conferred prestige and added to the credentials of the lawyers who attended. Not until the middle of this century did law schools provide the only means of preparing for a career as a lawyer.

The introduction of lectures on law at the College of William and Mary in 1779 was the result of the efforts of Thomas Jefferson who, as governor of Virginia, suggested the establishment of a professorship of law and police. "Police" referred not to law enforcement but to government. George Wythe, a judge in the court of chancery in Virginia, was appointed law professor. His course of study was limited to one year and consisted of lectures with frequent moot courts. In 1824 the college began conferring degrees. The law school suspended operation during the Civil War

and did not become permanent until 1922. Many of the leaders of the post-revolutionary bar of Virginia, including John Marshall, attended the lectures by George Wythe or his successor, St. George Tucker.

The second law school established in the Southeast was at the University of Transylvania at Lexington, Ky. The law department was established in 1799 and continued until it was interrupted by the Civil War. It affected the legal profession in several respects. It was the first to seek out and collect a law library, which was supported by fees from auctioneers in Lexington. The library was one of the largest antebellum law collections in the country. Many leaders of the American bar in the central area of the nation attended the school. The course of study was typical of the period, consisting of lectures and moot court arguments.

Many of the law schools established in the antebellum South began as private endeavors of lawyers or judges and later were incorporated into a college or university. Joseph Henry Lumpkin apparently had established such a "law school" in Athens, Ga., around 1843; the school was incorporated into the University of Georgia in 1859. Lawyers and judges found it profitable to teach students in their offices, but if these endeavors can be called "schools," it is difficult to establish their identities or determine the precise number that existed at any particular period. This continued to be true in states where unapproved law schools were permitted.

If these proprietary schools are disregarded, approximately seven other law schools were established in the Southeast during the period prior to the Civil War. Generally, the courses consisted of a one-year program made up of lectures and moot court participation. Although this education may be considered primitive by today's standards, it was generally of higher quality than many of the lawyers received through training in law offices or self-study. The justification for the schools was to promote a more thorough and systematic study of the law. This was not a barren period in the annals of legal education, for many of the founders of these law schools were intellectuals who experimented with various techniques of teaching.

Law schools continued to be founded at a slow rate in the Southeast after the Civil War, but events in another part of the country were shaping legal education and laying the foundation for law schools to become the only means of preparation for the legal profession. In 1870 Christopher Columbus Langdell introduced at the Harvard University Law School the case method system of teaching law. This system consisted of reading cases to extract "principles or doctrines" in a scientific manner to arrive at the fundamental legal doctrines. However, southern schools were reluctant to embrace this method of teaching and most held out for the lecture method into the next century.

Meanwhile, the American Bar Association was responsible for founding the Section on Legal Education, and later the same organization was instrumental in establishing the Association of American Law Schools in 1900. These organizations began to agitate for a three-year program of study and the attendance at law schools as a method of professional preparation. The University of Tennessee Law School was the only southern chartered member of the Association of American Law Schools, which indicates that school's early acceptance of the standards prescribed by these accrediting agencies. After 1910 such law schools as Texas, Kentucky, Tulane, Vanderbilt, and Virginia became members. At the beginning of this century many of the better law schools began to hire academic law teachers rather than rely upon practicing attorneys as professors; this strengthened the methods of teaching. During the decade of the 1920s other southern law schools became members of the Association of American Law Schools and began to meet the standards prescribed by the association.

These organizations did not have a significant impact on legal education until the 1940s when statistics were collected and inspections of the programs at each individual school began. ABA approval was made a necessity as more states adopted a statute requiring graduation from an accredited law school as a prerequisite for admission to the practice of law. Most of the standards were objective rather than qualitative, based on the theory that better teaching methods would be the result of better libraries and facilities. After World War II the number of law schools increased significantly as the demand for legal education mushroomed.

Unapproved law schools exist in the South only in Georgia and Alabama. Though unsupervised, these institutions continue to graduate a sizable number of lawyers.

Acting under the doctrine of separate-but-equal education, three southern states founded all-black law schools— at North Carolina Central in 1939, at Southern University in Louisiana in 1947, and Texas Southern University Thurgood Marshall School of Law (which began in 1947 and moved to new quarters named for Justice Marshall in

1976). The faculties of the state university law schools were often used as the faculty at these black law schools. Desegregation has had little impact on these schools, which have kept their identities and, generally, their limited student body. The Supreme Court case of *Sweatt* v. *Painter* (1950), which mandated the desegregation of the University of Texas Law School, was a landmark in overturning legal support for racial segregation.

By the beginning of this century women had won the right to become members of the bar, but their numbers were small, usually limited to under 5 percent of the student body. In the 1960s this changed drastically as women came to constitute as much as 40 percent of the total student body.

See also EDUCATION: / College of William and Mary; Georgia, University of; Kentucky, University of; Texas, University of; Tulane University; Vanderbilt University; Virginia, University of

Erwin Surrency
University of Georgia

David John Mays, *The Pursuit of Excellence: A History of the University of Richmond Law School* (1970); Alfred Z. Reed, *Training for the Public Profession of the Law* (1921); John Richie, *The First Hundred Years: A Short History of the School of Law of the University of Virginia* (1978); Robert Stevens, *Law School: Legal Education in America from the 1850s to the 1980s* (1983). ✩

Lawyer, Image Of
||||||||||||||||||||||||||||||||||||||||||||||

Two types of lawyers have traditionally appeared in American fiction—conscientious, elite practitioners and predatory shysters. Although southern legal characters tend to conform to these basic stereotypes, they also embody distinctive regional values that set them apart from Yankee and western lawyers.

The typical antebellum practitioner, such as Philpot Wart in John Pendleton Kennedy's plantation novel *Swallow Barn* (1832), is a transplanted English gentleman. Warmhearted, courtly, and a bit eccentric, he can quote passages from the Greek and Latin classics as readily as citations from Coke and Blackstone. With ties of kinship and professional service to the planter class, he also shares the patriarchal ideology of slaveowners. A staunch defender of slavery and states' rights, he recognizes the importance of unwritten law—local custom and community opinion—in regulating the behavior of white southerners.

Even extralegal violence, including dueling and vigilantism, may seem at times an appropriate means of settling personal disputes, and the lawyer is generally as willing to seek personal retribution in affairs of honor as the most thin-skinned of his clients. Judge York Leicester Driscoll in Mark Twain's *Pudd'nhead Wilson* (1894) thus reacts in characteristic fashion to the news that his nephew has taken an assailant to court: "You cur! You scum! You vermin! Do you mean to tell me that blood of my race has suffered a blow and crawled to a court of law about it?"

As a practitioner the antebellum attorney takes a special interest in the plight of the legally disadvantaged, including women, paupers, and slaves. Ishmael Worth, the lawyer-hero of Emma Dorothy Eliza Nevitte (E.D.E.N.) Southworth's *Ishmael; or, In the Depths* (1863), wins fame by vindicating the legal rights of women before all-male juries; Edward Clayton in Harriet Beecher Stowe's *Dred: A Tale of the Great Dismal Swamp* (1856) argues unsuccessfully for extending to slaves the legal protection granted as a matter of course to children and other dependents.

More paternalistic and emotionally involved in his client's affairs than his counterparts in other regions, the southern lawyer prizes equity above black-letter rules in all cases. Although he is quite familiar with abstract legal terminology and doctrine, he prefers to appeal directly to the feelings of jurors through spellbinding courtroom oratory in the manner of Patrick Henry. The image of the antebellum practitioner as a wise and chivalrous community leader has persisted in popular fiction, and it figured prominently in Hollywood's sentimental re-creation of the Old South in the movies of the 1930s and 1940s.

There was, however, a darker side to antebellum lawyering that found expression in fictional accounts of the frontier bar. Joseph G. Baldwin's humorous classic, *The Flush Times of Alabama and Mississippi* (1853), introduced a variety of lower-class backwoods attorneys who used their minimal legal skills to exploit a gullible public. Typical of the breed was Simon Suggs, Jr., who won his law license in a card game. Although the village pettifogger appeared in much northern fiction as well, he represented for southerners a peculiarly dangerous and subversive force. In a plantation society that cherished personal honor and customary practices, Suggs and his kind threatened to establish a new system of pecuniary values that had no place for patriarchal mores. As quintessential economic men, they repudiated all obligations except those dictated by

self-interest. A clear line of descent links them to William Faulkner's unsavory Snopes clan in the 20th century.

The archetypal imagery of a divided profession—patricians versus rednecks—reappeared in Thomas Nelson Page's *Red Rock* (1898), Thomas Dixon's *The Clansman* (1905), and other Reconstruction novels. The legal villains in these works tend to be poor white carpetbaggers and scalawags who are explicitly allied with Yankee businessmen in a conspiracy to "mongrelize" and industrialize southern society. Leading in a grass-roots resistance movement against these alien forces is a younger generation of elite attorneys, who preserve the paternalistic outlook of their elders. Schooled in the racist tenets of social Darwinism, they equate southern "civilization" with white supremacy and invoke higher-law sanctions to justify disfranchisement and other assaults upon the legal rights of blacks. "We will take from an unprofitable servant the ballot he has abused," declares Charles Gaston, the hero of Dixon's *The Leopard's Spots* (1902). "It is the law of nature. It is the law of God." Dixon's ideas, dramatized in D. W. Griffith's powerful film, *Birth of a Nation* (1915), reached mass audiences around the world.

Until the Warren Court precipitated a "Second Reconstruction" of the South by holding segregated schools unconstitutional in *Brown* v. *Board of Education* (1954), fictional lawyers continued to support the racist institutions they had helped create. The self-righteousness of Dixon and Page diminished perceptibly, however, in works that dealt with race relations from World War I to mid-century. Here the typical lawyer was a troubled liberal, who acknowledged the injustice of segregation and risked community censure by defending individual blacks who had been falsely accused of crimes. Yet he never attacked the system directly, because he believed that fundamental changes must await the erosion of custom and the growth of a more enlightened public opinion. Such ambivalence characterized the actions of Gavin Stevens in William Faulkner's *Intruder in the Dust* (1948), Atticus Finch in Harper Lee's *To Kill a Mockingbird* (1960), and Mary Winston— one of the few female attorneys in southern fiction—in Robert Rylee's *Deep Dark River* (1935).

As the civil rights movement intensified in the South during the early 1960s, the image of the tradition-conscious practitioner underwent a striking reevaluation. No reputable novelist of the Second Reconstruction had a kind word for diehard segregationists. In sharp contrast to the literary stereotypes of the late 19th century, legal characters who defended southern autonomy and customary racial practices were now perceived as villains, while NAACP attorneys and other latter-day carpetbaggers received praise for forcing state and local officials to comply with national civil rights laws. The pattern is clearly discernible in Jesse Hill Ford's *The Liberation of Lord Byron Jones* (1965), in which the mindless traditionalism of an aging small-town lawyer serves to radicalize his young partner, Steve Mundine, who resolves: "Never again will I stand aside, defer to age and bigotry. We'll take it [the civil rights struggle] into the streets."

Female and black lawyers did not appear regularly in southern fiction until the 1960s. In scattered earlier works they were often treated with humorous condescension, and for black practitioners the transition from clown to hero

was especially marked. Illustrative of popular attitudes in the 1920s were the *Amos 'n' Andy*-type sketches of black professionals in Birmingham, Ala., that Octavius Roy Cohen wrote for the *Saturday Evening Post*. From their comical antics it is a long step to the civil rights activism of David Champlin, the hero of Ann Fairbairn's *Five Smooth Stones* (1966). Champlin is as idealized a legal character as the virtuous Anglo-Saxons of Page and Dixon, whom he resembles in many ways. Like them, he uses his professional skills to liberate a worthy and long-suffering people.

With the nationalization of civil rights and the reemergence of two-party politics in the South, little remains of the shared values and siege mentality that once gave the region a sense of unique identity. Depictions of contemporary professional life reveal a notable absence of issues or practices that might be labeled distinctively southern. The television series *Hawkins* (1973–74), which starred James Stewart as a West Virginia attorney, contained no identifiably southern themes; and William Harrington's novel *Partners* (1980), which examines the careers of three women lawyers in Houston, Tex., might have been set as easily in any large city. Here, as in other respects, art mirrors the reality of changing political and cultural conditions.

See also EDUCATION: Classical Tradition

Maxwell Bloomfield
The Catholic University
of America

Maxwell Bloomfield, in *Law and American Literature: A Collection of Essays*, ed. Carl S. Smith, John P. McWilliams, Jr., and Maxwell Bloomfield (1983); James McBride

Dabbs, *Civil Rights in Recent Southern Fiction* (1969); Floyd G. Watkins, *The Death of Art: Black and White in the Recent Southern Novel* (1970). ☆

Police Forces

||||||||||||||||||||||||||||||||||||

Police forces in the South increasingly resemble their counterparts in other regions of the country. The civil rights movement of the 1960s and the influence of national standards of professionalism in law enforcement in the late 1960s and 1970s combined to eliminate the distinctive features of southern law enforcement. With respect to role, organizational structure, personnel practices, operational procedures, and community relations, police forces in all regions of the United States share a high degree of similarity.

Prior to the civil rights movement of the 1960s, law enforcement agencies in the South were primary instruments in the maintenance of the racial caste system. Racial discrimination existed in both personnel practices and law enforcement policies. The civil rights movement swept away the more blatant forms of discrimination, and the increasing acceptance of professionalism in law enforcement supported the ideal of equality under the law. Racial problems persist today, but they are largely indistinguishable from similar problems faced by law enforcement agencies in other regions.

The primary responsibility for law enforcement in the United States is borne by the 3,300 county sheriffs' departments and over 13,500 municipal and township police agencies. Size rather than region accounts for the principal variations among these institutions. The Atlanta Police Department with 1,100 sworn officers, for example, has more in common with other big-city police departments across the country than with the small-town departments in neighboring parts of Georgia. By the same token, the two- or three-officer police department in Georgia is very similar to the small-town police departments in other parts of the country.

Atlanta best exemplifies the impact of national influences on southern law enforcement. In the late 1970s the city of Atlanta hired Lee Brown as police commissioner. Not only was he black but he held a doctorate in criminology and had been the director of justice services (i.e., sheriff) in Multnomah County (Portland), Ore. The fact that he was from outside the South and had academic credentials was almost as significant as his race. By the early 1980s the Atlanta Police Department was one of the three in the entire country (Detroit and the District of Columbia were the other two) that had made substantial progress in the recruitment of black officers.

The county sheriff occupies a unique role in American law enforcement. The oldest law enforcement agency, with roots going back to the earliest English settlements, it has responsibility for all three branches of the criminal justice system. The sheriff polices rural areas, serves as an officer of the court, and maintains the jail. In addition, sheriffs in many states have important civil duties such as tax collection. An elected official, the sheriff has traditionally been one of the most important political figures in county politics. While the role of the sheriff has been greatly diminished in cities, where it is overshadowed by the municipal police, the office continues to be extremely important in rural areas.

The southern sheriff is a stock character in the entertainment and advertising media. The stereotype portrays a fat, uneducated, ill-trained person who is either a comic buffoon or a vicious racist. In fact, southern sheriffs are no worse than their counterparts elsewhere in terms of physical condition, education, training, attitudes, or performance. Regardless of region, larger agencies tend to have higher standards than the very small rural agencies.

Municipal police departments fall into two general categories—big city and small town. Big-city departments are large and complex bureaucratic structures dominated by a military-style command. Civil service systems and collective bargaining agreements impose a high degree of rigidity on all personnel decisions. Southern police departments are somewhat less likely to have collective bargaining agreements between officers and their employers than are departments in other regions. This reflects the general weakness of organized labor in the South.

Big-city police departments have the most complex role of all law enforcement agencies. In addition to enforcing the criminal law, urban police spend most of their time as "peacekeepers." Officers are confronted with all of the social problems found in the urban context: crime, delinquency, family disputes, alcoholism, drug abuse, mental illness, and other problems arising from poverty and racial discrimination. In addition, the crowded urban environment generates conflicts over different standards of moral behavior.

The convergence of poverty and racial discrimination produces the most difficult problems for police. As the real and symbolic manifestations of the established legal order, police are inevitably in conflict with powerless groups. This problem, generally labeled "police-community relations," is found in all urban communities. As a result of the civil rights movement and the drive to make law enforcement more professional, the police-community relations problem in southern cities is little different from that in other American cities.

Small-town police departments in the South, like their counterparts elsewhere, have a much less complex role. Even though the South as a region has a higher rate of criminal violence, particularly in terms of homicide, small towns have comparatively few serious crimes. Peacekeeping in small towns is primarily a matter of coping with minor acts of juvenile vandalism. Small-town police departments have an average of five or six officers. Professional standards, particularly in terms of personnel, are less stringent in small-town police departments than in big-city police agencies.

Samuel Walker
University of Nebraska

John F. Heaphy, ed., *Police Practices: The General Administrative Survey* (1978); National Sheriffs Association, *County Law Enforcement* (n.d.); Elliott M. Rudwick, *Journal of Criminal Law, Criminology, and Police Science* (July–August 1960); Southern Regional Council, *Southern Justice: An Indictment* (1965); U.S. Department of Justice, *Sourcebook of Criminal Justice Statistics* (annual); U.S. Department of Justice, Federal Bureau of Investigation, *Crime in the United States* (annual); Samuel Walker, *The Police in America: An Introduction* (1982), *Popular*

Justice: A History of American Criminal Justice (1980). ☆

River Law

||||||||||||||||||||||||||||||

River law deals with rights of seamen, harbor workers, shippers, adjoining landowners, and various states where the river constitutes a boundary. Because of the tremendous volume of the waters of the Mississippi River and the relatively soft alluvial floodplain through which it courses, the southern states lying within the lower Mississippi Valley account for a large portion of this body of law. No distinctive "southern" law exists in this field, but the laws of southern states do differ from those elsewhere.

One of the most important property rights is that of the riparian owner—the person living adjacent to a waterway. The value of land bordering on a navigable stream far exceeds that of a parcel located away from the waters. It is access by commerce to the waters that gives the riparian land its value. As Justice Holmes noted, "A river is more than just an amenity, it is a treasure."

Most of the states of the Union follow the common law of England regarding land titles, but in determining the locus of state boundaries marked by navigable streams, the courts have looked to international law for guidance. International law and European custom suggest that when a navigable river constitutes the boundary between two independent states, the line defining this boundary is the middle of the main channel of the stream. However, the courts of the various states in early decisions reached differing conclusions as to what constituted the middle of the channel of a stream, some holding it to be a line equidistant from the banks at ordinary low water and others holding that it was a line marking the deepest water in the channel. The controversy was laid to rest in the case of *State of Iowa* v. *State of Illinois* (1892), wherein Justice Field, writing for the United States Supreme Court, concluded that the boundary should be "the middle of the main channel of the stream." This line has also been defined as the deepest channel, the principal channel, the track of navigation, and the thalweg.

As the bed of the river changes because of the gradual caving away of its banks and the concomitant building up of the opposite shore by the deposition of alluvion—a process called accretion—the boundary follows the migration of the river. However, during periods of great floods the river sometimes leaves its old channel by cutting a new channel across the narrow neck of an elongated "point," followed in time by the adoption of the new channel by navigation.

Numerous disputes have arisen as to the apportionment of alluvion that has built up against a river bank resulting in the creation of an elongated body of land called a "point" or "point bar." While all courts hold that this alluvion belongs to the owners of the banks to which it is attached, they are not at all in agreement as to how it is to be divided between coterminous owners of the banks. Generally, they all seek an equitable apportionment. The rule most often followed is that of allotting to each landowner as much of the new bank as would be in proportion to his ownership of the original bank. Thus, if A owned

500 feet and B owned 1,000 feet of old bankline and the new point bar measured 1,300 feet, A would be given 600 feet along the new bank and B would be allotted 1,200 feet with the boundary connecting the old point of division with the new point of division by a straight line.

There is no uniformity among the states regarding the ownership of the beds of rivers, and each state determines its own laws. Thus, Mississippi holds that the riparian owner holds title out to the "thread" or "thalweg" of the stream, while in Louisiana, Arkansas, and Tennessee title is vested in the states. Again, there is no uniformity as to whether the "bed" stops at the low-water mark or high-water mark on the bank.

If an island forms on the bed of the stream by the deposition of alluvion, it becomes the property of the owner of the bed. However, if an island builds downstream to such an extent that it crosses the boundary of a downstream owner, the owner of the downstream bed gets title to as much of the island as is located on his portion of the riverbed.

All private rights in the bed and bank of a stream are subject to the superior right of navigation by the public. Therefore, the government can dredge or construct dikes in the interest of navigation. Structures that might cause an obstruction to navigation, such as piers and wharves, must first be authorized by public authorities.

See also ENVIRONMENT: River Life; Rivers and Lakes; / Mississippi River

M. Emmett Ward
Vicksburg, Mississippi

States' Rights Constitutionalism

States' rights constitutionalism holds that in the federal system the states retain certain rights and powers that cannot be taken from them. The doctrine has never been a whole cloth; generations of southerners have tailored their constitutional views to fit changing social and economic realities.

Diversity characterized southern attitudes in 1787 toward relations between state and nation. Led by James Madison of Virginia, southern Federalists wanted a strong central government of enumerated powers that was also responsive to local self-interests. Ardent states' rights proponents, such as Patrick Henry of Virginia, denounced the new Constitution because it left unclear the balance between state and national powers. They also rebelled at Madison's successful effort in 1789 in preventing the insertion of the word "expressly" in the Tenth Amendment as a limit on national powers. Southern Federalists won important concessions for the peculiar institution of slavery in return for their support of the national Constitution.

States' rights constitutionalism after 1787 evolved from a passive doctrine of resistance to national authority based on strict construction to an aggressive theory of state sovereignty. Southern proponents of the Constitution, like Madison and Thomas Jefferson, believed that the national government should remain sensitive to local self-interest and agrarian values. Thus, they resisted northern Federalist attempts to consolidate national power. Madison and Jefferson in 1798 most fully argued their position when they denounced the Alien and Sedition Acts. Their famous Virginia and Kentucky resolutions insisted on strict construction of the delegated powers of the national government and set forth the theory that a state might interpose itself between the citizenry and the national government in order to nullify a federal law. Few southerners supported the broad implications of the resolutions, and both Jefferson and Madison in the White House frequently adopted an expansive view of federal powers.

Economic depression and the large slave population in the Southeast during the 1820s radicalized states' rights constitutionalism. John C. Calhoun of South Carolina linked federal tariff policies to the region's economic woes. He pushed beyond the strict constructionism of Madison and Jefferson by asserting that the states could not only interpose their authority to nullify a federal law but also break from the Union altogether. During the nullification controversy of 1832 South Carolina's attempt to put Calhoun's theory into action faltered before Unionist sentiment in the Palmetto State, the leadership of Andrew Jackson, and the refusal of other southern states to lend support.

Under the pressure of the slavery expansion issue, states' rights constitutionalism emerged during the 1850s as a doctrine of power and not of right. Jefferson Davis of Mississippi replaced Calhoun as the South's most radical proponent of this view of states' rights. Confronted with a hostile antislavery movement in the North and declining power in Congress, Davis claimed that the federal judiciary was responsible for sustaining slaveholders' property rights in the new territories. Because the states were sovereign entities, Davis argued,

the national government had a constitutional responsibility to protect slaveholders' rights aggressively. Ironically, northern antislavery forces resorted to the traditional Jeffersonian notion of states' rights as a passive restraint on the national government to justify their attempts to frustrate enforcement of the Fugitive Slave Act of 1850. The Supreme Court in *Dred Scott* v. *Sanford* in 1857 confirmed Davis's arguments, but it was a Pyrrhic victory; the social calculus of the peculiar institution and the election of Abraham Lincoln in 1860 culminated in the most extreme form of states' rights—secession. The ideals of local self-government and strict construction did retain vitality, however; the Confederate wartime effort, under Davis's leadership, suffered because authorities in the southern states refused to cooperate fully with the Confederate government in Richmond.

Confederate defeat marked the end of exaggerated claims for states' rights constitutionalism. Southern Democratic leaders in the post-Reconstruction era reaffirmed the traditional passive meaning of the doctrine in their successful efforts to deny free blacks the national protection of the Fourteenth and Fifteenth Amendments. The Supreme Court abetted this process in a series of decisions that culminated in the 1896 case of *Plessy* v. *Ferguson.* The justices sustained segregation by race in public places as long as the states provided equal facilities.

Events inside and outside the South during the 20th century undermined this coupling of states' rights and a dual system of race relations. The Supreme Court beginning in the mid-1930s broadened the interpretation of the commerce and other "elastic" clauses of the Constitution and accepted limited incorporation of the Bill of Rights into the Fourteenth Amendment. The justices enhanced the powers of the national government at the expense of the states. Moreover, the moral legitimacy of states' rights ebbed as a result of southern resistance to ending de jure racial segregation. Following the Supreme Court's decision in *Brown* v. *Board of Education* in 1954, southern Democratic politicians orchestrated a strategy of massive resistance in order to prevent integration of public facilities. Governors Orval Faubus of Arkansas and George C. Wallace of Alabama resorted to Calhoun's exploded theories in futile attempts to block integration of public schools and universities. States' rights appeared in the South to be little more than a code word for racism.

The principle that the states retain certain distinct powers remains constitutionally alive within the American federal system. But the absorption of the South into the mainstream of American culture and the demise of the section's legally mandated dual system of race relations have made the South more like the rest of the nation and, therefore, less dependent on states' rights constitutionalism.

See also HISTORY AND MANNERS: / Davis, Jefferson; Jefferson, Thomas; POLITICS: / Calhoun, John C.; Faubus, Orval; Wallace, George C.

Kermit L. Hall
University of Florida

William Anderson, *The Nation and the States, Rivals or Partners?* (1955); Numan Bartley, *The Rise of Massive Resistance: Race and Politics in the South during the 1950s* (1969); Arthur Bestor, Jr., *Journal of the Illinois State Historical Society* (Summer 1961); Daniel Elazar, *American Federalism:*

A View from the States (1972); William W. Freehling, *Prelude to Civil War: The Nullification Controversy in South Carolina, 1816–1836* (1966); James J. Kilpatrick, *The Sovereign States: Notes of a Citizen of Virginia* (1957); Alpheus T. Mason, ed., *The States Rights Debate: Antifederalism and the Constitution* (1972); Frank L. Owsley, *States' Rights in the Confederacy* (1925). ☆

Supreme Court

||||||||||||||||||||||||||||||||||||||||||

Writing more than a half-century ago, Charles S. Sydnor observed that the two traditional sources of authority in the South were the Bible and the Constitution. Relying on the Constitution, the region's leaders developed a cultural constitutionalism intended to protect regional values and institutions from external forces. At the heart of cultural constitutionalism lay the political theory of states' rights, which preserved the powers of the states from any encroachment by the national government. The Supreme Court's interpretation of the Constitution remained compatible for a century and a half with the region's dominant values. But during the last half-century the Supreme Court has played a major role in reshaping the institutional structure of the region and forcing changes in the South's public values. As a result, Supreme Court decisions have become the focal point of many of the region's modern controversies.

By far the most significant subject of judicial interpretation has been the Supreme Court's definition of the constitutional terms of race relations. During the course of a century, the Supreme Court sanctioned slavery, legitimized segregation, and ordered integration of public institutions. Through the antebellum period, a series of Supreme Court opinions sustained the institution of slavery. These cases culminated in 1857 with the Dred Scott case. In that case, the Court decisively confronted the conflicting values that circumscribed the slaveowners' approach to the institution of slavery—the dilemma over whether slaves would be treated as property or as human beings. Dred Scott was a black slave who had been the property of an army surgeon. Scott had been taken by his owner into Illinois and into Wisconsin Territory, which was free territory under the Missouri Compromise. Scott eventually returned to Missouri with his owner. The surgeon died and title to Scott passed to a New York resident named John F. A. Sanford. In 1846 Scott brought suit in the Missouri courts to obtain his freedom. He claimed that he had become a free person because he had been taken into free territory. The Missouri courts rejected Scott's plea, and his attorneys initiated a new suit in federal courts. After years of litigation, the Supreme Court held on 6 March 1857 that Scott could not sue for his freedom and that he was still a slave. Chief Justice Roger B. Taney argued that Scott could not sue because he was not a citizen. He was not a citizen because he was black and a slave. In effect, Scott had no rights under the Constitution.

The abolition of slavery in the aftermath of the Civil War placed race relations in a state of flux. By the early 1890s an increasingly rigid system of legal racial separation was in place throughout the region. The Supreme Court was unwilling to challenge the new system. In 1896, in the celebrated case of *Plessy* v. *Ferguson*, the Court gave constitutional legitimacy to the so-called separate-but-equal principle. The opinion feigned a commitment to the concept of equality but consigned black southerners to a status little removed from slavery.

During the next half-century, carefully drawn constitutional challenges gradually chipped away at legal segregation by means of a slow and tortuous strategy. The Supreme Court did not abandon generations of inaction and aggressively assert the basic political and civil rights of all citizens until 1954. In *Brown* v. *Board of Education* the Court attacked the separate-but-equal principle by concluding that in public education separate facilities were "inherently unequal." Thus the segregated educational systems of the southern states violated the equal protection clause of the Fourteenth Amendment to the Constitution. Opponents of the *Brown* decision throughout the South placed blame not on the Constitution, but on the Supreme Court's interpretation of the Constitution. In 1957 resistance to *Brown* was encouraged by 101 southern congressmen who signed the "Southern Manifesto," whereby they pledged to "use all lawful means to bring about a reversal of this decision which is contrary to the Constitution and to prevent the use of force in its implementation." Eventually, force was used and the Supreme Court's interpretation of the Constitution prevailed. The Court's attack on segregated educational institutions proved to be merely the first step in a long struggle against all forms of racial discrimination in the public life of the South.

The South's system of race relations was not the only element of the traditional southern value system to come under Supreme Court review. Agrarianism, however defined, has been an essential element of the distinctive regional culture for the last 200 years. A major source of continuing agrarian dominance in southern public life has been rural control over state legislative politics. By the 1950s, burgeoning urban areas in the region were severely underrepresented in state legislatures, while the rural areas and adjacent small towns enjoyed representation far in excess of what their declining populations would warrant.

In the 1962 case of *Baker* v. *Carr* the Supreme Court abandoned its longstanding decision not to intervene in legislative reapportionment matters. *Baker* v. *Carr* challenged the 1901 Tennessee statute that had provided the method of periodically reapportioning the state legislature. Provisions of the law assured continued rural dominance of the legislature at the expense of the urban areas. The decision held that it was permissible to challenge the statute as a violation of the equal protection clause of the Fourteenth Amendment, but provided little in the way of a remedy. Two years later the Supreme Court embarked on a course of simple majoritarianism in reapportionment matters. In *Reynolds* v. *Sims* the court struck down a complex Alabama reapportionment plan and ordered the implementation of a reapportionment plan based on the principle of one person, one vote. The consequence of these decisions has been gradually to shift the locus of political power in the states from the rural areas to the cities. One other likely consequence may well be the gradual erosion of agrarianism as a dominant value in the culture of the region.

The third major element of the region's culture that has come under Supreme Court scrutiny has been religious fundamentalism. The flash points of the conflict between regional cultural values and the Supreme Court have been the issue of school prayer and the teaching of evolution in the public schools. In each case religious conservatives have been especially forceful in pressing their case in favor of school prayer and against the teaching of evolution. In like manner, Supreme Court opinions have stood as the major bulwark against the widespread adoption of both these practices in the public school systems throughout the region. Rulings in these cases have raised opposition to the Supreme Court opinions that was surpassed only by the desegregation cases. Unlike the desegregation and reapportionment cases, however, the school prayer and evolution cases seem unlikely to alter the South's tradition of religious conservatism. If anything, the zealous defense of religious values may strengthen their place in the pantheon of southern life.

Robert Haws
University of Mississippi

Richard Cortner, *The Apportionment Cases* (1970); Don E. Fehrenbacher, *The Dred Scott Case: Its Significance in American Law and Politics* (1978); Richard Kluger, *Simple Justice: The History of Brown v. Board of Education and Black America's Struggle for Equality* (1976); Charles Lofgren, *The Plessy Case: A Legal-Historical Approach* (1987). ☆

BLACK, HUGO

(1886–1971) U.S. Senator, Supreme Court Justice.

Through intelligence, grit, determination, and temporary alliance with the Ku Klux Klan, Hugo Lafayette Black rose from simple origins in the Alabama hills to the U.S. Senate (1927–37) and the

Supreme Court (1937–71). During 34 years as an associate justice, Black, whose only prior judicial experience had been as judge of Birmingham's police court, forged a reputation as an eloquent defender of First Amendment freedoms. The seeming paradox of a former Klansman evolving into an ardent civil libertarian remains an intriguing episode in Supreme Court annals.

Son of a small-town merchant, Black was born 27 February 1886 in Clay County, Ala. He completed his formal education in the two-year law school of the University of Alabama, Tuscaloosa, in 1906. By the early 1920s he was a highly successful damage-suit lawyer, suspected by Birmingham's establishment of being a "Bolshevik" because of his ties to organized labor. Black joined the Klan in 1923 by swearing allegiance to its principles, including white supremacy and anti-Catholicism. Thereby he allied himself with a large, highly disciplined organization soon to dominate state politics. The Alabama Klan of the 1920s reflected not only the prejudices, ignorance, and inherent violence of numerous poor, white Protestants but also their desire for a share in political and economic power from which they had long been virtually excluded. Undoubtedly, Black knew of the Klan's excesses against individuals; evidently, his personal ambition persuaded him to believe that, over the long run, the Klan's democratizing impact could prove beneficial to these less-privileged and underrepresented white Alabamians. With the crucial aid of Klan-controlled votes, Black achieved in 1926 the otherwise unattainable office of U.S. senator. Although he had resigned from the Klan for appearance's sake at the start of his campaign, he remained politically indebted to the In-

visible Empire until the early 1930s, by which time most Alabamians had become temporarily satiated with violence and appeals to prejudice.

Senator Black proved an ardent New Dealer, even alarming Franklin Roosevelt by advocating a 30-hour work week. As a Senate investigator he dramatically demonstrated his hostility to special privilege and entrenched interests. Black's progressive record, coupled with the Senate's tradition of confirming its members nominated to high office, led Roosevelt to make him the first appointee in an ultimately successful endeavor to reshape the Supreme Court in favor of federal activism in economic, political, and social spheres. Despite the initial skepticism of some of his judicial colleagues and a nationwide outburst over his former Klan membership, Black became a major intellectual force on the high

Hugo Black, U.S. Supreme Court justice, 1926

court, pressing his fundamental concept that the guarantees of the Bill of Rights are absolute and should bind states as well as the nation. To the acute dismay of many fellow southerners, Justice Black sided with the Court majority to strike down legal segregation in schools and public facilities; to advance the principle of one man, one vote; and to outlaw reading of official prayers in public schools. Through the unlikely instrument of the Klan, the Senate and the Supreme Court gained the services of a type of southerner rarely chosen for public office in the 20th century—a latter-day disciple of Jeffersonian and Jacksonian democracy.

> Virginia Van der Veer Hamilton
> University of Alabama
> at Birmingham

Howard Ball, *The Vision and the Dream of Hugo L. Black: An Examination of a Judicial Philosophy* (1975); Hugo Black, Jr., *My Father: A Remembrance* (1975); Gerald T. Dunne, *Hugo Black and the Judicial Revolution* (1977); Virginia Van der Veer Hamilton, *Hugo Black: The Alabama Years* (1972); Virginia Van der Veer Hamilton, ed., *Hugo Black and the Bill of Rights: Proceedings of the First Hugo Black Symposium in American History on the Bill of Rights and American Democracy* (1978). ☆

BLACK CODES
||||||||||||||||||||||||||||||||||||||

One legal response of southern white governments to the end of the Civil War and the passage of the Thirteenth Amendment was the adoption of laws purporting to bestow upon the newly freed men and women certain civil rights. Mississippi passed the first of these codes in 1865. They granted rights of blacks to hold personal prop-

erty, intermarry, sue in state courts, swear out criminal warrants, and testify against whites under certain conditions. The right to vote, however, was not given to blacks under these codes.

Black codes were primarily promulgated to control a newly fluid black labor force. For example, Section 1 of the Mississippi Black Code allowed blacks to sue and be sued and to acquire and dispose of personal property, but limited their property owning to incorporated towns or cities and severely hampered individual rural agricultural pursuits. Involuntary labor was authorized by statutes concerning vagrancy, peonage, work contracts, enticement, convict labor, surety, and emigrant agency. Law and terror were successfully combined to enforce what those who opposed black codes called a "new slavery."

Congressional Reconstruction required temporary abandonment of many of the black codes. After Reconstruction most states reconstituted the involuntary labor sections. These vestiges of the original black codes remained a part of southern social and economic life until the civil rights movement of the 1950s and 1960s.

See also VIOLENCE: / Peonage

> John R. Wunder
> Clemson University

William Cohen, *Journal of Southern History* (February 1976); Theodore B. Wilson, *The Black Codes of the South* (1965).

BROWN V. BOARD OF EDUCATION
|||||||||||||||||||||||||||||||||||||||||||||

On 17 May 1954 the U.S. Supreme Court ruled in *Brown* v. *Board of*

Education that separate educational facilities for blacks and whites "are inherently unequal." With that decision the Court overturned the precedent of "separate but equal" set by the 1896 *Plessy* v. *Ferguson* case and set the stage for the civil rights movement of the 1960s.

The National Association for the Advancement of Colored People (NAACP) played a major role in the instigation of the case, which centered around Linda Brown, a black child denied admission to a Topeka, Kan., elementary school because of her race. *Brown* brought together five related cases from South Carolina, Delaware, Virginia, Kansas, and the District of Columbia, all of which challenged racial segregation as a violation of the equal protection clause of the Fourteenth Amendment. The arguments heard by the Court centered on the intentions of the framers and ratifiers of that amendment.

In the brief, unanimous opinion delivered by Chief Justice Earl Warren, the Court ruled that the separate-but-equal doctrine, which held that racial segregation was permissible as long as equal facilities were provided for both races, was in violation of the equal-protection clause. The justices wrote that the segregation of white and black children in public education "generates a feeling of inferiority" among the black children that could have an irreversible detrimental effect on the rest of their lives. In the spring of 1955 the Court heard arguments about how their *Brown* decision might be implemented. At the end of these arguments the Court remanded the four cases back to the district courts with the order to take whatever steps were necessary to "admit to public schools on a racially nondiscriminatory basis with all deliberate speed the parties in these cases."

The *Brown* decision and the Court's demand for swift integration did not bring about the immediate desegregation of public schools. The only school boards legally bound by the *Brown* decision were those named directly in the cases on which the Court ruled, and the only laws held unconstitutional were those specific laws cited by the plaintiffs. Ordinarily, rules of constitutional law decided by the Supreme Court are universally accepted and implemented where they apply. Technically, however, compliance is voluntary, and there was intense resistance to implementation of the controversial *Brown* decision. The political branches of government were employed to speed integration. The threat by the Department of Health, Education, and Welfare (HEW) under the Civil Rights Act of 1964 to withhold federal education funds from school districts that persisted in segregation policies was one such way of encouraging integration. Many school districts began busing students from one neighborhood to another in an effort to achieve integration. Many southern states sought to obstruct integration through "massive resistance," and in 1965 less than 10 percent of the South's black students were in integrated public schools.

The *Brown* doctrine, which said that segregated schools are illegal, was extended to apply to other public facilities through separate court cases involving, for instance, the segregation of beaches (in Maryland), golf courses (in Atlanta), and recreation facilities (in Memphis). Probably the most famous case ever decided by the Supreme Court, *Brown* v. *Board of Education* was the first step in major reform of not only public education but also race laws and policies in almost all aspects of American life.

Karen M. McDearman
University of Mississippi

Robert Cushman, *Cases in Constitutional Law* (1975); Richard Kluger, *Simple Justice: The History of Brown v. Board of Education and Black America's Struggle for Equality* (1976); J. Harvie Wilkinson III, *From Brown to Bakke: The Supreme Court and School Integration, 1954–1978* (1979). ☆

ERVIN, SAM, JR.

(1896–1985) Lawyer and U.S. Senator.

Samuel James Ervin, Jr., graduated at age 26 from Harvard Law School in 1922. He subsequently practiced law with his father in Morganton, N.C., held various local and state offices, and from 1954 to 1974 served in the United States Senate.

Ervin's Senate career spanned a tumultuous era in the history of the South and the nation. Ervin viewed the South's dual system of race relations as a social reality that only the individual states could change. In the wake of the Supreme Court's 1954 decision in *Brown v. Board of Education*, he joined other southern members of Congress in signing the 1956 Southern Manifesto that denounced court-ordered integration. Ervin in 1960 filibustered the Eisenhower Administration's civil rights proposals. He also opposed the civil rights acts of 1964, 1965, and 1968. Yet Ervin was neither an apostle of massive resistance nor a racist. He rejected radical states' rights ideas of nullification and interposition. Moreover, on questions of civil liberties, where the racial issue did not threaten his political base in North Carolina, Ervin was liberal. He supported the 1966 Bail Reform Act and the 1968 Indian Bill of Rights.

Late in his Senate career Ervin emerged as a significant voice in constitutional matters. In 1971 he orchestrated the Senate attack on spying by

Sam Ervin, North Carolina country lawyer and U.S. senator, 1970s

army intelligence on civilians. More dramatically, as chairperson of the Select Committee on Presidential Campaign Activities in 1973, Ervin treated the American public to a lesson in constitutional government. His homespun stories, biblical quotations, and pointed questions captured the imagination of a national television audience. The common-sense wisdom of this southern country lawyer was more than a match for the Watergate conspirators.

Ervin believed that persons were only truly free when they accepted responsibility for their own lives. This notion paled before the historical realities of southern race relations, but it was an otherwise fundamentally correct insight into the nature of southern character. Sam Ervin the southerner, moreover, in his confrontation with Richard Nixon's White House, reaffirmed for all Americans the connection between this ideal and the value of limited constitutional government.

Kermit L. Hall
University of Florida

Paul L. Clancy, *Just a Country Lawyer: A Biography of Senator Sam Ervin* (1974); Dick Dabney, *A Good Man: The Life of Sam J. Ervin* (1976). ☆

FIFTH CIRCUIT COURT OF APPEALS

Spanning the Lower South from Florida to Texas, the Fifth Circuit Court of Appeals was one of the regional federal circuit courts created in 1891. Following the 1954 decision of the U.S. Supreme Court in *Brown* v. *Board of Education*, the Fifth Circuit was called upon to supervise the dismantling of separate schools and the elimination of racial discrimination in the region. Dominated by several prominent liberal judges, notably Elbert P. Tuttle and John Minor Wisdom, the court repeatedly insisted upon compliance with desegregation despite widespread public hostility. Indeed, the Fifth Circuit has been described as "the nation's greatest civil rights tribunal." This court took the lead in fashioning new remedies for school segregation and devising streamlined procedures to expedite discrimination cases. One of the most celebrated matters handled by this court was the admission of James Meredith to the University of Mississippi.

The judges who constituted the circuit bench held widely differing opinions on many issues. The tribunal was racked by a bitter schism over the handling of contempt proceedings against Governor Ross Barnett and by the allegations of Judge Ben F. Cameron that the Fifth Circuit's three-judge panels were being stacked in favor of liberals.

In addition to difficult racial cases, the Fifth Circuit was required to handle an extremely heavy volume of general litigation. In fact, the docket of the Fifth Circuit was dominated by cases involving economic issues such as labor law and taxation. Proposals to divide the Fifth Circuit were blocked by desegregation proponents who feared that the resulting new circuits might prove to be more conservative. Instead, Congress repeatedly enlarged the size of the tribunal until it reached the unwieldy number of 26 judges. This was by far the largest circuit court in the federal system. Finally, despite lingering opposition from civil rights activists, Congress voted to split the Fifth Circuit effective in October of 1981. Alabama, Georgia, and Florida were placed in the newly created Eleventh Circuit Court of Appeals.

James W. Ely, Jr.
Vanderbilt University

Jack Bass, *Unlikely Heroes* (1981); J. Woodford Howard, Jr., *Courts of Appeals in the Federal Judicial System: A Study of the Second, Fifth, and District of Columbia Circuits* (1981); Frank T. Read and Lucy S. McGough, *Let Them Be Judged: The Judicial Integration of the Deep South* (1978). ☆

FINCH, ATTICUS

A major character in Harper Lee's novel, *To Kill a Mockingbird* (1960), Atticus Finch represents the conscience of the white South in the years before the advent of the Warren Court and the civil rights revolution. As a descendant of local slaveowners, he well understands the deep-rooted racial prejudices that continue to exist in Maycomb, the small Alabama town in which he practices law during the Depression. Mild-mannered and scholarly, he is a stubborn idealist who believes in equality before the law for everyone, regardless of color or class. When Tom Robinson, a black man, is accused of raping the daughter of a poor white ne'er-do-well, Atticus is appointed by the court to defend him. Convinced of his client's innocence, he makes a determined effort to save his life, despite the growing opposition of the white community. His neighbors denounce him as a "nigger-lover," his children suffer insult and ridicule at school, and a mob threatens his life on the eve of the trial.

In the courtroom Atticus destroys the credibility of the prosecution's witnesses through skillful cross-examination. There is no proof that a rape occurred, he demonstrates, and strong circumstantial evidence suggests that the complainant, a lonely girl, was savagely beaten by her own father because she had made sexual advances to a black man. Reminding the white male jurors that "in our courts all men are created equal," Atticus pleads with them to abandon racial stereotyping and to decide the case on its merits.

After deliberating for several hours, the jury returns with a verdict of guilty, and Robinson is sentenced to death. The time has not yet come when southern juries will accept the word of a black man against that of any white man, Atticus explains to his children. Yet there are some indications that the grip of custom may be loosening. As a neighbor observes, only Atticus could have kept a jury out so long in a rape case. Through his gentlemanly appeals to shared southern values of honor and paternalism, he gradually persuades other white southerners to reexamine their inherited racial attitudes.

To Kill a Mockingbird received the Pulitzer Prize for fiction in 1961, and Gregory Peck won an Oscar for his portrayal of Atticus Finch in the movie version in 1962.

Maxwell Bloomfield
The Catholic University
of America

Gregory Peck as Atticus Finch in the film made from Harper Lee's Pulitzer Prize-winning novel To Kill a Mockingbird *(1963)*

FOREMAN, PERCY

(b. 1902) Lawyer.

As a defense lawyer, Percy Eugene Foreman combined his knowledge of law, his courtroom prowess, and his thirst for wealth to achieve legendary status in his native Texas and throughout the nation's legal community. His own celebrity status has attracted celebrated defendants and, in turn, been enhanced by his association with them.

Born in Polk County, Tex., in a backwoods area known as the Big Thicket, Foreman is the son of a former county jailer and sheriff. At eight years of age, he began earning money by shining shoes. He soon bought out his sole competitor in the town of Livingston and added a delivery business to his growing empire. By age 11 he was making as much money as most adults in the impoverished east Texas community. His next enterprise was loading cotton onto trains. While his bid of 25 cents per bale was low, he hired laborers at 8 cents per bale to do the actual loading. At 15 he quit school and at age 16, having saved $6,500, he moved to Houston. Subsequently he briefly attended Staunton Military Academy in Virginia before joining a chautauqua company as an advance man. He delivered his first public oration as an 18-year-old with the company in Burnside, Ky.

Returning to his native state, Foreman enrolled at the University of Texas. He attended classes part of each year but continued to tour with the chautauqua company as a circuit manager and lecturer. At age 25 Foreman completed law school, having served as president of the student body during his senior year.

In December 1927 Foreman formed a partnership with J. W. Lockett with offices across from the Rice Hotel in Houston. The Rice remained a favorite Foreman hangout through much of his career. A few months after forming the partnership, he went to work for the district attorney in Houston. In 1929 he returned to private practice when his boss failed to win reelection. In 1933 Foreman became an assistant district attorney with a special interest in keeping gamblers from nearby Galveston out of Houston. In 1935 he again left the district attorney's office for private practice. His 1940 bid for election as district attorney failed.

Foreman's legendary status owes much to his record in capital punishment cases. By the late 1960s he had represented over 1,000 defendants in such cases, only one of whom had been executed; only 55 had even served time in prison. His most celebrated defendants include Jack Ruby, James Earl Ray, General Edwin Walker, and Candy Mossler.

Although part of his celebrity status stems from his successful record and the clients attracted by it, some of it derives from Foreman's being a member of that small fraternity of lawyers who have become wealthy doing criminal defense work. He received both his Houston home and a New York City co-op apartment as fees. His obvious early interest in making money has not abated over the years.

Foreman is the most famous of a special breed of southern attorney; Richard "Racehorse" Haynes and Warren Burnett are other examples. Although Foreman has tried cases across the country, he has the physical stature—at 6'4"—and the down-home manner that make him the literal embodiment of that dominating courtroom presence, the Texas trial lawyer.

C. Martin Wilson III
Austin, Texas

Michael Dorman, *King of the Courtroom: Percy Foreman for the Defense* (1969). ☆

FRANK, LEO, CASE
||||||||||||||||||||||||||||||||||||||||||||||||

Described by Leonard Dinnerstein as "one of the most infamous outbursts of anti-Semitic feeling in the [history of] the United States," the Leo Frank case inspired formation of both the second Ku Klux Klan and the Anti-Defamation League of B'nai B'rith. The case began on Confederate Memorial Day in 1913 with the murder and mutilation of Mary Phagan, a 13-year-old employee of an Atlanta pencil factory. The mayor and an anxious populace, aroused by yellow journalism, demanded that the police find her killer quickly. They responded by arresting the victim's boss, Leo Frank. A Jew from New York, Frank rapidly became a focal point for the resentment toward factories and outsiders that rapid industrialization had ignited in southern traditionalists.

Frank's Atlanta trial took place in an atmosphere of public hysteria and amidst threats of mob violence. The prosecution, led by Solicitor Hugh Dorsey (who rode the publicity he gained from this case into the governorship), portrayed Frank as a lecherous employer who preyed on young factory girls. The state relied heavily on the testimony of Jim Conley, a black janitor with a criminal record, who claimed to have been asked by Frank to help him hide a body and to write two notes found next to Phagan's remains. Evidence available to police and prosecutors strongly suggested that he, not Frank, was the killer. Nevertheless, the jury convicted the Jewish factory manager. Although he believed Frank was innocent, Judge Leonard Roane denied his motion for a new trial and sentenced him to death.

A good deal of new evidence soon surfaced, which raised further doubt about Frank's guilt. Efforts to secure a new trial failed, however, despite an appeal carried to the United States Supreme Court. The Court also spurned a petition seeking Frank's release on a writ of habeas corpus. He gained a temporary reprieve when Governor John Slaton sacrificed a promising political career by commuting his sentence to life in prison. Then, on 16 August 1915, a group of respectable citizens from Mary Phagan's hometown, Marietta, Ga., abducted Frank from the state prison farm at Milledgeville and hanged him.

Frank's death and the events preceding it aroused intense interest throughout the country. Governors, state legislators, and members of Congress joined more than 100,000 other Americans in efforts to save Frank's life. This outpouring of public sentiment and the nationwide press coverage of the case owed much to the efforts of Jewish leaders, who viewed this incident as a threatening manifestation of anti-Semitism, comparable to France's infamous Dreyfus affair.

Concerned Jewish groups persisted in trying to clear Frank's name, and evidence continued to surface. In 1982 a former office boy at Frank's factory, Alonzo Mann, came forward and said that he had seen another man carrying Mary Phagan's slain body. As of 1983 Governor Joe Frank Harris publicly supported a posthumous pardon of Leo Frank, but the Georgia Board of Pardons and Paroles refused to take such action. The Anti-Defamation League, the American Jewish Committee, and the Atlanta Jewish Federation submitted another petition focusing on the denial of justice to Frank, and the Board of Pardons and Paroles reversed itself and granted the pardon in March 1986, 71 years after the lynching of Leo Frank.

See also ETHNIC LIFE: / Jews

Michael R. Belknap
University of Georgia

Leonard Dinnerstein, *The Leo Frank Case* (1968). ☆

Sit-in at Woolworth's store, Greensboro, North Carolina, February 1960

GREENSBORO SIT-IN
||||||||||||||||||||||||||||||||||||||||||||||||||||

The sit-in demonstrations in Greensboro, N.C., marked an important turning point in the history of the civil rights movement. In February of 1960 four black college students sat down at a Woolworth's lunch counter and demanded service. Woolworth's, like other chain stores in the South, sold merchandise to all customers but denied black patrons the use of its lunch counters. The demonstrations rapidly grew in intensity. More black students participated and occupied the lunch-counter seats. White counterdemonstrators soon appeared. The incidents captured national headlines and within a week sit-ins had spread to Winston-Salem, Durham, and other cities across the South. There was supportive picketing in the North against local branches of chain stores that denied service to blacks in the South.

At the end of February the students agreed to suspend their sit-ins while negotiations were in progress. When discussions failed to produce any resolution, direct action was resumed. Woolworth's then closed its lunch-counter operation. The students successfully mobilized the entire black community in support of their cause.

Local blacks participated in an economic boycott and refused to patronize stores that would not serve them food. In the face of mounting business losses, Woolworth's quietly opened its food service in July to all persons.

It was ironic that Greensboro was the site for such a watershed in race relations. The home of five colleges, Greensboro had long enjoyed a reputation for moderation on the racial issue. City leaders had early announced that they would comply with the school desegregation requirements of *Brown*. Blacks, nonetheless, shared a sense of continuous frustration in achieving equal rights. Only minimal school integration had occurred by 1960 and other institutions remained racially separate.

This spontaneous action by Greensboro students provided a catalyst for a decade of direct, active protests. The Greensboro sit-ins altered the nature of the civil rights movement in two important respects. First, the sit-ins suggested new and more dynamic methods by which protests could be expressed. Shortly thereafter the Freedom Rides began to challenge racial segregation in bus facilities. No longer were blacks content to await the often slow and elusive results of court decrees. Second, blacks were no longer willing to permit moderate whites to define civil rights objectives. Blacks were increasingly willing to jeopardize the goodwill of white moderates and liberals in order to follow their own agendas for social reform, which would culminate in the black-power demands of the late 1960s.

James W. Ely, Jr.
Vanderbilt University

William H. Chafe, *Civilities and Civil Rights: Greensboro, North Carolina, and the Black Struggle for Freedom* (1980); Miles Wolff, *Lunch at the Five and Ten: The Greensboro Sit-Ins* (1970). ✩

HERNDON, ANGELO, CASE

The most famous civil liberties and civil rights case in Georgia during the 1930s centered around Angelo Herndon, a young black Communist. A native of Ohio, Herndon moved to the Deep South in the early Depression years in search of work and traded his fundamentalist Christianity for communism in 1930 while living in Birmingham, Ala. Assigned by the Communist party to Atlanta, the 19-year-old Herndon organized a large interracial demonstration in June 1932, protesting the suspension of public relief. As a result, Atlanta police eventually arrested Herndon and charged him with attempting "to incite insurrection" against the state of Georgia, a capital offense. In his January 1933 trial, Herndon was represented by black attorneys Benjamin J. Davis, Jr., and John Geer, who boldly challenged the exclusion of blacks from local juries, while the prosecuting attorneys responded with an emotional condemnation of communism. An all-white jury quickly found Herndon guilty and sentenced him to 18 to 20 years in prison.

The seeming injustice of Herndon's conviction helped stimulate greater solidarity among Atlanta blacks and prompted a somewhat more assertive stance toward racial discrimination. Through vigorous publicity efforts the International Labor Defense, a Communist-influenced legal defense organization, eventually turned the affair into a national cause célèbre. A team of prominent attorneys headed by Whitney North Seymour of New York City twice appealed the conviction to the U.S. Supreme Court, which in *Herndon v. Lowry* (1937) declared the Georgia insurrection law to be unconstitutional. After his release from prison, Herndon moved to New York City, where he remained active in radical causes and later helped to edit a literary magazine. Toward the end of World War II he left the Communist party and eventually moved to Chicago, where he pursued a career in business.

Along with the more famous Scottsboro case in Alabama, the Angelo Herndon case symbolized the use of political justice to maintain racial subordination in the Deep South. Unlike Scottsboro, however, Herndon's prosecution under the insurrection law also raised a serious challenge to free speech and helped rally many civil libertarians to his cause. Although the Supreme Court eventually freed Herndon after nearly five years of proceedings, dramatic improvement in the status of blacks within the southern legal system had to await the advent of the civil rights movement in the mid-1950s.

Charles H. Martin
University of Texas at El Paso

Angelo Herndon, *Let Me Live* (1937); Charles H. Martin, *The Angelo Herndon Case and Southern Justice* (1976). ☆

JAWORSKI, LEON

(1905–1982) Lawyer.

Jaworski, who became nationally recognized as the special prosecutor of the Watergate affair, was born in Waco, Tex., on 19 September 1905. He was the son of the Reverend Joseph Jaworski, a Protestant minister of Polish birth, and Marie Jaworski, who was born in Vienna.

After deciding to devote his life to a career as a trial lawyer, Jaworski attended law school at Baylor University, receiving his LL.B. in 1925; he then spent a year at the George Washington University School of Law and was granted the LL.M. in 1926. Returning to Waco to begin practice as a trial attorney, he was immediately successful, and he soon moved to Houston. His reputation spread rapidly, and in 1931, at age 26, he was asked to join one of the leading firms in that city, Fulbright, Crooker and Freeman. He remained with this firm, becoming a senior partner in 1951. Fulbright and Jaworski became one of the largest and best-respected firms in Texas.

During World War II, Jaworski served in the Judge Advocate General's Corps, attaining the rank of colonel. He conducted the prosecution of Nazi prisoners of war in this country and then became the chief of the United States War Crimes Trial Section in the European Theatre in our zone of occupation, with headquarters at Wiesbaden. He personally prosecuted the first war crimes trials in Germany. In 1946 he returned to his law practice in Houston. His reputation continued to grow, and

he became increasingly involved in civic and social affairs. He was president of the American College of Trial Lawyers in 1961, president of the State Bar of Texas the next year, and president of the American Bar Association in 1971. He received numerous awards, including 15 honorary degrees, and was an elder in the Presbyterian church.

Jaworski's significant accomplishment was the successful prosecution of the Watergate crimes. He served as director of the special prosecution team in 1973 and 1974; his expertise as a trial lawyer and his professional, dispassionate conduct exposed the burglary and obstruction of justice by President Nixon and his close associates. Jaworski died 9 December 1982 in Wimberly, Tex. His four books of memoirs are *After Fifteen Years* (1961), *The Right and the Power: The Prosecution of Watergate* (1976), *Confession and Avoidance: A Memoir* (1979) [with M. Herskowitz], and *Crossroads* (1981) [with D. Schneider].

W. Hamilton Bryson
University of Richmond

J. Doyle, *Not Above the Law: The Battles of Watergate Prosecutors Cox and Jaworski* (1977). ☆

JOHNSON, FRANK M., JR.

(b. 1918) Federal judge.

Frank Minis Johnson, Jr., was born on 30 October 1918 in rural Winston County, Ala. During the Civil War, Winston and other northwest Alabama hill counties with few slaves had little sympathy for the Confederate cause. After the war, Winston became a lone Republican stronghold in Democratic Alabama. Frank Johnson's father was

active in GOP politics and was elected
probate judge and a member of the Alabama Legislature on the Republican
ticket. Following law school at the University of Alabama and military service
in Europe during World War II, Frank
Johnson, Jr., practiced law in Jasper,
Ala., and, like his father, also became
active in GOP politics. His services on
behalf of Dwight Eisenhower's 1952
presidential campaign led to his appointment, in 1953, as U.S. attorney in
Birmingham. In 1955 Eisenhower appointed him to the U.S. District Court
for the Middle District of Alabama in
Montgomery, where he served until his
appointment to a federal appeals court
in 1979.

While a U.S. attorney, Johnson successfully prosecuted members of a
prominent Sumter County plantation
family on peonage and slavery charges,
though such convictions had been rare
since Reconstruction. As a district
judge, he quickly gained a reputation
as a vigorous defender of civil rights.
During his first year on the federal
bench, he helped to form a majority outlawing segregation on Montgomery's city
buses. In the years that followed he issued numerous decisions on voting
rights and became the first judge to
order the names of qualified blacks
added to county voting rolls. He also
outlawed discrimination in Alabama's
transportation facilities, libraries, agricultural extension service, and political parties; wrote the first statewide
school segregation decree; and placed
numerous state agencies under permanent federal court order.

Judge Johnson's opinions on civil
rights perplexed and angered his fellow
white Alabamians, making him a
convenient scapegoat for George C.
Wallace and other race-baiting politicians. During his 1962 gubernatorial
campaign, Wallace—Johnson's law
school classmate and an associate of
more than passing acquaintance—condemned "lying, scalawagging" federal
judges, with Johnson his principal target. Court baiting remained a familiar
Wallace tactic for years after the 1962
election, and on at least one occasion,
a Wallace aide urged Alabamians to os-
tracize federal judges, their wives, and
children. Judge Johnson had become a
pariah in his native state, however, even
before the Wallace era in Alabama politics. Intermittently for 18 years, a
dusk-to-dawn guard maintained a vigil
at his home. His mother's home was
bombed, crosses were burned on his
lawn, and hate mail was directed to him.
In 1975 his adopted son committed suicide. His son's emotional problems,
some suggested, had their origins partly
in the pressures to which his family had
been subjected.

With increased black voter registration and the subsiding of race as *the*
issue in Alabama politics, the attitudes

of white Alabamians and the state's officialdom mellowed somewhat toward Judge Johnson. In the 1970s his landmark decisions mandating reform of Alabama's mental institutions and prisons prompted challenge from other quarters—critics who contended that Johnson and other activist judges were confusing their own social preferences with constitutional commands and encroaching unduly on legislative and administrative domains. Combined with his record on civil rights, however, such decisions served largely to enhance rather than damage his judicial reputation. His name was invariably mentioned when Supreme Court vacancies arose. In 1977 President Carter selected him to head the Federal Bureau of Investigation, but Johnson ultimately withdrew his name from nomination for medical reasons. In 1979 President Carter appointed Judge Johnson to the Court of Appeals for the Fifth Circuit. In 1981 the Fifth Circuit was split into two courts, and Judge Johnson became a member of the new Court of Appeals for the Eleventh Circuit, with jurisdiction over Alabama, Georgia, and Florida.

Tinsley E. Yarbrough
East Carolina University

Robert F. Kennedy, Jr., *Judge Frank M. Johnson, Jr.: A Biography* (1978); Tinsley E. Yarbrough, *Judge Frank Johnson and Human Rights in Alabama* (1981). ☆

LITTLE ROCK CRISIS

White southerners invoked the doctrines of states' rights and interposition to counter the NAACP's post–World War II campaign against de jure seg-

regation. A few places in the Upper South immediately complied with the Supreme Court's decision in the 1954 case of *Brown* v. *Board of Education*, which overturned the doctrine of separate but equal, but throughout states of the old Confederacy governments embraced a strategy of "massive resistance." The first major constitutional test of this strategy grew out of efforts to integrate the Little Rock, Ark., public schools.

The NAACP in 1956 brought one of its more than 50 post-*Brown* desegregation suits against the Little Rock Board of Education. Under federal court order the board in September of 1957 proposed to admit a small number of blacks to formerly all-white Little Rock Central High School. Governor Orval Faubus invoked states' rights and interposition as constitutional grounds to block the plan. Acting on the governor's orders, the Arkansas National Guard, accompanied by a jeering white mob, rebuffed black students. Faubus denounced as unconstitutional federal court orders directing compliance.

Republican President Dwight D. Eisenhower responded to this attack on federal judicial authority by asserting the supremacy of the national government. He directed the attorney general to obtain an injunction against Faubus, who in turn withdrew the national guard. The president on 25 September 1957 dispatched troops from the 101st Airborne Division to restore order and to force the admission of black students.

The tug-of-war between state and federal authorities continued until late 1959. The Supreme Court, in *Cooper* v. *Aaron* in September 1958, unanimously reasserted the supremacy of the federal government, denounced interposition, and reaffirmed the federal judicial power. Governor Faubus then implemented two statutes that authorized him to close the Little Rock schools. The Court in the 1959 case of *Faubus* v. *Aaron* unanimously declared these statutes in violation of the due process and equal protection clauses of the Fourteenth Amendment.

Little Rock Central High School reopened quietly in September 1959. Events of the preceding two years discredited die-hard segregationists' arguments that states' rights and interposition could thwart the massive social changes sweeping the South.

See also URBANIZATION: / Little Rock

Kermit L. Hall
University of Florida

Numan Bartley, *The Rise of Massive Resistance: Race and Politics in the South during the 1950s* (1969); Daisy Bates, *The Long Shadow of Little Rock: A Memoir* (1962); Benjamin Muse, *Ten Years of Prelude: The Story of Integration since the Supreme Court's 1954 Decision* (1964). ☆

MARSHALL, JOHN
‖‖‖‖‖‖‖‖‖‖‖‖‖‖‖‖‖‖‖‖‖‖‖‖‖‖‖‖‖‖‖‖‖‖‖‖‖
(1755–1835) U.S. Supreme Court
Chief Justice.

Born in Fauquier County, Va., Marshall was a prominent member of the Richmond legal profession before he accepted federal office, first as a minister to France during the X.Y.Z. Mission (1797–98), then as a member of the House of Representatives (1799–1800), and as secretary of state (1800–1801). Appointed chief justice of the United States in January 1801, he served for the remaining 34 years of his life during a period of unprecedented institutional change in the Court and unparalleled constitutional growth in American law. He is best remembered for his articulation of the doctrine of judicial review (*Marbury* v. *Madison*, 1803), the use of the contract clause to defend private property against legislative seizures (*Fletcher* v. *Peck*, 1810; *Dartmouth College* v. *Woodward*, 1819), and his classic expositions and constructions of the interstate commerce power (*Gibbons* v. *Ogden*, 1824) and the necessary and proper clause (*McCullough* v. *Maryland*, 1819). A former officer in the Virginia Continental Line during the American Revolution and a close friend of President George Washington, Marshall displayed in his jurisprudence an affection for a strong federal government and a desire to perpetuate the moderate Federalist concern for sustained economic growth and political cohesion among the various states.

Despite growing isolation from both his pro-Jeffersonian Virginia contemporaries and the "high Federalist" branch of his own party, Marshall remained a political power in his native state. This was due in no small measure to his personality and mannerisms, which won him friends and supporters. The simplicity of his behavior and carelessness of his dress have become legendary. Even in the last decades of his life he welcomed the opportunity to toss horseshoes with friends at a local Richmond tavern. His "lawyers' dinners" were famous throughout the Old Dominion, and he persisted in that hospitable practice even after his entertainment of Aaron Burr during Burr's treason trial had generated public criticism. Charming, chivalrous, and, in later years, flirtatious with women, the chief justice remained devoted to the ailing wife he had married in 1783, mother of their 10 children. Gifted with a self-deprecatory sense of humor, Marshall was liked by virtually every Virginian of note in his generation. He in turn treasured his association with other Virginians, missing their unadorned hospitality while he was living in Paris and seeking their company when compelled by judicial duties to reside in Philadelphia or Washington. Next to Virginia society Marshall loved the landscape of his native state, particularly the mountain region of his birth; in the months immediately preceding his sudden death he was planning his retirement to the Fauquier homestead he had retained throughout his active career.

A veteran of Virginia local politics, John Marshall may well have derived his sense of federal balance from the example of Virginia state government. In Virginia substantial local autonomy in the county courts was balanced by extensive legislative power in the general assembly and general judicial authority in the general court, which exercised appellate review over county courts and broad original jurisdiction. Marshall was not a nationalist but rather an advocate of a federal government adequate to perform the necessary functions of a national state.

Like his Virginia contemporaries the chief justice preferred an agrarian way of life, and hence an agricultural economy for the United States. But unlike them he foresaw the inevitability of economic diversification. Recognizing the potential evils of commercial development and industrial growth, he sought means by which government might encourage the accumulation of national wealth and soften the impact of such development upon the people. A contemplative and compassionate man, the chief justice brought to the national scene all that was exemplary in the Virginia of his day.

Herbert A. Johnson
University of South Carolina

Leonard Baker, *John Marshall: A Life in Law* (1974); Albert J. Beveridge, *The Life of John Marshall*, 4 vols. (1916–19); Robert K. Faulkner, *The Jurisprudence of John Marshall* (1968). ☆

MORGAN, CHARLES, JR.

(b. 1930) Civil rights attorney.

Born in Cincinnati, Ohio, in 1930, Morgan was reared in Kentucky and at age 15 moved with his parents to Birmingham, Ala. He graduated from the University of Alabama and received his law degree from the same institution. Morgan first achieved national prominence when he denounced the September 1963 Birmingham church bombing and blamed community attitudes for the tragedy. In the resulting furor Morgan left Birmingham. A year later he became the regional director for the American Civil Liberties Union in Atlanta.

Throughout the 1960s Morgan was involved in much of the litigation that altered political and social life in the region. He was instrumental in handling lawsuits challenging racial segregation in jury selection, state prisons, and the choice of delegations to political conventions. Perhaps Morgan's most significant impact came as a result of *Reynolds* v. *Sims* (1964), in which the Supreme Court mandated equal population districts for legislative bodies. Morgan was one of the plaintiffs and successfully argued the case before the Court. Subsequent litigation by Morgan forced a reapportionment of the Alabama Legislature.

Morgan has also demonstrated a commitment to civil liberties. He defended Captain Howard Levy at his court martial for refusing to teach dermatology to Green Beret medics. Morgan also represented Julian Bond in the early stages of his challenge to the 1967 action of the Georgia Legislature denying Bond his seat because of his antiwar political views. He appeared on behalf of Muhammad Ali, a conscientious objector, in his prolonged fight against conviction for draft evasion.

In 1972 Morgan moved to Washington and became head of the ACLU's national office. He was one of the first persons to call for the impeachment of President Richard M. Nixon over the Watergate scandal, and he persuaded the ACLU Board to adopt this position in September of 1973. Morgan resigned from his ACLU post in 1976 when he was criticized for publicly supporting fellow southerner Jimmy Carter's presidential bid. Always the maverick, Morgan then organized his own law firm and began defending corporations from assaults on their rights. In 1979 he instituted a lawsuit on behalf of Sears, Roebuck, and Co., which attacked affirmative action employment efforts. A skillful and dedicated advocate, Morgan once declared that "you don't hire a lawyer to lose."

James W. Ely, Jr.
Vanderbilt University

Philip Kopper, Washington *Post Potomac* (7 October 1973); Charles Morgan, Jr., *A Time to Speak* (1964), *One Man, One Voice* (1979). ☆

NAPOLEONIC CODE
||||||||||||||||||||||||||||||||||||||||||||||||||

To prevent the complete adoption of the Anglo-American common law after the Louisiana Purchase (1803), the largely French and Spanish residents of Louisiana sought to preserve their Latin legal tradition by the reception and enactment of a civil code modeled after the *projet* of the *Code Napoleon*. On 31 March 1808 the territorial legislature of Orleans adopted a "code" drafted by Louis Moreau-Lislet and James Brown, the *Digest of Civil Laws Now in Force in the Territory of Orleans*. Printed in both English and French, and patterned after the Napoleonic Code of France, this was indeed a digest, i.e., a compilation of existing law, rather than a definitive and final statement of the law, a true code. Unlike the French code upon which it was based, the Digest of 1808 was not enacted in revolutionary times, nor was it intended to effect a national legal unification or extensive social transformations through legislation. It was not a break with the past, it did not abrogate the preceding law, and many of the radical ends that the authors of the French code championed were the very things Louisiana's inhabitants sought to avoid. This precursor of the modern civil codes of Louisiana was mainly the result of a confrontation between competing cultures rather than a true codification effort.

The legislative act promulgating the Digest of 1808 stipulated that "whatever in the ancient civil laws of this territory . . . is contrary to the dispositions contained in the said digest, or irreconcilable with them, is hereby abrogated." In this clause, the earlier law was not necessarily abrogated. As the Superior Court of Louisiana observed in 1812, "what we call the Civil code, is but a digest of the civil law which regulated this country under the French and Spanish Monarchs." Moreover, unlike the products of legislative positivism associated with civilian codification movements at the time, the Louisiana "code" gave legal effect to custom. Spanish law, therefore, survived in Louisiana as an authoritative source of law as custom. The two major sources of Spanish law in Louisiana had been the *Recopilacion de Indias* and *Las Siete Partidas*. Indeed, because the Spanish had previously abrogated much of the former French law, the Digest of 1808 was largely a digest of Spanish law.

The Digest of 1808 did serve the purpose of preventing the erosion of the Roman civil law during the early high tide of the common law in Louisiana. It remained for Edward Livingston, sometimes called the "Bentham of American Jurisprudence," to awaken in Louisiana a zeal for true codification. Livingston, with Moreau-Lislet and Pierre Derbigny, drafted the Louisiana Civil Code of 1825, which repealed all previous civil laws and which was enacted by the state legislature. The authors asserted that "in the Napoleonic code we have a system approaching nearer than any to perfection." Although modified after the Civil War to reflect the abolition of slavery and reenacted as the Louisiana Civil Code of 1870, the version of the Napoleonic Code received by Louisiana in 1825 remains the fundamental basis of the state's system of private law. Thus, the Roman civil law has been preserved in Louisiana as a mixed jurisdiction in the midst of a basically American-style judiciary and in the face of general reception of the Anglo-American public law such as prevailed elsewhere throughout the South.

Ernest S. Easterly III
Baton Rouge, Louisiana

R. Batiza, *Tulane Law Review* (April 1971); George Dargo, *Jefferson's Louisiana: Politics and the Clash of Legal Traditions* (1975); Ernest Easterly III, *Geojurisprudence: Studies in Law, Liberty and Landscapes* (1980); Robert A. Pascal, *Louisiana Law Review* (December 1965). ☆

PLESSY V. FERGUSON

In *Plessy* v. *Ferguson* (1896) the United States Supreme Court ruled in favor of the "separate but equal" principle in public transportation facilities for whites and blacks. In doing so it affirmed the role of states in controlling social discrimination, and, many argue, the decision actually promoted enforced segregation. The number of Jim Crow laws increased rapidly during the following years.

The case originated in Louisiana, which had a statute requiring separate-but-equal accommodations for whites and blacks on railroad cars. In 1892 Homer Adolph Plessy purchased a train ticket from New Orleans to Covington, La. Plessy, seven-eighths white and one-eighth black, sat in a "whites only" car and refused to move to a "colored" section. He was arrested for violating the "Jim Crow Car Act of 1890." The "Citizens Committee to Test the Constitutionality of the Separate Car Law," a group of 18 blacks, had instigated the incident, choosing Plessy as the example and making sure train officials knew his racial status. Their attorney was Albion Winegar Tourgee, a carpetbagger during Reconstruction and author of the Reconstruction novel *A Fool's Errand.*

Four years later, the Supreme Court heard the case and voted seven to one (Justice David Brewer did not participate) against Plessy. In the majority opinion Justice Henry B. Brown wrote: "We consider the underlying fallacy of the plaintiff's argument to consist in the underlying assumption that the enforced separation of the two races stamps the colored race with a badge of inferiority. If this be so, it is not by reason of anything found in the act, but solely because the colored race chooses to put that construction on it." Furthermore, he wrote, "The argument also assumes that social prejudices may be overcome by legislation, and that equal rights cannot be secured to the negro except by an enforced comingling of the two races. We cannot accept this proposition. If the two races are to meet upon terms of social equality, it must be the result of natural affinities, a mutal appreciation of each other's merits and a voluntary consent of individuals."

Ironically, the only southerner then serving on the Court, Justice John Marshall Harlan, cast the sole vote against the final decision. In the minority opinion he asserted the equality of all men with regard to the civil rights "as guaranteed by the supreme law of the land." He stated, "Our Constitution is color-blind, and neither knows nor tolerates classes among citizens. In respect of civil rights, all citizens are equal before the law."

Not until the 1950s did Supreme Court decisions, most notably in *Brown* v. *Board of Education* (1954), begin to dissolve the Court's sanction of the concept of separate but equal. For more than a half century, the principle had dictated the social treatment of blacks, with "equal" facilities providing the legal rationale for segregation. Finally, though, what had been the minority opinion in *Plessy* became that of the majority, a belated response to Justice Harlan's statement that "the thin disguise of 'equal' accommodations for passengers in railroad coaches will not mislead any one, nor atone for the wrong this day done."

Jessica Foy
Cooperstown Graduate Programs
Cooperstown, New York

Henry J. Abraham, *Freedom and the Court: Civil Rights and Liberties in the United States* (1982); Catherine A. Barnes, *Journey from Jim Crow: The Desegregation of Southern Transit* (1983); John C. Livingston, *Fair Game?: Inequality and Affirmative Action* (1979); Frank T. Read and Lucy S. McGough, *Let Them Be Judged: The Integration of the Deep South* (1978). ☆

POWELL, LEWIS F.

(b. 1907) U.S. Supreme Court Justice.

A private lawyer possessing no elective or judicial experience is seldom appointed to the U.S. Supreme Court. Lewis Powell, nominated to the Court in 1971 by Richard Nixon, is an exception.

A lifelong Virginian, Powell was born 19 September 1907 in Suffolk, Va. He received his law degree in 1931 from Washington and Lee University. From 1937 to 1971 Powell was a member of a large, prestigious Richmond law firm. During this period he quietly established a reputation as one of the South's leading corporation lawyers, earned a handsome income, served as a director of 11 major companies, and was elected president of the American Bar Association and the American College of Trial Lawyers. During the 1950s he served as the chairman of the Richmond School Board, steering a moderate course in the slow-paced desegregation of the public schools.

Powell's nomination met with less resistance from liberals than did several of Nixon's other choices for the Supreme Court seats: unlike Harold Carswell, Powell was judged to be highly competent; unlike Clement Haynesworth, Powell was seen as a racial moderate; and unlike William Rehnquist, Powell was not regarded as an uncompromising ideologue. In Powell, Nixon found the highly qualified southern jurist that he so desperately wanted to appoint to the Court.

As a justice, Lewis Powell has not assumed a self-consciously "southern" stance. A regional orientation has not emerged in his opinions—even those touching federalism or race. Favoring a "balancing approach" in constitutional adjudication similar to that of his avowed idols, Felix Frankfurter and John Marshall Harlan, Powell has proven to be the swing vote in several close cases and the author of some of

Lewis Powell, U.S. Supreme Court Justice, 1980s

the Burger Court's most carefully wrought opinions. In 1972 he wrote a thoughtful majority opinion reaffirming the position that a wiretap is a search or seizure within the meaning of the Fourth Amendment. In his opinions on equal protection, Powell has resisted the expansion of "suspect classifications."

Only in his opinions involving big business—perhaps because of his long service to large corporations—has Powell been unable to maintain a stance of moderation. His aggressive support of big business is characteristic of the New South—a South no longer consumed by virulent racism but now willing to adopt strategies pioneered by northern corporation lawyers in the service of improved quarterly reports.

Powell's most famous opinion, *Regents* v. *Bakke* (1978), is characteristic of his balanced, trenchant, perceptive, and articulate legal analyses. In this landmark case that divided the Court and the country, Powell presented a lucid argument that invalidated racial quotas but upheld the concept of "affirmative action."

One scholar described Powell's work habits and temperament as being distinguished by "conscientiousness, thoroughness, craftsmanship, and sheer capacity for hard work." Powell is already being spoken of as a particularly distinguished "lawyer's judge" among the Supreme Court justices.

John W. Johnson
Clemson University

Leonard W. Levy, *Against the Law: The Nixon Court and Criminal Justice* (1974); Burt Neuborne, *The Justices of the United States Supreme Court* (1978); *Richmond Law Review* (1977). ☆

ROBINSON, SPOTTSWOOD W., III

||||||||||||||||||||||||||||||||||||||||||||||||||||

(b. 1916) Jurist and civil rights lawyer.

Robinson is one of the most prominent black jurists in the United States. Born in 1916 in Richmond, Va., he was graduated from Virginia Union University and then studied at Howard Law School, where he earned the highest scholastic average ever achieved at that institution. Robinson remained at Howard in a part-time faculty position for several years, dividing his time between teaching and the private practice of law in Richmond. His legal career was interrupted by military service during World War II. Robinson subsequently left Howard and devoted his energies to real-estate law in Richmond and civil rights litigation for the NAACP. In the late 1940s he filed numerous lawsuits seeking equalization of facilities and teacher salaries between white and black schools in Virginia.

Throughout the 1950s Robinson served as Southeast regional counsel for the NAACP. Noted for his clarity of expression and scrupulousness in handling details, Robinson played a major role in preparing and arguing *Brown* v. *Board of Education* (1954) before the Supreme Court. Following the decision in *Brown* he pushed actively for school desegregation across Virginia. From 1960 to 1963 Robinson was dean of Howard Law School. In 1961 President John F. Kennedy named him to the Civil Rights Commission. In October of 1963 he was nominated by President Kennedy as the first black judge of the Federal District Court for the District of Columbia. Three years later President Lyndon Johnson appointed Robinson as the first black judge on the U.S. Court of Appeals for the District of Columbia.

Robinson wrote more than 300 opinions while serving on the appellate court. He usually voted with the liberal wing of judges on this court, which has often been polarized along philosophical lines. In *Nixon* v. *Sirica* (1973) Robinson joined the majority opinion holding that the courts and not the president must determine the extent of executive privilege. He became chief judge of the D.C. Court of Appeals in 1981, only the second black to head one of the federal circuits. As chief judge, Robinson has handled the administrative duties of the court.

James W. Ely, Jr.
Vanderbilt University

Howard Law Review (No. 1, 1977); Richard Kluger, *Simple Justice: The History of Brown v. Board of Education and Black America's Struggle for Equality* (1976); *Washington Post* (27 May 1981). ☆

SCOPES TRIAL

|||||||||||||||||||||||||||||||||||||||||

See SCIENCE AND MEDICINE: / Scopes Trial

SCOTT, DRED

|||||||||||||||||||||||||||||||||||

(c. 1795–1858) Slave.

Captain John Emerson of Missouri in 1833 purchased Dred Scott, an illiterate slave born in Virginia. Emerson took Scott to Illinois, to that portion of Wisconsin territory embraced in the Missouri Compromise, and then back to Missouri. When Emerson died in 1843, putative ownership of Scott passed to John F. A. Sanford, Emerson's brother-in-law and executor. Three years later Scott sued in the lower courts of Missouri claiming that his sojourn in free territory had made him a free man.

Scott's litigation consumed more than a decade. The Missouri Supreme Court in 1848 held that the laws of Illinois and Wisconsin territory had no extraterritorial status in Missouri. Scott in 1854 filed suit in the U.S. Circuit Court for Missouri against John Sanford, who had moved to New York. Judge Robert Wells rejected Scott's substantive claim, but he left open the question of the slave's citizenship. Scott appealed this issue to the U.S. Supreme Court.

The Court on 6 March 1857 issued its opinion in *Dred Scott* v. *Sanford*. A proslavery, southern majority, led by Chief Justice Roger B. Taney, rejected Scott's claims. Taney struck down the Missouri Compromise, denied the power of Congress to abridge slaveholders' property rights, and held that a black person could not be a citizen of the United States within the meaning of the Constitution.

Taney's invocation of judicial authority complemented postnullification southern attitudes toward relations between nation and state. Southern leaders believed that declining influence over the political branches of the national government dictated a greater reliance on the federal judiciary to protect slaveholders' interests. Yet the cost of obeisance to the Court in *Scott* was further division of the northern and southern wings of the Democratic party and potential destruction of the Union.

Irony and tragedy have plagued the South's efforts to harmonize states' rights, the rule of law, and a dual system of race relations. Although freed by a new owner following the Court's decision, Scott died of consumption on 17 September 1858. The postwar freedom of other blacks, to which Scott's case

contributed, also proved ephemeral. After Reconstruction the South, with the blessing of the Supreme Court, reasserted the concept of states' rights to foster white supremacy, a concept that reigned until the civil rights changes of the 1960s.

Kermit L. Hall
University of Florida

Don E. Fehrenbacher, *The Dred Scott Case: Its Significance in American Law and Politics* (1978). ☆

SCOTTSBORO CASE

The "Scottsboro case" was the cause célèbre of American race relations in the 1930s. Touching on both the North's outrage at southern racism and the South's defensiveness about northern claims of moral superiority, this trial of nine black youths for rape in Scottsboro, Ala., reminded the nation of its failure to reconcile its image as the world's leader of democracy with the squalid reality of bigotry and repression daily faced by its black citizens.

On 25 March 1931 the deputy sheriff of Jackson County, Ala., reacting to reports of a fight among "hobos" on a Southern Railway freight bound for Memphis, stopped the train at Paint Rock, Ala., and arrested nine black youths, jailing them at the county seat of Scottsboro. The deputy also removed several white hobos from the train, including two white women. Minutes later, the women accused the blacks of rape, and only courageous action by the Jackson County sheriff saved the blacks from a lynching. The first rape trial took place in Scottsboro just three weeks later, and despite the trumped-up nature of the charges, the jury convicted eight of the nine and sentenced them to death.

The severity of the youths' sentences galvanized public opinion throughout America. When an appellate court overturned the verdicts, the state of Alabama immediately launched a second prosecution of the "Scottsboro boys" in 1933. During the second trial the International Labor Defense, an organization closely aligned with the Communist party, defended the youths, and the case became front-page news. Five years of legal maneuvering followed in both the state and federal courts. In 1937 defense attorneys and the prosecution finally reached a compromise, which freed four of the defendants while sentencing the others to long prison terms. Not until 1950 did the last of the Scottsboro boys emerge from the Alabama prisons. For many southerners, the Scottsboro case marked a low point in 20th-century race relations because it starkly revealed white southerners' oppression of blacks.

Carroll Van West
Center for Historic Preservation
Middle Tennessee State University

Dan T. Carter, *Scottsboro: A Tragedy of the American South* (1969). ☆

SLAVE CODES
||||||||||||||||||||||||||||||||||||||||

The first statute reflecting slavery in the South was adopted by colonial Virginia in 1660. That law recognized a class of blacks as life servants, and it established as a punishment for white servants who ran away with black life

servants the service time the black servant would have been required to render. This rather brief and simple act gave way within a generation to a complex code of laws concerning slavery in Virginia, which was a pioneer in this effort. In 1705 the Virginia Legislature passed a slave code, one of the first such codifications in the South.

The Virginia Slave Code of 1705 clearly established two themes that would remain a part of the slave codes in every southern colony and state. Slaves were defined by race, and this meant black persons; and slavery was associated primarily with a plantation economy. Provisions of the early Virginia slave code included sections concerning the torture and murder of slaves, the legal status of children whose fathers and mothers were slaves, penalties for failure to obey commands of a master, and restrictions on nonslave fraternization with slaves. For example, Chapter 49, Section 37, of the 1705 Virginia slave code provided that "any slaves, against whom proclamation hath been thus issued, and once published at any church or chapel, stay out, and do not immediately return home, it shall be lawful for any person or persons whatsoever, to kill and destroy such slaves by such ways and means as he, she, or they shall think fit, without accusation or impeachment of any crime for the same." The section further allowed dismemberment of any slave caught and returned alive.

The first codes and all subsequent codes encompassed three elements. First, the slave status was defined; second, the slave was regulated as a form of real property; and third, codes delineated slaves' social behavior and provided legal forms for social control of slaves. This latter element reflected the southern fixation on slave insurrections. As the Civil War approached, slave codes added further restrictions on personal freedoms of slaves, including the virtual abolition of manumission. By the 1850s slave codes in most southern states provided procedures for the expulsion of free blacks or their reinslavement with a master of their choice.

John R. Wunder
Clemson University

Eugene D. Genovese, *Roll, Jordan, Roll: The World the Slaves Made* (1972); Kenneth M. Stampp, *The Peculiar Institution: Slavery in the Ante-Bellum South* (1956).

TUCKER FAMILY

Over several generations the Tuckers of Virginia produced a number of eminent attorneys, jurists, politicians, and authors. From the early postrevolutionary years the family name was bound inextricably to the legal and political culture of the Old Dominion and of the South. St. George Tucker (1752–1827), progenitor of the main Tucker line in the Commonwealth, pursued a lengthy career as a state and federal judge, poet and political essayist, and successor to George Wythe as law professor at the College of William and Mary. On the bench, Tucker's able decisions set important precedents during the formative years of Virginia jurisprudence. His opinion in *Kamper* v. *Hawkins* (1793), for instance, forcibly stated the doctrine of judicial review by holding the state constitution to be the supreme act of a sovereign people with which all subsequent legislation had to conform.

Tucker's lengthy series of notes and annotations derived from his experience as a law teacher prompted him to prepare a five-volume American edition of *Blackstone's Commentaries* (1803). In appendices designed to identify and explain areas of American practice that had diverged from English substantive and procedural law, Tucker expressed admiration for the profound American innovations in constitutional government that had occurred during his lifetime. He took occasion, too, as he had done in student lectures, to assert his strong objections to the institution of slavery and his hope for its gradual elimination. Though keyed largely to Virginia's law and practice, Tucker's edition of *Blackstone's Commentaries* rapidly emerged as an essential reference tool for student and practitioner alike and found a receptive and loyal audience throughout the South until superseded by later editions at mid-century. But beyond its practical value, Tucker's work served as an important early exposition of Jeffersonian concepts of democratic government.

A distant Bermuda kinsman of St. George Tucker, George Tucker (1775–1861) acquired less fame as a lawyer than as an author and political economist. Written on the eve of Virginia's troubled constitutional debates, *The Valley of Shenandoah* (1824), his best-known work, castigates the financially irresponsible Tidewater aristocracy, frets about the cultural and political alienation of the western portions of the Commonwealth, and berates the legal profession. Most importantly, however, Tucker's book marks the first significant use of the plantation setting and the stereotyped southern slave in fiction. His later works on political economy, some written while Tucker was professor of moral philosophy at the University of Virginia, saw his strident opposition to slavery somewhat muted as his main focus turned to a deep concern for public prosperity and a growing anxiety over the economic future of his section.

Henry St. George Tucker (1780–1848), son of St. George Tucker, made his greatest contribution as the state's highest judicial officer and as a legal writer. Thoroughly skilled in the application of complex principles of equity, he led the Virginia bench in quest of justice over legal technicality and, unlike many of his contemporaries, refused to be hampered by precedent. With this enlightened approach he exerted further influence on the legal culture of the Old Dominion by training a remarkable generation of attorneys drawn from throughout the South at his own private law school in Winchester and later at the University of Virginia. From his lecture notes he prepared in 1831 the two-volume *Commentaries on the Laws of Virginia*. This encyclopedic work became a handbook for Virginia practitioners and students, as well as a valued legal text across the South.

The most prolific of the Tuckers, Nathaniel Beverley Tucker (1784–1851), parted from his father and brother to espouse extreme states' rights and pro-slavery positions in numerous essays and contributions to Virginia newspapers and southern periodicals. Eventually assuming his father's old post as law professor at the College of William and Mary, he imbued a restless generation of aspiring southern attorneys with his own fiery brand of southern nationalism and secessionist rhetoric. His anxiety over northern domination of the South led to the prophetic *Partisan Leader* (1836), a novel that perhaps most effectively captured the spirit of states' rights proponents who foresaw

clearly the coming conflict. But Tucker also took the training of law students as competent advocates seriously. His broad approach to legal education blended the practical with the theoretical, stressing the importance of the *Principles of Pleading* (1846) as firmly as did his *Lectures on the Science of Government* (1848).

After the Civil War, John Randolph Tucker (1823–97) assumed the family mantle of leadership in Virginia jurisprudence. Son of Henry St. George Tucker, this Winchester attorney served as Virginia's wartime attorney general and later became dean of the law school at Washington and Lee University and an influential Virginia congressman. Conservative southern Democrat and strict constructionist, Tucker mirrored the temper of his times in Virginia. Yet, at the same time, he led his southern contemporaries in renewing their devotion to the federal Constitution and understanding its usefulness to their section. He represented a group of Chicago anarchists before the U.S. Supreme Court in the case *Spies* v. *Illinois* (1887), which first contended that the Fourteenth Amendment incorporates the Bill of Rights. He explained his action by stating, "I do not defend anarchy, I defend the Constitution." One of the first southerners elected to the presidency of the American Bar Association (1892–93), Tucker wrote frequently on topics of concern to practitioners in the South. In a last great attempt to withstand the rising influence of Harvard and the developing case method of instruction, Dean Tucker stood as one of the leading opponents of such innovation in southern legal education. He continued to proclaim throughout the last years of his life the virtues of those attorneys who were formally educated but ultimately self-trained.

E. Lee Shepard
Virginia Historical Society

W. Hamilton Bryson, *Legal Education in Virginia, 1779–1979: A Biographical Approach* (1982); William R. Taylor, *Cavalier and Yankee: The Old South and American National Character* (1961); J. Randolph Tucker, *Virginia Law Register* (March 1896). ✩

TUTTLE, ELBERT P.
(b. 1897) Federal judge.

As chief judge of the Fifth Circuit Court of Appeals throughout the 1960s, Elbert Parr Tuttle provided leadership in the development of civil rights law comparable to that of Earl Warren on the Supreme Court. In a 1967 tribute to him Chief Justice Warren praised Tuttle for combining "administrative talents with great personal courage and wisdom to assure justice of the highest quality without delays which might have thrown the Fifth Circuit into chaos." Tuttle and three other judges—John Minor Wisdom of New Orleans, Richard T. Rives of Montgomery, and John R. Brown of Houston—were disparagingly labeled "The Four" by an outraged fellow judge, who saw them as destroyers of the Old South he cherished.

Tuttle, Wisdom, Brown, and Rives shared a quiet passion that reacted to injustice and translated the Supreme Court's basic school desegregation decision into a broad mandate for racial justice and equality under law. They battled to make the law work during a period of social upheaval. They not only accepted the constitutional philosophy that extended downward from the Warren Court but also reinforced it upward and outward, stretching and expanding the law to protect rights and liberties granted by the Constitution. They proved that change can come from below, provided there is an accepting climate in the structure above.

Born in California on 17 July 1897, Tuttle grew up in Hawaii, attending multiracial schools. He settled in Atlanta in 1923 after graduation from Cornell University Law School. In Atlanta he opened a law practice with his wife Sara's brother, William Sutherland, who had grown up in Jacksonville, Fla., and had clerked for Justice Brandeis. As a lawyer, Tuttle won a landmark case before the Supreme Court, establishing an indigent's right to counsel.

A World War II battlefield hero who became a brigadier general in the army reserve, Tuttle led a floor fight that seated the contested Georgia delegation that supported Dwight Eisenhower at the Republican National Convention in 1952. Following Eisenhower's election, Tuttle served as general counsel to the Treasury Department until 1954, when the president appointed him to the Fifth Circuit Court of Appeals. In his first 29 years on the federal bench, Tuttle wrote 1,225 opinions, reputed to be more than any federal judge in history, including 94 dissents.

Based on his belief in the theory of common law development, Tuttle believed that "the law develops to meet changing needs . . . according to changes in our moral precepts." In civil rights cases that broke new legal ground, Tuttle explained, "I never had any doubt that what I was doing would be affirmed by the Supreme Court. It was the easiest field of the law I could write in. . . . The truth is, the black person in the litigation I sat in on was entitled to the result he got, under what the Constitution required."

In 1965 Harvard University awarded Judge Tuttle an honorary Doctor of Laws degree, stating, "The mind and heart of this dauntless judge enhance the great tradition of the federal judiciary."

Jack Bass
University of South Carolina

Jack Bass, *Unlikely Heroes* (1981); Howell Raines, *My Soul Is Rested* (1977); Earl Warren, *Georgia Law Review* (Fall 1967). ☆

WHITE, EDWARD DOUGLAS

(1845–1921) U.S. Supreme Court Justice.

The first sitting Supreme Court justice promoted to the chief justiceship, Edward Douglas White was a jurist who carved a place for himself in legal history because of strong personality and longevity rather than legal brilliance.

The son and grandson of Irish Catholic judges, White was born in 1845 in Louisiana on his father's 1,600-acre sugar beet plantation. The young White was educated almost entirely in Jesuit institutions. After a brief, frustrating service as an aide-de-camp in the Confederate army, White apprenticed himself to a distinguished New Orleans lawyer and in 1868 was admitted to the Louisiana bar. White's affiliation with influential New Orleans law firms, coupled with the income from his Thibodaux plantation, provided him with the financial security to enter politics. His fortuitous association with the Redeemer governor Francis Nicholls ultimately won him the state legislature's selection to the U.S. Senate.

As a senator, White conformed to the dominant laissez-faire spirit of turn-of-the-century America except for a self-serving defense of the high protective tariff on imported sugar. In 1894 he was nominated for the Supreme Court by President (and fellow Democrat) Grover Cleveland. The choice of White to fill a Supreme Court vacancy in the midst of the Populist upheaval of the 1890s was intended by Cleveland as a device to bolster the southern wing of the Democratic party.

On the Supreme Court, White used his hearty friendliness and access to the best parties in Washington to create a place for himself as one of the Court's social leaders. Although not characterized by a rigorous legal mind, White was a hard worker and possessed an absorbent memory that allowed him, upon occasion, to deliver his opinions without notes.

In 1910 President William Howard Taft nominated White for the chief justiceship. Apparently Taft wished to place someone in the Court's center seat sufficiently advanced in age (White was 64 at that time) to allow the position to become vacant again in a few years so that Taft himself could be appointed to head the Court. Although Taft eventually obtained his coveted judicial position, he had to wait until White's death, 11 years later, in 1921.

The traditional southern states' rights doctrines that White articulated as a senator from Louisiana were occasionally enunciated in his Supreme Court opinions. However, his judicial orientation was not self-consciously southern. White's status as a Confederate veteran did not keep him from developing a close personal friendship with Justice Oliver Wendell Holmes, a Boston Brahmin and Union veteran.

One biographer has referred to White's opinions as following a "jagged pattern," the product of "judicial whimsey." White's positions on such dominant legal concerns of the time as substantive due process and federal regulatory activity showed little consistency. In the *Insular Cases* White introduced the novel but slippery doctrine that the Constitution followed the flag only for those overseas possessions properly "incorporated" by Congress. White's most famous contribution to public law was the creation of the "rule of reason" as a test for alleged restraints of trade: only those business combinations that were deemed "unreasonable," White argued, should be dismantled pursuant to the Sherman Antitrust Act. What White and his like-minded brethren meant by "unreasonable" was never articulated. This crude, pragmatic concept was White's principal doctrinal legacy.

John W. Johnson
Clemson University

Robert B. Highsaw, *Edward Douglas White: Defender of the Conservative Faith* (1981); John Semonche, *Charting the Future: The Supreme Court Responds to a Changing Society, 1890–1920* (1978); James F. Watts, Jr., *The Justices of the United States Supreme Court*, ed. Leon Friedman and Fred I. Israel (1969). ☆

WISDOM, JOHN MINOR

(b. 1905) Federal judge.

The "scholar" on the Fifth Circuit Court of Appeals during the turbulent battle over civil rights in the 1960s, Judge John Minor Wisdom "transformed the face of school desegregation law" in the absence of Supreme Court leadership.

Born 17 May 1905 in New Orleans, Wisdom received a B.A. degree from Washington and Lee and a LL.B. from Tulane. As a young man the New Orleans aristocrat became one of a handful of Republicans in Louisiana who openly argued that Huey Long's dictatorial control threatened democratic principles in the state. In 1952 Wisdom served as chairman of the 15-member Southern Conference for Eisenhower, which helped draft the former general to run for president. Wisdom played a significant role in the nominating convention, arguing successfully before the Credentials Committee for the seating of the contested Eisenhower delegation from Louisiana. President Eisenhower appointed Wisdom to the Fifth Circuit Court of Appeals in 1957.

In *U.S.* v. *Jefferson* (1967) Wisdom declared that school boards had "the affirmative duty under the Fourteenth Amendment to bring about an integrated, unitary school system in which there are no Negro schools and no white schools—just schools." The doctrine of affirmative duties developed by the Fifth Circuit shifted the burden from black plaintiffs to school boards and other public officials to end discrimination. It also helped lead to affirmative action programs to overcome the effects of past discrimination. "The Constitution is both color blind and color conscious," Wisdom wrote in *Jefferson*; "the Constitution is color conscious to prevent discrimination being perpetuated and to undo the effects of past discrimination. The criterion is the relevancy of color to a legitimate government purpose."

In his opinions in civil rights cases Wisdom combined literary flair with a scholarly depth that left a major imprint on constitutional law. In *Jefferson*, he placed school desegregation in a larger historical and philosophical framework. "*Brown*'s broad meaning, its important meaning," Wisdom asserted of the landmark 1954 Supreme Court decision, "is its revitalization of the national constitutional right the Thirteenth, Fourteenth, and Fifteenth Amendments created in favor of Negroes. This is the right of Negroes to *national* citizenship; their right as a class to share the privileges and immunities only white citizens had enjoyed as a class. *Brown* erased *Dred Scott*, used the Fourteenth Amendment to breathe life into the Thirteenth, and wrote the Declaration of Independence into the Constitution. Freedmen are free men."

Wisdom also wrote landmark opinions in cases that involved jury discrimination, voting rights, and affirmative action in employment, as well as in fields of law besides civil rights.

Jack Bass
University of South Carolina

Jack Bass, *Unlikely Heroes* (1981); J. Harvie Wilkinson III, *From Brown to Bakke: The Supreme Court and School Integration, 1954–1978* (1979). ☆

INDEX OF CONTRIBUTORS

Index

Picture Credits

||||||||||||||||||||||||||||||||||||||||

Ethnic Life

1 Hargrett Rare Book and Manuscript Library, University of Georgia, Athens

5 Historic New Orleans Collection (1985.41), New Orleans, Louisiana

15 New Orleans Museum of Art (56.34), New Orleans, Louisiana

20 From a drawing by Du Pratz, Louisiana, 1718–34, National Anthropological Archives, Smithsonian Institution, Washington, D.C.

23 Deaconness Bedell Collection, National Anthropological Archives, Smithsonian Institution, Washington, D.C.

36 William Ferris Collection, Archives and Special Collections, University of Mississippi Library, Oxford

40 Philip Gould, photographer, Lafayette, Louisiana

45 Eudora Welty, Mississippi Department of Archives and History (12.31.86), Jackson

55 University of Texas Institute of Texan Cultures, San Antonio

56 Library of Congress (L C - U S W -3-43130- K C), Washington, D.C.

63 Louis Schmier Collection, Valdosta, Georiga

72 National Museum of American Art, Smithsonian Institution, Washington, D.C.

Folklife

81 Doris Ulmann, Art Department, Berea College, Berea, Kentucky

89 William Ferris Collection, Archives and Special Collections, University of Mississippi Library, Oxford

100 William Ferris Collection, Archives and Special Collections, University of Mississippi Library, Oxford

104 William Ferris Collection, Archives and Special Collections, University of Mississippi Library, Oxford

115 Russell Lee, News and Information Service and Barker Texas History Center, University of Texas at Austin

126 Amon Carter Museum, Fort Worth, Texas

147 Private collection, Winston-Salem, North Carolina

170 William Ferris Collection, Archives and Special Collections, University of Mississippi Library, Oxford

174 William Ferris Collection, Archives and Special Collections, University of Mississippi Library, Oxford

178 William Ferris Collection, Archives and Special Collections, University of Mississippi Library, Oxford

187 William Ferris Collection, Archives and Special Collections, University of Mississippi Library, Oxford

191 William Ferris Collection, Archives and Special Collections, University of Mississippi Library, Oxford

194 William Ferris Collection, Archives and Special Collections, University of Mississippi Library, Oxford

210 William Ferris Collection, Archives and Special Collections, University of Mississippi Library, Oxford

217 William Ferris Collection, Archives and Special Collections, University of Mississippi Library, Oxford

Geography

231 Marion Post Wolcott, Library of Congress (L C - U S F -34-55745- D), Washington, D.C.

251 William Ferris Collection, Archives and Special Collections, University of Mississippi Library, Oxford

269 Georgia Department of Archives and History, Atlanta

272 San Antonio (Texas) Conservation Society

285 Ann Rayburn Paper Americana Collection, Archives and Special Collections, University of Mississippi Library, Oxford

286 Marion Post Wolcott, Library of Congress (L C - U S F -34-51787- D), Washington, D.C.

294 Russell Lee, Library of Congress (L C - U S F - 33-11410- M S), Washington, D.C.

History and Manners

301 Marion Post Wolcott, Library of Congress (L C - U S F -34-54814- D), Washington, D.C.

305 Gift of Edgar Williams and Bernice Chrysler Garbisch, 1963 (63.210.3), Metropolitan Museum of Art, New York, New York